AND THE ROOTS OF RHYTHM REMAIN
A Journey Through Global Music

Also by Joe Boyd
White Bicycles: Making Music in the 1960s

AND THE ROOTS OF RHYTHM REMAIN
A Journey Through Global Music

Joe Boyd

PUBLISHED BY
Ze Books of Houston, TX
(in partnership with Unnamed Press
of Los Angeles, CA)
3262 Westheimer Road, #467
Houston, TX 77098
zebooks.com

COPYRIGHT
Book and series design © Ze Books
Text copyright 2024 © by Joe Boyd
First published in 2024 by
Faber & Faber Limited, London

BOOK SERIES DESIGN
With Projects, Inc.

CREDITS NOTICE
Contributor credit for visual content is included at the end of this volume. All rights reserved, including the right to reproduce this book or portions thereof in any form whatsoever.

ISBN
9798988670025
Library of Congress control number available upon request.
Manufactured in North America.

FIRST ZE BOOKS PRINTING
September 2024
246897531
First Edition

For Andrea

For recordings and film clips of the
music assembled by the author, visit
joeboyd.co.uk or www.rootsremain.com

Contents

I	Mbube	001
II	Babalú-Ayé	073
III	Catch a Fire	213
IV	Latcho drom	287
V	Chega de saudade	389
VI	Mano a mano	487
VII	Szerelem, szerelem	535
VIII	Tezeta	655
IX	How we begin to remember	827

Acknowledgments	853
Notes on Sources	859
Bibliography	895
Index	923

This is the story of how we begin to remember
This is the powerful pulsing of love in the vein
After the dream of falling and calling your name out
These are the roots of rhythm
And the roots of rhythm remain

— Paul Simon, "Under African Skies"

Late one afternoon in 1999 in New Orleans, I found myself handing out $20 bills to a group of local horn players who were adding parts to an album called *Mardi Gras Mambo* by the Cuban all-star group ¡Cubanismo!. To Jesús Alemañy, the band's leader, their playing was never quite right and he kept demanding retake after retake. The group would roll their eyes, check their watches, mutter about having to get home to change before a gig that night, and I would bribe them to stick with it for another fifteen minutes. The problem was that they laid back on the beat with a sensual Big Easy cool. Cubans, on the other hand, generate their sexy grooves by sticking to the task with rigor, the rhythm section meshing together with the precision of a Swiss watch. When we finally got a take that made Jesús, if not entirely happy, at least ready to move on, I took a moment to ponder what I had just witnessed. The album was conceived as a celebration of links between the musical cultures of New Orleans and Havana; both were born in Africa, then shaped by colonial slavery and had borrowed freely from each other over the centuries. How did their rhythmic sensibilities come to be so different? I parked that question in the back of my mind. One day, I thought, I'd look for the answer.

Having grown up on the North American side of that divide, I'd immersed my youthful self in the holy trinity of blues, jazz, and rock 'n' roll, then added British folk to the mix when I moved to London and embarked on my career as a producer. I always loved the stories behind the music: Elvis shyly asking the Sun Records receptionist how much it would cost to record a demo for his mother's birthday, Louis Armstrong inventing scat-singing when he forgot the lyrics, James Brown lurking in the crowd at a Georgia roadhouse, watching Little Richard's every move, Mick Jagger and Keith Richards meeting by chance on a Dartford railway platform... I was also inspired by music's power to unsettle and outrage authority: Billie Holiday's shocking rendition of "Strange Fruit"; 1950s kids defying parents and preachers to flock to rock 'n' roll shows; and "We Shall Overcome" empowering demonstrators and infuriating cops during the Civil Rights era.

Music from over the horizon came to me in flashes: my mother's Édith Piaf and Carmen Miranda 78s, a bit of flamenco guitar, some of African drumming, bouzoukis on the jukebox in a Greek restaurant... As a producer, I never felt limited by genre or style, so when opportunities arose to work with South African, Indian, and Jamaican musicians in the 1960s and '70s, I took them eagerly. The circle widened when I started my Hannibal label in the eighties: Bulgaria, Mali, Hungary, Cuba, and Brazil. After forty years in the business, I took a step back and wrote a memoir about music-making in the sixties. I was often asked if the next one would be about the seventies. No, I thought, I'd rather write about the puzzle of that hard afternoon in the Big Easy instead.

The answers I found involved both Dizzy Gillespie and a 1552 Islamophobic edict by the king of Spain, which seemed like a pretty good start, so I decided to keep going. Along the way I discovered, among many other things, why the Soviets hated Bulgarian women's choirs, that afrobeat began with a subscription to an American jazz magazine, why so many artists, from Caetano Veloso and Gilberto Gil to Ivo Papasov and Fela Kuti, ended up in prison because of their music, how Frank Sinatra owed his career to a French tango singer from Buenos Aires, and why Charles Dickens wrote an angry polemic against a Zulu choir that visited London in 1853.

This is not an academic book; it travels back in history and across the globe—from Africa to the Caribbean and Latin America and through Europe to South Asia and back—following the circular flows of musical influence and the interconnectedness of cultures. Rhythms get traced back to their roots, then forward to show how they shape so much of the music we all know so well. This journey brings to life the little-known backstories and the personalities at the heart of the process, characters as colorful and unforgettable as the stars of Western popular music.

Modern technology has been a mixed blessing for music, but it has certainly brought more of it within reach than ever before. Just as knowing the stories behind them can bring sounds to life, hearing the music enriches the stories. Writing this book has expanded my listening—and my record collection—beyond measure. I now hear *habanera* syncopation, pentatonic scales, and notes between the notes everywhere. It may be rash to suggest that reading about music can be as enjoyable as listening to it, but my aspiration for this book is that it will open readers' minds and ears, as mine have been, to a wider, richer musical world.

1
Mbube

Malcolm McLaren was bored. It was 1982 and the glory years of punk were ancient history. Managing his new protégés Bow Wow Wow was turning into a tedious music-business job: promo meetings, tour schedules, B sides. He tried to liven up the group's sound by playing them Burundi drumming and Balinese gamelan records, but they weren't interested. For the album cover, he shot a pastiche of Manet's *Déjeuner sur l'herbe* with fourteen-year-old singer Annabella Lwin in the nude. Her mother reported him to the police, but the incident provoked little of the precious tabloid outrage generated by the Sex Pistols saying "fuck" on television.

At a New York music conference, Malcolm had met Afrika Bambaataa, who took him to a Bronx schoolyard for a Zulu Nation gig. The absence of any other White faces in the crowd made him nervous but the scratching, rapping DJs amazed him. Hip-hop was outsider music—*just like punk!*—and ripe for a well-connected impresario to make his fortune. But that would have been too simple. No, McLaren had to add his own surreal vision to the mix: *folk dancing!* His antidote to disco would have kids joining hands and dancing to ethnic beats remixed by Bronx DJs. He played a clip of Jimmy Stewart singing "Buffalo Gals" in *It's a Wonderful Life* to whoever would sit still long enough to watch it. And who would be the face of this musical revolution? Why not Malcolm himself? It was time to bring his light out from under the bushel of management. So what if he couldn't carry a tune? With his charm, the force of his personality, he could pull it off.

Malcolm signed a deal with the British Charisma label and enlisted Trevor Horn as engineer/producer. Horn was the perfect partner, a pioneer of electronic pop who, when asked about the possible negative effects of computers on music, responded: "On the contrary, technology will liberate us from the tyranny of technique!"

They took a Fairlight sampler to the city McLaren called the "cesspool of nations," recording Dominicans in East Harlem and rappers in the South Bronx. A trip to Appalachia for hoedowns proved fruitless, but back in New York they found a team of "double-dutch" rope-skipping girls from Harlem; Malcolm could see them starring in a promo video. He persuaded ex-girlfriend Vivienne Westwood to open a folk-dance-themed boutique called Nostalgia of Mud, inspired by a line from a play by Emile Augier (*"nostalgie de la boue"*), referring to sophisticates' inclination towards the primitive. But he still hadn't found the magic beat to set the project alight. Perhaps Bambaataa's group was on his mind; at some point Malcolm watched a video of *Zulu*, starring Michael Caine. The sight of thousands of warriors massed along a ridge, spears raised, singing in rich harmonies and stomping out complex rhythms before charging into the British guns at Rorke's Drift stirred something in the McLaren breast. "*That*'s a tribe that's worth meeting," he told Horn. After hearing some tracks of the Zulu wedding music known as *mbaqanga*, he boarded a flight to Johannesburg.

In Soweto, where Whites weren't allowed past sundown, Malcolm dodged police, slept on floors, hung out in shebeens, "slept with a few Zulu girls," booked a session with members of seventies mbaqanga outfit the Boyoyo Boys, and sent for Horn. They spent a couple of weeks cutting tracks, took everything back to London to mix, and registered the tunes in McLaren's name. (A music publisher had advanced him £60,000 against composer's rights on the album, so the songs needed to be credited to him.)

Their hip-hop version of "Buffalo Gals" reached the UK Top Ten, but British kids didn't respond to the Zulu beat of the follow-up, "Soweto," a remake of "He Mdjadji," by Mdjadji Shirinda and the Gaza

Sisters. A South African music publisher took note, however, and sued for copyright infringement. McLaren's mbaqanga-filled *Duck Rock* LP flopped; to this injury was added the insult of the Earthworks label's release of *Duck Food*, a compilation of the original versions of the songs Malcolm had appropriated. The whole shebang—square dance, hip-hop, mbaqanga, and McLaren's tuneless singing—sank beneath the waves of the American market with hardly a ripple. *Duck Food* inspired the Earthworks label's *Indestructible Beat of Soweto* series but Charisma lost their shirts. Vivienne Westwood's "Mud" collection launched her solo career as a fashion designer. McLaren moved on; opera, he decided, would be the next big thing.

∽

In the summer of 1984, an unmarked tape featuring those same Boyoyo Boys found its way into the box of cassettes that kept Paul Simon company as he drove from Manhattan to Montauk, Long Island, where he was building a house. Simon's 1983 reunion tour with Garfunkel had been a triumph, but his latest solo album, *Hearts and Bones*, hadn't sold. Over that summer, as he pondered his next move, the 1977 compilation *Gumboots: Accordion Jive Top Hits Vol. 2* became his favorite driving music. The tracks were all instrumentals and he found himself singing over them.

The tape sounded oddly familiar, like fifties rhythm and blues from a parallel universe. He figured it was African, but where? When he found out, his first thought (having turned down a Sun City invitation because of the anti-apartheid boycott) was "too bad it's not Zimbabwe." He asked Quincy Jones's opinion: "Don't worry about it" was the response, "it's not like you're going out there to cut a track with the white guys!" Harry Belafonte suggested he clear it with the ANC, but he preferred Jones's advice. Art, Simon believed, shouldn't need permission from politics to come into being.

In February 1985, straight off a flight from London, Simon sat in a Soweto bar with Boyoyo Boys sax player Barney Rachabane as the jukebox pumped out Parliament/Funkadelic. When he explained what he was after, Rachabane protested: "Why do you want that old-fashioned stuff?" He could put together a tight *modern* band for him, hot as Bootsy Collins and those American funk boys. His guys could play *anything*! Hux Brown, Jackie Jackson, and Winston Grennan, one of reggae's great rhythm sections, had voiced similar objections when Paul went to Jamaica to record "Mother and Child Reunion" in 1971. But Simon didn't care about "modern"; he liked classic styles, music with the spontaneous virtuosity and deep roots of the doo-wop and R&B he'd grown up with in 1950s Queens.

I first met Paul in the mid-sixties when he was an expat working the British folk circuit. He had developed an affection for English traditional music and was particularly taken with Martin Carthy's elegant way with a ballad. His good taste served him well: Carthy's arrangement of "Scarborough Fair" became "Parsley Sage Rosemary and Thyme" on the soundtrack of *The Graduate*. Simon also revered gospel quartets, recording "Loves Me Like a Rock" with the Dixie Hummingbirds and borrowing an invocation from gospel-show preaching for the title "Bridge over Troubled Water." Another old-fashioned melody that caught his ear was the turn-of-the-century Peruvian parlor song "El Cóndor pasa": "I thought there was no reason music from another culture couldn't be popular music."

Paul booked Ovation, the Johannesburg studio McLaren and Horn had used three years earlier, and summoned Roy Halee. Halee is Trevor Horn anti-matter, an engineer who loves recording groups live in the studio and produces rich, clear, three-dimensional sounds. Ovation had plenty of isolation booths, but Halee placed Simon and the others in a semi-circle in the middle of the room. Paul hadn't written any lyrics yet, so they just cut take after take of mbaqanga grooves, looking for a magic feel. The $600-a-day pay scale and Simon's assurances of fair composer credits had dispelled much of the lingering McLaren-inherited mistrust, but when Halee brought everyone into the control room for the first playback, the atmosphere shifted dramatically. The excited musicians had never heard their music sound so rich, so powerful—so world-class! Paul decided to extend his stay. It wouldn't be just a track or two, like that trip to Jamaica; he could hear a whole album sounding like this.

There were hiccups, of course. One accordionist went after Simon with a knobkerrie when asked to repeat the part he'd played correctly again and again. Paul struggled with the extra beats and bars the musicians added when the feeling took them. The more they played, the more intense, complex, and subtle the music felt to him. The tracks were so strong, they intimidated him: "It took a long time before I had the courage to start writing words over them." As a result, he says, some of the *Graceland* lyrics are "the best I ever did."

When he heard the accordion flourish at the front of the track that became "The Boy in the Bubble," he knew it would open the album. "It was like an announcement: you haven't heard *this* before!" Zulu songs often start that way, with mouth-bow or voice in the countryside, then acoustic guitar or concertina as the music migrated to the cities. As a fanfare heralding the birth of the "world music" phenomenon, it was perfect.

I ran into Simon at a party that autumn in London, where he was recording "Homeless" with the Zulu vocal group Ladysmith Black Mambazo. When he told me what he'd been up to I was skeptical. I owned a few Ladysmith records and had brought a treasured mbaqanga LP back from a trip to South Africa in 1970. In 1982, when my brother urged me to release a Ladysmith album on my Hannibal label, I had dismissed the idea as uncommercial. Now, as Simon talked, I felt the instinctive defensiveness of the aficionado when his arcane enthusiasm starts to become popular (particularly when said aficionado's label seems about to miss the boat). Paul sat me down next to him, put a cassette in the stereo, and—in a room full of chattering guests—proceeded to sing most of *Graceland* in my ear as the extraordinary backing tracks poured from the speakers. "Do you think it will sell?" he asked.

This music contravenes apartheid's determination to deny blacks not just a reasonable living but a meaningful identity . . . [A] rock and roll . . . of unimaginable vitality, complexity and high spirits was somehow thriving in apartheid's face.

—Robert Christgau on *Graceland* in the *Village Voice*, 1986

There is a theory, nicely documented in Leslie Woodhead's film *How the Beatles Rocked the Kremlin*, that the boys from Liverpool did more to bring down the Soviet Union than its delusional Five-Year Plans or Reagan's arms race. A Russian friend told me about his first fifteen seconds of hearing "Girl" on the banks of the Moscow River in 1974: "I realized immediately that whatever this music was, it represented the Truth, so everything I had learned up until that moment must be a Lie."

The South African government was initially delighted with *Graceland*, largely because anti-apartheid organizations were so appalled. The UN placed Simon on a blacklist of "sanctions violators"; Howard University's student body voted to condemn the "racist" project. (No one condemned the South African productions of Athol Fugard plays earning rave reviews in London and New York, though they seemed equally guilty of breaking the boycott.) Yet when White South African kids brought home the new Paul Simon album and put it on the turntable, housemaids looked up from scrubbing the floor and said, "That's *our* music." Smug grins were wiped off Boer faces as the world took *Graceland* and the culture it celebrated to its heart. Liberals were forced into awkward U-turns; no-nonsense activist Hugh Masekela publicly defended it (and would later join the *Graceland* tour), while one ANC official conceded that it was "strengthening the people in their resistance." The UN lifted Simon's blacklisting in time for the Grammys.

During their promotional visit to New York for the album's launch (including an appearance on *Saturday Night Live*), the nine members of Ladysmith Black Mambazo performed at the Brooklyn home of South African friends of mine. Their voices swooped and crooned, each one part of an elaborate mosaic. In a thrilling inversion of the Rockettes, their legs kicked for the ceiling on a grace note before stomping emphatically on the downbeat. I had imagined I knew their music, but that evening the full glory of its sophistication and strangeness was revealed, hand in hand with *Graceland*'s mass-media ubiquity as the "You Can Call Me Al" video appeared in heavy rotation on MTV. Chevy Chase and Simon enter a pink room; Chase lip-syncs Simon's vocal while the latter mouths some harmony parts and mimes playing a few instruments. The contrast between the bland White faces, the jokey set and clownish performances, and the powerful, exotic rhythms with an emphasis on growling bass notes, both vocal and instrumental, was surreal. When the touring began, Simon showcased not only the album but South African music in general, giving featured spots to Ladysmith, Miriam Makeba, Hugh Masekela, and to the backing band. "We used Paul as much as Paul used us," said the guitarist Ray Phiri. Ladysmith's leader Joseph Shabalala called Simon "Vulindlela"—the man who opens the door. The group was invited to appear in Michael Jackson's *Moonwalker* video.

The only non-*Graceland* artists to benefit from the bull market in South African music were Mahlathini and the Mahotella Queens, a combined powerhouse of talent and mbaqanga's biggest stars. Mahlathini was a "groaner" whose rough, deep tones were known in South Africa as his "goat voice" but marketed to northern hemisphere audiences as the "roar of the Lion of Soweto." France's Angoulême Festival invited them to headline the 1987 edition and they stayed on to record *Paris–Soweto*, an album that sold more than 100,000 copies in Europe. Volume after volume of Earthworks' *Indestructible Beat of Soweto* compilations—each containing a few Mahlathini tracks—flew out of LP bins.

If *Graceland* provided a taste of Zulu popular music, Mahlathini and the Mahotella Queens delivered a full dose of the real thing. The Queens decked themselves out in a stylized version of traditional Zulu garb, with dazzling headgear and brightly colored skirts a good deal shorter than those worn in Natal villages. On some album covers, Mahlathini looks like a smooth Township operator in dark suit and fedora, but he often appeared onstage in an off-the-shoulder lion skin like the one Louis Armstrong wears in the musically thrilling but otherwise embarrassing 1930 "soundie" *Rhapsody in Black and Blue*.

Mahlathini's harsh voice was a fantastic instrument, eclipsing the sandpaper standards set by Tom Waits or Satchmo himself with its power and musicality. The interplay between him and the Queens is pure African call-and-response while his domineering interjections evoke America's finest gospel preachers. The Queens' vocals veered from unison to a Zulu take on the Andrews Sisters, while behind them the Makgona Tsohle Band drove an even more powerful mbaqanga beat than Simon's rhythm section. For me and for many others, Mahlathini and the Mahotella Queens became the embodiment of South African music during the intense years of the late eighties and early nineties.

∽

"Intense" is an understatement. The Thatcher and Reagan governments tried to deflate the Anti-Apartheid Movement that had been active since the 1960s by declaring Mandela's ANC a "terrorist organization." But Jerry Dammers's magnificent 1984 single "Free Nelson Mandela" helped breathe life into the cause, as pressure on South Africa continued to build through cultural and sporting boycotts, economic embargos and disinvestment campaigns. Two months after *Graceland*'s release, in October 1986, Congress overrode Reagan's veto, enshrining sanctions in law and prodding other countries to follow the US example.

Simon was criticized for avoiding South African politics in his lyrics. "I'm not a good 'angry' songwriter," he says. "It was my job to express the utmost respect for these great musicians by writing the best songs I could. It wasn't my role to express their anger. I showed another side, where there was laughter, dancing, where life was being celebrated." The awed affection Simon felt during those Johannesburg sessions came through loud and clear in the rhythmic complexity and sensuality of the production. The world had heard South African music before, but mostly as novelty; *Graceland* was mass-market serious, even sexy. A culture that had been infantilized and suppressed was being embraced by a world most White South Africans longed to rejoin. For the fourteen million who bought the record and the crowds who went to the concerts and festivals, musical enthusiasm crossed effortlessly into political sympathy; how could they fail to want Nelson Mandela freed from captivity?

The anti-apartheid surge climaxed on June 11, 1988, as a worldwide audience of sixty-seven million watched the Mandela birthday concert at Wembley Stadium. Simon and the *Graceland* musicians weren't invited; the organizer Tony Hollingsworth told me that lingering bitterness within the movement for Simon's "sanctions busting" had ruled them out. A galaxy of stars—Eric Clapton, Dire Straits, Stevie Wonder, Peter Gabriel, the Eurythmics, Simple Minds, and Sting—

set out to unhook Mandela from the "terrorist" tag and succeeded brilliantly. The line-up was a sobering reminder of the mainstream's aversion to "foreign," though Mahlathini and the Mahotella Queens, Miriam Makeba, and Hugh Masekela were added as afterthoughts—the latter two out of respect for their long association with the movement and the former at the suggestion of music journalist Robin Denselow. Mahlathini's mbaqanga stood up against the rock phalanx a bit better than did Makeba or Masekela, but most broadcasters cut to news bulletins during the African sets or edited them out of delayed transmissions.

Horrified right-wing politicians pressured the BBC to drop the concert, but Hollingsworth's team had made their deals with the networks' entertainment departments and no executive wanted to miss out on the great ratings. Activists chafed against the "no political speeches" rule, but there was no arguing with the concert's impact. On February 11, 1990, Nelson Mandela was freed from prison and began negotiations with the South African government. Dammers, Hollingsworth, and *Graceland* had together created a "Walls of Jericho" moment. What was actually taking place on the streets of South Africa, though, was very far from what the northern hemisphere audience imagined.

Total number of plays for *Buena Vista Social Club* on commercial Latin radio in America? Zero. *O Brother, Where Art Thou?* (another Grammy winner) on country stations? Likewise, zilch. Once Muddy Waters had played the Newport Jazz Festival and toured Europe, how many Black DJs played his records? Cultures in which these artists blossomed had grown ashamed of such "old-fashioned" music. Their audiences were middle-class and White, radio exposure strictly NPR and BBC. The same was true for the South African phenomenon, only more so; to Mandela's ANC youth fighting on the streets of Soweto, Ladysmith and Mahlathini represented not just a shamefully acquiescent past, they also represented the enemy.

In northern hemisphere news reports, street fighting before and after Mandela's release was shown as Black youth against police and soldiers. But there was much African-against-African violence as well, with the Zulu Inkatha movement pitted against the ANC. Inkatha, created in the 1920s to defend Zulu hierarchies and traditions against both the White man and the modern world, had long received government support as a counterweight to the pan-tribal urban culture that threatened the "Homelands" system. Many Zulus defied tribal politics and joined the ANC, but Inkatha leader Chief Mangosuthu Buthelezi, insisted that "no one escapes being a member [of Inkatha] as long as he or she is a member of the Zulu nation."

Between Mandela's release and the 1994 elections, more than fourteen thousand South Africans (mostly ANC supporters) were killed. Not only did the government provide Inkatha with arms, they tilted regulations to help it seize the initiative in the Townships. Knobkerries, traditional Zulu clubs, were protected as ritual objects while all other weapons were outlawed. In October 1992, there was a massive *impi* (fighting team) march through central Johannesburg in full regalia; non-Zulu gatherings were forbidden. Government agents in blackface were spotted leading Inkatha battalions into ANC neighborhoods.

Township residents feared the "country" Zulus, most of whom stayed in hostels on short-term contracts. The migrant workers, in turn, hated the citified *isazis* (Zulu for "clevers"). Rural Zulus were often brought to the city specifically to fight the ANC, having been told it was a threat to their traditional ways and their honor; ANC-led strikes were seen as a plot to keep Zulu men from desperately needed jobs. Mandela and much of the ANC leadership were Xhosa, and for someone from that nation to fall amongst an Inkatha impi during those violent years was often fatal. Mandela, who had learned to respect Zulus and taken part in *indlamus* (Zulu martial ceremonies) while in prison, wanted to make a deal with Inkatha, but was overruled by the ANC executive committee.

While liberals in Europe and North America were discovering Ladysmith and Mahlathini, many right-wingers fell under a Zulu spell of their own. Laurens van der Post, Conrad Black, Jimmy Goldsmith, Prince Charles, and the zookeeper/gambler John Aspinall all visited KwaZulu-Natal and counted Buthelezi as a friend; by the mid-eighties, attending Zulu feasts and expressing enthusiasm for the culture had become a coded anti-ANC, pro-apartheid signal. Zulu objections to being subsumed in Mandela's "Rainbow Nation" put a positive spin on the government's ideology of "separate development."

By the mid-eighties, enthusiasm in South Africa for mbaqanga and *isicathamiya* (the a cappella form in which Ladysmith were the greatest stars) was almost exclusively Zulu. Like the regulars at the shebeen where Paul Simon and Barney Rachabane planned *Graceland*, ANC comrades preferred American funk and disco. English lyrics were seen as modern and anti-tribal, while tradition-based music played into the hands of the government's divide and rule strategy. These tensions invaded the *Graceland* tour: longtime exile and ANC stalwart Miriam Makeba resented Ladysmith's presence and cold-shouldered them throughout. Joseph Shabalala took Simon to a feast given by Buthelezi; Paul recalls being uncomfortable with the fierce tribalism—to say nothing of the on-the-spot cattle slaughtering.

Shabalala insisted he was never anti-ANC: "If you sing the truth, it is political. We give people back their melodies, their harmonies, and it gives them power." But in the wake of the student strikes of the mid-seventies, Township youth had rejected every aspect of tradition, burning down shebeens, smashing liquor bottles, and destroying halls where singing competitions took place. Their fury extended to *sangomas* (tribal healers), many of whom were "necklaced," meaning burned to death inside gasoline-filled tires. After 1976, Mahlathini and other "old-fashioned" singers had seen their bookings evaporate; a late-eighties Johannesburg concert to celebrate his success abroad drew fewer than a hundred people. Inkatha impis, meanwhile, often wore traditional costume, dancing and singing as they went into battle against the ANC.

In the decade before the 1976 uprising, 80 percent of South African recordings were Zulu despite only 26 percent of the population being from that nation. Habits die hard: mbaqanga instrumentals were sometimes used as backing tracks for defiant songs by marching students, much to Buthelezi's distress. His mother, Princess Magogo, was a singer and composer of praise songs, an ethnomusicologist who had instilled in her son a deep affection for Zulu music. As the violence escalated, he used it as a divider, condemning imported soul as anti-African and attacking Zulu musicians who performed anti-apartheid songs.

Zulu resistance to the modern world and their sense of entitlement goes back centuries, as does the world's fascination with them and their music. *Graceland* was not an aberration; it wasn't even the biggest-ever Zulu-based recording. A few months before Malcolm McLaren began his folk-dance crusade, a remake of one of the twentieth century's most popular songs hit #1 on the UK singles chart. Tight Fit's video is a ridiculous bit of camp from a very silly year. But no other piece of world music has ever come close to matching the popularity of this song about a young boy in the KwaZulu bush.

What is it about the male falsetto? On the greatest live rhythm and blues recordings women in the crowd can be heard screaming when B.B. King, James Brown, and Sam Cooke break their voices. You've seen footage of teenage girls fainting when Lennon and McCartney go "*oooo*" in "I Saw Her Standing There." I share Paul Simon's admiration for the late Rev. Claude Jeter of the Swan Silvertones, the greatest falsetto singer ever recorded. Is it androgynous sexual bravado, an evocation of orgasm, or perhaps the shamanic imitation of an animal's cry from a prehistoric hunters' ceremony? Did the Pharaoh's eunuchs sing in ancient Egypt? Did *castrati* remind aristocratic Europeans of our Rift Valley origins? None of these questions is answerable, but we can say that no falsetto vocal has been more widely imitated than Jay Siegel's on The Tokens' recording of "The Lion Sleeps Tonight."

"*In the jungle, the mighty jungle / The lion sleeps tonight.*" That melody originated in a one-take, spur-of-the-moment improvisation during a 1938 recording of "Mbube," a song about a Zulu boy braving lions in the Natal bush. The singer was Solomon Linda, leader of the Original Evening Birds, and he always sang *fasi pathi*—the falsetto part. Zulu men, more than those of any other southern African nation, left families at home and worked on temporary contracts in the cities; women being such a key part of Zulu musical tradition, falsetto vocals compensated for the lack of female voices in the new urban life.

Solomon Linda had come to Johannesburg from the remote Msinga Valley, where he grew up with the traditional Zulu vocal harmony known as *isigubudu*, after the way cattle horns curve inward, touching the body of the animal. Arriving in Jo'burg, he formed the Evening Birds to compete in the singing contests that were a staple entertainment for urban Zulus. Tall and a sharp dresser, Linda added slick footwork and a second bass voice to make his group stand out. The rural Zulu economy is based on cattle; they love singing about herd-boys defying and occasionally ganging together to kill a lion. "Mbube" is such a song.

Eric Gallo emigrated from Italy to South Africa in the late 1920s and started a business importing hillbilly records. While Whites may have had more money, they lacked Africans' passion for music, and Gallo soon built a recording studio and hired Sotho former choirmaster Griffiths Motsieloa as talent scout for his eponymous label. Motsieloa didn't have far to look: Solomon Linda was packing 78s in the Gallo warehouse.

Motsieloa felt the first two takes of "Mbube" didn't do it justice, so he invited the banjo, guitar, and piano players waiting for the next session to join in and give it extra energy. On the master take you can hear Linda hesitate before starting his golden descant over those two bassos riffing "*uyimbube, uyimbube.*" The recording was released on the day Hitler invaded Poland. By 1948, it had sold over 100,000 copies and that Zulu vocal style had become known as *mbube*. The Evening Birds were paid the normal pittance for the session and it never occurred to Gallo—or to Linda—to register the song or to calculate and pay composer royalties. The group became stars, but Linda kept his day job in the shipping room; "singer" was not a recognized employment category for the government pass he needed to avoid being sent back to Msinga.

Helped by "Mbube," Gallo grew to dominate the South African record industry. After the war, they secured local distribution rights to the American Decca label and, hoping for some reciprocal business, sent samples of their best-selling titles to Decca's New York office. The box languished in a corner until Alan Lomax, who was working on a field-recording project for the label, took it home to the apartment he shared with Pete Seeger.

Intrigued, Seeger brought "Mbube" to his group, the Weavers, and "Wimoweh" (Seeger's mishearing of *uyimbube*) became their showstopper. It might have topped the hit parade as their follow-up to "Goodnight Irene," but early in January 1952, just as "Wimoweh" reached #6, the House Un-American Activities Committee opened an investigation into the Weavers' politics. Nervous radio stations dropped it and the group went into a decade-long eclipse.

A few years later, the cover versions began: Yma Sumac, Jimmy Dorsey, and the Kingston Trio among many. In 1960, when the Tokens proposed recording it, the RCA producer insisted it needed an English lyric. The veteran songwriter George David Weiss ("Wonderful World," "Can't Help Falling in Love") turned Linda's one-line improvisation into the central melody and wrote some verses the group hated. Initially a B side, "The Lion Sleeps Tonight" started getting play in Massachusetts, spread rapidly down the East Coast, then soared like Siegel's falsetto to #1. The album cover featured a girl in a nightie with a large cuddly lion.

Over the years, "Wimoweh"/"The Lion Sleeps Tonight" has become one of the most-played, most-covered, highest-revenue-generating copyrights of all time, including serial visits to the Top Ten by falsetto-flaunting singers in America, Britain, and France. (The stuffed lion reappears in Tight Fit's 1982 video.) There were, of course, lawsuits. As an arranger of "traditional" material, Pete Seeger earned composer royalties on "Wimoweh" from the Weavers' and other 1950s versions. Gallo challenged, theoretically on behalf of Linda, although they had no publishing contract with him. They ended up with a share of "Wimoweh," and though Seeger asked his publisher, Howie Richmond, to make sure Linda got a taste, nothing made it past a Johannesburg law office until long after the singer's death.

Weiss's publishers took the view that "Lion" was an entirely new song, a position Richmond and Gallo contested. After years of skirmishing, everyone ended up with a share except Solomon Linda. When Disney included it in the score of *The Lion King*, the sums involved became astronomical. In 2000, *Rolling Stone* ran an account of the song's complex history by Rian Malan, scion of a powerful Afrikaner family (whose uncle was behind the "arms to Inkatha" scheme). This helped trigger a more equitable distribution of royalties and a sizable payment to Linda's niece, then living in poverty. The endless covers of "Lion" now include versions by Chet Atkins, R.E.M., and the New Zealand Army Band.

∾

The Zulu language is vast and complex: 19,000 words (as many as Shakespeare's English) with eight classes of nouns governing the inflection of verbs and adjectives. Zulu speech is measured and dignified; before urban migration, slang was non-existent, as it was considered shameful to speak ungrammatically. Zulu words often end in long vowel sounds, ideal for holding harmonized notes. Music is almost entirely vocal; without the large trees native to Central and Equatorial Africa, drumming has less prominence. The roots of the mbaqanga beat lie in the twanging of mouth-bows and the foot-stomps of singers as they celebrate a marriage or intimidate their enemies.

Like other Nguni peoples of southern Africa, Zulus sing in harmonies based on the mouth-bow's overtones and, like most cattle cultures, they sing a lot. Zulus mark weddings, births, deaths, feasts, battles, and every kind of military ceremony with music. Praise songs maintain tribal memory, and Zulu history, particularly around the turn of the nineteenth century, is worthy of Homer (with footnotes from the Kama Sutra).

Zulu boys and girls were expected to give each other sexual pleasure and, since penetration was not permitted before marriage, they learned to be inventive. When, in 1787, the young chief Senzangakona fell for the gorgeous Nandi at a secluded pool, that he should *amahle indlela* with her was unremarkable, but they got carried away and she fell pregnant. Senzangakona was obliged to marry her, but she suffered the disdain of his favored wives. Nandi and her son, Shaka, eventually moved back to her family kraal, where another chief, Ngomane, spotted the boy's potential for leadership.

Shaka's rise to power, the Oedipal victory over Senzangakona's impis, his revolutionizing of Zulu military tactics, and the vast conquests (stretching from the Indian Ocean to the Drakensberg Mountains and from the Tugela to the Usutu Rivers) parallel Napoleon's roughly contemporaneous career. There were further echoes of the great Corsican as Shaka undermined the power of the sangomas and attracted the fiercest warriors and most original minds from across southern Africa; generals he trained broke away to found the Matabele and Shona kingdoms and conquer lands as far north as Tanzania. The few Europeans to visit his capital were struck by its order and cleanliness (Zulus like to always "smell of water") and by the disciplined displays of his troops. Shaka was also a fine singer and composer, renowned for his punning wordplay; Mahlathini's and Shabalala's vocals provide modern evidence of how Zulus relish the sounds and subtleties of their language.

Apartheid apologists would seize on the movements of groups displaced by Shaka's campaigns to create myths about the Boers settling a land to which no African nation had an established claim. Portuguese sailors, however, had traded with Nguni-speakers on the Natal coast since the end of the fifteenth century. By the time Shaka was murdered in 1828 he had turned a scattering of chiefdoms into an empire; Brits and Boers, during the same period, were squabbling over control of the tiny Cape Colony.

An alternative view of the American Revolution is that it wasn't so much unfair taxes that angered the Colonists as the unnerving growth of the Abolitionist movement combined with British reluctance to break treaties and massacre inconveniently located natives. Licking their wounds after surrendering to the upstarts at Yorktown, the British took Cape Town from the Dutch in 1795. If they thought the Boers (Dutch for "farmers") would be more manageable than the obstinate and bloodthirsty Yankees (or have a different agenda), they couldn't have been more wrong.

Like many North American settlers, the Boers were religious fanatics in search of an Eden. The Cape was perfect: no jungles (the lyrics of "Lion" notwithstanding), no tsetse fly, endless stretches of arable land, and a climate mild enough for even the weediest Whites to survive and prosper. The fact that, like most such promised lands, it was already inhabited was unfortunate, particularly for the sitting tenants. Cheap labor was essential, but a slave economy worked best with ocean (or desert) between victim and homeland. Malay slaves were imported from the Dutch East Indies, but with limited success. Lascivious behavior among settlers, sailors, Malays, and local Khoikhoi (once known as Hottentots) turned Cape Town into a "Sodom" of inter-racial couples and their offspring, who, centuries later, would constitute a third classification under apartheid, the "Cape Coloureds." The horrified Boers fled up the coast and inland, seizing locals' land then "employing" them with ever harsher abuse and wage-cheating.

The British imposed a semblance of the rule of law, honoring (for a time) treaties with defeated kingdoms and allowing Africans to appeal against cruel treatment and non-payment of salaries. Though few colonial officials were seriously concerned with native rights, to the Boers it was an outrage to treat Africans as anything other than the subhuman children of Ham. The first Boer martyr was Cornelis Bezuidenhout, killed in 1815 by police after refusing to answer charges brought by his servants.

British settlers established libraries and a postal system and cherished their connections to the outside world. Boers yearned for isolation, were suspicious of schooling, hated books, banned music, and wanted to carry out God's plan for White domination without interference. Missionaries who converted and educated the locals infuriated them; respecters of African rights, souls, or traditions were accused of "Rousseau-ism," much like being called a "liberal" in today's America. (Archbishop Colenso, persisting in his view that natives who had died without hearing the Gospel were not *necessarily* burning in Hell, became one of nineteenth-century South Africa's most reviled figures.) Over the course of the century, the Dutch continued to move north and east, while back in London Parliament debated the cost of chasing them. In 1867, after an African girl spotted a sparkling stone in a creek bed, the argument was settled in favor of pursuit. Cecil Rhodes built railways, first to the vast troves of diamonds and then to the world's richest gold mines.

The Boers' counterpart to Rhodes was Paul Kruger, a man who read only religious tracts and helped found the Dopper Kerk, the most rigidly fundamentalist sect in a culture with plenty of competition. At the dawn of the twentieth century, the inevitable Boer War for control of South African diamonds and gold introduced the world to the concentration camp and the machine gun. Like post-Reconstruction American southerners, the defeated Afrikaners (as the more urban Boers now called themselves) imposed a vicious regime of racial suppression with few complaints from the exhausted victors.

☙

Charles Dickens's response to an 1853 London performance by a thirteen-strong troupe of Zulus was that they should be civilized off the face of the earth. "If we have anything to learn from these noble savages," he wrote, "it is what to avoid." The show, however, was a hit; English audiences loved the powerful singing as the company enacted a wedding ceremony, cooking a meal, and preparing for battle.

That last part was still very real. When Shaka's successor massacred Boer leader Piet Retief and a hundred of his party in 1838, "Zulu"—a name no twenty-first-century marketing consultant could better—became a byword for savagery. In 1879 at Isandlwana, a Zulu impi wiped out an 800-strong British regiment, surpassing the Sioux triumph over Custer at Little Big Horn three years earlier; widely reprinted drawings showed warriors with plumed headdresses, tooth necklaces, spears, cowhide shields, and feathered leggings. Like Sitting Bull and the Sioux, Zulus were thrillingly bloodthirsty and box-office gold. (Hollywood's take on Isandlwana is called *Zulu Dawn*, stars Burt Lancaster and Peter O'Toole, and includes tom-tom drumbeats straight from a *Lone Ranger* TV show.)

Throughout the late nineteenth and early twentieth centuries, Zulus starred in what Eric Hobsbawm called "giant new rituals of self-congratulation"; as European powers colored in the maps, expositions and world's fairs packaged and paraded Africans, South Sea Islanders, Orientals, and American "Indians." Crowds swarmed around the mocked-up villages while often ignoring engines, gadgets, and streamlined designs in the next aisle. No World's Fair was complete without a company of Zulus performing impi war dances and singing wedding songs while showing off their finery and their bodies. Astonishing victories over White armies had made them heroes to oppressed peoples; parades at the New Orleans Mardi Gras have been led for more than a century by Black celebrities chosen as that year's "King of the Zulus." A year before Isandlwana, a Zulu troupe performed in Paris at the Folies Bergère.

In 1892, a Zulu choir arrived in England for a concert tour. Half the program was performed in formal dress and featured beautifully harmonized Gilbert & Sullivan and Stephen Foster songs; after the interval, the group reappeared in blankets and headdresses, the women bare-breasted as they sang ceremonial songs. Critics were befuddled: some praised the strong, expert singing while deploring the nudity; others thought the "civilized" repertoire nowhere near as interesting as the traditional material; one was apoplectic in his conviction that they must be fakes, as no *real* Zulus would be tame enough to stand onstage in a coat and tie and sing to a hall full of Englishmen. At the Greater Britain Exhibition in 1899, De Beers presented a heavily guarded demonstration of diamond-processing; many of the skilled and well-dressed polishers, sorters, and clerks were Zulus. In a nearby exhibit, loincloth-wearing fellow Zulus acted out "primitive" village life; warriors and polishers no doubt met for a drink after work.

At the "Savage South Africa" exhibit the same year, military officials still smarting over Isandlwana tried to have the Zulus' battle dress and martial singing banned, but public demand forced them to back down. The savagery of Africans—*missionaries in a cooking pot!*—became a cliché of *Boy's Own* adventures, cheap novels, and history texts. This despite the fact that African warfare had consisted largely of ritual combat until clashes with heavily armed and merciless Europeans demonstrated the quaintness of that approach. As photography and new modes of mass communication brought the sickening reality of the Crimean, Boer, and American Civil Wars into the homes of the burgeoning middle classes, savagery needed to be deflected onto "un-civilized" peoples. Darwinism added a twist: if the wealthy nations could no longer claim to be "chosen by God," their material success demonstrated that, in their eyes, they were fitter for survival. The further back on an evolutionary scale colonized peoples could be placed, the more comfortable Europeans and Americans could feel in oppressing them. For some, "primitives" became a repository of the spirituality and connectedness that seemed to be evaporating from the industrialized world. Observers of the throngs around model Tahitian, Sioux, or Zulu villages began using the word *nostalgia* to describe a new form of sadness, a discomfort with the headlong pace of urban life.

The British took their revenge for Isandlwana, carving up the province they named Natal and giving the best land to White farmers. The proven policy of squeezing Africans onto small patches of infertile land, then hiring their desperate menfolk to work for starvation wages, was less successful with Zulus: many took one look at a mineshaft and refused to go down. They preferred becoming houseboys, clerks, janitors, or wagon drivers (to this day the Soweto taxi business is controlled by Zulus). In rural areas, "kaffir laws" meant agricultural work resembled slavery, including the right of farmers to punish with the whip. In 1906, Bambata (McLaren's Bronx mentor's hero) led an uprising against unfair taxes and land confiscations; in the suppression that followed, Zulus were hunted down like game.

Protestant missionaries arrived by the boatload; by the middle of the nineteenth century, South Africa was the most God-bothered land in all Creation. Many Africans were drawn to Christianity by the implicit promise of inclusion in a materially successful culture, and by the fact that churchmen tended to treat Africans slightly better than did most Whites. Music, including learning to play a Western instrument, was also an important lure. Getting to grips with the Sankey & Moody hymnal wasn't difficult; the Bantu people of southern Africa had been improvising harmonies all their lives. As one European (unusually open-eared for the nineteenth century) observed, "Many of the native songs . . . are very intricate compositions, in which the different parts are adjusted to each other with ingenious nicety."

First in the line of evangelical fire was the nation that, two centuries later, would take the lead in political protest and the singing that energized it. Just up the coast from the Cape Colony in the fertile Transkei are the Zulus' cousins the Xhosa. The two can understand each other's speech, though isiXhosa is studded with clicks ("Xh") borrowed from the region's original inhabitants, the Khoisan or "Bushmen" (and made famous by half-Xhosa Miriam Makeba's "Click Song"). When mines and factories began recruiting, many Xhosa moved permanently north since the Transkei was too far from the Rand for easy travel back and forth. They took quickly to urban life, loosening their connection to traditional ways; much of Black South Africa's political leadership has been Xhosa, as have many of the country's best jazz musicians and popular singers. The contrast between their response and that of the Zulus to the Anglo-Dutch invasion marked South African politics and culture from the start.

Xhosa monarch Ntsikana embraced Christianity in 1816, composing the hymn "Ulu Thixo mkhulu" (Thou Great God), based on a Xhosa praise song. Whites were horrified: "insufferable to the musical ear," "little better than a deadened howl," and a "low monotonous native air" were a few contemporary responses. In fact, it's a beautiful melody still widely sung, but most missionaries were deaf to African music. Just as the Xhosa were obliged to "cast off redness" (their traditional ocher body decoration) and adopt modest Western dress, they also had to abandon the sliding notes and pentatonic scales of Nguni song and learn to sing like Europeans. A Xhosa expression for conversion to Christianity was "to give up dancing." One Xhosa leader, Nxele, recanted his conversion, urging his people not to "pray with their faces on the ground and their backs to the almighty—but to dance and enjoy life and make love, so that black people multiply and fill the earth." He smeared his body in ocher and led ten thousand warriors against the British garrison at Grahamstown in 1819. Captured, he became one of the first prisoners of Robben Island and drowned "while attempting to escape."

Steve Biko, the murdered founder of the Black Consciousness Movement of the 1970s (a Xhosa, although he never emphasized that aspect of his heritage), described the missionaries' efforts:

> The missionaries stepped up their terror campaign on the emotions of the people with detailed accounts of eternal burning . . . [T]hey argued that theirs was a scientific religion and ours a superstition—all this in spite of the biological discrepancy which is at the base of

their religion! . . . [T]he converted . . . were taught to ridicule and despise those who defended the truth of their indigenous religion. With the ultimate acceptance of western religion, down went our cultural values!

Xhosa were the first South Africans to confront the contradictions of the "civilizing" mission of Christianity. Many learned English, dressed like Europeans, abandoned traditions (notably polygamy), and sang "correctly" in church. The more satisfactory Whites found their behavior, the more it marked "advancement." But neither social acceptance nor responsible jobs were ever on offer.

> *I turn my back on the many shames*
> *That I see from day to day;*
> *It seems we march to our very grave*
> *Encircled by a smiling Gospel*
> *For what is this Gospel?*
> *And what salvation?*
> *The shade of a fabulous ghost*
> *That we try to embrace in vain*

wrote Xhosa poet Jonas Ntsiko in 1884. Another African observed: "At first we had the land and the White man had the Bible: now we have the Bible and the White man has the land." The divide between Africans seeking White approval and those who had no interest in it found its most vivid expression in music. And with the arrival of a group of Black Americans in 1890, South African music was changed forever.

"Just our coons," explained the captain of the Confederate gunship *Alabama* in 1862, following a sensational impromptu concert by the (enslaved) crew at the Cape Town docks during a refuelling stop. Subsequent musical inroads from America were less authentic: by the 1870s, minstrel shows were all the rage in the Cape Colony. Whites blacked up; Xhosa incorporated their traditional music into the minstrel-show format and put on shows for workers from other parts of South Africa. For descendants of Malay slaves, the minstrel tradition continues to this day.

In post–Civil War America, music had become a cultural battleground. Southern and northern Whites united in their love of minstrelsy, which managed the neat trick of paying tribute to the music of the very people the shows were designed to ridicule. Countering this were the Jubilee choirs, their spirituals a symbol of Black dignity and aspiration. (They were named for the Old Testament's "Jubilee Year" tradition, in which slaves were occasionally set free.) Though relatively sedate compared to modern gospel music, the singing was inimitably African-American, safe from appropriation by Whites armed with a burnt cork.

When Orpheus McAdoo brought his Virginia Jubilee Singers to South Africa in 1890, the effect was electric. Here was a group of free Blacks, singing, in the words of a Cape Town critic, "as if they were lifting up their voices in praise of God with hopes of liberty." From the opening song of their first concert, they resolved the question of how hymns should be sung. As thrilled as Black South Africans were, White churchmen were horrified; the joyful noise of the Jubilee Singers bore little resemblance to the somber intonations they were teaching. Jubilee singing also, by implication, raised the issue of African languages and Christianity; the flowery cadences of Nguni speech had been hard to reconcile with the staid meters of Anglo-Saxon compositions, but this African-American style was liberating. (As Xhosa composers began merging traditional melodies and language with the structures of Christian hymns, Zulu preacher Isaiah Shembe inserted Christian phrases into shamanic chant while wearing the animal skins of a sangoma.)

Close on the heels of the Jubilee Choir came Black American preachers from the Abyssinian Baptist and AME (African Methodist Episcopal) churches. Over the next twenty years these new sects, their hierarchies free from White control, gained converts all over South Africa. Many Abyssinian churches practiced "lining out": call-and-response singing with roots in West Africa. This could lead—*heaven forfend!*—to improvisations, the building-up of rhythmic intensity, hand-clapping and foot-stomping. Missionaries became alarmed when even their own choirs began to "move," forcing some to permit "uniform movements under the control of a conductor." The Catholic Church in Brazil, Cuba, and Mexico had responded to similar pressures by tolerating African slaves and indigenous peoples grafting their gods and their music onto Christian saints and rituals. For puritanical Protestants, this was inconceivable. A scene in Malcolm McLaren's beloved *Zulu* has the missionary Jack Hawkins's daughter watching dancing Zulu girls suggestively offering knives to their chosen warriors; Ulla Jacobssen's expression sweetly combines horror and arousal.

∽

Zululand, shielded by the Drakensberg Mountains, contained little in the way of gold or diamonds and was also barren ground for missionaries; until well into the twentieth century, Christian converts were ostracized, no longer considered members of the Zulu nation. Those who did join a church referred to hymns as *iMusic*; their own songs were *isiZulu*, something entirely different.

As South Africa's growing economy inexorably drew them in, *gxagxa*, a halfway culture of Zulu migrant workers, emerged. Its symbol was the concertina, a good "walking instrument"; it was easier to hitch rides if you were playing one, and the dialogue between the left and right hands worked nicely with the rolling gait of the long-distance traveler. From the 1870s onwards, Italian and German manufacturers dumped cheap concertinas on the local market, with Africans gravitating to the "two-reeds-per-note" models that mimicked the dense texture of an Nguni male chorus. A striking image from the Boer War is of thirty Zulu concertina players leading a march of seven thousand workers fleeing starvation after the closure of the mines. The intro to "The Boy in the Bubble" evokes this adaptation of isiZulu to the squeezebox.

Nguni musicians had been dabbling with Western instruments since the sixteenth century, when Portuguese traders first swapped guitars for ivory. Mine overseers employed guitarists for the "gumboot" dance contests which had evolved out of coded foot-tapping, the only way miners could communicate in the deep, waterlogged tunnels. This guitar style was called *maskanda*, a Zulu adaptation of the Dutch word "*musikant*." Maskanda songs were often epics of Zulu history, accompanied by a strum that echoed rhythms derived from the mouth-bow, with chords alternating between two fundamentals a tone apart in cyclical patterns. The shift to the now-dominant picking (*ukupika*) style gives us a glimpse of a musical pioneer: John Bhengu, known as Phuzushukela, the "sugar drinker," who developed the percussive arpeggios used to this day in maskanda and mbaqanga recordings. Music is Exhibit A for the "Great Man" school of history; a list could extend from Bhengu to João Gilberto, via Scott Joplin, Louis Armstrong, Carlos Gardel, Oum Kalsoum, Sidiki Diabaté, and countless others, originals whose personal styles became accepted as "typical" of powerful musical cultures.

This growing mastery of Western instruments should have pleased churchmen and educators, but most were aghast, banning all instruments, traditional or modern, from churches and mission schools (with the exception of brass for Salvation Army–type bands). Their problem was rhythm; concertinas, guitars, and, later, pianos enabled African virtuosos to adapt traditional dance patterns into high-energy modern performances, creating a sensation among their listeners but, from the White point of view, dragging African society backwards towards "savagery."

To many Africans, the modernity of maskanda made renditions of the same songs by flute, mouth-bow, and voice seem quaint and old-fashioned. Clothing kept pace as Zulu women swapped traditional skins for European blankets, symbolizing their new power as they took charge in the villages while the men stayed away on longer and longer work contracts. Many Zulu women defied their chiefs, the government, and often their husbands by taking domestic work in the Rand. (Houseboy jobs for Zulus had evaporated as White husbands began having second thoughts about leaving their wives at home alone with a retired warrior from an impi with a high White body count.)

In the decades after the Boer War, governments supported traditional kings and chiefs as a counterweight to the growing urban politicization and as allies in the policy of keeping work in White areas "temporary." This could cut two ways: Zulu hard men were known to beat White employers who abused servants, then disappear back into the steep valleys of the Natal bush. The number of those identifying as Zulu grew far beyond Shaka's old boundaries; the appeal of Zulu music and culture cannot be separated from the proud virile image they conveyed at a time when African men were being systematically emasculated by ever more extreme governments.

The hymn sung at the founding convention of the African National Congress in 1912 was "Nkosi Sikelel' iAfrika." (The White-supremacist National Party was formed two years later.) Composed by mission-educated Xhosa Enoch Sontonga and based on the melody of a Welsh hymn, it is a plea—in Xhosa, Sotho, and Zulu—for God to bless the land. With added verses in Afrikaans and English it is now the national anthem. Like many South African hymns, it is set in a minor key; what, after all, did Africans have to be cheerful about at the dawn of the new century?

The other great song of the period is called simply "iLand Act"; it was sung at marches protesting the 1913 legislation assigning ownership rights over six-sevenths of the territory to one-third of the population. The contradictions that would eventually put an end to apartheid were all in play in the first decades of the twentieth century. For example, while the government was anxious to keep Africans at a safe distance on Native American–style "reservations," the riches of the Rand were too deeply buried to be extracted by Klondike-style prospectors, so only vast armies of poorly paid Africans would suffice. Despite mine operators resenting having to train new teams every season, Afrikaner ideologues insisted that all Black workers be temporary. As word spread of the harsh conditions and risible pay, recruitment had to stretch farther and farther afield, turning the Rand "Locations" (miners' shantytowns) into melting pots of men too far from home for seasonal migration. When White workers got wind of a plan to use low-paid Africans as clerks and managers, they threatened revolution, electing a government in 1924 that was committed to barring Africans from administrative work as well as from the education that would qualify them for it. Africans who'd converted to Christianity were alienated by laws that kept them in thrall to remote tribal hierarchies, sangomas and all. Location housing was often torn down on grounds of sanitation, as if that were the fault of the residents rather than the government's refusal to install sewers. As one official acknowledged, "We cannot afford a wage to make it possible for a [Black miner] to live in an urban area"; pay was sufficient only for "the bare . . . necessities of life as understood among barbarous and underdeveloped peoples."

Growing up in the Transkei, Nelson Mandela was taught that to be Christian was to be civilized. Yet he soon discovered that only the Communist Party was prepared to support Black aspirations without condescension or paternalism. With all attempts to ameliorate the harshness of White rule thwarted, music became the expression of African anger, hope, misery, and joy. As a pressure cooker brewing a rich and powerful musical culture, South Africa from the 1920s to the 1980s can only be compared to America in the bitter wake of the Civil War.

"*Ndunduma*" is the Zulu word for the dumps piled high with mine waste that dot the landscape around Johannesburg, and it also became the name for the mix of music heard in South African cities in the 1910s and early '20s: guitarists and concertina players entertained on street corners; *stockfel* bands, raising money for housing, local businesses, and bail, played a kind of Nguni ragtime as they marched through the Locations; a high-kicking Sotho courtship dance called *famo* became a kind of speed-dating craze in the Townships; in Cape Town, Xhosa, Malays, and Cape Coloureds danced to three-chord rags with a funked-up *vastrap* or *tiekiedraai* beat borrowed from the Dutch; in Durban, the hook from a popular song started the "*tula ndivile*" beat. Reuben Caluza, king of Zulu vaudeville, brought all these styles together, touring every corner of the land with a show that mixed ragtime, Jubilee-style choral singing, maskanda, slick choreography, and silent films. He was a unifier, teaching everyone "Nkosi Sikelel' iAfrika" and exposing them to one another's music; his was the ladle that stirred the musical stew that would become known as *marabi*.

Women had always been the brewers; many followed the men to town, setting up as shebeen queens in opposition to the government-monopoly beer halls. The halls were sad, impersonal, men-only places;

you went there just to get drunk. Shebeens hired musicians to pound away on harmoniums or pianos, with percussion from pebble-filled cans supplying a beat for dancing. In shacks with no electricity or plumbing, hidden behind corrugated iron, down shantytown alleyways, marabi was born. The relentless three-chord cycle of I–IV–V–I that marks South African jazz to this day became the mold into which anything could be poured: Zulu epics, Sotho chants, Xhosa wedding songs, Christian hymns, or Tin Pan Alley pop.

Since Africans were forbidden to buy spirits, corrupt policemen and poor Whites supplied the brand liquor, though most drank home brew: traditional millet and sorghum beers or a lethal concoction called *skokiaan*. (Some may recall Louis Armstrong's 1954 hit of that name, a cover of a shebeen anthem.) Modikwe Dikobe gives us the recipe:

> *Drink my dear*
> *This is pure brandy*
> *Brewed in Korea*
> *Bottled in Malay Camp*
> *Delivered by the flying squad*
> *Don't cough, my dear*
> *You'll scare the customers*
> *The ingredients are excellent:*
> *Methylated spirit, tobacco juice, yeast, marijuana*
> *And, of course, a pint of vinegar*
> *For colouring*

To "respectable" Africans, marabi was shameful and low; for everyone else, it was the birth cry of an urban working class. Sex was at the heart of the conflict: many churchgoing Africans bought into the Victorian ideal of women as chaste and dignified, while Zulu and Sotho girls were often happy to "wipe the spears" of the men after a battle (or a hard day in the mine or factory). And women could take their pick (or name their price): in 1900 there were twelve men to every woman in the Rand Townships, by 1927 six, and in 1939 it was still three. Even censorious observers acknowledged that great music was being created: "The atmosphere was obscene," reported Herbert Dhlomo, "and yet what naturally talented players the . . . concerts had! . . . [M]en who, like tribal bards of old, created beauty they knew not."

Marabi evoked the music of wedding feasts back home while its inexorable locomotive beat satisfied the Nguni taste for repetition. During this same era in South Side Chicago and Harlem, African Americans fleeing peonage in the South developed jazz and urban blues, while Pontic Greeks in shanty towns outside Piraeus and Thessaloniki were singing the hashish-infused songs of displacement that became *rembetika*. Adventurous labels created industries around those forms as well as building catalogues of *son* in Havana, tango in Buenos Aires, flamenco in Seville, and *thumri* in Calcutta. But since no one in the Locations could afford a gramophone, marabi went unrecorded. Legends grew around Ntebejana, Boet Gashe, Toto, Highbricks, and Nine Fingers, but their music has vanished beneath the waves of history.

After the "black peril" election of 1929 produced a resounding victory for the Right, the government declared war on marabi culture. Shantytowns were razed and shebeens closed; the authorities were determined to profit from their beer-hall monopoly. (Draining joy from city life and turning African men into stupefied drunks were side benefits.) Ragtime and jazz were condemned in the same "scientific" language employed in America—"pathological, nerve-irritating, sex-exciting." With such great marketing, the music's popularity continued to grow. Promoters, many of them women schooled in the hard world of shebeen management, began renting halls for the "concert & dance" evenings that would dominate African entertainment in the 1930s. Bigger stages meant bigger bands; back-alley keyboard virtuosos emerged as orchestra leaders and arrangers.

Hollywood musicals were the new sensation; kids pooled their pennies so one could watch a film then "do" it for the others from memory, complete with sound effects and songs. Zuluboy Cele's Jazz Maniacs took in a matinee of *Pennies from Heaven*, stayed for the second show, then dazzled dancers that night with a great arrangement of the title song. With swing 78s on the market, gramophones made their way into the

Townships, with Benny Goodman and the Mills Brothers topping the list of America's most influential musical exports. The Nguni ear for harmony welcomed challenges and the Mills Brothers' clustered chords fascinated singers; their influence can still be heard in Johannesburg's vocal sound. Goodman's presence would be felt for decades in the clarinet-imitating pennywhistle magicians of the *kwela* craze, while the best gumboot dancers were avid students of Fred Astaire's movies.

For the aspirational, America remained the arbiter; as McAdoo's Choir had given the green light to Africanized hymns, Duke Ellington, Louis Armstrong, and Teddy Wilson now linked jazz to glamour, wealth, and status. The Black bourgeoisie (or what passed for such in a society in which all were poor) was won over—but they weren't the only ones. Gangs had always been a feature of Township life; in the early years, Sotho *amalaitas* wearing conical hats and colorful blankets would surround a victim, covering him with a pale cloth that turned crimson as they beat him to death with clubs. Patterns of conflict were established that would last the century; the Zulu-led Russians (so named in honor of the Crimean War killers of the hated General Cathcart) fought pitched battles against the ANC over strikes they felt were unfair to temporary workers. Finger-popping *tsotsis* in zoot suits and fedoras prowled the Townships, demanding protection money from concert promoters, robbing workers dressed up for a payday night on the town and carrying off good-looking girls straight from the dancefloor. The toughest of these gangs was called, of course, The Americans.

Peter Rezant's Merry Blackbirds was the hot orchestra, setting the (Whites-only) dancefloor alight at the 1936 Johannesburg World's Fair. (Like Chicago in 1893, Johannesburg called its expo site "White City.") The musicians' prowess and the flashy glamour of the "concert & dance" scene alarmed the government but intrigued many Whites; downtown club owners began hiring Black groups. White players, suffering in the comparison, demanded a color bar; determined managers resorted to registering band members as busboys, hiding their horns and handing out mops when police appeared.

One thirties story involves a White orchestra who appropriated the name Jazz Maniacs, then sued Zuluboy for degrading the brand with his unschooled "native" musicians. Cele challenged them to appear in front of the courthouse, where both bands were handed a new arrangement; the Whites struggled but the African Maniacs sight-read it flawlessly. Case dismissed!

∽

Progressive Whites, unnerved by swaggering, urban-dwelling Africans in stylishly draped suits, tried to encourage traditional culture while also warning against a return to "savage" ways. Favored events included Welsh-inspired Eisteddfods, where prizes were awarded for politely arranged Nguni choral singing; officials remained blissfully unaware that many of the songs included metaphors that signified "We're going to kill you bastards." The Zulu writer and activist Mark Radebe championed folk traditions, but had a horror of music that sounded "too African" and believed that assimilation was essential. Well-meaning sponsors sent J. P. Mohapeloa, a Sotho composer who wrote strikingly original choral works combining African and Western harmonies, to music college, but when he returned his compositions were no longer so interesting.

Heedless of White approval or disapproval, traditions were alive in the Townships. Hugh Masekela remembered childhood Sundays filled with warrior dances by troupes of Sotho, Venda, Tswana, Ndebele, Pedi, and Zulu, as well as gumboot contests of astounding skill. These events served as newcomers' defence against city-dwellers' snobbery and condescension. In the countryside, song lyrics warned of innocent youths arriving in "iGoli" (Johannesburg, City of Gold) and being lost to *iqilika* (alcohol).

The government refused to build infrastructure for permanent residents, but found money for temporary workers' hostels. These became homes-from-home for Zulus, keeping them apart from urbanites who mocked them as "turkeys" (since, to them, formal Zulu sounded like "gobbling"). The Rand's lingua franca was now a slang-filled blend of English, Zulu, Afrikaans, and Sotho known as Tsotsitaal or Flytaal— gangster-talk or fly-talk. The new argot rubbed comfortably along with multilingualism: Solomon Linda's discoverer, Griffiths Motsieloa, had made his mark in vaudeville with a recitation of "Old Mother Hubbard" in English, Xhosa, Afrikaans, and Sotho.

The Jazz Maniacs would start their shows with popular American numbers to get the crowd dancing, then move to up-tempo versions of marabi classics; when crowds heard their own songs coming at them from a swinging big band, they went crazy. Encouraged by White jazz buffs, the hottest players dreamed of touring Europe, or even America. One band from Durban called Lucky Stars, whose repertoire consisted of big-band arrangements of Zulu melodies, received a firm offer, but the outside world never got to hear them; "Taking aborigines to London or other European capitals has not been very productive of any happy results in the past" was the rationale for denying their passport applications.

The war that began the day "Mbube" was released transformed South Africa; factories ramping up production brought tens of thousands more workers into the Rand. Hendrik Verwoerd, editor of *Die Transvaler* (and later, after his Nationalists won the 1948 election, minister of "Native Affairs" and "architect of apartheid"), was doubly outraged: not only were cities now surrounded by millions of Blacks who showed no signs of leaving, but their war effort was against his beloved Hitler.

Sophiatown had been built for poor Whites, but downtown Johannesburg proved too far and the open sewers too near, so it became "Little Harlem," filled with dance halls, clubs, and record shops. As the music scene grew, gangsters with the cash to buy instruments started "owning" orchestras. Musicians could be hired and fired on whims and often got caught up in violent feuds; Zuluboy Cele's body was found on a railroad track. Alcohol, prison, and disease added to the high death toll among musicians.

The war introduced bands in Durban and Cape Town to Black American servicemen and sailors; playing for these enthusiastic and knowing audiences was a thrill. In 1943, the ANC produced a pageant entitled *Progress of a People*, in which South African actors and singers portrayed Joe Louis, George Washington Carver, Paul Robeson, and Marian Anderson. The real Robeson responded with an article for *Bantu*

World urging Africans to focus on their own culture and stop chasing after American and European models.

Nothing showed more clearly how little control elites—White or Black—had over popular culture than the *tsaba-tsaba*. As outrageous in its time as booty-quivering Jamaican dancehall in the 1980s, tsaba-tsaba involved rubber-legged couples advancing and retreating, with plenty of grinding and grabbing in between. Meaning, roughly, "back off!," tsaba-tsaba swept all before it in the early 1940s; bands had no choice but to play its un-jazzy African rhythms. Meanwhile, the first glimmers of bebop began arriving via Black American sailors, which set Township jazz off on its journey—as in the US—into something for intellectuals, complete with earnest listening sessions and berets.

1944 saw the formation of the ANC Youth League; Mandela and Buthelezi were both charter members. With African pay still, despite the boom, at 10 percent of White rates, confrontations with the government escalated; in 1946, 75,000 striking miners were driven back underground at gunpoint. Following the 1948 election, Verwoerd's Nationalists began constructing their ideal society: all Africans must register as a member of a particular "tribe"; racially mixed concerts, plays, church services, and sex were outlawed; Bantu education was dumbed down so as not to "over-train" the natives; communal farming was outlawed on the grounds it was communistic (undermining the government's pet chiefs in the Homelands); Black entrepreneurs had to turn their businesses over to Whites (carrying on, if they were lucky, as employees). The Communist Party was the only opposition group not to have separate "Black" and "White" sections, thus proving that race-mixing was a Red plot. Dutch *Kerk* sermons resembled today's from Tehran (or perhaps Mississippi): authority must be obeyed, democracy is against God, evolution is a lie, music is sinful.

Africans, it was claimed, were "ill suited to city life." According to White photographer Jürgen Schadeberg, though, "Sophiatown was like a Mediterranean city—full of life and excitement; colonial Johannesburg was boring and dull . . . very much behind the times. You couldn't even get a decent cup of coffee in Johannesburg. Whereas Sophiatown Africans were modern people." The new *Drum* magazine chronicled the excitement: boxing matches, beauty contests, concerts, celebrities, pin-ups and gossip. *Drum*'s journalist Arthur Maimane found that "people felt very positive about the future . . . they did not take the apartheid regime seriously. It was so ridiculous, it couldn't last."

In a Zulu marriage, the bride price is often negotiated in song; at the wedding, the two families would try to out-harmonize each other. Before Shaka, war between clans was often averted by *ngomas*: song-filled competitive martial displays. Shaka himself would mark a victory by belting out a triumphant anthem with his generals in the home of the vanquished chief. Mine overseers began organizing ngomas as an alternative to fighting between groups of frustrated workers far from home. In Durban, pitched battles engulfed entire districts in the wake of disputed ngomas.

By the 1930s, Zulu workers had distilled ngomas into weekly singing contests. Competition bred complexity: nine to a dozen voices singing Wesleyan hymns, traditional wedding songs, minstrel melodies and Tin Pan Alley tunes in complex arrangements, with leads, basses, and *fasi pathi* (falsettos) entering at different points in an eight-beat cycle derived from Nguni ritual music. During World War Two, improvised interjections became known as "bombings," after the explosions seen in newsreel footage. Flimsy meeting-hall stages couldn't stand up to fierce Zulu stomps, so footwork became as intricate as the singing: elegant, delicate steps miniaturized the impi moves and the rapid "going home" tiptoeing of the AME church, or even conjured up the Cakewalk. This style of *ngom'ebusuku* (night music) came to be known as isicathamiya, after the "stalking approach" used to seduce audiences and judges.

Zulu warriors were known for their finery, so sharp, colorful matching suits with white gloves, white shoes, bow ties, and a white sash for the leader became de rigueur. Judging was vulnerable to dispute, so the safest solution was to entice an unchallengeable (and neutral through ignorance) White man with food and drink. A tramp was ideal since his clothes would be gratifyingly grubby compared to the participants'. Awarding a goat as first prize was not only of practical use, it avoided overvaluing the White man's money. This was the world Solomon Linda conquered and that was renamed *mbube* in his honor.

～

Linda's Original Evening Birds may have ruled the isicathamiya circuit, but they were barely mentioned in *Drum* and were never asked to endorse products aimed at the growing African market. Sophiatown's own harmony sensations, the Manhattan Brothers, became South Africa's first urban superstars; appropriately, one of the quartet was Xhosa, one Zulu, one Sotho, and one Tswana.

Like the Beach Boys or the Jackson 5, the Manhattan Brothers began as a kiddie act managed by one of the boys' fathers. Having discovered the group singing on a street corner, Gallo launched them as soon as pressing plants resumed production in 1946; their sound—Mills Brothers harmonies with Jubilee tones and isicathamiya flamboyance applied to circular Xhosa melodies with a Tin Pan Alley middle eight—was perfect for the post-war era. Recording in Xhosa, Sotho, English, and Zulu, their sales regularly topped 100,000. They wore custom-made suits from Levinson's but had to sneak into the exclusive shop for after-hours fittings so as not to upset White customers. Police often refused to believe they were stars, forcing them to sing and tap-dance in the station house before releasing them. Baritone Rufus Khoza's fake American accent was so skilled that he became the only Black South African able to purchase liquor from a store.

As a thirteen-year-old in New Jersey in 1955, I heard the Manhattan Brothers' biggest hit, "Lakutshona iLanga," re-recorded in English as "Lovely Lies," on *Bob Horn's Bandstand*; the kids liked slow-dancing to it, but it never got past #45 on the *Billboard* chart. I had no idea who they were or where they came from, but something about the harmonies and accents intrigued me enough to buy a copy. I heard The Weavers' version of "Wimoweh" around that time, but never imagined the two having anything in common. The bland English lyrics—"*You tell such lovely lies / With your two lovely eyes*"—had little connection to Mackay Davashe's brilliant original about a desperate search for a lover in police stations, hospitals, bars, gutters and morgues. Fifteen years later, I produced "Davashe's Dream," the Brotherhood of Breath's tribute to this great figure of South African music, and, largely unaware of his history, recorded Rufus Khoza singing on a Dudu Pukwana track in a London studio. The Manhattan Brothers paved the way for a generation of South African stars, but their path to an international career was blocked in the usual way: denial of passports until their moment had passed.

Something in the 1950s air made even White South African kids rebellious. Though the government refused to countenance television (so no equivalent of *American Bandstand* or *6.5 Special*), *Blackboard Jungle* was banned and radio stations wouldn't dream of playing rock 'n' roll, teenagers found something on urban street corners to excite their transgressive impulses: kwela. Groups of African pennywhistle and guitar players would perform as passersby filled a hat with coins, while boys with ducktail haircuts and turned-up collars hung around, intrigued by the sound. The music's name derived from the way police would shout "*kwela kwela*" (climb up, climb up) when loading street-corner groups into paddy wagons. (Busking was good cover for dice games.)

Township gangs in the 1920s liked to parade, but lacked the funds and training for brass instruments. Northern peoples such as the Tswana and Pedi had always played wooden flutes, so they took easily to the cheap flageolets imported after World War One, and a marching battalion playing whistles made an impressive noise mimicking (or mocking) the colonial soundtrack of brass or bagpipes. Willard Cele—no relation to Zuluboy—revolutionized pennywhistle techniques, placing the mouthpiece at a sharp angle between his teeth and blowing very hard, thereby thickening the sound and enabling him to bend notes.

Kwela's chord progressions stuck to the classic marabi I–IV–V–I, with multiple whistles evoking big-band horn sections and a guitar strumming the infectious beat. In a street-corner competition, flamboyance rules, and Benny Goodman's clarinet solos inspired the best players. In 1956, imagining that kwela might remind British listeners of skiffle, a UK record label made Elias Lerole and His Zig-Zag Jive Flutes' recording of "Tom Hark" the first South African track to reach a foreign Top Ten. When Ted Heath's orchestra covered it, clarinets completed the circle, imitating pennywhistles.

Kwela was perfect fifties crossover music: melodic, bouncy and devoid of overt sexuality. Plus, it was almost always instrumental, so no off-putting foreign words. In a nod to kwela's legacy, Paul Simon added a pennywhistle solo on "You Can Call Me Al." The hottest players were Lemmy Special and Spokes Mashiyane. In 1965, while working at the Newport Folk Festival, I collected Spokes at the bus station, then recruited a backing band for him among folkies with a vague idea of kwela rhythm. He and the audience didn't quite know what to make of each other; my most vivid memory of his visit is a jam session in the musicians' canteen with an Appalachian fiddler, a couple of guitarists, and Spokes improvising soaring solos on Celtic melodies.

He was a quiet, unassuming man who, I later discovered, had won a stunning victory against his country's racist systems. By the late fifties, Spokes was selling millions of records, the first Black artist to reach deep into the White market. Gallo was galled that he belonged to their upstart rival, Trutone, so when his contract was up they enticed him with a revolutionary concession: *royalties!* South African labels had always insisted that paying percentages to African musicians was somehow "illegal." Spokes's new deal changed everything; African composers even started registering their songs for copyright. Furious radio stations cut their quota of African records and insisted that Black songwriters were only due half the White rate.

Newport would have been as shocked by Spokes turning up with a saxophone as it was by Dylan's electric guitar. But by 1965, kwela was passé and back home Spokes was playing sax jive, the tougher, modern sound of urban South Africa. After the 1960 massacre at Sharpeville, the destruction of Sophiatown, and the removal of its residents to the distant South Western Townships (known to all by its acronym, Soweto), who could grin and bounce to pennywhistles?

Sophiatown had to die. It had aspired to an American aesthetic as seen through George Raft movies and Weegee photographs; gangsters drove huge convertibles and wore zoot suits while shebeens stayed open till dawn so customers could avoid the curfew police. Naturally, the government found the richness of life there and the fact that there was no clear pass-checking demarcation from neighboring White areas intolerable. For Africans its memory would live forever. "*Have you heard the white people say? / Let's all go to Meadowlands / Our beloved place,*" sang Nancy Jacobs and Her Sisters (in English) about the proposed move to Soweto. Another verse (in Tsotsitaal) was more to the point: "*We're not leaving; we're staying right here / Staying here in our beloved place!*"

Anthony Sampson, the White editor of *Drum* in the early 1950s, had the wit to hire the "Meadowlands" pianist, Todd Matzikama, despite his never having written an article: "He used to go at the typewriter the way he played piano. There was rhythm in his every sentence." Matshikiza profiled Sophiatown musicians, actors, boxers, and lowlifes in a style that became identified with *Drum*:

> Her first name is Amaren. Her second is locked up in her bosom . . . Her story is as deep as her dark eyes. Her grandpa was an Arab craftsman, sailor, musician and trader who sold black people to white people for calico! He sold mostly tall black people, because the taller you were the more calico he got for you. She lives her own young life among a closed circle of unknown [undivulged] friends. But she's a breeze of an actress, and what a voice! She loves the Rand like liquorice and wants to write a big book . . . Amaren was dancing, singing and acting professionally at sixteen. She has written a number of "jungle" songs on themes from East Africa, which she remembers from childhood. She has sung some of these over the air. Very emotional, yes, and easily upset; but brimful of life when the occasion arises. Amaren is an unabashed actress.

In 1956, Matshikiza revisited his first creative love, composing "Uxulu" (Peace), a cantata commemorating Johannesburg's seventieth anniversary. In the wake of this success—and with bulldozers advancing ever closer to the heart of Sophiatown—he created a stage musical based on the tragic life of boxing great Ezekiel Dlamini. Starring Miriam Makeba and the Manhattans, *King Kong* opened in 1959 at Witwatersrand University, an academic enclave where authorities could not prevent Whites from attending. Filled with Sophiatown characters, music, and style, it reveled in the energy of African urban life hidden by apartheid; after-show parties brought together rebellious characters from both communities, forging bonds that endured at the heart of the resistance movement in the bitter and violent years ahead.

Since those long-forgotten nineteenth-century tours by Zulu choirs, cover versions of "Mbube" / "Wimoweh" and "Skokiaan," the US release of "Lovely Lies" and the UK charting of "Tom Hark" were about as much as the outside world had heard of South African music. In 1959, that was about to change; Sophiatown culture, its sophistication still relatively intact, was headed to the northern hemisphere in the form of a movie, a singer, a trumpeter, and a stage musical.

A film-maker from New York named Lionel Rogosin told the authorities he was making a tourist short to promote holidaying in South Africa. The fact that he spent most of his time at the wrong end of Johannesburg seems to have escaped their notice; even the most paranoid Afrikaner couldn't conceive of a White man in love with an African slum. In fact, Rogosin was shooting a drama of life under apartheid with amateur actors, a crew of sympathisers and bootleg film stock. He lied to officials about what he was doing again and again, determined to document the daily outrages he witnessed in his exploration of life in Johannesburg's African neighborhoods. *Come Back, Africa*, shot in 1957 as Sophiatown was in its death throes, was smuggled out, edited in New York, and caused a huge stir at the 1959 Venice Film Festival.

This sometimes stodgy film comes to life in the shebeen scene, when Sophiatown's most famous singer pops in for a late-night jam session with the regulars. Without realizing it, I had heard Miriam Makeba's voice amid the harmonies on "Lovely Lies"; the Manhattan Brothers liked having a girl singer to add color to their shows, and their choices were astute. One, Thandi Klaasen, went on to form a popular "answer" group, the Quad Sisters, and after she left, they recruited Makeba.

Miriam spent the first six months of her life in prison, her Swazi mother having been jailed for brewing beer. Her older brother's record collection included traditional Xhosa music as well as Ella Fitzgerald singing "A-Tisket, A-Tasket," a range that pretty well defined Makeba's style. Her mother was similarly divided: as a young woman she had dressed in the latest fashions, but later, when she became a sangoma, or healer, she hand-stitched her clothes from traditional cloth and went barefoot.

Makeba had been singing around the Townships for a few years when the Manhattans spotted her. *Drum* soon put her on the cover and she became a pin-up for Coca-Cola before touring the country with the African Jazz & Variety Show, singing Xhosa folk songs in traditional dress. Back in Johannesburg, she joined the crowd outside the Gallo offices hoping to audition for the (always late) *uBaas*. Some of the best groups, including Makeba's Skylarks, were formed during those interminable waits. The first Skylarks line-up was short-lived; Miriam was a demanding leader, firing and hiring frequently and holding the team to the high professional standards she'd learned with the Manhattan Brothers. The Xhosa spin they put on Andrews Sisters harmonies propelled her into stardom, surpassing established glamour girls such as Dolly Rathebe and Dorothy Masuka.

Knowing that Makeba's performance was the high point of *Come Back, Africa*, Rogosin brought her to Venice, where her stunning looks, powerful voice, and the first Afro hairdo ever photographed for an Italian fashion magazine caused a sensation. Within weeks she was in New York, singing at the Village Vanguard and appearing on Steve Allen's TV show.

In 1952, Hugh Masekela's uncle helped him gain admission to St. Peter's boarding school, where Rev. Trevor Huddleston was headmaster. The school's founder, Raymond Raines, had spotted his successor at an episcopal retreat outside London. The young priest was startled by the proposal, but the choice was astute; Huddleston became so beloved of Black South Africans that his statue stands today in downtown Johannesburg.

At Huddleston's suggestion, Masekela composed a letter to Louis Armstrong that brought a battered trumpet in the post a few months later. Huddleston encouraged a jazz craze at school, with Hugh at its center; soon the prodigy was leading the Huddleston Jazz Band and joining a short-lived modern jazz surge in South Africa. "The government despised our joy," said Masekela. "They couldn't figure out how Africans could still find any pleasure under such harsh social conditions."

"Natives will be taught from childhood to realize that equality with Europeans is not for them," said Verwoerd, who loathed St. Peter's for its high academic standards. Huddleston was banished from South Africa in 1956, and the school, forced to choose between continuing under Bantu education regulations or closing, opted for the latter. Hugh and the band played at Huddleston's farewell concert; the funds raised helped establish Dorkay House, a musicians' center next door to the Bantu Men's Social Centre, a hub of Black cultural activity in downtown Johannesburg since the 1930s.

Destined to follow Sophiatown into the government's cross hairs was Cape Town's District Six, a mixed area reflecting the city's complex make-up: Malays, Cape Coloureds, Xhosa, and a few Whites, with a jazz scene centered around the Zambezi Indian restaurant. Masekela, trombonist Jonas Gwangwa (later leader of the music arm of the ANC-in-exile), and sax great Kippie Moeketsi traveled south in 1959 to join Dollar Brand's trio as part of South Africa's first "supergroup," the Jazz Epistles.

Adolph "Dollar" Brand (later known as Abdullah Ibrahim) was the leading figure in a Cape Town style influenced by Malay *Goema* music, *langarm* country dances, and complex Xhosa harmonies. The newcomers added Zulu melody, marabi chords, and kwela rhythm, helping lay the foundations of a distinctively South African form of modern jazz.

Newsreel footage shows a piano being lifted in the jaws of a crane from the ruins of a building and tossed onto the back of a truck, the keys breaking apart and falling into the dust. Thus ended the great era of Sophiatown music as government bulldozers destroyed lives and memories along with buildings.

Confrontations were multiplying: the 1957 *azikwelwa* ("we will not ride") bus boycott lasted six months and was marked by groups of commuters singing as they walked as much as twenty miles to and from work. The government ultimately repealed the fare increase. Troubadour Records A&R man Cuthbert Matumba recorded protest songs that spread across the country before the authorities could decipher their meanings and ban them.

In 1958, Black South Africans were stripped of their citizenship and assigned to the "Homelands" of their "tribes," despite many having been born to urban parents from different backgrounds. Training and experience counted for nothing; if a journalist or teacher lost their job, they had to accept menial employment or lose their pass. Arrests involved deliberate humiliation, including a pathological police obsession with penis measurement during strip searches.

The mounting tension reached breaking point at Sharpeville: on March 21, 1960, a month after British Prime Minister Harold Macmillan's "Winds of Change" speech to a shocked South African parliament, police opened fire on protesters, killing sixty-nine. The world recoiled in horror; isolating South Africa was suddenly a realistic goal. In January 1961, 156 members of the ANC, including Nelson Mandela, were found not guilty of treason after a five-year trial.

As singing became the weapon of choice at rallies, a Port Elizabeth labor leader with a beautiful bass voice named Vuyisile Mini began composing powerful anthems. Mini had been arrested in 1956 after leading a strike and freed two years later; in 1963, he was jailed again and sentenced to be hanged. On the gallows he sang his most famous composition, "Watch Out Verwoerd": *"Here comes the black man, Verwoerd / The black man is going to get you!"*

A London producer heard about *King Kong* and invited the show for a West End run; under heavy pressure from the British government, South Africa reluctantly issued passports. The cast were thrilled with life outside South Africa from the minute they stepped aboard the desegregated BOAC plane; soon after landing they came to the happy realization that it was not a criminal offense in Britain to have sex with White people.

In the wake of Sharpeville, the world was keen to learn about South Africa, but not yet ready for its undiluted music. At least that was the London producers' excuse for watering down *King Kong*'s arrangements, making them less African and more Broadway; as their version was the only one recorded, we'll never know if that was the reason it wasn't a hit. The show did inspire the Labour Party to organize a massive demonstration outside the South African Embassy that kick-started the Anti-Apartheid Movement, and also opened the door for long runs in New York and London by *Ipi Tombi*, *uMabatha* (*MacBeth* in Zulu), *Woza Albert!*, *Poppie Nongena*, *Sarafina!*, and the plays of Athol Fugard.

The Manhattan Brothers decided to stay. Todd Matshikiza also wanted to remain but found it hard to break into the London music scene. When South Africa refused to allow him back, he settled in Zambia, writing and broadcasting from there until his death in 1968. Bandleader Kippie Moeketsi, who had been badly beaten in a tsotsi dispute just before departing for London, was given electro-shock treatment in an English hospital and never regained the motor control needed to play the saxophone as beautifully as legend assures us he did.

Makeba, who had opted for Venice with *Come Back, Africa* over joining the cast of *King Kong* in London, triumphed in America; audiences were enthralled with her striking looks, powerful voice, and Xhosa clicks. Masekela, who had been carrying on an affair with her ever since he was a schoolboy, was desperate to follow his friends and his lover out of South Africa. With Huddleston's help, he secured a scholarship to Juilliard and was reunited with Miriam in New York.

Lionel Rogosin continued to run the movie house he had founded— New York's Bleecker Street Cinema—while making subversive documentaries on the side. Trevor Huddleston became a bishop, serving in London's East End, Maur itius, and Tanzania, and was elected head of the Anti-Apartheid Movement in 1981.

After Sharpeville, the South African Broadcasting Corporation (SABC) fired its jazz presenters, jettisoned most urban music, and built up separate "tribal" services. The newly built Townships included no performance spaces, while "rediffusion" speakers blasted out the radio signal appropriate to each neighborhood. Fort Hare University, the crucible of African leadership, was reshaped along ethnic lines; Xhosa Mandela and Zulu Buthelezi as classmates became a thing of the past.

The twisted contradictions of these policies were in evidence at Mandela's second trial in 1963–64 (which produced the required life sentence). When Africans at the court stamped and cheered for the star prisoner's appearance in a traditional Xhosa *kaross*, the government forced him—and his similarly garbed wife, Winnie—to change back into Western dress. The only consistency, it seemed, was opting for whatever would be the most inconvenient and humiliating for Black South Africans.

African attitudes were also conflicted. Anthony Sampson once polled a crowd at the Bantu Men's Social Centre for guidance about *Drum*'s editorial content: "Give us jazz and film stars, man! Hot dames! . . . anything American. You can cut out this junk about kraals and folktales and Basutos in blankets—forget it!"

Mandela kept a balanced view. He is remembered for turning up, during his rare periods of freedom, at Soweto shebeens and dancing the "Madiba Jive" until 4 a.m. In prison, he supported circumcision ceremonies for young prisoners over the objections of many in the ANC leadership. Mandela was the son of a Xhosa chief, the sort of leader the government wanted to encourage. Yet he renounced tribal power in favor of the larger struggle, while never losing sight of tradition as a source of strength.

A towering figure of a different sort was Yvonne Huskisson, the long-serving music director of the SABC; implacably tribalist, she once described jazz as "a particularly dirty basin of water." Huskisson ensured that only the most conservative music was played on the various SABC outlets. Africans called her programming *msakazo*—"broadcast music." She was equally fierce with White playlists, barring rock 'n' roll and gouging offending tracks in the SABC library with a razor. She tried to steer Boers away from American country music in favor of German *schlager*, promoting the sounds of Bert Kaempfert and James Last. Her proudest achievement may have been the triumph of isicathamiya and Ladysmith

Black Mambazo during the seventies, an uncomfortable fact for those of us who treasure our original Ladysmith vinyl from this period.

The great ethnomusicologist Hugh Tracey was another awkward figure. His English father had moved to Southern Rhodesia in 1923, when Hugh was a teenager, and he became fascinated with the music of miners and factory workers. By the time he died in 1977, he had released 210 LPs of African field recordings; his archive at Rhodes University in Grahamstown is a researcher's gold mine. But Tracey was a Huskisson ally, providing scholarly support for her rejection of urban modernity and collaborating with the government's idealization of tribal culture.

～

Of the many creation myths for mbaqanga, my favorite involves Todd Matshikiza waking up hung over one morning in 1948 while on tour with the Harlem Swingsters. The sax player started in with a simple riff and the rest joined in, sore heads rendering them incapable of playing anything more complex: "We dropped our corn bread and got stuck into Gray [Mbau]'s mood . . . We syncopated and displaced accents, gave variety to our 'native' rhythms. We were longing for the days of Marabi piano . . . It was . . . [Marabi] but . . . with a dash of lime." Players from different bands would jam at Sophiatown's Odin Cinema, finding common ground in Zulu melodies; this became a laboratory where ways of playing traditional rhythms with an American edge were tested and improved.

By the early sixties, in the wake of kwela's strong sales, Gallo and the other labels were taking the "native" music business seriously. With radio restrictions and a lack of performance spaces squeezing the jazz scene and the Bantu Education Ministry eliminating all music teaching jobs, no jazz musician could afford to turn down the payday of a "Township jive" session. Though they raised standards, these virtuosos were often condescending about what they were asked to play. Sax player Michael Xaba's disparaging epithet, "mbaqanga," denoted a type of simple Zulu dumpling, but as with many insults, it became a badge of pride. "It's a . . . very strong food," said producer West Nkosi. "You don't get hungry."

Mbaqanga had many parents, but the most exotic may have been Jet Harris of The Shadows. On a 1960 South African tour he sold his electric bass to Joseph Makwela, who used the country's first such instrument to transform the bottom end of African recordings. Drummers responded to its aggressive sound—played with a pick rather than fingers—by moving from kwela's brushes to sticks, while concertinas were replaced by bigger-sounding accordions.

Over the course of the sixties, textures evolved as producers got fed up with jazzers' arrogance and started using rural musicians newly arrived in 'Goli. Andrews Sisters and Mills Brothers harmonies faded; as lyrics focused more on life back home, tenor vocals an octave apart added authenticity. The gentle syncopation of kwela was replaced by the gracenote-and-downbeat Zulu stomp. Worldly Africans professed to hate mbaqanga, but many grudgingly admitted to enjoying it.

A key figure in its transformation was a street-corner pennywhistler-turned-sax-player from Pretoria named Johannes Hlongwane. He gathered up a team of Sotho garden boys and by the time they arrived in Johannesburg, he had become West Nkosi and his mates were the Makgona Tsohle or "Jack of All Trades" band, which included bass pioneer Makwela and guitarist Marks Mankwane, who had developed an electrified version of "Sugar-drinker" John Bhengu's ukupika patterns. As Gallo's equivalent of the Motown Funk Brothers, Makgone Tsohle provided backing on hit after hit for A&R man Rupert Bopape, the Berry Gordy of mbaqanga. The elements were now in place for the sound that would dominate the South African scene for the next fifteen years, before *Graceland* took it to the world.

Elias Lerole of "Tom Hark" fame had a brother, a "groaner" known as "Big Voice Jack." Jack was the final piece in the mbaqanga puzzle; his rasping basso connected Nguni listeners to traditional male singing, particularly the *imbongi*, the praise poet of the royal kraals. It is probably no coincidence that this fiercely masculine sound took off as the government was intensifying its humiliation of African men.

When Lerole blew out his voice, Simon "Mahlathini" Nkabinde, brother of a member of Jack's band, Alexandra Black Mambazo (meaning "axe"), stepped in. Mahlathini had been earning a living by choreographing isicathamiya choirs for Zulu weddings; he would later hone his *mqashiyo* style by adding the counterpoint of a female chorus: the Mahotella Queens.

> My father died when I was seven and I picked up his voice right up into my neck, right into my shoulders. I grew up in the good mood of music. With my parents dead, I had no one to help me with school fees, so I went to work in a 7-UP factory, then as a dairyboy, starting deliveries at 1 a.m. My wrist was broken when I was hit by a car, so the owner agreed to sign my passbook so I wouldn't be arrested while I looked for another job.
>
> I loved singing Zulu wedding songs—street corner singing, a cappella—but we were trying to get involved with guitar players. When I talk to people, I talk normally, but when I sing, the voice changes by itself. I didn't train for it; I can change the tones from my stomach.
>
> The youth should follow their culture, that's what I'm singing about. I don't write songs, I dream, I observe.

At a time when Africans were being forced into soulless identikit Townships, Mahlathini's songs told of a life where men were heads of families and leaders of their communities, in a voice that evoked the history of a warrior nation. His audience identified with his costume changes—from sangoma garb to sharp suits and back again—which evoked Reuben Caluza's vaudeville shows and the African Jazz & Variety tours. Returning from Europe in 1988 with the first serious money he ever made, Mahlathini bought a cow.

During the 1970s, as African entrepreneurship in the wider economy was being suppressed, Bopape, Nkosi, and other Black music producers created powerful assembly lines; Gallo may have owned the tapes but these promoters managed and booked the artists, controlled the instruments and sound equipment, printed the posters, and collected the ticket money. Tours followed the vinyl all over South Africa and into Lesotho, Zimbabwe, Malawi, and Zambia. Rival labels copied the Gallo formula; Teal's house band was the Boyoyo Boys.

While mbaqanga never set sales records outside South Africa, it remains the most familiar South African style for world music audiences, and not just because of *Graceland*. Mahlathini's recordings share a perfectly pitched balance between modernity and tradition with Mali's Rail Band (featuring Salif Keïta), Dakar's Super Etoiles (with the youthful Youssou N'Dour), the classic Kinshasa rumba of Franco and Tabu Ley Rochereau, and the Golden Era *Ethiopiques* series. The genius of Mankwane, Makwela, and Nkosi was to move the music simultaneously backward and forward, leaving behind the jazzy chords and swing inflections of kwela and sax jive in favor of rhythms and harmonies rooted in the wedding music of rural KwaZulu, while giving the sound a rock 'n' roll punch.

Mbaqanga was sung at first in many languages, with different versions of the same song being sent to each Bantu Radio outlet. But the Zulu tracks sold best, partly because Zulus were such avid consumers (of rural-friendly cassettes in particular), and partly because neighboring peoples were drawn to the Zulu image. Singers from other areas learned the language and the SABC was forced to modify its tribe-specific playlists in order to maintain listenership. Looking back, West Nkosi regretted the music's Zulu-ization: "We made one good solid rhythm that could appeal to all these different tribes. And it worked out very well. People could come together and start respecting one another." But mbaqanga's universality didn't last.

∽

Isicathamiya, meanwhile, was in decline; talent like Solomon Linda's was thin on the ground. Recordings in the 1950s and '60s had failed to keep up with changes in Zulu culture; longer work contracts meant leaving women to run the household back in KwaZulu while men spent most of the year in urban Locations. The Hanover Brothers singing *"the hurrying of people in Durban so disturbed him he caught the train back home"* echoed the government's position that Africans weren't meant to live in cities.

Joseph Shabalala came to Durban from the town of Ladysmith in 1960 in search of work, joining a local choir and taking part in competitions in the evenings. When the choir refused to sing his compositions—

and after a prophetic dream—he formed Ladysmith Black Mambazo, honoring Big Voice Jack while boasting that his own group also "cut like an axe." Shabalala set out to transform the mbube world, and he succeeded. Understanding the importance of radio, he taught his group to sing intimately, taking a cue from—*them again!*—the Mills Brothers. When Solomon Linda died in 1962, Shabalala sent gifts and messages of respect to his family.

Huskisson and Nkosi, by now the two most powerful figures in South African music, took an early interest. For Huskisson, Ladysmith Black Mambazo were a godsend, revitalizing a form she viewed as appropriately rural and tribal, with the flair to draw the listener numbers she needed to keep Bantu Radio afloat. Ladysmith's repertoire was perfect: officialdom heard the nostalgic rural message while the Zulu audience detected defiance and pride in their invocation of Shaka and other references too subtle for Whites to comprehend. The group connected modern life to the past, linking the sharp-dressed Township wide boy to the elaborately clad warrior and to Isoka, the Zulu rake of legend. After falling out with Mahlathini in 1971, Nkosi became Ladysmith's producer and manager, finding in Shabalala someone who shared his vision of bringing an mbaqanga edge to mbube. From the early seventies to the early eighties, he and Shabalala ruled the isicathamiya world.

Marilyn Monroe in *that* dress breathily cooing "Happy Birthday" to President Kennedy in Madison Square Garden is part of America's collective memory. Few recall that preceding her on the bill that night was Miriam Makeba singing "The Click Song"; it was a safe assumption in 1962 that a New York crowd who loved JFK and Monroe would be fans of the other MM, too.

On her arrival in America, Harry Belafonte had taken Makeba under his wing. She took a cue from his approach, tacking her Xhosa folk songs towards the slick, rhythmically bland folk of the pre-Dylan era. Other options were probably unrealistic: Americans would have had trouble getting their heads around the idea of such a "foreign" jazz singer, and most African Americans had an almost pathological aversion to Africa.

(When backing musicians Makeba had sent for landed at Idlewild Airport, at a press agent's suggestion they disembarked in full tribal regalia. Black baggage handlers recoiled, either ridiculing or fleeing the "savages.") Her arrival, though, did trigger interest in South African folk music: Pete Seeger brought the prisoners' anthem "Shosholoza" into the canon of workers' songs, while Ramblin' Jack Elliott learned "Guabi Guabi" off a Hugh Tracey LP. It also appealed to the opposite end of the music industry: Bert Kaempfert's hit LP *A Swingin' Safari* included "Skokiaan" and a cover of a Lemmy Special kwela tune.

Changes in Miriam's life came rapidly. Soon after Masekela's arrival, they embarked on a tempestuous marriage marked by collaborations, battles, betrayals, reconciliations, divorce, and affairs (pre-divorce with others, post-divorce with each other); their passionate connection extended from Sophiatown in the fifties through every decade and across three continents until her death in 2008. Following Makeba's eloquent speech to the UN in the wake of Sharpeville, she was barred from returning to her home country, even for her mother's funeral. J. Edgar Hoover considered her to be the devil incarnate and pushed the government to view anti-apartheid activity as subversive and communistic.

With the FBI discouraging promoters from booking her, she needed a hit. In 1967, with the help of the producer-composer Jerry Ragavoy ("Piece of My Heart," "Time Is on My Side"), she turned to "Pata Pata," a song with a long history. It was first sighted in 1941 as "Noma Kumnyama" by mbube group the Dundee Wandering Singers, with lyrics referring to the tsaba-tsaba craze. In 1959, Dorothy Masuka's "Ei-Yow" sparked a craze for the *pata pata* dance, in which the man mimics a policeman frisking (or "patting down") the woman. Gallo, anxious for one last hit before Miriam left for Europe, recorded her singing a kwela update of "Noma Kumnyama" under the "Pata Pata" title, but sales were poor. With a few English lyrics by Ragavoy and his sharp production, the new "Pata Pata" reached #7 on the *Billboard* charts, her biggest American hit. Predictably, the songwriting credits were disputed among Ragavoy, Makeba, her manager Sanford Ross, and South African guitarist Reggie Msomi. (Alson Mkhize, leader of the Dundee Wandering Singers, had died in 1961 and was not mentioned in any of the writs.)

In 1968, Makeba shocked her liberal supporters by marrying Trinidad-born Black Power pioneer Stokely Carmichael. The couple fled the furor, settling in Conakry, Guinea, where President-for-life Sekou Touré gave them a house. Makeba was astonished by the uncompromisingly African music Touré's government was supporting, blending saxophones, koras, and electric guitars. Abandoning the pop-folk style of her years in the US, she made some interesting records with local hero Sekou "Diamond Fingers" Diabate, but the West Africa / South Africa mix never quite gelled.

Hugh Masekela spent the sixties immersing himself in the American jazz and rock scenes, particularly their accompanying drugs and groupies. With his forceful personality and skillful playing he forged a career, but insisted on becoming musically as American as possible, treating his homeland's rhythms with the condescension typical of a Sophiatown jazzman. In 1964, Miles Davis told him, "If you play some of that shit from South Africa . . . you gonna come up with something that none of us can do. Fuck jazz, man . . . You know what I'm sayin'?"

A year after "Pata Pata," Masekela paid a visit to friends in Zambia —including a death-bed reunion with Todd Matshikiza—and took the opportunity to pick up the latest South African hits. In a Los Angeles studio, having begun his new album with Motown covers, he sifted through those records for ideas to finish off the project. Finding one particular mbaqanga guitar line he liked, he stretched the riff into a tune and took just two hours to record, overdub, and mix it. In a control room filled with marijuana smoke, everyone agreed it should be called "Grazing in the Grass."

One Sunday afternoon in 1963, a White South African girl named Maxine Lautré took in a jam session at Dorkay House:

> It was the only place in Johannesburg where Africans of artistic or literary bent could meet, keep in touch, discuss ideas, and attend various classes. Grubby, a shambles of old papers, cigarette butts, empty bottles and dust, there was nevertheless a tremendous energy alive in the building. Raucous joyful noise invaded you in every corner . . . it

was a window on a world bursting with . . . artistic wealth but with almost nowhere to give it expression . . .

So I saw him on that first afternoon, a tall, almost gaunt . . . [pianist], dark circles under his closed eyes, mouthing the sounds he would produce in his fingers a fraction of a second later, his hair falling over his brow with the continual sway of his body to the rhythm . . . Beside him was the ceaselessly moving body of Dudu, the alto saxophonist, cadence after cadence of tearing, vibrant sound pouring forth from deep in his lungs in continually inventive phrases of melody, bouncingly energetic, sometimes shocking, sometimes soothing . . . always surprising. Seemingly completely engrossed in his creation yet, like a hunter with one ear turned backward . . . he was very conscious of the piano, the drums. The drums, pitilessly, almost aggressively beating out their rhythm, building up the excitement, the sound so great that you had forgotten whether it was loud or not; you were within it, completely open to it . . . Now the altoist retired, the trumpeter stepped up . . . and after a short pause, a moment of suspense, the first long pure note of his solo; the tapping feet of the audience beginning with renewed vigour . . . I was completely fascinated, swept up by the force of the music, by the obvious rapport between the musicians and the incredible joy and life that was so immediately apparent. Such intensity was something I had never really come across before.

This was the Blue Notes, South Africa's first mixed-race band; the pianist was Chris McGregor, Maxine's future husband.

McGregor had grown up in rural Transkei, where his father ran a school even more at odds with the Bantu Education Act than St. Peter's. Chris attended a White academy but spent most of his time with his father's students. Music was everywhere: school kids learned the alphabet by singing, while their Xhosa mothers were always harmonizing, the lines overlapping, weaving together in the staggered cycles that would later inspire McGregor's compositions. By the time he was ten, he was playing organ for church choirs and sitting in on piano with local dance bands.

Chris arrived at Cape Town University in 1956; African students had just been banned and many Whites joined the protests. A large crowd of men from the Langa Location marched on Parliament, a peaceful, silent vigil against the new laws; when police blocked them off into a sealed area (the kettling tactic now so popular with British and American police), McGregor joined a group of musicians who snuck in to serenade the crowd. He later helped organize free music classes in Langa Township.

Sessions at the Vortex Club and the Zambezi introduced him to Dudu Pukwana (alto sax) and Mongezi Feza (trumpet), who would join him and the drummer Louis Moholo as the Blue Notes' core. Onstage, Chris always wore a hat so his lank brown hair wouldn't give away that he wasn't a "very light" Cape Coloured. Castle Lager, defying the government by sponsoring jazz festivals, backed a tour by McGregor's big band with the cream of South African jazz talent. Castle wouldn't risk bringing the show to a White area, but Maxine was too young to know any better and produced a historic concert in Braamfontein. South African critics were stunned to discover world-class jazz in their midst and puzzled by the White pianist so at one with the Black musicians. From childhood, Chris had never found any conflict between White and Black culture—or, for that matter, among jazz, Township jive, and Xhosa traditional music.

A Blue Notes tour of the Townships organized by Maxine was a nightmare of red tape, harassment, drunken musicians (and audiences), and unpaid or stolen fees, but the responses made it all worthwhile. Eventually, though, she and Chris concluded that while he might be willing to risk everything for a musical ideal—even changing his registration to "coloured"—his Black colleagues faced dangers far greater. A Parisian friend of Maxine's played a Blue Notes tape to someone at the Antibes Jazz Festival, who extended an invitation; flummoxed by this color-blind pianist, the government opted to give them all exit visas, in the hope they'd never come back.

Joining the Blue Notes on the bill at Antibes in 1964 (along with Ella Fitzgerald, Horace Silver, and Jean-Luc Ponty) was Dollar Brand. Brand had grown up in Cape Town, where his grandmother played piano at the local AME church. His conversion to Islam in the early seventies (and change of name to Abdullah Ibrahim) seems to have only intensified his connection to the Protestant hymns of his youth.

Brand left South Africa in 1962 for Switzerland, where Duke

Ellington heard him in a club and became his champion. When I saw him at the 1965 Newport Jazz Festival, I don't recall his playing sounding particularly South African, but that may say more about my youthful listening than about Brand's music (although he did tend to belittle African music in early interviews). But during a Cape Town recording session with former District Six colleagues in the mid-seventies, he recorded "Manenburg," a composition by legendary District Six sax great Basil Coetzee that would become his signature. "Manenburg" is instantly recognizable as South African, rooted in the interface between Wesleyan hymns and Xhosa chant. "Grazing in the Grass" made Hugh Masekela's fortune but few listeners connected it with South Africa. For most jazz fans, Abdullah Ibrahim's elegant playing has become the most evocative representation of the country's unique style. Of the psychic damage wrought by apartheid on both Black and White, Ibrahim once observed that "music saved us."

Many more listeners know Ibrahim's and Masekela's music than Chris McGregor's. I surrendered objectivity the moment I walked into a small club in London's Chinatown in 1967 and experienced the Blue Notes in their prime. I had toured with Albert Ayler and George Russell, but their American avant-garde sound seemed two-dimensional next to the Blue Notes' avalanche of free expression, gospel, Ellington, kwela, Mingus, and what I would eventually learn was Xhosa folk music.

I wish there was a triumphant story to recount, but the tale is a sad one, with scattered successes, the melancholy of exile, untimely deaths, and posthumous praise for reissued recordings. Perhaps their destiny was foretold at Antibes, where the music astonished audiences, promoters, and critics but no one knew what to do with them. The European jazz world of 1964 was conservatively hip, wedded to fifties bebop performed in elegant surroundings. With Django Reinhardt long gone and Jan Garbarek still in short trousers, few could imagine jazz sprouting from non-American roots. The Blue Notes' nightly jams at Antibes' Pam Pam bar attracted such raucous crowds that the police banned them, while their own appetites for alcohol and unruly behavior alarmed promoters. The best they could manage was a two-week stint subbing for Brand in Zurich and, after an agonizing wait during which they busked on the street, a short season at Ronnie Scott's in London.

The decision to base themselves in England made sense at the time: a common language and a community of expatriates, plus the world's strongest anti-apartheid movement. But the British musicians who cheered their originality grew distant and even hostile when the group settled in and began competing for jobs and girls. The Musicians' Union refused to make concessions: membership could be granted only after a year of (theoretically unemployed) residence. Most devastating for McGregor was the indifference: "That what you do doesn't really matter to anyone is difficult to adjust to."

My period in the late sixties as their manager and record producer was relatively unsuccessful. I got them a deal with Polydor, but *Very Urgent* didn't sell. Frustrated with the indifference of the British jazz world, I began working with Dudu on a "rock kwela" project. We pieced together a makeshift band of Ghanaians and South Africans and cut a few decent tracks. Early in 1970, imagining that things were changing in South Africa, I bought us both plane tickets to Johannesburg; I didn't know the word *mbaqanga* before I went but quickly learned it once I arrived.

Dudu and I slept in our separate racial enclaves but met every day at Dorkay House or the Bantu Men's Social Centre, where I played pool and ping-pong and discussed Harold Pinter and Miles Davis with out-of-work actors and musicians. I remember being struck by the shabby dark clothes of the men and women in the bus queues and thinking how interesting it would be when the looped earrings, colorful dashikis, and Afro hairdos of the American Black Power movement reached South Africa.

I brought back a great mbaqanga compilation called *Good Luck Motella* (Motella being a short-lived Detroit-aspirational Gallo subsidiary) and loaned it to Richard Thompson, saying, "Learn this." With Simon Nicol, also of Fairport Convention, Richard joined some memorable sessions with an impressed Pukwana. In 2020, Matsuli, a South African label, reissued the tapes I had licensed to Trutone to finance our flights to Johannesburg, plus the ones we made with Richard and

Simon when we got back. Dudu and I were convinced we'd failed, but fifty years later they sound great. (Dudu and Chris were very open to the folk-rock I was recording for Witchseason Productions, with Chris adding a wonderful solo to Nick Drake's "Poor Boy" and Dudu's sax gracing tracks I produced by Mike Heron, John Martyn, and Toots and the Maytals.)

In 1970, just before I moved to Los Angeles, we recorded the first Brotherhood of Breath album; with its blistering solos, graceful lyricism, powerful rhythms, and un-American texture, it has had, over the years, a big influence on European jazz. To Chris, the piano was a drum with notes; the British members got used to McGregor's way of rehearsing the marabi rhythms in Xhosa-like cycles, learning the charts on the fly as the inexorable beat never stopped for a wrong note; he knew they'd catch it next time.

Of the Blue Notes' recording "Don't Stir the Beehive," McGregor's brother Tony says it reminds him of "a Transkei evening with herders whistling and calling to each other, snatches of song and the random rhythms of insects in the thorn trees . . . I can almost smell the cooking fires and see the sun setting behind the hills in a dusty purple and orange haze. I certainly feel the longing for home that pervades the track."

Mongezi Feza, the brilliant, scrawny half-Xan trumpeter, came down with tuberculosis and was treated with drugs that made him painfully light-sensitive and paranoid. Sent to a mental home and dosed with Largactil, he died there in 1975. Bassist Johnny Dyani decamped to Copenhagen, where, after years of heroin addiction, he passed away in 1987. Chris and Maxine moved to the more congenial atmosphere of France, where he continued to perform as a soloist, with occasional tours by a sixteen-piece Brotherhood of Breath. Just prior to a 1990 tour, he was diagnosed with cancer and died within weeks. Dudu kept a band going for years in London before succumbing to a heart attack a month after Chris's death. Louis Moholo was the only original Blue Note to witness Mandela's swearing-in as president; he now teaches music in the Townships and performs in South Africa and Europe.

By the end of the sixties, the natives were getting restless—the White ones, that is. The government's refusal to allow "Godless" television meant being excluded from Neil Armstrong's "giant leap for mankind." The decade-long economic and sporting boycotts were starting to bite, while the now-integrated US Navy had stopped calling at South African ports. Things got so bad that in 1971 the SABC's highest-rated program was a radio adaptation of *The Avengers*; trying to imagine Emma Peel in trousers was becoming a painful distraction for the country's managerial class.

The Black population, on the other hand, felt more connected than ever. The end of the British and French empires had spawned independent nations from Zambia to Senegal. LM Radio, just over the border in Mozambique, was blasting out pop and rhythm and blues; everyone in the Rand could hear James Brown's Black Power message, while some Sowetans took to wearing their hair long, calling themselves "hippies," and forming rock bands. Inspired by James Baldwin and Miles Davis, writers and musicians were laying the foundation of the Black Consciousness Movement, which sprang to life in 1968, when Steve Biko led a walkout over unequal conditions at a National Student Union conference. The drab clothing I saw on my 1970 visit belied the fact that beneath the surface, the ground was rapidly shifting. Liberals may have been dismayed by the separatism implicit in Black Consciousness, but Biko insisted that "the first step is . . . to infuse [the black man] with pride and dignity." Jazz players gave up trying to hustle gigs at White venues in Hillbrow; Club Pelican in Soweto and the Galaxy in Cape Flats became the new hubs.

In January 1976, to the fury of the Dutch churches, the government launched a pair of TV channels, one for each White language. Boers were afraid superior anglophone boob-tube programming would hasten the decline of Afrikaans; White immigration had soared since World War Two, yet few Italians, Greeks, Jews, or Australians were interested in learning the founders' tongue. Conservatives also worried that Africans would use the new medium to deepen their unnerving connections to the wider world. To counter these trends and placate the Right, the government appointed Dr. Andries Treurnicht as deputy minister of education, with a brief to convert half of all African high school classes from English into Afrikaans. If immigrants could not be persuaded to speak the Boers' language, the country's Black population would be forced to.

On June 16, 1976, police shot twelve-year-old Hector Pieterson during a demonstration against Afrikaans classes; photos of his corpse were seen across the country and around the world. The ensuing uprising plunged South Africa into eighteen years of violence that ended with Mandela's swearing-in as president. Apollo 11 was the beginning of the end of apartheid.

> In confidence we lay our cause before the whole world. Whether we win or whether we die, freedom will rise in Africa like the sun from the morning clouds.

Nelson Mandela loved this quote from Paul Kruger about the Boer struggle against the British at the end of the nineteenth century. Another pungent line came from Dizzy Gillespie: "I want to join your revolution . . . The only thing we had was 'We Shall Overcome.' Every time I see South Africa on TV, they've got a new song." On news broadcasts outside South Africa, police bullhorns and gunshots couldn't drown out the glorious singing of the crowds. Perhaps, like their forefathers, the government still heard South African harmonies as a "cacophonous wail," but ANC and union leaders knew what a potent weapon they were.

With most music venues shut down either by police or by Township youth, churches and streets filled with harmony. Protest songs had evolved from the simple maid's request of "Madam Please" (*"Before you ask if your children are fine, ask me when I last saw mine"*) to newly politicized hymns. "Senzeni na" (What Have We Done?) was one of the most effective, a moving melody repeated over and over at mass rallies. Yvonne Huskisson complained that "an abortive attempt was made by the ANC to insinuate that ordinary Bantu singing 'Nkosi Sikelel' iAfrika' were doing so in support of its aims." Eventually, alarmed by the anthem's power, the government outlawed it. Other absurdities followed, like banning *Black Beauty* for its title and Thelonious Monk's "Crepuscule with Nellie" on grounds that its mysterious first word might represent something sexual. A Black classical singer was barred from the SABC for sounding "too white." Ray Phiri, later *Graceland*'s lead guitarist, was prohibited from staging his musical adaptation of *Volpone*; the censors couldn't accept that an African was capable of creating such a thing.

Hymns about Israelites in Egyptian captivity morphed into undisguised topicality, "putting in an AK-47 here, taking out a Bible there," as one veteran of the struggle put it. Rhythms became more aggressive after 1976 as fighters returned from military training abroad, bringing with them the *toyi-toyi*, a hunters' chant learned from Zimbabwean rebels. Soldiers in uMkhonto we Sizwe—the ANC's military wing, known as MK—kept up their spirits during long marches by adapting the Afrikaners' beloved "Marching to Pretoria" as a toyi-toyi. White policemen would later confirm how terrifying it was to confront huge crowds explaining in harmony and gesture how they planned to kill you.

At the funerals that took place every Saturday during the height of the struggle, graveside anthems turned each death into a renewed commitment. One comrade observed, "We didn't want the singing to be too sad—it might have demoralized us." Music transformed not only the world's view of the struggle but the participants' as well, buoying spirits and instilling bravery. The Nationalists didn't get it, but even if they had, what could they have done about it?

Another sign that apartheid's days might be numbered was how White teenagers would black up to sneak into Percy Sledge concerts. They weren't the only ones mesmerized by the Memphis/Muscle Shoals sound. As American releases were trumpeting Black Pride and emboldening Black leaders, the Atlantic and Stax recordings were transforming the popular musical landscape. The seventies soul surge followed the pattern of swing in the thirties; Sledge was (if such a thing can be imagined) even more popular than the Mills Brothers, while the role of Benny Goodman's clarinet was taken by Booker T's organ. Soul music reached deep into South African life, altering the sound of mbaqanga and steering youth towards all things American. African-American performers paid less attention to the cultural boycott than Whites; Wilson Pickett and Brook Benton were among many who toured in Sledge's wake. Black American stars were accused of political obtuseness, but by going directly to Black audiences were they transgressing any more than Paul Simon a decade later? For the young and hip, soul became the soundtrack of revolution.

We saw earlier how, after the 1976 uprising, musical and other traditions were attacked by militant youth for their ties to a "sell-out" past; but a fixation on US alternatives brought its own contradictions, as the pride of early-seventies soul gave way to the *get down and party* superficiality of disco. Masekela lamented, "We're trapped, man. Disco is a social tranquilizer," as ANC comrades defiantly embraced its modernity. In 1980, under pressure from business leaders who felt thwarted by their uneducated and demoralized workforce, government attempts at reform included repealing some pass laws and freeing Bantu Radio to play what listeners actually wanted to hear. Ratings-conscious DJs immediately switched from local music to American imports; except in Durban, that is, where Radio Zulu stuck determinedly to isicathamiya, mbaqanga, African bubblegum pop, and electrified versions of the ageless John Bhengu's maskanda.

Mbaqanga responded to the soul challenge by merging its wedding-dance beat with a machine-generated, four-on-the-floor disco feel and becoming even more Zulu-ized. The most prominent source of old-school mbaqanga was an unlikely hit television series starring the Makgona Tsohle Band as garage mechanics who brought out their instruments whenever the foreman wasn't around. The biggest record sales and tour receipts, meanwhile, were racked up by the Soul Brothers, who ruled the middle ground between mbaqanga and Memphis.

Few others made a success of touring in the eighties; most venues had disappeared, leaving music fashions to be defined by ever more artificially produced recordings. Traditional elements were fetishized, with overdubbed marabi saxes or maskanda guitar flourishes signaling that roots had not been entirely forgotten. Gadgets that could make a track at once shiningly modern and "bulldozer-like" were irresistible. A&R man Mose Dlamini claimed that Black musicians' ability to create great tracks in a few takes had deprived them of the benefits of modern hi-tech practices; now they were finally in a position to make records almost as bad as White pop. Tradition was relegated to urban backyards on Sundays, where Tswana, Sotho, Pedi, and Xhosa musicians would play for their own people. A market for regional productions still existed in remote areas, but professionalism counted for more than authenticity: Sotho John Moriri became a star by singing mbaqanga in Tswana with Zulu dance steps. Fears of violence and growing support for the boycott brought a halt to touring by Americans and drove multinational labels out of the country; into the vacuum came South African mimics of US styles, such as Brenda Fassie and Yvonne Chaka Chaka.

As South Africa tried to maintain control of its "near abroad" by sending the Defence Force to intervene against liberation movements in South West Africa, Angola, and Mozambique, the ANC did its best to bring the battle home. After 1976, occasional bombings of power lines were superseded by pitched street battles against the police, the army, and the Zulus of Inkatha. Musicians in exile, led by stalwarts Makeba and Masekela, performed in newly independent Lesotho and Botswana; South African crowds streamed across the borders to hear their shows. When Botswana's capital, Gaborone, became a hive of revolutionary and counter-cultural activity the South African army raided it, moving from house to house gunning down artists, musicians, teachers, and scientists as well as activists. Abstract canvases by murdered painter Thami Mnyele were shown on SABC-TV as evidence of the subversive intent of the victims.

Under the direction of Jonas Gwangwa, Masekela's former classmate at St. Peter's, MK's musical arm, Amandla, toured the world, though the quality of their performances was hindered by a politics-first agenda. Broadcasts into South Africa by Radio MK were often jammed and listening could lead to arrest. Former policeman Paul Erasmus later testified to the Truth and Reconciliation Commission about how he prowled record shops looking for subversive LPs and warning retailers not to stock anti-apartheid foreign artists. One fan was imprisoned for owning a cassette copy of a track by Makeba.

Another unsettling development for the government was dreadlocks, a border-transcending kinship of Blackness that defied definition or prohibition. Police would react angrily to manifestations of Rasta culture, and legend has it that some people were jailed for owning Bob Marley LPs, though his records were actually released locally and sold widely. Some surreal events cut the other way: when mbaqanga-singer-turned-reggae-star Lucky Dube found himself booked at an army camp, he improvised isiZulu insults over his band's expertly mimicked Jamaican beat while the unsuspecting White soldiers danced and cheered.

One evening in 1982, I attended an off-Broadway production called *Poppie Nongena*. In the previous decade I had seen *uMabatha* (the Zulu *Macbeth*) and *Sizwe Banzi Is Dead*, Athol Fugard's great play about a man who has lost his pass. I had also endured *Ipi Tombi*, the "tribal musical" produced by an apartheid supporter featuring cheerful, barely clothed natives. All three were huge successes, although *Ipi Tombi* was eventually shut down in New York by protests. *Poppie* wove traditional singing into the true story of a woman married to a man from another region whose family is torn apart by Homelands regulations. The cast were all South African and the evening culminated in a thrilling rendition of "Nkosi Sikelel' iAfrika," with the audience on their feet, many of them in tears. The English dialogue was interspersed with click-filled asides in Xhosa. It was a stunning evening of theater, with brilliant singing from Poppie (Thuli Dumakude, previously star of *uMabatha*) and her mother (Sophie Mgcina, a veteran of the glory years of Sophiatown).

When I discovered they had an invitation from the Edinburgh Festival but no means of getting there, my ambitions expanded from cast-album producer to theatrical impresario. From a week in Edinburgh, we progressed to a five-month run in London's West End, followed by seasons in Sydney, Melbourne, Perth, Chicago, and Toronto. I spent long stretches with the cast and the director, Hilary Blecher. Mgcina still lived in South Africa but the rest had followed the play into New York exile. Poppie's husband was played by Selaelo Maredi, a Pedi who, as a youth, had been part of a gang that robbed rural jewelry stores. One weekend, he told me, he begged off a raid to attend a family wedding; the police had been tipped off and his mates were all arrested and hanged. Selaelo decided to try another profession. While coaching soccer at a Township youth club, he helped the team present a drama in the community center and was bitten by the theater bug. When he, Fana Kekana, and Seth Sibanda (also members of the *Poppie* cast) created an award-winning three-hander, they were invited to an arts festival in Orange County, Southern California. On their first night outside South Africa, after a twenty-four-hour journey from Johannesburg, they left their motel in search of food. Two blocks down the street a police car screeched to a halt and they were thrown against a wall, spread-eagled, and frisked. Just to make them feel at home.

Blecher had created *Poppie* in a series of collaborative workshops with the show's cast at Johannesburg's Market Theatre, a progressive oasis that produced many powerful pieces under Barney Simon's supervision (including later hits *Woza Albert!* and *Sarafina*). I treasure memories of my time with the *Poppie* company; the ease and wit of the mixed-race cast (White villains being essential) made that period of my life immensely enjoyable. Most nights, I would go to the theater in time to hear the finale and enjoy the ovations. During the London run, Equity, the actors' union, became our enemy, demanding that Nigerian, Ghanaian, or Afro-Caribbean actors fill the roles, despite none of them speaking Xhosa or having any feel for the Xhosa way of singing. Appeals bought time, but eventually we closed rather than succumb to the union's mindless diktats.

The attack that never came was from the Anti-Apartheid Movement itself, soon to be so vociferous in its complaints about *Graceland*. What, in the end, was the difference between play and record? Both were created in South Africa, with a cast and production team of mostly South Africans, a clear violation of the cultural boycott. Solly Smith, head of the London office of the ANC, was a frequent visitor to the show and once shocked the cast by reciting Voortrekker ballads and recounting the respect his grandfather had for the toughness of the Boers.

The turmoil in South Africa transfixed liberals in the northern hemisphere while also presenting us with a gift—the exiled musicians, actors, politicians, writers, and ordinary refugees who came to live among us. The Blue Notes and the *Poppie Nongena* company showed me a commitment and an idealism that I treasure still.

∽

Sixteen-year-old Johnny Clegg was walking near his home when he saw Sipho Mchunu sitting on a wall, playing a guitar. Fascinated, he persuaded Mchunu to give him maskanda lessons. Thus began Clegg's journey into the heart of a culture simultaneously local and remote. "To be with the Zulus I had to become humble and learn how to behave." He studied the language and became a scholar of Zulu epic poetry.

Acoustic duets with Mchunu at the Market Theatre in the early seventies evolved into South Africa's first successful "fusion" bands: Juluka and its successor Savuka. White South African students—and the French—loved their combination of mbaqanga and rock, but timidity about the "Zulu sound" limited their international impact; while African producers were adding ever more bottom to their records, Clegg's label insisted he not make his mixes too heavy. I met Johnny in London once during the mid-eighties; encouraged by my interest, he grabbed a broom handle and a dustbin lid and belted out high-kicking Zulu chants to a bemused Sunday-lunch gathering of Brits in a Battersea flat.

Musical mixing spread; Black musicians hanging around studios met White bands who eagerly recruited their superior skills. Some were even pressed into service on Boer country music; one recalls being astonished at the luxurious treatment—*Cape Town by plane!*—plus a multiple of his normal pay scale for a radio broadcast. The authorities seemed relatively relaxed; their fury was directed more at White singers who protested against the military draft or supported the boycott. Bernoldus Niemand's anti-conscription song "Nobody" was banned outright, while the secret agent Erasmus would later testify about his campaign to destroy the career of the White singer Roger Lucey after he stepped out of line with his lyrics.

South Africa's military campaigns failed to prevent Angola, Mozambique, and Namibia becoming independent majority-ruled nations. In 1989, Prime Minister P. W. "Big Crocodile" Botha handed over the reins to F. W. de Klerk, who, to general bewilderment, un-banned the ANC. De Klerk could see that apartheid was doomed; he also understood that the Boers' old enemies, the Zulus, could be their allies. While most South Africans considered the Homelands system an unworkable mockery, de Klerk's promise to make KwaZulu-Natal a quasi-independent state appealed to many Zulus. Whites in Natal, moreover, tended to hold more complex views than most, often speaking a bit of the language and considering themselves "honorary" Zulus. As ANC strikes and demonstrations were being violently suppressed, Zulu marches got permits and arms were given to Inkatha gangs. Evaporation of the broad African audience for isicathamiya and mbaqanga during the 1980s was but a footnote to the greater conflict between forces battling for the soul of the country.

In the Xhosa traditions that exerted such a strong influence on the ANC, decisions are taken by a council of elders while the praise-singer who illuminates issues at their gatherings doesn't hesitate to criticize, even mock, the chiefs. Zulus, on the other hand, defer to a powerful king who brooks no dissent. Mandela's Xhosa reasonableness provided South Africa with the chance to emerge peacefully from two centuries of brutality, while Zulu defiance became one of the few cards left for the Nationalists to play. When Zulu Jacob Zuma was elected ANC leader in 2008 and went on to become president, he introduced media laws restricting the reporting of government corruption and malfeasance and sued the painter of a disrespectful portrait.

Paul Simon arrived in Johannesburg believing that "as cold as I am, I can do this privately, no one will be paying attention." Out, as he imagined, of the spotlight, he created a work that reveled in the contradictions inherent in the developed world's attraction to exotic music. The gap in values between New York's Upper West Side and the hills of KwaZulu-Natal was made clear. As Simon sings:

> *She's a rich girl*
> *She don't try to hide it*
> *She's got diamonds on the soles of her shoes*

In *isiZulu*, Ladysmith complains:

> How does it happen?
> Awa, awa, the girls are self-reliant

"Homeless" evokes sympathy for refugees:

> Strong wind destroy our home
> Many dead, tonight it could be you

Unbeknownst to anglophones, Ladysmith counters by boasting of gaining respect and revenge, recording in their ancient enemy's capital:

> We are the conquerors
> We fought the battle in the heart of London

Simon's and Shabalala's vocal tones represent contrasting notions of masculinity. Paul is the consummate "new man"—soft-spoken and reasonable—while Shabalala's intense nasal timbres reflect the fierceness of his complaints about changes in Zulu society. Mbaqanga and isicathamiya constituted rearguard actions against the loss of traditional male roles in South African society; *Graceland*'s production enhanced their power even as Simon's lyrics undercut their meaning.

Isigqi was central to the Zulu s' resistance to the "Rainbow Nation" ideal. Literally, it means "something like sound" and represents the essence of Zulu-ness: a deep voice, a high step, a resonant stomp, a gesture. Lured to Johannesburg by the isigqi urgency of the Boyoyo Boys, Simon, royal emissary from the Rainbow world, became an unwitting Zulu acolyte. Though fewer than half the *Graceland* musicians were actually Zulu, all knew the semiotic language; you couldn't prosper as a 1970s Johannesburg session man if you didn't. Roy Halee's use of samples and electronic augmentation—a Synclavier to deepen the opening accordion flourish, for example—was subtler and more sophisticated, but not fundamentally different from what West Nkosi and the others were doing as they churned out assembly-line mbaqanga.

The Johannesburg tracks challenged Simon to work harder, to listen more closely, to match their nuances with his own. Paul didn't need to propel the songs, he could ride them; the powerful playing inspired him to compose the lyrics of a lifetime, "the best I ever did." Perhaps this unfamiliar rhythmic terrain freed his right brain to give voice to dreamscapes and uncanny visions of the future ("the bomb in the baby carriage"). Few fusioneers since have worked so hard to meet an alien rhythm on its own terms, to focus on what they do best and leave the propulsion to the experts. More than any other recording of the decade, *Graceland* opened Western ears to music from far away. When Simon revisited the album in 2012, the touring show was greeted in London's Hyde Park by a huge throng. As I walked through the crowd, everyone was singing along, the twenty-somethings and the sixty-somethings; all seemed to know the words by heart.

In 1987, starting to sense victory, the ANC organized a "Culture in a New South Africa" conference in Amsterdam. South Africa–based musician-delegates (the government had given up blocking exit visas by then) were astonished by the level of international support for the Anti-Apartheid Movement; in those pre-internet years, little news of it had trickled past government censorship. Within three years, Mandela was free; 1994 saw his election as president as the ANC swept to power. Peace broke out in KwaZulu-Natal after back-room deals engineered by Jacob Zuma allowed Inkatha to avoid electoral humiliation and gain a few ministerial posts in the ANC government.

The end of apartheid led to the popping of musical bubbles; after years of struggle, audiences were looking for light relief. When disc jockeys Oskido and Christos slowed American house tracks down to 110 beats per minute, lyrics rapped in local "vernacs" could be more easily superimposed and *kwaito* was born, its tinny sound paying homage to the Casio-driven bubblegum hits of the seventies and eighties. The ANC government was quick to embrace this new musical landscape, inviting kwaito artists to perform at rallies, while Mandela encouraged them to write positive, optimistic lyrics. As the AIDS epidemic spread (and before President Mbeki's delusional betrayal of those efforts) the government used kwaito to increase awareness of the disease. In tune with their electoral triumph, ANC's disco trumped Inkatha's mbaqanga.

Nor could churches escape the transatlantic onslaught; modern R&B-inflected beats swamped local styles. (Zulu churches, of course, provided the bulk of resistance to electronic keyboards.) African Americans, Oprah Winfrey and Whoopi Goldberg among them, came searching for roots (at the wrong end of the continent). South Africans aspired to be like them, often affecting American accents.

South African mines once had trouble finding enough cheap labor, but by the 1990s the country was an immigration magnet. Johannesburg filled with Nigerians, Congolese, and Kenyans, though their arrival failed to trigger much musical cross-talk; South Africans have never seemed much interested in foreign culture if it isn't American. In 2008, Township-dwellers (reportedly led by Zulus) rioted against the immigrants, burning down businesses, looting and killing. The apartheid-era practice of enabling the powerful to seize the best land, squeezing locals onto barren margins, then forcing desperate breadwinners into infrastructure-starved shantytowns and poorly paid assembly-line jobs has become a business model emulated the world over.

Gallo and other labels tried to follow up the international successes of Ladysmith and Mahlathini, but only the golden voice of Vusi Mahlasela gained any traction outside the country. Artists who might have made an impact were hampered by the over-slick production and cheesy fusion impulses of local producers; music buffs in Europe and North America may have supported political modernity, but few had much time for drum machines and synthesizers. Hilda Tloubatla of the Mahotella Queens pointed out how essential music had been in pushing back against apartheid: "Then you had to stay an African and be black and never think of being white. But now the young musicians . . . have taken too much from the Americans."

Enthusiasm for the country's musical heritage now lies primarily abroad, though the new middle class did enjoy the Market Theatre production of *Sophiatown*, a nostalgic revue with modernized jive, retro sets, and period outfits. Hugh Masekela created *Stimela*, a stage show based on the trains that brought workers to the mines, which played to genteel audiences, both Black and White.

Mahlathini's death in 1999 triggered Gallo's first concerted attempt to mine the catalogue, which was hampered by having lost most of its master tapes in a warehouse fire. That collectors have been able to hear so much of South Africa's musical past is due, as in many such cases, to independent archivists. Rob Allingham, an American who grew up in California with matching passions for steam trains and jazz 78s, came to South Africa in the early seventies to work on South Africa's wonderfully antiquated railways. Between shifts, he went through the Townships buying 78s, 45s, and LPs; his vast collection is now the source for most reissues of South African music and his encyclopedic knowledge graces the booklets. The prime international outlet for the back catalogue has been UK-based Earthworks Records, founded by Trevor Herman and the late Jumbo Vanrenen, South African expats who first met while buying records from workers on Cape Town train station platforms.

When Zulu Jacob Zuma replaced Xhosa Thabo Mbeki as leader of the ANC and as president, it completed a transformation in the relationship between Zulus and Mandela's party. Since Inkatha's 1994 electoral defeat, more and more Zulus have joined the ANC, worrying some that they could become a dominant force in the organization. There have been accusations that, like their great-grandfathers who refused to go down the mines, Zulus disdain heavy work, preferring soft jobs and patronage earned by their new party allegiance.

City-dwellers have revived the tradition of sending boys to the country to be circumcised, a custom Shaka had ended for Zulus but which Zuma encouraged after politicians of other backgrounds mocked him for being uncircumcised. Traditional stick-fighting also made a comeback among Xhosa and Zulus, while middle-class Blacks began traveling to KwaZulu-Natal to buy beads and trinkets from bemused villagers (who were urged by local leaders and preachers—some things never change—to drop traditional garb and "modernize"). Not that such developments had much effect on the broad popular market for music, which remains in thrall to US R&B and hip-hop, though Ukhozi FM, the change-resistant Zulu radio station, retains the biggest listenership in the country. Neighboring Botswana, meanwhile, treats the Xan with the contempt White colonists once showed towards the Tswana, calling them "backward" and corralling them onto reservations.

When South Africa hosted the 2010 World Cup, the organizers seemed to think that having Angélique Kidjo, a Benin-born New Yorker, Tinariwen from the Malian Sahara, and the Colombian Shakira alongside African Americans John Legend, the Black-Eyed Peas, and Alicia Keys was an appropriate musical line-up for the opening ceremony. Protests brought a belated invitation for Vusi Mahlasela, but even after their 7-Up and baked-bean commercials, Ladysmith Black Mambazo were deemed too rustic for a global audience of football fans. The closest the world's mainstream media has come lately to any glimpse of South Africa's cultural roots were the 1970s *pantsula* outfits on dancers in a Beyoncé video.

Invoking roots in today's South Africa can be a tricky business; youth leader Julius Malema was expelled from the ANC for leading a "kill the Boer" toyi-toyi chant at a rally. He insisted he was simply honoring the crowds who had defied machine-gun-toting policemen with it during the years of struggle, but the claim was undermined by his threats to lead Zimbabwe-style seizures of White farms. Jacob Zuma's Zulu traditionalism—he married multiple wives—emboldened rural chiefs, who began flexing the power of tribal courts. There has even been a movement to enshrine this reactionary system in South African law. Women's rights activist Nomboniso Gasa sees it as an attempt to "turn rural people into subjects rather than citizens." The issues aren't entirely straightforward: South African jurisprudence can be remote, slow-moving, and corrupt, while tribal justice is at least nearby and everyone knows both accused and victim. From afar, we know which recordings we like, but on the ground music is more than an abstraction; it is a powerfully coded representation of social trends and political change.

In the summer of 2011, I attended a tribute concert to the late Miriam Makeba at London's Hackney Empire, starring Hugh Masekela.

The crowd was primarily expat Black South Africans, liberally scattered with Whites of undetermined nationality. The ingénues hoping to follow in Makeba's footsteps were Thandiswa and Lira, the cream of a new South African generation. From the opening set by Vusi Mahlasela, all the vocals were strong, while Masekela's playing was as brilliantly distinctive as ever. The crowd loved all of the "Mama Africa" songs and seemed not to mind that the rhythm section was mired somewhere in the American jazz-rock-fusion world of the 1980s, with hardly a flicker of South African feel. When Thandiswa sang "Pata Pata," Masekela got a big cheer for getting down on his knees and chastely miming the frisk. At the slightest hint of isigqi, the crowd roared; they clearly would have leaped to their feet and danced if the band had broken into an mbaqanga step, but that seemed the farthest thing from Masekela's Sophiatown jazzer mind.

On a brighter note, the documentary film *AmaZulu* is set in a high school in a Durban Township that starts each day with singing in the courtyard. The harmonies are pure Zulu, the voices powerful and uplifting, and the refrain translates as "*bring the weapons.*" But in this case, their weapons of choice are books, the students' own intelligence, and their Shaka-like determination.

One would think, given *Graceland*'s dramatic boost to the anti-apartheid cause in the late eighties, that talk of Simon's "betrayal" might have dwindled over the years. But the release of *Under African Skies* in 2012, a documentary about the album, triggered a chorus of the same complaints and denunciations, with no one attempting to articulate why *Graceland* was such a crime while all those theatrical exports were not. Perhaps the album's unspoken transgression was using music of the Zulus, seen justifiably by many in the ANC as their enemies.

My focus on *Graceland* risks evoking one of those Hollywood films where a White hero comes to the aid of suffering Africans. That's *Graceland* in a nutshell, you could say, with Joseph Shabalala in the role of "loyal African sidekick." Simon, however, has always made it clear he received more than he gave, though he certainly contributed a lot, financially, in credit, and in exposure. *Graceland* more resembles the tale of the Township music icon Benny Goodman and his "use" of the talents of Fletcher Henderson, Teddy Wilson, and Lionel Hampton to build a swing empire. One can't say that Ladysmith Black Mambazo, Ray Phiri, and the others went on to careers at the same level as those Goodman sidemen, but that has more to do with the era and South Africa's ambivalence towards its own music.

"You haven't heard *this* before!"; that accordion flourish certainly got the world's attention. But, like the cassette on the drive to Montauk, *Graceland*'s appeal lay as much in the familiar as the unknown. South African music—be it "Wimoweh" or "Homeless," "The Click Song" or "Grazing in the Grass," "Nkosi Sikelel' iAfrika" or "Manenberg"—has always caught the northern ear that way: more like our own than any other African music yet alluringly exotic at the same time. Despite the battles over singing styles, Wesleyan hymns struck a deep chord in South Africa, finding echoes in the texture, if not the fluidity, of local harmonies. South Africa is also the only African land to have experienced an industrial revolution. Despite the fact that most slaves brought to North America were from kingdoms as remote from Nguni country as Andalusia is from Norway, South Africa evolved a musical language intriguingly resonant of African-American.

South Africans plundered their conquerors' music with great sophistication, creating a culture of rich complexity. We, the faraway listeners, have been gifted with the artistry of Solomon Linda, Spokes Mashiyane, Hugh Masekela, Miriam Makeba, Dudu Pukwana, Abdullah Ibrahim, Chris McGregor, Mahlathini, Ladysmith Black Mambazo, Vusi Mahlasela, the casts of *Sarafina!* and *Poppie Nongena*, to say nothing of the crowds who defied machine guns and tanks with song while we looked on—and listened—from our northern hemisphere armchairs. Even as apartheid-era Africans aspired to the gains of Black Americans, it was the US Civil Rights movement—and the worldwide cause of human rights—that drew inspiration from South Africa and its music more than vice versa.

II
Babalú-Ayé

Humiliation was staring Desi Arnaz in the face. It was 1937, the opening night of his run at a Miami Beach nightclub, and despite the frilly sleeves on their shirts, the bumbling musicians Xavier Cugat had sent him couldn't tell a *clave* from the cleavage at the front-row tables. The tepid applause that greeted the opening numbers had faded to near silence; he had to do something.

According to Desi's autobiography, an image from his 1920s Cuban childhood came to him in that moment. He was on a reviewing stand beside his father, the mayor of Santiago, watching the carnival street bands known as *comparsas* parade past. They danced in a line, *conguero* in the lead and everyone following his rhythm. Arnaz's problem-solving brain would one day make him the first TV star to own syndication rights to his own hit show and thus one of the richest men in Hollywood. That night, it told him to grab a conga drum, start singing an Afro-Cuban chant, and invite the prettiest girl from those front tables to join on behind, hands on his hips; as more and more patrons fell into line, he circled the club—all the while dancing to Latin music's simplest beat—then led them out onto the sidewalk, startling Collins Avenue traffic as they thrust out a hip or a leg on the final stroke of that *1–2–3–4–cong-Á*.

The next night the club was packed. Desi's conga line became the talk of Miami, then the talk of New York, and finally, the talk of Hollywood.

He was on his way, the latest Latin star to light up US show business in the years before World War Two. Through the soft-focus lens of Desi's memoir, the Santiago carnival seems like a Cuban version of a Trinidad steel-band parade or a glittering Rio de Janeiro samba competition. But it wasn't like that at all.

Standing beside them on the reviewing stand that day was Alfonso Menencier, the Afro-Cuban ward heeler who delivered the Black vote. He wore an immaculate white suit and straw boater, held a silver-topped cane, and looked ill at ease. The barefoot, half-naked bodies passing before them were an uncomfortable reminder of the four short decades since slavery had been abolished in Cuba, of how blockade-running ships had continued to bring human contraband from Africa until the last minute, and that the conga line had originated in the chanting of slaves chained single-file as they were marched to the cane fields, where life expectancy was less than a decade.

These parades went back centuries to Kings' Day and pre-Lenten celebrations, when slaves were allowed a fleeting respite from the killing fields. Some onlookers would throw coins and cheer, while others recoiled from something they found "savage" or "barbaric." Before Emancipation in 1886, White Cubans could rest assured that the next day drummers and dancers would be back where they belonged, in the fields and *barracones*. Modern notions, that these shabbily dressed and very Black revelers were actually fellow Cubans and that some twenties intellectuals were making the case that this so-very-African music represented a national culture, made many Whites (as well as aspirational Afro-Cubans) uncomfortable.

No one was more uncomfortable than Desidero Arnaz, Sr.; in 1925, he banned the conga lines, describing his son's future meal ticket as "full of improper contortions and immoral gestures that do not belong to the culture of [Santiago] . . . [E]pileptic, ragged and semi-naked crowds run through the streets . . . they disrespect society, offend the morals, cause a bad opinion of our customs, lower us in the eyes of foreigners, and, most gravely, contaminate by example the minors . . . who are carried away by the heat of the display . . . engaging in frenetic competitions of bodily flexibility in those shameful, wanton tournaments."

Another prohibition issued by the mayor forbade the use of carnival masks. The idea that Whites in disguise—women, for example—could join the crowds dancing in the streets . . . well, the possibilities didn't bear thinking about.

∽

In a photograph of Machito and His Afro-Cuban All-Stars onstage in New York in the early 1940s, a painting of a conguero looms over them. He's huge, of indeterminate race, with bulging biceps, his hands poised over the head of a phallic-looking conga drum held by a strap at his waist, a precursor of the rock hero with guitar neck erect in note-bending solo.

By 1937, the conga drum had already entered the zeitgeist, Cuban revues having popularized it in Paris and London. Desi's role as Xavier Cugat's protégé resulted from the bandleader's search for a good-looking White guy who could both play it and sing. Like Sam Phillips in Memphis fifteen years later, who realized that finding a handsome cracker who could sing rhythm and blues would make him a fortune, Cugat sensed that anglophones were ready for someone sexy but safe to lead them onto the dancefloor and show them how to shake their asses like a Cuban.

Across the Florida Strait, the island had bowed to tourist pressure and reinstated the comparsas. Time and again, we see local culture reviled and repressed by an insecure bourgeoisie but embraced by outsiders. Grudgingly (and often avariciously), guardians of national culture admit that, well, if foreigners like it so much, there *might* be something there whose value they failed to recognize. In Cuba's case, this meant drums. As bars and nightclubs filled with Americans looking for somewhere to drink, gamble, and shed their inhibitions, it made sense to bring back the carnival in a more glamorous Rio/Trinidad mode, with formal competitions, cleaned-up costumes, and strict policing to make sure things didn't get out of hand.

One figure dominated the Havana parades of the late 1930s. Wearing a white tuxedo and sporting a top hat, conga drum strapped on, chanting Yorùbá and Abakuá ritual songs and playing complex rhythms, was Desi's opposite, the Blackest, most skilful conguero of them all, Chano Pozo.

While Arnaz's maternal grandfather had founded Bacardi, Pozo was born in a Havana slum. When his mother died, his father took up with Natalia, who already had a son, Félix Chappottín, the future revolutionary of Afro-Cuban trumpet. Their *solar*, or tenement, was called "El Africa" and it was as easy to fall into a life of crime there as it was to absorb music. Perhaps it was Chano's good fortune to be arrested at fifteen and spend a few formative years in a young offenders' institution where he learned to be charming when it suited. After his release, the owner of *El País* took a shine to him and gave him newspapers to sell. Soon Pozo was at the heart of the revived carnival scene, the most powerful drummer and loudest singer around, moving from comparsa to comparsa, whichever offered the most money. After falling for a dancer with Los Dandys, he settled on them, chanting, "*I hear a drum, Mama, they're calling me! Yes, yes, it's Los Dandys!*" so it could be heard for blocks around.

Like Desi, Chano adored women and had a powerful effect on them. He combined menial jobs—shining shoes, selling papers—with a strutting, idle life, wandering through the *solares* looking for trouble, usually in the form of angry husbands. He liked the fight game and joined the World Featherweight Champion Kid Chocolate's entourage. Pozo became as street-famous as *soneros* (*son* singers) of legend, such as Mulenze. Even after starting to make real money, he remained in El Africa, sauntering out to the communal sink in the late morning in a red silk bathrobe, his gold Cadillac parked in front.

Tourists loved the drum; Afro-Cuban percussion, chant, and mock-ritual dancing became a featured attraction at Havana's hottest nightclubs. Impresarios conjured up themed shows; Chano starred in *Tambó en negro mayor* and *Batamu* (which means "drum festival" in Yorùbá). In the latter he shared the stage with Rita Montaner, a sepia-skinned operetta star who had turned her back on that world to become an interpreter—and champion—of Afro-Cuban music. She took Chano under her wing, convinced of his greatness.

A Black Cuban would struggle to succeed in those days without help from light-skinned friends, sponsors, mentors, or lovers. After Rita and the *El País* publisher came Amado Trinidad, head of the island-spanning RHC Cadena radio network. He set Chano up with a shoeshine stand in the station lobby, where he would sing and play his conga, joining *conjuntos* and *orquestas* on air, probing the possibilities of blending his powerful drumming with dance bands. But his most important ally would prove to be an old friend from the solares who returned to Havana in 1937 like a prodigal son.

∽

Miguelito Valdés had grown up on those same street corners. As kids, he and Chano would hustle coins, Miguelito chanting in Abakuá as Chano played the conga. But Valdés was an anomaly in this world, where one of the defining hierarchies concerned the amount of African blood in one's veins; Miguelito had none.

Valdés's mother was Mayan from Yucatán, mistress to a retired Spanish general. His father paid occasional attention, though not enough to lift mother and son out of the solares. Miguelito grew up feeling Black but looking coppery, with high "Indio" cheekbones. He absorbed the ritual chants of the *orishas* and sang them with the same nuance and commitment as his neighbors. In years to come, he would bring these African gods with him as he ascended to the highest rungs of international show business; in the early years of his fame, he made a point of singing Afro-Cuban religious songs wearing a tuxedo.

Valdés not only shared Pozo's mastery of Afro-Cuban rhythm and melody but also had Arnaz's ability to stay a few steps ahead, outmaneuvering everyone. Miguelito, though, was devoted to his fellow musicians, opening doors for them, always boosting the music and the players, never turning his back on those who lacked his confidence to move effortlessly through the worlds of business and money, the world of Anglos. Within months of his return from a few years in Panama, he had formed a cooperative of top players and brought them to the Casino de la Playa, a new nightclub where tourists and high rollers drank, danced, and gambled. He secured sponsorship from a soap company for a daily radio show and got the band signed to RCA Victor Records.

Having surveyed the Havana scene, Valdés pulled some of its most brilliant strands into his vision for the Orquesta Casino de la Playa. Cubans had fallen for American big-band swing; imported and domestic groups played it across Havana every night. With one leap, Valdés gave Cuban music a brassy, optimistic American horn section while also reaching deep into the music of the Afro-Cuban bars and social clubs. This world was being transformed by *tres* player, composer, and bandleader Arsenio Rodríguez, "El Ciego Maravilloso" ("The Marvelous Blind Man"), and his incorporation of the conga drum into his seven-piece conjunto.

Valdés wanted Rodríguez to join his orchestra, but in 1937, no swanky Havana club would accept a musician that Black. And Arsenio wasn't just Black in complexion, he was uncompromisingly African in attitude and expression. In contrast to the Cuban stage tradition of *bozal* accents (think of Stepin Fetchit or *Amos 'n' Andy*), Rodríguez's songs were revolutionary in their use of authentic Afro-Cuban speech. Two years before Billie Holiday recorded "Strange Fruit," Rodríguez wrote (and Valdés recorded) "Bruca manigua," which means "Brutal White Man." The lyrics combine Spanish with handed-down Ki-Kongo and Afro-Spanish pidgin, proclaiming: "*Yo son carabalí / Nego de nación / Sin libetá / No pueo viví / Mundele acabá / Con mi corasón / Tanto maltratá / Cuerpo dan fuirí*" ("*I'm Carabalí / Black man of a nation / Without freedom I can't live / White man finished off / My heart / So mistreated / They kill the body*").

A Victor recording team booked three days in a room above the Rumba Club, June 15–17, 1937. Bands and singers came and went. When Valdés's Orquesta set up at the end of the last day, only six blank discs were left; the three double-sided 78s they produced changed the face of Latin music. Aside from arrangements showing that Cuban dance music could stand toe-to-toe with American swing, these tracks laid down enduring markers for individual performance. The tres, for example, is a particularly Cuban survivor of medieval Arabo-Spanish plucked instruments, with three widely separated pairs of strings on a body that resembles a cross between an oud and a mandolin. Arsenio was the master of this instrument, and his playing on these recordings set a benchmark for tres virtuosos to follow.

The day's other great solos were by pianist Anselmo Sacasas; with their cascades of octave-spanning arpeggios, they mirrored the octave-apart tunings of the top and bottom string-pairs of the tres. In the impressionistic cadenzas of Latin pianists from Bebo and Chucho Valdés to Eddie Palmieri and Gonzalo Rubalcaba, echoes of Sacasas's playing that day continue to resonate.

But the most striking feature was Valdés's vocals. As far back as the eighteenth century, popular contradanzas had featured sections of differing tempi. Late in the evening, when older dancers had retired, codas at the ends of songs provided an opportunity for the Black and mixed-race musicians (Whites weren't interested in such a lowly and ill-paid profession) to inject a more African feel and for young couples to step more freely and rhythmically. By 1937, these *montuno* ("from the mountain") sections had become a place to shift gears, for instrumentalists to stretch out over a repetitive groove and for soneros to improvise around the song's theme. Valdés combined operatic lung power and the attack of an American jazz singer with a deep knowledge of Abakuá and Yorùbá chant and Afro-Cuban argot. We'll never know if ghostly unrecorded figures such as Mulenze improvised as deftly as Valdés, but singers from Bogotá to the Bronx were transfixed by the Casino recordings; the legacy of Celia Cruz, Benny Moré, and Héctor Lavoe starts here.

In New York that year, Tito Puente was a rebellious teenager ready to reject the Latin culture of his Puerto Rican neighborhood in favor of becoming a jitterbug champion or a Gene Krupa–style swing drummer. In the Colony Music shop on Broadway one day, he took the Casino 78s into a booth out of curiosity. He bought all three, took them home, listened over and over, and started playing along with a set of timbales: "They are responsible for what I am today."

To bring his Afro-Cuban heritage into the music of the Orquesta, Valdés naturally sought out his old friend from the solares. Chano Pozo had begun creating songs, but had neither the musical training nor any idea how to register them for copyright. Miguelito brought him to Sacasas, the group's chief arranger, who set Chano's compositions down on paper.

Then he introduced him to the Havana office of Peer Southern Music, a publisher that had flourished by copyrighting bawdy vaudeville songs, Appalachian hillbilly ballads, Mississippi Delta blues, and Mexican *corridos* that other companies disdained. Valdés and the Orquesta proceeded to make a series of great recordings of Pozo's songs.

With Afro-Cuban drums moving to the forefront of Havana nightlife, other groups were looking for similar material. An encounter at the radio station led to Chano's first hit as a singer: "Blen Blen Blen" with the Havana Casino Orchestra. Like many Pozo compositions, it could be seen as little more than the vocalization of a drum pattern or a line of doggerel, but Chano had a wonderful sense of melody—of hooks, even—and a talent for fitting rhythm and words together. His use of African phrases took his songs far beyond any US equivalent; America's shift in the early nineteenth century to breeding its own slaves rather than importing them from Africa meant that by the middle of the twentieth century, few African Americans felt much connection to the lands of their ancestors.

Fleeing war-ravaged Europe, the post-Diaghilev Original Ballet Russe arrived in Havana in 1941, where it fell apart, unable to pay its dancers. The Tropicana, a spectacular new nightclub in a verdant Havana suburb, commissioned *Conga pantera*, a lurid pageant featuring the stranded ballerina Tania Leskova as a panther and Chano as the hunter. Surreal descriptions are all that survive: the conguero Mongo Santamaría up in a tree accompanying the pursuit of the Russian (very White, dressed in black) by the Cuban (very Black, dressed in white), while Rita Montaner and Bola de Nieve sang the narration surrounded by a chorus line of near-naked girls. In this collision of Busby Berkeley–style Hollywood glamour, Diaghilev sophistication, and Afro-Cuban sensuality lie the roots of the Las Vegas and Folies Bergère stage shows that define our notions of cabaret spectacle to this day.

Chano was the first to build a stand for three drums of differing pitches, helping him to meet the challenge of integrating congas into his new orchestra. He brought his stepbrother, Félix Chappottín, over from Arsenio's conjunto to play trumpet, taking the blind pioneer's ideas and making them bigger, louder, even more African. Hits ensued; at the end of World War Two, his triumphant "Pin Pin Cayó Berlín, Pon Pon Cayó Japón" became an anthem of victory across Latin America.

Like a later generation of rock heroes, the demands of Chano's hectic life plus the money to afford it drew him to cocaine and he became known as a *huele-huele* ("sniff-sniff"). His visits to the Peer Southern office demanding royalty advances became more frequent and less reasonable; refusal could trigger a furniture-smashing tantrum. Following one tirade, Peer's man in Havana told his aide to get a gun; when the drummer stormed back the next day, shouting demands and clenching his enormous fists, the assistant shot him. He survived with a bullet lodged in his spine largely because the radio station arranged prompt treatment at Havana's best hospital. Without such intervention, a Cuban as Black as Chano would have stood little chance.

Valdés was having hits, too, the biggest being his version of "Babalú," a song composed by the patrician Margarita Lecuona that borrows snatches of Yorùbá chant and recounts how the owner of a Santería fetish honors this West African god. After RCA sent him on a tour stretching from Mexico to the southernmost cities of Latin America, Miguelito's photo on the cover of the sheet music was pinned to female fans' walls across the hemisphere and he became known as "Mr. Babalú."

Desi heard the Valdés recording in New York, incorporated the song into his cabaret act, and began calling himself "Mr. Babalú," too. Comparing the two versions, it is tempting to assign Valdés the "Ain't That a Shame" role of Fats Domino, with Desi as Pat Boone. Beyond Miguelito's clear-eyed authenticity and nuanced singing versus Desi's eye-rolling mannerisms and broad-stroke vocals, the other great difference lies in the rapid-fire improvisations in the montuno that Arnaz doesn't even attempt. Valdés's cascade of Africanisms evokes the orishas in ways even the song's composer could never have imagined.

Valdés always had an eye on New York, but Arnaz's blatant pilferage forced the issue. He and Sacasas arrived in April 1940, ostensibly for a gig at the Riviera club just across the George Washington Bridge in Fort Lee, New Jersey. When the American Musicians' Union blocked

Sacasas's contract, Miguelito decided to bide his time and wait for a summons from Xavier Cugat, whose Latin orchestra had been a fixture at the Starlight Ballroom of the Waldorf-Astoria Hotel since 1932. Valdés turned down offer after offer, forcing the bandleader up to $150 a week, which was a huge sum then. Miguelito earned it, singing five sets a night, filling the house and drawing ecstatic media acclaim.

His other coup was probably even more painful for Cugat, a self-styled ladies' man. On opening night, knowing Valdés was a sensual performer, Xavier warned him not to "move around" too much onstage; his pride in presenting the star's New York debut was tempered by concern that he would get upstaged. Miguelito ignored the instructions. Frank "Machito" Grillo once described him as "this gorgeous hunk of a man, very handsome . . . The women were crazy . . . they would not stop screaming . . . He smiled through it all." Valdés didn't need a whole crowd of women, though, after a glamorous redhead in the front row that night summoned him to her table. Virginia Hill—a constant presence in New York gossip columns, friend to gangsters and mistress of Bugsy Siegel, with a taste for Latin lovers and the money to hold their attention—was too important a patron for Cugat to cross. Before the first week was out, she had given Valdés a diamond-studded watch and four thousand dollars (which he sent to his Havana girlfriend to buy a house). With Hill on his side, he could "move around" as much he liked and Cugat couldn't say a thing.

It can seem quite bizarre for a crowd of wealthy New Yorkers to be so enthralled by songs evoking Afro-Cuban life and Yorùbá religion. "Babalú," the showstopper (which later became a theme song of *I Love Lucy*), was, in the words of Cuban expert Ned Sublette, about a "smallpox-afflicted, Dahomeyan god who walks with a crutch, attended by dogs who lick the ulcers on his legs." But was this any stranger than millions of White American kids in the sixties lapping up an assortment of British art students singing about hard times in the Mississippi Delta?

Desi's light could have been dimmed by the arrival of the real Mr. Babalú, but the ever-resourceful charmer was never at a loss. Cast as a handsome Latin football star at an Ivy League college in the Broadway show *Too Many Girls*, he would run around the corner after the curtain call to his regular club, La Conga, and lead the line. Miguelito may have won Virginia Hill, but Arnaz had his pick of the Broadway and Hollywood starlets who frequented La Conga: Betty Grable, Martha Raye, Diosa Costello (a rising Latina star on her way to Hollywood), and many other beauties fell for him. When *Too Many Girls* was made into a film, Desi went west; in the cast of Hollywood co-eds, he found his own redhead—Lucille Ball.

After columnist Walter Winchell dubbed Miguelito Valdés New York's biggest star next to Frank Sinatra, the Starlight Room was no longer big enough for both bandleader and singer. When a jealous Cugat persuaded the director of *You Were Never Lovelier* to cut Miguelito's scene from the movie, divorce was swift. Valdés began his own run at La Conga, and business was so good that a number of midtown nightclubs had to close for lack of clientele. Having altered the course of Latin music with Casino de la Playa, he cut a series of sides with Machito's band that, with their powerful American brass section and higher fidelity sound, pushed the envelope still further. Miguelito returned to Havana in triumph in 1945 for a celebratory concert at Teatro Martí. Chano and the Orquesta Casino de la Playa accompanied him; backstage, he urged his old friend from the solares to follow him north.

∽

Pozo took his time about it, but eventually arrived in January 1947 and went straight to La Conga, where Miguelito was on a sold-out run. Valdés persuaded the club's owner to book the conguero and his dancer girlfriend as an opening act. Within a few weeks, Chano had established himself across the city. Down the street at the Roxy Theater, he appeared in Katherine Dunham's *Bal nègre* revue and joined the Sunday rumba matinees at the Manhattan Ballroom (where the orchestra would have to start playing and drown him out as he sat center-stage, skin oiled, chanting and pounding the conga with no sign of stopping). New York's top Latin stars showed up to back him (for no pay) as Chano Pozo y Su Ritmo de Tambores in a series of historic recordings.

Americans were amazed by Chano. Latin music had been edging into popular consciousness, but mostly as a pace-changing novelty for

Hollywood and Broadway. At the Waldorf, Cugat would play a foxtrot to fill the floor, then shift to a tango or a rumba, counting on Yankee pride to keep dancers from retreating to their tables. Americans tended to blur "Latins" (excepting the apparently all-White Argentines) into a cartoonish Mexican-flavored composite, in which women were sultry and men were moustachioed and either comically unthreatening or schemingly villainous. Desi rattled those clichés with his sexy but wholesome good looks. Miguelito took it further, exciting women as much as Rita Hayworth (originally Margarita Carmen Cansino) was arousing the men.

Pozo was something completely different; the intense Africanness of his drumming and chanting and his fierce masculine presence gripped audiences. There was nothing remotely resembling him in African-American popular music. Women didn't scream for him as they did for his old friend, but many fainted.

Due to the wartime ban on shellac, the bebop movement led by Dizzy Gillespie, Charlie Parker, and Miles Davis seemed to spring forth fully formed in 1945, at least so far as the record-buying public were concerned. This revolution had, so far, been largely harmonic. Now Gillespie wanted to change the beat; ever since sitting next to the Cuban Mario Bauzá in Cab Calloway's brass section a decade earlier, he had been fascinated by the possibilities of Afro-Cuban rhythms.

In 1947, capping two years of growing excitement around the new jazz, Dizzy was booked for a Carnegie Hall concert. He wanted to use the occasion to make a statement featuring Latin percussion, but hadn't found a conguero flexible and skilled enough to navigate between the 4/4 swing of jazz and Afro-Cuban rhythms. When Bauzá took him to East Harlem to meet the new drummer in town, Dizzy found shaking Chano's hand was "like being crushed between cinder blocks." He had found his man.

Rehearsals were difficult; Chano struggled with the straight American time, and Dizzy's rhythm section were nonplussed by the complexity of the Cuban's playing. For many in the group, the future would lead them far from bebop: pianist John Lewis, drummer Kenny Clarke, and vibes player Milt Jackson would later form the sedate Modern Jazz Quartet, while bassist Ray Brown became a central figure in the sort of mainstream jazz that emerged in the fifties as bebop's antidote. (Rehearsals improved when Al McKibbon replaced Brown on bass.)

This wasn't a sideshow. Dizzy later told writer Robert Palmer he considered it the most important thing he'd done. The new music had, after all, been named after his scatting evocation—*be-BÓP!*—of the sound made by the two ends of a Cuban bata drum. Ever since his childhood visits to the Sanctified Church in South Carolina, Dizzy had been fascinated by rhythm. He never wanted jazz to end up where it eventually did: in clubs and concert halls, with no dancefloor in sight.

Breakthrough came on the band bus. Chano handed out small percussion instruments—claves, bongos, cowbells, güiros—and got everyone playing a different pattern, the beats meshing together like the gears of a watch. McKibbon complained that the idea of playing a drum with his hands was alien—*too backward! too African!*—but he eventually got his head around it. Stan Kenton had tried this sort of fusion but the Cuban element tended to end up where Latin jazz would in the future—as conga-and-flute frosting on top of a jazz cake rather than a fundamental, danceable part of the rhythm.

For Carnegie Hall, Dizzy, Chano, and arranger George Russell created two centerpieces that sound quite different to what we now think of as Latin jazz: "Afro-Cuban Suite" and "Cubana Be, Cubana Bop." The audience had never heard anything like it. On the recording, the sound of Chano's voice flutters as it passes through the blur of his hands hammering out a machine-gun fire of blows to the conga head.

Dizzy's first studio sessions for RCA Victor (having become the first bebop artist signed to a major label) include the only hit single he ever had: "Manteca." Chano spoke just scraps of English, but he had a great ear and noticed little things, like the way men would greet each other in Harlem: "*Gimme some skin, man, gimme some grease.*" "Grease" in Spanish is "*manteca*"; when Chano approached him with an idea for a tune, he had, according to Dizzy, "already figured out what the bass was gonna do . . . how the saxophones were gonna come in . . . He had the riffs of the trombones; he had the riffs of the trumpets. But Chano wasn't too hip about American music. I wrote a bridge." The other famous track from those sessions is "Tin Tin Deo," another of Chano's onomatopoeic percussion titles. It, too, became a jazz standard, but would never again be recorded with the powerful foundation Chano gave Dizzy's band on that session.

༄

The success of "Manteca" allowed Dizzy's agent to book a series of tours—to Europe, to the West Coast (where Chano wowed a Hollywood audience that included Ava Gardner, Lena Horne, and Mel Tormé), and into the American South. Dizzy and most of his musicians (with the exception of John Lewis, who disapproved of Dizzy's clowning and hated his attempts to get audiences to dance) were excited by this new line-up. "Manteca" was the showstopper, often turning into a forty-five-minute jam featuring a long Chano solo complete with Abakuá chants.

Again and again, the South would prove a stumbling block for Latin music; most Latin orchestras contained a spectrum of skin tones, but southern hotels, restaurants, and nightclubs only saw things the binary, "one-drop," American way. (Miguelito Valdés would abandon the *Mambo USA* tour in the early fifties rather than stay apart from the rest of the band on its southern swing.) Dizzy's musicians were used to staying in cheap boardinghouses in the Black sections of cities, but Chano hated it. When his congas were stolen from a flimsily locked room in North Carolina, he boarded a train for New York, the only place to buy adequate replacements. Once back in Spanish Harlem, he was in no hurry to rejoin the tour.

Chano's idea of celebrating was to score some dope. He bought grass from Eusebio "El Cabito" Muñoz, a tough Cuban ex–US Army hustler known for always having spliffs available. Chano and his friends lit up while driving through Central Park and could tell immediately that their tokes were more oregano than sinsemilla. Furious, Pozo drove straight back to the El Rio bar and demanded his money back. When Muñoz refused, Chano decked him with one punch. That night, friends urged him to make peace; El Cabito was not someone to mess with. Chano brushed them off. The next day, he sauntered into El Rio and put a nickel in the jukebox to play "Manteca." As the opening bars filled the room, Muñoz appeared in the doorway, drew out a pistol, and shot Chano through the heart.

Dizzy and his band, Duke Ellington, Mario Bauzá, Machito, Cab Calloway, Tito Puente, Tito Rodríguez, and dozens of other musicians attended the funeral. Miguelito eulogized his friend in Spanish and English. When the body was flown back to Havana for burial, RHC Radio broadcast the pre-dawn arrival time of the plane; fifty vehicles filled with mourners followed the hearse from airport to funeral parlor.

When an emigrant dies violently, conspiracy theories back home can easily grow. The conguero's Cuban rivals were jealous, said some; US musicians resented his impact, said others. A popular notion in the solares was that Chano had offended the orishas by using their music to further his career. Even "Cachao" López, the calm, worldly master of the Cuban bass, insisted to the day he died there were secrets behind the killing he dared not disclose.

༒

Latin jazz lived on, of course, in Cal Tjader and Herbie Mann records, in the later career of Tito Puente, and in many of Dizzy Gillespie's own line-ups. Modern jazz drumming was transformed as Cuban rhythms infected, consciously or unconsciously, the wrists of Max Roach, Kenny Clarke, Art Blakey, and their successors. Horn players and bass players started syncopating, shifting accents and leaving spaces. But Dizzy couldn't find another conguero to carry on his project: "[A]ll those guys are like babes in the woods compared to Chano. On everything I played, he played something that transformed my rhythm . . . It's not the same without Chano." Bebop settled in nightclubs where tables hugged the stage apron, occupying what might once have been a dancefloor. John Lewis won the debate: modern jazz became a listening music.

Miguelito Valdés settled in Hollywood with Virginia Hill, who shuttled between him and Siegel. Bugsy was a key player in the transformation of Las Vegas and didn't seem to have Cugat's ego problems; Valdés became an early Vegas fixture. He sang for a while with Machito, then his own band, establishing himself in high-end, high-paying venues. By the mid-fifties, big-band touring was no longer viable, but Valdés was too good and too savvy to ever struggle. His style may have grown a bit dated next to Celia Cruz and Benny Moré, but he had a contract with the Hilton hotel chain that kept him comfortable for the rest of his life. When he died in 1978, Latin music was in a down cycle, remote from mainstream consciousness, and his passing brought few memorials or lengthy obituaries. Salsa great Charlie Palmieri insisted, "[Miguelito] Valdés is the one responsible for elevating Afro-Cuban music to respectability . . . [He] removed the racist barriers by making the music sound exciting with his innovations; his contribution to Latin music may never be equaled."

In a neighboring Beverly Hills canyon, Desi Arnaz and Lucille Ball lived their dual lives, the TV version and the real one. *I Love Lucy* created the concept of "comedic alternate reality" that lived on in *Ozzie and Harriet* (and their singing son, Ricky Nelson) and reached its apex with *Seinfeld*. Arnaz inherited Charlie Chaplin's mantle as the performer who did the most to seize control of process and proceeds, turning Desilu Productions into a behemoth that virtually single-handedly pulled television's center of gravity from New York to Hollywood. He even did the occasional tour with his own Latin band, which, he stated proudly, combined the easy-listening aesthetic of Mantovani and Andre Kostelanetz with a simpler version of the rhythm of Machito (whose sound he found "tinny"). I was visiting the set when he guest-hosted *Saturday Night Live* in 1976. Backstage he was charm itself, happily taking the piss out of himself in sketches and performing "Babalú" with the SNL Band.

In the late 1940s, the young Elvis Presley would never miss a new release by Dean Martin and Jerry Lewis. The classic explanation of rock 'n' roll as a meeting of blues and country tells only part of the story; Dean Martin's Italianate crooning is all over Elvis's vocal style, false bass and all, to say nothing of the slicked dark hair falling over his forehead. Cuban music is also cited as an ingredient, the basis for rock 'n' roll's syncopation, entering America's musical bloodstream via the left-hand patterns Professor Longhair developed while jamming with Cuban sailors in New Orleans dockside bars. But equally intriguing is a short film used as an opener for Martin and Lewis's films; watching *Desi Arnaz and His Orchestra*, I am struck by how Desi's hair, his stance, the way he holds his conga drum and "moves around" on stage reminds me of Elvis. A lot of America's musical heritage seems to have taken shape in 1949, in the dark of a Memphis cinema.

When Miguelito Valdés held court at La Conga after the war, he got to know a hustler named Federico Pagani. One night, he mentioned to Pagani that a big dance studio two blocks away, at 53rd Street and Broadway, could be rented, cheap. Why not try promoting Latin bands there on Sunday afternoons?

Midway between Dizzy's Carnegie Hall concert and Chano Pozo's death, the trumpeter's dream of bringing together Afro-Cuban and Afro-American music took shape in this dance hall, soon renamed the Palladium. Great bands, dancers, solos, jam sessions, every color in the New York City rainbow out on the floor and crowding the bar. No one called it Latin jazz or Afro-Cuban music; it was "dancing Latin," "mambo," "cha-cha-cha," "charanga," "casino," "salsa." The names came and went, but the true legacy of Desi's conga line, Miguelito's montuno improvisations, and Chano's clave lessons in Gillespie's bus could be found on dancefloors like the Palladium's and reached every corner of the globe.

The rhythmic chasm that ran down the aisle of Dizzy's bus was four centuries old. The Spanish and British colonial empires differed widely in matters of religion, finance, sex, race, and slavery . . . and in how to beat a drum. This latter difference stemmed from a phobia we know only too well—fear of Muslims.

1492 is considered a watershed because of Columbus's "discovery" of the "New" World. But in Spain, the explorer's feat was but a footnote to the year's major event, the Reconquista—the expulsion of an eight-hundred-year-old Muslim kingdom from the Iberian peninsula, "the moor's last sigh" as he looked back over his shoulder at beloved Granada. Columbus believed his destiny was to find enough gold to fund the coming "end of days" battle with Islam. The second expedition to what he insisted would prove a shortcut to the riches of the Orient was manned by a posse of greedy thugs. Cuban anthropologist Fernando Ortiz politely describes them thus: "With the Arabs expelled and then the Jews, in Iberia there was an excess of nobles and hungry soldiers, prevented from continuing their haphazard life and acquiring enemy lands at the point of a lance, and a bellicose clergy whose intransigence had been exacerbated by the continual struggle against the infidels." (Which sounds a bit like America at the end of the nineteenth century, when, after murderously brushing aside the continent's original residents all the way to the Pacific, we followed the sunset to Hawaii, the Philippines, and eventually Korea and Vietnam, with side trips to the Caribbean and Central America, in search of more non-Whites to subdue or kill.)

When the whistle-blowing priest Bartolomé de las Casas delivered his report in 1552 on how Caribbean natives responded to enslavement by dying or fleeing into the islands' forested interiors, Charles I decided to follow de las Casas's advice. Native Americans, he proclaimed, were unsuited to hard labor; better to use Africans.

The first slaves brought to the Caribbean were from Senegambia, a short sail down the coast from Cádiz. But they proved almost as problematic as the local Taíno "Indians," rebelling against their owners, refusing conversion to Christianity, fleeing into the woods, and, in 1538, sacking Havana. The problem, Charles's advisors explained, was that much of Senegambia had been converted to Islam. Spaniards, after their eight-centuries-long struggle against the Moors, wanted no part of Africans prepared to die for Allah. A royal decree banned the purchase of Muslim slaves and sub-contracted the supply of labor for the empire to the Portuguese, who did their slave-shopping thousands of miles farther south and east along the Kongo and Angola coasts. The contrast between the cultures of Kongo and Senegambia (where the British continued to purchase a majority of their slaves for the next two centuries) is as distinct as that between Sicily and Sweden. The arid Sahel region has an elaborate, string-based musical culture; the Kongos' forest kingdom provided perfect drum frames.

The Spanish may have suffered from Islamophobia, but their culture has been indelibly shaped by that religion's eight-century-long presence in their midst. Arabs had been buying Africans for centuries; in the Muslim practice of *mukataba*, slaves could earn money to purchase their freedom and their children were generally accepted as free members of society (particularly as the father was usually the slave-owner). To many Spaniards, such practices seemed natural and appropriate; in North America and the British Caribbean, slavery was a life sentence and slaves' children were viewed as a crop. Anglophone owners were as sexually predatory as their Spanish or Arab equivalents, but less willing to acknowledge the fact and quite happy to sell their own progeny "down the [Ohio or Mississippi] river."

British slave owners weren't afraid of Muslims but they were terrified of drums, convinced (correctly, no doubt) that early slave uprisings in North America had been organized through percussive conversations among plantations. Along with the suppression of drums, African religious practices were labeled "witchcraft" and strictly forbidden. Portuguese sea captains, on the other hand, found that allowing "the cargo" up on deck for an occasional dance was good business, as it reduced the number of prisoners dying from illness or despair. One survivor of the Middle Passage suggested, "If there had been no drum on board . . . not one *negro* would have arrived alive." Once on land, Spanish owners observed that slaves allowed to preserve languages and customs and share barracks with their own people worked better and lived longer.

Out of these policies grew the *cabildos*; centers where Kongos could meet and keep their traditions alive were established from one end of Cuba to the other. Later imports from other regions established their own societies on the Kongo model. In these lodges, drums were built and "blooded," African languages were common parlance, and resources were pooled for funeral ceremonies and other commemorations of ties to an impossibly faraway homeland. Catholic priests generally steered clear, deeming Africans unworthy of conversion. Thanks to intrepid

Portuguese missionaries, however, many Kongos had already been converted to Catholicism, or had at least a rudimentary idea of it, finding convenient parallels between Christian saints and their own gods. In Kongo culture, an even-sided cross symbolized the intersection of earthly and heavenly realms; syncretism came to be widely accepted in Cuba and throughout the Spanish Empire.

Religion means different things in different cultures. Protestantism demands adherence to a clearly laid-out (and endlessly disputed) belief system. Catholicism, with its emphasis on ritual, was more compatible with (and accepting of) the African way of invoking and pleasing gods, rather than obeying or worshipping them. The Roman Empire, Catholicism's role model, welcomed conquered people's deities, building shrines and temples for them in Italian cities.

Off days were rare on the plantations, but on certain fiesta days, slaves were allowed to dance and parade and their drums could see daylight. Cuban crowds loved watching these African celebrations, awarding prizes for the best costumes and the most agile dancers. Elections were held for a king, a *Rei Momo* (after Momus, the Greek god of revelry). The tradition of parading "in submission" on Kings' Day reached back into Iberian antiquity and to the Roman Saturnalia, or Feast of Fools, when the weak became powerful for a day and elected a leader.

> Havana, maritime capital of the Americas, and Seville, its Iberian counterpart, changed year after year, for three centuries, their ships, their people . . . the pleasures of their joyful souls . . . But another race spilled forth their passion, pleasure, and art . . . into the seething brews of Seville and Havana. For centuries, abundant torrents of muscular strength and spiritual spontaneity were extracted from . . . Africa and taken to white-controlled shores on either side of the Atlantic . . . Havana was famous for its diversions and libertine behavior . . . Songs, dances, and music came and went from Andalusia, America, and Africa: Havana was the center where they all came together with the greatest heat and warmth and with the most polychromatic iridescence.
>
> —Fernando Ortiz, *La clave xilofónica de la música cubana*

Through some bureaucratic sleight-of-hand, Havana remained beyond the reach of the Inquisition. Financially, the Spanish Empire ran on Mexican gold and Peruvian silver, but musically and sexually Cuba set the standard. Havana was a way station, the port where plundered treasure was gathered for fleets that braved hurricanes and privateers to reach Seville. Soldiers and sailors spent months there gambling, whoring, drinking, and enjoying the musical accompaniments to those activities. Rhythms, steps, and melodies flowed back and forth between Havana and Seville and across seas and over mountains to Veracruz, Caracas, Bogotá, Lima, and Buenos Aires, triggering dance crazes everywhere.

Black Cubans—enslaved and free—walked around towns, carried arms, and often lived something resembling a normal life. When liberated slaves reached Havana, they found Afro-Spanish *curros* well established in the bars and brothels; this hybrid culture originated in Seville, which had boasted an African population for centuries under Moorish rule. Curros were flamboyant characters in wide striped pants with silk tassels hanging from their hats, puffed-sleeve shirts, and gold earrings rattling with charms. Their gait was full of attitude and they wielded the knives at their belts with expert flair. Black sailors and freedmen aspired to the curro look; the ruffles of Latin dance orchestras in the thirties and forties were a homage to these legendary wide boys of old Havana. To this day, Cubans sporting a single left-lobe earring, wearing a broad-brimmed hat, and talking an impenetrable slang can be seen striding the streets of Havana.

In the latter part of the eighteenth century, the island was transformed by two invasions. First came the British, who occupied Havana in 1762 as part of their Caribbean campaign in the Seven Years War. Madrid had always kept the local economy on a tight rein, with little access to credit and all trade routed via Spanish ports. This interregnum opened Cuban eyes to the joys of Anglo-Saxon debt and financial freebooting as well as trade with North America and the nearby British and Dutch islands, to say nothing of the rest of the Spanish Empire. It also brought an addictive taste of Cuban tobacco to the wider world. The Spanish regained control a year later, but there was no going back: the number of ships docking annually in Havana soared.

A quarter-century later, thousands of French refugees arrived. The western end of the neighboring island of Hispañola had been abandoned by Spain in the early seventeenth century, becoming a lawless haven for pirates and privateers, most of them French. So wealthy grew this no-man's-land that Paris decided to assert control. With European appetite for sweets and stimulants surging, then-verdant Hay-iti (the Taíno name for the area) became the most profitable outpost of Louis XIV's empire. A virtuous circle of elevated Parisian tastes, fueled by colonial wealth and the resulting expansion of fashionable demand for sugar and coffee, paid for the indulgences of the Sun King's court. This required slaves and more slaves, and planters hadn't the patience to purchase females for breeding, preferring to buy endless boatloads of young men and work them to death. Eighteenth-century Haiti became a hellish outpost, marked by avarice, brutality, and White fear at being so outnumbered. It was also a pleasure-loving land where younger sons sent off to make their fortunes tried to re-create the château life of home. Decadence requires a soundtrack, and African musicians were pressed into service to play the English "country dances" (*contredanses*) that were so popular with the French aristocracy. The history of popular music sparkles with styles born out of failed attempts at mimicry. Brits trying to play American rock 'n' roll created something fresh, as did Jamaicans imitating New Orleans rhythm and blues, to name but the most obvious and recent of countless examples. In providing the music for French dances, Africans in Haiti planted the seeds of what we now call "Latin music."

In 1783, literal-minded slaves and mixed-race freedmen had the temerity to assume that the French Revolution's *liberté, égalité, fraternité* applied to them. A bloody and ultimately successful uprising ensued, sending French settlers—and as many of their slaves as they could hold on to—fleeing to Santiago at the nearby eastern end of Cuba, to Havana, and to New Orleans. The impact of the Haitian Revolution on Cuba's economy was immense: French planters brought a commercial mindset and the latest techniques for maximizing crop yields, while the vindictive boycott against the victorious Haitians opened up a huge market gagging for sugar. Cuba needed more slaves, fast.

Havana was rapidly transformed into a bustling international port with a far more varied population than the soldiers, sailors, priests, administrators, and camp followers of the past. Churches hired musicians and choirmasters, balls, concerts, and operas dotted the calendar, and there was dancing every night in the bars. Spaniards had always aspired to French sophistication in fashion and amusements, so what locals called the *contradanza* was already well established as a popular pastime. But Cubans had never heard it played this new, Haitian way.

The forests of Dahomey have been identified as the beating heart of African religion. Priests and *bokors* from what is now Benin and western Nigeria are reputed to have extraordinary powers; definitive rituals associated with many African deities, including those known as voodoo, can be found there. Around the turn of the nineteenth century, this region was plagued by war; wars generate prisoners, and prisoners can be sold. Sugar boom demand met West African supply, leading to the arrival in Cuba of millions of Yorùbá-speaking African captives.

A British traveler in West Africa contended that "there is not a more industrious people on the face of the earth." In Cuba, Yorùbá slaves were soon in demand for skilled jobs; many were put to work in mills or plantation offices rather than the cane fields. Yorùbá culture was ancient, highly evolved, urban, and, having resisted repeated attempts at conversion and conquest by Islamic rulers from the north, very confident. Muslim influence was nonetheless present: the Yorùbá Creator, for example, is Obatala, a hybrid of Orisha and Allah. In nineteenth-century Cuba, the Yorùbá galaxy of deities merged with images of Catholic saints to form the belief system known as Santería; Lucumí is its ritual language, in parallel with the Roman church's Latin.

Santería's syncretism mirrored the origins of Spanish Catholicism, which endowed its saints with the characteristics of Iberian pagan deities. Santa Barbara's axe, for example, links her both to pre-Christian European cults and to Chango. Santería also resembled the Franco-Iberian

Cathar heresy in its Manichean acceptance of good and evil in all things. Yorùbá orishas are not, however, the dignified, revered figures of Christian traditions. As Ned Sublette points out, "Jesus Christ does not get drunk and fall down in the road, but Elegguá has been known to." This devilish deity is associated with St. Anthony and with crossroads. (Perhaps it was Elegguá that Robert Johnson met during his apocryphal midnight stroll.) Ogun, like the Norse Thor, is a machete-wielding warrior-blacksmith, while the water goddess Yemaya undulates like the waves when she dances. Babalú-Ayé is the god of sickness (and modern-day guardian of AIDS victims); Ochún, the "Yorùbá Aphrodite," is the laughing patron saint of prostitutes.

Cuba became a virtual convention of orishas; each locality had its favorites and all were made welcome in this horrific, endless exile. In the cabildos, ways to honor them and the rhythms appropriate to each ceremony flourished, evolved, collided, and merged. In contrast to the secretive Palo Monte of the Kongos, Santería's colorful array of images and personalities made it the most visible and accessible of Afro-Cuban religions. To this day, it provides Cuban musicians, songwriters, and singers with a rich store of rhythms, imagery, turns of phrase, dance steps, hand gestures, and costumes.

In the second decade of the nineteenth century, the quest for slaves was extended east of the Niger Delta to the land of the Carabalí. Their Abakuá societies were even more closed than the Kongos', resembling a cross between a religious order, a Freemason's lodge, and a protection racket. Abakuá phrases entered Afro-Cuban patois and can still be heard in song lyrics and street jargon: "*chévere*," for example, meant "authorized" but has evolved to "cool," while on the streets of East Harlem, "*asere*" now equals "bro" and salsa singers shout "*Ecua je!*" (Get on it!) The Ki-Kongo language, meanwhile, has provided Latin music with countless words hinged on "mb" or "ng," including *mambo*, *tango*, and *bongo*.

Afro-Cuban ceremonial and recreational music was constantly being refreshed by new arrivals, with styles evolving as cultures rubbed up against each other. In the century following the arrival of the Haitians, Cuban music continued to absorb Spanish melodies into the structures of French dances while adding the ever more complex rhythmic patterns emerging from the cabildos. The huge ceremonial drums of the Kongos impressed everyone; eventually, ways were found to incorporate smaller, movable versions of these behemoths into the music of the cities and the dance bands. These drums would be called "congas," after the land that inspired them.

Unlike most Afro-Cubans, few African Americans could, before the arrival of DNA testing, identify where their ancestors were captured. Considering how their forebears were punished for speaking an African language, forbidden drums, barred from practising their religion, and how many were purchased not in Africa but in the British Caribbean, this is not surprising. Research has confirmed that a very large portion, particularly those imported early in the process, were from Senegambia and the Sahel, a region where scarce wood was more likely to be used as a neck or resonating chamber for a stringed instrument than for a drum. Many were captured far inland, in what is today northern Mali, where the music of Ali Farka Touré and Tinariwen shows the link between that area's music and American blues.

Africans proved musically adept and were soon pressed into service playing at White dances. European fiddles were no problem for virtuosos familiar with the savanna's bowed instruments and, by adapting the wood, gut, and fiber of the new land to re-create the dowel-necked *ngoni*, they invented the banjo. Forbidden both the drums and the privacy available to Afro-Cubans, North American slaves applied their skills to European instruments. They profoundly altered playing techniques, though it was in vocal music that the "imports" carved out the most striking new forms. Forbidden by their captors to practice Islam or any African religion, they gradually adopted Christianity. Senegambia has a long tradition of singing and storytelling, hence the attraction of Protestantism's participatory hymns and colorful Bible tales. While Afro-Cubans were adapting their galaxy of deities to Catholicism's array of saints and expanding the complexities of religious drumming, African Americans were singing at work and singing in church.

In the West African savanna, it is considered impolite to listen passively; *griots* expect audiences to interject and encourage as they sing their ancient tales. This cultural connection is obvious today in many African-American churches and it may have influenced the "Great Awakening" religious revivals that ebbed and flowed through White and Black America across the eighteenth and nineteenth centuries. The westward impulse that settled the anglophone New World was energized by Nonconformist desire to escape the heavy hand of staid Anglicanism. Replacing psalms with Dr. Watts hymns while adding emotional preaching and speaking in tongues, it all seems parallel to—if not inspired by—aspects of West African culture. The call-and-response patterns of Senegambian group singing invaded White Protestant churches, while the melismatic calls to prayer of the region's muezzins shaped the decorative gospel and blues singing that has found its most exaggerated form in today's R&B.

Folklorist Alan Lomax noted that collective agricultural work in West Africa was driven by singing and that these customs crossed the Atlantic to the American South. In *Land Where the Blues Began*, he describes the futile efforts of White laborers to clear mangrove swamps in the Mississippi Delta, the first major public-works project in the post–Civil War South. When one contractor turned in desperation to the newly liberated Black labor force, the chanting and rhythmic movement of the workers transformed and mastered the job.

West African *balafon* players have been known to sit in a busy marketplace and improvise sequences that mimic the voices around them. Blurring the line between instruments and voice is a West African technique clearly present in African-American music, be it Bukka White's bottleneck guitar finishing a line of sung blues or Louis Armstrong's leap from pioneering cornet solos to revolutionary scat-singing. Fresh ideas in phrasing and tone passed easily back and forth between singers and instrumentalists, while African vocal textures, from basso growling to falsetto, were a far cry (as it were) from the European desire to maintain a "pure" tone. All this can be drawn in a relatively straight line back to West Africa, but rhythm was another story; North America's drum-starved musical culture was reconnected to African rhythms through a back door opened by the jokers in this deck of musical cards, the French.

∽

In the initial period of colonial conquest, as Spain invaded Central and South America and the Caribbean, and Britain focused on the Caribbean and North America, France's explorations farther north would have an equally dramatic effect on musical history. During a westward push across the Great Lakes by fur traders and missionaries, they came across tributaries of a great river and staked a claim to its watershed. Following the Mississippi downstream, they established the port of Nouvelle Orléans at its mouth, a short sail from Havana. In 1769, after desultory attempts to create a trading center there, Louis XV persuaded his cousin Charles III of Spain to take the Louisiana Territory off his hands; Haiti seemed of far greater value then than the trackless wastes of the American West. Needing a buffer between gold-rich Mexico and the aggressive British, the Spanish king agreed. When Napoleon captured Spain in 1803, he reclaimed Louisiana for France, then quickly flipped it to the young United States for a cool $15 million.

During its three Spanish decades, New Orleans had changed dramatically. The city's "French" Quarter consists mostly of Spanish-Caribbean style buildings that replaced the wooden structures destroyed by huge fires in 1788 and 1794. Ned Sublette's *The World That Made New Orleans* recounts the growth of a distinctive African-based culture in the city; as the port grew, bars and whorehouses provided the same fertile ground for musical development as they had in Havana. When paranoid Cuba expelled Franco-Haitian refugees for fear of revolutionary contagion, New Orleans welcomed them. Touristic "voodoo museums" and the "legend of Marie Laveau" are but the most superficial legacies of these immigrants. With the Louisiana Purchase, America acquired much more than a vast expanse of territory; once absorbed into the new republic, the port acted as a valve, drip-feeding Afro-Caribbean music into the bloodstream of American culture.

With little demand for manual labor in the region, few slave ships had docked in New Orleans before the post-1812 cotton boom. Slaves arriving with their refugee owners, plus freedmen who had made their own way there, established a distinct, confident, African-American culture, a blender where Hispanic, Senegambian, francophone, Yorùbá, anglophone, Kongo, and even Mexican worlds met and mixed. North American visitors were astonished by New Orleans's raffish atmosphere, the many free persons of color there, and by the Sunday dances in Congo Square (now Louis Armstrong Park). These gatherings inspired vivid eyewitness reports: the previously unheard sound of African drums, the circle-dancing, the singing, the complex hand-clapping—all seemed very exotic and often quite repulsive to American ears.

New Orleans and Havana, each in its own particular way, have long refused to conform to Northern European notions of order and progress. The Louisiana port remains a place apart, the "Big Easy" that disdains the Protestant work ethic while providing the wellspring for what the world has come to view as "American music."

∽

There is a traceable arc in Cuban music, from the arrival of the first Haitian refugees in 1783 to Independence in 1898 (following what Yankees insist on calling the "Spanish-American War," as if Cuba had no part in it). As with so many modernizing societies during this period, rural people flocked to the cities, bringing along their music and adapting it to the pace of their new lives. But what was fertilizing the nightlife of Havana, Santiago, and other Cuban cities was something quite unique, a broad representation of some of the richest cultures from across the African continent.

In the early years of the sugar boom, Havana added theaters, ballrooms, and "dance academies" (which were essentially dating agencies for White men and light-skinned Afro-Cuban women). The soundtrack to this wide-open society was provided by Afro-Cuban ensembles playing clarinets, trombones, and percussion and performing the contradanzas that would eventually spawn the danza, habanera, and danzón while injecting progressively more Haitian-African feeling into the music. Young dancers cheered; older ones complained. At least the elders couldn't blame Black musicians for the shocking arrival of embracing-couple dances; moving to music in pairs was a European phenomenon, imported along with the waltz and mazurka, and something completely unknown in Africa. Across the decades of the nineteenth century, Cuban ballrooms grew freer and more sensual as the island became even more dance-mad than pre-revolutionary France.

In Europe, Roma musicians had come up with new styles while playing the dominant culture's music. Afro-Cubans' impact on French and Iberian forms was even more profound: they completely changed the guitar, for example, from being a plucked melodic instrument to a rhythmically strummed one, while adding a call-and-response *coro* to ancient song forms such as the *décima*. African polyrhythms in Hispanic music were "caged but not tamed."

> The power the black race has over us begins with dance.
> —*La Aurora de Yumurí*, 1881

> Africanism is the secret sickness of our social organization, a great danger to our civilization.
> —*El Triunfo*, 1882

Black women in Cuba could earn their freedom through needlework, prostitution, cooking, or attachment to a wealthy man. For Afro-Cuban men, one of the best ways to earn money was by playing an instrument. White Cubans felt a grudging admiration for the musicians who made Cuban feet move so joyfully on the dancefloor. "A European musician can play the notes, but he can never give them that air, the rhythm, that *flavor* a Criollo musician gives them," wrote one mid-nineteenth-century critic. "Who does not know that the bass notes of our danzas constitute an echo of African drums?" observed another. A classical contrabassist confessed of his inability to decipher a part "executed every night . . . by a Negro who couldn't read a note."

Fear of Africans kept Cuba from joining the Bolivarian revolutions that were throwing off Madrid's yoke from Mexico to Chile. The astonishing French defeat in Haiti had poisoned White attitudes to Black freedom throughout the New World, and many Whites were afraid of opening what they saw as a Pandora's box. For some White Cubans, their African-inflected music was a badge of national pride and defiance of Madrid, possibly even marking a path towards some kind of racial accommodation. For many, though, enjoyment of this music was a source of shame and anxiety.

When Afro-Cubans were accused of leading the failed "Conspiracy of the Ladders" revolution in 1844, there followed a general rejection of any music tainted with Blackness; Italian opera and Spanish *zarzuela* boomed. But Cubans soon got bored and wanted their *criollo* dances back. Continuing to chafe against their colonial masters, they welcomed Black courage and leadership in the Ten Years' War of 1868–78. One embedded US journalist reported that whenever there was a lull in the fighting, wives, lovers, and parents would appear as if from nowhere to join the troops for a dance at a clearing in the woods. The ranks, he reported, danced separately, but the races together.

Despite their defeat, Cubans were proud of the *mambís* who had fought so bravely and they revered general Máximo Gómez, who led their forces until the bitter end. As the years passed, Afro-Cuban music was embraced more and more widely as a badge of national identity. Recently arrived Spanish immigrants (who mostly sided with Madrid) were derided as *patónes*: "those who dance badly."

The skill and bravery of Black soldiers frightened the Spanish. When the Ten Years' War ended, they defied their landowning allies by opening a path to Abolition, hoping to get Afro-Cubans on their side. Conveniently, new technology meant less manpower was now required to produce sugar, so Emancipation saved slave-owners the cost of feeding their workforce all year round. Even so, Spanish officials and White Cubans couldn't get used to confident Blacks in their midst and deployed every means to suppress their culture.

Free and semi-free flocked to the cities; in the solares, the rhythms and rituals of African nations and Cuban regions blended in the urban cauldron, bringing the strongest to the fore. Seasonal jobs meant that workers returned to towns and cities after the *zafra* (sugar harvest) with money and time, perfect conditions for musical experimentation. Cubans who had always viewed African culture as something tribal were forced to confront a distinct Afro-Cuban world evolving before their eyes.

In June 1877, in the Alturas de Simpson (Simpson Heights) area of Matanzas, the bandleader Miguel Faílde Pérez conducted what has gone down in history as the first danzón, a truly Cuban form cut loose from the moorings of the contradanza and infused with habanera beats. Danzones had been heard before at "candle dances" in Black neighborhoods, but Faílde's big, brassy orchestra brought this sensual dance to a broad audience. His outfit was as loud as a military band, probably the loudest thing anyone had ever heard on a dancefloor. (Shades of Dylan at Newport; volume has often matched rhythm as a flashpoint for generational conflict.)

In its nascent form, danzón involved a roomful of embracing couples connected by long ribbons, all dancing the same pattern, stopping, starting, and turning in unison, cued solely by their knowledge of the music. What alarmed parents was the slow tempo, encouraging dancers to bring their bodies close together and lower their center of gravity. For the young, danzón became a proud Cuban soundtrack in the build-up to the War of Independence (1895–98), defying critics, such as the one who wrote: "[Cuban men] express fear and disgust . . . at the idea of marrying a woman who 'has danced a lot of danzas and danzones.'"

The world's best-known habaneras are the ode to love from *Carmen* (*"Prends garde à toi!"*) and the bridge section of "St. Louis Blues" ("*St. Louis woman with her diamond rings*"). For Americans of a certain age, the list could also include the *Dragnet* theme and Harry Belafonte's "Jamaica Farewell." Habanera can be thought of as dum-da-DAT-dah, with a stanza-ending flourish of da-DUM-dah-DAHHH. African-sourced rhythmic patterns can be hard to notate; confusingly for Anglo-Saxons, the *clave*, for example, extends across two measures and only incidentally lands on a quarter or eighth note. The habanera figure, on the other hand, is contained within one bar, is relatively straightforward to set down on paper, and isn't too difficult for non-Latins to grasp.

For centuries, along with tobacco and sugar, Cuba had been exporting dance beats. By the eighteenth century, rhythms such as the *zaraband* and *chaconne*, branded as lascivious Negro imports when first heard in Seville, had been tamed into polite templates suitable for Bach and Handel. Spanish *bufo* theater companies of the mid-nineteenth century embraced the rhythm of the *contradanza habanera* as a comedic signal for loose Cuban morals and Négritude. Popularized and simplified during its Iberian sojourn, the habanera made its way to Buenos Aires, where, dropped into the Argentine mix like a culture into milk, it grew the rich fermentation of tango. After infecting Mexico, it entered America via New Orleans, where it kicked off a musical revolution.

Franco-Haitian refugees had decreed that every fashionable New Orleans parlor must have a piano, and the habanera soon made itself at home in local players' left hands. It starts with a held first beat, with the next two played more hurriedly, as if to catch up. The right hand can play almost any melody but the feel is transformed by the habanera pattern in the bass. Americans called this "syncopation," and its influence has been felt across every sort of modern music. You hear it in the horn parts on the Bill Haley and Little Richard records that started the rock 'n' roll revolution—dumm-Dah-da, dumm-Dah-da.

The great explainer of Cuban music, Alejo Carpentier, put it this way: "The black musician was elusive, inventing between the written notes . . . Thanks to blacks, there was a growing hint in the bass lines . . . of a series of displaced accents, of ingenious and graceful intricacies . . . that created a habit and originated a tradition." Ned Sublette adds: "You could call it syncopation, though of course African musicians don't have [that] concept . . . They had their way of perceiving time, which the European called syncopation." What to a Cuban musician was simply an obvious way to make feet move was so alien to non-Cubans that it had to be codified and, for most White musicians, written down. This led to some clumsy stepping on the dancefloor, but it also inspired creative notions of how to render Afro-Cuban feeling in a more linear way. A good example of this is ragtime.

Around the corner from Congo Square in New Orleans, the Gottschalk household consisted of a Franco-Haitian refugee mother, an Anglo-Jewish father, and their children, including a piano-prodigy son named Louis Moreau, plus the father's mixed-race mistress and *their* children. After a childhood reveling in his mother's songs, the Creole melodies of his Haitian nurse, and Sundays at Congo Square, Louis Moreau set off at thirteen for advanced tutelage in Paris. In 1853, at twenty-four, he returned to America as a celebrated soloist and began touring and composing. Extended stays in Puerto Rico, Martinique, and eventually Cuba inspired him to create works based on the music he heard in the streets, dance halls, and bordellos of the Caribbean. Gottschalk had fallen not just for the melodies of Latin America, but for its women as well; musical and sexual adventures would propel him in his constant travels. In 1860, he astonished Havana by mounting an Afro-Cuban extravaganza on the stage of the opera house, bringing a *tumba francesa* troupe of Haitian-descended drummers, singers, and dancers from Santiago to join the orchestra.

Sandwiched between Caribbean travels were concert tours in America, where he entranced sold-out halls with his habanera-inflected compositions, before dying at forty in Brazil from yellow fever. His stardom wasn't as spectacular as Liszt's, but as a composer, his immersion in the folk rhythms and melodies from his side of the world was far ahead of his European equivalents and inspired pianists across the hemisphere, particularly North Americans.

> French opera and popular song and Neapolitan music, African drumming . . . Haitian rhythm and Cuban melody . . . creole satirical ditties, American spirituals and blues, the ragtime and the popular music of the day—all side by side in the streets of New Orleans.
>
> —Alan Lomax, *Mister Jelly Roll*

Sunday visitors to Congo Square often remarked on how "black" everyone was; no "yellow" or light brown participants at all. Free men of color and the offspring of Whites and their octoroon mistresses kept their distance from "African" dances; their culture, they felt, was a modern, international one. Before the Civil War, New Orleans boasted three opera houses, and all were dependent on mixed-race and Black patrons. Many of those fashionable pianos were in Creole homes, laying the ground for a keyboard culture that would stretch from Gottschalk through the legendary Tony Jackson, then Jelly Roll Morton and on to Billie Pierce, Professor Longhair, James Booker, Allen Toussaint, and Mac Rebennack (aka Dr. John).

But what really engaged every shade of the New Orleans public in the nineteenth century was brass bands. The myriad New Orleans nationalities all celebrated their particular holidays, and each required a parade. Crowds loved military pomp; technological advances meant that large brass sections could now play in tune and execute the trills and glissandos that had previously been the province of strings and keyboards. Theaters promoted competitions among trombone and trumpet virtuosos; the latter instrument was the electric guitar of the era (and Louis Armstrong would become its Jimi Hendrix). Marching bands also played for dances, of which there were almost as many in New Orleans as there were in Havana. "Tricolor" balls both evoked and mocked nostalgia for the years of French rule, as well as flaunting the "white-tan-black" mix among the dancers.

In the left hands of pianists throughout the Mississippi watershed, from the Gulf Coast to the Great Lakes, the *oom-pah* of low-register brass met habanera syncopations while right hands invoked the rippling fingers of banjo aces from minstrel shows and country dances. Another flourish of influence arrived with the 1884–85 Industrial and Cotton Exposition in New Orleans, where the band of Mexico's 8th Cavalry Regiment caused a sensation with their stunning arrangements of Mozart sonatas, Sousa marches, and Mexican folk tunes, all delivered with a habanera swing. An enterprising publisher created sheet music of the band's repertoire, with a heavy dose of spelled-out syncopation in the left hand, and it sold as fast as he could print it. By the 1890s, up the river in Missouri, Scott Joplin had begun putting the finishing touches on his immortal compositions built around the ragtime rhythms that were sweeping the country.

Multiple forces were coming together in New Orleans to create the soundtrack of the first half of the western hemisphere's twentieth century: popular rags arranged for brass band, the strutting cakewalk rhythm (essentially a form of tango/habanera), the French tradition (via Haiti) of instrumental virtuosity (on woodwinds in particular), and Mexican horn players who fell for the Crescent City and stayed behind after the Expo. Intriguingly, added to this list is the city's Onward Brass Band and their two-year stint in Havana with the invading US Army, 1898–1900; Onward soaked up many of the island's musical treasures and incorporated them into their playing.

When America ended its Cuban occupation, military bands were decommissioned and their brass sold off, usually in New Orleans, where the troop ships docked. Cheap, well-made instruments fell into the hands of players with Cuban, Mexican, ragtime, and martial beats running through their heads, while ex-slaves from across the southern states were arriving in the city carrying their own rich melodic and rhythmic traditions. Put it all together and, as Bing Crosby sang in *High Society*, "Now you has—*jazz, jazz, jazz!*"

In his Library of Congress recordings, Jelly Roll Morton recalls the turn-of-the-century musical atmosphere in New Orleans. He states emphatically (while idly doodling a bluesy habanera figure with his left hand) that the only pianists who qualified as real "jazz" players were those who had mastered what he called "the Spanish tinge."

Cuba's tortured relationship with its northern neighbor goes back a long way. America developed a taste for Hispanic land-grabs after buying the Florida peninsula from Spain in 1821. A quarter-century later, when newly independent Mexico refused to sell its northern provinces (Texas, New Mexico, Arizona, and the southern half of California), President Polk sent in the troops. America would have gladly added Cuba to its booty but the Spanish garrison there was larger than the entire US Army. An envoy arrived in Madrid with an offer of $100 million for the island, but the man's behavior was so boorish that the Spaniards refused to consider it.

After the Civil War, southern planters cast a dreamy eye onto the island where slavery was still a way of life. Many bought plantations there and the scale of investment ramped up after 1878, when Spain confiscated land belonging to rebellion-supporting growers and sold it off cheaply. Policy-makers in Washington were of two minds: on one hand they gave token support to the rebels, hoping to loosen Madrid's grip, while more conservative elements were appalled by the racially mixed guerrillas and their often Black officers. The US hedged its bets by selling armored ships and munitions to Spain.

Some Cubans were intrigued by the idea of becoming a US state, not least as a means of keeping post-Emancipation Afro-Cuban ambitions in check. American culture also caught the popular imagination; some wealthy kids came back from US boarding schools with baseball bats, balls, and gloves and the sport spread like wildfire, becoming an "anti-bullfight" symbol of defiance. In Matanzas, particularly, everyone loved baseball games; women brought drinks and food and cheered while the game was played—as it is in Cuba today—to the beat of Afro-Cuban percussion. Games were often followed by dances, particularly in Simpson Heights. Danzón and baseball was a hot combination for youth; entire teams would sometimes run off after a dance to fight with the rebels. Spain responded by banning the sport.

Throughout the last decades of the nineteenth century, musical and political revolutions advanced in syncopated time towards their twin destinies of independence for the island and the flowering of its music. By the time the War of Independence began in 1895, enjoyment of Afro-Cuban music was at the heart of an island-wide spirit in which Black and White fought side by side. Many pro-independence leaders, though, remained uncomfortable. One charge leveled against Spain was that it had allowed Cuba to become too Black, with former slaves and their offspring dominating trades such as carpentry, tailoring—and music. The struggle for independence was hindered by some White rebels' reluctance to ally themselves with the island's most effective fighting force. And many who admired Afro-Cuban battle skills were quick to join the chorus against the *comparsas*, not wanting the Revolution to be identified with "lewd" or "primitive" behavior.

Such concerns were often echoed by leaders of the Afro-Cuban community (like Alfonso Menencier, Desi's dad's ward heeler). The Afro-Caribbean writer Frantz Fanon remembers growing up in Martinique in those decades and being taught that everything clean, proper, and intelligent was White, while Blacks were sloppy, malicious, and instinctual. Even Haitian leaders Toussaint and Christophe had tried to prohibit drums in the interest of "improvement." Supporters of equality believed Black Cubans needed to demonstrate "civilized" behavior in order to advance. Poet-hero José Martí was the exception, celebrating the island's racial mix and its African heritage in poems and speeches: *We are all Cubans!* (Martí's idealistic proclamation would later be used by Castro's revolution to suppress Afro-Cuban culture in the name of collective progress.)

As the final war for Cuban independence began, the US, having crushed the last of the Native American resistance at Wounded Knee, was seeking new conquests. Teddy Roosevelt and the press baron William Randolph Hearst pumped up the expansionist hysteria but were held in check by a few crusty New England politicians and pundits who insisted that America was founded in opposition to the very idea of empire. (Native American lands obviously didn't count.) Plans for a canal across the Panamanian isthmus, though, made Cuba an even more valuable plum, and Hearst's papers encouraged sympathy for the noble rebels fighting the cruel Spanish.

On their own, the Cubans had fought Spain to a standstill but lacked the firepower to finish the job; with an excuse provided by what was later found to be an accidental explosion on the battleship *Maine* in Havana harbor, Roosevelt's Rough Riders and the US Navy arrived to deliver the *coup de grâce*. The only thing standing between the island and absorption by the US was that many found the Cuban population too Black, too lazy, and too degenerate to qualify as citizens. "To be brief and emphatic, they are nothing more or less than a lot of half-breed Cuban n——," observed one American. "To the faults of the parent [Spanish] race, they add effeminacy and a distaste for exertion which amounts really to a disease," wrote another.

The African-sounding music and general air of decadence in Havana shocked the invaders. "[Havana's] immorality is worn on its sleeve. The American visitor may learn more of its vices in a week than he has known about the dark shadows of his home city in a lifetime," observed one American, for whom lack of hypocrisy seems to have been the most troubling of Cuba's sins. An alliance of northern constitutionalists, southern racists, and Midwest sugar-beet barons backed the Teller Amendment, which barred America from absorbing Cuba without the approval of both the island's electorate and the US Congress.

The occupiers refused to allow rebels to march in victory parades or display the Cuban flag, then set about banning African drums, segregating the army, and hectoring Cuban leaders about the need to expunge "savagery" and "backwardness." Mixed-race and Black officers who should have been at the core of the first Cuban government were marginalized or cashiered. Occupation officials tried to bar Blacks from voting but post-Emancipation Cuban law was far more color-blind than America's and suffrage, though male only, was otherwise universal.

Reconstruction money flowed to the already wealthy; land promised to soldiers was sold off to rich Americans and White Cubans. As with so many twentieth-century US victories, occupation officials (led by Confederate General Robert E. Lee's nephew) felt more comfortable with former enemies than with their rebel allies. The Onward Brass Band may have been transformed by their Havana sojourn, but most Cubans were glad to see the back of American marching ensembles; endless parades featuring strict-time marches were among the countless reasons the islanders were fed up with their liberators. The new country's first free election in 1900 was as big a shock for the US as Labour's 1945 rout was for Churchill and the Tories; anti-American, "independent Cuba" parties swept the board. Following this electoral insult, America refused to leave until the Cuban Assembly passed the Platt Amendment, giving the US the right to intervene any time it felt the need (or whenever the moneyed classes felt threatened and sent for them). The most enduring legacy of the occupation was the ironically named Cuba Libre, rum mixed with Coke; the Yanks couldn't take it straight.

It could all have been different if Cuba's inspirational leader, José Martí, hadn't insisted on leading a cavalry charge as soon as he arrived back from exile. His death robbed the country of a vision of how to deal with its two most problematic relationships: with the US and with its Afro-Cuban citizens. Martí had spent fifteen years in New York and Florida. (Nineteenth-century Cuban exiles tended to be anti-imperialist liberals, rather than the most recent half-century's reactionaries.) He devoted much of his energy to the education of Black and mixed-race Cubans living in exile, believing that his country's future depended on literacy and skills for all. He was impressed by America but fearful as well; its people, he wrote, had "at once the characteristics of giants and of children." He knew that getting free of Spain was only half the battle; staying out of the clutches of the *Yanquis* would be an even greater challenge.

One positive legacy of the US occupation was the explosion of *son*. Like many imperial powers, the US believed in stationing soldiers far from home to mitigate corruption, desertion, and excessive sympathy with the locals. Regional styles had been gathering steam in the wake of emancipation and Spain's "strategic hamlets" policy; now they began spreading across the island via troops and refugees. American capital further stimulated the fluidity of the Afro-Cuban population, with new owners hiring mostly seasonal workers, sending yet more cane-cutters with money in their pockets to Cuban cities at the end of the zafra.

Son (from *sonar*—"to sound"), which combined the clear-voiced Spanish song traditions of Santiago with Afro-Cuban rhythms, surged out of that city's streets and cafés, progressing across the island from east to west, absorbing influences as it went. The hilly tobacco country of Oriente, with its small-scale farms, had always been marked by a slightly easier relationship between the races; the music played by Afro-Cubans in their neighborhoods was more blended with the region's Spanish heritage than that from the cane fields and dockyards to the west. Resistance to oppression, be it Spanish or American, was stronger at the Santiago end of the island and "Oriental" *sones* were often political, with coded references to the anti-colonial struggle. Many early *soneros* also served as the readers who entertained and informed cigar-rollers as they worked. *Son*, for all the shocking impact of its percussion-driven rhythm, began as a delicate, literate music.

From our twenty-first-century vantage point, it can be hard to grasp the surprise—mostly delighted but quite often horrified—with which *son* was greeted. Things we take for granted were then astonishing; like Gillespie's bass player forty years later, many found the idea of striking a drumhead with the hand horribly alien. Along with anti-comparsa laws, some municipalities enacted regulations requiring drums to be hit, if at all, with a stick.

Son's other revolutionary aspect was singing over a dance beat. Custom and lack of amplification meant that in the growth of urban popular music across the nineteenth century, you sat down and listened to a singer or perhaps tossed them a coin on a street corner; to hear a vocalist in front of a dance band was an amazing innovation, be it *tango canción* in Buenos Aires or an American swing band with a crooner. Sensual, pulse-racing beats with great singing on top—it was almost too much excitement to bear, like 1950s American teenagers hearing Little Richard for the first time.

Adapting its structure from the contradanza, *son* began with verse and chorus borrowed from Iberian song, then moved to vocal improvisations in the montuno section at the end, which owed a debt to both the wit and spontaneity of the décimas and to African call-and-response. Part of *son*'s appeal lay in its magpie-like inclusiveness: Taíno and Arawak phrases, quotations from European parlor song, touches of Jamaican mento and calypso-like topicality. *Son* also had the advantage of being portable; with no bandstand or piano, groups could move from street corner to street corner dodging the police. And always, at the base, that infectious rhythm, propelled by guitar, maracas, güiro, and bongo.

Emanating from Matanzas, Abakuá rumba sessions also established themselves in the solares as cities swelled with new arrivals from across the island. Initially sung in slaves' original languages, Africanized Spanish gradually became rumba's lingua franca; a previously hidden culture was flowering into urban popular music. Growing out of the rituals of the Carabalí, rumba was refined in the docklands, where labor was controlled by Abakuá societies. Packing crates straddled and struck like drums and pairs of shipbuilding pegs were used to mark the rhythm; all that was needed were singers and dancers. In the twenties and thirties, the word *rumba* would become a catch-all term for Cuban music; the French, muddling it up with their spelling of cane-distilled liquor, convinced many to write it "rhumba." But in the solares, a rumba was both a party and its percussion-based music, performed by people too poor to own tempered instruments.

In the decade after Independence, racial tensions grew. Afro-Cuban bitterness at the collapse of their dreams of equality collided with White paranoia about the ex-slaves' pride and the soaring popularity of Black music. Revived comparsas celebrated Black war heroes and chanted Afro-Cuban grievances; drums were called *mambís* in honor of the fighters and *son* was everywhere, on street corners, in bars and cabarets. In a musical Thermidorian Reaction, the once-shocking danzón sounded hyper-respectable, almost White.

In 1912, frustrated Black Cubans formed their own political party. White Cuba's panicked response was swift and brutal. Troops massacred Black demonstrators, race-based parties were outlawed, organizers hunted down and summarily killed, their heads impaled on posts. Police raided Santería ceremonies and confiscated drums; dancers were arrested, cafés shuttered, parades forbidden (except for polite masqued White versions, with many in blackface). When labor tried to organize, sugar barons brought in scabs from Haiti and Jamaica. *Son* was dismissed as a "*cosa de negros*" and forced back inside the solares along with rumbas and Afro-Cuban religions.

But, like after the Ladders Conspiracy sixty-five years earlier, they couldn't keep a good beat down. With Europe at war, demand for Cuban sugar surged and the island's economy boomed. In 1916, President Menocal's nephew heard a *son* outfit called Los Apaches on one of his sex-seeking prowls through a rough Havana quarter. He booked them to play for a dance at the Vedado Tennis Club and the fashionable crowd adored them; they and other *sextetos* were soon in demand for White dances across the island.

Anti-American resentment may have helped drive *son*'s popularity, but American culture also appealed to urban Cubans. When the US Congress enacted Prohibition in 1919, the island was only too eager to welcome pale, thirsty tourists who gave a much-needed boost to the island's post-war economy. When northern visitors brought with them dances such as the Charleston, Grizzly Bear, and Bunny Hug, the Cuban bourgeoisie was forced to concede that dirty dancing might not, in fact, herald the "end of Christian civilization." (Or perhaps it did, but there was little to be done about it.)

By the early twenties, *son* was again omnipresent. Thwarted in their political ambitions, Afro-Cubans focused on survival, religion, and music, possibly in reverse order. Thirty years later, descendants of the mambís who had led the nineteenth-century battles for freedom were conspicuous by their absence from Castro's guerrilla army.

༄

> [Cuban] music should not be sacrificed . . . in attracting the rabble—always disposed to vulgarity and regression—to the call of an African drum . . . we need to moralize it and not prostitute it.
>
> —Sánchez de Fuentes, composer

> If you are young, black, and poor, your activities are likely to strike the older, whiter, and richer power structure as subversive whatever they may be.
>
> —John Storm Roberts

Debates in the first quarter of the twentieth century about *son*, rumba, and Cuban culture exposed so many contradictions, ironies, hypocrisies, pretensions, and insecurities among different sectors of Cuban society that it is hard to know where to begin. Easiest to mock is the *guajirismo* movement, which, inspired by the "Indio" revival in Mexico, insisted that Cuban culture was a blend of Spanish, Taíno, and Siboney, with nary a shadow of Africa. The sixteenth-century Taíno King Hatuey (who, after being assured Heaven would be full of Spaniards, opted for Hell before being burned at the stake) was suddenly a national hero.

Considering how the invaders killed off most of the indigenous population within seventy-five years of their arrival and forbade the few survivors any cultural expression, the sudden reverence for Hatuey bordered on the surreal. Aside from a few words (including "tobacco," "hurricane," "canoe," and the island's name), what shards of Taíno legacy could still be found lay almost exclusively in the ring dances and rattling percussion instruments adopted by fugitive African slaves who found shelter in the hills and forests with natives. Some have suggested that rumba parties were inspired by the days-long *areíto* orgies/feasts early invaders witnessed—and often enjoyed—before obliterating the culture that produced them.

This desperation to deny any connection to Africa is bound up with the island's complicated bloodlines. Most Cubans are a genetic mix, but of which strains? The almost entirely male conquistadores "took" local women as mistresses, wives, or slaves; in the early years, these were largely "Indians," but over the centuries the vast majority of Cuban baby-mothers have been partly or entirely African. This inescapable fact tortures the Cuban psyche. Though the island's view of ethnicity is more nuanced than the Anglo-American "one-drop" attitude, it still leads to convoluted denials about how much African blood courses through the nation's veins. That Cubans of all shades were reveling in *son* in the 1920s and moving their behinds like Africans was hard for many to bear. The Ku Klux Klan opened a Cuban chapter.

Another response was to welcome back Spaniards expelled for opposing independence and to encourage boatloads of their countrymen to join them; the number of Spanish immigrants in the first three decades of the twentieth century exceeded the total for the entire previous history of the island. Galician peasants were no longer the butt of jokes. One immigrant Gallego farmer was Ángel Castro; he named his Cuban-born sons Fidel and Raúl.

Left-wing movements throughout Latin America were inspired by the Russian Revolution's short-lived enthusiasm for "music of the people"; progressives duly embraced *son* as a focus for their resentment of Yankee culture, but soon ran into the same contradictions that marked Stalin's policies on peasant music. The Left honored Afro-Cuban contributions to the War of Independence and hated *guajirismo* but favored an ideal of "elevated" Black culture as curated by sympathetic Whites. This exposed an uncomfortable twentieth-century fact: many, if not most, progressive movements have been prudish at heart, recoiling from both sensuality and authenticity. The Left found allies among Afro-Cuban leaders; *Adelante*, the journal of the Black bourgeoisie, insisted that Afro-Cubans must become "civilized" and "respectable" before they could hope for equality. *Sociedades de color* held to the most conservative of music policies—strictly come danzón. Some even accused Whites of fomenting the *son* craze as a trick to hold Afro-Cubans back.

When the anthropologist Fernando Ortiz began researching Afro-Cuban culture he discovered a gold mine of confiscated musical instruments and religious artefacts in the storerooms of police stations as well as inside the glass cases of museum exhibits purporting to demonstrate Black "primitivism." Ortiz felt that Afro-Cuban culture was so rich and interesting that he would devote his lifetime to its study; where others heard noise, Ortiz saw art. *Son*'s bongos and güiros, he contended, were as profound as the drumming in *The Rite of Spring*. He described Afro-Cuban music as a "group of highly original and complex aesthetic combinations of noises, tones, timbres, rhythms, melodies, harmonies, song and dance with universal values."

This was meat and drink to *son*'s elite supporters, the *minoristas*. They considered *son* to be a naturally avant-garde style grown in Cuba's backyard and relished the bourgeois outrage it inspired, seeing it as a form of modernism that defied a perceived American monopoly on the "new." But they, too, had blind spots; minorista author Alejo Carpentier complained that Afro-Cuban music lacked variation, and it took Ortiz, after years of study, to point out that trance is a key element in African music, that "repetition" is hardly the same as "monotony" and that dancers supply their own variations to a good groove. Ortiz and the minoristas were virulently anti-religion and made no exception for Santería or Palo Monte; myths are myths, be it Islam's Garden of Virgins, Christ's Resurrection, or Chango's cross-dressing. Ortiz was a true pioneer; today we salute quests for "authenticity," but in the early 1920s such research was viewed as an eccentric revelling in crudity.

Gerardo Machado, the most powerful and notorious politician of the 1920s, established a template for Cuban dictator-presidents by paying lip service to progressive values while abetting corruption and playing elites, the Black, and the poor off against the middle classes. He shocked the bourgeoisie—and gave *son* a huge boost—by inviting Sexteto Habanera, complete with bongo, to perform in the presidential palace, while also encouraging his allies (including Mayor Arnaz of Santiago) to ban drums and comparsas. Machado used coded symbols to woo Black voters, wearing all-white clothing as a nod to Santería and planting a ceremonial ceiba tree near the capital. Percussion-driven sextetos were often booked for late-night lock-ins where politicians partied with light-skinned Afro-Cuban girls.

Like many dictators, Machado conflated anarchism, communism, and the avant-garde, ordering a modern-art exhibit to be closed on grounds of subversion. The US opposed him at first, worried that he was, among other things, too Black-friendly, then reversed course in the interests of stability. In 1933, President Roosevelt finally pulled the rug out from under his corrupt rule; Arnaz fled to Florida in a private plane, along with Desi Jr. and bags of Machado gold.

Many Cubans despaired of politics in the turbulent twenties and sought diversions; dancing became, if such a thing were possible, an even greater national obsession. The wealthy liked booking groups too Black for most Afro-Cuban social clubs; the musicians, of course, had to use the back door. Nationalists were in a bind; across the last decades of the nineteenth century, they had flaunted Afro-Cuban music as a symbol of the island's cultural sovereignty. Once the country was (somewhat) independent, like other Latin republics, they lost interest in peasant roots and craved international acceptance as a sophisticated modern culture. Was Afro-Cuban music a source of national pride or shame? Cultural and political leaders seemed unsure.

As the twenties neared their end, all these many dilemmas were magically resolved. Black fingers and mouths needn't be confronted when disembodied music emerges from a wireless radio or shellac disc. Issues that had tortured so many minds were suddenly rendered moot by an explosion of modern media; from one end of the island to the other and across oceans and seas, everyone delighted in—and danced to—the sound of Afro-Cuban *son*.

～

Son de la loma
Y cantan en llano
(They're from the hill
And they sing on the plain)

—Miguel Matamoros, "Mamá, son de la loma"

In the 1920s, America sent Cuba thirsty tourists, armed threats, jazzy dance steps, and adventurous record producers. The Victor label, inspired by Ralph Peer's opening-up of markets for country blues, hillbilly songs, and Mexican music, brought *son* pioneers to New York or recorded them in Cuba, then sent thousands of freshly pressed 78s to the island. These grooves held the sounds of the country's first recording stars.

Cuba is 750 miles long, an east-west expanse of varied land and culture; Habaneros referred to *son* as "Oriental" music, after Santiago's province, and a group called Cuarteto Oriente was one of the first to record. By 1921, they had moved west, expanded, changed their name to Sexteto Habanero and become *son*'s most famous outfit. Columbia Records then entered the fray; when their Sexteto Occidental failed to topple Habanero from its perch, Occidental's songwriter, arranger, and bassist, Ignacio Piñeiro, formed Sexteto Nacional, a group that became a cornerstone of Cuban music. Piñeiro was a Havana *rumbero* who injected an Abakuá intensity into the sound while composing songs of everyday Cuban life that remain essential to the Latin music canon. The new line-up came from every region, the first truly "*nacional*" group. Their harmonies were ground-breaking, with high and low voices exploring intervals outside the usual thirds and sixths.

Piñeiro had learned to play the bass from a remarkable figure in this story: María Teresa Vera. This Habanera daughter of a Yorùbá mother and Spanish father began singing in theaters as a teenager and helped found Sexteto Occidental. Having just "made *santo*" (been initiated into Santería), she passed up the opportunity to join Piñeiro's new outfit, but the duo she later formed provides us with a contemporary connection to early *son*. Vera sang for many years with Lorenzo Hierrezuelo, a part-Siboney *trova* singer from Santiago who also partnered Francisco Repilado in Los Compadres. Repilado became known as "the second Compadre" or "Compay Segundo," composer of "Chan Chan" and totemic vocalist with Buena Vista Social Club. The other breakout stars of the era defied the rule that the road to fame lay through Havana: Trio Matamoros went straight from local renown in Santiago to a New York recording studio and international stardom. Lead singer Miguel Matamoros's earthy, nasal voice epitomized how *son* was transforming the sound of Cuban singing; next to him, Rita Montaner sounds like Jeanette MacDonald.

The most famous sextetos and trios may have been known from Pinar del Río to Guantanamo and from Mexico City to Paris, but stardom didn't make them rich. Royalties were low, if paid at all, and composers' rights were often sold for a few dollars. Piñeiro, whose signature line "échale *salsita*" ("put a little sauce on it") memorialized the food-sex imagery central to Latin music (and is the origin of the tag "salsa"), left the band for spells to work as a bricklayer, where he could make more money.

> With our music we Cubans have exported more dreams and pleasures than with our tobacco, more sweetness and energy than with all our sugar. Afro-Cuban music is fire, savor and smoke; it is syrup, charm and relief. It is like a sonorous rum, which brings people together and makes them treat each other as equals. It brings the senses to dynamic life.
>
> —Fernando Ortiz, *La Africanía en la música folklórica de Cuba*

Fernando Ortiz was a man of grand, sweeping ideas. In *Cuban Counterpoint*, he broke down his island's history into a dialectic between sugar and tobacco. Looking at Europe, he saw a continent transformed from the harsh medieval land of religious wars, plagues, and feudal dynasties into a pleasure-loving powerhouse, where coffee, sugar, tea, spice, and tobacco stimulated thoughts, appetites, and ambitions that could only be satisfied by technological advancement and conquest. Now, as the modern age dawned, Cuba was once again ready to cater to the needs of a continent grown decadent and jaded.

Paris had gone mad for tango on the eve of World War One and for American jazz in the years immediately after. Now, in the late twenties, the city was mesmerized by Josephine Baker and her sophisticated brand of primitivism. Across the globe, previously ignored working-class cultures—musical ones most of all—were bursting out of shantytowns and ghettos via records, radio, and print. In the artistic stratosphere, Bartók was basing his avant-garde approach to rhythm on Transylvanian field recordings, while Picasso's Paris atelier was filled with African masks; down the street, Pablo's pal Tristan Tzara was assembling an immense collection of Cuban and Brazilian 78s.

Alejo Carpentier arrived in Paris in 1928, after serving time in a Havana jail for signing a minorista manifesto that demanded a "revision of all false and wasteful values, for a vernacular art and . . . for Cuba's economic independence." From a distance, he had been enthralled by *The Rite of Spring*, cubism, and Les Six, viewing Paris as the epicenter of a modernist movement that was transforming the world. Instead, he found a city bereft of new ideas; in Latin America, he believed, the surrealism that obsessed European artists "is quotidian, current, habitual" and Afro-Cuban culture was its apex. As if on cue, Sexteto Nacional arrived in Seville for the 1929 Ibero-American Exhibition.

Word of their sensational impact spread to Paris and long-underpaid Cuban musicians flocked there to meet the demand. Carpentier promoted dances at bars and clubs that had hosted tango sessions fifteen years earlier. "There is nothing more contemporary, nothing more *now*, in Paris these days," he wrote, "than the abrupt and unexpected triumph of Cuban music." Back home, his countrymen reacted to *son*'s transatlantic success with delighted (or outraged) wonder. But the Cuban music Paris embraced was not exactly the sort heard in Havana bars; the central figures in this invasion had barely a drop of African blood among them.

Having charmed Cuban audiences in her teens as a pure-voiced coloratura, Rita Montaner shocked them by adding Afro-Cuban percussion onstage and swinging her hips to Ernesto Lecuona's and Moisés Simons's corny (but often brilliant) songs of Afro-Cuban life. The cry that opened the world's doors to Latin music was the one selling peanuts;

Montaner loved one of Simons's melodies and begged him to write words for her. As he sat one afternoon in a Havana café, a peanut seller's call provided the germ of a simple lyric. That's one story; another is that the melody was itself borrowed from a Gottschalk fragment inspired by a nineteenth-century *pregón*, or street-seller's song. In any case, when Montaner joined Josephine Baker's Paris revue and sang the soaring leap of "*man-íííííí*" (Spanish for "peanut"), it became the siren call summoning the world to the music of her tropical island.

Simons's prolific output as a songwriter was filled with broad portrayals of Afro-Cuban sexuality: the allure of women and the threat—or promise—of men, often expressed with food metaphors. (The lyrics to "El Manisero" urge women to eat a "*cone of nuts*" before they go to sleep.) That these songs were performed by genteel, White-ish singers and musicians playing watered-down arrangements was probably central to *son*'s Parisian triumph.

Abroad, Cuban music triggered many of the same clichés that had marked its centuries-long dialogue with Spain. (Since White guys were now playing it, the "Afro" prefix began to seem superfluous.) A woman swinging her hips expertly on stage, screen or dancefloor was clearly "fallen" (albeit sultry and desirable to sufficiently "manly" Europeans). A people that could produce such music must be "pleasure-loving," "lighthearted," and "living for the moment." Europe's cultural reactionaries anguished that Parisians were throwing "masterworks of the human spirit . . . into a bonfire around which savages will dance naked." Oswald Spengler reliably chipped in with a jeremiad that accused France of having "betrayed European culture. In the name of her own impotence she has awakened the African continent . . . the blood of Europe has been poisoned by the perverse miscegenation of France." (Shades of today's Great Replacement theory.)

Latin America had already taken Cuban music to its heart and now the "rhumba" craze spread, infecting Germany, Scandinavia, the Balkans, Egypt, Japan, and Manchuria. "Even the pallid daughters of Albion," wrote Carpentier, "forget for a moment their pre-Raphaelite poses by burying themselves in the sonorous sortilege of the Antilles." Ortiz and Carpentier, though, were far from delighted; the music got so diluted by the urge to seduce unpracticed ears and feet that they feared it had been made "hollow like a maraca." In London, for example, after an initial flurry of excitement, bandleader Edmundo Ros fired his Afro-Cuban percussionists in order to simplify the beat for the clumsy British.

The changes *son* endured in Paris may have been uninspiring, but New York, which would eventually transform Latin music in ways even Havana found exciting, was far slower to join the conga line. Xavier Cugat, moreover, the music's American trailblazer, was even less authentic than the suave bandleaders who had charmed Paris.

Cugat wasn't even Cuban; after Independence, his family had moved from Catalonia to Havana, where Xavier began to show promise as a violinist. He got work alongside Moisés Simons in a pit band playing for silent films, then in 1918 demonstrated his talent for wooing and winning beauties by marrying (briefly) the teenage Rita Montaner, the first of five glamorous wives. After failing to make an impact on New York in the early twenties, he headed west, showing off another of his talents by becoming a popular cartoonist for the *Los Angeles Times*. Always moving in celebrity circles, he landed a job as music director for Enrico Caruso during the tenor's Hollywood sojourn, then jumped on the Rudolph Valentino/tango bandwagon with a new outfit, Xavier Cugat and His Gigolos. At the Coconut Grove he catered to screen stars' appetite for sexy, exotic dancing minus the tricky footwork. "I gave the Americans a Latin music that had nothing authentic about it," he boasted.

In 1932, he began a thirty(!)-year residence at the Rainbow Room of New York's Waldorf-Astoria hotel. Cugat was never keen on *son*; his personal taste was for light classical. But even Latinos who rolled their eyes at his dumbed-down rhythms had to admit that he hired top musicians and his arrangements were always first class. Cugat's weak spot was his hypersensitive ego; when he discovered pianist Nilo Menéndez spending a post-rehearsal afternoon at the Rainbow Room piano helping Cole Porter add Latin flavor to "Begin the Beguine," Cugat sacked him. He was obsessive about presentation: vocalists were generally female and beautiful, from Rita Hayworth to Abbe Lane and Charo (Cugat wed the latter two), while his musicians ranged from White to shades of tan, but no darker.

Dozens of Havana musicians headed north in the 1920s hoping for better pay and, for the Afro-Cubans among them, a fairer shot. Given racial attitudes even more primitive than those back home, this was usually a pipe dream. And it wasn't just on the bandstand that Latin music walked a racial tightrope; Vicente Sigler, New York's first authentically Cuban bandleader, advertised his midtown dances "for Gallegos only." But from silent-movie houses looking for improvising pianists to jazz and dance orchestras needing well-schooled, sight-reading sidemen, Yankees learned that Cuban musicians were often far ahead of their northern counterparts in technique, experience, and flexibility. Compared to the polyrhythms they'd grown up with, they found jazz and other American forms quite straightforward. US musicians, on the other hand, were completely befuddled by Cuban beats.

Son's American breakout took place at an unlikely venue: the midtown Palace Theatre (part-owned by JFK's father, Joseph Kennedy). As in France with Montaner, a woman played a central role; Marion Sunshine was married to the orchestra leader Don Azpiazú's brother and persuaded the Palace to add Azpiazú's outfit—already in New York playing to uptown Cubans and Puerto Ricans—to a variety bill in the last week of April 1930. The curtain opened on a band of ruffle-shirted musicians and skimpy-skirted dancers in front of a palm-tree backdrop. The short set climaxed with singer Antonio Machín pushing a peanut vendor's cart onstage, dressed like a cartoon Cuban with red bandana and guajiro straw hat. Launching into "El Manisero," he tossed bags of nuts into the crowd, who were already going wild to the rhythms, the energy, the color, and now this irresistibly catchy song. Al Jolson jumped on the bandwagon by hiring Montaner to tour the country with him; he passed out peanut cones—*in blackface!*—while Rita repeated her Parisian coup. Sunshine volunteered to write some English lyrics and "The Peanut Vendor" became an instant standard, famous enough to be lampooned in the Marx Brothers' *Duck Soup*. Sunshine may have just wanted to give her brother-in-law a hand, but she ended up providing dozens of English lyrics for Latin songs, draining them of double entendres (the message of "El Manisero" became *"fifty million little monkeys can't be wrong"*), having hit after hit and making a fortune.

In an era when the song was more important than the singer, "Peanut Vendor" sold a million copies of both the sheet music and the recording. (It was only a modest success in Cuba, however, epitomizing a pattern in which foreigners' enthusiasms are rarely in sync with local tastes, Cugat, Desi, Pérez Prado, and Buena Vista Social Club being prime examples.) Hollywood's Belasco Theatre started serving "peanut vendor sundaes," Paul Whiteman, George Gershwin, and the Andrews Sisters "went Latin," and then-hoofer George Raft starred in a movie called *Rumba*. (America and Europe never could get the terminology straight, which is one reason the "salsa" catch-all ended up working so well.) Either Latin music was becoming a jokey novelty or the market was being softened up for something more fundamental and long-lasting. The arrival in America of clarinettist Mario Bauzá helped ensure the latter.

The first job Bauzá applied for when he got to New York was playing trumpet in "El Manisero" vocalist Antonio Machín's new orchestra. That he had never touched the instrument before was no obstacle for the supremely gifted Bauzá; he told Machín to hold the job for him, spent two weeks practicing in his hotel room, and became so fluent that he would later hold down a chair in the brass section of Chick Webb's great swing band. In Cuba, Bauzá had been considered light-skinned enough to work with the top orchestras, but he wanted to play with the best, which meant getting in trouble for hanging out with and hiring dark musicians. In America, he encountered the binary color bar, but also a flourishing African-American music scene with touring bands, clubs, dance halls, and recording dates that together could generate something resembling a living wage.

Webb taught Bauzá to lose the "bullfight" tones and pronounce his notes like an American; he predicted that the Cuban would become a force to reckon with, particularly after Mario tipped him off about a teenaged singer named Ella Fitzgerald. In the 1930s, swing was the world's dominant pop music; while Bauzá was plotting the creation of a Cuban orchestra with the energy and volume of the top American outfits, he was also subverting the 4/4 feel of groups that employed him, Cab Calloway's in particular. Some bandmates resented the way he captivated Calloway, Dizzy, and others with his beat-shifting notions, but to the extent that a few bebop drummers and bassists were ready for Chano Pozo's rhythm revolution, Bauzá is largely responsible.

He wrote to his wife's brother, Havana sonero Frank "Macho" Grillo, and urged him to "come starve with me" in New York. Once there, Grillo married a strong-willed Puerto Rican woman who shrunk his nickname, and together he and Bauzá formed Machito's Afro-Cuban Allstars. From the orchestra's first gig, dancers marveled that it sounded like "Count Basie with a *clave*." The band's name threw down a gauntlet. Cubans in America tended to downplay their racial ambiguity; Bauzá and Grillo were serving notice that, like Miguelito Vargas's Orquesta Casino de la Playa, they were moving in two directions at once, towards brassy sophistication and deep into Afro-Cuban authenticity.

Latin lite may have been the rule downtown, but in East Harlem, Bauzá and Grillo found plenty of allies in bringing the Real Thing to the Big Apple. Latin music owes much of its modern character to the US Army's need for cannon fodder in World War One. The Act of Congress that blocked Cuba from becoming a state or colony didn't prevent Puerto Rico, a smaller and poorer ex-Spanish territory, being absorbed into America's burgeoning empire as a "Commonwealth." The 1917 Jones Act made the island's natives eligible for the draft and, as a necessary footnote, gave them US passports. Congressmen were fine with sending Puerto Ricans (who had nearly as much African blood as Cubans) off to die in the trenches of Flanders, but were appalled when hundreds of thousands of them celebrated their new paperwork by moving to the mainland. Most chose New York, where they found a growing Latin neighborhood on the Upper East Side of Manhattan. Early Cuban arrivals had secured jobs managing Jewish-owned buildings in the area; with inside information about vacancies, they tipped off friends and relatives. As Jews prospered and moved to the suburbs, Latinos took over not just living quarters, but also storefronts theaters, and dance halls. Spanish Harlem as a destination, as an idea, and as launch pad for the music that would animate dancefloors across the world was born.

☙

> In black music, the drum has a rhythmic, melodic, and even speaking role, besides being sacred and thaumaturgic, and at times dynastic and pontifical . . . [O]ther instruments . . . are vassals to it and form its symphonic entourage.
>
> —Fernando Ortiz

> We still remember the marvelous stupor with which the people of our generation greeted . . . the instruments that came from the eastern provinces, and that are heard today, poorly played, in all the world's cabarets.
>
> —Alejo Carpentier

> With any kind of object, the long dry fingers (of Cuban blacks) find a way to produce unexpected sounds . . . Wood, metal, baked clay, dried hides, they offer an inexhaustible range of delightful timbres, from which they extract a true orchestration of sounds . . . evoking the universal consent of things moving to the rhythm of the dancing. Tell me: what worth do our timbales, our tambourines, our triangles, our cymbals . . . have when faced with Cuban percussion instruments, so full of nuance, so poetic, with their spellbinding hums, their caresses of torn silk, and their small silver anvil?
>
> —Émile Vuillermoz, *Candide* (Parisian magazine)

There is a near-Oriental formality to the structures of Afro-Cuban rhythm. Styles emerge from fixed groupings; experimental additions or alterations are noted, tested, then adapted or rejected in a Darwinian process that evolved across the thirties and forties. The roots of this elegant rigidity may lie in Yorùbás' obsessive organization, the strict regulation of Abakuá ceremony, or the rhythmically segmented forms of Spanish flamenco—most likely all three. Whatever the source, it provides a firm foundation for the interweaving of African and European cultures that constitute this music's flesh and blood.

The need for small, light, portable instruments that could replicate the rhythms of the *cabildos* led to the creation of the bongo drum and the adaptation of native Antillean instruments such as the güiro and maraca.

The deeper-sounding member of a pair—of maracas (gourd shakers), for example—is called *"el macho"* (male), the higher and smaller *"la hembra"* (female), though this order is reversed for bongos, where the *macho* "speaks" above the deeper *hembra*. The güiro, a notched gourd that replicates the ancient monotone glissando of an ass's jaw, is the bachelor of the rhythm section.

By the 1920s, many dance orchestras had added güiro and maracas. Neither involved fingers striking hide; before *son*, most Cubans only knew that sound from Kings' Day and pre-Lenten parades, where comparsas were led by men with the large *tumbadoras* that the music and tourist industries would later call congas. It was this connection to the Africanness of the parades that sent shock waves through urban Cuba when sextetos began adding bongos. Early recordings show *son*'s rhythm being driven primarily by the strum of the guitar and the stroke of a güiro or the rattle of maracas (usually played by a vocalist); bongos tended to improvise around the beat rather than define it. The sound of a wet finger sliding across the head revealed a *bongosero*'s familiarity with Abakuá ceremonial drumming (and got some early adaptors in trouble with those reclusive societies for betraying a hidden practice).

Pairs of bongos were originally connected by a short rope, but eventually locked together in a metal frame. The image of a seated player, spread knees gripping the small drums, would become an emblem of Cuban hipness in 1940s and '50s America. Armando Peraza's stints with Charlie Parker, Cal Tjader, and most famously George Shearing placed bongos at the center of beatnik culture. Marlon Brando became particularly obsessed, often flying to Havana for lessons.

As these instruments and their interactions were evolving in eastern Cuba, the docks of Matanzas and Havana saw the growing musical use of shipbuilding pegs that would become known by the name of the rhythmic patterns they marked. Claves are far more than simply two blunt sticks. Having cut down her own hardwood to build the galleons that conquered Latin America, Spain shifted boatbuilding (and deforestation) to Cuba. Carved from the same materials (rosewood, ebony, and granadilla) used to hold gold-laden ships together through stormy ocean crossings, when struck expertly (with the left hand cradling the hembra so as to create a resonant chamber in the palm for the blow of the slightly longer macho) claves create what Federico García Lorca called a "wooden raindrop" (*gota de madera*). This sound cuts subtly but clearly through vocals, horns, strings, and other percussion, providing musicians and dancers with a rhythmic "key" that is particular to Afro-Cuban music. (The word *clave* is close to *llave*, Spanish for "key.") Which is not to suggest that the sound of wood on wood originated in Cuba; it has long been a part of music-making in sub-Saharan Africa, as well as the Maghreb, where *qidab* sticks anticipate Spanish castanets. Nineteenth-century Chinese immigrant workers added to the mix; Cubans found their hollow *muyu* blocks intriguing, called them *guaguas*, and mounted them next to the cowbell on sets of timbales.

In 1942, John Cage published a manifesto that called for modern composers to develop systems of rhythmic organization as evolved as those pertaining to harmony. Cubans and their African cousins had been doing just that for centuries, but only in the wake of Independence, and the *son* revolution was the organization of beats around the clave codified. And when I say "codified," it was outsiders such as Ortiz and Carpentier who observed and described it, not the players themselves; they had no need to contemplate or analyze it, they just did it.

Somewhere deep in African culture lies a dialectical feeling about rhythm that manifests itself in "call and response," the clave and many other musical phenomena. Question and answer, yin and yang, *macho y hembra*—a binary that is so deeply ingrained as to obviate any need for codification. The twelve-bar blues can be seen as a distant relative of the clave, with a proposition repeated before a third four-bar line provides the resolution. When different African cultures began colliding and blending in late-nineteenth-century Cuba, it became necessary to have this skeleton—"one-two-three /one-two" (or, sometimes, "one-two /one-two-three")—clearly defined. What can flummox non-Africans about the clave is that although those five strokes can, in theory, be pinned down to points in the two bars across which they fall,

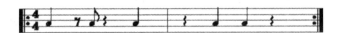

you really need to feel, not read them. Someone marking them with hand-claps or finger-snaps often starts to move against or around (rather than with) the 4/4 Cuban rhythm. The West's musical revolutions (at least through the early twentieth century) have been largely harmonic; since the Renaissance, Europeans have reveled in ever more complex vocal and instrumental harmonies and wider sweeps of melodic interval. Over the same centuries, Afro-Cubans were drawn to more and more complex layering of rhythms.

For Ned Sublette, the clave "does not even have to be played, since all the musicians are marking it mentally and playing to it . . . [T]here are any number of rhythmic formulas played by various instruments that are images of the clave, any of which is sufficient to tell the other musicians where the rhythmic key is . . . A European ear would analyse [the clave] as a two-bar pattern . . . This endless, unbroken two-bar sway . . . a feel that exists across a wide area of West Africa[,] became a fundamental structural principle of Cuban music."

Drums were generally forbidden in the dockyards but waterfront rumbas required more substantial propulsion than just clave pegs. Over time, certain types of shipping containers, or *cajónes*, emerged: a *bacalao* (codfish) crate for low macho tones, a particular candle box for hembra sounds. These dockside parties helped spread the popularity of Abakuá rhythms and the cajón became popular throughout Spain's former colonies as a percussion of the poor. It rarely found its way onto stages or into recording studios before flamenco guitarist Paco de Lucía's tour of Latin America in the early seventies. At a post-concert celebration in the Lima home of Peruvian diva Chabuca Granda, de Lucía's Brazilian percussionist was mesmerized by her cajón player, astride what looked like a simple wooden box. He bought the expertly crafted object, took it back to Seville like colonial-era booty, and incorporated it into his percussion arsenal. Within a few years, every *nuevo flamenco* group in Spain had to have one, and soon the world wanted that sexy high-low thud that only a cajón can provide. It eventually completed a circle back to Cuba, where some twenty-first-century Latin jazz and *timba* outfits employ one for its cool international sound.

In the solares, *tumbadoras* (congas) were common, their varying pitches comparable to the sounds of the different cajónes used on the docks. *Son*, as it moved west, absorbed elements of rumba, but it took a conceptual leap to bring the deep, powerful sound of the conga into sextetos, conjuntos, and orchestras. When Chano Pozo rigged up that three-headed set of congas, he was following the trail blazed by El Ciego Maravillosa, Arsenio Rodríguez.

Rodríguez's childhood prepared him well for the role of synthesizing genius of Afro-Cuban music. Born in 1911, when he was seven a kick in the head from a mule combined with poor medical care left him blind. Arsenio was schooled in Abakuá ritual by his ex-slave grandfather, while an uncle taught him to play the drums and took him to rumbas. When the family moved from Matanzas to Güines, near Havana, Arsenio picked up the Ki-Kongo language and traditions as well as absorbing Santería practices from a Yorùbá family who lived next door. A 1926 hurricane forced his family to Marianao, a then-shabby suburb full of bars, clubs, and whorehouses, where Rodríguez immersed himself in popular Afro-Cuban music, mastered the tres, and began composing. Throughout the 1930s, his style evolved in bordellos, in the slightly more respectable *academias de baile* and in Afro-Cuban social clubs. These tough environments taught him to look after himself and he grew into a muscular bull of a man, fiercely punching the air while advancing towards the sound of an offending remark.

Bands everywhere were growing in size and volume to match the bigger crowds and dancefloors and the clamor of modern cities. There seems, however, to have been no grand plan behind adding a conga drum to Arsenio's sexteto; he only wanted to give his brother Kike, who guided him everywhere, something to play. But when other musicians heard Rodríguez's new line-up, it was a revelation; the conga had become the beating heart of the music.

One American who visited Havana in the twenties to buy molasses for his bootleg distillery returned in the post-Prohibition thirties and set up a different sort of business: "I couldn't get that little island out of my mind," recalled Meyer Lansky. His casinos lured a new sort of American tourist, not so booze-thirsty but hungry for risk and exoticism.

A conga drum, a Carabalí chant, a semi-naked dancing girl—Havana in the late 1930s provided a classic example of outside fascination with perceived authenticity forcing local bluenoses to allow what every fiber of their being wanted to suppress. Cartoonish cabaret titillation was balanced by earnest concert-stage presentations organized by Ortiz and his minorista cohorts, though it is unlikely any cabildo would have allowed their actual sacred rituals to be staged for White people. The closest Havana came was a 1936 concert organized by Ortiz focusing on Yorùbá voice and drum, a good two years before John Hammond's groundbreaking plunge into roots with his *Spirituals to Swing* concerts at Town Hall in New York. Such events, combined with the explosion of tourist-friendly comparsas and cabaret pastiches of Abakuá and Santería ceremonies, helped accustom the public to the sight of hands striking the head of a conga.

The sanitized carnival parades of 1937 and onwards remained reassuringly chaotic and often dangerous; poor neighborhoods celebrated with street parties and rumbas late into the night. The teenaged Celia Cruz defied her parents to go: "The colors, the music, the sense of energy and living life to its fullest potential were intoxicating." Ortiz and Carpentier may have complained that the elite skills of earlier street percussionists had been lost, but for once the hyperbole of the tourist brochures wasn't wrong: Cuba, they proclaimed, was the most musical country on earth.

The natural inclination of African percussion is for conversation. By the mid-1940s, when tuning pegs had made them more band-friendly, triple sets of congas had become part of many Latin ensembles. Chano Pozo may have been the pioneer, but the man who shaped the conga's future was Carlos "Patato" Valdés. According to historian Raul Fernandez, Patato "stands out as the musician who, almost single-handedly, defined the function of the conga in the Cuban *conjuntos*; expanded its role by using more than one drum in dance ensembles; developed original *tumbaos* [rhythmic patterns] to go along with the larger conga set; and explored to the fullest the melodic and harmonic potential of the conga drums."

I saw Valdés at one of those legendary *Salsa Meets Jazz* nights at the Village Gate in New York in the 1980s. (His teasing schoolmates weren't wrong: Patato's face was a bit tuber-like.) A small, wiry man bursting with controlled energy, he seemed to dance as he played, peering over his conga set with a knowing glint. As ignorant of his history as I then was, he appeared to be operating on a different plane to the musicians around him. I now realize I was getting a privileged whiff of 1940s Havana.

Starting with Sonora Matancera (original home of Celia Cruz), Valdés seized the opportunity presented by tuning keys to fit the conga into the sound of an orchestra. A champion dancer in his youth, Patato gave Brigitte Bardot "rhumba" lessons in Paris before moving on to New York, then ending up in the San Francisco Bay area, where *bongosero* Armando Peraza and *batá* master Francisco Aguabella had already settled. It may not be entirely obvious from the recordings, but these drummers' influence—and occasional participation—provided a direct link from the Lucumí societies of thirties Cuba to the seventies West Coast sound of Santana, Malo, Cal Tjader, et al. By the late sixties, single, double, or triple congas had become standard equipment for many jazz, funk, and rock outfits, Trojan horses insinuating yet more polyrhythms into American music.

The final piece in the modern Latin percussion jigsaw was the incorporation of timbales, a smaller, cheaper, *macho y hembra* version of the classical tympani. Although the increasingly African way they were used in the nineteenth century was shocking, they had, like the danzón, grown respectable by the 1920s, being struck, after all, with a mallet or a stick, not a hand.

Tito Puente's playing has come to define most listeners' image of the timbales. Inspired by those Miguelito Valdés records to see his future in Latin music rather than jazz, he emulated Gene Krupa by moving his drums to the front of the bandstand and playing them with Krupa-like aggression and ego. Two key tools in Puente's arsenal were linked directly to Arsenio Rodríguez's innovations: he credits Arsenio with being first to give the clave such prominence and for having the clave player switch to cowbell on the montuno section, a shamanistic forged-iron signal for gear-changing as the intensity increased, invoking the pots, pans, and tire irons of the Santiago comparsas. Arsenio also encouraged his bongoseros to apply the "dry hit," a single blow placing an oblique accent rather than "chattering" as they did on most recordings from the twenties. In the clank of the cowbell mounted on his stand and in those sudden blows to the hembra, Puente was drawing a straight line to the influence of the Marvelous Blind Man and, through him, to Africa.

Cuban music is voices and drums, and the rest is luxury.

—Orlando Marin, bandleader and timbalero

Most early *son* ensembles included a *botijo* (jug) or *marímbula* (bass thumb piano), African instruments that had followed the captured slaves. By the 1920s, even to *son* enthusiasts, they looked and sounded crude; with the music's arrival in Havana, the European upright bass began to replace them.

Many of the most important innovators in Cuban music have been bass players; in the 1980s, Los Van Van's Juan Formell led his immensely popular and game-changing band from the bottom, just as Septeto Nacional's Ignacio Piñeiro had in the 1920s. But the key figure in the transformation of the instrument was Israel "Cachao" López. López was a prodigy; starting in his teens, he played with the Havana Philharmonic (including under the visiting batons of von Karajan, Kleiber, Beecham, and Doráti) while moonlighting with his pianist brother Orestes in Antonio Arcaño's *charanga* (flute-driven ensemble). Cachao's discovery of what Arsenio was up to led him to transform the undercarriage of danzón; taking his cue from the counter-rhythms of El Ciego's tres playing, he used the bass to drive the music forward with lines that, when they reached New York, also influenced jazz players. The López brothers were tasked with composing the band's material and came up with ever more African-sounding danzones; these would eventually lead to the form's collision with *son* in what became the worldwide phenomenon known as the mambo.

In an ideal world, recordings would allow us to follow the evolution of Cuban line-ups and playing styles across the thirties. But in 1929, Depression-shocked US companies abandoned the island, and with no labels of its own, Cuban recording didn't begin again until that 1937 RCA Victor expedition. We are forced to rely on memories, print archives, and triangulation to understand how the music evolved during the decade.

President Gerardo Machado's regime was careening towards a chaotic and corrupt abyss when the 1929 Wall Street Crash pushed it over the edge. To make matters worse, just as Americans began to realize they were too broke for a boozy holiday in Havana, the Hoover administration raised protective tariffs on sugar. The resulting economic collapse threw millions of Cubans out of work, many musicians among them.

Franklin D. Roosevelt's election in 1932 brought an end to Prohibition as well as a promise to jettison cousin Teddy's Big Stick approach to Cuba. As if. After the "Sergeants' Revolt" led by Fulgencio Batista, Roosevelt insisted on free elections that brought liberal Ramón Grau to power. Grau proved a bit *too* liberal for the Yanks, annulling the Platt Amendment, granting equal rights to women and Blacks, establishing minimum wages in the cane fields, and generally being a nuisance to American capital. Washington decided that Batista was more its type of guy after all and encouraged him to throw out the elected government and take over himself.

Batista was a genetic and political mix; his ancestry combined Native Caribbean, Chinese, African, and Spanish and he forged alliances with the poor, the army, the US State Department, the Mob, and the Communists. Never accepted by the Cuban establishment, while president he was famously refused entry to a Whites-only yacht club. Though he often brutally repressed dissent, his new Constitution enshrined (and failed to implement) many of the ideals that would later form the basis of Fidel Castro's Revolution.

Ortiz and Carpentier may have bemoaned the simplification of Cuban music for tourism and export, but based on the eventually recorded evidence, the island's music actually grew more interesting and complex across this "drawn curtain" period. The long silence amplified the impact of recordings by Miguelito Valdés's Orquesta and others released in the late thirties; a spectacular new world of rhythm, harmony, and singing suddenly appeared as if out of nowhere.

The suppression of street dances combined with the surge in unemployment across the Grau-Batista decade had forced Afro-Cuban music deeper inside the solares, where rumba mixed with Lucumí, Kongo, and Abakuá ceremony and fed streams of influence into the sounds of the bars and social clubs. One of the prime vehicles to carry this *solar* intensity into the mainstream was the tres and Arsenio's playing of it. Hand in hand with his more aggressive use of percussion, it was this rustic-looking descendant of the medieval *bandurría* that gave *son* its modern edge. In Arsenio's hands, wood and metal joined to create a sound that spread outward from the solares until much of the Latin world was moving to accents articulated by Rodríguez's fingers.

Despite looking like something out of a still life by Van Dyck, the tres had over the centuries become a very African instrument. Its widely separated pairs of strings, for example, don't chime sweetly like Roger McGuinn's or George Harrison's Rickenbacker twelve-strings, they buzz like a thumb piano, a fundamental instrument in Arsenio's grandparents' Kongo. Attacking it like a percussion instrument, Rodríguez's piledriving lines of counter-melody locked in with the conga to emphasize the second and fourth beats. The three-minute limit on 10-inch 78 rpm recordings means we can't experience his legendary cowbell-driven montunos, which could last until dancers were too exhausted to continue, while the poor sound quality of the early recordings forces us to turn up the bass to try and get an idea of the bottom-up power of Arsenio's band. The path from the melodic sweetness of twenties Cuban recordings to the hard edges of modern salsa begins here. Long after the instrument had become a rare sight in modern Latin bands, its influence insulated salsa against the electric guitar, preventing the feel of the music from drifting towards the rock.

In this, the piano was the tres's ally. Keyboards had been respectable presences in Cuban music from the mid-eighteenth century onwards, following rather than leading the contradanza's evolution into danzón. But during the 1930s, they took on a role carved out by the tres, becoming as much a rhythm instrument as an harmonic one, their cyclical arpeggios directly connected to the playing of the thumb piano in Central Africa.

Winds from the north, west, and east blew the sound of the trumpet into Havana, inspiring sextetos to become septetos. No individual musician in the late 1920s could match the global impact of Louis Armstrong, and the daily boats between New Orleans and Havana brought reminders of the trumpet's possibilities. From the west, Mexican radio signals carried the sound of mariachi bands (so named for their popularity at weddings); these had always been string-led, but when the blare of US jazz inspired one outfit to add trumpets, the new sound caused a sensation, first in Mexico, then spreading to Cuba. From Santiago came the ear-splitting blasts of the "Chinese cornet" in the comparsas of Oriente. (I once recorded this double-reed instrument in a Santiago studio; we had to park it and the tire iron down the hallway with the door open just a crack, and both were never less than prominent in the mix.) Classically trained Lazaro Herrera from Septeto Nacional pioneered *son* trumpet, but the style was eventually defined by two graduates of Arsenio's conjuntos: Chano Pozo's stepbrother Félix Chappottín (who stayed in Cuba) and "Chocolate" Armenteros (who brought his influential playing to America).

Arsenio's 1940 conjunto line-up synthesised the thirties evolution into a template for the future: a pair of vocalists doubling on maracas, güiro, and claves, two trumpets, piano, tres, guitar, bongo, and conga. Cuban groups might have wanted to grow larger, but, like rhythm-and-blues outfits in the American South, the size of working bands was limited by how many players and instruments could be crammed into a single battered sedan with a roof rack.

The material being performed by late-thirties bands ranged from

Rodríguez's very Afro-Cuban songs to the often cartoonish creations of Lecuona, Simons, and their ilk. Rita Montaner's recordings of her friends' compositions are rarely very interesting, but the effects of her passion can be felt everywhere. Her relentless promotion of Afro-Cuban music and its practitioners, from her blackface role in the hit 1927 revue *Havana 1830* to her tireless touring across the island and overseas in the thirties and forties, softened the resistance of White audiences to darker performers and to Afro-Cuban music in general. In the early thirties, she hired a dark-skinned piano accompanist named Ignacio Villa, who had gotten his start working in movie houses with Cachao López. He soon graduated to becoming Rita's opening act, singing all manner of parlor songs. ("I would have liked to sing opera, but I have the voice of a mango-seller.") Montaner gave him a ridiculously racist stage name that he eventually came to view as a stroke of good fortune: "Bola de Nieve," which means "Snowball." His recordings of "Babalú," "Siboney," "Drume negrita," and "El Manisero" dignified these outsiders' portrayals of Afro-Cuban culture almost to the level of greatness that Billie Holiday bestowed on cheesy American Tin Pan Alley songs.

Like Chano, Arsenio needed help getting his songs down on paper and published, but what songs they were! Celebrating Africa, its languages and religions, they quoted from folk tales, hailed comparsas, bemoaned the suffering of poverty-stricken solares and attacked Cuban politicians, landowners, and America while praising mambís and Martí. His lyrics may have sometimes been obscure to White Cubans but they were clear as day to his fellow Afro-Cubans. All this was accomplished with wry sophistication, turning bufo clichés back on themselves and mocking the assumptions behind even the best-intentioned of "elevating" minorista compositions.

Forces moved in multiple directions across the thirties, creating whirlpools of creativity and change. Many Cubans aspired to jazzy modernity, so bands added brass, pianos, basses, individualistic solos, and arrangements that referenced American swing along with hints of Debussy and Ravel. (The period's leading arranger, Félix Guerrero, had studied in Paris with Nadia Boulanger, whom we will encounter again and again in surprising corners of this book.) He in turn taught

Chico O'Farrill, the man responsible for many of the greatest Latin jazz arrangements of the forties and fifties and whose New York–based son Arturo is central to that music today.) Swing 78s were like gold dust in 1930s Havana, with musicians prowling the docks to meet sailors selling shellacs. Cuban baseball players were another source, arriving home for the off-season with suitcases full of Benny Goodman and Count Basie discs.

Arcaño's charanga (including the Lópezes) played Afro-Cuban venues for low fees while charging top peso for society gigs. They absorbed Arsenio's lessons and paid homage with songs dedicated to the different Black social clubs, including one called "Buena vista." One López brothers tune was "Mambo," which would provide a springboard for the dance craze of the early fifties; another, "Chanchullo," contained the riff that was the basis for Santana's "Oye cómo va." Cachao's bass lines, meanwhile, became more and more adventurous, pushing the beat with contra-rhythms and establishing his instrument as a central voice in the music.

"Ritual" cabaret shows and the heavier sound of the bands had a positive effect on Black employment. White musicians might excel on trumpet or piano and could appear convincing on maracas, but few dared compete with an Afro-Cuban conguero. The bigger sound also meant an evolution in vocal styles; only hard-edged voices could cut through brass, piano, and conga. The future would belong not to sweet-voiced Rita Montaner or Lecuona's Cuban Boys but to the likes of Benny Moré and Celia Cruz. And in Afro-Cuban music's salsa future, the nasal edge of Puerto Rican *jíbaro* singers would prove ideal for the modernist bravura that forties New York added on to the riches of thirties Havana.

> If Cachao and Arsenio Rodríguez hadn't been born, the Cuban music of the 50s . . . would have sounded like the [Cuban] music of the 30s.
>
> —Bebo Valdés, pianist and bandleader

Cuba was a radio pioneer; stations sprouted across the island in the late 1920s and broadcasts reached every corner of the Caribbean. Foreshadowing fifties American rock 'n' roll, disc jockeys from genteel backgrounds shocked older audiences by promoting *son*. After the flow of new records dried up, most music was played live on air and radio's reach meant that standards were raised across the island as local musicians learned from broadcasts by Havana's and Santiago's best. In 1935, Sensemaya Radio began a thrice-weekly series of lectures by Ortiz on the subject of Afro-Cuban music, illustrated by Rita Montaner, Bola de Nieve, and Merceditas Valdés. These shows lasted for a year and a half before pressure from the Catholic Church, outraged by Ortiz's legitimization of African religions, forced their cancelation.

One thirties radio slot that reverberates to this day was hosted by Joseíto Fernández, a sung magazine of the air which combined current events, readers' letters, snatches of Martí poetry, and the host's running commentary. Each afternoon from 3:30 to 3:45, Fernández would improvise verses over a signature *guajiro-son* (rural folk song over a *son* beat) that he called "Mi biografía." We know it as "Guajira Guantanamera." When Fernández finally retired in 1957, every Cuban had internalized the melody, with many fervently wishing never to hear it again. Pete Seeger dashed such hopes by making it a staple of his concerts—right after "Wimoweh"—and turning it into an anthem of the Left. Another early radio fixture was the talent contest; *The Supreme Court of Art* began in 1937 and had many imitators. Judges and audiences seemed to like female singers: Celia Cruz, Merceditas Valdés, Olga Guillot, and Elena Burke all got their starts in these on-air competitions. *X-Factor*, eat your heart out.

Havana boomed during the war years and race relations improved when Julio Cueva's catchy "Agua de tinajón" became the first hit to generate equal fervor with Black and White audiences, with everyone singing along and dancing to it together. Musicians themselves were generally color-blind; the light-skinned Arcaño y Sus Maravillas were regularly co-billed with Arsenio Rodríguez's group, and players of all shades met at Black social clubs that stayed open all night to spare patrons having to run the gauntlet of police checks on their way home.

The 1943 launch of the Communist Party's Radio Mil Diez (1010 on the dial) transformed Cuban airwaves. As in South Africa, the Party was the only political organisation prepared to treat Black citizens uncondescendingly. This attitude was manifest in 1010's programming, where they played bebop and blues as well as highlighting regional Afro-Cuban styles in a way never previously attempted. Every afternoon at five came a live broadcast by Arsenio, with Arcaño following at seven. The cross-talk which had begun with the López brothers' visits to Rodríguez's gigs deepened, with an Afro-Cuban edge added to Arcaño's sweet charanga and Arsenio's horn charts growing richer and more complex. With such exposure Arsenio's fame mushroomed; at one point, both he and Arcaño had three interchangeable bands, with the two leaders racing across the Havana night to play a set with each. The war years of the early forties marked a short-lived Yankee preference for anti-fascism over anti-communism. Once the Iron Curtain came down in 1947, under pressure from the US, Radio 1010 was gone.

The famous VJ Day photo of a Times Square kiss symbolized the joyful release that swept America at war's end. The country had no refugee camps, no rubble to clear, and apparently no reckoning to be made with war criminals, while vast spending on the conflict had swept away the Depression. But what would these unleashed party animals choose for their soundtrack, what rhythm would they move to, what steps would they dance?

America had swung into World War Two to a big-band beat, but those days were over; musicians had been scattered by military service and bands broken up by wartime travel and energy restrictions, while swing's bland popularizer Glenn Miller had vanished over the English Channel. The Musicians' Union expanded its power during the war; minimum wages now made it harder for orchestras to barnstorm the country. Many leading figures in jazz were intrigued by the modernist possibilities unleashed by wartime jam sessions at Minton's in Harlem; dancing to jazz was so pre-war.

Which brings us back to that 1947 conversation at La Conga between Miguelito Valdés and Federico Pagani. Pagani started slowly at the Palladium, with Sunday-afternoon dances alternating swing and Cuban. With crowds showing little interest in jazz and many wanting just to "dance Latin," the promoter initiated weekly Blen-Blen Club matinees (named after Chano's hit), with Machito and the All-Stars headlining.

Pagani had to walk a racial tightrope; this wasn't a Harlem or Bronx ballroom, it was right in the heart of midtown, a few blocks north of that VJ Day kiss, and neither the police nor the Mafia lurking behind the Palladium's ownership wanted to see Black crowds there after dark. The racial ambiguity of the Hispanic world, however, trumped American primitivism; what could you call these dancers who blended every shade from palest white to darkest black? Not only were there hundreds of thousands of Black and mixed-race Cubans and Puerto Ricans in the metropolitan area, but many African Americans had learned to love the music pouring out of storefronts and jukeboxes in Upper Manhattan, where the lines between ethnic neighborhoods were seldom other than blurry.

"You want the green, you gotta have the black," Pagani told menacing men with Sicilian names and blue-uniformed Irishmen looking for their cut. Tentatively, he expanded, first to Wednesdays, then Fridays, and finally all three weekend nights. Every show featured three bands providing non-stop music, with lessons for newcomers at cocktail hour and dance contests at midnight, plus competitions for "best legs," "loudest shirt," "weirdest shoes," and "healthiest female chest." What poured from the stage was no gimmick; numbers extended for fifteen minutes and more, with conga battles, horn solos, and montunos that rose to a sweat-soaked crescendo. The dancefloor was a revelation that could only have happened in New York: Cubans, Italians, Puerto Ricans, Jews, and African Americans, the rich rubbing shoulders with the poor, expert movers with awkward neophytes. The crowd became as big an attraction as the bands.

> Looking back, it seems [to have been] a place that was hipper than anything we now have, and more innocent. I don't mean that nobody ever snorted cocaine or smoked marijuana in the Palladium ... But there was something fresh and amazing about the dancing ...
>
> —José Torres, a Palladium regular

My feeling for Latin music grew . . . along with my developing interest in women. Looking at them and seeing them move. The rhythmic stuff of how music relates to sensuality. I started going to the Palladium . . . during my senior year in high school. It cost a buck-fifty to get in . . . throw my books in the checkroom, and dance for hours on end. Till three or four in the morning. Sometimes, I'd go right back to Brooklyn to go to school the next day.

—Bill Graham

Bill Graham took his first steps towards becoming the world's greatest concert promoter in 1966, when he met Ronny Davis, head of the San Francisco Mime Troupe, and volunteered to organize a benefit concert for them. He and Davis had discovered they had a bond; both "danced Latin."

The Palladium years from 1947 to 1966 have entered the annals of legend. The mobsters' and cops' worst nightmares were quickly realized: an interracial dancefloor led straight to the bedroom. Latinos from East Harlem and the Bronx couldn't believe how many eager "bagel babies" there were; by the mid-sixties, Palladium crowds included Jewish–Puerto Rican and Cuban-Italian kids whose parents had met on the Palladium dancefloor in the late forties.

To reach that floor, dancers climbed a narrow flight of stairs on the south side of 53rd Street, halfway between Eighth Avenue and Broadway, and entered a huge ballroom that could hold three thousand people. There was a long bar to the left and a low stage straight ahead; in the right-hand corner were a few sofas, with the area in front of them implicitly reserved for the best dancers. Women sat, men asked and were often refused; girls didn't come to the Palladium just to look for cute guys, they wanted to dance with the best.

A block away was "Swing Street," the highest concentration of jazz clubs in America. Musicians on a break would wander over to check out the new neighbour; Dizzy Gillespie naturally led the way and often sat in with his pal Bauzá. Producer Norman Granz took Charlie Parker with him one night to hear Machito's band, and a few weeks later they were all in the studio together recording *South of the Border*. In 1953, pianist George Shearing and his vibraphone player Cal Tjader were persuaded by their bassist, that very same Al McKibbon, to join him on a visit. They must have dug what they heard: Shearing quickly hired a bongo player, and Tjader left soon after to start the first Latin jazz combo.

Show-business celebrities followed the musicians: Marlon Brando, Kim Novak, Esther Williams, Van Johnson, Sammy Davis Jr., Shelley Winters, Henry Fonda, Lena Horne, and Cesar Romero were all Palladium regulars. Then came the disc jockeys: Dick Sugar was followed by "Symphony Sid" Torin, and both were entranced by the Palladium scene. Sugar launched the first English-language Latin music radio show, and Torin began adding Afro-Cuban tracks to his hugely popular jazz show before eventually "going native" and playing exclusively Latin, a betrayal many in the jazz world never forgave.

Radio's ripples spread the music across the region. Was it the looser limbs of a Mediterranean DNA that brought so many Jewish and Italian New Yorkers to the Palladium? Perhaps it was Sugar's and Torin's Brooklyn accents. Or maybe Afro-Cuban music simply filled a vacuum between the death of swing and the birth of rock 'n' roll; people needed to move and New Yorkers were the first to realize that Latin was the hippest rhythm around. Whatever the socio-genetic cause, some of the best Palladium dancers weren't Latins but "mambonicks." The music became so popular among Jewish kids that their vacation playground, the Catskill Mountains, was transformed into an outpost of the Palladium, with Latin bands booked all summer at Grossinger's, the Concord, and the Stevensville. This inspired better-off Puerto Ricans to develop Las Villas, a Hudson Valley resort modeled on the Jewish Catskills.

Tybee Afra and her "Grossinger's brat" best friend, Abigail Lasman, were archetypical bagel babies who threw themselves body and soul into Latin dancing. Afra was spotted by Frank Sinatra, who hired her for his Las Vegas show, then by Miguelito Valdés, who brought her with him to Havana as featured dancer when he played the Tropicana. Lasman was scooped up by Xavier Cugat; after marrying the bandleader she changed her name to Abbe Lane, learned Spanish, and became a star in Mexico, then on Broadway, and finally on American TV. Italians could claim Millie Donay, who partnered "Cuban Pete" Aguilar (actually a

Puerto Rican) in one of the most popular fifties dance teams. (Italian and Jewish musicians would also play key roles in the evolution of Latin music in New York.) For many African-American New Yorkers, Sunday nights at the Palladium capped a weekend ritual: swimming at Jacob Riis Park beach out past Idlewild (later Kennedy) Airport, a stroll across the boardwalk to the basketball courts to practice steps with portable radios, then jump on the A train straight to 53rd Street and Eighth Avenue and the Palladium's cheap early-entrance tickets.

For most non-Latins, dancing has always been the music's prime attraction; not understanding the lyrics has meant that singers have had limited appeal, while bandleaders can seem a blur of surnames ending in "ez." But in the early years at the Palladium, even Jews and Italians became obsessed with different orchestras and personalities. Machito's Afro-Cubans were at their zenith; when Grillo got drafted in 1943, Bauzá invited the sonero's foster sister Graciela to New York to take his place. With the siblings reunited after the war, the band found a new power and personality as Graciela and Machito matched sexy double entendres and extended montuno improvisations. Initially, their main rival was recent Cuban arrival José Curbelo, but it was two of Curbelo's Puerto Rican sidemen who ended up providing the Afro-Cubans' stiffest competition. First came singer Tito Rodríguez, who formed his own band in 1947, then Rodríguez's old buddy from East Harlem, the "other Tito."

Tito Puente had served bravely in the Navy during the war, being plucked from a fiery sea after his boat was sunk by a kamikaze plane. On leave in California, he witnessed how Hollywood was taking to Latin music; he and his childhood friend Diosa Costello (an ex of Desi's who had gone west with an MGM contract) put on a sensational dance show one night for a club full of stars and became—for a minute—the toast of Hollywood. Back in New York, Pagani heard Puente jamming with some fellow members of Curbelo's band, offered him his own spot, and it was soon "Tito versus Tito" in legendary Palladium battles. The rise of the Titos symbolized the start of an inexorable displacement of Cubans by Puerto Ricans in the hierarchy of New York Latin music. (As the first wave of masters aged and were supplanted by Puerto

Ricans and Dominicans, Curbelo remained a Very Important Cuban; he gave up leading the orchestra and became Latin music's most powerful booking agent.)

One evening, Rodríguez caught Puente switching the billing on the Palladium marquee to put his name on top; the two never spoke again, but the rivalry made for fantastic dancing as each pulled out all the stops to inspire the biggest ovations and wildest moves. Puente edged ahead when Rodríguez was barred following reports that the Palladium house manager's wife had succumbed to his legendary charms. Money talked louder than jealousy, however, and Tito #1 was allowed back after crowds flocked to hear him at other New York ballrooms. The midtown momentum, though, had shifted to Puente and he never surrendered it.

Tito the timbalero became a favorite of Jewish dancers, learning Yiddish phrases for his between-song patter in the Catskills and playing Latin versions of Eydie Gormé and Eddie Fisher hits. Bill Graham got to know him while working as a Catskills waiter in the early fifties and would later insist that booking Puente's orchestra into the Fillmore West in the early seventies was one of his peak moments as a promoter. More far-reaching, however, was how Graham encouraged a Bay Area blues guitarist to borrow his Puente albums and blend those rhythms into his band's sound. Carlos Santana wisely took the advice.

> My biggest ambition at the time was to someday dance in the corner at the Palladium where people sat at those tables and watched . . . After I got out of the service, I went to the Palladium the first Wednesday night . . . That night I not only danced in the corner, but I also entered the contest and *won* . . . You understand what this means? It means "Why should I ever want to be president of the United States?" Because I've accomplished something better. It was great. God, it was so great.
>
> —Bill Graham

> We began with the *danza*, then came the *danzón* . . . soon it will be the rumba, and . . . we'll all end up dancing like ñáñigos.
>
> —Nineteenth-century observer

Everyone has seen, if not actually danced, Latin. It was famously featured in *Dirty Dancing*, a film set in a Catskills resort where mambo and cha-cha were at the center of social life. In Britain, it's a regular part of *Celebrity Come Dancing* (and *Dancing with the Stars* in the US), featuring hot moves, spins, twirls, bends, flying skirts, and an occasional nod in the direction of the clave. Does this dance bear any resemblance to the danzón that shocked 1870s Matanzas? Tango seems to have arrived in Buenos Aires almost fully formed at the end of that century and has only been honed and elaborated upon since, but what about salsa?

Dancing at the Palladium represented a collision of Cuban and American moves and attitudes, two great-grandchildren of eighteenth-century English "country dancing" meeting in post-war Manhattan at the end of very different evolutionary journeys. After cleaned-up versions of the rustic original had become popular at the English court, one branch spread west to the US colonies in the form of barn- or square-dancing while another crossed the channel and started the contredanse craze in Paris. Aspirational Spaniards brought the dance to Cuba, where it was Africanized by Haitians. The miscegenated rhythms that accompanied dancing across the Hispanic and Portuguese empires never gained much of a foothold in America or any other British colony; bodily movement in the anglophone Americas was as restricted as the meeting of hand and drum.

A central movement in both square-dancing and contredanse is the female turning under the arm of the male. This was originally part of elaborate ballroom patterns not unlike the parade-ground maneuvers of marching battalions. The African moves that collided so spectacularly with these well-drilled gavottes could hardly have been more different, though each tradition placed either a couple (Europe) or an individual (Africa) in the middle of a circle or between two facing lines and let them show off their stuff before surrendering their place. European dance was all about giving couples an excuse to touch and smell and get a feel for one another's physical presence. In African societies, such coyness would have seemed ridiculous.

The European and African approaches were both knocked sideways by the waltz. This Austrian-Bavarian peasant dance had horrified Central

European parents as early as 1750, but didn't really hit its three-quarter-time stride until it stormed the gates of Vienna at the turn of the nineteenth century. The Romantic age popularized notions of sentimental love and the concept of the individual cast loose from society's strictures; what more perfect expression of that spirit than for dancers to abandon the group and pair off, pressing their bodies close together as a trigger for romance free from parental arrangement or approval?

Africans in the Americas learned to enjoy moving in pairs but refused to surrender the flamboyant moves and freedom of expression central to their approach to rhythm. The roots of most twentieth-century dance steps lie in the merging of individualistic African traditions with couple-dancing brought to the Americas from Europe.

> Our ideas of dance evoke but memories of sickly gymnastics, performed in the company of a beautiful woman . . . the dancing of blacks encompasses an entire poetic realm: shaking, serpentine undulations, a repressed passion, a feverish love; it is love, suffering, all linked up into a tumultuous and inflexible rhythm.
>
> —Louis Moreau Gottschalk

> [Afro-Cuban dance] always represents a series of courtship and coquetry, during which the lover expresses his feelings, partly by a tremor in all his joints . . . as he turns round and round his fair one, like the planet around its sun . . . enfolding his lady with both arms, but without touching her.
>
> —Swedish traveler, 1851

> What fondlings! What liberties! What shamelessness! Are there really parents who bring their daughters to these dangerous gatherings, where innocence must fend off the perverse wiles of young strangers?
>
> —*La Moda* (Cuban magazine), 1830

> The whole year is one big dance, the island one big ballroom.
>
> —French traveler, 1850

The contradanza stubbornly held its shape as a group enterprise across the first three-quarters of the nineteenth century, while its coda grew freer, more individualistic. White men learned their montuno moves from mixed-race and Black women at the "academies" (where Afro-Cuban males were not allowed); they would pass these steps along in turn to White girls at respectable balls. Parental paranoia was justified; *academias*, after all, had the primary purpose of advertising the sexual skills of women in search of short-term customers or long-term sponsors, and the dancefloor was their showroom: "The talent, for the female dancer, stems from the perfection shown in moving her hips and the lower part of her kidneys [*sic*], conserving the rest of her body in a kind of immobility . . . The dance . . . becomes a picture whose features go from voluptuous to lascivious."

Young dancers waited for the "swing-your-partner" section at the end of the contradanza, where they could grip one another by the waist and shoulders, touching for minutes on end. Dancefloors would fill when this montuno arrived, and Darwinian laws forced orchestras to extend the codas longer and longer. This led to interaction between dancers and musicians; great moves would inspire the band to increased intensity, just as at the Palladium a century later.

Claims that such dancing "unsettled innocent girls" only increased its popularity; candle dances in Afro-Cuban barrios drew scores of White female visitors along with the men. The danzón revolution dispensed with the early sections of the contradanza, devoting the entire evening to what youths once impatiently awaited. Couples would spin and turn under ribbons that threaded their way across the floor as well as under their partners' arms. The danzón pioneer Faílde Pérez was renowned for changing tempi in the middle of a tune, harking back to the sectional rhythms of contradanza and forward to Cugat's habit of luring dancers with an easy step, then shifting gears.

☙

Se armó la rumba.

(The rumba has broken loose.)

When the bourgeoisie embrace a working-class style, the source culture usually moves on in quest of a more extreme expression, hoping to carve out a haven into which the middle classes won't venture. Some vain hope, as the evolution from rhythm and blues to soul to funk to rap and hip-hop demonstrates; even the Whitest American suburbs follow doggedly in the wake of African America's ever more radical attempts to shake them off. One Black style that evolved in the late nineteenth century, however, has remained an almost exclusively Afro-Cuban enclave to this day, despite elements being superficially appropriated and its name being carelessly bandied about and misspelled from Mexico City to Shanghai: rumba.

A rumba is an event, it is a dance and it is the percussive music that propels that dance. Evolving within Abakuá societies and the solares and dockyards they controlled, rumba's roots have been traced back to a solo Kongo dance, the *yuka*. The best-known style, the *guaguancó*, emerged from the novelty of couple-dancing, a rooster-and-hen courtship in which the man makes sudden, fowl-like moves towards the woman as she attempts to evade his *vacuano* ("vaccination") by covering her crotch and dodging his thrusts. Though the dancers never touch, their movements seem highly sexual. I say "seem" because the jerking of the dancers' bodies evokes spirit possession and being "ridden" by an orisha as much as it does the sexual act. The dance appears quite African, though its structure—couples dancing in turns in front of the gathered community—has a paired-up European formality about it.

Rumba accompaniment is never more than percussion and voice: *cajones*, *shekere* (bead-draped gourds), claves, and, most important, the *quinto*, a smallish, single-headed member of the drum family that spawned the conga. "Accompaniment" is probably a misnomer; rumba in its truest form is a dialogue not only between male and female dancers, but between dancers and drummers, with each attempting to challenge and surprise the other with sudden feints or the startling blows that found an echo in those "dry hits" to Arsenio's bongos.

The (apparent) simplicity of rumba's drum-and-chant and the complexity of its dance is as good a way as any to separate White from Black. Even Ortiz and Carpentier struggled to hear the purest Afro-Cuban ritual music as anything but "tedious" and "repetitive." Nervous White ears crave melody, harmony, and progression from verse to verse. Much

African music, however, points towards trance; a complex groove, played for hours, varying slightly, growing and decreasing in the intensity of its dialogue between musicians and dancers—what more could anyone want? In the late nineteenth and early twentieth centuries, rumba was like a hidden spring, refreshing and nourishing Cuban dancing via the academias and candle dances, inspiring more and more complex moves by dancers of all hues. The extended montunos at the Palladium mark an exhilarating meeting point of European and African sensibilities. The modern rave and electronica scenes represent a pyrrhic victory for African trance in the wider world.

Surviving in parallel with the paired guaguancó is the *columbia*, a solo male rumba that can be compared to Brazilian *capoeira*, since both are derived from the Congolese *mani* or battle dance, in which one man holds the ring until literally beaten out of it by a successor. This ritual was eventually outlawed in Cuba and Brazil: too many valuable slave assets/lives were lost in these sometimes violent contests. Mani endured, however, in the form of terpsichorean shadow battles and demonstrations of agility and control. Columbia dancers often balance a glass on their heads or wear an elegant hat while flourishing a knife or a stick. For the great sonero Benny Moré, top hat and gold-topped cane were his trademarks, representing both sartorial elegance and deep roots in rumba.

Following Independence, Cuban authorities sounded an alarm about the Africanization of White dances, raiding solares to confiscate drums and arresting "lewd" dancers. On the bufo stage, audiences accepted some sexy moves, but only from the waist up and only when performed as mockery by White actors in blackface. In 1922, Lina Frutos scandalised her audience by executing a *culebra*. This rippling, snake-like movement culminates in a *quebrada*, or break, a snapping pelvic thrust that is pure rumba and leaves little to the imagination. The bluenoses surrendered in the 1930s, when cabarets and casinos began luring tourists with dumbed-down rumbas; most shows dispensed with the rooster and limited the dancing to a scantily clad hen, thus sparing delicate White male sensibilities.

New York experienced a pale replication of the dialogue between the rumba of the solares and popular dancefloors when Katherine Dunham brought an elevated version of Havana's nightclub aesthetic to Manhattan. Great Cuban dancers and percussionists performed in Dunham's company and many Palladium regulars attended her shows and classes, where they learned moves to try out on the dancefloor. Dunham's tours helped sow the seeds of Latin dance across the globe. Today, Los Muñequitos de Matanzas and other groups still give electrifying performances of classic rumba, while the physical language of guaguancó and columbia remain part of the fabric of many Afro-Cuban neighborhoods. At a rumba in Matanzas in 2016, I saw eight-year-olds executing startlingly deft quebradas.

> [Y]ou have to be born in the Caribbean, because it's a matter of blood . . . [I]n the United States . . . only the Jews, who have an incredible sense of rhythm, know how to dance it. You see a Jew dancing and you think he's a Cuban, but if you look closely, you realise he's studied it and does a good job, but he lacks the final cadence of the rhythm.
>
> —Cachao López

The first wave of the Latin music explosion in New York was thwarted by the talkies. Joe Kennedy's Palace Theatre found bigger crowds and fatter margins with the new Hollywood craze, so Don Azpiazú moved downtown to a Greenwich Village nightclub. What was needed, he decided, was a sexy girl to show stiff Yankees how to move. Out of the 150 he auditioned, the clear standout was the club's own cigarette girl Alicia Parla, daughter of a wealthy Havana family who had fled the repression of the Machado regime. Parla joined Lecuona, Carpentier, Simons, Ortiz, et al. in a long line of well-born Whites who championed Afro-Cuban music. Onstage, Alicia always performed solo; her "rotating hips and shimmying shoulders" wowed the downtown crowds and she ended up traveling the world and giving dance lessons to royalty: King Leopold of Belgium, the Prince of Wales, and Josephine Baker.

Hollywood and Tin Pan Alley joked about non-Latins trying to master the new steps, with lines like *"there's a great big crack / in the back of my sacro-iliac"* and *"Caramba! It's the samba, it's the one dance I can't do."*

Latin dancing between the wars, be it in the roughest Havana bars or under Cugat's genteel baton at the Waldorf-Astoria, was mostly about hips and feet, the turning figures of nineteenth-century candle dances having passed largely into the realm of nostalgia. Those country-dance twirls came storming back, however, with the arrival of "jitterbug swing." This acrobatic dance began in the African-American community of San Francisco in the mid-1920s and moved east with an "All-Negro" revue. It reached New York in the wake of Lindbergh's famous flight, and the sight of girls being tossed in the air (and landing safely) led to it being christened the "Lindy Hop." Most Lindy moves were simply Africanized elaborations on square-dance figures, but the excitement of the music and the spectacular swings and flips (plus their African-American provenance) endowed them with the aura of hip modernity. In New York, as well as in swing-crazy Havana, Cubans and Americans absorbed these jive steps into their dancefloor DNA.

As dancing became a bigger and bigger business, Cuba's racial attitudes were tested: the darker your skin, the harder it was to gain admission to popular clubs. And as the Arsenio revolution gained traction, further barriers were raised between expert and amateur dancers, which most Cubans perceived as a Black and White divide. While the brassy optimism of Miguelito et al. led to faster tempi, Arsenio's conjuntos maintained their deliberate pace, focusing on elaborate cross-rhythms and *diablitos* (breaks) where the band would stop to let one or two instruments challenge dancers with complex figures. The broad appeal of *son* drew Afro-Cubans towards more nuanced moves that befuddled tourists and pale Cubans. Arsenio relished his role as pied piper leading his people down that path.

At the edge of the once-elite Havana suburb of Miramar stands a huge outdoor dancefloor known officially as Salon Rosado but universally called "La Tropical." The last time I visited, the color scheme was bright green and pink. On Friday and Saturday nights, the place heaves with Afro-Cuban dancers; Whites and tourists look down from three stories of observation decks at the back. These days, *timba* and rap rule; when the dance hall opened in 1940, Arsenio was its king.

La Tropical was the only large Havana venue that welcomed all shades, and both Arsenio and Arcaño loved playing there. Arcaño complained that White couples liked to go off in corners and snuggle up while Black dancers wanted to be seen, to show off their moves. Arsenio's music was often called *estilo negro*, evolving in spiritual collaboration with his dancers; the more complex his music and their answering steps became, the less chance that White dancers could follow. (Mario Bauzá insisted that to dance to Arsenio's music you had to be "Cuban, a good dancer, and, to make sure, very black.")

From the opening of La Tropical in 1940 to Arsenio's departure for New York in 1947 was the most intense period for dance in Cuba. Fans followed their favorite bands from hall to hall by bus, train, taxi, and on foot. Cachao remembered how weekend dancers carried an extra set of clothes and didn't go home for days. In this pre-amplification era, dancing was serious and chatter was minimal; in a huge ballroom holding thousands, often only the shuffle of feet could be heard against the sound of the band.

Someone told Arsenio about a Manhattan eye doctor who could restore damaged sight. In 1947, he traveled to New York armed with an appointment, but a five-minute examination was all it took to determine that his case was hopeless. Rodríguez went back to the East Harlem apartment where he was staying, lay down, and took a nap. When he awoke, he wrote down the lyrics to his classic song, "La Vida es sueño": "*Life is a dream / And everything goes away / Reality is being born and dying / . . . / Everything is no more than eternal suffering.*"

Despite the disappointment, Arsenio decided to remain in New York. He had grown tired of the racism, corruption, and poverty in Cuba and perhaps envied the acclaim and riches America had brought Miguelito, Grillo, Bauzá, Curbelo, and others. What befell him in his new home is subject to debate. On one level, it is a sad tale of failure: from being king of an economically poor but culturally rich Afro-Cuban world in Havana, he went to scuffling for gigs, rejected by the Palladium and other major ballrooms for being too Black and too old, for playing too slow, for his conjunto being too small with not enough brass, for being too "primitive." The union wouldn't let him bring his own musicians, forcing him to use local players and watch from the sidelines as the mambo, a style he was generally credited with inventing, was ridden to wealth and fame by others. Arsenio died in 1970, all but forgotten.

But there is another narrative, which begins with his Radio 1010 broadcasts and subsequent touring that reached every corner of the Caribbean. In Puerto Rico, the Dominican Republic, and Colombia, he inspired local musicians to navigate their own rural forms—*jíbaro*, *bachata*, and *cumbia*—into the radio stations, recording studios, and dance halls of their capital cities; those who moved on to New York became Bauzá's and Machito's allies in El Barrio. The dancing public there may have been too enamored with speed and volume to appreciate the dense sounds of Arsenio's conjunto, but New York's Latin musicians revered him. His songs were recorded again and again and he remained a beacon for keeping the music funky. To those who say Arsenio died impoverished, Mario Bauzá countered that those compositions provided him with a good living: "Arsenio dressed like a prince, with fancy threads and a diamond on his fingers."

On the Palladium and other New York dancefloors in the late forties, all these forces converged: Lindy Hop acrobatics, the complex layers of Arsenio's Afro-Cuban rhythm, Italian and Jewish kids determined to match the sensuality and rhythmic ease of Afro-Caribbean dancers, America's post-war optimism and energy, the vacuum created by the death of swing, and the reluctance of jazz's brightest minds to factor dance into their musical vision. It can be argued that those early Palladium years mark a high point for Latin dance, that it's been downhill from then on, the decline gradual at first, then, in our new century, rapid.

Palladium dancers had the passion of the newly converted; they watched closely as dance teams, sometimes three men, often a couple, demonstrated new steps then showed off what they'd learned. Some credit Pete Aguilar and Millie Donay with the earliest and smoothest merging of Cuban footwork with American swing, while others say it was a legendary dancer called Al Israel. What is certain is that Afro-Cubans who relished slower, deeper, more complex rhythms were outvoted by New York crowds who loved the flashiness of the new steps. The Cuban rhythm meant that underpinning the spins and turns was a pattern of footwork that the Arthur Murray dance studios would explain to nervous learners as "quick-quick-slow," meaning that each four-beat, three-step measure started on an alternate foot, in a circular, two-bar-long cycle that Ned Sublette evokes in his explanation of the clave. To make things trickier for newcomers (as I discovered when I took lessons first in New York and then in Havana), New Yorkers (and most beginners) tend to start "on the one" while Cubans generally leave the first beat open and dance "on the two." (James Brown's philosophy of rhythm was based on the idea that the one is an optimistic "good foot," while the backbeat, the two, is pessimistic and holds Afro-Americans back.) Connecting that footwork to the turns and swings of jitterbug came easily to those growing up amid Afro-Cuban culture but could be a challenge for someone whose childhood soundtrack was "How Much Is That Doggie in the Window?" and "I'm Dreaming of a White Christmas."

To read Bill Graham's account of his teenage passion for Latin dancing is to be transported back to a time with no TV or smartphones, when an immigrant from Eastern Europe found himself surrounded by the noise of New York's multicultural streets, where radios were blasting Louis Jordan's version of rhythm and blues, bursting with syncopation borrowed from the Cubans. Why not fill your undistracted mind, body, and spirit with an all-consuming passion and get so good at it that girls will be eager to dance with you?

But that was New York City; this sensual intensity didn't travel far. America was hungry for something new, but as in so many things cultural, political, and racial, New York was—far more so then than today—a law unto itself; the rest of the country wasn't ready for what those cats were up to at the Palladium. What was needed was a simplified version of the sexy dancing in the Big Apple, and America duly found it; it was called the mambo and it swept the country (or at least the big cities). The Havana–New York axis that generated the Latin craze was too parochial, too self-referential, and too hip; Bauzá, Machito, the Titos, and the rest were so deeply immersed in the brilliant music they were creating and so committed to challenging crowds wanting to learn new tricks that they would never have come up with a simpler approach. That required turning that line into a triangle; enter, stage left, Mexico City.

⌇

Mexico in the forties was booming. While Argentina had been Latin America's film capital in the thirties, that country's alliance with Nazi Germany had forced Hollywood to shift support to America's long-disdained southern neighbor. Disney, the Rockefeller Foundation, and the US government sponsored "good neighbor" Latin tours and "fact-finding expeditions" by Hollywood stars and producers. Most Mexican movies, however, remained firmly in the sub-B category, with simplistic plots, caricature bad guys, and sultry dames. Two things stood out: many featured great musical interludes (often *son*) and, in flicks with titles such as *Night of Perdition*, *The Insatiable*, or *Victims of Sin*, there was an easy way to spot the Cubana: she would be the "bad" girl.

As far back as the sixteenth century, Mexicans had seen Havana as a den of delicious vice with a great soundtrack. Along the east coast, from Yucatán to Veracruz and up to the heights of the capital, Cuban music and culture infused the land. Mexicans had been obsessed with danzón since the nineteenth century and they still hold festivals today to celebrate it. Performers from the island toured regularly and some of its greatest stars were discovered there; when Rita Montaner stormed off a Mexican tour, Bola de Nieve finished it for her and triumphed. Trio Matamoros visited constantly; when they brought a new singer, Bartolo Moré, with them in 1944, he liked the place so much he married a Mexican girl and settled down. In Mexico, donkeys are often named Bartolo, so he changed his to Benny, in honor of the ubiquitous Goodman. The only thing preventing the Mexican music scene from being dominated by Cubans was the refusal of the Mexican Musicians' Union to grant work permits. (That and the spicy food. Benny Moré was about the only Cuban who loved his chili; most can't abide it.) If you were an arranger, though, Mexico might be a great place to work.

Cuba's new horn-heavy bands needed charts, and in the mid-forties, two of the most important arrangers in the country's history could be found in the Radio 1010 studios, caught up in the whirlpool of change swirling around Arsenio and Arcaño. Bebo Valdés was paid to be there; fast becoming Havana's most in-demand arranger, he was musical director at Mil Diez as well as house pianist at the Tropicana. Pérez Prado, on the other hand, was just hanging out; obsessed with the modernist sound of West Coast jazz figures such as Stan Kenton, he was on a mission to bring that dissonant edge to Cuban music. Both were fascinated by how the Lópezes were turning Arcaño's old-fashioned charanga sound funkier and Blacker while Arsenio was adding horns and sophistication to his. They loved Cachao's cross-rhythms and the frantic intensity of the montuno codas, and both were exploring ways to incorporate these patterns into their horn charts.

Bebo was indefatigable; after finishing work at the radio station and then the nightclub, he would head for a recording studio or an all-night jam session. His arrangements were modern but brimming with folkloric influence. (He returned from a trip to Haiti inspired by the neighbor's ceremonial drummers.) Valdés's effect was profound but he moved Cuban music forward at a measured pace, always respectful of the past. Prado cared not a fig for history. Fernando Castro, the powerful head of Peer Southern's Havana office, convinced that Prado's "difficult" sound would make Peer's songs less commercial and stigmatize valuable copyrights, barred its composers from employing him. When the boycott proved effective, Prado left for Mexico City.

Many factors combined to make Prado's move there a triumph. He adored brass, and lots of it, particularly the high-pitched variety; Mexico, of course, was full of mariachi trumpeters who loved nothing more than reaching for the topmost notes. Prado was also a joker; his eagerness to modernize the music was matched by a willingness to simplify and even mock revered Cuban traditions while clowning around with a baton in his hand. "Oriental formality" and measured evolution were not his style.

Soon after arriving he ran into a Cuban dancer named Ninón Sevilla, who often played the blond bombshell in Mexican films. On a trip home to Havana, she made one of her habitual visits to a solar, where she learned a new step. It was called the mambo and was both more African, in that pairs danced separately, facing or circling one another, and simpler, since steps need not be executed while spinning and turning from an embrace. Sevilla hired Prado to write music for a stage show based around the mambo.

Originally from Matanzas, Prado was familiar with this word, whose meanings stretch from "an important message" to the chant at the end of a ceremony. In the music of Arsenio and Arcaño, it usually referred to a four-bar riff that drove one of Arsenio's diablito breaks or a *son montuno* coda for Arcaño's charanga. The López brothers had composed a tune called "Mambo," and Prado often referred to his own arrangements as "mambos." Bebo Valdés was using these patterns in more and more of his big-band charts, writing blocks of horn lines based on how Cachao's bass and the conga interacted in Arcaño's *son montunos*. Cachao began using the verb *"mambear"*—"to mambo"—in writing his montunos.

"If there is such a thing as a magic word," writes Ned Sublette, "the best example I can think of is *mambo*. People who didn't even know how to dance . . . were attracted by the sound of the word." Prado made sure that when that word drew neophytes to one of his records (from "Mambo No. 1" up to "Mambo No. 9"), they heard music that was relatively easy to dance to. With a jazz drum kit driving his band, Prado turned Cuban music upside down, adding complex harmonies and mirroring some of Arsenio's diablito bass and conga patterns in charts for the horn sections while stripping the rhythm of much of its complexity. Arcaño's charanga may have been getting more rhythmic and "African," but its sound remained, as Sublette puts it, "smooth and suave"; Prado's, on the other hand, was "aggressive, jumpy, and violent."

⌒

Who invented the mambo that drives women mad?
Who invented this thing?
A short, stocky guy with a face like a seal's.

—Benny Moré, "Locas por el mambo"

Possibly the mambo is an outrage . . . And possibly also, the mambo is a danceable outrage . . . maestro Pérez Prado mixes slices of trumpets, chopped-up saxophones, drum salsa, and pieces of well-seasoned piano, to distribute throughout the Continent that miraculous salad of hallucinatory outrages.

—Septimus (journalistic alias of Gabriel García Márquez), 1951

Prado's band's nicknames for their leader included "Seal Face" and "Doorknob" for the way he would turn his fist while conducting. His meteoric rise is a textbook lesson in bringing avant-garde ideas into the mainstream. For a start he hired Benny Moré as his vocalist; Moré would go on to become a Cuban icon known for his flamboyant commitment to rumba and *son*, but he made his name singing broad-stroke commercial mambos in Mexico. Prado's comedic conducting style was modeled—like Miguelito Valdés's montuno vocals—on Cab Calloway. He would announce breaks or shifts in the rhythm with loud grunts: "*UNNNH!*" Half a century later, the Guinness brewery would build a spectacularly successful ad campaign around a Prado mambo. But amid the simplified beats and crazy showmanship, he hewed to his dream: the brass harmonies were far closer to Kenton than they were to Chappottín or Bauzá. (Bebo Valdés, on the other hand, took heed of an uncle's warning—"*Don't play . . . any American chords!*"—but did manage to sneak Debussy into some of his charts.) Irony alert: while Stan Kenton was helping lead jazz away from the dancefloor to the concert hall, his disciple Prado was flag bearer for the dance craze that upstaged jazz in early-fifties America.

Prado's mambos became huge hits; he and his orchestra were soon omnipresent on Latin American dancefloors and movie screens. By 1950, he was a household name from Tijuana to Punta del Este, with the Catholic Church playing a key marketing role by loudly denying absolution to mambo dancers. But there were two big exceptions to Prado's inexorable advance: Cuba and America. US recor...d companies were skeptical of the craze and it was mostly among Latino communities in California that Perez was known. Only after bandleader Sonny Burke heard "Qué rico el mambo" during a Mexican holiday and began including a limp version of it in his sets did anglophone America begin to take notice. In 1951, a Mexican-American promoter booked Prado for a concert at the Zenda, a nicely positioned downtown Los

Angeles dance hall where Hispanic neighborhoods to the east met African-American ones to the south and White areas to the west and north. The American Federation of Musicians, however, as hostile to foreign players as their Mexican brethren, blocked the visas for Prado's band. The ever-resourceful Cuban quickly assembled a great outfit using Stan Kenton and Sonny Burke sidemen, rehearsed for a couple of days, got the bongosero's mother to sew ruffles on their shirts, and triumphed. Mambo USA was on its way, with Prado leading the parade. Despite his rejection of the structures of its music, the absence of solos, and the simplicity of the beats, Cuba couldn't, in the end, ignore the prodigal son who had become such an international star. Cuban television's gala initial broadcast in 1953 featured Pérez Prado.

The naysayers that first night at the Zenda were dancers who had experienced the Palladium. They were unimpressed by the shuffle steps of the largely Mexican-American crowd; with their pegged trousers and zoot-length coats, the guys looked nothing like New Yorkers. Which points to an interesting divide: most of Prado's fans were linked to those western parts of the Spanish Empire which had imported comparatively few African slaves and where "Indio" culture remained strong. Cuban and Puerto Rican stars ruled North American cities where immigrants from the Caribbean basin and its slave-built economies lived. One can also speculate whether cocaine, the drug of choice on the Pacific slopes of the inter-American mountain chain, may have fueled Prado's nervous, hyper-energetic style, in contrast to the sensual, rum-soaked vibe of most Cuban music. Prado sold millions of records, topping the US charts with "Cherry Pink and Apple Blossom White" and helping create a dance craze that drove thousands onto dancefloors across America. But east of that other geological divide, the Allegheny Mountains, the music and the dancing were of a completely different order. New York never embraced Pérez Prado.

> I couldn't believe my eyes or ears. It was terrible. I mean terrible. It wasn't Cuban music . . . I said to my guys, "Let's get out of here."
>
> —Tito Puente after Prado's New York debut in 1951

Arsenio created the mambo. But I am the one who has made all the money.

—Pérez Prado, 1952

There was a lot of money to be made. Early-fifties American charts boasted titles such as "Papa Loves Mambo" by Perry Como, "Mambo Italiano" by Rosemary Clooney, "They Were Doin' the Mambo" by Vaughn Monroe, and "Loop de Loop Mambo" by The Robins. *Time*, *Newsweek*, and the *New York Times* Sunday magazine published feature articles on the craze. The mambo's success may have been due as much to the word's magical (or perhaps simply fun-to-pronounce) qualities as to the popularity of the dance itself, which never reached that deeply into the American heartland. One Philadelphian told of learning the steps on a beach near Atlantic City, hearing a track on the radio, jumping onto a New York–bound bus, and going straight to the Palladium. There, Machito and the Titos capitalized on Prado's impact, giving a burgeoning crowd of East Coasters a taste of what Arsenio, Bebo, and Cachao had created at the mambo's source.

Footage from the period shows couples facing each other, advancing and retreating "on the two," hips swinging in a simplified, speeded-up sort of guaguancó, with little embracing or twirling. As floors grew more crowded, space was at a premium, and rumba-inflected steps require elbow—and hip—room. The compact spinning and turning which came to be known as "casino" (after the 1950s Havana gambling palaces where Lindy-meets-*son* is said have been perfected) allowed dancers to show flashy moves on limited real estate.

For the Arthur Murray dance schools, the mambo craze was initially a boon, but ultimately demonstrated the formula's limitations. Murray (born Moses Teichman in Poland) had arrived at Ellis Island at the age of two. He began teaching in the 1920s, the golden age of popular dance crazes, and invented the "numbered feet" floor charts for beginners. He was so successful at popularizing between-the-wars fads such as the Lambeth Walk and the Big Apple that his operation grew into a kind of pyramid scheme, with top instructors offered franchises and the right to sell their own sub-franchises, and so on. As mambo exploded in the early fifties, Murray himself could be seen prowling the Palladium seeking instructors for his classrooms. Repeating his "1-2-3, quick-quick-slow" steps, however, didn't earn you much admiration on a Latin dancefloor.

For the millions of Americans wanting to get in on the Latin craze—and for entrepreneurs like Murray—a boost arrived in the form of the slower, gentler cha-cha-cha. Originally invented as a twist on the ramped-up intensity of the montuno, the cha-cha-cha was tagged on to energetic mambos to give sweating, worn-out dancers a chance to cool down. This dance, like the pre-war conga craze, had a flourish at the end of each phrase that was fun, simple, and unifying, with entire dancefloors anticipating the band's shouted three-note punctuation, mirrored by the sound of shoes doing that triple shuffle. While the mambo was, despite Prado's simplifications, quite Arsenio-African at heart, the cha-cha-cha grew out of the laid-back sweetness of flute-driven charangas such as Arcaño's. That the footwork could be formulaic and still look OK helped it reach parts of America the mambo never could. In Cuba, Benny Moré's hit "De la rumba al cha-cha-cha" provided a neat putdown of how the music was losing its African edge through commercialization. I remember Prado's million-selling cha-cha "Cherry Pink and Apple Blossom White" sounding very tame to my eleven-year-old ears; listening to the hit parade on Saturday mornings, I would wait impatiently for it to end, confident that the first shoots of doo-wop would be close behind.

The mambo and cha-cha years of the early fifties served as an opening act for the main American event: rock 'n' roll. Perhaps White America needed to get comfortable with something Brown before it could embrace the Blackness of rhythm and blues. The legendary Brill Building producers George Goldner and Bert Berns were Palladium regulars; in 1954, Goldner mounted an ill-fated *Mambo USA* tour that triumphed in the northeast before collapsing in the face of southern disinterest and racism. Berns, who had visited Havana at nineteen and been dazzled by the music, became obsessed with Arsenio Rodríguez, going so far as to record him performing "Hang on Sloopy" in Spanish. This is not as ridiculous as it sounds; the original "Sloopy" (composed and produced by Berns) is full of Afro-Cuban touches and syncopations, as are many fifties doo-wop and rhythm and blues hits, from "When You Dance" by The Turbans all the way to "Slippin' and Slidin'" by Little Richard.

Rock 'n' roll dancing emulated Latin in how it absorbed the Lindy Hop. Its biggest novelty number was a kind of slowed-down, Whitened-up mambo: "The Stroll" harked back to early French and African formations, with couples taking turns strutting between lines of fellow dancers. Buccaneering labels such as Goldner's Gone and Berns's Bang took their cues from the Latin and jazz labels of the 1940s, who proved that when it came to outlier music, the majors were at a bureaucratic loss. Columbia, RCA Victor, Capitol, and Decca would spend the 1950s trying to undermine the agile indies that had outmaneuvered them in rock 'n' roll's early years.

The borrowing went both ways. Latin music would eventually fight back with attitudes, harmonies and even rhythms copied from rock. But that came later, following a political-musical cataclysm that would forever alter the flow of influence, inspiration, and personnel between Cuba and America.

> [Havana is an] American playground, complete with gambling houses, whorehouses, and brightly lit cafes, every other one boasting a live orchestra.
>
> > —Ava Gardner (who was spotted climbing off the balcony at Hotel Nacional on the first night of her honeymoon with Frank Sinatra in 1951)
>
> We are in Havana, home of the pineapple and Meyer Lansky. And we're happy to be here.
>
> > —Steve Allen, introducing his TV show live from the lobby of the Hotel Riviera in 1957
>
> [Havana] was being debased into a great casino and brothel for American businessmen over for a big weekend from Miami. My fellow countrymen reeled through the streets, picking up fourteen-year-old Cuban girls and tossing coins to make men scramble in the gutter. One wondered how any Cuban . . . could regard the U.S. with anything but hatred.
>
> > —Arthur Schlesinger, historian

Meyer Lansky and Batista went way back; the mobster had delivered his first cash-stuffed suitcase to the former army sergeant in the early thirties. In 1950, when the Kefauver investigation turned its spotlight on bashful gangsters, states and localities began tearing up permits for Mob-controlled casinos. Lansky stepped forward as the Mafia's Moses, leading them to this promised (and unregulated) offshore land. When elections threatened his cozy arrangements, Lansky helped finance the US-backed 1952 coup that brought Batista back to power. The dictator returned the favor by appointing him to an official government post supervising the island's casinos and racetracks. The Mafia stashed its dirty money in Havana while Cuban politicians hid their bribes in Miami banks. Hotels sprouted, casinos multiplied, the party was on.

If the kitsch Norman Rockwell image of the Eisenhower fifties represented America's super-ego, then Cuba, just thirty dollars and half an hour by plane away from Miami, was its id. When Sky Masterson wants to loosen up the Salvation Army virgin in *Guys and Dolls*, he flies her to Havana. Many planes had on-board slot machines, and the music would begin before takeoff, washed down with a Cuba Libre compliments of La Tropicana. There were ferries, too, full of the big-finned American sedans that, to this day, lure tourists back to Cuba. Dollars poured out of Yankee pockets for sex, booze, and music, but fastest of all for gambling. As the Mob learned decades earlier in its New Orleans, Chicago, and New York speakeasies, good music opens suckers' wallets. (And suckers they were; Lansky ran a daily courier to a Miami check-cashing operation to pre-empt gamblers who felt cheated from stopping payment.)

With so many nightclubs, casinos, and hotels, visitors were spoiled for choice; all agreed that the Tropicana, a huge outdoor cabaret in a palm-filled glade on the outskirts of Havana, set the bar. Well-traveled celebrities (including Elizabeth Taylor, Liberace, Joan Crawford, Ernest Hemingway, Debbie Reynolds, and Tyrone Power) raved about the lavish and highly professional shows. The Tropicana was also unique in fifties Havana for being run by Cubans rather than US mobsters. Founded in a vacant lot in central Havana, with live music amid potted plants, Eden Concert had moved in 1939 to a nine-acre Marianao estate, where it added gambling tables and acquired a new name combining "tropical" with "Mina," the woman who owned the lush suburban jungle. The venue struggled through the forties, but hit its stride in the early fifties when a former numbers runner named Martín Fox bought it and hired Roderico Neyra as artistic director.

A novelist inventing "Rodney" Neyra would be mocked for abusing readers' credulity. He emerged from the secretive but very popular world of Havana porn shows, where you could find female tourists, their faces hidden behind scarves, watching "Superman" balance silver dollars on his erect member, alongside other novelty attractions. One of Rodney's biggest successes involved naked streetwalkers in stilettos getting "intimately searched" by a burly (also nude) policewoman.

Rodney's promising career as a dancer had been ended by scarring from a bad case of leprosy. Cuban authorities normally forced lepers into isolated colonies, but Rodney had been rescued by—who else?—Rita Montaner, who insisted that he direct her Tropicana shows. Neyra was both flamboyantly gay at a time when that was an illegal rarity and an expert on Santería and Abakuá ritual. He introduced authentic guaguancó to the popular stage and would prepare Tropicana performers for his orisha-themed revues by taking them to ceremonies and hiring skilled Black drummers to accompany the shows.

One memorable Rodney *coup de théâtre* was for a few muscular Afro-Cuban dancers to invade the audience during a Santería number, grab a touristy blonde from one of the tables, carry her kicking and screaming onto the stage, then chant their victim into a trance. With an unfocused gaze, she would strip off her dress and begin executing culebras in her underwear, leaving the audience speechless with shock before they realized it was all an act. Thrills and wish fulfilment for the tourists! With his limping gait, ugly scars, wicked tongue, and adoring entourage, Rodney was Babalú-Ayé come to life.

Other themed Tropicana shows invoked Hawaii, Broadway, Italy, and China, while a Weimar revue featured a Zeppelin crossing overhead on a guy-wire. Rodney introduced ultraviolet lighting effects a decade before psychedelia. All performances were backed by great players; the club's musical director, Armando Romeu, was a jazz fan who layered bebop chords over Cuban rhythms and brought top American talent to perform at the club. Sunday jam sessions lured visitors such as Zoot Sims and Stan Getz; the pianist Bebo Valdés sometimes turned over his chair to his young son Chucho. Fox had no hesitation in featuring dark-skinned singers: Celia Cruz and Bola de Nieve made their international names at the Tropicana. He drew a line at the chorus girls, however; *"mulattas"* and *"negritas"* had to wait until after the revolution to wear Tropicana spangles.

∽

Frank Sinatra, Tony Bennett, Maurice Chevalier, Édith Piaf, and Lena Horne were all brought to the island by Martín Fox and his competitors at the Hotel Nacional and the Sans Souci, but it was Nat "King" Cole's week-long engagement under the Tropicana palms in 1956 that marked the apex of the era's good times. If there was one singer on which Cuban and American audiences could agree, it was Cole. A good jazz pianist with a successful bebop-inflected trio, Cole's ballad recordings for Capitol Records generated hit after hit, keeping that label afloat during its lean rock 'n' roll years; the company's famous disc-shaped Hollywood tower is known as "the house that Nat built."

Everyone who was anyone was there for opening night. Cole and his entourage were dazzled by the lush gardens, the huge cast of beautiful showgirls, and the spectacular modernist canopy Fox had built to protect his stage and gambling tables from tropical rainstorms. For Cuba, the triumph of the dark and handsome Cole was the culmination of a half-century of racial revolution. Bola de Nieve was a Black star, but a camp and sexually unthreatening one. Cole's velvety voice spoke to women of all colors and he peered at them over the piano with bedroom eyes, the first Black male sex symbol to cross those lines. With Eartha Kitt often purring over at Hotel Nacional and pale Americans wooing or renting Cubans of all shades, mixed-race sex became a fundamental part of Havana's allure. (Bebo Valdés would augment his musician's pay by steering tourists to the best whorehouses; White southerners, he recalled, always wanted Black hookers.) Cole fell so hard for Cuba and its music that he recorded a series of *Cole Español* albums that sold millions across the Americas (with many tracks arranged by Valdés).

These albums represented the flowering of a second Cuban-Mexican-American musical triangle that had almost as great an impact as the mambo craze.

"*What a diff'rence . . . . adaymade*": Dinah Washington's eloquent pause in the first line of her 1959 hit draws a neat circle around this triad. The song itself is the anglophone version of a 1934 Mexican bolero, "Cuando vuelvo a tu lado," while Queen D's phrasing is very habanera. Boleros are a Cuban form that Mexicans adored even more than the danzón. Like *son*, the bolero came from the east, part of the repertoire of Santiaguero *trova* (troubadour) singers, who generally performed solo with a guitar. In the thirties, when most Cuban songwriters were preoccupied with dance numbers, the bolero baton passed to Mexican composers. As American torch singers absorbed Cuban vocal delivery, Cubans were adding jazz chords to Mexican songs and Spanish translations of American ballads. When some Havana singers became enamored of the oft-encountered English word "feeling," a movement was born and named: *filin*.

Much of filin's power came from Cuban singers' intimacy, in contrast to the operatic belting of Mexican balladeers. Cubans love words—books of poetry and literature have huge sales on the island—and the clear diction of Olga Guillot, Omara Portuondo, and Elena Burke was central to the success of filin. Until *Buena Vista* forty years later, Portuondo et al. didn't have much success in America and filin never became a byword outside the Latin world. In America, it blended with Neapolitan crooning to give us the "smoochie" records by Perry Como, Dean Martin, Johnny Mathis, Frank Sinatra, and Cole that fifties US radio played between mambos, novelty numbers, doo-wop, and rock 'n' roll.

Lansky and his pals were grinning like Cheshire cats as the chips piled up on roulette and baccarat tables; good times had truly arrived. There were sporadic reports of guerrillas in the mountains, and Batista's police stayed busy beating and jailing left-wing students, but Yankees in Havana remained oblivious. There was an alarming moment in 1957, when a bomb exploded in the foyer of La Tropicana, wounding a number of people and shattering glass doors. Fox and his wife visited victims in the hospital, paying medical bills for one girl whose arm had been blown off and giving money to her family. Years later, after they'd fled to Florida, the Foxes did a double-take. *Her arm?* The girl they'd helped so much, they realized, must have been the bomber.

This kind of disconnect ran like a virus through Havana. While Castro's men eluded the army and Batista's heavy-handed tactics drove more and more peasants to join them, life in tourist hotspots went on as normal: Ginger Rogers flew in to help Lansky launch the classily modernist Hotel Riviera, and Steve Allen followed with a week of TV broadcasts live from the lobby. Even when Lansky was told of the deteriorating military situation, he remained unruffled; how could the Cuban economy survive without tourists and gambling? Despite Castro's Sierra Maestra Manifesto targeting corruption and gangsters, Lansky was sure that, if the time came, it would be simply a question of finding the right man to pay. (By the late fifties, the president's monthly skim had reached $500,000.) Lansky and Batista had both grown up poor, craving wealth; neither grasped what it meant to confront a middle-class intellectual like Castro, who had made an emotional connection with honest peasants.

Cuban musicians were in a tricky position. In many ways, it was the best of times, with nightclubs, casinos, and cabarets putting more of them in employment than ever before. But pay and conditions were poor, with hardly any job security and nothing to fall back on. They were well aware of the battles in the mountains to the east and many quietly supported the Revolution. No one, however—mobsters, musicians, intellectuals, students, or workers—had any real notion of what was in store when, on New Year's Eve 1958, Batista grabbed cash and gold bars and fled to Florida, leaving Havana undefended and wide open to the rebels' triumphant entrance.

> I approved the proclamation which Fidel Castro made in the Sierra Maestra, when he justifiably called for justice and especially yearned to rid Cuba of corruption. I will even go further: to some extent it is as

though Batista was the incarnation of a number of sins on the part of the United States. Now we shall have to pay for those sins.

—President John F. Kennedy, interviewed by Jean Daniel, October 24, 1963

We shouldn't have killed Giovanni [John]; we should have killed Bobby.

—Mafioso Santo Trafficante, as quoted by his lawyer Frank Ragano

Pero ha de llegar el día
que tenga soberanía
el pobre proletariado

(But the day has to arrive
that the poor proletariat
has sovereignty)

—Early *son* lyric, 1910

Like mambo and filin, Castro's Revolution was a Cuban-Mexican-American joint venture. Fidel's harebrained assault on Santiago's Moncada Barracks in 1953 was timed to coincide with the city's (and its police force's) preoccupation with carnival, but incompetence and bad luck led to most of his comrades being killed, while he and Raúl meekly surrendered in the hills outside the city soon afterwards.

Castro's "history will absolve me" speech during his trial was memorized by legions of the young and the poor. Batista released him two years later in response to an amnesty campaign led by the Jesuits, with radio support from Rita Montaner, who now had her own talk show. In his Mexican exile, Fidel gathered around him radicals from across Latin America, including the Argentine doctor's son Ernesto "Che" Guevara. (A key salon for dissident exiles was mambo queen Ninón Sevilla's Mexico City mansion.) Most had direct experience of the brutal side of America's Monroe Doctrine; Guevara had been in Guatemala when the CIA brought down Árbenz's elected government, and Castro had witnessed firsthand America's role in Colombian political violence. All understood that the US would be an implacable enemy of the kind of wealth redistribution being planned. From the Veracruz coast they launched the good ship *Granma* (which was, indeed, named after the

Mexican owner's grandmother) and overcame a bumbling start to launch what would become a triumphant guerrilla campaign.

Despite the stylish revolutionary posters designed by the Havana branch of the J. Walter Thompson ad agency, capitalist America and revolutionary Cuba regarded each other across the Florida Straits with barely disguised hostility. Twenty-first-century politics has confirmed that image often "trumps" ideology, and Castro's look and behavior—the fatigues, the beard, the stay in Harlem's Hotel Theresa—spoke as loudly as his confiscation of American-owned property. The US loved sprinkling habanera sauce over its music, reveled in Havana's just-next-door foreignness, and laughed every Monday night at Desi and Lucy's Cuban-American misunderstandings, but the country failed to grasp how despised it was for its bullying arrogance. By the end of 1963, the Bay of Pigs invasion, the Russian missile crisis, and the Kennedy assassination (following JFK's refusal to fund CIA collaboration with the Mob to reinstate corrupt rule on the island) left only the charred remains of one of the most fruitful musical bridges in America's history.

> We are not only disposed to deport the gangsters, but to shoot them.
>
> —Fidel Castro

> Havana has become as sad as a tango.
>
> —*Bohemia* (Cuban magazine), 1959

> It is the same thing as squeezing a boil. Those who have left are the pus, the pus that was expelled when the Cuban revolution squeezed the society. How good the body feels when pus is eliminated!
>
> —Fidel Castro, 1962

For Meyer Lansky, the herd of pigs let loose in the lobby of the Riviera in January 1959 was not a good sign. The Revolution allowed casinos to continue operating for a while, but bearded, gun-toting rebels guarding the tables and the counting rooms didn't make for the sort of atmosphere to encourage high-rollers. Within months, Lansky's Riviera, Pan

American's Nacional, and the rest had all been confiscated and their casinos closed. Lansky searched high and low but couldn't find anyone to bribe.

Closing the casinos put many musicians out of work and the Revolution tried to compensate by guaranteeing them all minimum salaries. That was the good news; the bad news for the better known was the imposition of maximum payments. Groups returning from overseas were forced to turn over much of their earnings to the government; work visas to the now-hostile US became hard to obtain. A year and a half into the new era, Sonora Matancera and their vocalist Celia Cruz boarded a flight for Mexico City. Once the plane was airborne, the group's founder, Rogelio Martínez, stood in the aisle and announced that they would never return to Cuba so long as Castro was in power. In a "knowing-what-I-know-now-I-never-would-have-done-that" move, I approached the regal (and out-of-contract) Cruz in 1999 with the idea of recording an album of fifties classics, backed by ¡Cubanismo!, the all-star Havana orchestra I had put together. Celia's English was even sparser than my Spanish, but despite the lavish Thames-side lunch I laid on, the cordial tones and diplomatic phrasing on both sides, the answer was clear: *Are you out of your mind?* By the turn of the century, Celia had become a symbol of intransigence, the Afro-Cuban mascot of Florida's largely White anti-Castro contingent.

Cruz was a textbook example of the sort of character who would have trouble adjusting to Castro's regime. Her rise to the summit of Cuban music had been due almost entirely to wilful individuality and discipline, transcending class, sex, and race. Born into a respectable, working-class, Catholic, Afro-Cuban family in Havana, she was, from an early age, fascinated by the rituals of African religions. Over the furious objections of her father, who viewed a singing career as bordering on prostitution, she entered radio talent contests and usually won. Sponsors loved her voice (if not her look) and she made good money singing *son*-laced radio jingles praising washing powder and soft drinks. Rodney found her vocal power and knowledge of Santería ritual a perfect combination for his Tropicana shows. At some point during their work together, he introduced her to Rogelio Martínez.

Martínez's Sonora Matancera had succeeded in 1940s Cuba by applying lessons learned from Arsenio's conjuntos with a lighter touch (and lighter skins). When young Celia first heard a Matancera broadcast, she announced that one day she would be their singer; that moment duly arrived in 1950, when their Puerto Rican vocalist left for home. Sonora's record label was reluctant to record Cruz since they were convinced that female vocals didn't sell, but she persuaded them to try just one track, which of course became a huge hit.

Cachao declared hers to be "a voice of clarity, force, and permanence." Through the 1950s, Sonora and the devout Catholic Cruz helped drive Santería and its orishas to the center of Cuban popular culture. Through intense study and practice, her Lucumí pronunciation became impeccable. She took control of her repertoire, adding songs from across Latin America and working with Martínez to "Cubanize" them; as a result, Sonora Matancera was beloved throughout the hemisphere. Cruz was teetotal, drug-free, and monogamous and shared with Martínez an obsession with professionalism and punctuality. Like most Latin cultures, Cuba tended to divide women in the public sphere into mothers and whores; Celia's statuesque dignity and lumpy features succeeded in placing her outside that dialectic. She was her own woman on her own terms. Given how the Cuban Revolution intended to mold society, she was never likely to fit in. The comrades wanted everyone, high and low, to roll up their sleeves and help rebuild the country; Cruz's response was an offer to donate some jewelry.

Benny Moré's idea of "living the dream" was his farm outside Havana. There he would sit on the terrace with friends, lovers, family, and fellow musicians, serve pork, rice, and beans (chili sauce on the side), open a bottle, roll a spliff, and lay out some lines. He owned a treasured flock of rare-breed chickens, the blackest of which he named "Celia Cruz." After returning from Mexico in 1950, he had released "Mata siguaraya," a song about an herb used in Santería rituals that Cruz had recorded with Sonora. Benny's version was better and sold more, and Celia never forgave him; Benny and Celia were opposites that didn't attract. Moré had been brought up in the central Cuban countryside by a music-loving daughter of slaves who had sixteen other children with various fathers (Benny's being a White farm manager he rarely saw). As soon as he could walk, he immersed himself in the rituals of the local cabildo; at age five, he sang atop a table in a local bar and earned a hatful of coins. He didn't have to learn Lucumí; it was as much a part of him as breathing.

As his fame grew, he shared top billing at a 1952 Havana concert with Rita Montaner, whose onstage embrace was taken to mean she was "passing the torch" to her successor as the island's most beloved singer. Benny didn't let her down; within a year he had formed his own "Banda Gigante" and established himself as "El Bárbaro del Ritmo," Cuba's biggest star.

Moré never learned to write music but he heard arrangements in his head and knew exactly how he wanted the orchestra to sound. Riding on a Havana bus one day he spotted a large man with a trombone case; his name was Generoso Jiménez and he became Benny's chief of staff, setting the singer's ideas down on paper and leading the band through the endless rehearsals Benny insisted upon. No matter how infectious the rhythm, dancers would often stand motionless watching Benny conduct; many of his gestures were from Calloway via Prado and he mixed them up with moves learned as a boy in the cabildos. Generoso played straight man to Benny's clown, becoming an ace soloist who defined a Latin approach to the trombone that endures today. Together they infused the brassy sound of 1950s Cuba with motifs from deep in the *barracones* and cane fields. Benny's accent was halfway between Habanero and Santiaguero; all Cubans could identify with it and he became the most beloved star in Cuban history, "part American hep-cat and part Cuban field-hand," the island's equivalent of Édith Piaf, Carlos Gardel, or Oum Kalsoum.

Benny's habits were the opposite of Celia's: he drank, took drugs, stayed up all night, and was rarely on time. Like Jerry Lee Lewis, he married a teenage cousin. His dream of headlining the Tropicana eluded him until he convinced Martín Fox he could stay sober for a two-week engagement. He kept his word throughout that legendary November

1956 fortnight; after finishing the last set, he opened a bottle of the finest *añejo* rum and they had to stack all the tables and chairs to force him out the door at dawn.

It never occurred to Moré to leave Cuba when Castro took over, even though he had called Batista a friend. The Revolution left him and his beloved farm alone, as long as he sang at the occasional rally. In 1963, at the age of forty-four, Benny's exhausted liver gave out. Castro sent a wreath and 100,000 mourners gathered in his tiny birthplace of Santa Isabel de las Casas to see him off.

What could be less communist than a *descarga*? Unstructured, individualistic, and strongly influenced by American jazz, these jam sessions were part of a dialogue between Havana and New York across the 1950s. There were so many great players in Havana in those years that sessions with visiting Americans only added to the already high level of musical excitement. Sunday sessions at the Tropicana and after-hours jams at other nightclubs became so popular that it was only a matter of time before someone figured out that they would be perfect for one of those new "long-playing" discs.

Cachao López and Bebo Valdés were central figures in the descarga recordings that provided the Cuban contribution to what became known as Latin jazz, and the Revolution was quick to make both feel unwelcome. After Valdés lost his job as music director at a radio station when he refused to join the Party, he and López left, never to return. Cachao spent much of the sixties playing with top bands in New York and becoming a beloved figure at the Palladium, before eventually settling in Florida after the New York scene cooled. Valdés was denied a US visa due to his association with Mil Diez; for the next twenty-five years he earned his living playing cocktail piano in a hotel lounge in Stockholm. Both were "rediscovered" during the nineties and made triumphant, Grammy-winning returns to the limelight. Chucho, the son Bebo left behind in Havana, grew up to become a key figure in a new era of Cuban music and was eventually somewhat grudgingly reunited with his father.

Cachao's classic *Cuban Jam Sessions* recordings were made at Panart, the island's first purpose-built, locally owned studio. The room was taken over by the government in 1961, retitled with the bureaucratic acronym EGREM, and starred in the *Buena Vista Social Club* film.

～

> A truly revolutionary party is neither able nor willing to take upon itself the task of "leading" and even less of commanding art . . . Such a pretension could only enter the head of a bureaucracy—ignorant and impudent, intoxicated with its totalitarian power . . . Truly intellectual creation is incompatible with lies, hypocrisy, and the spirit of conformity. Art can become a strong ally of revolution only insofar as it remains faithful to itself.
>
> —Leon Trotsky

> What do our homeland's pain and people's mourning matter to the rich and fatuous who fill the dance halls? . . . There will be no lack of idiots who think we envy them and aspire to the same miserable idle and reptilian existence they enjoy today.
>
> —Fidel Castro in a 1955 letter at the start of his campaign

> The [buildings] revalidated individualistic and skill-based craftsmanship, they promoted sensuality . . . and alluded to ideas of *cubanidad* and Africanness that were unacceptable to the Revolution, which was proletarian, committedly internationalist, and resolutely opposed to any and all manifestations of decadence.
>
> —Alma Guillermoprieto describing the authorities' distaste for the modernist architecture of the National School of Art

The last years of the 1950s had been violent, chaotic, and exuberant. Cuban music soared through them on a sea of easy money, wild nightlife, and danger. By 1959, this music had become a paragon of authenticity, an internationally acclaimed marriage of tradition-based sophistication and mass taste. The Revolution quickly imposed a shotgun divorce. To the rebels, the glorious music of 1950s Cuba was simply a soundtrack for corruption and exploitation. They could not accept that such sounds might be society's cultural and emotional pillar. No matter that Cuba had withstood the onslaught of Elvis and rock 'n' roll far better than almost any country in the Western world, and had itself transformed four continents' attitudes towards music and dance. Radio broadcasts, records, and touring had made Cuba the cultural beacon of the Caribbean. Castro, the ultimate Gallego *patón*, wasn't interested; as one Cuban told me, "Fidel doesn't dance, not even one step."

The victorious Fidelistas confronted a quintet of intertwined, self-inflicted dilemmas: what was the appropriate relationship of the Revolution to the island's musical past, to dancing, to Afro-Cuban culture, to homosexuality, and to sounds arriving over the airwaves from the neighbor to the north? The story of the Cuban Revolution's battle for cultural control from 1959 to 2018 is one of slow, reluctant retreat ending in ignominious surrender on all five fronts.

Banning the music of exiles was step one; over the first few years, radio stopped playing most pre-Revolutionary tracks, save the occasional song by Benny and a few others who publicly supported the Revolution. The blacklist grew, as even those who had celebrated the demise of the old regime felt they had no choice but to leave. There was no work, at least nothing they recognized as such; tours were organized to "fraternal" socialist countries, but the government pocketed the fees and allowed musicians to keep only their nominal workers' salaries plus per diems.

Across the 1960s, justifying itself with the very real threat posed by the US and the anti-Castro exiles just across the Florida Strait, the Revolution set about seizing control of all means of cultural expression. As with so many revolutionary movements, "new" declared war on "old." Music that referred to glamour and sensuality or to African gods and rituals was forbidden, thus eliminating pretty much everything composed before 1959. Castro and his cohorts embraced worn-out notions of "elevation"; Fidel wanted a ballet school, a world-class orchestra, and art schools. All these he achieved; Cuban music may have been crippled by ideology but never by lack of technique. The Soviet approach turned out brilliant virtuosos with total command of their craft; today, internationally renowned painters, poets, and ballet dancers—as well as musicians—heap praise on the training they received during their

Cuban youth. One effect, however, was to turn out generations of highly skilled musicians with no place to play; the government was far too nervous of uncontrolled public gatherings to permit vibrant live music scenes to develop.

Along the Malecón, Havana's famed shoreline boulevard, some large billboard frames have survived that once advertised toothpaste or made-in-Detroit vehicles. Since 1959, a couple of them have boasted one jauntily lettered word: *Alegría!* (Joy!). The Cuban Revolution may not have been as puritanical as many twentieth-century communist movements, but it did struggle mightily with activities that, to most Cubans, came under the heading of joy. Dancing, for example.

Fidel's speeches in Revolution Square were legendarily endless. Reverence for El Jefe and his ideals (along with vigorous prodding from neighborhood committees) drove the vast crowds that came to listen and stayed to the end. What set these rallies apart from contemporaneous events in China, Albania, or Egypt was the percussion; as crowds gathered, the boulevards leading to the square filled with conga lines and informal comparsas, while speeches were often accompanied by an undertone of drums and shakers. A joke circulating in sixties Cuba had Fidel leading a parade and becoming annoyed with the constant pulse of the tumbadoras and what he saw as the undisciplined swaying of the crowd on what was supposed to be a serious revolutionary occasion. "*Que se acabe la rumba!*" ("Let's stop the rumba!") he shouts, and the crowd relays his request back along the length of the parade. The comparsas take up the call and soon "*Que se acabe la rumba!*" acquires a simple melody and a beat and becomes a chanted chorus up and down the boulevard. Cubans can't not dance; it's simply impossible.

Across the early years of the Revolution, though, dance venues steadily closed. Cabarets were accused of being nothing but "commercial structures designed to exploit frustrations and vices . . . a mere ostentatious exhibit of butts and thighs." Rules of supply and demand meant that as dance halls were shut, more and more people crowded into fewer and fewer spots, leading to fights at entrances; this served as a further excuse to close those remaining, on grounds that they were magnets for trouble. Dances, one official stated, "contribute to crudeness, bad taste, insolence, cheap sensualism, or sexual ambiguity"; another referred to dancers as "lumpen." Salón Rosado—Arsenio's "La Tropical"—was an early casualty. The one temple of decadence to survive was La Tropicana; the scale of its shows appealed to the same corner of the communist brain that adores 200-strong Russian choirs or massed Chinese calisthenics. Besides, they needed something other than the revolutionary atmosphere and a few scrawny beach resorts to lure the odd tourist and entertain "fraternal" visitors.

Supervisory boards took over the formation of musical groups and the vetting of lyrics; no more spontaneous gatherings of like-minded friends and, above all, no soloists! Guaranteed (but meager) salaries sweetened the bitter pill that every "career" must now be managed by a central agency staffed by clueless bureaucrats. EGREM was in theory set up to produce records, but lacked engineers or arrangers who understood how to make a good-sounding track. The state label issued patriotic and work-encouraging songs as well as LPs of kitsch Eastern European ensembles licensed from socialist allies. In the fifties, Cuban pressing plants had turned out millions of discs annually, a number more than matched by imports from the US and Mexico; in 1966, the nationalized plants produced a grand total of 140,000 platters and imports were barred. New songs were, as always, being created, but most were far too "incorrect" to be recorded. One popular 1962 street ditty mocked Krushchev for "blinking" under US pressure and removing his missiles: "*Nikita, you little faggot, what has been given cannot be taken back.*" Young Cubans adored Castro's fierce anti-American stance and most were committed to the Revolution's ideals; it is tempting to speculate how successful the Revolution might have been had it not drained away enthusiasm with its implacable opposition to the country's music. The rebels were operating in uncharted territory; no communist revolution had ever triumphed in a society where music was such a central part of life.

By 1970, Cuba was in crisis. Guevara, frustrated by bureaucratic inertia, had abandoned his dream of diversifying the economy and gone off to meet his fate in the Bolivian jungle. Like desperate gamblers at one of Lansky's casinos, the comrades put all their chips on one last throw of the dice to rescue the nation from abject dependency on Soviet largesse. The entire population, they announced, would join that year's sugar harvest; the target was ten million tons, far beyond anything achieved in the years of capitalist exploitation. With party journals hectoring the masses and workplaces busing staff to the cane fields, officials felt some rousing music would help. Castro asked a percussionist who performed under the name "Pello el Afrokán" to compose a paean to cutting cane for the motherland. Pello duly delivered and the track was a "hit," played so often on the radio that listeners who had enjoyed it at first grew heartily sick of it. The comrades were delighted, until someone explained to them the song's Afro-Cuban slang: "*How tasty the cane is, honey . . . bring your cart over here.*" They would have banned it, but by then it was too late.

It was also too late for the Cuban economy; the zafra target was always a fantasy and the effort fell far short. The island slid back into its time-worn role from days of old—an undeveloped agricultural economy toiling in the hot sun to feed the sweet tooth of a far-off and not particularly sympathetic empire. Planeloads of Russians arrived to oversee their investment, replacing Americans in popular contempt with their pasty skins, inability to hold their rum, hopeless dancing, and grim lovemaking. They soon earned the nickname "*bolo*" ("bowling pin"), for their complexions and shape. A subversive undercurrent of nostalgia for the old days began to be felt; at least Yanks could talk baseball, and some could even dance.

∽

In the mountains of the Sierra Nevada, Castro had a loyal Black bodyguard called Pombo. In early January 1959, Pombo and some mates were refused entry at a Havana nightspot on grounds of color. Outraged—the Revolution had made racial equality one of its central tenets—Pombo cleared the club at gunpoint. He was reprimanded: "[T]he Revolution had not yet progressed far enough for people to understand that there were neither blacks nor whites, but that we were fighting for all Cubans." Other comrades told Pombo: "I'll give my life for you, but I wouldn't let you marry my daughter."

In 1995, in Havana to record the first ¡Cubanismo! album, I sat one morning with our pianist, Alfredo Rodríguez, having breakfast in Hotel Inglaterra's gorgeous restaurant. Alfredo was a brilliant player who'd left Cuba in 1960 to seek his musical fortune abroad; this was his first trip back in thirty-five years and he could hardly believe we were staying in his old neighborhood. On journeys to school in the forties, he would cross the street to avoid the boot of a doorman on alert to prevent any Afro-Cuban feet treading the carpet outside this once-swanky hotel. Alfredo also told me how touring pianist Arthur Rubinstein had praised his performance at a school recital and handed him a note to show backstage so he could watch that evening's gala concert from the wings. Dressed in his best suit, Alfredo presented himself at the stage door, only to watch the guard tear up the note, call him the Cuban equivalent of the "n" word, and tell him to beat it.

It occurred to me that morning that in the eyes of most Florida Cubans, Fidel's greatest crime was probably not nationalizing the Bacardi distillery or confiscating someone's grandfather's *estancia*, but rather encouraging Afro-Cubans to walk around like they were equal and allowing the niece who stayed behind to date a Black guy. The rebel leadership certainly seemed unprepared for the backlash it got when color restrictions were lifted; the Party quickly realized that they had better ease up a bit on equality if they weren't to alienate poor Whites and light-skinned Afro-Cubans.

First, the Afro-Cuban social clubs were all shut down; the rationale was that race-based organizations had no place in this new, egalitarian, workers' paradise. To club members, the move smacked of the brutal 1912 eradication of Black political parties. Castro was determined to eliminate all organizations independent of Party control, and the question of Black identity seemed to particularly unsettle the rebels.

Next, they turned to the orishas. The Party was an equal-opportunity religion suppressor: Catholic churches and schools were closed in tandem with the cabildos. Whites could still be unnerved by Black customers at a hotel bar or dark-skinned officials in a government office, but at least the Party was seen to be cracking down on *cosas de negros*. Though the Revolution's leadership remained far lighter-skinned than the population at large, many high-ranking rebels quietly kept Lucumí shrines in their homes or, like Castro's personal assistant, consulted *babalaos*. Some hospitals even retained a *santero* as a specialized "caregiver," and the Party was not above stealing a few tricks from the Machado and Batista playbooks, like having white doves fly over Castro's head as he delivered his inaugural speech and choosing Elegua's red and black for the colors of the 26th of July Movement's flag. Revolutionary rhetoric, however, continued to dismiss Afro-Cuban religions and the music associated with them as "backward" and "barbaric," passé symptoms of "false consciousness." Official texts referred to it all as *brujería*—witchcraft.

Despite its egalitarian slogans, the Revolution, like politicians from a half-century earlier, viewed Afro-Cuban culture as unruly, crude, and somehow shameful. References to African history and slavery in school curricula were eliminated. Che said he saw no more reason to educate Afro-Cubans about their roots than teaching his own kids about Argentine history; Marxist-Leninist texts on workers' struggles should be the focus. Members of private study groups on African history were harassed and even jailed. When the government got wind of plans to propose an African Studies seminar at a 1968 Cultural Conference in Havana, the Afro-Cuban intellectuals involved were barred.

Having met Black Power leaders during his ten days in Harlem in 1960, Fidel loved how annoyed the Americans were when he invited Angela Davis and Stokely Carmichael to Havana. But the comrades were horrified when Davis turned up for a Youth Congress sporting a huge Afro and urging Black Cubans to take pride in their heritage. Officials watched aghast as Davis jumped into a spontaneous conga line, shaking her behind like an Afro-Cuban. The island had never had a Marcus Garvey or a Malcolm X; perhaps its broad spectrum of racial ambiguity made the emergence of such figures unlikely. That a Black Power movement might now arise in Cuba ranked among the Party's worst nightmares.

༜

Son, rumba, mambo—everything seemed passé. It was the dawning of an age in which many people believed they had to use their art solely in the service of the revolution. The melodies were Cuban . . . but the lyrics sounded about as exciting as a party newspaper.

—Alicia Castro of the all-female conjunto Anacaona

The fun-hating rebels recognized there had to be *some* music, so they authorized the formation of "folklore" companies. These resembled nothing so much as the drum-chant-and-dance nightclub shows that had so delighted US tourists in the thirties and forties (minus the sexy costumes and cleansed of any references to orishas). The great Lucumí singer Lázaro Ros was commissioned to form the Conjunto Folklórico Nacional, and it grew into a highly professional outfit, admired abroad and by visitors more than by Cubans. As professional as CFN became, it was crippled by the limits imposed by the culture ministry: no improvisation, no religion, no regionalism, and no sexuality. Further problems were caused by traditional percussionists' view that rum was an essential part of the process, that you played when inspired rather than to a schedule and you certainly never took orders from a woman, such as the first administrative director of the CFN, who was forced out by its members' machismo. Abroad, some emulated capitalist rock 'n' rollers by trashing their hotel rooms while others anticipated future baseball defectors by absconding. The very concept of folklore was itself a problem for communists; music and dance come alive in the specifics of a particular region but tend to become terminally bland when stirred into a "workers unite" pot. The Party was far more comfortable with Afro-Cuban traditions on this CFN reservation than as a living presence in Cuban society.

Since melody instruments made uncomfortable connections to the golden age, the folklore movement spawned a drum boom. Percussionists such as Pello El Afrokán were the stars of the new era, as Cubans found themselves dancing to watered-down versions of the kind of drum-and-voice rumbas that had once been hidden out of sight in the Blackest solares. Pello shocked the apparatchiks by using a White female dancer to execute dangerously sensual moves, while sneaking in Yorùbá phrases and oblique references to Santería. These groups' heyday didn't last long, however, and those that survived ended up mostly touring abroad.

Carlos Moore, a left-wing Afro-Cuban intellectual who emigrated rather than endorse government policies, complained that ritual music was "being *prostituted* and presented in theatres as 'people's folklore' . . . to emasculate the faith, through . . . a demoralization of its followers."

The government's attitude changed somewhat after the Soviets asked Cuba to assist in the liberation of Portugal's African colonies. Angola, the primary theater of operation, was the ancestral home to a large part of Cuba's population, and Castro decided that emphasizing the connection would help rally support for the campaign. So many soldiers returned home with a new feeling for Africa that a shift could be detected; Castro himself came back from a non-aligned nations conference in Addis Ababa enthused about the "new Africa" and with a fresh, though vague, willingness to acknowledge his nation's deep connection to the continent. In South Africa, the "Black" Cuban army's defeat of apartheid's praetorian guard in Angola was a psychological earthquake, often credited with strengthening the 1976 student uprising in Soweto.

The Revolution could always be relied upon to display its prudish side. El Jefe demanded that his commandants marry one of their mistresses and settle down (though exempting himself). Fidel took a personal interest in getting the singer La Lupe to tone down her energetic and highly sexual act. When she resisted, "Wolf-girl" was encouraged to leave. Despite it all, Cuba never achieved the somber, gray atmosphere of most Soviet client states. How could it? The weather, the sexy atmosphere of the streets, and the dancing on the few floors that remained . . . no, the Revolution could not bend *alegría* entirely to its will, no matter how hard it tried.

The social group that unnerved the rebel hierarchy as much or more than Afro-Cubans was homosexuals. The journalist Alma Guillermoprieto spent a year in the late sixties teaching modern dance at Cuba's Escuelas Nacionales de Arte, where she encountered a miasma of mistrust and obstruction at every turn. The fatigue-clad ex-guerrillas who ran the culture ministry saw "*maricónes*" (gays) behind every initiative in music and art; if a student wanted to stray from the party line, he or she must be "deviant." Failure to show appropriate enthusiasm for rifle practice could trigger whispered rumors, as could waiting too long to visit the barber. The comrades' image of the Revolution as a macho triumph was threatened at some primal level by any male who didn't fit their vision of masculinity. Those suspected of homosexuality—or simply deemed uncooperative—were sent, like lepers under Batista, to isolated colonies; enduring such "re-education" became a badge of honor, a secret handshake, and a way to form lasting friendships with like-minded subversives.

Much of the regime's remaining paranoid energy was devoted to building a sonic wall around the island to hold back foreign music. Cuba shared the communist world's anxiety about rock music in general and The Beatles in particular: English lyrics were feared, long hair forbidden, electric guitars unthinkable. As a result, the Woodstock generation's music held a far more potent allure for young Cubans than Elvis or Chuck Berry ever had for their pre-Revolution predecessors; bootleg tapes were passed around like *samizdat* in the USSR. Jazz was also anathema; the bebop-buff Czechoslovakian ambassador caused high-level consternation by holding salons where he'd spin his Monk and Miles LPs.

Hostility to New York salsa was even greater. Culture ministers couldn't make up their minds whether commercial Latin music was a capitalist plot to steal, rebrand, and exploit the nation's patrimony or a decadent aberration Cuba was happy to be rid of. It was hard to explain why the world insisted on paying such homage to this Cuban art form when the regime reviled it. When Pello used his post-zafra fame to popularize a rhythm he called "Mozambique," the New York pianist Eddie Palmieri recorded an album inspired by and named for it. Cuban officials flaunted their ignorance of the Berne Convention by trying to sue Palmieri for copyright theft, not grasping that a drum pattern cannot be registered. Not that Pello would have seen much benefit; the meager fruits of EGREM's attempts to claim international royalty payments on behalf of Cuban artists rarely reached any of the composers. Those inventive enough to join SGAE, the Spanish copyright agency, landed in jail.

Cuban nights were full of private parties where couples danced to old records or bootleg salsa recorded off static-filled radio waves from Miami, Venezuela, or the Dominican Republic. The country was becoming so alienated from its musical roots that behind some drawn curtains, dancers were executing rumba moves—*on the two*—to Creedence Clearwater Revival.

> It's clear that salsa has its deepest roots in Cuban *son* and that due to the blockade and the political climate of the 1960s, less information started to come out of Cuba. That break was a decisive factor in the birth of salsa, which emerges as a grafting of the musical folklore of other Latin American countries onto *son* . . . [W]hile *son* has a specific structure, salsa is pure freedom, which means it can start with a *guaguancó* and finish with a Puerto Rican *aguinaldo*, with a dash of Brazilian *batucada* or a passage from Mozart.
>
> —Willie Colón

> In Fania we had Dominicans, Puerto Ricans, Cubans, Anglos, Italians, and Jews . . . a diverse group of condiments that would make a good sauce . . . [S]ince the word "salsa" . . . had always been associated with this music, it seemed logical to call it that.
>
> —Johnny Pacheco, musician and co-owner of Fania Records

> His musicians were really scary-looking black guys who said they had their own cemetery in Cuba . . . [E]very time I got off the beat, Arsenio would shout "*machete*" and all the black guys would give me the meanest look you could imagine . . . But they were all great people and they taught me a lot.
>
> —Johnny Pacheco on jamming with Arsenio Rodríguez

By the mid-sixties, rents along Broadway were up and the landlord was squeezing Pagani. Police had been raiding the hated ballroom since the start of the decade and finding (or planting) drugs, guns, and knives, leading to frequent suspensions of its liquor licence. On May 1, 1966, Pagani threw in the towel; the Palladium era was over.

Latin dance music in the early years of the decade was having almost as hard a time outside Cuba as in. After an initial post-Batista surge, the flow of Cuban talent to the US slowed to a trickle; many New York bands had relied on new Cuban songs and arrangements throughout the forties and fifties, and suddenly there were none. Equally sad was the end of touring; no more Nat "King" Cole or Stan Getz in Havana, no Benny Moré or Orquesta Aragón at the Palladium. At the start of the sixties, bossa nova grabbed the spotlight, then Beatlemania reset the world's musical metronome to a 4/4 White-boy backbeat. Without a flow of ideas and talent along the Havana–New York axis, Cuban polyrhythms seemed helpless against the challenges of rock and soul.

It took a while for New York's Latin musicians to come to grips with the fact that Castro had, in effect, handed them the keys; most were still worshipping at the shrines of Arsenio, Cachao, and Bauzá. The salsa comeback of the 1970s would be engineered by a creative and commercial conspiracy that could only have been hatched in New York. Its seed was planted in the late fifties, when pianist Charlie Palmieri (brother of "Mozambique" fan Eddie) heard another band's percussionist practicing his flute in a Bronx dressing room. Flute-driven charangas had been the last Cuban style to storm New York before the door slammed shut, and Palmieri liked the percussive style he heard as well as the warm-toned wooden instrument Johnny Pacheco was playing. He invited the handsome Dominican to join his band and together they explored a high-energy, jazzy advance on the charanga sound.

Their collaboration lasted only long enough for the ambitious Pacheco to gain a name for himself so he could start his own group, creating a funky variant called "pachanga." In 1964, when he and his creation were big in the now-shrunken world of Latin music, Pacheco met an Italian-American ex-policeman-turned-lawyer named Jerry Masucci and the pair went into business together. For the next fifteen years the label they created, Fania, would dominate and transform Latin music.

Pacheco and Masucci were conservative revolutionaries. Masucci adored Cuba and had visited the island many times, even post-Revolution; both revered the classic Arsenio canon. When Celia Cruz came to New York to pick up an award for a record she'd made in Mexico with Sonora, they wooed her to join Fania, and she and Pacheco made a series of hit albums together. The changes the label made to the Latin sound began subtly, but eventually resulted in total modernization and Nuyoricanization. Cut off from the source and surrounded by the powerful melting-pot energies of the Big Apple, how could it have been otherwise? Puerto Ricans, for example, have always loved trombones, and the new sound featured as many as four in the horn section, something never heard in Cuban music. As Havana studios slid into obsolescence, New York rooms stayed up-to-date; multitrack recording, isolation booths, and close miking helped make Fania's sound bigger and punchier, while subtle cross-fertilization with jazz, rhythm and blues, and rock added an edge that made it feel less foreign. Fania's groups featured Jewish keyboard players, Italian trumpeters, and Anglo trombonists, sidelined the tres (as well as its Puerto Rican cousin the *cuatro*) in favor of electric keyboards, and did away with frilly shirts. In jeans and suits, Fania musicians looked masculine and confident; Carlos Santana winning over the Woodstock crowd with *son*-inflected rock wearing a tank-top didn't hurt.

In the late sixties, some Latin kids who had grown up with a stronger feeling for doo-wop and rhythm and blues than for their Cuban heritage challenged Fania with an R&B-Latin hybrid called "boogaloo." Whether boogaloo petered out through its own limitations (which were severe) or was brought down by a cabal of promoters and veteran musicians in league with Masucci and Pacheco depends on who's telling the story. Whatever the case, Fania surged into the seventies with a saucy new catchword—"salsa"—and a commitment to youth, while always adhering to their high standards of musicianship and reverence for roots. Latinos everywhere rallied to the sound, helping the hemisphere avoid getting swamped by rock and soul.

Among Fania's many brilliant ideas, the notion of assembling the leaders of all their groups as the Fania All Stars comes a close second behind the music's new name. Starting in 1968, regular concerts and foreign tours by this great line-up put the spotlight on the high quality of their roster and provided a platform to promote its lesser-known bands. In 1972, Fania booked the All Stars into a New York dance club and filmed two nights of great music. Augmented with footage of life in Spanish Harlem, the resulting documentary, *Our Latin Thing*, was shown largely by renting theaters and promoting it themselves. This echoed Pacheco and Masucci's early DIY days, when they would pile discs in the back of a battered station wagon and service shops in a twenty-mile radius of Times Square—pretty much the extent of the Latin market in those days. (Miami Cubans found Fania too "Black" and "low-class Puerto Rican"; only after years of Cruz's anti-Castro pronouncements did they embrace her, alone of the Fania roster.)

A half-century later, *Our Latin Thing* doesn't stand up as a classic, but it has energy, great music, and plenty of cultural pride. Without ever having a distributor, its reach extended from the tip of South America to Scandinavia, Japan, and Africa and back to North America; well-worn videocassettes helped create a footprint that was hard to erase. Fania's core artists—Pacheco, Cruz, Ray Barretto, Larry Harlow, Cheo Feliciano, et al.—were augmented by the label's willingness to take risks, bringing on board rebel trombonist-composer Willie Colón and singer Héctor Lavoe when both were barely of New York drinking age.

Two years after *Our Latin Thing*, Fania rented the vast Yankee Stadium in the heart of the Nuyorican Bronx and filled it for a gala concert. When the energy began to flag in the mid-seventies they turned to their office boy, a Panamanian law graduate named Rubén Blades, pairing him and his witty, political songwriting with Colón for the hit album *The Good, the Bad, the Ugly*. All in all, it was a pretty peerless fifteen-year arc of label management. They rarely paid royalties, of course, and many artists felt embittered by how they were treated, but Masucci and Pacheco would probably riposte by asking how many would trade those years of globe-spanning glory (and good gig fees) for a few royalty checks.

Where was the King of the Palladium during all this? Tito Puente suffered and sulked; he mistrusted the Fania boys and had grown weary of the small-time mentality and crooked promoters of the Latin dance world. He tried to match Pacheco's success with Cruz by teaming up with the exiled La Lupe, but fruitful collaboration with the self-destructive Cubana proved impossible. He ventured more and more into Latin jazz, starting with a memorable live broadcast from Birdland jamming with bebop greats. Jazz clubs might not have delivered his beloved sight of dancers filling the floor, but he found the money better and promoters easier to deal with. But the rock surge of the late sixties was rough on jazz, too; after *Our Latin Thing* proved Masucci and Pacheco to be the smartest kids on the block, a truce was arranged and Puente was welcomed into the Fania fold. They quickly wangled him a slot on Dinah Shore's popular TV show, which at a stroke revived his career. Matchmaking Celia with Tito for a series of acclaimed albums established the pair as the golden couple of salsa; their successful partnership outlasted Fania, which collapsed at the end of the seventies. Salsa experimented and grew, but it couldn't stray too far; after all, people still had to dance to it. Eddie Palmieri and Larry Harlow, along with Colón and Blades, led the way into the eighties. The Corso on East 86th Street emerged as the closest thing to a Palladium successor Manhattan ever had.

Puente's trumpet player Mario Rivera, meanwhile, began making clandestine visits to Havana, bringing back tapes, LPs, and reports that allowed New Yorkers to check out what was going on there, at least out of the corners of their eyes. Whenever Tito and Celia found themselves sharing a bill with Cubans at a European festival, she would insist on staying at a separate hotel while he snuck out to join the "communists" for late-night jams. New Yorkers absorbed a few uncredited melodies and riffs, but it would have been career suicide to acknowledge any link to Castro's Havana.

> Did we, the politicians, conceive of [the] movement? Did we plan it? No! These things arise, like so many others, that none of us can even imagine.
>
> —Fidel Castro on the *nueva trova* movement

The Santiaguero trova singer Carlos Puebla moved to Havana in 1952 and began a long residency at La Bodeguita del Medio, Ernest Hemingway's legendary hangout in Old Havana. Puebla's penchant for songs attacking Batista and his serenades to the triumphant guerrillas combined with trova's unthreatening beat earned him and a few *compadres* the right to keep singing through the sixties. Filin was another survivor; many of the genre's stars had quickly declared their support for Castro and few left the country. It may have sounded suspiciously jazzy, but like trova, at least no one danced to it. These two slow-tempo'd, literate forms combined to open the door a crack, enough to allow the growth of something fresh, interesting, and hard for bureaucrats to control.

The key figures in what became known as *nueva trova* got off to rocky starts. Aspiring filin singer Pablo Milanés had two strikes against him: he was Black and his hair was long. Authorities sent him away to deviant camp, where he languished until Omara Portuondo, who had started singing some of his songs, demanded his release. The other, Silvio Rodríguez, is White but also had suspiciously ample locks and a tattoo, besides. His sweet voice and the protective sponsorship of a veteran of the Moncada Barracks assault secured him a spot hosting a youth TV show. His look, irreverent attitude, and the fact that he chose Bola de Nieve for his first interview meant he was soon off the air. He got into further trouble by dedicating an early masterpiece, "Te doy una canción" (I Give You a Song), to the daughter of an army officer; the furious general had him briefly jailed and for a time succeeded in blocking his career. But he continued to perform at the House of the Americas, where he met and exchanged ideas with the Chilean songwriter Víctor Jara.

In the wake of the 1973 US-backed overthrow of the Allende government in Chile (which included the brutal killing of Jara), a light went on in the culture ministry; someone realized that encouraging Pablo, Silvio, and their friends would not only throw a bone to restless Cuban youth but also solidify the Revolution's connection to Yankee-averse movements throughout the hemisphere. A distinct melodic approach connected nueva trova to political songwriters from Chile and Nicaragua, the Brazilian Tropicália movement, and other musical manifestations of the Latin American Left, though the comrades weren't savvy enough to detect the influence of Lennon/McCartney, Dylan, James Taylor, and other alien anglophones. When I met Silvio in London in 1986, he astonished me by revealing that when he'd been wounded in Angola during his military service, his hammock companion while recuperating in a forest clearing had been a cassette of the Incredible String Band's *The Hangman's Beautiful Daughter* and he considered them a key inspiration.

Rodríguez and Milanes became stars across the Hispanic world and received privileged treatment at home: they were allowed to keep their hard-currency earnings, recorded abroad, bought cars and houses, and lived lives inconceivable even for high party officials. As painful as it might have been for the Revolution, Pablo and Silvio earned those perks; their popularity was a nightmare for the CIA, helping to keep Castro's Cuba relevant among Latin youth. Despite his most famous song, "La Vida no vale nada," (Life Is Worth Nothing) being initially banned, Pablo proved the more reliable Party man; Silvio's imagistic lyrics were so difficult to decode that he remained generally uncensored yet unloved by officials. Looking back on nueva trova's early years, Silvio recalled obstruction by "squares . . . who didn't trust the young . . . enemies of culture . . . cowards who were ruining the revolution that I carried inside of me."

Young musicians with more on their minds than acoustic guitars and thoughtful lyrics began moving through the openings created by nueva trova. The regime tried to channel the energies of conservatory virtuosos by authorizing the formation of a big band called Orquesta Cubana de Musica Moderna, whose brief carefully avoided the j-word (though the notion that an outfit containing Chucho Valdés, Arturo Sandoval, and Paquito d'Rivera would not be playing jazz was clearly delusional). Those three plus some like-minded cohorts soon threw out the rulebook by forming their own group; the name they chose sent a not-so-subtle message: "Irakere" is Yorùbá for the forest that slaves ran into after escaping.

While Irakere was establishing a beachhead for Cuban jazz, the man who would get the nation's feet dancing into the future began his own Long March. Juan Formell was a bass player with good Party credentials, having been a member of the Revolutionary Police Band before holding down a privileged chair in the lounge of the Havana Libre (formerly Havana Hilton). Like most musicians who prospered during the sixties, Formell cared not a fig for the past. He was very aware of what was happening elsewhere, however, developing a fascination with rock and soul and a desire to marry lessons learned from bootleg cassettes with the sensibilities of his country's youth, to unite the revolutionary generation in a distinctively Cuban way, and to do it on the dancefloor. In 1967, he joined Elio Revé's charanga as musical director; that the Party found this gently rhythmic style the least offensive holdover from fifties dancefloor decadence had helped Revé navigate a delicate political path. This well-established band was the perfect palette for Formell's experiments; to his own electric bass, he added a full drum kit, putting clear distance between them and traditional line-ups. (The irony of socialists presiding over the replacement of the collectivist rhythm section with the individualistic drum set seems to have eluded the cultural authorities.)

Formell's own instrument was also key to separating his approach from what was happening abroad. Ampeg had created the "baby bass" in 1959, and the New York Latin world embraced this rotund, plastic, cartoonish imitation of a wooden upright. The Ampeg's compact tone was perfect for carrying Cachao's innovations into louder modern ensembles, leaving sonic space above for the bongo, güiro, and timbale, and below for the conga. In Formell's rhythm section, the thud of a foot-operated bass drum occupied the basement, and with his own edgy Jaco Pastorius–like bass sound plus the top end of the drum kit, there was no need and no room for anything as old-fashioned as a bongo or a güiro.

In 1969, Formell led a few of his Revé colleagues down their own forest trail to form what would become the dominant Cuban band of the next half-century, Los Van Van. The name was portentous, indicating the bassist's ambition to create something in the oft-invoked *"vanguardia"* of the Revolution. It also signaled that they would make feet move through great dance beats rather than Party exhortations; *"van van"* means, approximately, "go go." By the late sixties, the Yorùbá word *"agogo"* had completed its journey from ceremonial percussion instrument to capitalist decadence via the Left Bank of Paris. Tagged on to almost any French or English word, it had become a signpost for a hot dancefloor.

Castro's embargo on Cuba's musical history triggered, in effect, two revolutions: as Nuyoricans were reinventing Afro-Cuban music from the outside, Van Van were able to create modern Cuban dance music on a virtually blank slate. On top of the drum kit and his complex, jazzy bass lines, Formell built the group around electric guitar, synth keyboards, and (in a nod to Nuyorican salsa) trombones. Cuban youth loved the electronics; they couldn't afford the gadgets visible through the windows of the hard-currency stores, but for *vanvaneros*, their beloved band sounded modern, gratifyingly more so even than the salsa they heard late at night through the radio static.

∽

> I admit that the graduates have achieved a very high level technically, higher than ours. But can you learn the *sabor*, the flavor of *son*, at a school? *Son* shouldn't be played with the head or intellectualized. *Sabor* is played from *inside*. When we're gone, there won't be any more real *son*.
>
> —Lázaro Herrera, leader of Septeto Nacional Ignacio Piñeiro

> The *songo* thing is just a distillation of two or three different rhythm-instrument forms, all put into two drums: the traps and the congas. No more bongos . . . [Y]ounger Cuban musicians . . . [are] not really exposed to the masters of those instruments . . . The [government] wanted the youth to think that everything that happened before the revolution was garbage.
>
> —Andy González, leading New York salsa bass player

By the 1980s, the floodgates had opened and music schools were spawning group after group, despite the fact that most teachers were classics-oriented Eastern Europeans with no feeling for tropical music. In the sixties, a conservatory student caught moonlighting at a dance or a rumba was often expelled; by the seventies, it was usually just a reprimand, and by the eighties, little more than a frown. In the nineties, schools began bringing in Afro-Cuban drummers to teach conga technique.

I heard Elio Revé's band in Britain in the mid-eighties and was disappointed. Having heard salsa bands in New York, I was eager for the "real Cuban thing" and found them highly technical and cold-sounding compared to the sensuality and feeling for roots of the New York bands. Revé called his style *changüí*, referring to a ritual music from the area around his birthplace in Oriente Province. Commercial savvy (yes, even in Cuba) dictated that creators of new styles looked to ng- and mb-hinged Ki-Kongo words for names. Out of changüí, Formell created *songo* with Los Van Van; this dense, complex, funk-inflected sound spawned a movement. By the 1990s, it was known as *timba*.

Timba is the logical fruition of highly trained musicians growing up surrounded by Afro-Cuban drumming, then focusing on Parliament/Funkadelic, the Ohio Players, and Weather Report rather than Benny and Celia, Arsenio and Chano. NG La Banda, one of the biggest bands of the 1980s, covered Moré classics, but the songs were barely recognizable amid dense synth riffs and beats that would have befuddled El Bárbaro del Ritmo.

~

We valorize most those cultural and artistic creations that serve a utilitarian function for the people . . . that support the revindication and liberation of humanity.

—Fidel Castro, 1972

The Revolution cannot wipe out this [Abakuá culture] just because it has reactionary elements. Even in socialist countries, there are some people who have a mystical way of seeing life . . . Life is full of contradictions. If you want to be a true Cuban or a Caribbean, you have to understand and live within all these elements.

—Miguel Barnet, Cuban writer, novelist, and ethnographer, 1985

It took a while for Celina González's loyalty to the Revolution to be repaid. Her music was a contradiction, a White country girl whose songs celebrated African gods. (Think of Dolly Parton covering "Got My Mojo Working.") González never stopped performing, but the culture ministry forbade her from including the core of her repertoire, particularly "A Santa Bárbara," with its earworm chorus of "*qué viva changó!*," a paean to the syncretic orisha and her altar ego, the axe-bearing Catholic saint. Nothing epitomized the thaw in the government's attitudes towards Afro-Cuban religion more than the island-wide mid-seventies popularity of González's recording of this irresistible song. Yorùbá and

Abakuá phrases and references soon began popping up everywhere. But unlike how Chano, Miguelito, Arsenio, Celia, and Benny had brought them out of the solares and onto the dancefloors and radio waves, this was mostly well-educated musicians appropriating Afro-Cuban religious imagery as part of an effort to authenticate and democratize the country's culture, whether the Revolution liked it or not. Los Van Van made wide use of Santería imagery and many bands would start a set with percussion and chant, before synthesizer and drum kit kicked off the dense timba beats.

Nueva trova's popularity with the Latin American Left had forced the regime to acknowledge Catholic liberation theology and to see possible upsides to religion. In 1991, it was decreed that believers could not only join the Party but were allowed to wear religious emblems in public. What no one could have predicted was that Afro-Cuban religions would generate far more popular enthusiasm than Catholic or Protestant revivals. The government now provides support to ceremonial societies, students (many of them foreigners) attend classes in Afro-Cuban history, and Yorùbá priests fly over the Middle Passage routes from Nigeria to study Lucumí rituals and language long forgotten in modern Africa. Rumba singers and percussionists have received "Treasured Artist of the Revolution" status and appear regularly on Cuban TV. Foreign visitors attend reasonably authentic performances of Yorùbá, Kongo, and Abakuá ceremonies (notably on tours organized by Sublette, before—and after—the Trump administration shut them down).

Beyond the use of African words and phrases, timba's lyrics strayed even further from the Party line than nueva trova's and in a completely different direction. No idealistic musings on the future of the Revolution for them; Los Van Van and others filled their songs with street slang, hard-nosed complaints about shortages, repeated references to *fruta* (pussy), and cynical portrayals of the hard lives of those with no access to hard currency (95 percent of all remittances from the US go to White Cubans). Another irony: the government's strict control of music culminated with the most successful group of the revolutionary era building their popularity around songs that are, in spirit, consumerist.

Timba's heroines are often *jineteras*, a word that means, literally, "female jockeys" and refers to women who "ride" tourists during their stays in Cuba. There is usually no agreed price for these services, but generous gifts or cash are expected before the foreigner boards his plane. One famous tale has Castro seated in first class on his way to an international conference and listening, aghast, as his neighbor, a well-traveled businessman, expounds on the pleasures of *fruta*-filled holidays in Havana. El Jefe immediately barred all Cuban citizens, male and female, from venturing beyond the lobbies of tourist hotels.

Colombian writer Silvana Paternostro published an article in *The New Republic* based on a lengthy interview with a young couple from a provincial city who, faced with a future devoid of any kind of material comfort, moved to Havana, where they stayed with the girl's grandmother and lived on the dollars she earned giving blow jobs to tourists. The lives of women like these are recounted and honored in timba's lyrics. Like Pello's zafra exhortation, groups often use such a dense and ever-shifting argot that the authorities can't keep up. Singers improvise and alter lyrics in live performance and audiences relish the rapid-fire, rap-inflected delivery that leaves censors nonplussed. During the "special period" of the early nineties following Russia's abandonment of the island, NG La Banda released a song fulsome with praise for the new all-soya "hamburger." Nothing in the words could be faulted, since they repeated the agriculture ministry's own hyperbole, but everyone knew the burgers were disgusting, bordering on inedible, so the ridicule was both completely understood and impossible to ban. In 1997, censors shut down Charanga Habanera for six months following a televised concert in which their vocalist sang about an "over-ripe mango falling from the tree," which many took to be a metaphor about Fidel's possible retirement—or worse!

A movement that was once so nervous about Afro-Cuban culture could only stand and watch as much of the music, clothing, slang, religious practice, street style, and "attitude" of a majority of urban youth, Black, White, and mixed, became essentially Afro-Cuban. By the mid-1990s, attendance at Party rallies without a popular timba group on the bill would be embarrassingly sparse; the government had no choice but to back off, defeated and powerless. When Raúl Castro's daughter emerged as a leading international spokesperson for LGBT rights, they were forced to abandon decades of anti-homosexual policies. Cuba has now become a world leader in sex-change surgery.

And as for prudery, dancing to timba follows the modern trend, being less about the couple and more about the individual. Its most notorious move, the *tembleque*, is a rapid-fire advance on the culebra. The rebels may have wanted the new Cuba to shun capitalist decadence, but these days, Havana dancefloors can make a New Yorker blush.

So, armed with the popular energy of the world's most musical island, timba went on to conquer the globe, right? Wrong. Van Van and a few others tour occasionally and have cult followings, but timba has disappointed its Cuban fans and failed to reward agents and promoters who have tried to break it internationally. In the US, it came up against two problems: Latin commercial radio is almost entirely controlled by Cuban exiles, who form a united front against giving any exposure to "communist music," while to Cuban émigrés, timba is not just communist, it's "Black" (which for many is the same thing). With the decline of Fania, the years beginning in the mid-eighties were dominated by slick, light-skinned Latin pop led by Gloria Estefan, Ricky Martin, and Marc Anthony. Timba was this music's polar opposite: a dense, colloquial sound whose true counterparts were rap and modern R&B, rather than salsa. Timba's fiercely "street" lyrics would never resonate outside Cuba, even to Latinos. World music audiences would happily listen to lyrics they didn't understand, but timba, with its crude yet aspiringly modern production style, was a far cry from what this crowd was after.

☙

Old-school New York salsa struggled but survived, aided aesthetically, if not commercially, by the phenomenon of *Salsa Meets Jazz* every Monday night at the Village Gate in Greenwich Village. The Gate was a historic venue; in the sixties, I saw John Coltrane and Nina Simone there, as well as the *Jacques Brel Is Alive and Living in Paris* revue, plus various folk singers and comedians. The owner, Art D'Lugoff, was a classic New York music buff, devoted to jazz, folk, and Broadway, who frequented the Greek tavernas along Eighth Avenue as well as, a few blocks farther north, the Palladium. Starting in 1962, Monday nights were given over to Symphony Sid's often historic (and occasionally recorded) descargas. After a hiatus in the seventies, *Salsa Meets Jazz* returned with a new formula: a pair of Latin bands played two sets each, while a guest jazz soloist joined for the final number of each set. There was a dancefloor in front of the stage, tables at the back, and standing room along the bar.

I went about a dozen times across the 1980s, heard wonderful music, and saw great dancing. Jazz emissaries ranged from the obvious (Dizzy Gillespie, Herbie Mann) to the inspired (Ray Charles's sax player David "Fathead" Newman, McCoy Tyner) to the weird and wonderful (David Murray, Lester Bowie). Bowie turned up in his Art Ensemble of Chicago lab coat and challenged Orquesta Broadway's trumpet section to see who could hit the highest note. Greenwich Village is a long subway ride from Spanish Harlem and Monday night isn't the weekend, so the crowd hadn't the sort of uptown dancers found at the Corso. It was mixed and hip; Latin American NYU students rubbed shoulders with brave Anglo salsa-class graduates, with the best movers taking over the floor as the evening progressed.

I stopped by Record Mart, the great Latin record store inside the Times Square subway station, to consult the experts, the owner Jesse Moskowitz and manager Harry Sepulveda, and they confirmed that recorded examples of this splendid music didn't really exist. "Latin jazz" discs were generally bebop with a bit of flute and conga, while commercial salsa was all about the vocals, with slick, compressed production and rarely any solos. The great descarga recordings of the fifties and sixties were long out of print, their resuscitation by YouTube and Spotify far in the future.

What a perfect challenge for my label! I decided that Manny Oquendo's Libre, with Andy González on bass, multiple trombones, and a Puerto Rican take on Arsenio-style arrangements, would be ideal for the project. It turned out they'd just finished recording a privately financed double LP, which had about one disc's worth of great tracks. Andy arranged a meeting with their Italian-American backer, but his expensive camel-hair coat, slicked-back hair, cigar, and exorbitant demands had me tiptoeing backwards out the door. The idea slid to the back of my mental drawer.

A few years later, I saw a Cuban band called Sierra Maestra at the 1993 WOMAD festival and was stunned; this was something completely different from Revé and Van Van. Cuba's loosened cultural reins, I later discovered, had unleashed not just critical voices from nueva trova and timba, but explorations of the forbidden past as well. Sierra Maestra's central figures, the tres player Juan de Marcos González and trumpeter Jesús Alemañy, had set out to revive classic *son*, seeking instruction and advice from members of Septeto Nacional and other golden era outfits, just as US folkies and Hungarian *táncház* bands had from aged blues singers and Transylvanian fiddlers. Dismissed with bemused condescension by their contemporaries, de Marcos's and Alemañy's subsequent successes with Buena Vista Social Club and ¡Cubanismo! would end up dwarfing Van Van's and Irakere's international accomplishments.

Nick Gold at World Circuit Records beat me to it, recording Sierra Maestra during their stay in London. But when the group returned to Havana, Alemañy stayed behind, embarking on a romance and eventually marriage to my friend the ethnomusicologist Lucy Durán, an expert on every sort of traditional music, particularly Cuban and African. Across Lucy's dinner table, I broached the idea of making an Afro-Cuban dance record with instrumental solos instead of lead vocals, and a horn section taking the place of the coro. I was convinced that, with this approach, Latin music could reach the middle-class "world" audience; for most such listeners, the slick pop texture of salsa combined with rapid-fire Spanish lyrics meant that no matter how much they might have liked Latin music, they had little clue which records to buy.

Jesús loved the idea. Could he assemble a group in Havana to make such a record? He could, and we did. My hunch was right; the first ¡Cubanismo! CD ended up selling a startling 150,000 copies in North America and Europe. But I wasn't anywhere near as right as Nick Gold . . .

༄

Engineer Jerry Boys, pianist Alfredo Rodríguez, and I arrived in Havana late one evening in 1995. The next morning, we walked through the potholed streets of central Havana to the door of a building with washing hanging from every window. Inside were sixteen musicians crowded into the entrance hall, seated with music stands, rehearsing arrangements for the album we would begin recording the next day. When they began to play, the tiled floor, walls, and ceiling made for an overwhelming acoustic effect. The musicianship at every chair was astonishing; it was old-school Afro-Cuban music, quoting from Arsenio, Miguelito Valdés, Cachao, and the heart of forties and fifties Havana, with touches of Fania-esque modernity. The reality went far beyond my wildest dreams.

Jerry and I paid a call at EGREM studios that afternoon. I had negotiated a rate by telex, and they were pleased to see me and my envelope full of cash. But the manager wanted to double-check: was I sure I wanted to use the large old room upstairs rather than the modern studio below it? We got a guided tour of the building; Studio 2 was a fashionably "dead" space, perfect for amps and overdubs, with soundproof booths and inputs on the console for electronic instruments and drum machines. Van Van recorded there. The high-ceilinged upstairs room was dusty, as if no one had crossed its threshold in months, possibly years. As we clapped hands to check the liveliness of the sound, Jerry's eyes lit up. It wouldn't be easy, but it was potentially a great room. Not even a question; we confirmed our intention to work upstairs.

The next day was one of the best sessions I've ever been a part of. We recorded four master tracks, including "Descarga de hoy" (Today's Jam), the opening and most oft-played track on the CD, completely live, solos and all. The only nod to modern technology was replacing a few errant bass notes. At the end of the afternoon, one of the young guys from the horn section approached me. "That was fun," he said. "Great demos! When are we going to record the masters?" I looked puzzled. "You know, go downstairs, lay down a track, overdub solos, add keyboards, all that . . ." When I explained that we weren't going to work that way, that what we had recorded would be mixed just as they were, his face fell. I think he had been looking forward to working with an "American producer" who could help Cuban music reach a worldwide audience, but he could tell I was a fool who had no clue.

The sessions were as challenging as they were exhilarating. The room was cooled by a gigantic Soviet air conditioner with no thermostat; when in operation, it hummed loudly and the temperature plummeted, and when it was off during takes the heat soared. The studio Steinway was a lovely instrument but years of neglect had loosened the pegs, so temperature swings wreaked havoc with the pitch. We hired a piano tuner to sit in the studio all day and wait for the call. It often came just as we had finished rehearsing a track and were ready to record; everyone would go off for a beer while he attended to the instrument, then the band would have to refamiliarize themselves with the charts. Nothing could dampen our spirits, though; the music was too wonderful to view such problems—as well as regular equipment failures—as anything but minor bumps in the road.

Once we were back in London, Jerry got a call from Nick Gold. He had an idea for a World Circuit project in Havana and wanted to know how it was to work at EGREM. Jerry reassured him; it was not without its problems, he said, but it was doable and, if you found a sweet spot for each instrument, the sound could be great. As we mixed, mastered, and got *Jesús Alemañy's ¡Cubanismo!* ready for release, far away in Bamako, Mali, fate was taking the international future of Cuban music in hand.

World Circuit's biggest success up to that time had been *Talking Timbuktu*, a collaboration between the Malian singer and guitarist Ali Farka Touré and Ry Cooder. Cooder and Gold had bonded over a shared fascination with Mali, its influence on American blues as well as the impact there of Cuban music in the decades before and after the former colony's independence from France. (In Chapter VIII, we'll see how Cuban *son* 78s helped shape the modern music of West and Central Africa.) My Hannibal label, by now part of the American indie Rykodisc, had licensed *Talking Timbuktu* for North America; it sold well and won a Grammy. Nick and Ry were keen to do another project together and decided that bringing Malian and Cuban musicians together—with Cooder in the middle—would be perfect. Leading the African delegation would be the Rail Band's guitarist Djelimady Tounkara, who had been at the heart of the rumba-inflected Malian music of the 1960s and 1970s, and the ngoni maestro Bassekou Kouyate; in Havana, Sierra Maestra's Juan de Marcos assembled a group of veteran performers to represent the Cuban side. To spread the cost of the trip, World Circuit also planned to record a big-band version of Sierra Maestra augmented with veterans of the golden era called the Afro-Cuban All Stars. When the musicians' plane left Bamako, however, they weren't on it; the reasons for this are better explained when we get to Mali in Chapter VIII. Suffice it to say that Gold now had two more weeks booked in EGREM, his illustrious co-producer/guitarist had just arrived, and a group of musicians were ready to begin a project that had gone up in smoke.

Luck, so they say, rewards the well prepared. A year earlier, Ry had, against his lawyer's advice, gone to Havana to record a track with Omara Portuondo and Irish group The Chieftains for a concept album about Galicia, land of patónes (who also happen to be Celtic cousins of the Irish). He'd been immersing himself in Cuban music ever since, particularly *son* and trova from Santiago. Nick had, in the meantime, not only recorded Sierra Maestra, but also released a Celina González compilation and brought the *guajira* diva to the UK for a tour; with expert guidance from Lucy Durán, he had done a great deal of listening to golden era Cuban recordings.

After a day of head-scratching paralysis, Nick, Ry, Juan, Jerry, and the musicians got down to work, figuring they might as well record *something*. Compay Segundo, Eliades Ochoa, Rubén González, "Cachaíto" López (Cachao's son), Puntillita Licea, and the others knew each other but had rarely played together; all had been shunted to the sidelines by government policy and popular fashion. What could be more enjoyable than sitting once again in the familiar studio and playing anything that popped into their heads?

Focusing at first on songs Ry knew, once they had a good take the musicians would break into smaller groups, reminding one another of old favorites. Ry circulated with his Dictaphone, grabbing snatches of music, then he'd stay awake half the night listening and figuring out what to record the next day. In an EGREM hallway, he bumped into Portuondo and asked if she'd like to sing something; she came back that evening, recorded two songs, and left the next day on tour. On another occasion, Cooder liked a song but thought it needed a gentler voice than Puntillita's; de Marcos strolled out the door and returned twenty minutes later with Ibrahim Ferrer, who hadn't sung for decades. After a week of growing delight with what was going down on tape, Ry and Nick devoted a couple of days to recording Rubén González piano solos, enough for a third CD.

The conjunction of good fortune and skilled preparation extended to the technical, distributional, and promotional aspects of the Buena Vista Social Club's success. Ry wanted a purist, old-fashioned approach to the recording, using ambient mics poised above a circle of musicians and singers. Jerry convinced him to adopt a "belt and braces" approach, with individual close-miking as well as the overheads. Cooder took the tapes back to LA, but the mix was disappointing. Jerry flew out to work with him but the result still lacked the punch of the rough mixes they'd made hurriedly at the end of each day's sessions in Havana.

Gold is nothing if not a perfectionist; weeks of experimentation and frustration turned into months. They knew they had a good record, but the mixes still didn't sound right. One day Jerry was thumbing through a directory of Southern California studios and came across a small outfit in the San Fernando Valley owned by a religious label that had an Amek control board identical to the one at EGREM. He and Ry drove out one afternoon, put on one of the multitracks, and *shazam!*, the elusive sound they'd been struggling for months to find magically burst forth from the speakers. "It was like washing the windscreen," said Jerry. They started mixing there the next day.

Despite our success with *Talking Timbuktu*, Hannibal/Rykodisc missed out on *Buena Vista* for North America. Nick wanted an overall label deal and the other Ryko directors weren't willing to give it to him. I was disappointed; I thought *Buena Vista* was a good record that would sell, but I can't claim prescience about the magnitude of what we missed. After the negotiations ended, I got a call from David Bither at Nonesuch Records wanting Nick's phone number; he loved Oumou Sangare, a Malian artist on World Circuit, and had heard there was a new album on the way. When Gold insisted Nonesuch take on the entire World Circuit catalogue for North America, Bither decided he liked Nick and the label and, on a hunch, agreed. After they'd signed the contract, Gold mentioned that he had three Cuban records ready for release next year: "I think you'll be pleased when you hear them." Talk about virtue rewarded; *Buena Vista Social Club* transformed the fortunes of Nonesuch, a specialist division of Warner Music that had been belittled and threatened with downsizing by the parent company. Rykodisc (and Hannibal) went into decline and were sold to a hedge fund, eventually becoming part of Warner Music's back catalogue.

Wim Wenders's documentary often gets credit for the success of *Buena Vista*, but the film wasn't even shot until the record had sold half a million copies, an unbelievable number for a world music release, or, for that matter, a Latin one. World Circuit put out all three albums at once and spent a year in preparation, flying journalists to Havana, creating great packaging, and lining up displays in retail stores all over the world. Having done the music for *Paris, Texas*, Ry knew Wim Wenders and sent him a copy of the finished record, which led, eventually, to the famous documentary.

Having Cooder's name on the cover didn't hurt, of course, but all the great promotion in the world won't help if the music and sound aren't right; *Buena Vista* was a magical combination of factors that were handled perfectly by Nick and the World Circuit staff, notably his second-in-command, Jenny Adlington, and Hannibal's former press officer, Sally Reeves. The songs were drawn from a huge reservoir of material generally unknown outside Latin America; most had been composed in the early years of Cuban recording and overshadowed internationally by the output of professional songwriters such as Lecuona and Simons. The album's texture was distinctive; with subdued percussion—just a bit of bongo, no conga—it sounded very different from what the world thought of as Cuban music. (Boys was tasked with barring the door on technical grounds to the congoseros and timbaleros who began turning up once word of the sessions got out.) You can't dance to *Buena Vista*; it's more trova than *son*, a very old-fashioned Santiaguero album. Ry was restrained in the mixing, blending his guitar and his son Joaquin's percussion subtly into the mix without hogging the spotlight or disturbing the Cuban feel.

For me, though, a key element is the sound. I watched people walk into the London launch party, where it was playing on the PA system; many glanced around, looking for the bandstand and the live musicians. Jerry and Ry had achieved the kind of warm, three-dimensional sound that can only happen when so many microphones are open (and perfectly positioned) in a big, "live" room, voices and instruments blending in the air before they reach the mixing board. If *Buena Vista* had been made downstairs in EGREM 2, it would have been lucky to sell ten thousand copies, let alone ten million.

¡Cubanismo!'s years of touring in the late nineties had many high points, but one I won't forget is the show at the Manhattan Ballroom on 34th Street, where Chano Pozo had performed a half-century earlier. Curious Nuyoricans, salsa students still on training wheels, liberal-minded Cubans, Latin jazz fans—it was like the Village Gate crowd that had inspired the project in the first place. In between numbers, dancers would approach one of the boxes to get an autograph from Orlando "El Duque" Hernández, then a star pitcher for the New York Yankees. El Duque's arrival in the Major Leagues had been as dramatic as any Cuban baseball defection; after showing their faces at a wedding party near a beach outside Havana, Hernández and his wife slipped quietly away and straight onto a small boat. They ended up stranded with no food and barely any water on a Bahamian atoll, where they were rescued by the US Coast Guard; a few months later, Hernández signed a multi-million-dollar contract with the Yankees.

In the short distance between El Duque's box and the stage lay one of the most eccentric contradictions of Castro's revolution. While one talented Cuban nearly died in a desperate gambit to offer his skills in the capitalist marketplace, others came and went easily, opening bank accounts in the Dominican Republic or Spain, buying rebuilt Ladas or new Hondas and parking them outside homes in the Havana suburbs stacked with newly added floors built with their foreign earnings. Why the difference?

Fidel never danced—*not one step!*—but he loved baseball. El Jefe took great pride in the success of the Cuban national team, watched broadcasts of the Cuban league, and turned up at stadiums unannounced to cheer for his favorite players. He cared nothing if the best bass players went off to France or New York, earning hard currency and bringing it home to Cuba. But let a star outfielder be seen speaking to an agent during an international tournament and his passport would be quickly confiscated. The ¡Cubanismo! sax player Yosvany Terry had already spent two summers teaching at Stanford when the group first toured the US; the only check on such activities came from the American side. Jimmy Carter tried to use music to loosen up relations with Cuba, with Irakere coming to New York and Dizzy Gillespie visiting Havana, but political pressure from Florida slammed that door shut during the Reagan and Bush Sr. years. Touring by Cuban musicians began in earnest during Clinton's second term, ground to a halt under Bush Jr., flourished with Obama, and shut down again under Trump. And all during these decades, of course, Cuban musicians were ubiquitous at European festivals and concert halls. Castro taxed their earnings but let them travel; if you're a baseball player or a boxer, though, the Revolution's manhood seems to have a stake in keeping you at home.

Cubans reacted to *Buena Vista*'s triumph with a mixture of sarcasm, fury, contempt, and a few cheers. It was as if the world had turned up its nose at Radiohead and Massive Attack, preferring to worship a group of Brit old-timers with banjos and accordions performing George Formby and Al Bowlly songs. Some of the outrage focused on the cover photo of a crumbling Havana street; the image seemed to flaunt the island's poverty, which most blamed on the US embargo, the very land that was buying millions of *Buena Vista* CDs. Cubans couldn't accuse the Florida exiles, though; they had as little interest as their island cousins. Latin radio ignored it completely; *Buena Vista* was strictly an NPR world music phenomenon, albeit one that reached almost as far into the mainstream as *Graceland*.

Groups playing a *Buena Vista*–ish repertoire had always been found in and around Havana's tourist hotels and hotspots, but now they multiplied like kudzu; *Buena Vista* helped propel a tourist boom, so there were now even more generous tippers to play for. Within Cuba, such music posed no challenge to timba, although Adalberto Álvarez y su Son and a few others explored an approach that, while slick and modern, did not ignore history. Álvarez's father once led a conjunto in Camaguey, and his son was a keen follower of New York salsa: "I decided . . . to do to their music what they were doing to ours." Adalberto's songs were more positive, idealistic, and patriotic than the general run of Cuban pop; his music was also highly danceable and for many years provided a counter-balance to Los Van Van.

Timba's strongest challengers, though, came from neighboring islands, particularly the Dominican Republic after its *merengue* was liberated by the death in 1961 of the country's dictator, Rafael Trujillo. Trujillo was obsessed with race and, despite merengue's Afro-Dominican origins, viewed this countryside dance as a bastion against "darker" musical forces. He declared it the Republic's national music but insisted on lyrics praising him and the anodyne virtues of the "homeland"; these were, needless to say, of little interest to outsiders. His assassin's bullet led to a flourishing of creativity that, with an assist from Dominican immigrants in New York, eventually turned merengue into an international success. At its best, it can be an appealingly jaunty and melodic music; for many, its strength lies in a deceptively simple beat and the sexy two-step embrace it inspires. As dancefloor moves that had won hearts and prizes at the Palladium began to seem like hard work, many Cubans also began to tire of timba's complexity. Despite the scarcity of foreign discs in Cuba and the rivalries among immigrant groups in America, in the late nineties you could hear merengue blasting from bars all across both Havana and New York. With the twenty-first century, a more formidable competitor for both timba and salsa arrived: *reggaeton*. Despite the name, this music has only the most tenuous of connections to Jamaica. Reggaeton evolved as a persecuted underground sound in Puerto Rico, with lyrics about ghetto life in the vein of timba and rap, backed by electronic beats with a Caribbean feel.

In a trend that mirrored how middle-class Whites took up blues in the early sixties as African Americans were moving on to soul, a generation of metrosexuals discovered Latin dancing just as Latinos began to lose interest. Salsa dance classes sprouted from New York to San Francisco and Paris to Tokyo, a small revolt against disco and techno, the same zeitgeist that inspired tango classes as well as jitterbug and swing evenings. A devotee of couple-dancing could visit any major city in the world and, on almost any night of the week, find a club dedicated to one of those styles. Such enthusiasts were rarely interested in the artists; it would have been unusual to find even the most fanatic Latin dancer with a big collection of Cuban or salsa classics, or even knowing the difference between Benny Moré and Tito Puente.

Spending $11 million on a Broadway musical about a Puerto Rican thug who killed two White boys in a Manhattan playground in 1959 seems a bit reckless, even if you are Paul Simon. I remember the tabloid headlines that zeroed in on the distinctive cloak that fingered Salvador Agron as the killer known as the "Capeman." For Simon, *Graceland* had proved a hard act to follow. Visits to Ghana and Brazil for the next album failed to provide the same magic as the journey to Johannesburg. How could they? Now, Simon's catholic musical taste led him back to home ground, the sounds of Latin New York that had spiced his boyhood in Queens.

The Capeman can be viewed as Simon's flawed, lost masterpiece. Impeccably researched, sensitive to its subject, crammed with great songs performed by top musical talent, including Marc Anthony and Rubén Blades, it was hobbled by English lyrics and a storyline that was never going to lure the busloads of suburban day-trippers essential to filling a huge Broadway theater eight times a week. I had the slightly surreal experience of seeing it in the company of David Calzado, the Charanga Habanera vocalist notorious for his "ripe mango" line, and Carlos Varela, Cuba's first rock star, a clever songwriter who had made similar waves with a song suggesting William Tell put the apple on his own head. Asked by a mutual friend to entertain them on their first night in New York, I blagged tickets to Simon's show and we ended up in a bar afterwards drinking until the early hours with Blades. I wished my rudimentary Spanish could have followed the nuances of a long, animated, and progressively inebriated discussion between two songwriters who attacked communist orthodoxy from within and a man considered the left-wing conscience of capitalist salsa. Varela and Calzado were dazzled by *The Capeman*'s staging and the quality of the music, but were, I think, as perplexed as the blue-rinse matrons from Westchester by the storyline.

Paul's musical closed after two months, with the cast album only released online many years later. The show's primary legacy may have been to inspire the Latin community to create their own stage musicals; I saw two excellent post-*Capeman* productions, albeit on equally depressing subjects: the short, sad, self-destructive lives of Héctor Lavoe and La Lupe. When subject matter becomes nostalgic and elegiac rather than forward-looking and provocative, it can be a sign that an era is ending.

In 2015, I went to a school gymnasium in East Harlem to see the Mambo All-Stars, veterans of Conjunto Libre, Orquesta Broadway, Tito Puente, and other anchors of the New York scene. It was a great but bittersweet night; the group was tremendous, the three vocalists (including one of my favorites, Frankie Vasquez) fronting a 'bone-heavy band. The dancing was also ace, but most couples were over fifty and some had difficulty navigating the steps to the raised dancefloor. The instant the music began, however, all were transformed into sylphs, moving gracefully and locked into the clave. On the way out, I shared an elevator with three couples who launched into an unprompted, misty-eyed reminiscence about the Palladium, the Golden Years of Latin dance and a lament about how their kids refuse to learn the steps.

A year later, I went to Cuba on one of Sublette's wonderful tours. A highlight was our two nights in Matanzas, "Rumba Central," the cradle of Abakuá culture. The first evening was spent in a sort of cabildo belonging to the Muñequitos de Matanzas, a rumba outfit that began performing in 1952, the first group to make a career of presenting authentic guaguancó onstage. Shut down by the Revolution, they regrouped in the seventies and began touring first Cuba, then the world. Los Muñequitos are a paragon of balanced authenticity, aware of the historic importance of what they do and brilliant at putting on a show while coming straight from the heart of a community and with none of Sierra Maestra's self-aware objectivity about them.

The next night was a street party organized by Rumba Timba, a group comprised of Muñequito offspring who perform guaguancó with a modernist, youthful edge, staying within the form while adding dashes of rap and timba. There may be other cultures besides Cuba, Brazil, and New Orleans where young musicians float effortlessly between up-to-the-minute modernity and undiluted traditions, but these three still set the standard. In so many communities, respect for the past is considered uncool. To many Cubans, trova and *son* can sound kitsch, while the more African sources remain vivid and alive. You can still find conga drums at the north end of Central Park on a summer Sunday in New York, but not the way you could in the sixties and seventies. The free market's inexorable assault on history has proved even more effective than *patón* Castro's strictures in diminishing a cultural legacy for a new generation.

Despite political barriers and the provincialism of timba, the flow of talent and influence out of Cuba has never really stopped for long. Refugees from Irakere made their mark on the international jazz scene in the 1980s and, with defection no longer necessary, Cuba's musical influence began once again to be felt across the globe. In the new century, videos of post-timba dance music, be it the slick "Bailando" or clips by X Alfonso, gained millions of YouTube hits. Groups from America and Europe traveled to Havana during the Obama years to shoot promos under the direction of young Cuban film-makers, while it is a rare international music festival these days that doesn't include a Cuban pianist. The exemplary Cuban musician of the twenty-first century could well be Yosvany Terry, who, in addition to his academic career at Stanford and Harvard, has also been, for many years, part of Eddie Palmieri's band in New York and whose own music has evolved to become a true synthesis of jazz and Afro-Cuban traditions. Or perhaps Dafnis Prieto, a drummer trained both at the National School of Music in Havana and in traditional Afro-Cuban rumbas who has won Grammy nominations as well as a MacArthur Genius Award and teaches young musicians at both NYU and in the belly of the beast at the University of Miami. Drum machines seem to be the only things capable of slowing the endless stream of polyrhythms from Cuba into the current of the world's music. It began in the sixteenth century, when the *zaraband* arrived in Seville, and has carried on for half a millennium.

In Cuba before and after World War One and in America in the 1930s, the words "jungle" and "primitive" were bandied about by those attempting to belittle Afro-Cuban music, pointing to the hand-struck drums as evidence. But the way Cuban musicians blended rhythms of disparate African lands, then invaded Spanish and French forms, creating music that swept the globe, is surely one of mankind's most elaborate and sophisticated cultural accomplishments.

III
Catch a Fire

Late one hot Saturday afternoon in 1958, three White teenagers, two boys and a girl, lay sprawled on the sand next to their small boat, its outboard motor beached and lifeless. Having left the dock in Kingston, Jamaica, without much water or fuel and been pushed far down the coast by tides and wind, they were hungry, thirsty, and exhausted—and now the sun was setting. At dawn, after a sleepless, mosquito-plagued night, the boy who had borrowed the boat (and gotten them into this mess) set out along the sandbar, separated from the coastal road by miles of marsh and mangrove swamp. After hours trudging through soft sand, he saw a fisherman's shack and a Black man with long matted hair peering out at him. Like every respectable Jamaican, Chris Blackwell had been taught to fear and avoid the strange tribe of outcasts who called themselves "Rastafarians," but thirst overcame trepidation and he hesitantly asked for some water. After explaining what had happened, he lay down and quickly fell fast asleep. When he awoke, it was dark and he was surrounded by Rastas. They fed him roast fish and told him the others had been towed safely back to port.

Thus did Blackwell come by his affection and respect for those who revere Ras Tafari, then Emperor of Ethiopia. When he started his first enterprise, a scooter-rental business, he was happy to rent to "dreads," and they always settled their accounts promptly. Fourteen years after that Sunday morning, when long, matted hair was still a startling sight, three Rastas turned up at his Island Records office in London. Blackwell knew their music; he welcomed them, chatted about the latest news from Kingston, listened to their ideas, and wrote out a check for £4,000, enough to finance reggae music's first album project. He trusted them to deliver on budget, and they did. Their names were Bunny Livingston, Peter Tosh, and Bob Marley, and the relationship between the world and Jamaican music would never again be the same.

Jamaica's character was formed in 1655. A marauding English fleet, having sized up Cuba and decided it was too well defended, veered south and captured this island, one-tenth the size of its neighbor. Spanish planters were invited to stay on, but most opted to leave. On their way out, as a thrust of the middle finger, they released all their slaves.

The northwestern and northeastern corners of Jamaica are covered in beautiful rugged hills and deep valleys, ideal for seclusion and ambush; most of the freed Africans settled there and over the years these remote communities attracted a steady trickle of runaways. For three centuries, the British struggled to assert control, but were never entirely successful. These "maroons" (from the Spanish *cimarron*, which was in turn borrowed from the Arawak *simarabo*, meaning "runaway") had earned a reputation as deadly shots; British soldiers were never eager to comb the bush for them. To this day, communities in Cockpit country around Montego Bay refuse to accept "outside" policemen. Tales, both true and mythic, of the "man in the hills" remain alive in story and song; heroes of Black resistance such as Cudjoe, Nanny, and Paul Bogle are commemorated with statues and plaques.

Many of the British who took the Spaniards' place were little more than pirates; over the decades they were joined by gamblers and chancers, often younger sons desperate to make from sugar the kind of money their siblings had inherited or married. Unlike the French in Haiti or the Spanish in Cuba, the British made little effort to transplant European culture: no opera houses and few music ensembles where slaves could learn European forms and instruments. Visitors to the island were often shocked by how the normal colonial balance seemed to have skewed, with owners and their wives more affected by African ways than vice versa.

In the eighteenth and nineteenth centuries, Britain's treatment of its own soldiers, sailors, workers, and prisoners was often crude and brutal; the punishments devised for its slaves in the West Indies were far worse, often grotesque and inhuman. By 1860, the 400,000 slaves imported over the centuries to what became the United States had grown into an African-American population of four million; of the two million captives brought to the British Caribbean, only 670,000 remained to be freed in the 1838 Act of Abolition. Jamaican slaves enjoyed few of the privileges granted to Cuban chattel; with nothing resembling the larger island's cabildos, Akan traditions from the Gold Coast of West Africa survived in curious and eccentric ways around the sugar plantations and up in Maroon country. Drums were banned wherever the British were in control, but they were never silent in the hills.

After Abolition, the sugar industry collapsed; few freed Jamaicans were interested in carrying on the back-breaking work of cutting cane. Desperate landowners contracted Yorùbá workers from West Africa, but many of these quickly abandoned the plantations and headed off into the bush. Chinese, Indians, and even Germans were also tried, without much success. Economic collapse was averted thanks to a plant that arrived from Bengal along with the indentured workers: hemp. London encouraged its cultivation and, for a time, Jamaica vied with Russia as a leading supplier of raw material for rope. Locals, meanwhile, adopted the Bengali word for the plant's smokeable buds and leaves: *ganja*.

The biggest singing star Jamaica ever produced isn't Bob Marley, it's Harry Belafonte. There are many ways to mark how the world changed from the 1950s to the 1970s, but the shift of the spotlight from Harry to Bob ranks among the most telling.

Belafonte always wanted to be an actor. Born in New York to a Jamaican mother, he spent much of his childhood in Kingston with his maternal grandmother but never manifested much interest in the island's culture. He wasn't that keen on singing, either, but found he could make enough money performing in cabarets and coffeehouses to fund acting lessons. He tried singing jazz (backed on one occasion by Charlie Parker and Miles Davis), then pop, before settling on the sort of folk music that flourished around left-wing political movements in New York. His sweet, strong voice, gentle Caribbean accent, and great looks got him a record deal, and in 1953 he released a single of the song that got the biggest reaction in the clubs, a calypso about "Matilda" who *"take me money and run Venezuela."*

Calypso hadn't hit America as hard as the mambo, but by the early fifties it was firmly established as an exotic novelty popular with sophisticated East Coast audiences. A comedian named Morey Amsterdam kicked it off after visiting the music's home island of Trinidad to entertain US troops during World War Two. Trinidad was a key source of petroleum and inventive locals scavenged the oil barrels, cutting them into differing depths, then heating and tempering the lids to create the steel drums which, assembled into orchestras, continue to dazzle crowds at carnival parades in Trinidad, England, and Brooklyn. The GIs themselves—"over-paid, over-sexed, and over here," as the British complained—provided fertile subject matter for the calypsonians, whose witty, intricate songs had been mocking authority at carnival time since the early nineteenth century. Amsterdam particularly liked one record, brought it home, fiddled a bit with the lyrics, registered himself as composer, and gave a lead sheet to his friends the Andrews Sisters.

The trio worked out a hurried harmony the night before a session and tried recording it when the producer said they had time for one more take. Haste needn't always make waste; "Rum and Coca Cola" became the biggest hit of the Andrews Sisters' career, spending ten weeks at #1 in 1945. The song's original author, Lord Invader, lived a lot closer to New York than Solomon Linda and had way more business savvy. The famous litigator Louis Nizer took it on and won Invader a then-huge $150,000 settlement for copyright infringement.

In 1956, Belafonte released an LP entitled *Calypso*, which contained very few actual calypsos. Most of the songs were Caribbean-flavored ditties composed by a Barbadian American named Irving Burgie who assumed a calypso-esque honorific—"Lord Burgess"—for his work with Belafonte. The singer's Jamaican origins might have remained a footnote in his biography were it not for side A, track one, the smash hit that established him as a star of the highest magnitude. Through his political activities, Harry knew an eccentric but brilliant audio innovator named Tony Schwartz, who pioneered the use of authentic sounds and the voices of ordinary people in advertising. Schwartz was also intrigued by the musical traditions of immigrant New Yorkers. One day he recorded a Jamaican cashier at Macy's department store singing a chant from the docks of her native Kingston: "*Day-o . . . daylight come and me wan' go home.*" Schwartz played the tape to some left-wing friends and the rest is history.

It seems appropriate that this most famous of all Jamaican folk songs was collected in New York, since the island's musical heritage is only sparsely documented. Unlike those from Trinidad, Cuba, or even Martinique, no Jamaican singers were brought to New York's studios during the recording boom of the late 1920s, nor did the island then have a music industry of its own. Visitors to its palm-fringed beaches were often serenaded by groups playing mento, a Jamaican variant of calypso, but the tourist board never succeeded in making this cheerful, melodic music central to the island's image the way calypso was to Trinidad's.

Ethnographers documented some "ring dances" that merged African traditions with English country dancing, and it was noted that Jamaican congregations particularly loved hymns composed by the Methodist Ira David Sankey. More recent research has shown that the culture of the hills is full of African retentions and was a key source for much of the island's musical energy; accounts from 1900 show Kingston residents complaining about the handclaps, tambourines, and exuberant singing of newly arrived "country folk." Tourists were occasionally treated to a performance of Burru drumming, a descendant of Akan traditions preserved in Maroon communities. To outsiders, Jamaica's image remained that of a sunny tropical isle, with bare-chested guys dancing under the limbo bar, rum cocktails served by smiling English-speaking "natives," and kids diving for coins thrown from the decks of cruise ships. "The Banana Boat Song" helped Jamaica blend in with the rest of Belafonte's Caribbean, one more "Island in the Sun."

⌒

But, as the British Colonial Office discovered when it tried to force the island into independence as part of a "West Indies federation," Jamaica was different. Twelve hundred miles west of the other British islands, larger than Trinidad and more populous, Jamaica had a longer and more brutal history, was far more African, and, lacking Trinidad's oil wells, much poorer. By the 1940s, the island's search for an economic engine had settled on bauxite, the raw material from which aluminum is forged. There was plenty of this high-grade dirt near the surface, but not enough electricity on the island to power a refinery, so raw bauxite was cheaply exported to be forged profitably into metal in British and Canadian mills. Digging up the earth also destroyed great stretches of tillable soil, driving displaced farmers to Kingston to look for work. The result was a certain amount of wealth for an elite and ever-increasing poverty for the rest.

The bauxite effect combined with 1951's Hurricane Charlie to change the face of Kingston; as the middle class moved out to the suburbs, the government rebuilt the devastated city by constructing "yards," where many families were housed around a central court. Another initiative by the colonial administration was to grant "rediffusion" licenses, allowing private companies to place loudspeakers in town squares and government yards, relaying a steady stream of bland music, news, talk, and advertising across the island.

Jamaicans took to the technology but preferred choosing their own music; radio ownership boomed and the island's location at the western end of the Caribbean made it easy to tune in US "clear channel" stations after dark. The poor state of the economy also drove many to look for seasonal work in Florida; travel and radio combined to broaden Jamaicans' musical horizons. If there had once been a superficial congruence between the tuneful, French- and Spanish-inflected music of Trinidad and that of Jamaica, the steady flow of rhythm and blues and jazz over radio waves and in the grooves of 78s and 45s turned Jamaica in a different direction.

> It seem like to be a teenager in Jamaica during that era was the best thing on earth.
>
> —Derrick Harriott, singer

Those rediffusion broadcasts sparked an idea that transformed Jamaican music. As the left-behind poor established themselves across much of central Kingston, the notion of blasting the sorts of music heard on US radio—Wynonie Harris, Jimmy Reed, Billy Eckstine, Louis Jordan, Fats Domino, Johnny Ace, and the like—over loudspeakers in open spaces known as "lawns" resulted in a "sound system" boom. Descriptions of these 1950s Kingston dances invoke the scent of bougainvillea mixing with ganja smoke under the moon while a DJ gauged the balance between energy and romance in his choice of discs. As the evening progressed, he would move from the wild to the smooth as boys began holding girls closer, "*greasin' da crease*" to a Jesse Belvin ballad. As Lloyd Bradley puts it in *Bass Culture*, the sound systems served as "a lively dating agency, a fashion show, an information exchange, a street status parade ground, a political forum [and] a centre of commerce," while also providing a community bulletin board, with DJs announcing who was out of jail or back from England. These were family affairs; some remember dancing as teenagers with their grandparents while stalls dished up curried goat, callaloo and salt fish, fruit juice and beer. Under the noses of the authorities, a vividly "Black" urban culture was emerging on an island whose self-image had been dominated by Whites and light-skinned Blacks and their very different vision of what Jamaica was supposed to look like as it moved towards independence.

Two factors dominated the competition between rival sound-system operators: volume and exclusivity. An early sign of the sonic wizardry that would later distinguish Jamaican record production was how Kingston sound mavens would wire higher and higher stacks of speakers to ever more powerful amplifiers, with the combined objective of giving patrons a visceral bass-heavy experience while drowning out smaller fry nearby. Dancers voted with their feet for systems that played great records they couldn't hear on the radio; by scratching off the labels, disc jockeys tried to keep competitors from discovering the artists and titles of tracks that got crowds moving. Seasonal workers often headed to Florida with shopping lists and could seriously augment their fruit-harvesting wages if they came back with a suitcase full of coveted discs. Visiting American sailors would barter records for cigars, rum, ganja, and women.

With Jamaican nights so hot and humid, high-energy rock 'n' rollers like Little Richard and Jerry Lee Lewis were never much of a factor; islanders preferred the late-forties/early-fifties jump blues that blurred the line between rhythm and blues and jazz, especially those coming from New Orleans or Memphis. "Bloodshot Eyes" by Wynonie Harris and "Later for the Gator," an instrumental by Willis "Gator Tail" Jackson, endured as totemic platters across the decade. When Jamaica began making its own records, sound-system tastes would be the guide.

An entrepreneur who generates stacks of cash in a poor neighborhood will require toughness and muscle to survive. Another truism is that for any music venue, alcohol is the key profit center. It should come as no surprise, therefore, that the giant among early sound-system operators was an ex-cop who owned a liquor store. Arthur Reid had been a corrupt and widely hated police sergeant; when his wife won the lottery, he retired from the force and opened Treasure Isle Liquors. The Reids sponsored the first rhythm and blues show on Jamaican radio, and the reaction was so enthusiastic that Arthur moved easily into running a sound system.

Styling himself "Duke," Reid would arrive wearing ten gold rings and a crown, with a bandolier of bullets across his chest, firing a shotgun into the air and sometimes juggling a hand grenade. His henchmen were known to smash rivals' speakers and turntables and threaten their patrons; it could be said that Duke Reid's with-me-or-against-me tactics, as they spilled over into post-Independence politics, established a violent pattern that poisons Kingston to this day. He did, however, have good musical taste and the cash to ensure a steady supply of the latest American records.

Clement Dodd's parents also ran a liquor store and were friends with Reid's wife. The young jazz buff took a few turns spinning discs at Duke's shows and earned some money bringing records and sound equipment back from Florida. Once he had amassed his own stack of tracks, Dodd became Reid's biggest rival, using a nickname derived from youthful cricketing exploits: "Sir Coxsone." His friend Blackie would invent dance steps and the two of them drew cheering crowds demonstrating moves that were emulated across Kingston.

Needing enforcers to protect his shows from Reid, Coxsone hired a young thug named Buster Campbell, who turned out to have extraordinarily sharp ears; eavesdropping on other systems, Buster could identify artists and often figure out the titles of their "secret weapon" 45s and 78s. Dodd later added another sidekick, Lee Perry, to run satellite systems for him out at the beaches.

As White American teenagers jumped on the rhythm and blues bandwagon in the mid-fifties, transforming it into rock 'n' roll, crowd-pleasing platters grew harder to find. The time had come for Jamaicans to make their own. Duke Reid, Coxsone Dodd, "Prince" Buster Campbell, and Lee "Scratch" Perry all became pioneering record producers, laying the cornerstones for a style of music with which this small island would conquer the world.

In 1960, when The Platters performed in Kingston, the start of their set was disrupted by a section of the audience demanding an encore by the opening act, a Memphis singer and pianist named Rosco Gordon. Gordon was embarrassed and puzzled by the attention, as he had never released any records in Jamaica and the clamor wasn't doing his relationship with The Platters much good. Keen students of Jamaican rhythms will sympathize with the audience's persistence; though Gordon was never a big seller, many of his tracks were Kingston sound-system favorites and are central to the history of the "skank," the off-beat pulse that lies at the heart of reggae's parent, ska (pronounced "skya" in one syllable).

The tributary streams that produced the flood of ska recordings in the early 1960s probably originated with a Lebanese-Jamaican jukebox operator's trip to Florida a decade earlier. Crossing a Miami street, Ken Khouri overheard two men haggling over a disc-cutting machine; on impulse, he trumped the discussion by pulling out the asking price in cash. Back in Kingston, he offered recording services straight to disc, Jamaica's first studio. Another Lebanese, a patrician Harvard anthropology graduate named Edward Seaga, who had done his dissertation on the music of Pocomania churches in Jamaica's hill country, started an operation called West Indies Records Ltd (WIRL). Each recorded a few mento sessions, while Khouri licensed some American pop tracks and imported record-pressing equipment. A mid-fifties survey determined that the biggest seller on the island was the pop-operatic tenor Mario Lanza.

In 1955, a radio announcer named Vere Johns decided Kingston was ready for the kind of talent contests he had organized during his time in the US back in the thirties. Audiences crowded downtown theaters to cheer as their friends and neighbors covered American favorites; the contests grew so popular that RJR radio began broadcasting them live. Some winners—as well as a few losers—immortalized their performances at Khouri's primitive studio. (Johns' contest winners would eventually include Desmond Dekker, The Wailers, Alton Ellis, Bob Andy, Jackie Edwards, and Laurel Aitken).

Prince Buster, by now operating his own sound system, was the first to play these acetates; crowds were amazed and delighted to hear their own accents and cadences blasting from Buster's gigantic stack of speakers. These discs truly were "exclusive"; only one copy existed and it would become unplayable after a couple of dozen spins. Coxsone began following Buster's example, but Duke Reid resisted, viewing local recordings as a silly fad. Women in particular seemed to love the new sounds; Reid's crowd of loyal rhythm and blues fans grew so male-heavy that his shows became known as "bull parties."

One day, a hustler on a motor scooter approached Coxsone wanting to buy 200 copies of a "soft-wax" track played at his dance the night before. Dodd was nonplussed: what did this guy want with 200 discs? The recording bore no resemblance to the type of music sold in the island's few record shops, but the buyer had the cash, so, using the acetate as a "master lacquer" (the first step in manufacturing vinyl), Dodd placed an order with Khouri. The salesman collected the discs a few mornings later and by lunchtime he was back for more. Jamaica suddenly found itself with a domestic record industry.

Anthologies of reggae's roots often lead off with Seaga's 1958 production "Oh Manny Oh" by Higgs and Wilson. It's a crude but effective track, with pounding piano triplets and doo-wop harmony; only the quirky flatness of the melody and the singers' accents (plus the raw production) give it away as not being American. This is often followed by an early Chris Blackwell effort, "Boogie in My Bones" by Laurel Aitken. Unlike most ska vocalists, Aitken was a well-established performer of mento, Latin, and pop; when he turned up at WIRL studio, he was startled to find a backing band consisting of four White Australians. At least he had brought along a Jamaican sax player for the solo.

"Boogie" was a hit, introducing both Blackwell's magic commercial touch and, lurking in the grooves, Rosco Gordon's influence. "Boogie" isn't a cover of a Gordon song, but it might as well be. A lengthy article in *Oxford American* magazine by John Jeremiah Sullivan traces the genesis of the skank; he identifies Earl Hooker's "Texas shuffle" guitar strokes, which put equal weight on the off-beats, as a key source, as well as a disc that Coxsone brought back from a Florida buying trip, "San Diego Bounce" by Harold Land, which converts left-hand boogie-woogie piano figures into horn riffs. (In the 1920s, Duke Ellington and the lesser-known bandleader Richard M. Jones both used a similar off-beat emphasis in their arrangements for "The Mooche" and "African Hunch" to signal *primitive!*)

For Sullivan, Gordon is a key figure; he bestowed a series of classic tracks on Kingston sound-system operators in the early fifties before vanishing, only to reappear in 1960 with The Platters. You can hear how those early Gordon sides would fit the sound-system aesthetic, serving as a conduit for Professor Longhair's and Fats Domino's New Orleans–style Afro-Cuban syncopations, filtered through a more straightforward Memphis approach. All three pianists enunciate the off-beats in a 2/4 bar (one-*and*-two-*and*) with the right hand, but Sullivan reveals that Gordon always played standing up (a role model for Little Richard and Jerry Lee Lewis, perhaps?), which, he suggests, led him to lean just that little bit harder on the right hand.

A band of Australians, though, can't provide evidence of a Jamaican cultural shift, and the backing of "Boogie" sticks pretty close to a straightforward Rosco feel. Following Blackwell's success, Coxsone entered the fray with "Easy Snappin" by Theophilus Beckford. Throughout the track, Beckford's right-hand chords are louder than the left, giving it the off-center feel that came to define ska. What makes ska sound foreign to those raised on African-American rhythms is the way its strong second and fourth beats are played absolutely in time, while in American boogie and bounce those notes get shifted ever so slightly later to become syncopated lead-ins to the third and first. The difference is microscopic but the effect is immense. The imbalance in "Snappin" could, to my ears, stem at least partly from microphone placement, but be that as it may, the great ship of Jamaican music had now been nudged slightly off its original rhythmic bearings towards Memphis and New Orleans. Just as an alteration of one degree will, over a vast ocean, divert a vessel thousands of miles from its original destination, so it was with Jamaican music.

Prince Buster had fallen out with Coxsone and never much cared for White people. Determined to improve on "Boogie" and "Snappin," his first session as a producer added another element to ska's basic ingredients. When Buster set up his own sound system, he located it far from the city center, out in Salt Lane, near the Wareika Hills Rasta community. He would later explain that he wanted to test himself at the bottom rung of society, the toughest of audiences; if it worked there, word would spread upwards. Buster often invited Count Ossie's Nyabinghi drummers from the Wareika camp to entertain the sound-system crowds during breaks; when he turned up for his first session at Duke Reid's new studio with Count Ossie's team in tow, the Rasta-averse Reid angrily canceled the booking. Buster was forced to rig up a makeshift studio around the corner; the resulting single by the Folkes Brothers, "Oh Carolina," sounds as if it was recorded in a shack, but that didn't stop it becoming a massive hit. The first time he played it at a dance, Buster got his revenge; crowds flocked to the sound of the drums in "Oh Carolina," draining Reid's nearby show of customers.

Nyabinghi drums are struck with an open hand, and though usually played in groups of three different-sized instruments, they don't mesh like the intricate gears of Cuban music. The drums themselves have a stark, dry sound; patterns are based on the Burru and Kumina styles of the Maroon hills, heavily syncopated and sparse. When Buster added them to piano, bass, and a bit of barely audible guitar, this Akan legacy from the slave markets of the Gold Coast joined the currents of Rosco Gordon's right hand, the banjo off-beats of mento, the Latin influence blowing in from nearby Cuba, Buster's beloved carnival march rhythm, the "two and four" handclaps on "Bloodshot Eyes" and "Later for the Gator," and Jamaicans' inherent cranky individuality. The ska blueprint was in place.

༄

There are differing stories about the term's origin. Buster claimed it came from his bellowed "*Scatter!*" aimed at his sound-system competitors, while Coxsone has described asking Ernest Ranglin to create a novelty dance step, with the name emerging as he urged the guitarist to play more of that "mm-ska-mm-ska" feel. Ranglin, a well-schooled musician who had been working for years with dance bands and jazz trios on the island, brought a clarity of attack and rhythmic precision to sessions as the sound of electric guitar up-strokes began drowning out piano vamps. The word's sibilant edge certainly has a closer onomatopoeic connection to steel strings than to ivory keys.

We look back on ska as the birth cry of one of the world's great musical forms, but at the time they were just trying to re-create the sounds of early-fifties American jump blues. To do that they needed horns; that excellent musicians were readily available was down to two heroic figures in this story, Eric Dean and Sister Mary Ignatius Davies.

Since the 1930s, hotels and resorts had employed dance bands playing Latin, swing, and calypso. Dean led the island's top orchestra, where he nourished a mother lode of young players eager to join the professional ranks. Many were drawn from the delinquents, orphans, and strays who had found their way to the Alpha Boys Home, where Sister Mary spotted and developed musical talent. Alpha Boys had, from the nineteenth century, been known for its excellent brass band, and since her arrival in the 1920s, Sister Mary had been matching talented youths with good quality instruments and the best instruction available. She amassed a large collection of jazz and classical records, which she would spin for her boys like a DJ. Sister Mary was also known to teach boxing and cricket and occasionally joined the Alpha Boys band on saxophone.

Some Alpha graduates would emigrate to theoretically hipper pastures, including Joe Harriott to London and Harold McNair to New York, but for most, playing in one of Dean's bands—he often had three or four performing around the island—was how they learned their trade. Between Sister Mary's disciplined regime and Dean's willingness to hire inexperienced youths, Kingston producers were able to choose from a pool of well-schooled players on every horn as well as bass, drums, keyboards, and guitar.

Over these early years, one group of musicians became "go-to" regulars. These included the legendary trombonist Don Drummond, trumpeter Baba Brooks, sax players Tommy McCook and Roland Alphonso, guitarist Jah Jerry Haynes, Lloyd Brevett on bass, and drummer Lloyd Knibb. Jazz fan Coxsone suggested they record an instrumental; in that post-Sputnik era the first proposal for a name was "The Satellites," but McCook objected: "It's ska we play." Thus was launched the Jamaican band that is still in orbit today—The Skatalites.

> [Y]ou can hear ska unfurl as another tendril out of the blues, the great mother root. It's as tidy a demonstration as I know of the fact . . . that black popular music in the twentieth century can't be comprehended except as a phenomenon of . . . the Atlantic world. In this case the old

West Indian world, of which Tennessee lay at the northern fringe... We gave Jamaica blues. Jamaica gave us ska. Jamaica gave us dub, we gave back hip-hop. It's been happening for four hundred years.

—John Jeremiah Sullivan

Almost overnight, music became a Kingston obsession; youths (mostly male) could be spotted on park benches and street corners, harmonizing and getting songs ready to audition. Subject matter ranged from Hollywood movies to sports to politics to *obeah* (Afro-Caribbean religion) to biblical quotations. Plus, of course, love. In Duke Reid's liquor store, aspiring singers had to compete with a speaker relaying sounds from the studio above the shop; when Reid heard something he didn't like, he would rush up the stairs cursing and shouting instructions then reclaim his seat behind the counter, selling booze and auditioning talent.

Contracts were verbal or rudimentary and royalties seldom paid, so singers would go from studio to studio and producer to producer in search of better deals. Seaga and Blackwell annoyed their rivals by paying fairly and treating artists with respect, but by 1962, Blackwell had moved to London, while Seaga got elected to Parliament and sold his studio, eventually becoming prime minister in the 1980s.

Recording standards evolved from acetates that were little better than "record-your-own-voice" fairground souvenirs to the ska, rocksteady, reggae, and dub classics that have influenced record production the world over. It was a magical formula: unselfconscious amateur singers and songwriters backed by a squadron of brilliant professionals led by the Alpha Boys alumni. Even the island's early attempts at mimicking American recordings sound, in retrospect, startlingly successful. The four sound-system pioneers established their own studios, upgraded their equipment and launched labels. Chinese-Jamaican Leslie Kong joined their ranks after being approached in Beverley's, his combination ice-cream parlor and record store, by then-unknown Jimmy Cliff with an idea for a song promoting the shop.

The years immediately preceding and following Independence in 1962 were full of great records (more releases per capita than any country in the world), with producers and singers united in an optimism that triggered a blossoming of creativity. (Disappointment, defiance, and delusion can also provide fertile ground for innovation, as later years would prove.) The ska surge peaked in 1964, but not before making two bold forays into the wider world. The first validated Chris Blackwell's decision to settle in London, initially acting as distributor of Jamaican-pressed 45s, then founding Island Records and licensing Jamaican tracks for British release. Island's market—which Blackwell often serviced himself with boxes of 45s in the back of his Mini—was in Brixton and along the Harrow Road in London, in Birmingham's Handsworth, Manchester's Moss Side, and Liverpool's Toxteth, communities where the *Windrush* generation had settled. Few White people, in the early years, took much notice.

Although extremely good at it, Blackwell has never been content to simply package and promote others' productions. It was time, he decided, to import more than just sounds, so he flew two Jamaican talents to London in order to launch them onto a bigger stage. He had always admired Ernest Ranglin's playing; the first Island Records production had been an LP of Ranglin's jazz trio. Chris cajoled Pete King, manager of Ronnie Scott's Jazz Club, into letting the guitarist play a set; King was so impressed that Ranglin spent a month there as an opening act and jamming with visiting American greats.

Chris also brought to London the teenage winner of one of Vere Johns's contests, a winsome sixteen-year-old named Millie Small, organizing elocution lessons for her as well as singing tuition and grooming sessions. Blackwell has devoted much of his life to promoting Jamaica and its talents, but even he wasn't prepared for the spectacular success of his first stab at producing ska in Britain. Adding Ranglin to a group of London session musicians, he spent an afternoon recording Millie's cover of an obscure fifties American track. Hearing the original "My Boy Lollypop" is a bit like stumbling on the Rosetta Stone; if there was ever a record that proves the link between the Memphis shuffle and ska, this is it. The fact that it was recorded in 1956, when ska was little more than a gleam in Buster Campbell's angry eye, begs more questions than it answers. The singer was a White teenager from Brooklyn named Barbie Gaye, whose only experience of "island life" was the boardwalk at Coney. A mobbed-up hustler named "Corky" Vastola heard Gaye singing on a street corner and took her to the notorious Roulette Records boss Morris Levy, who suggested "My Boy Lollypop," a song he had just bought off a member of The Cadillacs doo-wop group. At the session, a veteran team of New York players asked Barbie to sing them the song a cappella; all agreed that it needed a shuffle backing, a kind of "Rosco Gordon" feel. The result is a startlingly ska-like prototype of Millie's hit.

Millie's version was, as you know, a worldwide smash. Blackwell sensed it the minute they'd finished recording. He decided that his fledgling label couldn't bear such responsibility, so he licensed it to Philips, who pushed it into the Top Five on both sides of the Atlantic. Pepsi-Cola came on board to sponsor a world tour and Millie appeared everywhere from *American Bandstand* to Nigerian football stadiums. Chris was chastened by how success alienated Small from her impoverished family and friends back in Kingston, but despite her status as a "one-hit wonder," Small seems to have parlayed her moment of fame into a well-traveled and contented life, before her death in 2020.

As "Lollipop" was climbing the charts, Edward Seaga launched another front in the Jamaican music offensive. Now a government minister, Seaga decided ska was the way to promote the new nation's pavilion at the 1964 New York World's Fair. There is film of one of the shows, with Jimmy Cliff and Toots and the Maytals sounding a bit tame backed by Byron Lee's Dragonaires. The Chinese-Jamaican Lee was generally well liked, known to post bail for musicians, lend them money, and, after turning Seaga's WIRL into Dynamic Sounds, give them studio time on credit. But the sort of calypso-flavored ska-lite his band played still causes bitterness when musicians recall Jamaica's New York moment and how The Skatalites were passed over. Seaga also took flak from respectable countrymen horrified at his promotion of this "crude" music. The dancefloor was filled for the shoot with neatly dressed teenagers executing moves based on Blackie's and Coxsone's steps; Seaga and Lee believed those arms-pumping-on-the-off-beat moves could lead to ska succeeding the Twist as a dance craze, and their honored guest, Arthur Murray, seemed to agree. Perhaps if America had not lost its innocence with the Kennedy assassination and if its musical tastes weren't being scrambled by The Beatles, ska might have stood a chance.

But the main reason ska never rivaled bauxite as an export was that Jamaica itself was changing as dramatically as post-JFK America and post-Profumo Britain. Unlike those societies, however, the island's problem was not "young people with too much money and freedom." Quite the contrary.

Post-Independence optimism didn't last. The year 1964 began with the cheery "Lollipop" and ended in tragedy. A dancer named Margarita Mahfood had provided a footnote in Jamaican musical history by forcing a reluctant Vere Johns to let her bring Count Ossie's drummers onstage as her backing group. In 1963, Mahfood embarked on a tempestuous relationship with trombonist Don Drummond, by general consensus the island's most brilliant musician. An Alpha Boys graduate, Drummond captivated bandleaders, producers, fellow musicians, and audiences from the first moment they heard him; visiting jazzmen such as George Shearing were certain he could have succeeded on the world stage. But he was an unstable character who had more than once checked himself into a psychiatric hospital. On New Year's Eve 1964, Drummond stabbed Mahfood to death. Sent to a secure institution where he would eventually commit suicide, Drummond left a legacy of great Skatalites tracks as well as contributions to dozens of classic recordings.

The Drummond case was the tip of a violent tropical iceberg; records had begun to claim their role in Jamaican culture as chronicles and harbingers, and more and more songs were about "rude boys" and hard times. Ska and the distribution system Blackwell had helped set up before departing for London were part of the reason; the music spoke to youth across the island and many couldn't resist the lure of the capital and its sound systems. But jobs there were few and, if you couldn't sing and weren't a star on the cricket pitch, crime often seemed the only option.

For the anniversary of Independence on August 6, 1965, the government organized a parade through downtown Kingston. Three years earlier, the historic moment had been celebrated with choral and orchestral concerts, ballet performances, and recitations of inspirational verse. This time, ska ruled and the middle classes stayed away, put off by the music and by fears of violence. To everyone's relief, the celebration passed without trouble; many put the benign atmosphere down to the central float where The Skatalites performed, while Duke Reid's and Prince Buster's sound-system trucks provided the parade's head and tail. The vibe may have been joyful, but, as many observed, it was strictly a "sufferah's jamboree." Buster had the hottest record of the day, a new track called "Jail House" by the young Wailers, with a chorus that boasted *"we gonna rule this land."*

> The beginnings of ska expressed the exuberance of the people around the time of independence . . . [then] a sense of dread of the future . . . set in . . . [T]here was a tension in the bass instead of the free-walking bass style. This disillusionment was the beginning of the music being slowed down to rock steady.
>
> —Linton Kwesi Johnson

The shift from ska to rocksteady had numerous causes, symptoms, and signposts. Hopeton Lewis asking the studio band to cut the beat right down on "Take It Easy" is regarded as one turning point; "rudies" had, after all, been dancing in half-time for years, refusing to get caught up in the ebullience of the early sixties or to spoil their shirts with sweat (the summer of 1966 being the hottest within memory). The recording process was changing; studios now had two- or four-track recorders, with Buster leading the way in giving singers a bigger say in arrangements, while Coxsone was the first to welcome spliff-rolling on the premises. Horns declined and vocal harmonies flourished as more singers combined themselves into groups. Stateside rhythm and blues, at long last, was again coming up with the kind of cool sounds Jamaicans could relate to: Curtis Mayfield and The Impressions, The Temptations, Johnnie Taylor—anything with a high tenor or falsetto lead and an unhurried rhythm. America's influence, however, remained only moderate; Jamaicans were no longer trying to replicate its sounds, they were becoming ever more defiantly themselves.

It seems a reasonably safe bet that ganja had something to do with the revelation that you could emphasize a beat by not playing it, which is what happened to the "one." This drum pattern became known as the "one-drop," a curious echo of a British colonial-era expression indicating how a single "drop" of African blood meant you were "Black." (It would make equal sense, of course, that one "drop" of Anglo-Saxon blood would render you "White.")

Bass players began emulating Cuban dancers by starting their oblique runs "on the two," while percussionists and guitarists interacted like Burru drummers, often over a bed of organ chords rather than the pointed interventions of a piano. The single-note trills that became a hallmark of reggae guitar arrived in the wrists of Nerlynn "Lynn" Tait, who was emulating the treble rolls of steel pans from his native Trinidad. Mixes shifted, with vocals sung softer and closer to the microphone, horns pushed back (when not eliminated by cost-cutting producers), and bass and drum moved up almost level with the voice.

When Duke Reid asked Alton Ellis for a novelty dance song, Ellis responded with "Let's Do the Rock Steady," inspired, as sound-system regulars knew, by how "Busby" and his gang, always on guard against ratchet-knife attacks by rivals, would sway to the music without lifting their feet. Busby enjoyed his notoriety; he asked Derrick Morgan to make a song about him, and Morgan complied with "Rudie Don't Fear." Youths in the crowd would shout and smash bottles when the song reached the line *strong like lion, we are iron*," and Busby liked it so much he would make the DJ drop the needle on that line again and again. Others were not so happy; Busby was killed soon after the record's release. Into the gangster vacuum came "Johnny Buzz" (in homage to the departed Busby), who inspired The Slickers' rocksteady classic "Johnny Too Bad," immortalized on the soundtrack of *The Harder They Come*.

Dodd, Reid, Kong, and the others were, ultimately, creatures of the market, so when rudie songs became hits, more followed. When Rasta lyrics sold (despite a radio ban on such references), that also started a trend, though very reluctantly; these producers had no enthusiasm for "ghettoizing" the music. Buster was different; he led the way with Rasta-oriented lyrics, patois phrases, and "yard" references because he believed in creating a true "people's music," and his success forced the others to follow. Ska's tempo was an ideal foundation for the church-derived melodies and gospel phrasing of tracks such as The Maytals' "Six and Seven Books" and "Carry Go Bring Come" by Justin Hines; rocksteady was more meditative, like the Burru drum sessions in the Wareika Hills. Rasta influence was audibly growing when international politics intervened to speed things up. Not the tempo, of course, but the pace of change.

The next big date in the island's historical calendar is April 21, 1966, revered in many quarters as "Grounation Day," the moment when Ras Tafari, Haile Selassie I of Ethiopia, set foot on Jamaican soil. From the point of view of Ethiopian diplomacy, it was simply one stop on a four-country visit to the Caribbean; Selassie seems to have enjoyed touring the world in his status as monarch of this ancient—and sole uncolonized—African land. For their part, the Jamaican authorities evidently hoped that by showing the human face (and minuscule body) of the Ethiopian ruler they could deflate the troublesome Rastafarians who viewed him as a deity. Many government initiatives in the years immediately following Independence proved ill-conceived or delusional; if debunking Selassie's divinity was the primary purpose of the invitation, the imperial visit can claim a place near the top of that list.

The morning was stormy, with heavy rain and thick dark clouds studded with lightning. As the Emperor's plane appeared on the horizon, its flanks decorated with the royal lion, the clouds lifted and the airport was bathed in sunlight. When Selassie emerged onto the portable stairway, he was confronted with a sea of dreadlocks, thousands of his Jamaican followers chanting "*God come, God come, hail Ras Tafari!*"

At first delighted with the reception, Selassie soon grew alarmed, fearful for his frail body in that uncontrolled mass of humanity. The Rastas had overwhelmed the military police, sweeping past and around the flimsy fences and astonished soldiers dressed for ceremony rather than crowd control. The historic moment turned into a tense stand-off, with Selassie retreating inside the plane and refusing to emerge until a secure path to the terminal had been cleared and insisting there be no violence or harsh police tactics. The authorities gritted their teeth and summoned the Rasta leader Mortimo Planno to negotiate the Emperor's deplaning.

The government's Rasta problem went back forty-five years, to March 31, 1921, the day that other totemic figure, Marcus Garvey, returned in triumph to Kingston; as head of the United Negro Improvement Association (UNIA), Garvey's huge parades through Harlem and fiery speeches had made him famous. He was an electrifying orator and his message was revolutionary: Black men and women need not apologize for their color and should no longer aspire to integration with Whites. To the US government, this was subversive and dangerous; in Jamaica, colonial officials were so nervous about his arrival, they had a Royal Navy frigate standing by in Kingston Harbour. But, like Selassie in 1966, Garvey in 1921 was fast approaching a precipitous fall.

Marcus Garvey had been born into a Maroon family. As a youth newly arrived in Kingston in 1905, he fell under the influence of a preacher named Robert Love, who taught him elocution and enlisted his help in a campaign to raise a statue for George William Gordon, leader of the 1865 Morant Bay uprising. The British, having summarily hanged four hundred people in the wake of Gordon's rebellion, wanted no part in a statue. Feeling unwelcome in Jamaica, Garvey traveled around the Caribbean and then on to London, where he helped edit the *African Times and Orient Review*, which was run by an anti-colonialist Egyptian named Duse Mohammed Ali. Ali introduced him to the teachings of Edward Wilmot Blyden, a West Indian who had moved to Liberia and married into one of the elite US families who "returned" there after the Civil War. Promoting the ideal of Africa as the true home of Afro-Americans and Afro-Caribbeans became Garvey's life's work.

After founding the UNIA, Garvey moved to New York. In the years immediately following World War One, one in five Harlem residents was West Indian; many had helped build the Panama Canal but found all-White unions barring them from the jobs their skills warranted when they arrived in the US. Despite such obstacles, Caribbeans were the stars of Harlem, setting the pace with style and confidence. Growing up on an island as part of a racial majority was a very different experience from being a member of a reviled minority on the mainland; West Indians could often see what African Americans couldn't or had been brainwashed to ignore. In Marcus Garvey, they and their American allies found a leader.

The NAACP was alarmed by Garvey; using the word *Negro* in the title of his organization was itself a provocation, since the NAACP preferred the term "Colored," aspiring to integration and acceptance on White terms. And as for Africa, most Americans, Black or White, ventured little further in their knowledge of the "dark continent" than cartoon images of cannibals boiling a missionary in a pot. America's president at the time was Woodrow Wilson, a man who had invited D. W. Griffith to the White House for a command screening of *Birth of a Nation*, the racist epic that rekindled US enthusiasm for the Ku Klux Klan. Wilson's predecessor, Teddy Roosevelt, had railed against the idea that "lower races" could rule themselves. Post-war America seemed intent on proving that whatever the law might say, White superiority was fundamental to the way society operated.

The NAACP fought for Black rights, but politely. Not so Garvey. As the Harlem Renaissance poet Claude McKay recalled, "Garvey shouted words, words spinning like bullets, words falling like bombs, sharp words like poisoned daggers, thundering words and phrases lit with all the hues of the rainbow to match the wild approving roar of his people." The West Indian lilt to his received British pronunciation struck Black Americans as both exotic and aspirational. He linked the Negro cause to the hugely popular struggle for Irish independence, and compared his "back to Africa" crusade with the American struggle for independence. The UNIA bestowed "African knighthoods"—Order of the Nile, Order of Ethiopia, etc.—on illustrious members and published a *Universal Negro Catechism* that, in one of its many revisions, altered the King James description of Solomon's betrothed from "dark but comely" to "dark *and* comely." To Americans in the early 1920s, Black or White, these were startling ideas and the movement rapidly acquired enemies of all shades.

Garvey provided his critics with plenty of ammunition. Race-proud editorials in his newspaper, *Negro World*, were flanked by advertisements for hair-straightening formulae and skin-lightening creams; it was also public knowledge that Garvey had left his dark-skinned wife for a "sepia" secretary. These issues were dwarfed by problems at the Black Star Line, the proposed fleet that would carry Africans home. As the FBI and the IRS spied and plotted, Garvey purchased two aging vessels but didn't complete the payments. As with many such hydra-headed enterprises, money sloshed undocumented among organization, newspaper, shipping line, and Garvey's personal (and growing) expenses. Faced with losing the ships, he appealed to his followers to invest but failed to record stock certificates properly or ring-fence these funds from his other needs. The feds pounced, jailing him for fraud and deporting him back to Jamaica after a term in the Columbus, Georgia, stockade.

Garvey may have been brought low, but he arrived home in 1927 like a monarch in exile, awing Jamaicans with his flowery and fiery rhetoric, elegant clothes, and regal manner. He gave lectures, ran for city councilor, and mounted a theater piece called *The Coronation of an African King*. The authorities scrambled to discredit him; a judge barred him running for office on grounds he had impugned the probity of the court, while the *Daily Gleaner* mocked his prophecies about an African monarch.

A few years earlier, the same newspaper had been equally dismissive of a confection called the *Holy Piby*, put together by a preacher from the tiny island of Anguilla, which claimed to be based on an ancient Ethiopian Bible. These attempts at ridicule had the effect of ensuring that all of Jamaica became familiar with the two foundation stones of Rastafarianism.

> Some Afric chief will rise . . . Then dear repay us in some vengeful war, and give us blood for blood, and scar for scar.
>
> —Jamaican slave belief, noted by plantation owner Thomas Thistlewood, late eighteenth century
>
> And Babylon shall become heaps, a dwelling place for dragons, an astonishment, and an hissing, without an inhabitant.
>
> —Jeremiah 51:37, King James Bible

Princes shall come out of Egypt; Ethiopia shall soon stretch out her hands unto God.

—Psalm 68, King James Bible

African captives brought their religious beliefs with them across the Atlantic, adapting or incorporating whichever strands of Christianity they encountered. While Catholic saints were merging with Yorùbá and Kongo deities in Cuba and Brazil, North American Protestantism was turning captives towards Bible-based song and story. Jamaican slaves had developed only a rudimentary connection to Christianity and encountered few new arrivals after the late eighteenth century. Afro-Jamaicans, particularly those in the hills, were pretty much on their own, with an ample supply of ganja to assist in their meditations.

Leonard Howell is often called "the first Rasta." Like Garvey, he left Jamaica after clashing with police, traveling the world as a seaman, with a 1918 stopover at Russia's Arctic port of Arkhangelsk that cured him of an infatuation with communism. Arriving in New York a year later, he heard Garvey speak and was transformed. Running afoul of US police, he spent two years in Sing Sing prison before being deported. Back in Kingston in the early thirties, Howell found a whirlpool of social, economic, and spiritual turmoil. The Depression had struck hard, removing the safety valve of seasonal work abroad; across the island, the poor were desperate and looking for answers.

Garvey took a shine to Howell and tried to recruit him to the UNIA, but Leonard had other plans. The African ideal may have been a tough sell in the US, but it had always fascinated Jamaicans; when an army under the command of Selassie's great-uncle Menelik II defeated the Italians at Adwa in 1896, the victory was celebrated in poor areas across the island. The *Holy Piby* placed Ethiopia at the center of its retelling of Judeo-Christian mythology and anointed Garvey as a modern-day prophet. On November 2, 1930, following a violent putsch against his cousin the Empress, Ras Tafari was crowned Emperor of Ethiopia; he took the regal name Haile Selassie, meaning "Power of the Trinity" in Amharic. Jamaicans were never much interested in the high-church subtleties of Father, Son, and Holy Ghost, so they stuck with his original title (roughly, "Duke" Tafari) as they celebrated the coronation. Garvey's prophecy was fulfilled.

Howell was arrested for distributing cards with a picture of Selassie that advised Jamaicans to pay their taxes to Ethiopia rather than the British Crown. After a spell in jail, he headed for the hills of east Jamaica, where a group of *Piby* followers had settled after being hounded out of Kingston by outraged Baptists. They were welcomed there by Pocomania adherents, a term that blurs the "little madness" of spirit possession with a connection to Kumina, an African belief system from the same sharp bend in the African coast that was home to Cuba's Abakuá.

Garvey had no patience for those who would turn the Emperor into a god; to him, Selassie was a political symbol, the proud ruler of an independent African nation. Garvey also couldn't forgive Selassie for his government's dismissive treatment of the UNIA and refusal to grant his requests for a meeting. Garvey understood what Howell and future generations of Rastas never would: that Selassie and the rest of Ethiopia's Amharic ruling class didn't actually consider themselves Black. The royal family had kept Black slaves for centuries; their view of the darker-skinned peoples in the south of the country was not much different from British and French attitudes towards their African colonial subjects. In 1935, Garvey left Jamaica for the last time, exasperated by his countrymen's unwillingness to do the hard work necessary for the achievement of his ideals and by what he viewed as their simple-minded credulity about Ras Tafari's divinity.

> Red, fe de bloodshed inflicted on de sufferah since slavery deys! Gold, fe de wealth stolen from de sufferah since Solomon's temple was laid low! Green, fe de blessed land in Africa dat awaits de black mon's return.
>
> —Rasta fisherman explaining his boat's colors

> He causeth the grass to grow for the cattle, and herb for the service of man . . .
>
> —Psalm 104:14, King James Bible

From the dawn of talkies, Jamaicans loved going to the movies; classic reggae tracks would celebrate James Bond, *The Guns of Navarone*, and Clint Eastwood. But no gangster or cowboy film could ever match the impact of the 1936 newsreel of Haile Selassie addressing the League of Nations. Many had heard about this African ruler, but now there he was up on the screen, larger than life (a lot larger, actually), addressing an assemblage of the world's leaders and accusing them of standing by while Mussolini's troops invaded his ancient kingdom. Marcus Garvey was far away in the damp Bloomsbury basement where he would soon die, composing screeds against Selassie for failing to prepare for the Italian attack. Howell was free to take Garvey's prophecy and run with it.

Like Joseph Smith with the *Book of Mormon*, Howell "discovered" Rastafarianism's foundation document, *The Promised Key*, supposedly created in West Africa, but actually the work of Howell and some friends. In 1938, he persuaded his first wife (of an eventual Mormonesque thirteen) to pawn her jewelry so he could buy some land high in the hills above Spanish Town; Pinnacle, the first Rasta settlement, was born. At the apex of its twenty-year existence, Pinnacle was home to 2,500 people; they raised crops and families, played the drums constantly, and were, in the early years, a nerve center for workers' protests and anti-colonial agitation. The authorities viewed the settlement as an intolerable affront, sending police and army units up the steep, rugged hill to harass and arrest its members. The government was caught in a cleft stick: the more they drove people away from Pinnacle, the more the Rasta message spread. In those early years, the men cut their hair like everyone else, making it difficult to single out and harass them once they left the settlement.

Rastafarianism was never a fixed belief system; the only universal strictures involve cleanliness, patriarchy, and a more or less Kosher diet. The Roman numeral after the Emperor's title was read as a magic vowel, creating new words and transforming old ones: I-rie, (v)I-tal, I and I (for we), I-rations (vibrations), etc., while the first syllable of Jahweh, the Hebrew word for God, served as an honorific for any male Rastafarian deserving of respect. Beyond that, so long as one was committed to loving thy neighbor, honoring Selassie, and rejecting the trappings of Babylon, the details were left to each group or individual.

For Rastas, the only news worth reading was African news; in the 1940s came reports of Nyabinghi and Mau-Mau rebellions in Uganda and Kenya, accompanied by photographs (*and newsreels!*) of captured fighters with long locks of matted hair. The look struck a chord and soon became the de rigueur Rasta hairstyle, complete with biblical justifications: "there shall no razor come upon his head" and "he shall be holy and shall let the locks of the hair of his head grow."

And then there was ganja. Howell embraced the South Asian herb ("It helps you to think faster, think stronger, think right") and sought to weave in elements of Hindu mythology, signing his writings "Gangungu Maraj" and answering to the nickname "Gong." Some Rasta pantheons include Kali alongside Selassie, Garvey, and Jehovah. Rastas passing long hours in ganja-fueled "reasonings" resemble nothing so much as *sadhus*, long-haired Hindu holy men who reject the world and follow a meditative path outside normal society.

It is easy to pick apart Rastafarianism, with its Garvey and Selassie delusions, its Old Testament codes for the treatment of women, and the clouds of smoke from its chillums; but what really freaked out the British Colonial Office and the local police was how Rastas walked proud and straight, bowed to no man, held no hand out in supplication, and never sought acceptance by the White and lighter-skinned-Black establishment.

Jamaica had grown used to ganja, but Britain hadn't, and Tory politicians were alarmed by its growing UK presence in the wake of Caribbean immigration. No less a figure than Winston Churchill intervened to make it clear there would be no talk of independence until Jamaica cracked down on "drug traffic." Pinnacle, by the early fifties, had become a busy purveyor of the weed and made a less awkward target than the well-connected, bribe-paying dealers who undertook most of the exporting. Police raided the settlement again and again, and Howell was eventually locked away in an asylum rather than granting him the platform of a trial. In 1958, the government, citing a technical error in the title deed, confiscated the land. Pinnacle was over; the words of its founder in the mouths of its members spread out across the island. By 1966, the sight of dreadlocked Rastas was not unusual, but they didn't seem particularly numerous; their jargon and their message resonated in the yards and in the hills, among musicians and the very poor, but few Jamaicans perceived them as an existential threat. At least not until Grounation Day.

⌘

I want you to know that I am the man
Who fights for the right, not for the wrong
Going here, I'm going there
Talking this and talking that
Soon you will find out the man
I'm supposed to be
. . .

This man, I don't trouble no man
But if you should trouble this man
It will bring a bam bam
Bam bam, what a bam bam

—Toots Hibbert, "Bam Bam"

These islanders are disturbed. They already have black government and black power, but they want more. They want something more than politics. Like the dispossessed peasantry of medieval Europe, they await crusades and messiahs.

—V. S. Naipaul

What somebody should have foreseen was that the more you make people suffer for their beliefs the more they will be willing to suffer, until the suffering becomes the belief.

—Michael Thomas, *Babylon on a Thin Wire*

Mortimo Planno asked the Rastas to clear a path to the terminal for His Majesty, and they did. Crowds lining the roads into the capital were unnerved to find so many dreadlocked men in their midst blowing "abeng" horns or holding long wooden staffs; as the motorcade proceeded into Kingston, what the government intended as a showcase for their modern diplomacy appeared incongruously biblical. The price of Planno's intervention was to include him and his dreadlocked cohort at the official banquet in King's House that evening, where he and Selassie discussed a plan to grant land in Ethiopia for a community of Rasta immigrants.

If there had been any question about how central Rastafarianism was becoming to Jamaican culture, Selassie's visit put an end to it. Soon afterwards, "Bam Bam" by Toots and the Maytals won the Jamaican Independence Festival Song Competition. The words are about how Jamaican society misunderstands Rastas, how they are genuinely peaceful men of goodwill, but that you'd better not mess with them since they won't hesitate to start a "bam bam" if provoked.

One could have imagined that the combination of Rasta obscurantism, ganja smoke, and Nyabinghi rhythms would steer Jamaican music into ever more self-referential circles, closing the island's fledgling record industry off from international markets. But instead, the opposite happened: a flowering of some of the most sophisticated local music ever to grace the world stage.

In the late nineteenth century, the lazy heirs of a minor Irish landowner named Daniel Power Trench abandoned the land he had bequeathed them outside Kingston; over the years it became a squatters' shantytown. After the 1951 hurricane, the government built dozens of compounds in what had become known as Trenchtown. In the area around Wilton Gardens known as "Rema," five of reggae's greatest international stars came of age in the early sixties and began their careers.

Jimmy Cliff set off this chain of events by walking into Beverley's, the Kong family shop, and persuading Leslie Kong to go into business as a producer with a shameless plug of a song called "Dearest Beverley." Cliff then got a deal with Kong's new label for his friend from down the street, Desmond Dacres. Dacres didn't have any hits until he changed the spelling to Dekker, but in the meantime, he in turn set up an audition with Kong for Rema's precocious "yellow bwoy," Robert Marley. When his first singles failed to chart, Marley moved around the corner to Coxsone's Studio One label and brought along his stepbrother Bunny Livingston and their neighbor Peter McIntosh (later shortened to "Tosh") to record as the Wailing Wailers.

Of these five kids from Rema, Cliff was the one with the ambition, the angles, and the not-quite-Belafonte good looks. His early singles were innocuous stabs at topicality: a paean to "Miss Jamaica" and a Rasta-lite, Disney-foreshadowing ditty about a lion called "King of Kings." Cliff

South African choir that toured Britain 1891–93, with their English manager and musical director

Solomon Linda's Original Evening Birds, with Linda on the left, c. 1941

Guitar pioneer John "Phuzushukela" Bhengu

top Miriam Makeba and the Manhattan Brothers, 1956

center left Hugh Masekela unpacking the trumpet sent to him by Louis Armstrong, 1954

center right Todd Matshikiza, c. 1955

bottom The Blue Notes: Dudu Pukwana (alto sax), Louis Moholo (drums), Mongezi Feza (trumpet), Johnny Dyani (bass) and Chris McGregor (piano), London, 1956

Mahlathini and the Mahotella Queens, 1988

Ladysmith Black Mambazo with Paul Simon on *Saturday Night Live*, 1986

Three congueros:
above Miguelito Valdés
center Chano Pozo
bottom Desi Arnaz

Sexteto Habanero, 1925

Arsenio Rodríguez, 1950s

top Benny Moré and his Banda Gigante on the *Cabaret Regalías* television show, 1950s

center left Bola de Nieve (Ignacio Villa)

center right Celia Cruz with La Sonora Matancera, 1950s

bottom Tropicana nightclub, Havana, 1952

top "Cuban Pete" (Pedro Aguilar) and Millie Donay demonstrating the mambo at the Palladium Ballroom in New York City, 1955

center left Frank "Machito" Grillo and his sister Graciela, New York, 1950s

center middle The young Tito Puente, 1950s

center right Chano Pozo jamming with Dizzy Gillespie, 1948

bottom Celia Cruz and Johnny Pacheco, 1977

top Duke Reid with his Trojan sound system, Kingston, 1954

center left Bunny Livingston, Bob Marley, Rita Marley, and Peter Tosh, 1967

center right Chris Blackwell, 1966

bottom Toots Hibbert (center) and the Maytals, c. 1970

top Marcus Garvey in a parade in Harlem, 1924

center Haile Selassie is greeted by Rastafarian crowds as he arrives at Kingston Airport, 1966

bottom Bob Marley on stage with Haile Selassie image, 1977

Lee "Scratch" Perry in his Black Ark studio, Kingston, 1970s

King Tubby (Osbourne Ruddock), 1970s

Joe Strummer, Don Letts, John Lydon ("Johnny Rotten"), and Paul Simonon during a video shoot for Big Audio Dynamite, 1986

top Sultan Akbar and Tansen in the forest listening to Swami Haridas, Mughal miniature painting, c. 1750

center Double-exposure photograph of Uday Shankar's dance company showing Ravi (left and right) as both musician and dancer, England, 1936

bottom Allauddin Khan with sarod

top The Beatles, their wives, and entourage with Maharishi Mahesh Yogi at Rishikesh, 1968

center left Alla Rakha and Ravi Shankar at the Monterey Pop Festival, 1967

center right Mike Heron of the Incredible String Band on stage with sitar, c. 1974

bottom Ravi Shankar and George Harrison

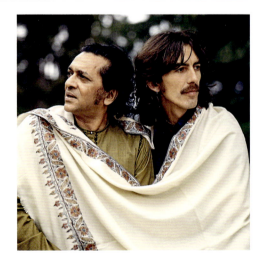

top Nazakat and Salamat Ali, c. 1945 (left) and c. 1961 (right)

center left Nusrat Fateh Ali Khan and party performing at WOMAD, 1985

center right Lata Mangeshkar and Asha Bhosle

bottom (left to right) Terry Riley (tabla), La Monte Young (tanbura), Pandit Pran Nath (vocal) and Marian Zazeela (tanbura). Pandit Pran Nath, Morning Ragas, Rothko Chapel, Houston, November 15, 1981

top left János Bihari, portrait by János Donát, 1820

top right Taraf de Haïdouks, 2000

center Esma Redžepova with Stevo Teodosievski (second from left) and band

bottom Quintet of the Hot Club of France: Stéphane Grappelly (violin), Eugène Vées, Django Reinhardt, and Joseph "Nin-Nin" Reinhardt (guitars), Louis Vola (bass), Casanova Club, Paris, c. 1937

Flamenco dancers at a café cantante, Seville, 1888

El Farruco (Antonio Montoya Flores)

Manolo Caracol with Pepe Pinto

El Chocolate (Antonio Núñez Montoya)

top Camarón de la Isla and Paco de Lucía, 1974

center left Manitas de Plata (Ricardo Baliardo), with his portrait drawn onto the guitar by Pablo Picasso, 1968

center right Ketama, photographed by Mario Pacheco, 1987

bottom Wooden statue of Saint Sarah, Les Saintes-Maries-de-la-Mer, France took advantage of Kong's rapport with Chris Blackwell to follow Millie's path to London; there, Island released a few of his pop-reggae songs, produced a couple of Cat Stevens covers with him, and had a degree of success in the international crossover market.

Desmond Dekker, meanwhile, stayed true to his family's church background by releasing a series of morally uplifting tracks, starting with "Honour Your Mother and Father." After singing backup on Derrick Morgan's "Tougher Than Tough" in 1967, though, Dekker's songwriting shifted towards rude boys and the plight of those at the bottom of society. Walking through a park one evening he overheard a couple arguing about money; this inspired "Israelites" with its timeless, percussively enunciated opening line: "*Get-up-in-the-morning, sla-ving for bread, sir / So that ev-er-y mouth can be fed.*" Cliff was trying hard and Blackwell was backing him, but Dekker soared effortlessly past them into the Top Ten in both the US and the UK, giving a sign that reggae's future lay not in calculated compromise but in its strangeness.

For most record executives, "Israelites" represented little more than a novelty, the kind of one-off smash that periodically confounded pluggers and programmers, like "Hello Muddah, Hello Faddah," "Sukiyaki," or "Dueling Banjos." No one would have predicted that it represented the advance brigade of the all-conquering sonic army taking shape in Cliff's and Dekker's old neighborhood.

> Brook Benton and Sarah Vaughan, me saw. Dinah Washington . . . Nat King Cole, Billy Eckstine, ya know? Even Frank Sinatra and Sammy Davis in a certain period of my time . . . But Fats Domino and Rick Nelson and Elvis Presley, a whole heap of lickle other music come on one time strong . . . [S]tarting listening to jazz. Except me couldn't understand it . . . and me meet Joe Higgs . . . who schooled me . . . Me try to go in the mood of a mon that's blue . . . understand the feelin' they express.
>
> —Bob Marley on his early influences

> Me don't dip on the black man's side nor the white man's side, me dip on God's side.
>
> —Bob Marley

Joe Higgs and Roy Wilson won an early talent contest with "Oh Manny Oh," and the song engraved their names as Jamaica's very first homegrown hit-makers. When Wilson emigrated to the US in the early sixties, Higgs continued working as a songwriter, singer, and session musician, but his impact on the history of reggae was far greater than any list of credits. He was a "baldhead" (short-hair) who preached a Rastafarian vision of universal love and lived it through his devotion to neighborhood youth, coaching them in singing, harmony, and songwriting and connecting them to record producers. His friend and neighbor in Wilton Gardens was Mortimo Planno and their most avid pupil was Bob Marley.

Marley, of course, looms over Jamaican music like a colossus and there are many books and films about him, particularly Timothy White's *Catch a Fire*, Christopher Farley's *Before the Legend: The Rise of Bob Marley*, and the documentary *Marley*, by Kevin Macdonald. There is a museum and visitor center now at Nine Mile, the remote hamlet deep in the hills where he was born to a White father and a Black mother. "Captain" Norval Marley married Cedella Malcolm when she became pregnant, but they never lived together and Norval soon left, allowing big-picture conceptualizers such as myself to link their son to innovative greats such as Carlos Gardel, Benny Moré, and John Lennon, who were also raised by struggling single mothers. Marley's racial mix injected another factor, as he stood out among the dark faces in the poor communities where he lived and was always driven to prove himself a part of those societies, first in the hills, then in Trenchtown.

The Wailers' first hit, "Simmer Down," was the fruit of Higgs's tutoring and, with its great horns and strong rhythm section, of Coxsone's production savvy. It was also a sign of Marley's very original mind at work. Cedella had moved to Kingston to be with Bunny Livingston's father and was, like many Trenchtown mothers, disturbed by her son's keeping company with rude boys. In "Simmer Down," Marley accomplished a deft balancing act, assuring his mother he knew right from wrong while sending a signal to ghetto youth that he was one of them. Despite its admonitions, the record became a huge favorite with rudies and was blamed for a city-wide surge of aggression. Like so many Marley compositions, it is written from both an outsider's and an insider's point of view; many of his greatest songs contain instructions—"Get Up, Stand Up," "Lively Up Yourself," "Keep on Moving," "Bend Down Low"—"mentoring" his listeners (as Higgs and Planno had mentored him, perhaps) while making it clear that he knows their lives and is one of them.

Like most who met him, Coxsone was immediately drawn to young Bob, offering him a cot in the office in return for sifting through the packages of American singles that arrived weekly at the Studio One office. (No more trips to Florida for Coxsone and the other foundation DJs; they now received the latest American 45s by post.) On the turntable in Studio One's back office, Marley absorbed another important pair of influences: Harvey Fuqua and Curtis Mayfield. Like many on the island, Bob loved doo-wop. That may have contributed to ska's slowing down to become rocksteady, or perhaps it was the modest tempi that encouraged languorous lead vocals and sweet harmonies. Marley was particularly drawn to that most sophisticated of fifties vocal groups, Fuqua's Moonglows, with their complex jazz-inflected arrangements that always included a nod to Harvey's uncle's outfit, the doo-wop mothership, The Ink Spots.

Early Wailers shows at the Majestic Theatre must have been memorable: dressed in the gold lamé suits Coxsone bought them, the trio veered from rude-boy anthems to sweetly harmonized love ballads. Their 1964 Christmas show caused a riot as the box office was besieged by downtown youths demanding free entrance. Coxsone tried to steer the group away from Rastas and rudies towards becoming a Jamaican Moonglows, but Bob's ear had also been caught by a more modern and more political group: Curtis Mayfield's Impressions.

You can hear echoes of Mayfield's songs ("People Get Ready" in particular), as well as his idealism and commitment, in much of Marley's work. When Bob's mother joined her brother in Delaware in 1966, he spent a year there with her, working on an assembly line and absorbing American Black radio. The US government has never been keen on non-White immigrants, but always welcomes non-White cannon fodder; after a year there, and with the Vietnam War raging, Bob received his draft notice. He quickly returned to Kingston, ready for a new start and determined to control his musical destiny.

～

> When the people hear what I-man do them hear a different beat, a slower beat, a waxy beat—like you stepping in glue. Them hear a different bass, a rebel bass, coming at you like sticking a gun.
>
> —Lee "Scratch" Perry

> He was the one who taught Bob Marley to sing. The way Bob sing is the way Scratch sing really . . . Scratch is not really a singer, but Scratch can express himself . . . That style is effective because you hear what he's saying more, so Bob Marley pick up that style and work with him.
>
> —Jimmy Riley, reggae singer

Marley's first efforts upon returning from Delaware were solo releases that went nowhere. When Bunny finished a term in jail the group reformed, but they'd been away too long and their sound seemed out of touch. Bob, meanwhile, had met the American singer Johnny Nash and his manager Danny Sims, who needed help connecting with local studios and musicians. Nash recorded some Jamaican material, including a few of Marley's own songs, but Sims's promised door-opening to the US market proved illusory and Bob ended up not only disappointed, but entangled in contractual and copyright issues which would plague him until his death. One compensation was Sims's record collection; it was full of Sly, James Brown, and Hendrix, and Bob absorbed it all.

Planno, meanwhile, was taking Bob to Grounation ceremonies in the hills, filling his chillum and leading him through the teachings of Garvey and Howell. Marley stopped going to the barber. A track called "Watch This Sound" by Slim Smith, a copyright-theft cover of "For What It's Worth" by Buffalo Springfield, caught his attention; Bob dug the bass part and went looking for the player. Aston "Family Man" Barrett had come by his nickname by gathering the musicians he worked with around him like a family (and would further justify it by fathering forty-one children). Aston and his drummer brother Carlton had a group called the Hippy Boys and were working for Lee Perry;

when they all joined forces, this combination would create the golden age of reggae.

Having fallen out with Coxsone and then with the producer Joe Gibbs, "Scratch" Perry's biggest sixties successes as an independent artist-producer were revenge songs; "Run for Cover" and "People Funny Boy" attacked Coxsone and Gibbs respectively. The latter track marks the birth of sampling, with looped wails from Scratch's baby mixed into the drum track. Further decorated by Lyn Tait's "steel-pan" guitar trills and underpinned by the Barretts' chugging beat, "People Funny Boy" laid the foundation for what would come to be known as reggae. (The word first appeared in a Toots and the Maytals track called "Do the Reggay," a 1968 "dance-craze" song written by Toots for Leslie Kong on a scrap of paper in a few mid-session minutes.)

Perry not only fought with other producers, he had vowed never again to work with singers, resenting how they were praised and rewarded for tracks he created. Family Man lobbied to make an exception in Marley's case; when a suspicious Scratch met Bob, he immediately recognized a kindred spirit. Marley was "from country" (Scratch had no time for city-born singers); the most original and creative producer in Jamaica agreed to take on Marley and his fellow Wailers.

The three were quickly immersed in Perry's methods; he would drive them around the city for hours with the car windows down, telling them to keep their ears open, listen to conversations, observe quarrels, and take in the atmosphere. Back at the studio, they'd write songs inspired by what they'd seen and heard; Scratch would summon the Hippy Boys and record while a song was still fresh. He put a stop to sweet harmonies and falsetto leads; natural voices with clear, urgent diction became the rule. Early fruits of this collaboration were "Duppy Conqueror" and "Small Axe," songs that put the group back atop the Jamaican charts. The latter, originally conceived by Perry, then reworked with Marley, conflates the music business and slavery, punning on the "big t'ree" record labels they felt were stifling independent producers. There were endless later arguments about composer credits, but "Small Axe" can be heard as Perry's combative (if not paranoid) fixations made poetic, elegant, and universal by the genius of Marley.

There was plenty for songwriters to be angry about in late-sixties Jamaica. Edward Seaga, who had repatriated Garvey's bones for a reverential reburial and never passed up an opportunity to honor Afro-Jamaican traditions, showed the other side of his political character when, as minister of housing, he ordered brutal slum clearances, leveling the biggest urban Rasta encampment at "Back-a-Yard" and sending in the army to guard the bulldozers. The view among the poor was that Jamaica was being sold out to America, with the profits going to the haves and leaving have-nots to suffer. At the turn of the decade, the discrepancy between the music people were buying and what the government would permit on the radio was growing wider.

Other producers took the revelations of "People Funny Boy" and ran with them, developing a style that retained many of rocksteady's innovations, including the one-drop, but at a faster tempo (dancers having grown tired of slow motion). Drummers tightened their snares until they sounded as dry as timbales and emulated their salsa brethren by injecting Puente-like paradiddles and fills. The way these rhythms interacted with guitars, keyboards, and vocalists was shaped in Wareika Hills sessions where schooled musicians jammed with Count Ossie's drummers, exploring and developing reggae's distinct grooves. For Jamaicans, the new sound was simply the latest installment in the evolution of their popular music; in a few years they would be ready for something new. For the rest of the world, the beats developed in Kingston at the end of the sixties and the start of the seventies would become frozen in time, like a fossil in amber, unalterable. This is not just a metaphor; cuts that Scratch and the Barretts produced with The Wailers during 1969 and 1970 would end up as basic tracks on Wailers and Marley LPs released by Island across the seventies—and posthumously into the eighties—and heard constantly around the world ever since.

Jamaican producers and artists have always had a flexible attitude about the sanctity of tracks, going back to how DJs would shout and improvise over rhythm-and-blues discs. By the mid-sixties, singles were being released with a song on one side and its instrumental backing on the other (usually titled "Version"); over those B sides, DJs could toast, sing, or make announcements, a Kingston take on "Music Minus

One," the American series that let musicians and singers practice or busk along with backing tracks. Poverty taught Jamaicans to recycle their goods, using them again and again, and record producers were no different; Scratch and the others would add vocals and create a new song months or years after a track had been the foundation for a hit by a different artist. Marley and Blackwell would return the favor, keeping all or part of tracks recorded with Perry years earlier, adding new vocals, guitars, and percussion, tailoring their mix for the ears and feet of a worldwide audience.

This being Jamaica and this being the music business, the practice led to endless disputes about payment, credit, rights, and respect. When The Wailers began touring the world, they took the Barretts with them, robbing Perry of his favorite rhythm section. Scratch would release a 12-inch single in the mid-seventies with a drawing of Blackwell as Dracula sacrificing a chicken on the cover, his fangs dripping blood. But despite accusations, lawsuits, and periodic estrangements, Scratch and Bob always spoke of each other with love and respect; the work they did together endured, becoming part of the world's soundtrack. Bereft of his team and of his ideal collaborator, Perry would turn a page and create a new revolution, as influential in its way as Marley's and possibly more enduring.

Jamaican music was still not on the map. The early seventies saw a three-pronged push that opened the door, not just for reggae and Marley, but for everything that followed: dreadlocks on blond Californian surfers; female sex tourists on the beach at Negril; anonymous reggae playing quietly in the background as you sip your latte or buy your granola; and Poles, Maoris, Ivorians, and Apaches carrying the flame for music invented thousands of miles away in cramped studios on unpaved streets in one of the world's poorest countries.

First came a film idea developed in Kingston by a White commercials director and a Black playwright. Perry Henzell and Trevor Rhone constructed a plot based around the true tale of a 1940s criminal named Vincent "Ivanhoe" Martin, who escaped from prison and eluded police for weeks in a murderous crime spree that transfixed the island. Moving the story to the present and turning Martin into an aspiring singer frustrated by the corruption of Kingston record producers, Henzell and Rhone created a script ready to be woven through with reggae music. They got Chris Blackwell and his checkbook on side by casting Jimmy Cliff as Ivanhoe and doing a deal with Island for the soundtrack album, then raising more funds from local businesses and friends. Everything, of course, proved more complicated and expensive than anticipated, and production stopped and started many times. The upside of this was that it allowed Henzell to edit as he went along, laying a bed of his favorite 45s under the film as a way of injecting atmosphere and excitement into the screenings he held for potential backers. By the time *The Harder They Come* was finished, it had become a brilliant blend of hero-on-the-run drama and music video (before music videos existed). Henzell not only assembled a great cast of actors, comedians, musicians, and local characters, he encouraged them to use their normal accents and patois, a decision that helped give the film its vividly authentic atmosphere (and forced the US distributor to add subtitles).

It premiered in 1972 at the Carib, a huge barn of a theater with 2,000 seats and 7,000 Jamaicans outside clamouring to get in. At the back of the crowd, wearing white hot-pants and white boots, was Sally Henzell, the director's wife and collaborator, helplessly waving her invitation. Forty years after the event, Sally told me what happened next: the crowd collectively decided that while they might not be able to squeeze in, she certainly should. She was hoisted up, passed along overhead, and deposited at the entrance; she watched the film sitting in an aisle of the crammed cinema. The audience was electrified from the first frames showing Ivan's bus bouncing over potholed country roads on its way to Kingston, a ride most had taken themselves. At the sound of *patwa*, they erupted, cheering even louder than the sound-system crowd fifteen years earlier when Prince Buster played the first local acetate.

The Harder They Come was an earthquake in Jamaica, but a head-scratcher in Britain and America. It was critically praised and there were packed screenings at a few festivals, but it didn't do well at the box office, save a few good runs in West Indian neighborhoods in England. In the

US, New World Pictures' Roger Corman tried to promote it as part of the seventies wave of Blaxploitation movies, but the idea went nowhere, the first of many doomed efforts to sell reggae to African Americans. Henzell took back the rights and traveled around the US, cajoling college-town movie houses into midnight screenings; audiences watched it over and over again, getting past the strangeness and coming to realize that Henzell had crafted a masterpiece. *The Rocky Horror Picture Show* and other late-night film cults followed in its wake.

And then there was the soundtrack album. Perry and Sally were from old planter families and had grown up listening to music on local radio, at sound systems, and to the singles they constantly played at home. Adding to the best five tracks Jimmy Cliff ever recorded ("Many Rivers to Cross," "You Can Get It If You Really Want," etc.), the Henzells "picked the eyes" out of late-sixties reggae and rocksteady: "Rivers of Babylon," "Pressure Drop," "Johnny Too Bad," "Sweet and Dandy," "Draw Your Brakes," and "007 (Shanty Town)."

The next move came from Paul Simon, fifteen years pre-*Graceland*. Simon loved Jimmy Cliff's singles, and for him, "Israelites" was way more than a novelty. He booked the cream of Jamaican musicians for a session at Dynamic Sounds, with a plan to reinvent "Why Don't You Write Me?" (a track from *Bridge over Troubled Water*) as a reggae. Hearing the musicians run through the song, however, Simon had to admit it didn't sound very convincing; chastened, he listened as Hux Brown, Jackie Jackson, Winston Grennan, and the others took him through the evolution from ska to rocksteady to reggae. His realization that he was in the presence of great musicians and shouldn't leave without recording something inspired the method he would later use in Johannesburg: they found a groove and a chord progression and recorded dozens of takes, then Paul took the tapes back to New York and wrote lyrics to fit the track. "Mother and Child Reunion" was the first single off his eponymous solo album and it reached #5 in the *Billboard* chart.

A New York band called Tidbits were paying attention; if Dynamic was good enough for Paul Simon, it was good enough for them, so they headed to Kingston to record. Their manager, Arthur Gorson, fell in love with Jamaica and chose the island for his upcoming nuptials;

his best man was the journalist Michael Thomas. Chris Blackwell's best mate in Jamaica, Dickie Jobson, a charmer who was never known to miss a good party, turned up at the reception. He and Thomas hit it off and the two set out on a tour of the island, focusing not on mountains and beaches, but on shantytowns, Rastas, and music. Back in New York, Michael pitched an article to Jan Wenner at *Rolling Stone* and the result was "The Wild Side of Paradise," a huge spread on Jamaica, its music, culture, and politics, the first major piece of its kind. Thomas's prose threw readers headlong into the heart of Trenchtown, vividly and without condescension. (The piece would later be expanded into a book, *Babylon on a Thin Wire*.) With *The Harder They Come* turning into a cult (Brattle Theatre in Harvard Square showed it every Saturday at midnight for two years), the soundtrack album booming out of college dorms and head shops, "Mother and Child Reunion" on the radio, and hundreds of thousands reading the *Rolling Stone* piece, the stage was set for Chris Blackwell's master plan.

Of the Jamaicans who followed Blackwell to London during the sixties, one of the least known, but possibly the most important, was Jackie Edwards. He did everything at Island, from packing boxes of 45s to singing duets with Millie. On a trip to Birmingham selling ska, Blackwell had heard the Spencer Davis Group and their fourteen-year-old lead singer, Steve Winwood. Chris signed them to follow Millie into his distribution deal with Philips, and in 1966 they had a worldwide hit with a Jackie Edwards composition, "Keep On Running." In Kingston, it would have been perfect ska material, but the group and Blackwell turned the process around, reshaping it as an R&B shuffle with a toned-down skank; Edwards also composed the follow-up hit, "Somebody Help Me," which established the group as stars. When Winwood left in 1967 to form Traffic, Blackwell decided he was ready to break away from Philips, shifting the reggae catalogue to a new company, Trojan, and reinventing Island as a rock label.

Through the late sixties, Island became the hippest, hottest label in Britain, with an artist roster that included Traffic, Cat Stevens, Jethro

Tull, King Crimson, and Free, as well as the artists I produced for them: Fairport Convention, Fotheringay, John and Beverley Martyn, and Nick Drake. Blackwell bought an old church off Portobello Road and turned it into a combination studio, office, and his own living quarters; all label employees (including the boss) sat around a circular table where communication, feedback, criticism, and praise were instantaneous. I got spoiled; no relationship with a record company would ever equal those early years with Island.

Chris was riding high in the charts and being courted by US record companies eager to do business with him, but Jamaica was never far from his mind; he had a plan to make reggae cool and relevant, and Jimmy Cliff was the key. But the singer had extracted a promise that if his royalty payments hadn't reached a certain target, he'd be free to accept a deal from a major label. Just as *The Harder They Come* was getting ready for release, he held Blackwell to his word. Chris was crushed; he knew EMI wouldn't have a clue how to make Jimmy a star (they didn't), but Cliff was determined to leave. A few days later came a phone call from someone Blackwell didn't know, who sounded a bit dodgy, asking if he'd be willing to meet Marley, Tosh, and Livingston. "A week earlier," Chris told me, "I would have said no."

In terms of Jamaican music, I wasn't much different from most White Anglo-American music buffs in 1971. I may have been a bit more open-eared than most, with firmly established enthusiasms (and the vinyl to back it up) for mbaqanga, flamenco, Carlos Gardel's tangos, Indian ragas, Bulgarian choirs, calypso, Mexican *jarocha*, and the Balinese monkey chant. But reggae? Not on my radar.

For many in sixties Britain, Jamaican music had two strikes against it. We were aware that ska provoked wild enthusiasm among skinheads, which constituted a puzzle not sufficiently interesting to solve: why would racist working-class English boys be fans of Black music from Jamaica? And if *they* liked it so much, why would we? When I stumbled on the Jamaican duo Bob & Marcia singing a soft-reggae cover of an American song backed by a cheesy string section on *Top of the Pops*, it seemed to confirm that of all the major African-derived musics of the "New World," Jamaican was among the least interesting.

Having moved back to the US in 1971, I paid Blackwell a visit at his home in Nassau one autumn weekend. My fellow guest was Paul Rodgers, then lead singer with Free (and later for Bad Company and Queen). After a day on the beach, a great dinner, and some high-quality ganja, Chris casually asked us if we had ever heard Toots and the Maytals. Our two heads shook in sync: *No.*

Blackwell slid a disc out of its cheap-looking sleeve and dropped the needle onto side A, track one. For the next thirty-five minutes, Rodgers and I sat side-by-side on the sofa, open-mouthed, transported, thrilled, and astonished (and, to be fair, stoned). When I returned to New York on Monday, I went straight to a West Indian shop in Brooklyn and bought *Slatyam Stoot*, the LP Chris had played for us in Nassau. Over the half-century since, no artist has spent more time on my turntable than Toots.

When I was next in London, Blackwell handed me a crude-looking, white-label 45 on the Roosevelt label: "I Just Want to See You Smile" by Paul Rodgers, with "Version" on the flip side. Paul, it turned out, had shown even more commitment, joining Chris on a flight to Kingston and spending an afternoon in the studio with the Harry J All Stars cutting one of his own songs in pure Jamaican style. With Rodgers's characteristically restrained phrasing, it worked perfectly. (For years, I considered my copy a treasured rarity of inestimable value, but the track can now be found in a Free box set as well as on Spotify.)

Blackwell's plan to turn The Wailers into rock stars fell quickly into place. It got a boost from Johnny Nash, who hit the top of the US hit parade in November 1972 with the reggae-ish "I Can See Clearly Now" and a chart album featuring four of Marley's sexy love songs, including "Stir It Up" and "Guava Jelly." Bob brought the Wailers' master tapes to London shortly thereafter and he and Chris set to work mixing at Island's studios. When they discovered an American band recording upstairs, they got a couple of them to overdub some bluesy guitar lines and Muscle Shoals piano chords.

Catch a Fire appeared in the spring of 1973, clad in an elaborate mock-up of a cigarette lighter complete with a (margin-busting) hinged lid. The title seemed like a casual exhortation to light up a spliff or simply get moving; anyone paying attention to the title song's lyrics, however, would find a darker and deeper meaning, evoking the slave master's whip and condemning him and his present-day heirs to burn in hell. It received heaps of critical praise and radio play and the group set off on a US tour, part of which involved opening for Sly and the Family Stone (who sacked them when they went down too well). Encouraged, Island sent them straight back into the studio. *Burnin'* was released only six months after *Catch a Fire*, had fewer un-Jamaican dilutions, and sold far better, boosted by Eric Clapton's respectful hit cover of one of the tracks, "I Shot the Sheriff."

Those were the headlines. Beneath the surface, there were conflicts and complications aplenty. To clear the way for the first album's release, Island had to fight a costly court battle with CBS Records, with whom Nash's manager Danny Sims had done an earlier deal for the group. While Marley seems to have bought into Blackwell's vision for giving the first album a more international sound (and would later recruit the American guitarist Al Anderson to provide similar textures on recordings and tours), the other two Wailers weren't so happy. Nor were they pleased with the Bob-centric publicity or the touring finances; rock bands were used to getting nothing but a per diem food allowance, hotels, and travel for label-funded, loss-making promotional tours, but Tosh and Livingston saw the arrangement as modern-day slavery. Though the group stayed together to finish *Burnin'*, when Marley left on a world tour to promote it, Family Man and Carlton went with him but Peter and Bunny stayed home. Bob replaced them first with his old mentor Joe Higgs, then added the I-Threes, a female trio that included his wife, Rita, and the Marcia I'd seen on *Top of the Pops*. It was now Marley's show.

On July 17, 1975, at the Lyceum Theatre in London, Island recorded the live album that would mark Marley's emergence as a major international star. It featured "No Woman, No Cry," perhaps his greatest song and certainly the one that brought him to the attention of many who had yet to be won over, particularly women. The song is credited to Vincent Ford, a wheelchair-bound ghetto hero who ran a Trenchtown soup kitchen, but it is generally agreed that Marley wrote the song and gave Ford the credit in order to support his mission, while keeping the copyright out of the clutches of Danny Sims, who still controlled Bob's composer rights. The song's poetic simplicity is unusual for Marley, more descriptive than prescriptive, mixing a romantic nostalgia for younger days with giving Marley's middle-class audiences a glimpse of the reality of Jamaican poverty.

It has been suggested that Marley's racial mix made him more comfortable dealing with the White music-business world than were his darker partners, but a far more likely source of the calculating ambition and fierce will to succeed were his Jamaican grandparents. Omeriah and Alberta Malcolm were powerful figures, well known across the hills around his birthplace as landowners and coffee producers; Omeriah in particular was revered as a Mayalman, someone who used his spiritual powers for good rather than evil.

Reggae is where it's at!

—Paul McCartney

It might not be an exaggeration to say that Bob Marley changed the world. His success certainly transformed Jamaica; Rastafarianism and dreadlocks became (almost) respectable overnight. The island's tourist board may have been horrified when scruffy young pilgrims began flocking to the west and north coasts, staying in cheap hostels or sleeping on the beach and buying ganja from local Rastas, but they soon got used to the influx of cash that came with them. The middle classes were likewise apoplectic initially, but eventually came to accept that their male children were unlikely to ever see the inside of a barbershop again.

In the "developed" Western world, sixties music icons who had (briefly) transformed a generation with their high-minded individualism were, by the mid-seventies, mostly coked-out, sold-out, dead, or Dylan. Marley provided a beacon for a new generation to reclaim that lost idealism. Within a few short years, his image was adorning college dorms, shantytown walls, boutique windows, and political rallies from Cape Town to Berkeley, Stockholm to Caracas.

A few musicians from the "developing" world brought Marley's approach home to nourish their own roots and rhythms, but most either tried to play like Jamaicans or sang his message while drowning their own musical heritage in Anglo-American beats. In Kingston, pride in Marley's success stood in contrast to a turning away from his style of music almost as emphatic as when African Americans cast off the blues the minute White people began to get the hang of it. "Roots reggae" now belonged to the world and Trenchtown needed a new soundtrack.

Osbourne Ruddock was a "techie," a nerd; he loved tinkering with gadgets, building radio sets and amplifiers. Setting up a repair shop in Kingston, he was quickly in demand to fix sound-system equipment, then, later, studio gear. Exposure to the music scene drew him in and he began developing his own ideas, eventually building his own sound system with great speakers and the highest-quality amps. Audiences clearly loved DJs messing with a disc, repeating a verse, talking and rhyming over the "Version" side, singing a song their own way, stopping or starting in the middle of a track. Not being much of a toaster, Ruddock would keep crowds entertained by twirling his EQ dials, ramping up the bass until its booming drowned out the vocal, then the other way around, making the singer piercing and thin, with great whooshes of sound as he swung the dials from one end of the spectrum to the other, throwing in a heavy repeat echo at just the right moment. Drawing on his live experience, he built new equipment and modified old gadgets, tailoring them to the kind of sounds Jamaicans loved. He needed a stage name to suit his burgeoning career; his mother's family were called Tubman, so slim, trim Osbourne Ruddock became King Tubby.

When he started cutting masters for Duke Reid, he would fill the order, then start fooling around, creating soft-wax acetates with the master tapes, slapping on reverb for a few bars, dropping out the instruments and leaving the singers on their own or vice versa—and doing it all in real time, straight to disc. Sound-system crowds loved the resulting exclusives. Other producers began stopping by Tubby's house, where the front room had become a pirate's den of effects and gadgets; together, they explored a new sound they called "dub."

The producer most intrigued by these developments, naturally, was Scratch Perry. He began recording vocals and mixing at Tubby's place, which inspired him to build his own studio, the Black Ark. The two pioneers made quite a contrast: Scratch worked standing up and barefoot, dressed in whatever he threw on when he got out of bed that morning, spliff always in hand, while Tubby was a short-back-and-sides man who dressed like a stylish accountant and polished his dials and faders until they gleamed. *Blackboard Jungle Dub*, generally considered the genre's first great LP, was produced by Scratch and mixed by Tubby.

Dub worked better with toasting than with singing. Volumes could be written about the African origins of rhythmic talking, or speech delivered over percussion, with a side journey to the Black *commandeurs* or "callers" who ruled eighteenth-century quadrille dances in the French and Spanish Caribbean. Jamaicans credit the island's particular style to the fifties sound-system host Count Machuki, a keen student of the way US rhythm-and-blues disc jockeys would hand out a line of jive over instrumental intros and interject between verses. Machuki didn't use "Version" simply as a bed to talk over, he bounced in and out of the rhythm, dancing across the beats with jokes and wordplay. Toasting took a leap forward when King Tubby started making dub plates for U-Roy, a DJ working at his sound system. Tubby would spin a well-known hit, then segue to his own twisted dub version as U-Roy made his entrance with a torrent of patwa and the crowd going wild.

For years, dub and toasting were considered strictly live phenomena. Labels couldn't imagine record buyers listening over and over to such a transitory event. But the labels were wrong; mid-seventies Kingston was ready for a change and dub suited the mood. Most of the top singers and musicians now had international recording contracts and touring agents and were often away "in foreign"; violence had rendered live music almost impossible in Kingston, so they had little incentive to stay at home. Political change had arrived, with

Seaga and the Jamaica Labour Party (JLP) losing the 1972 election to Michael Manley's People's National Party (PNP). Manley, almost as light-skinned as Seaga, campaigned wielding a "rod of correction" while Delroy Wilson's "Better Must Come" blared from PNP campaign trucks. Manley's early years promised much, with the economy improving and the government showing a commitment to helping the poorest. But when he tried gathering the (mostly poor and undeveloped) bauxite-producing countries into an OPEC-style cartel to push up prices, Alcoa and Reynolds simply shrugged and began digging up Australia and Brazil instead. Jamaica's economy cratered as a crackdown on ganja exports removed the one remaining financial lifeline. When the PNP tried to stabilize the currency by outlawing the use of US dollars, dealers began swapping herb for guns, ratcheting up the level of violence on the island even further. Things got worse during the petrol crisis of 1974; when Manley opened an embassy in Havana and had his picture taken with Castro, the US cut off financial aid and the CIA began a violent campaign to run the PNP out of office, funneling guns and money to JLP-linked gangs. As far as most Rastas were concerned, it was all "politricks" as usual in Babylon.

To cap it all, a revolution in Ethiopia dethroned Haile Selassie; kept under house arrest for a time, in 1975 he was reported to have died. Rastas refused to believe it; within twenty-four hours, Marley had recorded and released a defiant single, "Jah Live."

What was the appropriate soundtrack to such events? Certainly not cheery melodic songs. Even before Scratch and Tubby brought mixing boards and special effects front and center, reggae's sonic atmosphere had grown steadily darker. Now, booming bass lines and repetitive drum patterns, interrupted by parts of the track dropping out, replaced by ghostly echoes and repeats, sounded even more ominous. Eighteenth-century planters had found their slaves' drums and chants mysterious and menacing, which was pretty much how the Jamaican ruling class now felt about the sounds emerging from the slums. The hairstyle wasn't called "dread" locks for nothing.

The word *dub* is, on one level, a straightforward term for an audio copy, dubbing from one medium (tape) onto another (disc). But the term also resonates with the Jamaican word for "ghost"—"duppy"—and how dissolving images of the original vocal or bass line appear as "spirits" of their original selves in a miasma of echoes and effects. It also didn't hurt that *dub* had become rude-boy slang for sex, referencing the dropping of the stylus onto virgin shellac. Sound systems, at least those that weren't shut by violence, flourished and DJs became stars. Musicians, initially resentful of the ascendance of studio effects and track recycling, learned how to mimic dub sounds with their instruments.

Despite the ubiquitous posters of Bob in his locks, there remained a degree of restraint when it came to hair; many still had to turn up for a job of pay, and in any case, serious growth takes many years. Which is why a dance at the Carib Theatre in 1973 is considered a defining moment in Jamaican cultural history. A toasting DJ, Big Youth, was wearing a large "tam" (from the Scots "tam-o-shanter") or bonnet; at a certain point in the show he pulled it off, freeing a spectacular waterfall of dreadlocks to tumble past his waist. The place went crazy; hair like that had never been flaunted onstage before. From that point on, Jamaican music was set on a path somewhere between Rastafarian advocacy and a hard-edged rude-boy aesthetic, with tracks crafted by producers, engineers, and DJs more than by singers or musicians. All were united in condemnation of Babylon, which had retreated behind the barbed-wire-topped walls of suburban houses and the government's Gun Courts that locked away indefinitely anyone found with a weapon (excluding, of course, politically connected gangsters).

When Blackwell turned over a large wooden house he owned on Kingston's Hope Road to Marley, the singer moved right in, vowing to "make a ghetto uptown." The short decade of Marley's triumphs was filled with the contradictions that Hope Road represented. Jimmy Cliff had tried to please an international audience with smoother productions than were fashionable in sixties Jamaica, but Marley may have been the first to confront the obverse problem of "outside" audiences wanting something more "roots" than what worked back home. For their part, the Jamaican establishment had reacted to Marley's success with a predictable mixture of amazement, admiration, envy, scorn, and outrage. Songs such as "Burnin' and Lootin'," "I Shot the Sheriff," and "Get Up Stand Up," to say nothing of the spliff-smoking, locks-flaunting album covers, were grenades thrown at the heart of Jamaica's self-image.

Tosh and Livingston tried to hang on to the lucrative outlet Island represented, but after Blackwell passed on Tosh's solo album, the singer would always refer to him as "Whiteworst." Bunny, meanwhile, produced the masterful *Blackheart Man*, which Island did agree to release; during the negotiations, Livingston insisted on a "key man" clause, meaning the contract was void should Blackwell leave the company—or die. Alluding to his notorious *obeah* powers, Bunny expressed satisfaction with the deal since the clause meant he could "get out of the contract any time I want." None of the three Wailers would ever again trouble the Jamaican charts; the closest any of them came was Tosh's 1977 "Legalise It," which became a stoner anthem and an underground Jamaican hit despite a government order banning it.

Though Marley often doled out cash to the *sufferahs* from his former haunts who paid regular visits to Hope Road, "the ghetto" never felt at home at Bob's new place and never dominated the atmosphere the way, say, Elvis's good ol' boys ruled Graceland. The choicest spots in the shade were usually occupied by Marley's new American manager, Don Taylor, and his entourage, or by Cindy Breakspeare, the light-complexioned former Miss Jamaica who had become Bob's "number two wife," or by local soccer hero Allan "Skill" Cole and his friends.

During the Hope Road years, Bob grew obsessed with football, ending each day with a pick-up game in which the wiry and agile singer tried (with some success) to hold his own against Skill and his crew. On September 30, 1975, the New York Cosmos arrived for an exhibition match against Cole's club Santos, the Jamaican champions. The Cosmos were part-owned by Warner Brothers and run by Atlantic Records' Nesuhi Ertegun, a friend of Blackwell's. This connection seems to have played a role in all of Hope Road believing that the game would lead to a Cosmos contract for Skill; he and Marley would conquer America together! Practice matches that week were correspondingly intense and Bob insisted on taking part, playing in his habitual bare feet. Myth has it that the wound he suffered the day before the Cosmos game triggered the melanoma that killed him, but medical opinion insists that while a gash may reveal a cancer, it can't cause one. The doctors who examined Marley's festering toe were sufficiently alarmed to recommend amputation and chemotherapy. Confronted with soccer-free, tour-canceling months of recovery, plus the (possibly permanent) loss of his hair, Marley refused and, encouraged by his Rasta entourage, focused on mystical and alternative cures. The Cosmos, meanwhile, failed to show any interest in Cole, much to the chagrin of Hope Road.

"Skilly" was also central to the other violent drama of Bob's last years. Cole's circle of friendships included a toxic mix of gamblers and political thugs, and these overlapping networks became involved in a betting scam at Caymanas Racetrack; the coup failed to produce the expected riches, leaving murky debts unpaid and threats directed at Skill and his famous ally (who was rumored to have tried to settle matters with compensatory cash). This affair became conflated with the CIA's desire to return the island to JLP control and the views of some sinister Americans that Marley was too close to the PNP as well as being a dangerously influential ally of the poor and the stoned around the world; how much these two threads overlap remains a subject of conjecture, rumor, and paranoia. But, as the saying goes, just because you're paranoid doesn't mean someone isn't out to get you; gunmen arrived one evening at Hope Road, spraying the kitchen, yard, and veranda with bullets. Amazingly, no one was killed, though Marley and Don Taylor were both wounded. No one was ever tried for the crime, though word in Trenchtown was that dead bodies left on the streets in the months following accounted for all of the attackers (though not those who ordered and paid for the raid). Bandaged and hobbled, Marley defied expectations by performing a full ninety-minute set at the *Smile Jamaica* concert two days later, but left for London after the show and didn't return to the island for two years.

Bob Marley played Adelaide in early 1979. The dust raised by that tour never really settled.

—Rose Ryan, Adelaide DJ

Something in the rhythm connected to the traditional music I'd been raised on. And the message of awareness and responsibility made me open my eyes.

—Casper Loma-Da-Wa, Hopi reggae musician

In his words I heard my own story and felt a growing pride. I am a survivor, a black survivor. For the first time I identified myself as a black man in a sea of whiteness. Marley cheered me on.

—Lemn Sissay, British-Ethiopian poet fostered in a white household

I ventured cocaine already and realized that it's not for me. It's not right. It does something very different than herb. It's negative.

—Ken Booth, reggae singer

On one level, the world outside Jamaica provided the solace of adoration, gratification, and income for Marley. His records sold millions, his tours drew larger and larger audiences, and he could claim a place among the era's biggest musical stars. But "the singer" (as he is called in Marlon James's Booker Prize–winning novel *A Brief History of Seven Killings*, based around the attack on Hope Road) always had wider ambitions than the average pop star. He wanted to fulfill his destiny as a follower of Garvey and Selassie, and insisted on performing in Africa even when costs outweighed income. He was also determined to realize the dream born during those Delaware nights listening to his mother's transistor radio: to have as great an impact on African-American listeners as he was having on White college kids and stoners.

Africa, however, proved a repeated source of heartbreak. On a visit to Ethiopia, Bob was crushed to discover that Selassie was (a) really and truly dead and buried in an unmarked grave, and (b) considered by most of his countrymen to have been a tyrant with little love for the poor and downtrodden. In Gabon, chatting to officials after a concert, he discovered that his fee was far greater than he had been told by Taylor, who was revealed to be skimming even more than he was already taking in commissions. Then in April 1980, a year prior to his death, Marley flew to Harare to perform during Zimbabwe's Independence celebrations. Having been assured that ordinary people could buy affordable tickets, he was confronted by a sea of luxurious armchairs filled with immobile, coat-and-tied government officials, while his fans were off in the distance behind chicken wire. When he encouraged them to break down the fence and fill the empty spaces in front of the stage, police beat them brutally and the stadium was filled with tear gas. Africa, it seemed, was as sad and unjust as Jamaica.

In America, his audiences remained as White as ever. Hustler after African-American hustler joined the entourage, promising keys to unlock the "urban" door. But despite an opening spot on a Commodores tour, the only way Marley and Black America grew any closer lay in the singer's increasing taste for cocaine. Pious Rastas were horrified to witness Marley and his contingent chanting praises normally directed at the herb towards lines of white powder.

Marley was encountering a phenomenon that would challenge world music artists and producers starting in the next decade: only the educated middle classes of Western Europe, North America, Australasia, and Japan have ever shown much enthusiasm for exotic rhythms and lyrics they don't understand. For most of the world's population, music provides a soundtrack to their lives, reflecting the rhythm of *their* streets, the cadences of *their* speech, and the nuances of *their* argot. Unless the unfamiliar rhythms were American or British (and therefore represented modernity), "foreign" music rarely attracted and often repelled the average listener. In the seventies, most Black Americans wanted a ticket to Las Vegas, not Africa. A few African-American homes may have sported a Marley poster, but almost none contained a Marley LP; to this day, urban radio programmers give his music a wide berth.

But the extraordinary thing about Marley's achievement is how, despite his music's failure to gain traction among African Americans, working-class audiences in the rest of the world embraced it with even more passion than their bourgeois neighbors. Long after the ephemeral spotlight of world music fashion had passed from isicathamiya to Bulgarian choirs to Buena Vista to Cape Verde to Mali, bands on Apache Reservations in Arizona, in Maori districts in New Zealand, and in Polish steel towns continued to faithfully plow Marley's furrow. It's not easy to grow dreadlocks with East Asian hair, but Japanese reggae artists somehow managed it. In Africa, Lucky Dube and Alpha Blondy became stars by mimicking Bob's attitudes, cadences, rhythms, and idealistic songwriting, Africans looking to a Jamaican who was looking to Africa. Marley, one Kenyan observed, showed how it was possible to be both African and modern.

Cuban *son* and American funk may have had a greater impact on dancefloors around the world, but their influence on local musicians was more oblique; emulating Benny Moré or James Brown, they often missed the target yet created something almost as powerful. Marley's reggae, on the other hand, inspired slavish replication by fanatics addicted to its alchemical beat. Reggae isn't so easy to "fuse"; the beat is either turned inside out or it isn't. Like death metal or Dixieland jazz emulators, roots reggae devotees rarely make music that is particularly interesting to anyone outside their home culture (and certainly not to Jamaicans), but their devotion speaks volumes about the extraordinary accomplishments of Marley, Perry, Tosh, Livingston, the Barretts, et al. at the turn of the seventies. As remarkable as this following was, though, in terms of Jamaica's worldwide influence it was but a big drop in an even bigger bucket.

There were three bands on board HMS *Empire Windrush*, the boat which brought the first wave of West Indian immigrants to Britain in 1948, and they played every night. When the ship docked at Southampton, photographs of the Trinidadian calypsonian Lord Kitchener strolling down the gangplank singing "London Is the Place for Me" made the front pages. No one paid much attention to the Royal Navy destroyer that shadowed the *Windrush* all the way from Kingston with orders to turn it around at the first sign of "trouble," but perhaps that was an equally prescient foreshadowing of future relations between the arrivals and their hosts.

Unsurprisingly, Trinidadian music overshadowed Jamaican in the first decade; no posh fifties ball was complete without a strolling steel-pan trio, and calypsonians popped up now and then on television, improvising verses about current events. With the arrival of the first ska 45s, though, the spotlight began to shift; along with the music came a new wave of immigrants as Jamaica's weak economy drove many off the island to look for work while Trinidad's oil boom kept its workers at home. Jamaicans in Britain saw ska as a cultural lifeline; their enthusiasm made licensing UK rights a profitable business for both Blackwell's Island and Emil Shalit's Blue Beat labels. (But not as profitable as it was for Kingston producers, who rarely told their artists about UK releases, much less shared any of the proceeds.)

The English had mixed feelings about the newcomers. Many, if not most, were unnerved by them, but younger ones were often attracted to the music and the style. As skiffle fans and blues fanatics picked up African-American music and ran with it, forming bands out of art schools and revolutionizing the country's (and then the world's) popular music, pockets of working-class youths held back, not so keen on Beatlemania and its offshoots and looking for their own place in the exploding world of teenage culture. Ska caught the ear of many such rejectionists.

Mods loved the Jamaican style; many British men looked as if they hadn't yet replaced their post-war demob suits, while West Indians always seemed to dress sharp. White boys often went for the whole package, music and fashion; Laurel Aitken's snap-brim fedora and Desmond Dekker's high-water trousers became sartorial icons. Great Black dancers wearing cool threads also attracted English girls, which built up a reservoir of resentment on the part of badly dressed, stumble-footed English guys.

Skinheads embraced ska's rude-boy aura but preferred instrumentals where they didn't have to deal with "foreign" accents or patwa; Prince Buster's "Al Capone" and Harry J's "Liquidator" became their anthems. (The latter is still used as a run-out theme at football grounds.) Skinhead get-togethers often resembled Duke Reid's "bull parties": heavily male, aggressive, and filled with music that, as the sixties blossomed, served as flower-power anti-matter. Outsiders were puzzled about how a love of Jamaican music could be compatible with "Paki-bashing" and xenophobia; Eric Clapton provided an answer of sorts when he delivered an expletive-filled, anti-immigrant onstage speech soon after reaching #1 with "I Shot the Sheriff."

Aitken, Dekker, Buster, and other Jamaican artists often toured Britain, and some settled down. Trombonist Rico Rodriguez proved the most durable, a familiar dreadlocked figure in the front row of the house band on BBC 2's *Later . . . with Jools Holland*. Rico had been tutored as a teenager by the master, Don Drummond, who took him along to jam sessions at Count Ossie's camp. Arriving in 1961, he got involved straight away in the scene around the Flamingo Club in Soho, playing with Georgie Fame and other jazz and rhythm-and-blues outfits, backing visiting American and Jamaican singers, and performing on every kind of recording session. Over the decades, Rodriguez became a touchstone, an iconic figure connecting the British music scene to an idealized Jamaican past. In 1977, Rico proved his authenticity; given a budget by Island to record an instrumental version of Marley's new hit, "Exodus" (and having barred the label's Trinidadian A&R man from the studio), he delivered a terrific version of the wrong song. He had covered the theme from the 1960 film *Exodus*, a favorite of Alpha Boys jazzmen and in Wareika Hills jam sessions. After all, what true Jamaican paid any mind to what Marley was up to "in foreign"?

Immigrant kids, including those from other islands (but few Trinidadians), followed Kingston fashions, egged on by a network of below-the-radar, mostly indoor sound systems. By the early seventies, a schism had opened, marked by the glimpse I caught of Bob & Marcia with strings on *Top of the Pops*. As the first *Windrush* wave began taking out mortgages, raising families, and hearing about violence and poverty in Jamaica, the idea of ever going back began to fade. Their children loved Jamaican music, but Rasta mythology and rude-boy braggadocio rang hollow for many; they had the same cravings as any English teenagers, just no interest in pursuing them to a White soundtrack. Trojan Records grasped the dichotomy; they licensed Bob & Marcia's "Young,

Gifted and Black" from Harry J, overdubbed strings, and brought the duo to Britain for a promotional tour that took it into the Top Ten. This was by no means Jamaica's first chart success, but earlier hits by Prince Buster, Desmond Dekker, The Ethiopians, Dave and Ansel Collins, and The Skatalites (as well as Max Romeo's banned but huge-selling "Wet Dream") were considered one-offs, exceptions that proved BBC Radio's rule that reggae didn't count as a significant popular form. Over on BBC Television, of course, the most popular Saturday-night variety program remained *The Black and White Minstrel Show*, featuring an army of blacked-up singers and dancers with painted-on piccaninny grins.

Like their parents' generation in fifties Kingston, when the supply of pleasing tracks began to dry up, young West Indians in seventies London took matters into their own hands. One record kids particularly liked was a slow, sexy Scratch Perry production called "Hurts So Good" by Susan Cadogan; it inspired producer Dennis Bovell and sound-system operator Lloyd "Coxsone" to produce home-grown tracks with a similar feel. Like Kingston's move to ska in the fifties, the lovers' rock revolution was driven by girls and sound-system promoters who wanted to lure them to their dances. Out went the dark, menacing atmosphere of roots events throbbing with dub, in came sexy lighting and romantic numbers sung by teenage girls with Anglo-Jamaican accents.

Discs by UK roots bands such as Aswad, Matumbi, and Steel Pulse never sold as fast as lovers' rock, even though the latter's discs were all released on small independent labels. The divide between the two was, to a certain degree, a false one, since musicians from Matumbi and Aswad provided the backing for most lovers' rock hits and Jamaican artists even began flying to England to record with them. But there remains a quizzical bitterness among Anglo–West Indian musicians and producers about how lovers' rock was ignored by British radio and by the labels busy capitalizing on Marley's success by signing Jamaican and British-based reggae artists. "As soon as they had to stop feeling sorry for us, they didn't want to know," observed Bovell. Dreadlocked *sufferahs* singing about Babylon and stoner-fodder dub were more exciting to White A&R men than what Afro-Caribbean kids in Britain were dancing to. Perhaps it was just business; labels knew what they could promote, and lightweight pop songs, even those with a nifty "one-drop," would be a tough sell to Island's or Virgin's target market in the hipster wing of the rock fraternity.

∽

Across the first three post-*Windrush* decades, Jamaican influence on British musical sensibilities ranged from the cartoonish (Paul McCartney singing "Ob-La-Di Ob-La-Da") to the arcane (collectors cross-examining visiting Jamaican artists about who played bass on their most obscure singles). As the Jamaican presence in British society entered its third decade, one engine that drove its growing influence was the Notting Hill Carnival. What is now "Europe's biggest street festival" began modestly in the early sixties with an annual indoor party for the Trinidadian community. In 1966, with help from John "Hoppy" Hopkins at the idealistic London Free School, it came out onto the streets around Portobello Market over the August bank holiday, with costumed children and a steel band. The following years remained heavy on the Trinidadian vibe, but little by little, helped by Marley's success and John Peel playing reggae on Radio 1, Jamaican-run sound systems began to drown out the steel-band floats.

In the watershed year of 1976, carnival arrived at the end of a summer of record-breaking heat filled with confrontations between Black youths and police using the "sus" laws to stop anyone they didn't like the look of. Encouraged by the soundtracks of confrontation coming from Jamaica and America, Black Britons had been growing in political awareness and confidence. Dreadlocks were a further trigger for clashes with parents, who wanted their kids to succeed in "Babylon," as well as with police, who were as enraged as Jamaican authorities by the defiant racial pride such hair represented. The violent police attacks on the 1976 carnival drew White sympathizers on the political Left to the Black cause, sweeping up dozens of young, angry, anti-establishment White musicians who felt (almost) as alienated as Afro-Caribbean kids.

Much has been made of the empathetic connection between punks and rockers in the late seventies, and certainly Johnny Rotten's and Joe Strummer's devotion to Jamaican music (dub in particular) helped drip-feed those sensibilities into punk and its offspring. The Boswell of the punk/dub connection is a dreadlocked son of Jamaican immigrants named Don Letts, whose career represents a remarkable feat of culture-straddling. Already embedded in the proto-punk scene, following an epiphany at Marley's Lyceum show in 1975, Letts embraced the spiritual aspects of Rastafarianism (including the locks) and became an articulate spokesman for both worlds. By Don's own account, though, the cultural traffic was mostly one way; his West Indian mates may have sold dope to the punks, but he seems to have been the only Black face at their gigs and most cross-talk involved Letts blasting out dub and reggae from a jukebox at his stall in a Chelsea antique market or between sets at the seminal punk club the Roxy. For many, those dub sets provided welcome relief from the frantic amateurism of the bands; the more astute punk musicians credit dub with teaching them about the use of "space" in music, a concept previously foreign to most of them. When Letts met Marley, the singer mocked him for his weird get-up, but recanted after Don took him to a Clash gig; the energy and defiant attitude impressed Bob and he responded with the song "Punky Reggae Party."

Rotten and Strummer had been keen students of Jamaican music with big collections even before they began hanging out with Letts, but both held muddled notions about Black culture. They loved being among the very few White faces at "blues dances" in Harlesden (where, the joke went, a White guy had to know a few regulars to get in, but he'd have to know *everybody* to get out), but when Strummer paid his famous visit to a big reggae show —"(White Man) In Hammersmith Palais"—he was shocked by how few dreadlocks there were amid the party frocks, coats, ties, and smoochy dancing to lovers' rock.

Repulsion at Clapton's rant and blowback from the police riot at the '76 carnival kicked off the Rock Against Racism movement in 1977. A huge march from Trafalgar Square to Victoria Park in Hackney, past glowering skinheads and tattooed thugs, was climaxed by a concert featuring The Clash and Aswad, while Steel Pulse and Elvis Costello performed at a concurrent event in south London. (I was on that march and remember feeling buoyant with the certainty that we represented the future and the ugly racists along Bethnal Green Road the past. That seems not to have turned out quite as we expected.)

A good idea attempted is better than a bad idea perfected.
—Don Letts on what he learned from the punks

Punk was London-centric; when musicians in other parts of Britain formed punk-inspired bands, the music was often more interesting, freed from the diktats emanating from Malcolm McLaren's SEX boutique and the Roxy club. In the unlikely Midlands outpost of Coventry, Jerry Dammers assembled a racially mixed group that tried to split the difference between punk and reggae. They would alternate the two at gigs, until they figured out how to combine them; the common ground, they realized, was ska.

They called themselves The Specials, after the dub-plate exclusives that sound-system DJs guarded so assiduously. Some of the original Afro-Caribbean members couldn't get their heads around playing their parents' old-fashioned beat and quit. There was clearly a retro aspect to it but ska was itself, after all, a throwback, with Jamaicans mimicking American records of the previous decade. Punk's "do-it-yourself" ethos inspired them to start their own label, and Dammers turned out to have a deft feel for graphics, marketing, and image; 2-Tone, with its black-and-white sleeves and logo, released a series of the group's own Top Ten hits as well as big records by Coventry mates The Selecter, The Beat from Birmingham, and the first hit by London's Madness.

Dammers's vision was to lure skinheads using their favorite music, then dance the races together. Fans came up with some neat moves that combined punk pogoing with the off-beat pumping motions of ska; the movement represented a genuine attempt to forge a multiracial English identity. But Specials' audiences, like Marley's, remained stubbornly White; most Afro-Caribbean kids couldn't have been less interested. Fascist groups did show up, however, recruiting in the crowd and sometimes throwing rocks or bottles at the group's Black members. The Specials' legacy was defined by their final single, 1981's elegiac "Ghost

Town," a requiem for what might have been, a grim harbinger of Britain's Thatcherite future and a masterpiece of British pop, complete with Rico Rodriguez trombone solo.

Like Marley's reggae, the ska revival established outposts of fanatics around the world. One of the more surreal sights I have witnessed was the 1989 London debut of the Russian ska outfit Avia, with a troupe of girls dressed like Aeroflot stewardesses executing robotic skanks on terraced risers behind the band. A decade later, I attended a concert of the Indonesian ska variant known as *dangdut* in Yogyakarta, where a group of skull-capped and bearded sharia students crowded in front of the stage to stare up the lead singer's miniskirt.

There was a valiant attempt to spread the ska revival to America; dozens of like-minded bands formed in the 1980s, mostly in New England and California, but the movement never advanced much beyond an excuse for both sexes to wear Doc Marten boots, drainpipe trousers, braces, and snap-brim fedoras. One West Coast ska outfit, however, secured a major-label deal. They were called No Doubt and their first LP flopped; the hugely successful follow-up played down the ska and focused on their charismatic singer, Gwen Stefani. Gadfly film-maker Michael Moore has shown that, after Stefani became a multifaceted star, her huge contract as a judge on *The Voice* so outraged Donald Trump (being significantly richer than his for *The Apprentice*) that he decided to enhance his brand with an obviously futile run for president.

Across the 1970s, a world away from the anger, poverty, and political violence of Kingston, reggae established itself as a fundamental part of the pop music landscape, often as a change of pace or a new flavor to spice up an album or a live set. After the Rolling Stones covered Eric Donaldson's rocksteady classic "Cherry Oh Baby" on *Black and Blue*, Boney M swept to the top of the charts across Europe with their slick version of The Melodians' "By the Rivers of Babylon." Blondie marked the high-water point of the cover trend with a 1980 #1 on both sides of the Atlantic, "The Tide Is High," a straight-up replica of a 1966 track by John Holt and the Paragons. Reggae had by then joined the habanera, bossa nova, mambo, and tango as a colorful rhythm, the rudiments of which needed to be in the repertoire of any self-respecting jobbing musician.

The Police began life masquerading as a punk band. Their arrangement for "Roxanne" originally had a bossa nova feel, but they chickened out of playing it at a punk club and switched the rhythm to a kind of "bastardised reggae" (as Stewart Copeland put it) and never looked back. Their early hits combined snatches of one-drop and dub effects, while Sting sometimes strayed into a cod–West Indian accent as the group marched triumphantly across the world's arenas and pop charts for the better part of a decade.

When a friend excitedly pointed out Bob Marley to the young Boy George, he had no idea whom they were talking about. He soon began listening and studying, however, lovers' rock in particular, and his subsequent success with Culture Club, was down, in his words, to "reggae that wouldn't frighten white people." Of the ska bands, only Madness kept making hits far into the eighties, fueled by the singer Suggs's cheeky-cockney attitude and Stiff label boss Dave Robinson's wonderfully surreal videos.

In 1964, during my spring of "total immersion" in British folk music, I spent time in Birmingham with the Scots singer Ian Campbell and his family. I made myself useful by taking his young sons to the local playground and pushing them on the swings. Robin and Ali grew up surrounded by Jamaican sounds and eventually applied the clear diction and nasal tones they inherited from Dad to a purist approach to reggae with the racially mixed band UB40 (named after Unemployment Benefit Form 40). An initial burst of political songwriting gave way to a more commercial repertoire combining Jamaican classics with American pop, set to a well-honed reggae pulse; over the next two decades they became the world's largest-selling reggae artists.

The biggest pop-reggae hit of the eighties emerged from what could be an episode of one of those feel-good BBC comedies about Pakistani or West Indian immigrants. Just down the road from UB40 in Birmingham, a Jamaican dad with thwarted musical ambitions hoped to turn his cute kids into Jackson 5–type stars. Their sanitized cover of a reggae song about passing the ganja chillum to the left (like the port in an English gentlemen's club) took Musical Youth into the Top Ten in both the US and UK. They had the wit to hire Don Letts to direct their promo video, which secured the first-ever airing of a Black group on MTV. But after their label (MCA/Universal) sacked Letts and insisted on filming the follow-up at a yacht club and making sure the group's trousers were neatly pressed, they vanished from sight.

Where did the idea of holding a dance and not booking any musicians originate? Jamaica, obviously; with no ballrooms or nightclubs to speak of, the island's bands performed mostly at tourist resorts or in the studio. Thanks to DJs, though, there was dancing in Kingston every night.

But that's the wrong answer. In Nazi Germany in the late 1930s, musicians caught playing "obscene Jewish jungle music" could end up in a concentration camp; "swing kids," the Reich's youthful dissidents, knew that only thick walls, heavy curtains, absolute secrecy, and someone's jazz 78s played at modest volume could allow them a few precious hours of jitterbugging. This practice seems to have been stowed away in the Wehrmacht's baggage on the march to Paris, where references to *discothèques* pop up in accounts of Left Bank life both during the Occupation and in those storied years following Liberation. What could possibly be hipper than a nexus where Juliette Gréco and Jean-Paul Sartre meet Prince Buster and Scratch Perry?

With louder PA systems, the practice of dancing to records began to spread, and it was the French model that dominated: fashionable "discos," velvet ropes, guest lists, and DJs whose skill lay in choosing records in a sequence that determined the mood of the night. But today's vast expanses of dancers in warehouses and fields owe far more to the "lawns" of Kingston than the A-Go-Gos of Paris; celebrity DJs such as David Guetta playing exclusive remixes (and earning many times more than the musicians they sample) fall in a direct line from gold-crowned Duke Reid firing his shotguns into the Jamaican night.

The notion of disc jockey as royalty gathered strength as another group of outcasts joined Germany's swing kids and Jamaica's urban underclass in particularizing their dancing experience. In the remote dunes of Fire Island in the early seventies, New York's gay dance scene honed the art of the mixtape. Tom Moulton was a pioneer who edited tracks together and looped the best bits using a pair of scissors and Scotch tape. He seems to have been unaware of the existence of Kingston "selectors," but by the end of the decade, New York's most famous downtown DJs were pronouncing Scratch's and Tubby's names with awed reverence and applying lessons learned from them in constructing their 12-inch remixes. There would seem to be a conceptual link between Kingston's promiscuous use and reuse of tracks and the postmodern, context-free appropriation of music from across the globe by the innovative kingpins of the gay dance scene. Rhythms remained the biggest difference between the two worlds; the tropical isle's fascination with ever more inventive and complex beats was very far from the jackhammer, four-on-the-floor pulse that provided a perfect accompaniment to the anonymous sex of the pre-AIDS seventies on those northern islands, Manhattan and Fire.

Meanwhile, about ten miles north of the Meatpacking District, on that southward-jutting peninsula of the US mainland known as the Bronx, something far more portentous was taking place.

> The sun hadn't gone down yet, and kids were just hanging out, waiting for something to happen. Van pulls up, a bunch of guys come out with a table, crates of records. They unscrew the base of the light pole, take their equipment, attach it to that, get the electricity—Boom! We got a concert right here in the schoolyard and it's this guy Kool Herc. And he's just standing with the turntable, and the guys were studying his hands. There are people dancing, but there's as many people standing, just watching what he's doing. That was my first introduction to in-the-street, hip-hop DJing.
>
> —Nelson George

Kool Herc was born Clive Campbell (no relation to Buster) in Kingston; he emigrated to New York as a kid in 1967, but not before experiencing sound systems. As a Bronx teenager in the early seventies, he hosted after-school parties in the recreation room of the building where his family lived at 1520 Sedgwick Avenue. This anonymous "project" tower is identical to hundreds of others, but New York State has designated it as a "site of historic interest"—the spot where hip-hop was born.

Spinning records for his friends, Campbell (nicknamed Hercules on the basketball court for his height and strength) noticed how they loved the drum breaks on old James Brown records. Borrowing an idea from King Tubby, he linked two turntables so he could jump from the end of a break on one copy to the start of it on another, effectively looping Brown's drum fills. Another trick that arrived in Herc's carry-on bag from Jamaica was to toast over those breaks. His classmates had never heard anything like it and soon his parties were overflowing the small indoor space and he had to move them to nearby basketball courts and playgrounds.

Two among those Nelson George describes watching Herc's hands were Joseph Saddler and Lance Taylor, children of Barbadian immigrant families and later known as Grandmaster Flash and Afrika Bambaataa. Despite the pilfered electricity and the booming sound from his ever-bigger speakers, police tolerated Herc's dance parties since they kept kids in one place and had a dampening effect on crime. During the first half of the seventies, the Bronx had been wracked by gang wars, arson, and random shootings; the second half of the decade was peaceful in comparison, largely due to the craze for spinning records, "scratching" back and forth between turntables, the break-dancing Herc encouraged with contests and prizes, and the toasting (which Yanks called "rapping").

Jamaican sound systems as the prototype for a Bronx musical revolution didn't end there. Herc also taught his friends about dub plates; rap's multibillion-dollar recording industry began, like ska and dub, with enterprising DJs cutting tracks, rhyming over them, and, eventually, pressing and releasing them, raps included. By the time "Rapper's Delight" and "The Message" arrived at the end of the decade, Herc was out of the spotlight, working in a record store, battered by violent jealousies, casual arson, and younger DJs with more advanced techniques.

Links between Trenchtown and the South Bronx had been forged, and they weren't just musical. The CIA had pressured Jamaica to crack down on ganja exports; this led to a boom in home-grown American dope and a Jamaican shift from weed-growing to becoming a conduit for Colombian powders. Cocaine traffic coursing through Kingston on its way from South America to the US East Coast created fabulously wealthy gangsters. The Jamaican record business began to resemble medieval African kingdoms where musicians, like griots, toiled in the service of "big men" who rewarded praise songs that glorified their exploits; Kingston dance tracks were now mostly crafted on computers, financed by drug dealers and tailored to please them. In perhaps Jamaica's ultimate "gift" to America, a Trenchtown drug lord named Vivian Blake is credited with the introduction of crack as a means of improving cocaine's profitability.

> A happy face, a thumping bass, for a loving race.
> —Jazzie B's Soul II Soul slogan

> There is a downside to affordable technology—mediocrity.
> —Don Letts

Over time, Britain has had almost as much influence on the evolution of the world's dance music as America, with the second generation of London's Afro-Caribbean kids leading the way. Many key figures were offspring of the original sound-system operators who set up shop in the post-*Windrush* decades. With the lovers' rock revolution, these producers, operators, and DJs showed that they had learned Kingston's lessons; musical vitality grew out of a feedback loop in which producers learned, through the constant dialectic of leading and following, of trial and error, precisely what works.

London sound systems in the 1970s were a far broader church than their Kingston cousins; Ohio Players, O'Jays, Ramsey Lewis, and Sly Stone rubbed up against dub and dancehall from home as well as their own lovers' rock, Aswad, and Steel Pulse. In the years after Rock Against Racism, White faces began to appear, influencing the music's direction and turning the scene into a peculiarly British phenomenon. Soul II

Soul was the prototype, a savvy bunch who parlayed their pirate radio station and sound system, a line of clothing, and their leader Jazzie B's non-ideological dreadlocks into a style-setting behemoth; when they finally ventured into the recording studio, they knew exactly what to do, ending up with Top Ten records on both sides of the Atlantic. Britain was where tectonic musical plates—Jamaica, Europe, America, Africa, and Asia—collided, pushing up the crust and creating mountains.

White British DJs returned from Ibiza at the end of the summer of 1987 armed with the revelation that even the most boringly repetitive tracks can sound transformative given the right drugs. Inspired by "Balearic beats," they collided creatively with Black British sound systems; early raves often featured Black DJs aided by White law students flinging legal jargon at police trying to shut them down. Over the next three decades, White and Black British dance scenes would repeatedly come together to create something new, then swerve away as the tastes of their respective dancers grew apart. One consistent theme seems to be that for White kids, drugs are a key part of the experience, while new moves, lyrical content, and rhythmic innovation come first for Black crowds. (For some "unknown" reason White youths are arrested for drug possession a small fraction of the times Black kids are.) Afro-Caribbean dancing in the nineties became progressively more exotic and erotic, with Jamaica's toe-touching and booty-quivering outraging the island's government while remaining beyond the abilities or desires of most White dancers in Britain. Another divide was sonic: Black sound systems are all about bass, while White raves are brighter, with more mid-range and treble. Jungle, acid house, drum 'n' bass, garage, grime, and techno would wax and wane in the decades that followed, triggered by that distinctively Jamaican process—innovation, special remix, dub plate, DJ improvisation, audience demand, record release, commercial success, and, finally, a new underground variation introduced via dub plate.

The headwaters of the modern world of electronic dance music as well as the meticulously layered crafting of pop hits are often traced to German bands such as Kraftwerk, the first to swap guitars for computers. But Scratch's crying-baby loop was probably more important.

Out of "Version" and the dub plates grew the notion that the primary function of recording sessions involving living, breathing musicians is to provide raw material for DJs and producers, to be molded like clay or pasted on as decoration. The serious work of the music industry today is the construction of flawless, heavily compressed tracks using drum machines, sequencers, samplers, and computers. For this we may thank or blame both Germany and Jamaica.

Why do you look so sad and forsaken?
When one door is closed, don't you know another is open?
In this life (in this life)
In this (in this life, oh sweet life)
Coming in from the cold

—Bob Marley, "Coming in from the Cold"

The ominous lyrics of Culture's "Two Sevens Clash" put the fear of Jah into JA. Stoned readings of the Old Testament gave weight to prophecies and forebodings for 7/7/77: seven seals, seven plagues, seven vials of God's wrath. Streets and highways throughout the island were deserted, but July 7 passed apocalypse-free. (Soon afterwards, though, Scratch Perry burned down his studio.)

That winter, Bob Marley's London exile was interrupted by a visit from Bucky Marshall and Claude Mossop, leaders of the two political gangs that were tearing the ghettos apart. Following a chance meeting in prison, the two had decided to broker a truce, and Marley agreed to return to the island to headline a historic Peace Concert. The British critic Robin Denselow describes it as the longest and most extraordinary concert he has ever witnessed, with a parade of Jamaican talent starting in the afternoon and ending long after midnight. The climactic set reunited the three Wailers, who then brought onstage Manley, Seaga, Mossop, and Marshall, all joining hands in an ecstatic finale.

The ensuing ceasefire lasted a fortnight; in a surge of violence Mossop and Marshall were both killed, while Tosh, who had outraged police during the concert by blowing ganja smoke at them and hectoring the politicians to *"legalise it,"* was arrested and beaten. Seaga won the 1980 election, the economy collapsed, and Jamaica suffered for the next decade under the heavy manners of the IMF.

As Marley's health declined, he continued to record and tour, under pressure, some said, from hangers-on with their snouts in the trough. When he delivered the masters of his final studio album, *Uprising*, Blackwell balked at releasing it, telling him the songs weren't strong enough; Bob returned a few weeks later with two of his greatest tracks, "Coming in from the Cold" and "Redemption Song." He died on May 11, 1981, in Miami, was mourned with a lavish Kingston funeral conducted by an archbishop of the Abyssinian Church, and buried at Nine Mile. The Jamaican establishment, long repulsed by his locks, his creed, and his fame, rushed to sanctify his memory and build the island's tourist image around his safely interred persona and now-archived music. The memorial album *Legend* sold as fast as parallel compilations from The Beatles, Eagles, and Floyd. Rita dealt with Bob's offspring scattered around the world with admirable tolerance, stating that such unjudgmental love was part of her Rastafarian ideals. She and Blackwell devised a Solomonic division of the estate that avoided lawsuits.

On February 23, 1985, at a dance on Waltham Park Road in Kingston, a producer named Lloyd "Prince Jammy" James launched a single by Wayne Smith titled "Under Mi Sleng Teng." "Sleng Teng" is a landmark, its rhythm track the accidental fruit of the percussion switch on a Casio keyboard—cheesy, simple, irresistible for dancers, and an instant hit. To old-school listeners, the record was a sacrilege: there was no bass! Even Jamaica was now succumbing to the rhythmic dumbing-down set loose upon the zeitgeist by disco.

With ragga and dancehall, Jamaica flaunted the local eccentricities that, with occasional exceptions, finally succeeded in cutting its music off from all but its own diaspora. Some tracks by Buju Banton, Shabba Ranks, and Shaggy did break through with hip-hop audiences in America, while influence, along with the drug trade, continued to flow back and forth, with each culture seemingly egging the other on to become more hard-edged, violent, misogynist, and homophobic, driven by feuds and revenge.

In a nod to the island's heritage, many of dancehall's electronic beats contained elements of Burru and Kumina drum patterns, seldom recognizable as such to outsiders, but sounding proudly Jamaican to islanders. Over the past four decades, Jamaican music has grown progressively jerkier, harsher, more staggered, often sounding as if put together by someone with a computer and a short, coke-fueled attention span; crowds of dancers are kept off-balance and nervous, and they seem to like it that way. Lyrics celebrate bling-laden materialism; Africa, Garvey, and Jah don't get many name-checks.

The government proclaims its support for "music and the arts," but—as recounted in Josh Jelly-Schapiro's book *Island People*—at a recent school prize-giving the culture minister scolded a neatly uniformed contestant for moving her hips during a performance. There must have been some raucous laughter in the girls' room after the ceremony; many, if not most of them, will have spent at least one recent evening in tightest spandex, bent over on a dancefloor, moving a lot more than just their hips. Jamaican girls who pass the age of seventeen without having a child are often mocked as "mules." The disconnect between government policies and people's lives seems almost total and election turnouts have plummeted.

Alpha Boys still teaches students how to play instruments, but sessions requiring their services are few. It remains customary, however, to play a Marley track at the close of every dance; in an instant, the mood shifts, becoming nostalgic, even gentle, with many in the crowd, even the youth, singing along.

In March 1976, I got a call from Chris Blackwell asking if I would take his place finishing off a Toots and the Maytals album. I doubt I have ever said a more rapid "yes" to anything.

Island began releasing Toots's records internationally in the early seventies and he gradually became a cult figure for those who explored beyond Marley and dub. In 1976, Blackwell proposed working with him the way he worked with his biggest star. Toots and the producer Warwick Lyn flew to London with two reels of twenty-four-track tape for a fortnight of overdubs, editing, and mixing at Island's Basing Street Studios. Marley got wind of it, however, and wasn't happy. He rang Blackwell from Nassau, saying he had some tracks ready and why didn't he come down and get to work? Torn, Chris felt he had no choice but to board the plane to Nassau, hence the call to me.

Lyn, a Chinese Jamaican with a startling resemblance to Jeff Chandler as Cochise in *Broken Arrow*, was a delight to work with. Toots was politely engaged but a bit distant, leaving me and Warwick to choose and edit tracks and book musicians. When I asked about Raleigh and Jerry, the other original Maytals, Warwick told me Toots had been singing the harmonies and backing vocals himself for years.

One memorable night, Rico arrived to add trombone parts to "Rastaman," a remake of "Bam Bam," the prize-winning song from 1965. Toots and the trombonist settled themselves out in the studio with a pyramid of herb wrapped in newspaper. Once the headphone mix was balanced to their satisfaction, we played them the opening bars. Toots would hum the line he had in mind and Rico would rehearse it until Toots was happy, then we'd try recording. Once we had recorded the line perfectly, we'd proceed to the next four-bar section and repeat the process. When we reached the end of the verse, we'd go back and start again for the harmony part. (Toots and Lyn had rejected my proposal to hire two trombonists.) The pair never left the studio; playbacks were heard through headphones. Neither called for food or a break and only occasionally requested water. When they emerged at about 4 a.m., blood from Rico's split lip was running down his chin. I consider it among my canniest moves as a producer that I asked the engineer to record Toots's humming on two separate tracks as he demonstrated the parts. When we mixed a week later, I replaced the second trombone line during the instrumental break with Toots's voice; the result is one of my favorite moments on any record I have been involved in.

Warwick and I added a few non-Jamaican touches but kept them subtle: a solo by Dudu Pukwana on one track, a Hammond organ part from Steve Winwood on another. *Reggae Got Soul* was released in July

1976 and did reasonably well, but failed to provide the big breakthrough Blackwell had been hoping for. Chris did, however, say it ranked among his favorite Toots records, and that was enough for me.

Forty years later, my wife, Andrea, and I went to hear Toots at the Barbican in London. On our way in, we spotted half a dozen former skinheads, plump and prosperous, the guys in suits with open-neck shirts revealing tattoos, their Essex wives in new hairdos and stilettos. We saw West Indian men with graying goatees and dreadlocks, women in go-to-church dresses, clusters of middle-aged *Guardian* readers and world music fans with ponytails and bald patches, two dozen or so young Black couples, bunches of White student types, and even a few Africans and Asians. All two thousand seats were filled.

When Toots strode out to join the band—the same musicians who had been backing him for most of those forty years—he went straight to the classics: "54-46 Was My Number" (written after spending a year in prison on a police-vengeance marijuana charge following the victory of "Bam Bam" in the 1965 song contest), "Pressure Drop" (his condemnation of a man who refused to pay him the money he was owed), "Take Me Home Country Roads" (an inspired transformation of the John Denver ballad), "Monkey Man" (about a muscly guy going out with a girl Toots fancied and from whom Toots asked permission before composing it), "Time Tough," "Six and Seven Books," "Rastaman." The great songs just kept coming, relentlessly. As the encores finished, I turned to look around the hall. Of course everyone was standing, cheering and clapping, but the most striking image was the ear-to-ear grins splitting every face.

Since that first Bahamas evening, I have listened over and over to Toots's records. Unlike so many Jamaican vocalists, he was never drawn to the light falsetto of Curtis Mayfield or his doo-wop predecessors; Toots's passionate, full-throated singing has been compared to Otis Redding's, a singer with similar roots in the Pentecostal churches of John Jeremiah Sullivan's "old West Indian world." Winston Grennan's drumming on the sixties tracks is a further source of endless fascination and delight, the way he upends Anglo-American sensibilities, turning our sense of time inside out while still speaking a musical language we understand.

Toots's records kept up with shifting fashions to a degree, but their melodic, joyful mood never really changed from the early days, after he left May Pen for Kingston and began writing songs while training to be a barber. He never cut much hair, but he had a hairdresser's ear for the trials and tribulations of the people he encountered. "I don't write nursery rhymes," Toots declared, making clear his chagrin at the simple-mindedness of modern dancehall lyrics. He was as idealistic as Marley, but his songs rarely instruct or generalize, they simply describe. "Sweet and Dandy," the song he is seen recording in *The Harder They Come*, tells of a groom struggling to pay for his wedding celebration:

>*Etty in the room a-cry*
>*Mama say she must wipe her eye*
>*Papa say, "She no fi foolish*
>*Like she never been to school at all!"*
>
>*It is no wonder*
>*It's a perfect ponder*
>*Why they were dancing*
>*In that bar room last night*
>
>*Johnson in the room a-fret*
>*Uncle say he must hold up him head*
>*Aunty say, "He no fi foolish*
>*Like it's not time for his wedding day!"*
>
>*One pound ten for the wedding cake*
>*And plenty bottle of cola wine*
>*All the people them dress up in a white*
>*Fi go eat out Johnson wedding cake . . .*
>
>*Well they were sweet and dandy*
>*Sweet and dandy*

His and Marley's recordings (along with hundreds of others) provide a testament to the people and culture of this small island where most have so little, yet retain such pride and such originality. Over the centuries, Jamaica's neighbor Cuba built a powerful engine for growing sugar and tobacco, scoured the coasts of Africa for countless millions of captives from widely varying cultures, developed a complex, sophisticated musical form that entranced the world, and lured tourists and dancers to its rhythms. Over that same period, Jamaica cut itself off from Africa, its economy shrank, and the island turned in upon itself, too big to be a palm-fringed dot on the tourist map and too intense, poor, and strange to draw visitors to its cities. Yet in the last decades of the twentieth century, as if by a trick of magic, reggae suddenly appeared, standing alongside Afro-Cuban music in the spotlight. At the cusp of the digital age, sounds created by these two islands stood toe-to-toe with African-American music in defining the global soundtrack. Digits would, in turn, wave their own darkly magic wand, creating a vast appetite for mechanical beats and turning the world's ears away from the complexities and eccentricities that geniuses from these two islands had produced. But even amid the most brittle of machine-generated rhythms, the DNA of Cuban and Jamaican music still resonate, shaping them and providing whatever complexity and subtleties they retain.

IV
Latcho drom

Late in the first half of Ravi Shankar's first New York recital on February 2, 1957, at Town Hall, Dick Bock fell asleep. Shankar's brilliance that evening inspired critics to compare him to Western classical masters and jazz greats, but Indian music's immense impact on the West in the late sixties can be traced directly back to Bock's doze.

Richard Bock was an early iteration of the West Coast hipster, a hash-smoking bebop buff who had started the Pacific Jazz label a few years earlier to record Gerry Mulligan's new quartet with Chet Baker. He was in New York that week to meet with George Avakian, the head of jazz at Columbia Records, hoping to talk him into becoming a partner; together, Bock felt, they could dominate the expanding jazz market. When Avakian went to check out the sitar master Yehudi Menuhin was raving about, Bock tagged along.

With only about a third of the seats filled, the concert was a commercial flop, but the audience was enthusiastic and Avakian so intrigued by the parallels with jazz that he offered Shankar a deal to make an album for Columbia. It was Bock, though, who would be the key to Ravi's international future. Had he dropped off out of boredom? Not at all; Indian music, he explained, "put the listener in a relaxed mood and calm state of mind, which carries [him] into an area of serenity." Bock may have then lacked the sixties vocabulary, but he responded as millions would a decade later; he had "tripped out" on Indian classical music.

Having arranged to meet when Shankar's tour reached Los Angeles, Ravi and Dick hit it off in the California sunshine and Bock got an OK from Columbia to do some recording of his own; Avakian knew that Indian music was the epitome of a niche product, and the more labels joining in to promote it, the merrier. Ravi's ragas joined an eclectic Pacific Jazz catalogue that included lessons in meditation and talks on Zen Buddhism as well as dozens of jazz albums. Columbia soon lost interest, but Shankar released album after album under Bock's World Pacific logo, with cool artwork and deft promotion. Ravi loved Southern California, and Pacific Jazz's backroom studio became a base where he gave master tutorials and relaxed between concerts.

As your author knows only too well, keeping an indie label afloat is far from easy, and in the early sixties, after the collaboration with Avakian failed to work out, Pacific Jazz nearly went under. To the rescue came an ex-GI, transpacific sailor and music buff named Jim Dickson, who came up with a pair of instruction albums for the twelve-string guitar, which sold like hot cakes. Bock showed his gratitude by giving the producer a key to the often-empty studio and inviting him to use it anytime.

Dickson's quest for hits led him to the coffeehouses of LA's early-sixties folk scene. There he came across Jim (before he was Roger) McGuinn, whose stock-in-trade was applying a Beatles feel to folk material; inspired by seeing George Harrison holding a Rickenbacker electric twelve-string guitar in *A Hard Day's Night*, he'd purchased one and had been studying Dickson's how-to albums. McGuinn and his friend Gene Clark had begun rehearsing and recording demos at Pacific Jazz when Dickson brought David Crosby into the mix. Crosby was a Lambert, Hendricks, & Ross fan who relished challenging music, particularly if it gave him ideas for unusual harmony parts. The three came up with a distinctive vocal sound: McGuinn and Clark in unison on the melody, and Crosby finding thirds, fourths, and even sixths above it.

Late one evening, as joints were being passed around the studio, Dickson put on a test pressing of Bock's latest Ravi Shankar album; he'd attended the session and wanted to see what his new charges made of it. David and Jim were stunned. Crosby hijacked the disc and played it at home endlessly, finding "the slow and reflective beginning and the gradual build . . . is very emotional and sexual . . . It takes you on its trip . . . Then it keeps picking you up and taking you further and further until the intensity is almost unbearable." McGuinn, who was as intrigued by the physicality of instruments as Crosby was by harmonies, loved how the sympathetic strings of Shankar's sitar seemed to echo the overtones of his Rickenbacker.

Dickson had found his hit-makers; as The Beefeaters, they released a single that flopped, but he persuaded Albert Grossman to give him an acetate of a song he'd heard Bob Dylan sing at the 1964 Newport Folk Festival. McGuinn, Clark, and new additions Chris Hillman and Michael Clarke loved Dickson's idea of covering "Mr. Tambourine Man," but Crosby was dead set against it. The indefatigable Dickson finally brought David around by bringing the man himself over to Pacific Jazz during a rehearsal. According to legend, after hearing their version, Dylan exclaimed, "Wow, man, you can dance to that!" The group decided to call themselves The Byrds (echoing the Fab Four's creative misspelling of an animal), Bock helped them open a door at Columbia Records via a supportive phone call from Miles Davis, and the rest is folk-rock history.

∽

Following their pyrrhic triumph at Shea Stadium on August 15, 1965, The Beatles rented Zsa Zsa Gabor's Beverly Hills mansion for some mid-tour R&R. Parties were non-stop, with plenty of girls, fellow celebrities, grass, and LSD. On the night of August 25, John Lennon and George Harrison ended up in Zsa Zsa's enormous (empty) bathtub, listening with stoned fascination as McGuinn and Crosby extolled the wonders of Indian music, of Ravi Shankar and of the modal scales McGuinn demonstrated on a guitar, a moment that has gone down in history as the start of Harrison's lifelong bond with India and its music.

A month earlier, British critics and audiences had given The Byrds a bruising on their promotional trip to London; perhaps the fact that Dylan's electric Newport moment hadn't happened yet had something to do with it. But they arrived back in LA pleased to have at least bonded with The Beatles and particularly happy with one bit of booty: a prototype cassette player and a couple of blank cassettes, a technology completely unknown then in the US. When the group set off that October on a cross-country tour, they traveled in a mobile home rigged up with a sound system using the cassette player and a guitar amp; John Coltrane's *Impressions*, featuring "India," filled one tape, with a couple of Ravi Shankar ragas on the other. Every day for weeks the music of the two geniuses invaded their brains. As soon as they got to New York, they recorded "Eight Miles High," featuring McGuinn's drone-based, Coltrane-meets-Shankar guitar solos. (Coltrane and Shankar had, in fact, met in 1961, introduced by Dick Bock, of which more later.)

During the war, when George Harrison's mother was pregnant with him, she had been entranced by the Indian music she heard late at night over Armed Forces Radio. As soon as The Beatles got back to London, her son went out and bought all the Ravi Shankar albums the HMV shop had in stock; a couple of weeks later, he stopped by Indiacraft near HMV on Oxford Street and bought a sitar that came with an instruction booklet. When the group began recording *Rubber Soul*, Lennon suggested George try shadowing the melody of "Norwegian Wood" on that "Indian thingy" of his. Getting the song down on tape involved a fateful hiccup when, during the evening session, Harrison broke a sitar string. Producer George Martin suggested that their best bet would be to ring the Asian Music Circle, and he just happened to have the number in his address book. Martin knew that the AMC's "office" was actually the north London home of Ayana and Patricia Angadi, a left-wing, Anglo-Indian couple devoted to keeping a flame of interest in Indian music alive in Britain. Starr volunteered to make the call, and when Ayana answered with "Ringo who?" his wife and their teenage daughter frantically intervened. A few minutes later, string in hand, the three were on their way to Abbey Road Studios. The group showed their gratitude by inviting them to stick around for the remainder of the session.

It is a peculiarly English footnote to this story that one of its unsung elements is class; Harrison's girlfriend at the time, Pattie Boyd, was a reasonably well educated, vaguely posh Home Counties English girl; that description also fit Patricia Fell-Clarke, who had spotted the handsome Angadi from across a road and married him over strenuous parental objections. The two women got on like the proverbial house on fire; not only did the Angadis find George a sitar tutor, but the couples began having regular foursome evenings, supper at one home or the other and outings to Indian music recitals. When George and Pattie got married in January 1966, amateur painter Patricia presented them with their portrait as a wedding present. This social bonding climaxed that July, when the Angadis hosted the supper at which George met his hero.

Ravi Shankar had heard about this Beatle and his interest in Indian music, but hadn't listened to "Norwegian Wood," was generally dismissive of Western pop music and wary of any link between his art and popular fads. That evening, though, the unassuming and thoughtful Harrison confounded Ravi's expectations. Within days he had been to George's home to give a masterclass, followed by supper and a private performance attended by the Lennons and the Starkeys (Ringo's real surname). That evening marked the start of two intense and eventful years that forged a lifelong friendship and brought Indian music into the heart of Western culture.

Many Indian musicians on tour in the West transform their hotel rooms into an outpost of the subcontinent: sticks of burning incense, spicy food on a hot plate, a small statue of Ganesh draped in blossoms or a copy of the Koran on the bedside table, and a closet filled with traditional clothing. That was emphatically *not* Ravi Shankar. Speaking fluent English and French, he wore Savile Row suits and Ivy League blazers, loved exploring new cities on foot, relished Italian, Mexican, and Japanese food, and was disappointed if the post-concert greenroom get-together didn't result in a female admirer accompanying him back to his hotel room.

Like father, like son. Ravi didn't actually meet his dad until he was eight years old. He'd grown up in the holy Hindu city of Benares with his mother, Hemangini, the Indian wife of Shyam Shankar, a London barrister with a sideline in creating Indian-themed stage shows as well as a second, English, wife. Ravi was the youngest of his parents' five children, conceived during an increasingly rare visit. Shankar Sr. returned to Benares in February 1929 to fulfill a promise to his recently deceased English wife by scattering her ashes in the Ganges. He checked into the city's most British hotel and invited his son to breakfast; joining them were Shyam's late wife's sister and his current mistress, a Dutch woman. Ravi had never used cutlery before and remembers being mortified by his struggles with the eggs. Hemangini had taught her boy the legends of the Hindu gods and the folk tales of Bengal, and he loved the rituals enacted daily on the ghats along the banks of the Ganges, but that morning's whiff of the foreign ladies' perfume would never be forgotten, a siren call that drew him inexorably west.

He didn't have long to wait. Uday, Ravi's two-decades-older brother, had moved to London in 1919 to help their father with one of his productions. When the great Russian ballerina Anna Pavlova spotted him, she declared that Uday was "endowed with one of the most perfect bodies I have ever seen in a man in any country." He performed with Pavlova and choreographed a few India-themed pieces for her company, but she persuaded him that such fusions were unworthy, that he should develop his own program of authentic Indian dance. Uday moved to Paris in the mid-twenties, where, out of the many women mesmerized by his beauty, two ended up as permanent fixtures: "Simkie" Barbier, a ballerina who darkened her skin and became a convincing performer of Indian dance, and Alice Boner, a Swiss heiress who bankrolled the project. Returning home after a decade away, Uday traveled the country auditioning performers. When the troupe set sail from Bombay in October 1930, Ravi was on board; after a few weeks of rehearsal, he'd earned a featured spot as a dancer and would become an audience favorite.

The West wasn't exactly gagging for a show of this kind. Prior to the Great War, there had been a flicker of fashionable interest in India triggered by Schopenhauer's pronouncement that all Western religions originated there and culminating in the awarding of the 1913 Nobel Prize to Bengali poet-savant Rabindranath Tagore. But, as with so many of the era's fads, the brutality of the trenches had shunted India into a siding along with tango and séances. Pre-war revelations that endured included yoga, which continued to grow in popularity, and explorer

Richard Burton's notorious translation of the *Kama Sutra*; sex always sells, and, in those years, sex sold best if it involved the exotic "other."

Uday Shankar and his Hindu Ballet toured the world in the early 1930s, drawing particularly good crowds and reviews in Germany and making its Paris debut at the Théâtre des Champs-Élysées, where *The Rite of Spring* had startled the world two decades before. The British were the toughest sell. As that prodigious chronicler of Indian history and culture William Dalrymple has pointed out in *White Mughals*, early adventurers from the East India Company may have immersed themselves in Hindu, Buddhist, and Muslim traditions and been fascinated by Indian music, but the stiff-necked Victorian imperialists who replaced them viewed Indian culture as obscure and backward and heard its music as "an alarming cacophony" and "a maze of noises." They stigmatized temple dancers as prostitutes and convinced middle-class Indians to shun the art. Americans harbored no such prejudices, and 1933 found Uday's troupe on a triumphant transcontinental tour promoted by Sol Hurok. They made the rounds of fashionable parties in Hollywood, where Ravi (now thirteen) met his idols Clark Gable and Myrna Loy and was fussed over by Marie Dressler, who tried to adopt him.

In between seeing the world, becoming an excellent dancer, and losing his virginity to Barbier, Shankar found time to pick up the company's seldom-used sitar and make a convincing stab at playing it. When the group returned to India in 1934, Ravi and his brother attended a stunning performance by the master musician Allaudin Khan, whom Uday promptly invited to join the company on the next European tour as musical director and multi-instrumentalist. Ravi was filled with admiration and respect for this virtuoso master; he got a kick out of tricking the devout Muslim into accompanying him into a Parisian burlesque theater but made up for it by taking him to Notre-Dame for an organ recital that moved Allaudin to tears. At the end of the tour, Khan told the teenager that his immense talent would be wasted if he continued traveling around and practicing in his spare time. If he were truly serious about music, he should give it all up and come study with him in rural Maihar.

As he turned eighteen, Shankar put behind him the life he had led since setting sail from Bombay eight years before; everyone in the company had been impressed by how well he was playing the sitar, but Ravi knew the master was right. He moved from swank hotel suites to a small back room in Khan's house where he waged a daily battle against the cockroaches, spiders, and scorpions—and occasional snakes—who felt they had equal claim. He became fast friends with his fellow student, Allaudin's son Ali Akbar Khan; they rose every morning at four and played for three hours before breakfast, Ravi on sitar, Ali Akbar on *sarod*, and his sister Annapurna on *surbahar*. Lessons were whenever the guru decided, often at midnight. Ravi stayed for more than seven years.

The term *raga* comes from the Sanskrit *ranga*, meaning "color" or "mood." Each raga has a time of day when it is appropriate to be played, and its own particular scales. I use the plural since the sequence of notes used while ascending always differs from those on the way down. All these scales are contained within our twelve-tone octave but are not limited to what Western music calls whole or semitones. Two ragas may contain identical sequences of notes but differ in which are emphasized or whether a tone is reached by sliding from above or below. Raga scales probably originated in Vedic chants brought by Aryan invaders from Central Asia around 1500 bce; the earliest used just three notes and expanded over the centuries until reaching the seven that comprise most ragas today. "Classical" Indian music was largely a vocal tradition; a third-century bce musical theorist named Bharata suggested that each note was derived from the cry of a particular animal, that "music is a form of listening to the world."

All changed with the Mughal invasion in the sixteenth century. The new rulers, notably Akbar, knew good music when they heard it and summoned the best performers into their palaces. The Mughals were part of a broad Persian culture and brought with them elegant love-centered poetry as well as Persian instruments, including the *si* (three) -*tar* (string), a lute which Indian musicians would enlarge over the centuries. The clearest differentiation that exists today between the Hindustani music of north India and the Karnatic traditions of the south lies in the matter of improvisation. South Indian music is more formal, closely tied to songs and folk traditions, and lacks the adventurous soloists who have made north Indian music famous. This is because the Mughal invasion was halted in the middle of the central Deccan Plateau; improvisational skills were developed as a way of showing off to a generous sultan. In the south, music remained primarily in the temples.

The father of modern Indian classical music was Mia Tansen, a singer and musician who was invited to perform for Akbar; the sultan was stunned by his voice and appointed him official court musician. When Akbar asked who had taught him, Tansen made the sultan dress like a peasant and follow him deep into the forest. Suddenly, they heard the most beautiful music, unlike anything Akbar had ever experienced; following the sound, they came upon an old man dressed in rags, seated cross-legged beneath a tree, singing. When Akbar asked why *he* never sang like that, Tansen responded: "That's simple, dear king. I sing for you. He sings for God." Tansen is credited with developing the secular *dhrupad* repertoire coupling ancient techniques and scales with Persian-inspired lyrics. Hindustani music may have left the temples but, at its best, it has never shed its original, divine aspiration.

For centuries, every palace had resident musicians, usually from one family and led by a "master." Distances in northern India are vast, and with pre-railway travel extremely difficult, distinct styles and repertoires evolved in isolation; nothing was written, everything was passed down aurally. These "schools," each with its own ragas and particular nuances of singing and playing, are known as *gharanas*. As Indian classical music encountered the concert halls, radio broadcasts, and recording studios of the twentieth century, every performer's style and repertoire could be traced to a particular gharana. Most were closed shops, exclusive to clans, just like other crafts and trades in a land that remained, in many ways, medieval. The mythology of Indian music is marked by tales of exceptional men and women who defy family, tradition, and caste, overcoming many obstacles before finding a master who would take them on and becoming a famous singer or instrumentalist. Allaudin Khan's story is one of these.

Nada Brahma.
(Sound is God.)

—Sanskrit expression

Though Allaudin Khan was born into a family of musicians, his mother had vowed that her son would attend a normal school and not follow the difficult path of a performer. Music, however, had been the boy's passion from the time he learned to walk. When he was eight, with both parents deaf to his pleas, Khan ran away from his home in East Bengal (now Bangladesh) and made his way to Calcutta, where he slept in the streets, begging for food and music lessons. His passionate determination, combined with extraordinary pitch for such a young age, eventually won him a corner to sleep in and instruction from a singing teacher. When Allaudin was sixteen, the guru died; his next mentor was the leader of a dance band who taught him Western notation and harmony and how to play the piano. At nineteen, he joined the court at Rampur, where his ability to commit ragas to memory after one hearing astounded everyone and drew master musicians from across the region to play him theirs, like registering them in a raga database. At Rampur he picked up Indian instruments for the first time; according to Ali Akbar, his father owned and played at least two hundred different ones, classical and folk. Most classical masters look down their noses at folk music, but Khan's years in the slums had instilled in him a love for and appreciation of the music of ordinary people.

A successful concert tour in 1918 made Allaudin's name and led to an offer from the sultan of Maihar to provide an income, a home, and a base for teaching. One of his first acts when he arrived was to form the Maihar Band of homeless street kids; he persuaded the maharajah to give them somewhere to live and the band became famous in the region. Khan taught his son and daughter from an early age, but Ravi was not the only outsider he took on. None was ever asked for payment; so long as they had the talent and were willing to work hard, they lived as guests with the family. Everyone sang; all music begins as vocal music and there was nothing played on an instrument, said the master, that couldn't be sung. Instrumental techniques were learned quickly, then repeated endlessly until they became as automatic as breathing; improvisation relied on absolute technical assurance and a deep feeling for each scale, achieved through the intimacy of singing them.

Khan not only mastered many instruments, he also altered and improved them. The sarod that his son would one day play in the world's grandest halls, for example, had been a simple Afghan folk instrument; Allaudin added a resonator, widened the fretless neck, and established it in the classical realm by performing ragas on it in concert. Most sitars today have six melody strings; Shankar's had a seventh, a low-pitched one added by Khan.

Ravi learned many things at Maihar that he would never have been taught elsewhere. A distinctive feature of his career was an emphasis on rhythm and percussion; the tabla master Alla Rakha would become Shankar's onstage foil and co-star, the interplay between the two a highlight of their international concerts. In Hindustani music the tabla had been more of an accompanying instrument, but Khan was fascinated by the Karnatic music of the south and its many different types of drums. Ravi the dancer and Allaudin the drummer would spend long evenings in Maihar focused entirely on rhythm. Khan also enjoyed adapting southern melodies to northern raga structures, another distinctive aspect of Shankar's music absorbed from his guru's teaching.

Allaudin Khan was ecumenical in more ways than north and south, classical and folk; the walls of the room where he prayed to Allah five times a day were decorated with portraits of Krishna, Christ, Beethoven, and other admired figures. Many, if not most, Hindustani classical musicians are descended from Hindu forebears who converted to the Islamic faith of their Mughal patrons. Hindu historians usually see this as purely a career move, but it seems equally likely that they were drawn to a religion that would free them from the confinement of caste. Monotheism may have also provided a welcome contrast to the eccentric galaxy of Hindu gods. Whatever the motive for their conversion, most court musicians continued to perform in Hindu temples and, like millions of ordinary Indians, pay reverence to Sufi saints, Hindu deities, and Allah without perceiving any conflict.

If David Crosby had attended a classical recital in Bombay in the thirties, it is unlikely he would have experienced that "very emotional and sexual" build. The different sections—the *alap* and *jor*, followed by medium-tempo *gats* and climaxing in the rapid *jhala*—had always been considered separate pieces. Concerts could last for six hours and there would have been no tabla solos or *konnakol* vocalizations of the beats that Western audiences found so thrilling. What the world (and, eventually, India) would experience in a Ravi Shankar concert was developed during long evenings in Maihar by two worldly men who understood more about other cultures than most Hindustani musicians. When the call of the West came, Ravi would be ready.

Yehudi Menuhin wanted to show his hosts that when it came to Indian culture, he knew which end was up; in the middle of a black-tie reception in Delhi in 1952, he removed his shoes and socks and performed a perfect yoga headstand. Not to be outdone, Prime Minister Nehru did the same. Menuhin had always been fascinated by India and had jumped at the chance of a country-wide concert tour organized by Mehli Mehta (father of teenage prodigy Zubin). Part of the welcome arranged by the culture ministry was a private performance of a morning raga by the bright young star of Indian music, Ravi Shankar.

Ravi knew all about the honored guest, having attended a Menuhin recital in Paris when he was thirteen (and Yehudi all of seventeen). Now, two decades later, the violinist was as dazzled by Shankar as his fellow prodigy had been at the Salle Pleyel; the two talked animatedly for hours—about music, about East and West, about possible collaborations, and about the importance of bringing this great musical culture to the world. Menuhin was as good as his word; back in Europe, he bent the ears of impresarios and agents, insisting they organize a tour for Shankar. The initial offer was perfect: a New York concert timed with the opening of Satyajit Ray's film *Pather Panchali*, the first great classic of Indian cinema, for which Ravi had improvised the score. To Yehudi's shock, his new friend turned it down.

It wasn't that Shankar didn't want to go, but he had problems that needed resolving before he could embark on an international career. His emergence from the cocoon of Maihar had begun slowly, accompanying the master on the *tanbura* drone in recitals before graduating to a supporting role on his sitar. Eventually he started leaving the guru's home for performances with Uday's company, collaborations with a Bombay theater group, small solo recitals, and a series of sitar-sarod *jugalbandis*—duets—with Ali Akbar that received an ecstatic response. In 1948, as the excitement and optimism of Independence was being overshadowed by the horrors and disillusion of Partition, many *ustads* (the Muslim honorific for "master") were torn between India and Pakistan. Allaudin remained in India; he and Ravi were committed to disseminating the great classical tradition to the millions in both new nations who had never had a chance to hear it over the centuries when it had been kept as a treasured possession of the elite. Radio was the perfect medium; Shankar moved to Delhi to work for the new All India Radio, eventually becoming its director of music, while traveling across the country every weekend giving recitals. Ravi always took on far too much, yet finished every task brilliantly, finding time to record for the Gramophone Company of India, compose for theatrical productions, and create film scores.

Amid all these accomplishments, he committed the grave error of marrying Allaudin's daughter, Annapurna. This was not a case of passionate glances over their instruments during the years of youthful study in Maihar; it was a typical Indian marriage, suggested and encouraged, if not actually arranged, by the two families. It was a rare one as well, with the Muslim bride converting to Hinduism with her family's blessing. Ravi had a fondness and respect for the unworldly girl and was honored to be welcomed into the family he so adored. But it was not in his nature to be a devoted husband and Annapurna seems never to have recovered from learning of her husband's previous sexual adventures, to say nothing of his ongoing flirtations. By the time the American invitation arrived, the couple had a young son and a marital crisis that, owing to his great respect for Allaudin, Shankar was not (at least initially) prepared to manage as his father had—by simply leaving his Indian family behind and journeying west.

When he proposed that Ali Akbar Khan take his place, neither friend was happy; the reluctant young sarod master had to be frogmarched to the plane and Yehudi given the most effusive guarantees about the brilliance of the unknown replacement. The result was a triumph that had almost as great an effect on Western music as Shankar's own career. Khan was pleasantly surprised by the attentive New York audience and captivated by the city's energy. For the rest of his life, he would spend the better part of each year in America, where his College of Music in Northern California tutored members of the Grateful Dead, The Doors, and Shakti among many influential figures in jazz, rock, classical, fusion, and avant-garde music. In the early sixties, Harvard Square folkies' favorite pun was "If Ravi Shankar can't do it, Ali Akbar Khan." We had no idea how apt that was.

> [T]he eruption of Indian music on the Western musical landscape modified radically our general perception of music . . . [I]t has, in any case, greatly contributed to questioning the West's biased assumption of supremacy . . .
>
> —Laurent Aubert, *The Music of the Other*

I joined a few of those folk singers one evening in 1962 for an Ali Akbar Khan recital at Boston's Jordan Hall. Indian music by then had a toehold in most of my friends' record collections, part of a cornucopia that was becoming available on long-playing discs: jazz, blues, country, cajun, calypso, Scots ballads . . . we were curious about it all. It was clear that evening, though, that what Ali Akbar Khan was playing wasn't "folk," that it represented a form at the highest level of tradition, sophistication, and complexity. Indian notions of spirituality were also spreading; Allen Ginsberg was rumored to be living in Shankar's home city of Benares, while travelers back from San Francisco reported that you could tell which Sausalito houseboat belonged to the Zen poet Alan Watts by the Indian music wafting from it. (Amazing how meditation could stop the needle from skipping as the tide came in.) The music seemed to speak to us not just across decades, like blues and old-time country music, but across centuries, perhaps millennia.

Our little group was a harbinger of the new audiences that Shankar began to notice as the fifties gave way to the sixties. He was dubious at first, worried that our long hair and slack dress code would lower the tone, and he once complained that the crowd at hippy-friendly Antioch College in Ohio was "smelly." What unnerved him most about the young fans, though, was the revelation that they found his records ideal for getting stoned and having sex to. (Bock once offered to initiate Ravi into psychedelics, but he politely declined.)

From sex and drugs, it was a short step to rock 'n' roll. "Norwegian Wood" was the opening salvo of a free-for-all in which Anglo-American popular music opened its doors to Indian music. Brian Jones had taken lessons from one of Ravi's disciples and came up with a sitar riff for "Paint It Black," a tune Mick Jagger once described as sounding like something "for a Jewish wedding." The Kinks' Ray Davies used a melody he heard fishermen singing during a Bombay stopover as the basis for the drone-anchored "See My Friends." That wasn't a big hit, but The Yardbirds' "Over Under Sideways Down" was, a song that began life as an homage to "Rock Around the Clock," then added a Middle Eastern guitar riff by Jeff Beck and an Indian tag to the chorus. In America, The Byrds continued to build many of their songs around South Asian modes, but the most emphatic statement came from an unlikely quarter, the Paul Butterfield Blues Band. Their guitarist, Mike Bloomfield, was an upper-middle-class Jewish kid who had studied old blues recordings like a rabbi poring over the Talmud; in 1965, he turned that intense gaze onto Indian music, borrowing a scale from Raga Bhairavi for the lengthy instrumental title track of the group's second album, *East–West*. The Doors, meanwhile, came into being when three Southern California musicians met at a Buddhist meditation seminar; the guitarist, Robby Krieger, based his solo in "The End" on a raga scale and the famous guitar break in "Light My Fire" on sitar fingering he had learned in a masterclass with Shankar.

The Stone, the Yardbird, and future Zep Jimmy Page were all taking lessons, but the only prominent sixties group to actually use a sitar onstage was the one I was producing and managing, the Incredible String Band. The ISB's Robin Williamson often composed drone-based, Middle Eastern–flavored melodies and played his guitar in open tunings with a lowered bridge that made the strings buzz like a tanbura; I thought a sitar might fit nicely with "The Mad Hatter's Song" on the group's second album, so I booked a friend of the Angadis, Nazir Jaraizbhoy, for the recording. Mike Heron, the other half of the duo, liked the result so much he bought a sitar and a dozen lessons from Nazir. Mike seated cross-legged on the stage and singing as he played became an emblematic image of the group as they toured across Britain, Europe, and North America in the last years of the decade. My view is hardly objective, but I feel the way Heron wove his deft playing into the group's songs was the most effective use of Indian music by any sixties outfit.

Except The Beatles, of course.

Did anyone realise they didn't change chords?

—Paul McCartney after the group listened together to a Ravi Shankar LP

The Indian drone as brought into First World culture by this track challenges not only seven centuries of Western music but the operative premise of Western civilisation itself. When Lennon's voice rises out of the seething dazzle of churning loops, the first words it utters, "Turn off your mind," are a mystic negation of all progressive intellectual enterprise . . . "Tomorrow Never Knows" launched the till-then elite-preserved concept of mind-expansion into pop, simultaneously drawing attention to consciousness-enhancing drugs and the ancient religious philosophies of the Orient, utterly alien to Western thought in their anti-materialism, rapt passivity and world-sceptical focus on visionary consciousness.

—Ian MacDonald, *Revolution in the Head*

My heart melted with love for him. His quest was beautiful . . . his interest in and curiosity for our traditions, mostly in the fields of religion, philosophy and music, was quite genuine. And he adored Indian food!

—Ravi Shankar on George Harrison

This music is thousands of years old; it makes me laugh the British going there and telling them what to do. Quite amazing.

—John Lennon

August 5, 1966, was both my twenty-fourth birthday and the day *Revolver* was released. I made myself a present of a copy, took it back to the office, and played it over and over. There were so many remarkable tracks that I don't recall being particularly struck by the two with obvious Indian connections, but they added to the overall impression that after *Revolver* things would never be the same. "Love You To" is extremely Indian, recorded with just Harrison and musicians provided by the Asian Music Circle; the other Beatles were a bit taken aback, but impressed with the result and happy to place it third on side one. "Tomorrow Never Knows" shows Lennon's very different response, using Indian drones and scales to open the door to a darker, more subversive form of rock 'n' roll. George's guitar solo on "Taxman" aggressively flaunts the modal zeitgeist, while in some ways the most interesting track is "I'm Only Sleeping," with its characteristic Lennon/McCartney chord sequence interrupted by raga-sounding backwards tapes and broken chords that evoke the strum of a tanbura.

The press conference and interviews marking the release of a new Beatles album once revolved around the Liverpudlian humor with which the group teased hacks from the popular press; that summer's encounters were different, marked by mutual incomprehension and hostility. Far worse was to come when the group hit the road. Twenty-first-century politics has been marked by confrontations that first emerged in the late sixties as large sectors of society reacted with alarm and hostility to changes taking place among youth, women, minorities, and in the developing world. In Tokyo, violent right-wing demonstrators tried to stop the Beatles' concert, and the group narrowly escaped from an enraged Imelda Marcos and her security police in Manila. By the time they got to America, hellfire preachers had seized on Lennon's offhand observation that the group were more popular than Jesus, causing bonfires of Beatles records to be lit across the country; they were barely able to finish their Memphis show and get out of town alive. On the plane home, they told manager Brian Epstein: *no more tours.*

George knew what was needed; he and Pattie took up Ravi's offer to show them around India, eager to leave the agonizing past months of Beatledom behind them. Their arrival brought out teenage Indian pop fans, much to the horror of the Hindu equivalents of American evangelicals, to say nothing of the four travelers (including Ravi's Indian girlfriend). After getting pestered in Benares, at the Taj Mahal, and in other favorite spots, they found refuge on beautiful Dal Lake in Kashmir, where they spent peaceful, anonymous weeks on houseboats. Those blissfully empty days—waking early, playing the sitar, meditating, eating vegetarian food, reading *Autobiography of a Yogi* by Paramahansa Yogananda, and contemplating life without the madness of pop stardom—altered Harrison forever. On the lake, he realized he would never master the sitar, that to imagine he could parachute into this culture and learn to create beauty on one of its most challenging instruments was a fantasy. Returning to London for the start of the *Sgt. Pepper* sessions, he felt detached from the process and bored by the endless overdubs made possible by Abbey Road's revolutionary eight-track recorder. George may have never played the sitar seriously again, yet as a musician he was transformed; through Ravi and India he had developed his own distinctive guitar style and become a very different, far more powerful songwriter.

The sixties cultural revolution had an exciting period of ascendance followed by a tortuous decline; Western youth's fascination with Indian music and culture moved arm-in-arm with other phenomena of the period, up that slope and down. The ascent began in the summer of 1965 with Dylan's electroshock treatment of Newport, followed three weeks later by the disconnect between a rapidly evolving Beatles and their screaming teenage fans at Shea Stadium, leading up to the meeting in Zsa Zsa's bathtub. After two almost unimaginably exciting years, a pair of seismic events kicked off the "Summer of Love." They turned out to be the beginning of the end.

On May 25, 1967, EMI released *Sgt. Pepper's Lonely Hearts Club Band*; within days, the album was everywhere. The idea that stores and restaurants might serenade their customers with recorded music had been largely unknown; this practice's soporific ubiquity today can be traced to a sense that summer that few shoppers or diners wished to go for too long without hearing *Sgt. Pepper*. Harrison's contribution, "Within You Without You," stands somewhat apart, another Beatles-free track recorded with an AMC pick-up band that managed somehow to fit into the stylistically disparate songs the group performed—and Martin produced—with such confident elan that the album felt somehow unified and indivisible.

Three weeks later, the Monterey Pop Festival took place in California. History has plowed over the fact that this was originally planned as a Ravi Shankar concert. His agent came up with the idea of an afternoon raga at the Fairgrounds, a popular spot where the Monterey Jazz Festival took place each September. When the notion of adding an evening show by some local bands was floated, all the San Francisco groups raised their hands to be included, Hollywood honchos Lou Adler and John Phillips muscled their way in, and suddenly no one from London to LA could bear to be left out. Ravi's original $3,000 fee was the sole payment made to any of the performers and his Sunday recital was the weekend's only stand-alone event. D. A. Pennebaker's film *Monterey Pop* is filled with indelible moments, from Jimi Hendrix's guitar immolation to Otis Redding asking, "This is the love crowd, right?" to entranced (or stoned) hippies listening with closed eyes and blissful grins to Shankar and Alla Rakha. For his part, Ravi was impressed by the fans and by much of the music, but horrified at the violence meted out to their instruments by Hendrix and Pete Townshend. (Shankar once scolded Harrison for stepping over his sitar to answer the phone.)

Many books have been devoted to what subsequently went wrong, but the exploding mass market for psychedelic drugs had certainly led suppliers to "cut" more than corners, turning an experience originally perceived as a spiritual adventure into a way for millions to get well and truly hammered. Both Harrison and Shankar visited San Francisco's Haight-Ashbury district and were horrified by the vacant stares, unwashed bodies, and desperate begging; poverty and squalor in Benares seemed somehow less disturbing. Trippy imagery was gleefully appropriated by Madison Avenue, turning what had once been counter-cultural into mainstream overnight. The electric sitar made its inevitable appearance, sounding not too bad on the Box Tops' "Cry

Like a Baby" and "Paper Sun" by Traffic. For Indian music, a tipping point arrived when Dick Bock made one of his few missteps by licensing a Shankar recording for a national ad campaign by a down-market shoe chain. Bible-thumping condemnation couldn't derail the hippie juggernaut but capitalist endorsement accomplished it with ease, as flowery fashions, long hair, drugs, rejectionist attitudes, and Indian music all became too popular for their own good. In the wake of Monterey, Shankar's bookings surged, but by the time he performed at Woodstock two summers later, tickets for his shows often went begging. And what, after all, did turmoil in youthful White psyches really matter beside the life-and-death struggles of African Americans, as violent political spasms claimed the lives of Martin Luther King, Fred Hampton, and Bobby Kennedy, to say nothing of the Vietnamese dying in America's game of Asian dominoes. The hundred miles and two years separating Monterey from Altamont encompassed a collapse of idealism and the death of many dreams.

> When you get the message, hang up the phone.
>
> —Alan Watts

Maharishi Mahesh Yogi was born in an obscure village, far down the caste ladder from most gurus. Having set out to get a physics degree, his life changed when he met the spiritual master Saraswati. He made himself indispensable to the holy man, and when Saraswati died, Maharishi claimed exclusive knowledge of the guru's method of meditation. On his first trip abroad, he grasped that a formula for "instant karma" would appeal to impatient Westerners and quickly got the hang of charming the wealthy; a $1 million donation from the tortured tobacco heiress Doris Duke funded the building of a Transcendental Meditation retreat at Rishikesh in the foothills of the Himalayas.

When some who had dived deep into psychedelics began looking for a way out, Eastern spirituality beckoned. The Beatles had been intrigued by their first encounters with the Maharishi, and they were on a retreat with him in Wales when news came of Brian Epstein's fatal overdose, leaving them adrift and in need of guidance. (The Incredible String Band and I met the Maharishi during a tour of Sweden that winter but were unimpressed with his insistence that meditation only worked if you bought one of the very expensive mantras he was selling.) That spring, all four Beatles and their partners headed east, settling into hastily spruced-up celebrity quarters in Rishikesh alongside Mia Farrow, Donovan, and Mike Love of The Beach Boys, while paparazzi camped outside the gates, hoping for glimpses and gossip. The world seemed transfixed by the sight of its biggest stars turning their backs on glamour to pursue an obscure Indian spiritual practice. The group's first weeks at Rishikesh represent peak India in the West's consciousness.

There were certainly some positive outcomes: all benefited from the sort of peaceful distance from Beatlemania that Harrison had found in Kashmir, and, by one count, forty new Beatles songs were composed during their time beside the fast-flowing waters of the young Ganges. First to depart were Ringo and Maureen, the Liverpool girl unable to stomach the food or cope with the insects. Paul and his girlfriend, the actress Jane Asher, were next; she never bought what the Maharishi was selling, and though Paul benefited from the meditation, the yogi's rules and strictures sparked a schoolboy urge in him to disobey, often sneaking out behind the compound with Lennon to smoke joints. One creative highlight before the couple grew bored and left was "Back in the USSR," composed during a raucous breakfast with Mike Love as they riffed on "California Girls" and "Johnny B. Goode." John, George, and Pattie were the most committed, putting in many hours of meditation and paying attention during the evening lectures. Cynthia Lennon seemed content just to have John to herself for a while; the past months in London had been dominated by her husband's growing fascination with the Japanese performance artist Yoko Ono, to whom he wrote multi-page letters from Rishikesh.

The finale of this strange sixties tale was like a scene from *Help!*; the film's plot has the four pursued by a comically sinister guru (played in dark make-up by Leo McKern, later famous as Rumpole of the Bailey) who wants to chop off Ringo's finger and reclaim a sacred ring. Rishikesh ended with the Maharishi and his team chasing the Harrisons and Lennons down the road, waving and shouting as they bolted from the compound in covertly hired taxis. The rupture was pure showbiz, stemming from the discovery that the Yogi was using a documentary proposal from The Beatles' Apple Corps to bid up a rival American project. In years to come, the group avoided bad-mouthing the Maharishi (bar Lennon's lyrics for "Sexy Sadie"), and John and George, at least, continued to meditate and chant. The West greeted the break-up with a collective sigh of relief and put away its Krishna posters, yoga mats, books on meditation, and Ravi Shankar records.

No one, of course, put away their Beatles records. Over the decades, however, it is an observable phenomenon that documentaries and books about the group, often full of images from their early mop-top stage and the later beardy period, rarely include shots of them with hands clasped in *namaste* position, garlanded in flowers.

∽

Raindrops on roses and whiskers on kittens
Bright copper kettles and warm woollen mittens
Brown paper packages tied up with strings
These are a few of my favorite things

—First verse of "My Favorite Things" from *The Sound of Music*

Could there be a cornier, Whiter song than "My Favorite Things"? In John Coltrane's hands, it became one of the most pervasively cool recordings of the early sixties, a pioneering track that applied Indian modes, scales, and instrumental techniques to an African-American jazz take on a Broadway show tune. Coltrane was way ahead of the rock 'n' rollers, having looked east for musical and spiritual connections when the lads from Liverpool were still The Quarrymen.

When Coltrane died of liver cancer on July 17, 1967, the musical world was stunned; few had even been aware he was sick. The tragedy was all the more poignant for its likely origin in a bout of hepatitis linked to a heroin habit he had, with the help of (non-Maharishi) meditation, long since put behind him. His transformative journey had begun a decade—almost to the day—before his death, when he joined Thelonious Monk's group for what would become a legendary six-month residence at New York's Five Spot Café. Over the course of that half-year, intrigued by Monk's way of searching for notes located between those on the tempered European scale by striking two adjacent keys at once, he began expanding the tonal possibilities of his saxophone. When the Five Spot gig ended, Coltrane joined the Miles Davis outfit that would make jazz history with *Kind of Blue*; in employing modes rather than harmonic progressions, Davis was following on from Dizzy Gillespie's explorations with Chano Pozo. Many African-American jazz musicians were striving to free themselves from the limitations imposed by European harmonic structures; the first place they looked, naturally, was Africa, where scales often involved tones found between those specified by keys, valves, and frets. Coltrane, too, was drawn to Africa, studying Yoruba rhythms with Nigerian drummer Michael Olatunji, but ultimately his search led him farther east. He was fascinated to discover that European concepts of harmony and pitch were local, not universal, that most of the world's musical cultures were linked by what he called a "pentatonic sonority" of modes. In that landmark 1960 recording of "My Favorite Things," he introduced the soprano sax, a rarely heard woodwind primarily associated with the traditional New Orleans jazz master Sydney Bechet. In Coltrane's hands, it sounded more like an Indian *shehnai* and he used it to transform "My Favorite Things" into a revolutionary advertisement for modal jazz.

Modes led to drones; when Bock organized a meeting with Shankar in December 1961, Coltrane had just completed a run at the Village Vanguard, where he'd performed "India," an extended piece based on a Rajasthani folk melody using a tanbura and two basses, one holding the drone while the other played freely in a higher register, an idea inspired by the interplay of Indian drums. Coltrane and Shankar connected immediately at a deep level; both regretted that, due to such busy schedules, their dialogue would be conducted mostly by telephone. Shankar was impressed by Coltrane's dedication, discipline, and understanding of the musical world outside America and by his spiritual journey. Many African Americans searching for an alternative to the Protestantism forced onto their forefathers by slave masters had turned to Islam; Coltrane (along with others including Don Cherry and Charles Lloyd) was drawn to Hinduism. In 1965, he named his second son Ravi.

Shankar always listened to Coltrane's new releases and saw him perform when he could, but was sometimes disturbed by what he heard—accurately—as anger expressed through music. Coltrane saw all his music as a devotional offering, and his recordings across the sixties demonstrate a remarkable range of mood, from exquisite ballads with Duke Ellington and Johnny Hartman to the furious "sheets of sound" of his later solo work. What direction might jazz have taken had it not lost Coltrane at such a crucial moment, when the rock surge was capturing the sort of hip young listeners who once might have been drawn to bebop? As it turned out, the way forward was shown not by this deeply spiritual African-American seeker, but by a deeply spiritual Brit from the sixties London world that spawned Jimmy Page, Jeff Beck, and Cream. John McLaughlin also owed a huge debt to Indian music, just not the same one acknowledged by John Coltrane.

⁓

McLaughlin had grown up in Yorkshire listening to guitarists with dazzling techniques: Django Reinhardt, Sabicas, and Tal Farlow in particular. He made his way to London, where, like various Rolling Stones and other British blues luminaries, he apprenticed with Alexis Korner and Georgie Fame. In 1963, he formed a quartet with organist Graham Bond plus two future thirds of Cream: Jack Bruce and Ginger Baker. Based on his first solo album, *Extrapolation*, Miles Davis's drummer Tony Williams invited him to New York for a collaboration; he was soon recording and touring with Davis (and becoming a devotee of Indian guru Sri Chimnoy). Some readers will certainly dispute my view that for this other John to succeed Coltrane as a key influence on Miles Davis was a bad omen for the future of jazz; the immense popularity of *Bitches Brew*, the Mahavishnu Orchestra, *My Goal's Beyond*, and Shakti shows that I'm probably in the minority. McLaughlin's entry in *Rolling Stone*'s list of the "100 Greatest Guitarists" cites his combination of "complex rhythms of Indian music with jazz harmonies and rock power chords . . . blizzards of notes, clearly influenced by the sheets of sound of his idol, John Coltrane." Musician friends of mine used to call this approach "note salad."

Before jazz and rock could hook up at the Raga Motel and conceive the devil's spawn known as "jazz-rock fusion," rock needed to become a bit more jazz-like. While Pink Floyd were launching twenty-minute-long space journeys at UFO in London, a San Francisco group was kicking off America's "jam band" movement. According to drummer Mickey Hart, "The Grateful Dead was a rhythm machine . . . This was what it was all about: invention, adventure, exploration, complexity." Hart used to meet up with Alla Rakha and play a game: Rakha would lay out a ten-beat cycle on the tabla then shout out a number—"seven!" perhaps, or "nine!"—and Hart would have to overlay that number of beats evenly on top of Rakha's ten, meeting him precisely on the "one." For Hart, Rakha was "the Einstein of rhythm"; watching him with Ravi Shankar at Monterey "allowed for modal playing . . . being able to stay on one chord and develop things . . . Jam bands came from raga as far as I'm concerned. It gave us license to jam, made it legal." Indian music may have surrendered its place in the mass market, but its effect on Western music was permanent and profound.

Fate took a hand in September 1969 as Shankar was preparing to fly from Bombay to New York for a one-off concert at Fillmore East; Alla Rakha was taken ill and proposed his eighteen-year-old son as deputy. Although this would be Zakir Hussain's first venture outside India, he was already a fusion prodigy, having worked on Bollywood sound stages alongside pianos, violins, and Western drum kits. Zakir dazzled New Yorkers with his tabla skills, and before his Air India flight could depart for home, he was offered a teaching post at the University of Washington in Seattle. From this West Coast base, Hussain would launch a remarkable career, joining McLaughlin in the arch-fusion outfit Shakti and collaborating on endless cross-cultural projects with musicians from around the world while also finding time to perform and record with traditional Hindustani classical virtuosos. In 1991, he joined Mickey Hart and drummers from Puerto Rico, Brazil, Nigeria, and India for the *Planet Drum* project that won the very first World

Music Grammy and sat for months atop *Billboard*'s new World Music chart. Musical miscegenation as a concept and a marketing force was off and running.

Among the more annoying developments of the late sixties was the appearance on crowded city streets of bedraggled teams of shaven-headed Hare Krishna chanters, banging drums, clinking finger-cymbals, and singing repetitive praises to their favorite Hindu deity. Which made it all the more astonishing that two of that era's most appealing and addictive singles were George Harrison's productions of the "Hare Krishna" chant (which reached #12 on the UK charts) and its follow-up, "Govinda." Both are masterclasses in record production; Harrison ran his guitar through a tremolo-generating Leslie speaker, made a down payment on the modal debt owed to India by laying some wonderfully cheesy chords under the sweet, anonymous vocals by members of the Radha Krishna Temple, and mixed it all together with an unerring pop sensibility.

For his next trick Harrison invented the good-cause megastar concert. The 1947 Partition had placed Allaudin Khan's Bengal birthplace in Pakistan's eastern half; for two decades, the new nation's politics and economy had been dominated by the distant western section. When a devastating hurricane hit Bengal in 1970, the Islamabad government's abject response led to an uprising by what would become independent Bangladesh, defeating a brutal campaign by the Pakistani army that slaughtered hundreds of thousands and left millions homeless. Shankar and Ali Akbar Khan wanted to raise funds and awareness and honor Khan's family by organizing a charity concert. When Ravi asked George for advice about publicizing the modest event, he got more than he bargained for: his friend rented Madison Square Garden for afternoon and evening shows on August 1, 1971, and put in a call to Bob Dylan. Neither Dylan nor Harrison had set foot on a US stage in five years and the concerts sold out within hours. The shows were as exciting as hoped, the live album won a Grammy, Bangladesh's plight was publicized, and Nixon and Kissinger's cynical support for Pakistan humiliated. The huge crowd even kept relatively quiet for Shankar and Khan's opening raga (though some earnestly applauded the tune-up). Wattstax, Live Aid, Mandela's Wembley birthday party, and the rest can all trace their origins to that day.

Those weren't the only gestures of support Harrison made to Ravi; when a documentary about the sitarist ran short of funds, he got Apple Corps to step in and finish the film. (The experience stimulated George's interest in film production; his Handmade Films would later produce *Monty Python's Life of Brian*, *The Long Good Friday*, and *Withnail and I*.) For 1974's *Dark Horse* tour, the first live solo venture of his post-Beatles career, he turned the show's opening half over to Ravi and a troupe of Indian virtuosos, providing unsuspecting crowds with a crash course in exotic music that brought complaints but also opened many ears.

The affection George felt for Indian music and culture was sincere and deep and the debt he owed was real. Lead guitarists for sixties British bands—Harrison included—usually got started by listening to Carl Perkins, Chuck Berry, and Buddy Holly, then branching out to lesser-known rural and urban blues players for further inspiration. This doesn't appear to have interested George so much; during The Beatles' early years, his playing was basic yet somehow quite distinctive. Following the revelations in Zsa Zsa's bathtub, George kept his Indian fascination and his guitar-playing separate for a time, but this changed when he gave up the sitar. His solo on "Something," for example, is unique; straddling two worlds of influence—America and India—it has become one of history's most famous guitar breaks.

In the 1880s, about as far from India and Liverpool as you can get, a young guitarist named Joseph Kekuku tried laying the instrument across his lap, putting it in an open tuning, and sliding a metal bar along the strings to pick out a melody and change chords. The style swept the Hawaiian Islands, and when a troupe toured America before World War One, it started a craze for the music generally and the "Hawaiian guitar" in particular. Polynesian melodies with ukulele-driven rhythms and slide-guitar solos popped up on between-the-wars hit parades in America, Britain, Germany, and Japan, as guitarists everywhere experimented with different ways of utilizing this ear-catching gadgetry. In post-war

Nashville, when they connected the lap guitar to an amplifier and added string-stretching foot controls, "pedal steel," with boosts from Hank Williams and Bob Wills, became a signature sound of country music. The most dramatic impact, though, was on the blues; singer-guitarists in the Mississippi Delta figured out that you could hold a guitar in the normal way, slip the neck of a broken beer bottle or piece of metal tubing over a finger, and get the Hawaiian effect on an upper string in counterpoint with normal blues finger-picking on the others. Dextrous players used it to hunt between the frets for notes from African scales, a quest which produced the "blue notes" that are a signature of the form. The sustained tones of the electric guitar allowed many—led by T-Bone Walker and B.B. King—to dispense with the slide and use fingers and frets to bend and stretch notes in much the same way a sitarist does.

Indian melody is full of slides and slurs; how a singer or instrumentalist "worries" a note (as they say in American gospel) is as important as the note itself. The sitar is among many Indian instruments designed to allow maximum "bend"; its wide, arched frets can stretch a string across two or even three full tones. With a few lessons from Delaney Bramlett under his belt, Harrison began playing bottleneck guitar in 1968 and almost overnight become one of the best and most distinctive slide players in rock, using blues techniques to evoke nuances of Indian music. His famous solos on "My Sweet Lord" and "While My Guitar Gently Weeps"—as well as the one on "How Do You Sleep" that Lennon called "the best he's ever fucking played in his life"—encompass notes that would never occur to blues players and can only have come from hours of listening to Shankar and his peers.

This all came full circle when a student of Ravi's from Delhi named Mohan Bhatt tuned his guitar like a sitar, added some sympathetic strings, laid it across his lap, and began playing ragas on it using a metal slide. An afternoon spent with Ry Cooder at a California studio earned the two of them the third World Music Grammy in 1994 for *A Meeting by the River*. The slide guitar has now become a reluctantly acknowledged but regularly heard import into the world of Indian classical music.

[Ravi looks like] a man who has patiently endured all the praise-without-comprehension an alien culture can bestow. He has been Martian-in-residence for years.

—Richard Goldstein, *Village Voice*

Melodically and rhythmically, Indian music long ago achieved a complex sophistication which only in the twentieth century, with the work of Bartók and Stravinsky, has Western music begun to adumbrate.

—Yehudi Menuhin

Ours is the song of personal solitude, Europe's is that of social accompaniment. Our music takes the listener outside of the limits of man's everyday vicissitudes to that lonely land of renunciation that is at the root of the entire universe, while Europe's music dances variously to the endless rise and fall of man's joys and sorrows.

—Rabindranath Tagore

Ravi Shankar had learned to love Indian culture in his brother's flat in Paris; the apartment was filled with costumes, instruments, and devotional objects, and each held a story that fascinated the boy. One reason Ravi became such an effective ambassador is that he never lost his outsider's gaze. Two-hour concerts were unheard of in India but Western audiences' endurance, he knew, was limited. At home, critics and rival musicians attacked him for distorting and diluting the tradition, but before long his compact programs, complete with tabla solos and scholarly explanations, were filling Indian concert halls, too.

The collapse of Beatles-driven Hindumania and the rise of fusion were the best things that could have happened to the pure classical form in America. After a few years performing to half-empty halls in places where his concerts should probably never have been booked in the first place, Shankar signed with a classical booking agent and went back to playing for genuinely interested and reasonably knowledgeable, if smaller, crowds. After a few stabs at jams with jazz musicians organized by Dick Bock, his collaborations became focused on the classical world.

Shankar and Yehudi Menuhin had become close friends. Yehudi had long dreamed of performing jugalbandis with him and they won

Grammys for their *West Meets East* collaborations, but Ravi always had to compose Menuhin's parts for him; improvisation simply wasn't in the conservatory-trained prodigy's mental universe. Ravi's dream was to import European symphonic forms into Indian music, and he founded a Bombay school to develop the required skills; most graduates, though, ended up sawing away in unison on Bollywood sound stages and the school eventually closed. (Perhaps Shankar should have taken note of what Philip Koutev was up to in Bulgaria with his orchestra of Balkan instruments.) Ravi composed a sitar concerto and performed it with André Previn and the London Symphony in 1971 and later a second with the London Philharmonic and Zubin Mehta, but it remains unclear why listeners would go out of their way to hear an Indian virtuoso in the straitjacket of a written score with one eye on the conductor's baton when they could enjoy an evening raga by a master musician playing freely within his thousand-years-old tradition.

Movies were a different story. Shankar the workaholic could never resist an offer from a film director, and he created some memorable scores. A chance meeting with Satyajit Ray led to the acclaimed music for the Apu Trilogy, and he continued composing for many of the small number of "parallel" Indian films made outside the garish clichés of Bollywood. His music for Richard Attenborough's *Gandhi* earned an Oscar nomination, and he even scored one Hollywood feature with no subcontinental connection: *Charly* (in which Cliff Robertson won an Oscar for best actor). Ravi never took more than two days to record a score, usually improvising in front of a screen accompanied by a trusted team of Indian virtuosos. When strings or other Western instruments were required, he would hire someone to take musical dictation, setting out the parts on his sitar. One such collaborator, David Murphy, said that Ravi "had the most incredible ability to compose a sublime melody at the drop of a hat. It just came pouring out, in the same way that Mozart and to some extent Beethoven could do." Shankar's hunger for work and for challenges (though not for money; he never seemed to concern himself about it and managed his very badly) led him to accept the task of scoring Conrad Rooks's *Chappaqua*, about the film-maker's escape from heroin addiction. It was a strange job to take on, considering Ravi's horror of any link between his music and drugs or psychedelic imagery (which *Chappaqua* is full of), but his need for someone to transcribe string parts in a Paris studio triggered a musical revolution.

The closest thing Western music had to a gharana was located in Nadia Boulanger's Paris apartment. There, this remarkable French guru tutored a long line of students including Burt Bacharach, Daniel Barenboim, Aaron Copland, Quincy Jones, Michel Legrand, Dinu Lipatti, and Astor Piazzolla, to name but a few. Rooks's budget was thin, so he put out the word among anglophone music students, and who should answer the call but nineteen-year-old Philip Glass, a Boulanger pupil with zero experience of Indian music. Glass was bemused at first by Shankar and his working methods, but soon became fascinated by the interplay between him and Alla Rakha, and began a deep dive into the study of Indian music as well as forging lifelong friendships with both masters.

Glass's years in Paris shaped him as a composer. After Ravi showed how it was possible to be both composer and performer, he came to believe that exposure to audiences was essential, that twentieth-century Western music suffered from domination by ivory-tower intellectuals with little feel for how audiences responded to their creations. Western music, he observed, takes a block of music and slices it "like a loaf of bread" into smaller units, while Indian music takes beats and "strings them together like beads" in cycles of twelve, sixteen, or more. Glass has also observed that his Paris exposure to Samuel Beckett's spare, plotless plays dovetailed perfectly with the cyclical approach to rhythm he learned from Alla Rakha to produce his "intentionless" works.

In 1990, Shankar and Glass collaborated on *Passages*, an album that qualifies as one of the more satisfying fusions of Western and Indian music. The recording's structure is neat: three tracks are Glass arrangements of Shankar melodies and three the obverse. Ravi chose his Western musical friends well, sharing affection and respect with Menuhin, Coltrane, Harrison, and Glass. The latter two also made immense practical contributions to his legacy: Harrison plumbed Ravi's archives curating *In Celebration*, a massive 1996 box set that includes rarities and long-out-of-print ragas, while Glass set his music-publishing company the task of cataloguing each and every Shankar recording and composition and hoovering up royalties for him that were lying around in bottom drawers at record companies and copyright societies.

After the end of his marriage to Annapurna, Shankar also grew wiser in his romantic life. No longer would he promise fidelity, openly conducting a series of affairs and long-term relationships across three continents; two of the twenty-first century's brightest musical talents, Norah Jones and Anoushka Shankar, are products of them. In 1989, nearing seventy and with a slower pace to his incessant traveling, he married Anoushka's mother and settled, somewhat, down.

> The frequencies in the raga are in tune, and our bodies are made of receptors that have harmonic relationships—synapses and so on. When we sing and play these wonderful intervals, they vibrate and tune our entire being, so that we can become altered—physically, psychologically, spiritually.
>
> —Terry Riley

For a while in the early seventies, I shared a house in the Hollywood Hills with John Cale. He rarely spoke of Lou Reed or the Velvet Underground, and then mostly in Welsh-accented monosyllables. But John loved talking about his work with the minimalist pioneers Terry Riley and La Monte Young; their influence, via Cale, on the Velvets, and through them on rock music, was profound, and much of that inspiration came from Indian music.

Before he even knew the word, La Monte Young loved drones. As a boy growing up in the Idaho woods, he was fascinated by the moan of winter winds through the cracks in the walls of his family's log house and the summertime buzz of crickets, and he enjoyed humming along with telephone wires. At music college in Los Angeles, Young played saxophone with cutting-edge beboppers but changed direction after hearing the tanbura on an Ali Akbar Khan LP. On a music-theory course in San Francisco, La Monte found a lifelong friend and ally in Terry Riley. Riley's work was based on *talas*, the rhythmic structures of ragas, while Young remained fixed on drones. In New York in the early sixties, he organized electronic-music nights at Yoko Ono's loft (in the neighborhood not yet known as SoHo) that can be seen as precursors of the trance marathons of a half-century later. With his perfect ear for pitch, Young was obsessed with tunings and how the equal temperament of Western instruments is actually a fudge to get around the fact that the notes of each scale require slightly altered tunings to be mathematically true. Instruments—pianos in particular—are "tempered" or averaged in a way that makes the keys work, sort of, for every chord or scale. This means that no notes except the As are precisely correct (concert A is normally tuned these days to 440 Hz); we're so accustomed to it that few are aware how nearly all music we hear is ever so slightly off. Most Indian instruments, on the other hand, are "bendable," enabling intervals in a raga scale to be played "true." Young's signature work, *The Well-Tuned Piano*, was both a homage to Bach's *Well-Tempered Clavier* and a minimalist landmark for which the piano must be specially retuned to create a perfect scale in the key of E flat.

Riley's seminal work *In C* was composed in 1964 while he was supporting himself playing ragtime piano in a tourist saloon in San Francisco and experimenting with tape loops. His notable innovation was to create live performances of *In C* in which teams of musicians (including Cale) emulated tape loops. The title of The Who's "Baba O'Riley" combines Terry's name with that of Pete Townshend's spiritual guru, Meher Baba; Riley had a similar impact on Brian Eno and Tangerine Dream.

In 1967, La Monte heard a tape of Pandit Pran Nath, a Punjabi vocalist whom a Bay Area yoga teacher was attempting to bring to America for a tour. Young sent Riley a copy and Nath became their shared obsession. When the singer eventually arrived, both were drawn to him "like iron filings to a magnet"; they became the Pandit's servants, gharana-style, preparing food for his special diet, catering to his every need, and waiting patiently for lessons. They kept this up until Nath's death twenty-six years later. He didn't radically alter the two minimalists' musical paths but rather confirmed them in the direction already begun and enriched their live performances.

Like Allaudin Khan, Pran Nath was born to prosperous parents who were horrified that their son wanted a musical career. Fleeing home at thirteen, he spent six years performing menial tasks in the Lahore gharana of Abdul Wahid Khan before being accepted as a student. Wahid Khan adhered to the Kirana school, founded in the thirteenth century by Gopal Nayak, a singer at the court of a Hindu maharajah, whose music was heavily influenced by Sufism. Khan once stated that he would have been content to spend his whole life exploring one piece—"Todi"—if it hadn't been inappropriate to sing a morning raga after lunch. The Kirana approach focuses on the alap, the slow exposition of a scale that Western audiences usually encounter as the opening section of a raga. Khan would slowly savor the tone and texture of each note, approaching it from different directions, in no hurry to "progress" to the next.

Young found Nath's meditative and pitch-perfect exploration of ancient raga scales to be an ideal riposte to the compromises of Western tuning systems. In the singer's vast repertoire, no two ragas were anchored to precisely the same starting point on the sonic spectrum, giving each its own distinct atmosphere and sound. La Monte considered Pran Nath (whose name means "master of breath") "the greatest living musician of our time."

Nath never had much of a concert career, partly because the notion held little interest for him, but also because Indian vocal music struggled to follow instrumental ragas into the concert halls and record collections of the West. The combination of foreign lyrics and the sound of the voice used in such an abstract way made the music somehow too alien. Nusrat Fateh Ali Khan, who broke through in the nineties with power, passion, and fusion production, used vocal techniques that can be traced back to that same Kirana gharana, but Pandit Pran Nath was a very different sort of singer. On recordings, his unearthly voice can seem to the uninitiated to be located far beyond the charms of the exotic. Converts, though, become mesmerized by his unhurried relishing of each note and the unfamiliar intervals he nails with such bullseye microtonal accuracy. Riley pointed out that "once Indian music came to the West, it got involved with Western musical taste, which was faster and louder. Pran Nath was never affected by this."

My first encounter with South Asian vocal music came on a frozen January night in 1965 in a grubby brownstone on the Lower East Side while smoking a very strong joint. The friendly hippie from across the hall had a gleam in his eye as he removed a disc from its flimsy sleeve with the logo of the Pakistan Gramophone Company on the back and a photo of two intense-looking young men holding drone instruments on the front. My infatuation with the music I heard that night survived coming down from the high; Nazakat and Salamat Ali may have sung a little "faster and louder," but they were absolutely brilliant and there was an aching gap in my record collection until I managed to track down an album of theirs when I moved to London.

Four years on, more good Ali Brothers fortune came my way when I got a call from a London music publisher named John Fenton. I have forgotten how the Ali party came to be staying with him following an appearance at the 1969 Edinburgh Festival, or why John thought to invite me to meet them, but I joined a few guests that evening at his Knightsbridge flat; we sat on the floor eating delicious Punjabi food prepared by the Alis' *sarangi* player, then leaned back against a wall for three hours of some of the most extraordinary music I have ever heard.

The brothers mostly sang verses from the Koran, but the divine was sought more through sound than texts, as their voices wound around each other in complex spirals, the sarangi following close behind. They began with an alap, exploring a scale slowly, like Pandit Pran Nath doubled, then increased the speed and intensity until we were all dizzy with amazement at the vocal control and ecstatic explorations of the rhythms of the tala. The next day they came to Sound Techniques studio, where I had evicted Fairport Convention or Nick Drake from a scheduled session in order to get the Alis down on tape before they flew back to Lahore. It probably qualifies as one of the best recordings I have ever produced (if you can call sitting in a control room listening to brilliant music go down on tape "producing"), but no record companies were interested and it would be twenty years before the tapes were finally released on my Hannibal label.

Salamat was ten and Nazakat twelve in 1945, when their appearance at a music conference in Calcutta astounded the Indian music world.

The power of their performance forced the assembled scholars to agree that these prodigies from a minor Punjabi gharana were already masters of the *khayal*, the form that had evolved centuries earlier in the collision of Persian and Hindu cultures under the Mughals. Following Partition, the Alis settled in Pakistan but continued to perform in India, despite the tensions between the two countries. In 1954, they gave a command performance in Delhi for Prime Minister Nehru, a symbolic moment representing the culmination of more than a thousand years of collaboration and exchange between Hindu and Muslim cultures in South Asia. With politicians in both nations stirring up and leveraging sectarianism, the spirit represented by that famous event has been in decline ever since. At the heart of this issue lies a movement that makes religious and political leaders on both sides of the divide nervous: Sufism.

෴

There are many ways to the Divine.
I have chosen the ways of song, dance, and laughter.

—

All day and night, music,
a quiet, bright
reedsong. If it
fades, we fade.

—

Let your throat-song
be clear and strong enough
to make an emperor fall full-length,
suppliant, at the door.

—Verses by thirteenth-century Persian poet Rumi

Sufism is more of an attitude than a sect or a category. There are Sunni Sufis and Shiite Sufis; millions of Hindus and Sikhs worship Sufi saints at Sufi shrines and listen to Sufi music. From Senegal to Java, many if not most of the best-known musicians in the Muslim world are Sufis, though the term also includes purists who condemn the use of musical instruments. The word itself comes from the Arabic for "wool," referring to the coarse garments worn by the first Sufi mystics. Like early Protestantism, the core of Sufi belief involves a direct path from the believer to God rather than through the mediation of priests or mullahs. For many Sufis, the door to ecstatic communion with the divine is through music, and Sufism is central to the Muslim-Hindu connection that spawned the great classical music of the subcontinent.

In my twenties, when I began attending friends' weddings, it was almost a given that someone would read from *The Prophet* by Kahlil Gibran. In the noughties, it was more likely to be a poem by Rumi. Jelaluddin Rumi was the son of a Sufi imam who set up a madrassa at Konya in Anatolia after fleeing west in the early thirteenth century, when the Mongols invaded what is now Afghanistan. As a youth, Rumi was drawn to a pillar in the center of his father's mosque; holding it with one hand and twirling around opened his mind to God's grace, and poetry would come to him. When he became a teacher, his students emulated his spinning, leading to the spread of whirling dervishes within Sufism. Rumi's verses were beloved and sung across the Persian, Turkic, and Hindi worlds. When he died in 1273, Christians, Jews, and Muslims of different orders and brotherhoods all helped carry his body through the city and contributed to the building of his tomb.

As some were heading west, others from the region fled east to escape Genghis Khan's horde; among them was Khwaja Moinuddin from the town of Chishti, near Herat. Moinuddin and his brotherhood of Chishti Sufis shunned the powerful and the wealthy, devoting themselves to the lowly and poor. They established a network of *khanqah* community centers throughout northern India that were open to all, regardless of faith or caste. Many Chishti sheiks became revered as saints, with shrines to their memory in Pakistan and northwest India that to this day draw thousands of Shiite, Hindu, Sunni, and Sikh pilgrims. Chishti Sufis were at the heart of centuries of cross-faith collaboration: Muslim singers performing Vedic chants in Hindu temples, Hindus singing Rumi's poems in sultans' palaces, Persian traditions of elaboration and decoration applied to ancient Indian ragas.

Someone who sings the words of the Prophet is known as a *qawwal*. For centuries, Islamic religious music was performed unaccompanied, but by the 1940s, *qawwali* singing by "parties" of men was often backed by drums, handclaps, and harmoniums, with a simple, infectious Punjabi rhythm that became hugely popular across the subcontinent and was at the heart of annual celebrations at the tombs of Sufi saints. Ustad Fateh Ali Khan, father of Nusrat, elaborated on qawwali's traditional style using some of the khayal vocal techniques employed by Nazakat and Salamat Ali. With his powerful and expressive voice, Nusrat became the form's biggest star in the seventies, with a series of Pakistan-produced cassettes distributed and bootlegged across the subcontinent and throughout South Asian communities, both Muslim and Hindu, in Britain and North America.

There weren't many Christians among Nusrat's millions of followers, but his path took a dramatic turn when it intersected with a tale from the Bible. Conservative Christians were so busy being outraged by the sex scenes in Martin Scorsese's *The Last Temptation of Christ*, they barely noticed that the music accompanying Christ's brutal cross-bearing climb up Calvary and the hammering in of the nails was Nusrat Fateh Ali Khan singing an Islamic text. Scorsese had always wanted Peter Gabriel to create the music for *Last Temptation*, and the world music pioneer delivered a defining blend of bland synthesizer chords with exotic instruments and voices that would dominate world music fusion in the coming years. Since no such category existed in the late eighties, Gabriel's soundtrack album *Passion* was awarded a Grammy for Best New Age recording (which tells you something about the music).

Nusrat's impassioned singing laid over Gabriel's electronics stimulated imaginations; being rhythmically much simpler than Hindustani classical music, qawwali is easier to lay on top of machine beats. The decade between the release of the film and Fateh Ali Khan's sudden death from heart failure in 1997 saw a feeding frenzy by producers from disparate musical worlds chopping, sampling, blending, adapting, and pilfering his music for purposes far removed from the devout gatherings that constituted its original audience. First up was a young DJ named Baljit "Bally" Sagoo, who'd grown up not far from the UB40 kids in the English Midlands and been similarly entranced by the omnipresent sounds of reggae. He convinced Oriental Star, a Midlands-based distributor of South Asian music, to let him try a Kingston-style remix on one of their Punjabi releases. When he applied the same dance-hall sensibilities to Nusrat's qawwali, he and the (initially oblivious) singer had hit after hit. Gabriel, meanwhile, brought Nusrat and party to the WOMAD festival in the English countryside and his Real World label released *Shahen-Shah*, a well-recorded album of unadulterated qawwali. But the remix temptation was too great and Gabriel hired Canadian guitarist Michael Brook for the task. It is illuminating to compare *Mustt-Mustt*, the album that made the singer famous in the world music arena, with *Magic Touch*, Sagoo's collection of Nusrat remixes. Released around the same time and using similar technology, Sagoo's is geared towards the dancefloor tastes of young Anglo-Asians, while Brook's bluesy slide guitar and earnest attempt to meet the qawwali rhythm halfway is aimed at a middle-class world music crowd. For his CD's bonus track, Gabriel doubled down on the remix notion by turning Massive Attack's postmodern dub loose on the title song. Both albums were huge successes, though the two audiences were barely aware of each other's existence. In terms of sheer numbers, though, the remix markets were dwarfed by qawwali's and Nusrat's biggest platform of all.

When Hollywood invented "talkies," its first productions were musicals with songs woven into the plot; the lineage from Papageno introducing himself in Mozart's *The Magic Flute* to Ko-Ko singing "Behold the Lord High Executioner" in *The Mikado* to Gene Kelly splash-dancing his way home from a date in *Singin' in the Rain* is pretty direct. The Hindi film industry aspired to the dazzle and glamour of Hollywood, but its antecedents lay elsewhere, in epic Hindu pageantry, where tales of misbehaving gods would be interrupted by intervals of singing and dancing that had little to do with the story. In what came to be known as Bollywood, they'd hit the "pause" button on the plot line a half-dozen times during a film and treat the audience to a lavish production number with actors lip-syncing voices clearly not their own. From the start in the 1940s, Hindi film music had always been a hodge-podge: Bengali and Punjabi folk tunes backed by lush Hollywood strings with jazz (take another bow, Benny Goodman), Latin, country and western, surf guitar, and the Twist all thrown in over the years and delivered with a vague nod in the direction of India's own classical traditions. Over time, Western beats began crowding out local rhythms. On Bombay sound stages, writers, actors, directors, composers, and musicians from all regions and religions collaborated in the construction of a cultural behemoth that, with its powerful blend of familiar and foreign (mostly US) styles, slowly suffocated local folk music.

All India Radio hated it. Its Ravi-inspired brief was to educate the country about its own traditions, so, just as the BBC in its early decades turned up its nose at the hit parade, Bollywood's mongrel sounds were banned from state radio. The film industry's growing power, however, ended up not only marginalizing AIR but smothering at birth all attempts to create a popular music industry. The only vinyl records or CDs to sell in large quantities were Bollywood soundtracks and they shifted millions. There were regional film centers for Bengali, Tamil, and Malayalam productions (and a Pakistani "Lollywood" in Lahore), but Bombay set the standard.

The exception that proved the rule was qawwali. Directors enjoyed using it as a plot device, though to an outsider, it can seem a bit surreal watching young Hindus making eyes at each other during a performance of what are primarily Islamic texts. Such scenes occurred regularly in the early years and their frequency multiplied as Nusrat's fame grew. A year before his death, he and his musicians appeared in *Aur pyaar ho gaya* (And Love Happened), a film about a wealthy Hindu girl who travels to Switzerland (big-budget Bollywood loves Alpine scenery) for a covert peek at the husband her family has arranged for her. Mistaken identities, romantic hijinks, and scandals climax at a lavish Hindu wedding where a heavily pancaked Nusrat and party (in bright blue garb rather than their normal black and white) pound out a jolly love song to which bride and groom perform a kind of Pan's People bump and grind and mime-sing a few verses. Like those gospel tunes "Swing Low Sweet Chariot" and "Michael, Row the Boat Ashore" around a New England campfire, qawwali, it seems, can be party music, and Sufis have always insisted that seductive lines to a sweetheart can also serve as words of love for God (which is how St. Francis of Assisi explained his youthful obsession with yearning troubadour ballads).

By the time of Nusrat's death, Bollywood had become addicted to qawwali's loping, clappy beat, making it virtually the only South Asian rhythm able to stand its film-score ground against the breakbeats blowing in from the west. Nusrat always insisted that hearing the Sound of God was good, no matter the context, and didn't seem to mind even the most blatant theft (though he finally lost his temper when one composer turned the prayerful classic "Allahu" into "I Love You, I Love You"). Hollywood didn't use Nusrat very often but appeared to show greater respect when it did; his duets with Pearl Jam's Eddie Vedder on the *Dead Man Walking* soundtrack are among the most successful cross-cultural performances in any context.

There's dancing, behind movie scenes,
Behind those movie screens—Asha Bhosle.
She's the one that keeps the dream alive . . .
From the morning, past the evening, till the end of the light.
Brimful of Asha on the 45.
Well, it's a brimful of Asha on the 45.

—"Brimful of Asha" by Cornershop (Norman Cook remix), a UK #1 in February 1998

In the late '60s, my Witchseason Productions office was in London's Charlotte Street opposite the old Scala Cinema, then a bastion of reruns, B movies, and "four-wall" rentals, often to immigrant groups enjoying a film from home. After a week in the studio, I'd go in on Sundays to catch up on paperwork and sometimes catch a whiff of curry wafting from the Scala. That signalled "Indian Film Day," when families arrived with pots of food they would eat while watching the latest arrivals from Bombay, Lahore, or Calcutta. This ritual was repeated across the globe, wherever enterprising South Asians had migrated to improve their lot (and usually that of the local economy as well): Africa, Southeast Asia, Northern Europe, America, Polynesia. The British remained as aloof as Uday Shankar had found them in the twenties, but Africans and Asians were intrigued and then entranced by Bollywood's spectacular musical numbers and feel-good plot lines. Soviet bloc commissars loved how

Indian films provided light-hearted diversion without poisoning minds with glimpses of Western material excess. Bollywood became a global phenomenon, its scores regularly quoted in Balkan and Arabic music and its influence felt in modern pop from Lagos to Shanghai.

Aside from Anoushka Shankar's star-studded jazz and classical collaborations, the twenty-first century's highest-profile East-West musical meeting might be *You've Stolen My Heart: Songs from R. D. Burman's Bollywood*, the Kronos Quartet's collaboration with Asha Bhosle. Burman and Bhosle represent a pair of patrician families who loomed over the world of Indian film music for half a century. Asha's grandfather was a Brahmin priest with a *devadasi*—a sacred dancer—for a mistress at his temple in Goa. Their son, Deenanath Mangeshkar, became a playwright and theater director before dying in 1942 and leaving five young children, who were looked after by his many friends in the film industry. All grew up on sound stages and became singers or musicians. Two of Mangeshkar's daughters would dominate Bollywood "playback" singing, with each ending up in the *Guinness Book of Records* for having recorded well over ten thousand songs in thirty-six different languages. Continuing to record well into their eighties, both Lata and Asha (who had eloped at sixteen with a man named Bhosle) always sounded like cheeky schoolgirls. (Female vocalists in Eastern cultures often sing in high-pitched voices, linked, one suspects, to the virginal innocence demanded of feminine icons in Asia.)

Lata Mangeshkar's career was launched through her early collaborations with a prince from the Tripura dynasty. Sachin Dev Burman had spurned his regal heritage, becoming a successful Bengali folk singer before moving to Bombay to compose film scores. After years of success together, Lata and S.D. fell out and the composer turned to her rival younger sister, elevating Asha to the pinnacle of Bollywood fame. This led to Asha's second marriage, to the composer's son, Rahul Dev, who had apprenticed with his father and become a top composer in his own right. Burman *père et fils* were technically astute modernizers who threw all manner of foreign sounds into the mix, reflecting the aspirations and frustrations of generations wearied by their country's conservative culture, protectionist economy, and stifling bureaucracy.

By the mid-nineties, both Burmans had passed from the scene, but the sisters carried on, recording hit after "playback" hit.

The biography of the new century's dominant composer, A. R. Rahman, reads like a movie plot or a modern film score—filled with samples and borrowings. Like R. D. Burman, his father was a film composer who died young, as had Asha's and Lata's dad. Enduring a series of Allaudin Khan–like struggles and rejections, he had to hustle to gain his musical education; once he got started, he took the Burmans' magpie skills to new extremes, bringing hip-hop and electronic dance music into his state-of-the-art studio in Madras. Rahman was central to the ultimate East-West fusion moment, the 2009 multi-Oscar-winning *Slumdog Millionaire*. Indians couldn't decide whether to be proud or furious about a movie that blended Bollywood swagger with British realism and sarcasm, paying homage to India while exposing its terrible poverty and the corruption of its institutions. Rahman's score was one of the Oscar winners, prompting the Indian government to bestow on him its highest civilian honor. Today's Hindu nationalist rulers wouldn't dream of such a thing; born a Hindu, Rahman's conversion to Sufi Islam makes him a symbol of everything Modi and the BJP hate about Bollywood: too many Muslim stars, too many scripts that challenge the BJP narrative, *too much qawwali!*

> There's been a significant amount of Islamophobia and a lot of bad marketing towards Pakistan in general—associations with terrorism and pain and Afghanistan-adjacent confusion—while the narrative around a lot of other south Asian countries is like "Oh my God! Beauty! Exotic landscapes! Yoga!" And the west loves that shit.
>
> —Singer Arooj Aftab, quoted by Fatima Bhutto in the *Guardian*, 2022

In the spring of 2021, Bollywood-Rahman anti-matter hit the internet with stunning force. The *Guardian*, Barack Obama, *Pitchfork*, and many more across the globe acclaimed Arooj Aftab's "Mohabbat" as one of the tracks of the year; Aftab earned a Grammy nomination as Best New Artist and won the Best Global Music Performance award (the World Music category's successor). Aftab's journey is a very modern one, from an internet-viral performance of Leonard Cohen's "Hallelujah" to a scholarship at the Berklee School of Music in Boston to working in New York as a sound engineer, where she learned not so much how to use the latest digital gadgets but rather to record beautiful sounds with acoustic instruments.

"Mohabbat" is a daunting piece for a Pakistani to take on; the words are by Hafeez Hoshiapuri, a twentieth-century poet held in Rumi-like reverence across South Asia, and there are many classic recordings of it, most famously by the great ghazal singer Mehdi Hassan Khan. Aftab hesitated to tackle the song, but alluded in interviews to how the sudden death of her brother may have given her the determination to approach these verses about love and loss in her own way. Using a singer-songwriter guitar strum instead of a drone seems to enhance rather than detract from the measured, intense emotion of the vocal. One Western critic interestingly compared her singing to Norah Jones's, while another praised her "effortless command of intertonal pitching; the precision ornamentation; and the awesome breath control." Could it be that South Asian vocal techniques have arrived to rescue Western popular singing from its obsession with African-American melisma?

Few expected this breath of fresh musical air from a land so rife with intolerance, whose democracy gets regularly pistol-whipped by the army and which has spent much of the new century supporting the music-hating Taliban. But, as a 2022 *Guardian* essay by Fatima Bhutto (niece of assassinated former prime ministers Benazir and Zufkir Ali) pointed out, Pakistani culture has actually become more vibrant and open in recent years, which is more than can be said of its Indian neighbor. At the heart of the musical side of these developments is the Great Satan's favorite refreshment; in 2008, Coca-Cola began sponsoring a show modeled on *MTV Unplugged* and featuring contemporary musicians paired with some of the country's greatest traditional artists. The first *Coke Studio* episode opened with a beautiful alap sung by Ustad Hussain Bakhsh Gullo, a nephew of the Ali Brothers, to drone accompaniment from electric guitar and synth before moving into a ghazal, with Gullo and the lead singer of the backing band trading verses. The show was such a hit that Coke extended the franchise to India,

Bangladesh, and the Middle East. The copies don't seem to work as well as the original, though; the Indian version looks overproduced and includes collaborations with rappers and K-pop starlets. The Pakistani version has continued to delve deep into regional traditions, with a *Coke Studio Explorer* sidebar traveling to remote corners of the country for encounters with minority music, showing instruments and styles few city-dwellers have ever seen or heard before.

Whether *Coke Studio* can hold back the inexorable tide of DJs at South Asian weddings remains to be seen. Musicians in the region have always relied on nuptials as a key source of income, but these days only the very rich and the very poor can be relied on to pay for live music at their marriage festivities, leading the offspring of many musical families to abandon the trade in search of a more secure future. As cultures across the globe modernize, India and Pakistan are hardly unique in this respect, but in one corner of the subcontinent the implications extend deep into a society where musicians are keepers of family histories and provide much of the glue that holds rural communities together. To lose these traditions would profoundly alter a vast area where few watch television or drink Coke.

> *O Pabuji, the cows' little calves are weeping,*
> *The cows' little calves are calling out to Pabuji.*
> *O Pabuji, may your name remain immortal in the land;*
> *O Pabuji, may your brave warriors remain immortal!*
>
> —Rajasthani epic

Pabuji was a minor fourteenth-century Rajput prince who led poor farmers into battle against rapacious landlords and cattle thieves. Told and retold over the centuries, Pabuji's legend has expanded like the plot of a Bollywood epic, adding snake goddesses, talking birds, and other magical transformations. The core of the tale, however, remains unwavering: protecting poor farmers and their animals against drought, plague, and the uncaring powerful. Across the parched expanses of Rajasthan in India's northwest, the story is seen as curative and prophylactic;

performing it over the course of a few evenings can prevent theft, cure sick cattle, and recover lost livestock.

In 2007, in a small garden behind the walls of the giant fort looming over the city of Jodhpur, Pabuji's tale unspooled before me on a *phad*, a fifteen-foot-long painted scroll. It was recited and sung by a *bhopa* named Mohan, who accompanied his narrative on the *ravanhattho*, a one-string spike-fiddle, while his wife pointed to the relevant section of the vividly illustrated phad. There are cave paintings in Central Asia many thousands of years old showing monks reciting in front of backdrops like this, with someone holding a lamp and pointing. Mohan had been the star of a celebrated 2006 *New Yorker* piece by William Dalrymple called "Homer in India," which linked Alfred Lord's groundbreaking 1930s research on Balkan oral histories to Hindu epics recited from memory. Aristotle worried that the spread of writing would put an end to bards and their tales but he didn't foresee how illiteracy would persist across the centuries and ensure the continued flexing of mankind's memory muscles. Dalrymple described a bhopa in south India who could, over the course of many days and nights and encouraged by shouts and cheers from his audience, recite the entire Mahabharata, a text six times longer than the Bible. In the years following Independence, under the onslaught of literacy, Bollywood, and now the internet, such skills have begun to evaporate.

That was certainly happening in Rajasthan, but more slowly. Rajasthan is the most "traditional" state in India. On the plus side, there are more hereditary craftspeople, acrobats, bards, and musicians than in any other region; on the minus side, *suttee* (widow burning) took place until fairly recently, while the gap between rich and poor and the percentage of landless peasants remain among the largest in India. Under British rule, the region was generally left alone, allowing local rulers to keep things much as they had always been; Indira Gandhi took away their power in 1971 but let them keep their vast tracts of land.

My encounter with Pabuji took place at the first annual Rajasthan International Folk Festival. With Mick Jagger on the board (and omnipresent during that first festival), the event is the highest-profile manifestation of a process that began in Jaipur in 1970, when a biker and chicken farmer named John Singh met Faith Hardy, an English girl intrigued by Rajasthani traditional crafts. Singh sold his share of the family silver to fund Anokhi, an enterprise the couple started based on traditional hand-block printing on organic cotton cloth. The Singhs transformed this ancient trade, providing material to skilled village women, shielding them from usurious middlemen and paying them fairly. Liberty's of London stocked their clothes and the Monsoon chain was built around selling Anokhi's goods across Britain. After inviting local musicians to perform at a celebration in Jaipur in 1988, when international buyers and press came to experience the culture behind the cloth, the Singhs became intrigued with the possibilities of applying to Rajasthani traditional music what they'd learned in the rag trade.

The situation was dire: modernity-obsessed local, regional, and national governments were dismissive of tradition, be it in architecture, craft industries, or music. Performers received pittances for appearing at official functions, while landowning families, whose links to musical clans go back centuries, were employing them less and less often. John decided to address the situation from the ground up, just as he and Faith had with Anokhi, launching the Jaipur Virasat Foundation in 2002 to provide funds for stages, sound systems, and payments to musicians. Most decent-sized Rajasthani towns had market days and festivals where musicians would perform informally, collecting whatever money listeners felt like giving. The JVF began staging events on those days that drew thousands of cheering spectators; the shows got coverage in regional newspapers and on television, helping turn musicians into local celebrities and increasing what they could charge for performing at births, deaths, and marriages. The good sound and impressive staging lent prestige as communities began to celebrate their local heritage. The number of events has continued to grow over the years, forcing governments and institutions to start paying more respect—and larger fees—to local musicians, thereby keeping the next generation interested. Children from these families rarely received much non-musical education, but the JVF has also raised money to support schooling for them. Since that first RIFF in Jodhpur, the music of Rajasthan has raised its international profile to the point where many

Rajasthani performers now tour the world and have become better known than their Hindustani classical peers.

In 2011, I traveled with Singh to a meeting with members of the Manganyar musical clan, in a village near Jaisalmer in the west of the state. The busiest Rajasthani musicians are either Langas or Manganyars, networks of Muslim performers who have for centuries kept the family histories of Hindu farmers, performing ritual music at all their births, weddings, and deaths. John organized these regular get-togethers so that musicians could compare notes, hear and encourage young musicians, and air shared problems. Those days resonate in my memory for the relaxed camaraderie, the brilliant music, the astonishing skills shown by pre-teen virtuosos, the delicious food scooped out of buckets onto tin plates, and the delicate light over the desert in the early evenings. On the final night, we were joined by a delegation of the Manganyars' employers, Hindu farmers whose links to the musicians extend back many generations. In what John told me was a first, they sat with the musicians and serenaded them with traditional songs of their own, a perfect coda to the preceding days and to the work the JVF has done to strengthen the ancient bonds holding these communities together in the face of sectarianism and the impatient energies of modernity. Caste is an awkward concept for an outsider to view with sympathy. Singh didn't disagree, of course, but pointed out that in today's India, liberation from hereditary trades often leads to an urban slum and work in a sweatshop or some other soulless job, with a cultural diet of soap operas and video clips sustained by junk food. The JVF works to provide those remaining within this ancient system some fair treatment, education, and dignity.

The Thar Desert around Jaisalmer has been at the front line of religious and cultural confrontation for millennia, crossed and recrossed by invading and defending armies. Many of the Manganyars I met there have traversed it to board a plane bound for Europe or America, where they command arts center and festival stages with the same relaxed confidence they demonstrate when singing the history of a landowning family at a wedding. The tourist-brochure cliché about India is that it is "timeless"; while resisting the reductive simplicity of that slogan, I couldn't help but ponder the fact that it was groups very much like these

Manganyars who headed west sixteen hundred years ago and would end up completely reshaping European musical culture.

⌇

The Shahnameh, a Persian epic written in the eleventh century, recounts a tale from around 450 CE. The great King Bahram found his subjects' drunkenness disturbing. He had no problem with wine as such, but the notion of drink without music offended him and he felt they were missing out on one of life's essential pleasures. Knowing India to be a land of music, he wrote to his Mughal father-in-law asking him to send musicians. According to the tale, ten thousand *luri*, or lute players, were duly dispatched westward to Persia, where Bahram presented each family with an ox, a donkey, plenty of seed, and some money to start a farm, on condition that they provide music for their local communities. When most returned a year later asking for another ox, another donkey, more grain, and more money, Bahram was furious, demanding to know why they weren't growing their own food with the seed he'd given them. But these *luri* weren't farmers and, in the rigid and already ancient Indian caste system, their ancestors never had been and their descendants never would be. Bahram banished them from his kingdom and most headed west. (Less poetic histories note that the Persian Empire often encouraged or forced itinerants and peasants to move west in order to settle newly conquered territory.)

Experts have analyzed the language spoken by these wanderers and conclude that they must have spent several centuries in Armenia (then a huge empire covering what is now eastern Turkey, parts of Iraq, and much of the Caucasus), followed by long years in Turkey and Greece. By the time they reached Central Europe in the fifteenth century, they'd learned that the best answer to the question of where they came from, the one that prompted the friendliest welcome and the biggest handouts, was "Egypt." Thus did these bands of Indian musicians, metalworkers, basket-weavers, and fortune-tellers become known as "Egyptians" or, in its colloquial shorthand, "gypsies."

Since the word has developed derogatory connotations, the preferred term now is "Roma," which different clans and branches across

Europe and the wider world have slowly embraced. All Roma speak some form of Romani, which, should any doubt remain, settles the question of their origin; like Hindi and Rajasthani, it is a Sanskrit language and the root word *rom* comes from a term meaning a man of low caste living by singing and playing music. Greeks muddled the Roma up with a long-established caste of musicians and palm readers called *atsinganoi*. That name also stuck, evolving over the miles and centuries into *tzigane* or *zigeuner*, terms still used in continental Europe. They are divided into distinct clans that speak widely varied dialects and who rarely intermarry or collaborate, including Manouche, Sinti, Lautari, Kalderash, Tshurara, and Matchvaya. Some specialize in horse-dealing (or now used cars), some in metalwork, and some make baskets, but nearly all have fiercely resisted being tied to one place and none ever till the soil or go to sea. Roma maintain an elaborate system of taboos and are deeply wary of *gadje* (non-Roma) mores, culture, and hygiene. The women of most clans excel at reading palms and telling fortunes (though only of gadje, as Roma don't believe in such things for themselves). Roma musicians take it upon themselves to master local gadje styles and usually transform them in the process.

The earliest recorded payment to Roma musicians was made in 1489, when they performed at a Hungarian princess's garden party on an island in the Danube near Budapest. The Ottoman invasion that surged through the Balkans and came to a halt in 1529 at the gates of Vienna had carried the Roma into the heart of Europe. "Egyptian" musicians were in demand on both sides of the line during the century-and-a-half stand-off; one Magyar nobleman's journal brags about capturing a great cimbalom player from the Turks, while a sultan noted giving a fat purse to a Roma violinist considered to be a champion of "Serbian" fiddling. When Queen Isabella of Spain visited Hungary in 1543, she raved about the music performed for her by "descendants of the Pharaohs."

After long years of turmoil brought on by war and plague, Europeans needed cheering up, but neither the Catholic nor the new Protestant churches were much help, hectoring the faithful about their transgressions and placing music and dance near the top of a list of sins. The Roma ignored such scolding, earning them fierce hostility from the churches and gratitude from nearly everyone else. Authorities had loathed these newcomers from the moment they first appeared, churchmen threatened by the popularity of their fortune-telling, spells and cures, and the liveliness of their music, and governments unnerved by their anarchic and itinerant way of life. Laws passed over the centuries could make for comical reading if their effects had not been so devastating: children taken from parents, men and women whipped, exiled, chained to ships' galleys, and even executed for the crime of being a "gypsy." The futility of these diktats can be inferred from the frequency of their repetition. When the Habsburg heiress Maria Theresa became Empress of Hungary in 1740, she declared them to be "New Hungarians" and banned the use of the term "gypsy." Though falling short in many ways, her reforms did bring a large number of Roma into a more settled way of life; many learned Magyar and became one of the few groups in Europe to lose fluency in Romani along with their tents and caravans.

The half-century reign of Maria Theresa and her son Joseph drew Roma musicians out of nobles' castles and remote villages and into urban spaces. A 1790 account of a Budapest ball describes two orchestras, one made up of neatly dressed Germans playing from written parts, the other of raffish-looking Roma with no music stands. No sooner had the Germans finished than the Roma band struck up a dance that filled the floor, and they continued in that vein for hours. Our witness notes that "the German musicians almost chewed up their music in their rage."

Now part of the Habsburg Empire, Hungary was obliged to provide its share of troops for the imperial army; what worked best was to send a recruiting sergeant and a few nimble and smartly uniformed soldiers around to popular taverns, accompanied by a group of Roma musicians. As everyone sang patriotic verses, the band would build up an infectious, accelerating rhythm that climaxed in a manly, boot-slapping dance that inspired half-drunk teenagers to enlist. This started a dance craze called *verbunkos*, after the German word for "recruitment," with melodies normally played on a bagpipe performed as they'd never been heard before, with violins, cimbalom, and drum.

The hottest verbunkos group was led by János Bihari, a showman who knew all the tricks. At dances, his band would start without him, James Brown–style, playing slow and ponderous melodies as the size of the crowd and the anticipation grew. With tension at its highest, Bihari would suddenly appear, take up his violin, and kick off a lengthy set of wild dancing. Afterwards, he'd go hat-in-hand through the crowd, starting with the most conservatively dressed burghers, whom he knew to be the stingiest. Their parsimony outraged the wealthy, who would ostentatiously toss gold and silver coins into Bihari's hat. After a year playing for post-negotiation dances at the Congress of Vienna, Bihari was famous across Europe. In the peaceful post-Napoleon years, Hungarian Roma bands were lionized in London, Paris, and Berlin, an early onset of the world music phenomenon.

Roma musicians and the great German and Austrian composers were full of mutual admiration. Bihari and his peers aspired to play music "like Haydn," while Hungarian dance melodies can be spotted in works such as Papa Joe's D-major piano concerto and G-major piano trio, Mozart's A-major violin concerto, and the last movement of Beethoven's Third Symphony. In his book *The Gypsies and their Music in Hungary*, Franz Liszt wrote glowingly about Bihari, though he was probably born too late (1811) to have heard him in person. (Bihari stopped performing in 1824, after breaking his shoulder in a carriage accident.) A Roma musician, Liszt observed, "takes the theme of a song or a dance" and "lavishly enriches [it] with runs, appoggiaturas, leaps, tremolos, chord stopping, diatonic and chromatic scales."

A couple of generations earlier, musical embellishments had been sufficiently controversial that J. S. Bach's son Carl Philipp Emanuel felt compelled to defend them, insisting that they "bind the notes together, they introduce life into them, they fill the notes with expression, they give them atmosphere and meaning, they breathe charm into them. They enlighten the emotions, whether sorrowful or happy, and they are thus important factors in the artistic impression." It is tempting to connect these dots to E. T. A. Hoffman's essays linking music, "the most romantic of all arts," to the birth of Romanticism. Italians and their increasingly loud and expressive violins are usually given the credit for transforming post-Baroque European music. But northern Italy had also seen a large influx of Roma soon after they reached Hungary; did Roma musicians across the Habsburg Empire help to inspire the shift from Haydn's elegance to Beethoven's drama and passion?

No speculation is needed to credit these players with a role in the surge of Hungarian nationalism. The decades leading up to the Revolutions of 1848 were filled with pride in one's own language and culture. Like those tipsy youths enlisting in the army, the sound of Roma bands playing heart-stirring traditional melodies inspired Hungarians of all classes to demand independence from Austria. In the years following the crushing of the rebellion by Russian troops, you could end up in jail for singing a Magyar song too passionately. Roma bandleaders moved with the times, shifting their music towards a more polished, sentimental sort of Hungarianness, the kind of sound that drove Béla Bártok mad when he arrived in Budapest at the end of the century. Ballads were bowdlerized and a bland style of fakelore called *nota* was created, matching parallel efforts from Saint Petersburg to Cincinnati (home of Stephen Foster). This period also saw the formalization of what came to be known as Hungarian "gypsy music"; a Roma named Pista Dankó, who rivaled W. C. Handy in his ability to reduce raw folk sources to something played pleasantly in park bandstands on a Sunday afternoon, marked out the territory. His style of sentimental kitsch is performed to this day throughout Central Europe by unctuous violinists hovering over your table at white-tablecloth restaurants.

Liszt's book scandalized many by claiming that Roma musicians had rescued the country's folk music from mediocrity. Bártok, on the other hand, made a point of avoiding them in his recording expeditions to the countryside. Later, between the world wars, he not only rejected the kitsch "gypsy violins" Admiral Horthy's fascist government adored (even as they imposed brutal repression on the Roma and sent tens of thousands to Nazi extermination camps) but also criticized Liszt's indebtedness to their flamboyant ancestors. Bártok held that the purest music was sung; instrumentalists (the best of whom were Roma) could only copy melodies and decorations developed by vocalists. Before soloists performed premieres of his new works, however, he would often insist they listen to field recordings of Roma violinists.

The two composers were not entirely at odds on the subject; in the years following the controversies around his book, Liszt had grown disillusioned with how Roma musicians were "elevating" Hungarian music: "When they think to be able to improve and perfect their art . . . they deprive it of its original and special character, and make it into a stunted phenomenon devoid of individuality." Bártok had been born too late to hear the playing that inspired Liszt's *Hungarian Rhapsodies*. Budapest's Roma musicians seem to have trodden a path a bit like Nashville's journey from Bill Monroe and Hank Williams to Garth Brooks and Shania Twain.

> They excite the *hatred* of the bourgeois even though inoffensive as sheep . . . [T]hat hatred is linked to something deep and complex; it is found in all orderly people. It is the hatred that they feel for the bedouin, the heretic, the philosopher, the solitary, the poet, and there is fear in that hatred.
>
> —Gustave Flaubert

Before Maria Theresa's reforms, Roma musicians in Hungary had often "belonged" to various noblemen; that sounds sinister, but wasn't much different from Haydn "belonging" to Prince Esterhazy (or, for that matter, Lionel Messi once being "owned" by Barcelona or Prince by Warner Brothers). To the southeast, in the Ottoman-protectorate principalities of Transylvania and Wallachia, however, Roma really *were* property. Slavery was common in the Turkish Empire, and that cartoon villain Vlad "the Impaler" Dracula seems to have kicked it off in 1445 by purchasing a job lot of twelve thousand Roma at a Bulgarian market; for more than four centuries, they and their descendants would remain, by law, slaves.

Roma were so much better than the locals at playing music, training horses, fixing pots and pans, predicting the future, and advising barons on their love life that rural big men couldn't bear to let them wander off as they were so prone to do. Roma women, moreover, were often so beautiful that wealthy bullies couldn't resist buying a charming young girl at an auction, then selling her on when he got bored. Modern Romanian history books have very little to say about this; with no written history of their own and a tendency to consign bad memories to oblivion, few modern Roma know much about it either. Slavery was finally abolished in 1844 by a progressive-minded Moldavian princeling, forcing other regions to follow suit. Liberated slaves were often offered land if they'd stick around, but most didn't wait to find out what the local version of "freedom" might be like, they just hit the road. Thus began the second wave of Roma migration into Western Europe.

The first, in the fifteenth century, hadn't been large in numbers but it got everyone's attention. Colorfully dressed groups of Roma had turned up in Germany, France, Italy, Britain, and the Low Countries waving *laissez-passer* documents (both real and forged) and claiming to be on a pilgrimage. Paintings by Caravaggio and Hieronymous Bosch show Roma picking pockets while distracting yokels with cards and palm-reading. (The original meaning of *gadje* is "dim-witted peasant.") Fake news six centuries before Murdoch and the internet accused them of murdering blond children and drinking their blood. Paranoid exaggeration came easily to peasants still recovering from the bubonic plague and the Hundred Years War, though it's also the case that many Roma didn't consider petty pilferage immoral; chickens, in their view, were no different from apples hanging from a low branch on a roadside tree.

Deep in most bourgeois hearts lies an envy of open-road freedom; how many folk songs celebrate or bemoan the wife who leaves her "*goose-feather bed*" for a life with the "*raggle taggle gypsies, oh*"? And how many children were frightened into good behavior by tales of kidnappings and cannibalism and shown storybook pictures of "witches" dressed like Roma grandmothers? Despite all the fulminations of local lawmakers, the violent attacks, and the imprisonments, more and more Roma began traveling European roads in the wake of Romanian emancipation, selling horses, fixing pots, reading palms, and playing music for the high and the low (but rarely the middle).

The sudden appearance of a train of Roma caravans, horses, and goats was usually a cause for celebration; men with their violins and cimbaloms and women telling fortunes and wearing long, brightly colored skirts were a source of wonder and delight. Such camps were a regular sight across northern Europe up to the start of World War Two and sometimes drew so many gawking visitors that the clan could charge admission. Roma liked being near borders so they could slip across when necessary, and the wooded hills of the Alsace and the Ardennes were perfect; with French, Belgian, Luxembourgian, German, Dutch, or Swiss frontiers never far away, the region became a hub of European Roma life.

In the early 1930s, the Belgian artist Jan Yoors's unconventional parents let him run off with a group of Roma at age twelve. His book *The Gypsies* describes this lost world, one he would rejoin every spring after boring winters at his Antwerp school. He adored his adopted Roma clan; loaded with cash from horse-trading, scrap-metal dealing, fortune-telling, and music, they would arrive in a city and head straight for the Jewish quarter, where they swapped banknotes for gold and silver coins, got fitted for suits they would wear for the coming year like second skins, and pick out the fedoras they would set at a distinctive tilt.

Around the turn of the last century, a Manouche family named Vées made their way to Belgium, probably from Wallachia via Bavaria. They found a winter home in a field near the village of Liberchies, where townspeople welcomed them with open arms. Messages could be received and money exchanged at Chez Borsin, an inn where Jean-Eugene Vées led a band for village dances and the group would put on burlesques to entertain the locals. Jean-Eugene's wife was known as Négros because of her dark skin; when she gave birth to their son in 1910, he was registered as Jean Reinhardt, taking her family name rather than his due to some outstanding warrants for draft-dodging and other offenses. Reinhards had their own notoriety in the region; two ancestors had been strung up for leading an outlaw gang that terrorized the Rhine Valley in the eighteenth century, so the Belgian official added the "t" just to be on the safe side. Like most Roma, once back at the campsite they forgot about the child's gadje name; to them he was always "Django," which means "I awake" in Romani.

On our first day in Paris in the spring of 1964, the French TV producer who was presenting the show I was tour-managing, *The Blues and Gospel Caravan*, asked if we'd like some music along with our lunch. Muddy Waters, Sister Rosetta Tharpe, Otis Spann, and a few of the others joined, and we were driven to the Marché aux Puces, just outside the Porte de Clignancourt on the northern edge of the city. Our guide led us through a rabbit warren of alleys lined with stalls selling crockery, knick-knacks, dodgy oil paintings, and crumbling furniture until we came to a small café. As we slid into a couple of booths and the producer asked if we'd all be happy with *saucissons, frites*, and a beer, we could hear guitars being tuned. The gray-haired, crimson-bow-lipped waitress began singing in a Piaf-esque voice as she handed around the beers, and we were carried off by the unmistakable *pompe* of *manouche* jazz. It was completely sublime. I remember thinking that it was the most French thing I'd ever experienced.

It wasn't, though; it was pure Roma. One of the guitarists was Joseph "Nin-Nin" Reinhardt, Django's surviving brother, and the café was in the middle of what had once been La Zone, a waste ground outside city limits where the Vées's and other Roma caravans gathered after being forced out of their familiar back roads, fields, and woods to make way for World War One. Before running off with another woman, Jean-Eugene showed his young son a few positions on the violin, enough to give the boy a head start when a friend of Négros gave him a beat-up banjo fitted with a guitar neck. By the time he was nine, Django was playing in the streets and bringing home coins for the family. At age twelve an accordionist heard him in a bar and offered the kid the astonishing sum of ten francs a night to accompany him in the *bal-musettes*.

Back into the mists of time, Auvergnois, like rural Hungarians, had danced to the music of a solo bagpipe. When Hausmann's *grands boule-*

vards revolution swept away centuries-old alleyways and half-timbered housing in the 1850s and '60s, it brought red-kerchiefed men in their thousands from the Auvergne to Paris to rebuild the city. Their bagpipe was known as a *musette*, and in the last decades of the nineteenth century, long after Budapest had heard its last squawk from a refashioned goat carcass, these economic migrants from *la France profonde* still danced to pipes every weekend in the Rue de Lappe. When the musette's usurpers arrived, they weren't Roma armed with violins and cimbaloms but Italians with squeeze-boxes. For a few years, the greatest Auvergnois piper shared the stage with an ace accordionist, but by the time Django was born, dance halls named after those pipes, the *bal-musettes*, were moving to accordions, violins, and banjos and bandleaders had discovered that the best sidemen in Paris were Roma from La Zone.

Django started working the dance halls just as Auvergnois music was bursting out of the backstreets to become a Parisian craze. "La Java" was the original dirty dance, taking its name from the way "*ça va!*" sounds like "*cha va!*" in that provincial accent, and its notoriety from the way couples would dance the bouncy up-tempo waltz while holding one another firmly by the buttocks. From the start, Django astonished his new bandmates with his witty runs and improvisations; he "played incredible, complicated things the other banjomen who worked with us could not have even imagined," one recalled. "Although he was our accompanist, it was we who were unable to follow him!" And that was even before the fateful night when the boy stood outside a Left Bank nightclub and heard an African-American band for the first time, playing the latest exotic sound to sweep Paris.

Jazz hit Django like a hurricane. *The rhythm! The freedom!* Next to this, the music of the bal-musettes felt stodgy and mundane. Django had always looked to other instruments, not other banjo men, for guidance. Like João Gilberto, who would import chords and figures from accordions and drums onto the guitar, Django began mimicking what those expats were doing with the trumpet, the clarinet, and the piano.

Buzz about the whiz kid spread. One evening in 1928, at a rough, working-class dance hall in Belleville, an elegant-looking gentleman smoking an expensive cigar, with a lavishly decked-out and perfumed girl on each arm, arrived to check this Reinhardt out. Jack Hylton, leader of Europe's most successful "orchestral jazz" revue, was passing through Paris on his way to a season in Berlin; like America's Paul Whiteman, Hylton's version of the new music was a lot tamer than what was being played in Harlem or on Chicago's South Side, but he was a huge star, selling millions of records and putting on hundreds of elaborate shows each year with singers, dancers, and comedians. Hylton was impressed and invited Django to come by his hotel the next day to sign a contract. The world was opening up for the Roma kid from La Zone.

Back at their caravan, Bella was awaiting him; at eighteen, Django was already on his second wife. Roma clans differ in their rules around courtship and marriage; for most groups, money must change hands between families, the girl's virginity needs to be tested by an old woman who specializes in the task, and the bloody sheet must be shown before a wedding ceremony can start. With the Manouche, elopement was the custom and bonds were looser. Django had run off at fifteen with Naguine then left her two years later for Bella. The couple toasted their bright future that night with perhaps too many glasses. A candle fell, curtains caught flame, and the plastic flowers Bella was garlanding for a funeral the next day turned the caravan into an inferno from which Django barely escaped, with severe burns on his hands and arms.

Roma herbs and spells have been known to work miracles, but not this time. Bella retreated to her family to recover while Négros scraped together the money to take her son to Paris's top specialist. Skin grafts and modern medicine salvaged two fingers on Django's melted left hand. When he finally emerged from the hospital it was not Bella but Naguine who greeted him with a bouquet of tulips: "These ones are real. They won't start on fire." She would remain with Django for the rest of his life.

Slowly, painfully, he began playing the new guitar Nin-Nin had bought him. Though the fourth and fifth fingers on his left hand were useless, he could at least wrap his scarred thumb around the neck to fret the bottom string while using his second and third digits to articulate chords and runs. Miraculously, Django was able to reinvent himself as a three-fingered guitarist.

When the good weather arrived, like many Parisian Manouche, Naguine and Django headed south. He earned money passing the hat, playing on the streets of Provence and occasionally putting together a band. In a Toulon bar one night, a painter and photographer named Emile Savitry, freshly returned from the South Sea islands where he had been working on F. W. Murnau's film *Tabu*, heard Django and was astounded. He invited the Reinhardts back to his flat, where he kept a huge collection of jazz 78s. Savitry's real name was DuPont and he'd spent his inheritance wisely: all the Armstrong Hot Fives and Hot Sevens, Ellington, Beiderbecke, Earl Hines, the Mills Brothers, Fats Waller, you name it. Django's experience of this music had so far been limited to hearing jazz through the windows of nightclubs, plus a few after-hours encounters. He moved onto Savitry's sofa, spending days listening to record after record, shaking his head in amazement and playing along. At summer's end he headed back to La Zone, ready to get started with his new musical life, the solos of Satchmo, Dodds, Bix, Bigard, Nance, Hines, and Waller running through his head.

In Paris, a battle was raging between those adding jazzy touches to the music of the bal-musettes and those fighting tooth-and-nail against it. An ally revealed himself to Django backstage during a break at a Claridge Hotel tea dance; when the band's violinist broke a string, he tested the new one by playing a jazzy lick, and Django answered with a run of his own. The two started jamming and their duets became a regular dressing-room event while waiting for the other outfit to finish their set.

Stefano Grappelli was born to a father from the land of the violin and a French mother who died when he was five. When his dad went off to war, the boy spent some time in Isadora Duncan's luxury commune outside Paris before being moved to a grim Catholic orphanage when Duncan went back to America. After the war, Stefano took up the violin, playing with Roma street musicians and Frenchifying his name to Stéphane Grappelly. Wealth and aristocracy seem to hover over this tale of "Django the gypsy" like medieval Transylvanian barons: Isadora Duncan was from a US banking dynasty, the DuPonts were, well, the DuPonts, and now along came Charles Delaunay, son of the painters Robert and Sonia Delaunay and grandson of a countess and a pre-

Revolution Russian oligarch. Like Django, Delaunay had been electrified by jazz; he'd assembled a record collection even bigger than Savitry's and was on a crusade to convert the masses via the Hot Club of France, a society he formed with another aristo, chateau-dweller Hugues Panassié. Alerted to those backstage sessions at the Claridge, Delaunay quickly became Django's and Stéphane's manager, producer, and champion.

He launched them with a series of shows as the Quintet of the Hot Club of France, which consisted of Reinhardt, Grappelli, two rhythm guitarists, and a bassist. The going was slow at first and all had to keep their regular dance-hall gigs. For most French enthusiasts, jazz had to be a) Black and b) played with horns, drums, and a piano. The slightest whiff of tzigane sensibility redolent of a Budapest restaurant or one of the Russian cabarets dotted around Paris meant instant disqualification. The guitar, moreover, wasn't seen as a solo instrument. Lonnie Johnson and Eddie Lang had made some small-group recordings in America, but the sound was too timid to be heard amid a full-on jazz outfit in those pre-amplification days. An Italian luthier working with the Selmer company finally came up with a big-sounding instrument that Django loved. Though never having been to Spain, he instinctively used flamenco techniques, holding his arm away from the guitar as it rested on his knee, attacking the strings with a downward stroke, rather than the upward or up-and-down motions of an American player, and replacing the Spaniards' lacquered fingernails with a tortoiseshell pick he guarded with his life. Propelling the quintet was the *pompe* (pump) we heard thirty years later at the flea-market café, a powerful, forward-leaning four-stroke engine rooted in Django's love for Fats Waller's striding left hand. The two rhythm guitarists (constantly changing but always Manouche) added syncopated grace notes, giving it a continental edge and opening up some rhythmic distance between their music and Harlem. The quintet's repertoire, particularly at the start, was almost entirely American, but the way Reinhardt's arrangements and solos moved between major and minor evoked the lurking Roma sadness and imprinted his people's indelible watermark without ever resorting to schmaltz.

By New Year's Eve 1937, the Quintet ruled Paris. When the German army marched down the Champs-Élysées two and a half years later, many cafés had posters of Django on the wall beside pin-ups of Édith Piaf and Maurice Chevalier. A performance of his most famous composition, "Nuages," at the Salle Pleyel a year later brought the house down and the group had to repeat it twice; the piece seemed to capture a national mood that combined relief at survival with the *tristesse* of defeat. This triumph was his alone; Grappelli had remained in London as Django rushed home when the war broke out during a UK tour.

Having known only the broad outlines of the story, I'd found Django's stardom during the German occupation bewildering. The Nazis hated jazz—*Jewish jungle music*—and often arrested its German fans, while *Zigeuner* were at the top of Hitler's extermination list alongside Jews, gays, and communists. How could Django have flourished under such a regime? The answer is as strange and chilling as most details of Nazi rule: the Wehrmacht dangled the carrot that every soldier would, at some point, enjoy a week in Paris; the French capital was designated as the army's whorehouse and they saw jazz as the appropriate soundtrack for a brothel. Lurking amid the twisted contradictions that seem to inhabit most right-wing psyches is the fact that German soldiers and officials in Paris were crazy for jazz. They packed the nightclubs and listened avidly to Allied broadcasts by Glenn Miller, all while going efficiently about the business of rounding up Jews, Roma, and other *Untermenschen* and sending them to extermination camps. The unofficial exemption that applied to Roma musicians didn't extend to Jewish ones; Reinhardt's regular bass player, Georges Effrosse, died in a camp. His own closest shave came when a Nazi official set up a tour of Germany for him. Understandably reluctant, he made a dash for it, was caught with fake papers at the Swiss border, and arrested. Luckily, the local commandant recognized him, gave him a good scolding, and sent him back to Paris. Estimates of how many Roma died at Nazi hands vary, but the lowest figure is five hundred thousand and some put it at close to a million.

When the Allies liberated Paris in 1944, Django didn't break stride, performing at US bases and over Armed Forces Radio as well as in celebratory concerts across France. Questions were raised about his wartime comfort level with the occupiers, but Django appeared so genuinely guileless that the matter was dropped. The biggest post-war controversy lay in the grooves of discs that began arriving from across the ocean as bebop opened a bitter divide between Delaunay and Panassié and among European jazz fans generally. Django was on the side of the radicals, having already ventured into the sort of Debussy-inflected harmonies Parker and Gillespie were exploring. His dream was to move to America, be courted by Hollywood, and play with his heroes. But when Duke Ellington brought him to the US in 1946 for a tour, it proved an anti-climax. Audiences were thrilled to hear him in person, but Django could read neither words nor music, spoke no English, and lived by Roma rules, which included not turning up when the mood wasn't right; the Musicians' Union strike meant that he never recorded with Ellington, and he returned to Europe deflated and frustrated.

Django died of a cerebral hemorrhage one morning in 1953 just as he was finishing his coffee, fishing rod in hand. He was forty-three. He had lived the ultimate Roma life, running musical rings around the gadje while embracing every cliché: ignoring contracts, taking months learning to scrawl a signature, spending his substantial earnings the instant they crossed his palm, buying one new automobile after another then wrecking them while driving without a license, and listening with childlike wonder and disbelief as Grappelli read to him from books on science and history. During the Ellington tour, he once interrupted a rehearsal claiming to hear an error in one of the horn parts that no one else noticed; to everyone's astonishment, the Duke's charts were wrong and Django was right.

In Reinhardt's charred hands, the oppressed cultures of African Americans and Roma were joined. He was proud of his heritage but aspired to Blackness, worshipping first Armstrong and Ellington, then Parker and Gillespie as gods. He would have been gratified had he known that west to east wasn't the only direction influence flowed across the North Atlantic; a young American guitarist stumbled on some Hot Club 78s in 1947 as he was starting to explore the instrument's possibilities: "Django's ideas . . . lit up my brain . . . He was light and free and fast as the fastest trumpet . . . running through chord changes with the skill of a sprinter and the imagination of a poet . . . I loved Django because of the joy in his music, the light-hearted feeling and freedom to do whatever he felt." Which nicely sums up how B.B. King, the author of that quote, transformed blues guitar.

※

O Lord, where should I go?
What can I do?
Where can I find
Legends and songs?
I do not go to the forest,
I meet with no rivers,
O forest, my father,
My black father!

—Composer, singer, and poet Bronisława Wajs, known as Papusza

Porajmos, "the great devouring" of Roma by the Nazis, barely got a mention at Nuremberg, and Roma themselves have hardly discussed it until recently. In the years immediately following Germany's defeat, those who survived were in their element; Europe had become a continent of refugees and Roma knew better than anyone how to travel and live that way. It took a while for those on the east side of the Yalta agreement to realize what they were up against. To Communist governments, Roma exceptionalism was an aberration; whatever hardships they had suffered in the past could only have been due to the evils of capitalism. Eliminate capitalists and the problem disappears. Housing and schools would be provided and Roma would be smoothly integrated into the new workers' paradise.

Wrong. One small example of the challenges lay in the matter of toilets. The very idea of indoor loos was, to most Roma, disgusting, and absolutely beyond the pale was the notion of men and women sharing one. Schooling was another very high hurdle. Gadje reporters who have spent time in Roma households have been mocked for reading and have even had books snatched out of their hands; closing oneself off from the warmth of family life to silently absorb words that no one else hears is seen as bewilderingly rude, and that also applies to a child doing his or her homework. And as for "her," she should be married off as soon as puberty approaches; the idea that a daughter might become the object of leering schoolroom desire on the part of spotty gadje teenagers was too offensive to contemplate.

Today, most Roma travel in cars and vans rather than horse-drawn wagons. These often sport bumper stickers, the favorite being a stylized *niglo* (hedgehog), a signal to fellow Roma and a badge of pride. The creature is both a favorite food (all the more delicious since gadje never eat them) and, with spines that only Roma know how to remove quickly and easily, a perfect symbol for a culture that remains fiercely defended against the gadje world, that keeps its indoor spaces spotless (a Roma kitchen floor gets scrubbed so often you could eat off it) while often littering the surrounding area with rubbish. Roma are a unique group of migrants, carving out roles in societies from Iran to California while retaining the hermetic coherence of an Indian caste, complete with taboos, customs, and views of gender and sexuality that have remained unchanged for a thousand years.

The Roma integration project moved particularly slowly in socialist Poland, in part because there were so few left following the organized slaughter of the war years. Through the early fifties, their traditional life carried on much as before. One exception was a girl named Bronisława Wajs or "Papusza" (Doll), who inexplicably insisted on trading chickens (often stolen) for reading lessons. Despite her parents' determination to destroy any books she acquired, Papusza became a Roma unicorn, a literate, reasonably well-read teenager. Married against her will at fifteen to a virtuoso harpist who bragged that he had once performed in Moscow for Lenin, she poured her frustrations into composing songs that she sang with her husband's group.

Jerzy Ficowski, a young poet, heard Wajs's band in 1949; when he discovered that Bronisława had composed the songs, he persuaded her to make him a copy of the lyrics, then arranged for them to be published as poetry along with a Romani–Polish dictionary and Ficowski's own study of Roma history and way of life. Papusza received much acclaim and was celebrated by Warsaw intelligentsia, but her fellow Roma were outraged. Publication coincided with the start of the Great Halt, when Poland's government decreed that the itinerant life had to stop and all Roma must move indoors. A *kris* was held—a kind of "supreme court" of the community—and Papusza was cast out for betraying tribal secrets. Feeling torn between worlds and exposed by Ficowski, she lived to seventy-nine in a small urban flat, far from her beloved woods and rivers and separated from those she never ceased to view as her true family. *Papusza*, a Polish film from 2013, eloquently recounts her story.

At the opposite end of Eastern Europe, another gadje man and Roma girl played out a parallel drama but with a wildly different outcome. In the late fifties, Stevo Teodosievski was a musician in the house band of Radio Skopje in the Yugoslav province of Macedonia. Like Ficowski, he believed Roma culture should be appreciated by a wider public and was determined to help make that happen; when he heard a girl singing a Romani song in a radio talent contest, he spotted her special talent. Esma Redžepova hadn't told her parents she was competing, and when she won first prize, the secret was out. Roma girls aren't supposed to sing outside a family ensemble, and her furious father vowed to quickly marry her off to protect the family's reputation.

Fortuitously, Esma's dad died before he could shake hands on a deal for a husband; with the family's cautious blessing, Teodosievski became her manager, arranger, and producer, wisely presenting her as a performer of traditional Macedonian material with a few Romani songs thrown in. She would stand as still as a statue onstage until Stevo convinced her it was OK to move as she would among the other girls at a Roma wedding; to maintain propriety, the hand drums propelling these movements were always played by prepubescent boys. He never booked her for weddings or restaurants, only concerts and television, making Redžepova the first Yugoslavian Roma performer to establish a career at that level. Having proved his acumen and tact, Stevo convinced her brothers and uncles to allow Esma to go on the road with his touring ensemble, which seems to have been understood as a Roma-style elopement.

The couple took a lot of flak. Macedonians attacked Teodosievski for "wasting" his talents on Roma culture rather than his own, while Redžepova's community couldn't accept her running off with a gadje and behaving in such a liberated fashion. Life would be simpler, the pair decided, if they moved to Belgrade. When "Romano horo," the single they released in answer to the Twist craze, was a massive hit, President Tito began inviting Esma to perform at official functions. Tito had always admired the Roma fighters who battled bravely alongside his partizans during World War Two and welcomed the chance to pay them some respect. Esma also performed abroad for Yugoslav guest workers, filled the Paris Olympia, and by the mid-sixties, had become the country's biggest star.

The couple returned to Skopje in triumph in 1968, formalizing their bond with days of feasting and a gigantic dance, the wildest wedding the city had ever seen; a Roma girl may have, at some point, married a prominent Balkan gadje, but not within living memory. With Stevo at her side, Esma went from strength to strength, accustoming Yugoslav ears to the sound of Romani lyrics on the radio and Roma-izing songs from across the Yugoslav mosaic, all the while insisting that she was first and foremost a proud Macedonian. Redžepova became the first prominent Roma to embrace the India connection, touring there in the seventies and convincing Indira Gandhi to commemorate the historic link. With her husband, she opened a music school for orphaned and abandoned Roma boys that led to dozens of professional careers, raised funds for Kosovar refugees, and was a pioneering champion of women's rights in the macho Balkans. Truly, there has never been anyone like her.

Nostalgia is virtually unknown amongst Roma. If it existed, it would probably be for the centuries spent roaming the Ottoman Empire selling horses, fixing pots, and playing music for everyone from pasha to peasant (and being careful not to stray into Wallachia or Transylvania). Istanbul governed with a relatively loose rein; as long as the various groups paid their taxes and didn't mount rebellions against the Sultan, all, even Roma, were encouraged to supervise themselves. To this day, more Roma live in the former Ottoman areas of the Balkans than any other part of the globe. Many settled down, owing both to pressure from post-Ottoman governments and because they were able to establish their own *mahalas*—improvised neighborhoods—in Slavic towns and cities. Skopje was for centuries an important stop on the trade route between Turkey and Europe, and the continent's biggest mahala—Esma's birthplace—was located near its central market. When an earthquake shook the city in 1963, cheaply built high-rises collapsed, killing more than a thousand people, while the mahala's simple low housing survived and Roma casualties were few. Authorities used the post-quake rebuild as an excuse to move them to a field on the edge of town called Shutka, which is now the world's only urban district officially run by Roma. (The city drew its boundaries carefully, making sure to exclude tax-generating factories and offices.)

Those who have seen Emir Kusturica's *Time of the Gypsies* will have an idea of life in 1980s Shutka. The film's style has been described as "magical realism," but going by the accounts of writers who spent extended time living among them, "Roma realism" may be closer to the mark. The few Roma who watched the film were reportedly impressed by the accuracy of its mise en scène.

Kusturica's film, combined with Esma's success and the cross-border popularity of Bulgaria's Ivo Papasov (whom we shall meet again in Chapter VII), moved Balkan Roma culture to center stage just in time for the fall of the Berlin Wall. In the free-market explosion that followed, Roma music was turbo-charged, celebrated and plundered. Which was only fair considering how Roma had been appropriating gadje music for centuries. (They usually played it better, though, while reverse borrowings have been mediocre at best.)

Going back to when Roma brought violins, cimbaloms, and other newfangled devices to the Hungarian countryside, Roma musicians have always been modernizers, and they were among the first in the Balkans to get the hang of synths and drum machines. Former cultural commissars from across thepeaceful region watched in horror as electronic *kyuchek* or "belly-dance" beats under songs sung in Romani and various southern Slav languages (with Roma attitude) began blaring from radios and ghetto blasters. For Serbs particularly, slick, Roma-flavored dance music provided an alternative to the cultural hegemony of hated America.

Kusturica's choice of ex-rocker Goran Bregović to compose the music for *Time of the Gypsies* had a huge impact. Bregović's clever score triggered an export surge in many directions: rock bands (Gogol Bordello et al.), trance tracks (*Electric Gypsyland*), and pretentious concert performances (Bregović himself, as well as Kusturica's own No Smoking Orchestra). The *Time of the Gypsies* score hadn't been particularly Roma-tic, but for *Underground*, a 1995 Kusturica film (which was not about Roma), Bregović made extensive use of a curious musical junction where Turkish history, Roma virtuosity, and Serbian nationalism meet in an unholy cluster and which spawned yet another strand of Balkan fascination for the world.

Turks have always loved the sound of brass. The army museum in Istanbul has a concert every afternoon celebrating the janissary bands who provided a soundtrack for the Ottoman conquest of the Balkans. Serbs hated the Turks but loved their brass, and the trumpet became an emblem of their nineteenth-century struggle for independence. Since 1961, the small town of Guča in western Serbia has held an annual brass band competition. It grew slowly, then took a leap following the success of the *Underground* soundtrack, which was filled with Boban Marković's Brass Orchestra. Marković so dominated Guča in the late nineties that he retired from the fray after winning first prize yet again in 2001. The festival draws hundreds of thousands of revelers every year, who drink beer, eat kebabs, dance, wave Serbian flags, and buy T-shirts honoring the genocidal war criminal Ratko Mladić. It's a surreal combination, particularly since most of the competitors and nearly all the winners are Roma, who have suffered so much over the centuries at the hands of Serbian chauvinism. (The phenomenon is reminiscent of the 1988 US presidential election, when George Bush Sr.'s campaign manager, Lee Atwater, who had frightened voters with his racist "Willie Horton" ads, booked Bo Diddley and Percy Sledge for the inauguration party.) Balkan brass has caught (some of) the world's imagination; Marković tours the globe playing adventurous and interesting music, as does the

Kočani Orkestar from Macedonia and Romania's Fanfare Ciocărlia, all of them Roma.

⌇

> In every village there are Gypsies who make the music for the people, swarthy rascals with music dancing in their blood, who can make their instruments say everything that is in the hearts of men, the birds and of the very earth itself.
>
> —Donald Hall, *Romanian Furrow*, 1933

> You don't learn this job, you steal it. A true lautar is one who, when he hears a tune, goes straight home and replays it from memory. The one who plays it certainly won't teach you!
>
> —Nicolae Neacşu, Taraf de Haïdouks violinist

Mercedes-Benz sedans were a common sight in Yugoslavia; few guest workers dared return home from Germany without one. In Romanian, Albanian, and Bulgarian villages, however, the first Mercs to appear after the fall of the Wall triggered outrage since most were driven by Roma. Free enterprise came as naturally as breathing; within months of regime change, Roma started arriving back from Turkey with vanloads of consumer goods, the kinds of things communist economists never figured out how to get onto retail shelves. Envy thus joined other resentments built up over the years—pilferage, dark skins, litter, enjoying life too much, and general "otherness"—and burst out across the ex-Soviet sphere in explosions of anti-Roma violence. Romania suffered the worst of them; some Roma were killed, homes were burned, and there were many attempts to run them out of towns.

A decade after *Time of the Gypsies*, part-Roma director Tony Gatlif made a wonderful film called *Gadjo dilo*, set in a Romanian village. *Dilo* means "crazy," and you know what a *gadjo* is. The film includes a deadly attack on a Roma community, but the story centers around a foreigner who comes looking for a legendary fiddler and falls for the Roma girl who helps him. The violence draws on the kinds of things that happened in Romania during those post-Wall years, but the romance is a true story.

Clejani is a peaceful hamlet not far from Bucharest, with a music-loving, Roma-friendly mayor. It was founded in the sixteenth century by a Serbian prince who built housing there for his slaves; over the years, it became a hub for music, where wedding parties and dance organizers could be certain to recruit a band of top players. The French ethnographic label Ocora released an album in the late eighties called *Musique des Tsiganes de Valachie: Les Lăutari de Clejani*. Within days of the fall of the Wall, a pair of Brussels music buffs who had worn out their copy of the Ocora disc got in a car and headed for Clejani. One, Michel Winter, was the son of Transylvanian Jews who had escaped the annihilation of the 1940s. The other, Stéphane Karo, was the drummer in a post-punk band. After their initial visit, they went back to Brussels, persuaded a bemused bank manager to lend them money "to bring gypsy musicians to Belgium," and, after Ceaușescu fell, returned to Clejani. Settling in the village, their mission created turmoil, with musicians serenading them around every corner; the first ones chosen insisted that their brother, cousin, or in-law absolutely must make the cut. After two months of nerve-wracking auditions and negotiations, they had their team and a name: Taraf de Haïdouks, which means, roughly, "outlaw band." And Stéphane and Margareta, the Roma girl who helped them navigate the minefield of selecting the band, had each other.

Backed by the intrepid Brussels label Crammed Discs (whom we'll encounter in Brazil and again in Africa), the management, promotion, and recording of Taraf de Haïdouks represents a kind of world music masterclass. The celebrated highlights of the group's career—Johnny Depp's wedding, Danny Elfman's birthday, Yamamoto's runway, films, concert tours, festivals—ought to have led to a decline in artistic standards or at least to slicked-up and mannered recordings and performances. That never happened; one of Taraf's most impressive albums, *Maškaradă*, in which they perform their own versions of Roma-inspired works by Bartók, Khachaturian, and de Falla, was recorded nearly twenty years after Karo and Winter's arrival in Clejani and by the same team that produced their first. Some might complain that Clejani's housing stock and infrastructure have little to show for all those Hollywood parties, but at least the Roma habit of spending earnings the instant they touch the recipient's hand kept village jealousies to a manageable level. An Englishman named William Blacker drove to Transylvania around the same time as Winter and Karo, fell in love with a Roma girl, and wrote an excellent book, *Along the Enchanted Way*, about living among Romanian Roma. (Non-Roma Romanians hate how the term "gypsy" has been replaced with one so easily conflated with theirs.) Having learned the language, Blacker overheard references to a local "gypsy millionaire." Where, he asked, was the mansion, the fleet of limos? Nowhere, was the reply. He doesn't *have* a million, he just *made* a million, spent it, and now lives like the rest of us.

Films played a big part in Taraf's success. They met Depp when he shared a scene with them in *The Man Who Cried*; later, they were featured in *Gypsy Caravan*, an excellent documentary chronicling a US concert tour by a package of Roma artists (Esma included) that followed them back to their homes in Europe and India. Best of all, though, was the first. Gatlif's 1993 *Latcho drom* (A Good Road) opens in the Rajasthani desert with a traveling group making camp for the night, building a fire, and getting out their instruments. It's beautifully shot and recorded, many notches above your average music doc. And it's not really a documentary, at least not as we normally find them; there are no voice-overs, no texts, no subtitles, we simply follow clues from the music and the surroundings to figure out that it's taking us from Rajasthan to Egypt, then Turkey, Romania (and the Taraf), Hungary, Slovakia, and France. But a film about "gypsy music" surely can't end there. Isn't there something missing? Indeed there is; the final reel of *Latcho drom* takes us over the Pyrenees and into Spain.

When I was a schoolboy, we were taught to write a dollar sign with two vertical strokes; in these streamlined days, you seldom see more than one. Those lines in the old symbol for the Spanish dollar that formed the basis for America's currency represented the Pillars of Hercules: Gibraltar on one side and a peak in the Rif mountains of Morocco on the other. Silver coins from Peruvian mines were stamped with symbolic columns entwined with a ribbon that Americans took for an "S." Andalusian music can't be traced back as far as the Tenth Labor of

Hercules, when the mythic hero opened the channel between the Mediterranean and the Atlantic by smiting a rock, but almost. The island of Erytheia, where Hercules stole cattle from a ferocious giant, became the port of Cádiz, a cradle of flamenco. The city's cathedral sits on the site of a Phoenician temple to Moloch; the Greeks replaced that with one for Cronos, and the Romans followed with a shrine to Saturn. The name Cádiz comes from "Gadira," Phoenician for "fort." Phoenicians were the first to venture south along the African coast and north to Brittany and Ireland, and the city's harbor was the last safe haven before sailors braved the storms and currents of the Atlantic. Ports have always meant bars and music, and Herodotus, Martial, and Juvenal all reported that in Rome, slave girls from Gadira were celebrated as irresistibly sexy dancers, with anklets that rattled like castanets and songs more lewd than what you might hear from "a naked slave standing in a . . . brothel archway."

Between ecstatic celebrations of deities and drunken shore-leave nights, the region around Cádiz has been filled with music for three thousand years. Melodies, instruments, verses, and rhythms arrived from across the Mediterranean, along the Maghreb, over the Pyrenees, and through the salt flats and sand dunes of the Western Sahara; at key moments in the region's history, they've come from far-off Baghdad and India. The Pillars drew armies, navies, adventurers, traders, and opportunists of all kinds to what seemed like the last outpost at the end of the world—or the gateway to a new one.

When the Roman Empire began falling apart, the Pope imposed order on the Iberian peninsula by inviting the Visigoths to invade and rule. As part of the deal, they agreed to stamp out all vestiges of paganism, particularly the use of drums, by which the Church seemed particularly repulsed and frightened. Which explains why Christian defenders and their horses were so terrified by the sound of Turkish kettledrums at the gates of Vienna and why explorers and slave traders were alarmed by African percussion; drums had been largely absent from European music for a thousand years.

In Spain, this led to a culture of song. Texts on the subject speak about the legacy of the Islamic conquest and the reverence for poetry and melody in the great Moorish cities of Seville, Cordoba, and Granada, while Ned Sublette's book on Cuba calls attention to the melismatic singing of the Visigoths and its influence on the invading Arabs and Berbers. In Al-Andalus, as Moorish Spain was called, slave girls remained a center of attention but these *qiyans* were prized more for their skill in memorizing and singing poetic texts than for booty-shaking (at least that's what the chronicles say). A qiyan who knew thousands of songs might change hands for a small fortune and each came with her own all-female backing band.

Al-Andalus found its first musical superstar in 822 with the arrival of Abu al-Hasan Ali ibn Nafi. Known as Ziryab (the blackbird), he was born a slave in Baghdad with probably at least one African parent. At an early age he was taken under the wing of the city's greatest music teacher, but when he upstaged his mentor in front of the caliph, he was advised to get out of town. Ziryab made his way along the Maghreb to the new center of culture and learning in Cordoba, at the opposite end of the Muslim world. His list of accomplishments is too impressive to be taken literally—designing male dress styles still in use today, developing a fusion cuisine combining Middle Eastern and Andalusian recipes, creating styles of interior decor that endured for centuries, and inventing toothpaste—but it seems certain that Ziryab was a musical giant. He improved the oud by adding a fifth pair of strings, and his vast repertoire of songs and beautiful way with a melody resonated over the years, influencing not only the Islamic world but also the Provençal troubadour movement via the numerous French students who came to Cordoba to study. Ziryab's time in Al-Andalus is considered a golden age.

While many Europeans were keen to learn from the scholars and libraries of Al-Andalus, Spanish rulers considered Muslim control of Iberia's south to be an affront to Christianity and they launched a crusade to put an end to it. No sooner had King Ferdinand and Queen Isabella expelled the Moors than they got rid of the Jewish community that had existed comfortably alongside Christians and Muslims for centuries. The music and culture they took with them into the more friendly environment of the Turkish Empire they called "Sephardic," from a Hebrew word for "Spanish," and left behind them a powerful influence on singing styles and melody.

Moors and Jews who had converted to Christianity were also expelled when Isabella decided she couldn't trust their sincerity. This left gaping holes in many sectors of society, since most butchers, tanners, metalworkers, masons, and horse-traders had been Muslims. Guess who showed up to fill those gaps? A number of Roma groups had crossed the Pyrenees in the general direction of Compostela in the late fifteenth century, claiming to be pilgrims. But here things get a bit confused; some historians insist that all Gitanos (the word *Roma* is rarely used in Spain) entered the peninsula through France. Others contend that Andalusian Gitanos came from North Africa, having made their way along the Maghreb from the Middle East. The name "Gitano" may be derived from "Tingitano," an antiquated term for a resident of Tangier. Most Roma view Andalusian Gitanos as a group apart and with a certain amount of awe. Their language, Caló, is also distinct, with a Sanskrit-Romani vocabulary and Latinate grammar. What is unarguable is that Gitanos did in Andalusia what Roma have done everywhere else: they mastered the local music and transformed it.

> There is no such thing as a stupid gypsy man or a foolish gypsy woman. Since it is only by being sharp and ready that they can earn a livelihood, they polish their wits at every step.
>
> —Miguel de Cervantes, *La Gitanilla*

> The poor payos don't understand that we are the last sons of God and that they are slaves to a system that reduces their life to meaninglessness . . . We symbolize everything they lack: integrity, individuality, freedom.
>
> —Elderly Gitana woman to Donn E. Pohren, *El Arte flamenco*

Watching a national football team sing their pre-match anthem can be comical or embarrassing or, on rare occasions, moving. But not the Spaniards; their anthem is an instrumental, so they stand silently as it plays. Why no lyrics? Because the regions can never agree on a text. Spain didn't unite, like Germany or Italy, out of nineteenth-century nationalistic fervor; it was brought together in a medieval alliance simply to fight the Moors. Catalonia and the Basque Country have always been notoriously separatist, but Andalusia, too, has never felt a part of the modern Madrid-centric state. The country's finest seafood can always be found at lunchtime in one of the capital's many tapas bars; each dawn, markets on the south coast put their freshest catch onto Madrid-bound express trains and locals get what's left. The same once applied to Mexican gold and Andean silver: straight from Cádiz and Seville to the royal vaults, with Andalusia mostly ignored, its people viewed by the Castilian ruling class with centuries-old condescension and suspicion.

Gitanos suffered in Spain, perhaps even more than elsewhere in Europe; at times they were hunted for sport, with rewards for kills. When Spanish naval galleys were short-handed, Gitanos were rounded up and chained to the oars. Bourgeois aversion, clerical revulsion, and the authorities' general disapproval kept them on the move; the one place they felt even somewhat at home was Andalusia. Bernard Leblon describes the Andalusian temperament as "prodigality, a hair-trigger temper, insane passion and a contempt for 'polite behaviour' and for material values." No wonder they got along. With the departure of Moors and Jews, the region had little in the way of a bourgeoisie; it was a land of horses and seasonal farm work, both of which were near the top of a list of Gitano money-earners. In the late eighteenth century, when Charles III emulated his cousin Maria Theresa and ordered the Gitanos' integration into Spanish society, Andalusia was the one area where this diktat had some modest effect. The king forbade the word *Gitano* and ordered them to be called *flamencos*. The term means "from Flanders" and was used proudly by those who had fought for the Spanish crown in the Low Countries and in defence of Cádiz and Gibraltar against the British; all-Gitano flamenco battalions earned a reputation for valor.

The end of the eighteenth and the start of the nineteenth centuries saw the first *payos* (Spanish gadje) sneaking into gatherings at the back of Gitano shops and forges and bringing *cantaores* (singers) for *juergas* (musical evenings) in their own homes. Listening to the singing of the flamencos became a defiant pastime of Majos and Majas; the woman who famously posed naked for Goya was part of this movement of young rebels who expressed their defiance of French and British invaders and their Spanish collaborators by embracing the most unfashionable and least "European" things, a bit like early-sixties American folk and blues buffs. Such evenings weren't exactly entertainment; there were no guitars, no dancing, just harsh, intense singing, with complex rhythms marked out by the cantaor's *palo seco*, a cane pounded on the ground to mark the beats.

For most non-Spanish aficionados, flamenco guitarists and dancers are the draw; vocalists sit or stand at the back of the stage, clapping out complex rhythms and punctuating dances with cries of "*olé*" and snatches of song. But for Andalusians, Gitano and otherwise, flamenco has always been and still remains *cante*—song.

Seville's Triana district on the west bank of the Guadalquivir River became the Gitano Harlem in the early nineteenth century, filled with stables, forges, markets, and the cafés where flamenco would evolve and formalize. Today, nearly all leading flamenco artists come from twenty-five interconnected Gitano families who live inside a triangle formed by Seville, Ronda, and Cádiz. When this music first began attracting audiences to the *cafés cantantes* of Triana over a century and a half ago, most performers were from those same twenty-five families.

Flamenco's past and present are linked by lines that connect, cross, and entwine; they involve great *cantaores* and *cantaoras*, virtuoso guitarists, famous dancers, touring companies, poets, and intellectuals. There have been opposing schools of criticism, changing attitudes of governments and battles between modernizers and traditionalists. It's a complex subject about which a vast library of books has been written, and mine is long enough as it is. But threads are there to be pulled and followed and that is what I intend to do. We'll start with a cantaor.

Diego El Fillo was a blacksmith and, like many Gitanos in that trade, he sang as he worked. His mentor was an older man from Cádiz they called El Planeta because he saw the future in the stars. We don't know what El Planeta's voice sounded like, but El Fillo's was rough; so rough, in fact, that the harsh quality that has often marked the deepest and most "Gitano" of singers came to be known as *voz afillá*, after Diego.

El Fillo lived a peaceful and eccentric life surrounded by violence. He sang about his brothers, both of whom died in knife fights; his wife, a singer known as La Andonda, always carried a blade and wasn't afraid to use it. El Fillo had a prodigious memory for lyrics and for the structures of the different song forms. Scholars tell us that virtually all that are sung today—*alegrías, siguiriyas, soleares, tarantos*, and dozens more—were part of El Fillo's repertoire in the middle decades of the nineteenth century. (It is worth noting here that there's no such thing as a flamenco *song*. Every performer has their cante, how they perform a *palo* or "post," meaning a particular metric structure. He or she will bring into that cante classic stanzas that, like blues verses, have been used for decades or even centuries, while also adding original verses of their own.)

Verses that have endured over the decades include these, among thousands:

> *That night in January*
> *who'd you go to see,*
> *like a colt with the bit in his teeth?*
>
> —
>
> *I climbed up to the town walls*
> *And the wind said:*
> *"Why so many sighs*
> *if you can't change anything?"*
>
> —
>
> *Your mother keeps on saying*
> *she doesn't like me 'cause I'm deaf,*
> *and I don't like you all that much,*
> *little girl, from all I hear said.*
>
> —
>
> *Man goes through his days*
> *like a stone through the air,*
> *waiting to fall.*

A teenager heard singing coming from El Fillo's forge one day and stopped to listen. Entranced by the sound, the payo boy convinced Diego to teach him. He astounded the cantaor and his Gitano friends with how quickly he mastered the cantes and how his voice could shift from the harshest tones to become smooth as honey. His name was Silverio Franconetti, son of an Andalusian mother and an Italian soldier stationed in Spain (not unusual at a time when the Spanish crown ruled half of Italy). Silverio was soon celebrated in *juergas* and in the Triana cafés that were starting to draw a paying public.

In 1854, Franconetti vanished. Reappearing ten years later, he told tales of time spent as a *picador* in Uruguay, in the gold fields of California, and on the docks in Havana. His golden voice was stronger than ever, with an added New World edge. He never discussed the reasons for his departure, but it was understood to have involved a woman and a knife. He opened a bar called Café Silverio that became a stronghold of old-school cante at a time when a fashion for *fandangos* was invading Triana. A young singer of pure flamenco called Antonio Chacón often sang there, and Franconetti became his mentor and champion. Chacón was probably a payo, though no one knew for certain; he'd been abandoned on a doorstep as an infant and raised by a humble Andalusian couple who tried to discourage his musical interests. That he was so drawn to cante suggests it might have been in the blood, but his bland features and pale skin argued otherwise.

Chacón rose to flamenco fame at a time of great change in the first years of the new century. A quirk of the tax code punished cafés and rewarded theaters, causing many performers to move into a kind of "flamenco opera" using zarzuela musicals as a model. Chacón's approach was tasteful, but that of others less so. With Spain supplying both sides in the Great War, the economy flourished, entertainment boomed, and flamenco became the subject of debate. The poet Federico García Lorca led the agonizing over the loss of authenticity as the music strayed ever further from its now-legendary heyday of backstreet juergas. Gitanos took the music very seriously but it was, after all, a livelihood. At juergas, they were rewarded for depth and complexity; theatrical producers paid them for accessibility.

Lorca formed an alliance with composer Manuel de Falla, who had returned from Paris at the start of the war fired up by Diaghilev, Debussy, and Ravel to look to his native Spanish culture for inspiration. His response was to create the famous ballets *El Amor brujo* and *The Three-Cornered Hat*, then he and Lorca set out to rescue flamenco. They organized a Concurso de Cante Jondo in Granada in 1922 which aimed, among other things, to bury the term "flamenco" in favor of their preferred *cante jondo* (deep song) and to turn the music away from contrived theatricals. To encourage anti-commercial authenticity, only "amateurs" could perform, which meant that the greatest voices, such as Manuel Torre and La Niña de los Peines (The Girl of the Combs), were absent. Serving on the panel of judges, Chacón recruited the twelve-year-old son of a Gitano family of bullfighters and cantaores (whose forefathers included El Planeta) as a contestant. The boy, Manolo "Caracol" (Snail), won first prize of 10,000 pesetas and his career was launched (foreshadowing Nazakat and Salamat Ali's 1945 triumph in Calcutta). As for the Concurso, the publicity it generated simply increased the demand for *opera flamenca* and a disappointed de Falla turned away from Andalusia to seek inspiration elsewhere. Right-wing nationalists never forgave Lorca for his insistence on the importance of Moorish, Gitano, and Jewish contributions to Spanish culture; he was arrested in Granada at the outset of the Civil War against the Republic and shot.

Antonio Chacón was the epitome of a dignified and austere artist; he researched traditions across Andalusia and other cantaores paid him great respect. Aficionados were happier, though, when Chacón avoided the darker *cante grande* and focused on *cante chico*. His young protégé was the opposite; Caracol has been described as "the drunkest, wildest, most argumentative flamenco of them all." From his first tours in the mid-twenties until his death in a car crash in 1973, Manolo's lavish lifestyle, tempestuous partnership with the beautiful dancer Lola Flores, and incessant carousing kept him in the public eye. Footage reveals him to be a jowly, genial man with a powerful voice who never strains or grimaces, delivering the most intense passages almost offhandedly, like a flamenco Big Joe Turner.

In the sixties, Caracol opened a *tablao* in Madrid that became a center for flamenco activity in the capital. Family always had first claim on jobs, and Manolo gave one to a great-nephew named José Monje Cruz, singing and making *palmas* (handclaps) for the dancers. Cruz eventually began performing his own cante under the name El Camarón de la Isla (The Shrimp from the Island). Manolo and the public were impressed, but it was when Camarón bonded one night over a Madrid pool table with the young guitarist Paco de Lucía that his life and the late-twentieth-century world of flamenco were forever altered.

> There is nothing more delicate than a rhythm, the basis of all melody; nor anything more difficult [to notate] than a singer of the people who . . . sings in quarter- or third-tones, for which there are no signs in written notation.
>
> —Federico García Lorca

> [The guitar] has lurked upon the dark, oriental, Jewish, and Arabic substance of the song, which babbles in its old age like a child. The guitar has made [*cante jondo*] into something Western. It has created unequalled beauty out of the Andalusian drama—the struggle of the Orient and the West—which has made Baetica [Andalusia] an island of true culture.
>
> —Federico García Lorca, *In Search of Duende*

The Iberian peninsula is famous for stringed instruments. Ziryab revolutionized the oud and turned Cordoba luthiers into the Fender, Selmer, and Gibson of the early Islamic world. Spain and Portugal seeded their colonial empires with all things plucked and strummed: trés in Cuba, cuatro in Puerto Rico, cavaquinha in Brazil, and guitar everywhere. In the wake of the Moors' expulsion, playing an oud could land you in big trouble with the Inquisition, so around the courts most musicians turned to the *vihuela*, a small guitar-shaped instrument with six pairs of strings tuned like a lute. Africans (of whom there were many in Andalusia, enslaved and free) were, meanwhile, showing the lower classes what a great instrument the guitar could be.

When the Gitanos arrived, Spain was a percussion desert. Rhythmic concepts they carried with them from India provided a structure that grew more and more complex in their a cappella world of voice and cane. In replacing the *palo seco*, guitarists brought centuries of Arabic, African, and courtly traditions to their dialogue with cantaores that would come to define the art of flamenco singing. A flamenco cliché holds that in order to prepare for a concert career, guitarists must spend twenty years playing for dancers, another twenty for cantaores, and only then might they be ready for their first recital. Outsiders (as I know from experience) can be puzzled when impressive soloists earn less praise from knowledgeable Spaniards than those who accompany singers. It takes a while to grasp how complex that task is.

Hispanophiles are correct when they contend that few palos are Gitano in origin. Some are derived from Byzantine chant or Hebraic liturgy, others from Moorish song, a few have been adapted from the music of African sailors and slaves, and many come from Spanish folk music. Melodies are often in the Phrygian mode, a scale first identified in ancient Greece as representing the music of slaves. Styles collided and blended in galleys, where Africans, Moriscos, and Gitanos pulled oars side by side. In one example from history, when Cádiz was besieged by Napoleon, a battalion from Aragon serenaded the city with their folk songs; the residents "flamenco-ized" them and sang them back across the walls. Getting "flamenco-ized" involves fitting a style's rhythm into the structure of a *compás* or rhythmic cell; these Aragonese songs became *alegrías*, one of Andalusia's most beloved forms.

Watching a cantaor and a guitarist seated with a half-dozen family and friends gathered around, it is nigh impossible for an outsider to grasp the rhythm of, say, a *siguiriya*. There is no steady pulse; the guitarist's emphatic chords and *falsetas* (melodic interjections between lines) are clearly following a structure, but what is it? Watching the tapping feet doesn't help since patterns differ from person to person, while handclaps arrive at unpredictable intervals (to non-Andalusians, anyway). A clue is provided by the singer's or the jaleador's hands, which resemble nothing so much as a Hindustani classical vocalist marking the emphasized beats of a tala, notably the final one at the end of a twelve- or sixteen-beat cycle and the open-handed gesture that starts the next.

In some palos, the *palmas* (rapid clapping) of the jaleadores multiply the beats just as a tabla player would.

Guitarists say that the most important thing for an accompanist is to follow the cantaor, but singers also follow their guitarists and rely on them to provide a secure platform for his or her improvisations (which don't extend as far or as freely as those of a Hindustani ghazal singer, but there are clear similarities). As with Indian music, there are emphasized beats across a multi-measure cycle, while chords change on certain beats—the third and tenth in a *soleá*, for example. Chords also follow a structure, but guitarists must be alert to melodic signals from the singer that demand a variation, sometimes moving into a surprising and uplifting major rather than the anticipated minor.

Among the first to master this puzzle were two turn-of-the-century guitarists: Ramón Montoya, a Gitano, and Javier Molina, a payo. Studying them closely was a young Gitano prodigy named Niño Ricardo; for half a century starting in the mid-1920s, Ricardo was the paragon of guitar accompaniment. His elegant and precise playing was sometimes criticized for lacking the "soul" or *duende* of such as Montoya. The latter's passion, however, sometimes distracted from the cante, whereas Ricardo always provided the perfect foundation for singers to express theirs.

In the late 1930s, Ricardo became friendly with a payo guitarist from Algeciras named Antonio Sánchez. Over the years he often visited Sánchez's home and met his Portuguese wife and their three guitar-studying sons. Niño became the totemic figure in the Sánchez household, the standard by which the young players judged themselves and were judged by their father, who gained a reputation similar to Mozart's father, Leopold, or Venus and Serena Williams's dad, Richard: the iron-willed parent who drills his offspring so that they can achieve the success he never did.

The youngest, Francisco, turned out to be the best. He was also the most irreverent, perfecting Ricardo's falsetas, then shocking his brothers by deconstructing and elaborating on them. Turning professional at fourteen, he chose his stage name the way many nineteenth-century figures had, with a nickname and a connection to his beloved mother: Paco de Lucía. After finding work with José Greco's touring dance company, de Lucía spent a season in New York, where he hung out with flamenco's pioneering soloist, Sabicas. Sabicas was living in self-imposed exile, having left Spain at the start of the Civil War, and had carved out an international career that brought flamenco guitar virtuosity to the world. Though he himself had spent many years accompanying singers and dancers, Sabicas encouraged Paco not to let tradition intimidate him, but to express himself freely, to strike out on his own path.

De Lucía did just that. With his father as producer and manager, he modernized flamenco guitar and built an unprecedented following in Spain; before his emergence in the late sixties, instrumental concerts had held more appeal for foreign audiences than for Spaniards. His father had it all mapped out, but he couldn't have foreseen what would happen when his son met Camarón de la Isla in that billiard hall.

My own relationship with flamenco and Andalusia began with two great strokes of good fortune. The first arrived in Marrakesh in 1970, when I honored one of the era's hippie rituals by taking my beer to the roof of the Café de Paris to watch the Atlas Mountains turn pink in the glow of a desert sunset. I struck up a conversation there with a blond Spaniard (obviously more Visigoth than Moor) named Mario Pacheco. Mario and I would remain the dearest of friends from that moment until his death forty years later; during that time, he started a record label, became a transformative producer of *nuevo flamenco*, and was my guide to all things musical in Spain (as well as much else in the wider world).

The second moment of serendipity arrived in 1974, when Mario and I met in Lisbon to scout locations for a feature film based on a book I'd optioned about the death of García Lorca. Franco was then still running Spain, so it was impossible to shoot in Granada, where the murder took place. (The film was never made.) Once we'd finished in Lisbon, I proposed going to Seville to hear some flamenco. Mario was pessimistic; the *tablaos* there, he said, had become too touristic. But hey, what was I if not a tourist, so we visited one on our first evening. As Mario had predicted, there was a lot of skirt-swishing, foot-stomping, *torero*-posing, guitar-strumming, and shouty singing. After supper at the normal Spanish hour of 11:30 and a stroll through the deserted streets of Barrio Santa Cruz, we arrived back at our hotel around two in the morning. The lobby was deserted except for an old guy pushing a mop across the stone floor; Mario went over to him and they exchanged a few words. "He's Gitano," said Mario. "I asked him where we should go to hear music."

The next evening our cab driver balked. "You don't want to go all the way out there," he said. "If you want flamenco, I'll take you to an excellent tablao by the river." Mario snorted and reached for the door. After much complaining, the driver dropped us in front of La Trocha, a dingy-looking cement bunker on a commercial street some distance beyond the end of the picturesque old city. Outside was a sign with block letters in the style of a boxing poster: "EL CHOCOLATE Y EL FARRUCO." We joined about fifty customers for a show that began with a comedian whose Andalusian-dialect jokes all seemed to concern a *maricón* (a derisive term for a gay man) who joins the army. This was followed by a performance of Sevillanas, the local folk dance, executed by a group of young women backed by an electric keyboard. Mario nodded in satisfaction; we were in the right place.

El Chocolate, so named because of his dark complexion, was from the Montoya clan. He'd grown up listening to Manolo Caracol and Manuel Torre and devoted himself to the oldest forms of Triana cante. His 2003 album, *Mis 70 años con el cante*, would win a Latin Grammy. That evening there were no microphones, just chairs for him and the guitarist and a small table for a bottle of *fino*, and everyone listened with silent intensity for over an hour. After the final cante, El Chocolate rose, helped the guitarist move the furniture to one side of the stage, and introduced "someone who will listen to me sing."

Into the simple overhead spotlight came a shortish man built like a fire hydrant and wearing a rumpled suit, an open-collared shirt, and a tilted wide-brimmed hat. He did just that, standing motionless for what seemed like quite a long time as El Chocolate and the guitarist performed. Suddenly he moved, the most violent, astonishing combination of gestures I had ever seen. I wasn't a particular fan of flamenco dance before that and the next forty minutes made it even more difficult for me to enjoy it in future, unless the dancers were El Farruco, his family, or his students.

Ramón Montoya was Farruco's grandfather and Chocolate his brother-in-law. Spanish critics speak of him with reverence as the purest bearer of the flame of *baile gitano*. Farruco said he never took lessons, that he came from a family that once made baskets from the rushes growing along the Guadalquivir River; his mother sang, but his father ("a Republican Gitano") wasn't interested in music. Farruco just *knew* how to dance. He rarely performed, but his school in Seville has provided dancers to many companies, none more notable than his grandson, El Farruquito, currently the world's most famous flamenco dancer. The two appeared together in Carlos Saura's film *Flamenco* and in the Broadway production *Flamenco puro*. I went to see Farruquito at Town Hall in 2003 and was impressed, but nothing will ever match that night at La Trocha.

> Their swarthy complexion brings out the clarity of their oriental eyes, which are tempered by I do not know what mysterious sadness, like the memory of an absent motherland and of a fallen grandeur . . . Nearly all of them have such a natural majesty in their carriage, and freedom in their bearing.
>
> —Théophile Gautier, *Voyage en Espagne*

When dance became one of the attractions in the *cafés cantantes* of the late nineteenth century, French and British tourists ate it up, imagining they were seeing Carmen come to life. The image of the "fiery gypsy temptress" inspired countless painters and has colored outsiders' response to flamenco dance and to Gitano culture ever since. Carmen, though, wasn't actually a Gitana. Prosper Mérimée based the novella that inspired the opera on a tale he heard while wandering around Spain in the 1830s; after his translation of Pushkin's poem *The Gypsies* was a big success, he changed his lead character into a Gitana and the rest is cultural-misunderstanding history. If Mérimée had dug a bit deeper, he would have known that Carmen's libertine life ran completely contrary to Gitano rules and ethos. That, however, wouldn't have suited the image the Romantic movement had built up about these colorful free spirits. Much of which is true, of course, just not the part about Gitanas and sex.

Flamenco dance actually has more to do with bulls than sex. The expressive parts of a flamenco dancer's body are the hands, arms, and feet; hips rarely move. Many gestures have echoes in Egyptian statuettes, Knossos bull dancers, and other ancient Mediterranean traditions of animal sacrifice. The elegantly anachronistic brutality of the *corrida* still takes place across Spain at five o'clock on seasonal afternoons. and many movements and poses seen in *baile* are linked to it. Gitanos are active in bullfighting at every level, from star *toreadores* to dragging away the carcasses, so they know the body language.

Then there's the India connection; many flamenco gestures resemble Kathakali, which, along with other Asian dances, shares with flamenco the deflection of femininity and sensuality away from hips to the arms and hands. Andalusia, on the other hand, has been full of hip-shaking dirty dancing going back to the time of the Phoenicians. The Gitanos arrived when the zarabanda was giving popes and inquisitors apoplexy and inspiring threats of excommunication and worse, which didn't stop this Afro-Cuban import spending decades as a low-life favorite before being gradually tamed into a polite template for Baroque composers. The direct impact of such popular barroom dances on flamenco is subtle at best, though, creeping into *bulerías* and a few other forms.

Gitanos have always danced, but mostly for themselves, in private, accompanied by palmas. Market forces brought a change, as family groups began appearing at the cafés cantantes. Dance pilgrims visited Triana, got inspired, went home, and spiced up their choreography. Baile's most famous early ambassadresses were a pair of non-Gitanas called, confusingly, La Argentina and La Argentinita, who helped audiences—and dancers—around the world fall in love with what they called "flamenco dancing" and with castanets (a Spanish folklore item no Gitana had ever touched). With the exception of Orezzoli and Segovia's wonderful production *Flamenco puro*, which reached Paris and Broadway, foreign stages have rarely been exposed to the "real thing." Like cante, baile is first and foremost a spontaneous individual expression of mood and moment; the notion of choreography—or even a set list—is antithetical to it.

In the 1930s, Carmen Amaya and her family troupe gave Paris, London, and the Americas a full-on dose of what was touted as "authentic" flamenco dance. Amaya was certainly a real Gitana, but from Barcelona, which is a long way from Andalusia. Her machine-gun stomping had fire and passion but bore little resemblance to what happens at a Gitano celebration in the southern triangle.

The grace and beauty of baile influenced dance companies everywhere as they brought its moves and gestures into their choreography. There have been some outstanding productions of "Spanish" pieces, but they represent an injection of flamenco into ballet, more than vice versa. In the fifties, dancers from around the globe began making pilgrimages to Seville for lessons, which has been good for the local flamenco economy. Another benefit, as the historian Claus Schreiner pointed out, was to deflect attention away from cante, to let the coarsening effect of foreign fascination dilute flamenco dance and guitar and allow singing to remain in its own local corner, unaffected by the outsiders.

As the rest of the world began to look for ways to relax and enjoy life after the war, Spain's fascist rulers realized that their moribund economy badly needed tourists. They built cheap hotels along the Costa Brava, and Brits in particular flocked there, but the country lacked a seductive image; cue travel posters with flashing skirts, wide-brimmed hats, high-waisted trousers, guitars and castanets. Traditional Andalusian fairs and fiestas returned, providing Gitanos with opportunities for horse-trading and music. Tablaos opened in big cities and resorts, flamenco was warily allowed onto the new medium of television, and intellectuals were once again free to argue about its origins and influences. As far as Franco and the Falangists were concerned, Spanish culture was rooted in the Visigoths' rigid vision of Christianity, and many were furious at this implied endorsement of what Lorca had been saying all along; times had changed, however, and money talked louder than reactionary racist outrage.

Not all the music was dumbed down; there were still juergas where wealthy aficionados and earnest experts kept the flame of cante jondo alive. Some great recordings were made and classics from earlier decades reissued, though sales were limited to payos who could afford record players. In a blow that struck at the heart of Gitano life, the government began tarting up Triana for tourists and moving residents out to the Polígono Sur (Southern Polygon) and its notorious Tres Mil (three thousand) new, cheaply built high-rise apartments. There was no consultation and no appeal; after all the other hardships, rejections, and cruelties, for Gitanos this seemed like the final indignity.

Following their mythic pool-hall encounter, Paco de Lucía and Camarón de la Isla decided to record together. Paco's father got them a deal with Philips and the first album was released near the end of 1969, just after La Niña de los Peines died. The cover marked it out as something different; guitarists were never credited on flamenco album covers, but this one had a photo of the two men, with both names in bold letters. The opening track confirmed that it was not a normal release; Paco begins by fiercely attacking the bulería with unusual flourishes, setting it apart from a traditional approach. Then Camarón opens his mouth. El Chocolate once suggested that cante began when a Gitano was thrown to the ground; his cry became the first note of their song and that song has been a cry of pain ever since. In Camarón's throat, the cry was so profound that it could be described as a summation of all the pain in all the cante that had gone before. Outsiders may appreciate it, but Camarón's voice speaks to his own community with shamanic power. That voice filled stadiums, sold millions of cassettes, and almost single-handedly reinvigorated *cante Gitano* and inspired the music's unique form of modernity. When they made that historic first album, Camarón was eighteen, de Lucía twenty-one.

Franco tried to keep the sixties from crossing the Pyrenees and, for a while, seemed to succeed. He didn't realize, though, that the deal with Eisenhower for US bases in the heart of flamenco country had opened a back door. Off-duty airmen and sailors started turning up in Seville and Cádiz bars and clubs, playing rhythm and blues and rock 'n' roll and spinning their record collections over base radio stations. The ears of Andalusian youth, Gitano and payo, perked up.

El Caudillo's most notorious mistake, of course, was anointing young Juan Carlos as his heir because he found the prince's father "too liberal." The low hum heard across the peninsula in the winter of 1975–76 was the sound of Franco spinning furiously in his tomb as King Juan Carlos I initiated free elections and put an end to censorship. This was followed by La Movida (The Movement): a cultural explosion that brought heavy metal, newsstand porn, and Almodóvar films to what had been a conservative backwater country. In Andalusia, La Movida dovetailed nicely with air-base rock and the annual releases by Paco and Camarón to inspire a flamenco revolution.

The uprising began when a Gitano named Manuel Molina joined a hippie rock band from Seville called Smash, contributing some flamenco-flavored vocals and guitar lines. Molina turned out to be quite an original musician who met his perfect match in Dolores Montoya from that royal flamenco family. Their three late-seventies albums as Lole y Manuel changed the face of Andalusian music; she sang with flamenco feeling minus the agony and enunciated Molina's words with simple clarity. Her partner's lyrics were both very flamenco and also contemporary, like nothing heard before in cante. Having spent some of her childhood in Casablanca, Lole even sang a few tracks in Arabic.

At the end of the seventies, when Paco de Lucía transformed his sound by adding cajón and Carles Benavent's fretless bass and went off to pursue international dreams with John McLaughlin and Al Di Meola, Camarón turned to Lole y Manuel's producer, Ricardo Pachón. When *La Leyenda del tiempo* (Legend of Time) came out, Gitanos thought Camarón had lost his mind; not only was it full of non-flamenco sounds like electric keyboards, but the title track (with lyrics by Lorca) was an actual song with a repeating melody and a catchy chorus. Almost as disturbing was the cover photograph, a moody black-and-white silhouette of the singer's newly bearded face. In 1979, Gitanos never wore beards. *Leyenda* turned out to be one of those records, like early Velvet Underground, Leonard Cohen's *Various Positions*, or, dare I say it, Nick

Drake's albums, that become influential in ways no one at the time foresaw. Within a few years, Gitanos, particularly those living in the Tres Mil, were playing keyboards and cajónes, writing edgy lyrics, singing harmonies . . . and growing beards. *Leyenda*—and its cover photo—had become legendary.

Mario Pacheco took that portrait. He was then mainly a photographer; his wife, Cucha Salazar, was the one in the music business, doing promotion for BMG in Madrid. At her suggestion, Mario took a job with a Catalan record label that was struggling to adapt to a post-Franco world with no repressive government to defy. When Mario grew frustrated with his bosses, Cucha found investors to fund a label; they called it Nuevos Medios and, since one of the backers was a grandson of Juan Miró, the master himself drew them a logo: "NM" in the shape of a bird.

I watched in wonder from London as Mario and Cucha built a small empire. Spain was virgin territory for hip international labels, and Nuevos Medios introduced the country to ECM (and Keith Jarrett), Rough Trade (and The Smiths), Factory (and Joy Division), Fantasy (and Creedence Clearwater), Greensleeves (dub reggae), and a bit of Hannibal. They made New Order's "Blue Monday" a dancefloor hit in 1983, and when Ibiza-partying Brits went home and demanded it, the 12-inch became that format's biggest seller of all time. While Spain's major labels were signing hair bands and power chords, NM did well with underground groups, using income generated by their foreign labels to explore Spanish corners the big boys were ignoring. One night in Candela, Madrid's coolest music club, Juan Carmona handed Mario a demo by his band that had been turned down everywhere. Ketama was named for a Moroccan valley famous for its *kif* and its members were from Gitano families with long flamenco pedigrees: Granada's Carmonas, the Sorderas from Jerez, and Madrid's Heredias. Mario quickly said yes and from that seed grew all the many flowering branches of what came to be known as *nuevo flamenco*.

The kingpins of Spanish media in those years insisted that Spain was backward, that foreign was best and flamenco was "music they were ashamed to listen to." Mario and Cucha felt the opposite, that if flamenco was well recorded, presented with confidence, and promoted with the same flair as top-table rock, it would succeed. It took a few years, but Ketama became Spanish superstars. (Since that story involves Africa, you'll read more about it in Chapter VIII.) In the meantime, Ricardo Pachón brought them Pata Negra, a group from the Seville housing projects who epitomized what the movement was about.

From the late eighties onwards, traditional forms everywhere were being updated, electrified, and synthesized, beats were being simplified for (supposedly) easier cross-cultural consumption, and techniques honed in LA and London studios were being applied in the "developing world." Nuevo flamenco may have had one ear cocked towards the wider musical world, but it was an entirely self-contained Spanish phenomenon, with no French bass players or British rock stars telling them how to reach a broader audience. And when you have palmas, who needs a drum machine?

Pata Negra was Raimundo and Rafael Amador, brothers who had grown up hanging out with English hippies and US soldiers, listening to The Doors, Hendrix, Santana, and Camarón. They brought B.B. King's Roma-inflected blues back full circle, throwing flatted sevenths, jazz chords, blues riffs, and even a drum kit into their *compas*. The older Gitano generation hated what the youth were up to at first, but when they realized how true to the spirit and history of the music the records were, most came around. Nearly all the important nuevo flamenco artists made their first albums for Nuevos Medios, and Mario's respect for the culture meant the recordings felt very Andalusian, very flamenco, and very Gitano.

By the early nineties, the major labels had woken up and began offering money NM couldn't match. Mario was philosophical; taking his cue from Manfred Eicher at ECM, whom he considered the Zen master of label management, there were no long-term contracts and artists came and went as they pleased. I was saddened when a Nuevos Medios artist turned up on Universal and chided Mario for fattening frogs for snakes; first and second albums, Mario countered, were almost always the best.

At the same time that Madrid film-maker Fernando Trueba was editing *Calle 54*, his documentary on Latin jazz featuring Bebo Valdés, he was finishing off a promotional video for the cantaor Diego el Cigala. Juxtaposition led to inspiration and the result was *Lagrimas negras*, an album of Cuban boleros sung by the rough-voiced Cigala accompanied by Bebo's piano. It won a 2004 Grammy, sold tons everywhere, and constitutes the most intense exposure non-Spaniards have ever had to *voz afillá*. With alluring melodies to hang on to, plus Valdés's elegant playing, it works pretty well. El Cigala can be seen as the Nusrat Fateh Ali Khan of cante, a figure who opens doors for a form Western ears usually find difficult. For most foreigners—and even many non-Andalusian Spaniards—cante, particularly of the *afillá* variety, remains forbidding terrain.

Nuevo flamenco's vocalists, on the other hand, were mostly clear-sounding tenors, their songs often had choruses and harmonies, and, though critics in Paris, London, New York, and Amsterdam praised them, the groups rarely ventured outside Spain. A socialist government had come to power in 1982 and Felipe González, the new prime minister, was a flamenco fan from Andalusia; national, regional, and local governments began supporting festivals and concerts and they paid very well. Why should anyone leave home for the small fees offered by world music promoters?

I have a big collection of flamenco recordings and count myself an enthusiast but I got disapproving looks from Mario and Ricardo Pachón when I revealed that my favorite cantaor was Pepe Marchena. "El Niño" de Marchena, as he was known until he got too old to be "the kid" anymore, was flamenco's first broadly popular star, touring across Spain from the twenties through the sixties and starring in those notorious operas. He specialized in *cante chico* and *ida y vuelta* (go and come, out and back), Spanish songs that returned from the colonies Latinized and Africanized. Marchena had a light voice and reveled in melody and decoration, and experts generally dismiss him now as barely worth a mention, the kind of singer Lorca hated. In one critic's condemnation, I discovered a source of my affection: Marchena stood accused of importing "a 1920s-style tango voice" into flamenco. Indeed, in Marchena, I can hear echoes of the wonderful Carlos Gardel. It's not that I dislike voz afillá, though I'm generally drawn more to melody than to intensity; my other favorites, the great cantaoras La Niña de los Peines and La Paquera de Jerez and the blind Porrina de Badajoz, all sang with raw, lung-bursting power while conjuring heart-stopping turns of melody amid the intensity.

In writings about flamenco, the word *duende* inevitably appears. Its literal meaning is "goblin" or "disembodied spirit"; foreign authors often compare it to "soul," but it's more about transcendent moments of startling intensity and brilliance than the inherent qualities of one musician. Lorca traces the concept back to Arab culture, where moments of musical magic were greeted by cries of "Allah, Allah." (One motive for his murder may have been the poet's suggestion that "Allah" was the root of *olé*.) His famous lecture on the subject doesn't provide much clarity; on the one hand, he said, it represents a uniquely Spanish intimacy with death: "The duende does not come at all unless he sees that death is possible." On the other, Lorca notes approvingly how a great cantaor, upon hearing some well-played Bach, exclaimed, "Olé! That has duende!"

The cantaor Juan Talega once asked an interviewer, "Where did you foreigners ever get this idea of duende? From García Lorca maybe?" Flamenco doesn't need duende to set it apart from other musical forms; nowhere else in Europe is there a musical tradition that has no academies, that can't be accurately transcribed, yet which is so formal and complex and takes so long to master. The most vivid and insightful book by an outsider, in my view, is Gerald Howson's *The Flamencos of Cádiz Bay*, about his time there in the early fifties, studying guitar, befriending a great cantaor, and attending many juergas. Towards the end of his stay, he noted down a conversation with Don Benito Cuesta, a man of moderate means who had hosted many juergas: "[W]hat can a history student say of an art that has no history? What theories will they advance to explain why flamenco should just appear in this one corner of Spain, and grow and grow in the hands of a few illiterate paupers, ignorant of the laws of music or even of the names of the notes, and continue to grow to this day into something glittering and gorgeous, and occasionally profound and terrible, inspired by—what?"

What indeed? As the great Tía Anica la Piriñaca once said, "When I sing as I please, I taste blood in my mouth."

> *The Castilians on the corners*
> *with their lamps and lanterns*
> *are saying in loud voices,*
> *Kill him, he's a Gypsy cur.*
>
> —Flamenco lyric

∽

In 1991, Ray Heredia, a founding member of Ketama who left before the first album came out, died of an overdose just as Nuevos Medios released his solo album. Heredia was strikingly handsome, a golden boy whose haunting song "Lo bueno y lo malo" has become an immortal Spanish classic. He was beloved; his fellow musicians and everyone at the label were devasted.

Camarón de la Isla, a lifelong heavy smoker, died of lung cancer a year later. One hundred thousand people filled the streets of Seville for his funeral. His last years had been tortured; wherever he appeared, mothers brought children for him to touch, like a living saint, and his concerts were always filled to overflowing. The pressure of such near-hysterical affection weighed on him heavily as his strength ebbed.

Cucha passed away in 1997, then Mario in 2010. Their daughter María keeps the Nuevos Medios catalogue alive and she and her filmmaker husband, Simó Mateu Pons, recently produced a film about her father for Spanish television called *Revelando a Mario*. In it, friends of Camarón and Paco de Lucía talk of how both artists regretted, because of their contracts, not being free to work with Mario.

Enrique Morente was the ultimate payo cantaor. One might even call him a twentieth-century Silverio Franconetti, passionate both in his reverence for the great singers of the past and his commitment to experimentation and exploration for the future. Almost alone of flamenco singers, he persevered in bringing cante jondo to the outside world. He was married to a Gitana *bailarina* and their daughter, Estrella Morente, has followed in her father's footsteps, seducing foreign ears with sung flamenco. A few days after his friend Mario's funeral, Enrique underwent a minor surgical procedure; something went wrong and he never regained consciousness.

Four years later, Paco de Lucía died of heart failure while on holiday in Mexico. For most non-Spaniards, his is probably the only familiar name on this mournful list. The others may not have made flamenco known across the globe, but they forever altered Spain. If there was such a thing as the perfect therapy for the Spanish spirit as it overcame the wounds of the Franco years, the music they and their colleagues made was surely it.

The rest of the world eventually got a full dose of Gitano music. But it wasn't really flamenco, and the musicians who made it came from over the Pyrenees in France.

***

Oh Mary, don't you weep, don't you moan
Pharaoh's army got drowned
Oh Mary, don't you weep

—African-American spiritual

When the Romans were trying to rub out witnesses to Christ's Resurrection, they put "the two Marys," Jesus's cousins who'd seen the empty tomb, onto a rudderless boat on the Palestine coast and cast them off to drown. Their loyal servant, a dark "Egyptian" woman named Sarah, tried to board the vessel but the soldiers blocked her, so one of the Marys threw her a cloak on which she floated out to join them. Miraculously, the craft made it all the way to the south of France, landing near the mouth of the Rhône. Another version has Sarah as a dark-skinned Provençal queen who rescues the Marys from a storm, brings them ashore, hears the word of the Lord, and converts her people to Christianity.

You won't find this voyage in the Bible, but the apocryphal tale (with and without Sarah) became so popular in the Middle Ages that an order of monks built a church honoring the beatified pair where they supposedly came ashore in the land of wild horses, the ethereal wetlands known as the Camargue. The Roma latched on to the version with Sarah, and the fact that the Church doesn't acknowledge her makes it all the more appealing; Sarah became *their* saint. Every year on May 24, Roma from all over Europe gather at Les Saintes-Maries-de-la-Mer, as they have been doing since at least the mid-nineteenth century.

There are statues of the Marys in the nave of the cathedral, but Roma pilgrims head straight for the crypts; there, in a dark corner, is a large wooden carving of Sarah. They drape her in cloaks and scarves, carry her into the light, bring her down to the sea, and give her a good soak in the Mediterranean. Her cheeks are worn smooth from thousands of good-luck touches. There are theses waiting to be written on the links between this and the high Catholic rituals in Andalusia where saints' images are taken for a walk once a year, escorted by buglers and drummers (and, at Easter in Seville, flamenco singers), and the journeys Hindus make to the Ganges with images of Kali. (Roma refer to their saint as "Sara-la-Kâli"—Sara the Black.)

Then the party starts. May 25 was a big date in Django Reinhardt's calendar, but it keeps growing and growing and the town now gets completely overwhelmed. There are jam sessions in every bar and on every corner, a wild mix of Balkan, Russian, Hungarian, Manouche jazz, and flamenco. It would make a nice coda to report fantastic music emerging from this Roma musical summit, the best of many worlds, but the most-played tune there is usually "Ochi chornye" (Dark Eyes), the corniest bit of schmaltz imaginable, with "Hava nagila" running it a close second. Which isn't to say there aren't great musicians there every year playing the hell out of "Ochi chornye."

∽

Your daddy he's an outlaw
And a wanderer by trade
He'll teach you how to pick and choose
And how to throw the blade
He oversees his kingdom
So no stranger does intrude
His voice it trembles as he calls out
For another plate of food

Your sister sees the future
Like your mama and yourself
You've never learned to read or write
There's no books upon your shelf
And your pleasure knows no limits
Your voice is like a meadowlark
But your heart is like an ocean
Mysterious and dark

One more cup of coffee for the road
One more cup of coffee 'fore I go
To the valley below

—Bob Dylan, "One More Cup of Coffee (Valley Below)"

In the spring of 1975, Bob Dylan was in France with time to kill. Bored in Paris, he headed south to stay with David Oppenheim, painter of the abstract image on the back of *Blood on the Tracks*. Oppenheim figured the best entertainment for his eminent guest would be a visit to Les Saintes-Maries during its annual Romafest. They paid a respectful call on the local "king," or clan leader, and were given the best seats by a campfire, where they stayed until dawn listening to Ricardo Baliardo, the hottest guitar in town. "One More Cup of Coffee," Dylan says, came to him in a dream the following night.

Baliardo was better known as "Hands of Silver"—Manitas de Plata. A decade earlier, with his cousin and jaleador José Reyes beside him, he hadn't been just the hottest player in Les Saintes-Maries but one of the hottest in the world. It all started with a photographer named Lucien Clergue, who'd known Baliardo and Reyes growing up in Arles and began his career by documenting Roma life in the south of France. Clergue's work was bought by big-time museums and galleries and he became a pal of Pablo Picasso; he hired Manitas and José for gallery openings in Arles, then in Paris and New York. Lucien knew all the right people and the pair soon had offers from promoters and record labels. Manitas was a stickler for Roma rules, however, and refused to consider recording until ten years had passed since Django's death. After 1964, though, there was no stopping them: the Paris Olympia, Carnegie Hall, the London Palladium . . . The pair filled what could be described as an international flamenco gap between Sabicas and Paco de Lucía. Not *real* flamenco, mind you, *rumba flamenca*.

Spanish rumba isn't Cuban rumba. It's a child of the nineteenth-century habanera craze, when Spanish theater companies made fun of Afro-Cubans and used a bit of syncopation to cue the audience to laugh at the blackface characters. But audiences, as we've seen, don't always follow the script and many enjoyed the music unsarcastically. Rumba flamenca (the Spanish seemed to like saying the "r" word as much as everyone else) made its way into cante—La Niña de los Peines is reported to have sung one in 1910—and it took a firm hold among Catalan Gitanos, who played it with a cheerful, energetic, unsubtle strum that was a good earner on the streets of Barcelona. A cottage rumba industry grew up there in the sixties, led by a clever singer and guitarist named Peret. He and a few others had hits across the sixties and seventies, earning the ultimate accolade/condemnation in 1974, when Peret was chosen to represent Spain in the Eurovision Song Contest.

Peret and Manitas, though different in presentation and target audiences, were linked through rhythm and by the ties connecting Catalan Roma on both sides of the border, particularly after so many fled north during the Civil War. By the time of Dylan's visit, both Manitas's and Peret's fame had subsided and a new breeze was blowing through the streets of Les Saintes-Maries as the cassette revolution of the 1970s transformed the Roma world. Though Django had long been revered as a guitar god, few had ever actually heard him play; with the release of cassette compilations, his music spread like wildfire. Portable players didn't mind the bumping and lurching of a horse-drawn wagon and every young Roma guitarist learned to play the pompe.

A key nexus of Roma musical exchange was up the road in Arles at Chez Nenes, a tiny bar in an alley behind the ancient bullring. It served as a stopping point on the way to Les Saintes-Maries and as a clubhouse for Baliardo's and Reyes's sons and nephews as they began performing for weddings and parties. The kids followed in their fathers' and Django's footsteps along the Riviera, getting booked for soirées in St. Tropez, where Brigitte Bardot would dance. They played the family rumba, adding a bit of Manouche pompe along with a *soupçon* of salsa and a dash of *horo* they'd picked at Les Saintes-Maries. Their lyrics were a melting pot, too; in 1988, their first record release mixed French, Romani, and Catalan. You know the song; it's called "Bamboléo" and they're the Gipsy Kings.

∾

> When the party is on, everyone wants to be a gypsy, but when it is over, they don't want to know anything about you.
>
> —Musician Rafael Ruiz

The Gipsy Kings unified the Roma, after a fashion. Balkan and Central European Roma bought acoustic guitars and began *pomping* away while the different clans finally accepted that they might all be in this European mess together. The horrors of post-communist persecution pricked a few gadje consciences and there were symposiums and conferences and agreements about replacing the terms "gypsy" and "tzigane" with "Roma." Promoters invited Rajasthanis in for collaborations and the film of the *Gypsy Caravan* tour shows them all getting along famously and admiring one another's music. It could be the start of a feel-good story, but there have been as many dark shadows as sunny uplands.

The modern world makes it almost impossible for Roma to fly under the radar. As their room to roam has grown inexorably narrower, most have been forced into public housing. Despair ensued, triggering a new scourge: hard drugs. Roma were never likely to be candidates for Narcanon or rehab clinics, but they found a cure that works. Though they'd always paid lip service to the local Muslim, Orthodox, or Catholic faith, few ever worshipped regularly or took seriously any beliefs besides their own ancient superstitions, charms, rituals, and Sarah. But many bought into the evangelical Light and Life Church's message, with its Roma preachers, all-Romani services, and hymns based on Django Reinhardt melodies. Healing is a focus of the movement, very important for a congregation that avoids doctors and hospitals like the plague.

Music has been hit hard. Once someone joins, he or she must give up all non-religious singing or playing. Across horizons and centuries, Roma fulfilled the original Persian brief, often in joyful defiance of religious strictures, transforming every musical culture they touched. Now, at both ends of that journey, in India and in Europe, modern society has combined with ancient prejudice and superstition to erode this unique culture. But not, however, before it embedded itself deep into the DNA of European music.

V
Chega de saudade

In December 1541, Francisco de Orellana and a cohort of sixty hungry Spaniards left Pizarro's Andean expedition in search of food. On their irreversible meander down a fast-flowing river that grew ever wider until the far bank was often out of sight, Orellana claimed they fought off attacks by fierce battalions of female warriors before eventually arriving at the Atlantic Ocean, the first Europeans to traverse what is now Brazil. His story was widely mocked back in Madrid but the colorful image of women warriors stuck and could not be dislodged, despite the conquistador's insistence that the great river should be named the "Orellana."

More than four centuries later, the *New Yorker* writer Alex Shoumatoff set off to track down archaeological evidence of those Amazons and invited along his friend Benoît Quersin, a Belgian bass player and musicologist known for his work in the Congo. Quersin had spent years in Africa, recording in cities, villages, and in the forest, but had never visited Latin America. In June 1986, the two men flew to the small city of Santarém at the junction of the Amazon and Tapajós Rivers; next morning they boarded a boat and headed into the Amazonas Reserve. At the end of that first day, they experienced an equatorial sunset, where the sun drops below the horizon in a flash and the sky goes dark like someone flicked a switch. The African rainforest is hardly silent at night, but it can convey a feeling of emptiness; cries of predator and prey, mating calls, and territorial claims emerge from a spacious, sometimes eerie soundscape. Not so Amazonia. After sunset, all hell breaks loose; chattering, croaking, screeching, cawing, clicking, humming, and rubbing, an avian, reptilian, and insect symphony that lasts until dawn. On the deck of the boat, Quersin turned to Shoumatoff: "Ah," he said, "now I understand samba."

Who invented Brazil?
It was Mr. Cabral!
On the 21st of April
Two months after Carnival

—Lamartine Babo, "História do Brasil"

Fathering the infamous Lucrezia didn't prevent Rodrigo Borgia becoming Pope Alexander VI in 1492; before he could get comfortably seated on the Chair of Saint Peter, the pontiff was confronted with a brewing conflict. Portugal, then Europe's most aggressive seafaring nation, had been claiming islands in the Atlantic and extending its reach ever farther down the coast of Africa, purchasing slaves and putting them to work both at home and on Cape Verde and Azores plantations. That same year, Christopher Columbus (who learned to navigate while serving on Lisbon-based slave ships) claimed Cuba, Hispañola, and a few other Caribbean islands for Spain. This put the cat among the Iberian and Catholic pigeons; anything to the west and south of the peninsula was supposed to be Portugal's. Alexander's papal bull drew a vertical line in the Atlantic one hundred leagues beyond the Azores, awarding the Spanish everything on one side and the Portuguese everything on the other. The settlement laid down a wager; Madrid would head west in search of a passage to the East Indies, while Lisbon bet on the route south and east around Africa. Both were winners; the Spanish found all the gold they could plunder in the Aztec and Inca empires, while the Portuguese established trading posts along the coasts of Africa and India and as far as Timor in the Indonesian archipelago, buying and selling spices and slaves as fast as they could get their hands on them.

It seemed but a footnote when a fleet of Portuguese caravels were blown off course and, as the song says, Pedro Cabral and his men landed on the shore of a massive protuberance extending over a thousand miles into the Portuguese side of the line. The traders met a few natives, bartered a few trinkets, chopped down some brazilwood trees known for their valuable red dye, sent one of the flotilla home to report the discovery, and kept on sailing to the Indies.

Afterwards
Ceci loved Peri
Peri kissed Ceci
To the sound of the Guarani!
From Guarani to guaraná
Then came the feijoada [black bean stew]
And later, the Paraty [white rum]

   —Lamartine Babo, "História do Brasil"

If the Pope's ruling constitutes one cornerstone document of Brazilian history, a book by an obscure anthropologist from Recife provides another. 1933 was a good year for Gilberto Freyre to publish *The Masters and the Slaves*, a treatise on the country's multiracial roots; President Getúlio Vargas had just fought off a rebellion by regional power-brokers and seized dictatorial control of the country. His stated agenda was unity—of regions, classes, and races—and *The Masters and the Slaves* made the case that miscegenation, far from being Brazil's problem, was its strength, and that the country's multiracial mix could provide a pioneering example to the world. (It is easy to forget that this was a time when "civilized" people in France, Britain, and the US still took seriously eugenicists' theories about "improving" the gene pool through selection, sterilization, and worse.) Inspired by Mussolini and Freyre, Vargas vowed to build a strong, united Brazil and align it with that bold new force, the Axis powers of fascist nationalism.

Something must have gotten lost in the translations of the Italian and German speeches and manifestos provided to the president. Besides limiting the power of Brazil's regions, Vargas's long-term goals included blurring the nation's races into one light-brown people. A key element would be radio, inspired by that medium's role in unifying Hitler's

Germany, but with a Brazilian touch: the glue Vargas would employ to hold this vast and disparate land together was the music that had lately emerged from the Rio de Janeiro slums: samba.

In 1936, Brazilian National Radio arranged a link with German state broadcasters to provide an hour-long show, live and direct from Rio to Reich. The program consisted almost entirely of music by the Portela *escola de samba*, a carnival society made up of Black and mixed-race musicians, singers, and composers. Quite what the elite in Berlin made of this most un-Aryan moment has not been recorded. But before the decade was out, the Nazis were caught backing a coup against Vargas, Uncle Sam dangled his dollars, and Brazil switched sides.

> Sex across the divide of race and ownership seemed to be at the very center of plantation life. Sometimes, reading Freyre, you wondered how they ever got the cane harvested.
>
> —Peter Robb, *A Death in Brazil*

> Gilberto's work leaves us all more Brazilian.
>
> —Jorge Amado

The Masters and the Slaves delves into Portugal's medieval past, when the country was notorious for how little shame was attached to sex—or even marriage!—between White and Black, gentile and Jew, Moor and Christian. A century before Cabral's starboard sighting, Lisbon dives throbbed to a mixture of Arabic, Iberian, and African music, while Portuguese slave traders paid extra for captives who were good musicians. The road to samba began there.

The Crown eventually realized that cornering the market in brazilwood would never provide a big enough return on the cost of keeping guard over such an enormous possession. To profit from Europe's growing sugar cravings, Lisbon carved its new colony into cane-growing fiefdoms, appointing well-connected courtiers and commanders as *coronéis* (colonels) to run them (thereby establishing the regional power bases that bedevil Brazilian politics to this day), and brought in boatload upon boatload of African captives to do the work. Much of Freyre's book is devoted to the plantation household, where Portuguese settlers, comfortable in the tropical climate but disinclined to hard work, settled into unambitious, indulgent, and decadent lives. Freyre describes a Portuguese sexual ideal, evolved over centuries of Arab rule, of the dark-eyed beauty bathing at a secluded river bend; indigenous and African women had been doing just that for millennia.

Brazil enjoys comparing itself to other nations forged out of colonial conquest, particularly the US, which was likewise born along the eastern shore of an immense landmass. The once-British colony was, however, settled by hard-working Protestants keen to establish small family farms and who made a great show of taking the Ten Commandments seriously. (Brazilian priests were largely unconcerned by rape and pillage so long as the perpetrators didn't eat meat on Fridays.) The overarching fact of the Portuguese Empire was demographic: there weren't very many of them, so in order to control such an expanse, the chancers, criminals, and riff-raff who disembarked from the caravels were urged to breed and breed quickly, with indigenous women, African women, and the mixed-race offspring of earlier arrivals. Africans and Natives, meanwhile, proved equally fascinated with each other.

> There began . . . those lewd dances which the inhabitants of Brazil have borrowed from the Africans . . . Nearly all were whites . . . they did not think they were demeaning themselves by copying the ridiculous and uncouth contortions of the [Negroes]. The Brazilians show a good deal of indulgence to their slaves, with whom they mingle so often . . .
>
> —Auguste de Saint-Hilaire, French naturalist

> While most instruments may have been imported, they have a national character today . . . The nasal sound of the Brazilian voice and instruments is natural and climatic; it is the *physiological* influence of Indian blood.
>
> —Mário de Andrade, poet and musicologist

> A mestizo culture is taking shape, so powerful and innate in every Brazilian that in time it will become the true national consciousness, and

even the children of immigrant fathers and mothers, first-generation Brazilians, will be cultural mestizos by the time they are grown.

—Pedro Archanjo, hero of Jorge Amado's novel *Tent of Miracles*

One way to get a feel for the vastness of Brazil's geographic, demographic, and cultural landscape is with lists. When the 1976 census invited respondents to state their skin color, there were 134 different responses, starting with *acastanhada* (nut-like), *agalegada* (Galician-looking), *alva* (pure white), and *alverenta* (like a shadow in the water). Inventories of Brazilian instruments and musical categories are almost as long; the former begins with *afoxé* (beaded gourd), *agogô* (double-headed iron handbell), and *apito* (whistle) and ends at *zabumba* (bass drum from the Northeast), while the latter extends from *aboio* (wordless cowboy melody), *acalanto* (lullaby), and *Afro-samba* (late-twentieth-century roots version of the national music) to *xote* (a 2/4 northeastern step derived from the schottische). A catalogue of indigenous groups starts with Aikanã and ends 222 entries later at Zuruahã.

Rhythmically, Brazil's roots are quadrilateral; the complexity of a carnival *batucada* (rhythm section) has its origin in Moorish tambourines and *krakeb* clappers and the aggressively struck stringed instruments of Portugal, stirred, along with the gourds and rattles of the Native peoples, into a *feijoada* stew of African percussion. It has often been assumed (by me, anyway, before I did the reading) that those most Brazilian of instruments, the octave-squeaking *cuíca* and the low-twanging *berimbau*, were indigenous contributions. Wrong; both are Angolan imports.

Early on, most music in the colony was provided by voice, percussion, and handclaps; rings of dancers known as "samba circles" were a regular sighting from the late sixteenth century onwards. The high frequencies of Brazilian percussion were shaped by more than just the forest; the Portuguese allowed no Cuban-style cabildos to house and maintain large drums, so instruments needed to be light and easy to carry, while the nasal tones of indigenous voices blended nicely with clanking and rattling objects. Influences were circular: Brazilian melodies, for example, often feature octave jumps that mirror the sound of the cuíca.

During their first three centuries, the colonists built no libraries, weren't allowed newspapers, and few of them kept diaries, so we are reliant largely on the letters and journals of bemused visitors. A German noted that "the Negroes appear to possess a high degree of aptitude for music. With little training they quickly achieve some virtuosity on any instrument." Travelers were astonished to encounter all-Black choirs and orchestras deep in the countryside performing the Stabat Mater or a baroque concerto. (This talent was often dismissed as "natural," an almost unfairly granted aptitude, much as some today account for Black skill at sports.) Reports complain (and occasionally celebrate) that the musicians were apt to "swing" European music. Travelers were further struck by the enthusiastic and sensual dancing of the Whites, many of whom seem to have wholeheartedly embraced African movements.

A few blinks of a tectonic eye ago, the Brazilian bulge fit snugly into the Central African bend like a jigsaw puzzle piece. Aeons later, the two continents still lie close enough for Cabral to make his discovery while taking a wide turn around Africa's Guinea bend. This relative proximity meant more back-and-forth interaction than elsewhere in the Americas: slave-trading African kings made promotional trips to Brazil to "develop their markets," while a prosperous freedman in Bahia could order his favorite soap from Benin. One wealthy African arrived in Salvador carrying gold to buy a captured cousin's freedom, got distracted by a Brazilian girl, had children, bought slaves and, according to local legend, "treated them very well."

Other recorded surprises include a slave teaching his owner Arabic script, another advising on crop rotation, and enchained Africans showing Portuguese how to pan for gold. Many prisoners were Kongo Catholics whose region had long been proselytized by Portuguese missionaries. An English visitor wrote that "a stranger . . . might imagine that the slaves were [Brazil's] proper inhabitants, and their masters its casual visitors." Another concluded, "Africa has civilised America."

> [A]n original sort of music different from any I ever heard, the most seducing, the most voluptuous imaginable, the best calculated to throw

saints off their guard and to inspire profane deliriums . . . [The *modinhas*] consist of languid interrupted measures, as if the breath was gone with excess of rapture, and the soul panting to fly out of you and incorporate itself with the beloved object. With a childish carelessness they steal into the heart before it has time to arm itself against their enervating influence . . . I confess I am a slave to *modinhas*, and when I think of them cannot endure the idea of quitting Portugal. Could I indulge the least hopes of surviving a two months' voyage, nothing should prevent my setting off for Brazil, the native land of *modinhas*.

—William Beckford, English visitor to Lisbon, 1787

Across the centuries of colonial expansion, Lisbon continued to be home to more Africans than any other European city. Many were sailors who plied the routes between Portugal, Africa, and Brazil; at every stop they would perform the latest songs and styles from wherever they had set sail. The first documented star of this Lusophonic triangle was, appropriately, the Brazilian son of a Portuguese father and an Angolan mother. Domingos Caldas Barbosa took vows as a priest, but soon began composing and performing *modinhas*, a variant on traditional *cantigas* that began, as would *tango canción*, with X-rated bordello anthems. Barbosa brought a repertoire of somewhat more refined songs to Lisbon, where his love-obsessed ballads, studded with syncopations, pregnant pauses, flatted sevenths, and exotic Ki-Kongo expressions, became a craze among Portuguese youth and even inspired settings by Viennese composers. The highest levels of society caught the bug; when the Portuguese royal family fled Napoleon in 1807, immediately upon arriving in Rio they requested a modinha concert.

Portuguese rulers had never before set foot in the colony that had been bankrolling them for centuries. The land was consistently generous; after the brazilwood and sugar booms came an eighteenth-century gold rush in the hills of Minas Gerais, and just as the nuggets were panning out, North Americans developed a ravenous thirst for Brazilian coffee. The government-in-exile arrived with British fiscal chaperones; Brazilian gold had been banked and invested in London, providing the capital to fuel the British Industrial Revolution. A few years later, in the wake of the Bourbon restoration, French craftsmen, tailors, chefs, musicians, and courtesans turned up in Rio, fleeing their reactionary new rulers. The city had, just a few years earlier, been a sleepy backwater in a spectacular landscape; now it was fast becoming a hive of commercial, social, architectural, and musical activity. Lisbon may once have ordered heavy-handed strictures against intellectual activity in its distant colony, but once King Dom João VI had settled in, he wanted newspapers, bookstores, theaters, and, most of all, music.

Perhaps the royal retinue and the French, who together transformed Rio, were picking up the scent of history. Rio's Guanabara Bay had been first "discovered" by French pirates in 1504; a colony survived there for a while, riven by its own internal conflicts (Catholics against Huguenots, puritans versus hedonists) but generally living in peace with the locals. For many, it was a paradise three and a half centuries ahead of Gauguin's Tahiti, complete with tropical beauty, sun, sex, easy living, and constant parties; many "went native" and raised families with indigenous wives. Only the fierce disapproval of their own devout leaders and the eventual arrival of the Portuguese navy put an end to a sybaritic life that, according to one report, included local women shaving themselves "Brazilian style." Three centuries later, Rio emerged as the love-obsessed city that shaped and blended Brazilian music. Dom João was enamored of the local sounds and regularly celebrated his colony's distinct musical identity (which helped inspire its demand for independence). British banks and French style abetted the royal enthusiasms, but a key element was the growing presence in the city of free Brazilians of color. To Cariocas (Rio natives), Salvador de Bahia, the original capital, was a Black city, theirs a White one. But across the nineteenth century, as the gold rush faded and prospectors set free the slaves they could no longer afford to feed, as droughts hit the cotton and cane fields of the Northeast, as authorities in Bahia grew ever more hostile to Afro-Brazilian culture and religion, and particularly after King Dom Pedro II abolished slavery, Black Brazilians headed for Rio.

> The best way to explain: it's the music of sailors, Galicians, and serving lads, of revelry and tumult, uproar and roguery . . . [It] entices your heart,

makes your body shake, and tears up your toenails by stealth; so hurrah! The Bahian *fofa* makes many people get married . . .

—Mid-eighteenth-century Lisbon pamphlet describing the dance also known as *lundu*

Let's face it. The reason Brazil is musical is because Brazil is an African country. And African people . . . create music for working, to teach the children, to make love or make war . . . Just like in Africa, we keep the history of the soul, the body, the mind.

—Gilberto Gil

These internal migrants' favorite dance was called the *lundu*. Yes, another fun-to-pronounce, two-syllable, consonant-hinged Ki-Kongo word. We've seen this before: Brazilians danced it in a circle, then the polka, waltz, and mazurka lured them into couples, generating new steps. The resulting *maxixe* gained some international renown; just before the tango exploded in 1913, those pied pipers of dance, Vernon and Irene Castle, announced it as the next big thing. But the maxixe, which involved couples locking legs and arms in a manner that shocked even the late twentieth century when it resurfaced with the lambada, was far too abstract and difficult (to say nothing of too intimate) for non-Brazilians and its star quickly faded. Another problem with the maxixe was that Black Cariocas saw it as a White notion of Afro-Brazilian dance; if the lundu was going to evolve, the belated end of slavery in 1888 gave them license to blend the music and moves of three continents in their own way. The new style would eventually fasten itself to the word *samba*, a Ki-Kongo expression meaning, among other things, a "flirtatious belly-bump."

In a time-honored demographic pattern, White families abandoned the center of Rio to escape the fumes of industry and the encroachments of free Blacks, with many relocating to the nearby fishing village of Copacabana. Stately downtown mansions built in the boom years of the early nineteenth century filled with the newcomers. One such address—177 Rua Visconde de Inhaúma—acted as a musical fulcrum. A Black doctor named João Batista da Silva lived there with his remarkable wife, Hilária Batista de Almeida, better known as "Tia Ciata." Their house was a stone's throw from Square Number Eleven—Praça Onze. The name may sound mundane but it resonates for Brazilians as "Storyville" or "the Left Bank" do north of the equator; the neighborhood became the heart of Black Carioca life and music, and Tia Ciata seems to have been at the center of everything. Like many of her fellow migrants from Salvador, she sold Bahian food on the streets and in the markets of the capital. These vendors wore distinctive full-skirted dresses, adorned themselves with charms and bangles, sported colorful headscarves, and were often called Tia (Auntie). A half-century later, Carmen Miranda's lurid elaboration on this look helped make her world-famous.

Tia Ciata and her husband held open house most nights; regular visitors included friends from the neighborhood, many of them Bahian musicians, as well as White politicians, journalists, and *flâneurs*. In the front parlor, visitors ate, drank, talked, and played or listened to music. Samba circles formed in the backyard, where dancing would go on far into the night. Only adepts ventured farther, to a shack at the rear where Candomblé ceremonies took place. Before leaving Salvador at twenty-two, Tia Ciata had been initiated as a *mãe-de-santo*, and her house was a center of Afro-Brazilian religion in Rio, shielded from police harassment by her well-connected guests. The property's layout was like a musicological diagram: from the ritual chant and percussion at the rear, rhythms blended into the patterns of handclaps, instruments, and dancing in the circles, which in turn fed jam sessions at the front, where news, poetry, and gossip were transformed into song.

Scandal was never in short supply. In the years before football took its place beside music and sex in the holy trinity of Brazilian obsessions, that space was occupied by gambling. Along with the many whorehouses and bars, the neighborhood around Praça Onze was full of illegal roulette and poker games, protected or menaced by policemen of varying levels of corruption. Politicians may have been powerless to stem the southward flow of Black migration, but it wasn't for lack of trying. Vagrancy laws were employed to stop outsiders settling down unless they had a job and, like England's "sus" laws or US "stop-and-search" statutes, were used against anyone the cops didn't like the look of. In smaller cities and distant suburbs, this process was, no doubt, brutal, but there was so much lucrative action around Praça Onze that police palms could afford to be greased. This milieu provided endless material for a generation of *cronistas*, Damon Runyan–like journalists who titillated readers with tales of Rio low life, often harvested at Tia Ciata's.

In 1913, one such visitor copied down some stanzas he heard sung there about a cop on the take ringing up an illegal gambling den to warn of a raid; the lyrics were rich in Carioca slang, internal rhymes, and wordplay spiced with a healthy dose of cynicism about the authorities. Two years later, another observer encountered a group at Tia Ciata's market stall performing the same song. By 1916, the tune could be heard across the city, and by the time the 1917 carnival kicked off, it had become a massive hit the really old-fashioned way, without a recording. The song's title was "Pelo telefone" (Phone Call), and when a toned-down, less subversive version was recorded and released in the spring of 1917, its huge success laid the foundation for what would become the samba industry. The registered co-authors of "Pelo telefone" were a White newspaper columnist named Mauro de Almeida, who wrote under the nom de plume "Cold Foot Turkey," and Donga, a Black singer and musician and key figure in samba history. Both were attacked: Almeida by rival journalists for involving himself in such a "seedy" (read Black) affair, and Donga by fellow *sambistas* for taking credit for a song that had been evolving around the scene for years, as well as by leftish intellectuals and ethnographers for extracting it from the folk process and dragging it into the grubby realm of commerce.

Cold Foot's partnership with Donga was prophetic; the early samba decades were full of composer couplings in which the darker half usually came off worse. Poor musicians from the *morro* (hillside slums) sold songs to lighter-skinned journalists-turned-composers or shared credit with popular singers who recorded their songs (shades of Colonel Parker's requirements for Elvis's songwriters). White authors made such a habit of buying tunes off poorer, darker songwriters that they were often called *comprositores*—a pun combining *compositor* with *comprador* (buyer). But Donga, who, like many key figures in early Rio samba, was the son of a Bahia-born Tia, never had trouble holding his own; he and his childhood friend, Pixinguinha, soon created the ensemble that would bring respectability to this ghetto music and, much to the distress of conservatives, take it to the outside world.

In 1919, the Palais, Rio's newest and biggest cinema, invited Pixinguinha and Donga to assemble a band to entertain crowds in the lobby. They called themselves Oito Batutas (Eight Aces), and were not only the first upscale group to include street percussion, but were neatly divided, four Black and four White. Among many entranced listeners was Arnaldo Guinle, a wealthy businessman who took them under his wing, funding a series of national tours and encouraging them to keep their ears open for local sounds. Not unlike Reuben Caluza's circuits around South Africa, the group brought the country's urban music to the sticks and vice versa. Oito Batutas were invited to Paris in 1922 as part of that city's post-war hunger for all things exotic and "primitive"; though they went down a storm, the group failed to convince the French to dance the samba rather than the tango or Charleston. Their triumph kicked up a lot of dust back home, though, as pundits either celebrated or agonized over the fact that these half-Black cultural ambassadors were playing what seemed a very African-sounding music, "pedantic . . . negroid and ridiculous," according to one, who "didn't know whether to laugh or cry." Historian Pedro Calmon complained that "they will take us for Guinea Blacks . . . rather than . . . a cultivated and ambitious civilization." The popular author José Lins de Rego shot back that "samba . . . is a far more serious thing than our literature and our vanities."

When Blaise Cendrars's boat docked in Rio in 1924, the first thing he did was eat a plate of feijoada, the black-bean-and-offal stew now on the menu of every tourist-friendly Brazilian restaurant, but viewed then as something strictly for the poor and the Black. The famous poet had already enjoyed this dish in the Paris apartment of Brazilian painter Tarsila do Amaral; eating "authentic peasant food" went hand in hand with the mania of French bohemians for collecting African sculpture and dancing to exotic rhythms. Joining Cendrars at the simple dockside café were Brazil's most prominent modernist writers and artists. This literary superstar intrigued them; he gave voice to the view that modernism should draw its inspiration from "roots" rather than from high-blown theorizing. Brazil, Cendrars contended, was unique, a growing economic power and at the same time a treasure house of barely diluted African and Amerindian culture.

Cendrars's next stop was up on the *morro* to visit Donga. He had enjoyed Oito Batutas during their Paris sojourn and the two found they had a friend in common. Composer Darius Milhaud had spent the war years in Rio as private secretary to France's cultural attaché (the poet Paul Claudel), profiting from the opportunity to delve deep into Brazilian popular music. Like Bartók, Milhaud treated traditional musicians as respected equals, with the difference that he didn't share the Hungarian's preference for rustic purity and loved urban popular styles. Milhaud wrote articles explaining how "serious" composers could learn from their vernacular colleagues, particularly on the subject of syncopation. Back in Paris he composed a suite based on traditional Brazilian melodies, including one from which Jean Cocteau took the name of his famous avant-garde cabaret on the Left Bank: "Le Bœuf sur le toit." The indefatigably acquisitive Donga gave Cendrars a letter for Milhaud that included a claim for a cut of said "Bœuf." Cendrars's visit inspired local intellectuals to look anew on the music and art in their own backyard and to reassess its value. This shift helped to lay the foundation for both Freyre's anthropological revolution and Vargas's political one.

Pixinguinha, meanwhile, was on his way to becoming Brazil's most famous instrumentalist. It could be argued that this isn't saying a great deal, since samba glory mostly found its way to singers and songwriters. Although Brazilian musicians were intrigued and influenced by jazz, neither samba nor its tributaries and offshoots ever left much room for solos and there is no Brazilian Louis Armstrong or John Coltrane. By general agreement, samba's greatest instrumental feats have involved brilliantly nuanced accompaniment to vocals (stand up and take a bow, João Gilberto). Which is not to belittle Pixinguinha's accomplishments; he stood out for many reasons, including the fact that he was both very Black and solidly middle-class, provided by his parents with the best teachers as well as any instrument he fancied, before settling on the flute. Critics struggled with his well-schooled brilliance since he failed to conform to the stereotype of the "natural" Black musician tapping out complex rhythms on a tabletop using only a matchbox; one described him as "a black Pan [playing] among frightened Nymphs." It remains a testament to Brazil's ability to be, at times, color-blind that Pixinguinha became not only one of the country's most beloved composers, but also the go-to orchestra leader and arranger for broadcasts, recording sessions, and carnival balls right through the twenties and well into the thirties, an era when Blacks and Whites in the US hardly dared share a bandstand.

Labels on most early 78 rpm discs include a single descriptive word below the title: "foxtrot," "waltz," "march," and so on. The point of these categories was often more to do with marketing than accuracy. In the wake of "Pelo telefone," any song that grew popular in carnival season would be labeled "samba." At the time, and in the years since, critics and musicians have argued over whether "Telefone" was really a samba. How do you define samba?

For non-Brazilians, the problem is similar to the dance's absence of step diagrams; there is no easily identifiable equivalent to the tango's habanera beat, *son*'s clave, or reggae's one-drop. Various rhythms have worn the "samba" handle; they generally inhabit a 2/4 structure with an emphasis on the second beat, overlaid with complex interlocking syncopations. As on the dancefloor, where the samba has persisted in its inherited African resistance to paired-up steps, a Brazilian can easily identify one, but may struggle to define it. In a famous interview, the great percussionist Ismael Silva explained, "Samba was like this: *tan tantan tan tantan*. It wasn't any good . . . So, we started to play like this: *bum bum paticumbumprugurundum*." Is that clear?

Silva was describing an upgrade that arrived from down the road, a newer, poorer area known as Estácio. In the late twenties, this way of playing invaded the bars and whorehouses around Praça Onze and caught on immediately; it was edgier, more percussive, a bit more African, and was named after its birthplace. In *Hello, Hello Brazil*, Bryan McCann describes Estácio samba as "a more syncopated style of samba, throwing in off-beat accents liberally . . . [T]he new style was merely catching up to the dancers . . . moving their bodies suddenly at odd angles and in unexpected directions, often on the weak beats."

The timing was good; recording techniques were evolving, with the electrical process producing a more vivid sound. Brazil, like Argentina, was growing fast, a big enough market to lure American, British, French, and German record companies into setting up local operations. The result was a flourishing industry that released dozens of discs a month. The downside was that foreign producers were as racist as can be expected and worked diligently to make the music less "African" and give the recordings a smooth "modern" sound. Across the 1920s, samba grew more respectable; at least this removed some of the rationale for police harassment of dark-skinned musicians.

A sonic corner was turned in the early thirties, when the Candomblé percussionist Tio Faustino joined a session. The RCA Victor producer told him to put away his *omele* (a low-register cuíca), but Faustino threatened to sacrifice a chicken then and there and summon the *orixás* to defend their rhythm. The omele stayed. It still took the all-White Bando de Tangarás to finally break down studio resistance to rhythm sections; one of the group, Almirante, insisted on bringing in a full carnival batucada—*pandeiros*, tambourines, cuícas, *surdo* drums, and rattles—for his song "Na pavuna." The German producer was horrified, but the singer stood his ground and samba recording never looked back.

Almirante was part of a generation of middle-class songwriters transforming the genre. Argentine tango and American torch songs of the time were usually about heartbreak and longing, but for these Carioca composers, love was a game, with break-ups fading quickly in the rearview mirror. A beach, after all, was always nearby. Leading characters in samba lyrics were often the *malandro*, a bad boy from the morro, and the *mulata*, a mixed-race temptress. There were "answer-song" battles, one in particular waged by Wilson Batista and Noel Rosa, with Batista's records warning the White star to mind his bourgeois business and leave the *malandragem* (roughly, "thug life") to Batista and his mates. Rosa should have listened; he died in 1937 aged twenty-six, from over-indulgence in drugs, women, and alcohol, a true malandro death.

Though White artists got better recording deals and radio contracts and were more easily accepted into the authors' society, a spirit of cooperation was generally the rule, with singers and songwriters—White, Black, and in-between—working together to make hits and helping out on each other's sessions. They would meet at Café Nice to swap tips, recruit sidemen, and try out ideas. (The café served no alcohol, music being far too serious a business to discuss while drinking.) Samba remained very much a male-dominated affair until the 1930 carnival season, when young Carmen Miranda's "Taí" became the first hit to rule the streets and airwaves all the way from one year's carnival to the next.

Carnival! How did we get this far without bidding *"carne vale"*—the pre-Lenten farewell to meat? One excuse is that I strive to avoid repetition and, up to the end of the nineteenth century, Brazil's carnival story is not so different from Cuba's. Spain, Portugal, and their respective colonial empires had long histories of costumed street pageants; with prohibitions and condemnations, Cuban and Brazilian authorities tried to keep a lid on Africans joining in too exuberantly. In the 1890s, though, after Abolition had loosened controls, the two countries' stories diverge. Mayor Arnaz's horror at the prospect of masked White women joining the Santiago parades was answered in Brazil with sly jokes and ribald songs. One Rio tale featured a masked celebrant dancing with a seductively veiled houri who turns out to be his cook. In another version the mysterious temptress is his wife. The devil, say Brazilians, is loose on the streets during carnival; no one belongs to anybody.

During the respectable "Venetian" carnival era of the late nineteenth century, Tia Ciata and her fellow Bahians did a brisk trade renting out Baiana costumes to wealthy White ladies as Black music and imagery infiltrated downtown parades. Joining Tia Ciata and Carmen Miranda in a female triumvirate that helped shape Brazilian music in the century's early decades was Chiquinha Gonzaga, a free-spirited composer who had ditched a husband who tried to curtail her musical career. Her 1899 song "Ô abre alas" (Make Way) is credited as the first specially commissioned carnival *marchinha*, a singalong samba variety designed for moving slowly along a boulevard while vibrating every part of your body. Other highlights in Gonzaga's long career include a stint as conductor of the army brass band, performing her lubricious song "Corta jaca" (Cut the Jackfruit) at the presidential palace and being a vocal campaigner for Abolition.

In 1907, a racially mixed group of Tia Ciata regulars founded a carnival society called Ameno Reseda (Delightful Myrtle). They were so elegantly turned out and well behaved that they were allowed to parade through the heart of the city; within a few years, Ameno Reseda had established a template for carnival's future with themed floats and costumes on subjects such as "Asian Court Life" and "The Planets." The next leap forward arrived in 1929, when the Estácio district spawned Deixa Falar (Let Them Talk), the first neighborhood samba school. Why "school"? Because they persuaded a local academy to let them build floats and store costumes in the gymnasium and rehearse in the playground, and groups in other neighborhoods followed their example. The fact that a vast throng of costumed celebrants moves through the streets of Rio like so many fish provides subtext, as does the way Deixa Falar set out to teach the city what carnival and samba were really all about.

And teach Rio they did. Initially lacking a permit, Deixa Falar samba'd through Estácio and Praça Onze and then kept going, their costumes, singing, dancing and the exuberance of their followers rendering futile any police attempt to block their way. By 1933, dozens of neighborhood associations were emulating Deixa Falar's annual song competitions and were being bankrolled by lottery operators and other deep-pocketed (often criminal) sponsors. President Vargas was completely on board, issuing supportive diktats and clearing the way for them to march through the heart of downtown Rio.

Presidential endorsement came with conditions. By 1934, there was an official competition with prizes and rules. Outlawing wind instruments in the streets was one far-reaching regulation that placed carnival music on a separate track from the samba of radio and recording studio. Formations were set in stone; each school was required, for example, to have a Baiana wing of ladies wearing those signature outfits, an appropriate bow to the headwaters of samba. Since then, the remarkable eccentric creativity of Rio's poor neighborhoods has been poured into a molded structure that allows the schools to be judged like-for-like.

∽

> [Music had] the pre-national and national spirit of the Luso-American people, whether aristocratic, bourgeois, plebeian, or rustic.
>
> —Gilberto Freyre

> I'm one of those who have always believed in our true national music. I don't believe in foreign influences on our melodies. We are a new people. And new peoples generally triumph over the older ones. Brazil, with its new music, its own music, is going to triumph.
>
> —Oswaldo Aranha, government minister, 1933

> The negroid music in Brazil offers the Brazilian composer a limitless source of materials.
>
> —Pamphlet issued by the Pan American Union in 1938

During the second week of August 1930, a diverse group assembled in a Rio graveyard: poets, drug dealers, politicians, prostitutes, *sambistas*, intellectuals, lottery dons, journalists, thieves, music publishers, actors, macumba priests, chauffeurs . . . They came to bury José Barbosa da Silva, better known as Sinhô; his death from tuberculosis marks the end of the "heroic" age of samba. Three months later, the military settled the disputed presidential election by installing Getúlio Vargas as "interim" president. If there had been any doubt that Sinhô's vision of samba would be interred with him, Vargas's ascension settled it.

Across the 1920s, the deceased had waged musical war against the samba establishment. Sinhô's prolific composing drew a line back to an African tradition of satire and insult; Manding villages in West Africa can spend years preparing elaborate musical dramas to ridicule a neighboring town, and Sinhô spared no effort in letting rivals feel the force of his scorn. "Três macacos no beco" (Three Monkeys in an Alley) was aimed at Pixinguinha, his brother China, and Donga. It seems that even before Oito Batutas's trip to Paris, the group had become enamored of ragtime and jazz and were outspoken on the need for samba to "elevate" itself, to shed "backwardness" and leave the ghetto. Despite playing such a key role in recording and broadcasting samba, Pixinguinha never concealed his preference for *choro*, the music's polite instrumental cousin. Sinhô, on the other hand, through his carnival *marchinhas* (which were often banned) and the celebrations of malandros he composed for his popular Praça Onze stage shows, showered contempt on those who would water down the music that had migrated south from Salvador and which continued to evolve "up on the hills," in the shack-filled ghettos known as "favelas."

Vargas was never going to achieve his surreal goal of creating a caramel-colored race of Brazilians, but he did succeed in engineering a caramel-colored samba. The dictator was drawn to Germany's model of a state radio monopoly, but, foreshadowing his eventual elopement with American capital, he couldn't resist the well-funded flair of broadcast entrepreneurs. Their aims were in sync: a smooth version of samba that every corner of the country could love, evolving along a parallel track with big-band swing and network radio in the US. Both featured light-skinned front-men (plus a few women) backed by brilliant arrangers, songwriters, and musicians of all shades. Thirties Brazilian radio rarely played records. It worked the other way around; broadcasters put musicians, singers, and arrangers on salary with daily shows, special guests, and intense competition for the newest stars and the catchiest songs. Labels would then release what radio had already made popular.

A transplanted American named Wallace Downey created the perfect companion to the expansion of radio, a series of musical films that showed fans across the vast country what their favorite singers looked like in action. Downey's films, combined with signals relayed from Rio and São Paulo radio stations, created a far-flung samba market that led artists (Carmen Miranda foremost among them) to embark on arduous tours; roads were bad and there were few railroads or internal flights, so travel was mostly up and down the coast and the rivers by boat. (Vargas would succumb to his German and then his American allies' mania for the automobile; Brazil never developed its railways.)

Vargas's first month in office saw a torchlight vigil outside his residence by songwriters and musicians demanding better royalties and the opening up of authors' society membership to Black composers; before the radio boom, even famous sambistas often needed a day job. Vargas's long rule delivered on many of his promises to the poor and the dark-skinned; he improved schools and hospitals, made it easier to buy property, start a business, or join a (government-recognized) union, and he poured money into the music scene, instituting "Brazilian content" quotas for the airwaves as well as the stages of Rio's fancy new casinos. But, as with carnival, there were strings attached: all songs had to be cleared by government censors.

A 1930s visitor observed that the Vargas regime represented "despotism mitigated by sloppiness." The censors certainly took a while getting up to speed; in the early thirties, malandros and mulatas still ruled. The former relished their role as hyper-masculine "true Brazilians" who would never be Americanized, while the latter were objects of desire for both the slumming White guy and the dark-skinned malandro. Men from the morro were rarely allowed (in song, anyway) to seduce White women; "deflowering" was a criminal offense, but rarely punished unless the man was darker than the girl. Transgression sold records, though; pale chanteuse Marília's first hit demanded that her malandro *"take me, carry me to the hill to give me my diploma."* Across the mid-thirties, the screw tightened against suggestive lyrics, glamorization of criminal behavior, and morro slang. Wilson Batista fought a rearguard action with a series of songs purporting to celebrate the "reformed" (i.e., legally employed) malandro while mocking the notion through puns conflating *operário* (worker) with *otário* (sucker).

Samba's stars covered a racial spectrum—Francisco Alves was White, Orlando Silva mulato, Sílvio Caldas a *caboclo* (African-Indian mix)—but stopped short of the very Black. By the end of the decade, few Brazilians could imagine a time when samba was not the country's soundtrack; the story of the music's journey down the coast from Salvador, up into Rio's hills then down again to its radio stations, record studios, and casinos was engrained in national mythology. Samba's popularity implicitly rejected the notion that Black blood was holding the country back; the sort of complaints triggered by Oito Batutas's Paris triumph could now be dismissed as unpatriotic.

While Simón Bolívar was leading the fight for liberty in Latin America's Spanish colonies during the early nineteenth century, Brazil was too busy fawning over its exiled royal family to pay much notice; its Declaration of Independence from the colonial parent represented defiance by the young prince rather than any popular enthusiasm for self-determination or democracy. The republic came into being in 1889, when moneyed Brazilians got fed up with King "Pedro Bananas" and his interfering daughter Isabel and put them on a boat to Lisbon; freeing the slaves by royal decree was seen as the final straw in a litany of eccentricities. The vast, disconnected land had never developed much sense of itself as a nation; when strutting jingoism became the 1930s zeitgeist, Vargas understood that instilling pride in Brazilianness would be a challenge. It was time for the president to call in favors from the composers; *samba-exaltaçâo* unleashed a cascade of songs singing the country's praises. Few have stood the test of time, with one shining exception.

Ary Barroso had arrived in Rio to study law, then drifted into the music scene around Praça Onze, playing cinema piano; needing money to properly court a girl, he wrote a successful carnival samba, and by 1935 had become Carmen Miranda's favorite composer. His response to Vargas's call was "Aquarela do Brasil" (Watercolor of Brazil); now known the world over as simply "Brazil," it follows close on the heels of "Girl from Ipanema" as the country's most oft-performed musical export. Vargas may have envisaged samba anthems to rival Germany's brownshirt favorite, the "Horst Wessell Song," but Barroso's lyrics could hardly have been less in line with the Nazi ethos, praising Brazil as a *"tricky mulato"* of a nation. The song's first recording was released in 1939, just before the country switched affections from Axis to Allies, and would provide a key plank in the "good neighbor" bridge to the US. The English-language version, of course, avoided all of Barroso's paeans to miscegenation; they would have gone down as badly in America as in Germany.

The other long-lasting fruit of samba-exaltaçâo is that exquisite curiosity *Bachianas Brasileiras No. 5* by Heitor Villa-Lobos. Like Barroso,

Villa-Lobos had done time accompanying silent movies; while Ary fancied himself a Brazilian Gershwin, Heitor was aiming even higher. After showing Darius Milhaud around Rio's nightlife and doing some ethnographic explorations of the interior, he followed Oito Batutas to Paris, hanging out with the avant-garde and telling anyone who would listen, "I don't use folklore, I am folklore." (Few then saw anything wrong with "serious" composers adapting and copyrighting music collected from the folk, but when the folk attempted to register the songs themselves, they were scolded for "commercialization.") Back in Rio, he threw himself wholeheartedly into the Vargas project, claiming that his folk-based compositions had "exalted" Brazil even before the dictator called for it. Villa-Lobos seems to have been a tiresome self-aggrandizer, but time only burnishes the luster of his tropical take on Bach, particularly in the recording he conducted himself with the Brazilian soprano Bidu Sayão; there's nothing quite like it.

By 1939, carnival in Rio had become a tourist attraction, with the cruise liner SS *Normandie* steaming into Guanabara Bay in time to catch that year's parades. The ship's biggest stateroom belonged to the Broadway impresario Lee Shubert, who had also reserved the best table for the show at the shiny new Urca casino; Lupe Vélez and Tyrone Power had both recently passed through Rio and urged Shubert not to miss its sensational star.

Carmen Miranda's routine that night had taken a decade to evolve. "Playing the Baiana" was a favorite dress-up for White Brazilians, and Carmen had often donned a colorful headdress and some bangles, applying burnt cork to her face and treating the whole thing as a lighthearted joke. The first hits Barroso composed for her were inspired by a visit to Bahia; he returned full of romantic notions about samba's birthplace and the seductive mulatas who swayed their hips along Salvador's narrow streets. (At least he didn't go as far as US composers of the era, who couldn't stop gushing about "darkies" yearning to take the "*Chattanooga choo choo*" back to their "*dear old Southland*" and "*beat their feet on the Mississippi mud*.") During one of her mid-thirties tours,

Carmen played a theater in Salvador; in the audience was nineteen-year-old Dorival Caymmi, dazzled by Miranda but underwhelmed by her Baiana songs; he was sure he could do better and was determined to go to Rio and prove it.

From the early thirties, when Miranda lived around the corner from a radio station, and later, after she bought a big house in a fashionable neighborhood, there was always a pan of feijoada on her kitchen stove next to a pot of coffee awaiting musicians stopping by for a meal or composers pitching songs. In 1938, as Carmen and Wallace Downey were discussing her material for his new film, they had a last-minute crisis: Barroso had rejected Downey's offer for his latest Baiana number. Carmen then remembered a song that nice young man from Salvador had played in her kitchen, "O que é que a baiana tem?" (Oh, What Is It the Baiana's Got?) Caymmi's composition inspired Miranda to her most vivid and creative take on the Salvador Tia character (*sans* blackface), and it worked so well in the film that she based her show at the Urca around it.

Sonja Henie, Olympic-skater-turned-film-star, sat with Shubert that night and she was adamant: if the impresario didn't sign Carmen Miranda to a Broadway contract, he was a fool and would always regret it. Shubert bought the act, clothes, headdress, songs, and all. From then on, the world would know "what the Baiana had got"; the Baiana had Carmen and would never let her go.

> I say money, money, money and I say hot dog. I say yes, and I say no, and I say money, money, money. And I say turkey sandwich and I say grape juice . . . I say mens, mens, mens.
>
> —Carmen Miranda's dockside response to a New York reporter asking how much English she knew

The night before she sailed, Miranda starred in a radio show that ended with her singing the beautiful "Adeus, batucada," a farewell to the sound of carnival; she and the audience wept together. The next day, all of Rio, it seemed, turned out to wave goodbye. One reporter asked if she planned to "annex the USA to the kingdom of samba." President Vargas, still clinging to his man-crush on the fascist powers, wished her success "behind enemy lines."

Brazilians cared deeply what the world in general and anglophones in particular thought of them. Faced with Britain's ban on slave trading in the 1830s, they camouflaged their human-trafficking industry *"para inglês ver"*—"for the English to see." The phrase entered colloquial speech, encapsulating the country's tortured relationship with the northern hemisphere. In 1931, it became the title of a hit variety show created by Lamartine Babo (composer of "História do Brasil"). The show's theme song mocked the invasion of foreign phrases and consumer products in a collagist style that foreshadowed the postmodern antics of the Tropicalistas three decades later.

The equator can act as a reality-bending prism, giving European and American cultures a funhouse-mirror quality as they enter Brazilian consciousness. (And vice versa, of course.) Her countrymen wanted to believe that Carmen had packed their collective anxiety about how they were perceived in her steamer trunk along with the turbans, dresses, shoes, and boxes of costume jewelry but had no grasp of how ill-equipped Broadway, Hollywood, and the American public were to absorb samba. When Brazilians saw and heard the compromises Miranda would make in order to succeed, they turned away in shock; despite periodic reconciliations, she would never really be forgiven.

In fact, she remained far truer to samba than anyone had a right to expect, fighting a fierce battle with Shubert to bring the Bando do Lua (Band of the Moon) along as accompanists. Like most Americans, the impresario couldn't tell a samba from a rumba or a tango and assumed that Miranda would strut her stuff backed by the sort of run-of-the-mill, chart-reading musicians that, around that same time, nearly sank Desi Arnaz's career before it began. The fact that the Bando do Lua's leader was her covert boyfriend probably had something to do with her unyielding stance, but it did mean that when she made her debut in the out-of-town run for Shubert's new Broadway revue, the audience was treated to a pretty authentic version of samba.

Our hyper-connected modern world provides little context for what transpired that first night in Boston. The audience had never heard samba, never seen a photo of a Baiana, and never experienced a performer with Miranda's sort of energy as she exploded onto the stage in the second-to-last set before intermission (the same spot as Bob Dylan's electric turn at the 1965 Newport Folk Festival). Brazilian Portuguese is rarely spoken slowly, and Carmen sang it a mile a minute, consonants bouncing off the music like water cascading over rocks. Thirties America loved tongue-twisters; tobacco auctioneers, Jerry Colonna's wacky vocals, scat singers Louis Armstrong, Cab Calloway, and Slim Gaillard—all had helped prepare the ground. Back home, part of her appeal had been how slyly she packed double entendres and internal rhymes into dense but clearly enunciated lines. She grasped that it didn't matter if US audiences couldn't understand the words; the fact that it was all "foreign" made her vocal gymnastics somehow more impressive. And then there was the look: bandana, fruit, bangles, necklaces, and skirt, on top of her very own invention, platform shoes, to say nothing of the mischievous smile and vibrating hips. Miranda pulled off the remarkable trick of being sexy while adding a self-deprecating wink that made women adore her even more than men. First-act closers Abbott and Costello were so traumatized by the audience's ovation for her that their career almost didn't recover.

Woodrow Wilson coined the term "Good Neighbor Policy" to perfume America's brutal interventions in Nicaragua and Haiti. Franklin Roosevelt vowed a softer approach, appointing Nelson Rockefeller to run a cultural charm offensive under the same heading and to enlist the help of the film industry. Once Brazil had signed on as an ally, only Argentina remained on the fence and, with war imminent, the US was determined to keep it that way.

Hollywood had dipped a toe in Brazilian waters with 1933's *Flying Down to Rio*, a film to which history is grateful for providing a first glimpse of Fred Astaire and Ginger Rogers's dancefloor magic, as well as the screen debut of the two-piece bathing suit (on Dolores del Río) plus a surreal song-and-dance number on the wing of an airplane (with

Guanabara Bay back-projected on an RKO soundstage), but not much else. It did reasonable box office in America, but Brazilians were unimpressed by the cheesy rhythms and the extras who looked (and no doubt were) Mexican.

Rockefeller recruited a pair of cinematic giants to bring the two countries closer. The music publisher Ralph Peer had already sold Walt Disney on Mexico, so the Mickey Mouse mogul needed little arm-twisting to include Brazil in a feel-good cartoon celebration of pan-American brotherhood (bankrolled by the government). The other luminary, Orson Welles, was then at the height of his fame following the triumph of *Citizen Kane*, but was struggling to finish the eagerly awaited *Magnificent Ambersons*. Welles didn't fancy making a documentary about the 1942 Rio carnival, but Rockefeller wouldn't take no for an answer and forced RKO (of which he was a major shareholder) to keep upping the ante. The studio liked the idea of getting Welles out of town so they could "rescue" the overlong *Ambersons* and made him an offer he could have refused, but fatefully didn't. It remains unclear whether Welles's change of heart was triggered by the size of the fee or the stories whispered in his ear about wild times with Carioca girls.

In Disney's *Saludos Amigos*, Brazil was represented by a wise-cracking parrot named Joe Carioca singing duets with Carmen Miranda's sister Aurora. It was a reasonable success for the studio and a triumph for Ary Barroso; not only did the film include "Brazil" (which spent sixteen weeks on the US hit parade, becoming a worldwide standard and part of the "book" for any self-respecting dance band), but he got hired as a Disney staff composer. Barroso would spend a decade in Hollywood before returning in triumph to Rio and living out his years as a football announcer.

Welles's documentary, on the other hand, proved a disaster for all concerned. Jazz-buff Orson was immediately charmed by samba, recognizing its African roots and parallels with American music. While Disney's writers and animators averted their eyes from Rio's slums and its ubiquitous racially mixed couples, Welles was fascinated. He focused on a hit song from that year's carnival, "Praça Onze," a eulogy for the fabled district being bulldozed to clear Black residents from the city center and make way for a new shopping district. His forays into Rio's poorest areas to film carnival balls set off alarms with the Brazilian authorities, who begged the equally unnerved RKO execs to pull the plug. RKO editors, meanwhile, butchered *The Magnificent Ambersons* and it flopped on release.

The film-maker fell hard for Rio and its women, sometimes disappearing for hours with a local beauty in the middle of a shoot; he ended up spending six months and hundreds of thousands of RKO dollars before the studio finally cut off funding and forced him home. The project was never completed, and there's a documentary called *It's All True* about its failure. Welles's production team ended up like those sixteenth-century Frenchmen, split between those who happily "went native" and others who sternly disapproved. Welles also gorged on plate after plate of feijoada followed by rich Brazilian desserts; newsreel clips show him arriving in Rio looking fit and handsome, but by the time he left, his girth was approaching the gargantuan dimensions he would retain for the rest of his life. The twin failures of the documentary and *The Magnificent Ambersons* destroyed his reputation and his bankability. The RKO board sacked the studio's management; the new lot unveiled a slogan pointed straight at the great man: "Showmanship Instead of Genius."

Hypocrisy was rife at both ends. The Vargas regime was furious that Welles had peered behind their facade of a race-blind society—*para inglês ver*—while Hollywood was equally determined to keep audiences from getting a clear look at Rio; neither the racial equality in sex nor the brutal inequality of living conditions would have played well stateside.

Carmen Miranda spent her first carnival February away from Rio, morose and freezing in New York. Wrapped up against the chill, wearing flat shoes and a simple housedress, she walked unrecognized along Fifth Avenue past department-store windows filled with mannequins flaunting copies of her outfits. Hollywood soon came calling; Darryl Zanuck at 20th Century Fox wanted to get in on the government's "Good Neighbor" subsidies and saw signing Carmen as the perfect move. They quickly churned out *Down Argentine Way*, *That Night in*

Rio, and *Week-End in Havana*, all featuring her as a "Latina," singing (mostly in heavily accented English) and dancing watered-down rumbas, tangos, and the odd samba. The movies were hits in the US, but painful embarrassments in the "neighborhood." Most scenes were shot on a Fox backlot, with Buenos Aires represented by a bit of stock footage from a nightclub and a racetrack, while in on-screen Havana (then a booming modern city with traffic jams) characters went about in horse-drawn carriages. Local men were crooked, stupid, leering, or ugly while the women were either sultry or maternal. *Down Argentine Way* probably increased local sympathy for Hitler before it was banned.

The films made Miranda an American household name; New York's glitziest new nightclub was named Copacabana in her honor while the outfit she wore to the 1941 Oscars established the ritual of extravagant red-carpet gowns. In Brazil, there was a spectrum of reactions, none positive. To the extent that Carmen had managed to sneak in some sambas, she was reviled by reactionaries for flaunting the "Black" side of Brazil and by everyone else for doing it so inauthentically. Pride in this Brazilian triumph was overshadowed by outrage at the cheesy American songs over vaguely Latin beats and the ludicrous plots.

On the Fox sound stages, Miranda startled directors by being so well prepared she usually only needed one take. She learned good English but was ordered to stick to her cartoon Brazinglish in public. Her relationship with Shubert constituted fiscal abuse, with the impresario claiming 50 percent of her earnings even after her career had shifted to Hollywood. Carmen spread her wealth among family and friends as well as helping out struggling musicians and composers back home. Her house in Beverly Hills was open for any passing Carioca to swim in her pool and eat her food. Vinícius de Moraes, the bard of bossa nova and lyricist of "Girl from Ipanema," practically lived there during his years as cultural attaché in LA. Onstage, she forced US audiences to deal with Brazilian racial attitudes; during a month-long run at the Roxy, she linked arms with the Nicholas Brothers (who were Black) for a "samba-boogie" finale, and when insults were shouted, shot back, "You are jealous, yes?" Miranda never took herself too seriously, even helping dress Mickey Rooney as a mock Baiana for the musical *Babes on*

Broadway. By the war's end, Fox had lost interest, but Carmen kept the money flowing through constant touring, bolstered by the amphetamine pills that were destroying her health.

༶

Mickey Rooney wasn't the only famous fake Baiana of the war years. Geraldo Pereira took aim at Carmen (and others) with his hit "Falsa baiana" about a costumed White woman dancing in a samba circle during carnival and a true (Black) Baiana showing her how it should be done. Pereira's sardonic songs provided an antidote to samba-exaltação: "Golpe errado" tells of an elegantly dressed malandro who spends days with his mulata while his dark-skinned wife cleans and cooks for a White family, then rushes home to put supper on the table for her unfaithful man.

Vargas's Estado Novo (New State) and samba-exaltação ran out of steam in tandem, with a military coup putting an end to the dictatorship in 1945. Nothing quite so dramatic happened to samba, but its status as the nation's official soundtrack bred complacency. In the mid-thirties, the role of top arranger had passed from Pixinguinha to the even more wonderfully named Radamés Gnattali; Gnattali led samba in a slicker direction, mimicking how Tommy Dorsey Whitened his sound by shifting some rhythmic responsibilities from drums to the horn section.

With the street ban on wind instruments steering carnival samba onto a separate track from the radio version, the *escolas*' annual song competitions kept the music rooted in communities and the batucadas kept it reasonably true to its rhythmic origins. But the need for sing-along melodies and committee-approved lyrics meant little remained from the satiric edge of earlier years. Every January, carnival sambas took over the airwaves, but by the post-war years they had become largely pale and formulaic.

The post-coup election matched one military man against another. The victor, Eurico Dutra, was a puritan; he shut the casinos, putting musicians out of work while depriving samba of a high-end showcase for its most sophisticated manifestations and leaving claque-dominated, downmarket, live radio shows as the music's prime engine. Dutra was very pro-Yankee, so American songs in both original versions and limp local covers flooded the country. Samba began to sound *quadrado* (square); its place atop the Brazilian music pyramid was no longer secure.

⌒

As a kid, Luiz Gonzaga would tag along when his father played the *sanfona*, a primitive accordion, for dances deep in the countryside of northeastern Brazil. In the army, he learned music theory and graduated to the modern version of the instrument; off duty, he picked up extra money playing in bars. One night in Rio, as Luiz was performing his usual mix of sambas and choros, a group of students from Pernambuco heard his accent and demanded something from home. When he reached into his childhood memory bank and pulled out one of his dad's songs, the crowd went crazy. The next day, guesting on a daytime radio show, he played the *sertanejo* tune again and it went down a storm. The *baião* boom had begun.

To non-Brazilians, all those "b" words can confuse. The *baiana* culture of Bahia (the state named after Salvador's Bay of All Saints) is Black; *baião*, the "broken" rhythm Gonzaga turned into a nationwide craze in the late 1940s, comes from the mestizo (White mixed with Indian and Black) culture of the *sertão* and its etymology lies with *baile* (dance). In the early decades of the century, both were considered simply "folklore" from "up north." Oito Batutas performed so many songs from the *sertão* that their critics dismissed them as being sertanejo almost as often as they were accused of flaunting African roots. Dorival Caymmi was dark and Bahian, but his lyrical songs, based around melodies he heard among the coast's fishermen, fit nicely into the romanticization of a generalized "North."

Gonzaga knew that to walk through the door that had just opened, he needed songs as clever as Caymmi's, to say nothing of competing with the best of samba-canção. Cometh the hour, cometh the man: Humberto Teixeira was a fellow northeasterner who had migrated to Rio in the mid-thirties and, like many songwriters, established himself by winning a carnival-song competition. Subsequent success had proved elusive, so he carried on with his studies and, by the time he met Gonzaga in 1945, Teixeira was a qualified lawyer.

Their initial collaborations were recorded by other artists; the label resisted letting the rough-voiced Luiz sing, but his first solo release, "Baião," proved a sensation that even caused ripples in North America. The music sounded rustic, like a Brazilian zydeco crossed with calypso (from just along the coast in Trinidad), but was actually a sophisticated take on the 2/4 rhythm of home, adapting its guitar strum for the accordion and basing melodies around a blues-tinged scale with flatted thirds and sevenths. (The syncopated sway of "Do You Know the Way to San Jose?" and "Save the Last Dance for Me" are, according to some, based on baião.)

Gonzaga had always admired the Northeast's legendary bandit Lampião. In the army, he had taken part in sweeps of the sertão badlands to rid them of Lampião-inspired outlaws and he remained fascinated by their *cangaceiro* culture. With its huge herds of cattle, the region's interior is not unlike America's Wild West, but sertão cowboys don't dress like the American version; sharp-thorned shrubbery forces them into head-to-toe leather topped by rawhide hats with Napoleonic front-lifted brims. There are photos of young Luiz performing in tuxedo and bow tie, but the Lampião look would become his trademark, with a touch of elegance comparable to Hank Williams's take on the American cowboy during the same period.

In sync with Americans escaping the racism-plagued South in the first half of the twentieth century, Brazilians were fleeing the drought-plagued Northeast. These demographic surges supplied the labor for manufacturing booms in both countries as well as an audience for urbanized versions of the music of home. It seems easier to imagine longing for Carolina or Mississippi (which might be quite nice places if racist rednecks magically disappeared) than for the harsh sertão. In the song that defines the era and marks the apex of their partnership, Teixeira's words combine nostalgia with the fantasy that rain will one day transform the land into a lush green paradise. "Asa branca" (White-Winged Dove) uses a fragment of melody from Gonzaga's youth as its heart-rending core; it has often been covered, notably by Caetano Veloso and David Byrne (whose accompanying video includes explanatory animation), and certainly deserves to compete with "Desafinado,"

"Mas que nada," and "Manhã de Carnaval" for the bronze medal in the battle of Brazil's best-known melodic exports.

July 13, 1950, saw the sunset flash of samba unity; it was the penultimate match of the first football World Cup since the war, and host country Brazil, was sweeping away all opposition. As 200,000 fans (yes, that many) in Maracanã Stadium watched their team demolish Spain 6–1, the crowd began chanting the percussive chorus of a famous carnival *marchinha*: "*Boom parará chim poom boom, boom parará chim poom boom.*" Everyone knew it and everyone sang it, an ecstatic communal moment never to be repeated. Three days later, the Maracanã watched in horrified silence as Uruguay beat the *Seleção* 2–1 and were crowned World Champions. The country's optimistic spirit began to ebb away.

Getúlio Vargas was flexible; if fascist dictatorships were passé, he would run in a democratic election—and win! If, when he reclaimed the presidency in 1951, Brazilians were no longer dancing as one to the samba, he was nonetheless grateful to the regionalisms that had led the resistance to what he most dreaded, the Americanization of his country. Caymmi and Gonzaga were given their own radio programs. Caymmi's show festishized Bahian music, culture, and food; Carioca ladies learned to decorate themselves with *balangandãs* (clusters of beads, rosaries, chains, and amulets) while the whole country salivated as Caymmi sang the recipe for *vatapá*, the ur-Bahian treat made from shrimp, chili, peanuts, palm oil, and coconut milk. On Gonzaga's program, listeners were invited to send in their own local traditions; Teixeira played the scholarly anthropologist, analyzing their significance while a sertanejo bumpkin ridiculed his posturings in a barely comprehensible accent and was roundly mocked in return. Gonzaga and Caymmi both toured constantly, with triumphant concerts in Rio, São Paulo, and Belo Horizonte packed with their fellow migrants from the Northeast.

You may recall Almirante (Portuguese for "Admiral," because he served briefly in the navy), the man who forced the batucada into Rio's recording studios; his hit radio show, *O Pessoal de velha guarda* (The Old Gang), launched yet another musical splinter. This one centered on choro and rescued Pixinguinha from under-employment to lead a Buena Vista–like studio band performing music from an imagined genteel past. (At the same time in the US, there was an equally popular Dixieland revival.) The program gave Almirante a bully pulpit to rail against singers imitating Bing Crosby and Frank Sinatra. He also led a campaign in support of Vargas's determination to keep US oil companies out of newly discovered offshore deposits (which was a bit ironic given the radio station's ownership by Standard Oil's local partner).

European and American dancers had been enjoying the mouth-feel of saying "rumba" and "tango" for years and had just begun having fun with "mambo." Brazilians took equal pleasure in pronouncing "boogie-woogie"; when "Boogie woogie na favela" hit the charts, one hillside shanty town changed its name to Favela Boogie Woogie. But in wealthier Rio districts and in pockets of aspiring cosmopolitanism around the country, young Brazilians were becoming obsessed with a different sort of Yankee music.

Vocal harmonies weren't a natural feature of Brazilian music, but many were drawn to its sound; Anjos do Inferno (Angels from Hell) carved out a nice career in the thirties sounding like a cross between America's Ink Spots and Germany's Comedian Harmonists. When sixth notes, flatted fifths, and augmented chords were stirred into the Yankee harmonic pot after the war, Brazil responded with Os Cariocas, modeled on America's Modernaires. Few recordings better express the conflicted relationship with the northern behemoth than their "Adeus, América," in which vehement rejection of all things Yankee is delivered in jazzy all-American harmonies. (How far Os Cariocas' tongues were into their cheeks is, from this distance, unclear.)

Another key figure in the half-in, half-out Americanizing was singer Dick Farney, who made his name with the 1946 hit "Copacabana." That recording showed how far arranger Radamés Gnattali had drifted from Dorsey and, like Pérez Prado, fallen under the spell of Stan Kenton. Farney was a Sinatra acolyte and many found his suave style a relief from the energetic delivery of most sambistas. He went off to try his luck in

Hollywood, where he passed many an afternoon by Carmen Miranda's pool, the two opposite poles of Brazilian singing chatting amiably in the California sun.

Farney didn't do too badly. He earned a regular spot on Milton Berle's TV show and got top billing at various nightclubs, but it wasn't enough; both he and his fans in Brazil had expected more. In 1948, Carmen sold him her huge Cadillac convertible and he shipped it—and himself—back to Rio. There he came across a group of cool Carioca kids in the middle-class suburb of Tijuca who had formed a Sinatra-Farney Fan Club; to them, the two crooners represented everything that was modern and un-samba. During carnival they remained defiantly indoors listening to Kenton and Modernaires records. Farney began dropping by; a half-dozen kids would pile into the Caddy and he'd regale them with tales of Hollywood as they cruised along the beaches of Guanabara Bay: Leblon, Ipanema, Copacabana . . .

> [I]ndependent prostitutes, pederasts, lesbians, marijuana dealers, cocaine addicts, and ruffians of the worst kind.
>
> —Antônio Maria, describing evenings in Rio's Copacabana neighborhood

Antônio Maria, a mid-century cronista, radio producer, lyricist, and fierce defender of all things samba, saw Copacabana as enemy territory. By the early fifties, it had welcomed an invasion of French and American stars to sing in its nightclubs, hotels, and casinos: Maurice Chevalier, Bing Crosby, Édith Piaf, Nat "King" Cole, Henri Salvador, Ella Fitzgerald . . . Away from the swankiest nightspots, a cabal of jazz-besotted Brazilian musicians began regular stints in small bars with low cover charges. The best of these were located in a narrow passage off Rua Duvivier known as "Bottles Alley" after the glassware hurled down in the wee hours by residents kept awake by loud talking, fighting, and impromptu harmonizing. On the other side of the Christ-topped mountain in Tijuca, meanwhile, the Sinatra-Farney Fan Club was flourishing; some members had become adept on musical instruments and begun exploring their own approach to the West Coast sounds they so admired. Most were now old enough to drink in Bottles Alley and a few began gigging there; two of them—Johnny Alf and João Donato—would play key roles in bossa nova history. Donato's parents, along with countless others seduced by Gonzaga and baião, had forced accordion lessons on their child. Unlike most, João did not drop the uncool instrument the minute he left home, but dug deeper into its possibilities, seizing any chance to jam with the pianists and singers of Copacabana (and keeping a photo of Stan Kenton by his bed). Johnny Alf was an SFFC exception; his widowed mother cleaned house for a Tijuca family and her employers let her son play their piano and helped enrol him at an academy with a strong music department. He was soon hired as resident pianist at the Plaza Club in Copa and would go on to become one of the few dark-skinned soldiers in the bossa nova army.

With the benefit of hindsight, two characters stand out from the early-fifties Copacabana milieu: Antônio Carlos Jobim and Vinícius de Moraes. Jobim had intended to study architecture but fell under the influence of a German émigré music scholar at the Goethe Institute, a Schoenbergian twelve-toner named Hans-Joachim Koellreutter. Jobim learned a lot from Koellreutter, but the minute he heard Villa-Lobos, the Viennese School lost him. "I could write a piece using the twelve-tone scale," Jobim remembered, "but Brazil, with all its rhythms, was more important." It was time to change mentors and he couldn't have asked for anyone less German than Radamés Gnattali. By the early fifties, Jobim was house arranger for Continental Records by day and playing piano in a Copacabana bar after dark. In his spare time, he sat at his upright and composed, watched over by a bust of Chopin.

It seems strange that these two great figures from the petri-dish era of bossa nova never met before their legendary 1955 encounter. Perhaps it was because de Moraes, poet, critic, and Brazil's "official bohemian," rarely turned up in Bottles Alley until sober family man Jobim had left for home. For Vinícius, man's best friend was distilled, not canine, particularly scotch, which he referred to as "bottled dog." His faithful elixir would sit by his side as he watched the sun rise over the Copacabana waves after the last bar had coaxed him out the door. Another reason they might not have met was because poetry and criticism didn't pay well enough to maintain a family and a harem of mistresses; just as Jobim was building a reputation as the best pianist at the beach, de Moraes rejoined the diplomatic service that had sent him to Hollywood after the war. He was offered a posting to Paris as cultural attaché and was too broke to turn it down. Life was hard.

Everything was now poised to change; if this section were a film, it would be called *Three Births and Two Funerals*. We'll start with the funerals.

The mid-twentieth century saw a number of burials in which the beloved musical figure brought forth as big an outpouring of national grief as the popular political leader, the most obvious examples being Carlos Gardel and Evita Perón, Édith Piaf and Charles de Gaulle, and Oum Kalsoum and Gamal Abdel Nasser. A case could be made for Elvis and JFK, but the King was too diminished by the end and Memphis isn't exactly Paris or Cairo (plus, a sizable percentage of Elvis fans refused to accept he was actually dead). Winston Churchill's terminal pageantry might have been matched by an outpouring of grief for John Lennon, if Yoko Ono hadn't scattered her husband's ashes without a ceremony.

Brazil's twinset of mournings began when Getúlio Vargas realized that holding the highest office in a democracy wasn't as much fun as being a dictator. Unable to force the media and military intelligence to back off in their investigations into the assassination of a rival, Vargas wrote a self-pitying letter warning against "foreign" (meaning US) interests undermining his country's independence and, on the afternoon of August 24, 1954, put a bullet through his heart. Vargas had been genuinely loved by most of his countrymen and huge throngs filed past his glass-covered coffin.

When Carmen Miranda was a schoolgirl, she was fascinated by movies and dreamed of being a film star. Early in her career, she broke up with her first love because he wanted kids and a stay-at-home wife. Over the years, she watched her sister, her girlfriends, and various ex-lovers settle down and raise families. Tortured by her self-perceived spinsterhood, she embarked on a disastrous marriage to a Hollywood hustler who took over her management and worked her like a mule. Pills kept her going, and few doctors then realized what damage they can do. On August 5, 1955, her heart gave out. She was forty-six years old.

In death, Cariocas gave her the love they had withheld since she sailed for New York. Half a million escorted her to the graveyard; Pixinghuinha and Donga began playing "Taí" beside the coffin, but were too overcome with emotion to finish. On a previous trip home, she had recorded "Disseram que voltei americanizada" (They Said I Came Back Americanized) and remained bitter to the end that her hard work had gone so unappreciated by her countrymen. Her fantasy had been to arrive at the start of carnival, dance incognito with the crowds in the streets, perhaps becoming that masked houri of legend for a day, then fly back to California on Ash Wednesday morning.

⌒

Juscelino Kubitschek was the son of a Brazilian father and a part-Roma mother from Prague. As mayor of Belo Horizonte, then governor of Minas Gerais, he built roads, schools, and hospitals. Kubitschek shared Vargas's populist instincts and concern for the lives of the poor but without the authoritarian impulse. He won the 1956 presidential election with a promise of "fifty years' development in five"; a new era of outward-looking optimism was born.

The circumstances of the birth of the songwriting duo that came to define bossa nova has entered Brazilian cultural apocrypha. During one of Vinícius de Moraes's visits home, he was reading a book about Greek mythology when a batucada drummer on the hill behind his house began practicing. A light went on in the poet's head; in Paris, he pitched producer Sacha Gordine an idea for setting a film based on the Orpheus legend in Rio during carnival. Gordine loved it, paid de Moraes a modest sum for the rights, but then couldn't raise the budget. On Vinícius's next trip back, he sold the same idea to Rio's Theatro Municipal, polishing off the script in a few weeks.

While lunching at the Villarino bar with his friend Lúcio Rangel, Vinícius mentioned that he was going that afternoon to meet someone Gnattali had recommended for the task of setting music to *Orfeu da*

Conceição (Orpheus of the Conception). Rangel spotted "Tom" Jobim at a nearby table and asked de Moraes if he knew him. No, but he'd heard him play once or twice and been impressed. Rangel called the composer over. When asked if he would be interested in setting Vinícius's play to music, Jobim's famous first response was to ask if there was any money in it. After Rangel scolded him, saying that was no way to talk to the great man, he sat down and listened to de Moraes's idea.

Their collaboration began the next day, but progress was painfully slow. De Moraes had always liked the idea of writing song lyrics, but had never actually done it. Eventually, they got rolling and crafted a fully formed piece of musical theater; *Orfeu da Conceição* opened on September 25, 1956, with a stark modernist set by Oscar Niemeyer, the architect who would shortly begin designing Kubitschek's new capital, Brasília. *Orfeu* was a huge success, but there was no established path for moving it to a commercial run the way plays transfer from London's National Theatre and New York's Public Theater to the West End or Broadway. Following a four-week season, it was never performed again, and, for reasons I will explain, you have never heard any of the songs. You may think you have, but you haven't.

The music of *Orfeu da Conceição* was samba. A step towards what came to be known as bossa nova arrived just as Vinícius was packing to fly back to Paris, when Jobim rang and asked him to stay a few more days to work on a new song. While visiting his parents in the countryside, the composer had been intrigued by the humming of a woman who cleaned their house. Her old-fashioned melodies were complex, far more interesting than the formulaic samba being played on the radio. Inspired, he drove home to his piano and Chopin and wrote the mysterious, meandering melody of "Chega de saudade" (No More Blues). Vinícius found the task difficult, but eventually managed to fit words to Jobim's complex creation, completing what would become the foundation stone of bossa nova before boarding his rebooked flight back to France.

The song lay on Jobim's desk for a year and a half; he finally found a place for it on an album he was arranging for Elizete Cardoso, a veteran singer from the heyday of samba. All the songs were by Tom and Vinícius, but it was "Chega de saudade," with its unusual melody and arresting opening, that stood out. The intro was by a guitarist who had recently reappeared in Rio after a long absence. The Copacabana crowd were puzzled; he was like a different person—and a different musician—to the one who had left Rio two years earlier. Our third "birth" is actually a rebirth, the rebirth of João Gilberto.

Musical stories in Brazil always seem to start in the Northeast, and Gilberto's is no exception. He grew up in the Bahian town of Juazeiro, where he and his teenage friends would gather round a microphone and harmonize during breaks at dances; they watched Fred Astaire movies and listened to Dorival Caymmi records, and João vowed that one day he would be a star. In Salvador, he befriended a guy just back from New York with a stack of Billy Eckstine and Sarah Vaughan records who also, unusually for a jazz buff, collected everything by Brazilian singer Orlando Silva. Gilberto didn't make much of an impression in Salvador, but a member of the Garotas da Lua harmony group heard his strong, confident voice and brought him to Rio to replace their lead singer, whom radio producers thought sang too quietly . . . (cue ironic background music). Rio was somewhat impressed, but João proved unreliable, missing rehearsals and turning up late for sessions; when the group threatened to sack him, he quit. By now he had discovered marijuana and would hang out with fellow tokers behind Bottles Alley bars, reluctant to venture inside since he was rarely invited up onstage.

Sometimes he performed at parties for food and drink and often freeloaded at "gaúcho" singer Luís Telles's flat. When a bar did hire him, he would walk off stage mid-set if the audience wouldn't stop talking. His hair was long and lank when everyone else had short back and sides. By November 1954, his life was a mess and getting worse. Telles had been impressed by Gilberto from the start and got him occasional work as a fill-in for his gaúcho group's regular guitarist, Luiz Bonfá. What João needed was a change of scenery; Telles took him south to Porto Alegre, where the gaúchos come from, paying his rent and introducing him to the local music scene.

Listeners in Porto Alegre hadn't been exposed to the cool new Copacabana sounds and they took to João right away; their effusive affection brought him back to life. After six months, Telles needed to get back to Rio and play gaúcho but dared not leave João unattended or let him slide back into his bad old ways in Rio. Gilberto's favorite sister, Telles discovered, lived in a small town in Minas Gerais called Diamantina, which was then in the news for being the candidate Kubitschek's birthplace. Big-hearted Luís paid for João to travel there; his sister was dumbfounded when he arrived out of the blue after so many years, but happily moved him into the family's small guest room.

It is rare to get such an intimate glimpse of the birth of a musical form; Ruy Castro's book *Bossa Nova* contains the following passage on what took place during the eight months João Gilberto spent sitting every day in his sister's tiled bathroom:

> He discovered that the acoustics . . . were ideal for listening to both himself and the guitar . . . If he sang more softly, without vibrato, he could speed up or slow down at will, creating his own tempo. To do this, he needed to change the way he projected, using his nose more than his mouth. His mind was like a radio whose dial was spinning apparently at random, tuning in to everything he heard and loved. The natural enunciation of Orlando Silva and Sinatra. Dick Farney's velvet tone and style of breathing. The timbre of trombonist Frank Rosolino with Kenton's orchestra . . . The colorful harmonies of the vocal ensembles—how was it possible to use one's voice to alter or complete the guitar's harmony? . . . It was possible to speed up and slow down in relation to the rhythm, as long as the beat remained constant. Johnny Alf's syncopated beat on the piano and, particularly, João Donato's on the accordion—how would that sound on the guitar? The new João Gilberto was being reborn from those experiences.

The author Alma Guillermoprieto spent six months embedded in one favela's preparations for carnival. In her book *Samba*, she describes watching a woman who appeared to be dancing to one particular percussion instrument in the batucada, then picked out a different drum in the cascade of sound and shifted the movement of her hips and feet to that one. João Gilberto altered his guitar-playing in similar fashion, selecting one instrument from the thicket of samba percussion, or perhaps just the left hand of João Donato's accordion part on "Eu quero um samba." Guitarist Baden Powell suggested, "João Gilberto did the following: he took the rhythmic figure of a [Brazilian *pandeiro*] tambourine from an *escola de samba batucada*, left out a few beats, and shifted the rhythm from one to two 2/4 measures." The twenty-first century is filled—plagued, even—with deconstructions of classic forms; I know of no other occasion when this process has been used to invent something as sublimely original as bossa nova.

One can be forgiven for assuming that João's beloved spliffs were central to this process. In fact, they weren't; one aspect of his stay in Diamantina was that grass was very hard to come by, and rather than let that upset him, he realized he felt better without it. Those months in the tiled bathroom were Gilberto's first dope-free time in years.

A cousin persuaded him to join her on a trip back to Juazeiro, but the visit proved a disaster that almost undid all the progress in Porto Alegre and Diamantina. His family and friends were completely nonplussed by this new way of playing and he became so depressed that they checked him into a psychiatric clinic in Salvador. The doctors, however, declared him sane and Gilberto fled back to Rio and his old life of couch-surfing and scrounging but minus the dope and alcohol.

One night at a party he ran into guitarist Roberto Menescal; they retreated to a back room, where João played him a few things in the new style. Menescal had never seen anyone play that way, with thumb and index finger held completely straight, picking out figures against chords plucked by the other three. He called his songwriting partner Ronaldo Bôscoli and told him to get out of bed, they were on their way over. (Bôscoli was well connected: his great-great-aunt was Chiquinha "Corta Jaca" Gonzaga, and Vinícius de Moraes was married to his sister.) João entranced the two of them until dawn with old sambas that burst into new life as he played them. He sang them just as he spoke, never prolonging syllables unnaturally; voice and guitar felt like a single entity rather than a singer and accompaniment. To Bôscoli, Gilberto's music seemed to answer questions the young generation were asking without realizing; it was unmistakably modern, but unlike the playing of the cool-jazz wannabes in Bottles Alley, completely Brazilian.

João moved onto Bôscoli's sofa, then made his host stand for ages at the far end of the flat as part of an experiment to see how quietly lyrics could be sung and still be understood. The singer hadn't forgotten those long-ago weeks in Salvador listening to Orlando Silva records; like João, Silva had a powerful voice but used it gently. Bôscoli and Menescal persuaded Jobim to grant an audition; the composer was suitably astonished and began trying to plot how to get Gilberto into the recording studio.

Playing guitar on two tracks of the Elizete Cardoso LP was a start, but Jobim had bigger plans and he found an ally in André Midani, a Franco-Syrian hipster posted to Brazil by the Paris headquarters of Odeon Records. As a youth, Midani had watched the post-war Left Bank scene evolve around Juliette Gréco and Boris Vian and felt Brazilian youth were on a similar search; the minute he heard João, he knew he'd found what he was looking for. Barring the way was Odeon's head of A&R, Aloísio de Oliveira, the boyfriend Carmen Miranda had insisted on bringing to America. As leader of Banda da Lua, he had remained at her side long after the romance was over and only returned to Rio after Miranda's death. He couldn't get his head around what Gilberto was up to, but when they told him João had no need for the usual orchestral backing (and after Dorival Caymmi added his endorsement) he surrendered to Jobim's and Midani's enthusiasm and agreed to fund a low-budget single. The song they chose was "Chega de saudade."

> Third-world countries usually produce raw materials that are then transformed into capital by first-world nations. This happens in industry, but it also happens in the arts. What was revolutionary about bossa nova is that a third-world country was creating high art on its own terms, and selling that art around the world. It remains a dream of what an ideal civilization can create.
>
> —Caetano Veloso

> No, I haven't got a good voice. What I've got is *bossa*!
>
> —Carmen Miranda on American radio, when asked if she'd had voice lessons

The session wasn't easy. First, João made the unheard-of demand for two microphones, one for voice, one for guitar. Then he tried to fire both drummers, eventually allowing one to tap along quietly (thereby establishing the template for bossa nova percussion). Even more shocking, he would stop in mid-take when he heard a wrong note, which was often, as the seasoned professionals struggled with what they called Gilberto's "*violão gago*" (stammering guitar). Halting a track was supposed to be the producer's job, not the singer's, and certainly not some unknown making his first record.

The timing of the release in July 1958 could hardly have been worse; Brazil had just won its first World Cup and the charts were filled with celebratory sambas. But then something stirred in the radio waves from São Paulo, prompting João to pay the city a visit, make some TV appearances and shake hands with buyers and DJs. (He could be extremely charming when he set his mind to it.) Slowly at first, then faster and faster, the record began to sell, not just in São Paulo, but in Rio, Salvador, Minas, and Recife. Midani was right; the youth of Brazil, or at least its educated, middle-class subsection, started going crazy for João Gilberto.

The guitar had never been a prominent Brazilian instrument; samba was generally strummed on the four-stringed cavaquinha, and from the mid-nineteenth century pianos had been the instruments of choice in respectable Brazilian homes. But now everyone was trying to play violão gago and finding it impossible. Some of João's jam sessions at the Plaza Club (he was now welcomed with open arms on Copacabana stages) were recorded and copies made the rounds as Rio guitarists started, stopped, and rewound their reel-to-reel machines trying to figure out what the hell he was doing. The struggle went on for months, then suddenly it was over; all at once, everyone got the hang of it and Gilberto's way of playing the guitar became a fundamental part of Brazil's musical landscape. Roberto Menescal and Carlos Lyra had started a guitar school largely as a way to seduce parent-defying girls who refused to learn the accordion; suddenly, the two found themselves engaged in the serious business of teaching bossa nova guitar. The accordion went into a near-total eclipse. The name arrived with a concert organized by the University Hebrew Group of Brazil, advertised as a *"bossa nova evening"* featuring vocalists backed by "a bossa nova group." No individual has been identified as the term's originator; perhaps it was just obvious that the music represented a "new wave" or a "new shtick," the latest iteration of whatever "it" was that Carmen Miranda knew she had.

∽

> ["Chega de saudade"] sounded like a message from an undiscovered country.
> —Julian Dibbell, US critic

> How fabulous, Brazilian music with no tambourines . . .
> —Telmo Martino, Brazilian journalist

> Bossa nova is serene, it has love and romance, but it is restless.
> —Tom Jobim in the album notes to the *Chega de saudade* LP

> [Bossa nova lyrics] must never speak about death, blood, or daggers.
> —João Gilberto

> He was like Oscar Niemeyer . . . whose architecture escapes symmetry without abandoning beauty.
> —Artur da Távola, journalist

Chegar is a versatile Portuguese verb that literally means "to arrive"; in certain contexts, the imperative form comes close to the Anglo-Yiddish "enough, already!" While de Moraes's impassioned lyric for "Chega de saudade" demands the return of a loved one, Caetano Veloso has suggested that the title can also be seen as drawing a line under the Portuguese legacy of mournful songs and attitudes often summarized as *saudade*. As Gilberto himself observed, his music is never about *tristeza*, only sorrow's diminutive, *tristezinha*.

Optimism swept the country; Kubitschek's electoral victory was followed by the World Cup triumph, Maria Bueno's two Wimbledon titles, the opening of a huge Volkswagen plant, and now this brilliant creation flowing into the ears of an entranced public. Jobim couldn't wait to get started on Gilberto's LP. The composer was himself too "restless" to wait for Vinícius's next visit, so he turned to his childhood friend, the mysterious, nerdy Newton Mendonça; their collaborations are wonders of quirky, colloquial songwriting. "Desafinado" was triggered by the tedium of accompanying out-of-tune amateurs taking their turns on Bottles Alley stages, as well as by critics who claimed the new music was dissonant; they turned it into an eloquent plea about a lover's difficulty in being "attuned" to the object of desire. "It's mine!" shouted Gilberto as soon as he heard it, and the song became his second huge hit. Mendonça and Jobim's similarly clever use of musical structure as a metaphor for love's pitfalls, "Samba de uma nota só" (One-Note Samba), would have to wait for João's second LP. The remainder of the first album was made up of Jobim–de Moraes and Bôscoli-Menescal compositions, plus a favorite Caymmi ballad and some slowed-down sambas.

By the time they returned again to the studio, Gilberto was a certified star and bossa nova was everywhere. This being Brazil, its success was exhaustively parsed, debated, celebrated, and mocked. Did it represent surrender to America? Or was it the country's glorious riposte to creeping Americanization? Was it "authentic"? Or "fake"? The issue that lurked at the fringes of the discussion concerned the music's racial identity. The fact that the success of "Chega" began in São Paulo, a city that viewed itself as an oasis of Whiteness, could be taken as a sign. A cursory overview might conclude that White, middle-class Brazilians, fatigued by three decades of embracing the notion of a race-blind national samba, craved something of their own, that Gilberto's aversion to drums was emblematic of Whites' desire to distance themselves from Blackness. Consciously or unconsciously, they wanted to make the leap Veloso described, to create an international high art that transfigured Brazilian traditions as thoroughly and elegantly as Bartók transformed Carpathian village music. Or, more to the point, as thoroughly as Stan Kenton transformed Duke Ellington and Machito following a map drawn by Debussy. As Jobim put it, "We're not going to 'sell' the aspect of the exotic, of coffee, of Carnival anymore . . . We're going to move from 'agriculture' to 'industry.'" Critic Augusto de Campos weighed in, complaining that purists would have Brazil export "macumba for tourists . . . It's necessary to put an end to this defeatist mentality which holds that an underdeveloped country can only produce underdeveloped art."

Ever the contrarian, Gilberto denied that he even *played* "bossa nova"; for him, it was all samba. Perhaps his reverence for older singers and composers said more about the fallen state of fifties samba, with its cheesy radio shows and hearty marchinhas, than it did about any notion that he was leading a middle-class exodus from Afro-Brazilian music. That being said, the jazz that opened the Copacabana door through which bossa nova entered was extremely White. Ever since the twenties, America's national music had been represented in Brazil mostly by the likes of Paul Whiteman, Benny Goodman, Tommy Dorsey, Glenn Miller, and, yes, Stan Kenton, with the occasional flash of a Nat "King" Cole or an Ella Fitzgerald. The jump jive and rhythm and blues animating the "lawns" of post-war Jamaica went mostly unheard in Brazil, nor did Charlie Parker's bebop revolution resonate much below the equator; post-war American jazz culture had a huge effect across the globe, but in Brazil it was embraced mostly in the Whitest of its manifestations.

Perhaps Brazil was simply ahead of the curve. The dominant musical trend of the sixties would be the capture of the high ground of popular music by children of the bourgeoisie. Across the globe, popular music careers had been seen as a route out of ghetto poverty, like becoming a professional athlete or a gangster. Dylan and The Beatles changed all that by engineering a confluence of self-expression with the rhythms and forms of commercial popular music. Gilberto, Jobim, and de Moraes may have simply gotten there first.

At the end of the fifties, meanwhile, a tidal wave of brilliant African-American jazz was pouring forth from Miles Davis, John Coltrane, Art Blakey, Thelonious Monk, et al., threatening to put White American jazz musicians irrevocably in the shade. For many of them, bossa nova would prove a godsend.

> [Bossa nova turned] classic samba into an almost Mondrianesque construction of clean, angular melodic lines and daringly off-kilter rhythms—the most self-assured bid for modernity Brazil's culture had ever produced. ·
>
> —Julian Dibbell

> We were looking for new ways to play the samba—because we couldn't play the samba!
>
> —Roberto Menescal, guitarist and composer

> I'd really like to know what it felt like being rich.
>
> —Tom Jobim, responding to a reporter's question about what it felt like to be famous

President Kubitschek triggered America's paranoia. Well, he was a socialist, wasn't he? Isn't that almost like being a commie? As the CIA began plotting against the new Brazilian administration, less sinister arms of the US government took a leaf from the old anti-fascist playbook and started sponsoring tours by American musicians. Three of them—Herbie Mann, Paul Winter, and Charlie Byrd—would fly back to the US in the early 1960s bearing the seeds of bossa nova's fleeting capture of the US imagination.

Both Winter and Mann went on to record successful bossa nova albums, but it was Byrd who dropped the first and biggest boulder in the pond. Running into Stan Getz one evening at Washington DC's Showboat Lounge, the guitarist invited him over and they stayed up all night listening to the albums Byrd had brought back from Rio. Getz was fascinated and, a few months later, they began recording. It took some trial and error to get the right combination of musicians; American jazzers relate easily to bossa nova's sophisticated harmonies, but the subtleties of the 2/4 samba feel tend to elude them and most end up playing bossa nova in mildly syncopated 4/4 time. Creed Taylor, then head of A&R at Verve Records, seems to have found the words *bossa* and *nova* too foreign-sounding, so the record was titled *Jazz Samba*.

Maybe Taylor knew what he was doing; the album spent seventy weeks on the *Billboard* charts, sold more than a million copies, and won Getz a Grammy for his playing on "Desafinado."

To grasp the evolution of Brazilian music's relations with the outside world, a minimal understanding of music publishing is required. Copyright 101: a singer recording a Dylan song earns "artist" royalties for his record sales, but nothing when the track is played on the radio. Dylan and his publisher get a separate, parallel royalty for the other artist's record sales, plus further payment for radio, jukebox, shop, and restaurant plays as well as stage performances. Recoupable production and marketing costs and variable percentages can inhibit the flow of royalties to an artist but publishing royalties are set by law and channeled in relatively undiluted form to whoever controls those rights. When I was a young record producer attending my first MIDEM convention in Cannes in 1968, an industry veteran placed an avuncular arm across my shoulders as we strolled along the Croisette. Gesturing towards the boats moored in the harbor, he said: "You see those yachts, kid? They all belong to music publishers. Don't ever forget that." (I confess, dear reader, that at key moments in my career it slipped my mind.)

Wallace Downey needed no schooling in the value of copyrights. While making those Brazilian music films in the 1930s, he also represented the giant New York publisher Robbins Music, and forced composers to sign with them as a condition of including their songs in his films; Ary Barroso's refusal started the chain reaction that brought Carmen Miranda to America. A few weeks into the Broadway run of Shubert's revue, Robbins Music realized they owned "O que é que a baiana tem?" as well as another of Carmen's showstoppers, and lodged a claim for fees and royalties. Shubert was apoplectic and threatened to cut the songs from the show. Eventually, the parties settled; Robbins, Shubert, and the lawyers all banked large sums but precious little made its way down the chain to Dorival Caymmi and Almirante. (Ary Barroso, on the other hand, never complained about Ralph Peer's company, Peer Southern Music, and the great job they did with "Brazil.")

In 1958, when Sacha Gordine finally raised the money to turn *Orfeu* into a film, everyone was delighted, particularly Vinícius de Moraes. But there was a catch involving publishing rights: Jobim had assigned the songs from the stage production to his Brazilian publisher, who insisted on getting paid if they were used in a film. Gordine went bananas and demanded that the pair write a new score to which he would own all the rights. So, as previously noted, readers who saw *Black Orpheus* (*Orfeu Negro*) heard a completely different score from the stage original, this one composed over the telephone between Jobim in Rio and de Moraes at his new diplomatic posting in Uruguay. The director, Marcel Camus, then complained that he needed more songs, but Jobim was tired of the whole thing and busy elsewhere, so former gaúcho Luiz Bonfá, who had been hired to pre-record the guitar part that makes the sun come up, was asked to create something. Bonfá was also preoccupied but found a couple of melodies written years earlier gathering dust in a drawer and played them to Camus and Gordine. Camus hated them, but Gordine loved them and it was his money, so he asked journalist Rubem Braga to write some lyrics. These afterthoughts became "Manhã de Carnaval" and "Samba de Orfeu," the two most famous songs from the film, ubiquitous over the years and steady sources of income for Gordine—with perhaps a bit left over for Bonfá and Braga.

De Moraes was so horrified by Camus's finished film that he stormed out in the middle of a screening. Brazilian critics and, to a lesser extent, audiences were also uncomfortable with its outsider's eye, but the movie won the Palme d'or at Cannes and the foreign-film Oscar in the US, where it was an art-house smash, softening up American ears for the bossa nova surge that was about to arrive.

Sidney Frey felt it coming. He had fallen in love with Rio when his US Navy ship docked there during the war and kept coming back to hang out in Copacabana bars. Frey had built a business around the new concept of stereo sound; his Audio Fidelity label never had the budget or the clout to sign big-selling artists, but he understood the value of a copyright and hatched a plan to grab a share of the imminent bossa boom. With backing from the Brazilian consulate in New York, he booked Carnegie Hall for the evening of November 21, 1962, then flew to Rio to assemble an all-star cast. The Copacabana crowd were all up for it, at least until they read the fine print about signing with Frey's publishing company. (Jobim and Gilberto were invited regardless.) The issue was endlessly debated in Bottles Alley; wise heads called it a rip-off and warned that with so many singers and players invited, the concert was bound to be a shambles. No one could disagree, but the magic words *New York* and *Carnegie Hall* proved irresistible.

The doom-mongers were both right and wrong. The concert was indeed shambolic; singers and musicians were shuttled on and off a stage cluttered with a rainforest of microphones for Frey's live recording, the Voice of America, Brazilian radio, and other outlets. The last thing the producers thought about was the Carnegie Hall audience (which included Tony Bennett, Peggy Lee, Miles Davis, Gerry Mulligan, Dizzy Gillespie, and Herbie Mann), for whom the sound mix was a muffled jumble. The notion that the concert had been a disaster appealed to many back in Brazil, for both anti-American and pro-samba reasons, plus the general begrudgement of success that afflicts all but the most self-confident of cultures. A lurid newspaper article the next morning (based on hearsay) triggered an avalanche of negative publicity. A few nights later, the gleeful mockery froze on journalistic faces when highlights were shown on Brazilian TV and the stylish crowd could be seen clapping and cheering and bringing Jobim, Gilberto, and Bonfá back for ecstatic bows.

Those three plus Sérgio Mendes all launched successful North American careers at the after-party, where agents and A&R men huddled in corners with performers, enunciating proposals slowly and precisely so the Brazilians could understand. Jobim landed an arranging job with his US publishers Leeds Music, Sérgio Mendes secured the first engagement of his long international career, and Gilberto decided the offer of a three-week booking at New York's Blue Angel nightclub justified tearing up his return ticket. (He would not live in Brazil again for eighteen years.) At some point during those hectic post-concert weeks, João had agreed to make a record with Stan Getz for Creed Taylor at Verve, so when the Blue Angel engagement was over, he and his young wife, Astrud, decamped to suburban Connecticut to stay with Getz and his Swedish wife, Monica, and plan the recording.

> Her marvellous passing would leave us speechless over our beers . . . moving with a swaying, gentle, geometric rhythm that was almost samba but whose precise formula would have eluded even Einstein . . . It would take an Antônio Carlos Jobim to ask the piano, with great and intimate reverence, to reveal its secret.
>
> —Vinícius de Moraes on "The Girl from Ipanema"

In early 1962, having finally reconciled themselves to the success of the film version of *Orfeu*, Jobim and de Moraes thought perhaps they ought to compose another musical. They began meeting at a café near the beach in Ipanema to trade ideas and soon became aware of the daily (and soon to be immortal) stroll past their table of a girl named Heloísa Eneida de Menezes Paes Pinto ("Helô" for short). During their legendary seven-week residence at a club that winter (summer in the north, don't forget), a live recording reveals Jobim, de Moraes, and Gilberto chatting onstage about love and music, expressing the view that a romantic sentiment can be best brought to life if it is sung by João with poetry from Vinícius and set to Tom's music. João finishes off the routine by concluding, "it would be better if all three of us sang," and together they give the audience its first taste of the immortal opening lines of "Garota de Ipanema."

They headed off to New York that November with what would become the world's most oft-covered song still unrecorded. Jobim was painfully aware of the pitfalls of English-language versions and insisted on working with Leeds Music's New York office to choose a lyricist for this weighty task. One can make a case that Norman Gimbel (who would go on to write words for many great songs, including "Killing Me Softly") didn't do too badly; his words aren't nearly as corny as Ray Gilbert's efforts on previous Jobim compositions (nor did he claim the lion's share as Gilbert often did). But the Brazilian critic-composer Arthur Nestrovski felt that "[the] poetry was all but destroyed in the English lyric . . . If you sing *'Tall and tan and young and lovely*,' everything is on the beat, like a military march. Vinícius's Portuguese lyric *'Olha que coisa mais linda / Mais cheia de graça* . . . ' scans very differently. It's languid, swinging, irregular. The rhythm is displaced. It has an extraordinary mobility which mimics the movement of the girl passing by." Nestrovski isn't wrong, but in the recording that made the song famous, the simplistic pulse probably helped it reach American ears. Plus, of course, the breathy, amateur, foreign-accented young girl's voice and the yearning tones of the sax; those didn't hurt, either.

In October 1966, almost four years after that Connecticut confluence of Getzes and Gilbertos, I was working as a tour manager for the Newport Jazz Festival in Europe; Stan Getz and Astrud Gilberto were among the headliners, performing together after a gap of two years. Late one night in the bar of our Barcelona hotel, I found myself having a drink with Monica Getz. The tension between her and Astrud was palpable, with catty comments passing back and forth about each other's wardrobe and dress sense. I was blissfully unaware of the history so Monica filled me in.

As the only one who spoke both English and Portuguese, Astrud had been indispensable during rehearsals. Monica told me it had been her idea to have Astrud perform the English-language demo for "Girl from Ipanema," since she could at least carry a tune and pronounce Gimbel's words correctly in a sweet Brazilian accent. That demo inspired the idea for Astrud to sing the English lyric on the actual recording after João had sung the original verses in Portuguese. For the single, Monica claimed it was again she who convinced Creed Taylor to get out his razor blade and leave Astrud's as the only voice on the track.

Something about the album, be it Astrud's tentative pitch or the un-jazzy Brazilianness of the music, made Taylor hesitate; he sat on it for a full year, until the spring of 1964. The single then proceeded to hit the *Billboard* Top Five, sell two million copies, and drive the *Getz/Gilberto* LP to the summit of album charts around the world. Some have cited it as a kind of post-assassination elegy for the Kennedy years.

Concert offers came pouring in, but that year of waiting had complicated matters. In a Rome café, Gilberto had fallen for "Miúcha" Buarque de Holanda, daughter of the famous Brazilian intellectual Sérgio Buarque de Holanda and sister of Chico Buarque (who would be one of Brazil's greatest post-bossa-nova singers and composers). There was now no question of Astrud and João touring together, but—*surprise!*—American promoters cared little for João's transformative genius, they just wanted Astrud's girlish tones singing in seductively accented English backed by Getz's languid sax.

Monica, who was, in effect, her husband's manager, was an enthusiastic supporter of this package, since the money was far better than what Stan was making on the jazz-club circuit. So, after gauging audience response to the first two shows, she returned to Connecticut to look after their children. Under the Law of Unintended (But Predictable) Consequences, no sooner had she departed than Stan and Astrud began sharing hotel rooms; Monica got wind of it and put a block on future dates. The 1966 European reunion was strictly about money; on their own, neither could command the fees they earned in tandem, hence Monica's combative, eagle-eyed presence, while Astrud arrived on the arm of a muscular Brazilian a head taller than Getz.

Jobim had always hated the English versions of his compositions, but when Frank Sinatra rang him out of the blue one afternoon and asked if he'd like to make an album together, literary misgivings were put aside. The collaboration was a huge success, reaching the Top Twenty on the LP charts and gaining a Grammy nomination (before losing out to The Beatles and *Sgt. Pepper*). "The last time I sang so softly was when I had laryngitis," cracked Frank. By then, the high notes of bossa nova's arrival on American shores—the Carnegie Hall concert, Jackie Kennedy's gala evening at the White House, "Ipanema" and other big and nearly-big bossa nova releases by the likes of Wes Montgomery, Gerry Mulligan, and Oscar Peterson—had, like virtually every other strand of popular music (with the possible exception of soul), been eclipsed by the British Invasion and the rock revolution. This musical uprising overturned many pieties, including the time-honored tradition of translating the lyrical poetry of one culture into the simplistic pop of another.

A pair of massive sixties hits proved to be the last gasp of this old Tin Pan Alley ideal. While sunning himself on an Italian beach, Paul Anka heard "Comme d'habitude" by Claude François on a nearby transistor, brushed off the sand, flew to Paris, bought the melody, stayed up all one night at his typewriter, rang Sinatra the next morning, and sang him "My Way" over the phone. Dusty Springfield heard "Io che non vivo" at an Italian song festival, secured anglophone rights, and recorded a powerful backing track without having any lyrics to sing over it. Her manager, Vicki Wickham, and their friend Simon Napier-Bell wrote "You Don't Have to Say You Love Me" in the back of a late-night taxi between Chelsea and Mayfair, and Dusty recorded it the next day.

So much for taking special care with translations; over the coming decades, Brazil's music would continue to have a huge international impact, but almost exclusively via the sophistication of its melodies, rhythms, and instrumentalists, and the brilliance of its untranslated singers and composers. Amid this new vogue for authenticity, Sérgio Mendes proved himself to be the canniest of all those ten-minute-set wonders from the Carnegie Hall concert by producing a hit record and building a career with "Mas que nada," which emphasized a funky take on samba and the sexy charm of Brazilian Portuguese. "Girl from Ipanema" marked an end, not a beginning; appreciation of bossa nova's often brilliant and subtle poetry would remain a secret handshake among lusophones.

༄

> I'm part of the bourgeoisie. I don't create popular culture, I create bourgeois culture.
>
> —Carlos Lyra

> I'm the bravest woman I know . . . [Y]ou can call me *Nara Coração de Leão* [Nara the Lion-Hearted].
>
> —Nara Leão

> After João opened up the gates . . . anyone can sing, sing with a tiny voice, no voice at all . . . be a Nara Leão, be a Chet Baker!
>
> —João Donato

Astrud Gilberto had a long career north of the equator, but Brazilians were never much interested. From the start of the bossa nova era, the role of token female star was occupied by Sylvia Telles, an early girlfriend of João. Telles was a big-voiced singer who tried, never entirely successfully, to sing quietly. By 1960, she had become romantically involved with her producer, Carmen Miranda's ubiquitous ex, Aloísio de Oliveira, who had changed his mind and become bossa nova's greatest champion. He took Sylvia to Los Angeles to make a Julie London–style record backed by every Copacabana jazzman's hero, guitarist Barney Kessel. If one wanted to make a case against exporting melodies while leaving their natural rhythm behind, this could be Exhibit A: great songs, pitch-perfect singing, elegant but pointless backing. The record also supports the view that without Gilberto's hyper-Brazilian, anti-jazz rebellion, Bottles Alley's musical legacy would in all likelihood have remained local and inconsequential.

One of bossa nova's many ironies is that most audiences—even Brazilian ones—didn't distinguish between João Gilberto's artfully understated vocals and the gentle artlessness of amateurs. The female vocalist who ended up having the biggest effect on bossa nova and who played a key role in shaping the future of Brazilian music had none of Sylvia Telles's vocal chops. Nara Leão may have seemed a bit like Astrud at first, another girlfriend tagging along with the boys, but she would prove herself to be far more than that. Nara first appeared on the scene when her family's spacious flat overlooking Copacabana Beach became a musical hangout. Roberto Menescal recalls, "Nara whipped our butts. At eleven, she taught me about jazz and we started to play guitar because of the things she showed me." Her bohemian parents nodded their approval when, at fifteen, she became Ronaldo Bôscoli's girlfriend, then his fiancée. It seems possible that Nara's anti-bossa-nova campaign was triggered by torch singer Maysa's dramatic announcement that Ronaldo was going to marry *her*, not Nara. Furious Nara certainly was, but whatever her initial motives, she became an astonishingly effective battering ram against bossa nova's pretensions. Then, as an after-thought, she opened the door to Brazil's next culture-shaking movement.

After years singing at late-night gatherings in her parents' flat, Leão turned professional in a revue created by Vinícius de Moraes called *Poor Little Rich Girl*. In overcoming her stage fright, she found she could shut up a noisy audience by singing even more quietly; João would have been proud. Her new boyfriend was a left-wing film-maker who schooled her in injustice and inequality and mocked bossa nova's elitism. When it came time to make her first album, she found an ally in her former guitar teacher, Carlos Lyra, who had grown weary of songs about "love, sea, flower." They invited *samba de morro* songwriters to collaborate, which the bossa nova boys saw as a betrayal. Not, of course, because their sweet little muse had chosen to work with Black men instead of with them; no, it was that she was collaborating with old-fashioned representatives of everything bossa nova was against. Or so they said.

To celebrate the loss of her amateur status, Nara signed on for a tour of Japan and France with Sérgio Mendes, sponsored by a Brazilian fashion house that thought she looked good in their clothes. It meant singing "Girl from Ipanema" every night, but at least she was earning her own money and seeing the world. The tour lasted four months; by the time they got back, Brazil had become a different country. A one-term limit on the presidency meant that the disorder of democracy resurfaced every five years. The sort of leader military men felt comfortable with (i.e., Dutra and Jânio Quadros, Kubitschek's short-lived successor) had proved completely incompetent; their failures paved the way for first Kubitschek and now João Goulart, liberals of the sort that authoritarian minds abhorred. This new president was the most alarming of all, shaking hands with Fidel Castro, supporting a campaign to unionize the lower ranks of the navy, and lifting a ban on the Brazilian Communist Party. The generals' eyes narrowed, their jaws set, and they started asking the CIA for advice about how best to rid the country of this dangerous leftist. On March 31, 1964, tanks appeared on the streets of the major cities and Goulart was shown the door.

Prison and torture were reserved, initially, for peasant activists in the Northeast and a few radical students; musicians, journalists, film-makers, authors, and painters carried on as if freedom of expression was somehow eternal. Nara's second album, *Opinião de Nara*, was full of protest songs and old samba-canções, topped off with a couple of the Afro-sambas Vinícius de Moraes had composed with guitarist Baden Powell. Vinícius claimed to be "the blackest white man in Brazil" and a "son of Xangô"; when he locked himself and Powell away for three months with a dozen cases of whiskey for sustenance and emerged with a song cycle based on the African gods of Salvador, it represented yet another blow against bossa nova's "love, sea, flower" ethos.

Opinião hit a nerve and sold well; reporters discovered that Leão could be counted on to deliver fluent quotes on everything from the Pope and the pill to the new Pierre Cardin collection or the coup in the Dominican Republic. Most of all, she enjoyed attacking bossa nova: "I want nothing, and I mean *nothing*, to do with a musical genre that . . . isn't even genuine . . . I don't want to spend the rest of my life singing 'The Girl from Ipanema,' much less in English. I want . . . to be a singer of the people." Bôscoli sounded hurt: "[S]he is denying a part of herself and is being ungrateful to those who helped to promote her career." If bossa nova lyrics had been about anything, it was a love of women; now their sweetheart-mascot had turned against them. Menescal acted nonchalant: "We'll all go on singing in apartments, making a little bossa nova to sell."

Nara quickly upped the ante, turning *Opinião* into a stage revue featuring the Afro-Brazilian protest singer Zé Keti and João do Vale, a sertanejo who sang of harsh peasant lives in the Northeast. Leão became the first female singer to perform sitting on a stool holding a guitar. Nearly half a million tickets to *Opinião* were sold between December 1964 and the following August, far bigger numbers than anything bossa nova could boast. The military threatened to shut it down and arrest her but never did. Leão's articulate tirades from the *Opinião* stage put the final stake through the heart of already-fading bossa nova. A live recording demonstrates the irony that her instrumental backing was actually very bossa nova; once guitarists had absorbed violão gago, it was hard to go back.

Having made her point, Nara grew tired of performing every night and looked for a replacement. A year earlier, the fashion house sponsoring the Sérgio Mendes tour had flown her to Salvador for a photo shoot in the city's picturesque backstreets. The indefatigable Leão had set about exploring this cradle of Brazilian music and quickly determined that the hippest local scene was at the Teatro Vila Velha, where a group of young singers and songwriters had mounted a show called *Nós, Por Exemplo* (Us, for Example). On February 13, 1965, a member of the Vila Velha troupe replaced Nara on the *Opinião* stage in Rio. The singer in question had been hesitant to embark on such an adventure, but agreed on condition that her older brother, also a member of the group (and who insisted he was a visual artist, not a musician), came along for moral support. His name was Caetano Veloso, hers was Maria Bethânia; their journey south marked the start of what was to become "Tropicália," the movement that would reset the compass for Brazilian music across the rest of the twentieth century.

> [I] thought he was a very interesting guy—very simple, very humble. Very thin!
>
> —Gilberto Gil on first meeting Caetano Veloso

> [W]e were being faithful to bossa nova in doing something that was its opposite.
>
> —Caetano Veloso on Tropicália

When Gilberto Gil was four years old, he heard Luiz Gonzaga on the radio singing "Baião" and announced, "I am going to do that when I grow up." Gil duly learned the accordion, but switched to guitar after hearing "Chega de saudade."

Not too far away, in another provincial Bahian town, Caetano Veloso's teenage friends were excited by rock 'n' roll; he thought Elvis looked like "a cross-dressed Katy Jurado" and was more interested in "Chega." For Veloso, bossa nova opened a door, but more to samba's roots than to modernity, hearing "the big *surdo* drum of the street samba, beating with a relaxed bounce" in João Gilberto's guitar. When the Velosos moved to Salvador in the early sixties, Caetano and Maria met a girl in their new high school with a wonderful voice named Gal

Costa. Then, one day in the street, a mutual friend introduced Veloso to Gil. Gilberto would later say that he felt he had found in Caetano "a true companion." These four would create *Nós, por exemplo*.

Maria Bethânia's youthful playlist had been more Édith Piaf than bossa nova and she was never a quiet singer. That suited Nara, who had always wished she could sing louder. Another reason she chose Maria was her look: dark olive skin, moorish features, and a huge mane of curly black hair. Whatever the logic, the choice was astute; her replacement took on "Carcará," João de Vale's angry anthem about the brutality of life in the sertão, and turned it first into a showstopper, then a hit single.

Like bossa nova, Tropicália had to travel inland to get rolling. Bethânia was invited to São Paulo for a TV show called *Tonight We Improvise* and brought her brother along. The show's producer heard Caetano teaching his sister a song during rehearsals and insisted that he appear as well. Deftly inventing verses based on suggestions from the audience, Veloso stole the show. Gil, meanwhile, not imagining he could support his young family by playing music, took a civil service job in São Paulo. Caetano decided to stay.

> A crisis of insecurity . . . [has] taken hold of Brazilian popular music, threatening to interrupt the march of its evolution . . . revealing itself in fear and resentment at the musical phenomenon of The Beatles.
>
> —Augusto de Campos

A diagram of the conflicts in mid-sixties Brazilian music might resemble the map of a Middle Eastern war. Nara and the generals had driven a wedge between the "love, sea, flower" and politically engaged factions in bossa nova, while the sambistas still resented both. All three felt threatened by rock 'n' roll, which, having blunted bossa nova's invasion of North America, was now threatening to capture young Brazilian ears as well. Galvanized by the coup, the Left rallied behind protest songs and against American culture, with particular hostility towards the electric guitar. Pop fans were divided between those defending the nation's music and those embracing the latest imports, while regional sounds from the Northeast were deemed uncool and old-fashioned. The military were theoretically pro-USA; they encouraged a surge of airplay for American records but became alarmed by the subversive turn taken by much of the new Yankee music. Nor could they decide whether to be pleased or unnerved by street demonstrations defending Brazilian music against foreign infection. Everyone (save his massive following) hated Roberto Carlos and his "samba-rock" compromise.

Disputes that might once have been argued in Rio bars or in the editorial pages of newspapers and magazines were now being watched by millions as studio audiences roared approval or hooted condemnation. Ratings for the music programming pioneered by São Paulo–based TV Record went through the roof; broadcasts of their song competitions left Brazilian streets as deserted as for a World Cup final.

One of the first weekly shows was *O Fino da bossa* (The Crest of the Wave), hosted by the young singing sensation Elis Regina. Among her early hits was a Gilberto Gil composition, so first Gil, then Veloso made regular appearances. Roberto Carlos's *Jovem guarda* show may have represented the enemy camp, but Gil and Veloso were cuckoos in *O Fino*'s nest, instinctively drawn to Carlos's transgressions. When Caetano won a prize for best lyrics at a 1966 televised competition, the image of him with his shaggy mop, wearing a borrowed suit and sitting cross-legged in an aisle awaiting his turn, "went viral," to borrow a phrase from the future. When Veloso got fed up with the pressures of fame and announced he was quitting music to pursue his original career as a visual artist, Gil forbade him: "If you leave, I'll leave, too." Caetano realized he would never find a wider, more open canvas than writing and singing songs, but craved an overarching project, something to reconcile the fragmented factions of Brazilian music. In April 1967, he visited a gallery showing an installation by Hélio Oiticica; Veloso enjoyed the exhibition, but, most of all, he loved Oiticica's title: *Tropicália*.

São Paulo is the samba's graveyard.

—Vinicius de Moraes

É que aprendemos com João / Pra sempre ser desafinado
(We learned from João / Forever to be out of tune)

—Caetano Veloso, "Saudosismo"

São Paulo prides itself on being unlike the rest of Brazil. Built on the riches of coffee-growing, it long resisted the government's centrifugal impulses. The region attracted more European and Japanese immigrants than it did ex-slaves and tended to view the music of Rio and the Northeast as something exotic, almost like world music. Elderly sambistas found a bigger nostalgia market with Paulistas than among Cariocas. It was also home to an avant-garde scene that loved concrete poetry and conceptual art. São Paulo was the sort of city where a songwriter could be eating his lunch and someone he'd never met would shout from across the restaurant that his songs were too wordy and he ought to read Ezra Pound. (Veloso took this advice and credits the encounter with making his lyrics more compact.)

The near-empty downtown flat where Veloso lived with his new wife, Dedé, became a hub of social activity; the most prominent piece of furniture was the constantly spinning record player that played Mahalia Jackson, James Brown, The Beatles, Frank Zappa, John Lee Hooker, João Gilberto (of course), Ray Charles, Pink Floyd, and The Doors, plus a new Brazilian LP by Jorge Ben. They were drawn to French culture as an alternative to American modernism, fascinated by the films of Godard and those of his local acolyte, Glauber Rocha. In 1967, all four of the Vila Velha gang (Gal Costa having by now also moved south) released albums. Caetano and Gal's shared debut, *Domingo*, was an exercise in bossa nova and samba nostalgia, though Veloso's album notes proclaimed a very different future. Gil's was inspired by a trip to Recife, where he spent days at the beach listening to guitars and flutes and nights engrossed in "Strawberry Fields Forever," a track he heard combining memory and tradition with a lurch into uncharted territory. LSD was scarce in Brazil; Gilberto and Caetano settled for drinking the Amazonian hallucinogen ayahuasca.

As much as the two adored João Gilberto and shared his aversion to jazz, they were not opposed to some orchestral backing. Clips from the era's TV shows usually feature a studio orchestra sawing away on violins and blowing trumpets behind the acoustic guitars and percussion. In his memoir *Tropical Truth*, Caetano admits, "We were influenced by the Beatles, but the Beatles after 'Eleanor Rigby,' when they became sophisticated." The Bahians were determined to find their George Martin, and they did; leading the pit band in a São Paulo theater was Rogério Duprat, fresh from studying in Europe with Boulez and Stockhausen. Duprat introduced them to a group of precocious Paulista kids called Os Mutantes (The Mutants), who built many of their own electric instruments (and were nervous around Bahians). With another northeastern singer, Tom Zé, joining them in São Paulo, Maria Bethânia opting out, and Nara Leão awarded honorary membership, the Tropicália team was now complete.

> In Tropicália, anything went: rock and samba, *berimbao* and electronic instruments, folk music and urban noise, the erudite and the kitsch.
>
> —Chris McGowan, *The Brazilian Sound*

> The critics thought we were rock and rollish. But you listen now and... [i]t doesn't sound like rock at all. It was hippie, because we had long hair, but you can't identify us as just part of the world counterculture. It was ... a different thing.
>
> —Caetano Veloso

Brazil's first bishop arrived in 1551. His hatred of the natives and refusal to convert them shocked even the hardest-nosed settlers and he was soon recalled to Lisbon. On the voyage back, his ship ran aground and he was captured by a group of Tupis. They celebrated with a feast at which the bishop was guest of honor, i.e., the main course.

The prelate's fate amused Tarsila do Amaral, the artist who served feijoada to Blaise Cendrars. Her painting *Abaporu* (Tupi for "the man who eats") became an emblem of the "anthropophagy manifesto" she created with her friend Oswald de Andrade, which proposed devouring imported techniques, then reinventing them on Brazilian terms. "The idea of cultural cannibalism," said Veloso, "fit tropicalistas like a glove." The Beatles and Hendrix were being "eaten," not imitated.

Tropicália made its debut at TV Record's 1967 Song Festival, an event spread out over several evenings with elimination rounds, a judging panel, and Eurovision-style suspense about the final order of finish. When Caetano revealed that he would perform backed by an Argentine rock band he'd met in a São Paulo bar, the producers feared a Dylan-at-Newport collision between audience and amps. Nothing, however, could have been further from Dylan's "Maggie's Farm" scowl than Veloso's irresistibly wide grin. "Alegria, alegria" (Joy, Joy) is a cannibal buffet of a song, combining references to Coca-Cola, Jean-Paul Sartre, and Chacrinha (a wacky local comedian) with a lilting melody and marchinha-worthy chorus; the rockers' guitars, drum kit, and lank hair seemed more conceptual decoration than a fundamental part of the music. After a few scattered hoots, the audience joined in on the chorus and cheered lustily at the end.

The following night was Gil's turn. "Domingo no parque" (Sunday in the Park) was a very different animal, with Os Mutantes's clever backing vocals and Duprat's charts as central as Gil's excited singing. The song blends baião beats and snatches of sertanejo melody with capoeira flourishes, all laid over an arrangement worthy of Jimmy Webb or Van Dyke Parks. The audience went wild.

Both made it to the final round, with Veloso finishing fourth and Gil second. Protest songs, both subtle and overt, had been a hallmark of the competition from the start; that year, "Ponteio" by Edu Lobo became the last political song to win.

> You are the youth who will always kill tomorrow the old enemy that died yesterday. You can't understand anything.
>
> —Caetano Veloso, responding to booing at the 1968 TV Globo Song Festival

> Both. And even more than that, it's a fad.
>
> —Caetano Veloso, answering a reporter's question about whether Tropicália is a movement or a philosophy

Just over fourteen months passed between the night of the finals on October 21, 1967, and December 27, 1968, the day Tropicália ended. During that time, the team released an album, launched a theatrical revue, and hosted a brief TV series. The album included Caetano's "Três caravelas," a deadpan mambo that celebrated or mourned (probably both) Columbus's discovery of America and the birth of Brazil. Escalating the level of provocation, they turned performances into "happenings," dressed in lurid outfits, and adopted a slogan photographed on a Paris wall during the May uprising: *It is prohibited to prohibit*. Their affinity for Roberto Carlos and electric guitars continued to upset both musical nationalists and the Left, while their surreal behavior and affection for Carmen Miranda and Luiz Gonzaga unnerved their allies. It was even suggested that Tropicália was a ruse by the government to confuse and distract the opposition. Veloso confronted the critics: "If you're the same in politics as you are in music, we're done for." Like Paul Simon eighteen years later, the Tropicalistas shared the Left's aims, but refused to accept that politics should rule art. When they brought their revue to Rio, a judge in the audience was so outraged that he ordered it shut down. A TV network fearlessly gave them their own program, *Divino, maravilhoso*; on the series' final night, they held a funeral service for Tropicália. No traditions should be preserved as sacred, especially not their own.

Gilberto had once asked Caetano if he realized the gravity of what they were doing. Everywhere that year, youth was challenging authority and many paid with their lives: the Mexico City Olympics, May '68 in Paris, the Prague Spring, Kent State . . . On December 13, a cabal of hard-liners staged a "coup within the coup," banning demonstrations, suspending habeas corpus, and asserting control over all media. Two days after Christmas, Veloso and Gil were arrested and placed in solitary confinement.

∽

Pay attention
To the windows up high
Pay attention
To the blood on the ground

  —"Divino, maravilhoso" by Gilberto Gil and Caetano Veloso

Why them? Their songs weren't "political," they hadn't campaigned against the government or championed the poor. But as recent years had so vehemently confirmed, Fats Waller and Marshall McLuhan nailed it: *It ain't what you say, it's the way that you say it*. One of Caetano's jailers told him he considered the Tropicalistas' deconstructions a far greater threat than any left-wing agitation; another revealed how proud he was to have helped beat up the cast and audience of a play the government found offensive. Perhaps, as Veloso has suggested, the generals were simply too thin-skinned to tolerate disrespect, particularly when they couldn't understand the joke but knew it was on them.

Though the Brazilian junta was never quite as brutal as their friends in Chile and Argentina, between 1968 and 1974 they tortured, imprisoned, or "disappeared" hundreds of student and labor activists. After six months of dithering, they ordered their two musical prisoners to leave the country, allowing them to stage a benefit concert in Salvador to raise the money for air tickets to London.

When I returned from a trip in the autumn of 1969, the Incredible String Band told me they'd had tea with a couple of very friendly Brazilian singers. Caetano and Gilberto tried to make the most of their time in London, exploring the sounds and sights of the city, reveling in the unarmed policemen and endless grassy parks, watching *Monty Python* on TV, and meeting musicians, artists, and Notting Hill Gate locals. The neighborhood had a lasting effect, particularly on Gil; his love affair with reggae endured long after rock's influence had faded. London helped cure them of over-elaboration; singing to their own guitar accompaniment, backed by a few sympathetic musicians, was how they would record in future. They performed at Queen Elizabeth Hall (with mostly Brazilians in the audience), played a set at the first Glastonbury Festival, and Caetano wrote and recorded some songs in English. Britain was otherwise engaged, though, and barely noticed their presence.

Most Brazilians didn't realize they were gone; the media was forbidden to report such things. When Veloso was allowed home for a brief family visit in 1971, the military required him to appear on television and pretend everything was normal. Soon after that, with nods and winks, it was made clear that the pair were free to return. The generals' slogan was *Um país que vai pra frente* (A country striving forward) but for many it was *Um país de absurdo* (A country of the absurd). If political activists had imagined Caetano's ordeal would radicalize him (in their sense of the word), they were to be disappointed. In that first TV appearance, he sang Carmen Miranda's gorgeous and sentimental "Adeus, batucada," the kind of thing the Left hated.

During the exiles' absence, Gal Costa, Maria Bethânia, and Elis Regina all released recordings of their songs. These three became Brazil's first big female singing stars since Carmen Miranda, as if the country had needed a generation to recover. Their choices of material helped shape what became known as MPB: *Música Popular Brasileiro*. They recorded bossa nova, Tropicália, samba-canção, samba-rock, protest songs (in code), and baião. They sang loud (Regina and Bethânia) and soft (Costa). Vocals were delivered naturally, which encouraged lyricists to be more colloquial and honest. MPB professed to represent a rejection of bossa nova, but thanks to Jobim, Gilberto, et al. its harmonies were richer and instrumental backings less grandiose than commercial samba; Brazilian music had been irrevocably altered by bossa nova's self-confidence. By 1970, the battles of the mid-sixties seemed somehow settled; though Tropicália had never been a broadly popular movement (much of the population was barely aware of it), its omnivorous approach infected everyone. MPB felt modern yet not American, still vehement in its opposition to outright "rock," but no longer fainting at the sight of an electric guitar.

One electric guitar that brought only joy belonged to Jorge Ben, the singer whose debut LP spent so much time on Veloso's São Paulo turntable. An A&R man had discovered Jorge in a Rio club singing "Mas que nada," and Ben's song was a hit in Brazil before Sérgio Mendes's cover version brought it to America and the world. Son of a carnival musician father and an Ethiopian mother and raised in a poor Rio suburb, Ben seemed to accomplish effortlessly what the Tropicalistas pondered and discussed at great length. He had clearly consumed platefuls of soul and rock but his style was completely Brazilian and all his own; some called Ben's guitar style "rhythm & samba," but no one aside from him ever managed to play it properly. The widest global reach of his music probably came via Rod Stewart's "Da Ya Think I'm Sexy," whose melody was pinched from the chorus of Ben's "Taj Mahal" (and paid for, after a lawsuit).

French and Italian dancefloors were filled with Jorge's music across the seventies. I saw him in 1975 at the Paris Olympia; the curtain opened on the dark-skinned, white-suited singer and his rhythm section: four very pale guys in dark suits, two of them blond, with a white piano, white guitars, and a white drum kit. Brazil's racial dynamics rarely failed to confound northern hemisphere assumptions.

One of Ben's songs, "País tropicál" (Tropical Country), showed the minefield MPB had to navigate under the military regime; his colloquial pronunciation, rapid-fire delivery, and dropped word-endings led paranoid censors to imagine he was sending coded signals to terrorists and the record was banned. Another star who caused the government endless headaches was João Gilberto's brother-in-law, Chico Buarque (who had written the play Caetano's guard bragged about trashing). Buarque established himself by winning the TV Record Festival with "A Banda" (The Band) the year before Caetano entered with "Alegria, alegria." Many saw the latter as a riposte to the nostalgia of Buarque's song because of oblique references to it in the lyrics. Buarque may have had little interest in the sort of modernity Tropicália flaunted, but he shared with Veloso and Gil a love of their country's musical history and all were agreed that the key to this door lay with bossa nova.

Throughout the years of military rule (1964–85), Buarque persisted in writing complex, allusive, and subversive songs that audiences often understood better than did the censors. "Apesar de você" (In Spite of You) sold 100,000 copies before the generals realized it was about them. Buarque was never actually exiled, though he spent extended periods in Rome (where he had lived for much of his childhood), as well as a few years writing under a pseudonym after the censors got fed up trying to decode his lyrics and simply banned all songs by Chico Buarque.

The government perceived threats from all musical directions: regional songs told tales of hardship and injustice, samba nostalgia venerated a time before the junta, while the music that television was beaming into every household flaunted the sort of openness to the world the generals abhorred. They would probably have been comfortable with kitsch stylizations of "traditions" or a modern take on samba-exaltaçâo, but MPB had become far too dynamic and imaginative to generate such things. Many songs were suppressed during those bleak years, but André Midani, who continued to oversee many of the era's best recordings, has insisted that repression provided Brazilian music with the healthy stimulation of an enemy. A common sentiment expressed in seventies lyrics was "*one day . . .*"; what the singers were waiting for remained unsung, but listeners understood.

One of this period's greatest compositions is "Cálice" (Chalice), co-written by Buarque and Gil. They planned to sing it as a duet during a 1973 celebration of their label, Philips, imagining that the song's biblical narrative—*father, take from me this chalice stained with blood*—could mask the thrust of verses about the country's crucifixion, to say nothing of the pun in the (three-syllable) title ("*cale se*" means "shut up") as well as an allusion in the lyrics to the horrible death of an activist under torture. Corporate execs insisted the pair alter the text, then cut off their microphones when they reverted to the original lyrics. The song was quickly banned, then unshackled five years later as part of a "lightening" of the censors' heavy hand. For the 1978 recording, another great figure from this remarkably fertile era took Gil's place in the duet: Milton Nascimento.

Like Johnny Alf, Nascimento was the son of a maid working for a White middle-class family in Rio. When Milton's mother died, the family adopted him and moved to rural Minas Gerais. Teenage Milton decided to become a songwriter after seeing *Jules et Jim* at a local cinema club. Influences can have curious effects when the source is elusive; Nascimento's hometown lay in a valley with poor radio reception, so he caught only a fleeting, static-filled glimpse of "Chega de saudade" when it first came out. Reception remained sketchy for weeks while he taught himself both the song and violão gago from memory and got everything beautifully wrong. When one of his early compositions made its way to Elis Regina, she turned it into a hit; television then made him a star.

Nascimento also became a thorn in the government's side. He released a wordless LP—just humming in layered harmonies—in protest against censorship; in 1984, his "Coração de estudante" (Heart of a Student) was chanted by huge crowds demanding (with some success) an end to the dictatorship. The music of his long and international career has remained very much of that post-bossa generation, yet always with a very individual sense of rhythm and harmony that cannot be explained simply by growing up Black in a White community or by the musical peculiarities of Minas Gerais; credit may also be due to the signal-blocking hills around Três Pontas.

> It would be better to play rock 'n' roll than that retarded jazz.
>
> —João Gilberto

> Sprung from an ultra-cool attitude to the samba and some rather tenuous connections with modern jazz, [bossa nova] has in fact developed into the "whitest" of styles, in which the rhythmic impetus and cross-rhythms of the samba have been schematised into a formula that (a giveaway, this) can pretty easily be handled by non-Brazilian musicians.
>
> —John Storm Roberts

> [T]he kind of soul and harmonic beauty that we loved in jazz . . . a very quiet, gentle music that had an equal amount of magic.
>
> —American musician Paul Winter explaining his attraction to bossa nova

Elis Regina was furious with her husband, so she decided to hit him where it hurt. Opening the door to their balcony overlooking Copacabana Beach, she frisbeed his Frank Sinatra collection—LPs, 45s, 78s, and memorabilia—out over the boulevard towards the waves. Her spouse was none other than Ronaldo Bôscoli, that experienced wooer of beautiful singers. They had met when TV Record hired him to liven up *O Fino da bossa* as it was struggling to keep pace in the ratings with Roberto Carlos's *Jovem guarda*. Back in Rio with his bride, Bôscoli missed his Bottles Alley pals, who, like the treasured Ol' Blue Eyes records, were now scattered to the winds. (The marriage, amazingly, lasted a few more years.)

Tokyo, Paris, and LA might still have fancied a bit of bossa nova, but in Brazil even the middle class was no longer interested, forcing many of its practitioners to follow the music and the money abroad. For Europeans unmoved by anglophone rock (and who had probably ignored the May '68 rebellion), the soundtrack of the late sixties was Francis Lai's infectious mock-bossa score for *Un Homme et une femme*. In America, things had moved on from "Bossa Nova Baby" (Elvis) and "Blame It on the Bossa Nova" (Eydie Gormé). With the sophisticated wing of Tin Pan Alley demoralized by The Beatles and Dylan, and only a limited supply of Burt Bacharach tunes to go around, many singers of standards looked, as Sinatra had, to Brazil; once they had all covered "Girl from Ipanema," they moved on to "Desafinado" and "One-Note Samba." Jazzers, meanwhile, were discovering what the Copa cats already knew: that Brazilian melodies and harmonies, particularly those composed by Jobim, were brilliantly suited to improvisation. The future of the "Brazil effect" would ultimately, however, lie less with the songs than with the players. An unlikely trio of trumpeters helped open the door for Brazilian virtuosos into the heart of American music.

Herb Alpert's father was a tailor and part-time musician who escaped Eastern Europe and landed in Southern California. Young Herb aspired to jazz fluency on the trumpet, but changed course after hearing mariachis at a Tijuana bullfight. He brightened his tone, learned how to multitrack in a makeshift garage studio, changed the title of a friend's catchy tune from "Twinkle Star" to "The Lonely Bull," and overdubbed a cheering crowd. Released on his then-tiny A&M label, the single sold a million copies.

Alpert understood as well as anyone how to turn Latin American music into a commercial North American sound. He sweet-talked Atlantic Records into letting Sérgio Mendes out of his contract to record for A&M; their first project together was "Mas que nada" and they never looked back. (Mendes's apotheosis was reached on May 5, 1968, at a concert in Chicago where Stan Kenton opened for *him*.) Sérgio Mendes and Brasil '66 and Herb Alpert and His Tijuana Brass sold so many millions of records that A&M was able to buy the old Charlie Chaplin film lot on Hollywood Boulevard. There, Alpert built a studio beloved by top rock bands and the label grew into a force, the US home to The Carpenters, Cat Stevens, Joe Cocker, Carole King, and The Police (as well as my own Fairport Convention and Sandy Denny).

Alpert wanted his first love, jazz, to share in the success, so he funded Creed Taylor's new CTI label. (It may be a stretch to count "the Man from Ipanema" as one of our brass trio, but he did play trumpet for Duke University's jazz band before heading to New York to become a record producer.) Taylor understood the crisis that confronted jazz in the late sixties better than most; dozens of jazz clubs had been converted into restaurants or rock venues, and the sort of kids who, a decade earlier, would have donned black turtlenecks and lit up a Gauloise while nodding their heads to Monk, Miles, and Coltrane were now wearing tie-dye, dropping acid, and tripping out on Hendrix and the Grateful Dead. John Coltrane may have explored Eastern music and mysticism, but by the late sixties, most African-American jazz players were, with good reason, too angry for meditation. While some channeled that aggression into compelling new forms, Taylor proposed a U-turn, a smooth sound inspired by the jazzy end of bossa nova, the Bottles Alley aesthetic writ large.

CTI's first big hit was by arranger and keyboardist Eumir Deodato, a former sideman to Roberto Menescal, and the label's catalogue was studded with the likes of Jobim, Milton Nascimento, and Rio's Tamba Trio. But even recordings by CTI's American stars—George Benson, Paul Desmond, Wes Montgomery, Quincy Jones, and Grover Washington, Jr.—were infused with a laid-back Copacabana cool, with a Brazilian or two often among the backing musicians. One could say (and I will) that "elevator jazz" was spawned in Bottles Alley.

But the moment with the greatest long-term implications for Brazil's musical influence on the northern hemisphere arrived courtesy of our third bugler: in August 1969, Miles Davis hired Airto Moreira for the *Bitches Brew* sessions. Moreira was a multi-instrumental prodigy who had reluctantly followed his girlfriend, jazz singer Flora Purim, to New York, only to be immediately embraced by the city's musicians.

Miles was so fascinated by his *pandeiro*'s box of exotic toys and his ability to come up with intriguing noises that he drafted Airto into his touring band. Thus did America get its first glimpse of those "percussion trees" that have cluttered up the world's concert and club stages ever since.

Davis was outraged when his agent booked him to open for a rock band at the Fillmore, but he soon began enjoying the new audiences and the resulting surge in record sales. *Bitches Brew* and *Live at the Fillmore East Vols 1 & 2* define the early stages of "jazz-rock fusion"; Airto and keyboard player Chick Corea left Miles to join Purim in Return to Forever, while other Davis alumni founded Weather Report and the Mahavishnu Orchestra. Samba rhythms were easier than the Afro-Cuban clave to blur into an American 4/4 bar; Herbie Mann (whose fusion pedigree is as long as your arm) noted that "in all fusion bands, the drummers slip into a Jazz-Brazilian groove almost automatically." Airto was ubiquitous throughout the seventies, forcing *DownBeat* magazine to add a "Percussionist of the Year" category to its annual poll; he monopolized the award for eight years, until the torch passed to another Brazilian, Naná Vasconcelos.

Vasconcelos was definitely not a Carioca. Growing up in Recife's bohemian neighbor, Olinda, he started playing percussion in his father's band at twelve. When he moved south, as all the best musicians from the Northeast were once required to do, it was to join the band of Nascimento, another provincial outsider. Vasconcelos was a virtuoso on just about anything that could be struck—Brazilian, African, or Oriental—but best known as a master of the berimbau. This is the instrument that looks like an archery bow, the taut string plucked to produce a low buzz that can be modulated by altering the tension on the bow. In Brazil, it is closely identified with capoeira, the circle dance/sport/fight that was once considered a subversive menace for how it honed Afro-Brazilians' fighting skills and celebrated their ties to Angola. For centuries it was suppressed and practitioners brutally punished, until Vargas began encouraging it as a pastime and tourist attraction and suggested that police take lessons from its masters. Capoeira's *bateria* of accompanying percussionists and vocalists celebrate its rituals while controlling the rhythm of the dance (or fight) and providing a running commentary.

Starting in the late 1940s, it grew popular outside the country as a form of martial arts, to the point where it may now have more adherents worldwide than there are fans of Brazilian music.

Vasconcelos became a beloved figure on three continents, central to a high-class European response to CTI's smooth sound, appearing on dozens of ECM recordings by Jan Garbarek, Pat Metheny, Egberto Gismonti, Collin Walcott, and Don Cherry. Mendes, Deodato, Airto, and Vasconcelos were but the tip of an iceberg-sized contingent of Brazilian percussionists, keyboard players, guitarists, arrangers, and producers whose names appear on the back of American and European pop, jazz, R&B, and fusion records from the late sixties through to the end of the century. Deodato produced hits by Kool & the Gang, Earth, Wind & Fire, and Roberta Flack, while a generation of songwriters, including Nascimento, Ivan Lins, João Bosco, and Djavan, were covered almost as widely as their illustrious predecessors. The success of Sade, Michael Franks, and Basia would never have happened without this wave of Brazilian sound-shapers.

Two of the world's biggest-ever rock concerts took place on Copacabana Beach. The neighborhood where nightclubs and casinos had welcomed foreign singers in the 1940s was swamped by millions-strong crowds for Rod Stewart (1994) and the Rolling Stones (2006). Defenders of Brazil's musical purity had proved as ineffective in repelling rock's reductive backbeats as indigenous bows and arrows were against Portuguese germs and blunderbusses. Yet, as popular as it became, rock never succeeded in derailing Brazil's own rhythms. In 1962, as The Beatles were auditioning for George Martin in London, a summit conference of sambistas gathered in Rio and declared that samba lived in the rhythm, which must not be diluted. Veloso acknowledges in his memoir that he never got the point of Little Richard or Jerry Lee Lewis; fifties American kids were thrilled with those transgressive sounds, but Brazilians of that generation, having imbibed far more complex African-based rhythms with their mothers' milk, were not so easily stirred. By the late sixties, however, like youth everywhere, many had been seduced by irreverent

British creativity and drawn inexorably to the spirit of rebellion rock represented.

There was never a peace treaty in Brazil's war of musical sensibilities, but there were white-flag moments. One arrives near the end of *Taking Iacanga*, a documentary about Águas Claras, a series of rock festivals held in the countryside north of São Paulo. In 1983, the organizers of what had become a highly eclectic annual event approached João Gilberto on a whim, never imagining that the notoriously reclusive and fussy star would agree to appear on a rickety outdoor stage miles from nowhere. But turn up he did, just before dawn on the final night; warily eyeing the crowd of over 50,000, he complains about the sound, starts and stops a few times, then cracks a hesitant smile as the audience, most of whom hadn't been born when "Chega de saudade" was released, begin to sing along. They seem to know every line; Gilberto looks as stunned and delighted as the organizers in the wings and the kids in the field, everyone beaming in a moment far smaller, perhaps, than that 1950 "*boom parará*" chorus in the Maracanã, but a beautiful snapshot of unity, nonetheless.

> Because everyone enjoyed the Negro singing so much—enjoyed the circle samba . . . the rhythmic drumming, the bewitching beauty of the *afoxés*—of course they had to be forbidden.
>
> —Jorge Amado, *Tent of Miracles*

The twentieth century held one big final twist in the tale. Brazil's musical narratives had followed what seemed like a law of gravity, with music spawned in the Northeast sliding down the coast to the favelas, bars, radio stations, recording studios, carnival schools, and television shows of Rio de Janeiro and São Paulo; the final twenty-five years of the millennium would be dominated by the upending of that pattern. And just as Nara Leão had cracked open the door that put the Tropicalistas in the spotlight, they in turn supplied the three records that triggered this seismic shift.

Salvador has been called "the Negroes' Rome," so full is it of African religion, to say nothing of its more than 350 Catholic churches and their mostly dark-skinned congregations. From the earliest years of slavery, the Church and the Africans had an implicit understanding: slaves pretended the saints were *orixás* and priests played along. Catholicism and the African religions known as *macumba* are both, after all, based more on ritual practice than belief. As in Cuba, tens of thousands of Yoruba captives arrived at the port of Salvador in the early nineteenth century; included among them were religious leaders who proved more doctrinaire than the Vatican, refusing to accept Black Brazilians' assurances that Saint Anthony was a stand-in for Ogum, Saint Sebastian actually Oxóssi, and so on. The newcomers caused so much trouble that some were shipped back to Africa. The row triggered a revival of African religion in Northeast Brazil contemporaneous with the "Great Awakening" of non-conformist Protestantism in North America.

The result was Candomblé, a very Yoruba form of worship with elements borrowed from Angolan traditions, indigenous Amerindian practices, and Catholicism. Many Whites (including officials on record condemning it) were drawn to Candomblé for herbal cures or charms to win lovers, but some joined ceremonies at *terreiros* (houses of worship—literally, "clearings"). Candomblé's ritual music can induce spirit possession, where the worshipper is "ridden" by their deity, though White adepts experience this far less often; one of the most renowned, the photographer and ethnographer Pierre Verger, when asked if he had ever been possessed this way, responded: "Alas, I am far too French for that."

Whites in Salvador were hyper-conscious of being in the minority and determined to repress African culture or at least keep it out of sight. As Rio's carnival grew, taking over that city's centre, Salvador's shrank; wealthy Whites retreated to indoor balls, while afoxés (Candomblé rituals brought into the street, pronounced "ah-fo-shay") were attacked by police and restricted to districts far from the city's picturesque heart in Pelourinho Square.

Change began during the 1950 carnival season. Osmar Macedo and Adolfo "Dodô" Nascimento were, respectively, an auto mechanic and an electrical repairman by day and musicians whenever they had the chance; between them they could build or fix almost anything. "Thank

God, I wasn't born up north or I might have invented a missile," said Osmar. As it was, they constructed an electrified cavaquinho and an odd-looking *pau elétrico* (solid-body guitar), stood on a flatbed truck in a crowded carnival street, and began playing loud, energetic *frevo* ("fervor"), a Recife dance based on the rhythms of capoeira circles. Most electric guitars in 1950 were polite-sounding (Barney Kessel, Django Reinhardt, Les Paul . . .), but Osmar and Dodô were rockers *avant la lettre*. When they added a drummer the following year, their following exploded and the *trio elétrico* phenomenon was born.

The trios (even when groups became much larger they were always "trios") were inclusive; Bahians of all shades formed carnival bands and everyone (save the wealthiest) danced behind the trucks. They remained a provincial Bahian phenomenon until 1969, when Veloso's label released his "Atrás do trio elétrico" while he was in prison. The single was so successful that he recorded follow-ups for 1970 and 1971, bestowing on Salvador's carnival some countrywide fame.

> In Bahia, the conditions in which the lower classes live are so terrible . . . that merely staying alive in such conditions constitutes extraordinary proof of strength and vitality. For this reason, the preservation of custom and tradition, the organising of societies, samba schools, parades, bands and *afoxés*, and the creation of new dance rhythms and songs . . . takes on the character of a veritable miracle.
>
> —Pedro Archanjo in Jorge Amado's *Tent of Miracles*

> [A Filhos de Gandhy procession] makes you feel like crying. You feel all that tranquillity, that shiver running through your body, taking hold of you. This is the spiritual side of Carnaval, its balance.
>
> —Gilberto Gil

A couple of years before Dodô and Osmar, a group of Afro-Brazilians, inspired by a newsreel about the Mahatma, formed a carnival association called Filhos de Gandhy (Sons of Gandhi). They dressed elegantly in white turbans and sky blue robes and paraded so decorously that police let them pass. The movement soon petered out, but one Bahian hadn't forgotten; in 1975, Gilberto Gil recorded "Filhos de Gandhi," about being inspired by them as a youth. The record was a hit, and at the following year's carnival they reappeared, stronger than ever.

The third disc is a Jorge Ben release from 1974 entitled "Zumbi," about the legendary leader of Palmares, Brazil's largest and longest-enduring *quilombo*. *Kilombo* is an Angolan word meaning "war camp," and for centuries there were settlements of escaped slaves scattered across the country's vast interior. Palmares was almost 100 kilometers from end to end and virtually an independent state through most of the seventeenth century, trading with nearby towns and providing sanctuary not just to runaways, but also to army deserters, indigenous peoples, and peasants who had run afoul of landowners or the law. The Portuguese army, preoccupied with a simmering war against the Dutch East India Company, left Palmares pretty much alone at first. After the Dutch were expelled in 1654, they turned their guns on it, but it took another forty years and the deaths of many thousands of soldiers before Palmares, led by the inspirational Zumbi, finally succumbed.

Ben's song was a smash, the right record at the right time; dark-skinned Brazilians—plus the more aware White ones—had taken note of the Black Power movement in America, danced to James Brown's "Say It Loud, I'm Black and I'm Proud," cheered the success of anti-colonial movements in Mozambique and Angola, and looked with fresh eyes on their own country's supposed racial equality. Within a few years of the record's release, November 20 (the date Zumbi was beheaded) had become an annual "Black consciousness day," the ruins of Palmares were turned into a historical park, and Rio had erected a statue of Zumbi outside the new Sambadrome.

Salvador's Liberdade district responded by forming a *bloco afro* called Ilê Aiyê (roughly "House of Life" in Yoruba). Ilê Aiyê was uncompromising from the start; it turned the Anglo-American "one-drop" idea on its head, barring membership to anyone with a trace of White blood. Their carnival parade was percussion-heavy and based on Candomblé ceremonial music. Police tried to block them at first, but by the late seventies, with Filhos de Gandhy clearing the way, Ilê Aiyê and other blocos afros were bringing a very un-Rio sensibility to Salvador's carnival streets. Ilê Aiyê honored a different African nation each year, while paying homage to their forerunners, the turn-of-the-century afoxés that had been so fiercely suppressed.

During the 2001 carnival, I watched Ilê Aiyê set off on their procession through the city; orixás were invoked and hundreds of doves fluttered into the sky as a well-drilled explosion of drumbeats ricocheted off the walls of Liberdade Square. The pulse was clearly Brazilian, but invoked none of the rainforest chatter of a Rio samba school. Low-pitched surdos were struck with mallets, while smaller drums were played with sticks and tuned high and tight like timbales, complete with Nuyorican-style syncopated fills. There was also something else, an unhurried, back-of-the-beat feel unlike the forward propulsion of Carioca samba. The nature of this ingredient was made clearer by another bloco I saw in Pelourinho Square. At the start of the eighties, some members of Ilê Aiyê had split off to form Olodum, the group Paul Simon deployed on a few tracks of *The Rhythm of the Saints*. "The Obvious Child" opens with a military-sounding salute before settling into the swaying march, both imposing and sensual, that has come to define the blocos afros. Brazilians call this groove "samba-reggae."

Gilberto Gil had experienced Jamaican sound systems up close during his time in London but he was not the only Brazilian captivated by reggae. For many Black Bahians, Rastafarian attitudes, hairstyles, and rhythms were a revelation. Gil's 1977 album *Refavela* contains tracks that set out samba-reggae's stall, sharing with the music of the blocos that self-assured pace, longer melodic lines, and hints of an inside-out Jamaican sense of time.

We're postmodern, postpunk, postyuppie, posttropicalista.

—João Jorge, cultural director of Olodum

The 1980s weren't a great decade for MPB and samba; home-grown rock bands and their foreign role models dominated the charts (and kept many record labels alive). In 1982, after the military allowed local elections in preparation for a national ballot, Rio de Janeiro persuaded

Oscar Niemeyer to return from self-imposed exile to design his first big project since Brasília. The Sambadrome is a massive ravine of brutalist viewing stands built over the grave of Praça Onze; it allows the city to more effectively monetize and televise carnival competitions. Neighborhoods took the cue and started charging admission for what had been free and open street celebrations; disillusioned party animals began heading for Salvador, where the reborn carnival was gaining a reputation for being edgy and a bit dangerous, with street parties that went on until dawn. Young Brazilian ears developed a taste for the blend of Candomblé and samba-reggae known as *axé* ("ah-shay").

In 1975, a former salesman named Wesley Rangel opened a small jingle studio in the city; by 1988, WR had grown into a busy modern recording complex with its own label. A local singer, Luiz Caldas, a Veloso protégé, made hits there based on *fricote*, a pop-ish take on the rhythms of the trios. Rangel later recorded local girl Daniela Mercury backed by Olodum on "Swing da cor," a track that heralded "*pop axé*," topping the Brazilian charts in 1991 and launching Daniela into stardom. Boosted by royalties from Paul Simon and Mercury, Olodum expanded its horizons, establishing political and educational projects in poor neighborhoods, founding a theater company, and bringing musical joy back to Pelourinho Square, which myopic city governments had tried to turn into a lifeless tour-bus stop.

A week before the 2001 carnival, I joined a few Carioca music people for dinner at Rio's Copacabana Palace. The ground floor of this massive art deco hotel (facing the famous beach) has the sort of expensive shops found in similar outposts of luxury the world over. Outside the jewelry store was a huge photograph of a bare-chested, dreadlocked guy wearing an enormous diamond necklace that sparkled against his black skin. This was Carlinhos Brown, the kid from a Salvador favela who had borrowed the Godfather of Soul's last name and, by the end of the century, become one of Brazil's most important musical figures. My hosts regaled me with tales of his talent for hustling corporate sponsors into donating impressive sums for development projects in the Candeal neighborhood where he grew up and learned to play percussion (defying his mother, who viewed drums as tools of the devil).

He apprenticed at WR, producing clever radio jingles that showed off his immense talent. Brown's compositions soon found their way onto records by Luiz Caldas and Caetano Veloso, before the eagle-eyed Sérgio Mendes hired him to arrange his Grammy-winning *Brasileiro* album. Carlinhos earned a lot of air miles—Paris, LA, Rio, New York—but always returned to Salvador, where he founded a bloco called Timbalada that introduced slick, modernized axé into Brazil's musical mainstream. During the nineties, between composing, collaborating, producing, and performing, Brown accounted for thirty Brazilian #1s, funneling large chunks of the proceeds into Candeal.

I knew Arto Lindsay from the downtown New York music scene, but had only lately become aware that he had grown up in Brazil, absorbing the music and the language. Arto invited me to pay him a visit at Brown's new studio in Candeal, where he was producing a record by Marisa Monte, a singer who had soared to stardom in the last decades of the millennium. The taxi driver was suitably impressed by my destination and full of praise for what Carlinhos had achieved. We climbed through Salvador's hilly outskirts, then paused for a moment before making a vertiginous plunge into a steep bowl crammed with jerry-built housing clinging to the hillsides. After getting dropped off at the bottom, I followed Arto's directions up another incline, overlooking newly built, brightly colored housing surrounding a large open space, with a stage at one end in front of a clubhouse and a music school. I later watched *Miracle of Candeal*, a documentary that shows how the community took the lead on spending the money Carlinhos had raised. (What a novel idea, applying development funds directly to a project, with no corrupt diversions or bloated admin costs and involving the people most affected from start to finish!)

Having released two albums by his discovery Virginia Rodrigues, as well as one by his son Moreno Veloso, I had gotten to know Caetano by the time of my 2001 visit to the Salvador carnival; I'll try not to sound smug when describing the vantage point from which he invited me to view its Monday-night epicenter. *Trios elétricos* have come a long way from Dodô and Osmar's flatbed truck; half a century on, gigantic custom-built vehicles with fully equipped dressing rooms, a rooftop stage, and a PA system move through the crowds at snail's pace. Veloso and Gil had chosen that year to revisit their Salvador history together atop a "trio" bus, trading hit after hit, memory after memory. I'm pretty sure the hundreds of thousands jamming the seaside boulevards were singing along because I could see mouths moving in rhythm, but I couldn't really hear them from where I was, seated onstage propped up against the rhythm-guitar amp. The two giants performed songs from every phase in their careers, including "Filhos de Gandhi" and "Atrás do trio elétrico"; they might have even played "Zumbi" but I can't say for certain.

A few days earlier, I had watched Caetano perform in an even more inspiring setting, if such a thing is possible to imagine. Projeto Axé was founded in 1990 to provide a home and a life to Salvador's abandoned street children. The kids are taught how to make carnival costumes, play an instrument, paint, draw, dance, and learn the discipline of capoeira; every aspect of their education is grounded in the Afro-Brazilian culture of their city. Veloso has supported Projeto Axé from the start and returns every year to play at the center and listen to the music the kids have created. Salvador, Havana, and New Orleans seem to be exceptions among modern cities in their unselfconscious love of tradition. Rap and machine beats are as ubiquitous as anywhere else, but that doesn't mean youths look down on older styles. I have watched musicians in all three places switch effortlessly from the latest sounds to flashing skills in second-line, rumba, or axé; you rarely see anything like that in New York or London.

On carnival's final night, everyone—trios, blocos, and special guests—paid tribute to Dorival Caymmi. The homage completed a circle: when Caymmi set off in 1939 to pitch his songs to Carmen Miranda, all musical roads led south. By 2001, even Rio seemed to have recognized the shifting dynamic; one of its leading samba schools, Mangueira, had made Salvador's status as a great musical city the theme of a recent carnival parade.

The cover of Daniela Mercury's 1996 album *Feijão com arroz* (Black Beans and Rice) shows her gazing at us over the shoulder of a Black male body as apparently naked as her own; even in Brazil the photo raised eyebrows, but the fuss only made her a bigger star. Looking at the axé surge from three decades on, one can imagine complaints of "cultural appropriation"; axé's biggest stars, after all, were the European-descended Mercury and the similarly complexioned Ivete Sangalo. But as with most things involving race in Brazil, it's not so straightforward. Ilê Aiyê's leader, Vovô, calls Daniela "the mother of axé," and there is clear affection and respect—and much collaboration—passing back and forth between the city's blocos and its lighter-skinned pop stars; all seem to think of themselves first and foremost as Bahians.

And it wasn't just axé that enabled the Northeast to lead Brazilian music through the nineties; Chico Science and Nação Zumbi used computers to stir Recife's carnival music and regional dance rhythms into an anthropophagical feast called *manguebeat* (or *mangue* "bit" as it was originally) that had national impact. Chico Science was lost to the country's musical future in a 1997 car crash, joining a sad roll call of truncated lives that extends from Sinhô and Noel Rosa through Carmen Miranda and Sylvia Telles (killed in her prime in an auto accident) to Elis Regina (dead at thirty-six from a drug overdose) and eighties star Clara Nunes, who died at forty during surgery.

> As for Brazilian music, let's just say that it's very seductive, sensual, smart, well done, and intelligent.
>
> —Gilberto Gil

These late-century musical dramas caused few ripples outside Brazil, at least compared to Carmen Miranda or bossa nova. Ironically, it was rock—or at least one distinguished exemplar of it—that tried to remedy the situation. The minute David Byrne moved to Manhattan in the mid-seventies, he began exploring the city's endless opportunities to buy exotic vinyl; he and I share a particular nostalgia for the Soho Music Gallery on Greene Street. It has since been revealed that the shop was a front for laundering Mob money and bootlegging records, but at the time, its numberless bins, filled with music for every niche of taste, were a constant temptation for wallet-thinning splurges.

Byrne and fellow audiovore Brian Eno would meet up and listen to recordings from across the globe (one result being *My Life in the Bush of Ghosts*, of which more in this book's conclusion). In 1986, when he was invited to Rio for a festival showing of his film, *True Stories*, David booked a stopover in Salvador. Knowing no one, he gravitated to record stores, where, just like everywhere else in the world, he found heroically friendly, knowledgeable nerds behind the counters. They gave him a guided tour of Brazilian sounds and the boxful of discs he returned with monopolized his turntable for months. In Brazil, Byrne felt, he had discovered "pop utopia," a sophisticated mass culture based on deep roots. He teamed up with Yale Evelev, a former manager at Soho Music Gallery, to start Luaka Bop records, launching it with a series of Brazilian compilations.

At the film festival, David met Caetano, and they have been enjoying one another's music and company ever since, sharing the Carnegie Hall stage for a memorable 2012 concert and live album. But when he asked for help selecting material for the discs, Veloso declined, saying it would be more interesting to hear an outsider's choices. With help from some friends' mixtapes, Byrne assembled two volumes, one focused on the Tropicalistas and another on gems from lesser-known (at least to outsiders) singers from the eighties. (They were followed later by a third devoted to *forró*, the up-to-date term for baião.)

"Umbabarauma" (six syllables, emphasis on the two "u"s) is a football stadium chant celebrating skill on the ball; it bursts from the throat of Jorge Ben at the start of *Volume 1* and for eighteen tracks (fourteen on vinyl) the energy and quality never flag, a sinuous dribble through the music of the Tropicália generation: four Velosos, three Gils, three Bens, three Nascimentos, two Buarques, and a Bethânia-Costa duet (roughly matching their word-count ratios in this chapter). *Volume 2* also grabs you by the ears from the off with Clara Nunes's glorious call-out to Iansã, goddess of the wind, searching for her lover Ogum, the iron god. The rest of the album tracks the eighties artists who prepared the ground for axé by pulling MPB back to the roots: Nunes invoking orixás, Alcione blending her Northeast rhythms into samba and Martinho da Vila showing why his samba-school anthems became chart-topping classics.

World music launched a thousand compilations, but *Brazil Classics* remains the gold standard; *Volume 1* made it to almost half a million, with *Volume 2* nearing 200,000 sales, astonishing figures even for "the good old days," surpassed in terms of impact only by the soundtrack to *The Harder They Come*. By 1990, Talking Heads was over and Byrne was making his first solo album, *Rei Momo*, with Latin and Brazilian musicians. On the subsequent world tour, he invited along the Afro-Bahian axé singer Margareth Menezes as a special guest.

So, with brilliant compilations selling like hotcakes, massive love from a rock star, and the world music scene exploding, MPB should have picked up where bossa nova left off. One obstacle was explained to me by a concert promoter who had tried to build a North American audience for Gal Costa. He booked her into New York's Town Hall on an October Friday night, then persuaded the *New York Times* to send a reporter to Brazil for a profile to appear the weekend before the show. Costa's multinational record company agreed to promote her latest album in the US, everything went off as planned, and the show sold out. The problem was that when the tickets went on sale six weeks ahead, Brazilian expats—always on the alert for any music from home—quickly bought them all. The promoter's target audience (the kind of fans who turned up for Nusrat Fateh Ali Khan, Buena Vista Social Club, or Le Mystère des Voix Bulgares, plus jazz buffs nostalgic for bossa nova) began calling the box office when they read about her in the *Times*, only to be told there were no seats left. The whole exercise probably expanded Costa's US profile by 5 percent, while the Brazilian audience mostly bought bootlegs, so the label got nothing for its trouble.

More recently, I heard Caetano Veloso and Gilberto Gil at London's Hammersmith Apollo, sitting trading songs with just their guitars. Seven thousand people saw them over two evenings and it was, of course, stirring and wonderful. The crowd, though, was 90 percent Brazilian; Caetano said a few words in English at the start, but from then on it was non-stop Portuguese. The audience sang along, waved their hands in the air, and shouted their affection, while the two singers beamed and bantered back. I wouldn't have missed it for anything, but like the other non-Brazilians, I felt a bit of an interloper at a family party. I have had similar experiences at Brazilian concerts in America, plus once in Berlin at a Chico Buarque show. Audiences are more mixed in southern Europe, but Brazilians far from home embrace their music with such passion that it can be hard for others to get a foot in the door.

Things can also work another way around; in one such case, reality mimicked fiction. Amado's *Tent of Miracles* begins with the arrival in Rio of a celebrated US academic to deliver a speech. He reveals that his fondest wish in coming to Brazil is to visit Salvador and meet the great author Pedro Archanjo. "Pedro who?" says everyone, and the book unfolds with eminent Brazilians gradually and reluctantly acknowledging dark-skinned brilliance in their midst. When Bill Clinton was invited to speak at an economic forum in São Paulo in 2001 and his hosts enquired if he had any special requests, he told them he wanted to hear Virginia Rodrigues sing. *Virginia who?* Minions scurried to locate this mysterious performer. She turned out, of course, to be, like Archanjo, Black and from Salvador, only non-fictional; the organizers grumbled but flew her south for the day and she thrilled Clinton with a serenade.

Virginia Rodrigues has a large body and a large voice with a timbre many associate with spirituality; from a young age she sang at Catholic, Protestant, and Candomblé ceremonies. Veloso heard her performing with the Olodum Theater Company and supervised an album I released on Hannibal in 1998. *Sol negro* is a wonderful collection of songs across a range of composers, with beautiful "chamber samba" arrangements. Showcase concerts we organized in Paris, New York, and London drew the prototype world music audience (including Jimmy Page) but few Brazilians (which was good, I guess). Rodrigues was perfectly placed to develop into an international star, but her career foundered on the sort of misunderstanding that can plague relations between artists from developing countries and those engaged in the tenuous business of selling global music in "the West." She was thrilled to have Caetano's guidance and very happy with our promotional efforts on her behalf, but couldn't comprehend how a rave review in the *New York Times*, curtain calls in London, and the US president's purchase of 100 copies of *Sol negro* for Christmas presents hadn't made her wealthy. Her family and friends in a poor Salvador neighborhood found this even harder to accept, which led to a breakdown in the relationship with her management and hence with us. In Brazil, she struggles to find a spot in the many-shelved MPB cupboard and success has been modest. (The two Hannibal CDs sold reasonably well, but not enough to salvage my job running the label once the parent company's ownership had passed to a hedge fund.)

By contrast, another Brazilian born in poverty who slept on the streets as a teenager has proved more than capable of navigating the currents of northern hemisphere show business. Seu Jorge is known in Brazil and has thrived outside it. He carved out a niche for himself from the crow's nest of Bill Murray's boat in Wes Anderson's *The Life Aquatic*, singing samba'd-up David Bowie songs in Portuguese (avenging, perhaps, all those bad bossa nova translations, though we anglophones will never know).

An unlikely cast of characters converged at the end of the nineties to produce Brazilian music's most spectacular "only-above-the-equator" success: a Serbian living in São Paulo, a Paulista relocated to New York, a pair of Washington DC bossa nova obsessives, a Belgian label owner, and a daughter of music royalty looking for a way to forge her own path. A November 2000 article by *New York Times* critic Ben Ratliff analyzed how these disparate characters joined up at the perfect moment, when dance clubs were adding "chill-out" rooms and DJs were mixing cool, laid-back beats with—what else?—bossa nova. The result was *Tanto tempo*, an album by Bebel Gilberto, which launched Ziriguiboom, a Brazil-themed subsidiary of Belgian label Crammed run by Béco Dranoff (the Paulista) and Marc Hollander (the Belgian). The tracks were created in large part by Suba, the tragic Serb who died trying to rescue tapes from a fire. The mix was finished off by a Washington pair known as Thievery Corporation and the resulting album sold a million copies across the noughties, outdoing not only Astrud, but possibly topping the international numbers for her father, João's own releases. To complete the circle, *Tanto tempo*'s most-played song was "So Nice (Summer Samba)," the one track with English lyrics, written by none other than Norman Gimbel.

MPB's other export problem was that whatever Europeans and Americans were doing while they listened to Brazilian music, it wasn't dancing the samba. Alma Guillermoprieto, however, refused to remain seated; during the run-up to the 1986 carnival, she learned how to move like a Carioca. In *Samba*, Guillermoprieto explains how to do it (and kindly granted permission to pass along the instructions):

HOW TO SAMBA (WOMEN'S VERSION)

1: Start before a mirror, with no music. You may prefer to practice with a pair of very high heels . . .

2: Stand with feet parallel, close together. Step and hop in place on your right foot as you brush your left foot quickly across. Step in quick succession onto your left, then your right foot. Although your hips will swivel to the right as far as possible . . . your head and shoulders should remain strictly forward . . . Practice this sequence right and left until you can do it without counting.

3: Test yourself: Are your lips moving? Are your shoulders scrunched? No? Are you able to manage one complete left-right sequence per second? Good! . . . [Y]ou're ready to add music . . . The key thing at this stage is speed: when you are up to two complete sequences per second you are well on your way to samba. Aim for four.

4: A samba secret: Add hips. They're probably moving already, but if you are trying to hit required minimum speed they may be a little out of control. You want to move them, but purposefully. When you step on your right foot your hips switch left-right. When you step on your left they switch again, right-left. Two hip beats per foot beat, or about twelve beats per second, if you can manage.

5: Stop hopping! Keep your shoulders down! Face front! The magic of samba lies in the illusion that somebody is moving like crazy from the waist down while an entirely different person is observing the proceedings from the waist up . . .

6: You've mastered the mechanics of samba. Now you are ready to start dancing . . . Dress appropriately for the next stage. Preferably something that emphasizes the waist, so that hip movement is maximized. Go for shine. Twelve hip beats per second will look like a hundred if you're wearing sequins.

7: Arms: If you are up to two to four sequences per second with a book on your head and your hips swiveling at least forty-five degrees in each direction . . . you're ready to ornament your dance by holding your arms out and ruffling your shoulders as you move. Think of a fine-plumed bird rearranging its wings . . .

8: Smile: The key rule is, don't make it sexy. You will look arch, coy or, if you are working really hard, terribly American. Your smile should be the full-tilt cheer of someone watching her favorite team hit a home run. Or it should imitate the serene curve of a Hindu deity's. The other key rule: There is no point to samba if it doesn't make you smile.

9: Sweat: Obviously, you will produce lots of it. You will soon discover that it looks wrong when it is dripping off the tip of your nose. Don't let this upset you . . . [K]eep at it. Practice. When you find that your body is moving below you in a whirlpool frenzy and your mind is floating above it all in benign accompaniment, when your torso grows curiously light and your legs feel like carving little arabesques in the air on their own for the sheer fun of it; when everything around you seems to slow for the rush that's carrying you through the music, you'll probably discover that sweat is clothing your body in one glorious, uniform, scintillating sheet, flying around you in a magic halo of drops, and you'll know that you have arrived at samba.

HOW TO SAMBA (MEN'S VERSION)

Find yourself a street corner . . . Practice just standing there. You should feel loose, but pleasantly expectant. Check how much time elapses before you feel the need to look at your watch. When you can complete a two-to-three-hour stint without having to know the time, you are ready to start practice.

1: The first thing is attitude. You should look and feel relaxed, yet vigilant, playful and ready to pounce. A slouching posture is easiest, but some crack sambistas manage a straight-backed nonchalance that is highly prized.

2: Put the music on. Listen to the beat. It is the road you will walk on, but whatever flow develops in your movements will come from the little plinking cavaquinho pegging away just behind the singer. Your task is to follow the drums with your feet and spell out their rhythm by flinging your legs as far away as possible from your torso on every beat. Master this, then practice the same movement with your torso casually thrown back at a forty-five-degree tilt.

3: As your legs cut circles in the air with your torso planed back away from them, it is critical that your head remain level, as if you were dancing wedged under a shelf. Hopping up and down is tasteless. Also, don't fall down.

4: If you have mastered cakewalking in place, swinging your legs under and over each other as if you were climbing an invisible spiral staircase, and pulling up to a sharp halt after sliding sideways very fast with your feet, you are ready to time your performances. Timing is the difference between dancing to devastating effect and looking like a fool.

5: Remain in your street-corner mode until a woman approaches. Let her walk by. Let a few more women pass. Remember, you're not desperate.

6: Wait until a woman you really like comes along, and let her go just past the point where she can see you out of the corner of her eye. Break into samba. If your energy is strong, she will perceive your movement with her back and turn around. Stop. Smile. (Not at *her*!) Tug your clothes sharply into place. Wait for another woman. Repeat many times. With luck, a woman will eventually walk by who turns your spinal column to jelly and sets your ears on fire. She will stop and look at you and smile and avert her eyes and look at you again and start to walk away and turn and grin and throw caution to the wind and break into samba and you'll move right up and dance a couple of circles round her and shrug up behind her real slow and catch her by the hips and circle her down to the floor and spatter a starstorm of steps around her feet and grab her and carry her home and ride her and catch her screams in your ears and lie back and breathe easy and watch her wash up and sing and cook and ask you for a cigarette and give you the eye.

If none of this happens, you can always form a circle with the other men and really dance.

One Brazilian dance did become a worldwide craze but it wasn't samba. In 1988, Parisian producer Jean Karakos heard a baião-crossed-with-merengue beat cleverly married to a Bolivian song. Karakos got some Paris-based African and Antillian musicians to copy the record, sold it to Orangina as an advertising jingle, and created a mania for the lambada. This dance contains none of the samba subtleties described above; it mixes century-old maxixe moves with newer ones inspired by the film *Dirty Dancing*, as its jaunty beat propels loin-locked couples in bouncy loops around the dancefloor. This craze lasted a bit longer than most (the copyright lawsuit dragged on even longer) but when it was over, the world's themed club nights were still "salsa," "tango," and "swing," with nary a "samba" or "lambada" in sight.

> Only intellectuals like misery. What poor people go for is luxury.
>
> —Joãosinho Trinta, director of Beija-Flor samba school

> That's something very strange and hard to understand about us . . . why we are willing to sacrifice so much for carnival. But we are.
>
> —Ana, member of the Mangueira samba school, talking to Alma Guillermoprieto

> Samba . . . propels and ignites the lower body . . . Any activation of the hips-sex-butt-pelvis relates to the source of all life, the womb. This music is definitely a respectful prayer in honor of the sweet, the feminine, the great mother—the sensuous life-giving aspects of ourselves and our lives—and to the Earth, the mother of us all. To shake your rump is to be environmentally aware.
>
> —David Byrne, album notes to *Brazil Classics*

Samba dancing has always been at its most ubiquitous, of course, during the Rio carnival. Each school's parade is led by a pair of *passistas*, whose performance can tip the scales in the judges' scoring. Guillermoprieto describes how the girl dances virtually naked while the man sports an elegant *malandro*/pimp outfit, gesturing towards his partner's body like he's showing her off to a john. TV cameras, omnipresent since 1960, have perfected the money shots: bums, breasts, crotches, and slo-mo of the sexiest gyrations and quivers, like replays of a Ronaldo goal. Everyone from Manaus to Porto Alegre tunes in and, for a week anyway, samba still rules.

The schools take a few months off, then begin the cycle again, composing songs, designing themed floats and glittery costumes, making everything by hand, and getting ready for next year's battle. Wealthy wannabes paying for their costumes and a spot in the parades are a good source of income, a far cry from the nineteenth century, when bourgeois ladies would rent baiana outfits to wear at private balls but wouldn't dream of dancing in the streets with people from a favela. Despite the lucrative new contract negotiated in 1988 with Riotur (the body that rakes in the television and ticket money), many schools continued to rely on the support of "animal game" bosses. These lotteries always operated at the margins of legality and during Dutra's term they were criminalized. Little changed, of course, other than adding extra layers of bribery that drove many neighborhoods further into the arms of criminals. Most of the work and much of the cost is still borne by people surviving hand-to-mouth whose lives revolve around carnival.

In Rio's more prosperous districts, the bossa nova effect had threatened to loosen samba's grip on the hips, feet, and imagination of the middle classes. Starting in the mid-'80s, however, the former red-light district of Lapa (where Carmen Miranda was raised above her father's barbershop) was transformed by hip bars with live samba bands and crowded dancefloors. Samba enthusiasm had skipped a generation but returned with a new intensity. At the turn of the millennium, a mixed group of pop musicians (including Moreno Veloso) and veteran sambistas added a new twist when they formed Orquestra Imperial, which began playing Monday nights at a disused ballroom. The group's eclectic repertoire was based in the tango-inflected *gafieira* style from the 1940s, the closest samba has come to a structured ballroom dance.

I had assumed *favela* was simply a slang word for "hillside shanty town," but a favela was originally a plant that grew in such profusion on a mountain in northeast Brazil that this historic spot became known by that name. Among the many ways Brazil can be compared to its northern counterpart, the most damning may be in the distribution of the land seized from the native peoples. America lured settlers westward by handing out deeds to family-sized plots like confetti; the Portuguese Crown gave massive swathes of territory to the already rich, and their successors have been exploiting and evicting tenants ever since. In 1897, there was a violent collision between the sertanejo poor and the government at a town called Canudos, built on the slopes of Mount Favela by the landless followers of a messianic preacher. The authorities assumed it would be a small matter to bring this outlaw settlement to heel (and tax it). Under the new republican constitution, Brazilian newspapers were free to publish what they liked; headlines went into hysterical overdrive as thirty thousand Canudos residents repelled three army assaults, killing hundreds of soldiers with ancient rifles, axes, and pitchforks. With headlines clamoring that the country's honor was at stake, a massive force complete with artillery was sent in; thousands were massacred, survivors executed in cold blood, and the town destroyed. When it was over, many discharged soldiers and sertanejo refugees ended up on a morro in Rio and named their shantytown after the scene of the crime.

History never stops repeating itself, certainly not in Brazil. A century later, many of Rio's favelas function like quilombos, off the water and power grids, their inclines too steep and narrow for ambulances or police vehicles, living by their own laws or those imposed by drug barons, unless a military assault re-establishes governmental authority. Police execute "bad guys" in the street like Canudos prisoners or runaway slaves.

By the mid-'90s, the soundtrack for this had become *baile funk*, a style based on American sounds fashionable in the eighties in upscale

Rio discos. A 1992 funk party on the beach ended in a melee followed by a police ban and the removal of such events to *praças* up in the hills where authority rarely ventures. Cocaine had by then worked its sinister magic in Brazil, as it had in Jamaica and everywhere else, making the narcotics trade even more lucrative while shortening tempers and attention spans. Baile funk became music to sell drugs by, its lyrics growing more violent and misogynist along the way. Whenever the government regained control of a favela, musical tastes tended to shift back towards samba. São Paulo, as usual, reacted differently, generating a politically astute, "conscious"—and very popular—rap scene as well as *samba-suingue*, an attempt to have the best of both worlds. As leading rapper Marcelo D2 observed, "To reach the people, rap needs to use samba."

A Rio group called AfroReggae has tried to bring the idealism of the Salvador blocos south and use roots music as an inspiration for change. The documentary *Favela Rising* shows dozens of uniformed police officers of both sexes learning to play the surdo and march/dance in a procession; the lessons loosen up the stiff young officers and engender empathy between them and their dreadlocked instructors. Unfortunately, the only police force willing to embark on such an exercise was in Belo Horizonte, three hundred miles north of Rio; despite AfroReggae's inspired work in its home city, the confrontations and killings go on. In a recent twist, drug lords converted to evangelical Christianity have started killing macumba priests and destroying their terreiros.

>Why complain? I drive a VW bug, live in a tropical country, have a black girlfriend—and once a year, there's Carnival!
>
>—Jorge Ben, "País tropical"

>[M]oney makes you white . . . and poverty makes you black.
>
>—Jorge Amado, *Tent of Miracles*

>Brazil is the country of the future and always will be.
>
>—Common saying supposedly first uttered by Charles de Gaulle

Compared to most northern hemisphere racial attitudes, Getúlio Vargas's ambition to make all Brazilians the color of milky coffee might seem progressive, even radical. But it implies a hierarchy in which—pure White being out of the question—lighter is better. One of carnival's all-time most popular marchinhas was 1932's "O Teu cabelo não nega" (Your Hair Can't Lie), which accuses a pretty mulata of being more African than her skin-lightening cream lets on. Edu Lobo's father had a big hit in 1950 with "Nega maluca," which complains that *"The bomb blew up in my hand / Everything happens to me."* The song tells of a White *bon viveur* confronted by a Black girl holding a brown baby and demanding he take responsibility. The song inspired cartoons in which the girl was drawn with a halo of vertical "piccaninny" braids and bulbous lips. To this day, many Brazilians think little of using slangy identifiers that categorize people by skin tone and imply a denigration of Blackness. A brown-skinned actress complained that people thought calling her *moreninha* (not very Black) was a compliment, but she's proud of her heritage and resents the implication. Conversely, an American sociologist reported that his mixed-race daughter responded to a questionnaire about whether she thought of herself as "Black" with a "yes" while her much darker Brazilian boyfriend ticked "no."

Among the most contentious categories is "mulata." An old samba line goes: *"Who invented the mulata? Portuguese men!"* A woman dancing for tourists in a sequined bikini and fishnet stockings is said to be working "as a mulata"; back in the favela, she's simply Black. Attitudes have begun to shift; a feminist carnival bloco removed Caetano Veloso's song "Tropicália" from its repertoire because it uses the term. "I think of myself as mulato," responded the composer: "I love the word." Veloso's confrontations with mid-'60s TV-studio audiences weren't limited to the times they booed an electric guitar. One TV Record show featured an elegant elderly sambista named Clementina de Jesus, who had been rediscovered after years working as a domestic. When the audience booed her black face and called her a monkey, Caetano cursed them and stormed off the set.

Early in his first term as president, Lula da Silva established the office of Secretary for Promoting Racial Equality. Some critics felt the initiative was more effective in dampening the debate on racism than combating the problem. Far more effectively, Lula instituted the Bolsa Família, which gave poor homes a basic income on condition they send their kids to school and have medical check-ups. Post-Lula, politicians tried to dismantle the program, albeit stealthily, given the Bolsa's popularity. In a 2015 interview, Carlos Lyra suggested that Brazil had never recovered the Kubitschek/bossa nova optimism crushed by the 1964 coup d'état. Good fortune has certainly been in short supply ever since. Perhaps that is why, since the seventies, Cariocas of all shades and classes dress in white and gather on New Year's Eve at Copacabana Beach to float bouquets in the waves, hoping to bring luck by honoring Lemenja, Yoruba goddess of the sea.

There is no folklore. Everything is culture.

—Gilberto Gil

On August 6, 2001, having found an excuse for another trip to Brazil, I was back in Salvador. Caetano performed that night in an open-air amphitheater for a popular audience who'd won their tickets in a promotion by a local bank. As the performance reached its climax, news arrived backstage that Jorge Amado had died. Returning for his encore, Veloso relayed the sad news, then embarked on what amounted to virtually a further concert. He sang his "Milagres do povo" (Miracles of the Poor), based on Amado's response when Caetano asked him about God and Candomblé, then another song he'd composed for a film based on an Amado novel, a few more of the writer's favorites, and, finally, Amado's own words set to a Dorival Caymmi melody, "É doce morrer no mar" (It's Sweet to Die in the Sea). For nearly an hour, the crowd never left the edges of their seats, cheering and calling out encouragement, a palpable feeling of communion flowing between stage and audience. An outsider might have expected such literate emotion from a bourgeois crowd in expensive seats, but these were ordinary people from all shades and strata of the Brazilian spectrum. Could one imagine an anglophone parallel? Paul Simon at Forest

Hills the night Philip Roth died? Jarvis Cocker onstage when we lost Harold Pinter?

Brazil has created its own musical world. The Portuguese and their successors never suppressed African and indigenous cultures as the English and Americans did; when music became a business, the economy was big enough to support its own vibrant and distinct industry. One could say that Byrne's vision of Brazil as a pop utopia and Veloso's dream of "creating high art on its own terms" have been achieved, though "selling that art around the world" has proved more difficult. Between the Portuguese language and the particularity of its dancing, the world has taken it up only in oblique ways, hiring its musicians, performing its melodies (minus the rhythms), sampling its recordings, and obsessively collecting and reissuing its fifties and sixties vinyl. American music is an open-source program for any culture to use in its own way. Brazil's firewalls are not so easy to get past; we press our noses up against the glass, looking, listening, and, if we're brave enough, trying to samba.

VI
Mano a mano

Jean de Reszké was once the world's most famous tenor; Caruso followed in his footsteps. After retiring in 1904, he bred racehorses, coached opera singers, and seduced a countess away from her count. The couple spent every "season" in their Paris apartment, holding fashionable salons where the countess liked organizing games her guests were expected to play. One April evening in 1912, she decided that everyone would sing, play, or dance a piece of music, each from a different country. When it came the turn of an Argentine dandy named Ricardo Güiraldes, he asked a fellow *porteño* to go to the piano and play a tango called "El Entrerriano."

Wealthy Argentines were thick on the ground in pre-war Paris. In the years either side of 1900, the Argentine economy had exploded; clearing the native peoples off the pampas had opened up the land for cattle and wheat, and refrigerated ships meant Argentine steaks began appearing on expensive menus across Europe. Sons of wealthy trading families followed the beef, becoming ubiquitous at Parisian cabarets, racetracks, balls, and salons.

As his friend played the sensual syncopations of the Argentine version of the habanera rhythm, Güiraldes walked over to the prettiest girl in the room, Yvette Gueté. Sharp intakes of breath were heard as he took her into the tango embrace; in polite society of 1912, no man held a woman that close on the dancefloor. Ricardo was pleased by how easily the shocked and delighted girl followed his lead as he spun and froze, paced and turned, at times entwining his leg around hers, a move he'd learned in Buenos Aires brothels. Güiraldes fancied himself a bit of a poet and would later publish this verse:

> . . . *silhouettes that glide by silently*
> *as if hypnotised by a blood-filled dream,*
> *hats tilted over sardonic sneers.*
> *The all-absorbing love of a tyrant,*
> *jealously guarding his dominion*
> *over women who have surrendered submissively,*
> *like obedient beasts . . .*
> *Sad, severe tango . . .*
> *Dance of love and death . . .*

That first moment at the de Reszkés' may not have risen to such a level of melodrama, but it certainly caused a sensation. The following day, no one in Paris "society" spoke of anything else. Hostesses scrambled to ensure Güiraldo or another Argentine *niño bien* attended their salon. Virtually overnight, Paris went tango mad.

Cause and effect are not entirely clear-cut; tango was already being danced in certain Parisian milieus. Argentine ensembles had traveled there to record and picked up extra money playing in dives similar to the ones where they performed back home. Nods of fraternal camaraderie had been exchanged between *tangueros* and Parisian *apaches*, who danced out a cartoonish exaggeration of tango attitudes. Nonetheless, the pre-war tango craze of 1912–14 was a top-down affair; once the toffs went for it, everyone else joined in.

> The tango is in Buenos Aires a primitive dance of houses of ill repute and of the lowest kind of dives. It is never danced in polite society nor among persons of breeding.
>
> —Argentine embassy official in Paris in 1912 explaining why the music was never performed at embassy functions

> Argentina? . . . Oh yes, the tango!
>
> —Tsar Nicholas II on being introduced to the country's new ambassador to St. Petersburg in 1913

[A country] which has such a national dance really must be a collective of monkeys . . . [O]nly somebody with the temperament of a negro can face such a spectacle without repugnance.

—Editorial in *Mercure de France*, 1914

Is one supposed to dance it standing up?

—Countess de Pourtalès on first seeing the tango

Slums in the center of Buenos Aires had been knocked down to build wide, Paris-inspired boulevards. With the help of British capital, Argentina had constructed a vast rail network bringing cattle, grain, and travelers to port. Its cities boasted opera houses, daily newspapers, museums, and tree-lined streets filled with mansions and fashionable shops. The booming economy made the country the second most popular destination after the US for Europeans in search of a new life: over six million emigrated there in the final years of the nineteenth century. Did Parisians speak of such accomplishments? No, all they wanted were tango lessons and they mocked visitors as prudes when refused. Young men in Buenos Aires didn't blink; hundreds, possibly thousands, traveled to the French capital hoping to make their fortunes teaching Europeans how to dance like a porteño and, while they were at it, seducing an heiress—or perhaps her mother.

Two years earlier, the Orientalism of Diaghilev's Ballets Russes had overturned centuries-old ideas of how fashionable women should dress; corsets were softened, then covered with loose, flowing garments that flattered the natural contours of the female body. Fads arriving from America had brought couples into closer contact through "animal dances"—the Turkey Trot, Bunny Hug, and Grizzly Bear—which seemed more athletic and silly than sensual. At first, even the French found the tango too risqué to be danced at night, so every afternoon at 5 p.m., cafés and dance halls held *thés dansants*. In her memoir, Adry de Carbuccia (whose uncle founded Maxim's and claimed the title "Tango King of Paris") wrote that "tango transformed conventions and scruples: women . . . lost the fear instilled by their mothers; and allowed themselves to be closely embraced by dancing partners who were often unknown to them." A silk manufacturer found himself with a warehouse filled with a dyeing error, stacks of orangey yellow cloth he couldn't give away. In desperation he advertised it as "satin-tango" and it sold out within days; this strange hue became the dance's official color.

By 1913, there were "tango balls," "skating tangos," and, that summer, "tango trains" to Deauville, where the casino held weekly contests with cash prizes. The dance spread eastward across Europe, fighting café-by-café, ball-by-ball, editorial-by-editorial, and sermon-by-sermon battles that reactionaries saw (not incorrectly) as a life-and-death struggle to preserve time-honored assumptions about social decorum, female behavior, and human sexuality. The Pope, the Tsar, and Queen Mary all received demonstrations. Kaiser Wilhelm refused to look, decreeing that any officer caught tangoing in uniform would be court-martialed; distraught German hostesses were forced to choose between having handsome men in military regalia at their balls or the tango.

In London, *Dancing Times* recalled how "our grandmothers fought tooth and nail against the introduction of the polka and the valse into England." The island's resistance collapsed when a tango was danced at the Hampstead ball given by Grand Duke Michael of Russia and attended by the season's grandest assemblage of titles. H. G. Wells declared 1913 to be "the year of the tango." *Dancing Times* took one final pre-war swipe the following spring: "The tango as danced in England by English people, is petulant rather than passionate, as mild and mellifluous as a spray of hawthorn swaying to and fro in a breeze." The *Times* complained not that it was immoral, but that it was unsuited to the national temperament, noting that British tango dancers could be seen counting under their breath while still being out of time with both the music and each other. "Whether we like it or not," the piece concluded, "we are English."

Vernon and Irene Castle, who had taught Europeans those animal dances, brought the tango back with them when they sailed to New York in 1912. American bluenoses were as aghast as the English, but the Castles' chain of dancing academies made a fortune teaching a watered-down version they advertised as "respectable" while winking at the dance's scandalous reputation. Tango controversies reinforced America's image as a land both democratic and litigious: Nutley, New

Jersey, split bitterly down the middle in a referendum on whether to allow the tango at its annual town dance, while a New York mother petitioned the court to commit her daughter to an asylum to stop her "ruining" herself at tango tea dances.

The surge came full circle when Baron Demarchi gave a ball for the cream of Buenos Aires society and most of the guests roared in approval when a fashionable young couple demonstrated the contentious dance. Tango had now completed its journey from the abattoirs and whorehouses of the *arrabals* (outskirts), via the salons and cafés of Paris, Berlin, London, and New York, to finally arrive in the mansions of Buenos Aires.

[T]heir brazen, immoral, abdominal localisations drive the dancers into a frenzy. It is an infernal tango. It is the most lascivious device that the choreography of the primitive races knows.

—Dr. J. Mejía, *Rosas and His Time*

Within the chaste contours of the tango figures, rages the desire of sex ... So intense is the current within the man and the woman, that it leaps in the air and copulates.

—Author Waldo Frank during his 1917 visit to Buenos Aires

Del fango viene el tango.
(Tango comes from the mud.)

—Argentine saying

Tango was also danced by carters, fairgoers, garbage collectors and port workers: it was the music of seamstresses, laundrywomen and ironers of the tenement houses and it was also sung in the dark brothels. However, it was also the gentle breeze of the gardens, the mirth of the corners, the guitars played in the storehouses, the music of [street] organists, the horn of trolleys.

—Daniel Vidart, Uruguayan essayist

Argentina is the Whitest country in Latin America; walking the streets of central Buenos Aires you encounter few non-European faces. Darker complexions generally belong to descendants of Spaniards with Roma,

Moorish, or Sephardic genes or migrant workers from Peru and Bolivia. The land's original occupants were "cleared" during the 1870s by General Roca; he didn't bother with discreet North American methods, such as diseased blankets or reservations located far from traditional hunting grounds, he simply gunned them down, men, women, and children.

The disappearance of the country's Black population is more complicated. While the land never had a slave-labor-intensive industry such as sugar or cotton, African captives were brought to the mouth of the Río de la Plata to be used as domestic servants or mule drivers for the wagon trains bringing silver ore down from the eastern slopes of the Andes (hence the country's metallic name). The economy expanded in the early nineteenth century after a brief occupation by the British, who introduced the sort of bank financing Madrid had always denied the colony. Afro-Argentines fought heroically against these invaders, weaving and ducking to avoid shot, then springing forward lance in hand to dispatch the enemy. Their exploits were celebrated for a few years, but gratitude was short-lived; in the early 1820s, newly independent Argentina banned public displays of African music and dance because, as one official explained, "Maidens and other innocents [might see and learn] things they should not." It was also important, added another, for Blacks to have "a proper understanding of their own lowness." Afro-Argentine culture went underground, preserved in societies called *candombes* (from the same root as the similar-sounding Brazilian religion), which means "in regard to us as black people" in Ki-Kongo.

After the abolition of slavery in 1853, the army was one of the few willing employers of newly freed Blacks, who were pushed into the front lines of the Paraguayan war, where they fought bravely and died in their thousands. Many more perished in 1871 as yellow fever swept through poor neighborhoods and doctors refused to treat dark-skinned patients. When waves of immigration from Italy and other European countries poured into Argentina later in the century, the Black percentage of the population plummeted. They could still be seen in the dance halls, bars, and brothels, though. And, music being one of the few rewarding careers open to Afro-Argentines, they could still be heard.

The Paris embassy official who described tango as a "primitive dance" was speaking in code; what he meant was that it was tainted by Blackness. Once northern hemisphere popularity had forced the country to embrace it, however, the idea that tango owed anything to Afro-Argentines was suppressed, ignored, or forgotten. Most books on the subject include a bit of potted history: gaúchos, stockyards, *compadritos* (the Argentine equivalent of *malandros*), Italian immigrants, and German bandoneóns, etc. Further back, the story fades, with a few references to the "traditional" tango of Andalusian Gypsies and stamping *zapateado* contests in dusty pampas bars. Some make reference to an African ingredient but don't examine it very closely.

Fortunately, one historian wrote a thoroughly documented response to every question about tango's origins and evolution. Professor Robert Farris Thompson of Yale specialized in tracing the African roots of the cultures of the Americas; he visited Argentina often over many years, dancing tango, interviewing its virtuosos, consulting experts, and delving deep into original sources. The result was *Tango: The Art History of Love*, a book that examines both dance and music in vivid detail, with names, dates, and eyewitness accounts. He also spent time in Central Africa investigating the great kingdoms that astonished Portuguese slave-traders and missionaries in the early sixteenth century.

Farris Thompson makes it clear that the word *tango* is neither Spanish nor gypsy but—like its cousins *rumba*, *samba*, and *mambo*—pure Ki-Kongo. Most Argentine slaves came from that Central African kingdom, which he describes as a largely urban realm with a complex system of laws and highly developed trade, in which dance was supremely important as both ritual and celebration. He explains the word's root and shows us its colorful branches: *tangana* (to walk), *tangama* (to take long steps or walk like a crab), and, best of all, *tanga dongulu* (to swagger).

At some point in the story of Kongo slavery in the Spanish Empire, *tango* entered the vernacular to mean music played or danced "in an African manner." How this word came to describe what the world was dancing up to the edge of the mass grave known as World War One can be divided into two parts: the music and the moves. We'll start with the music.

As in Cuba and Brazil, Black Argentines picked up European instruments with relative ease and played them for White occasions, while dancing in the candombes to drums, handclaps, and singing. White folk music was mostly played on guitars and other European instruments, such as the sanfona (the primitive squeezebox Luis Gonzaga's father used), which was popular in the north, where German immigrants had settled. Itinerant singers called *payadores* (many of whom were Black or mixed-race) challenged each other in décima contests, improvising song battles with roots in medieval Europe. Then, in the middle of the nineteenth century, the country's musical landscape was transformed by an import that everyone, Black and White, found irresistible.

When its empire was still intact, Spain had always insisted that goods grown, mined, crafted, or plundered anywhere in its far-flung colonies be brought to Seville to be taxed before being exported. No colonial product ever followed these tortuous trade rules more correctly than the habanera. This infectious rhythm began life as an Afro-Cuban bass line borrowed from a Kongo drum pattern, graduating from the marimbula to the contrabass before infecting pianists' left hands. After propelling Cubans onto Havana dancefloors it was carried to Spain, where it quickly grew ubiquitous and was named after its point of origin. Gitanos in Andalusia called it "tango" because it sounded Black, and we've seen how it invaded theaters high and low, evoking cartoon Blackness in the bufos and a "gypsy temptress" at the opera.

Like many goods in the old empire's trading network, the habanera arrived in Argentina both officially and by the back door. By the time those Spanish theater troupes got to Buenos Aires, sailors had already brought the habanera to waterfront bars, where it was straight away employed as the rhythm for a popular song style called the *milonga*. This is a key word in the history of tango; some have claimed that it's Spanish slang for a "lock-in" or "elongated" session at a bar where tango was danced, but *milonga* is another Ki-Kongo word, meaning "dialogue" or "argument." Central African dancers used it metaphorically for "call and response," one line facing another, one step or gesture answered by another.

It is tempting to imagine Black and White Argentines describing the fruitful musical interplay between their cultures as a milonga, but all we know for certain is that there was a popular song form by that name that began moving to a habanera beat sometime after mid-century. When touring Spanish companies introduced it to a broad audience, the beat invaded every corner of Buenos Aires; sheet music diagramming a rigid version of it sold like the proverbial hot cakes. A group of rich kids formed a band called Los Negros that for years dominated the city's streets during its (rather tame) carnival, dancing and singing to the new beat beneath girls' balconies. In blackface, of course.

Another invasive musical species, the polka, showed how much fun couple-dancing could be when the tempo was fast. In combination with habanera-inspired styles such as ragtime and cakewalk from America and maxixe from Brazil, polka inspired the milonga to become a cheerful, fast-paced dance music, laying the foundation for what, in the new century, would become tango.

This music was usually performed by trios in some permutation of piano, guitar, clarinet, flute, and violin. The shadowy pioneers waving to us across the decades from tinny cylinders and early shellac 78s, who defined the feel of this music and set the standards for playing it, included many Black or mixed-race artists: violinist, arranger, and bandleader Carlos Posadas, guitarist Luciano Ríos, violinist "El Negro" Casimiro, clarinettist "El Mulato" Sinforoso, and, perhaps the most important of all, bassist and arranger Leopoldo Thompson. (Thompson may have been the first anywhere to deliver percussive slaps to this normally bowed instrument.) The better-sounding recordings of *trios típicos* along with later vocal discs have the intensity and swing of early *son* or country blues records, driven by guitarists such as Ríos. Many ended verses with a flourish: *da-dum da DAA*, the final two beats often emphasized with a shouted Ki-Kongo exhortation, *tshia-tshia* (dance, dance), that evolved to *chin-chin* and, later, in Cuba and America, to *cha-cha*.

It was Posadas, ironically, who had the bright idea that would forever alter the music. "Ironic" because over the coming decades, this addition became the primary weapon with which White Argentines and Italian immigrants would *agringar*—"gringo-ize" or Whiten—the sound of tango.

> The bandoneón is a hellish instrument. It was made and developed in Germany, at a time when things were meant to last, a time when plastic didn't exist. The materials were noble: wood, metal, leather, mother-of-pearl... For a bandoneónist, the instrument becomes one's alter-ego—it is partly oneself, partly one's wife... One feels possessed and possessor, one caresses it, is aware of its temperature.
>
> —Rodolfo Mederos, bandoneón player

The bandoneón is an oversize concertina with buttons at either end, just outside the player's line of vision. The positioning of these "keys" seems to follow no comprehensible logic; there can be as many as 75 of them producing 150 "voices," half made by pushing the bellows closed, the other half by pulling it open. The instrument's inventor, Heinrich Band, saw it as a portable church organ, hence its low, sonorous tones. When the bandoneón arrived in Argentina sometime after the middle of the nineteenth century, it was viewed as a *cosa de gringos*—something for Whites—played around pampas campfires or in bars.

Carlos Posadas may have gotten the notion to add one to his trio from the bellows-y sound of the *organitos*, barrel organs that were a common sight on Buenos Aires streets; their punched rolls of programmed music included the odd tango, and when passersby heard one they might start dancing. The bandoneón's velvety sound was far lower and thicker than an organito's, though, the last thing one could imagine suiting tango in its larval milonga stage, when instruments needed to be agile and light on their feet. The virtuoso who mastered this puzzle was another Afro-Argentine: "El Pardo" (the Dark One), Sebastián Ramos Mejía, the instrument's tango pioneer, who taught many of the great players who followed.

The bandoneón is even heavier than it looks, so Mejía and most other Argentine players discarded the neck strap in favor of playing it seated, with a lap rug to keep from chafing their thighs. Gaúcho and stockyard life was never gentle and Argentines handled the instrument roughly, in ways that would have horrified its inventor; they bounced it to give the notes more "bite," struck the frame for percussive effect, and kept time by stomping.

In that pre-cell-phone era, rendezvous were arranged for a time and a street corner. When one party was stood up, porteños (natives of the port of Buenos Aires) called it being "cornered," on the receiving end of "El Esquinazo." An instrumental by that name helped establish Posadas's vision, becoming the first huge tango hit, the catchy melody driven by Luciano Ríos's "dancing thumb" on the guitar's lower strings and fleshed out by El Pardo's bandoneón, including his evocation of a lover's impatient foot-tapping by hitting the frame. The tune's exuberant melody was so infectious that it was banned in many establishments, as customers would celebrate the final *chin-CHIN* by smashing glasses on the Moorish-patterned tiles of the city's many barroom floors.

Ángel Villoldo, the composer of "El Esquinazo," was the renaissance man of early tango, a bridge between nineteenth-century payadores and the dawn of the Argentine music industry. He published instructions on how to play the guitar, collected *criollo* melodies in a popular songbook, worked as a circus clown, entertained bar patrons Dylan-style with guitar and harmonica rack, was a great dancer, and kept busy during the day by using his sturdy horse to pull trams up hills or set them back onto their rails. Another enduring Villoldo composition is "El Choclo" (The Corncob), a prototype of the bawdy tango with unprintable lyrics that has been continually recycled, often with new, more polite words, for over a century.

The dance that conquered Paris was in a state of transition. Instrumental line-ups were becoming fixed: bandoneón, piano, violin, and bass, with the piano mimicking the patterns of tango guitar (thus rendering the latter superfluous). The rhythmic structure, which for the music's first decade had largely been major-key melodies over a habanera line picked out on bass or guitar, was starting to flip. Even Farris Thompson couldn't identify who first pounded out *el cuatro*, the four-by-four beat played against a syncopated, minor-key, habanera-shaped melody that would define tango as it moved on into the twentieth century.

The music was also slowing down to accommodate the growing complexity of the dancing, the older, more respectable crowds that were joining in, and the bandoneón. The new instrument made other contributions aside from its rich tone, one being the *arrastre*, a tantalizing slide that delayed—and emphasized—the opening note of a verse or chorus;

as players grew more adept they added a *carraspeo* or "throat-clearing" growl to augment the drama of the arrastre (which had its roots in Kongo dance moves and foot-dragging gestures in zapateado contests). It is hard to put a finger on what it was in the bandoneón's timbre that spoke so movingly to Argentines, the usual answer being that it was particularly well suited to tango's mournful minor-key melodies. This instrument was not the only thing setting tango apart from dance forms evolving in other cultures at the dawn of the new century; another was its lack of drums or percussion. Is the dance's slippery rhythm—holding back, catching up, hesitating, stopping, then striding forward again—a cause or an effect? In tango, melodic instruments generate their own dancing pulse, giving the music a fluidity to which jazz, *son*, and samba have never aspired.

Tango evolved in a conversation (or, I should say, a milonga) among three groups: the criollos (native-born), the (mostly Italian) immigrants, and the Black Argentines. Criollos tried to keep tango to themselves at first, imagining that immigrants would find it too difficult. As those two groups wrestled for dominance, each referred to the third for inspiration and support. The fact there were so few Afro-Argentines may have made it easier for White dancers and musicians to look so openly in their direction. Many Black musicians were well schooled in the northern hemisphere's classical and popular forms, so were able to abet the Europeanizing impulse as well as the native feeling, while maintaining the rhythmic vitality that ensured tango remained broadly popular and not marooned in polite salons. Even after authorities and pundits began denying the African connection, the best dancers and musicians always knew where the music's headwaters were located. All three groups may have responded to and encouraged the music's mournful tones, sharing as they did the sorrow of exile, from the pampas, from Europe and from Africa (the brutality of the last displacement, of course, being of a completely different magnitude).

The post-Paris decade would be dominated by three orchestra leaders, one a native Argentine (Roberto Firpo) and the other two (Francisco Canaro and Julio de Caro) from Italian immigrant families. As tango became the mainstream music of Buenos Aires, each helped to forge a balance between "tango *liso*," the smooth Italian-leaning style, and the African root, or, as Farris Thompson puts it, between "*Weltschmerz* and cool." All had one thing in common: in the early years of their orchestras, each had employed Leopoldo Thompson as bassist and arranger. Thompson died in 1925, aged only thirty-five; his passing was tragic for tango but the rhythmic signature he created remained astonishingly intact for more than a century. Due, in no small part, to the fierce demands of those who danced it.

Tango is a sad thought danced.

—Enrique Discépolo, composer

The basis is rhythm, the goal is love. Sensual, easy, undulating, full of surprises in the movements that accompany the syncopated music, each dancer, each couple, is a picture of changing attitudes.

—1896 description in *La Nación* of a dance attended by "blacks and foreigners"

The tango appears to be in the genre of European, embraced dances. But danced by Argentines, it displays differences . . . Limbs of both male and female dancers seem to move independently of their own bodies. Torsos remain motionless while legs perform what appear to be completely unrelated figures.

—Julie Taylor, *Paper Tangos*

My girl's got a gift
For the real creole tango,
And all its quick stops.
There's power in her hips,
She's a motor, she's tops.
See her work out.
Doing fours or half-moons
She's tango deluxe.
The perfect woman of my youth.

—Ángel Villoldo, "Cuerpo de alambre" (Wiry Body)

By 1901, things were getting too hot for Butch Cassidy and the Sundance Kid. The American West was being carved up by cattle barons; police and Pinkertons were everywhere and there was clearly no future for old-fashioned outlaws. With the loot from one last train robbery in Montana, they bought passage to Buenos Aires and headed out into the pampas, looking for a fresh start. To their great (and soon fatal) disappointment, the colorful world of the gaúchos, so vividly invoked in the Argentine national epic, José Hernández's *The Gaúcho Martín Fierro*, had long passed into mythology. Just like in the prairies of the American West, the pampas only needed inconvenient natives to be cleared away and the moneymen were ready to move in.

Culturally, with its mix of Iberian, indigenous, and Black, the pampas were more like the Brazilian sertão than Wyoming or the Dakotas. The hero of Hernández's poem is a payador turned outlaw; he engages in a décima duel with a Black singer and later witnesses a zapateado contest in one of the pampas bars known as *pulperías*. This hyper-masculine foot-stomping comes from Andalusia and, before that, the Berber culture of North Africa. The gaúchos called such battles *malambos*; it seems they pound their feet in Central Africa, too, in a dance by that name that represents the "burying" of a dispute.

African culture was hiding in plain sight everywhere. Regulations prohibiting Blacks dancing in public seem to have been as ignored there as they were in Cuba or Brazil; Whites wrote of watching circles or facing lines of dancers, with individuals taking it in turns to show off complex, acrobatic moves. Afro-Argentines picked up European dances as readily as they played European instruments; an 1840 newspaper account of a Black ball reports: "The quadrilles were danced with a rigid, almost Britannic seriousness. The etiquette of the waltzers left nothing to be desired."

"Seriousness"—perhaps that is Kongo's most enduring gift to tango, the idea that in dance, nuances are matters of supreme importance. When Blacks took up the waltz and the mazurka, they would embellish them by stepping out of the embrace to add moves borrowed from candombe. In 1865, an English visitor reported seeing mazurkas "with stop-pattern flourishes . . . horizontal breaks and passages with knees deeply bent." Black dancing seems to have been a source of delight and fascination for many White Argentines; Manuela Rosas, daughter of the notorious mid-nineteenth-century dictator, shocked polite society by not only attending Black balls but enthusiastically joining in.

Once tango had been embraced by the wealthy, Argentine journals began exploring its history. In a lengthy 1913 article, "An Old Tanguero" recalled how the whole thing began for him in 1883, when he and a group of friends went to a Black party in an arrabal, paid close attention to what the dancers called "tango," then went back to their own barrio and spent all night practicing what they'd seen.

In the last decades of the century, the pampas came right up to the edge of the city. Arrabals were filled with stockyards, slaughterhouses, tanneries, pulperías, and flimsy shantytown housing, sometimes just a tent pitched under a tree. In that rough-edged community, immigrants and criollos competed for jobs and women. Single girls were scarce; those who weren't working in brothels often served in cafés or dance halls, where definitions were blurred. With the odds so wildly in their favor, even professionals could be choosy, and mastering the tango became the most telling way for men to gain female approval. Newcomers might spend as long as two years in all-male *practicas*, where veterans would school them like apprentices until they were ready to dance with a woman without making a fool of themselves.

Tango's milonga parent resembled Brazilian maxixe in that there were few fixed patterns, with dancers carried along by the fast-flowing music. In 1883, Argentine folklorist Ventura Lynch wrote that compadritos "[gloried] . . . in quick subtle tricks . . . a burlesque of the dances that blacks perform." As the music slowed down, the moves became more complex: candombe-derived "cuts," "breaks," and "freezes," sweeping foot gestures from the rural El Gato folk dance, steps borrowed from polka, mazurka, and European circle dances, as well as *ochos* (figure eights), the women's twists and turns so named for marks left in the dust of the streets by Black dancers during carnival. Captions to photos of dancing couples in a 1903 magazine include "This is called being stuck together, even if we have no glue" and "This corte will leave Uncle cross-eyed!"

Around 1900, Black dancers developed a style called *canyengue* (Ki-Kongo for "melting into the music"). Modern tango stage shows often include a canyengue number to demonstrate what many consider the dance's fundamental root. This style was marked by bending at the knees and at the waist, leaning back, then dipping forward. The *"enganche"* position mocked by *Some Like It Hot* and Groucho Marx—knees bent, arms straight out in front, cheek-to-cheek with both facing forward—is pure canyengue.

In an essay written in 1955, Jorge Luis Borges endorsed the idea that tango developed in brothels, and his stature as the country's greatest man of letters put the seal on a notion that has, over the years, become accepted as fact. It was certainly true that plenty of tango could be heard in Buenos Aires whorehouses; one famous nineteenth-century bordello, El Teatro de Alegría (Theater of Joy), hired Black dancers and musicians to entertain customers waiting their turn. But therein lies the problem; outnumbered sex workers were far too busy to waste unpaid time that way, so tango in brothels was probably danced mostly by male couples. Tango really developed in dance halls whose atmosphere echoed the rough pampas pulperías; on weekends they filled with payday workers, pimps looking for recruits, and the girls both sought. Pimp style guided men's sartorial choices, including stylish silk scarves and "homburg" hats. Pimp priorities also affected the dance; they wanted to show they could dominate their women and at the same time advertise how great the girls looked and how freely and sexily they moved.

Accounts of tango's early years confirm that Afro-Argentine style set the standard; tough guys danced Black. The erect posture comes from Spanish flamenco, but the cool, mask-like face (as Farris Thompson wrote and lectured about so eloquently) is an essential feature of many African cultures. Pibe Palermo, a famous dancer of the modern era, insists that to really dance tango, you need "to season it with candombe." To this day, couples at a milonga circulate counter-clockwise, the universal African direction, mirroring the path of the sun.

The Great War may have brought a halt to Europe's tango craze, but the injection of bourgeois money into the local scene transformed life for Buenos Aires's best dancers and musicians; some could now give up their day jobs (many were streetcar or taxi drivers), opening tango academies or taking well-paying gigs at fashionable cafés and society balls. With creative competition among orchestra leaders, arrangers, composers, and bandoneón virtuosos, to say nothing of dancers, Argentine tango was poised to carry on where it left off, once the world emerged from the carnage of war and the even greater death toll of the flu pandemic that followed. But while it remained hugely popular in many countries—Japan, Russia, Turkey, Finland, and France foremost among them—it was never again a craze. There was more competition, particularly from jazz, then rumba, but equally important was that tango itself became distracted, no longer so focused on the dance.

Berthe Gardès was one of many single women to ship out from Europe in the last years of the nineteenth century and head for the Río de la Plata. Some were experienced sex workers drawn by a booming economy with a surplus of men; others were following sweethearts who had sent letters full of promises. Many of the latter would end up disillusioned and, in order to survive, join the former in Buenos Aires's many brothels. But Berthe had already endured her heartbreak; abandoned by a married lover, she sailed from Bordeaux in hopes of giving herself and her baby boy the chance of a better life.

While his mother took in laundry, young Charles reveled in the noisy, chaotic streets of his new home. Italians played Caruso recordings as loud as early technology permitted, and some could belt out Neapolitan songs and Verdi arias pretty well themselves. He also loved the payadores and the organitos, while tango, of course, was always in the air. By the time he reached his teens, his first name had been localized to "Carlos" and Gardès had become "Gardel." He joined a claque who earned free entrance to the opera by cheering for particular singers and, according to some accounts, he occasionally sang in the chorus.

In 1912, Gardel teamed up with José Razzano; they dressed like dandified gaúchos and sang duets filled with nostalgia for the rural life, their look and musical texture closer to Gene Autry than to Luiz Gonzaga or Hank Williams. They hung around with compadritos and gamblers and were sometimes hired for private parties where a gangster picked up the tab. Gardel was handsome and not bashful; he got wounded in a fight over a woman by one Dr. Guevara, father of Che. One night in 1913, he and Razzano were part of a rowdy assemblage at Madam Jeanne's (the city's most expensive brothel) that moved en masse to the nearby Armenonville cabaret, commandeering the stage and demanding a song from Carlos and José. When the pair brought the house down, the club's owner offered them a contract. In a few months, they were stars.

With fame, Gardel's nightlife milieu expanded to include journalists, politicians, and poets as well as the criminals and bookies. (Carlos loved the racetrack almost as much as he loved music.) One evening at the Café Raffetto he heard a thin-voiced payador named Pascual Contursi singing lyrics set to a popular tango melody. Gardel couldn't get the song out of his head; for weeks he hung around the Raffetto hoping Contursi would turn up so he could hear it again. But the payador, it turned out, had moved back across the Plata to Montevideo, where Gardel ran into him many months later when he and Razzano played a theater there. This time, he made sure to copy down Contursi's verses about the tortured end of a love affair; the words were elegantly poetic but also colloquial, peppered with Lunfardo expressions. Gardel wanted to add it to their repertoire, but Razzano adamantly refused.

Tango may have crossed over into the Argentine mainstream, but strictly as dance music. There had been sung tangos, but they were, as a rule, humorous and bawdy singalongs. Lunfardo was a street language, a blend of Spanish slang, Genoese dialect, Romani, and Cocoliche, an argot used by Italian criminals. The nostalgic world of gauchos and pampas that Gardel and Razzano's singing celebrated was linked to a jingoistic reaction against the mongrel chaos of the new Buenos Aires; for the pair to sing a tango would have been like Merle Haggard following up "Okie from Muskogee" with a Sly Stone cover.

Gardel, though, would not be deterred. On July 31, 1917, on the stage of the Teatro Empire, accompanied by Afro-Argentine guitarist José Ricardo, he sang Contursi's song and the audience went crazy, leaving his nervous record label little choice; they released the song Gardel called "Mi noche triste" (My Sad Night) on January 12, 1918, and could barely keep up with demand. Just as "Pelo telefone" had kicked off the samba industry and Mamie Smith's "Crazy Blues" was about to launch the American blues business, Gardel's recording marked the start of *tango canción*. It didn't happen overnight; Gardel knew he needed to find or generate songs at a similar level of quality. He challenged his nocturnal companions to write words, set some to music himself, and match-made lyricists with composers. By the early 1920s, the duo was history and Carlos Gardel was on his way to becoming the greatest star in Latin America.

Listening today, Gardel's voice remains a thing of wonder. With the timbre and occasional bombast of a Caruso-era tenor, the seductive undertones of a baritone, the nasal intensity of a street singer, and the clearest diction imaginable, he relishes the words, chortling at the adventures, passions, and disappointments of the characters animating his songs. He is worldly but never cynical, drawing the listener into his love for the barrios of his youth and the people who inhabit them.

In 1930, at the height of Argentina's passion for tango canción, Jorge Luis Borges predicted that future generations would recognise in those lyrics "the true poetry of our time." As an outsider with limited Spanish (and, needless to say, non-existent Lunfardo), it's not for me to judge whether he was right or wrong, but most Argentines seem to concur. I can at least affirm that the stories told in 1920s and '30s tango songs are rich and strange in ways not commonly found in such broadly popular music.

One example of Gardel's astute opportunism came in 1920, when he spotted a verse published in a newspaper, introduced its author to a composer, and had a hit record with the result. The aspiring poet was Celedonio Flores, a mixed-race twenty-year-old from Gardel's old barrio whose main occupation was prizefighter; the two became friends and Gardel recorded many of his earthy, Lunfardo-laced songs. The closing lines of the most famous of them all, "Mano a mano" (We're Even), were inscribed on Flores's grave in the Chacarita cemetery, a few paces from Gardel's.

From the moment I first heard it, Gardel's recording of "Mano a mano" has been a favorite of mine, not just in tango canción, but anywhere. (There's a wonderful film clip of him performing it.) With the help of Argentine friends, I came to understand the song's text and the story behind it. It seems that Flores frequented the same bar as an old man named Fernando Nunziata and once visited the simple room where Nunziata lived, decorated only with a photo of a long-lost love. "Mano a mano" tells his side of their story.

She was born poor: "*You dribbled* [gambeteabas] *the football of poverty in and out of the door of your tenement.*" (In the twenties, on the terraces of Boca Juniors, the notorious ur-*porteño* football club where Diego Maradona began his career, the verb *gambetear*—"to prance"—meant a clever dribble.) The couple were happy for a time: "*Your high-living* [bacana] *style lit a flame in my life, and you were even faithful.*" (Bacan is Lunfardo for "flash guy," *bacana* the female equivalent; the word also pops up in Brazilian samba of the same period.) Nunziata had no money and she was eventually lured away: "*Now your head is full of pitiful illusions . . . partying with high-rollers, where pretensions and vanity prevail.*" There are no hard feelings, though: "*We owe each other nothing, we're even . . . The favors I had from you have all been repaid, and if there's anything I may have overlooked, your sugar daddy can cover it.*" He wishes her well, but he's not optimistic: "*The guy that feeds you, may his bankroll stay fat, and may you keep away from all those pimps . . . And tomorrow, when you start to fall apart like old furniture . . . If you need some help, or perhaps a piece of advice, remember your old friend, who will put it all on the line for you and help out in any way, should the occasion arise.*"

The tortured emotions coursing through "Mano a mano" might explain why Buenos Aires has more psychiatrists per capita than any city on earth. It's not the shrink-consulting middle classes, though, who feature in tango canción, but the immigrants and former gaúchos for whom the "Argentine dream" rarely worked out. The boom years of 1880 to 1910 were long faded and the country had failed to capitalize on either the northern hemisphere's Great War or the subsequent recovery; when Wall Street crashed in 1929, Argentina's economy tanked along with the rest of the world's. Suffering and poverty were everywhere.

The harsh truth was that it was far easier for a poor but pretty girl to catch the eye of a wealthy guy (probably at a milonga) than for a man to escape poverty while remaining honest; song after song repeats that story. And when the girls grow older, in tango canción anyway, they get discarded like in "Un Viejo coche" (An Old Carriage), another classic song of the period.

The late historian Simon Collier, who pioneered Latin American studies in both British and American universities and wrote books on Gardel and tango, provided pithy song summaries in his notes to the Gardel compilation *The King of Tango*. For example:

> "Mano cruel" (Cruel Hand): "In the neighbourhood, you knew how to captivate people. More than one young man sighed for you. In the shadows, lying in wait, was the vile crook who tarnished your enchantment with his cruel hand. You yielded to his passionate words. We saw you no more."

> "Malevaje" (Underworld): "Good God! What have you *done* to me? The underworld gives me strange looks, it sees me losing my grip—me! And only yesterday my daring deeds were famous! Your love has trapped me. I don't know who I am anymore."

> "Seguí mi consejo" (Take My Advice): "Live like a swell. Avoid overwork. Get by on champagne. Always live your life at night. Find girls who are already fixed up and it won't cost you money. Avoid milk, it's bad for the heart. Make whiskey your friend instead. Take my advice!"

> "La Cumparsita"/"Si supieras" (If You Knew): "The morning sun no longer comes in through the window as it did when you were here. And the little dog, my companion, which stopped eating because you had left me, seeing me alone the other day, has left me, too."

Gardel's French blood beckoned him; from the mid-twenties onward he toured Europe often, spending long periods on the French and Spanish Rivieras. His records made him a star in Spain and sports-mad Carlos became an unofficial mascot of the Barcelona football team, traveling with them to international matches, serenading them in dressing rooms, and being presented with an automobile by the grateful club. His breakthrough in France arrived in 1928, when he stole the show from Josephine Baker at a star-studded benefit concert in Paris for the victims of a hurricane in Guadeloupe.

With the advent of talkies and the success of Al Jolson's *The Jazz Singer*, film studios were looking for photogenic vocalists; Paramount's Paris office signed Gardel in 1930, producing the first in a series of music-heavy features that filled movie houses across the Spanish-speaking world. After a Gardel song, audiences would sometimes storm the projection booth to demand a rewind and a second viewing.

The wafer-thin plots were the work of a Paris-based Argentine named Alfredo Le Pera, who also began collaborating with Carlos on song lyrics. Le Pera convinced him that in order to become a truly international star, he needed to drop the Lunfardo phrases and local references. It worked; Le Pera's lyrics graced hit after international hit across the first half of the thirties. These recordings were part of an evolution: on his first tango tracks, Gardel accompanied himself on guitar, before José Ricardo took on the task; then there were two strumming behind him and eventually four he called his "brooms." After moving from Odeon to RCA, his 1930s recordings often had orchestral backing, including violins and the occasional bandoneón. The look changed, too; gaúcho and compadrito were left behind as Gardel became a groomed and dapper man of the world.

When Paramount realized Gardel was box-office gold, they shifted production to their studios in New York; during a break from filming in early 1935, the NBC radio network arranged a live broadcast designed to reach America's growing Hispanic population, the increasing numbers of gringo tango fans, plus Mexicans and Cubans in range of NBC's powerful signal. In the studio audience that night was a girl from Jersey City and her boyfriend, a hoodlum with a good voice whom she was trying to persuade to go straight. After the show, the couple managed to get backstage, where she asked Gardel to give her beloved some advice. He told the young singer that he himself had started out on the wrong side of the law but had chosen to work hard on his musical gifts, and look at him now! Gardel then grabbed a passing NBC exec in charge of their *Original Amateur Hour* show and persuaded him to let the kid try out for it.

You can guess the rest. The skinny thug was, of course, Frank Sinatra; he won the contest, got a contract to sing with Harry James, and the rest is history. When Sinatra performed in Buenos Aires in 1981, he brought flowers to Gardel's grave and told local journalists that meeting him had saved his life.

In Buenos Aires, people sat and listened to singers in cafés that once hosted milongas. Sheet music sold in the tens of thousands. Francisco Canaro was the first bandleader to bow to the inevitable and add a vocalist, and the rest soon followed (though generally allowing them just one refrain per song). Many female vocalists made their names singing with orchestras in the twenties and early thirties, some appearing in trousers, tie, and trilby; after all, tango composers were almost all men and wrote songs from a male point of view. Porteño culture, it seems, wasn't quite ready for women to sing about their own passions and heartbreak.

No one danced to tango canción; combining the two, it was felt, did justice to neither. There may have also been a subtext; in many songs, the man is the broken-hearted victim of a duplicitous woman. How could he play the proud leading role the dance required while listening to such lyrics? With the economy in free fall, many Argentines succumbed to *mufa*, a Lunfardo word for a peculiarly Argentine state of self-pity, often savored in a café with a nice glass of wine or a cup of good coffee. Though the twentieth century was only one-third of the way along, and with far worse yet to come, songwriter Enrique Discépolo's hit dismissed the era as a "Cambalache" (Junk Shop): "[A] *real showcase of mischief . . . Today there's no difference between straight and treacherous, ignorant, wise, thieving, generous . . . nothing's better or worse."*

Tango was born nostalgic. Those early years when the dance was central to Argentine identity seemed long ago and far away. Poet Carlos de la Púa insisted,

> *. . . through your complicated tango steps . . .*
> *You will live on in the deeds of others,*

as long as a slum tough makes light of the cops . . .
as long as there's a poet, a thief, and a whore.

Past times and lost loves always seemed better than whatever the present had to offer, with only the slimmest of chances the future would bring improvement. Yet 1935 brought a pair of cataclysmic events that would usher in the start of a golden age.

I do not like the woman to talk to me while I dance tango . . .
When she says to me, "Omar, I am speaking," I answer, "And I, I am dancing."

—Buenos Aires dancer

Carlos Gardel and Alfredo Le Pera became good friends. Among the many things Alfredo had done for him was helping the singer overcome his dread of airplanes; Gardel had always traveled by boat, train, and auto, but could now cover a lot more ground by flying. As fate would have it, Le Pera was with him on a tour of Colombia; on June 24, 1935, their plane collided with another while taking off from Medellín Airport and burst into flames, killing everyone on board.

Gardel's body lay in state in Rio de Janeiro and Montevideo on its way home, before being escorted through the streets of Buenos Aires to the Chacarita cemetery by hundreds of thousands of black-clad mourners. Today there are Gardel murals everywhere and a larger-than-life statue in his old neighborhood. He remained the biggest-selling artist in Latin America for decades after his death. Bing Crosby said he had never heard a voice more beautiful, that Gardel had achieved the "fourth dimension" of song, making listeners truly feel it. Porteños still pay homage: "*Gardel?*" they say. "*Cada día canta mejor*" (He sings better every day).

The other musical cataclysm of 1935 was not tragic, nor did it make headlines, but it propelled dancing into the vacuum Gardel's death left in the heart of tango. And it, too, was an accident.

After the pianist Rodolfo Biagi got back to Buenos Aires following an overseas tour, he began hanging out at the Chanticleer cabaret listening to his favorite orchestra, Juan d'Arienzo's. One night the band's regular pianist failed to turn up and Biagi didn't have to be asked twice, quickly making himself at home on the stool he had been eyeing up for some time. The routine at the Chanticleer was that the band played four sets every evening, the first one more of a warm-up enjoyed by the staff, some teatime stragglers, and a few early birds; d'Arienzo himself often didn't bother with it, arriving in time for the second set as the dancefloor started to fill up. One fine spring evening that November, with the boss nowhere in sight, Biagi and the band began fooling around. The pianist's own favored style was aggressive and highly rhythmic; he and the others began egging each other on, pounding out a very emphatic sort of tango, exaggerating the crescendos and the arrastres, quite a change from the polite sound that had evolved across long years of respectability and playing second fiddle to vocalists. This was a more syncopated style, crashing down on certain beats like those drinkers of thirty years earlier smashing their glasses on barroom floors to the final notes of "El Esquinazo." It was just for a laugh, but the slim crowd went nuts, bartenders dancing with waitresses, elderly couples strutting around the dancefloor like spring chickens. When the second set began, they demanded more of the same; d'Arienzo shrugged and let them carry on. Suddenly his band was the hottest show in town, young dancers were flocking to the Chanticleer and other orchestras were taking note, cranking up the tempi and filling their own dancefloors. The golden age of tango dance had begun.

Orchestras ruled for the next twenty years: newspapers had columns listing each night's milongas, football teams held dances at their clubhouses, booking agents' datebooks were filled a year in advance... Each band had its followers, many with their own distinctive looks. Older styles—the original milonga and canyengue—were revived and practicas returned; everyone wanted to be a great dancer. An experienced eye could tell which neighborhood couples came from by their moves. The heart-to-heart embrace, for example, with female mouths within whispering distance of male ears, was common in the working-class districts of the city's south, but considered gauche on the well-to-do north side. The era's leading dancer, nicknamed "Petróleo" after his consumption of spirits, and his mentor, "El Negro" Navarro, kept inventing dramatic new steps, pushing the boundaries.

D'Arienzo's main competitor was Carlos di Sarli. One might assume that the ultra-smooth di Sarli would be a favorite of the northern districts while d'Arienzo ruled the south, but it wasn't like that; poor people loved an elegant tango, too. Di Sarli was a pianist and his charts were often a dialogue between keyboard and violins, with the bandoneón hardly getting a look-in. Tango DJs in Buenos Aires today keep going back to di Sarli's recordings because he's such a pleasure to dance to.

The bandoneón, though, would have its moment. The instrument's great virtuoso and champion, Juan "Pacho" Maglio, died just before the era began; he'd spent his life in a cloud of black tobacco smoke and his lungs gave out when he was fifty-four, but his influence would be felt. In 1929, Maglio had given a precocious fifteen-year-old named Aníbal Troilo his first chair; over the next decade, Troilo played with everyone, learning as he went. He used that experience, along with a sensational, cocaine-fueled technique, to dominate the 1940s. The singer Francisco Fiorentino left d'Arienzo to join him and together they worked out how to make the vocalist truly a part of the band. Given full verses rather than just refrains, Fiorentino sang with bandoneón-like twists and accents in playful counterpoint with the instruments, inspiring dancers to remain on the floor. Troilo also led the way into adventurous new harmonic territory while never letting up the intensity of his rhythm.

The last twelve years of the golden age coincided with the time of Juan Perón. This period began inauspiciously when the military putschists who took over in 1943 banned Lunfardo and anything they considered disreputable or seedy, which covered most tango lyrics. Colonel Perón used his position as labor minister to build a following, then won the 1946 presidential election and repealed the censorship laws.

Like Vargas in Brazil, Perón was a populist and nationalist, with Mussolini as a role model. However much we may condemn his postwar welcome for fugitive Nazis and his vicious secret police, compared to our own era's Xi/Orbán/Trump/Putin versions, Perón's populism seems like a lost idyll. He championed workers' rights, higher wages, and better living conditions, earning the enmity of the wealthy, the Church (for his legalization of divorce), and the military brass, who had a distaste for the "lower orders." Historians usually put Perón's concern for the common man down to an obsession with replacing communism in proletarian hearts, but he did far more than talk; Argentine workers revere his memory and still tend to vote for anyone who campaigns as a Peronist.

Perón wasn't a dancer, but after falling for tango-loving actress Eva Duarte, he embraced the music as part of an idealized working-class culture. He imposed a 50 percent local content rule on radio, giving a boost to both tango and traditional folk music. His support for music and his anti-communism collided, however, in the matter of Osvaldo Pugliese, the fourth great bandleader of the era.

Pugliese led his orchestra from the piano; his arrangements were complex but passionate, full of light and shade and blue notes, not so easy to dance to, but once mastered, his devotees wanted no other. The core group of musicians with whom Pugliese began in 1937 were still with him thirty years later; having joined the Communist Party during the Spanish Civil War, he never wavered, running his orchestra like a cooperative and sharing profits among the musicians. His popularity didn't prevent every post-1943 regime from arresting him, but it ensured that they didn't keep him locked up for long. Whenever their outspoken bandleader was in jail, his orchestra carried on as normal, with a red carnation lying across the piano bench; Pugliese would emerge with new arrangements written on prison paper. In 1949, Perón's thugs were said to have wrapped him in chains and made as if to throw him in the Plata, before eventually letting him go. Many years later, when Perón returned from exile and reclaimed the presidency, Pugliese received the Orden de Mayo; as he was pinning on the medal, Perón muttered something about forgiveness. The unflappable tanguero shrugged and responded that there was nothing to forgive. Not every performer could negotiate the country's volatile politics with such sangfroid. In 1946, the singer Libertad Lamarque clashed with Eva Duarte during a film shoot; when Duarte became First Lady Evita Perón in 1948, it was made clear that Lamarque had no future in Argentina. Fortunately, the Mexicans adored her, so she moved there and became a star. Nelly Omar, on the other hand, was Evita's great pal and her tango "We Are the Shirtless Ones" became a Perón campaign anthem. After Juan was removed in a coup in 1955, Omar was blackballed and didn't work again for almost twenty years. The first act by the post-Perón government was to reinstate censorship and ban gatherings of more than three people; goodbye milongas, farewell tango. A darkness that was to last nearly thirty years descended on the music.

∽

Tango, once you were happy
As I used to be . . .
Ever since that yesterday
So many things have happened to the two of us
Critical departures and the pain
Of loving and not being loved back.
I might have died
But you kept extending the Barbary shore of our lives.
Keep in deep memory, O Buenos Aires,
The tango you were and will be

—Jorge Luis Borges, "Alguien le dice al tango" (Someone Says to the Tango), 1965

Qué booa? Qué booa? On the evening of March 21, 1979, Caetano Veloso stood on a stage in Buenos Aires staring out at the crowd that had been cheering him to the rafters a few minutes earlier. He'd been booed during the early days of Tropicalismo, of course, but now he was supposed to be a hero to the young porteños. They had spent much of their lives under the heel of a military dictatorship and had paid good money to see an artist who had himself been jailed by the Brazilian junta; his songs exuded an unbending and internationally admired sophistication Argentines could but envy.

It was just a few scattered hoots, a bit like Dylan's single-voice "Judas" moment in Manchester fourteen years earlier, but they still came as a shock and no one in that audience would ever forget them. Veloso's crime had been to strum the unmistakable opening bars of "El

Día que me quieras" (The Day That You Love Me), a Carlos Gardel classic. Tango was terminally unhip in 1979 Argentina, danced only by the audience's parents, perhaps, and by a few generals and their mistresses. The 1955 ban on milongas had long been lifted, but the years since had been filled with curfews, restrictions, censorship, and a generalized suppression of the kind of free and bohemian life tango represented. 1979 found the country in the midst of a "dirty war," a euphemism for torture, disappearances, and killings intended to stamp out all opposition, including musical. Long hair seems to have been particularly unsettling to the junta; the police would periodically back their wagons up to the door of Obras Sanitarias, Buenos Aires's leading rock venue, and arrest everyone inside. Rock, along with Chilean and Cuban political song, was the focus of defiant youthful energy, while tango had drifted into irrelevance; for two long decades, there had been no practicas, a few early-evening milongas but no orchestras, and no experienced bandeónists and dancers passing on their skills to the young. Club Michelangelo gave Osvaldo Pugliese's reduced ensemble a regular gig, keeping his profile high enough to stop the generals from doing away with him. What survived of the tango world was not particularly oppositional; most tangueros were short-back-and-sides men, sharing the generals' hatred of long-haired rockers.

Veloso sang Gardel's song through to the end, with a warning to the audience not to lose sight of their own traditions or abandon their roots. Few could disagree with the principle, but the idea that milongas might once again light up the Buenos Aires night seemed delusional. Some interesting music had emerged from the small groups that survived—Aníbal Troilo's quartet, for example—but what little fresh air remained in tango was mostly breathed abroad.

Carlos Copes and María Nieves, for example, were champions who refused to stop dancing; they traveled the world, appearing on the Ed Sullivan and Arthur Murray TV shows in the US, including once when they danced an entire tango on a tiny tabletop. Cut off from its root, international tango took on strange, often gimmicky forms that dragged it into the clichés that still rule in risible outposts such as *Strictly Come Dancing*. Unlike with post-Castro Afro-Cuban music, there was no large pool of talent in expat or fraternal cultures to take the music in fruitful new directions. Once again, though, Paris came to the rescue.

※

In 1934, Astor Piazzolla's father paid the producers of one of Gardel's New York films twenty-five dollars to secure a small part as a paperboy for his son. Gardel was so taken with the bandoneón-playing kid that he invited him along on that fatal last tour, but his father, who had moved the family (and his huge collection of tango records) to New York in the mid-1920s, wouldn't allow Astor to miss that much school time.

The Piazzollas returned to Argentina in 1936 and young Astor was soon soaking up the golden age excitement and impressing everyone with his virtuosity. In 1938, he auditioned for Troilo with a solo rendition of "Rhapsody in Blue," was hired on the spot, and soon became the band's chief arranger. Growing up in Greenwich Village had given him an outsider's perspective; Piazzolla was never content with tango as it was, not even Troilo's adventurous version of it. Away from the milongas, he experimented with less danceable, more abstract compositions inspired by Bartók, Ravel, and jazz; performing them with a small ensemble in theaters and cafés, he raised eyebrows by playing standing up, one knee on a stool and the instrument draped over it. When Troilo heard one of his new compositions and said, "No, my boy, that isn't tango," Piazzolla decided it was time to leave.

Resolving to become a "serious" composer, he headed for the City of Light in 1953, to study with Nadia Boulanger. One day, after they'd been working for a while on his chamber music, Boulanger asked to hear the music he played for a living. "Now that," she said after listening to one of his tangos, "is the *real* Astor Piazzolla." He took her words to heart, picked up his bandoneón once again, and embarked on an intense period of creativity: "jazz-tango" tours and recordings with Gerry Mulligan and Argentine saxophonist Gato Barbieri, a tango opera, and a chamber-tango ensemble. In 1970, he returned to Paris, where he wrote one of his most moving compositions, *Suite Troileana*, following his mentor's death. For some, Piazzolla was keeping the music vibrant, rescuing it from torpid nostalgia and taking it into the future; for others, his work constituted an assault on everything tangueros hold dear. He became for tango what John Lewis and the MJQ were to jazz, "elevating" it from the dancefloor and giving it concert-hall respectability.

Since 1951, Paris had also been home to Argentine writer Julio Cortázar, whose 1963 novel *Rayuela* (*Hopscotch*) is often credited with launching international interest in Latin American literature. The longer Cortázar spent in exile and the worse his homeland's political situation became, the closer he felt bound to his culture and to tango. In collaboration with fellow Parisian Argentines, composer Edgardo Cantón and singer and musician Juan "Tata" Cedrón, he wrote and recorded an album called *Trottoirs de Buenos Aires*, which received much French acclaim but was barely noticed in Argentina. With more and more exiles turning up in Paris, and French tangophilia again stirring, Cortázar and Cedrón decided the title of their album would be a good name for a nightclub. Located between Châtelet and Les Halles in the Rue des Lombards, a nocturnal street known for its jazz clubs and bars, Trottoirs de Buenos Aires opened on November 19, 1981, with a residency by chamber-tango stars Sexteto Mayor.

Over the next few years, the club booked many of the leading practitioners of "serious" tango, with one particularly memorable engagement by a group led by the great Afro-Argentine pianist Horacio Salgán. Paris audiences were bemused by the distinction between listening and dancing and requested a bit of floor space, along with some proper rhythms. Cedrón asked Sexteto Mayor to oblige and they nervously agreed, never before having played for dancers; the result was Paris's first regular Buenos Aires–style milonga. For the next thirteen years, Trottoirs de Buenos Aires served as the epicenter of a renewed French passion for tango and a meeting point for homesick porteños.

Perhaps the club's popularity influenced how Michel Guy reacted to a suggestion from an Argentine theater director, Jorge Lavelli. Guy, director of Paris's Festival d'Automne, was bemoaning the fact that he found himself choosing, year after year, from the same pool of theater companies around the globe; where, he asked his friend, could he find a fresh, original voice from outside this cozy circuit? Lavelli suggested

Claudio Segovia, a Paris-based Argentine director who had been trying for years to stage a theatrical revue of classic tango. Guy met with Segovia and his producing partner, Héctor Orezzoli, and they showed him footage of a Spanish production of theirs from a few years earlier called *Flamenco puro*.

Flamenco puro was exactly what the title implied: authentic, traditional flamenco dance and song produced with flair and confidence, perfect sound, a beautiful set expertly lit, and a firm conviction that the "real thing" could appeal to a broad audience. Impressed, Guy agreed to present their tango show at his festival in November 1983. But there was a catch: the funds available were nowhere near enough to cover pre-production expenses for Orezzoli and Segovia's vision. For months, they pitched this great opportunity to investors and presenters in Europe and Argentina but found no takers; one impresario handed over a big check, but it bounced. Segovia's mother finally came to the rescue, contributing the proceeds from Claudio's late father's life insurance policy, just about enough to cover the shortfall.

The Argentine junta, meanwhile, was running on empty, beset by strikes, international condemnation, and weekly demonstrations by the Mothers of the Plaza de Mayo demanding information on their missing children. In a desperate gamble the generals seized Las Malvinas, islands in the South Atlantic known to the anglophone world as the Falklands. The international sympathy that might have attached to a southern hemisphere nation battling an arrogant post-colonial power was trumped by the detestable nature of Argentina's government; the defeat suffered in that "bloody little war" was the beginning of the end. As democracy returned, curfews were lifted, bars reopened, and life slowly returned to the Buenos Aires night. The military tried to tilt the October 1983 election to the Peronists, who had reportedly cut a deal to spare the generals an investigation into their rule, but Raúl Alfonsín and the Radical Civic Union stunned everyone by winning a clear majority.

With such dramatic goings-on, few could be bothered with Orezzoli and Segovia's project; rehearsal space was hard to come by and many dancers, musicians, and singers, doubting it would really happen, turned them down. In the end, it was mostly those with firsthand experience of Paris who signed on: Horacio Salgán and Sexteto Mayor (who had enjoyed playing for the milonga after all). Dancers Carlos Copes and María Nieves, who knew the international circuit well, were excited by the show's possibilities and were the first to commit, with Copes coming up with many of the show's choreographic ideas.

One problem remained: Segovia's funds had run out before he could buy the air tickets. An appeal to the new government brought an offer they couldn't refuse, hitching a ride with an Exocet missile being flown to France for repairs. This is the weapon that had given the Argentines their only moment of hope in the Malvinas War, when one of them sank a British destroyer. An Exocet is twenty feet long and weighs nearly a ton; thirty-three cast and stage crew sat on benches alongside the missile all the way to Paris, holding packed lunches in paper bags and averting their eyes from the scowling soldiers escorting it, who clearly felt allowing these decadents on a military plane was a bad omen for civilian rule.

What followed changed the history of tango: a seven-day *succès fou* at the huge Châtelet theater was extended again and again, with long queues forming each dawn outside the ticket office. The show was called *Tango argentino* and it toured the world, filling top-flight venues and culminating in a triumphant year at the Mark Hellinger Theater on Broadway. The *Financial Times* credited it with "the kind of vivid, meticulous, serious staging that we associate with Diaghilev." Revivals, spin-offs, and rip-offs continue to this day.

I bought tickets during the Broadway run out of curiosity and attended a revival of *Flamenco puro* a few years later. After Orezzoli's death, I saw Segovia's *Brasil brasileiro* at Sadler's Wells in London in 2005 and regretted never catching *Black and Blue*, their tribute to 1930s Harlem. Studying Orezzoli and Segovia's productions should be mandatory for anyone involved in presenting "world" or "roots" music. They treat the music and the culture from which it comes with total respect: no apologies, no dilutions, no fusions, no kitsch storylines, no narration, just top-of-the-line sets, sound, and lights and elite performers. They had the confidence to demand top Broadway ticket prices; they expected sell-out crowds and they got them.

Audiences and critics were particularly astonished by the dancers; the creators knew that no young performers would have been properly trained in practicas, that only veterans from the Golden Age would do. Most were in their fifties or sixties and none had sylph-like bodies, but they moved beautifully. Decades of vulgar tango clichés evaporated in front of audiences' entranced eyes.

☙

Back home, as proud as the country was of *Tango argentino*'s triumphs, milongas remained scarce. With long hair and electric guitars no longer life-threatening, heavy rock boomed. On a visit to Buenos Aires, I talked with an Argentine woman who had been in her late twenties during those first post-junta years. Beyond the 650 Argentine soldiers and sailors killed in the Malvinas debacle, another 30,000 people (90 percent of them men) had been disappeared and almost a quarter of a million (75 percent male) had left the country in search of freer air. For a single woman, particularly if her politics were on the left, pickings were thin. One day a friend told her of a visit to one of the few tango salons that had survived the years of curfew. She hadn't met Señor Right, but had passed a lively evening in male company, dancing, chatting, and being treated with the gallantry for which tango is the perfect soundtrack. Word spread among the women of Buenos Aires: perhaps their parents and grandparents had the right idea all along. Similar reports circulated among the men: if you're a decent dancer, you'll be spoiled for choice at a milonga! As each year passed, the number of dances grew and grew.

☙

Tango in Argentina is like ice to an Eskimo.

—Daniel Melingo, musician

Tango is against anything that may be considered mechanical or collective. Tango is a display of many of our essential characteristics, of our passiveness, of our fundamental sorrow, of our languid sensuality, of our negligence, of our desolation.

—Manuel Gálvez, *Hombres en soledad*, 1938

In 1976, after they killed one of his actors, then tried to kidnap him, filmmaker Fernando Solanas knew it was time to leave; he joined the exiles in Paris, watching, waiting, phoning home, hearing of more and more disappearances and finding musical consolation at the Trottoirs. The two films Solanas made after the return of democracy constitute a kind of milonga about those terrible years: first, he told his own Parisian story in *Tangos: El exilio de Gardel*; the next, *Sur* (South), is a tale of ordinary people who had no choice but to remain and try to survive. Both films are infused with tango. Solanas persuaded Piazzolla to compose a score for the first and asked the veteran tango singer Roberto Goyeneche to perform a kind of Greek-chorus role in the second, singing with a few musicians on a cobblestone street outside a bar in a gritty barrio.

Sur won prizes in France, prompting a label there to ask Litto Nebbia to produce an album for them with Goyeneche. It would be hard to imagine two more different musical personalities than Roberto Goyeneche and Litto Nebbia. The former was an inveterate tanguero, having sung initially with Salgán, then Troilo, Pugliese and Piazzolla; Nebbia had been leader of the hottest sixties Argentine rock band, Los Gatos (The Cats). When Goyeneche began singing at eighteen in 1952, his blond hair (perhaps from a recessive Visigoth gene mixed with his Basque heritage) earned him the nickname "El Polaco" (The Pole). He stayed put during the dark years, rarely leaving his working-class neighborhood of Saavedra, drinking at the same bar and standing on the terraces of his beloved Atlético Platense, the perennially second-rate local football club. When the call finally came, he was ready, touring as vocalist with *Tango argentino* and providing the highlight of Pugliese's triumphant 1985 comeback concert at Teatro Colón. Mop-topped Nebbia, meanwhile, didn't wait around to find out if the 1976 coup would be bad for his health, he fled to Mexico City. (The generals locked up Los Gatos's other vocalist in a mental hospital, subjecting him to repeated electro-shocks; when finally released, he threw himself under a train.)

Nebbia had always loved roots music, be it American blues, Latin American political song, or tango. When his mother (who had once played piano in an all-female tango orchestra) encouraged him to build a recording studio in the back of her house, he used it as a base for Melopea, the label he named for a musical structure employed in ancient Greek tragedies. His first foray into tango worked pretty well; he heard something in a demo tape from an unknown folk singer and with his guidance, Adriana Varela became one of the stars of the tango revival.

Nebbia and Goyeneche ended up making three albums together before the singer's death in 1994, stripped-down productions with a hip sensibility. Goyeneche was the ideal figure to connect a new generation to tango; where Gardel's love of melody had propelled him, smiling, through the most heartbreaking lyrics, Goyeneche, as he put it, sang "every comma, every period, every accent, every rest," savoring the lines like the storyteller he was. The poet Horacio Ferrer, lyricist of Piazzolla's "Balada para un loco" (Ballad for a Lunatic), which Goyeneche sang in its definitive recording, provided him with an epitaph (using porteño backslang for tango, *gotan*):

> *Very young, in that backyard,*
> *your sorrow made its debut in an orchestra of blackbirds*
> *As the angel of asphalt blooms in your throat's tremor*
> *And when the bandoneón blows its breath-taking gale*
> *Tango becomes a poetic delirium in your voice*
> *Your sand-clock face, the clothes that cover your pain,*
> *Your masterly way with a tale*
> *Always faithful to the milonga of your joys and sorrows*
> *In an ecstasy of Troilean love*
> *The ghosts of gotan are not dead*
> *Roberto, lend them your mystery*
> *Let them come back, enjoy, vibrate, suffer and love*
> *Hey, Polaco, just like you do*

༺

I heard my first Carlos Gardel record on Tom Schnabel's radio show in Los Angeles in the early seventies; by the end of the first line, I was a convert. To my younger ears, orchestral tangos seemed a bit corny, the bandoneón too accordion-like for comfort. From a hemisphere away, it seemed my team had lost, that guitar tango had died with the great man.

I wasn't too far wrong; after 1935, those "brooms" were mostly hung up in a closet.

Perón's national content law for radio was designed to boost not only tango but also the country's traditional folk music; to the leader's chagrin, the great figure who rose with this tide was a committed and very active communist. Like Goyeneche, Héctor Chavero Aramburu was of Basque stock, with a genetic wild card from the indigenous people on the slopes of the Andes, where General Roca's massacres hadn't been so thorough. When he began collecting and performing folk songs in the thirties, Aramburu borrowed a stage name from a pair of Inca kings: Atahualpa Yupanqui. In 1949, after one too many arrests and beatings from Perón's police, Yupanqui fled—guess where!—to Paris; with vigorous cheerleading from Édith Piaf, audiences there embraced him and he remained based in France for much of his life. Yupanqui was an elegant guitarist, composing and performing the sort of airily wistful Andean melodies the world knows through tunes such as the Peruvian classic "El Cóndor pasa."

The year 1935 saw both Yupanqui's radio debut and the birth of Mercedes Sosa; by the 1960s, these two were at the forefront of a politically aware Andean music that provided connective tissue for leftist and indigenous-rights movements around the world (as well as inspiring the panpipe groups who for decades could be heard busking at virtually every Paris Métro stop). Their music was particularly beloved by Argentines outside Buenos Aires to whom it came to represent a purity of spirit lacking in the tango-obsessed capital. When martial law was imposed in 1976, Sosa refused to leave despite police once handcuffing her onstage in front of a packed house. She remained a heroic figure for activists and audiences in Argentina and around the world until her death in 2009.

While Yupanqui and Sosa were filling concert halls in Europe and the Americas, fresh ways of playing tango on the acoustic guitar were being explored in Buenos Aires by Roberto Grela, co-founder of Aníbal Troilo's new quartet. Grela's playing is clear and melodic but reminds you more of Django Reinhardt than of Gardel's sidekicks or Yupanqui. (When Django met Grappelli, both were playing in Louis Vola's tango orchestra in France in the early thirties.) Grela grew up surrounded by bandoneóns, and his style reflects it, evidence, perhaps, of tango's Europeanization gaining the upper hand over its criollo roots.

How these various strands of Argentine music were related grew clearer for me while watching one of Gardel's movies; *Cuesta abajo* has a silly plot but some excellent musical numbers, particularly a mid-film sequence with an unlikely group of gaúchos gathered around a bonfire on the grounds of an American mansion where Gardel is attending a party. He goes outside, eager to hear music that is "*ni milonga, ni tango*"; the strumming and finger-picking of their *guitarras criollas* feels very Argentine in its blend of Andalusia, Africa, and the Andes, while the vocal harmonies evoke the Gardel-Razzano duo from the years before "Mi noche triste." As Gardel looks around for his girlfriend (who's busy making eyes at one of the guitarists), a pair of gaúchos flash some zapateado footwork in a malambo; the rapid steps, seemingly independent of the upper body, mirror the footage of early tango dancing. Gardel (wearing a tuxedo) joins them to sing a folk song, his phrasing and attitude hardly different from when, elsewhere in the film, he performs the latest hit written for him by Le Pera, backed by an unseen orchestra. The sequence is like a diagram, connecting the dots of Argentine music, urban and rural, Andes and pampas, modern (as of 1934) and nostalgic.

I had my own moment of being lured away from a party by the sound of an Argentine guitar; at a dinner thrown in 1996 by a London wine-dealer friend to celebrate the arrival of a planeload of Mendoza Malbecs, I was astonished to hear a Gardel song coming from the rear of the flat. Even more surprising, the singer was backed by a guitarist whose fingerpicking could have come straight off a twenties recording. Dolores Solá and Acho Estol turned out to be porteño ex-punks, friends of the Buenos Aires chef flown in to take charge of the steaks. They had a passion for the sort of old-fashioned tango they felt shared rock's original spirit of spontaneity and rebellion. Later that year, they sent me the first album by their group, La Chicana: *Ayer hoy era mañana*

(Yesterday Today Was Tomorrow), featuring a mix of twenties tangos, early milongas, and original songs.

La Chicana were viewed at first as eccentric outliers, but by the time I visited Buenos Aires in 2005, there was a thriving underground of guitar-based tango. More than a few ex-rockers, it seems, had taken to heart the porteño maxim that "tango is waiting for you when you grow up." The best known of such figures is Gustavo Santaolalla, whose name might ring a bell since he's won film-score Oscars for *Babel* and *Brokeback Mountain*. Gustavo told me his journey of discovery began after he left the country—and a successful rock band—in 1977; on his travels, he encountered Ketama, the nuevo flamenco group Mario Pacheco was producing in Spain, and resolved to look for ways to engage with Argentine traditions outside the Anglo-American model.

Santaolalla made his name in Hollywood with *The Motorcycle Diaries*, a score filled with the familiar-but-different-sounding *charango* and *ronroco*, Argentine cousins of the guitar. He had learned to love these instruments during a journey the length and breadth of the country with the singer-songwriter León Gieco in a caravan kitted out with recording equipment. The resulting album won many awards and shares its title with Santaolalla's theme for *The Motorcycle Diaries*: *De Ushuaia a la Quiaca*, after towns located at the country's southern and northern extremities. Santaolalla soon turned his postmodern eye to tango, making a *Buena Vista*–style album and film called *Café de los Maestros* with a group of Golden Era veterans and forming Bajofondo, a modernist techno-tango outfit. Of all his endeavors, my favorites are the records he produced with a couple of young tango revivalists. One, a reformed punk named Javier Casalla, plays the Stroh violin, with its antique-looking sound trumpet mounted on the bridge; the other is Cristóbal Repetto, whose borderline falsetto vocals are modeled on Ignacio Corsini, a singer with a similar range whose career was overshadowed by Gardel but who left some wonderful recordings, ranging from tangos to waltzes to payador ballads. Repetto recreates the feel of Corsini's old records with the fierce dedication of a US folk-revival blues singer channeling Blind Willie McTell. Neither Casalla's nor Repetto's albums sold particularly well, but Santaolalla keeps them busy performing with the popular Bajofondo as it tacks back towards traditional tango and attempts to educate its young audiences about the music's history.

Solá and Estol stick to their guns; though La Chicana eventually added a bandoneón, the rhythmic base is still Acho's guitar and always very Argentine. I asked him if anyone dances to their music, and he told me of a 2019 festival in Patagonia, where for two hours they had the huge crowd executing cortes and quebradas to their century-old sound. "Tango doesn't need reviving," he says, "it simply exists."

～

> [T]he French or Spanish composer who . . . correctly crafts a "tango" is shocked to discover he has constructed something that our ears do not recognize . . . that our bodies reject . . . [W]ithout the evenings and nights of Buenos Aires a tango cannot be made.
>
> —Jorge Luis Borges

When a well-traveled rock musician named Daniel Melingo was hosting a cable TV show in the late nineties, he asked pop-star friends to come on the program and sing their favorite tango. The audience response was so ecstatic that it set Melingo to thinking; he now tours the world with a band he calls Los Ramones del Tango, channeling turn-of-the-century compadritos with a louche stage persona located somewhere between Tom Waits and Emir Kusturica's No Smoking Orchestra. No surprise, then, that he has a cult following in Central Europe. When a previously unknown cousin turned up at an Austrian concert, she told him their family has roots in Greece, which made sense as the singer recalled hearing his grandfather noodling rembetikas on his guitar in the family kitchen when he was a kid.

When Melingo followed up this news with a visit to Athens, he got a shock; there seemed to be almost as many milongas there on any given night as in Buenos Aires. This surge followed the 2009 economic meltdown; restaurants and cafés were either shut or unaffordable, so many neighborhoods began holding free outdoor milongas. Observers have pointed out parallels between Greece's and Argentina's Mediterranean sensuality and their shared sense of tragedy; others have noted Greek admiration for the way Argentina defied the dollar, the IMF, and Wall Street bond traders and how they wished they could have been equally defiant of the European Central Bank.

Greek love of tango goes back a lot further than cynicism about the euro. Global enthusiasm never again reached pre–World War One levels, but in Greece, as elsewhere, tango put down deep roots. Rembetiko's genesis in refugee shantytowns bore many similarities to tango's own and snatches of habanera can be heard in early Greek recordings. Authorities even tried using tango to lure the Greek public away from rembetiko, which they loathed for its hashish-infused Oriental sound and low-class origins. Next door in Turkey, Kemal Atatürk was determined to break the tradition that only non-Muslim women—Armenian, Jewish, or Roma—could appear on Turkish stages; with his support, the tango singer Seyyan Hanım became a star and a pioneering symbol of his liberal reforms. One could map out a "tango corridor" from Egypt, Lebanon, and Turkey through the Balkans and Central Europe into Russia, eventually reaching the most tango-obsessed land of all, Finland. The Finns caught the bug in 1913, when they were still part of Russia and developed a flourishing tango industry between the wars; the Soviets, naturally, decided the dance was subversive and banned it. (They knew enough, though, to blast "El Tango de la muerte" through giant loudspeakers all night at German lines during the Battle of Stalingrad.)

One of the music's most colorful European stars was a dancer named Pyotr Leshchenko, who found himself on the Romanian side of the Bessarabian border as the Russian Civil War ended. When his vocalist wife (and professional tango partner) fell pregnant, he grabbed the microphone and became a singing star among Russian émigrés and Eastern Europeans of all stripes. Leshchenko's recordings are among the most enjoyable of all non-Argentine tangos, many of them embellished with the Hawaiian steel guitars that often fill a bandoneón-sized hole in far-from-home tangos. (Only porteños, it seems, can master this impossibly difficult instrument.) Smuggled Leshchenko records were treasured in the USSR—the original *samizdat*—while his Bucharest nightclub became a hotbed of White Russian intrigue and exile nostalgia. He should have been doomed when the Red Army marched into

Romania in 1944, but the general in charge of the occupation turned out to be a closet tango fanatic, providing protection in return for private concerts. Shifting ideological winds made Leshchenko welcome in the post-war USSR one minute, then thrown into a Romanian jail the next; he died in a prison camp in 1954.

For decades, Japan released more tango records per annum than any country in the world, including Argentina; Japanese tours can still provide an economic lifeline for Argentine tango singers, dancers, and orchestras. In parts of China, tango is a morning exercise ritual. Wherever one looks in the northern hemisphere, there's a tango tradition of some kind. Tango has taken its place alongside jazz, rock 'n' roll, salsa, and reggae as an international musical currency onto which cultures have projected their particular notion of modernity and sensuality, often seeking an escape from their own folk traditions. Which is remarkable considering how, to the uninitiated, tango can seem more athletic than erotic and, in any event, dauntingly eccentric and difficult.

> The man who cannot make the woman feel like a queen on the dance floor will never be king.
>
> —Professional tango dancer

> I'm delighted that we have lots of international people here now, it gives me work. But they bring confusion. They want to dazzle and shine with crazy shit instead of just walk and enjoy simple steps, which is the real art. So you end up with dance floors like slaughterhouses.
>
> —Tango instructor in Kapka Kassabova's *Twelve Minutes of Love*

Post-1983, the tango world changed as much outside Argentina as inside. *Tango argentino* hit foreign dancers like a bombshell, showing them an elegant, complex form quite different in spirit from how tango had evolved in exile, cut off for so long from any meaningful contact with Buenos Aires's shuttered milongas. Tango had aged everywhere, as young people rarely took it up. Trottoirs de Buenos Aires may not have had the global profile of *Tango argentino*, but its ripple effect was, in the long run, at least as meaningful. Trottoirs was the first tango club aimed squarely at a young, international crowd; when bars and clubs elsewhere began having weekly tango nights, whether they knew it or not, the atmosphere of the Parisian venue was a prime influence.

Most one-night-a-week dancers, be it of salsa, swing, or tango, care little about the artists' names on the records the DJ spins; eventually, though, the world music movement's quest for authenticity did impact the tango zeitgeist. Demand grew for genuine Argentine instructors; in New York, Paris, Berlin, Tokyo, Milan, and London people wanted the "real thing." For the seriously committed, this could lead to the purchase of a round-trip plane ticket to Buenos Aires, or, in extreme cases, a one-way.

Once landed, the dedicated pilgrim could take two three-hour lessons between lunch and supper, attend a practica at nine, then, starting at midnight, "relax" for a few hours at a milonga. For many, the journey is about more than simply improving one's skills; dancing tango has come to represent something deeper. Once they enter "the embrace," the dance can confront dancers with fundamental questions about intimacy and about themselves. Much has been written on this subject, and the new century saw a series of books describing outsiders' firsthand experiences in Argentina. I read three—*Paper Tangos* by Julie Taylor, *The Meaning of Tango* by Christine Denniston, and *Twelve Minutes of Love* by Kapka Kassabova—and each has a different take.

All agree that the first step in acclimatization is getting used to the eye-lock and the nod. No Argentine man will cross the floor, stand in front of a seated woman, ask her to dance, and risk being refused. Male eyes scan the room, settle on a potential partner, attempt eye contact, and, if found and held, he nods, she nods, and they join together for a twelve-minute *tanda*, the four-tune set that marks the unit by which time is measured at a milonga. Taylor, an American sociologist, struggled with it; after several agonizing evenings of not being asked at all, she realized her New York reflex when a stranger met her gaze was to quickly lower it. She had to train herself in what locals call the *cabeceo*.

Each author confronts the issue of the degree to which the dance is inherently macho. Denniston, a matter-of-fact British playwright, harks back to turn-of-the-century practicas, in which young men learned to follow as well as lead and regularly practiced with great dancers; today, lessons are filled with neophytes and it has become almost impossible to learn directly from a great dancer. She writes eloquently about the "heart-to-heart" posture, in which a pair move together with no pulling, pushing, or steering, but rather a Zen-like impulse that starts in the leader's chest. Partners who fail in this she dismisses as ill-taught or ill-mannered. Freedom and grace, she learned from Golden Age veterans, can only be achieved when the leader "follows the follower."

Taylor, after a traumatic childhood and years of analysis, is having none of it. She meets with other tangueras to share complaints about instructors who tell women their job is to become the man's shadow and about men who keep women prisoners in their embrace, her breaks simply reflections of his elegant moves. She remains grateful to tango, nonetheless, for "giving her back her body" following years of alienation after abandoning ballet for an academic career.

Bulgarian-born, New Zealand–raised, Scottish-settled Kassabova is the frankest of the three about tango's erotic core and her own attraction to it. She is also the most thorough in connecting the dance's history to its present (as of 2011). Most couple dances, she says, make you "laugh and forget your troubles" whereas tango is "all *about* your troubles" and "makes trouble exciting." One of the through-lines of the book is her quest for the perfect partner and the perfect dance or, as she calls it, the "tangasm." For her, as for many, this leads to a conflation of the terpsichorean and the personal and a series of unsatisfactory relationships. Tango, she points out, has from its earliest years been a way for men lacking worldly power to radiate it on the dancefloor, attracting women who would not otherwise be interested. She also understands the responsibility that weighs on guys; many non-Argentine male adepts, she discovers, are techies, mathematicians or engineers in their professional lives. Tango is unique among social dance forms in its lack of any fixed pattern and its need for constant improvisation, so if you're not a porteño who took it in with your mother's milk, you may require a mental diagram or a system if you're going to lead it. "At its best," she says, "the milonga makes women feel wanted and held, and it makes men feel accepted and competent."

Male writers have also had their say; Richard Martin saw tango as a duel in which "dance partners exchange leadership ... Dominance is always fragile and unsure; subjugation merely a quiescence in which to plot the regaining of the upper hand." In an interview following the publication of his book, Farris Thompson insisted that love was the essence of tango: "How do you take responsibility for the happiness of someone else?" The best dancers, he insists, show affection rather than domination, "[taking] the woman's hand just by the fingertips, so that she can leave whenever she wants to." When questioned on the matter, porteño veterans Copes and Nieves deadpanned that for them, control was "always fifty-fifty."

During the years when these authors were immersing themselves in the milonga culture of Buenos Aires, tango was still finding its post-junta feet; the music was seldom played on commercial radio, but you heard it everywhere else. Each night, all across Buenos Aires, there were concerts, club gigs, and milongas, and tango blared from loudspeakers in neighborhoods where tourists looked for landmarks mentioned in Gardel songs. Music at milongas was mostly classic tracks spun by DJs; live bands were rare. In 1999, Buenos Aires saw the opening of its first modern tango club, La Catedral, where women danced in jeans and dreadlocks swayed. Some DJs even tried to get porteños moving to the Gotan Project, a Paris-based electronic tango outfit. The dance got a further boost during the turn-of-the-century financial crisis, when the country disconnected its peso from the US dollar and defied the IMF; many Argentines stopped listening to foreign music on principle, reverting to tango and other national traditions. When pot-banging protests began again in the Plaza de Mayo, many demonstrators would instinctively finish their evenings at a milonga.

According to Kassabova, the best dancers came from the same rough neighborhoods they always had, where they "move differently from the rest of us ... The men's sleekness, quickness, smoothness and roundness makes you think of Maradona ... The women's ... suppleness of body and gracefulness of leg-flick makes you think of Botticelli." Outsiders like her, she felt, could never achieve that indefinable quality locals call "cobblestone."

The elegance of the remaining tango parlors belies the gritty reality of much of the dance's history. In his short story "The Gates of Heaven," Julio Cortázar described an evening at a late-1940s milonga where "the cigarette smoke and the barbecue laid down a low cloud which distorted the faces." Around eleven, the "monsters" arrive, dark-skinned men from obscure suburbs, "bound into tight black suits . . . the hard hair painfully plastered down," who dance "slowly without speaking." Such scenes have disappeared into the tango's rearview mirror; the great-grandchildren of Cortázar's "monsters" now dance cumbia. This jaunty blend of Colombian folk dance and Afro-Cuban rhythms (that some may remember from 1980s UK coffee commercials) has spread through working-class neighborhoods along the west coast of Latin America, following the spine of the mountains from Mexico to Bolivia, then down the old silver trail to Buenos Aires. Drum machines don't work for the slippery rhythms of tango but they can make cumbia sound impressively modern and gratifyingly primal. Despite the massive evidence to the contrary, in some quarters there's an even fiercer resistance to acknowledging cumbia's African roots than there is with tango.

When Copes and Nieves were on a tour of America with a tango troupe, the Pittsburgh promoter was horrified that one of their dancers was Afro-Argentine: "Don't come back here with that n——," he said. "That isn't tango." Most non-Argentine enthusiasts would be surprised to learn of the dance's Kongo roots, which are woven so subtly and deeply into the fabric that it would be easy to see tango as something obliquely European, the most sophisticated, sensual, "White" dance of all.

When Kassabova was at a low ebb during one stay in Buenos Aires, a friend decided a visit to Montevideo would cheer her up, bought her a ferry ticket, and put her in touch with musicians and dancers there. I haven't said much about the Uruguayan capital, though it plays an important role in tango's history. For talented composers, singers, and bandoneónists who wanted to make an impact, the journey across the Río de la Plata resembles the one made by so many comedians, actors, and musicians from Toronto to New York. One side effect of Montevideo's backwater status is that the Black population there was never made to disappear as it was in the booming metropolis over the water. Uruguay's most renowned painter, Pedro Figari, left a vivid record from the 1920s of Afro-Uruguayan life and music: balls, candombes, funerals, and feasts from a rich culture that seems to have been entirely unhidden.

One evening, Kassabova was invited to join her new friends for a candombe celebration in a neighborhood just a few blocks from the center of Montevideo. From her description, it sounds like a New Orleans "second-line" march without the horns: thirty hand-struck *tamboriles* and a crowd of singing, dancing Afro-Uruguayans. The intense beat swept her up; she couldn't stop moving, stepping rhythmically, one foot for two rapid beats. She realized the drums were forcing her feet into "the staggered, shuffling, cheeky, sexy double-step of the milonga." She recalled the lines of an old song: "*Milonga is daughter of candombe / And tango is son of the milonga,*" and thought of what she had read about slaves arriving at the mouth of that river, when "the only thing that united them, apart from suffering, was music." When the celebration was done, someone told her that in the eighteenth century those drums had a different name; back then, they were called "*tangó.*"

> Tango is a product of crisis of identity. In the old days, it was the identity of the nation, now it's masculine and feminine identity that's in crisis.
>
> —
>
> Freud said that the aim of psychotherapy is to replace neurotic misery with common unhappiness. I had a psychotherapist. It didn't work. But tango works.
>
> —Buenos Aires dancers in *Twelve Minutes of Love*

In 1912, the tango embrace was shocking and radical, opening the door to a risqué modernity that swept across the globe, scandalizing as it went. In the century since, most forms of social dancing have changed beyond recognition but not tango, which now finds itself again an outlier, a stubborn form that could almost be called reactionary. "If nostalgia is a country," wrote Farris Thompson, "tango is its capital." Once the yearning was for a distant homeland, now it mourns a lost aesthetic of seduction and intimacy; rock, disco, hip-hop, and raves have combined to make dancefloor embraces seem quaint and old-fashioned. Some wonder, though, at what cost; a tango teacher told Farris Thompson of a girl bursting into tears at her first lesson; "I've never been held like that before," she explained.

Argentines used to worry about measuring up to their self-image as the most "European" of Latin American countries. These days, there's little difference between the porteños filling Buenos Aires's milongas and the devotees who have come to learn their secrets. At the entrance to dance halls, salons, and rehearsal spaces there are leaflets for yoga classes, mindfulness sessions, and personal trainers, while the best foreign dancers, I am told, have so much "cobblestone" that you can't tell them from the natives. Postmodern cravings have converged with porteño nostalgia to put tango DJs out of work, with most milongas now employing live bands.

Tango doesn't get much airplay or sell many records outside Argentina; even Gardel has become a pretty recherché taste, but you can find a milonga, a lesson, or a partner any night, in any city in the world. The cabeceo may be simply an analogue antecedent of the Tinder swipe and tango could be nothing more (and nothing less) than an elegant way to find romance. Yet for many, the dance touches something more profound; perhaps it's not just Argentines for whom tango awaits "when we grow up."

VII
Szerelem, szerelem

> While music will obligingly serve to animate marching men or Young Pioneers, it also anchors individual memory and group consciousness ... placing them out of reach of the state.
>
> —Mark Slobin, *Retuning Culture*

Albert Grossman flew back to New York from Europe in the spring of 1965 with a tape in his briefcase. His first task was to close a deal with Elektra Records for the Paul Butterfield Blues Band, the latest addition to Bob Dylan, Odetta, and Peter, Paul and Mary in his management stable. When Jac Holzman presented the label's final offer, Grossman responded, "OK, on one condition—you have to release this as well," and placed the mysterious tape on Holzman's desk.

In a Paris flat, Grossman had heard a 10-inch LP called *Music of Bulgaria* by the Philip Koutev Ensemble. The next day, he walked into the Chant du Monde office and paid two thousand dollars cash for the US rights. When Holzman heard the tape, he happily added it to his Nonesuch subsidiary's new Explorer Series (as a rather stingy 12-inch LP). It was released that autumn, just as I started work opening Elektra's London office.

I will never forget hearing it for the first time: thirty-five women singing (yelling?) in unearthly, not-quite-dissonant harmonies and vibrato-free, "open-throat" voices. The music jumped out of the grooves at you, thrilling and strange, a Wall of Sound beyond anything Phil Spector could dream up. The album quickly became a badge of open-eared hipness; Boston folkies, the Incredible String Band and their Edinburgh friends, Lower East Side stoners—all loved donning headphones and tripping out on the Koutev Ensemble. No one imagined actually going to Bulgaria; the music seemed disembodied, the context impossible to visualize.

A decade later, copies had worn out or slid to the back of cupboards, Grossman's license had expired, and the record was out of print. I occasionally heard snatches of other Eastern European ensembles, but they bore no resemblance to the rich intensity of Koutev. I saw an article in a KLM in-flight magazine touting Bulgaria as a holiday destination and contemplated a visit, but the description of local food as mostly pickled put me off.

᎐

The Swiss metallurgist Marcel Cellier had no such qualms. Setting out in the early 1960s to map Balkan mineral deposits, he developed a fascination with the region's music. His first motherlode was a Romanian panpipe virtuoso named Gheorghe Zamfir. An amateur keyboardist, Cellier recorded an album of organ-panpipe duets that sold well and created a demand for Zamfir's exotic (if slightly new-agey) music in film scores, eventually including *Once Upon a Time in America* and *The Karate Kid*.

In 1975, Cellier released an album by the Women's Choir of Bulgarian Radio under the title *Le Mystère des Voix Bulgares*, consisting of arrangements by Koutev and Koutev-trained composers. The record had a certain impact in France and Germany but lack of distribution restricted it to cult status elsewhere. Unlike the Nonesuch disc, which alternated choir tracks with instrumentals, this was exclusively vocal, and a full-length LP besides. Cellier was credited as producer and liked to present himself as a sort of Balkan Alan Lomax, but Bulgarian Radio assured me that the *Mystère* recordings had all been produced in their German-equipped studio long before Cellier darkened their door.

In 1982, my brother Warwick took a break from his work as a civil rights lawyer to help out with my struggling Hannibal label. One of his first suggestions was that we license Anglo-American rights to the

Cellier disc and release it along with a Ladysmith Black Mambazo compilation and the recording I had made in 1970 with the Ali Brothers; these would be the start of an "international vocal harmony" series. (The term *world music* had not yet been invented.) I was preoccupied with trying to scrape together funds to press more copies of Hannibal's first hit, *Shoot Out the Lights* by Richard and Linda Thompson, and dismissed his idea as an uncommercial waste of our limited resources.

In my frantic transatlantic commuting that year, I missed an Anglo-Bulgarian moment that might have made me pay closer attention to my brother. In Collet's (the British Communist Party's London bookshop), *Folk Roots* magazine editor Ian Anderson had purchased a Balkanton LP by Koutev's leading soloist, Nadka Karadjova; the backing is bland and orchestral rather than choral, but her voice—one of Bulgaria's finest—sounds glorious. When a friend of Anderson's was asked by a BBC presenter to name the unheralded record she would most like other people to hear, she chose the Karadjova disc. Ian loaned it to the BBC for the occasion and a track, whose title translates as "A Lambkin Has Commenced Bleating," was played one Sunday afternoon on Radio 4. Phone calls and letters poured into Broadcasting House; within the week, a tape dubbed off Anderson's LP was in heavy rotation on Terry Wogan's massively popular Radio 2 Breakfast Show and every record shop in Britain was getting orders for a single that didn't exist. By the time Ian (who also ran a small label) tracked down the rights via the British legation in Sofia, the moment had passed and the UK release sold only a few thousand copies.

Fairport Convention always invite a broad variety of guests to their annual Cropredy Festival in Oxfordshire. At the 1985 event, as I was wandering away from an uninspiring set by Euro-folk fusion outfit Mosaic, I was halted in my tracks by a piercing, open-throat voice: Márta Sebestyén, the Hungarian member of the group, was singing a Bulgarian ballad. Afterwards, I complimented her on mastering that technique. "Oh, if you like that music, you should join us next summer." She told me about Koprivshtitsa, the great festival of Bulgarian music that takes place every five years; she and some friends were going. "Meet us on July 25 in Budapest and come along." I resolved to do just that.

As I was making travel plans the following spring, the 4AD label, home to the avant-pop duo Cocteau Twins (whose wordless vocals hinted at a familiarity with Balkan music), released Cellier's *Mystère* LP clad in abstract Cocteau-style packaging. John Peel started playing it every evening on Radio 1 and the record sold 200,000 copies in Britain, adding another half-million after Nonesuch picked it up for the US. (Never ignore your attorney's advice, especially if he's your brother and has a better record collection.)

The boat ride down the Danube from Vienna held the next surprise. My image of the Austrian capital as a *Gemütlichkeit*-filled party town and Budapest as a grim Soviet outpost was turned on its head. After the baroque self-importance of the Austrian capital, my walk from the stunning Pest-side riverfront along tree-shaded avenues flanked by crumbling art nouveau buildings to the flat of Nikola Parov, Márta's half-Bulgarian ex-husband, was an eye-opener; the streets buzzed with youth, life, and very short skirts. A few whirlwind days introduced me to the "dance-house" scene (of which more later), but my Hungarian companions took one look at my video camera and said I'd have to fly, as Romanian border guards were certain to confiscate it. A ninety-minute flight in a Tupolev jet landed me in Sofia, where I rented a Lada and headed north into the Balkan Mountains; Bulgaria at last, and not a gherkin in sight.

In Koprivshtitsa, I was directed to a steep path on the side of a hill looming over the village. After a ten-minute ascent I beheld a stunning spectacle: as far as I could see, there were woods and meadows filled with crowds in wildly colorful traditional garb. Eight stages were scattered across the plateau, each one representing a different district. It was overwhelming, almost too much to absorb. I wandered from region to region, taking in the raw material from which Koutev had forged music that now seemed staid and formal compared to what was going on around me. In glades between stages, professionals from the state ensembles jammed with village virtuosos. That night, singers serenaded crowds on the stone bridges arching above the town's fast-running river. The Hungarians and I joined an excited throng following the piercing sound of the double-reed *zurna* accompanying young men dancing barefoot across glowing coals, a trance-assisted feat older than Zoroaster.

In the campgrounds, *gaidas* (bagpipes), *kavals* (wooden flutes), and *teppans* (drums struck on the heads with mallets and with thin sticks on the rims) played for dancers circling huge bonfires. I had seen such circles before; in Princeton, New Jersey, there was a folk-dance group that met in a park near my home on summer evenings. The girls wore sandals and corduroy skirts while most of the men had pocket guards and slide rules and appeared in need of the latter to follow the time signatures of the music emanating from the record player. No one was counting 9/8 or 11/8 under their breath in Koprivshtitsa; like the playing, the dancing was exuberant, complicated, and sensual.

The next day, Rumyana Tzintzarska, head of folk music for Radio Sofia, introduced me, my video camera, and my translator to an elderly woman glowing with intensity and character. "Go into the woods and interview her," said Rumyana. "You will find it interesting." Under a pine tree the woman recounted how Philip Koutev had visited her village in the early 1950s; after an audition, she was invited to join the ensemble but her father refused to allow his teenage daughter to leave home. She was crushed; the memory of that missed chance had haunted her life. She sang a *hajduk* (Ottoman-era outlaw) ballad for my camera in a frail but clear voice. My last day was spent in a dream-like series of musical encounters, captured indelibly in my mind's eye and ear; thirty-five years on, they resonate still.

After World War Two, Bulgarians were unabashedly grateful to their linguistic and religious brethren from the Soviet Union for liberating them from Hitler and eager to cement an alliance that would insure against their ever again falling under the "Turkish yoke." Elsewhere in Eastern Europe, things were not so straightforward. One explanation for the rape and pillage meted out by the Red Army in its advance on Berlin was the soldiers' fury and disbelief at the luxurious living standards they found amid the wreckage of bombed cities: *Private telephones? Flush toilets?!* Surviving owners of such homes were rarely happy at having fallen on the communist side of the Yalta deal done by Stalin, Roosevelt, and Churchill, while in the countryside the peasantry was almost as resistant to collectivization as rural Russians and Ukrainians had been in the 1930s. The Soviets knew they would confront capitalist revanchism and bourgeois elitism in their newly conquered lands; unlikely as it may seem, state folk ensembles were considered an important weapon in this struggle.

The choice of Philip Koutev to lead Bulgaria's was easy; a lifelong Communist and head of the composers' union, he had dreamed of such a project since 1932, when, as a student at the Sofia Conservatory, he attended a recital by a Russian folk choir. Koutev's wife, Maria, an ethnographer and close friend of the wife of Todor Zhivkov, head of Bulgaria's Communist government, would partner him in shaping a company on the same grand and colorful scale as their cohorts in the Soviet Union.

Koutev died four years before my first trip to Bulgaria, but I did meet the veteran arranger Kosta Kolev, who accompanied Koutev to Moscow in the late 1940s. There, along with counterparts from the rest of the new Soviet bloc, they received instruction in the formation of a national folklore ensemble from Igor Moiseyev, director of the famous Moiseyev Ensemble. Each returned home charged with creating a company glorifying the "people's culture" of their homeland. Elena Kouteva told me that her father's ensemble toured widely during the fifties and sixties, but performed only once in the Soviet Union and was never invited back. The problem, it seems, went back to Koutev's 1932 epiphany: *he had been inspired by the wrong choir!* Made up of actual peasants, the Pyatnitsky Ensemble sang in the open-throat style of Slavic villages; when they returned to Moscow following that Balkan tour, they were subjected to a mock trial broadcast by Soviet state radio where their style and repertoire were "convicted" of being harmful to socialism. The group had come up against Stalin's decision to reshape the countryside and create a "new" peasantry. The era's slogan was "make war against the past"; folk music was to be reshaped in the kitsch image of Moiseyev's gigantic company. Did this anti-authenticity crusade spring from the fevered minds of Joseph Stalin and his cultural commissar

Maxim Gorky? Or do its roots lie deeper in Russian history, long before Lenin first cracked opened a copy of *Das Kapital*?

∽

The Bolshevik vision of a new society was not the first ambitious plan for the transformation of Russia. Peter the Great grew so frustrated with "medieval" Moscow that in 1703 he shifted his capital to the shores of the Baltic Sea in an attempt to make his kingdom a part of Europe. Tens of thousands of serfs perished creating the Italianate city of Saint Petersburg on a necklace of swampy, often frozen islands in the Neva River. The emulative creations of Brasilia, Canberra, Naypyidaw, Astana, and Washington DC were child's play in comparison.

Moscow *boyars* were ordered to up stakes and follow—and to cut off their beards while they were at it. Many saw Peter's reforms as the coming of the Antichrist; this was, after all, a society that had burned a Protestant in Red Square as recently as 1689 and where, for reasons similar to those offered today by Iranian mullahs and the Taliban, the Orthodox Church forbade the use of musical instruments. Peter's nobles did as they were told, fronting their new mansions with classical Mediterranean facades; but to his fury they insisted on keeping pigs and cows in the courtyards and letting them graze along the canals. When Peter left town, the men stopped shaving.

He didn't live to see it, but before the century was out, educated residents of Peter's capital were conversing and corresponding in French and, thanks to a parade of Italian musicians arriving in the wake of the architects, opera was now their favorite entertainment. But just as society was becoming more urbane, contrarian winds began wafting in from the West. Catherine the Great sponsored a French opera company whose productions were set in rural idylls with romantic shepherds and picturesque villages, implying that the true spirit of a land lay outside city walls. Such notions originated with a student of Emmanuel Kant named Johannes Herder, a deeply eccentric character who had a profound influence on Goethe and the German Romantics. Herder took Rousseau's "noble savage" idea one step further, insisting that the untutored outpourings of a people, shaped by blood and geography, were of greater significance than the works of an intellectual elite.

On April 27, 1791, Grigory Potemkin, Catherine's infamous lover, organized festivities to celebrate a victory over the Turks. The highlight of the evening was a group of "carolers" led by a royal counselor named Mitrofanov, who was a fount of folk songs, many of which ended up in a Herder-inspired *Collection of Russian Folk Songs and Their Tunes* by Mitrofanov's aristocratic friend Nikolai Lvov. The songs were set in parlor-keyboard mode, the only way anyone could imagine doing such a thing in the pre-recording era. Lvov's book was a huge hit and laid the foundation for Russia's notions about its folk music; Beethoven was among the many who plundered it—for the melodies of his *Razumovsky* string quartets, among others.

Nationalism was originally a liberal concept, built on the radical notion that everyone was part of a people, rather than simply a subject of whichever ruler happened to have inherited that slice of territory. Victories by Napoleon and his citizens' army over royal mercenaries added to the momentum. While other crowned heads trembled, Tsar Alexander kept his vow to overthrow the French Republic and restore the monarchy; the Russian troops who fought alongside the British at Waterloo stayed around to occupy Paris. The liberalizing effect this adventure had on a generation of Russian officers has been the subject of countless novels and histories; many had been so moved by the character and bravery of their serf soldiers that they returned home determined to see them freed from bondage. Disgusted by the French Revolution's descent into bloodletting, they were certain that the Slavic soul would never tolerate such savagery when the time came for *their* revolution.

Aristocrats began spending more time at their country estates, even joining the peasants in church, something once assiduously avoided, since many nobles saw Orthodox Christianity as an obscure religion for the simple. The Russian Church is filled with pagan remnants such as the "onion" domes that evoke the sun, and the pre-Christian ritual of sun-mimicking clockwise processions. The Orthodox pay little attention to Mary's virginity, identifying her with Rozhanitsa, the ancient Slavic fertility goddess. Many serfs viewed priests as black-robed shamans, seeking their blessings to make land and women fertile and to ward off evil spirits. Russian Romantics saw this naivety as evidence of a purity long lost in the decadent West.

At Saint Petersburg balls during the 1820s, formal European gavottes gave way to the *pliaska*. *Natasha's Dance*, Orlando Figes's history of Russian culture, takes its title from the scene in *War and Peace* where the city girl returns to her childhood village and breaks into a wild peasant whirl. Much nineteenth-century Russian literature would dwell on the dichotomy between Saint Petersburg sophistication and the ancient customs, folk cures, shamanic practices—and music—of the countryside. Many wondered if Russia could become modern and European, or if it would remain forever primitive and "Asiatic"; the elite are both defiantly proud and fearfully ashamed of the Oriental heart of their country. The balalaika resembles the Central Asian *dombra* much more than it does the guitar; in dances, heads and hips remain still as shoulders, arms, and hands move, while traditional Russian rhythms have closer cousins in Asia than in Europe. *Obshchina*, the Tatar-influenced custom of collaborative allocation of land and work, functioned far better than would any future socialist notion of agricultural organization.

Kievan Rus, the country's medieval predecessor, had a typically feudal hierarchy, with upward obligations in a pyramid of power. As Europe was growing out of its Dark Ages, Russia plunged further in; a 1649 law criminalized the movement of serfs and forbade them from marrying outside the estate without the lord's permission. (*Pravo pervoy nochi* is Russian for *droit du seigneur*.) By the nineteenth century, peasants were still property; as in the American South and the Caribbean, they represented a large proportion of the capital assets of the landowning classes. Pressure on Tsar Alexander II to free the serfs had been growing, but what may have tipped the balance was the mid-century popularity of serf choirs. Russian singing can be every bit as thrilling as its Bulgarian cousin; with vibrato-free, open-throat "head" voices belting out improvised harmonies roughly equivalent to open fifths, the sound of a group of rural Russian women can be both startling and exhilarating. As urban audiences confronted the character-filled faces and powerful voices of chattel who could be whipped or sold at the whim of an owner, many wondered how such an institution had survived for so long. When emancipation finally arrived in 1861 (two years ahead of America), it was, according to Dostoyevsky, as earth-shaking a moment as Kievan Rus's conversion to Christianity nine centuries earlier.

Idealists flooded the countryside, volunteering as teachers or doctors and preaching socialism. Many were shocked and disillusioned by the superstitious, submissive, and drunken peasants they encountered. For their part, villagers were often so scandalized by the invaders' books and rhetoric that they demanded police arrest them. For a former serf, that he might share "nationality" with his *barin* was beyond imagining. Conservatives clung to the notion that, free or not, peasants remained at the foot of a societal pyramid with the Tsar at the top; their *narodnost* (patriotism) was set against the liberals' *narodnichestvo* (people-ism), but both were delusional. The clearest-eyed appreciation of rural culture emerged from Decembrists exiled after their failed 1825 revolt. In remote corners of the vast land, many developed great respect for their neighbors, documenting the songs, customs, and work-sharing traditions of these proud people who saw no need for grandiose theories of progress.

Strolling down Nevsky Prospekt in the middle of the nineteenth century, one would have heard organ-grinders pumping out Viennese songs and delivery boys whistling Italian arias; people read books in English, French, and German and attended Italian operas. The capital's attitude towards "Russianness" bordered on the hostile; Peter's window on the West had been flung open, but through it, wrote Dostoyevsky, Russians "saw all the wrong things." Herder had urged composers to seek inspiration from their own *Volkslieder*, but few Russians followed the example of their German counterparts. When Mozart or Beethoven quoted a folk tune, even a Russian one, the result was considered "universal"; to Anton Rubinstein, the dominant figure of nineteenth-century Russian music, local melodies sounded "ordinary." A Russified Italian named Catterino Cavos was the first to make the counter-argument, composing *Ilya Bogatyr*, a magical opera filled with Russian melodies. (Yet another example of foreigners' enthusiasm nudging natives towards a reluctant appreciation of their own music.)

Post-emancipation, the Five (also known as "The Mighty Handful")—Mily Balakirev, Modest Mussorgsky, Nikolai Rimsky-Korsakov, Alexander Borodin, and César Cui—began defying Rubinstein by scouring the countryside for inspiration. Balakirev's collection of melodies from the Volga region was an advance on Lvov's with its valiant attempt to render the songs' un-European harmonies; it also set the tone for the decades leading up to Stravinsky by focusing on wedding and other ritual songs. The most dramatic contributions to musical narodnichestvo came from Mussorgsky in his 1874 work *Pictures at an Exhibition* as well as that most Russian of operas, *Boris Godunov*, which featured a Dostoyevskian cast of unprecedentedly introspective and morally conflicted characters. His influence resonated across boundaries and eras: Debussy adored Mussorgsky, likening him to "an inquisitive savage . . . free from artifice or arid formula."

It would be unreasonable to fault the pre-technology Five for not having delved more deeply into authentic folk music; Bartók's immersion in the rhythms, harmonies, and instrumental techniques of the Carpathian Basin would have been impossible without the wind-up recording machine he took with him on his travels a quarter-century later. The Mighty Handful would certainly have heard serf choirs, but even had they studied rural music more closely, they would have struggled to notate it. Russian harmonies, like much of the world's music, are based not on a tempered Western scale, but on overtones, and would have sounded awful rendered by the vibrato-filled voices of an opera company. Nonetheless, at the margins of continental Europe, folk melody was starting to be viewed as a weapon of resistance to the Teutonic musical hegemony that, in the wake of the 1870 Franco-Prussian War, was becoming geopolitical domination as well.

A group of painters known as the Wanderers, inspired by the Mighty Handful, shocked the art establishment by depicting the lives of ordinary rural people. The folkish mysticism of Viktor Vasnetsov had a huge influence on Chagall and Malevich, as well as on *The Rite of Spring*'s set designer Nikolai Roehrich and the Slavic "master race" advocates we shall meet presently. In Moscow, brightly colored, tent-shaped wooden houses sprang up around Red Square, forcing the authorities to abandon rules requiring all-brick frontages. (The GUM department store and Yaroslavl train station are echoes of this era.) A further spur in this embrace of the narod was the Crimean War; just as Serbs in the 1990s struggled to comprehend why the West wasn't their ally against the Muslim Bosniaks, Russia turned bitterly inward, feeling betrayed by its fellow Christians' alliance with the Turks.

"The study of the people is the science of our times," announced folklorist Fedor Buslaev; ethnographic museums sprouted in Moscow and Saint Petersburg. "But," as Dostoyevsky put it, "we, the lovers of the people, regard them as part of a theory, and it seems not one of us loves them as they really are." Except Tolstoy, of course, who loved the reality of peasants so much he fathered a dozen children with servant girls on his estate (to go with the thirteen he had with his wife). But even Tolstoy picked a fight with Chekhov over the latter's unflatteringly realistic portrayals of village life. Chekhov, who never missed an opportunity to annoy the master, observed, "There is more love of humanity in electricity and steam than in vegetarianism." The playwright was himself discomfited by raucous new audiences cheering lustily as his cherry orchard got the chop. Young men heartily sick of age-old customs and hierarchies would provide the backbone of the Bolshevik Revolution.

On a flight from Moscow to Tokyo in the mid-nineties, I watched a Russian film about heroic arms smuggling during the Boer War (supplying the cruelly oppressed Afrikaaners, naturally). The Russian spy passed messages through a cabaret singer who closed her show each night with a song about moonlight on the steppe. Boer characters spoke Russian with a Dutch accent, villainous Brits spoke it with an English accent, and the few Black actors spoke with Slavified "African" accents. As the credits rolled, I had enough Cyrillic to deduce that it was shot in Kazakhstan. *How ludicrous!* was my first thought. But then I recalled all those Hollywood movies in which Mexican-American Anthony Quinn masquerades as a leathery Greek, Arab, or Italian while "locals" deliver their lines in comically accented English. Neither country likes to admit the similarities, but the evidence is inescapable: have the French ever set a lavish film in an Indian-looking backlot, with actors speaking a Bengali-accented version of the language of Voltaire?

The provincial arrogance of the two huge empires has rarely played out with such symmetry as during the Westward/Eastward-ho! conquests of the nineteenth century. Apache and Buryat, Shawnee and Tuvan, Sioux and Tadjik—all succumbed to the inexorable expansion of these brutal outliers of European civilization. Outcomes differed, of course: Russian agronomists failed to turn the taiga into the country's breadbasket, Vladivostok never lived up to its mirror destiny as the glamorous film capital of Asia, and no one sang about wearing flowers in your hair when you visited Magadan. Riding California-ward into the sunset is a journey filled with (often delusional) optimism; Isaak Levitan's painting *The Vladimir Highway* portrays the stark gloom of the journey east to a land of frozen tundra, swamps, mosquitoes, and north-flowing rivers. Perhaps the only advantage Siberia has is its indigenous music, which might explain why Russia produced magnificent Orientalist operas while the American West gave us dime cowboy novels and John Wayne.

> In Europe we were hangers-on and slaves, but in Asia we are masters. In Europe we were Tatars, but in Asia we too are Europeans.
>
> —Fyodor Dostoyevsky

Starting in 732, when Charles Martel defeated the Moors at Tours, Europe could boast the occasional success against armies from the East: a few during the Crusades, the "moor's last sigh" triumph of Los Reyes Católicos in Spain, and Venice's naval victory at Lepanto, for example. Russia, however, felt shamed by its failure to repel the Mongol and Tatar invasions that, according to some histories, reduced its population by 50 percent. The lone point of Russian pride lay in resisting conversion to Islam; as tenth-century Prince Vladimir put it, "Drinking is the joy of the Russes. We cannot do without it."

Thanks to fur, the commodity that financed the building of the great cities of the American East Coast, tables were eventually turned. Profits from pelts enabled the Stroganov family (Russian equivalents of the fur-mogul Astors) to fund a Cossack river pirate named Yermak, whose mercenary army subdued the Khans in the late sixteenth century and opened up the lands beyond the Urals. Explorer Ivan Moskvitin gazed out over the Pacific Ocean in 1639, 166 years before Lewis and Clark could wave back from the other side. Russian tactics in Siberia provided a blueprint for the Yanks: cheap trinkets, diseased blankets, fur quotas, and booze worked efficiently to destroy ancient societies. There was similar ambivalence in both cultures about converting the "savages." Under Russian law, Christian tribes were exempt from tribute; in reactionaries' long catalogue of Peter the Great's sins was his insistence on offering barbarian souls the spiritual comforts of the Orthodox Church. Like America, Russia insists to this day that its expansion bears no resemblance to European colonialism, that it was simply inviting backward neighbors into the embrace of a more civilized "older brother" (or fulfilling a "manifest destiny"). But the rare Siberian group that evaded Russian occupation maintained a far higher level of health and life expectancy than those forced to accept the invitation.

Things got more complicated when the Russians came up against the Khanates of Bukhara, Samarkand, and other kingdoms along the Silk Road. This was the rough equivalent of the Spaniards encountering Aztecs and Incas; only geography spared anglophone pioneers the awkwardness of stumbling upon cultures as wealthy and sophisticated as their own, but lacking gunpowder.

When, in 1783, Catherine the Great visited her latest acquisition, Tatar Crimea, she pronounced it "a fairytale land from *A Thousand and One Nights*." According to Orlando Figes, this Antoine Galland compilation of Arabic and Persian stories created in the Russian mind an image of the Muslim "other" inhabiting "a hedonistic kingdom of sensual luxury and indolence, seraglios and sultans . . . everything, in fact, that the austere north was not." Across Europe, composers responded to their imperially enhanced awareness of faraway peoples with pageantry; ballet surged as opera companies employed dance to represent the colorful life of exotics, particularly Muslims. Representing the *actual* East, however, was never the point of Orientalist music; it was about the *idea* of the East.

For Rimsky-Korsakov and the rest of the Five, "these new sounds were a sort of revelation for us then, we were all literally reborn." Looking back from 1882 on a quarter-century of Russian music, the critic Vladimir Stasov saw the turn Eastward as the dominating idea in Russian music and credited the Mighty Handful with leading the way. While it was no coincidence that this new direction coincided with wars of conquest in Central Asia, it was also in line with other trends: the growing resentment of German musical domination, a newly confident nationalism, and the fashion for "program music," with Mussorgsky's *Pictures* leading the way. As César Cui wrote after hearing a Rimsky-Korsakov piece, "Only a Russian could have composed it, because it lacks the slightest trace of any stagnant Germanness."

After leading his colleagues down folkloric Russian paths, Mily Balakirev now introduced them to the pentatonic scales found in most Asian music. They employed the Phrygian variant, adapted from the Middle Eastern Hijaz mode with its raised second note; the scale bestowed melodic qualities on Russian composition that are among its most distinctive features, from the "Polovtsian Dances" of Borodin's *Prince Igor* to Stravinsky's *Rite of Spring*. For Russians, that scale signals—*the East!* For everyone else, it means—*Russia!*

Borodin created *Prince Igor* intermittently between 1869 and 1887, as Russia engaged in a brutal struggle against the Khan of Bukhara and the Muslim Holy League. Stasov's libretto is based on the twelfth-century *Lay of Igor's Campaign*, about a clash with an Asiatic enemy. Russian affection for the novels of James Fenimore Cooper prompted him to add a "good Indian" to the plot as well as a love-interest princess; subversively, Stasov portrayed the Polovtsians as more civilized than the Russians. The 1953 Broadway musical *Kismet* (including the hit "Stranger in Paradise") was lifted from *Prince Igor*'s first act and other Borodin pieces. The American words of the Polovtsian theme—"*Take my hand, I'm a stranger in paradise*"—actually succeed in conveying the spirit of Orientalist opera: an intrepid but square Westerner finds a beautiful guide to show him the ropes in this world of pleasure and indulgence. Local men are always ugly and cruel and clearly deserve to have their women and kingdoms taken away from them. *Igor* reverberated down the decades: the young Stravinsky got an early taste for musical exoticism watching his father sing the bass role on opening night in 1890, while the Soviets turned to it during World War Two for reassurance about Russian character and determination.

The Orientalist paintings of Ingres, Delacroix, Holman Hunt, and Alma-Tadema make clear what the East represented in the nineteenth-century European imagination: sex. The expanding bourgeoisie craved titillation, and sensuality was more acceptable if set in a far-off land. In reality, the Islamic world was nearly as puritanical then as it is now, though the European travelers whose writings sold so well seemed always able to find the bordellos. Harems were great for sales and became the repository of male fantasies; musically, this manifested itself in the *nega*, a sensual passage signaling ecstasy, marked by ascending and descending chromatic waves often led by a French horn (for the sound of the hunt, perhaps). The great expert on Russian music, Richard Taruskin, rhapsodized over Borodin's "languorous undulation" in the nega from the "Polovtsian Dances." Nineteenth-century Russian elites liked to imagine they were descended from blond Vikings and represented the purest strain of European civilization. Russia's location with one foot in Asia had, they believed, kept it from falling into the spiritual corruption that engulfed Europe following the Protestant Reformation. The ancient *byliny* from which many operatic plot lines were sourced are oral epics once considered to be close relatives of Norse sagas. In a famous essay, Stasov pointed out that byliny make no mention of snow, winter, lakes, mossy riverbanks, or wooden buildings. In great detail, he traced the parallels between them and the *Mahabharata* and *Ramayana* as well as Mongolian and Persian legends. He also found references to Asiatic shamanism and linguistic links to Sanskrit. To great nationalist outrage, he concluded that Russia's true roots lay not with the Vikings, but in Asia. Stasov felt that Oriental culture pervaded Russian life and that reflecting that influence was the most natural thing for its composers, who "had been surrounded with Oriental impressions all their lives . . . To see in this only a strange whim . . . would be absurd."

The debate about Russia's cultural wellsprings was fierce, at least among intellectuals. Wassily Kandinsky spent a year living in a Finno-Ugric community near the Urals; their pagan imagery and rituals were a major influence on his painting, and he gave lectures in Saint Petersburg on Russia's connection to Finno-Ugric culture. By the final quarter of the nineteenth century, Herder had been updated: neighbors, invaders, immigrants, and traders, most ethnographers agreed, did as much to forge national identities as land and blood. But *narodnost* folklorists stuck to the conviction that byliny were "the finest living relics of our people's poetry . . . without the slightest trace of outside influence." Like Federico García Lorca in the cultural battles that preceded the Spanish Civil War (and the poet's resulting murder), Stasov was accused of slandering Russia by celebrating its non-Christian influences.

Russia's southerly conquests ground to a halt in the mountains of Afghanistan; further limits were defined in 1904, when the Tsar's forces were trounced in the Russo-Japanese War. Rimsky-Korsakov's reaction was to create *The Golden Cockerel*, in which a buffoonish ruler is bamboozled by a wily Oriental queen and her troupe of girls in harem pantaloons. The plot is based on one of Washington Irving's *Tales of the Alhambra* that Pushkin transposed to Russia's borders. For European audiences, Muslims from Morocco to Cairo to the Caucasus to Samarkand were pretty much interchangeable; some historians have suggested that the very notion of Europe as a cultural entity took shape more as "not the Islamic world" than through any cohesive identity of its own.

The Mighty Handful eventually grew weary: "We had enough of the Orient," said Mussorgsky. "Art isn't a pastime and time is precious." Musical Orientalism had attempted to bridge Dostoyevsky's divide, distancing Russia from the East through caricature while separating itself from the West by flaunting its own foreignness. For the West, the most enduring bit of Russian Orientalism must be Rimsky-Korsakov's *Scheherazade*, which would become a key to Diaghilev's conquest of Paris and has never left the mainstream of the world's ballet repertoire. But perhaps its most telling legacy lies in the music we have come to associate with America's own wide-open spaces, the sweeping orchestrations that (with help from a few beats on a tom-tom) evoke smoke signals on the horizon and scalp-hungry braves hiding behind rocks. A pupil of Rimsky-Korsakov's emigrated to Hollywood, where he scored *Rio Bravo, Gunfight at the OK Corral, Giant,* and *The Alamo,* and won an Academy Award by borrowing an old shtetl melody for the theme song of *High Noon*. In his 1952 Oscar acceptance speech, Dimitri Tiomkin explained: "A steppe is a steppe is a steppe. The problems of the cowboy and the Cossack are very similar. Their courage and philosophical attitudes are similar and the steppes of Russia are much like the prairies of America."

As the nineteenth century neared its end, urban Russians no longer needed to head for the countryside in search of the "folk"; the "folk" were coming to them by the millions. In the countryside, obshchina was breaking under the weight of soil degradation and increased population, while factories were hungry for workers. Emancipation plus the new railways made possible previously unimaginable migrations. Poor neighborhoods mixing Caucasians, Jews, and ex-serfs became a feature of the urban landscape. Lingering fantasies of peasant nobility were dashed by the novelty-craving, porn-loving, heavy-drinking newcomers. In a land where theater had been a private domain of the ruler a few years earlier, many found the phenomenon of illiterate crowds flocking to the cinema profoundly disturbing. The safest "folk" to study were the Old Believers hiding out in isolated corners of Siberia as a result of a seventeenth-century dispute with the Patriarch over whether to cross yourself with two fingers or three. The outside world placed freed serfs in a pantheon of primitives that included Zulus, Sioux, and Tahitians, but the Tsar angrily blocked proposals to include Russian peasant villages in late-nineteenth-century expositions.

Rimsky-Korsakov branded the work of a man named Melgunov "barbarous"; his crime was to transcribe songs exactly as they were sung, "Oriental" decorations, pentatonic dissonances, and all. The hoary Lvov collection was reprinted and distributed throughout the expanding rural school system, with the result that collectors began encountering Mitrofanov's recycled repertoire alongside genuinely ancient songs. Regional distinctiveness evaporated as urban ditties spread to villages through the increased back-and-forth lives of workers, aided, as the twentieth century dawned, by railroads and cylinder players. The conductor Serge Koussevitsky tried to inject some class into the new openness of the countryside by giving "elevating" orchestral concerts from a boat that plied the Volga every summer from 1910 to 1914.

Thanks in part to the Church's hatred of instruments, most rural music had always been sung a cappella: communal rituals, wedding songs, bandit ballads, comic ditties, and chants to help pull barges or bring in new seasons. In the cities, vocalists teamed up with accordions or the recently invented balalaika. Like touring Zulus singing Gilbert and Sullivan, serf choirs began adding Neapolitan songs and Lvov "folk" arrangements. Song collectors found themselves in uncomfortable alliance with reactionary priests and village headmen, aghast at the erosion of traditional culture and the "coarsening" effects of education, mass media, and improved infrastructure.

One body of song previously ignored by collectors was suddenly omnipresent: Jewish. Refugees fleeing rural pogroms led the migration from the Pale of Settlement first to Odessa then on to Moscow and Saint Petersburg in sync with blues arriving in New Orleans from the Mississippi Delta, then heading north to Chicago and New York. Jews brought the satirical couplet to the city; a form called *chastushka* became Russia's blues, delivered with exaggerated grimaces and poses, celebrating outlaws and rebels and full of anti-establishment attitude. Many Jews from the Pale—Irving Berlin among them—moved on to America, bringing shtetl melodies and sentiments with them to Tin Pan Alley.

Another once-marginal group now taking center stage were the "gypsies." Russia didn't have a particularly large Roma population, but generals returning from Balkan campaigns started a fashion by bringing their favorite singers and musicians back with them. Like White American singers aspiring to "soul," many of the most popular *tziganshchina* performers were Russians playing up the accelerating rhythms and flourishes of Roma music and horrifying the Church with their erotic movements and salacious lyrics. The overstated emotions of the style became deeply embedded in Russian song, elbowing aside the nuanced, unaccented, open-throat cadences and subtle ornamentation of rural singing and, to this day, defining what the world—and most Russians—think of as "Russian" ballad-singing. Notions of exceptionalism persisted; sexuality was always "foreign," with actors blacking up to portray lusty savages and female impersonators mocking Roma *chanteuses*.

An apocalyptic atmosphere pervaded the period following the October Revolution of 1905; optimism faded as slums and disease multiplied. Narodniks, once true to the "people's cause," were alienated by peasants seizing land, burning farms, and demanding economic justice. "In our hearts," wrote the poet Alexander Blok, "the needle of a seismograph has twitched." As many liberals moved to the right, others, such as Maxim Gorky (who had been badly beaten trying to protect a village woman from her violent husband), aligned themselves with the Bolshevik view that peasant culture must be destroyed in order to renew it.

The between-revolutions period from 1905 to 1917 provided a dress rehearsal for many aspects of musical life under the Communists. Vasily Andreev, for example, created a vehicle for the instrument he had helped invent, touring the country with a tuxedo-clad balalaika orchestra playing classical compositions in cod-folk style, borrowing the instrument's now-ubiquitous tremolo strum from Neapolitan mandolinists. Dmitri Agrenev-Slavianskii's chorus provided a blueprint for the Moiseyev Ensemble, "improving" serf choirs by dressing them in historical court costumes, giving them a "pan-Slavic" repertoire with Western harmonies, and quadrupling their size. Gorky created a dry run for the *dom kulturi* of the Soviet era by organizing lending libraries and workers' dramatic societies. Music halls began including folk songs accompanied by the dreaded accordion in their shows, even as imported crazes for the tango, foxtrot, and cakewalk spread to remote corners of the country.

Running counter to these trends was Philip Koutev's hero and role model, Mitrofan Pyatnitsky, collector of genuine folk songs and folk singers. In the wake of the 1905 turmoil, he formed a workers' chorus in Saint Petersburg along the lines of nineteenth-century serf choirs. Wearing handmade clothing and standing in front of painted backdrops of idealized rural settings, they sang traditional songs from regions left behind in the search for jobs in the city. Local success propelled them to Moscow, where their debut on March 2, 1911, was cheered by a packed house that included Sergei Rachmaninoff and the great *basso* Fyodor Chalyapin. Soviets would later attack Pyatnitsky for his obsession with "ugly" authenticity and praise Agrenev-Slavianskii for capturing the "true spirit" of Russian song.

Groups in traditional dress, including Pyatnitsky's, flourished during the Great War as the monarchy tried to rally support for its foundering campaign by appealing to national stereotypes. (Stalin would attempt the same twenty-five years later.) The war years' most unlikely star was a woman named Maria Krivopolenova from an Arctic village near Arkhangelsk; she sang ancient songs and told handed-down tales, and huge crowds came to see her when she performed in Saint Petersburg. The Left was already busy demonizing traditional music, trying to inspire workers with "modern" compositions that fell on stony ground. The most popular wartime songs were ballads about bandits Razin and Pugachev; the notion that virtue lay with outlaws and rebels helped set the stage for the Bolsheviks. The elite, meanwhile, flocked to cults that tapped into anti-rational ritual and sought transcendence: theosophy, kabbalists, neo-pagans, Rosicrucians, Swedenborgians, Madame Blavatsky's seances, and so on. The Tsarina's obsession with Rasputin was simply part of the aristocratic zeitgeist.

A foretaste of what lay around history's corner came in a 1915 proclamation by the Suprematist painter Kazimir Malevich: "I say to all: abandon love, abandon aestheticism, abandon the baggage of wisdom, for in the new culture, your wisdom is ridiculous and insignificant."

Has any revolution produced a more compelling image than Lilya Brik shouting "*KNYGY*" (*BOOKS*) into Rodchenko's constructivist megaphone? Eisenstein's films, Mayakovsky's poems, Meyerhold's theater, Tatlin's tower, Rodchenko's photographs: to this day, the artistic energy unleashed in revolutionary Russia's first years holds our imagination, while capitalist ad agencies plunder its archives for hip graphics. But when the Party sent this new "popular culture" out around the country via propaganda trains, posters, circuses, and fairs, it fell flat. Beautifully designed magazines and newspapers got used for cigarette papers or fish wrapping. Composers of "new" folk songs tried to adopt a village style and rural argot, but the results were mocked. Before decamping for Italy, Gorky expressed his disgust: "[T]he whole of the Russian intelligentsia . . . has manfully attempted to set on its feet the ponderous Russian people, lying lazily . . . on a fabulously rich land on which it managed to live astonishingly poorly."

That was the nub: the land! Soviet cities were hungry and the Party was convinced that the kind of collective organization being applied to industry would transform the countryside into an agricultural powerhouse. It was a cultural and economic stand-off: urbanites hated and feared the "dark" and backward peasants they relied on, while villagers fiercely resisted collectivization; from long experience, they knew that "trouble always comes from town."

"Any peasant who . . . has emerged from his muzhik darkness, will agree . . . *that all surplus grain without exception* must be turned over to the workers' state." Lenin's words typified the Party's attitude; they hoped to turn "poor" peasants against the *kulaks* (a Ukrainian word for "fist," implying "tight-fisted"), those who had responded to the land reforms of 1906 with the most initiative. But peasants saw little difference between themselves and those with a bit more land, and in any case hated being called "poor." Feelings of empathy or common cause between agricultural and factory workers were virtually non-existent.

Lenin was a pragmatist. When it became clear that attempts to force an agricultural revolution were propelling Russia into a terrifying famine, he introduced the New Economic Plan (NEP), which placed buying grain from the hated kulaks at the heart of the food supply. He accepted that transforming the countryside would be a long, gradual process. The peasants reveled in their triumph and the NEP era became a time of unprecedented prosperity for villagers; taverns, drugs, prostitutes, record players (and 78 rpm shellacs of "gypsy music" to play on them), American movies, crime, and venereal disease spread to regions where such things had been unknown. Landless peasants fatefully transformed themselves into kulaks by taking over acreage vacated by landowners exiled, dispossessed, or killed during the Revolution.

A decade later, those who had supplied the cities with the most grain would be rewarded with execution or Siberia, but pre-1928, Soviet officials limited their resentment to occasional tax raids or anti-hoarding grain seizures. Villages avoided ostentation; road repair or church renovations would bring unwelcome attention from Party apparatchiks. Rural women, alarmed by the drunkenness and whoring, clung ever tighter to their traditions, reviving ancient practices and gathering together to sing old songs.

The Party celebrated the Pyatnitsky Ensemble as appropriate representatives of "people's music." Lenin himself loved music but was wary of its power and rarely mentioned it or made it a government priority: "I can't listen to music too often. It affects your nerves, makes you want to say stupid nice things, and stroke the heads of people who could create such beauty." Though sparing rural music, urban culture, he felt, was too important to be left to its own devices. Film studios, theaters, talent agencies, print media, and radio stations were all brought under Party control, with song lyrics subject to particularly rigorous scrutiny. Producers and performers fled abroad in droves, leaving large swathes of show business in the hands of the Proletkult and Forward movements, who cherished a dream of elevating the masses. When audiences failed to respond to machine sonatas and avant-garde dance performances, Party officials began the long march towards the planned mediocrity of socialist realism.

There is evidence that the dying Lenin tried to save the Party from falling into Stalin's hands; his failure to do so sealed the fate of the countryside. In 1928, as industry stagnated and agriculture flourished, Stalin ordered price controls; outraged peasants withheld their grain. This was the trigger he had been seeking; like Margaret Thatcher with the miners, he had never forgiven the peasants for their defiance. Kulaks would now be eliminated and collectivization enforced at the point of a gun.

A stated objective of Stalin's first five-year plan was to "defeat peasant darkness" and "overcome rural backwardness." Returning from his self-imposed exile to take up the post of culture commissar, Maxim Gorky predicted that "the half-savage, stupid, ponderous people of the Russian villages . . . will die out, and a new tribe will take their place—literate, sensible, hearty people." Resistance was implicit in rural music; its strange dissonances, bawdy innuendos, and religious themes made it an inappropriate soundtrack for this brave new world. As for tradition's original enemies, the avant-garde, their creations were now as ill-fitting as *babushkas* belting out a religious chant. Party modernists had set out to obliterate not only folk song but sentimental, aristocratic "rubbish" such as Glinka. But Glinka, they were horrified to discover, was music-loving Stalin's favorite composer.

Orders went out to the cultural bodies: all art must be uplifting and unifying. Individual performance, obscure regionalisms, dirges, and songs that celebrated superstition, religion, or shamanic ritual were banned. There would be no *lapti* (birch-bark boot) wearers on Soviet stages and no babushkas in scarves. The Pyatnitsky aesthetic was recast as a subversive, possibly fatal, error: kulak art. Having died in 1927, Pyatnitsky himself was spared the sight of his once-great choir churning out fakelore designed to obliterate his beloved peasant culture. This, unashamedly, was the new cultural policy.

> Communism was modernity in its most determined mood and most decisive posture; modernity streamlined, purified of the last shred of the chaotic, the irrational, the spontaneous, the unpredictable.
>
> —Zygmunt Bauman

Marx had condemned "the idiocy of rural life" and asserted that as a class, the peasantry were as redundant as capitalists. Mayakovsky seconded the motion: "A way of life which has not changed at all and which is our greatest enemy." When collectivization officials arrived with armed guards, many peasants saw it as the Apocalypse, the coming of the Antichrist or a return to serfdom. They weren't far wrong on the last point: *kolkhoz* workers were not allowed to leave the farm without a signed paper and needed permission to study or marry. Despite an inbuilt resistance to negative information, Soviet archives show 13,000 "riots" in 1930, involving two million peasants. Another file contains accounts of 2,796 assaults on Party officials the same year. In the first two years of the new plan, nearly a thousand Party workers were killed; officials were warned to stay away from windows and not venture out at night.

Rural Russia had been dealing with unreasonable absentee landlords for centuries, but not even Peter the Great shut churches and melted down their bells for the iron. By 1931, 80 percent of Russia's houses of worship had been closed. Government hostility to religion terrified the peasants; the holy sacrament of marriage seemed to have become little more than a mechanism for creating more workers. Reports spread of lights in the sky and holy visitations; doom-laden prophecies were being fulfilled.

Entire villages insisted on going into exile with families convicted of kulak-ism; peasants suspected of informing on stashes of grain or hidden animals were often lynched. Not wishing to be branded as kulaks (and loath to share meat with urban workers or lazy neighbors), farmers butchered livestock before it could be registered and seized. In one report, a family turned over a beloved horse to the collective, only to see a supervisor treat it so brutally that it died; they held an equine funeral and fought off kolkhoz officials attempting to halt the ceremony. Promised tractors rarely materialized, and when they did, fuel and spare parts would fail to arrive, leaving fields unplowed and peasants starving. In cities, new housing was built without kitchens on the grounds that vast, efficient workers' canteens would feed entire neighborhoods, freeing women for factory work. Those canteens were stored with the tractors' fuel, somewhere in Soviet officialdom's imagination.

Women needing to put food on their families' tables were at the forefront in dealing with the new reality. Peasants found that troops were less likely to fire on a female protest, so crowds of shouting, singing women would invade collectives, tear up documents, and seize grain and livestock. A chorus of Russian women in full voice is remarkably loud, with startling harmonies and dissonances; one can imagine the impression it would have made on an urban Party worker sent to collectivize a village. Officials tried to characterize protests as "March fever"; organized resistance was put down to *muzhik i babi* (yokels and old women) primitivism. An oft-used expression was *babi bunt*: "granny riot." No wonder the spine-tingling female harmonies of the Pyatnitsky Ensemble had to be eliminated. (In 2011, Russian officials found another female musical protest—Pussy Riot—similarly alarming.)

Attention turned to markets, mills, and artisan workshops; anything that reminded peasants of old ways or provided them with a gathering place outside the kolkhoz had to go. Like other skilled craftsmen, musicians were branded as parasites. Music was also used in evidence: if you had the funds to support a seasonal or religious celebration, you must be a kulak. Brawls broke out when a village procession encountered an official gathering, one singing traditional chants, the other Party anthems. Reporting such events required a contorted circular logic; village rather than class-based solidarity was, by Marxist definition, impossible. Any peasant who resisted was, therefore, a kulak, so all subversion must be the fault of kulaks. As starvation set in, the campaign turned even more vicious. Every grain, every piece of chaff, must be sent to the cities; only when the quota—an unreachable one, with so many exiled, fled, or killed and no animals or fuel to pull a plow—was fulfilled could peasants put something aside for their families. Many of the most able farmers simply gave up and moved to the cities or escaped into the woods, living as brigands and raiding collective farms for supplies. At least two million were exiled and thousands committed suicide; execution statistics have been disputed, but from 1928 to the start of the Great Patriotic War, no fewer than half a million peasants were killed by firing squad or hanged. Stalin singled out Ukraine for particularly vengeful policies; over three million starved to death there. One way or another, between 1928 and 1932, more than five million left the land.

The countryside gradually became a land of women. To male victims of repression and starvation in the early 1930s and soldiers killed in World War Two can be added the millions of veterans who chose not to return to their villages after demobilization. Women who once wove, sewed, and carved (singing all the while) now worked the fields and had no time for such frivolities. Soviet propaganda recognized the gender shift: most worker-glorifying posters and statues show a man in factory garb and a woman wielding a scythe or hoe.

∾

> Folk songs . . . [have] nothing in common with the tasks, worldview, and psychology of the contemporary industrial proletariat.
>
> —Iu. I. Laane, *Sovetskoe iskusstva* (Soviet Art), 1927

Reshaping the musical landscape began slowly. As late as 1935, state-sponsored ethnographers were still in the field collecting songs; with most proving unacceptable, however, storylines had to be altered and new verses imposed on the singers. Like churches built on the site of former pagan temples, saints' days and holidays were Sovietized: October 14, Holy Virgin's Day, became "Collectivization Day." Well-known songs were given new, "uplifting" lyrics; wood nymphs morphed into tractors. Spontaneous music was forbidden; most decent-sized towns built cultural centers where singing and dancing could be funneled into competitions, with lyrics monitored and "improved." New folk songs were created by composers with no interest in the tonal mutability, heterophony, or parallel fifths of traditional music. The Pyatnitsky Choir eliminated improvisation and regional dialects and fired anyone who couldn't read music. All listeners could now, theoretically, "recognise themselves, their thoughts and feelings" in the group's repertoire.

The way forward was signaled when a 30,000-strong ensemble sang at the 1932 Moscow Olympics. Immense choirs took the place of small groups of open-throat singers improvising around one another's overtones; informal village dances were replaced by exercises set to music modeled on the folk arrangements of Glinka and the Handful. Soviets insisted they were simply "polishing the gem"; anything hard for urban masses to understand—complex rhythms or harmonies, metaphorical lyrics, subtle phrasing, or regional dialects—was suppressed in the interest of "raising the level." The standard was defined by nineteenth-century Western classical music and sold to audiences with grandiosity and volume.

The man destined to forge the prototype for state folk ensembles was, in the early 1930s, a principal dancer in the Bolshoi Ballet with a sideline in choreographing pageants in Red Square. Born in Paris in 1906 to a Russian father and a Franco-Romanian mother, Igor Moiseyev had joined the Bolshoi directly from its ballet school in 1924. His dream was to elevate the level of athleticism in dance. In 1936, he was asked to produce a folk-dance festival; when a spectacular multi-ethnic number he choreographed was the hit of the show, Commissar Molotov asked him to form an ensemble, eventually known as the Moiseyev Dance Company.

Moiseyev's approach merged the fantasies of nineteenth-century ballet with the synchronized athleticism of a May Day stadium show. He hated traditional music and dance; his aim was to raise the standard of folk dance, but the starting point lay in his own imagination filtered through classical training and Party ideology. Moiseyev recruited from ballet schools and conservatories, never villages. The company's orchestra was strictly "Western symphonic"; other nationalities within the Soviet Union included traditional instruments in their state ensembles, as would Eastern bloc allies after 1945, but in Russian ensembles, native instruments appeared only as stage props.

Dancers were taught classical ballet techniques, though solo turns were rare other than for stock comic characters or villains (usually fat with mustaches). The company's stages were brightly colored, sexless places where boys and girls played "fun-in-the-village" games. Moiseyev's favorite combination was three dancers in red, three in blue, three in yellow, and three in green. Male and female dancers were all of uniform height and most were blond and blue-eyed; according to one account, even smile widths were matched. History does not reveal whether Moiseyev watched Busby Berkeley films, but the spirit echoed that of Depression-era Hollywood: *We're modern! We aren't poor! We're all in it together!*

Storylines were moralistic, upholding collectivist values against threats from reactionary villainy with the subliminal message that one man's will—Moiseyev's or Stalin's—could control a vast army of dancers/ workers like so many marionettes. This notion had a basis in the work of the Russian psychologist Ivan Sechenov, a predecessor of Pavlov, who had written about the brain as an electromechanical device. Lenin had been contemptuous of Russian workers' skills and intrigued by the idea that they could be programmed. He shared with Meyerhold and other theatrical pioneers a fascination with the work of US time-and-motion expert F. W. Taylor; imposing factory whistles and eight-hour days on collective farms may have had a disastrous effect on agriculture, but mechanistic choreographic displays could be spectacular. As Taylor was being earnestly studied in Russia, Fritz Lang's *Metropolis* and Charlie Chaplin's *Modern Times* were taking the piss in Europe and America.

Gigantic choirs became hugely popular, with their dramatic swings from *pppp* to *ffff*, comedic interjections, and melodramatic lyrics. In 1938, the Pyatnitsky Ensemble put the final nail in the coffin of their founder's vision by adding a full orchestra of Western instruments to their now-bloated company. Collective farms were required to have choirs, but as the new "village" music needed sheet music, a conductor, and instrumental accompanists, they were often resented as a drain on scarce resources. "Folklore" was originally (according to Party dogma) a creation of "the people"; Gorky now decided it was "literature" and could be created by individuals—so long as they were loyal Party members.

This gargantuan pageantry was in sync with the huge construction projects of the thirties: Moscow's magnificent Metro system, its wide boulevards, and the deep canal connecting the Moscow and Volga Rivers. Official imagery was filled with healthy workers, tables groaning with food, and modern, bustling factories. Behind the scrim, the Soviet Potemkin village was beset with missed targets, moribund industry, and rural starvation. "Real" music risked a brush with Truth; there would instead be a half-century of socialist realism, authenticity's polar opposite.

In sixties London, the *International Times* attributed its masthead slogan to Plato: "When the mode of music changes, the walls of the city shake." A more restrained translation from the ancient Greek might read "the music and literature of a country cannot be altered without major political and social changes." The Soviets took that message to heart and to a certain extent they succeeded; in the end, peasant resistance produced little more than torpor and pilferage. When a new transformation beckoned in the post-Soviet nineties, few farm workers could recall the vibrant rural culture of the past and most had little enthusiasm for mad schemes of privatization and individual farms; this was just more trouble arriving, as usual, "from town."

In 1906, the year Igor Moiseyev was born in Paris, that other great impresario of make-believe Russian folk traditions, Sergei Diaghilev, began his journey in the opposite direction, with an exhibition of Russian art in the French capital. One would let loose upon the world an avalanche of kitsch; the other commissioned some of the greatest music of the twentieth century.

Sjeng Scheijen's richly detailed biography begins with Diaghilev's birth in 1872 near the Ural city of Perm, his mother's untimely death, and the arrival of an inspirational stepmother: "You must forget the phrase 'I can't,'" she told him. "When people want to, they can." Reading the account of Diaghilev's Ballets Russes company, triumph alternating with near disaster, I was awed by this fellow producer's ability to keep the theatrical equivalent of an indie label going at such a level for nearly a quarter-century, all the while nurturing the composers who would shape twentieth-century music.

As a young man in Saint Petersburg, Diaghilev moved in elevated circles, visiting Tolstoy to discuss modernity, hearing Mussorgsky perform his latest works at family gatherings, and showing his own youthful compositions to Rimsky-Korsakov, who delivered a cold-water splash of dismissal that helped steer Sergei towards his true calling. He joined a group calling themselves the Nevsky Pickwickians, who embraced the Saint Petersburg yen for connection to wider European culture but with none of Rubinstein's shame about Russia's own heritage. In founding the magazine *Mir iskusstva* (World of Art), Diaghilev assembled the brains trust that would propel Ballets Russes onto the world stage, including designers Leon Bakst and Alexandre Benois. *Mir* championed a diverse palette of non-establishment Russian art, including the Wanderers, rural and urban folk art and old-fashioned provincial landscapes and portraits. It also supported the mystical visions of Nicholas Roerich, *The*

Rite of Spring's set designer. Another foreshadowing was the profligate absence of budgeting, resulting in a small collectors' treasure of colorful and exquisitely printed editions, followed by bankruptcy. All remained loyal to their youthful commander; as Benois recalled, "Diaghilev's boundless energy made us forget the risks and our exhaustion . . . a true leader whom you would follow through thick and thin . . . [He] had an individual gift of creating a romantic working climate, and with him all work had all the charm of a risky escapade."

A bequest from his mother allowed him to live comfortably despite such setbacks and he licked his wounds with a tour of Europe; Wagner's operas at Bayreuth stunned him, as did Mozart and Verdi in Vienna. Venice, he declared, was where he intended to die, but not before proving that Russia could match the greatest Western Europe could offer. The trip stimulated his curatorial instincts; producers, he felt, must be ruthless, improving great works by trimming the flab. Despite his pride in Russia's riches, he was never a simplistic nationalist: "[W]hat could be more destructive than the wish to become a national artist? . . . [U]ntil we see in Russian art an elegant, grandiose harmony, a majestic simplicity . . . we will have no real art . . . The demand that art should serve society . . . is completely incomprehensible."

Diaghilev nonetheless admired how Finland (then a Russian province) had revived its sense of identity through folk-tinged art and the music of Sibelius. His 1898 exhibition of Finnish painting set what Scheijen sees as a template: "subversive art in a lavish setting." His catalogues, how works were hung—everything was at a level of professionalism, opulence, and attention to detail rarely seen before in Russia. At a subsequent exhibition, Diaghilev delivered a speech in which he spoke of "things . . . coming to an end in the name of a new, unknown culture, one which we will create but which will in time also sweep us away . . . And the only wish that I as an irredeemable sensualist can make is that the coming struggle will not insult the aesthetics of life." Some hope . . .

When an exhibition of Russian art they brought to the 1906 Paris Salon was only mildly successful, he and his team decided to mount a Paris production of *Boris Godunov* starring Fyodor Chalyapin; music, they reasoned, would have a greater impact than painting. Wealthy

French allies mesmerized by Diaghilev's ability to combine tradition with modernity, Europe with Asia, and an artistic temperament with business acumen lent their support. *Boris* was a smash; one Chalyapin ovation went on so long that the conductor walked off in disgust. *Le tout Paris* flocked to added concerts where the great *basso*, accompanied by Alexander Scriabin on piano, sang Mussorgsky, Rimsky-Korsakov, Tchaikovsky, Glinka, and Borodin. Like turn-of-the-next-century audiences absorbing Malian music at WOMAD, Parisians lapped it all up. In the years leading up to the Great War, France craved exoticism, be it the Orient as evoked in the writings of Pierre Loti, the shock of the Argentine tango, or the spirit world conjured up by mystics such as Allan Kardec (whose Père Lachaise grave is still more visited and beflowered than Jim Morrison's or Édith Piaf's).

Despite its success, *Boris* was a financial trainwreck. Diaghilev, Benois, and Bakst decided that ballet—far cheaper to produce than opera—was the sensible way to present the magic of Russian music; they would draw on the rich trove of as-yet-unheard works by the Mighty Handful and other Saint Petersburg composers. Their timing was perfect; the fringes of European theater were bristling with radical ideas that established dance companies ignored. Diaghilev and his friends had adored Isadora Duncan's 1904 performances in Saint Petersburg and pledged to "carry the torch that she lit." Dance also appealed to another aspect of Diaghilev's ahead-of-its-time personality: as possibly the first unabashed "grand homosexual," he saw an opportunity to glorify the male body, to steer ballet away from its frilly feminine aura and forge a new, athletic image for "sensitive" men. Unlike Saint Petersburg, where elite society had hounded Tchaikovsky to his death, Paris was a free and easy city where he and his friends could (somewhat) openly express their sexuality. Diaghilev and Oscar Wilde drew an admiring crowd as they walked arm-in-arm down the Champs-Élysées.

In Saint Petersburg, most ballerinas had "sponsors," rich men who organized cheering claques and were repaid with sex; wealthy homosexuals were similarly (if less openly) linked to male dancers. The cultural history of the twentieth century changed course when Diaghilev's infatuation with Vaslav Nijinsky triggered an arrangement with the young dancer's sponsor to "transfer" him, both as star of the newly formed company and as lover. Nijinsky, eager to escape Russia after scandalizing the royal box with form-revealing tights, readily agreed. The Paris opening of *Les Sylphides* on May 19, 1909, was a sensation. Poet Anna de Noailles wrote: "It was as if Creation, having stopped on the seventh day, now all of a sudden resumed . . . Something completely new in the world of the arts . . . a sudden glory." The diarist Harry Kessler chimed in: "I could never have dreamt of a *mimetic art* that was so beautiful, so refined, so far beyond theatrics . . . These [dancers] seem to have descended from another, higher, more beautiful world, like young living gods and goddesses . . . We are truly witnessing the birth of a new art."

Bakst's art direction was central to the success, fusing the exotic with the erotic; even in Paris, it was safer to present sex in a fantastic and/or distant land. Set design had been an isolated and lowly craft, largely consisting of stock images; Diaghilev, in contrast, presided over a round table at which designers, costumiers, choreographers, conductors, and composers debated every detail of a production. In the first year of the company's existence, this team had created eight completely new works, all premiered over three Paris evenings in the spring of 1908. A highlight of the first season was the "Polovtsian Dance" excerpt from *Prince Igor*, whetting French appetites for a Russian vision of "East" while remaining comfortably within Degas-esque traditions, i.e., a stage full of leggy girls. Male dancers had previously served mostly as foils for the ballerinas, but in the following year's *Scheherazade*, Nijinsky changed everything with his interpretation of the Golden Slave, in a sexually charged *pas de deux* with Ida Rubinstein during the "sultan-is-away" orgy scene.

Before long, Paris's leading couturier, Paul Poiret, was inviting customers to lounge on Persian carpets and cushions as they viewed his collection of harem pants, loose, uncorseted garments, turbans, and Chinese cloaks. "To enter Poiret's salons in the Faubourg St Honoré," observed Cecil Beaton, "was to step into the world of the Arabian Nights." Interior designers took up the cue, transforming bourgeois apartments into seraglios; Diaghilev's Orientalism had become the rage of Paris. Staff at the Théâtre du Châtelet, meanwhile, were as horrified by the Russian technicians and performers as Parisians had been by the Tsar's occupying army a century earlier (whose imperious demands for quick—*bistró!*—service had given Paris's everyday restaurants their name). These new brigades were equally aggressive and demanding, but raised all the bars for professionalism in French theaters.

Having launched his company with Orientalist fantasies, Diaghilev was determined to present Russia's own folk traditions with equal elan. For inspiration, he turned to Alexander Afanasiev's collected tales (which would later provide the narrative for Prokofiev's *Peter and the Wolf*). The impresario sat with choreographer Michel Fokine by an Italian lake to plan *Firebird*, which wasn't, in the end, so very different from the Orientalist pieces that preceded it: an exotic palace, a despotic ruler, a captive princess, a fearless Russian intruder . . . They hired a promising Petersburgian named Anatoly Lyadov to write the music, but some weeks later, when a friend of Diaghilev's ran into the young composer on the street and asked how the work was coming along, he beamed and replied, "Oh excellently. I've already bought the music paper!" The hapless fellow was sacked and the impresario sent for a young man he remembered performing a piece called *Fireworks* eight years earlier at a "new music" evening. Igor Stravinsky was only too eager to take up the task; he had been at a loose end since the death of his mentor Rimsky-Korsakov and depressed at being eclipsed by his rival pupil Maximilian Steinberg.

Stravinsky quickly grasped what this "fairy tale for grown-ups" needed; he had spent much of his childhood in western Ukraine, not far from the Carpathian Mountains and Slovakian valleys whose traditional music had inspired Bartók and Janáček. Stravinsky loved the music's wildness: singing that resembled shouting, instruments which, to the uninitiated, sounded like so much noise. He turned to the "barbarous" Melgunov transcriptions that had so upset his mentor thirty years earlier, as well as to cylinder recordings by Yevgeniya Linyova, a pioneering Russian ethnographer. The raw material from which he forged

Firebird bore no resemblance to the polite Lvov and Balakirev sketches employed by the Mighty Handful. For many late-nineteenth-century composers, the lodestar for rendering folk tunes into orchestral form remained Wagner and his way of cloaking melodies in a "sonic halo." Stravinsky charted a new course inspired by his Orientalist mentor, plus fresh favorites Debussy and Ravel. Like his Czech and Hungarian contemporaries, he plundered the complex beats and harmonies of folk dances as well as their melodies; modernism was drinking from ancient streams.

Firebird was a triumph, as was *Petrushka*, another Stravinsky creation for the Ballets Russes. Whether the next production, *The Rite of Spring*, was Stravinsky's own idea or Nicholas Roerich's is a matter of debate. The composer's version was that while completing *Firebird*, he saw a vision of "a solemn pagan rite: sage elders, seated in a circle, watched a young girl dance herself to death . . . to propitiate the god of spring." Roerich's early canvases are filled with pagan imagery inspired by taking part in excavations of ancient burial grounds unearthed by the boom in railway construction. The painter claimed to have suggested the subject and was certainly at Stravinsky's side throughout; for once, the idea for a landmark Ballets Russes production came about independently of the fertile mind of Sergei Diaghilev.

Stravinsky insisted later that he wrote the piece in a trance: "I am the vessel through which the *Rite* passed." The work marks a midway point between *Firebird* and *Les Noces*; many of its "primitive" elements are complete inventions, while its musical scale has no direct ethnic provenance, though the famous opening bassoon figure is taken from a book of Lithuanian wedding songs and some of its melodies echo Rimsky-Korsakov's folk-song arrangements or tunes recalled from Stravinsky's childhood. Rhythmically it is inspired by the complex beats of Slavic dances. More questionable is the central drama itself; there is no basis for the "dance-to-death" as a fertility rite, although Roerich's research did contribute some details, drawn mostly from Finno-Ugric settlements near the Ural Mountains.

When the composer played it for Diaghilev in Venice, the impresario was unnerved by the pounding chords and strange harmonies and asked if it would go on "this way" much longer. "Till the end, my dear!" shouted Stravinsky, not missing a beat. Shocked he may have been, but Diaghilev understood the work's significance and, equally important, its potential for publicity-generating controversy.

The process of guiding *The Rite of Spring* to its Paris opening the following May is one of the most interesting and complex theatrical geneses ever documented. With Fokine having left the company, Diaghilev was only too happy to hand the choreography over to Nijinsky, whose talent for scandal had followed him from Russia. (In *L'Après-midi d'un faune*—Debussy's very French take on Orientalism—he mimed copulation with a nymph's veil.) When the company's regular conductor, Pierre Monteux, heard it, "The old upright piano quivered and shook as Stravinsky . . . attacked the score . . . I did not understand one note . . . My one desire was to flee that room . . . Then [Diaghilev] turned to me and with a smile said, 'This is a masterpiece, Monteux, which will completely revolutionize music and make you famous, because you are going to conduct it.' And of course, I did."

> I am an Egyptian. I am a Hindu. I am an Indian. I am black. I am Chinese. I am Japanese. I am an outsider. I come from elsewhere . . . I am the tree . . . I am the roots . . .
>
> —From Vaslav Nijinsky's diary

Nijinsky's concept for the *Rite*'s choreography had no precedent: classical ballet—the French school in particular—was all about upward movement, lightness and grace. He alarmed the company straight away by leading them through furious "eurhythmic" exercises developed by Émile Jaques-Dalcroze, based on Arab dances. Nijinsky wanted their movements to reflect the pounding of Stravinsky's score, but he faced open rebellion not only from the *corps de ballet* but also from the composer, who felt dance and music should not act together but in counterpoint and attacked Nijinsky for his lack of musical understanding. The dancers found the downward stomping patterns horribly ugly, a perverse rejection of everything they had been trained to do.

They were further outraged when they tried on their sack-like shifts. Roerich based his designs on research conducted at Princess Maria Tenisheva's folklore collection and on the Uzbek outfits he had bought for *Prince Igor* in Saint Petersburg's street markets. His *Rite* costumes were painstakingly dyed, stenciled, painted, printed, and tailored by Caffi, Russia's leading costumier. He also created a curtain decorated with images of stags inspired by artefacts found in Scythian grave sites and associated with Yarilo, the fertility deity. Neither Nijinsky nor Roerich would budge. By opening night on May 29, 1913, *The Rite of Spring* had been rehearsed for an unprecedented 120 hours.

Diaghilev had a pretty good idea of what was in store. Did he program *Les Sylphides* as the evening's first half to sugar the pill, or to heighten the contrast? The second half's opening melody, straining far above a bassoon's normal register, signaled (to musical sophisticates in attendance, anyway, including the astonished Saint-Saëns) that the *Rite* would resemble nothing seen or heard before. Eyewitness accounts emphasize that it was the dancing, more than the music, which outraged the audience. Paris in 1913 was eager to be shocked. The cover of that season's Ballets Russes program showed a dark Oriental man throwing a White ballerina around, Apache-style. The tango craze that had begun a year earlier was, like Nijinsky humping the veil, one of many sexy scandals of the pre-war years. Parisians expected, at the very least, to see under ballerinas' tutus as they were borne aloft by a muscular male dancer. What they were absolutely unprepared for was a stage full of girls in shapeless beige shifts stomping on the floor and gesticulating jerkily to a pounding, unfamiliar, inelegant rhythm.

According to Harry Kessler, it was "the most dazzling [audience] I've ever seen in Paris, aristocracy, diplomats, the demi-monde." Many women sported headdresses: tiaras, bandeaux, or Oriental turbans. This glamorous crowd descended rapidly into a noisy mob. The bassist, the only member of the orchestra facing the hall, reported top hats smashed down on heads and canes brandished like swords. One wag called for a doctor and was quickly trumped by calls for "a dentist!" then "two dentists!" Stravinsky was horrified; he rose from his seat and ran backstage: "During the whole performance I was at Nijinsky's side in the wings.

He was standing on a chair, screaming 'sixteen, seventeen, eighteen' . . . Naturally the poor dancers could hear nothing by reason of the row in the auditorium and the sound of their own dance steps." Monteux, he remembered, was "nerveless as a crocodile. It is still almost incredible to me that he actually brought the orchestra through to the end."

The time signatures were irregular: a bar of four beats followed by two bars of five, then three, etc. Stravinsky had improvised long stretches of the *Rite*, then struggled to divide it into measures; the rhythmic complexity may have been inspired by folk dance, but the time signatures bore no resemblance to even the most elaborate 11/8 horo. The costumes, moreover, were made of heavy wool; later productions recrafted the originals in silk and no one could imagine how the 1913 company hadn't collapsed with exhaustion. The arm movements captured in photographs and drawings and described by witnesses are central to our only access to the original choreography, the 1987 re-creation by Millicent Hodson for the Joffrey Ballet; among the most problematic elements in the recreation were the awkward positions of the limbs. During the troupe's 1912 season in London, critic Edwin Evans had made Nijinsky a present of a jointed wooden toy duck that would come to rest in awkward, angular positions. After the *Rite*'s London opening, Nijinsky asked Evans: "Did you recognize it?" "What?" asked Evans. "Why, the duck, of course."

⌒

> The prize bull that inseminated the whole modern movement.
> — Robert Craft, Stravinsky's biographer, about *The Rite of Spring*

Heading for a late supper after the opening with Stravinsky, Nijinsky, Bakst, and Jean Cocteau, Diaghilev declared that the audience response was "exactly what I wanted!" Competing analyses of *The Rite of Spring*'s meaning and significance began almost immediately. The French may have thought they relished "primitivism," but the *Rite* had proved far too extreme a version of it. Jacques Rivière in *La Nouvelle Revue Française* called it *"un ballet biologique"* and added, "There is something profoundly blind in this dance . . . like an animal that turns in its cage and never tires of butting its forehead against the bars." Rivière's analysis bordered on the telepathic, since Nijinsky had prepared much of his choreography in a tiny Saint Petersburg apartment where, with little room to move, he compressed his steps, intensifying the meaning as he limited their scope. And prescient as well, since Nijinsky's career would be cut short in 1919 by mental illness and he would spend the rest of his life in and out of asylums.

Which begs the question about the *Rite*'s importance: did Nijinsky's choreography point a knowing finger towards modernism's future, or was it simply the "outsider art" of a disturbed mind? After attending a London performance, T. S. Eliot commented, "The spirit of the music was modern, and the spirit of the ballet was primitive ceremony . . . It was interesting to anyone who had read *The Golden Bough* . . . but hardly more than interesting . . . Whether Strawinsky's music be permanent or ephemeral I do not know; but it did seem to transform the rhythm of the steppes into the scream of the motor horn, the rattle of machinery . . . the beating of iron and steel, the roar of the underground railway, and the other barbaric cries of modern life; and to transform these despairing noises into music."

The Golden Bough is James George Frazer's study of ritual and myth, which provided an intellectual spine for the turn of the last century's fascination with the primitive. Once its implications were fully grasped, this lengthy tome was deeply subversive; for Frazer, Christ's springtime crucifixion was but the most recent in a long line of sacrifices intended to placate gods whose whims determined crop yields. Later critics would ponder whether the *Rite* might contain a premonition of the slaughter of youth in the trenches of World War One. It was even suggested that Stravinsky was responding to the crescendo of brutality—lynchings in the American South, pogroms in Russia's Pale—that preceded the war. That seems doubtful; in correspondence the composer revealed himself as a nasty anti-Semite, still bitter about Rimsky-Korsakov encouraging his daughter to reject him in favor of teacher's pet Steinberg.

Stravinsky was delighted when Monteux conducted an orchestral performance in the spring of 1914. The audience remained silent and listened intently. "I realized that I prefer 'Le Sacre' as a concert piece," said the composer. Taruskin saw the work as "the perfect musical approach to the primitivist ideal—the resolute shedding of conventional complexities . . . and their replacement by long spans of unchanging content . . . [R]ational complexity is far less disquieting than a mystifying simplicity." The musician most attuned to the cross-fertilization of folk and classical, Béla Bartók, praised the piece as "a kind of apotheosis of the Russian rural music . . . Even the origin of the . . . musical structure . . . which is so completely different from any structural proceeding of the past, may be sought in short-breathed Russian peasant *motifs*."

Stravinsky may have used "primitivism" to distance himself from nineteenth-century art music, but he was also breaking free (for a time) from Germanic ideas of modernity as represented by Schoenberg and his disciples. Debussy heard jazz influences in the *Rite*, which may say more about the Frenchman's tastes than the composition (although Charlie Parker adored it and quoted the opening bassoon phrase during a solo when he spotted Stravinsky in a Birdland audience in the early fifties).

For Diaghilev, the sophistication of Debussy's *Jeux*, premiered two weeks earlier, with its jazz-inflected score and *sportif* costumes, was of a piece with the *Rite*; together, they laid down a marker for "ultra-modernity." The two productions would, however, soon part company; the impresario may have been "modern" about his lovers' infidelities with other men, but he became hysterical when Nijinsky began an affair with a female dancer and inconsolable when his favorite got married during a Latin American tour. Nijinsky was peremptorily fired and his productions dropped from the repertoire; Diaghilev would soon commission Picasso and Matisse to create designs and Léonide Massine to choreograph dances more in tune with the public's idea of "primitive" than the *Rite*'s somber ritual.

The brilliance of Stravinsky's music camouflaged its subtexts, which were as totalitarian as Moiseyev's. The Maiden dances to her doom without sensuality, passion, or resistance; in her submission to the elders, she echoes the conformity demanded by tsars, commissars, and now Putin. Stravinsky always resisted any attempt to analyze the thinking behind the *Rite*, which is unsurprising given Taruskin's research, which reveals the composer to have been a fervent member of a sinister cult known as Turanianism. Of all the turn-of-the-century mystical Russian movements, this was the one that survived revolution and exile to flourish among the émigrés. It involved a murky concoction of ideas drawn from Nietzsche, Spengler, Madame Blavatsky (who popularized the Hindu swastika in Europe), Oriental religious texts, and *The Protocols of the Elders of Zion*, along with Dostoyevsky's suggestion that the dilemmas of the modern age could be solved by Russians' particular ability to reject reason and logic.

Turanianism can be seen as a response to Stasov's revelations about Russia's Asiatic roots; reactionaries clung to a vision of the Russian people as a pure Aryan race descended, if not from Vikings, then from Scythian horsemen who had roamed the steppe for thousands of years. Ancient travelers' reports of these warriors are sketchy but impressive: Herodotus wrote of their fierce tactics, drawing Persian armies northward, then burning their own crops and cities and falling on the starving invaders as they retreated. Napoleon is reputed to have said, as he watched Moscow go up in flames, "What extraordinary resolve! What men! These are Scythians!" The poet Alexander Blok (an avid Turanian) wrote: "*Yes, we are Scythians, Yes, we are Asiatics . . . / Russia is a sphinx, triumphant and mournful*" and "*You have forgotten such love exists / which burns, and destroys!*" Turanians revered the paganism of the early Rus, but believed the Orthodox Church was an essential institution for the cohesion of society, asserting that the rot had set in for the West with the unity-shattering Reformation; their villain was Peter the Great and his opening to the spiritual cesspool that was Europe. They interpolated the little known about ancient Siberian cultures to conjure up a society willing, even eager, to accept submission and conformity, like the Maiden in *The Rite of Spring*.

Such ideas found fertile soil among émigrés unnerved by the decadent liberalism surrounding them in Western Europe and feeling closer to Herder and his vision of folkloric unity than to the ideas-driven Enlightenment. Their repugnance was comparable to some more recent Muslim immigrants' abhorrence of Western sexual freedom and secularism; the Turanian view of religion and society resembles that of Al Qaeda and ISIS and their quest to restore the caliphate under sharia law, and now animates Putin's confrontation with the West. Pre-Revolution Moscow was viewed as the "new Byzantium" and Russian Orthodoxy preferred to the corrupted Greek version. Peasants, with their raw emotion and plain speech, were superior to so-called citizens. Turanians felt no loyalty to the Tsar, whose reign had been poisoned by German influence, but loathed Kerensky and the Provisional Government of 1917 for its cosmopolitanism and concerns for minority rights; as for Bolshevism, it represented the culmination of two centuries of Europeanization promoted by Jews. Like Hitler, Turanians admired Madame Blavatsky and her belief in a group of "Masters" who held the key to ancient wisdom, while sharing with American "know-nothings" a paranoia about an alliance between the Pope and communism. Suspicious of reason and facts, they believed anyone deviating from the thoughts of the community could be done away with in the interests of stability and harmony.

In a September 1914 interview, Stravinsky stated that Russia possessed a "beautiful, healthy barbarism, big with the seed that will impregnate the thinking of the world," and that the ancient Rus represented "an organic, preternatural unanimity of popular aspiration" that was preferable to the dubious virtues of Western "legalism." He railed against Bolshevism as a Jewish plot led by Lev Bronstein (Leon Trotsky) and complained that Jews were often taken by the outside world to be "authentic" Russians. The further Russia receded into Stravinsky's past, the more devout an Orthodox believer he became, drawn to its focus on form and ritual devoid of complex subtexts or long-winded theories.

Between 1911 and 1924, Stravinsky created the greatest works of Turanian music, brilliantly true to the spirit of this sinister cult. His vision was anti-Romantic and anti-European, adhering to repetition and simplification to "quell the voice of reason." He emphasized his rejection of modernity during this period by annotating scores with pseudo-archaic calligraphy modelled on a pre-Petrine alphabet. His aim was to create a new Russian folklore "realer than the real." Another revelation that inspired him was the ethnographer Yevgeniya Linyova's analysis of vocal emphasis in Russian village music; rural singers give every note equal weight regardless of meaning, with no histrionics, no emotionality, the opposite of "Russian gypsy" style. For Stravinsky, this confirmed his vision of a culture that submerged personality within a collective. His ur-Turanian masterwork *Les Noces* would have only the most tenuous connection to Russian wedding music but would be firmly anchored in Linyova's theories. He used an "anhemitonic" (full tones only) pentatonic scale based on the Turanians' favored mode, one found in Finno-Ugric and Altaic cultures, which they felt encouraged orderliness, regularity, and repetitiveness and was free of Islamic influence. Any music that used a Western scale, even Orthodox chants, was, for them, corrupt. They also believed (like many Soviet culture commissars) that line- and circle-dancing were culturally correct, while couple-dancing was a lascivious, corrupting import.

Les Noces took Stravinsky ten years to complete. Taruskin characterizes it as having an "incomparably compelling aesthetic integrity and ominously compelling political allure." The dance critic Alastair Macaulay has called the piece a "harsh implacable machine." There is certainly no place in it for the ribald jokes and boisterous festivities of an actual Slavic wedding. Stravinsky himself called the result "perfectly impersonal, perfectly homogeneous, and perfectly mechanical." In the original 1924 Ballets Russes production, the choreographer, Bronislava Nijinska, carried forward her brother's vision of a company of dancers fused into one movement like an orchestra, with designer Natalia Goncharova's vast collection of objects purchased in Russian street markets giving it an aura of folkish authenticity. *Les Noces* sent Stravinsky's fellow Turanians into ecstasy. The publisher of the movement's house journal wrote: "The knowledge that you live on this earth helps me to go on."

Like Calvinism and Marxism, Turanianism began as a prediction of how societies and individuals were destined to evolve. With Russia so clearly failing in its "inevitable" rejection of communism, Turanians redirected their enthusiasms towards strong-willed dictators who could enforce the correct outcome. "I don't believe that anyone venerates Mussolini more than I," said Stravinsky. "He is the savior of Italy and—let us hope—the world." He then announced himself the "Mussolini of music," abandoning folk influences and embracing neoclassicism. This had nothing to do with nostalgia for baroque elegance and everything to do with stripping away frills and individual emotion and embracing a brutal simplicity of form. The composer would later describe his work in this period as "tonal masses . . . sculptured in marble . . . to be regarded objectively by the ear." When Nazi Germany included him in a schedule of "degenerate" composers unsuitable for performance, Stravinsky appealed, claiming that his politics were in total agreement with Hitler's, and was duly removed from the list.

Taruskin concludes that, like Wagner's operas, Stravinsky's Turanian work is powerful for the very reason of its passionate wrongheadedness. By the time he arrived in America in 1939, Stravinsky had been intimidated into serial complexity by advocates of Schoenberg's version of modernity, the antithesis of folkishness, real or concocted. Debussy hated his friend's change and urged him to remain "a great Russian artist. It is a good thing to be . . . attached to the earth like the humblest peasant!" Today, Stravinsky's Turanian compositions resonate more strongly than work from later periods; much credit for this is due Diaghilev, who at the very least demanded engagement with the audience, unlike the isolated and cerebral Schoenberg school. Once he relocated to America, Stravinsky thought it best to take the Dylanesque position that "[m]usic needs no help . . . Don't look for anything else in it beyond what it already contains."

> He was . . . a Dionysian pagan—not an Apollonian. He loved everything earthly—earthly love, earthly passions, earthly beauty . . . That doesn't mean he had no religious feeling. But that feeling was pagan rather than Christian. Instead of faith, he had superstition; instead of the fear of God, terror of the universe and its secrets; instead of Christian meekness, a delicate, almost childlike tenderness.
>
> —Walter Nouvel, secretary of the Ballets Russes

When, on August 19, 1929, Diaghilev fulfilled his vow to die in Venice, the world lost its most fruitful advocate for a modernism that could reach wide audiences and influence popular culture. Many of Diaghilev's collaborators—Debussy, Picasso, Ravel, Matisse, Stravinsky, Bakst, and de Falla among them—found inspiration in what was perceived as the "soil," the "primitive," the "folk." The mysticism of the late nineteenth century, augmented by encounters with distant cultures, had opened up the possibility that magic was real, that rituals, fetishes, incantations, and ceremonies possessed actual power. Consciously or unconsciously, painters and composers sought to unlock these secrets. With the aid of photography and sound recording, the explorations that accompanied colonial conquest provided them with vivid raw material. Picasso collecting African masks mirrored Debussy being mesmerized by a Javanese gamelan at the Paris Exposition of 1899. The trend soon became more adventurous, Kandinsky spending a year in a Ural village and Bartók venturing into remote Transylvanian valleys with his wax recording device.

Nowhere were the fruits of this revolution presented more effectively or to such a wide and influential audience than in the productions of the Ballets Russes. Even after the Great War opened a brutal trench between Europe's present and its past, Diaghilev continued to seek originality inspired by tradition—Neapolitan *commedia dell'arte*, Spanish flamenco, and Siamese temple dances as well as the reliable Orientalism of *The Golden Cockerel*—embracing past, present, and future with equal vigor. Stravinsky once accused Diaghilev of understanding nothing about music; the impresario responded calmly that composers and painters had been making similar accusations for twenty years, but they kept coming back to work for him. He was an opinionated bully with impeccable taste—perfect qualities in a great producer.

When Matisse began work on *Le Chant du Rossignol* in 1920, he was astonished: "There's absolutely no fooling around here . . . no one thinks of anything but his or her work." Diaghilev himself ran all dress and lighting rehearsals, which usually lasted until dawn: "[T]he art of man isn't simply birdsong. Above all it's work. A thing must be well made . . . [W]e can't pin all our well-being on the audacity of the new." He had neither nostalgia for the past nor the urge to jettison it for a brave new future; he simply understood what worked. He is rightly credited for constantly unearthing new talent, but he needed to; success with the Ballets Russes often made composers and dancers too expensive to keep. To replace Nijinsky, he found first Léonide Massine, then George Balanchine; for the departed Bakst and Benois, he substituted Picasso, Matisse, and Goncharova while commissioning new works by Debussy, Satie, and Prokofiev. In *The Story of Music*, Howard Goodall compares Diaghilev's effect on twentieth-century music to that of the Eastern European Jewish immigrants who transformed America's Tin Pan Alley and thus the world's popular music. During the Ballets Russes's heyday, there was another form of musical modernism running alongside, pale, shadowy, and intellectual, with its own promoter and publicist. The German philosopher Theodor Adorno served as the outspoken champion of twelve-tone and serial music. He hated jazz, despised popular culture, and derided any music that expressed emotion. In *The Rest Is Noise*, Alex Ross provides intriguing clues to the movement's frigidity, fingering Schoenberg's discovery of his wife in bed with a painter and the death of Webern's adored mother as triggers for the twelve-tone syndrome.

Popular music responded to the carnage of the Great War with the joyful outpourings of the jazz age and the explosion of urban dance music around the globe. Why, then, was the high ground of Western classical music seized by the grim sounds of Adorno's beloved Second Viennese School? What seemed like a footnote might well have been the key: at the end of the twenties, Sergei Diaghilev died.

On April 14, 1930, after being criticized for "bourgeois individualism" at a writers' union meeting, Vladimir Mayakovsky went home and put a bullet through his heart, an appropriate ending for the Revolution's avant-garde era. A year earlier, culture commissar Anatoly Lunacharsky, innovation's champion, had been put (non-violently) out to pasture. Privacy evaporated as living spaces were collectivized (simplifying the monitoring of anti-socialist behavior while also dealing with a housing shortage); the individual's time was over. "Gypsy music" was banned for promoting "decadence and unhealthy exoticism, so-called free love, and drunken tavern debauchery." Silent-film text cards were altered, statues given detailed plaques explaining their revised significance, and workers subjected to speeches on the dialectical process. A century earlier, narodniks had heralded the spontaneous natural spirit of the Russian people; 1930s commissars were determined to eliminate anything that smacked of unpredictability.

From 1929 to '32, the RAPM (Russian Association of Proletarian Musicians) suppressed not only traditional music, but tango, foxtrot, and jazz, everything but the "mass music" created by its members. The Revolution's vanguard had espoused sexual freedom, but the new apparatchiks loathed anything "animal" or erotic. Jazz was a source of particular discomfort: an extended spat between *Izvestia* and *Pravda* debated whether it was the noble expression of a race downtrodden by capitalism or an alien, filthy product of Tin Pan Alley. Echoing Methodists in nineteenth-century South Africa (who could tolerate choirs "moving" only when such motion was "conducted"), authorities tried to popularize "mass dances" where the desire for rhythmic movement could be de-eroticized. Prime prig Gorky returned from overseas to report that jazz promoted homosexuality and drugs; he proposed a ban on saxophones.

In 1932, alarmed by the lack of popular enthusiasm for its brave new culture, the Party changed course. Cinemas and theaters were suddenly awash with sentimental melodramas. Prokofiev was lured back from exile as attending classical concerts became de rigueur for careerist officials. Worried by audiences' crude behavior, culture workers lectured the masses on "proper" (quiet, seated) comportment. To generate catchier tunes, the Soviets turned to Jewish songwriters from Odessa, who combined *estrada* and *chastushka* styles with correct political messages. (In New York, their cousin Irving Berlin was adding yet more patriotic verses to his "God Bless America.") The "gypsy orchestra" that had serenaded Rasputin at Moscow's famous Praga restaurant was restored to the bandstand. A cautious green light was even given to big-band jazz, so long as it was more Paul Whiteman than Count Basie. Jewish orchestra leaders jazzing up Roma and shtetl melodies became the "kings" of Russian jazz. Moiseyev attempted to satirize this decadent development, but audiences cheered his jazz parody so unironically it had to be dropped.

Shostakovich's opera *Lady Macbeth of Mtsensk* arrived in Moscow following a successful season in Leningrad. One evening, the composer was alerted that Stalin would be using the Party box; when the Great Leader failed to return for the second act, Shostakovich knew he was in trouble. Sure enough, *Pravda* launched a furious attack on him for the opera's sympathetic portrayal of a murderous adulteress and for the music's "formalism." Stalin seems to have been outraged by the female independence and sexual appetite on display. Soviet Russia's greatest composer would spend the rest of his life dodging threats and living in fear of the Party's interpretation of his work.

By 1937, the idealists who had driven the Bolshevik Revolution were mostly dead or in exile, replaced by men with normal lowbrow tastes and no desire to be "elevated." The soundtrack to the purges and show trials of the late thirties was a relentless barrage of "life is gayer and better" songs.

> The proletarian culture does not abolish the national culture: it gives it content; and, inversely, the national culture does not abolish the proletarian culture: it gives it shape.
>
> —Joseph Stalin

In 1938, in Odessa, the First All-Ukrainian Congress of Banduristy was announced. Bandura-playing bards, whose epic songs had kept alive a rich oral history of Ukrainian culture, brought their instruments cautiously out of hiding, amazed by this sudden change of policy. Once gathered together by the Black Sea, they were all shot.

Eliminating the *banduristy* was a sign of the Soviets' alarm about anything legitimizing the Ukraine as having a stand-alone culture, echoing tsarist attitudes from a century earlier. The meaninglessness of Stalin's pronouncement was clear in every direction, be it Russia's lack of respect for "autonomous" ethnic groups within its borders, the smothering of culture in the various Soviet republics under the pillow of "international proletarian brotherhood," or, after 1945, suppressing national traditions among its Eastern European "allies."

It hadn't begun that way. The Soviets were initially more tolerant of minority cultures than that of Russian peasants. (More was expected, they said, of their own.) Under Lenin, the Soviets recognized and "developed" 192 different linguistic groups, creating alphabets for those lacking them, promoting local leaders to high Party positions, and encouraging indigenous literature, art, and music. The process was often, of course, heavy-handed; Muslim societies, for example, were not best pleased at having their alphabet switched from Arabic to Cyrillic. Officials arriving in Tashkent and other Asian cities behaved like typical colonials, living across the river from the town center and treating local customs with contempt. A few Russians were fascinated: a group of painters spent the twenties in Turkmenistan and Uzbekistan, blending impressionism with local colors and design, and insisting that Asians and Russians had much to learn from each other.

Under Stalin everything changed. Resistance to collectivization in Uzbekistan and Turkmenistan was savagely suppressed, and when it came to the subtle and ancient Silk Road music of Bukhara, Samarkand, and Tashkent, the Soviets could not grasp the Islamic conflation of real and spiritual; metaphor confused them and religion was, of course, counter-revolutionary. Amorous verses could be about a lover or, perhaps, Allah; nothing could be further from dialectical materialism. Lyrics had to be registered and every performed verse noted down. Despite their opposition to ethnic separatism, the Soviets refused to accept the blurred Uzbek/Tajik tradition of *maqams*, where verses alternated between the two languages; bureaucratic diktat required that all must be sung in either one or the other. They were further confused by the fact that the greatest instrumentalists and singers in Uzbekistan were Jews. When, in the early thirties, a cultural group organized a Moscow concert by a Bukharan Jewish ensemble, Jews in the audience complained that the music sounded Islamic. Stalin personally ordered the company to return their fee as punishment for "masquerading as Jews" and the group was disbanded.

Nor could the Party get to grips with a culture in which the Khan's court and the poorest road sweeper enjoyed the same music and understood the same nuances. The beautiful poetry of the *shash maqam* had grown out of defiance towards arrogant rulers of the past, but by the

1920s, the about-to-be-abolished royal courts had become the music's sponsors and protectors. Every aspect of Central Asian culture—music, carpets, textiles, mosaics, written and oral poetry—was based on "handing over" from one generation to the next, anathema to a party committed to "fight against the past." The Soviet solution was to drain every ounce of life out of musical forms they couldn't comprehend; a form that had remained vibrant and alive for over a thousand years was effectively dead within a decade of Communist rule.

Religious music was banned, owning a Koran became a crime, and Islam went underground. Musicians were beaten by Party thugs if they objected to alcohol at a wedding, and keeping a pig became an essential sign of political reliability. Lenin had cultivated modernizing reformers known as *jadids*; Stalin had them shot. The greatest Bukharan singer, Leviche Babakhanov, died of poisoning, probably at the hands of the secret police.

"Experts"—mostly second-rate Russian composers or conductors in need of a job—were sent to reorganize the music. The shash maqam, once an improvised form full of individual expression by vocalists and instrumentalists, had to be set down on paper. Pitches were altered so that singers of different ranges must trade off, preventing any individual from shining like Babakhanov. (Instrumental and vocal virtuosity were deemed "remnants of bourgeois ideology.") An Armenian named Petrosian was brought in to design frets for the necks of traditional instruments, eliminating the microtonal subtleties of the masters. The intention was to make Asian culture "more Russian," but the effect of these changes was to make the music, at least, more "Western European."

Uzbek composers were sent to conservatories and taught to Borodinize the maqam. Singers were trained in bel canto technique; it was said of one that he "went away a nightingale and came back a sparrow." Concert halls were built everywhere; the Tashkent opera house was designed by the Lenin Mausoleum's architect (with appropriately dead acoustics). Performances by the new ensembles were, according to one witness, "like you're listening to funeral music." Respectable women in Muslim cultures never danced onstage; female roles had always been taken by young boys in drag or Jewish girls. The Soviets were horrified by the former and not at all keen on the latter, so professionals were sent from Moscow.

Non-Muslim cultures didn't fare any better: "[A] Russian girl in our school dances Moldavian dance much better than a Moldavian girl," said Moiseyev, who seemed to believe he could find the essential gesture of any group and use it to portray them in dance; the images he chose were reliably caricaturish. For the Russian rulers of the USSR, the "idea" of folklore was essential in mobilizing the diverse population. Every minority was given its moment in a stage show; representation was supposed to serve as compensation for conquest and subjugation, but minorities were always shown as rustic naïfs, in contrast to the modern Soviet man and woman.

The Buryats from around Lake Baikal, after some teething troubles at the time of collectivization (during which they killed a number of Soviet officials), adapted to communism as they had adapted to life under the Tsar, moving from yurts into high-rise apartments and becoming bureaucrats and enforcers for the Russians. Most other Siberian groups "failed to flourish" and were subjected to fierce repression. In the early 1930s, the Committee of the North, formed under Lenin to facilitate the integration of tribal peoples into the Soviet world, tried to explain to Party bosses that owning a hundred reindeer did not make you a kulak, but they were brushed aside.

It is hard to say who aroused Soviet ire more, shamans and those who believed in them or ethnographers who wrote papers explaining the importance of ancient beliefs for Siberian natives. Buddhism had found it easy to coexist with local rituals, allowing shamans to park their fetishes in temples and conduct ceremonies there, but communists showed no such tolerance. Shamans, who described their hallucinatory spiritual journeys as "flights," were taken up in planes and told that this was their opportunity to really fly, then flung to their deaths. Members of a Khanty village who objected to the construction of a fish-processing plant on a sacred lake were shot. Ethnographers who could have helped ease the transition were exiled, often to the lands they had once studied.

Once the initial violence subsided, Soviet treatment of its "first nations" was not much different from the American, Canadian, or

Australian versions of the same thing: children torn from parents and sent away to school; harsh punishments for speaking their own language; proud, self-sufficient herders, hunters, and fishermen transformed into browbeaten, often alcohol-dazed, laborers. Buddhists also suffered; Soviets razed ancient monasteries and, alarmed by the fashion for Zen meditation in "decadent" urban circles, arrested and exiled leading masters. Stalin was an aficionado of vengeance. Any group that had shown sympathy for the White Armies in the Civil War was treated with special savagery. Likewise, after the Great Patriotic War, peoples such as the Chechens and Crimean Tatars, who had failed to resist the Germans with sufficient determination, were exiled en masse.

There are a few glimmers of light in the sad tale of Soviet rule in Central Asia and Siberia. One involves a music student named Alexei Kozlovsky, who was among a group of avant-gardists repressed when the cultural winds shifted in the late twenties. While many of his cohorts were shot, he was exiled to Tashkent and became fascinated by the way women danced and sang all day while doing chores. Inspired by street cries and the music of secret dervish ceremonies, he created works that avoided Orientalist clichés and showed great respect for the culture in which he found himself. Kozlovsky's Uzbek-language opera *Ulugbek* initially confused the locals and was heavily censored by cultural commissars, but revived in more liberal times it has become a beloved favorite in Uzbekistan.

Patriotic fervor during World War Two stripped away the pan-ethnic facade of the Soviet Empire; Russianness was back with a vengeance as Stalin embraced quasi-Turanian fantasies of Slavic exceptionalism. Red Army choruses and Moiseyev-style ensembles multiplied to serenade the troops, new editions of Tolstoy were rushed into print alongside every kind of sentimental narod tosh, while a treatise on Mozart's influence on Glinka was pulped. The new Soviet anthem, with lyrics by Sergei Mikhalkov (father of film-makers Nikita Mikhalkov and Andrei Konchalovsky), acclaimed the *"union of free republics sealed forever by the Great Rus."* After the paranoia of the show-trial years, the war was almost a relief as everyone united against a common foe. Delusional imagery and kitsch patriotic songs may well have been essential to the Soviet Union's come-from-behind triumph over Nazi Germany.

Returning troops and POWs who had seen too much of the West were exiled or shot, mirroring paranoia in the US with its (far less lethal) red-baiting and horror of un-American influences. Anti-Semitism was rife; Moiseyev never seems to have suffered for his Jewish name, although it is worth noting that he waited until after the collapse of the USSR to add a "Jewish folk dance" to the repertoire. Social dancing was too popular to ban, so they settled for name changes; foxtrot became "quickstep," tango "slow dance," waltz "ballroom dance." Composers were under orders to create "popular" music, but the challenge was terrifying: anything smacking of jazz or Western pop could land them in big trouble, but the masses only responded to music with swing.

By the fifties, non-conformist impulses had coalesced around the poetic, gypsy-esque balladry of Alexander Vertinsky, Bulat Okudzhava and Vladimir Vysotsky. The authorities were able to co-opt much of the energy of this very Russian-sounding music; some of the lyrics may have been a bit off-message, but at least the style was comfortably familiar. Vysotsky in particular moved easily between official concerts and private performances in dissident apartments.

Soon after Stalin's death in 1953, word of Bill Haley's "Rock Around the Clock" spread like wildfire among urban youth. Such was the demand that primitive styluses were employed to cut spirals onto discarded X-ray plates that became celebrated as "Rock on Bones." Greased-back tough-guy haircuts, tight dresses, and jitterbug dancing alarmed the commissars; the words may have been harmless, but the beat was threateningly alien and erotic. A policeman is reported to have shouted, "All this energy could be invested in building a hydro-electric power station rather than wasted here on a dancefloor," as he pulled the plug on an illicit party. Always up-to-date, the Moiseyev company introduced a rock 'n' roll parody entitled "Back to the Apes."

Soviet jazz had ground to another halt with the banning of instrumental solos as the show trials began in the late thirties. Over the next half-century, jazz would be revived during the war in solidarity with

Glenn Miller–loving allies, forbidden again post-war, persevere as an underground quasi-dissident pastime through the fifties, and enjoy cyclical thaws and suppressions on into the eighties. Love of jazz and its accompanying hipster jargon became a lingua franca in Siberian prison camps. A telling moment arrived in 1967, when Willis Conover, longtime host of a Voice of America jazz show, visited Leningrad as a tourist. When a few enthusiasts discovered his presence, he was persuaded to appear at a local concert: "No one knew him by sight, but his voice was definitely familiar to everyone in the audience. When he announced the next number something unbelievable happened—the entire crowd charged toward him."

When Rudolf Nureyev emerged from his dressing room for the 1958 opening night of *Don Quixote* wearing tights rather than the usual baggy shorts, officials refused to raise the curtain. After a lengthy stand-off, during which the sold-out house muttered and consulted its watches, the Kirov surrendered; a thrilled gasp rose from the audience when they beheld his perfect male form, a near-exact replica of the scandal over Nijinsky's tights at the Mariinsky Theatre in 1910.

During the Khrushchev thaw, Igor Stravinsky returned for the first time in over fifty years. The Bolshoi honored him with its first production of *The Rite of Spring*; censors were unhappy with the plot, however, so a new ending was added in which a worker-hero leaps to the rescue of the sacrificial Maiden.

As post-war Soviet audiences became bored with the state ensembles, foreign enthusiasm grew. With hard currency scarce, loyal companies such as Moiseyev's, the Red Army Choir, and the Cossacks were encouraged to earn their keep by touring abroad. Sol Hurok and other capitalist impresarios booked them from London and New York to Sydney and Buenos Aires. For crowds with little experience of Russian music, the Moiseyev company was a sensation. US concert halls were packed with dance buffs, lefty "comsymps," and rubes wanting to see for themselves if Russians had horns; they were a perfect fit for *The Ed Sullivan Show*. As one member of a Los Angeles audience recalled, "In the 1950s the impact of the one hundred Moiseyev dancers, performing never-before-seen synchronised choreographic feats with the power and ease of circus acrobats, created an electrifying impact . . . that is difficult to imagine for those not present." The torch for this sort of spectacle was carried into the future by Michael Flatley; his *Riverdance* even included a featured spot for borrowed Moiseyev dancers.

Greece, the Philippines, Mexico, Iran, Turkey, and many others started their own Moiseyev-style companies as an antidote to the tsunami of American culture sweeping the post-war world. Reactionary governments liked the idea of a noble Rousseauian spirit in an imaginary rural setting and loathed authenticity as much as the Soviets did. Repertoires were keyed to a sentimentalized region (often the rustic birthplace of the current strongman), dances slickly choreographed, and costumes simplified and brightened. America tried to get in on the act by enshrining square-dancing as the "national dance," but the bill failed to muster enough votes in Congress. (The late forties was probably the wrong moment to endorse something whose signature call—*allemande left!*—gave props to enemies past and present.)

Islamic countries were torn between presenting a modern image and their horror of sensuality; Egyptian belly-dance and Turkish dervish-whirling were barred from national company repertoires. Some Middle Eastern countries turned to friezes on ancient ruins for ideas on movement and costume—anything smacking of current popular practice was too fraught with uncomfortable implications. Recently established states, smarting from centuries of marginalization in vanished empires, repeated the offense by meting out similar treatment to their own minorities—the old story of the bullied turning into bullies at the first opportunity.

While many governments eagerly embraced a kitsch aesthetic, for those in Eastern Europe, it was mandatory. (The transition was actually quite smooth: hostility to individualism, authenticity, spontaneity, regional cultures, Jews, and gypsies had been hallmarks of the German occupation as well.) Communists took music very seriously as a tool of social management; changes in repertoire or choreography needed approval at the highest level. Leftist intellectuals who welcomed the Red

Army were in for the same shock experienced by the Russian cultural vanguard at the end of the 1920s; Soviet communism, they discovered, was no longer progressive but brutally lowbrow.

Few urban Czechs or Poles cared much about folk song, but traditional music was central to Baltic identity. The craze for polite choral singing in all three states seemed reasonably compatible with the Moiseyev aesthetic; but even after bowdlerizing the lyrics, the passionate participatory enthusiasm of all ages and classes made the Soviets paranoid. They struggled to impose communist anthems on the annual choir festivals that had been a part of Estonian and Latvian cultures since the nineteenth century, while sending tens of thousands into Siberian exile and replacing them with out-of-work Russians.

The Khrushchev thaw, a subversive taste for things American, and the fact that Pete Seeger was being persecuted for his communist connections—these all combined to allow wisps of the Yankee folk revival into the USSR. Folk songbooks reappeared in the late fifties; they were always front-loaded with ballads celebrating Lenin, tractors, or electricity, so everyone opened them from the back. Local "houses of folk art" were established and universities gave ethnomusicology studies a tentative green light (though few dared take it up). Religion was also granted a bit of breathing space, but so many flocked to the reopened churches that the shocked Party promptly shut most of them again.

In 1958, a Moscow choir director named Vyacheslav Shchurov began visiting nearby villages in search of inspiration for his choral arrangements. He was so taken with the long-forgotten songs and vocal styles of the elderly women he met that he began bringing them to Radio Moscow late at night for clandestine recording sessions. In 1966, he organized a series of concerts, the first documented encounter between traditional singers and the urban intelligentsia since the Pyatnitsky "trial" of 1932. The initial concert drew 100 listeners, the second 500, including composer Alfred Schnittke. "Finally they've shown us Moscow invalids some real people," said one authenticity-starved listener.

By the early seventies, Shchurov was head of a new "folklore commission," had a weekly late-night radio show (where he played Pete Seeger, Paul Robeson, and Josh White, interspersed with his tapes of Russian traditional singers), and once a month was given a slot on a popular TV variety show. The routine was for Shchurov to introduce a rural singer or group and explain the cultural background of the music. After a brief dose of the real thing, the show would revert to massed balalaikas or accordions playing "Ochi chornye" (Dark Eyes). One evening in 1973, Khrushchev's successor, Leonid Brezhnev, was relaxing in his Kremlin apartment, channel-surfing between Russia's two TV stations. It was at this moment that the highest level of Soviet authority encountered the passion of Vyacheslav Shchurov. Brezhnev rang the head of Soviet television at his home and bellowed, "I will NOT have men with beards babbling about babushkas wearing *laptis* on my television! Get rid of him immediately!" Thus ended Dr. Shchurov's media career.

In the audience at Shchurov's first concert was the man who would become the anti-Moiseyev, the champion of Russian village music. Dmitri Pokrovsky was then a student at Moscow's Gnessin Institute, where he found professorial allies in Yevgeny Gippius and Alexander Yurlov, who had fought long bureaucratic battles to be allowed to teach folklore. Together the three began exploring regional singing styles, fascinated by the effect of topographical acoustics—forest, steppe, rivers, valleys, mountains—on vocal traditions.

Shchurov's choirs had defied Soviet practice with less bombastic singing and no Moiseyev-style gimmicks, but it had never occurred to these urbanites to attempt the open-throat voice. Pokrovsky borrowed some recordings to play to his small ensemble (which at the time was performing well-known songs with an accordion in hotel lobbies). A month later, the group presented the fruits of their work at the institute. Ethnographer Ivan Kabanov recalled: "I remember where they were standing . . . I was sitting [here], and Gippius was there . . . So, imagine, one, two, three, four young men . . . and Tamara [Pokrovsky's wife] . . . I remember that the *sound itself* amazed me. [It had] the effect of a huge chunk of emotions tumbling down . . . hysterical, aggressive, but one's own, completely engrossing . . . It was something tremendous."

Pokrovsky and the others had absorbed the voice still practiced in a few villages, yet completely absent from official ensembles. Technique and style quickly became more important than lyrics; each singer had to listen to their neighbors' overtones and find a harmony, to improvise and make it their own. Their first public performance was in a Georgian restaurant in Moscow. The diners loved it; so unfamiliar was the sound, they assumed the group must be from the Caucasus.

The Pokrovsky Ensemble's reputation grew in underground and dissident circles; their admirers weren't sure what to make of them, but the music was so different from the official canon that it must be healthily subversive, not least because they stood in a circle with no conductor. After several years in semi-professional limbo, Pokrovsky applied for official status; he got the government stamp, but no sooner had they opened their throats at a public event than they were banned. There was no statute defining what sort of art or music or literature was acceptable, but authorities recognized transgression when they heard it.

In the late seventies, they were taken under the wing of a mysterious sponsor who arranged for them to be signed to Roskoncert, the agency for state ensembles. Their prime appeal, Pokrovsky felt, was that they were only six in number so salaries and expenses were low; choir concerts had a book price and the agency could pocket the difference. Their benefactor turned out to be a KGB agent; Pokrovsky never discovered his motive.

Roskoncert events, like Uzbek cotton production during the same era, often existed only on paper and in the fees skimmed by corrupt officials, leaving Pokrovsky and his colleagues plenty of free time for teaching and collecting. The ensemble's tours, mostly to Siberia, routinely involved a brief concert in front of a few nonplussed officials in a virtually empty hall followed by private sessions in the homes of local enthusiasts. Then they would spend a few days traveling the countryside, looking for strong-voiced *babi* with long memories. Pokrovsky began lecturing on the shared pagan roots of Slavic peoples and how traditional music was as rich and complex as the Stravinsky and Mighty Handful compositions it had inspired.

Central to how he connected with his growing band of followers was sex. A woman who encountered the group in the seventies remembers that they were "[s]uch *men* . . . through those songs they showed all their virtues—I had never seen such an energetic mix . . . [Pokrovsky], with his open sexuality . . . he opposed the folk chorus, which was completely sexless!" Singers were taught to engage the lower abdomen, to feel it in their genitals; pure singing, Pokrovsky told them, was "like vomiting," and he sometimes made students get down on all fours and bark. Wherever they went, they would learn local dances and bring villagers onto the stage with them. They told folk tales in dialect and outlined the pre-Christian origins of local traditions.

By the early eighties, the ensemble had gained a measure of popularity with students and intellectuals; they even appeared on television occasionally and their concerts drew good crowds. Their success encouraged traditionalists in Georgia and the Baltic states as well as in Russia itself. For many, learning village songs was an outgrowth of passion for jazz or rock—anything that felt authentic as opposed to the falsity of official culture. Former Moiseyev apologists began revealing what they really thought, that those songs were "stillborn forgeries of folk creation that cannot be regarded as folklore." Others pointed out that adapting Western singing styles was unpatriotic. A parallel literary movement called "Village Prose" grew in opposition to socialist realism, Solzhenitsyn's early story "Matryona's House" being a prime example. Pokrovsky made a memorable appearance singing "the old way" in *Farewell*, a film about a town obliterated by a dam. He was always careful to identify songs by region rather than as "Russian," but the group was nevertheless embraced by a nascent nationalist movement eager for a soundtrack. One could say that the receptivity of audiences to this musical realism heralded the psychological shift we have come to know as perestroika, but it was also a harbinger of the neo-Turanian fantasies that have emerged in post-Soviet Russia.

The contrast between the Pokrovsky and Moiseyev aesthetics parallels (in a funhouse mirror sort of way) the Boston versus New York battles of the American folk revival two decades earlier. The former was marked by studious analysis of specific banjo or blues guitar styles from the rural South, while the latter's leading figures, Pete Seeger and The Weavers, sang songs from around the globe in campfire harmonies, all propelled by the same hearty strum, demonstrating that men the world over really are brothers. The Weavers' folky-fifties approach never recovered from Newport '65, but it took the fall of the Berlin Wall to put a stake through the heart of the Moiseyev style.

On January 25, 1982, during a concert in Novosibirsk, Pokrovsky denounced the razing of "economically useless" villages and the cultural bonfire such destruction represented. The ensemble's contract with Roskoncert was canceled and tapes of past TV appearances erased. Glasnost brought them back into favor, even to the extent of being awarded a state prize in 1988. Leaders of official ensembles were outraged; one attacked Pokrovsky for bringing to the stage "something that's appropriate in a kitchen or in a forest." Their supporters from the nationalist Pamyat movement, on the other hand, attacked them for performing a composition by the Jewish Schnittke with a text by the quarter-African Pushkin. Like the British National Party selling Sandy Denny CDs on its website, Russian nationalists tried to appropriate the symbols and surfaces of the folk revival while averting their eyes from its humanist spirit. The ensemble began touring abroad in the late eighties. Pokrovsky had thought that to reach foreign audiences it would be necessary to add drums and electric instruments, to "Fairport Convention–ize" the music. To his delight, however, Western Europeans and Americans were even more enthusiastic about the a cappella "real thing" than Russians. Dmitri had no illusions about the revival; he knew convincing the Russian countryside to reclaim its heritage was virtually impossible. His aim was to provide a choice, keeping songs, rhythms, and techniques alive so that those who were interested could listen and learn. A genuine rebirth of traditional musical culture would require a revolution in rural life; the sad state of Russian agriculture in the new century is testament to the remoteness of such a possibility.

Authorities criticized Pokrovsky for performing music deemed "too complex." He pointed out that folklorists have always struggled to annotate the elaborate harmonies and between-the-keys scales of the different regions, the complex time signatures of the dances, and the subtle wordplay of the endless (unwritten) ballads; nuances that come naturally to those born to a culture can, indeed, be hard work for outsiders. What could not be disputed was that his audience remained an elite minority. When Pokrovsky died of heart failure in 1996, he left behind too few recordings. One in particular stands out: the ensemble's performance of *Les Noces*, sung open-throat rather than bel canto. Pokrovsky and Taruskin cordially disagreed on how the composer would have felt about such a rendition; Pokrovsky believed that Stravinsky had employed "folkloric thinking." Some listeners (naming no names) find the traditional wedding songs that make up the rest of that Nonesuch CD as rich and exciting as Stravinsky's masterwork, if not more so. Thomas Adès often conducts *Les Noces* this way, with surviving singers from the Pokrovsky Ensemble. Lincoln Center proposed this approach to Russian conductor Valery Gergiev when he was scheduled to conduct the piece there; Putin ally Gergiev was horrified and refused to even consider it.

> The wound is still open which the revolutionary shrapnel of modern society, guided by symbols of future and progress, inflicted on the rural, indigenous past. Through this wound the political culture wheezes ... it devises a profile of contemporary man that corresponds, point by point, with the myth of paradise subverted.
>
> —Roger Bartra, *The Cage of Melancholy*

The journalist's facial expression passed from curiosity through skepticism to incredulity, finally settling on contempt. It was 1987; we were in a hotel bar in Sofia, Bulgaria, and hes had asked if I was the same Joe Boyd who produced the early Pink Floyd recordings. When I confessed I was, he demanded to know what possessed me to waste my time on Yanka Rupkina and the Trio Bulgarka when I could be producing proper music—*rock!*

As the popularity of *Le Mystère des Voix Bulgares* soared in the West, most young Bulgarians were sick to death of the arranged *narodna* sounds emanating from state radio and television. I tried to convince him that Yanka (lead vocalist on many of the *Mystère* tracks) was one of the world's great singers and that her Trio Bulgarka were as brilliant as most (post-Koutev) state ensembles were mediocre, but he was having none of it. Neither of us could then imagine that the communist system was just two years away from collapse; nor could we conceive of decades of carefully constructed Bulgarian musical identity being swept away in an avalanche of heavy metal, Serbian turbo-folk, hip-hop, and synth-pop kitsch.

Bulgaria's self-image is built around its five-centuries-long resistance to the "Ottoman yoke." Like many smaller European countries, it is a nineteenth-century, post-Herder creation; before 1877, there was little distinction among southern Slavs, while the Russian and Bulgarian languages were usually referred to simply as "Slavonic." Balkan Slavs looked to Russia as the fatherland, their liberator from Turkish tyranny and inspiration for the Slavophile movement that emerged in the wake of pan-Germanism (and which in turn inspired Zionism). Progressives from every corner of the Balkans made pilgrimages to study with Herder, who can be said, for better or worse, to have built the idea of nationalism on cornerstones of folk tales and folk songs.

Like Britain's, Bulgaria's post-Ottoman royal family may have been German immigrants, but it was Russian that became mandatory in schools, while language police tried (vainly) to purge the vernacular of Turkish words. Bulgaria was eager to join the modern European world and Slavophilia was seen as an asset. Music teachers and choirmasters arrived from Germany, Czechoslovakia, and Russia, along with imported trumpets, violins, and clarinets. Roma (whom most didn't view as real Bulgarians) and Ottoman-era boys kidnapped to Istanbul who had ended up playing in janissary marching bands were among the few previously known examples of the concept of "professional musician."

After World War Two, as most Eastern countries tried to avoid ending up on Stalin's side of the Iron Curtain, Bulgaria actually applied to become a part of the USSR. The "little brother" Bulgars were rewarded with special rights and duties within the Soviet bloc: their secret police were expected to carry out dirty jobs (the assassination attempt on the Pope in 1981, for example) but they were given leeway to ignore strictures that other COMECON countries daren't. Sofia publishers, for example, translated some banned Western literature;

curious Russian intelligentsia could combine a Black Sea holiday with a book-buying spree.

Bulgaria's paranoid nationalism, which saw threats on every side (while itself claiming the formerly Bulgarian-speaking city of Thessaloniki, much of the former Yugoslav province of Macedonia, and Romanian lands south of the Danube delta), was also tolerated by the "workers-of-the-world-unite" Soviets. The need to build up a strong cultural identity informed the choice of Philip Koutev as leader of the State Ensemble; his brief was to enlist music in the effort to defend the country against the Turks and Greeks.

Koutev and his wife traveled the Bulgarian hinterland collecting songs and learning about the cultures of the different provinces. In the ensemble, singers and instrumentalists were encouraged to celebrate regional traditions and melodies (so long as they didn't sound too "gypsy" or too Turkish). Koutev's first orchestra comprised one gaida, three kavals, six *gadulkas* (vertical fiddles with sympathetic strings), two *tamburas* (three-stringed lutes shaped like bouzoukis), and a teppan. Though this line-up struck a blow for authenticity, nothing resembling it had ever been heard in a Bulgarian village; back into the mists of time, dancing had been propelled by a single instrument, sometimes assisted by a teppan. Although he added a cello and a bass to anchor the arrangements, Koutev refused to consider urban folk instruments such as accordion, violin, or clarinet, and it would have been unthinkable to include popular Turkish-rooted instruments such as the zurna or oud.

Witnesses to early concerts report wildly exciting performances. Though time would smooth down the ensemble's edges, Koutev largely succeeded in his goal to create a colorful and exciting show that would "elevate" rural music and please urban audiences while staying true to the music's spirit. Koutev had studied Bartók, Grieg, and Janáček and written symphonies based on folk themes, but for the ensemble he stuck to the instruments, playing techniques and rhythms he had heard on his domestic travels, with a repertoire consisting entirely of traditional songs. He celebrated the distinct cultures of Rhodope, Thrace, Pirin, Strandja, Dobrudzha, and Shop and would later help establish regional ensembles in all of them.

Bulgarian men do sing, but the ensemble's fame grew from the sound of its women's choir. (Bulgarian resistance tales are full of heroic women who prove braver than their male cohorts.) The key to the sound of Bulgarian voices lies in the *burdon*, or drone, a tradition particularly strong in southeastern regions of Pirin and Shop. In a group of village women, all bar one remain on the drone note while the *okachka* sings a melody that can approach the burdon to approximately a major or minor second above or seventh below. The open-throat voice is pure and straight, devoid of any vibrato that would blur these near-dissonant combinations into unlistenability.

∽

In 1963, a German opera singer named Gerald Messner entered a competition in Sofia. When he developed a sore throat, he was advised to spend a few days in Bistritsa, a nearby mountain village known for its healing waters and healthy air. During his visit he heard some local women singing; the effect was so profound that he gave up opera to devote his life to studying the vocal techniques of the region. (His subjects would later tour the world as the Grandmothers of Bistritsa.) Messner's research, supported by the Bulgarian government, was the first serious analysis of the so-called *Mystère*. In what he termed "interferential diaphony," Messner believed he had stumbled upon an ancient practice rooted in pre-Christian Thrace, Greece, and Asia Minor. In a world devoid of musical notation or the mathematics of a tempered scale, singers would tune in to the overtones of other voices and find pleasing (if, to us, jarringly close) notes around the drone. Messner found that the women in Bistritsa had an aversion to the octave, the third, the fifth, and the sixth, preferring to stick close to the burdon. Bulgarian farmers have similar inclinations, carefully selecting bells for their livestock that ring ever so slightly off pitch from one another, creating a satisfyingly dissonant vibration.

Within a few years, early music pioneers David Munrow and Thomas Binkley were sending vocalists to Bulgaria to learn how European singing might have sounded before the Italians sullied it with all their trills and vibrato. (Lutenists were packed off to Syria to study with oud masters for similar reasons.) Bulgaria's ruling comrades, meanwhile, blared symphonies over village PA systems to help peasants out of their backward ignorance of "developed" music. (Once again, the "West" was craving traditions while the source culture pursued modernity.)

By incorporating these patterns into his choir arrangements, Koutev was living dangerously; the drone is the basis of much Islamic music, precisely what Bulgarian authorities wished to expunge from the national consciousness, even though "Oriental" influences could have derived from the Asiatic origins of Slavs and Bulgars as much as from the conquering Turks. Other composers would have underpinned traditional melodies with comforting German-Italian chords, or followed Bartók and Stravinsky into using folk music as a road to edgy modernism. Instead, Koutev turned to the choral traditions of the Orthodox Church with its open fifths and octaves, leaving space for those arresting seconds and sevenths without causing harmonic trainwrecks. Koutev's radicalism lay in the simplicity of his vision; what he avoided was as important as what he did. He also rose to the challenge of teaching barely literate women from rural Bulgaria to read written arrangements and sing in chords without altering their vocal technique.

Instrumentalists were always men, their skills passed from father to son, just as songs were handed down from mother to daughter. In the early years, Koutev heeded his musicians; if they didn't like an arrangement, he let them alter it. But traditional techniques were on a collision course with the needs of a professional ensemble. The gaida, for example, like most bagpipes, sounds two notes, a drone and a melody; a voice can easily modulate, but for a gaida to change keys, the drone pipe must be blocked off, radically curtailing the sound. Likewise, the elaborate ornamentations of the best *gaidari* and *kavali* clashed with fixed arrangements and had to be eliminated. For all his good intentions (and often brilliant results), Koutev played a central role in the erosion of Bulgarian musical traditions.

Collectivization and quotas meant there was no place for the seasonal rituals that once brightened hard lives in the Bulgarian countryside.

Winter had always been a time for energetic dancing "to keep warm," while tempi slowed in the sultry summer months. No one danced during Lent: the earth is pregnant, so tread gently. Tradition demanded each song be sung exactly as in years past to avoid tempting fate to bring drought, flood, or war. To the Party, this was all criminal nonsense. Forcing music into structured ensembles and competitions was a metaphor for the way agriculture was being modernized, with centuries of subtle skills and hard-earned knowledge discarded in favor of theories developed in Soviet laboratories. Although Bulgaria never experienced famine on the scale of the USSR in the 1930s, collectivization brought about shortages that mirrored the decline of village music.

Many musicians "lost the heart" to play after their fields and animals were confiscated. Women had once sung throughout the day, weaving, embroidering, cooking, or tending their gardens; but girls now went to school, no longer sharing songs with their mothers. Bulgarian rural customs should not be over-romanticized; girls had sung about their fears of being kidnapped (traditional courtship often involved rape) or married off to a man from another village. They also sang of their dreams of being taken by their real or longed-for lover—referred to in song as the "dragon." Traditional wedding ceremonies bordered on fertility rites.

The Koutev Ensemble staged pantomime weddings and festivities that—musical quality and authentic costumes aside—were almost as fake as Moiseyev's. Village nuptials and dances could last for days; songs on the radio or in concert were rarely more than a few minutes long. Bulgarian dances are beautiful, particularly seen from above, with lines spiraling in, then out, resembling both an exotic crustacean and a Zoroastrian symbol. For the concert stage, Madame Kouteva had little option but to reshape them into rows and arcs.

One may bemoan how communism broke the chain of rural tradition, but the industrialization of Western Europe had an even harsher effect, often with less effort devoted to preserving the disappearing music. At different times in both Western and Eastern Europe, cities have swelled with migrants happy to leave the countryside—rituals, music, and all—behind them.

In 1964, a school of folklore was established in the beautiful Thracian capital of Plovdiv; from now on folk music would be learned in a classroom. "Oriental" embellishments and "gypsy" improvisations were not taught. In the early years, experienced musicians joined the beginners to learn notation and students were sometimes sent to the countryside to learn from veterans; eventually, though, village virtuosos proved too individualistic for the school to tolerate, either as tutors or as students. Interaction continued in spaces beyond government control (the jam sessions I witnessed in the woods at Koprivshtitsa, for example), but the clash between tradition and dogma-driven systems of instruction was the shoal on which good intentions foundered. The conflict was subtler than (but not fundamentally different from) encounters between Christian missionaries and the "heathen" practices of "natives" they wished to convert.

Even the most positive aspects of Bulgarian music policy eventually crumpled under the weight of bureaucratic inertia and ineptitude. Party hacks were given cushy jobs in the culture ministry; one way to augment a slim state income was having your compositions performed on the radio, so Koutev's great creations were often pushed aside in favor of an assembly line of mediocre work by composers with friends or kickback recipients in state radio and the culture ministry. Older musicians referred to the ever more boring arrangements as *notno* (a dismissive reference to parts read from sheet music), in contrast to *izvor* (the spring), the art of the aging masters; they found Plovdiv graduates' playing cold and unsubtle. Nor could veterans get used to performing for seated audiences; a village hall or square full of dancers was what they craved. They felt the color had been bled from the tradition, its soul emptied. Not only did the folk orchestras become less interesting but choirs lost their luster as village singers were gradually replaced by Plovdiv graduates. There is a characterful warmth and sweetness amidst even the harshest of harmonies in the early Koutev recordings; the new singers sound shrill in comparison. "Serious" composers, creatively frustrated and needing to earn a living, often took up conducting and composing for folk ensembles; the result was a growing intellectualization of the music, treating the burdon as a vehicle for modernist experimentation.

One positive development was the opening of instrumental instruction to women. Even this was limited; Plovdiv professors couldn't get used to the sight of a woman putting a kaval or gaida in her mouth (though a man doing the same seemed not to trouble them). Prior to 1944, music had been communal and free of careerists—*melodic socialism!* After twenty years of communism, it had become a means of earning a living, with rivals fighting over the spoils—*just like capitalism!* New works were commissioned from on high, like the old European system of royal patronage. Nothing (with, as we shall see, one huge exception) bubbled up from below.

⁂

Urban audiences grew bored with force-fed folk; and while many rural listeners enjoyed the big, polished sound of the ensembles, they hated the truncated verses, complaining that stories no longer made sense. While kids in villages who learned an instrument were still admired, carrying a kaval around in the city drew ridicule from peers. "The people don't like the people's music," observed a veteran musician.

Music was but one of many examples of the system's inability to respond to reality; records were pressed and distributed based on what officials decided ought to sell. There was no provision for shops to return surplus vinyl, nor any method for rapid restocking when a record sold well. Musicians referred to the state record label Balkanton, the Plovdiv school, and the culture ministry collectively as "Vinprom," after the government wine behemoth that blended distinctive regional varieties into cheap plonk.

Yet even in this regimented landscape, traditions continued to flourish. In a five-year cycle of local and regional competitions, amateur village singers, dancers, and instrumentalists were winnowed down to finalists for Koprivshtitsa. The result was the joyful celebration I beheld in that unforgettable summer of 1986, the sixth since the event's inauguration in 1961. Koprivshtitsa is a beautiful town in the Sredna Gora mountains of northern Bulgaria, chosen for both its nineteenth-century

Balkan-revival architecture and the fact that the first shots of the 1876 rebellion that expelled the Ottomans were fired there. Koprivshtitsa competitors were small groups or solo performers; large ensembles were mostly professional and therefore ineligible. As dazzled as I was by the richness and variety, over time I realized that the heavy hand of the ensemble arrangers, combined with the conservatism of the judging panels, was slowly squeezing the life out of village music. Koprivshtitsa did, however, energize performers in every corner of Bulgaria and kept alive virtuoso skills and ancient songs far longer than in almost any other European country.

My head still spinning from the festival, I called on Rumyana Tzintzarska in Sofia to ask if she would help me put together a small group of artists to perform in the old, free style. Unlike the journalist, Rumyana did not hold my past against me; walking over to her LP cabinet, she pulled out a battered copy of *The 5000 Spirits or the Layers of the Onion* by the Incredible String Band. She agreed to help me construct an Incredible Bulgarian String Band.

We began with the singers. Yanka Rupkina is the golden-haired lead on the most famous *Mystère* tracks, a Balkan Dolly Parton, the Radio Choir's diva to rival the Koutev Ensemble's Nadka Karadjova (of "A Lambkin Commences Bleating" fame). Her home region of Strandja borders both the Black Sea and Turkey, so her vocal decorations have a strong "Oriental" flavor, while the region's songs, when arranged for orchestra, bear an uncanny resemblance to Percy Sledge ballads. Yanka had once been married to an Olympic weightlifting champion, but was then living alone in a Sofia flat with a photo of Stalin in the front hall.

She and two other soloists from the Radio Choir had formed the Trio Bulgarka with a repertoire of stripped-down renditions of Koutev's arrangements. Stoyanka Boneva was from the mountainous Pirin region; her distinctive voice gave those harsh harmonies a velvety undertone. Eva Georgieva, from Dobruja, near the Romanian border, sang lighter songs in a sweet contralto. When blended together, with Yanka usually in the lead and the other two singing harmonies below the melody (like the Staple Singers), they formed a sonic three-in-hand knot that remained honeyed and warm no matter how unnervingly close the notes.

Trakiiskita Troika—"the Thracian Three"—provided the core of the instrumental backing: gadulka, kaval, and tambura. Ognyan "Jimmy" Vasilev, the *teppanista*, was the life of our party; he had started as a dancer with the Koutev Ensemble in the fifties, performing with them until, having put on too much weight, he switched nimbly to percussion. It has been noted that many jazz and Latin percussionists are also excellent dancers, and Jimmy proved the rule. The *gaidari*, Kostadin Varimezov, was the most impressive figure, having been central to UCLA musicologist Timothy Rice's studies of Bulgarian music, guiding Rice through its history and the intricacies of its politics, assisting lectures in Los Angeles and performing at the Folklife Festival in Washington DC.

We called the group Balkana. Our first concert was in London in 1987, for an audience that knew the *Mystère* LP and was fascinated by the sudden appearance of actual Bulgarians from behind the Iron Curtain, but had little idea of the richness of the country's musical culture. Bulgarian groups, including the Koutev Ensemble, had been to Britain before, but previous audiences bore no resemblance to this crowd, drawn by the music rather than spectacle or politics. Everyone loved the instrumentalists, but Yanka and the Trio were the stars. I had to convince them to gather around a single microphone rather than each having their own; harmonies blend much better in the air than in a mixing board's transistors.

On their first visit I got a glimpse of the conditions under which official touring took place; grabbing Eva's suitcase as she alighted from the airport minibus, I staggered with the astonishing heft of it. What on earth had she packed? In the hotel room, she revealed it to be full of tinned cheese and meat. When the Radio Choir toured outside Eastern Europe, the agency confiscated all the hard-currency fees, so musicians would eat in their rooms and pocket the per diem allowances provided by local promoters, their only way of returning home with anything of value. (We paid fees and royalties directly to the musicians, not via the state agency; on future tours, Eva traveled lighter.)

Encouraged by the London show, I decided to try America. We booked New York's Town Hall for May 15, 1988, and an agent began organizing a follow-up tour for the autumn. The concert was sold out; John Rockwell in the *New York Times* called it "a gripping, stirring evening of music, one that validated the very notion of fashion." After the show, we moved downtown to the space now occupied by City Winery, where Martin Koenig (a veteran Balkanologist who had made field recordings of Bulgarian village music twenty years before I ventured there) had organized a dance. Gone were the hesitant steps I remembered from Princeton's folk-dance club; these New Yorkers were almost as deft and confident as the Bulgarians circling those Koprivshtitsa bonfires.

I was pleased when Nonesuch Records, who were enjoying a hit with the *Mystère des Voix Bulgares* LP in North America, purchased a Town Hall box and brought along a phalanx of New York luminaries including David Byrne and Natalie Merchant. But seeing their choir's lead singers in the flesh removed some of the intimidating mystery about the music's source. A few weeks after our triumph, the agent called me to sheepishly announce that she had taken on the Mystère choir as clients; with tour support from Nonesuch and record sales soaring, they were a more attractive proposition to arts centers around the country than Balkana. Our "breakthrough" tour now canceled, within two years of its formation my all-star team was on its last legs.

One afternoon in the Hannibal Records office, a colleague answered the phone and shot me a funny look as she pushed the hold button: "Someone who says she's Kate Bush." Indeed it was Kate Bush; she wanted to add Bulgarian harmonies to her new record and had heard that I was the man to talk to. I explained that it wouldn't be a simple matter of flying in the Trio Bulgarka and working out parts with them, as you would normally do with backing singers. Kate is notoriously averse to flying, so I was impressed when she hesitated only a few seconds before agreeing to join me on a Balkanair Tupolev for my next visit. The aircraft was rickety, the flight bumpy, and to add to the strangeness, the airline had recently decided to enter the modern age by creating smoking and non-smoking sections: smokers on the left, non-smokers to the right.

Kate, Del Palmer (her engineer and boyfriend at the time), and I joined the team in the music room of a Sofia high school: Yanka, Eva, and Stoyanka, Rumyana, the arranger Dimitar Penev, and Borimira Nedeva, a classically trained pianist and fluent English-speaker working for Jusautor, the Bulgarian copyright bureau. Once they got down to work, Kate would play a passage on her ghetto blaster and Rumyana would come up with a Bulgarian folk melody that fit the harmonies of Kate's song; she knew that the Koutev sound Kate was after could not be uncoupled from its source and would require a characteristically Bulgarian melody line. Once a fragment was chosen, Dimitar would go to the piano to create an arrangement, with Borimira providing the musically literate translations without which the project would have foundered.

That evening, the three singers hosted a welcoming dinner for Kate, Del, London journalist Nick Coleman, and me in a Sofia restaurant. Surrounded by the Trio and the Troika in a small, acoustically excellent back room, Kate, Del, and Nick all described the evening as unforgettable. Coleman later wrote that being sandwiched between Yanka and Eva as they harmonized was easily a match for previous close encounters with Miles Davis and Marvin Gaye.

Saturday morning, Nick and I left them to it and headed for a rendezvous in the southern mountains (more about which presently); we returned on Sunday night to find an exhausted but exhilarated team still hard at work in the schoolroom. Kate told me her favorite moment had been when the Trio wanted to sing her something and Stoyanka picked up a telephone to get their burdon note from the dial tone. A few weeks later, the team arrived in London to record "You're the One," "Why Should I Love You?" and "The Song of Solomon" for Kate's *Red Shoes* album. I filmed the process for a documentary about Bulgarian music as part of BBC Arena's *Rhythms of the World* series.

That was not, of course, the last time Bulgarian singing leaped across into the realm of capitalist popular music—nor was it the first. Joni Mitchell had trumped everyone by multitracking Bulgarian harmonies on "Rainy Night House" on 1969's *Ladies of the Canyon*. David Crosby cited the Koutev LP as an inspiration for many of his parts with The Byrds and CSNY, while one of Balkana's last concerts was a private performance for George Harrison at his Sussex manor. By the end of the century, Koutev and Mystère choir recordings had been used to sell cars and computers and heard in countless film scores. The sound that won the heart of Albert Grossman in Paris in 1965 had been woven into the sonic wallpaper of hip consumption.

As the Mystère phenomenon ran out of steam, the Koutev Ensemble and the Radio Choir both needed foreign income to survive in the post-communist world, and battles began among Cellier and various former Bulgarian radio officials over who had the right to the Mystère des Voix Bulgares name. The situation wasn't helped by Jaro Records, the German label that signed the choir in 1991, encouraging post-Koutev arrangers to venture ever further into cold and dissonant avant-garde territory. (I am not aware of any Schoenberg-like romantic disappointments or Webernesque bereavements that might explain this.)

When Tim Rice visited Yambol province in the summer of 1969, the district's culture commissar said he'd come at a bad time, since all the local musicians were away working at the seashore. That evening, hearing the sound of a gaida as he drove through a village, Rice discovered a wedding party in progress. Invited in, he drank *rakiya* and reveled in the music and bacchanalian dancing until the wee hours. The next morning, he was summoned by the commissar and expelled from the district: "I thought I told you there was no folklore in the Yambol district!"

The Achilles heel for government control of music was its citizens' persistence in getting married; the state may have driven ceremonies themselves out of the church and into a registry office but nothing could stop the celebrations that followed. And since local amateur groups were fast disappearing, the primary musical option (particularly in the densely populated Thracian heartland) was Roma bands. Bulgaria has both Christian and Muslim Roma; the crisis of the mid-eighties stems from the fact that almost all of the country's Roma musicians are Turkish-speaking

Sufi Muslims whose ancestors arrived in the fourteenth century with the Ottoman conquest.

In the early 1980s, faced with empty shelves and a disgruntled urban workforce, the government gave farmers permission to sell surplus produce at street stalls. The effect of these hugely popular markets (most city-dwellers hadn't seen fresh vegetables for years) was like taking a Bulgaria-shaped tray and tilting it so all the loose change slid into the Thracian breadbasket. With this money, however, there was little to buy; waiting lists for automobiles and refrigerators were many years long and only the most daring hung around rest stops on the Istanbul highway making off-the-back-of-a-lorry deals with German truckers. As cash piled up under rural mattresses, the only way to flash it was on lavish wedding parties.

With this surge in business, Roma musicians began buying the loudspeakers, amplifiers, saxophones, electric guitars, and drum kits needed to play the sort of high-octane folklore invading the country on radio waves from Greece and Yugoslavia. Onto the 2/4 and 7/8 time signatures of traditional *horos* and *ratchenitsas* they threw jazz and rock, plus Turkish, Romanian, Greek, and Serbian melodies and Roma flair. Dancers went wild; the government was apoplectic.

Many older musicians shared the authorities' distaste for showy "Turkishisms" and loud volume, but the Roma were proud to play "*s bus*" (with gusto, from the Turkish word for "fast"). Soon there was more work than they could handle, so Plovdiv graduates and members of state ensembles began working the wedding circuit on weekends, playing with and emulating the Roma and discovering they could earn more at one wedding than a month's salary in an ensemble.

These developments collided with Chairman Zhivkov's lunge towards ethnic nationalism; a 1985 decree outlawed the use of non-Bulgarian names. Hundreds of thousands of Roma and *pomaks* (Turkish-speaking Bulgarian Muslims) were forced to re-register with suitably Slavic handles. The official line was that the new names were simply a response to a "resurgence of Bulgarian identity" among Muslims, who were equally enthusiastic, no doubt, about bans on listening to Turkish radio, importing Turkish periodicals, circumcision, studying the Koran, or wearing baggy trousers. Many Balkan Slavs are convinced that they are frontline defenders of European civilization against the Muslim hordes; they hold the Ottoman captivity responsible for the area's missing out on the Renaissance and the Industrial Revolution and its resulting backwardness.

Roma musicians presented a tricky issue, since many of the greatest Bulgarian players—Kostadin Varimezov among them—openly credit the influence of their Romani-speaking mentors. It had long been customary to hire such groups for important festivities; their playing was admired, even revered, but they remained social outcasts—"the brown ones." Roma playing styles were officially deemed "too individualistic" and "un-Bulgarian." Even as Zhivkov banned the Roma language and "gypsy" entertainment at up-scale restaurants, these musicians continued to perform at wedding celebrations every weekend.

It was a toss-up as to which infuriated the government more, that their flamboyant style was so popular or that they were making so much money. ("Gypsies," one official told Rice, "lack the stable moral basis to handle wealth.") When pronouncements excoriating "foreign" playing styles failed, it was decided that all wedding bands must be licensed and that the government would publish a fixed schedule of fees. Groups playing traditional acoustic instruments were allowed to charge more than those using modern ones, but it hardly took much ingenuity for bandleaders and wedding organizers to sign an official contract in triplicate, then pass extra cash under the table. Through the mid-eighties, Thracian weddings grew more and more elaborate; booming PA speakers, drum kits, and saxophones were matched by vertiginous piles of gifts and tables groaning with food and alcohol, enough conspicuous consumption to give a good communist indigestion. The ancient tradition of bridal necklaces of gold and silver coins was replaced by sheaves of thousand-lev notes pinned to wedding gowns.

And it was no longer just weddings: housewarmings, baptisms, and military draftee send-offs began hiring bands. Nothing could stop the music at these celebrations becoming more and more "Oriental," as dancers demanded the Turkish kyuchek beat by licking banknotes and sticking them to players' foreheads. Crowds roared their appreciation of the wildest solos and the loudest ensembles. Crashing weddings became a new pastime for urban youth; music students swapped awed tales of hearing this or that accordion or guitar virtuoso as they might talk about a new midfielder for Lokomotiv Plovdiv. Teachers who railed against this evil influence in class were spotted by their students at weddings, each pretending not to recognize the other. Policemen sent to shut down a party one Saturday night would turn up a week later at another, out of uniform and dancing. Officials didn't know which way to look: while the intonations and embellishments made the bands "too Eastern," the volume and electric guitars made them also "too Western."

Attendance at official concerts slumped, as did sales of Balkanton LPs. Since the label refused to record wedding bands, a market in bootleg cassettes flourished. As one arm of the government barred wedding musicians from health and social services and kicked them out of the musicians' union, another, the network of Stereo Zapis shops, was happy to profit from duplication services for anyone with a cassette.

Manol Todorov, a professor at the Plovdiv Institute, was among the first to call for a rethink: "[I]t's about time the government paid attention to [this music] . . . [W]e can't preserve folklore unchanged." Ethnographers began publishing hand-wringing analyses of the paralysis gripping official music and tried to place wedding bands into historical perspective. It was decided to hold a competitive annual festival of instrumental music, with cash prizes for the best modern bands; by laying down rules and specifying Bulgarian-only melodies, the authorities hoped to channel the craze into a more acceptable direction. The first Stambolovo Festival in 1985 was either a triumph or a fiasco, depending on your point of view. Twelve thousand fans arrived, camping out for the duration and shouting support for their favorite ensembles and soloists; the jury, however, awarded no prizes since no group had adhered to the nativist script. Some judges, drawn from the ranks of academia and bureaucracy, had their first exposure to wedding-band music at regional semi-finals and were so shocked they could barely bring themselves to recommend anyone for the finals. Tim Rice witnessed one deliberation where the judges spent most of the time equating the aggressiveness of the music with the bad character and ethnic menace of Turkish-speaking Roma. Stambolovo did force Balkanton into signing wedding bands, but they released only bland, highly arranged recordings with no improvisation and no un-Bulgarian melodies.

A concert of Stambolovo finalists in Sofia the following year is remembered as a defining event in the collapse of Bulgarian communism, the country's Dylan-at-Newport moment; after it, great swathes of urban youth were no longer reachable by Party propaganda. To the kids and the musicians, wedding music represented freedom; the frightened government saw it that way, too. One traumatized official admitted that for young people, "Bulgarian folk music . . . [has] become an organic necessity for moral-aesthetic improvement and for patriotism." Another added, "They have created a style which successfully combats foreign invasion." Communism, as Václav Havel famously put it, "is a world of appearances trying to pass for reality."

The first time I heard a Stereo Zapis wedding-band cassette was in 1987 in a suburban house near Princeton, New Jersey. Brad Hill, a musician my mother knew, had spent a year studying in Plovdiv and got in touch after hearing that I was producing Bulgarian music. He played me a tape by the kaval maestro Teodosi Spassov's group and it was extraordinary: impossibly fast tempi propelled by mad drumming, James Brown–esque guitar, and topped off by kaval-playing that sounded as if it must have been recorded at half speed then doubled. While arranging the recording sessions for the Trio Bulgarka LP (and only dimly aware of the cultural-political turmoil described above), I asked Sofiakonzert if they could arrange for me to hear Spassov's band.

On a rainy morning, the agency representative collected me at my hotel and we drove to the grim outskirts of Sofia. On the way, I was informed that the requested group was unavailable so we would hear the Plovdiv Folk-Jazz Ensemble instead; and since Spassov himself had been unable to travel from Plovdiv, they had arranged for an "equally good" soloist to take his place. In a shabby House of Culture surrounded by cement high-rises, we found a very un-Roma band setting up onstage. The whole thing began to seem like an annoying waste of time.

The first two numbers did nothing to allay my impatience: tepid jazz-rock built around Bulgarian folk melodies, with the dubious addition of conga drums played in 7/8 time. My translator (whom I had hired outside official channels) whispered that she had overheard a conversation revealing that Spassov (a non-Roma making good money on the wedding circuit) had refused to perform without a fee and didn't give a toss how "important" the American visitor might be. At the start of the third number, a large man with an impressive pot belly, a small beard, glinting eyes, and thinning dark hair strode onto the stage clutching a clarinet. He played along with another boring arrangement, then took an astounding solo; witty, inventive, and dazzling, I'd never heard anything like it. After another number with an equally remarkable clarinet break, he wandered off as casually as he'd strolled on. I told the translator I wanted to talk to him—alone. In a backstage hallway, I was introduced to Ivo Papasov; when I asked if he always played with the Plovdiv Folk-Jazz Ensemble, he rolled his eyes and said he had his own band. They were playing a wedding that weekend in the village of Yabalkovo, two and a half hours' drive from Sofia. I said I'd see him there.

Yabalkovo (Apple Town) sits in the middle of the Thracian plain. Mountains loom to the south and north, while the land stretches east to the horizon. Horses, cattle, and goats were tethered outside a large wedding tent. Inside, a bandstand was set up at one end; trestle tables and benches filled most of the remaining space, with a small dancefloor wedged in between. Girls circulated with platters of meatballs, tomatoes, bread, and beer, all delicious. The band consisted of drum kit, electric guitar, amplified gadulka, accordion, saxophone, and clarinet, plus occasional vocals by Ivo's wife, Maria Karafizieva. They galloped through complex arrangements involving stop-on-a-dime shifts of tempi, time signatures, and keys; it was some of the most thrilling music I had ever heard. The drummer, in particular, was mesmerizing; stripped to a sleeveless T-shirt and grinning like a madman, he brought every corner of his kit into rapid-fire play on time signatures that ranged from 2/4 to 11/8, 7/8, and possibly 13/8. When Ivo took a break and sat down at our table, I pointed to the drummer and gave a thumbs-up. Papasov grinned and said, "*Bool-gar-ee-yah-beel-ee-cobe-am.*" I glanced quizzically at my translator before it dawned on me that I had just been informed that the object of my admiration was "Bulgaria's Billy Cobham." By evening, when I reluctantly began the drive back to Sofia, the group had moved to the village square and was propelling ecstatic lines of dancers winding in and out of those dizzying Zoroastrian spirals. Recording this band and bringing them to the West became my obsession.

Ibrahim Hapasov was born in 1952 in Kardzhali, near the Bulgaria-Turkey border. His father and grandfather were Turkish-speaking Roma who played zurna and clarinet for weddings. His mother tied off his umbilical cord with a piece of string used to tighten clarinet keys; by the age of nine, Ibrahim could "play like a man." In 1974, he formed Trakia, which soon became the most in-demand group in the region. By government diktat in 1984, Ibrahim Hapasov became Ivo Papasov. A year later, while playing at a wedding in Stara Zagora, he was arrested for speaking Turkish in public and playing Turkish music. When the judge pointed out that neither was actually a criminal offense, the charge was altered to "hooliganism" and he served twenty-five days in prison. (His 2011 CD, *Dance of the Falcon*, is named after the tune he was playing when police arrested him.)

Papasov is a showman; one of his favorite routines is to perform "a musical stroll around Bulgaria," visiting the different regional styles while mimicking the sounds of the gaida, the Rhodopian *kaba gaida*, the kaval, and of course the zurna. He solos while dismantling his clarinet and can play it and a sax together, like Roland Kirk. Saxophonist Yuri Yunakov described playing with him: "Have you ever seen how a hunted wild rabbit runs? . . . zig-zag, stops, returns . . . That's how Ivo plays. And we chase him like hounds with our tongues hanging out."

Ivo takes the view that Bulgarian music has always been a mix of East and West. In the nineteenth century, he says, wedding parties were entertained by *chalgadzhii* groups, comprising gypsies and non-gypsies, Bulgarian speakers and pomaks. He's not fond of playing for seated audiences: "A wedding," he says, "is equal to a dozen concerts." Papasov keeps the structure of a maqam in his head to guide him through his solos, which are further inspired by hours of listening to Charlie Parker and Benny Goodman records. The beautiful singing of his wife, Maria (wooed away from a former accordion player in his band), is based on an ancient style from Yanka's Strandja region and employs a Persian vibrato technique outlawed in the mullahs' Iran. The conflict between government and wedding bands might not have grown so severe were it not for Papasov's brilliance; Trakia's exciting playing defined the style and inspired the others.

As I walked through Plovdiv with him one afternoon, people repeatedly approached us wanting to book a wedding. As Ivo pulled out a crumpled notebook, one man thrust a huge wad of banknotes into his fist and they shook hands on a date the following autumn. I heard of couples who risked scandal by marrying when the bride was eight months pregnant because Trakia weren't available earlier. One academic told me he was convinced that in the years leading up to 1989, the only Bulgarian as wealthy as Papasov was Todor Zhivkov. Ivo was that most exotic of characters in 1980s Bulgaria, a true star.

Once I had permission to take the group into the studio, my only disappointment was a slight change in the line-up. At Yabalkovo the rhythm was propelled by drummer Salif Ali (or Stefan Angelov as we had to credit him) and guitarist Yuri (formerly Gyurai) Kamzamalov. Kamzamalov's technique combined bass runs with machine-gun funk, his thumb wrapping around the neck Django Reinhardt fashion to fret the bottom string. In the studio a year later, Kamzamalov had been replaced (after a row over money) by his brother Andrei (formerly Aidan) on guitar and Radi Kazakov on fretless bass.

Though I admire Jaco Pastorius and his pioneering way with this instrument, I have often encountered the fretless bass's malign influence in developing countries. Like auto-tuned vocals, it bestows an unmistakable modernism; the fact that it blurs traditional rhythms as they migrate into urban recording studios only seems to increase local enthusiasm for its sound. I persuaded Radi to limit the effects and slides, and Andrei is an excellent guitarist, so the recording roars powerfully along; but my mind's ear always yearns for the agile single-jet propulsion of that day in Yabalkovo. Also standing by Ivo's side at that first wedding was the accordionist Neshko Neshev, as sphinx-like as the rest of the band is animated. During the recording, as I became familiar with the harmonic patterns of the music, Neshko's solos began to feel more and more psychedelic.

One aspect of the band's sound I was happy to leave outside the studio was PA effects. Having discovered the reverb switch, Roma bands and their audiences couldn't get enough; the endless dizzying bounce of repeated notes was one area where I might have sided with the Stambolovo judges. What was fascinating, however, was hearing the heavy tremolo of Maria's vocals beating at the same wavelength as the Echoplex. She gives open-throat singing a surreal twist, with throbbing waves far slower and heavier than bel canto vibrato; it was sometimes hard to tell where the pulses of her beautiful long notes left off and the reverb began.

The player I initially found most difficult to approach was Yunakov. A former boxer with shoulder-length jet-black hair, gold incisors, and the Cyrillic equivalent of "love" and "hate" tattooed on his knuckles, Yuri could play the exotic assassin in a Bond movie. Naturally, he turned out to be the sweetest of characters. Three junctures marked his journey from a poor Thracian village to his current home in New York City. The first came when I walked with him across midtown from NBC Studios in Rockefeller Center (where the group were rehearsing for David Sanborn's *Night Music* show) to Manny's on Seventh Avenue, to purchase a new saxophone, the transaction solemnly observed by autographed photos of Coleman Hawkins, John Coltrane, and King Curtis. The next came when he received his fee for the second LP, recorded in Cologne, Germany. Adding it to savings from recent tours, Yuri bought a used Mercedes and set off, tears of delight rolling down his cheeks, to drive back to his village near Kardzhali. The third was when I turned up at a Turkish restaurant on Third Avenue where he was performing with a pick-up band of Turks, Albanians, and Macedonians shortly after becoming the first (and to date only) recipient of political asylum granted by the US government to a Turkish-speaking Bulgarian Roma on grounds of racial persecution.

Ivo and the band gathered around a television in a London pub and watched the Berlin Wall come down. Soon after their return to Bulgaria, Zhivkov was ousted; unlike his neighbor Ceaușescu, he survived for years under house arrest and died a natural death. Historians credit his downfall to the manic anti-Turk campaigns that alienated Gorbachev as well as Zhivkov's own Politburo. In the Bulgarian Parliament today, the balance of power often lies with the pomak party, the Movement for Rights and Freedoms.

Ivo's tours in the West bestowed respect at home; Bulgarian radio interviewed him live from the NBC studios as we sound-checked for *Night Music*. It wasn't just Sofia broadcasters who were astonished by his appearance on the show; David Sanborn and the house band's ace rhythm section—Marcus Miller, Hiram Bullock, and Omar Hakim—watched open-mouthed as Ivo and the guys rehearsed a breakneck 11/8 ratchenitsa. In the show's finale Bullock, Nona Hendryx, and Pops Staples traded verses on "Take Me to the River" while Sanborn, Ivo, and Yuri provided a slightly surreal impression of a Stax horn section. As the credits rolled Ivo took off on an interplanetary solo, while I sat grinning in the control room. An ambition born on the Thracian plain, fulfilled.

⌖

a bell, sunken in a mountain lake,
which suddenly begins to ring,
the pilgrim's staff began to bloom,
the flute that caused to sound whole orchestras

—Géza Képes, "Bartók's String Quartet No. 5"

In the late 1960s, an ethnographer named György Martin proposed a radical idea to the Bartók Ensemble (a Hungarian folk-dance company sponsored by the Chemical Workers' Union): that they go to the countryside and see how the actual "folk" dance. The group was fascinated by their first glimpse of village style and made repeated visits, unlearning everything they had been taught, finding freedom where there had been regimentation. There were, however, no musicians in Budapest who could replicate village dance music and no well-recorded discs of the music.

They eventually came across avant-gardists Béla Halmos and Ferenc Sebő. A theater director had asked them to set some ancient Chinese texts to music; they tried, as avant-gardists will, hitting the strings of a Chinese instrument with a stick. Someone pointed out that the *gardon*, an instrument shaped like a cross between a small cello and a guitar, was still struck that way in rural Hungarian communities in eastern Transylvania. Like a good academic, Sebő went to the library and attempted what he assumed would be the straightforward task of learning about traditional instruments from a book.

He and Halmos soon realized that you can't play folk music off the page, at least not so that anyone can dance to it. Hungarian radio had long banned authentic folk music on the grounds that it was "unpleasant," but a rock musician named Péter Éri led them to his father-in-law's apartment, where they huddled around a tape recorder like dissidents listening to a talk by Andrei Sakharov. The field recordings they heard astonished them; thus began a journey that led to a "dance house" in Szék, across the border in the Romanian province of Transylvania, where many villages still had such things. By the fourth day of a big wedding, the local musicians were so exhausted they would have been happy for any kind of assistance and allowed Halmos and Sebő to sit in. As Halmos triumphantly reported, "They did not beat us up."

Once the pair began playing for the Bartók Ensemble, crowds flocked to their shows, outraging other ensembles, who accused them of primitivism. They challenged members of the state ensemble to a now-legendary 1972 dance-off where a huge crowd turned up to witness the official group's humiliation. The delighted audience demanded to learn the steps as well, so the Bartók leaders announced that the following week, lessons would be given at 6:30, followed by a dance starting at 7:30. The dance-house—or *táncház*—movement was born.

We must drink our fill not from your silver goblets, but from cool mountain springs.

—Béla Bartók

In 1825, Count István Széchenyi horrified the nobles of the Budapest Diet by addressing them not in German but Hungarian. Gradually, Magyars began to realize that only by embracing their native language could they prevent the complete Germanization of the Habsburg Empire. Music was at the heart of this resistance, with Franz Liszt as central to the Hungarian national question in the nineteenth century as Béla Bartók would become in the twentieth.

Liszt had studied in Paris with an unsung hero: Anton Reicha was a pal of Beethoven's, a frustrated composer-turned-teacher who urged both Liszt and Berlioz to study folk music. Reicha was ahead of his time in recognizing the inadequacy of written transcriptions; he told Liszt to go to the countryside and listen to musicians play rather than read melodies off a page. Franz wasn't much of a country boy, but he did seek out Roma virtuosos, including the violinist János Bihari, who inspired the *Hungarian Rhapsodies* and provided a flamboyant example for Paganini and Liszt to follow. As the pianist embarked on the concert tours that made him the world's first megastar (complete with autograph hunters, fainting female fans, and bodyguards) he never ceased to talk up Hungarian music, language, and nationhood. The youthful revolutionaries of 1848 he inspired would end up being crushed by the royalty-defending Russian army (foreshadowing the commissar-defending Soviet suppression of Hungary's 1956 Revolution), but they left a legacy of a Hungarian-speaking parliament in a reformed Austro-Hungarian Empire and a class-wide pride in all things Magyar.

Béla Bartók was born in 1881 in Nagyszentmiklós ("Greater St. Michael," then part of Hungary but Romanian since 1920) to a Hungarian father and a German mother. Languages spoken in the local marketplace included Hungarian, Romanian, Serbian, German, and Romani. In 1899, he enrolled at the Royal Academy of Music in Budapest. The capital repelled him: the noise, the bustle, and, not least, the Hungarian aristocrats, German officials, and wealthy Jews who dominated the capital's cultural life. (Though Bartók resented the power of Jewish patronage, he always rejected anti-Semitism; as Stravinsky was petitioning to be removed from Hitler's list of banned composers, Bartók demanded to be added to it.)

Having just celebrated the thousand-year anniversary of the Magyar invasion and settlement of the Danube valley, turn-of-the-century Hungary was full of strutting national pride. Bartók's patriotism was fierce but often at odds with the official version. In searching for a musical reflection of his feelings for the homeland, he began by deciding what he disliked most. His hostility towards Budapest's fashionable elite may have stemmed in part from being made to feel like a country bumpkin, but he particularly loathed the "gypsy" music that most urbanites heard as perfectly Hungarian. His resentment of the subservient position of Hungary in the Austrian-dominated Habsburg Empire found its expression in a growing aversion to the Germanic musical forms he had been taught. (His first published work had been a piano arrangement of Richard Strauss's *Ein Heldenleben*.) He joined the battle over the right of Hungarian soldiers to receive commands in their own language and forbade his mother to speak German at home.

During a stay in Paris he opened the door to non-Germanic role models by immersing himself in Debussy. At the Louvre, he discovered Murillo's *The Beggar Boy*, "fine" art whose subject was peasant simplicity. In a perfect irony, reading *The Lower Depths* by Maxim Gorky (the man who tried to eradicate rural culture in the Soviet Union) turned Bartók's gaze towards the music of the Hungarian countryside. The final key to his musical destiny was turned in 1906, when he moved to the village of Gerlicepuszta and hired a Transylvanian servant girl who sang as she worked. Bartók was fascinated; her melodies were beautifully strange and pentatonic, nothing like the *nota* and other kitsch heard in Budapest. He announced a new objective: "I shall collect all the most beautiful Hungarian folk songs and raise them to the level of art songs by providing them with the best possible piano accompaniments."

"National" composers such as Grieg, Szymanowski, Janáček, and Sibelius had already embarked on this path, but Bartók's mission quickly grew more ambitious: to document not just the melodies of Hungarian villages but, by listening closely to rural singers and instrumentalists, how they were actually performed. It hadn't occurred to anyone that rural music might be worth hearing before it passed through the pen of a trained composer; for Bartók, folk music "attains an unsurpassable degree of perfection and beauty to be found nowhere else except in the great works of the classics." He had an advantage over other collectors; his perfect ear and quick mind could notate the rural musicians' complex rhythms and nuances of melody on the fly. When portable recording equipment was developed, he quickly acquired a set.

His fellow collector and lifelong ally Zoltán Kodály had already ventured into the countryside. Both were shocked by how deeply corny nota compositions had penetrated village life and how rapidly the ancient songs and rhythms seemed to be disappearing; in 1907, the pair launched an appeal for funds to preserve untainted music. Like Paul Simon in Johannesburg, Bartók found traditional musicians' metric structures to be challengingly flexible, expanding and contracting as the mood struck. As Alex Ross observes in *The Rest Is Noise*, Bartók "came to understand rural music as a kind of archaic avant-garde." He loved the elaborate time signatures of the dances, the improvisational freedom, and the ancient sound of their harmonies, and believed that the strangeness of folk art could disrupt accepted notions of what constituted modernity.

Schoenberg and the Viennese School insisted that their twelve-tone system represented an inevitable future and that anything melodic or easy on the ear was a retreat into the sentimentality of an obsolete world. For much of his composing life, Bartók vehemently rejected this, marrying classical structures to the melodies, rhythms, and eccentricities of peasant music. His field recordings guided him to a new approach to harmony just as folk-hating Schoenberg was developing his twelve-tone scale. Rural music, said Bartók, "showed me how I could free myself completely from the hegemony of the system of major/minor."

He found kindred spirits in other disciplines. Architects Károly Kós and Ödön Lechner, whose buildings help give Budapest its distinctive character today, were creating structures based on rural designs. Aladár Körösfői Kriesch, painter of the gorgeous murals in the Liszt Academy concert hall, wrote that "the art of the Hungarian people, like all true art, is a fully organic part of the life of the people. It is called primitive because it is innocent of falsehood and opportunism."

In Paris, Bartók had befriended a group of Hungarian painters known as the Eight; he would later give piano recitals at their Budapest openings and hire them to create sets for his operas. Led by Bartók and the Eight, Hungarian modernism became a new way of looking at the ancient spirit that grew from the soil, just as Herder said it would. He wanted to create music in which Hungarian listeners could recognise the voice of their own culture. Unsurprisingly, these efforts often fell on deaf ears; working-class audiences at his free concerts found it incomprehensible and refused to keep quiet.

> [W]e are dealing with an individual gone astray, a perverted, pathological, disingenuous traitor to the fatherland, a decadent and a sansculotte.
>
> —Gyula Fodor, reviewing Bartók's *The Wooden Prince*

Bartók's patriotism placed no limits on the range of his musical interests; he traveled to Algeria on a collecting venture and remained fascinated by Romanian, Bulgarian, Turkish, and African music. Such open-mindedness clashed with the mood of inter-war Hungary, so bitter about losing much of its territory in the 1920 Trianon Treaty. (Queen Victoria's favorite granddaughter, Marie of Romania, looking gorgeous in low-cut gowns, had cut a swathe through the gathered diplomats, negotiating a doubling of her country's size with the addition of the largely Hungarian-speaking region of Transylvania.) Bartók defied the nationalists by celebrating "racial impurity" and the mingling of cultures, styles, and people. He taught himself Romanian and Slovak so he could follow songs as they migrated across ethnic boundaries. His sympathies were always with the underdog: Hungary against the Habsburgs, peasants against the gentry, the village against Budapest, minorities against the fascists.

Throughout the twenties and thirties, Bartók maintained a combative relationship with critics and listeners. Not only did audiences often find his work difficult, many were offended by its glorification of the peasantry; the idea that their culture might be represented abroad by such works appalled them. Singers sometimes refused to perform his compositions: "These melodies are meant for the tavern." Others were repelled by his openness to Romanian, Turkish, and Arab music: "Bartók has become the servant of alien spirits . . . devoured by foreign influence," claimed *Budapest News*. To progressives, he was a hero; for inter-war intellectuals, attitudes towards Bartók became a means of self-definition.

∽

I never liked his music anyway.

—Igor Stravinsky on hearing of Bartók's death in 1945

Stravinsky and Bartók met twice. At their first encounter, in Paris in 1921, the Russian told the Hungarian he was done with folk music; from now on, all his compositions would be "completely objective" and "devoid of human expression." Bartók thought this neither possible nor desirable; even Bach, he insisted, was emotional—and human! In 1926, the Budapest Symphony invited Stravinsky to perform his *Concerto for Piano and Wind Instruments*. Bartók and his wife, Ditta Pásztory, were impressed but conflicted by the all-Stravinsky program. "Now I know quite exactly what the new direction is," wrote Pásztory, "there is absolutely no room for feelings . . . bare rhythm, bare hammering . . . truly one gets caught up in his miraculously beautiful-timbred machine music." Bartók supported Stravinsky's rejection of Wagner-Strauss Romanticism but had no desire to create "machine music."

Stravinsky, for his part, was condescending: "I never could share his lifelong gusto for his native folklore. It was real and touching, but I couldn't help regretting it in a great musician." As the thirties wore on, Bartók seems to have been intimidated into moving towards the Vienna School despite himself: "All the tangled chaos that the musical periodicals vomit thick and fast . . . come to weigh heavily on me: the watchwords, linear, horizontal, vertical, objective, impersonal, polyphonic, homophonic, tonal, polytonal, atonal, and the rest . . . one . . . becomes quite dazed when they shout it in our ears so much." Among the many points Hitler and Stalin agreed upon was a horror of modernist music; with such enemies, joining the serialists must have been hard to resist, even though audiences had failed to respond. For modernists, the public was at fault for their "discomfort with the truth" and failing to confront "the apparently 'logical' consequences of the historical evolution"; Adorno viewed tonality as "shameful" and "a narcotic illusionism and an aesthetic inducement to collaboration with real evil." Getting booed was a necessary stage in restoring music's "ethical power." Schoenberg agreed: radical modernism was essential "to make our souls function again as they must if mankind is to evolve any higher." Adorno and Schoenberg hated Bartók for seeming to embrace modernism while clinging to the melodic and harmonic "clichés" of folk sources. Their arguments seemed to mask a conviction that the "inexorable European tradition" was whatever German composers said it was, looking down from their Teutonic heights on composers from "small" cultures.

When Bartók's mother passed away in 1940, he and Ditta decamped to America, escaping Europe just as two decades of bitter battles on political and cultural fronts climaxed in war. Despite the death sentence of a leukemia diagnosis, Bartók's American compositions approach the tonal sweetness of his early years. He even mocked the twelve-tone police with a "serial" composition (in which the theme includes every note of the Western scale used once and not repeated) that is beautifully melodic. Bartók's death in 1945 spared him witnessing the repression of Hungarian culture by its post-war communist government, which lionized him as an anti-fascist hero but criticized his music for "formalism."

The post-war decades in Western Europe were salad days for dissonance as the US State Department sponsored the annual Darmstadt Festival to curry favor with European intellectuals. The event became a feeding frenzy for the avant-garde, where Pierre Boulez, Edgard Varèse, Karlheinz Stockhausen, and Luigi Nono flourished; Bartók's music was shunted into the unfashionable or impermissible long grass on both sides of the Iron Curtain. Only in the wake of the failed 1956 Revolution was Bartók celebrated as a national hero and compositions from all phases of his career performed again in his homeland.

In his obituary, Bence Szabolcsi wrote that Bartók

> burst into Western music with the folk music of Eastern Europe, as if leading an army of Huns . . . Bartók only learned what he knew already . . . [that folk music] only appears to be simple . . . The one thing he could never abandon . . . was the Timeless Music of the peoples and of the great masters of old, in which he always recognized his kin . . . [H]e did so just in time to save the real soul of Europe, in time to be the representative of our perishing world's nobler, more immortal portions . . .

∽

"Freedom of national cultural expression" was a key item in the sixteen-point student manifesto of October 22, 1956, that triggered the Hungarian uprising. Soviet archives reveal that Khrushchev was prepared to grant many of their demands, but nationalist stirrings in Romania and Bulgaria made Soviet generals—like US militarists in Vietnam—paranoid about a domino effect. The "middle way" imposed on post-1956 Hungary seemed, for a time, a workable compromise. Russian troops remained, but seldom left their bases. (Those who ventured out alone sometimes ended up facedown in a ditch.) The economy was liberalized, but for music, bland state ensembles and corny violins were as much "national cultural expression" as the regime allowed. In 1964, after much academic arm-twisting, the state record label, Hungaroton, released a limited-edition box set of Bartók and Kodály field recordings; the thousand-copy printing sold out immediately and they were forced to re-press.

The táncház movement that followed befuddled the authorities: it had no precedent, wasn't conceived at a party meeting, and didn't fit into the dialectical process. Hungarian youth were creating something entirely on their own, based simply on the experience of taking part in a movement that was vibrant, sexy and organically rather than conceptually communal. A fundamental problem for the government was that the source for much of this music lay in Romanian Transylvania; Stalin's long-term plan after World War Two was to absorb Eastern bloc countries into the Soviet Union, just as the Baltic, Central Asian, and Caucasian states had been. To accomplish this, the Soviets needed to break down cultural distinctions, so any over-stimulation of national or minority identity was anathema.

Transylvania is Hungary's equivalent of America's Deep South, the wellspring of what it means, musically at least, to be Magyar. In the early seventies, it was a land ignored by time, where peasants wore handmade clothing out of a Breughel painting. Handmade music, too, was woven into the fabric of life; though the songs themselves were not subversive, the influx of educated young people, spreading out across northwest Romania with fiddles and tape recorders, made both governments very uneasy. That the Hungarian-speaking population lived side by side with Romanians, Roma, and Saxons (descended from German mercenaries sent to guard the Hungarian kingdom against the Turks in the twelfth century) made ethnic questions even more sensitive.

In 1978, there were twenty-five urban traditional bands in the dance-house movement; by 1983, the number had soared to sixty. Eager to distance themselves from "restaurant music," they adhered to the "lack of sentimentality" Bartók had noted in village musicians. The culture ministry always presented folk music as something easy to sing and simple to dance to, so emphasizing the complexity of the real thing was defiant as well as challenging. Tánchaz workshops and summer camps sprang up; everyone wanted to get really good at it. What other urban folk revival could claim to have spawned music with the same social functions as the original?

When Dániel Hamar was a young classical bassist, his dream was to visit the West and meet girls. He figured his best bet lay in joining one of the official folk-dance ensembles and putting up with the boring music in return for the chance of a trip outside the Eastern bloc. His reward arrived in 1973 with an invitation to an Italian Communist Party youth festival in Sicily. There was a performance on the first day by an Argentine company and Dáni couldn't believe what he saw—*the freedom! the sexiness! the exuberance!* Nothing in his ensemble's repertoire came even close. Back in Budapest, he found his way to the Bartók Ensemble's weekly táncház, where he witnessed Hungarian moves as exciting as those of the Latin and African companies he had experienced in Italy. Official Hungarian choreography was childishly bland, danced to toned-down rhythms devoid of sensuality. Village dancing *in situ* is fiercely flirtatious, despite the multilayered skirts covering girls' legs to mid-calf; the whole point of many maneuvers seemed to be to send those skirts flying. According to the culture ministry, village dancing was "vulgar" and "not art." Dániel wanted in, but like all other dance-house musicians, he would have to learn the steps and become a dancer; only then could he join a band.

At first Dáni felt uncomfortable playing with his new friends; there were no written parts! After repeated listening to field recordings, the music "came into my heart, it was so good." One by one, the young men who would join him in creating Muzsikás, the group that would define the dance-house era, emerged into view. Péter Éri, whose father-in-law had played those field recordings to Halmas and Sebő, encouraged his rock band to try playing a folk dance, and the music's power astonished them. Sándor Csoóri, a celebrated poet who often wrote of the old ways, had moved his family to Transylvania, where they lived as peasants. When a Budapest violinist, Mihály Sipos, visited Szék to hear the music at source, he met Csoóri's son, *kontra* player Sándor Jr., who offered to teach him the dance steps. Sipos was struck by how participatory everything was; even during instrumental passages, dancers would sing the well-known songs, and seemed to bloom as they did, growing more radiant by the verse.

Each of these four came at the music from a different angle; when they decided to form a band, they were committed to learning the context of what they played, understanding the cycles of village life from which this music grew. The name they chose is Transylvanian dialect for "musicians." There is no escaping that these were middle-class intellectuals—a geophysicist, a mathematician, an artist, and an ethnographer—drawn to a culture closer to the soil than they could ever be. But their rapport with village musicians was always collegial, treating them as masters at whose feet they came to study, just as one would learn from a jazz or classical virtuoso.

Muzsikás made their first record for Hungaroton in 1978. When authorities noticed that the songs were sourced from all corners of the Magyar-speaking lands, including the western fringes of the USSR, label bosses were reprimanded and it would be eight years before another Muzsikás LP appeared. By then they had begun touring abroad, pleased to discover that audiences anywhere could appreciate Hungarian dance music. The next two additions to the Muzsikás team would lift them into international stardom.

~

> People think folk music is for old situations. I think that's rubbish because the basic human and emotional situations are still the same. If you say people have to respect this music of your ancestors—people shit on that. But if it touches the heart it will be remembered forever.
>
> —Márta Sebestyén

Zoltán Kodály devoted much of his life to implanting the study of Hungarian folk music in school curricula. In 1937, the Catholic Church attacked him for corrupting innocents by exposing them to folk songs, but his prestige, determination, and diplomatic personality helped avoid confrontations with both fascists and communists. The latter, predictably, stripped his courses of all reference to rhythms, and students were never allowed to hear recordings of actual performances.

Ilona Farkas, a teacher who worked closely with Kodály, immersed her daughter Márta in Hungarian song from an early age. Her economist husband, József Sebestyén, brought home a set of Smithsonian Institute recordings of Hungarian folk music after attending a conference in Washington. Most schoolchildren learned a dozen or so folk songs; by the time she was twelve, Márta could sing almost two hundred. Her prize for winning a national competition was a copy of that Bartók and Kodály box set.

The voice emanating from the gramophone after Ralph Fiennes's seduction of Kristin Scott Thomas in *The English Patient* belongs to Márta Sebestyén. By the late seventies, she had become táncház's star; to her mother's influence and the recordings she studied so intently, she added Bartók and Kodály transcriptions and, eventually, rural treks in the composers' footsteps. She met aged singers and learned how they delivered the songs. Like Bartók, Sebestyén has an extraordinary ear; she can imitate—sometimes in wicked mockery—almost any accent, pattern of speech, or melodic decoration. From this mix of talents, influences, and hard work (plus perfect pitch and a rich, clear, and distinctive voice), she forged a style that came to define how most Hungarians now hear their folk songs. It is difficult to find a young vocalist in the country today who does not wear Márta's influence on their sleeve. By the late seventies, Muzsikás was táncház's dominant group, and inevitably Márta began performing with them. For more than twenty years, they toured and recorded together, a musical collaboration made in heaven (but a mix of temperaments cooked up in another location).

The other new contributor came from an unlikely place. In the mid-eighties, Levente Szörényi, lead singer of Illés, Hungary's most famous rock band, approached Muzsikás about making a record. On the strength of his involvement, Hungaroton's pop department agreed to lift the unwritten ban on the group. (State organizations were not monolithic and high-level sympathy for táncház was widespread, if not loudly shouted.) Szörényi added production savvy; the new record could never be accused of being fusion, but he recorded them with a close-mic'd warmth rare in pure folk recordings and added subtle touches that give it a hip edge. (When someone applying for a job at Hannibal Records told me the electric bass entrance halfway through that LP's "Fly Bird" was one of her all-time favorite musical moments, I hired her.)

After listening to the copy I brought back from my trip to Budapest and Koprivshtitsa in 1986, I approached Hungaroton about licensing it and began arranging Muzsikás tours of the UK and US. "Muzsikás featuring Márta Sebestyén" was the billing we agreed on, and with their combination of personalities and intense virtuosity, they became that rare phenomenon, a group celebrated both within their culture and outside.

While most young urban Hungarians revered the group, a review of *The Prisoner's Song* (Hannibal's title) in New York's *Soho News* revealed a sobering truth. The critic had a second-generation Hungarian pal; they took a train out to Magyar-filled New Brunswick, NJ, and played the album for a gathering of his parents and their friends, most of whom had left Hungary in 1956 or earlier. This focus group absolutely hated the record, finding the music vulgar and shamefully "peasant-like." When they wanted to be reminded of home, some Roma violins or schooled voices singing nota would do just fine. But the son—and the reviewer—loved it.

∽

When Hungary began deportations to Auschwitz in the spring of 1944, the Jews of rural Transylvania were the first to go. Few survived. In 1946, Zoltán Kodály found some Roma musicians in the Máramaros region who had performed for Jewish weddings and purims before the war, all that remained of what had been for centuries a vibrant culture. Following Kodály's trail nearly five decades later, Muzsikás came across Árpád Toni and Gheorghe Covaci, two elderly Roma who remembered the songs and dances they'd performed with their fathers at Jewish functions in the 1930s. I encouraged Muzsikás to make an album with them and the result was *Máramaros: The Lost Jewish Music of Transylvania*. Toni, a dapper man with a Lothario's mustache, joined the group in London for a *Máramaros* concert; he attacked the table-sized *cimbalom* with gusto, stealing the show with Django-esque solos. *Máramaros* became the first CD stocked by the Holocaust Museum in Washington DC, and Muzsikás's best-selling recording.

With his limited equipment, Bartók had only documented solo vocalists and instrumentalists, giving little hint of the power of a Carpathian band in full cry. In 1995, Muzsikás took part in a Bartók festival at Bard College in New York state; the classical audience had never heard those familiar melodies performed by a traditional group and went wild when the *csardas* rhythms kicked in. This encounter inspired *The Bartók Album*, a collaboration with the Balanescu Quartet built around songs and dances the composer had recorded and adapted, juxtaposing original village versions with what the composer had crafted from them. By the end of the century, sharing bills with classical pianists, string quartets, and orchestras had become central to Muzsikás's work, which was useful, since by then the group and Márta were barely on speaking terms. They continued to appear together occasionally, but a US tour with the Takács String Quartet (including a memorable 2008 Carnegie Hall concert) marked the sad end of their long and fruitful partnership.

Such encounters brought into focus the huge gap in feel between village music and how classical adaptations are normally performed. In 2004, a concert in Glasgow featuring Muzsikás and the BBC Scottish Symphony called for the group to intersperse traditional Transylvanian dances with orchestral performances of the Bartók, Kodály, and Ligeti works they inspired. I arrived that afternoon to find Dániel and the conductor, Ilan Volkov, looking glum; despite two days of rehearsal, both felt the orchestra had failed to grasp the spirit of the music. Those preparations hadn't included the two dancers, who arrived around the same time I did. Zoltán "Batyu" Farkas and his wife, Ildikó "Fecske" Tóth, had met in the Hungarian State Folk Ensemble and left in 1984 to start their own company, the Kodály Chamber Dance Ensemble. Batyu and Fecske are the terpsichorean equivalent of Muzsikás and Márta, bringing athleticism and training plus an outsider's determination to an ancient folk art; their spins and twirls crackle with sexual energy.

What transpired that evening was alchemical. Muzsikás set up to one side in front of the orchestra, leaving space for the dancers. You could see both audience and orchestra move to the edge of their chairs as Fecske began to whirl and Batyu started his boot-slapping and high kicks. When Volkov mounted the podium to conduct Bartók's *Romanian Folk Dances*, the orchestra was the opposite of uninspired. The dancing had transformed everyone's perception of Bartók's music. In the *Glasgow Herald*, Michael Tumelty wrote:

> Amazing scenes last night... as two Hungarian folk dancers pounded the floor and scythed the air ... a hair-raising climax to one of the most original events of recent times... Ilan Volkov and BBC Scottish Symphony Orchestra added Bartók's own virile, driving orchestration of the folk dance to what was already an irresistibly thrilling brew. To say the performance was high-voltage is to come nowhere near catching the electric atmosphere ... an event that had the capacity Tramway crowd stomping the floor and baying for more. Even those of us who think we know where Bartók was coming from ... must

have been gobsmacked as we heard the originals played by Muzsikás, each number underlining how the genius of Bartók preserved . . . the essence and spirit of the . . . original.

Volkov told me afterwards how stunned he was by the change from afternoon to evening. Pianists, string quartets, conductors: all who have collaborated with Muzsikás vouch for how the experience has altered their approach to Bartók's music. Silent film exists of the composer staring at village dancers' feet, and you can hear it in many of his compositions. I doubt he could ever have imagined a group of trained urban musicians—people like him, in other words—absorbing village playing styles and bringing them to the concert stage. He also would have been startled by how alive the sources remained nearly a century after he and Kodály sounded their tocsin over the disappearance of village traditions.

By the 1970s, Transylvanian villagers who had once eyed folklorists and tune-hunting composers with suspicion were greeting táncház youth with open arms; Ceauşescu's Romanian government was doing everything it could to stifle rural culture, so outside enthusiasm was invigorating. Hearing themselves back on recordings helped raise performance standards in the countryside, while both sides benefited from urban-rural jam sessions. In 1989, I visited a Budapest táncház that had bused in virtually an entire village to join them for the evening. Transylvanian musicians joined the revival band, men in handmade traditional dress danced with miniskirted students, and the women sold crafts, embroidered fabrics, preserves, and homebrew; urbanites and villagers seemed equally moved by the experience.

The basic line-up of the Carpathian basin (which extends from southern Poland and western Ukraine down through Hungary and Romanian Transylvania into Serbian Vojvodina, taking in bits of Croatia and Slovakia) consists of one or two violins, one or two *kontras* (flat-bridged violas), and a bowed bass. Vienna, lying at the western edge of the region, absorbed this template for the classical string quartet. Aside from "written" versus "improvised," classical and folk part company in the rhythm provided by bass and kontra. The latter's flat bridge facilitates bowed chords; the aggressively traded strokes of kontra and bass provide the pulse that gives the traditional version of this music its danceable essence.

At a festival in Budapest in the early nineties I heard a Transylvanian group from Szászcsávás, a regional center for Roma musicians; when anyone needs a band for a wedding or dance, they recruit there like a straw boss rounding up day laborers on a Texas street corner. While it is tempting to compare táncház bands to White blues players in America, the cultural leap is never as great for an urban Hungarian as it is for a middle-class White kid trying to channel the Delta. That evening, though, I realized that the rhythmic gap can be similar; the Transylvanian bassist leans as far back on the beat as one of James Brown's or Al Green's drummers. Like blue-eyed soul boys, táncház players lack the laid-back certainty to wait that nanosecond longer on the stroke.

One night during the festival, I spent an hour with Ferenc Csángáló, the Szászcsávás Band's kontra player, as he jammed with a mix of brass and string players. Rarely have I experienced such intense musicianship at close range. In one vertical stroke across the strings, flicks of Csángáló's wrist could articulate ten rapid-fire beats. He was impatient to go in search of a drink and kept handing his instrument to a junior member of the band, but could never make it past the doorway. He'd pause, listening to how his sub was faring; cursing, he would charge back into the room and seize the instrument. The instant it was in his hands, the music's rhythmic intensity would elevate several notches. Unforgettable.

On a summer evening in 1987, I walked up four crumbling flights of stairs to a hall in an old building on the campus of Budapest University. The first half of the evening was a brilliant combination of jazz and modern dance, with a slightly surreal, subversive feel about it. The second part was pure tradition, with Muzsikás and Márta providing the music and the same dancers now wearing folk costumes and performing csárdás. The finale was an old Transylvanian wedding song; when the

Hungarian girl I was with heard the opening lines, she—and many others in the audience—gasped. Under her breath, she explained the words of "Eddig vendég" (The Unwelcome Guest): *You've drunk all the wine, eaten all the food, spoiled the party, so please now leave.* The taunting of the crumbling Soviet empire was daringly in the air.

It is tempting to overstate the Party's opposition to tánchaz. There are tales of tapped phones and organizers being followed by men in trenchcoats or summoned for questioning. But many officials were quietly proud of the movement's Hungarianness, and no one ended up in a gulag. True believers of an older communist generation were certainly hostile; they understood what the dancers also sensed, that (curious as it may seem to Westerners for whom folk dance almost defines "square") tánchaz touched the same nerve as rock; it was honest, free, and sensual and its popularity held ominous implications for the future of Soviet rule in Hungary.

Roy Guest, a concert promoter friend of mine from London, spent the summer of 1968 in Bratislava, Czechoslovakia, celebrating the Prague Spring by organizing an outdoor stage for folk and rock concerts. In early August, he and his team were forced to stand aside when Leonid Brezhnev convened an emergency meeting of COMECON leaders in the Slovakian city and their stage got submerged under a reviewing stand for the obligatory military parade. Roy had a close-up view as dark-suited Gomułka, Ceaușescu, Ulbricht, Kádár, Zhivkov, and Brezhnev emerged from black ZiL limousines and took their places, sweating grimly in the sun with their burly bodyguards, awaiting Alexander Dubček. When a small Škoda pulled up, the Czech leader emerged from the driver's seat wearing a blue linen suit with a flower in the lapel. There were no bodyguards. He strolled over to the crowd, kissed a few babies and their mothers, then skipped up the steps to the podium. Roy glanced at the assembled leaders; their facial expressions, he told me, made it clear they would opt for military intervention. He and his crew began dismantling the stage the next day and left for London just before the tanks rolled in.

In August 1990, my first visit to the Soviet Union found me, slightly dazed after consecutive overnight flights, wandering near a large yurt outside Alma-Ata (now Almaty) in Kazakhstan and gazing up at the snow-capped Altai Mountains. Marijuana was growing everywhere. (Excavations of Siberian burial mounds have revealed kings interred with sacrificial wives and horses along with large sacks of pot to keep them cool in the afterlife.) Behind the yurt, a small flock of sheep chewed contentedly on the hemp, providing a sedative buzz, I hoped, in advance of their impending fate; each time I came out for air their number had shrunk as the jury and officials of the Azia Dausy music festival feasted on roast mutton. Our host was Zamanbek Nurkadilov, mayor of the city, founder of the festival, and chairman of the jury. In the wake of the Wall's fall the previous autumn, he had grown concerned that local bands were using their new freedom to slavishly emulate Western hard rock and pop. He decided that a competition rewarding the most imaginative updating of Soviet Asian traditions might help stem the tide: first prize a Lada sedan.

The mayor had the good sense to ask Artemy Troitsky for help in winnowing down the entries into a first-round selection of forty-two groups and soloists. Troitsky is a unique figure in Russian musical history; after organizing underground events in the early eighties, he became glasnost's musical ambassador, chronicling Soviet rock for readers at home and abroad. (He now lives in exile.) Troitsky convinced the mayor that a foreign judging panel was essential since everyone knew that politics, cronyism, and bribery were integral to the deliberations of any Soviet jury. I received a crackly telephone invitation, followed by an Aeroflot ticket.

The outlanders included two Yanks, two Brits, a Moroccan, a Pole, a Mexican, a Canadian, and a Japanese, plus Troitsky and the mayor. We quickly rejected Roza Rymbayeva, a local singer whose idea of modernizing Kazakh music was to wear an elaborate traditional costume while singing derivative disco. It was subsequently revealed that not only was she Kazakhstan's biggest pop star, but also the mayor's mistress. Nurkadilov accepted the vote without complaint, unlike the delegation of angry Muslims complaining about our elimination of a singer from Turkmenistan who sang lyrics from the Koran.

Being a jury member was not child's play. For four nights, an evening concert in a huge ice-skating stadium in the mountains above the city would be followed by hours of deliberation. At midnight an enormous banquet was served, consisting largely of dried, cured, and roasted horsemeat. Courses were interspersed with ritual toasts, translated line-by-line into whichever two of English, Russian, and Kazakh the speaker hadn't used. As we waited for the last vodka-chased speech to finish around three in the morning, my fellow juror, former Pink Floyd manager Peter Jenner, cracked that we were being "held toastage." At nine the following morning, a bus would arrive to take us on a tour of a local rug factory or historic monument.

Finalists included two Kazakh bands, a Mongolian group featuring throat-singing over feedback guitar, a Daghestani girl, two Uzbek outfits, an Alma-Ata-based Russian, a Kirghizian, two Tuvan entries, and a Yakutian heavy metal band. The last represented a curiosity from the final years of the USSR and the random perseverance of folk traditions across its vast territory; Choron were the tip of a Yakut heavy metal iceberg.

Yakuts are a fascinating, tragic people. Their capital, Yakutsk, located in the far north of Siberia, is said to be the world's least hospitable city. The average January temperature is thirty degrees below zero (the point where Centigrade and Fahrenheit cross on the way down), while broiling summers inspire remarkably aggressive mosquitoes and blackflies. Why would anyone live there? Gold and silver have been the lure since the nineteenth century, but the tale of how the Yakuts ended up there was told to me during the festival over an endlessly refilled mug of vodka and confirmed by Anna Reid's excellent Siberian history, *The Shaman's Coat*.

As Genghis Khan's Golden Horde pushed westward in the thirteenth century, Yakuts were among many groups displaced from their traditional grazing pastures on the hilly steppe north of Mongolia. Desperate to escape, they built a fleet of rafts by the banks of a rapid west-flowing river, loaded the entire community onto them, and set off. When the river took a northward turn, they weren't too bothered—rivers meander, don't they? But as the Lena grew wider and faster, it was clearly headed for the Arctic Ocean. Eventually, they gave up and disembarked, trapped with no way back through the impenetrable forest.

Over time, their traditions blended with local rituals, often involving psychedelic fly agaric mushrooms. When Gorbachev's reforms took the bridle off Soviet popular culture, Yakutian heavy metal complete with shamanic chants, dry-ice fog, and pentatonic power chords gripped the imaginations of many Soviet youths.

Choron lost out to a group whose tape Troitsky had plucked from the "unsolicited" pile. Kars, from a poor town in south Uzbekistan, were among the least-connected and most obscure of the contestants. At the closing-night party (where we danced to an excellent Chuck Berry cover band), jury members were smothered in embraces from contestants, journalists, and fans who could scarcely believe such an impartial competition had taken place. The finalists' music had all been pretty good, imaginatively fulfilling the brief, despite the Soviet mindset and technical limitations that meant most performances were mimed or sung to backing tracks.

One exception was a young man with long black hair and dark glasses who walked alone to the microphone holding a small knife and a flat stone. After building up a rhythm scraping the blade across the rock, he began growling the harsh, impossibly low tones of Tuvan chant. This was my first encounter with Albert Kuvezin, throat singer and rock star. That night he seemed to be something of an eccentric outlier; certainly no one would have imagined that of all the music from the (soon former) USSR, Tuvan throat-singing would become the biggest success in the international arena.

The course of the Soviet bloc's musical traditions since then has been mostly catastrophic, with the few bright spots largely down to the intervention of reformed rockers or quixotic idealists. (Kuvezin qualifies as both.) The post-Soviet fate of music, of course, is but the least of it. Following independence, Nurkadilov, the forward-thinking mayor who chaired our jury with such an even hand, became disillusioned with his friend President Nursultan Nazarbayev and took a leading role with an opposition party. In 2005, just before a national election, a gunman entered his home in the middle of the night and shot him dead. No one has ever been charged with the crime.

When Indiana Jones reaches Kali's underground lair in *The Temple of Doom*, the soundtrack threatens danger with a chanted *basso* drone. The rumble of the human voice at the bottom of its sonic well seems to evoke alien spirituality as much as menace; the Christian equivalent is often expressed by the boy sopranos of an Anglican church or the falsetto-studded passion of African-American gospel singing. (Russian Orthodoxy shows its Asian roots with the prevalence of the bass voice.) The best-known cellar-dwelling chants are Buddhist; Mickey Hart of the Grateful Dead produced a recording of the Tibetan Gyuto monks that became a world music hit in the late eighties.

Some Tibetan monks can sing a triad. No, really. It requires a good twenty years of meditation on the overtones of their *Om*, but individuals have been known to bring first one, then two higher notes into audible focus. This is no party trick but a metaphor for achieving higher planes of spirituality. (Scientists have confirmed the extraordinary level of larynx control possessed by these monks.) Kuvezin was bringing his overtones into focus that night in Alma-Ata, one of them a high whistle that seemed to come from a ghost standing behind him, or perhaps a collaborative avian hiding in his cloak.

My favorite stamps in a short-lived childhood collection were the colorful triangles from Tannu-Tuva. As a map fiend, I was aware of the location of this briefly independent country just inside the Russian border north of Mongolia; culturally, however, it was terra incognita. The Nobel Prize–winning quantum physicist Richard Feynman was similarly intrigued; those exotic stamps plus the fact that by one calculation, Tuva lay at the geographical center of Asia (and had a capital named Kyzyl) inspired Feynman and his friend Ralph Leighton to write a letter "to whom it may concern, Kyzyl, Tuva, USSR." The quest became an obsession; Feynman's California license plate read "TOUVA" and he would sign off correspondence with "*Tuva or Bust!*" though, as the region was not on any Intourist itinerary, the Soviets kept refusing their visa applications. From 1977 to 1988, Leighton and Feynman kept up a barrage of subterfuges and pleas; just as the visas were finally approved, Feynman died of cancer, aged sixty-nine. Leighton persuaded the organizers of Pasadena's Rose Parade to invite three Tuvans to ride in the 1993 event in memory of Feynman, who had taught at nearby Caltech. One of the equestrian trio happened to be Tuva's leading throat singer, Kongar-ol Ondar. For his next trick, Leighton arranged a San Francisco concert for Kongar-ol's ensemble Huun-Huur-Tu, which means "sunbeams" and included Albert Kuvezin. (Tuvan authorities were so outraged at both their loss of control and the export of "authentic" music that they had the group arrested on their return.) A burst of airplay from Bay Area non-commercial radio ensured the concert was sold out, with an overflow crowd filling the lobby of the Asian Art Museum. When Kongar-ol emerged to sing a few songs for the disappointed fans, he was confronted by a blind singer performing a highly creditable rendition of Tuva's *kargyraa* form. Kongar-ol was so astonished he invited the man to take part in a throat-singing competition the following year in Kyzyl.

Paul Pena came from the large Cape Verdean immigrant community in New England, singing fado and morna as he grew up, then moving to blues as his eyesight deteriorated. He played rhythm guitar with T-Bone Walker before forming his own band and moving to San Francisco, where he opened occasionally for the Grateful Dead and wrote a song, "Jet Airliner," that Steve Miller turned into a hit single. Pena left the road when his wife became ill, devoting his nights to shortwave radio. After stumbling on Tuvan throat-singing, he tracked down recordings and books and taught himself the language along the way. After his wife's death in 1991, he poured his energy into developing this new craft, channeling the harsh tones of his blues-singing heroes, Charlie Patton and Son House. Ralph Leighton was, of course, fascinated; getting Paul Pena to Tuva for the competition became a way of honoring his late friend's quest. The documentary film about their journey, *Genghis Blues*, with its scenes of the American wowing Tuvan judges and audiences with his mastery of their singing, instruments, and language, was nominated for an Academy Award in 2000.

There is a tale about a Tuvan khan whose favorite horse died. Aware of the risks run by messengers with bad news, no one dared tell him.

Eventually, a musician entered the royal chamber and played galloping equine rhythms under a melody of such utter sorrow that the khan got the message (and the messenger survived).

Seventeenth-century Russian explorers arrived in Tuva with the sort of cheap trinkets they traded for pelts in the tundra to the north. To their astonishment, they found an elaborate traveling court furnished in silk and gold with a spectacular jeweled throne for the khan. Tuva epitomizes what the Russians could never grasp about many of the Asiatic cultures they colonized: it is both elegantly sophisticated and primordial. Tuvan singers and musicians are attuned to nature—flora, fauna, weather, and topography—to a level almost impossible for us to contemplate. Overtone singing predates the rituals of the Tibetan Buddhism they eventually adopted; a Tuvan's "higher plane" is to commune with and become a part of nature. Singers and musicians sit beside rivers and streams or atop mountains, tuning their voice or their instrument to the sounds of water and wind. Equally ancient are their evocations of animal cries, perhaps to soothe a quarry's soul before a hunt or encourage healthy herds. Bestial spirits inhabit the instruments themselves: horseheads are carved into the stock of horsehair fiddles; rattles are made from sheep's knee bones inside a dried bull's scrotum.

It takes time for Western gourmets to get accustomed to the Oriental focus on "mouth-feel" as much as on taste. Similarly, Tuvan and other Asian musical traditions can be as concerned with texture as they are with melody or rhythm. In *Where Rivers and Mountains Sing*, Theodore Levin uncovers how each note opens up fan-like possibilities of textural variation. Asian visual arts often reveal how, over the millennia, images of nature became stylized, like pre-Columbian Inca art grown from the same roots, with depictions of animals or plants evolving into elaborate symbolic shapes. What may be true of all music—that its origins lie in the sounds of nature—is manifestly so with Tuvan forms.

When Tuva was absorbed into the Russian Soviet Republic in 1944, one might have imagined that a country where the land already belonged to everyone would be granted a peaceful adjustment to Soviet collectivism. Of course not. Once-free herders were transformed into badly paid laborers and livestock numbers plummeted. Shoehorning

Tuvan music into the Moiseyev formula was doomed from the start; finding it altogether too strange, the Soviets allowed throat-singing onto the newly built stages in something approaching its natural state, but only if performed collectively by a large ensemble. Which did, of course, successfully ruin it.

Kongar-ol Ondar grew up in a small village listening to herdsmen throat-singing around a campfire after a few cups of fermented mare's milk. He did time in prison for fighting, but used it to strengthen his vocal cords and hone his technique. After meeting Ralph Leighton on the Californian's first visit to Kyzyl in 1991, he formed Huun-Huur-Tu with Kuvezin and Sayan Bapa, a Russian-born, half-Tuvan rock musician who had returned to look for his roots. Their repertoire combines throat-singing with spectacular instrumental virtuosity, including Hendrix-style back-of-the-hand dombra glissandos.

With the help of their manager Sasha Cheparukhin (who began his career organizing concerts for environmental causes and went on to manage a branch of Pussy Riot), Huun-Huur-Tu have been touring since 1993. Their voices and instruments are a magnet for fusion hounds, from Willie Nelson and Frank Zappa to the Kronos Quartet and Russian classical orchestras, while their recordings have been used in commercials for the Greek state lottery and an AT&T digital recording system ("Singing two notes at once may not be revolutionary for the people of South Siberia, but . . ."). The group view most Western music with bemusement, unnerved by what they call "conflict"—metal strings against wooden necks and other "violent" juxtapositions.

Music as a part of everyday Tuvan life was eliminated by the Soviets, and the post-communist world is even worse, lacking even the distorted pre-1991 support. Some throat-singing has survived, but individual eccentricities have given way to uniform techniques; the notion that music is for the spirits rather than audiences has virtually disappeared. Local radio has collapsed and venues are closed, making it impossible for a musician to build a Tuvan career. The return of the Tuvan language after years of Soviet suppression has led not to pride, only isolation and depression. There are a few bright spots: before his death in 2013, Kongar-ol created a school program to teach traditional music, one fruit of which is the country's first all-female throat-singing ensemble.

～

For many years, an English bass player named Lu Edmonds has divided his time among Kuvezin's electric band Yat-Kha, John Lydon's Public Image Ltd, and the Mekons; in the early years of the new century, his day job was traveling Central Asia on a grant from the Christensen Fund, digitizing radio archives in Kyrgyzstan and Tajikistan. Buried amid the dross of state ensembles were hours and hours of well-recorded virtuoso music that had never been broadcast or released on disc. Officials barely registered his presence at first, happy to have some mad Englishman cleaning up and cataloguing their archives. But when Edmonds kept returning and talked of possible box-set anthologies, bureaucrats became uneasy, paranoid that they were missing out on some mysterious capitalist gold mine and fearful they would be shamed by acclaim for something they had dismissed as valueless. Cultural ministries seized control of the project and Edmonds was barred. The work ground to a halt, the tapes continue to deteriorate, and anthologies are unlikely to ever see the light of day.

Architecture has been caught in parallel struggles. The Uzbek city of Khiva was once a bustling regional center with an ancient bazaar that attracted intrepid tourists. Authorities expelled the bazaar's residents and merchants, turned it into a lifeless Silk Road theme park, and were bewildered when visitors evaporated. A few middle-class Uzbeks live in beautiful traditional houses and some have made tasteful restorations. But the newly wealthy more often choose to build homes resembling what they see in Mexican soap operas on land where old houses once stood.

But all is not lost. The Ismaili branch of Islam is led by a man with the hereditary title of Aga Khan. His followers once made annual donations of gold equal to his weight and they continue to tithe a percentage of their income to the charities he administers. The current occupier of this throne is an enlightened gentleman who has poured huge sums of money into the art and music of Muslim countries. In

Central Asia, Fairouz Nishanova, director of the Aga Khan Foundation's arts program, had the good sense to hire Theodore Levin to lead the project's musical direction.

Levin is a Dartmouth professor who speaks Russian and Uzbek along with some Tajik and Kyrgyz, has traveled widely in Central Asia, written books about his experiences, and has a deep understanding of the region's musical history. In October 2004, the opening-night gala at the WOMEX (World Music Expo) conference in Essen, Germany, was *Voices from Central Asia*, organized by Levin to showcase the Aga Khan's program. It was quite something to experience the fruits of ample funding combined with impeccable taste and total confidence in the music. The performers appeared in front of beautiful backdrops that evoked the cities and landscape of the region. The sound and lights were perfect, performances just the right length; Kyrgyz, Tajik, Uzbek, and Afghan master musicians and singers enthralled the audience for two hours, a textbook lesson in how to present traditional music.

The wonder of that concert stood within a circle of hostile forces, all pulling away at the foundation's goals: local officials who view tradition as "backward"; audiences that gravitate towards digitized modern renditions of something vaguely resembling their heritage; and "global music" presenters who haven't the budgets or the imagination to present music with this sort of elegant simplicity and focus instead on collaborations with Western jazz, rock, or classical musicians or modernizations that assume—as the commissars once did—that the music by itself is "too difficult."

Levin has released a series of albums through the Smithsonian Folkways label that are exquisitely recorded, packaged, and annotated, with elegant portrait photographs on the covers (no yurts or yaks) and well-written, enlightening notes. When one album won a Grammy, the Tajik government declared a national holiday, but it had little impact on listening preferences in local bazaars. The foundation is playing a long game, to build habits of hard work, study, and respect for the musical heritage of a region whose culture has been viewed with condescending incomprehension by Russians, Chinese, Persians, and now by Western presenters. Many of their most passionate participants are refugees from classical orchestras and reformed rockers. Time will tell if the Aga Khan's aims will be realized.

∽

The fall of the Wall was not kind to Bulgarian wedding bands. Turbo-folk and hard rock flooded the country as most things Bulgarian, be they state ensembles or wedding music, were jettisoned. A 1989 visit by the Gipsy Kings led many Roma groups to try rumba guitars and handclaps. Poverty returned to the countryside as economic upheaval brought a halt to Thrace's agriculture bonanza. Papasov began turning down gigs because he worried families would bankrupt themselves to pay his fee and he didn't want to play for less. Cash-laden musicians were targeted in a rash of post-wedding robberies.

Over the course of the nineties, Bulgarianness re-emerged, but in a form that horrified what was left of the country's cultural establishment. The big stars were Roma playing electrified Turkish kyuchek rhythms, taking Ivo's energy and attitude and crossing it with programmed beats, slick production, and blatantly sexual lyrics. There was even—*the horror!*—a huge hit ("Doko doko" by Kondio) sung entirely in Romani. Bulgarian Roma, long reviled as "backward," have always been the most quick-footed modernists in the country, incorporating the latest styles and equipment with elan. In 1999, as a condition of its application to join the EU, Bulgaria wrote laws to improve Roma schooling and enforce equal treatment by police; once membership was secured, the government forgot about implementing the statutes. Papasov winning the 2005 BBC World Music Audience Award led to a brief flurry of official recognition and acclaim, but in 2012, when a Brussels theater invited him to celebrate his sixtieth birthday with a gala concert, the Bulgarian embassy in Belgium refused to participate. Ivo is proud that young Roma kids are now encouraged to play an instrument after long years when music seemed a vocation in decline. He feels that wedding bands helped keep Bulgarian music strong enough to resist the barrage of Serbian and Anglo-American music that swept into the country after 1991.

In 2000, London's Barbican Theatre presented the Koutev Ensemble as part of a festival of Eastern European music. For years they had been overshadowed by various iterations of the Radio Choir under the Mystère banner, so it was good to hear the master's arrangements in person and enjoy the slick but firmly traditional choreography. The hall was packed and it was a great show, but the ensemble doesn't tour often and has become a part-time job for its members. Some Mystère singers have been quoted saying they would prefer to sing Koutev's arrangements, but American, German, and Japanese audiences want the modern compositions. Do they really? All over the world there are amateur choirs singing Koutev's arrangements, with local enthusiasts leavened by relocated Bulgarians. But recordings and concerts under the Mystère trademark continue to delve ever deeper into intellectual modernism; no wonder audiences have declined.

In 2005, I made a sentimental return to the Koprivshtitsa Festival. That year's event was drenched by rainstorms, forcing many performers to rush home and attend to flocks and crops, but even allowing for the tempests, it was clear that much had changed, and not for the better. Twenty years earlier, evenings in the town were filled with singing and the wail of the gaida; chains of horo dancers wove in and out of bars and restaurants and formed huge spirals in the campgrounds. This time I was assaulted by turbo-folk blasting from stalls selling bootleg CDs. Along the river, tents with huge PAs sold beer and kebabs while wedding bands played a hybrid of simplified Serbian and Thracian beats at deafening volume.

Late one evening, a moment of revenge arrived when a pair of zurna players and a couple of *teppanitsas* led a huge horo down the main street. The ear-splitting screech of the double reeds and the pounding drums sent stallholders running for cover, while the surreal improvisations of the players and the interlaced rhythms of the dance briefly opened a window onto a time when complexity and eccentricity were badges of pride in a culture as musically rich as anywhere on the planet.

In the early nineties, Olga Solovyova made a series of documentaries for the Second Channel of Russian state television. She followed Pokrovsky's trail, interviewing elderly singers in Russian villages and chronicling what was left of pre-Soviet musical traditions. One day her boss got a call from the head of music at the First Channel. "You mustn't broadcast this nonsense," said ninety-year-old Igor Moiseyev. "Such music does not exist."

Yes, the old man was still alive and powerful and his dance company continued to tour the world. Cycling down a back road in an obscure corner of Gascony during a French holiday in the mid-nineties, I spotted a poster for a Moiseyev show nailed to a telephone pole. I couldn't resist; that evening, in the square of a small working-class town with a Communist mayor, I found a shabby stage faced by a couple of hundred folding chairs, about half of them occupied. The music was mostly canned Handful, with dancers in garish costumes performing scenes from "folklore" and Orientalist opera. Even the accordion music for the fun-in-the-village dance was a playback. On a side street stood an ancient bus, with dancers' laundry drying in the windows. No more week-long runs at the Royal Albert Hall, but when Moiseyev died at 102, Putin went on national television to praise him and all he stood for.

Dmitri Pokrovsky's posthumous achievements were greater than he could ever have imagined; by the late 1990s, estimates of the number of participants in the "authentic" folk revival in Russia ranged from one to three million. Many of his victories, however, were pyrrhic, as the US academic Laura Olson noted in her book *Performing Russia*. Music schools, for example, began teaching open-throat singing, but without the intensity of his methods: no improvisation, no spiritual dimension, no barking.

Sex, though, was still a big draw for the revival. As one enthusiast told Olson, "This is sex together with culture. With wisdom. Everything's here. It has such an incredible strong effect, which you can only dream of." Academics who cautiously embraced the movement continued to bridle at the steamy lyrics found in many rural songs, insisting that, like trouble, sex comes from the city. Shchurov regretted the self-censorship in his arrangement of "Porushka-Parania," a song that became the "If I Had a Hammer" of the Russian folk revival; his bowdlerized version is sung everywhere, including by a Russian "red grass" group appearing at the Grand Ol' Opry in Nashville.

No longer mocked, old-style singing groups were suddenly in demand by local authorities for official gatherings and holidays. Folk festivals sprouted across the country, with authentic-style music sandwiched between Moiseyevian ensembles and many audiences barely noting the difference. Like the mayor of Alma-Ata's girlfriend, ensembles often focused on costumes rather than music. In 2012, a group of babi from the village of Buranovskiye, singing ancient Udmurt songs to a disco backing, finished second in the Eurovision Song Contest.

Villagers often struggled with their own traditions; after decades of dictated lives, many found improvisation impossible. Some older Russians, bewildered by the sudden end of the Soviet system, clung to Moiseyev-style ensembles much as babi had clung to traditional singing in the 1930s. Polina Shepherd, a Russian who teaches the technique in England, told me that students often find open-throat singing frightening and that breakthroughs can be intensely emotional. The brilliance of some post-Pokrovsky ensembles proves it can be done, but it is hard to deny that ultimately peasant singing grows from what anthropologist James Scott calls "an alternative symbolic universe," of which urbanites can never be truly a part.

As the prudish Soviet years disappeared in history's rearview mirror (for audiences at least, if not for academics or the government), the revival's vision of Russianness replaced sensuality as the extra-musical attraction; audiences and performers were drawn to something seen as both anti-Soviet and anti-Western. Like nationalism at the dawn of the nineteenth century, Russian traditionalism began for many as a liberal idea; but once the USSR was no more, darker impulses flooded into the vacuum. One revivalist singer was horrified when a journalist complimented her on "strengthening the foundations of the nation" and insisted that "foreign sounds negatively impact a person's brain and health." A liberal Russian friend of mine found himself mourning the end of the USSR. He had loved sharing a passport with so many nationalities; now he feared being marooned in a state run by Russian nationalists who hate "dark" or "foreign" peoples. Right-wingers are often perplexed by the folk revival, being instinctively more comfortable with the fakery of Moiseyev. Their musical tastes generally echo the former Moscow mayor Yuri Luzhkov's architectural policies: raze old buildings and erect grotesque memorials to a sentimental view of Russian history in their place. With the fall of communism, Russia seemed to pass from an idealized and fantastical vision of its future to an idealized and fantastical vision of its past.

One outstanding Pokrovsky offshoot is Sirin, a small choir that performs medieval Orthodox chants. I heard one performance in a beautiful Moscow chapel and spoke with them about the vocal practice that predates Patriarch Nikon's reforms of 1653. As you may have noticed, I am a sucker for history and for dedication to tradition, so my response was enthusiastic (and in any case, the singing was wonderful). Then I began encountering that date in other contexts. Nikon's attempt to reconcile differences between the Russian and Greek Orthodox churches involved discarding the medieval Znamenny chant and bringing in notation and harmony from Poland and Germany as well as "perspective" in religious painting. Coupled with Peter the Great's opening of the "window" a half-century later, 1653 represents for many nationalists the death knell of true Russian culture, a sentiment that seems to animate Putin's view of Russia's relationship to the West.

> The Cossack revival is a disaster of the human ecology. Not all the ecological catastrophes of the Black Sea happen in water.
>
> —Neal Ascherson, *The Black Sea*

In Putin's attempt to set Russia's course away from Western ways, Pokrovsky unwittingly provided him with a key tool. Dmitri had always been fascinated by the polyphonic improvisations in Cossack song but had taken pains to avoid the clichéd and violent imagery associated with that culture. When revivalists began setting up village groups, women were easiest to recruit; to lure boys and men, a winning approach turned out to be the inclusion of Cossack songs and dances. The manly image and distinctive uniforms (particularly in the wake of a Soviet era that seemed bent on the emasculation of rural Russian men) were far more appealing to the male psyche than any regional heritage. Simplified Cossack songs became central to the growth of the revival; with folk festivals providing a platform, it didn't take long for Cossacks to reclaim their central role in national mythology.

Experienced Russia-watchers grew alarmed when Vladimir Putin started having photo ops with Cossacks and Orthodox biker gangs after reclaiming the Russian presidency in 2012. He clearly recognized the importance of both as symbols of anti-Western masculinity and relished the implicit rebuke to liberalism. Cossack gangs served as commandos and enforcers in Chechnya and Ingushetia (as well as less glamorous work as security guards in shopping malls). In southern provinces, Cossack vigilantes became the scourge of "dark" migrants (who, as Russian citizens, have as much legal right as anyone to live in Vladikavkaz—or in Moscow, for that matter). Cossacks have traveled eagerly to Moldova, Bosnia, Kosovo, Abkhazia, and Ukraine to defend "Russian interests." The Cossack leader Yevgeni Yefremov told *The Times* that sending his men into battle was "like drinking a cooling glass of water after a long walk through the desert."

After his return to Russia in 1994, the Nobel Prize winner and dissident hero Alexander Solzhenitsyn shocked the West when he advocated barring Protestant and Catholic missionaries from Holy Russia. He claimed his homeland was in a mess because it had "forgotten God" and reiterated his view (often expressed during his years in America) that the country should shed its non-Slavic regions and create a new superstate by annexing Ukraine, Belarus, and the Russian-speaking parts of Kazakhstan.

Another perplexing figure for the West is film-maker Nikita Mikhalkov. His Oscar-winning *Burnt by the Sun* is a brilliantly acted tour de force with a fascinating plot and vivid characters that harbors an oblique justification of Stalinism. I told Russian author Viktor Erofeyev that I had loved the film but felt somehow soiled by my enthusiasm. He beamed and said, "Now you understand this country!" Mikhalkov's father was a famous writer of children's books and author of the Soviet anthem's lyrics during the purges of the late thirties. The son was an early supporter of Pokrovsky's work and his films are suffused with a deep feeling for the Russian land and its traditional culture. He is also a fervent Putin supporter.

There is a grim inevitability about the rise of Russian nationalism. Yeltsin's magic trick of making the USSR disappear triggered explosions of long-suppressed minority consciousness within and around its borders (Ukrainian in particular) that many Russians found menacing. Throw in the US response of sending Harvard Business School graduates to place privatization limpet mines below the waterline of the Russian economy while recruiting former Soviet and Eastern bloc nations to join NATO and *presto!*—a perfect formula for bruised pride and chip-on-the-shoulder xenophobia. Whether the camouflage is Ottoman, Habsburg, or Soviet, Eastern European ethnic nationalism doesn't die, it just lies dormant, festering and mutating like a Japanese movie monster waiting for a seismic trigger. At the start of his second presidency, Putin pointedly endorsed many racist Slavophile groups and embraced the notion of Holy Russia as a bastion against barbarism. At the time we thought he meant Islam; now we know he means us.

In the wake of Russia's move into eastern Ukraine in the spring of 2014, *Foreign Affairs* published an article entitled "Putin's Brain," about Alexander Dugin's growing influence in the Kremlin. Dugin is Russia's leading apostle of "Eurasianism," which is another name for Turanianism. He sets up Russia as successor to Rome and in opposition to America: "The USA is a chimerical, anti-organic, transplanted culture which does not have sacral state traditions and cultural soil, but nevertheless tries to force upon other continents its anti-ethnic, anti-traditional [and] 'babylonic' model." This description is not inaccurate, but where others see virtue, Dugin sees evil. His stand against mongrel America has resonated across Western Europe, making Putin the pin-up boy for right-wing nationalists everywhere. From the Turanians to Dugin is a straight (and proudly acknowledged) line, but the latter has access to far more power than the former could have ever imagined. There are reports that Dugin has persuaded Putin to fund a mission in the Altai Mountains to hunt for the "door to Shambala," the seat of Mme. Blavatsky's "Masters." If Russia is to provide the alternative to a corrupt

West, its Eurasia can't be Mongol or Turkic, it must be the home of an (imaginary) Aryan master race.

Putin's hysterical response to Pussy Riot echoed the Stalinist horror of singing women. Here lies another irony: the Scythians and Sarmatians who form the basis of the male-dominated Turanian fantasy worshipped the goddess Mixoparthenos, whose image, aquatic legs spread, decorates handles, prows, and wagons found in digs all over "Turania." Steppe peoples were often led by powerful queens, whose burial mounds are filled with jewels and the sacrificial carcasses of horses and toy boys. (Ancient Greek travelers speculated that this might be connected to the low libido suffered by steppe horsemen spending too long in the saddle.) Parallels between Russia and America are many and colorful, but there is one huge difference: Americans have always mythologized individualism and "freedom"; Russia romanticizes unity and submission. Russian nationalists share with the Soviets a horror of individuals separating themselves from the authorized collective. "Freedom of conscience" is so engrained in our thinking that we are astounded when someone is sentenced to death for apostasy, underestimating the priority many societies give to unity of ritual. We can mock Russia's Dostoyevskian "rejection of reason," but with the rise of Trump the jokes die in our throats.

In the summer of 2008, I attended the Sayan Ring Festival in Siberia. Just being there felt remarkable: four time zones east of Moscow and still only halfway to the Pacific! The first two days were intriguing: Altai throat singers, local fakelore ensembles, and Inna Zhelannaya, Russia's answer to Sandy Denny. But it was the last day that resonates; wandering near the stage during microphone checks, I was drawn to the sound of three fierce open-throated voices, two female, one male. The young group sported a defiantly clunky name—the Irkutsk Authentic Music Society—and were making some of the most beautiful harmonies I have ever heard. They told me their repertoire was drawn from a village destroyed by the Bratsk Dam northwest of Lake Baikal; the group had discovered a trove of recordings made by ethnographers in the 1960s as the waters advanced towards the doomed town. They then tracked down relocated villagers and recorded them in depressing high-rise blocks in the new town built at the edge of the vast man-made reservoir. I felt like those astonished Gnessin Institute ethnographers on that memorable day; here was Pyatnitsky's vision and Pokrovsky's dream at its most thrilling—the power of open-throat voices, the improvised harmonies, the idealism, the songs keeping alive memories of another time, pre-Lvov, pre-Balakirev, pre-Stalin, pre-Putin.

> My guiding philosophy has always been the ideal of different nations uniting into brotherhood, in spite of all the wars and hostility. I have tried to serve the aims of this idea, as best I can, in my music, so for that reason, I do not shrink away from any influence, be it Slovak, Romanian, Arab or any other source.
>
> —Béla Bartók, quoted in the notes to Muzsikás's *The Bartók Album*

An orchestra's worth of violinists, kontra players, and bassists with their bulky instruments strapped to their chests marched slowly through the cemetery, bowing in unison as the crowd sang mournfully along. The wooded grounds provided an acoustic chamber, holding the immense sound in a delicate embrace. The music was characteristically Hungarian, with unexpected intervals, jerky pauses, and exquisite snatches of melody followed by dark modulations. When the procession reached the grave, the mourners crowded around as Béla Halmos's coffin was lowered down while the musicians continued their lament. I'm not sure I have ever experienced a more moving musical moment.

I had come to Budapest for Muzsikás's fortieth-anniversary concert in August 2013 and stayed for the funeral of Halmos, the man who kicked off the táncház movement by striking a *qin* with a stick. The evening before the interment, I attended an all-night vigil for him at Heritage House as soloists and groups took twenty-minute turns to pay tribute to the man who had been a beacon to them all. The anniversary concert the previous night had celebrated not only Muzsikás, but the Transylvanians they learned from, the stage filled with dancers, violinists, pipers, and singers. Márta Sebestyén was conspicuously absent but the group had the good sense not to ask any one singer to fill those shoes; a pair of young women sang a few of her famous numbers in unison. There was an inspiring collegiality about it all, watched by a big crowd who'd paid good money for tickets. Hungary's folk revival, by general agreement, is streets ahead of any other in its impact on the culture, breadth of participation, quality of results, and empathy between urban apprentices and rural practitioners. Even the hardest-core Hungarian heavy metal headbanger will acknowledge a fondness for Muzsikás, Márta, and táncház.

After the concert, *pálinka*, the powerful local *eau de vie*, was served backstage and musicians continued to play as the group and their friends socialized. I watched a pleasant-looking woman wearing shorts, a backpack, and sandals approach, leading her three daughters. They embraced the group animatedly and the girls, aged about ten to fourteen, enthused knowledgeably about their favorite moments of the show. Just then, Muzsikás's manager grabbed my arm, saying she wanted to introduce me. I shook hands with the woman and gulped as I heard the quickly thrown name. It was Anikó Orbán, wife of Prime Minister Viktor Orbán, champion of Europe's new "illiberalism," beacon for reactionary and proto-fascist movements across the continent.

The party Orbán leads, Fidesz, began as an underground, liberal, anti-communist group that surfaced after the fall of the Wall, finally winning power in 1998. As a young activist Orbán was often spotted at Muzsikás concerts, although his fiercest passion is football. (In 2013, he ordered a 15,000-seat stadium to be built in his home village, population 3,000 . . .) In one speech he talked of his vision of a modern state that was true to its roots, insisting that Hungarians needn't choose between "Muzsikás and Tina Turner." During the nineties, most táncház musicians gravitated to Fidesz as an alternative to the Socialists, many of whose leaders were former Communists. After Socialist victories in 2002 and 2006, a fierce new Fidesz emerged, purged of liberals and moderates and determined to win not just the 2010 election, but to fix the electoral, judicial, and treasury systems so that they could never again lose power. Lurching to the right on social issues, they sealed that flank by pandering to the supporters of Jobbik, a violent anti-Semitic, anti-Roma party that had gained 17 percent of the vote. In 2013, they erected a statue to Hitler's ally Admiral Horthy in central Budapest.

Many folk musicians were reluctant to shed their loyalty to a party that had made such a refreshing change from the tradition-hating communists, and some grew defensive about Fidesz, resenting outsiders' criticisms. But following Fidesz's 2013 electoral triumph, I heard mostly disillusionment and resignation. "All politicians are liars. We can't rely on political parties," said one. In a discussion of his country's xenophobic drift, Dániel Hamar told me of visits to villages in Transylvania where Romanians and Hungarians lived side by side. They were often too poor to have more than one dance on holidays, so the two communities would pool resources and hire Roma musicians; when the melody was Hungarian the Romanians sat and watched their neighbors, then the Hungarians would stand by while the Romanians danced. "In those villages, you were judged by whether you told the truth, paid your debts, and didn't beat your wife, not by which language you spoke or where you went to church."

In later years, when Muzsikás gave concerts in Transylvania, he found the communities had grown more separate and mistrustful of each other. Politicians, he felt, were the cause of nationalism. At the source, where melodies flow from strings and voices, music brings people together in respect and harmony. It is downstream, in the political sphere, where it is put to sinister use. There is no escaping the fact, however, that like Pokrovsky and the Cossacks, táncház helped provide cultural cover for Fidesz's ugly nationalist turn.

Hamar loves the "less pure" music of the farthest reaches of the Magyar-speaking territories for the very reason that it has absorbed more outside influences and taken strange turns. When in doubt, he always refers back to the words of his beloved Bartók, quoted above. Hungary's 1848 hero, Sándor Petőfi, foreshadowed Orbán by claiming that minorities were "ulcers on the body of the motherland." Bartók liked to counter this view by quoting Hungary's founder, Saint Stephen: "[G]uests . . . bring with them various languages and customs . . . All these adorn the royal court, heighten its splendor. For a country unified in language and customs is fragile and weak." Try telling that to Viktor Orbán.

It can be difficult for a melting-pot American to get to grips with the intensity of Eastern European nationalism. For us, ethnic pride has meant the St. Patrick's Day Parade down Fifth Avenue, eating sausages in Little Italy during the Feast of San Gennaro, and listening to steel bands at the Caribbean Carnival in Brooklyn. The clichéd Irish cop kisses the Trinidadian carnival queen and pockets a bribe from the unlicensed Italian street vendor and everyone's happy (except for the easily offended Italian-American Civil Rights League, who sue me for that last part). One can credit the Bolsheviks for trying to defuse rivalries and hatreds that cling to the hills, valleys, and cities of Eastern Europe. But by attacking two of the most fundamental connections that bind any group—rural land and the music played on it—they destroyed essential assets; without them, people seek more sinister expressions of their identity.

In the cultural life of the West, Eastern European music isn't much more than a colorful footnote. "Global music," for most, means African rhythms transfigured via slavery in the Americas or taken straight; the lack of such obviously danceable beats strips most European folk music of its broad appeal. But when Slavic or Hungarian music reaches our ears undiluted, it can entrance listeners and dancers. For that we must thank Béla Bartók, Béla Halmos, Márta Sebestyén, Muzsikás, Mitrofan Pyatnitsky, Sergei Pokrovsky, Philip Koutev, Rumyana Tzintzarska, Ivo Papasov, and so many others, who from inside their cultures recognized their music's unadorned beauty and were unafraid to say so.

VIII
Tezeta

When he heard the postman drop a heavy envelope into the mailbox, Tony Allen opened one eye. He'd been out late the night before watching a Ghanaian highlife band, but he knew what that sound meant so he roused himself, got up, and brought the package into his family's Lagos kitchen. When he opened it, the latest issue of his sea-mail subscription to *DownBeat* fell out onto the table, followed by a small booklet: *Max Roach's Guide to Playing the Hi-Hat*.

Telling me the story a half-century later, Tony still marveled at the serendipity. It had been just over two years since he'd sat behind a drum kit for the first time, aged seventeen. He'd come across it while repairing a radio antenna for someone who sponsored a local band and kept their equipment in his garage. Allen had tried other instruments before, but never felt comfortable blowing or plucking. When he took a seat behind the kit, though, it just clicked; he knew that was where he belonged.

Graduating rapidly from playing "sticks" (or *claves*, as Cubans call them) to becoming, in 1959, the drummer for Lagos highlife band the Cool Cats, Tony was determined to master the craft. There were two places to look for inspiration: one was Ghanaian bands, since the style had originated there in the 1920s; the other was jazz recordings. Highlife's rhythm-feel was closer to calypso, but the instrumentation and playing techniques weren't far removed from jazz (and Louis Armstrong was still among the most revered musical heroes in both Ghana and Nigeria).

The first US drummer to impress Allen was Gene Krupa, whose flamboyant solos for the Benny Goodman Orchestra had made him a star. But after hearing Art Blakey, Philly Joe Jones, and Max Roach, Krupa's pounding seemed overblown; the nuanced polyrhythms of the beboppers were more to Tony's taste. Subtlety appealed to Allen; he always believed that what you left out was as important as what you put in.

Accra was just a day's drive along the coast, so Ghanaian bands often played in Lagos and Tony always made a point of going to hear them. But the previous evening had been, like others before it, something of a letdown. Walking home after the show (Lagos was then a very safe city), he puzzled over the repetitive simplicity of highlife drum patterns and how rarely the hi-hat was put to use; the drummer that night had barely touched his. After devouring Roach's booklet, Allen began spending every spare moment practicing the exercises. When he found he could keep one beat going on the snare while marking accents and counter-rhythms on the hi-hat (or, even better, the other way around), he was delighted. Other highlife drummers were dumbfounded.

He would learn to use pedals that way, too, throwing in accents on the bass drum in response to a solo or a shift in the conga drum pattern. Tony's playing always seemed relaxed and effortless; he never pounded, never broke a sweat. Brian Eno was one of the first outsiders to notice; in 1985, he pronounced him the world's greatest drummer. When Allen died in Paris in the summer of 2020, artists from across the musical map queued up to sing his praises. Drummers told of how impossible they'd found trying to play as he did, how Tony was the only one who could ever really manage it.

> We should have been playing . . . like that in Nigeria. After all, it originally came from here. They took it, went there to the Americas, polished it, and sent it back to us in Africa.
>
> —Tony Allen

The Ghanaian flag hoisted above Accra's Osu Castle on March 6, 1957, was, like the Rastafarian banner, red, green, and gold. Both were inspired by the one that flew above the battlefield at Adwa in 1896 during the

Ethiopian army's momentous triumph over the invading Italians. In the coming years, as European colonial powers scuttled out of Africa as fast as they'd scrambled in seven decades earlier, those three colors would dominate the flags of the new nations. Like the former Gold Coast, many would add a five-pointed star; Ghana's is the only black one, in honor of the emblem painted on the smokestacks of those ill-fated steamboats Marcus Garvey had hoped to fill with settlers returning to their ancestral home. Kwame Nkrumah, Ghana's first president, urged African Americans to take up Garvey's call and "come back" to Ghana; Maya Angelou stayed for a few years, and Garvey's nemesis W. E. B. Du Bois settled there in old age, but not many followed.

Ghana's future looked pretty good that March day; palm oil and cocoa prices were surging and Nkrumah was an agile politician who had outsmarted the British, earning their grudging respect and the adoration of his people. Ready or not, the remaining British and French colonies were being lined up to follow Ghana out the colonial door; empires had turned virtually overnight from a proud asset into a costly and somewhat shameful liability. One might suppose that imperial rulers would try to prepare these arbitrarily carved-out entities for independence, but only in the Gold Coast and Senegal had African cadres been given any meaningful experience in the mechanics of governing. Unsurprisingly, most new nations struggled; the next half-century would be marked by civil wars, coups, endemic corruption, ethnic rivalries, and exploitation by foreign capital (or, in some cases, inept economic plans imposed by Eastern bloc sponsors). A century earlier, the world had seen Africa as a land of raw resources ripe for plunder. Today, six decades after independence, financial hegemons still tend to view it in much the same way.

There was one raw material, though, that evolved into a fully fledged creation, something in which countries could take pride and, in some cases, profitably export, developed in a dialogue with the outside world, through a give-and-take of mutual respect. This product was music. Its foreign advisors didn't settle in air-conditioned compounds, drive expensive cars, and earn salaries many times that of their African colleagues; influence arrived via disc and radio, from intrepid adventurers, and, eventually, from ocean-spanning tours and recordings. The dialogue was almost entirely between Africans and their long-lost cousins, whose ancestors had been taken in chains from these same lands. Their descendants had propelled and provoked the "developed" world into musical modernity; now it was Africa's turn.

Patterns of influence and connection were seldom as linear as Max Roach's hi-hat instructions. Tracking them is a bit like tracing dye dropped off the stern of one those ghostly Black Star Liners somewhere between Recife and Conakry. Take, for example, the drum kit itself, first assembled as a money-saving device in New Orleans, where Cuban and Haitian immigrants with their rich traditions of African percussion had collided with an Anglo-Saxon culture bent on suppressing every drum save the European marching variety. By the 1920s, players with one-man kits built from military drums were making bottoms shimmy from San Francisco to Paris; the Roaring Twenties soundtrack was based on rhythms handed down from those nineteenth-century Sunday get-togethers in Congo Square that had shocked onlookers because they sounded so African.

In Africa, the Gold Coast had always seemed a few steps ahead. Among the very few things its inhabitants enjoyed about British rule were the parades; by 1900, brass bands were so popular that locals had formed their own marching societies. Employment with colonial authorities or British trading companies created an African elite who could afford to emulate the occupiers; before long, the sound of brass was heard in the evenings playing for dances while impecunious crowds gathered outside, eavesdropping on the "high life" being celebrated within. This music soon shed its European pretensions as the rhythms grew more local, more Akan, but with a twist: many of the leading players were West Indians working for the British who had brought along their calypso 78s and a Trinidadian feel to how they played. Locals were surprised by how familiar that beat felt, but they needn't have been, considering how many Akan captives had been brought as slaves from that same stretch of coast to British islands in the Caribbean.

One Gold Coast drummer, named Guy Warren, had enjoyed his posting to London during the war and was eager to go back; on a visit in 1948, he found the English had gone crazy for conga lines, so he brought

top left   A Baiana, believed to be Tia Ciata, c. 1885

top right   Carmen Miranda in one of her trademark Baiana stage outfits

center   Oito Batutas with Pixinguinha (left with flute) and Donga (fourth from left with guitar), c. 1919

bottom   Luiz Gonzaga, 1955

Orson Welles at the Rio de Janeiro carnival, 1942

Vinícius de Moraes
and Tom Jobim

João Gilberto

Astrud Gilberto and Stan Getz
at Birdland, New York City, 1964

top left Nara Leão with *Opinião* co-star Zé Keti

top center (second down) Gilberto Gil and Caetano Veloso during their London exile, 1969

center Milton Nascimento at the International Song Festival, Rio de Janeiro, 1967

bottom left Jorge Ben

bottom right Album cover of the 1972 reissue of *Tropicália ou Panis et Circencis*

top left Afro-Argentine guitarist José Delgado (center), Buenos Aires, c. 1930

top right Tango-dancing couple, Argentina, c. 1913

center Tango dancers in front of the Panthéon on Bastille Day, Paris, 1912

bottom Men's tango *practica*, Buenos Aires, early twentieth century

top Julio de Caro and his Sexteto Típico, c. 1927

center left Osvaldo Pugliese

center right Carlos Gardel

bottom left
Roberto Goyeneche

bottom right Aníbal Troilo and Astor Piazzolla

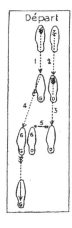
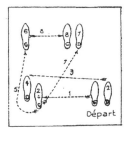
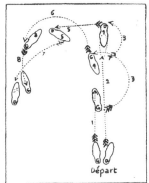

top Poster for *Tango argentino*, created for the 1983 Salon d'Automne in Paris

center 1920s tango foot diagram

bottom La Chicana: Acho Estol and Dolores Solá

top Mitrofan Pyatnitsky (top center) with the Pyatnitsky Russian Folk Chorus, 1918

center left "The Adolescents," from the original Ballets Russes production of Igor Stravinsky's *Rite of Spring*, Paris, 1913

center right Sergei Diaghilev, New York City, 1916

bottom left Igor Moiseyev, Moscow, 1947

bottom right Moiseyev Dance Company, London, 1964

top Dmitri Pokrovsky and his ensemble, Russia, 1977

center left Shaman Idamchap Xomushtu making an offering to the spirit masters during a recording session, Tuva, 1987

center right Albert Kuvezin

bottom Philip Koutev with members of the Koutev Ensemble choir, 1962

Trio Bulgarka: Stoyanka Boneva, Eva Georgieva, and Yanka Rupkina, with Kate Bush, 1989

Ivo Papasov and Yuri Yunakov, 2003

top Béla Bartók reviewing field recordings, 1918

center Muzsikás: (right to left) Mihály Sipos, László Porteleki, Péter Éri, and Dániel Hamar with vocalist Márta Sebestyén and dancers Zoltán Farkas and Ildikó Tóth

bottom "Dance-house" *(táncház)* gathering, Budapest, 1982

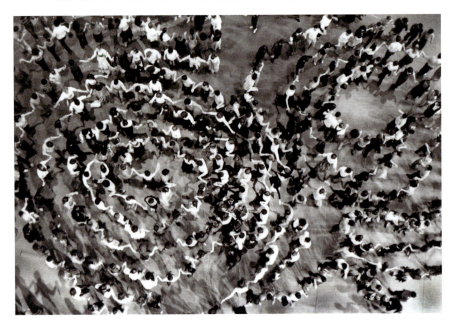

top Fela Kuti, 1986

center Nineteen-year-old Tony Allen with the Cool Cats, Nigeria, 1959

bottom left Fela Kuti in 1978, with some of the twenty-seven wives he married that year

bottom right Tony Allen, 2016

top left Docteur Nico (Nico Kasanda)

top right Franco (François Luambo Makiadi), aged sixteen, 1956

center Tabu Ley Rochereau at the Paris Métro stop Denfert-Rochereau

bottom left Konono N°1, Kinshasa, 2014

bottom right *Sapeur* Willy Covary walks the streets of Brazzaville, Congo, 2008

The Rail Band, Salif Keïta third from the right, 1970

Manu Dibango, c. 1970

Youssou N'Dour, 1986

top Toumani Diabaté and his father, Sidiki Diabaté, Mali, 1987

center left Ali Farka Touré, c. 1990

center right Oumou Sangaré, 2007

bottom Malick Sidibé's photograph of a dancing couple on Christmas Eve at the Happy Club, Bamako, Mali, 1963

top Second Police Orchestra, Ethiopia, c. 1965

center left Aster Aweke, 1991

center right Mahmoud Ahmed, 1999

bottom Emahoy Tsegue-Maryam Guebrou at home in Debre Genet, the Ethiopian monastery in Jerusalem

top Guillaume Apollinaire on his divan at home, Paris, 1909

center Head-strapped *aulos* player with dancer, detail from a drinking cup found at Vulci, Italy, from c. 510 BCE

bottom left and right Master Musicians of Joujouka

back a trunk full of Cuban percussion—bongos, güiros, maracas, and claves—that caused a sensation in highlife circles. The music's image still demanded that it be played on imported instruments by musicians in neat British-style suits with anglicized names; no one would then dream of bringing an Akan or Asanti drum, bell, or rattle onto a highlife bandstand. But what were these "Latin" objects if not variants of traditional African percussion endowed with a jaunty modernity by Edmundo Ros and his frilly-shirted "Cubans"? These instruments arrived just as rumba fever was spreading from Central Africa, fueled by Radio Brazzaville's powerful signal broadcasting Cuban discs and live performances by the Congolese imitators who had recognized their own rhythms in the exciting sounds arriving from Havana. Anglophone colonies weren't jumping in as wholeheartedly as the French, Belgian, and Portuguese territories, but Latin flavors—including those "wooden raindrops" Tony Allen played at the start of his career—also found their way into highlife.

When Louis Armstrong toured Africa in 1956, he was greeted at the airport in Accra by trumpet star E. T. Mensah and his band playing one of their signature tunes, "All for You." Armstrong recognized the melody as one sung in the streets of New Orleans by the descendants of Haitian refugees. The tune is also close to the calypso "Sly Mongoose," which was a hit in Trinidad in the twenties and was brought to both the US and West Africa by Caribbean immigrants. (The mongoose is a familiar character in West African folklore, known for his cunning and resourcefulness.) Mensah often toured Nigeria, starting in the early fifties, and his recordings became prized possessions in Yoruba and Igbo households. When they lowered the Union Jack in Ghana, Nigerians knew their turn was next and celebrated their neighbors' freedom by going mad for their own local highlife bands.

The bebop drummers that Tony Allen found so inspiring were part of a movement to make modern jazz too complex and Black for White musicians to copy the way they had with Dixieland and swing. Shifting to scale- rather than harmony-based improvisation was one strategy; stirring in Afro-Cuban rhythms was another. Then there's the 1948 photo of Dizzy Gillespie greeting Benny Carter by holding up one hand with fingers spread, the other below it, palm down. This was Gillespian sign language for "flat five," the note Dizzy liked to invoke when touting bebop's harmonic innovations. The flatted fifth lies at the exact midpoint of the octave; inserted into a dominant seventh chord, it sounds both dissonant and cool. Its use in modern jazz has been credited to bebop's admiration for Debussy, Stravinsky, and Schoenberg, but Gerhard Kubik, an Austrian musicologist, identifies it (along with those other "blue notes," the flatted thirds and sevenths) as an attempt by African-American musicians to reconcile the tempered Western twelve-tone scale with pentatonic and heptatonic African ones, in which notes often fall outside the intervals built by Europeans into their keys, valves, and frets. Scales, melodies, rhythms, instruments, and folk tales, all swirling around in that mid-Atlantic gyre. And that's just highlife; the second half of the twentieth century would be filled with rich and wonderful African popular music forms, each with its own tales of interaction with what Paul Gilroy has dubbed the "Black Atlantic."

> I'm telling you—it was fantastic, man! . . . What we had there in Nigeria . . . was really like a paradise!
>
> —Tony Allen

Antony Oladipo Allen grew up on the island that gave the city of Lagos its name. It had been home to a community of fishermen since at least the fifteenth century, but when the Portuguese took a fancy to it and the big lagoon—or *lago*—behind it, they turned the fish market into a slave-trading emporium. After the abolitionist British captured it in 1851, a cosmopolitan town developed around the port, with the original population augmented by "Saros," Yorubas who'd been sold into slavery, freed on the high seas by British frigates and taken to Sierra Leone. (The Allen name comes from Saro ancestors, and the family still own property in Freetown.) Many made their way back along the coast to Lagos, where they were joined by slaves fleeing from the Islamic sultanates to the north. Long before Marcus Garvey preached his "back to Africa" gospel, adventurous freedmen from Brazil, Cuba, and the United States had emigrated to West Africa, with many settling in Lagos. Drawn by the harbor and the many mission-educated Christians, the British chose the town for their Nigerian headquarters.

The island has an Aguda district, built by Brazilians, who brought with them a distinctive style of architecture introduced by the Dutch during their occupation of Northeast Brazil in the seventeenth century. Catholic Agudas and Protestant Saros dominated the cultural life of turn-of-the-century Lagos, which included Shakespearean theatricals and chamber music. Saros liked to dress in Victorian finery with top hats and handlebar mustaches, while Agudas were the party animals. In Antonio Olinto's *The Water House*, a novel set in nineteenth-century Lagos, a Brazilian immigrant declares: "We are civilised people, different from these others. It was us who taught the people here joinery, we taught them how to build big houses, and churches, we brought cassava, cashews, cocoa, dried meat, coconuts. They stare at you with big round eyes and don't know how to enjoy themselves."

By 1957, Lagosians had learned to enjoy themselves; with wages from his electronics-repair job in his pocket, Tony Allen was ready to join them. There were nightclubs and dances everywhere; young people took waltz, foxtrot, and jitterbug lessons and got all dressed up for a night on the town. Tony fixed up a rudimentary PA system, borrowed his uncle's collection of highlife and Cuban 78s and 45s, and began DJing at all-night street parties. When his eureka moment behind the drums arrived, he was ready to commit himself to music. His parents were skeptical but didn't try to stop him; on October 1, 1960, the day the flag of independent Nigeria was raised in Tafawa Balewa Square, Tony Allen embarked on his career as a professional musician.

The Cool Cats were in demand, busy most nights playing around the city or out in the bush, where they used 12-volt batteries to drive their PA system and amps. Their young drummer was just starting to gain a reputation when the group fell victim to a problem that often plagued African bands: money passing carelessly through the hands of a leader who failed to set aside enough for salaries or a share for the sponsor (mirroring how many newly independent African nations would be governed in the coming decades). After the Cats' acrimonious meltdown, Tony began playing weekends for a cover band in Ibadan, which meant adding rhythm and blues, pop, and Latin styles to his arsenal. Through it all, the cautious Allen kept his day job, often turning up for work having barely slept. Never far from a radio, he was quick to notice a new show on NBC (Nigerian Broadcasting Corporation), a Friday-evening jazz program that played Miles, Monk, Bird, and plenty of Blue Note. The show's presenter was an exuberant young Yoruba just back from earning a music degree in London named Fela Ransome-Kuti.

At that time, Ransome-Kuti considered himself primarily a trumpet player; he liked being paid to spin records, but what mattered most was his jazz quartet. He'd found a good keyboard player and a bassist, but drummer after drummer had disappointed. He was at the point of giving the whole thing up when someone suggested auditioning Tony Allen. Setting themselves up in an unused NBC studio, the group was less than a minute into the first number when Fela shouted to his manager, "*Are you hearing this!?*" He demanded to know where in Britain or America Tony had learned to play like that, refusing to believe that Ibadan was the farthest extent of his travels.

For a year and a half the group played private parties at homes or on boats in the lagoon and occasionally in clubs or restaurants, but generated little income or enthusiasm; Nigeria, it seemed, wasn't ready for modern jazz. NBC grew tired of Ransome-Kuti's casual time-keeping and "inappropriate" on-air language and sacked him. At this critical juncture, Fela's mother sat him down and told him that if he was going to succeed as a musician, he had to give Nigerians something they could understand, something recognizably their own.

Many musicians have gathered strength and confidence from maternal love and support, but none has ever had a mother like Funmilayo Ransome-Kuti. A 1951 profile in *West Africa* magazine described her "air of authority, a compelling manner not common with Nigerian women . . . a resolute, tenacious woman who has made even rulers totter." Those rulers would have been Oladapo Ademola II, Alake (chief) of the

Ransome-Kutis' home city of Abeokuta, and his imperial overlords the British. In 1948, after the colonial administration had encouraged the Alake to fund local improvements by taxing the women who operated the city's market, Funmilayo organized an occupation of his palace grounds. A thousand market-women kept the royal court awake for two nights chanting about the Alake's *"penis of a poison rat"* and vowing that *"vagina's head will seek vengeance."* The government backed down; the creative use of *"yabis,"* a Yoruba term for insults, seems to have run in the family.

Funmilayo had been the first girl in Abeokuta to graduate from grammar school and the first Nigerian woman to drive a car. Kwame Nkrumah became a close friend who sought her advice; she visited Russia and China, shook hands with Mao, hung out with Paul Robeson, and would have traveled more widely if the Americans hadn't refused her a visa and pressured the British into confiscating her passport. Her formidable husband, the Rev. Israel Oludofun Ransome-Kuti, was a composer of religious music and a tyrannical school principal who refused to fly the Union Jack or allow colonial inspectors past the front door. Fela's paternal grandfather, Josiah, a renowned singing minister, had been the first Nigerian to record in London for His Master's Voice. "Reverend JJ" fought street brawls with traditional religious leaders over the right of Christians to parade on days set aside for the orishas. All of Fela Kuti's extraordinary qualities, with the possible exception of his gargantuan sexual appetite, can be traced to inherited nature and parental nurture. To complete the image of fruit falling close to the tree, the Egba people of Abeokuta are, according to the musicologist Christopher Waterman, viewed by other Yorubas as "sophisticated, magically powerful, and inordinately ostentatious."

Abeokuta is a small city lying midway between the massive urban conglomerations of Lagos and Ibadan. It was founded in 1830 by Egba refugees, a group seeking sanctuary from the warfare of the early nineteenth century. (The city's name means "hidden by rocks.") The conflicts were the result of tensions generated by the usual suspects, money and religion; as you may recall, these wars triggered an influx of Yoruba slaves that transformed music and society in Cuba and Brazil. Fulani and Hausa Muslims may have been conducting a jihad against *kaffirs*, or unbelievers, to the south, but they were also fighting to protect a lucrative slave trade menaced by competition from coastal rulers whose European clients were ready to pay as much or more than customers in Arabia and the Middle East.

The culture of this region (which covers much of southwestern Nigeria, extending into neighboring Benin and a bit of Togo) has been largely urban for a thousand years, long before Fulanis began referring to its inhabitants as "Yoruba." Their cities were among the largest in pre-colonial Africa, wealthy trading hubs with efficient markets run entirely by women. The area resembled pre-Risorgimento Italy, with each city-state having its own ruling caste and dialect; when the British adopted the Fulani term for its inhabitants and Protestant missionaries set about translating the Bible for them, they designated the version spoken in the Oyo kingdom as "standard Yoruba," around the same time as Italy was settling on Florentine as the official Italian language.

The British model for expanding its empire was to subcontract the process to private enterprise. It had worked quite well in South Asia (for the British, anyway), as the East India Company established a hugely profitable trading network and a semblance of British rule before handing it all over to the Crown following the 1857 Mutiny. The British granted George Goldie's National Africa Company a similar monopoly along the lower Niger River, but the firm managed only a two-decade run (in contrast to the East India Company's two centuries) before the government had to step in at the turn of the twentieth century to prevent a chaotic breakdown of law and order. A central problem was that palm oil, an ideal substance for lubricating the gears of the Industrial Revolution, had long been traded through a complex and sophisticated system in Yoruba and surrounding lands; interposing itself as sole buyer, Goldie's operation dismantled these centuries-old networks, destroying the delicate infrastructure that harvested the oil and also cultivated the burgeoning cocoa crop. Once in control, the Colonial Office forced Yoruba agriculture to focus on cash crops for export, undoing centuries of self-sufficiency in which urban dwellers grew their own food in carefully maintained fields just outside city walls. They also shut down long-established freelance tin mining, granting exclusive mineral rights to British firms and transforming proud, independent miners into miserably treated employees. The British found it difficult to take African culture and traditions seriously. After defeating the Yoruba's cousins in the kingdom of Benin, they refused to believe that those exquisite bronze heads could have been created by Africans; recognizing their extraordinary beauty, though, they seized them anyway and brought them back for the British Museum.

Abeokuta aligned itself with the British, both for protection and because many of its leading citizens were Saros, freed, educated, and converted by the British in Sierra Leone. The city, though, was never dominated by one religion; Christians, Muslims, and devotees of the Yoruba orishas rubbed along together quite peacefully, save for the occasional street fight involving a Ransome-Kuti. The Yoruba have generally pursued what has been termed "utilitarian syncretism," mixing and matching whatever works, in matters commercial and spiritual. Which was just as well, given their location, with the vast lands of the Bantu to the east and south, Fulani and Hausa Muslims to the north, the formidable Benin and Asanti kingdoms to the west, and predatory Europeans sailing in from the south. Fela Kuti came to be seen as a radical outlier, a musical original, but his openness to diverse influences is typical of his culture. To get his musical revolution under way, though, he needed that push from Mom.

> I don't think anyone kicked my ass as much as my mother. But I dug her. I liked to hear her talk . . . The more she got into politics the less time she had to beat me. So I, too, began liking politics.
>
> —Fela Kuti

The Ransome-Kutis were pillars of the Abeokuta establishment; they lived in a large compound and owned the city's first car. When he was twelve, Fela swiped the keys and taught himself to drive; rather than thrash him, his mother was so impressed that she appointed him chauffeur for her shopping expeditions. Years later, Fela's band members would dread road trips, as their leader always insisted on taking the wheel and driving hyper-aggressively at white-knuckle speeds for hours at a stretch. As a boy, recalled one friend, Fela "looked like a . . . perfect square. But inside he was a ruffian," adored by schoolmates and deeply unpopular with their parents. His own were firm believers in the British practice of corporal punishment; Fela confessed to feeling, at fifteen, more relieved than sad when his father died from prostate cancer. Freed from the reverend's oppressive control, he began to spread his wings. It was, as Tony Allen said, the best of times in Nigeria, with traffic mostly pedal-powered and nights full of adventure. J. K. Braimah, a friend who had been to school in Ghana and knew many of Accra's highlife musicians, brought Fela along to meet them whenever they played Abeokuta, and some invited the precocious kid onstage to sing a chorus or two.

Fela played piano in his father's church and for family gatherings; at the keyboard, "I forgot everything and went into my own little world." Prosperous Yoruba families considered musical education to be part of a good upbringing, but none could imagine it as a profession; music was considered a low-class occupation, not far removed from begging, since most performers relied on tips in return for singing the praises of the wealthy. In his early teens, Fela took up the trumpet; in those years preceding the triumph of the electric guitar, it seemed the most manly and assertive of instruments. As he developed a good embouchure and a confident sound, Fela became intrigued by the idea of music as a career. Had his father been alive, Fela would never have been allowed to attend Trinity College of Music in London. His brother Beko, already in Britain studying medicine, persuaded Trinity to offer Fela a chance to study there; when he got cold feet and told his mother he'd rather stay in Lagos, she thrust the plane ticket she'd bought into his hand along with the passport she'd organized, drove him to the airport, and frog-marched him to the departure gate. Funmilayo may not have grasped the fine print in Beko's letter, that admission depended on passing an audition. It did not go well: "I was playing the piano like a fucking monkey," Fela recalled. But, as would so many in the coming years, Trinity's principal succumbed to the Ransome-Kuti charm; rather than force the boy into a humiliating return to Lagos, he offered him a place.

Classmates were fascinated: "[A]n extraordinary fellow in every sense . . . clad always in some garish garb . . . Fela regularly held court among the bedazzled students . . . and seemed to regard the whole collegiate establishment as comical." He learned a lot about music at Trinity, but equally important in charting his future was what he absorbed cruising around town with J.K., his Abeokuta mate who was also in London studying law. The most salient lessons from those years were, first, that being a musician gave a huge boost to his success rate with girls, and second, what it meant to be a Black African ("Oh wow. These white people don't like us too much!").

Accounts of musical London at the turn of the sixties tend to focus on the 2i's coffee bar and skiffle's reverberations in the pop world, but the city had plenty of jazz clubs, plus Caribbean and African students who partied hard, often with live bands. Out and about in the evenings, Fela would carry his trumpet, more as a ruse to avoid paying door charges than any burning desire to get up and jam. ("I kept blowing nonsense . . . The more I tried to impress my audience, the worse for me.") Eventually, he and J.K. formed a highlife band to play the student-party circuit; they called it Koola Lobitos, a name Fela always refused to decode, but which seems to comprise a Pidgin take on "cool" and the Spanish for "wolf cubs." The Koola Lobitos version of highlife was propelled by a Bermudian drummer and a revolving line-up of Nigerians, Trinidadians, Ghanaians, and the occasional Brit, so it hardly broke any new ground. Their repertoire included topical calypsos by Mighty Sparrow and Lord Kitchener as well as songs from Fela's favorite Frank Sinatra and Louis Prima LPs. His first love was always modern jazz, but he was appropriately hesitant to solo in front of savvy London audiences; that would have to wait until he got back to Nigeria. Many African students tried to put off returning home, deliberately flunking final exams so they'd have to stay another year. Not Fela; he couldn't wait to leave behind the racism and the damp, chilly weather.

At a party thrown by the West African High Commission, he had chatted up Remi Taylor, daughter of an African-American father and a Nigerian mother. Before 1962 was out, Remi was pregnant and they were married. ("It was really colonial, inside a court . . . Can you imagine me standing in front of a white man to get married?") Prior to the wedding, he warned her that he would never be a faithful husband. "[G]irlfriends, he always had them," Remi remembered. "It didn't really bother me . . . He never brought any woman to my house." She bore three children in the first years of their marriage (including today's afrobeat bandleader, Femi), moved to Lagos with him, and maintained a dignified silence through the tumultuous years to come.

∽

Following the failure of the quartet, Fela recycled the name Koola Lobitos for a "highlife jazz" band designed to camouflage his bebop crusade behind a danceable front. During auditions, Tony Allen would chuckle behind his drum kit as musician after musician struggled with Fela's dense, complex arrangements; most were quickly dismissed, and of those who passed muster, some failed to turn up for rehearsal while others walked off in the middle of a show. Audiences often responded the same way; "it was far too complicated . . . a bit like showing off," Allen felt. Some critics were impressed, but the "Peter Pan" columnist in the *Lagos Daily Times* wrote: "Fela Ransome Kuti knows music but he doesn't play it. Rex Lawson [a rival bandleader] does not know music but he plays it."

Koola Lobitos were rarely short of work, though, and got signed by EMI Records. In the studio, Fela was a perfectionist, stopping takes when detecting flaws neither Tony nor the producers could hear. Fela fell into the usual pitfalls of running a band and was rarely able to pay salaries on time. Some musicians got fed up and left; in previous bands, Tony had always played shop steward, leading rebellions and strikes to hold leaders to their commitments. This was different. Allen understood that Fela would always be, well, Fela, and he resigned himself to a chaotic and insecure life; he recognized Fela's unique brilliance and believed the musical rewards would be great. Fela, likewise, understood that his musical ambitions would be almost impossible to achieve without the rhythmic foundation Tony provided. The Koola Lobitos years were the time of closest friendship between the two; Tony would often pick the Kuti kids up from school, and when Fela turned up for supper and found good Nigerian food on the table, Remi would admit that Allen had cooked it.

The country, meanwhile, was evolving in ways Fela would spend the rest of his life fighting against. He was his mother's political son, and Funmilayo was a staunch ally of Nigeria's first president, Dr. Nnamdi Azikiwe. "Zik," a rarity among politicians for speaking fluent Hausa, Igbo, and Yoruba, worked tirelessly for his vision of a unified nation in which ethnic and religious differences would fade away. Highlife, Fela believed, was the musical expression of that ideal; but by 1965, as Koola Lobitos played their first gigs, Zik's dream and Nigerian highlife were both in terminal decline.

So many African nations have been crucified by their colonial borders that it feels inappropriate to single one out, but a case can be made that Nigeria was dealt the worst geopolitical hand of all. Greed augmented by rivalry with the French led the British to capture the Muslim city-states in the north. Using their South Asian model, they left feudal sultans to run them how they pleased, so long as they paid taxes, cut back on the slave-trading, and kept the French at bay. Northern leaders' view of the rest of the country was eloquently expressed by the Sardauna of Sokoto following his first visit to Lagos: "The whole place was alien to our ideas and we found that members of the other regions might as well belong to another world." They were determined not to allow that infidel world to infect theirs. (This century's Boko Haram terrorism is a manifestation of that historic tension.)

In the run-up to independence, Britain divided the country into three regions, effectively giving the populous north veto power. When the 1963 census threatened to reveal the north's population falling below 50 percent, books were cooked to maintain the status quo. In January 1966, this and other outrages triggered a coup led by an Igbo officer in which the prime minister, a northerner, was killed. The Muslim north was already paranoid about Igbos; while the Hausa-Fulani educational system focused on religion and keeping the modern world at bay, Igbos were eager and worldly students and even better entrepreneurs. Following independence, they started businesses and filled government jobs in every corner of the country, a bit like Greeks and Lebanese in the

Ottoman Empire, Chinese in Southeast Asia, or Sikhs in East Africa, earning wealth and local resentment in equal measure.

The backlash was swift; Igbo businesses were destroyed and thousands massacred. Tony Allen remembers emerging at dawn from clubs in the middle of Lagos and seeing dead bodies in the streets following clashes between Hausas and Igbos. By autumn that year, a group of northern generals had organised a counter-coup and Igbos were fleeing for the safety of their homeland in the southeast. The final straw came when the new rulers re-drew political boundaries to dilute Igbo influence; the southeastern region declared independence under its pre-colonial name, Biafra. Might the country have allowed Biafra to walk away if vast quantities of petroleum hadn't been discovered under its earth and off its shores? In the minds of the generals, future oil income was already factored into the national budget (and into their Swiss bank accounts). The bloody civil war was on.

Away in London during the early years of independence, Fela may have missed the shifting of Nigerian musical tastes. For those flocking into Lagos, Ibadan, and other burgeoning cities, it was *juju* rather than highlife that filled evenings and blared from radios and record players. Juju is a Yoruba form that had long been considered a low-class music of the poor, absorbing elements from across Nigeria and speaking directly to ordinary people. If highlife began as a foreign style that grew progressively more African, juju was the reverse, a very African music that evolved by adding foreign elements.

Guitars, played in the "palm wine" finger-picking style, were juju's cornerstone. I realize this doesn't sound very indigenous, but the Portuguese had introduced them so many centuries ago that, along the coast at least, they had become part of the cultural fabric. Those intrepid Iberian traders brought members of the lute family with them wherever they sailed; even remote Hawaii has the Portuguese to thank for its love affair with the guitar. In West Africa, the Kru from what is now Liberia became the guitar's masters and disseminators. Kru were expert sailors, manning trading vessels from Dakar to Cape Town and omnipresent along that stretch from Freetown to the mouth of the Congo River. Using thumb and forefinger, they developed a distinctive style based on the interweaving arpeggios of traditional thumb pianos, the small portable sets of metal tongues that were among Africa's most common melody instruments.

Guitars and lamellophones (the technical name for thumb pianos) were often played together; the Isale Eko district on Lagos Island was full of palm-wine dives where "coast boy" guitarists jammed with thumb-pianists from the bush, stirring in recycled sambas from the Agudas plus whatever passing sailors might add to the mix. By the late twenties, the magic of 78 rpm shellac was bringing in more influences; highlifers picked up on Louis Armstrong's jazz and Attila the Hun's calypsos, while palm-wine and juju players were fascinated by Jimmie Rodgers and the crazy things Hawaiians got up to with their guitars. Everyone loved Cuba's Trio Matamoros.

Competition between highlife and juju had sociopolitical undertones; those who did well under British rule tended to enjoy the modernity of highlife and were often also interested in folklore from the countryside, but never mixed the two. Incomers resentful of the racial ceiling colonial authorities imposed on civil service positions saw juju and other modern iterations of traditional music as a defiant soundtrack in the move towards independence. Highlife musicians and fans disdained "dashing"—tipping in return for name-checks and praise—but for juju audiences the practice helped create networks of affinity and obligation; "big men" and politicians would throw parties and prove their bona fides by showering musicians with cash.

What really got the money flowing at juju shows were the tambourine acrobats who could toss one in the air or roll it across their shoulders, catch it on the beat, and slap it into a fingertip spin, always in time; then they'd rub damp fingers across the head to create a low-register buzz, a sound credited with giving the music its onomatopoeic name. The zills, those metal rings mounted into the frame, connected the tambourine to a sonic quality often found in African music: rattling tabs attached to drums, balafons, and other instruments, the buzzing of elevated strings on plucked instruments, and the rasping edge of voices such as

Mahlathini's all invoke shamanic ritual and the magical power of blacksmiths. The tambourine was a perfect mid-century Nigerian instrument, its clean, European-manufactured lines and association with Protestant missionaries balanced by sonic connections to ancient African spiritual practice.

On Independence Day in 1960, I. K. Dairo and His Blue Spots put on a triumphant show in Ibadan and never looked back, becoming *juju*'s first national stars. I.K. played accordion and blended the accordion's modern sound with harmony-singing based on Christian hymns, while also giving prominence to the *dundun* or talking drum. Dairo was a genius at shifting tempi and changing keys depending on where he was performing, understanding the different musical cultures of perhaps not all Nigeria's 250 ethnic groups, but a large number of them. Modern technology didn't have to be an enemy of tradition; juju groups with microphones and PA systems were able to balance vocals and electric guitars with the sounds of traditional percussion. (A little "shamanic" amplifier distortion was also welcome.) Juju was always receptive to novelty and change; Dairo's domination of the music in the sixties would be followed in the seventies by King Sunny Ade with his Hawaiian steel guitar and afrobeat-inflected rhythm section. As one juju musician put it, "Our Yoruba tradition is a very modern tradition."

Fela couldn't help but notice that jazzy complexity was not where Nigerian music was headed. In highlife, the most interesting new wrinkles were coming not from him, but from Ambrose Campbell, who, after many years in London, was back in Lagos and blending traditional village music with highlife. But what finally forced Koola Lobitos to change direction were shifts in the US that were being felt in Nigeria. The 1965 Newport Jazz Festival doesn't reverberate through history like the Folk Festival three weeks later, but it marked a watershed in its own way. Just as rock swept folk aside, jazz quickly fell from those Miles-Monk-Coltrane heights to be overshadowed by soul and funk. Great records out of Memphis, Muscle Shoals, and Detroit got much of the attention, but in Africa, it was all about James Brown.

The music of Black America had always held an appeal for Africans, but the way Brown's grooves seemed in no hurry to change key and how the harmonies on his extended riffs bordered on the modal were something different. Brown's musical director at the time, Pee Wee Ellis, has described how they borrowed from Afro-Cuban music, adding congas and a clave feel while extending repetitive figures into a kind of funk montuno. John Chernoff, an American percussionist who spent many years in Ghana performing with traditional musicians, noted, "[Brown's] rhythms . . . are extremely open and stable . . . To an African ear . . . his arrangements bear close comparison with African ones." The connection was noted on both sides of the Atlantic; the African-American author Thulani Davis felt that Brown's music provided "proof that black people . . . had to be from somewhere else, that Africa was really over there." Africans sensed the cultural confidence Brown's music engendered in Black Americans, and it boosted theirs as well.

Soul bands sprouted all along the coast. In Sierra Leone, a highlife bandleader named Gerald Pine, having caught Latin fever from listening to too much Radio Brazzaville, changed his name to Geraldo Pino and his music along with it. A year later, he made another U-turn and began channeling the Godfather of Soul. Pino's show was so spectacular, complete with choreographed moves, a stabbing horn section, screamed vocals, and even velvet capes, that he conquered every anglophone dance hall from Freetown to Calabar. He completely traumatized Fela: "This man was tearing Lagos to pieces . . . After seeing this Pino, I knew I had to get my shit together."

After he adopted a harsher vocal style, added some funk guitar, and even performed a few James Brown covers, crowds kept demanding more. Fela grew frustrated, giving one audience the first of many hectoring lectures: "A lot of the local bands are hiding under the cloak of soul music . . . to establish a name for themselves . . . I am sticking to my brand of highlife." One day at rehearsal he asked the bass player to try mimicking the pattern of a large Yoruba ceremonial drum while the guitarist played that signature James Brown riff and Allen kept up the distinctive jazz-highlife feel he'd been perfecting on the drums. The rhythm that would eventually triumph began to take shape. Fela's interest in traditional music was new; he would later express regret that his family's religion and social status had kept him away from orisha and Muslim parades and ceremonies when he was growing up. (His father would have thrashed him.) Tony was a few steps ahead; he'd long been fascinated by village drummers and had already incorporated many of their patterns into his playing.

Though Ghanaian bands often came to Lagos, Nigerian bands rarely made it to Accra. Fela decided to reverse the flow; audiences there, he figured, were used to Guy Warren's highlife-jazz experiments and would be more receptive, so he booked a tour. The band adored Ghana; everything was so orderly, the food was great, the crowds enthusiastic, the promoters honest, the venues well equipped, and the women friendly. Since they had begun a regular residence at a club in Lagos they called the Afro Spot, one of their Ghanaian promoters suggested they call their new style "Afro beat." And so they did.

☙

Ghana was just what Koola Lobitos needed; word of how well they did got back to Lagos and boosted their reputation. Hired to back up Chubby Checker and "My Boy Lollipop" Millie on the last big stadium tour before the Biafran War, they impressed everyone with their musicianship. But when the conflict began, army patrols proved even more dangerous to Lagosians (particularly women) than criminals, so no one wanted to be out after dark and live music suffered; the Afro Spot's "afternoon jumps" (an idea picked up in Accra) became the hottest events in town. Fela invited top bands—juju, soul, and highlife—to share bills; these head-to-head battles pushed groups to their limits and were still vividly recalled decades later.

Tony would turn up at the club at around eight in the morning during those months to work on new licks and techniques. Fela's songwriting also improved, including a glimpse into the future with an early version of "Chop and Quench"; the title is Pidgin for "eat and rinse" and refers to the corruption that was engulfing the country (and which would never cease, even after the war ended). Dancers loved the new afrobeat groove and were beginning to appreciate Fela's dense arrangements, but martial law made everything difficult. Juju thrived as generals lavishly "dashed" their favorite bands, while the highlife scene emptied out as many of its best musicians fled home to Biafra. So when Tunde Fademolu, a Nigerian student back from America on vacation, proposed bringing Koola Lobitos to the US for a tour, Fela's impulse was "let's get our asses out of this place"; if his band's reputation had been enhanced by success in Ghana, just imagine the glory when they returned in triumph from America!

Such dreams died quickly. Fademolu booked them up and down the East Coast, playing for African student parties and in small clubs. Fela was beside himself: "Look, I never came all the way from Africa to America to play for a handful of Nigerians. Is this a joke?" Their amateur agent managed to get them to the West Coast for some small gigs in San Francisco and Los Angeles, and there they came to rest: no income, no bookings, a very long way from home, and their leader vowing not to leave until he had something to brag about. They wangled a house in the Watts area of South LA; local kids intrigued by the sudden appearance of Nigerians in their midst would invade the kitchen in the mornings hoping to catch them before they were dressed. Why? Because they had a wager on whether Africans had tails. American ignorance about the "dark continent," African-American ignorance in particular, was a source of wonder and outrage to Koola Lobitos.

Then, one night at a party, Fela met Sandra Smith. He hadn't yet reached his harem stage, but Fela was an indefatigable seducer and Sandra was up for it. At this point in his life, assessing how far he'd come in his quest for fame, one would have to conclude that Fela was one of many mildly successful post-independence African bandleaders. Perhaps the group would have gone back to Lagos and become more popular, but would Fela have become the icon he is now? Would his music be sampled and spun for twenty-first-century dancers around the world? Would university courses study him and books be written? That night would change everything.

By the following morning, it was clear Fela had gotten more than he bargained for; Smith turned out to be a former Black Panther who had done jail time for assaulting a policeman during the 1967 LA Riots. After getting a blank look when she mentioned Malcolm X, Sandra gave Fela a copy of the *Autobiography* and ordered him to read it. The man was stubborn, vain, and often blinkered, but his mind was a sponge; he read, he listened, he took a view on everything that passed in front of him and Smith, and the Malcolm X book gave him a lot to think about. "I felt ashamed that a woman could be involved in black radical revolutionary politics and I was singing useless songs." Sandra never overtook Fela's mother as the greatest influence in his life, but she ran Funmilayo close.

Smith was connected in Hollywood, too. She got the group a gig at a club on Sunset Boulevard called the Citadel, and when the owner liked what he heard, she convinced him to let them park their equipment there and become the resident band. With income now just about covering outgoings, an incipient rebellion in the ranks calmed down. At the club, they met Muhammad Ali, the American football legend Jim Brown, Diana Ross, and a record producer who offered them a deal but backed off when Fademolu insisted the contract go through him. As Sandra schooled Fela about the Panthers, about slavery, civil rights, police brutality, and inner-city resistance, he began to see his ambitions as egotistic and shallow. Sandra urged him to start a revolution; that his country's oppressive rulers were now African rather than British didn't make the cause less important, quite the contrary.

She also turned Fela into a pothead. He had smoked a joint once before, backstage in a London club just before going onstage; the musician who handed it to him said it would improve his trumpet solo, but he panicked and played so badly he imagined the audience and his fellow musicians all laughing at him. Ever since, he had avoided drugs and forbade their use in Koola Lobitos (though Tony had long been a quiet toker). When Sandra lit up in bed one night, Fela was taken aback, but was so impressed by its sexual effect that he tried a joint at the club and was amazed at how his musical perception opened up, how seamlessly everything seemed to fit together. "Man, I used to just stand there stiff as a stick. My feet were glued to the floor. This night I started jumping, dancing, flying. The music poured out. From now on, I said, we all turn on." Fela never did anything by half; from then until the end of his life thirty years later, with the possible exception of time spent on airplanes, in prison, or asleep, he smoked dope non-stop. Tony should have been pleased, but for him, "the old Fela was gone overnight—his personality changed *completely* . . . It's like now he has to be the king of grass, giving it out to everybody."

With his new perspective, Fela became a proud African. He saw Black Americans wearing dashikis and sporting natural hair, while back home Nigerians were playing secondhand funk and dressing like White people. He changed the group's name to Africa 70 and, with a place to practice every day and play every night, started composing again. A promoter he met at the club had complimented the band but said he thought Fela was over-thinking the arrangements; if he kept it simple, he'd make a fortune. Now, through his marijuana filter, the wisdom of the man's comment seemed blindingly obvious.

"My Lady Frustration" begins with just bass and drum; Fela's chant and the horns enter next, following a very un-American pentatonic line, while the guitar scratch is full of James Brown attitude but never wavers from a three-plus-two clave, all combining to form an irresistible groove. For Fela, "It was the first African tune I'd written . . . [The club owner] was behind the bar and almost jumped over it. 'Fela, where did you get this fucking tune from?' The whole club started jumping and everybody started dancing."

It wasn't just Fela whose approach was transformed by America. The only woman in the touring party was their dancer, Dele, who was considered an essential part of the show. In Washington, some friends took them to a strip club; such things were unheard of in Nigeria (perhaps only in cold climates do people wear enough clothes to build a whole act around taking them off). They were amazed by the way American women took African moves and turned them into a provocative bump and grind. In San Francisco, a girl jumped onstage to dance with them, and Dele was so knocked out with her style that she asked for lessons. Dele's new routine, combining traditional Yoruba, Frisco hippie, and Sunset Strip go-go, became a showstopper for Africa 70 in both LA and Nigeria. (In the seventies, foreign visitors to Fela's Shrine club would be astonished by the *Shindig*-style dancer cages and ask if this was originally an African thing.)

Tony was psyched to be in a town with plenty of jazz clubs and checked out as many drummers as he could. One, Frank Butler, who had played with Coltrane, came by the Citadel and was intrigued by Allen's style. Tony returned the gesture and was equally impressed watching Butler. When he asked how to improve his technique, Butler told him that every morning, as soon as he woke up, he should practice on a pair of pillows: "[R]oll, land on the other pillow, and come back ... Land and come back, without breaking the roll ... [D]o everything with my wrists ... It sounded simple, but ... [i]t's not easy for a stick to bounce on a pillow ... [I]t started to change my playing. My wrists loosened up and became less stiff ... One night Frank came into the club ... and he ran up to me and said, 'You fucking got it!'"

It was time to go home. Fela now understood "that I should not try to impress foreigners. I should impress my own people first. When my people accept me then foreigners will see a need to accept me." Back in Lagos, J.K. saw straight away the change in his friend: "Because of Sandra," he said, "Fela became black."

The group arrived home at the end of 1969 as the Biafran War was ending. Hoping to prove Black government didn't work, South Africa, Rhodesia, and Portugal had all supported Biafra, as did France, which viewed a unified Nigeria as a threat to its domination of West Africa. But in the wake of the Suez blockade Britain desperately needed Nigerian oil and put all its many chips on Lagos. More than a million died before Biafra finally collapsed.

General (now President) Gowon was ruthless in waging the war but generous in victory, welcoming Biafran soldiers back into the army, restoring Igbo property and civil service jobs, and declaring that there had been "no victor and no vanquished." Despite such gestures, Azikiwe's dream of a unified, pan-ethnic Nigeria was over. With oil money flowing and cocoa and palm oil prices falling, the urban population ballooned as rural areas went into decline. In crowded city neighborhoods, people became even fiercer in their regional, linguistic, and religious loyalties than they had been in their villages.

The post-war years are seen as a golden age of Nigerian music, a time of ferment and change; juju, highlife, funk, *apala*, *fuji*, and afrobeat from 1970 to 1977 are all subjects of intense study (and great compilations). Like other former British colonies (and in contrast to their *dirigiste* francophone neighbors), Nigeria had scarcely any cultural policies or budgets, but with the economy booming there were plenty of places to play as well as studios and record labels. Wads of dash were also there to be pocketed, though whenever anyone approached Fela onstage waving banknotes he would hide behind the amps and call his guards to eject the offender. Africa 70 was all about the music and the message, and those years would be their greatest.

The audience for Koola Lobitos had been mostly middle-class students; Africa 70 spoke to the street and its crowds became a real Lagos curiosity, combining intellectuals and hipsters with youth from the lower end of society. Fela started writing songs in Pidgin, the lingua franca of the cities; everyone else's lyrics were either in English or a local language. His songs were never about love: "We have so many women, you don't need it . . . Our music . . . should be about reality." Sung insults and critiques are part of the culture, but most artists used allusion and metaphor and completed the thought with the dundun talking drum; Yoruba being a tonal language, audiences would get the message. Fela "threw the drum to the ground" and expressed issues directly. Then there were the girls; the songs, he declared, were "like a symphony," with a long instrumental section followed by the vocals, with Fela singing in a complex call-and-response dialogue with a half-dozen vibrato-free, unison female voices, their lines supporting, contradicting, or mocking his. It was knowing and street-smart, raucous yet wonderfully musical, the Yoruba bush colliding with Motown.

New songs came about like this: Fela would suddenly tune out from whatever was going on around him, stare off into space, grab a pen, and jot something down. Next afternoon at rehearsal he would have everything ready, not on paper, just in his head. Starting with the rhythm section, he built up a groove using three guitars like parts of a traditional Yoruba percussion ensemble, each with its own role, much like Afro-Cuban music. After the horns had nailed their parts, he would drill the girls. This all took place in front of a crowd; rehearsals were open to the public and many fans went regularly, finding it even more entertaining than the evening shows. An American visitor compared it to a revival meeting, with Fela passionately explaining the meaning of each new song. A friend from Abeokuta was struck by how Fela's gestures reminded him of his father putting the church choir through its paces. The songs' structures reflected what he had been taught at Trinity and the band performed them exactly the same way at every performance, like classical pieces.

Soon after their return to Lagos, Fela had hired Igo Chico, reputedly Nigeria's finest sax player. Igo didn't last long; his drinking and unreliability were incompatible with Fela's strict rehearsal schedule. But Chico made him realize that saxophone was a better fit with his new sound than trumpet, so Fela taught himself to play it and jettisoned his old instrument. Like many northern critics, when I heard Fela live I was unimpressed with his solos. I have since come to understand the close connection in many African cultures between instrumental performance and tonal languages such as Yoruba. Nigerians can detect insults, praise, religious expressions, and other allusions in the varying pitches of dundun, *gangan*, and other traditional "talking" drums, while wind instruments are also heard as a kind of speech, rather than an exercise in musical dexterity. While Fela will never be considered a great soloist, I now enjoy his playing a lot more.

∽

> Like a great boxer, he knows when to jab with his bass drum . . . when to momentarily scatter and reconsolidate the flow with a hi-hat flourish, when to stoke the tension by laying deeply into the groove, and when to break and restart that tension by interjecting a crackling snare accent on the downbeat.
>
> —Michael E. Veal, *Tony Allen: Master Drummer of Afrobeat*

> I sit straight. I'm not leaning on any side. I'm right in the middle . . . Some [drummers], their body is playing more than what the drums are doing! . . . But maybe that's what he thinks will make him a drummer . . . Maybe he thinks he has to show [the audience] a lot of action . . . Don't fight the drums, just deliver coolly.
>
> —Tony Allen

As Fela's arrangements became simpler and clearer, Tony Allen's rhythmic underpinning grew in complexity, bringing into play everything he had studied and observed over the past decade. Other great drummers around this time were transforming dance beats by applying jazz techniques to the rhythmic traditions of their culture: Sly Dunbar and Carlton Barrett in Jamaica, Ziggy Modeliste in New Orleans, Clyde Stubblefield with James Brown, and (stretching the thought to include timbales) Tito Puente in Latin New York. Though none lacked subtlety, all struck their instruments with force. A remarkable thing about Africa 70's power as a dance band is the delicacy with which Allen played his instrument.

Tony encouraged Fela to add a conga drum to the ensemble but he never wanted shakers, rattles, or other high-frequency percussion. Allen's own strokes on the cymbal, hi-hat, and snare mirrored the dialogue among wood, hide, metal, gourd, and beads in traditional African music. When Fela stated, "I had been using jazz to play African music, when really I should be using African music to play jazz," it was Tony who made that shift possible, anchoring Africa 70 in the timeless forms he knew well. The haze of pot smoke and Fela's offstage focus on his growing harem (sex three times a day) meant the two were no longer so close, but the musical bond between them was stronger than ever. After Fela appointed him bandmaster, Allen would lead the group through rigorous afternoon rehearsals and long instrumental sets at night, with Fela nowhere to be seen.

The sundering of this great partnership took years to arrive, but it probably began with the name-change business. Funmilayo had long embraced jettisoning "slave" names in favor of African ones, but it was Mobutu's Zairization campaign in 1974 that prodded Fela to drop "Ransome" and replace it with "Aníkúlápó." Given the Yoruba predilection for blurring metaphor and meaning, the new word could signify "with an arrow in his quiver" or possibly "having death in his pocket." The band was ordered to follow suit, but Tony refused; he was comfortable with "Allen" and had no wish to distance himself from his family. "Today I'm not the slave of anybody," he said. Others might have been sacked, but Fela swallowed Tony's defiance; in one recording where he name-checks everyone in the band, he calls the drummer "Mr. Alien."

> 3 P.M.: Fela Kuti . . . wakes up. In white briefs, he leaves his poster and bill-plastered room and enters [the living room], a room with broken armchairs, dirty mattresses and jumbled sheets. One of his followers, whose only function is to serve Fela beverages, hands him a drink. Another man brings him a dish of rice, that being his only function . . . [A] third man presents himself and opens a black box. Fela takes a joint out of the box . . . as thick as one's thumb and as long as one's hand. He makes himself comfortable, takes a drag, and man, now he's ready. Ready to start the day, a day which will only end at 6 A.M. the next day.
>
> —Carlos Moore and Sylviane Kamara

In 1973, Fela moved the group's headquarters from its original Afro Spot location to the Empire Hotel across the street from his mother's house where he and his entourage were living. It was normal for successful groups to have a regular place to play: King Sunny Ade, I. K. Dairo, Ebenezer Obey, Victor Olaiya, Sikuru Ayinde Barrister, and others all had similar bases. Fela called his the African Shrine; it was open all day, with a café, a selection of magazines, books on African history, posters showing Afro hairstyles, and an altar with photos and information about his heroes: Kwame Nkrumah, Malcolm X, Martin Luther King, and . . . Idi Amin! The Shrine was modeled on Mbari Arts Club, a student center at Ibadan University co-founded by Fela's cousin the Nobel Prize–winning author Wole Soyinka.

Fela's club was partly covered by a corrugated tin roof and held a thousand people; shows lasted until dawn, both because Fela was nocturnal and since it was no longer safe to be out in Lagos after midnight. The Shrine was unique in many ways, but the most striking involved girls and dope. It was generally accepted that unaccompanied women in a Lagos nightclub were almost certainly prostitutes. Not at the Shrine; making single women feel safe and welcome certainly altered the vibe, with the added virtue of allowing Fela to recruit additions to his seraglio as he wandered through the crowd (and band members to chat up girls who didn't interest the boss).

Marijuana had been an accepted part of Nigerian culture until the British established a fierce intolerance that the post-colonial government inherited; possession was punishable by ten years in prison. Fela's yabis during the early Shrine years were mostly directed towards societal hypocrisies rather than Gowon's government or the army, so defiance of the drug laws marks the opening salvo in his twenty-year war with the authorities. He smoked openly onstage, waving a massive spliff as he conducted the band, while encouraging dealers to sell loose joints in the audience. With his popularity approaching peak adulation, the government was wary of confronting him. (When Fela turned up at a stadium packed for a Jimmy Cliff concert, for example, the crowd roared their acclaim, hoisted him on their shoulders, and carried him around the running track, forcing Cliff to abandon the rest of his show.)

In April 1974, with the tabloid press running lurid stories about sex, drugs, and Fela, someone in power decided enough was enough and ordered a raid on his home. He was kept for a week in a large holding cell with a group of prisoners who were thrilled to have the great man among them, electing him president of what they called the "Kalakuta Republic" (from the "Black Hole of Calcutta"). When he was finally bailed, Fela installed barbed wire around his house and erected a sign declaring it the "Independent Kalakuta Republic." Two classic compositions emerged from the experience: "Alagbon Close" (the address of the police station) and "Expensive Shit" (about the attentive wait for the prisoner's first bowel movement, as it was suspected—wrongly—that an analysis of his feces would incriminate him). The most far-reaching implication of these events was to ratchet up government paranoia; calling his compound a republic smacked of separatism, a sensitive matter for this post-civil-war regime, and they were not amused.

Things got worse when a Lagos police inspector's fourteen-year-old daughter ran off to join the harem. Her brothers were turned rudely away by Fela and his guards when they came looking for her, but they returned with a squad of Daddy's police, who gave Fela the first in his long Calvary of savage beatings. After seventeen days in hospital, he returned home in triumph; one court had reprimanded the police and refused to press charges of kidnapping, while another declared him not guilty of drug possession.

⌇

> Tell our parents we were going to the Shrine? No way! Everyone said it was a place where people on the run from the law hung out, criminals, hemp smokers, prostitutes, school dropouts . . . We went anyway because there were a lot of progressive things happening there.
>
> —Fan quoted in Michael F. Veal's *Fela*

> He is . . . certainly not handsome, slight in stature, with a narrow face, high cheekbones and widely set eyes. But when he moves on stage, in restrained, graceful motions like a coiling snake, and when he sings, hunching over the microphone and spitting out the words, the magnetism is unmistakable in any culture: superstar.
>
> —John Darnton, *New York Times*, 1977

> When you are the king of African music, you are the king, because music is the king of all professions.
>
> —Fela Kuti

> We were the only white people there and it was very intense, but when this music broke, I ended up just weeping.
>
> —Paul McCartney describing his visit to the Shrine

Among the many off-duty soldiers who visited the Shrine was Murtala Mohammed. A complex figure in Nigerian history, Mohammed was a rigid, Sandhurst-trained northern general responsible for atrocities against civilians during the civil war. Serving in the Gowon government, he grew increasingly uncomfortable with its corruption and incompetence; oil income meant the economy was surging, but passengers arriving at Lagos Airport had to bribe their way through a chaotic customs hall while freighters queued offshore for months, waiting to unload cargo as shipping companies tried to figure out whom to dash. In the summer of 1975, with Gowon away on a diplomatic trip, a group of younger officers seized power and Mohammed was named head of state.

Fela was pleased, and not just because the president was a fan. (The new Lagos police chief was also a Shrine regular and a friend of Funmilayo's.) During his brief time in office, Mohammed purged the military and civil service of many of the corrupt and the useless, returned stolen land to its rightful owners, cleared the backlog at the docks, and told Henry Kissinger not to bother stopping off in Lagos on his African trip. For our story, though, Mohammed's most fateful acts involved FESTAC '77.

By 1975, the idea of a high-minded festival of African arts and music felt like a relic from another era. The first FESTAC, held in Dakar, Senegal, in 1966, had been a well-organized celebration of "Négritude," President Leopold Senghor's concept for the future of African culture. With African unity an agreed goal, the second was set for four years later in Nigeria, the most populous of the anglophone nations; owing to the small matter of the host country being busy with its civil war, however, the event was postponed. 1974 came and went without a festival, and one of Mohammed's first acts on taking charge was to push the new 1976 date back a further year, a sensible move considering how little had been organized yet. The general then took the remarkable step of appointing Fela to the selection committee.

What might the future have held for Nigeria and for Fela under this strong-willed, afrobeat-friendly reformer? The notorious Lagos traffic, however, proved fatal for Mohammed; inching towards his office on February 13, 1976, in a jam too dense for the sirens of the motorcycle escorts to part, his limousine was riddled with bullets by a group of disgruntled officers. The assassins were quickly caught and executed, and Mohammed's colleague General Olusegun Obesanjo took over. A career soldier, Obesanjo had no sense of humor and little interest in music. He was a contemporary of Fela's from Abeokuta, where he had attended the Baptist Boys Academy, often going to class barefoot; at his father's elite school nearby, Fela always wore expensive shoes. The two and a half years between Mohammed's killing and Fela's famous delivery of "Coffin for Head of State" to Obesanjo was the most event-filled and dramatic period of the singer's life (which is saying a lot).

> [H]e weaves local and world events into a magic carpet of jokes and humorous anecdotes while playing with language, which, were he to have chosen the field of comedy, would have put him up among the elite in this field. He has the full range of comedy skills, including mimicry and superb timing.
>
> —Michael Archangel, *Rule by Love*

> One can easily and without exaggeration characterise contemporary urban culture in Nigeria as hostile and alienating. It is a culture of violence . . . Dominant in it are corruption, confusion, bewilderment, and insecurity.
>
> —Eme Ekekwe, political scientist

> *Pen get power gun no get*
> *If gun go steal eighty thousand naira*
> *Pen go steal two billion naira*
>
> —Fela Kuti, "Authority Stealing"

> *Some will rob you with a six-gun,*
> *And some with a fountain pen*
>
> —Woody Guthrie, "Pretty Boy Floyd"

Fela capped off the mourning period for Mohammed with a day-long concert in the national stadium, dedicated to the general. He then dutifully turned up at a meeting of the FESTAC committee, but was so appalled by the venality and bad taste on display that he resigned. From then on, Fela was FESTAC's implacable enemy and the government grew increasingly uneasy about this massively popular dissident in their midst.

Though NBC refused to play most of it, Fela's music was everywhere; the mid-seventies represented the height of his power as a recording artist, before pirate cassettes began crippling the music industry. He released between six and ten 12-inch discs a year, each containing a pair of epic songs and dressed in cartoonish cover art mocking the army, the government, or some heretofore unchallenged assumption of Nigerian society (skin-lightening creams, for example). One reason for Fela's enduring legacy is how good the records still sound; Africa 70 would rehearse a song for weeks, perform it for months, then record take after take until their perfectionist leader was satisfied. Once a song was committed to vinyl, Fela refused to ever play it onstage again. Africa 70 was hugely popular in surrounding countries, particularly Cameroon, but after a visit to Douala in which Fela, despite being showered with favors and moved to a five-star hotel, wouldn't perform "Lady" for the culture minister, the group were never invited back.

The combination of Mohammed's sitting-duck murder, a surge in car-window stick-ups, and the prospect of thousands of visitors arriving for FESTAC '77 forced the Obesanjo administration to address the Lagos traffic problem. Their creative solution was to issue traffic police and soldiers with bullwhips; when a hapless driver was pulled over for an infraction, lashes were delivered curbside. This and other examples of the military government's contempt for its citizens inspired "Zombie," perhaps Fela's most enduring composition, the lyrics mocking military discipline with simple commands: "*Go and kill / Go and die*." It became the street soundtrack in the lead-up to FESTAC and soldiers played it in the barracks whenever officers weren't around. The government was beside itself.

Fela's onstage yabis continued to hit the mark. One example: because a key FESTAC event was being held hundreds of miles away in Kaduna, the government purchased two thousand people-movers to ferry performers and dignitaries; within weeks of delivery, most had disappeared into the country's chaotic free-enterprise transport system. A later investigation revealed nearly half of FESTAC's $140 million budget to be unaccounted for. Fela underlined his contempt by leafleting the city with his accusations of corruption and riding around on a donkey outside the national stadium during a concert wearing only underpants and blowing his saxophone.

A constant humiliation for the regime during the month-long event was visiting celebrities asking to meet Fela; official guides were under orders to refuse, but no one could stop Stevie Wonder or Sun Ra slipping away from a post-concert reception, jumping into a cab, and heading for the Shrine. When Guinea's President Sékou Touré arrived with Miriam Makeba and Stokely Carmichael, they invited Fela for a meeting; his car was intercepted by military police, but Makeba and Carmichael became Shrine regulars during their stay. Fela was in dazzling form, performing every evening at midnight rather than the usual three times a week at 2 a.m., and delivering hilarious mockeries of government incompetence to a club packed with visiting performers, politicians, and journalists. Hugh Masekela, Archie Shepp, Randy Weston, and Michael Olatunji all sat in with Africa 70, while Stevie Wonder spent evenings there drinking palm wine and shouting his approval.

> [T]he man turned Nigeria completely upside down! He had the whole country in his hand . . . Fela at the time was a law unto himself and did whatever he pleased in Nigeria, until he met an equally lawless group—the army.
>
> —Fan quoted in *Fela*

By 1977, the street between the Shrine and the Kalakuta Republic was Fela's territory; his entourage had expanded to include a gang of street kids who fought off local thugs and took control of the area. The police, mostly Lagosians, were generally friendly to the singer and his boys, offering an escort when he ventured out late at night and never invading the "Republic." The army was another story. Wary of creating a rival power, military governments underfunded local police and encouraged the army to undertake many law enforcement duties. Soldiers were drawn from across the huge country, particularly the north, where military service had long been a favored career choice. Not wanting to risk his predecessor's fate, Obesanjo ran the country from army headquarters at Dodan Barracks, located not far from the Kalakuta Republic. The mostly rural, poorly educated, and often devout soldiers couldn't help being aware of

Fela's scantily dressed girls, to say nothing of his contemptuous yabis against those "un-African" religions, Islam and Christianity.

Once FESTAC's distinguished visitors were out of town, retribution came swiftly. On February 16, 1977, a car with one of Fela's men at the wheel knocked over a lance corporal on his motorbike; when a group of soldiers from Dodan Barracks arrived at the compound to arrest the offending driver, Fela refused to surrender him. (Friends had often warned about letting his arrogant "boys" roam around Lagos causing trouble, confident Fela would protect them.) "Zombie" blared from a window as girls danced mockingly around the departing soldiers. Soon they were back, this time with hundreds of comrades, most of them Hausa Muslims; every male they encountered on either side of the street was beaten with a club or rifle butt or slashed with a bayonet. Fela was knocked unconscious by a blow that broke his jaw, and he would have been killed had another soldier not intervened. The women were brutalized: raped, beaten, stabbed between the legs. Both buildings were trashed and burned, but not before both Funmilayo and Fela's brother Beko had been thrown from a second-floor window, with both suffering broken arms. Fela and his music would survive and carry on for another two decades, but nothing would ever be the same after that day.

෴

Fela had a Diaghilev-like ability to fall on his feet (not to mention extraordinary physical courage). No sooner was he discharged from the hospital than he filed a lawsuit against the government and found a new base for Africa 70. The Crossroads Hotel's landlord was an army officer, providing some insulation against government efforts to shut him down. Eventually, however, army patrols harassing fans on their way there put a drain on attendance; Fela and the group (as well as his mother, whose hair had turned white since the attack) needed somewhere to recover physically, emotionally, and financially. Where better than Ghana?

The move to Accra was going well until he sent for his harem. Ghana was also now run by a military junta, who were growing almost as nervous as their Nigerian colleagues of Fela's songs and speeches and refused to grant the extra visas. His solution was to fly back to Lagos and marry all twenty-seven so he could bring them in as wives. It was a spur-of-the-moment bit of sleight-of-hand, but he made the most of it, announcing that he had long intended such a gesture, particularly after the terrible ordeal they had all been through. Unfortunately, it didn't work; Ghana's border remained closed to the entourage and the authorities there made it clear they'd be happy to see the back of Fela, too. Funmilayo was the first to leave, deciding she'd be better off in Lagos, where her other two sons were doctors and her daughter a nurse, and the rest soon followed.

Fela was always an awkward subject for hero worship; including Idi Amin in his pantheon of Black saints was the least of it. He opposed schooling of any kind, insisting Nigerian kids should all be sent to the country, Khmer Rouge–style, to learn through traditional husbandry of the soil. For many, his attitude towards women remains the biggest obstacle. I once heard an Anglo-Nigerian woman shut down critical talk about his ménage by insisting it was simply cultural, that she had an uncle there with a dozen wives and that such things were customary for Yoruba "big men." Few Nigerians seem to agree, pointing out that he never presented himself to the girls' families, paid no bride prices, and failed to take any responsibility for wives who fell out of favor and onto hard times. He may have adored and respected his mother and Sandra Smith, but on the home front—and in song—he was a tyrant. "Lady" ridicules women wanting to be treated as such, while "Mattress" expresses his view of their most important function. Funmilayo, it must be said, blessed the multiple marriage and calmly took part in the chaotic life of the compound.

1978 began promisingly with a generous offer from the Berlin Jazz Festival; Fela and the band (who were owed many months of back salaries) looked forward to regaining financial and emotional equilibrium in the German autumn. But in April, Funmilayo died, sending Fela, the family, and much of the country into mourning. She had never recovered from the defenestration, and her death marked a point of no return in Fela's battle with the authorities. "Sorrow Tears and Blood," originally inspired by the student uprising in South Africa, became the opening shot in this war, the call of the title underlined by the response of the chorus, aimed at the Nigerian army, "*them regular trademark.*"

Berlin delivered fresh blows. Film from the concert shows the band playing well, demonstrating clearly the originality and brilliance of Fela's arrangements in a tight, well-structured set. But Germany in 1978 had little experience of African popular music; the world music surge, when African groups dazzled audiences across Europe, was years in the future. Some were expecting a purely African music based on timeless rituals from an exotic culture, while others, particularly the festival's regular contingent of critics, were looking forward to hearing what "African jazz" had to offer. No one was prepared for funk guitar, go-go-style dancing girls, a garishly dressed leader with pop-star attitude, and instrumental solos that bore little resemblance to bebop improvisation. The performance took place at the gorgeous (all-seated, no dancing allowed) Haus der Kulturen der Welt, with the audience looking earnest at the start and bewildered by the end. Onstage, the band was focused but unsmiling.

That afternoon at the soundcheck, Tony Allen had announced his departure. The satisfaction of helping someone he considered a genius to create a new form of African music had kept him on board for years, enduring repeated broken promises and watching dozens of hangers-on added to the payroll and the food budget while the musicians' salaries fell further into arrears. The Berlin touring party was over seventy strong, with the extra airfares and hotel costs (including room service) deducted from the fee. To cap it all, Fela revealed that whatever profits remained would be set aside not for the band, but to finance his new political party. Tony booked a flight to London for the next day.

A German promoter had been waiting in the wings with an offer for a two-week post-festival tour, but after scathing reviews he backed out. Eight more walked off into the city, preferring to take their chances as illegal immigrants rather than endure life in Lagos with Fela.

∾

"*KA-LA-KU-TA, KA-LA-KU-TA.*" With Fela away in Germany, thousands of his followers turned out to try and prevent it, but could do nothing except chant and jeer as heavily guarded bulldozers reduced both Republic and Shrine to rubble. Fela's career now resembled that wreckage: Africa 70 was completely broken, with one member after another following Allen out the door, while his international reputation lay in tatters, with no promoter interested in booking a tour. The government, to no one's surprise but Fela's, barred his Movement of the People party from taking part in the upcoming elections.

Yet setbacks only seemed to energize the man and make him more determined. He quickly formed a new band and, having learned how dark and African-looking ancient Egyptians actually were, named it Egypt 80. If you listen carefully, you can tell their recordings from Africa 70's: the conga is higher in the mix and there's no *tsh-tsh-tsh* from the Allen hi-hat whispering the beat along. The post-1978 tracks are denser, too, the arrangements more complex, the call-and-response vocals even more inventive. Tony stopped by the New Shrine on a visit to Lagos and thought Egypt 80 were great, that Fela had created something new and special. A Lagos critic wrote: "[He] has lost nothing musically. Money, cars, and some 'queens' he has lost, yes . . . [I]f anything, he has had time to reflect and improve on his composition, arrangement, and even his dancing." Fela told his drummers exactly what patterns to play and warned them to forget trying to sound like Allen. He went through a lot of them; at one point there were two taking it in turns, so exhausting was the task, particularly on nights when the frustrated leader would turn to his audience and ask if there were any drummers in the house.

Fela the lyricist focused his attacks on the government. The official inquest into the 1977 assault found that "an exasperated and unknown soldier" had set fire to the building, mildly criticized the army, and recommended that Fela be compensated for the destruction. The High Court, however, ruled that there was no provision in law for such a payment, so Fela remained desperately broke. (Shrinking the household seems not to have been considered.)

On the day before the 1979 election that restored Nigeria (temporarily) to the ranks of parliamentary democracies, Fela, accompanied by wives and entourage, marched to the Dodan Barracks with a farewell gift for Obesanjo: a replica of Funmilayo's coffin. Such representations of the dead can have huge symbolic power in Africa, and the guards reacted with predictable outrage; shots were fired as the group surged through the gates, but miraculously no one was killed. Fela was arrested and beaten, as he would be more than two hundred times in the coming years: repeatedly for marijuana, once for a "currency violation" (the cash float for a foreign tour), another time for emptying the contents of a sewage truck onto the front yard of the president of Decca Records, again for harboring criminals, and finally, in 1994, on a trumped-up murder charge. Mostly, he would be released on bail and the charges eventually dropped, but he spent nearly two mid-eighties years in prison on the currency conviction before a change of government led to his release. A surreal footnote to Fela's legal troubles was that the only one who could come close to replicating his distinctive vocals was his lawyer, a man named Feelings, who would deputize for him onstage whenever he failed to get his client out on bail.

Depending on who was president, authorities seemed more or less sanguine about the political threat Fela posed inside the country, but all were unnerved by the image he projected abroad. A *New York Times* reporter who insisted on attending the Kalakuta inquest was expelled from the country, while Fela's arrests were often timed to sabotage a foreign tour. Despite the government's best efforts, though, quite a few did take place; as Tony Allen would also discover, the audiences most receptive to afrobeat were not their fellow anglophones, but the French.

> The gods do not want the music to break into the international scene as a fashion . . . [but] as a serious cultural episode.
>
> —Fela Kuti

Egypt 80's international career was launched as the result of a plot to sabotage it. In 1980, the Italian Communist Party decided to include Fela's band in its annual series of youth festivals around the country. After messages were passed between Lagos and the right-wing government in Rome (eager to embarrass the Communists), the group's equipment was impounded and Fela locked up while Italian customs officials searched for the drugs the Nigerians assured them were there (since they'd planted them). Somehow, the plot was exposed and Fela was freed.

A few lines about the incident in the *International Herald Tribune* caught the eye of Martin Meissonnier in Paris. Meissonnier is a man of many parts, at that time a presenter on Radio France, journalist with *Libération*, energetic promoter at the progressive edge of jazz and funk, and longtime admirer of Fela Kuti. He was part of a coterie of *soixante-huitard* enthusiasts for exotic music and culture, the nexus of which was *Actuel* magazine and its dynamic editor, Jean-François Bizot. It is tempting to suggest that the French are so open to music from distant lands because they're useless at rock 'n' roll; one might also question why Parisians got so excited about afrobeat when sublime sounds from Senegal, Mali, Algeria, and the Congo could be heard by crossing the Boulevard Periphérique and venturing into the *banlieues*. But credit where credit is due; Meissonnier jumped on a plane and flew to Naples, where the freshly bailed Fela was performing, and made him an offer he couldn't refuse: six concerts across Europe starting in Paris (with a budget big enough to accommodate the full entourage) and a record deal with Arista/BMG.

In many ways, Meissonnier's tour was a success. His brilliant advance promotion covered all the bases: photos of Fela and his wives were splashed on the front pages of popular dailies, there were deep analyses of the music in the specialist press, plus television news coverage and an ARTE documentary, resulting in sold-out houses everywhere. For the rest of his life, Fela would compare the promotion of subsequent tours unfavorably with Meissonnier's. Egypt 80 seemed to embody everything the *branché* flank of French society was looking for in 1981, so Fela probably had only himself to blame for the tour's failure to launch him into European stardom. He and the group couldn't rouse themselves to attend a lavish reception laid on by the new record label, while owing to the singer's recent discovery of a cannabis tincture that left him moving and talking in slow motion, the onstage Fela was a subdued shadow of his usual self.

When Chris Blackwell approached Meissonnier about signing Fela to Island, he was told it was too late, and the two worked out a deal for Martin to produce King Sunny Ade for the label instead. Nigerian music would get its cool global outlet, but Fela wouldn't become Bob Marley's successor. Even after the offended Arista execs dropped him, Blackwell decided against signing Fela when he learned of the singer's refusal to travel without the full complement of wives and hangers-on. A follow-up tour in 1983 was an anti-climax; audiences, media, and Meissonnier were no longer quite so interested.

Fela's forays into anglophone territory were also problematic. Targeting Black audiences on a couple of short US tours, he offended both Christians and Muslims with his anti-religion diatribes, ridiculed his Nigerian fans for crossing the ocean to perform menial tasks for White people, and turned off dashiki-and-Afro-sporting families at an afternoon show in Brooklyn with his "slack" talk about women and sex. (Jamaicans in the crowd loved it.)

The international outlet for his recordings was now Celluloid, an aggressive independent label founded by a group of May '68 veterans, including *Actuel*'s Bizot and the future lambada man, Jean Karakos. In 1985, while the singer was languishing in prison, Karakos turned over multitrack tapes of "Army Arrangement," Fela's attack on Nigeria's sham democracy, to Bill Laswell, a musician and producer now at the cutting edge of dub-influenced remixes. The minute he was free Fela furiously denounced the new version, which had stripped away most of the African rhythm (Laswell's "regular trademark"), leading to a war of words between the two. Laswell's riposte—"I would never work with musicians at that low a level"—sounded as obtuse then as it does today.

I saw Egypt 80 at London's Brixton Academy in 1986 along with a mixed crowd, African and British. The audience for their 1983 show at the same venue had been mostly Nigerians; those three years had seen the explosion of a middle-class audience for music from afar, particularly Africa. The Greater London Council (about to be abolished by Thatcher) underwrote a series of concerts in the spring of 1985 at a dance hall in Victoria: Youssou N'Dour and Touré Kunda from Senegal, Kanda Bongo Man, Sam Mangwana and Les Quatres Étoiles from Zaire, Fela's fellow Nigerian Segun Adewale, Pierre Akendengué from

Gabon, and the Ghanaian African Brothers. Fela did not fit neatly into the exuberant, seductive sounds on show across those unforgettable evenings. He may have craved international acceptance, but his music remained defiantly local, the coiled anger of sound and words aimed squarely at his corrupt and violent government and his submissive fellow citizens. Outsiders could listen and move, but truly grasping what Fela was up to wasn't so easy. Decades on, afrobeat has become a relatively familiar sound, but in 1986 it seemed an intriguing but curious blend of Yoruba authenticity and African-American showmanship that was difficult for critics to categorize or describe.

Those GLC concerts, curated by Robert Urbanus from Stern's, London's pioneering African record store, may have been an opening fusillade in the West's fascination with African popular music, but they also marked a pinnacle, an all-too-brief moment when European and African dancers would happily move to the same beats. Many music buffs were seeking refuge from years of assault by disco, punk, prog rock, and glam rock, styles that repudiated much of what had drawn us to music in the first place: virtuosity, spontaneity, roots. Popular forms from faraway cultures, particularly African ones, seemed to offer a chance to regain some of what had been lost. The moment didn't last; while we were learning to tell a *soukous* from an *mbalax*, African musicians and audiences were falling hard for drum machines and synthesizers. Fela should have been our hero; he hated electronic beats as much as we did. But the impossible demands he placed on promoters, track lengths as awkward for radio as Indian ragas, the battles with his government that often stopped him touring . . . these things kept northern hemisphere audiences from fully embracing him during his lifetime. Three and a half decades on, you hear Fela's music far more often than that of those other African visitors to London.

In truth, Fela's enduring legacy owes less to the world music scene than to dancefloor pioneers such as Gilles Peterson, who loved mixing afrobeat with American funk, acid jazz, and modern samba. Fela's studio perfectionism and Tony Allen's impeccable timekeeping meant their tracks sit comfortably in sequences that include machine beats. It was open-eared DJs, with an assist from political movements inspired by Fela's defiance and admiring figures such as Brian Eno and David Byrne, that kept Fela's flame burning through the decades.

Foreign audiences may have been slow on the uptake, but many musicians got the message. The guitar lick on Marley's "Could You Be Loved" shows that Fela must have been on the turntable at Hope Road. Paul McCartney tried to hire members of Africa 70 for the recording of *Band on the Run* in Lagos, but Fela wouldn't allow it. Talking Heads' Eno-produced *Remain in Light* has a clear afrobeat feel. Bootsy Collins often spoke of his unforgettable and transformative evening at the Shrine. The American vibraphonist Roy Ayers lugged his bulky instrument all over Nigeria so he could join Fela for a tour; recordings they made together prove that jazz virtuosos can sound great playing to afrobeat. Trumpeters Lester Bowie and Hugh Masekela both traveled to Lagos to play with Fela at low points in their lives and left feeling inspired and rejuvenated.

As thrilled as visitors were to experience his music *in situ*, they were often taken aback by the offstage Fela; Masekela described a day spent talking music and politics being regularly interrupted by women demanding (and getting) sex. Though there was hardly any corner of life in which Fela did not challenge custom and authority, the most notorious was in the realm of sexuality. Sociologists might classify Yoruba society as "sex positive," but the subject is rarely discussed. When Fela and the girls sang "Na poi" (*"Put it in, please / That's not the right spot / It's the wrong place / Move it forward—gently, gently / It's sex! / Do it!"*), it was even more shocking than his yabis against big men and religion. Fela enjoyed showing off his legendary equipment by parading around his home in the skimpiest of briefs or, on occasions such as the arrival of a government minister for a meeting, completely naked.

In the end, sex proved Fela's downfall. Like many Africans in those years, he refused to confront the reality of HIV even as he grew thinner and weaker, clinging to the fantasy that it was strictly a European disease and that acknowledging it was unmanly and shameful. On August 2, 1997, with French concert promoters and festivalgoers awaiting the start of his biggest European tour ever, Fela passed away. Beko Ransome-Kuti, a dissident doctor who had spent more time in prison than his brother, was one of Nigeria's leading crusaders for AIDS awareness. Defying Fela's—and the government's—wishes, he quickly announced the true cause of death, an action that increased the sense of national urgency. The funeral took place in Tafawa Balewa Square in front of a crowd of 150,000, including a group of students who tried to steal the body so they could embalm and preserve it at their university, like Lenin in Red Square. Femi, Fela's son with Remi, and Seun, whose mother, Fehintola, was one of the harem wives, vowed to (and did) carry Fela's music into the future. Egypt 80 and the cream of Nigeria's musicians serenaded the coffin and the crowd until sunset.

Every day, every day, I dey hungry
Every day, every day, no house to stay
Monkey dey work, baboon dey chop
Baboon dey hold de key of store
Monkey dey look, baboon dey laugh
De day monkey eye come open now
Baboon dey vex

—Fela Kuti, "Unnecessary Begging"

I have opened the eyes of the people to oppression in our continent. The people know I did it. I'm honest and consistent. That's enough.

—Fela Kuti

At his first press conference after returning from America in 1970, Fela raised his fist in the Black Power salute; no one in Nigeria had a clue what it meant. He spent the rest of his life trying to awaken his fellow Africans to its meaning in their lives: composing impassioned street-slang lyrics, raining down hilarious yabis from the stage, touring his band throughout the region, giving lectures, buying space in the *Lagos Times* for his "Chief Priest Say" editorials, and ceaselessly subverting the norms of Nigerian society. As conditions grew steadily worse, culturally ingrained deference to power meant that Fela and his music were among the very few high-profile avenues for protest. Aside from his shrinking fan base, not many paid attention; by the time Fela died, Nigeria had become one of the most corrupt and unequal countries on earth.

As frustrating as it must have been to watch thieves building their luxurious, high-walled compounds, the growing power of religion must have been even more painful for him. Fela felt the burden of his grandfather's Christian proselytizing—"I have to undo what he has done." By the mid-nineties, though, evangelical churches stood where many nightclubs (including the Shrine) had once been, while more than a few music stars (King Sunny Ade and I. K. Dairo among them) had turned to preaching. On northern tours, Fela would get into shouting matches with Muslim crowds; the millions of naira spent every year on the hajj, he insisted, brought Nigeria only "sick pilgrims and brainwashed Africans." Perhaps Fela's attacks contributed to a feeling that Islam needed defending; since his death, the northernmost twelve of the thirty-six states have incorporated sharia law into their legal system. Femi Kuti says that if his father played Kano today, he and the band wouldn't get out of the city alive.

Fela insisted that the answer to his countrymen's spiritual needs could be found in traditional African religion ("Me, I'm a born-again 'pagan'!"), but the beautiful face and body paint on the women in his troupe and the rhythmic patterns at the base of afrobeat were among the few positive manifestations of those beliefs. The self-styled Chief Priest grew dependent on a Ghanaian faith healer called Professor Hindu, who combined carnival tricks with potions supposed to protect his patron from violent harm and sickness. Even Fela's most devoted followers rolled their eyes when he banged on about the charlatan's shamanic powers.

On one level, Fela followed the path outlined in Franz Fanon's *The Wretched of the Earth*, a book always on the reading table at the Shrine: study the colonial mentality at close hand, celebrate one's own traditions, then turn a critical eye on the failures of post-colonial society. As a privileged decadent who created Africa's first counter-culture, though, Fela's approach was as much Sly Stone or Prince as it was Fanon and Malcolm X.

With Fela's awkward self out of the way, wider and wider circles of listeners came to appreciate the genius of his music. An unlikely figure in this posthumous growth industry was a US political science undergraduate named Martín Perna, who heard his first Africa 70 record while DJing in the early nineties; having grown up with Latin music, Perna was drawn to afrobeat's clave feel. In the late nineties, he formed Antibalas ("bulletproof" in Spanish) to play afrobeat in Brooklyn bars. By the turn of the millennium, Antibalas had carved a niche for itself in the jam band circuit built around Deadheads, campus pot enthusiasts, political activism, and a nascent rebellion against machine beats. When Femi Kuti couldn't navigate his band through the minefield of the US visa application system, Antibalas backed him on a US tour. Slowly but surely, Fela and his music became talismanic for hip crowds across America.

For twenty-something stoners to fall for afrobeat made perfect sense; no one, however, could have predicted that a stage musical called *Fela!* would run for more than a year on Broadway and win three Tony Awards. In 2009, the Chief Priest of Lagos joined Buddy Holly, Tina Turner, and Freddie Mercury in that pantheon of stars transformed into comic-strip characters and portrayed by a succession of actors singing original lyrics over reverential backing (in this case by Antibalas) and spouting biopic dialogue. The show, though, never recouped its investment; selling Fela to African Americans proved as futile as getting them to buy into Bob Marley's reggae.

∽

A resident of west London needs a good reason to drive across the city to Hackney for an evening's entertainment. I have made many such journeys over the years, and two of them, twenty-five years apart, were to hear Nigerian music. The first seemed quite surreal at the time; in a small room up some rickety stairs in an alley behind Hackney Downs station, about a hundred very dignified Nigerians in starched *bubas* were standing around holding cans of lukewarm beer or Coke. After a very long wait, the small stage was suddenly filled with what can best be described as a rabble of percussionists in scruffy Western clothes, exuding a heady perfume of sweat and marijuana. This was Sikiru Ayinde Barrister's fuji outfit, over the last quarter of the twentieth century probably the most popular band in Nigeria. As the music built up a fevered intensity, the audience remained virtually motionless. I assumed *fuji* to be a Yoruba word but have since discovered that Barrister took it from a poster advertising flights to Japan; his music, he knew, was like that mountain, towering above the landscape. Outsiders can struggle to recognize anything familiar in fuji: dense percussion from hand drums, bells, and rattles that Tony Allen must have studied, supporting scattered, almost throwaway vocals that follow an unusual pentatonic scale containing hints of a muezzin's call to prayer. That's it, there's little else save the lyrics, which are reputed to be slang-filled and witty; there are no melody instruments. Fuji is afrobeat's defiant opposite, an intensely local blend of Muslim, Christian, and Yoruba traditions oblivious to influences from across the Atlantic. The fact that it became so popular across Nigeria is a reminder that however much we may love afrobeat, juju, and highlife (and fuji, too, once you get into it), distant cultures must always remain, at some level, opaque.

A quarter of a century after that night, I found myself in a decommissioned church near London Fields, overlooking a dancefloor filled with a young, White crowd that reflected how Hackney (like Brooklyn) had changed as well as the evolution of afrobeat. Dele Sosimi, once an Egypt 80 keyboard player, leads one of the few remaining London outfits that play live for dancing (the others being mostly Latin or Irish ceilidh bands). Other than on the bandstand, Nigerians were not much in evidence; their preference for dancing these days is "afrobeats," an apologetic "s" separating this new music and its mostly machine rhythms from Fela and Tony's original. They take justifiable pride in the fact that records made in Lagos spread at digital speed around the globe; Burna Boy and the others have won an audience among African Americans and Europeans that Fela never managed. Some of their beats reference patterns heard at the Shrine, but the vibe is hard-edged and electronic-modern while the singing is filled with the sort of auto-tuned grace notes that dominate modern international vocal performance. Live, old-school afrobeat (even when played by Femi's band or Egypt

80 under Seun's leadership) is of as little interest to most of them as *Fela!* was to African Americans. The Ezra Collective winning the 2023 Mercury Prize has injected new life into the form, but probably won't change the dancing habits of many Nigerians.

They're prominent everywhere these days, Nigerians, filling rosters in the National Football League, the English Premier League, and the NBA, to say nothing of the internationally renowned authors, actors, academics, scientists, and bankers. This can be partly explained by the chaos and corruption at home that drive the talented to seek fortunes abroad, but I doubt any psychological profile of modern-day Nigerians can avoid the term *self-confidence*. Even as they move to a different beat at home and in the diaspora, the ghostly, inspirational figure of Fela Aníkúlápó-Kuti leads them on.

☙

> It was almost like he created a beat that was ahead of the drum machine, it was so constant. And if you're used to dancing on the fourth beat, you can fall into a four within his beat, but if you want to dance to the offbeat, you can find that too. There's several different rhythms to latch on to, depending on what you like. And that's really powerful—he's managed to incorporate the swing and the hypnotic, two very different areas. You really have to mess up, or the crowd has to really suck, if they don't dance to Tony Allen records.
>
> —Gilles Peterson

Tony Allen gets what a boy can do
He really got me dancing

— "Music Is My Radar," by Blur

> Questlove, Chris Dave, Moses Boyd—these are all people I know are directly influenced by Tony too, but none of us can make a beat sit down and groove like he did. It's so weird, because it's not even that hard. You'll look at the notes, what he's doing, and you're like: right, I can play everything in the right place. But when he does it, it just sounds better. Like when a really great narrator reads a sentence, it just has an authority to it that you couldn't give, even if you read the same sentence. He had a special gift.
>
> —Femi Koleoso, drummer with the Ezra Collective

But before I let your steam drill beat me down,
I'd die with a hammer in my hand

—"John Henry," American folk song

Tony Allen's legacy may turn out to be even more durable than Fela's. After some initial hard times in Europe, he lived out his fourscore years in progressively greater comfort, happily settled in Paris with his French wife, Sylvie, and their three children. Once he overcame the *idée fixe* that Africans only play drums with their hands, Tony was in constant demand; the last years of his life were filled with praise, recognition, income, and, on occasion, backing for his own projects as bandleader. In Blur's Damon Albarn, he found a visionary supporter who included him in one high-profile project after another and paid him well. And yet . . .

Tony was always up for an adventure and for a while he found working with drum-machine-loving producers, who track instruments one at a time and use ProTools to sample, cut, and paste, an interesting challenge. But Tony told me that ultimately, he found it "totally boring, really, really boring, everything sounds the same." Whenever we met, Tony and I talked about making a proper "Black Atlantic" record: an afrobeat rhythm section with top American jazz soloists. But Tony's French management preferred high-profile pop and R&B projects, Blue Note didn't answer my emails, and we never got it done. I felt sad and frustrated that we hadn't managed to make the kind of record that would have brought Tony full circle to that teenage *DownBeat* subscription and given some great bebop soloists a chance to play over Tony's inimitable beats.

There were attempts by European promoters to maneuver a reunion with Fela. On one occasion he turned up at the Glastonbury Festival, sticks at the ready and a contract guaranteeing payment directly by the agent, but when Fela overheard the guys from Weather Report saying how excited they were to hear Tony play, he freaked out and called the whole thing off.

One of Albarn's projects was Africa Express, a fulcrum where African artists (including Baaba Maal, Amadou & Mariam, Femi Kuti, Salif Keïta, and Oumou Sangaré) perform with high-profile pop musicians (Flea, John Paul Jones, Brian Eno, Paul Weller, Johnny Marr, Fatboy

Slim, and 3D from Massive Attack among them). In 2008, Tony joined an Africa Express assemblage performing as part of a "Felabration" week at the New Afrika Shrine. A packed house of Lagosians saw the show open with the Senegalese Baaba Maal backed by a line-up including a British rock drummer. Backstage, Allen was nervous; in less than a minute, the first bottle flew past the drummer's head—*This is the Shrine! You play afrobeat here!* More projectiles followed; when a stone struck the drum kit, Tony rushed on from the wings, pushed the drummer off the stool, and took over. Nigerians usually don't seem too bothered when afrobeat gets simplified or ignored, but the Shrine is different; on such an occasion, only Fela's shamanic blacksmith, the remaining half of the team that forged the magic, would do.

In the first week of January 1960, a nightclub in Brussels called Les Anges Noires (The Black Angels) hired a young Cameroonian saxophonist named Manu Dibango to lead the house band. His group would be expected to play Latin music, and when the dancers got tired, he could move on to bebop. Dibango was a committed jazzer; having left home to attend school in France at fifteen, he had little memory of, or interest in, African music. His dream was to turn Les Anges Noires into a jam-session magnet for the top American and European players when they came through town.

The club was already established as a late-night hang for hip Belgians, as well as for some of the Black faces occasionally seen on the streets of the city. Africans who turned up might be from any corner of the continent; anywhere, that is, except the Congo. Belgium had a policy of keeping its colonized population isolated; few Congolese were educated beyond the rudimentary schooling provided by Catholic missionaries and none were allowed to travel. One group visited Brussels for Expo '58, but the price was high; they had to spend every day in loincloths and fetish necklaces, holding spears in a "jungle village" at the fairgrounds, an installation critics called a "human zoo."

Towards the end of Manu's first month there, well-dressed Congolese suddenly began turning up; the Belgian government had organized a round table to discuss the colony's future, and many of the ninety-strong delegation found their way to Les Anges Noires. When they asked if a band that had traveled with them could come over and play some late-night sets, Dibango figured, why not? The group were called African Jazz but they didn't actually play jazz, more a laid-back sort of Latin music, and Manu was astonished by how good they were; he had dim memories of hearing tinny Congolese sounds over the radio in Douala in the late forties, but this music was sublime. When they played one of their scheduled sets at the conference headquarters in the Plaza Hotel, some Belgians complained they must be miming to a tape; Africans couldn't possibly play that well.

The club was soon packed every night; close behind the delegates came CIA and KGB agents, plainclothes policemen, mining speculators, journalists, and, as a member of African Jazz later put it, women who wanted "to see if [my color] came off." The atmosphere was electric; the conference may have been conceived as simply a gesture to show Belgium wasn't entirely out of step with modern times, but it rapidly evolved into a geopolitical moment where the future of a continent (and the uranium America used in its A-bombs) seemed up for grabs.

The leader of African Jazz was Joseph Kabasele, a member of what passed in Léopoldville for an elite, a nephew of the city's Catholic cardinal who'd learned to sing like an angel in the church choir. His close friend among the delegates (and at whose rallies African Jazz often performed) was Patrice Lumumba, the one all the spooks had their eyes on. Lumumba was easy to spot: the tallest man in the room, handsome, with a distinctive parting in his natural hair and a charisma that drew everyone to him. Jailed for organizing demonstrations a few months earlier, he'd been freed when delegates refused to come to Brussels without him. Lumumba quickly forced the issue, letting the Belgians know that once this door to independence had cracked open, it couldn't be closed or even delayed. Reluctantly, the Belgians set elections for May and the handover at the end of June; they had seen the violent, divisive, and costly drama their French neighbors were going through with Algeria and had neither the resources nor the stomach for anything like that. Thus was this immense land, without a single university graduate, no lawyers, a couple of doctors, and no one with any experience in government administration, cast loose to sink or swim.

One could argue it was the networking and scheming that took place during the small hours at Les Anges Noires which set the course for much of Africa's post-colonial history. The future of African popular music certainly began there; a Belgian record company offered African Jazz some studio time, and the recording they made, "Indépendance cha cha," became the first continent-wide hit, establishing Congolese rumba as every new nation's template (Ghana and Nigeria excepted), and inspiring people across Africa to dance their way into the new era.

Kabasele introduced other Congolese bands to his new distributor, Fonior, and to the efficiency of Belgian studios. A flight to Brussels followed by a day or two of recording became a rite of passage for Congolese groups. They'd return home with one copy of the tape (often containing as many as twenty songs) for the local pressing plant, while the Belgians went into action with another, shipping singles to every corner of Africa south of the Sahara and north of apartheid. Congolese groups weren't just streets ahead of the rest of Africa in musical sophistication, but also in terms of business and logistics. Across the sixties and seventies, tours would follow the vinyl in wider and wider loops, eventually reaching the West Indies, Europe, and Japan. Some musicians and composers would even become wealthy, controlling their own master recordings and joining Belgian or French authors' societies. Congolese music grew into a behemoth, a paragon of the successful exploitation of a homegrown product created by a nation and its people. Music, however, was about the only thing that went well for the new Congo.

> [I]t was not the natives who needed to be civilized; it was the newly arrived white man.
>
> —Ali Mazrui, political scientist

Belgians aren't entirely wrong when they blame it all on Leopold II. The French Revolution had planted the idea that "peoples" should be "citizens," not "subjects," but most newborn states—as Belgium was in 1830—felt insecure without a figurehead, so Leopold's father, an unemployed member of the Saxe-Coburg family, was recruited to be monarch. Leopold I's ambitious and greedy son made a fortune in Suez Canal bonds but wanted more and craved being head of an important state. After assuming the throne, he proposed that Belgium emulate its French and Dutch neighbors by starting a colonial empire, but Parliament wasn't interested; they had enough trouble dealing with their own quarrelsome tribes, the Flemings and the Walloons, without trying to manage the hundreds of different groups inhabiting the huge swathe of Central Africa their monarch proposed seizing.

Leopold wasn't easily deterred, though, and he had Europe's cleverest diplomat, Germany's Otto von Bismarck, whispering in his ear, *Why not just do it yourself?* Bismarck relished the idea of a scramble for African colonies that would keep Britain and France busy while newly unified Germany built up its strength. Henry Morton Stanley, the Welsh-American journalist who had found Dr. Livingstone deep in the Central African rainforest, began touring Europe in the 1870s with self-aggrandizing tales of exploration (bankrolled by Leopold) and insisting that Africa desperately needed "the three Cs" (Christianity, Civilization, and Commerce), while the popular press crowed about riches and glory. Britain and France fell into Bismarck's trap. Leopold, meanwhile, paid Stanley to cruise up and down the Congo River bribing local rulers to put their mark on a bit of paper they didn't understand, then claimed an area more than double the size of Germany, France, and Britain put together and called it the Congo Free State.

Leopold never set foot in his private domain. As Adam Hochschild showed in his shocking and groundbreaking book *King Leopold's Ghost*, having proclaimed himself a champion of free trade in order to secure British and US support, the king proved the least free trader ever, monopolizing the export of ivory and rubber and using the most brutal and inhumane methods to force the Congolese to bring these goods out of the forest. In 1908, when the world discovered a fraction of the truth, Leopold was obliged to turn the territory over to a reluctant Belgian government, which imposed a slightly less brutal administration over the vast land. In the twenty-three years of his rule, over ten million Congolese died or fled their home regions. Exhibit A in the case for humanity's resilience in the face of unimaginable horror, for its ability to create beauty in defiance of monstrosity, is the extraordinary sounds created by Congolese musicians even as their land was being plundered.

༄

> The Belgians were awful in Congo because they had no grandeur themselves. This was the Zaire of Europe, a ratty little country divided amongst itself... incapable of aspiring to the heights.
>
> —Diplomat quoted in Michela Wrong, *In the Footsteps of Mr Kurtz*

On the balance sheet of Belgium's post-Leopold rule, there are few credits and many debits: forced labor, arbitrary punishment with the *chicotte* (a rhino-hide whip that wasn't outlawed until 1959), refusal to allow Congolese students to attend universities or to become doctors or lawyers, and a 9 p.m. bugle call in Léopoldville that commanded all Africans to leave the city's "White" district. The few entries in the credit column include building more infrastructure than in most British or French colonies, but perhaps the one with the most lasting effect was musical. Along with their guns and whips, Belgians brought with them thousands of pianos, guitars, violins, accordions, brass, and woodwinds. By the 1930s, there were Congolese guitar players working the riverboats that brought people and goods from the interior to Léopoldville, while accordionists and fiddlers played for dances in riverside parks or bars in the city's "African quarter." Adapting the music of the country's two hundred linguistic groups to Western instruments produced some appealing sounds, but everything changed when the GVs appeared.

The HMV label's GV series was initiated by some bright spark in the London office who licensed African rights to Victor's and Odeon's Cuban recordings. They sold like hotcakes across the continent, particularly in the francophone territories; Trio Matamoros, Sexteto Habanera, "El Manisero"—when Africans heard them, they would nod their heads, move their feet, and say, "That sounds like ours." The connection was felt particularly strongly in the Congo; after all, it was to the coast either side of the mouth of the Congo River that Portuguese traders came in the sixteenth century, when tasked by the Spanish with supplying them with non-Muslim slaves. Kongo culture, as we have seen, became deeply embedded in Cuba. To the Congolese, the GV discs sounded not just familiar but also wonderfully modern, opening a door onto the wider world. Afro-Cuban records gave local musicians a template, a basis for fitting any sort of melody, from traditional village songs to French pop, into a structure and a rhythm everyone could relate to.

Another welcome discovery was how well these rhythms worked with Lingala, the "language of the river," a trading jargon that had evolved long before the arrival of White colonists. With Lingala, we meet the first in a long line of Belgian Congophiles who make cameo appearances throughout this tale and who seem not to have shared their countrymen's general contempt for Africans. Égide de Boeck was a Catholic missionary who, in 1901, took it upon himself to set down a Lingala grammar and vocabulary and bring some order to the various strands of this vibrant "slanguage."

Jean Hourdebise was next up, an entrepreneur who established Congolia, Léopoldville's first radio station, in the late thirties. When he heard the rumbas being played in the streets by small groups of guitarists, accordionists, and percussionists, he astonished his fellow colonials by putting them on air. (Hourdebise seems to have been the first in all of Africa to whom such an idea had occurred.) Steered by a combination of the "coastman" picking style on the guitar (an instrument Cubans mostly strummed if they played it at all) and the sound of Lingala (as singers began using it instead of phonetic cod-Spanish), Congo's rumba cast off its Caribbean moorings and became a style all its own, one that everyone within range of Congolia's signal found to be the most wonderful and amazing thing. It didn't matter that not everyone spoke Lingala; the way its syllables seemed to glide through or bounce off the beats delighted every ear. A half-century later, my own ears came to relish the sound of *motéma*, a word that pops up as regularly in Congolese music as *corazón* in Spanish or *coraçao* in

Brazilian or *s'agapo* in Greek or *habibi* in Arabic music, all expressing the same romantic yearning.

☙

When Stanley set up camp on the south bank of the great river at the point that became Léopoldville and is now Kinshasa, he was horrified to spy a blue, white, and red tricolor on the opposite bank. It had been planted there by Pierre Savorgnan de Brazza, a French explorer whose character could not have been more different from Stanley's. The soft-spoken Brazza respected Africa, its people, and its cultures, and tried to keep the French side of the river from falling into the swamp of brutality that defined Leopold's realm. Brazza died of a fever in 1905 on board a France-bound steamer, with a blistering report on inhuman practices in his country's African colonies in his briefcase. The French government tried to bury the report along with the explorer and celebrated his timely demise by renaming the trading post opposite Léopoldville "Brazzaville."

For more than a century, a short ferry ride has connected the two cities; the US journalist John Gunther described Brazzaville as "still an African city, loosely constructed, colorful, relaxed, to which has been magically added a dash of Paris." These two colonial backwaters were thrust into the world's spotlight in 1941, when the German blitzkrieg overwhelmed first the Belgian army and then the French. Britain, desperate to keep the Congo's rubber, minerals, and cotton out of Axis hands, gave the Belgian government-in-exile a desk and a telephone in London and sent cruisers to patrol the coast and scare off the Germans. The only recorded battle between Vichy and Free French forces took place next door in Gabon; the (mostly Black) Gaullist troops defeated the (all-White) pro-Nazis, whose leader was so mortified he committed suicide. Berlin was further dismayed to discover that while they had little trouble jamming broadcasts from London, they were unable to block nocturnal shortwave signals from Africa; as a result, Brazzaville became a nerve center of the French resistance. After the war, Radio Brazzaville's powerful antenna found a new calling: beaming Cuban records and home-made Congolese rumba across Africa.

☙

There's a joke about Neil Armstrong stepping out of Apollo 11 and being met by a Greek selling moon-rock souvenirs. Belgium sent plenty of bureaucrats, priests, mining engineers, and soldiers to the Congo but hardly any shopkeepers; as in much of Africa, networks of Greek families with retail in their blood moved into the vacuum. Their stores were among the first to stock the GV discs, and they sold so well that music-loving Nicolas Jeronimidis was inspired to set up a recording studio behind his shop. Ngoma would be the first of four Greek-run labels in Léopoldville; a fifth, the only one with a Greek name (Olympia), was started by a Belgian.

Major labels were active across the globe but showed little interest in recording Africans, thereby leaving the field open to local indies. In 1949, Ngoma came up with the first big hit, "Marie-Louise," composed by their in-house guitarist, Henri Bowane, and sung by the music's first star, Wendo Kolosoy, who had worked his way down the river to Léopoldville as a boat mechanic. The record created such a sensation that the Catholic Church threatened to excommunicate anyone buying a copy. There was nothing particularly risqué in the lyrics, but the ban declared the disc to be "demonic," a recognition of the power of recorded rhythm to reach people in ways beyond religious or governmental control.

Another adventurous Belgian arrived in 1953 bearing agents of change almost as powerful as the GV discs: a pair of Gibson Les Paul electric guitars. Bored in Brussels, Bill Alexander took on the task of opening a new studio, backed by a Belgian company that realized there was money in Congolese music. Playing with the house band on promotional tours and using a small amp and a never-before-seen plectrum, Alexander's sound beguiled the Congolese and prompted the other studios to invest in Gibsons of their own.

By 1956, acoustic guitars were a thing of the past, as Congolese rumberos strayed ever further from the original. Effortlessly seizing the Cuban pulse (and familiar clave), they overlaid beautiful un-Cuban melodies. The vocals were pure and open; Islam had made only a few converts at the edges of the vast country, so the nasal Arabic style that influenced much of West African and Spanish singing had made few inroads. Harmonies paid homage to Cuban trios and sextetos but were also shaped by church choirs and Bantu traditions of group singing. Léopoldville record companies were inventive: color photos of artists on the label, sharp-looking sleeve designs, energetic promotion, and sponsored tours. Singers were brought in from Gabon, Cameroon, and Ubangi-Shari (now the Central African Republic) to record in their studios; in 1956, Congolese labels sold 600,000 78s and 45s in a region with a very limited number of phonographs.

Keen to escape the European winter, Alfons "Fud" Candrix, a saxophonist who had played with Django Reinhardt, brought his combo to Léopoldville for a season at the city's newest hotel. Fud joins our list because a Greek producer hanging out in the hotel bar booked him for a session and the Congolese loved his sound, so much cooler than the usual clarinet. Visiting bass players gave lessons and sometimes sold their instruments before leaving. Electric guitars, saxes, and basses (plus a bit more Cuban percussion) pumped up the rumba's volume; by the late fifties, there was live music every night in big dance halls on both sides of the river.

The growing excitement matched the demographics; like Lagos during those years, Léopoldville was expanding fast as people abandoned the countryside to fill jobs in the burgeoning urban economy. And it wasn't only Africans; looking to relieve pressure on its own sluggish economy, Belgium encouraged citizens to move to their fast-growing colony. With its mineral wealth and fecund climate, they saw their Congo becoming the economic powerhouse of Africa. At the dawn of independence, Lagos and Léopoldville were by far the two largest cities between Cairo and Johannesburg.

⌒

In 1941, Roosevelt and Churchill had announced an "Atlantic Charter" that affirmed "the right of all peoples to choose their own government." Did they really mean *all* peoples? Even *Africans*? At the time the British and French clearly didn't. By the fifties, though, the wind had begun to shift; having an empire was no longer such a good look and besides, they were losing money. The British spent a fortune crushing the Mau

Mau rebellion in Kenya and the French were hemorrhaging blood and money in Algeria; maybe it was time to cut and run.

Belgium remained oblivious to the change in mood. The Congo had always been profitable to a degree, but it was now coming into its own; by the late fifties, the colony was producing 10 percent of the world's copper, 50 percent of the cobalt, and 70 percent of industrial diamonds, along with tons of cotton and the purest uranium. To support their ambitions, the Belgians built roads, airports, and railways. Managerial posts were all filled by Europeans; it never occurred to them to train the Congolese or encourage an educated middle class.

It was becoming harder and harder, however, to sustain the isolation in which Belgium had held the colony. Cuban music wasn't the only thing opening Congolese connections to the world; outdoor cinemas showing Hollywood westerns and Bollywood musicals drew huge crowds. Neighborhoods began taking their names from American frontier towns while the street slang of Kinshasa's rude boys was called "Hindu-Bill," a linguistic mating of sacred cows and buffaloes. The Belgians' biggest problem, though, was the Brazzaville ferry.

Léopoldville bands were full of musicians and singers from the other Congo and everyone agreed that the best nightclub by far was Chez Faignond, over on the French side. For years, Paris had been sending the brightest *lycée* students from their side to universities in the home country; when they returned on holiday, these star pupils loved nothing more than jumping on the ferry and flaunting their *rive gauche* threads. In 1958, the constitution of the Fourth Republic established a path to independence for France's African colonies, with Brazzaville set to become capital of the new Congo Republic. The contrast could not have been starker.

The Belgians grew nervous; an innocent record called "Mokili ekobaluka" (roughly, The World Is Changing) was banned and the singer jailed. Then they confiscated a journal that issued a modest call for expanded civil rights; who knew Africans could write such a thing, much less publish it themselves? The colonists made a fatal error in 1957, when they brought a Stanleyville labor organizer to Léopoldville for his appeal against a conviction on trumped-up charges. This was the dramatic entrance of Patrice Lumumba into African history; chanting crowds outside the courtroom spooked the judges into reducing his sentence. When he was released a few months later, a brewery hired him to travel the country plugging their beer and he seized the opportunity to promote his new political party at the same time, with Kabasele and African Jazz often along to swell the crowds and pump up enthusiasm for lager and for liberty.

Hindsight allows historians to point out the rash moves that would seal Lumumba's fate: interrupting the handover ceremonies to scold King Baudouin I ("We are no longer your monkeys"), appealing to Moscow for help in putting down a rebellion in the mining region of Katanga, and being unable to resist giving speeches while on the run from house arrest, thus alerting enemies to his whereabouts and ensuring his capture and execution. But the most lethal misstep of all may have taken place in Brussels during the round table. Some say it was Kabasele, who, one night at Les Anges Noires, introduced Lumumba to a Brussels-based Congolese journalist named Joseph Mobutu; impressed with what a clever fellow he was, Lumumba hired him as his assistant, never stopping to wonder how Mobutu had been allowed to stay on in Brussels for two years after Expo '58 and not be sent back to Léopoldville.

It seems his visa was approved by Belgian *securité*, who helped him out with expenses and later passed him along to their friends at the CIA. When, as prime minister, Lumumba fired the Belgian officers who were trying to maintain White control over the army, he placed Mobutu in charge; from then on, every move the military made was guided and supported by the Americans, including Lumumba's arrest and murder. The ensuing years would be violent, chaotic, and disastrous for the country's future, but America had achieved its goal of keeping out the communists. For the Congolese people, about the only thing they could rely on was the weekly flow of great new records.

⌒

> [The guitars'] lustrous melodies . . . transmuted the euphoria of nationalism and independence into musical sound . . . These heady sonic

constructions, Baroque in their structural complexity, were driven mainly by the utopian visions of nation-building . . . enabling popular styles to become agents of social change.

—Michael E. Veal

[T]he best way to achieve happiness, is it not through one's culture? Isn't a happy man the one who sings and dances? . . . It is when people are able to communicate what they feel deep inside, when they can sing and dance, then they are truly happy.

—President Mobutu

Kabasele always had a keen eye for talent; an early masterstroke was recruiting a pair of guitar-playing brothers to come by the studio every day after school. Nico Kasanda and Charles "Déchaud" Mwamba's fraternal dialectic would chart the course for the future of Congolese music. They modeled their style on a guitarist from Ubangi-Shari called Zacharie Elenga, better known as "Jhimmy l'Hawaiien," who made his name in rumba's early years by evoking the sound of the Pacific islands. Jhimmy tuned the D string to E, raised the pitch with a capo, and used his agile fingers to give every note a tremolo others envied but couldn't match. In 1954, Ngoma released a recording by a pair of traditional *likembe* or thumb-piano players; the way the two weave rhythmic and melodic patterns around each other is just how Nico and Déchaud played, only with the clarity and sweet sustain of their electric guitars plus some melodic inspiration from Cuban trumpeters. Their hypnotic, dance-propelling style paved the way for Congolese rumba to conquer a continent. When a Belgian disc jockey heard Nico take a solo one night at Les Anges Noires he pronounced him "a doctor of his craft" and the honorific stuck; soon he would be known from one end of Africa to the other as "Docteur Nico," the continent's most famous and influential musician.

Guitars—two, three, four, or even five to a group—gave Congolese music its power. Nico and a few others stood out for their inventive solos, but there seems to have been an inexhaustible supply of players who mastered the plectrum style that, as one critic suggested, "eroticised the rumba." Outsiders' attempts to unlock its secrets have met with scant success; Bob White, a skilled American guitarist, spent years in Kinshasa working with local bands and found it impossible to replicate the elusive nuances and improvised accents scattered among the arpeggios that make everything flow. When that intrepid ethnomusicologist Gerhard Kubik asked one Congolese player to demonstrate his part so it could be recorded and transcribed, the musician couldn't do it; the part only worked in dialogue, and without a second guitar, he had no idea what to play.

Taking advantage of the shift from 78 rpm discs to longer-lasting 45s and eventually LPs, groups began adding a montuno-like coda at the end of songs featuring an upward shift of tempo and key that, as the years went by, might last longer than the body of the song itself. This was called the *sebene*, and there are various theories about the word's origin. I like the one involving those guitar-proselytizing (and often anglophone) Kru coastmen, many of whom took jobs around the Léopoldville docks. When one wanted to extend a good groove, he'd shout "*Seven!*" meaning everyone should go to the seventh chord, giving the music a feeling of being elevated and suspended, ready to go all night. One description of a Kinshasa band during the sebene describes a stage awhirl with intense energy, everyone dancing and moving. Except the guitarists: they stand motionless in concentration, eyes fixed on the fretboard, concocting elaborate arabesques that have the crowd shouting, cheering, and throwing money.

An insignificant matter: you talk with your wife about it.
An insignificant matter: you talk with your brother about it.
An insignificant matter: you boast about it to your in-laws.
The secret matter: you share it with the prostitutes.
If you want to keep it in your heart, don't share it with anybody.
If you want to keep it at the bottom of your heart, don't get drunk.

—Tabu Ley Rochereau, "Mass Media"

Ellington and Basie, Beatles and Stones, Marley and Toots, Rochereau and Franco; like many musical movements, Congolese rumba came to be dominated by a pair of giants, one on the elegant side, the other more elemental. Pascal Tabou was the only one in his high school class able to name the "Lion of Belfort," a French officer who held out heroically against a Prussian siege. Pierre Denfert-Rochereau's memory lives on in the form of a massive bronze beast in the center of the Paris *rond-point* where Boulevard St. Michel meets Boulevard Raspail—and in the nickname "Rochereau" that the boy could never shed after classmates teased him for being a swot.

Tabou was indefatigable as a youth, not only a star student but also a composer of songs he would send to his idol "Le Grand Kallé" (Kabasele's nickname). The African Jazz leader liked them so much that the group recorded a few before ever meeting the prodigy. Pascal eventually took a few turns subbing for absent singers, and when African Jazz returned from Brussels in the spring of 1960, he was officially installed as a member.

Across the sixties, African Jazz experienced defections, betrayals, schisms, and name changes; at one point, Tabou and the Kasanda brothers abandoned Le Grand Kallé (or vice versa, depending on who's telling the story) and went their own way. Pascal tried to evade destiny by calling himself "Tabu Ley," but Rochereau was too good a name and he eventually embraced it, split from Docteur Nico, and became leader of the country's new champions, African Fiesta. Fela Kuti insisted that Africans had no use for love songs since, unlike Europeans, they could get laid whenever they wanted; like Kolosoy and Kabasele before him, Rochereau refuted Fela's macho posturing by building his career around songs of love in all its complexity, and singing them in a pure, romantic tenor that drew legions of followers, male as well as female, across Africa.

Reggae fans are often perplexed when they discover the cult following in Jamaica for that cheesiest of Nashville balladeers, Jim Reeves. It seems equally curious that a major influence on the likes of Kolosoy, Kabasele, and Rochereau would be Tino Rossi, a thirties French crooner with the blandest style imaginable. But whenever you hear a high Congolese tenor—and you hear them everywhere—you are hearing the ghost of Rossi, the Congo's favorite non-Cuban singer.

Rochereau never lost the outward-looking curiosity of his student days. When African Fiesta performed at the 1967 Montreal Expo, he spent every offstage minute watching other performers and becoming the first African bandleader to get the full-on, in-person experience of the James Brown Revue. By then, the influence of another stray Belgian had shifted the rumba's foundation. Charles Hénault was a jazz drummer who helped Kabasele with equipment and logistics in Brussels during the round-table month and was so intrigued by the music that he took up an offer to join them on the plane back to Léopoldville. He fell in love with the city and the music scene there and began playing with African Jazz, while teaching others how to use a drum kit; by the time Rochereau experienced the Godfather of Soul in Montreal, Afro-Cuban hand percussion had been shifted to one side and most bands were playing with a full kit, forcing the other sections to grow in size and volume to maintain the balance. African Fiesta's first post-Expo appearance back in Kinshasa boasted a horn section, backing singers, and dancing girls, a full-on "show" inspired by Brown; other bands had to ramp up to keep pace.

The band toured to every corner of the Congo, as far east as Dar Es Salaam and Nairobi (where he performed Swahili versions of a few of his songs), and west to Douala, Lagos, Abidjan, Bamako, and Dakar. Ready for the next challenge, Rochereau took aim at Paris; for months he lobbied Bruno Coquatrix, hard-nosed boss of the Olympia, to let him play the legendary venue. On December 1, 1970, the moment arrived; it was a triumph, with more than half the audience well-turned-out French and the rest even-better-dressed Africans. Critics raved, word of mouth was great; it was the highest-profile concert to date by a popular African band outside the continent. But lacking visionary agents or promoters to carry the momentum forward, Congolese music remained omnipresent in the banlieues but rarely heard inside the Périphérique.

One exception proved the rule; Father Guido Haazen, another in our cast of Belgian éminences *grises*, had been sent to central Congo in 1953 to run a school at Kamina, in the heart of Luba country. Mission schools often had choirs and many musicians learned a great deal from that experience, but Father Guido seems to have followed his own rules. Encouraging the students to improvise around their own traditional melodies and rhythms, together they created a strikingly original mass.

He played the politics of fifties Congo by calling the choir Les Troubadours du Roi Baudoin and convinced Philips to release a recording of their *Missa Luba*. By the mid-sixties, the record could be found in student dorms and on the LP shelves of genteel households across the northern hemisphere. A less successful *Missa Criolla* from Argentina and *Misa Flamenca* from Spain followed. The "Sanctus" from *Missa Luba* helped Lindsay Anderson's *If...* win the 1969 Palme d'Or at Cannes and make Malcolm McDowell a star, and the piece has entered the canon of choir repertoires around the world. Having not heard it in almost half a century, I was prepared for something a bit dated, possibly even twee, but it's actually a wonderful record, the harmonies reminiscent of some early rumba recordings and its rhythms not unduly softened. Rumba might have reached at least some of that market, but the francophone labels controlling distribution and marketing had trouble imagining anything but an African audience for it.

At an age when Tabou was boning up on the Franco-Prussian war, François "Franco" Luambo Makiadi was hustling in the market, drumming up business for his widowed mother's *beignet* stall. Tagging along with a street singer named Albert "Papa" Luampasi, he learned a style of guitar-picking using his thumb and forefinger the way traditional musicians play the region's small, kora-like harps. At age thirteen, he knocked on the door at Loningisa, a studio run by the Papadimitriou brothers, and so startled them with his talent that they gave him his first guitar and invited him back the next day for a session.

Loningisa was located above the brothers' store, which specialized in the colorful wraps worn by most Congolese women; they would play their latest recordings in the shop and choose releases by how their customers reacted. Henri Bowane was Loningisa's musical director and he became Franco's mentor; by 1956, the youth was firmly established as primary guitarist in the studio band. (All roads lead back to "Marie Louise"; Bowane composed it and played guitar, while Kolosoy, Rochereau's role model, sang it.) A nearby bar took its name from the initials of its half-Belgian, half-Congolese owner, Oscar Kashama; like the Shrine, OK Bar was known for its mixed clientele: dockworkers, students, prostitutes, and *intellos*. Kashama hired some of the younger Loningisa musicians to play there in the evenings, and when he got them bookings in other parts of the city, they became his OK Jazz band. Soon there was no stopping them; as their early hit proclaimed, "*On entre OK, on sort KO*" (You come in OK, you leave knocked out).

The minute he had some money in his pocket, the tall, handsome Franco spent it on clothes; at fifteen he was a girl magnet, with fans waving their kerchiefs when he took a solo and queuing up to show their admiration in a more personal way. On the electric guitar, he steered away from the Kasanda plectrum technique, perfecting his own two-fingered style; Franco's powerful playing led OK Jazz back towards the country's own traditions and away from light-hearted rumba. In the early years, Franco's was the only Congolese band with just one guitar. Like The Wailers in Scratch's car, he would wander through the streets listening, observing, and taking notes; his compositions covered every aspect of people's lives, earning him one critic's description as a "Congolese Balzac." While Rochereau and African Fiesta were seen as favorites of the *evolués* (a dubious term meaning "evolved," or "Westernized"), Franco and OK Jazz were heroes of the poor, those newly arrived in the city and the Hindu-Bill street kids. While Rochereau's love songs were yearning and romantic, Franco's recounted tales of sex and betrayal.

When Lumumba was killed, Franco recorded a lament the government banned, forcing him to hide out in Brazzaville until things calmed down. From then on, his political criticisms became oblique, couched in the allusive tradition known as *mbwakela*. OK Jazz always had a team of great singers and songwriters; only when one of his own compositions had an important message would Franco put his powerful, rough-edged voice up front. I grasped the breadth (rather than the depth) of his songwriting skills when I looked up a track that had caught my attention on a compilation many years ago; "Azda" is an earworm, its unique melody line and chorus of "*vay-way, vay-way*" insinuating itself pleasingly into my brain and welcomed back as an old friend each time I heard it. The title turns out to be the name of a Kinshasa car showroom and *vay-way* the local rendering of VW; the dealer was so pleased when it became a hit that he gave each of Franco's twenty-eight-strong team of musicians, technicians, dancers, and composers a car. (One of Rochereau's most gorgeous melodies is for his paean to washing powder: "Savon Omo.")

Franco was nothing if not enterprising; in 1967, when OK Jazz found itself buried under a mountain of debt, he stepped calmly away from the financial debris (somehow holding on to all the instruments and equipment) and reinvented the group as TPOK Jazz—*Tout Puissant* (All Powerful) OK Jazz. He ran a tight ship, but wasn't threatened by others' talent; the great composer Simaro Lutumba remained at his side for decades, while Sam Mangwana, who would have more careers in more capitals than any other African vocalist, got his start with Franco and was welcomed back many years later to sing the lead on yet more celebrated recordings.

Kabasele had introduced Franco to Fonior and his records were massive sellers; OK and TPOK Jazz toured constantly, but focused mainly on the Congo and its neighbors. In 1970, following a trip to Chad, the central tragedy of Franco's life unfolded. His younger brother Bavon was a talented musician whom Franco had always praised and often helped, though Bavon preferred to follow his own path rather than become a member of OK Jazz. Some details of the story remain murky, but it seems fraternal bonds weren't as strong as Franco's womanizing habits, his companion on the tour being Bavon's fiancée. On their return, his brother confronted them, forced the girl into his sports car, and drove off at high speed. A short way down the road he collided with a truck; Bavon was killed and the girl lost both her legs. Franco was never the same after that. He continued to produce masterpieces—"Kinsiona" (Grief), a mournful tribute to his brother, is an extraordinary recording featuring his own haunting vocal—but in the coming years he grew ever more remote, dictatorial . . . and fat.

> I cannot sleep at all on a plane and I am terribly scared of sleeping pills. To accuse me of wasting money—no, I am sorry. Just think of the time I save.
>
> —President Mobutu on chartering Concordes for all his travel

He [Mobutu] was so different at the start. I can remember him as a dynamic, idealistic young man who was determined to have an independent state in the Congo, and really seemed to believe in all the things Africa's leaders then stood for.

—Larry Devlin, CIA station chief in Léopoldville at the time of independence

There are no opponents in Zaire, because the notion of opposition has no place in our mental universe. In fact, there are no political problems in Zaire.

—President Mobutu

[W]e are proud and very, very pleased to have you with us today.

—President (and former head of the CIA) George H. W. Bush welcoming Mobutu to the White House

The corruption of Mobutu Sese Seko, as the president now called himself, was legendary: the skim from the copper and diamond mines of Katanga paid directly into his personal bank accounts, the palace in the jungle, the Concorde chartered to fly a hairdresser in from Paris for a day, the Cap Ferrat compound just along the road from Leopold's. For the outside world, his image is dominated by such tales, along with the leopard-skin Nehru hat, dark glasses, and expressionless gaze. Few outsiders realize how charismatic Mobutu was or what a witty and dynamic speaker he could be. Diplomats and spies who were in Brussels during the round table insist it was he, not Lumumba, who was the most impressive character there. While Havana crowds were looking at their watches during Castro's endless harangues, huge audiences at Mobutu's rallies were laughing at his wordplay and cheering the clever putdowns of his and the country's enemies. Some have even suggested that his pun-filled command of Lingala was a match for Fela's way with Pidgin.

Words alone, though, couldn't hold the vast country together. Money tried, and to an extent, succeeded; in her book *In the Footsteps of Mr Kurtz*, Michela Wrong tracks a torrent of cash as wide and deep as the Congo River and concludes that only a fraction actually went into

Mobutu's many bank accounts; most was delivered in crates to regional big men and warlords, keeping them on side and holding the country together. This may have worked while the economy was growing, but when the price of copper sagged in the early seventies, something more was needed. Mobutu admired and feared musicians; he once asked, "Does Rochereau realize the magnitude of a song?" Rochereau certainly did: "[T]he newspaper will only be bought by the old lady in the street to wrap her doughnuts. But a song goes everywhere." From Matadi near the mouth of the great river to Elizabethville in the mineral-rich southern finger poking into Zambia, rumba was everywhere, giving people the feeling of being part of something uniquely Congolese. Like Vargas in Brazil, Mobutu decided that culture would be both his legacy and the country's glue.

It started soon after the 1965 putsch that gave Mobutu total control: Léopoldville became Kinshasa; Stanleyville, Kisangani; Elizabethville, Lubumbashi. Then came October 27, 1971, "the day of the three Zs," when the nation, the currency, and the river were all renamed Zaire. Individuals were next; Fela changing Ransome to Aníkúlápó was inspired by Mobutu's order that all citizens drop their Western names in favor of African ones. Musicians who had spent years building careers were beside themselves; changing names could be almost like starting over.

Perhaps it was when the biggest stars (such as Franco) were allowed to evade the new rules that it all began to crumble. Most never took seriously the president's subsequent order that they address one another as *citoyen* and *citoyenne*. After he commanded them to abandon Western dress and introduced a curious, Asian-looking coat for men during a frantic speech in which he shouted, "*À bas le costume!*" (Down with the suit), the garment was mockingly dubbed the *abacost*.

The campaign (now officially known as "Mobutuism") reached its disastrous climax in 1974, when the Great Leader confiscated all foreign-owned businesses and turned them over to cronies and political allies. A few of the new proprietors managed to keep experienced managers in place, but most simply plundered the assets and let the businesses fall apart. "They were giving cattle herds to people who couldn't sex a bull," observed one businessman. The Belgian-owned pressing plant went to Franco, and it continued to thrive until bribe-hungry customs officials made importing raw vinyl impossible. Mobutu became the country's biggest grower and rancher while doing all his personal shopping abroad: French champagne, Italian marble, German cars, US weapons, and daily airlifts of haute cuisine. A man who never forgot the name and ethnicity of a once-met face had zero grasp of finance and would leave the room when ministers brought the subject up. School principals and army officers started holding on to funds meant for salaries, causing soldiers to rob citizens at gunpoint and teachers to abandon their classes in order to hustle on the streets. It was generally agreed that the country's constitution contained a hidden "Article 15," the obligation to *se débrouiller* (fend for oneself). Mobutuism steered the economy into a nosedive from which it has never recovered. Even the new names that kicked it all off turned out to be bogus: "Zaire" was a fifteenth-century Portuguese mishearing of *nzadi* (Ki-Kongo for "big river"), while the impatient Stanley had scribbled down the riverside village of Nshasha's name as "Kinshasa." Mobutu imagined the campaign would make him the toast of Africa.

When his fellow tyrants ignored it, he was crushed. Bitterly abandoning any ambitions to build a positive legacy, he focused on survival, comfort, and profit. Rumba certainly did more to keep the country unified than any of Mobutu's schemes and campaigns.

> This is going to be the greatest show on earth. The festival will be greater than anything that was seen at Monterey or Woodstock . . . This is a spectacle, an extravaganza, a blockbuster that should not be missed by anybody. Billions throughout the world via satellite will see it. Yes sir, Don King put it all together with His Excellency the President of Zaire, the honorable Mobutu Sese Seko. Yes sir, Don King, a little black boy from Cleveland, putting together the greatest spectacle on earth, make no mistake about it!
>
> —Boxing promoter Don King announcing the "African Woodstock"

It wasn't only African dictators who were suffering from delusions of grandeur. The march of Peruvian powder through the music business during the seventies led to more than a few deals that drained investors of capital and industry figures of credibility. It was one such that provided Kinshasa with a bit of relief from the misery of Mobutuism.

The idea may have been delusional, but it wasn't lacking in elegance. When Hugh Masekela and his producer, Stewart Levine, heard that wild-haired boxing promoter Don King was holding the 1974 heavyweight championship match in Kinshasa—the famous "Rumble in the Jungle" between George Foreman and Muhammad Ali—they came up with the idea of an "African Woodstock: Three Days of Music and Fighting" (a riff on the original's "Three Days of Peace and Music"). King saw no reason to object, so long as he got his 10 percent. Not of the profit, mind you, nor even of the gross, but 10 percent of the *budget*. (Don King could see around corners.)

Since going into exile, Masekela had spent a lot of time in West Africa and was tight with Stephen Tolbert, the president of Liberia's brother. Tolbert had access to a substantial pot of money (source unknown, best not to ask) and agreed to back the project. Jerry Masucci was immediately on board with Celia Cruz, Johnny Pacheco, and the Fania All-Stars, giving the venture a resonant *raison d'être* by connecting Congolese music with its Afro-Cuban backstory. Contracts were signed with James Brown and Bill Withers among a planeload of American stars, while Rochereau, Franco, Miriam Makeba, and Manu Dibango would represent Africa. A world-class stage was built, flights and hotels booked, press conferences held.

When Mobutu learned that tickets were priced at $10, he issued a presidential decree making the shows free; no ordinary Kinois, he knew, could afford even one US dollar, much less ten. With no box-office revenue and no satellite TV deals on offer, Tolbert's $2 million would have to be recouped from the film they were making. *Woodstock*, of course, had been a blockbuster, but the early seventies had seen a parade of money-losing music documentaries (including my own *Jimi Hendrix*). One of them, *Soul to Soul*, had followed a similar collection of American stars to Ghana in 1971. Perhaps Masekela and company weren't even aware of it; that it made barely a ripple in *Variety*'s box-office charts might have given them pause. But perhaps not; as Hugh admitted in his autobiography, *Still Grazing*, everyone involved was coked out of their heads most of the time.

    A week before the event, George Foreman cut his eyebrow in a sparring match and the fight had to be put back six weeks. The music couldn't wait, though, since the artists had all banked their deposits and had busy touring schedules. The stadium was indeed packed for three nights, but the world barely noticed. Thanks to a Don King lawsuit, the film *Soul Power* had to wait thirty-five years before being released, then went straight to DVD. Leon Gast, the director, stayed behind after the musicians left; his documentary about the fight, *When We Were Kings*, won an Oscar in 1996. After all these ill winds, luck may have been with Masekela and Levine after all; Tolbert went into a predictable rage about his vanished money, but before he could do anything unpleasant about it, he was killed in a plane crash that is generally viewed as a CIA hit. (The Tolbert brothers had been flirting with the Soviets and threatening Firestone Rubber, the primary US business in Liberia, and Washington was not amused.)

    The early seventies seems to be when African Americans discovered Africa. *Soul to Soul* and *Soul Power* are both primarily performance films featuring big-name American stars, but between numbers the focus is on cultural interaction. Both movies include the inevitable conga drum jam session, and Fania's Ray Barretto seems genuinely thrilled to be trading licks with Congolese drummers. Tina Turner has a nice moment learning some moves from local women during an Accra walkabout, and the musicians' visit to the fort where slaves were held before being taken in chains onto ships is somber and emotional. The Accra concert was funded by the Ghanaian government; even after Nkrumah was deposed in a 1966 coup, the country remained wedded to his Garveyite ideals. (The event took place in a packed Black Star Square.) Wilson Pickett in *Soul to Soul* and James Brown in *Soul Power* are duly lionized as headliners, with cutaway shots of bemused but enthusiastic Africans moving to the Yankee beats with interestingly different foot, arm, and hip action. The most ecstatic moments in both films, however, are the Latin ones: Santana in Accra and the Fania All-Stars in Kinshasa. The clave seems to be the one sure key to unlock

African feet and ears, transcending the fact that these were the least Black of all the performers.

Norman Mailer's bizarre, race-obsessed book *The Fight* describes the competing arrogances of wealthy African Americans and Congolese hotel staff; many encounters between Africans and their American cousins seem collisions of mutual incomprehension. In *Soul Power*, Muhammad Ali expresses his delight that Kinshasa has an airport, wide highways, and tall buildings; he seems to have been expecting the fight to take place at a clearing in the rainforest.

Manu Dibango's response was more to the point. In 1962, his new friend Kabasele had invited him to join African Jazz on a month-long tour of the Congo, back when the country's highways and airports made such a thing possible. In his autobiography *Three Kilos of Coffee*, Manu describes the thrill of arriving in Léopoldville and finding "the beauty of a New York in miniature. Homes were made of marble; hotels were comfortable. The colonialists had built an ultramodern metropolis to last an eternity. I had dreamed of an Africa that looked like this." Twelve years on, he found the city tragic, a crumbling, sprawling shadow of its former self. *Kin' la Belle*, as some called it, had become *Kin' la Poubelle*.

> With Lumumba's assassination the Congolese will to be modern was shattered, and a rich tradition of leadership with the potential for responsibility was put in the hands of people whose only legacy was to drive the country into the ground.
>
> —Bob W. White, *Rumba Rules*

Mobutu and Franco. In books and articles on Zaire, linking and comparing the two is a temptation few authors can resist. Both survived hardship-filled childhoods that forged rough-edged characters and iron wills. Franco, they say, ran his band the way Mobutu ran the government (or vice versa): constant changes of personnel, departures, returns, exiles, and reconciliations. The rewards of service in both operations were such that even former political prisoners who had been brutally tortured returned from exile to take up government posts when they were offered. Franco didn't waterboard his bass players, but he, too, believed in keeping rivals close and allies off balance.

Both ended up with bloated payrolls. Each time Mobutu shuffled his cabinet, the new ministers would hire relatives and people from their home region; these would then remain in their posts after the next round of appointments, with salaries paid to multiple cadres doing (or, more likely, not doing) the same jobs. Franco, for his part, stockpiled guitarists, percussionists, and singers until TPOK Jazz resembled Real Madrid's *galactico*-era squad or the LA Dodgers' pitching staff; at one point he was paying four complete orchestras. Both men were ravenous sexual predators, assuming *droit du seigneur* over any woman within reach of their power, with Mobutu making a particular point of sleeping with each of his ministers' wives.

The personal relationship between the two remains opaque, though the leader bestowed many favors on the musician: the pressing plant, the escape from bankruptcy, putting him in charge of the musicians' union, and providing land for a huge office-nightclub-studio complex. In return, TPOK's recordings never criticized the president, though when performing at Mobutu's rallies Franco might improvise lyrics bemoaning problems plaguing the poor or complaining about petty corruption. The president would appear startled, but then he'd pick up the theme in his speech, expressing outrage that people were experiencing such hardships and vowing to put an end to the problem (though never actually doing anything about it). Each seemed respectful and wary of the power of the other; in private, Franco was known for his wicked imitations of Mobutu.

There were plenty of differences, too; Franco was a canny businessman who had learned to keep a firm grip on his vast enterprise, while Mobutu was one of those (and there are many) with an aversion to clarity, giving vague, often contradictory, instructions to ministers and generals, forcing them to come back to him to resolve the inevitable disputes. Nor did Mobutu have any head for numbers, getting constantly ripped off in purchases both personal and national. Another contrast was electoral; in 1980, Franco won a free and fair newspaper poll for the most popular musician in the country, a feat Mobutu never dared emulate. Not that there was much in the way of dissidence or organized opposition, other than a resigned *when are the Americans going to take Mobutu away?* feeling. The two shared a distaste for modernity, the outside world, and the *evolués* who craved a progressive, democratic, and sophisticated Congo. As Mobutu pressed forward with Zairization, he promoted traditional village music with concerts and subsidies for folklore troupes, while Franco delved deeper into rhythmic patterns from those same local dances. The two recognized in each other the traditional type of Central African big man who may have been briefly (for less than a century) upstaged by Leopold and the Belgians, but whom they (and most Congolese) felt was what a boss ought to be. One musician observed: "If as a leader you're not hard they call you *yuma*, meaning someone who is afraid and weak . . . We learned this from Mobutu . . . If you listen to him talking to his subordinates, it sounds like he's always angry, but that is the only way people will respect you."

Some have suggested that Franco's many songs about people trapped in unhappy marriages are political metaphors, but that is probably a stretch. More telling about the state of Congolese society are the treachery-filled relationships described in his lyrics: the woman who works hard to support a man who tells everyone *he* is keeping *her* ("Mario"), the girl who works to pay her boyfriend's college fees only for him to refuse marriage, since now that he's a graduate she is beneath him ("Treize ans"), the woman who warns her married friends that their husbands all come to see her ("Ngai Marie nzoto ebeba"), and "La Vie des hommes," about a man who betrays his wife then becomes fearful she will take revenge, so leaves her and stops supporting their children.

As Franco's weight ballooned (a journalist once witnessed him gulp down twenty-five slabs of cassava dough, a whole chicken, several kebabs, and fried greens) and the quality of his songwriting waned, Kinois often commented on the two men's similarities. In the end, though, a more apt parallel is probably Mobutu and Leopold, rulers who treated the country as a private estate. Comparing and contrasting Zairean music and politics can, nonetheless, be illuminating; as the economy continued to plummet across the eighties, two outlier statistics consistently trended up: the number of musical groups and the volume of beer consumption.

∽

> We imagine corruption to be like a tick on a dog. There are some places in Africa where the tick is bigger than the dog.
>
> —John Robertson, Zimbabwean economist

> Inside each of us there is a little Mobutu.
>
> —Lye M. Yoka, Zairean political analyst

> [I]n their desire for splendour, the masses join in madness and clothe themselves in the flashy rags of power so as to reproduce its epistemology; [and] power, in its own violent quest for grandeur and prestige, makes vulgarity and wrongdoing its main mode of existence.
>
> —Achille Mbembe, Cameroonian political theorist, on the symbiotic relationship between power and popular culture

> Most peoples measure their national history in rulers . . . Many Congolese like to reflect on five generations of musicians, whose languorous rumbas and faster modern beats, adored across Africa and beyond, have served them better than any government.
>
> —*The Economist*

If you visited Kinshasa during the decade following the Ali-Foreman fight and only ventured out after sunset to tour the city's nightspots, you could have believed that Zaire was flourishing. Clubs and bands proliferated, shows grew wilder and more grandiose, people dressed up for a night out; in 1978, a newspaper counted 1,200 working bands in the country. Not only was Zaire one of the few African nations with its own recording studios and pressing plants, it was also unusual in treating music as a respected craft and musicians as a kind of elite. Rochereau's and Franco's styles continued to rule, with new bands sticking close to the template, though often with faster tempi, keyboards instead of horns, and less virtuosic nuance. The novelties that did emerge were in form rather than essence, based around two words: *animation* and *ambiance*.

Mobutu had adored the vast choreographed stadium shows they put on for him during a visit to China and North Korea; he tried to mount a sort of mass rumba along those lines, but it didn't work very well, so he settled for a campaign called *animation politique* designed to pump up enthusiasm for *authenticité* and Mobutuism with slogans, songs, posters, and rallies. When the hottest new band of the late seventies, Zaïko Langa Langa, recruited two boys from a folklore group to show off their cool *zekete* step, one of them got the crowd going with the sort of banter and shouted encouragement associated with this village dance. He was given a pair of maracas and a spot next to the dancing girls and soon made Zaïko's sebene his own, name-checking members of the audience in return for tips, ramping up the energy with a pre-rap line of jive that soon became an essential part of every group's live shows. This role is traditionally known as the *atalaku*, but, with tongues at least part way into cheeks, they became *animateurs*, while the excitement of the sebene, as it extended longer and longer, became *animation*, a post-modern moment when centuries-old dances and incantations were dropped into the maelstrom that was the Kinshasa sebene.

Politicians loved hanging around the clubs; they got to meet the many girls aspiring to show off their moves onstage (and who were expected to be accommodating to the bands' backers and political protectors if they wanted an audition) as well as getting free *libanga* (name-checks). Big men (and big car dealers) had always been able to buy praise from Congolese bands, but with the ascent of the animateur, the practice came to dominate the sebene, with cash being passed to the stage and the wannabe's praises shouted out as the music cranked up another notch while the poker-faced dancing girls' hips traced ever more complex cycles that defied geometric analysis.

As the tale of tango makes clear, Kongo culture takes nuance and detail very seriously. With foreign currency impossible to obtain and greedy customs officials making importation impossible, maracas disappeared from the market; around the same time, Kinshasa's pest-control and rubbish-disposal systems collapsed, turning the city into a breeding ground for mosquitoes. Trial and error arrived at a recycled Mobil-brand pesticide can punched with a particular pattern of holes and a certain number of seeds from a local hardwood tree inserted through a small triangular flap at the base of the can; this provided animateurs with an uncannily maraca-like sound. We can't check the accuracy of this account because *animation* was strictly a live phenomenon in the mad years leading up to the collapse of the regime and was never recorded.

Where did all this money come from? Businesses that could generate cash for the boss to splash on dash were few and far between, the infrastructure was in a state of collapse, electricity was intermittent (the best clubs had their own generators), and much of the economy had sunk into a lethargic state of barter. The US, the IMF, France, and the World Bank, though, seem to have decided that whatever Mobutu was, he was preferable to the alternative, and besides, a budgeted quota of development funds needed to be "pushed out the door" and start clocking up interest. (Executives signing off on the loans would have banked their bonuses and moved on long before the recipients defaulted.) A vast flood of aid money poured into the country, much of it earmarked for grandiose projects that never broke ground; Mobutu played the bankers and diplomats like a thumb piano. The funds made their way via corrupt, nepotistic, and gun-barrel-directed channels into streets made desperate by the terms of those same loans, which had put an end to food and fuel subsidies.

Experience tends to teach Africans that success arrives not through hard work and diligence but rather via family, bribes, big men, or magic. The ecstatic glitz of the sebene, with the animateur crowing exhortations and braggadocio, the barely clothed girls, and the ever faster, louder, dumbed-down rumba, came to symbolize a country in which little was of substance and everything was a show performed at the edge of an abyss no one would admit existed. With a bit of a squint, one can detect parallels with the last years of the great Kongo kingdom of the early sixteenth century, when European cloth, trinkets, and weapons triggered a fever to capture and trade anyone—war prisoners, rivals, neighbors, even cousins—to Portuguese slave merchants in exchange for those wonderfully novel goods.

A sapeur's walk is an art form in itself, a mixture of swagger and stroll as individualistic as a graffiti artist's tag.

—Michela Wrong, *In the Footsteps of Mr Kurtz*

Ambiance, as any *sapeur* will tell you, is the opposite of *animation*. La Sape is one of those acronym puns the Congolese are so good at: a devotee of the Société des Ambianceurs et des Personnes Élégantes becomes not only a French word for "fireman," but also encompasses *sapé*, Parisian argot for "well-dressed" (rooted in the Latin *sapa*, meaning "cut"), along with a passing swipe at the IMF's Structural Adjustment Program, which forced African governments to sell state assets to well-connected thugs and foreign investors.

Zaïko Langa Langa's singer Shungu Wembadio always liked to dress well. He sang in a pure, high tenor touched with a melancholy absorbed, perhaps, from his mother's work as a professional funeral mourner. When he broke away to form Viva la Musica and renamed himself Papa Wemba, he became one of Zaire's biggest stars. Kinois musicians could still make serious money in the 1970s, and Wemba used his to build a compound near the airport, where he assumed the role of big man for the quarter. Inspired by a movie about yet another quixotic Belgian, he named his neighborhood Molokai, after the Hawaiian island where Jozef de Veuster (better known as Father Damien) achieved sainthood by creating a refuge for lepers. Wemba then decreed that Molokai would set itself apart by keeping its streets clean and that its residents should always appear in neat and stylish clothes. Many credit this as the start of *la sape*; the movement's true origins, however, lie a half-century earlier on the other side of the river.

Early on in their colonial adventures, the French found Africans to be fierce fighters and great shots and decided to put those skills to use. In the early 1920s, André Matsoua from French Congo joined the all-African Tirailleurs (Marksmen) battalion that had served with honor in the Great War; after being wounded fighting rebels in the Rif Mountains of Morocco, Matsoua recuperated at a hospital in Paris and arrived home on leave wearing the latest in fashionable French attire. This may seem a simple statement, but at the time it was like an earthquake; neither the awed Congolese nor the outraged colonial authorities had ever seen an African dressed like a sophisticated, urbane White man before. Matsoua's nightly riverside promenades might have been forgotten were it not for the fact that once back in Paris he became as painful a thorn in the French side as Marcus Garvey was for the Americans. Attempting to form a Black trade union, he led strikes and pickets and demanded equal rights for immigrant workers. The French stole a leaf from the Yanks' book and jailed Matsoua for supposedly defrauding the Africans who had sent small sums to support his movement; after a series of trials, jailbreaks, and dramatic adventures, André died in a Brazzaville prison in 1942, following a brutal beating by French colonial police. His legend grew to the extent that he is now the subject of a popular cult, the Church of Matsouanism.

Servicemen returning from the war in 1946 signaled their support for Matsoua's ideals by dressing sharp; that impulse later blended, as we have seen, with the desire of Congolese students studying in France to show off their sartorial sophistication when they got home. Over the ensuing years, impeccably turned-out men emerging from scrap-metal shacks in Brazzaville *bidonvilles* became an engaging (if eccentric) footnote to the life of the capital, with a growing number of adepts across the river among the Kinois. Papa Wemba blew on this glowing coal and it burst into flame.

∽

Listen my love
On our wedding day
The label will be Torrente
The label will be Giorgio Armani
The label will be Daniel Hechter
The label for the shoes will be J. M. Weston

—Papa Wemba, "Matebu"

La sape is a movement of contradictions and paradoxes. It juxtaposes symbols of excess and conspicuous consumption amidst some of the most agonising scenes of urban poverty. It has strong religious and moral undertones and codes, while at the same time verging on the blasphemous by flouting its unstinting devotion to worldly symbols of money, "bling" and consumerism.

—Paul Goodwin, Introduction to *Gentlemen of Bacongo*

A series of coffee-table books and fashion-magazine articles have introduced *sapeurs* to the wider world. And an extraordinary sight they are, wearing immaculately tailored, brightly colored, perfectly pressed suits, accompanied by well-chosen hats, socks, shirts, ties, neatly folded pocket handkerchiefs, and brilliantly shined shoes, their hands holding gold-topped canes or Cuban cigars, stepping delicately around rubbish and muddy puddles or snaking their way through crowded markets. They rarely visit nightclubs, as anything involving sweat is to be avoided. Sapeurs insist they dress for themselves, though many earn fees for turning up at weddings, receptions, or concerts. For the fully committed, *la Sape* is not just for weekends but every time they step outdoors. The rules are strict: no more than three colors in any outfit, no drugs, no touching, no politics. The *ambiance* exuded by the sapeurs may qualify as the ultimate expression of Farris Thompson's "African cool."

During the eighties, Congolese bands touring or recording in Europe would fly home with suitcases crammed with designer-label gear. At the height of Wemba's (and the movement's) popularity, Kinois gangs would descend on Paris or Brussels, piling into exclusive shops and running out with their arms full of clothes and straight onto the next flight home. Congolese tailors became so expert at knocking off famous brands that it was hard to tell fake from real. One bragged, "We are not scared of Parisians, the Sape in Brazzaville is a giant."

Sapeurs are defiant; their predecessors challenged colonial attitudes that Africans were uncivilized savages, while the eighties generation helped to undermine Mobutu's *abacost* nonsense. *La Sape* outlived the president and thrives to this day; every few years there's a new book of photos, a magazine feature, or a TV documentary on the subject. One could wish such extraordinary creativity be directed towards something more productive, but in twenty-first-century Kinshasa or Brazzaville, what would that be? George Orwell observed similar impulses in working-class Lancashire in the thirties (as have we with the Rio carnival);

spending time and money on fantasy, he concluded, is part of what makes us human.

As for Papa Wemba, he always took the stage in designer gear and was lionized by the Japanese for how he wore his Yamamoto. He starred in *La Vie est belle*, a likeable-enough movie about an aspiring singer arriving in Kinshasa, and toured with Peter Gabriel in 1993. He later did time in a French jail for immigrant smuggling, with evidence reportedly provided by disgruntled Congolese who felt he'd been overcharging. He died from an onstage heart attack in Abidjan in 2016. Wemba had an original musical mind and an appealing voice and his records sold well during his lifetime, but he left few classic tracks. Though always proclaiming great affection for Zaire's musical traditions, his use of drum machines and synths started early and was a constant throughout his career; the cheesy keyboards make his recordings sound dated, leaving behind a legacy more sartorial than musical.

Walking through a poor Kinshasa neighborhood, Michela Wrong asked a near-naked urchin playing in the dust if he had a favorite designer; the boy thought for a moment, then said, "Versace for jackets and Girbaud for jeans."

Music was everywhere in eighties Zaire, but musicians were struggling to survive. With vinyl as scarce as maracas, the make-do was melting down old discs, resulting in blurry, crackly pressings. Cassettes began their insidious invasion; easy to bootleg and, with the help of ghetto blasters, playable on the move, they would bring domestic record industries the world over to their knees. Since most ordinary Kinois were broke, libanga earned more than gig fees, with a resulting malign effect on the music. No wonder Rochereau lost half his band during a visit to Abidjan; why go back to Kinshasa when there was a flourishing economy in the Ivory Coast, complete with decent recording studios and audiences across West Africa crazy for Congolese rumba?

While francophone countries to the north and west had fallen early and hard for it, the anglophone ones to the east and southeast took a bit longer. Most eventually embraced the rumba in their own way, blending harp and mbira traditions and, to the south, some maskanda-style guitar-picking with the irresistible Congolese propulsion. Nairobi, Mombasa, and Dar Es Salaam became home to popular orchestras led by Congolese expats, while in Zimbabwe, local bands developed a kind of rumba-rock hybrid.

One of these was the Bhundu Boys, an appealing group of kids with a style called *jit*. An enterprising Scottish label licensed enough tracks for a full LP and sent copies to BBC DJs Andy Kershaw and John Peel, who played it incessantly. In 1986, a year after that series of great African shows (and just before *Graceland*), the Bhundu Boys arrived for their first UK tour, and I went along to the Town & Country in north London to check them out.

The place was full and the audience cheered them to the rafters. I found the music enjoyable if a bit lightweight compared to those GLC concerts, but it was clear that African music was on the rise in Britain. I had been particularly impressed the year before with the Congolese artists—Les Quatres Étoiles, Sam Mangwana, and Kanda Bongo Man—and, as I left the hall that night, I made up my mind to track Kanda down and try to make a deal with him for my label. My life has had its share of good fortune and extraordinary happenstance, and near the top of that list has to be walking up Kentish Town Road that night in the middle of a crowd, glancing to my left and finding Kanda and his distinctive gap-toothed grin standing next to me.

Kanda Bongo Man took his name from a percussion-ace grandfather in the lakeside town of Inongo in northern Congo. His musical style had also lately taken on an assumed name: *soukous*. As far as non-Congolese were concerned, the name *rumba* was always problematic; despite the word's Ki-Kongo origins, Cuba's claim on it would always take precedence. Among a series of catchwords for eighties dance steps, *soukous* (from the French *secouer*, "to shake") emerged as the tag of choice for this music. Kinshasa never took to it much, but as more and more musicians decamped to Abidjan, Paris, or Nairobi, it became synonymous with the faster, slicker style that evolved when the transplanted musicians lost their close connections to the rough but rich soil of Zaire. Propelled by drummers who had discovered the hi-hat thanks to Tony Allen and disco, soukous tracks often start off at the pace of a sebene and stay there, earning the nickname "TGVs," after France's new high-speed rail network.

Fed up with the crumbling infrastructure and the cut-throat Zairean music world, Kanda was among the first to leave for Paris. He was also a pioneer in looking over rumba's horizons; the British scene interested him, so he crossed the Channel to investigate, which is how he came to join his host, the journalist Chris Stapleton, at the Bhundu Boys concert. Kanda and I made a deal the next day at Chris's flat; over the next seven years, Hannibal released four of his albums and all sold well, boosted by the tours we helped organize in North America and around northern Europe. Kanda used a great Paris band for his recordings, built around the Congolese guitarists Diblo Dibala and Rigo [sic] Star and drummer Ty-Jan from Guadeloupe. What I loved about Kanda and his music was how out of step he was with the latest sounds emanating from Kinshasa, Paris, and Abidjan; he couldn't afford horns, but eschewed the now-ubiquitous synths and keyboards, recording with a classic three-guitar, bass, drums, and percussion line-up, adding a pair of dancers and an animateur for the tours.

I have a vivid memory of standing in SOB's in New York as the packed house, mesmerized by the guitars, the TGV beat, and the dancing girls and egged on by the animateur, heaved and roared while Kanda delivered one of the best sets I've ever seen. One name on the guest list that night was Andy González, the great salsa bassist; he had been paying attention to the music coming out of Kinshasa and was fascinated by the bass parts, which were often taken from traditional drum patterns. Kongo rhythms had been crossing the Atlantic since the sixteenth century; now the process was coming full circle, with the Congolese studying González's playing and Andy learning from theirs.

I had to prod the PA engineer that night to keep the second and third guitars up nearly level with the lead; even the best-produced Congolese records rarely do justice to the way three soukous guitars can sound when balanced so those interlaced parts chime together perfectly. For me, it's one of the great sounds in music and was always best live, when the notes bounce off each other in midair, creating eddies of overtones amid the dizzying cascade of arpeggios. The guitars need space to work properly; sustained chords from an electric keyboard or synth smother the effect, which is one reason why, once Europe had discovered soukous, it never really took off. Peter Gabriel's Real World label released a heavily promoted Papa Wemba CD that sounded so keyboard-pop it did little to elevate the magic of soukous.

Another memorable—though sobering—moment took place at the 1989 New Orleans Jazzfest. Having persuaded Quint Davis, the festival's producer, to book Kanda, I lobbied for the ideal Sunday-afternoon slot on a big stage in the center of the Fair Grounds. In most respects, everything went according to plan; there was a core group of soukous fanatics and some important critics, the crowd grew and grew, and everyone danced and cheered like crazy, but the field in front of our stage was never really packed. That same afternoon, crowds were swarming to see Aaron Neville, Allen Toussaint, Irma Thomas, Art Blakey, the Rebirth Brass Band, and other great African-American performers. The NPR/PBS shoulder-bag crowd who accounted for much of the Jazzfest audience (and the bulk of potential US consumers of soukous) had access to so much of America's own roots music that they didn't see much need to explore the unfamiliar. It was a shame that Kanda and a few other old-school artists began touring outside Africa just as the Congolese sound shifted and modernized. Rochereau and Franco had big, expensive orchestras that world music promoters and festivals couldn't afford (and no incentive to cut their fees in search of new audiences). The slick style of the younger groups seemed to suit African clubgoers in Paris, Brussels, Kinshasa, and Abidjan well enough, but gave the music little chance of establishing itself outside that world. Looking back, Rochereau observed: "What we'll never be able to recapture is the spontaneity, the concentration, of the musicians of that era . . . [O]ut of this sprang stuff . . . that was unbelievable, which we no longer see."

Why did we fight against the white man's rule?
Did we shed our blood for independence . . .
The country is in ruins.
What a humiliation before the world!
A country so rich, with leaders so careless of its future.

—Tabu Ley Rochereau, "Le Glas a sonné" (The Bell Has Tolled)

Evening arrives, the day disappears
Night falls; it is the hour of sorcerers and fetishists . . .
The white man has made cannons to destroy the world,
But to destroy the truth,
The white man has not been able.
Oh the earth.

—Simaro Lutumba, "Mabele (Ntoto)," sung by Sam Mangwana with TPOK

It was those two world-altering phenomena of the eighties, AIDS and Glasnost, that brought down Franco and Mobutu. Right up to his death in 1989, even as his massive body had been reduced to skeletal fragility, Franco remained as insouciant as Fela, calling the disease "Syndrome Imaginaire pour Décourager les Amoureux" (after the French word order, "SIDA"); he left eighteen children from fourteen mothers. Rochereau (who kept his distance from Mobutu and the excesses of Kinois life) lived to the ripe old age of seventy-three. He received threats after releasing "Le Glas a sonné"—and spent much of his later life in exile. The vast catalogues created by these two, along with Docteur Nico and Joseph Kabasele, stand with the greatest music created in any culture, endlessly rewarding repeated listening.

Mobutu, meanwhile, bitterly resented US pressure to hold elections once the threat of Soviet influence in Africa had abated; as the political process opened up, the chaos he had predicted duly ensued as parties split into factions, then forged a jumble of new alignments, just like rumba bands. Everyone wanted to be the big man, but few besides Mobutu and Franco could pull it off. The currency collapsed, banks closed, and desperate people sought superstitious answers; as in Lagos, nightclubs were transformed into churches. The president spent his last years isolated in the jungle compound, his ego so bruised by demonstrations in favor of the opposition that he couldn't face Kinshasa. At the end, Mobutu didn't resemble Franco or Leopold so much as Mr. Kurtz in Conrad's *Heart of Darkness*. When, terminally ill with cancer, he flew off to die in more luxurious surroundings, his guards took potshots at the plane and began looting his palace the minute the wheels were off the ground.

The signal for the start of the 1994 Rwanda massacres was a Congolese-style rumba with anti-Tutsi lyrics played repeatedly on a Hutu radio station. Zaire's musical hegemony continued its outward spiral, but in the real world of geopolitics, the obverse was happening. Having supported the Hutus, Mobutu paid dearly when the struggle spilled over into eastern Congo, violence opening the door for greedy incursions by Uganda, Angola, Zimbabwe, and, finally, the now-victorious Rwandan Tutsis. A combined force of Ugandans, Rwandans, and Zambians crossed the immense country from east to west on foot through the forests; when they reached Kinshasa, Mobutu's army evaporated, barely firing a shot. Zaire became a nation in name only, its mineral wealth mortgaged in Mobutu's failed attempts to hold on to power or siphoned off by invaders from the east and south.

The faraway island of Cuba, so influential on Congolese music, also had its fingerprints on the next regime. A brothel-keeper, kidnap-gang leader, and occasional guerrilla named Laurent Kabila was chosen by the invaders as their figurehead largely because Che Guevara had praised him during the rebellion Castro tried to mount in 1964 among Lumumba's followers in the east. Three decades later, Kabila resurfaced as the sinister, if somewhat ridiculous, leader of a new Congolese era.

Towards the end of 1999, I got a collect call from Montreal; it was Kanda, whom I hadn't been able to reach for several years. He sounded exhausted and depressed, but cheered up when I said we were holding a nice four-figure sum in royalties for him. He'd had a pretty good nineties, successfully extending his anglophone incursions into East Africa and single-handedly creating a post-apartheid soukous buzz in South Africa. Having vowed never to go back while Mobutu ruled, the minute the new government was in place, Kanda flew to Kinshasa; officials had promised to let him start a copyright structure for the country. The new bureau collected some money, he told me, but not a *centime* ended up in songwriters' pockets; the Kabila regime proved as hopelessly corrupt as Mobutu's. Kanda eventually settled in Britain, assembled his usual great band, and kept old-school soukous moving forward into the twenty-first century.

⁂

> Kinshasa is a very loud town. I wanted to be heard around a large circle, to make some publicity for my group. Guitar pickups didn't work, so I broke car alternators with a hammer, took the magnets out of them, and wound copper wire around them. It's so powerful, the output overdrives any amplifier. No guitar pickup can compete.
>
> —Mingiedi Mawangu, founder of *likembe* group Konono N°1

Mingiedi Mawangu and his family arrived in Kinshasa from the Angola-Congo border region of Bazombo in the early seventies, bringing with them *likembes* (thumb pianos) of various sizes and pitches with scavenged metal strips for "tongues"; as Mawangu describes, they added amplification to be heard above the urban clamor. (Mingiedi was a truck driver and auto mechanic, so knew his way around car parts.) The group played *zombo* music that was traditionally performed with hocketing elephant-tusk horns; the likembes mirrored the horn parts just as rumba guitars mirrored likembe patterns. They played for funerals and other ritual events in neighborhoods where Bazombo and other Bacongo people lived, using old Belgian police loud-hailers as speakers. The sound was both big and distorted, which appealed to the "rattle and buzz" sensibility of Central African ritual. In addition to varying numbers of likembes, the group featured call-and-response vocals and percussion, including a minimalist drum kit with a hi-hat made from pot lids. The word *konono* describes the stiffness of a dead body; the Bacongo always massage the deceased to delay rigor mortis and give the spirit time to adjust to its altered state.

The seventies were a good time for village music in the capital; Mobutu's *authenticité* campaign provided support for folklore groups and encouraged city-dwellers to retain rituals and rhythms from home.

In 1976, a French radio presenter named Bernard Treton (who had instilled in the young Martin Meissonnier a love of African music) moved to Kinshasa to teach aspiring sound engineers; while exploring the city he came across Konono N°1 and made recording them a class project. They also taped other *tradi-moderne* groups (the Kinois term for the application of technology to folk music) and the results were later released on an LP called *Musiques urbaines* à *Kinshasa*.

A Brussels bass player named Vincent Kenis taped Treton's 1980 Radio France broadcast about Konono and played it over and over; hearing them in person became his quest. Having played with African musicians in Latin bands, he began buying Franco and Rochereau records in the city's Congolese district. He also met our man from the Amazon sunset, Benoît Quersin, who played him his field recordings from the Congo hinterlands. In 1989, Kenis visited Kinshasa, staying with Quersin and his Congolese wife on their farm outside the city and prowling Bacongo neighborhoods, vainly searching for Konono. After another fruitless visit in 1996, he finally tracked them down at the turn of the millennium.

If this were a film, we'd now have a scene with Kenis and his fellow Belgian Tony van der Eecken (who organized European tours for African artists) standing in a Kinshasa shantytown watching Konono N°1 perform. The camera would follow the power cable from their amp to the battery of a derelict car. Then we'd jump-cut to a sequence of clips: Konono playing to tens of thousands of kids at a pop festival, Konono receiving a BBC "Newcomer of the Year" award, Konono collaborating in the studio with Herbie Hancock and then with Björk. This is not a screenwriter's invention; it happened. And that's not all. Kenis and van der Eecken heard five groups in a Kinshasa neighborhood of immigrants from Kasaï Province and persuaded the leading figures from each band to form a collective; the Kasaï Allstars have toured widely, released a series of successful albums, and collaborated with hipsters Deerhoof, Juana Molina, and Animal Collective. There's a tribute album of their and Konono's songs covered by indie bands. The Kasaï Allstars performed in *Félicité*, a film based on incidents in their singer's life, which won the Grand Prix at the 2017 Berlin Film Festival. Wait, there's more.

Kenis came across a group comprised of polio victims and abandoned street kids called Staff Benda Bilili, and recorded them in the Kinshasa Zoo, where many of the band live. The album sold even better than Konono or the Allstars, and their single "Allons voter" is credited with increasing the turnout for the 2006 election, Congo's most successful to date. A documentary about Staff Benda Bilili was selected for the 2010 Cannes Film Festival and the group performed at the opening gala.

The average Kinois knows little of this, and those who do are often bemused, puzzled, or outraged, not least about their country being represented in Cannes by handicapped musicians (African cultures being generally ashamed and/or contemptuous of disability). Why would northern hemisphere audiences and media, who paid so little attention to the genius of Franco, Rochereau, and Docteur Nico, make such a fuss over provincial nobodies who can't even get a booking in downtown Kinshasa? Do images of poverty, disability, and naïf art fit more easily into Western prejudices about Africa than artful, million-selling sophistication?

Audiences can only respond to what's put in front of them; after the collapse of Fonior, the bulk of classic Congolese tracks ended up in cheap packaging, scattered around various Parisian and African labels with virtually no promotion. (Stern's brought order—and royalties—to the catalogues for a while, but after their licenses expired, chaos returned.) Kenis, moreover, loves Congolese music in all its forms and has played onstage and in the studio with both Franco and Wemba. It can sometimes be easier for outside producers to work with artists unappreciated at home than with those who rule their base market and see no reason to experiment. Kanda Bongo Man is unique; he had little interest in following modern rumba trends yet remained popular in Africa while also exploring uncharted soukous markets. We have seen ample evidence that outsiders' takes on a musical culture are often at odds with those of the locals: Paul Simon's debate with Barney Rachabane in the Soweto bar, Fania's devotion to the classic Cuban songbook the Castro government viewed as reactionary, Marley's late triumphs everywhere bar Jamaica, the sold-out concerts for the Mystère choir when most Bulgarians couldn't stand the sound of them, the Brazilian eclipse of bossa nova even as it continued to conquer the globe . . . the list is long.

∽

There were other, more high-profile efforts to connect northern audiences to Congolese music. Damon Albarn's Africa Express came to Kinshasa in 2008 with a group of West African and Anglo-American stars and spent a week jamming and recording with local musicians. Clips from their visit are full of northerners speaking of the trip as "eye-opening" and "life-altering," but there doesn't seem to have been much knock-on benefit to the Congolese and the resulting CD made little impact. The US band Vampire Weekend came together at Columbia University through a shared love of African music; one of their best-known songs, "Cape Cod Kwassa Kwassa," references a Kanda Bongo Man track in the title, the guitars make a nod in the direction of soukous, and the lyrics give Peter Gabriel an ambiguous name-check. The backing, however, is stodgily rockish (barring one Kinshasa-style bass-guitar slide) and neither they nor any other anglophone bands (Antibalas excepted) have delved into African beats with the sort of acuity sixties rock bands brought to the mining of American blues.

What stands out here is the work of Kenis and his collaborators, Crammed Discs. We met the label and its founder, Marc Hollander, in the Brazil and Roma chapters, when they were home to Bebel Gilberto and Taraf de Haïdouks, and we'll encounter them again when we get to Ethiopia. The savvy with which Hollander and longtime colleague Hanna Gorjaczkowska promoted the three groups, the respect with which they treated them and their music, and the originality of the projects they and Kenis developed with them stand out amid the rather mixed history of European and US labels' dealings with African artists. Crammed refused all requests to do remixes because they wanted listeners to focus on the musicians' own version of modernity.

I went to their *Tradi-Mods vs Rockers* concert in London and all my fusion aversions melted away at the sight and sound of the indie musicians following gamely and interestingly along with the powerful playing of the Kasai Allstars and Konono N°1. To my ears, most fusion projects get it backwards, laying down a culture-neutral backing track for the "exotic" musicians to play over (the egregious *One Giant Leap* being the most glaring example) rather than letting them set the beat. This was something quite different, a continually entertaining and surprising evening, with Black and White musicians appearing equally delighted with the adventure. My ideal fusions, of course, would have been for Celia Cruz and Bill Withers to sing a few numbers with Rochereau's band at the Rumble in the Jungle. Or, a decade and a half later, perhaps, that same band brought to New York for a Central Park SummerStage show and joined by David Byrne and Héctor Lavoe for a song or two each. A Boyd can dream, can't he?

Tony van der Eecken told me he was inspired to go to Kinshasa by the grand buildings in Brussels: "All of the money to build them came from Congo; I felt a responsibility as a Belgian." Belgium once imagined its colony would be the most powerful country in Africa, a beacon of economic strength. Such dreams died long ago but music is another story; for a quarter of a century (with assists from a motley crew of Belgians, whose efforts don't compensate for their country's crimes but at least made a start), Congolese music prodded and inspired other new nations of Africa as they carved out their own musical identity. During that period, Congolese rumba went through evolutions as complex and interesting as Anglo-American rock 'n' roll while having none of the West's historic infrastructure or commercial momentum. For inquisitive Western ears, those fecund years, plus Crammed's adventures in the new millennium, provide a mine as rich as the copper, uranium, and diamonds of Katanga.

∽

In 1940, a German officer, spotting Black faces among a group of French prisoners of war, ordered them to be taken out and shot; as the condemned men raised their fists and shouted, "*Vive la France, vive l'Afrique noir*," a Vichy aide-de-camp talked the officer out of giving the fatal command. One of the spared soldiers was Léopold Senghor; in 1960, he became the first president of independent Senegal.

Senghor had gone straight from smoking Gauloises and talking philosophy with Jean-Paul Sartre and Aimé Césaire at the Brasserie Lipp into the front lines. He was the paragon of a French ideal, in which African elites became *citoyens* and colonies were gradually absorbed into Greater France, as Guadeloupe, Martinique, Guyana, and Algeria had been. Son of a wealthy Dakar trading family, Senghor was sent to study in Paris, where he learned to be more French than the French. After the war, when he was elected to represent Senegal in the National Assembly, that august body chose Léopold as their language monitor, policing the grammar used in drafting bills and official communiqués. Over the course of his career, Senghor would prove a master straddler, between France and Africa, modernity and tradition, Christianity and Islam, rural and urban.

Compared to the brutal Belgians and the arrogant British, French colonialism has been given a relatively easy ride by historians. But when Geoffrey Gorer was traveling in the late 1920s across French West Africa, as he approached the border of a British colony (Gambia, Sierra Leone, Gold Coast, or Nigeria), he found empty villages and a deserted countryside. Intrigued, he discovered that people so loathed the French that they would pick up and move just to be under the laissez-faire British instead. The French didn't chop off hands like the Belgians, but they imposed an annual head-tax in a land with little access to money; those who couldn't pay had to work in what amounted to chain gangs or spend years in military service, including providing cannon fodder in Europe's savage wars. Accepting that most colonies had little economic upside, the French got Africans to do most of the (unpaid) work, administering an area of 2.3 million square miles and a population of 24 million with a staff of five hundred. Senegal stood apart. The dominant group there, the Wolof, had long experience accommodating European intruders, having made their first commercial agreement in 1488, with the Portuguese. In the centuries that followed, they often served as middlemen in what Europeans had hoped would be a trade in gold, but from which both sides would profit by trafficking in humans. (Wolof influence on African-American culture—and through that, the world's—includes some of our most popular slang: *dig*, *jive*, *hip*, and *cat* all evolved from Wolof expressions.) As a colony, Senegal became a test tube for assimilation, with residents of its four largest cities granted French citizenship and the right to elect representatives to the Assembly in Paris.

When the storm clouds of independence began swirling around French Africa in the late fifties, Senghor helped draft the measure that would keep colonies inside a Greater France. Economics, he believed, was the key and he saw little chance of the impoverished lands of French West Africa and French Equatorial Africa thriving without European support. Nor was there much enthusiasm for independence within colonies that had barely any infrastructure and little potential to pay their way. Senghor also believed that European culture was badly in need of Africa's humanizing influence.

Provoked by Nkrumah's dash for Ghanaian independence, the French gave their African "subjects" a chance to vote for Senghor's plan. When Guinea returned a solitary but overwhelming *Non!*, de Gaulle was so outraged that he scrapped the whole idea. (European big men often have fragile egos.) Two years later, fourteen French colonies were shown the door, with most in a Congo-like state of unreadiness. Learning from Brussels's mistakes, Paris managed to maintain a good deal of economic and political control while no longer having to pay the upkeep. An orchestra from Brazzaville called Les Bantus de la Capitale, led by ex-members of OK Jazz, performed at one inaugural party after another from Bangui to Bamako; rumba was the soundtrack of independence.

The Senegalese national anthem (lyrics by Senghor) begins, "*Everyone strum your koras, strike the balafons*," but reverence for tradition did not run deep among the country's elite. French intellectuals often have a trademark idea and Senghor's was Négritude, an aesthetic connection uniting Africa with its diaspora whose paramount manifestation was jazz. (Senghor liked reading his poems in Left Bank dives, backed by small combos.) For decades, there had been clubs in Dakar and Saint Louis where évolués expressed their aspirational modernity by listening to jazz and dancing Latin, while the griot tradition was seen as old-fashioned and backward. Always more interested in culture than economics, Senghor's efforts to promote Négritude were perfectly expressed in the headline accomplishment of the nation's first decade, the Festival Mondial des Arts Nègres (FESMAN), held across three and a half weeks in the spring of 1966.

Funded by France's Ministry of Culture and UNESCO, FESMAN represented the dying gasp of a particular vision of traditional music and art. America sent jazz in the form of Duke Ellington, while the evening galas were filled with earnest historical dramas and choreographed dance ensembles. The opening address was by André Malraux and there were *son et lumière* evenings at the slave prison on Gorée Island. Senghor's beloved Harlem Renaissance was front and center, with the poet Langston Hughes the star of the show, giving impromptu talks and interviews in which he endorsed Négritude as another word for soul. Critical voices, though, could also be heard; *Ebony* magazine's Hoyt Fuller wondered why James Baldwin, Thelonious Monk, Leroi Jones, and Miles Davis weren't there (the CIA had vetoed them) and complained about the "Disneyfication" of the slave trade. Senghor had invited his friend Katherine Dunham onto the selection committee, but during the festival she complained about Africa's music and dance traditions becoming over-arranged and gentrified. (You may recall Chano Pozo joining Dunham's Broadway revue.) The choicest dart hurled at the Senghor ethos came from Fela Kuti's cousin Wole Soyinka, author and director of a theater piece from Nigeria, who pointed out that tigers don't announce their *tigritude*, they "simply pounce."

On New Year's Eve 1958, Ndeye Sokhna Mboup was a happy woman; she had sung her way through her Dakar neighborhood, just as her griot parents had done, opening her powerful throat, praising the different families and earning dash. This was the first time her husband had allowed her to do it; Elimane was a Serer, a group related to the Wolof, while Ndeye was a Tukolor (connected to the Fulani) whose family had been unhappy when she announced her desire to marry not just "out," but to a non-griot. On that auspicious night, her husband shared her joyful spirit and they conceived their first child; she knew right away it would be a boy and that he was destined for greatness.

Elimane and Ndeye's son grew up, to his mother's delight and his father's bemusement, with an extraordinary singing voice. Surrounded by Wolofs, he immersed himself in their traditions, learning the rituals, rhythms, and songs. Pioneering musical figures have often been born between cultures: Miriam Makeba, Miguelito Valdés, Bob Marley, Carmen Miranda, and Carlos Gardel, to name a few, and many readers will by now have anticipated the reveal—that this couple's family name is N'Dour and that their son is called Youssou.

The boy seized any chance to perform; at thirteen, he sang at the funeral of a revered Senegalese jazz musician and was asked to repeat his musical paean on national radio. Elimane, however, was determined that his son would have a more respectable and reliable career than singer, a profession tainted by the low opinion in which many held *griotisme*. When Youssou ran off with a touring band, Elimane alerted the police and they delivered the boy back home. In 1976, when he was sixteen, N'Dour was invited to join the resident Star Band at Club Miami, the most famous venue in Dakar; the momentum was now irresistible and his father reluctantly gave his assent.

The Star Band had been going for sixteen years. Their style lay firmly within the African/Afro-Cuban template established by the Congolese, with the sort of differences one might expect 2,600 miles closer to New York. I came across one of their LPs in the early eighties and found it fascinating, particularly the track "Bouna N'Diaye," sung by N'Dour. The vibe is funkier and more punchy than Kinshasa's rumba, the feel more Arsenio than Trio Matamoros (including *tres*-like figures on the electric guitar), with a distinctive, stuttering beat and chord changes reminiscent of Brill Building pop; the *sabars*, Wolof talking drums, add flourishes not unlike timbale fills in salsa. Youssou's vocal, though, is what brought me back to that track again and again: pure of tone but melismatic, youthful yet confident, nasal, exuberant, and dazzlingly strange. I found the singer's name in the small-print credits and made a point of remembering it.

So crowd-pleasing was Youssou's way with traditional melodies that within his first year the balance of Star Band's repertoire shifted from Latin covers to Wolof songs. Dakar was experiencing a similar transformation, an influx of madrassa-educated youths from rural areas that challenged the évolués and their modernizing aspirations. The time was ripe for a musical revolution and N'Dour was clearly the one to lead it, but it needed a final push. That impetus duly arrived from a hundred miles to the south, across one of colonial Africa's strangest borders. In 1765, at a time when European powers were regularly hijacking each other's galleons and raiding rival colonies, the British established a few slave-trading outposts along the Gambia River, much to the annoyance of the French just up the coast at Saint Louis. Later, after the Scramble, London practically begged Paris to take this pointless sliver of pink off its hands, but the French never offered much in return and British pride wouldn't let them just hand over the keys gratis. As a result, the tiny independent nation of The Gambia lies today along its languid, eponymous river, like one of those measly slices in an old-fashioned British bread-roll sandwich, with Senegal playing the part of the roll.

Nightlife in Banjul, the Gambian capital, was never the equal of Dakar, but the country had a worthy rival to the Star Band called the Super Eagles; being anglophone, they were big admirers of Geraldo Pino and proud of their mastery of both funk and salsa. Funded by a fan who traded diamonds for a living (and wearing knock-off *Sgt. Pepper* uniforms), the Super Eagles ventured to London in the early seventies to play some club dates; they were startled to find English audiences cheering their adaptations of traditional songs and not much interested in the James Brown and Fania covers. The group decided to take time off; they traveled the Gambian hinterlands, learning old songs and instrumental techniques (like American folk revivalists venturing into the Appalachians), incorporating them into a style they called "Afro-Manding Blues" and changing their name to Ifang Bondi (which means "be yourself"). What made the new sound revolutionary was the rhythm; jettisoning Cuban and American templates, Ifang Bondi dived deep into the Mandé culture of the Mali empire that had ruled much of West Africa for more than four centuries. When Youssou and some of the younger members of Star Band heard what the Gambians were up to, they were blown away.

I'm not the one who changed the face of Senegalese music. But I think I'm the one who took these changes to their furthest limit. Others were moving . . . towards a more traditional sound, but they hesitated, they didn't dare go quite far enough.

—Youssou N'Dour

We are people of the dance, whose feet regain strength as they strike hard ground.

—Léopold Senghor

[I]n griot families, we sing with the stomach, to give out something from inside. I sing with a great deal of effort. My mother and her relations, the *gawlos*, learned to sing like that.

—Youssou N'Dour

When Wolof boys complete their circumcision ordeal, they celebrate with a party; propelled by teams of drummers, they perform leg-wiggling, crotch-clutching *hoti* dances to announce their renewed interest in the opposite sex. Girls get together separately to show off their own wild, haunch-twirling *ventilateur* moves. Youssou had sung at these parties from an early age and knew the rhythms backwards; when he and some mates quit Star Band to form Les Étoiles du Dakar, circumcision-party beats formed the basis of their *mbalax* revolution (pronounced mm-BAH-lakh), with electric guitars and keyboards following the *sabar* drum patterns. They recruited Assane Thiam, master of the *tama*, the drum that "calls to the dance," and turned Star Band's formulae upside down, with Latin and Anglo-sounding melodies over undiluted Wolof rhythms. Borrowing a trick from reggae, they would sometimes leave out the first beat in order to emphasize it. Les Étoiles made traditional rhythms sound like the most up-to-date thing imaginable; moves previously seen only at neighborhood parties were being danced at their shows by both sexes. N'Dour's lyrics also broke new ground by praising women and singing about romantic love in ways previously unheard, earning him the adoration of female fans (and the condemnation of conservative mullahs). Their first cassette release was *Xalis*, whose title song celebrated being young and having money to spend; its impact lifted them to the summit of Senegalese music on the shoulders of the country's youth. Older Senegalese were aghast; for many, mbalax was both far too traditional and, at the same time, unnervingly modern, not at all the decorous future for Senegalese culture envisaged by Senghor. For heads of traditional families, the sexes dancing together in a nightclub came as an almost unimaginable shock. Once Senegal and Gambia were converted, other lands beckoned.

N'Dour took his group (now called Super Étoile—à la Franco—after a purge of members he felt had let success go to their heads) to Bamako in Mali, a concert that caused a spike in the local divorce rate after so many women defied their husbands to attend. The next foray was to Paris in 1983 for a concert organized by a group of Senegalese taxi drivers. The group stayed on to record what many feel is their best album, *Immigrés*, the title song inspired by the plight of so many countrymen forced to work far from home. During his Paris sojourn, Youssou met the singer Jacques Higuelin, the first of many northern stars drawn to working with him.

For artists such as Peter Gabriel, Sting, the African-American-Swedish Neneh Cherry, and Higuelin, N'Dour was the perfect African collaborator: strikingly handsome, with an irresistible voice, ambitious, intelligent, diplomatic, authentic, original . . . Working with him provided instant exotic credibility, while they offered Youssou worldwide exposure. Thus was launched his curious international career, combining triumph and failure, acclaim and frustration in equal measure.

> Have all these albums he's recorded for the Western majors with the input of his rockstar friends actually made a dent in the market . . . ? Have they fuck. Because they are, in fact, extremely dull. His live shows are full of colour and spectacle, and a controlled African "wildness" he thinks the West wants.
>
> —Mark Hudson's novel *The Music in My Head*, about a character based on Youssou N'Dour

> Big record companies don't know how to deal with African artists.
>
> —Youssou N'Dour

If you reach for your sunglasses while strolling on a Riviera beach or walking down Fifth Avenue and find you've left them back at the hotel, there will very likely be an African selling shades not far away. It's a safe bet that this enterprising vendor is a Senegalese Mouride, a member of the country's largest Sufi order, sometimes called "Muslim Protestants" for their work ethic. You can walk into a Mouride money-trader's office in Dakar, put cash on the table, and, with a single phone call to almost any large city in the world, that amount will be placed in the hands of your designated recipient. A fellow Mouride arriving in any of those cities will be given food, a place to stay, and help finding a job or starting a business.

When the French colonized Senegal, they viewed Islamic religious leaders as their enemies, with the Mourides' founder, Cheikh Amadou Bamba, among the most powerful and therefore toxic. He was exiled in 1895 but brought back fifteen years later, in part to stem the unrest his banishment was causing and also because the French had come to realize that the Cheikh was committed to leading an orderly and hard-working following. Based at Touba, the city he founded a hundred miles inland, Bamba built an economic powerhouse around peanut farming, self-help and micro-finance; France would eventually award him the Légion d'honneur. When he died in 1927, the Cheikh's followers numbered some seventy thousand; today there are more than three million, including many of the country's leading businessmen and most of its musicians. President Senghor treated them with respect and they reciprocated, helping to make Senegal a peaceful, relatively prosperous and stable democracy (until recently). Mourides are devout (but not puritanical), energetic, practical, and worldly; they see no reason to limit their horizons to Senegal. Youssou N'Dour is a Mouride.

When Peter Gabriel saw Les Super Étoiles' 1985 London show, he was so impressed that he followed them back to Dakar. Youssou ended up dueting on Gabriel's next album and learning about modern hi-tech recording at the British singer's Real World Studios in Wiltshire. After opening on a few Gabriel and Higuelin tours, N'Dour was invited to join Sting, Bruce Springsteen, Tracy Chapman, and Gabriel on the 1988 *Human Rights Tour* of twenty major arenas around the world.

Senegalese musicians are very conscious of the difficulties of selling *mbalax* to outsiders. It has none of the seductive Latin sway of soukous or the limb-loosening groove of afrobeat; it's dense, jagged, and complex. Youssou decided early on that the music he presented to the rest of the world would be different from his local releases. Intrigued by the latest technology, N'Dour loved the way everything could be separated, the sound of each instrument controlled, tweaked, replaced, or added later; he was also excited by the size of the crowds on those tours with big-name artists. To reach that Western audience, he would use Western technology; Virgin Records signed him up, eager to be part of the process.

The Virgin deal lasted all of two expensive and disappointing albums. The first, *The Lion*, was co-produced by Gabriel and recorded at Real World; it has the glossy bombast of an eighties Phil Collins record and left most critics and African music fans bemused. Before embarking on the next, a Virgin A&R man approached an experienced "roots-style" producer, who proposed recording in Dakar, mostly live-in-the-studio and without all the gadgetry. N'Dour reacted with outrage, accusing the producer of wanting to "keep me as an exhibit in a museum." If Michael Jackson used the latest technology, why shouldn't an African artist? Conducting this dialogue via the A&R man, the producer explained that he was simply being practical; the potential audience for an artist singing in Wolof would never be the size of Michael Jackson's and most listeners open to "foreign" music want spontaneous virtuosity and something that sounds authentic (whether it is or not). Hi-tech modern pop production, he contended, erects a barrier between an African artist and his or her potential audience. Besides, it's expensive, and the market for African music isn't big enough to recoup that sort of budget. Youssou was offended by the idea that his market was limited and remained unmoved; *Set*, the second album for Virgin, was produced in much the same way as the first, with a slightly more African feel, its funk-rock base decorated with mbalax flavoring from sabar drum overdubs.

Eyes Open, the first record under his next deal with CBS, doubled down on the gadgets and the celebrity connections, with Spike Lee as executive producer and director of the big-budget videos. If Youssou harbored any doubts about this approach, they were swept away by the success of his one-off duet with Neneh Cherry. With nothing remotely African about its rhythm, "7 Seconds" became a massive 1994 hit, staying at #1 in France for months, charting in many other countries, and Youssou's voice sounding great on Top 40 radio. Though originally Cherry's track, "7 Seconds" was shoehorned into N'Dour's next album, *The Guide*, which helped make it his biggest seller to date. His concerts (in Europe, at least) were always packed and across the nineties he entered a kind of jet stream where every world music award nomination, commission (for the 1998 World Cup theme song, for example), or collaboration came his way as if by default. Album sales, though, continued to fall far short of justifying their costs. A casual listener asked to name a great African singer would be likely to say "Youssou N'Dour," but probably couldn't name any songs beyond "7 Seconds."

Readers who suspected that the producer whose ideas Youssou found insulting might be me were correct. While history supports my pessimism about his approach, I am now less confident that a pure mbalax recording would have done much better, given the difficulties foreign ears have with that rhythm (though it would likely have recouped its lower costs). A decade after that exchange, I spent an evening with a long-term member of N'Dour's band; he told me that "7 Seconds" was "the greatest catastrophe to ever happen to Senegalese music," confirming Youssou in his vain pursuit of mainstream success. John Collins, the Accra-based scholar of African music, has another take; he credits Youssou as a pioneer for creating different releases for home and abroad, but thinks he got them the wrong way around. African audiences do seem to enjoy high-tech sounds; a Banjul disc jockey once told Lucy Durán that he loved the way N'Dour made a synthesizer sound like a balafon; most of the singer's Western fans would prefer to hear an actual balafon. Another Senegalese artist followed a similar path to Youssou one notch down in the world music pecking order. Baaba Maal is a striking-looking Tukulor with a distinctive tenor voice and magnetic stage presence; he came to the northern hemisphere's attention in the late eighties, when Ian Anderson, editor of *fRoots* magazine, assembled *Djam Leelii* from some tapes Maal's producer brought to London and released it on his small Rogue label. The album is a hypnotic duet between Maal and the blind griot Mansour Seck, mostly just two guitars and voice. It became a cult hit, prompting an invitation to perform in London, where Baaba was quickly snapped up by Chris Blackwell's Mango label.

Blackwell had set out to do for African music what he'd done for reggae, and with the early-eighties signing of King Sunny Ade, Mango had a head start on other big labels. Around that same time, they released a stunningly good series of compilations called *Sound d'Afrique*, featuring dancefloor-friendly rumba and rumba-influenced tracks from across francophone Africa. In the end, though, Mango's African effort focused on singers who had become stars through live performance and who stuck doggedly to the challenge of mixing high-end pop production with singing in African languages while trying to stay connected to their roots.

Maal once said, "Mansour Seck will always be the one who pulls me by the skirt and says come back to the road we are on," but he remains intrigued by the notion of "fusing" African roots music (often via samples of his own field recordings) with various forms of Western music. Though his acoustic albums *Djam Leelii* and *Baayo* have been his biggest successes, most of Baaba's releases are based in rock or electronica. (Mango and its successor, Palm Pictures, seem to have been more forgiving of unrecouped production costs than Youssou's various labels.) My own favorite "cross-cultural" moment of Maal's is his extraordinary rendering of "Bess You Is My Woman Now" on a Gershwin tribute album.

One Senegalese group, meanwhile, had the problem solved all along, without even trying.

> We are like the baobab tree, even when it's chopped down it just can't help growing.
>
> —Rudy Gomis, vocalist with Orchestra Baobab

In a corner by the bar, next to the huge indoor tree that gave Club Baobab its name, was a jukebox filled with records from all over:

Congo, Egypt, America, France, Cuba, Britain, Morocco, Jamaica . . . The resident band would amuse themselves during afternoon rehearsals by picking a track at random, then learning the song and the style. As with most great bands, Orchestra Baobab's take on rumba, funk, *son*, or reggae ended up sounding more like nuanced versions of themselves than the style they were mimicking.

Club Baobab was located up on the Plateau, the Dakar district overlooking the sea, where the elite live, work, and shop. It was opened in 1970 by a group of well-connected businessmen and politicians (including Senghor's nephew) who had watched the success of Club Miami down in the scruffy Medina quarter and decided that the lower orders shouldn't have all the fun. They paid well, luring a trio of Star Band defectors up the hill. One was a Togolese law student named Barthélémy Attisso, who taught himself guitar because music seemed a good way to earn money in the evenings, leaving his days free for classes. Attisso took his heroes—Docteur Nico, Django Reinhardt, Wes Montgomery, and Carlos Santana—one by one, listening repeatedly until he figured out how they got their sound. Balla Sidibé was another recruit, a percussionist-turned-singer who specialized in adapting Mandinka songs to Latin rhythms. The third, Rudy Gomis, grew up in Casamance, the Senegalese province south of Gambia near the border of Guinea-Bissau (where his parents came from), surrounded by music from the old Portuguese triangle. They added a handsome lead singer in the form of Laye M'boup, whose soaring vocals transformed how traditional Wolof songs could be put across with a modern outfit (and who perished in a car crash in 1975, just as Youssou was joining the Star Band). The rest of the group were nearly as polyglot as the jukebox, with members from Gambia, Guinea, Mali, and Morocco around the Senegalese core.

Orchestra Baobab quickly became the country's most popular band, their recordings constantly on the radio throughout the seventies. Their sound was an elegant distillation of the examples set by African Jazz, Les Bantus de la Capitale, and the other great bands from Congolese rumba's early years; Attisso's arrangements blended Cuban beats with local melodies, French *chanson*, harmonies from Casamance, and, very important to my ears, the seductive chords of *morna*, the music of the Cape Verde islands just off the Senegalese coast (which you'll know from your Cesária Évora CDs). The group were all proud to be Senegalese—either native or adopted—and they composed and sang in several of the country's different tongues (as well as French and Spanish), but declared their cosmopolitanism by never, ever using a sabar drum. The contrast between their rhythms and those that drove mbalax is the difference between an older crowd that doesn't want to spoil their outfits by working up a sweat and energetic youths from down the hill showing off their acrobatic moves. When the new style surged at the end of the seventies (as Senegalese men went mad for watching women dance the *ventilateur*), Baobab began to sound old-fashioned; they held on for a few years, then disbanded. Attisso achieved his ambition by opening his own law office back in Lomé.

Many Baobab tracks have the Santiaguero sweetness and gentle propulsion of *Buena Vista Social Club*, which helps explain why it was Nick Gold from World Circuit who brought them out of retirement. He began in 1997 by releasing a compilation of seventies tracks called *Pirate's Choice*, the title referring to the fact that with their records mostly out of print, Baobab's music was being kept alive by bootleggers. When the album sold well and Gold set about getting the group back together, Youssou N'Dour demonstrated the legendary camaraderie of the music scene in seventies Dakar by cajoling stragglers to join the party and helping produce their comeback album, *Specialists in All Styles*. With the group assembled at World Circuit's studio in north London in 2001, Ibrahim Ferrer stopped by to say hello. They quickly worked out an arrangement based on an old Afro-Cuban favorite, and "Hommage à Tonton Ferrer" became an electrifying live studio moment, with first Ferrer, then Youssou joining the youngest (Ndiouga Dieng) and oldest (Rudy Gomis) of Baobab's singers on vocals and Ferrer improvising over a very African *coro* during the montuno.

Having been nominated on four fruitless occasions, Youssou finally won a Grammy in 2005 with an acoustic album he'd recorded for religious reasons, unsure if his new label Nonesuch should release it, particularly in post-9/11 America. *Egypt* is dedicated to Cheikh Bamba and the Mourides and recorded in Cairo and Dakar with ouds, koras, and a string orchestra, its style an *hommage* to his father's favorite singer, Oum Kalsoum. I suspect that many fans and critics, despairing of ever hearing that glorious voice again in a naturalistic setting, would have embraced almost any N'Dour album that broke with the overproduced past, though with its passion and originality, *Egypt* earned the acclaim.

Baobab just picked up where they'd left off two decades earlier, a few waist sizes larger, but with voices, fingers, and spirits intact. Their promiscuous repertoire might have diluted their impact, but musical magic can't be easily categorized; Attisso's sinuous, Nico-worthy solos, the impassioned singing of Gomis, Issa Cissoko's languid saxophone, and the tight yet relaxed rhythm section add up to far more than the sum of the parts. Having sold a quarter of a million copies of *Specialists in All Styles* and toured the world to adoring crowds, they returned to Senegal and Youssou's new studio in 2007 (along with Gold and *Buena Vista* engineer Jerry Boys) and produced an equally triumphant *Made in Dakar*. The two weeks they spent recording there were bracketed by N'Dour's months-long construction of *Rokku mi rokka*, an album that cost many times more and sold far less. One benefit of our new digital era is how Spotify's statistics make the contrast clear: as of this writing, *Made in Dakar*'s tracks have been played roughly eight million times, *Rokku mi rokka*'s about two million. The biggest tally on the Baobab album is for "Nijaay," which features a guest vocal by Youssou that evokes the pre-mbalax days of the Star Band. If a *really* clever producer could have persuaded him to make that the sound of his international releases, N'Dour would have been unstoppable.

Much of this book has been written at a desk facing shelves filled with obsessively organized vinyl (alphabetical by country) mounted on top of a long cabinet containing drawers full of similarly ordered CDs in labeled envelopes (the jewel boxes having been chucked to save space). As you might imagine, I feel an affinity with collectors, particularly when their passions have an impact on the music around them. Senegal was blessed with a pair of them, two visionaries who helped shape the country's music—and, in the second case, the entire continent's.

Ibrahim Kassé ran Club Miami, bought the instruments, produced the records, and, in effect, owned the Star Band; in the early years, he shared his collection of Latin discs with the musicians, schooling them in the Afro-Cuban tradition and suggesting songs to cover or adapt. His evenings were spent operating the club's PA system, cutting off their microphones when someone played or sang a wrong note. It was Kassé who invited that precocious teenager to join the band, then encouraged him and the others to pay attention to what the Super Eagles were doing and to dig deep into their own rhythms. More than one musician has called Kassé "the father of Senegalese music."

The other collector was Ibrahima Sylla; he appeared on the scene at the end of the seventies, hanging out at Club Baobab and doing odd jobs in a recording studio owned by Senghor's son. When Ibrahima's father learned of his son's ambition to become a record producer, he got a hard slap across the face and the two didn't speak for years. That rebuke wasn't like getting push-back from just any father; Karamoko Al Hassan Sylla was a powerful *marabout* of the Tijaniyyah Sufis, a sect comparable to the Mourides within Senegal and a powerful force across West Africa. The role of marabout goes back thousands of years, pre-dating Islam in the Sahel; these diviners and priests of the royal courts adapted to the arrival of the new religion by becoming Koranic scholars, interpreters, and counselors while retaining a reputation for possessing shamanic powers.

Ibrahima's mother was one of thirteen wives (and he one of sixty-two children), but she must have been a favorite since Karamoko often brought her young son along on his trips across Africa to advise politicians, generals, and other big men. Wherever he went, Sylla kept his ears open, absorbing local music, becoming an aficionado of salsa and rumba, and building up a collection. After three years at a Koranic boarding school in Chad, he was sent to Paris to study business administration and law. He quickly discovered the Pasdeloup record store near the Jardin du Luxembourg, spending far more time there than at the law library; he made compilation cassettes for his friends and vowed that music would be his future. Returning to France after the rupture with his father, he opened his own record store near the

Gare du Nord specializing in Caribbean and African music; there he experienced firsthand the dramatic changes wrought by the invasion of cassettes and portable players.

Sylla saw the early eighties as a moment of opportunity; cassettes were far easier for the mass African audience to afford but perilously simple to copy. The majors avoided what they saw as a chaotic market, while independent labels had little cross-border distribution and were suffering from the assaults of the bootleggers. Sylla stepped into the void left by the demise of Fonior with a Paris-based modus operandi that involved dealing directly with artists, keeping master tapes under the tightest security with no news of upcoming releases allowed to leak out; then he would duplicate tens of thousands of tapes overnight, ship them to every corner of West Africa in a lightning strike, and sell out the initial run before pirates even realized there was a new release to pilfer. His sister Binetou managed to keep hidden from their father that she worked closely with Ibrahima, supervising local distribution and new recordings from Dakar to Kinshasa, while he organized things back at headquarters. Artists appreciated their efficiency and success provided Syllart with the means to finance new recordings. Like Manfred Eicher and Mario Pacheco, Sylla dealt with artists one project at a time, challenging them to come up with interesting ideas and never signing anyone to a long-term contract. The company became so successful that Karamoko was forced to forgive his son. Syllart released many of the most important African records of the eighties and nineties, with musicians eager to work with them despite a reputation for having a Fania-like aversion to paying royalties.

Success allows people to act out youthful dreams (think Bezos in orbit); such ventures often bring disappointment, but Sylla's pet project succeeded beyond even his wildest imaginings. When I stopped by Ned Sublette's office on Manhattan's West Side late one summer afternoon in the mid-nineties, he suggested we go for a beer in the Dominican bar across the street. As we walked in, a record was blasting from the jukebox; it sounded fantastic, not compressed like most modern salsa or merengue, but full and open, the rhythm-feel very old-school Afro-Cuban. But what language was that? Not Spanish, that was clear.

Ned told me the track was a favorite in the bar and pointed to the listing on the jukebox display: "Yay Boy" by Africando.

Africando was Ibrahima Sylla's sweetest dream, a heavenly marriage of his favorite salsa records and African rumba discs. Recorded a few years before those other high-concept Latin projects, ¡Cubanismo! and *Buena Vista Social Club*, the first of an eventual six albums brought three of Senegal's greatest singers to New York to work with an ace Latin rhythm section. The arrangements were by Boncana Maïga, a Malian flautist who had studied music in Havana during the country's post-independence "socialist alliance" years; while his horn charts are perfectly within the spirit of Afro-Cuban music, they're full of unusual phrasings and harmonies and bear scant resemblance to modern salsa. Across the series, the vocals vary widely in tone and texture, with lyrics in Wolof, Maninke, Mina, and Lingala as well as a bit of Spanish; the result is music that achieves a producers' pinnacle, both comfortingly familiar and startlingly fresh, appealing to multiple audiences: Latin dancers, world music fans, and Africans at home and abroad. Africando sold like crazy on four continents, creating a powerful touring brand and a template into which was plugged, album after album, a parade of great singers ranging from Rochereau to Guinea's legendary Sekouba Bambino. All knew the music well—they'd grown up on it! After decades navigating away from the Afro-Cuban format to create a distinct identity for their own cultures, African stars could turn nostalgically back to the starting point with musicians who could play the original Cuban grooves in their sleep.

For his next trick, Sylla revisited the pool between Kinshasa and Brazzaville, putting together Kékélé, an acoustic Buena Vista–like group of rumba veterans that had a good run at world music festivals and even gained a following among older generations of Congolese. Ibrahima was a unique figure, more A&R man than producer, since he wasn't always in the studio for the records he backed; he generated music beloved by outsiders and insiders, dancers and critics, FM radio presenters and drinkers propping up shantytown bars. Syllart kept up a steady flow of releases across francophone Africa over a quarter-century, including an important list of albums from the vast nation to the east of Senegal, the land that would come to embody the notion of "African music" to more Europeans and Americans than any other.

☙

On July 18, 1324, a Malian king named Musa arrived in Cairo en route to Mecca. His entourage reportedly numbered sixty thousand courtiers, wives, soldiers, and slaves, many decked out in gold cloth and carrying large fans with golden handles. Musa had brought stacks of ingots plus a staggering number of bags filled with gold dust, which he lavished on virtually any Egyptian of stature he met. Word of this spectacular apparition from out of the Sahara (and of the rampant inflation triggered by his largesse) spread across the Mediterranean, implanting in European minds the image of West Africa as a land with an unlimited supply of gold and slaves.

This was old news to the Arab world, which had been trading across the desert for salt, gold, and slaves for centuries while spreading the Prophet's Word. The first call to prayer was, after all, chanted by Bilal, Mohammed's African slave. Islam's spread was a top-down affair: traders, royalty, and shopkeepers were the first to convert, ordinary people the last. In the forests to the south, Islam lost momentum; trees mean drums and, like the Christian missionaries who followed, Muslim clerics were horrified by them, both for their evocation of sensuality and for the "pagan" ceremonies in which they were used. It was easier for societies whose music was sung and plucked to embrace Islam. The feeling wasn't always reciprocated; the history of the Sahel is marked by repeated attempts by fundamentalists to force African societies into a no-fun, no-music, women-under-strict-male-control version of Islam. This battle has ebbed and flowed for centuries and continues today.

It took the Portuguese a while to figure out how to profit from the Cairo reports, but by the middle of the fifteenth century Lisbon-based traders were swapping trinkets, cloth, and weapons for gold along the West African coast. This bonanza triggered a nouveau riche shopping spree that jolted Europe's moribund medieval economy into life. Jealous Spaniards eventually found their own treasure in Mexico and Peru, sending the Occidental economy through the roof. When the golden flow began to ebb, sugar—planted, harvested, and processed by enslaved Africans—inspired and financed a colonial expansion stretching from the Andes around the globe to Polynesia. With the Dutch, British, and French joining the gold-trading, slave-buying frenzy, African coastal kingdoms were in a constant state of turmoil as European rivals formed alliances, sold guns, and purchased captives.

The inland Sahel remained a bit calmer, retaining many of its ancient ways, including music. Coast-boy guitars rarely reached the royal cities of Segou, Djenne, Timbuktu, and Gao, while wars, raids, and trade meant that many captives from the Mandé and other Sahel cultures ended up in North America. Which may explain why Malian music resonates for so many anglophone listeners; elements of American "swing" can be found in its rhythms, while narrative song backed by stringed instruments is a hallmark of both Mandé and American music. To say nothing of all those "blue" notes . . .

The glory days of the Ghana, Mali, Songhai, and Bamana empires were long over when a French force led by one Colonel Desbordes invaded the interior in 1881. Desbordes was exactly the sort of maniac Bismarck had in mind when he prodded King Leopold to get the African Scramble rolling. The glory-hungry colonel saw himself as a modern Caesar bringing civilization to dark-skinned Gauls and was contemptuous of his superiors' caution. He repeatedly presented the government in Paris with facts on the ground and with the need to rescue allies or punish enemies as he pushed eastward along the Senegal River, breaking treaties like the US Cavalry and building a fort on the Niger River where the city of Bamako now stands. Under pressure from a nationalist and racist yellow press, the Quai d'Orsay succumbed to Desbordes's ambitions, announcing plans for a Dakar-to-Djibouti corridor linking the Atlantic Ocean with the Red Sea.

In the summer of 1896, as Bismarck lay on his deathbed, the British delusion of a north-south, Cairo–Cape Town chain of railroads and riverboats collided with French east-west fantasies at Fashoda, a swampy outpost in what is now South Sudan; rather than open fire, the opposing battalions began popping champagne corks and beer-bottle caps and arguing about which was the better evening tipple in the tropics.

Realizing the absurdity of the situation, the two governments agreed a treaty clarifying respective areas of control (including France's suzerainty over what is now Mali), which eventually led to an alliance against Germany. In *The Scramble for Africa,* Thomas Pakenham makes the case that Bismarck's African plotting, far from making Germany safer, set it on the disastrous collision course that became the Great War (to say nothing of condemning most of Africa to seventy-five years of colonial misrule).

~

The name Mali comes from Malingke, another word for Mandé, a grouping that includes the Mandinka-speakers of Gambia and Senegal as well as the related Bamana-speakers of Mali, Guinea, and the Ivory Coast. Throughout the colonial decades, as its borders and name were repeatedly altered by bureaucratic whim, Mali never forgot its imperial lineage. In the fifties, the Kaira movement sent *jalis* from village to village teaching people about their history and their culture and performing ancient epics.

Jali—also spelled *jeli* or *djeli*—is the term Malians prefer to *griot,* a word derived from *criado,* a Portuguese import meaning "court jester" or "bard." Andy Morgan has described the jali's functions as resembling a "Swiss Army knife": "musician, oral archivist, genealogist, diplomat, emissary, match-maker, instrument-maker, blacksmith, poet, advisor, spokesperson, flatterer, and repository of traditional knowledge." Disputes were often turned over to jalis for resolution, much as litigating corporations or divorcing couples hire lawyers. Historians take note of their epic verses but with a certain skepticism; relying on patronage as they do, flattery and spin are implicit in the jali versions of history.

When independence arrived in 1960, proud though they were of the country's heritage, Modibo Keïta's socialist government pushed Kaira to the side; they were wary of jalis, who represented a caste system out of step with the new egalitarian vision. Malians might have come to accept the marginalization of the jalis and the hereditary district chiefs who were often their patrons, but they chafed at the nationalization of commerce. For thousands of years, the area had been a hub of trans-

Saharan trade; its people are as deft with goods and money as those from that other timeless trading nexus, the Levant, and didn't take kindly to Cuban-trained bureaucrats placing themselves in charge of every sort of business. In 1968, with the economy in free fall, patience expired; the army moved in and replaced Keïta with Moussa Traoré.

Many musicians, even jalis, look back to the Modibo Keïta era with fondness. Following the lead of neighboring Guinea's *dirigiste* regime, Keïta's government sponsored regional and national music competitions and gave financial support to the winning bands. The template was similar to most newly independent francophone states: rumba blended with local tradition (including the jali canon of historical epics), though with an added Latin twist since many Malian musicians received musical training in Cuba. In the wake of the coup, with subsidies abolished and ideological controls lifted, musicians once again looked to patrons, weddings, and ceremonies for income. The Traoré era would see a flowering of remarkably diverse music in this poor, landlocked, and divided country, an output whose richness can be safely said to put every other African nation in the shade.

There's a black-and-white photo you have probably seen in an exhibition, a coffee-table book, or on the agnès b. T-shirt: a young couple, bodies apart but heads nearly touching, he in a slim-cut suit, she barefoot in a full-skirted dress, both smiling but focused, gazing down at their dancing feet on a stone floor. The man who took the photo, Malick Sidibé, described that period in Mali at the end of the sixties: "We were entering a new era, and people wanted to dance. Music freed us. Suddenly, young men could get close to young women, hold them in their hands. Before, it was not allowed. And everyone wanted to be photographed dancing." Cosima Spender's 2005 documentary, *Dolce vita africana*, follows Sidibé as he travels to Venice to receive the Golden Lion Lifetime Achievement award from the Biennale and views him at work in his Bamako studio; she also filmed the friends who were subjects of his iconic photos as they reminisce about those good times and the beach parties beside the Niger River. The innocence of those days was overtaken in the seventies by a growing worldliness as the country opened up. Manthia Diawara, then a university student in Bamako, describes how he and some friends organized a "Woodstock Festival":

> [We] knew the names of all the musicians . . . [T]he speakers were blaring "With a Little Help from My Friends" by Joe Cocker . . . [People] were dressed like Jimi Hendrix, George Harrison, Richie Havens, Buddy Miles, Sly Stone, Frank Zappa, Alice Cooper, and James Brown. But there were some who had donned traditional hunter suits; tight-fitting trousers and mud-cloth blouses oversewn with cowrie shells and mirrors . . . "Voodoo Child" filled the air, and by then we were on top of the world.

In Bamako during those years, you might walk a few meters from a bar playing a James Brown, Sly Stone, or Johnny Pacheco record and find yourself at a wedding or a circumcision where music was being performed that had barely changed in centuries. Mali's leading seventies band split the difference between the two.

At the edge of downtown Bamako sits a typical French provincial railway station. Once upon a time, it represented colonial ambition; having laid track (or rather, used forced labor to lay track) from Dakar to Bamako, the French sent an expedition north along the Niger to map out an extension across the Sahara to Algiers. When the surveying party got massacred by Tuareg rebels, the plan was abandoned. A century later, after the IMF ordered Mali and Senegal to privatize the railway, it fell into disrepair and, in 2012, ceased operations; the station became a symbol of decline.

To most Malians, however, *La Gare* means music. The Ministry of Information and Malian Railways joined forces in 1970 to create a band that would define the mood of the decade and send the first in a long parade of Malian artists out into the world: Rail Band du Buffet Hôtel de la Gare. Music played at the station bar defined the country's modernity; politicians came by to be praised, businessmen threw cash, and the Buffet Hôtel was packed every night.

The Rail Band's story contains elements of déjà vu: charismatic, big-lunged vocalist defies father to pursue a music career, achieves fame at home but looks abroad for bigger audiences, more expensive sounds, and Whiter beats. It's doubly repetitive since the outline fits not just one, but two of the Rail Band's singers. There's also a guitar hero to join Nico, Franco, and Attisso in our African pantheon.

Mory Kanté's decision to stray from his jali family's balafon tradition and take up the kora registers but faintly on the scale of filial defiance. Salif Keïta's path, on the other hand, was brave and arduous. Albinos in African societies have a history of ostracism at one extreme and fetishistic fascination at another; Keïta's family (aristocrats with a lineage going back to Sundiata, the thirteenth-century founder of the Mali empire) used their young son as a kind of scarecrow to frighten monkeys away from the garden. Salif's love for music further horrified his father; royal families *hire* musicians, they never perform themselves. After being barred from teacher's college because of poor eyesight (a common side effect of albinism), Keïta followed his music dream to Bamako, cutting himself off from his family. With his powerful voice and love for the jali repertoire, he was a perfect fit with the Rail Band and quickly became a star.

Strong-willed and ambitious, Salif bridled at the group's position as, effectively, civil servants working for the railroad, and after a few years, he left to join Les Ambassadeurs, a rival band based at a Bamako motel. With drought and a plummeting economy making life in mid-seventies Mali more and more difficult (and after the group's political protector was arrested for excessive corruption), Les Ambassadeurs moved to Abidjan, West Africa's new music hub in the then-prosperous Ivory Coast. A chance encounter with an A&R man from a US disco label led to a trip to Los Angeles to polish and mix an album, during which Keïta acquired a taste for high-tech production. With the pan–West African hit "Mandjou" under their belts, the group headed for Paris in 1984 to play a concert for African taxi drivers, one of the few occasions when Salif was a step behind Youssou N'Dour (who, you may recall, had played a similar event the year before). Unlike his Senegalese peer and rival, he stayed on in France to launch an international career.

The ubiquitous Martin Meissonnier persuaded CBS Records to fund a demo for a solo album; when the label was unimpressed with the result, Keïta turned to that other heavyweight producer, Ibrahima Sylla.

During my visit to his home outside Paris in 2012, I asked Sylla about that moment; he smiled and shook his head, remembering how Salif spent money like water, hiring the French keyboard and computer whiz Jean-Philippe Rykiel (son of fashion queen Sonia) and sailing rapidly through the allotted budget; the album ended up costing more than anything he'd ever produced, but Ibrahima kept his nerve, convinced it was worth the risk. He was right; *Soro* proved a massive hit, making Keïta a star and N'Dour envious. In his novel *The Music in My Head*, Mark Hudson eloquently sums up the album's impact (and has confirmed to me the identity of the thinly disguised characters):

> A Mandé-style girlie chorus with just the right amount of authentic sing-song nasality, traces of the old . . . Mandinka guitar, synthesised kora, digitally funky Afro-Paris rhythms a . . . few "African" sound effects—the buzz of insects, howling hyenas—the sort of thing no African musician in Africa would have thought of putting into their music—and BIG synthesisers, huge and magisterial chords, evoking the sheer scale and majesty of Africa as seen on wildlife documentaries, out of which [Keïta's] voice, "the raw cry of Africa, full of pain and mystical anguish," came at you in widescreen dimensions. As cinema-style hokum it worked remarkably well, and it did contain moments of genuine beauty. [N'Dour] in particular became obsessed with it . . . But repeating, let alone surpassing or finding a commercially viable variant on the magic formula of [*Soro*] proved surprisingly difficult. [N'Dour] never managed it and [Keïta] certainly didn't.

With *Soro*'s success—it enjoyed massive sales across Africa, France, and Britain (and even did well in North America)—the high-tech compass was set for Salif and Youssou as well as for Chris Blackwell's Mango, which released it in the US and a few other territories. Neither singer, nor any of Mango's other African artists, would ever again see that sort of impact. Like Baaba Maal, Salif has a sincere ambition to merge African and Western music and modest sales haven't deterred him; once at a concert in London, I saw him lean his head on the French guitarist's shoulder during a rockish solo, mimicking the famous Mick and Keith pose.

> Unlike . . . Fela Kuti, [Mory] Kanté doesn't give interviews backstage in his knickers, but instead dons a dapper white silk suit and a silk scarf with a Pierre Cardin monogram.
>
> —*Melody Maker*, 1988

With Keïta departed, Mory Kanté took over as the Rail Band's lead singer. After a few great years with them, he followed in his predecessor's footsteps to Abidjan and Paris. Like Salif, he was never able to match his early solo triumph, but the hit was big enough to fuel a career that kept him performing until his death in 2020. Kanté's 1987 million-seller "Yé ké yé ké" is a tremendous track, the right record at the right time, when Europe—France, in particular—was discovering African music and disco DJs were lighting the way up the charts. The song originated in a flirtatious girls' chant from Kanté's home region near the Guinea-Mali border and the record is full of sexual exuberance, with Mory and the female backing singers' Bamana vocals just exotic enough, the beats a perfect balance between eighties Euro-disco and a Mandé rhythm, the production bursting with dancefloor drama. Coming on the heels of *Soro*, the crossover success of "Yé ké yé ké" opened the sluice gates for major labels to invest in African music, for good and for ill.

The Rail Band, meanwhile, continued to hold forth at La Gare, with guitarist Djelimady Tounkara now the central figure; Banning Eyre has described how Tounkara "worked the crowd like Buddy Guy while playing ancient praise melodies." Those jali epics may have been central to the band's repertoire in the early years, but Tounkara's solos never had much to do with the blues; he taught himself by following Cuban horn parts over the radio from Brazzaville and trying to figure out Congolese guitarists' tunings, not realizing they were using capos. Tounkara's inventive response led to what is known as "griot tuning": raising the low E string to F and the B to C.

The Rail Band's role in Mali is comparable to Orchestra Baobab's in Senegal. Both began losing their audience as the seventies turned into the eighties, but unlike Baobab, the Rail Band never stopped. When audiences grew thin at La Gare, they moved to a club called Djembe, where a young crowd eventually discovered them. Another difference was the nature of their competition; while Baobab was pushed aside by full-on, high-volume mbalax, the Rail Band was eclipsed by a generation of young women, many of them backed by little more than a six-string harp.

❧

> *Sundays in Bamako are wedding days*
> *These are wedding days*
> *Djembés and doundouns resound everywhere*
> *Baras and n'tamas resound everywhere*
> *The kora and the ngoni are present too*
> *Sundays in Bamako are wedding days . . .*
> *Men and women are wearing their beautiful boubous*
> *Jewels and shoes are present*
> *Bazins and bogolans are present*
> *The bride and the groom are present too*
> *Sundays in Bamako are wedding days*
> *Sotramas, dourounis, taxis, cars*
> *Brothers, sisters, passersby, griots*
> *Sundays in Bamako are wedding days*
>
> —"Beaux dimanches" by Amadou & Mariam, from their 2005 album *Dimanche à Bamako*

Modibo Keïta wanted Malians to forget the French and become self-sufficient in every way, but one colonial holdover he couldn't shift was how couples in this Islamic country always got married on a Sunday. Historically, wedding music had been mostly in the jali tradition, but by the seventies, wedding parties, particularly the brides, were ready for change. A leader of the new wave was Fanta Sacko, who sang beautiful melodies in a high-pitched voice, with lyrics about love rather than history; others followed, with songs admonishing husbands to treat wives, particularly second and third wives, with respect.

An iconic image in the annals of African-American gospel music is of Rev. C. L. Franklin lifting his small daughter Aretha onto a chair, then watching with pride as her powerful and expressive voice astonished churchgoers. Bamako saw a parallel moment in which the tiny Oumou Sangaré climbed onto a chair by herself, filling in for her ill and depressed mother when she was little more than five; by the time she was ten, Oumou had become an in-demand wedding singer in her own right. Many cultures have a particular region that captures the imagination and becomes identified as the wellspring of a nation's musical soul; in America, it's the Lower Mississippi River, encompassing Memphis, New Orleans, and the Delta, Italy has Puglia and the tarantella, then there's the lost Hungarian province of Transylvania, Andalusian flamenco, Salvador for Brazil . . . the list is long. Oumou Sangaré grew up in Bamako but her family is from Wassoulou, a fertile region of green hills in southwestern Mali near the Guinea border, where the key instrument is a six-string "hunter's harp," the *donso ngoni*. Despite the name, it is unrelated to that ancient jali lute the *ngoni*; with its calabash base and six elevated strings, it looks more like a child's kora. Its origin couldn't be more different from either of those courtly instruments, being emblematic of the clans of hunters who once brought hides, meat, claws, and fur to sell in the cities. As the desert's southward creep destroyed much of the cover for them and the animals they hunted, Wassoulou became a stronghold where they could continue their ancient traditions. Like American cowboys, the *donso* have maintained an aura of romance into the modern age, their music cloaked in the mystery of secret ceremonies. In the sixties, a version of the donso harp called the *kamelengoni* or "youth harp" became popular as an accompaniment for non-jali singers in Wassoulou; its twang is earthier than the jali instruments, evoking *gnawa* music from southern Morocco and the American diddly-bow.

In a world where hormonal rebellion is linked to loud amps and pounding drum kits it may be hard to imagine a youthquake driven by this hand-held acoustic instrument. But village elders in Wassoulou were as horrified by the kamelengoni's throb summoning teenagers to dance in the moonlight as older Americans were by Little Richard. Sangaré wasn't the first wedding singer from Wassoulou to compose songs based around this instrument's pentatonic scale and propelled by its distinctive drive, but when she released *Moussolou* (Women) in 1991, the broad reach of cassettes pushed this musical revolution to a new level and made her a star. One track in particular, "Diaraby nene" (Shivers of Love), caused controversy:

Wait for me, my love, and don't think too much . . .
When I talk of shivers, I'm not talking of the cold season, or the rains
I'm talking of the shivers of love, my sweet one
My fathers, you can "tut" at me
My mothers, I am to blame
Life is pleasurable, I swear to God . . .
No need to talk, my love opened the door, no need for words
I put my leg on his leg, his leg is cold
I put my hand against his arm, my skin is gooseflesh on my love's arm
I put my hand on his chest, his chest is cold, my love's chest
My chest is shivering
I put my hand low on his stomach, on my love's stomach
Mmm, the shivers of love!
There are many pleasures, but not all are the same!
Ah, baby, I'll see you in the morning

The fact that Sangaré was twenty-one and unmarried when *Moussolou* was released compounded the shock. She led a parade of young women who seized the initiative, their cassettes piled high in markets from Senegal and Gambia to Burkina Faso and Niger and south into Guinea and Côte d'Ivoire. Producers often added drum machines, electric guitars, and cheesy reverb to the basic platform of a kamelengoni or other traditional acoustic instrumentation. It represented a triumph for the female point of view and for youth, but it also threatened to marginalize jali traditions, just as during the same period in many African cultures musical history was being pushed aside. An outside intervention, however, helped to shift the Malian dynamic and open the door to new careers for jali musicians.

⌒

Lucy Durán had come to Anthony King's office at SOAS (London's School of Oriental and African Studies) to deliver proofs of texts on African music that King was editing for a new edition of the *Grove Dictionary of Music*, her employer. Opening King's door, she was engulfed by some of the most beautiful music she had ever heard: "The music of the spheres," she recalls saying to herself. When Lucy asked what it was, King responded, "Just leave the proofs on the desk, please, I'm busy now." At twenty-five years old in 1973, Durán had probably heard more different kinds of music than anyone else her age. Her father, Gustavo Durán, was a Spanish pianist and composer and, during the Civil War, the youngest general in the Republican army; wounded, he was evacuated to Dartington Hall School in Devon, where he met Lucy's mother. The family, including two older sisters, moved during the forties and fifties from Britain to Cuba to Chile to New York to Athens, with every sort of music constantly on the gramophone or sung around the family piano. King's College in London tailored a music degree specially for Lucy and she was tutored for her master's by the Cambridge ethnomusicologist Laurence Picken. She wrote her dissertation on the *rizitika* songs of Cretan resistance against the Turks and had sat by the Ghadames oasis in southern Libya listening to the music of Tuareg women. But she had never heard anything like what was playing that day on King's stereo.

Durán didn't achieve all she has in the male-dominated worlds of music and academia by accepting brush-offs and refused to surrender the proofs until King identified the music. By the time she left, she knew that the instrument was called a kora, had been shown one propped up in the corner of the office, and had an appointment with King the following week for her first lesson in how to play it. Five decades on, the kora has become ubiquitous, the most widely known of traditional African instruments, the sound of its plucked strings downloaded, broadcast, and streamed in restaurants, health-food shops, and boutiques from Santa Monica to Helsinki, solo and duet, as part of a traditional ensemble or (more and more often these days) blended with strings, jazz instruments, or classical harp. All of this can be traced back to the determined quest of Lucy Durán.

[T]here's life in the kora. There's the skin of an animal. There's a tree. There are strings. There's a calabash. The animal world, the spirit world are all represented there. It's as if it was a living thing.

—Seckou Keïta, kora player

The kora is a complex harp-like instrument. A large calabash is cut in half and covered in cowhide, with two parallel rows of strings (one of ten, the other eleven) secured by leather rings to a round, vertical hardwood neck, stretched over a raised bridge and anchored to a wooden base that resonates in the acoustic chamber of the calabash; handles on either side of the strings allow a player to hold it firmly while playing intricate patterns using thumbs and forefingers. Traditional tunings follow a pentatonic scale; a metal resonator attached to the bridge had the virtues of adding a buzz to the notes while also amplifying them.

Harps have been found in pharaonic tombs and are common to many African cultures fanning out south and west from Egypt, but none are as sophisticated as the kora. Despite hyperbolic claims about multiple generations of griots playing the instrument back into the mists of time, studies place its origin in the late eighteenth century amid the Mandinka culture south of the Gambia River. Legends portray it as a gift from the spirits, with the skills to play it bestowed in a Robert Johnson–at-the-crossroads-type encounter with the supernatural. The kora was employed at royal courts and, until recently, played only by male jalis.

Durán abandoned her study of the sitar to focus on the new instrument; when she had advanced as far as she could under King's tutelage, he proposed that she travel to Gambia and take lessons from a master there. They approached Amadou Bansang Jobarteh (the anglophone rendering of Diabaté), a jali from a Malian family that had moved to Gambia in the early years of the twentieth century seeking patrons. Jobarteh was willing and, with a few Mandinka lessons under her belt, Lucy spent eight months living close by his compound, sharing meals with him and his family, taking lessons and going along when he played for patrons or took part in ceremonial events.

The kora was rarely heard on its own in public, being used mostly to accompany singers or the jali's own spoken or sung narrative. A turning point came in 1968, when Moussa Traoré, Mali's new leader, lent his support to a project documenting the country's many musical forms and styles. The German Bärenreiter label released a series of those recordings, including *Cordes anciennes*, an album of kora duets and trios centred around Amadou's cousin, Sidiki Diabaté, who had moved back to Bamako in the late forties and become a leading figure in the Kaira movement. Diabaté was a brilliant player who brought a more aggressive style to the Malian kora tradition; it was his idea to record without vocals and, importantly, to remove the metal resonator, allowing the notes to ring out cleanly. For Durán and other admirers of the instrument, *Cordes anciennes* became a touchstone, the kora recording by which all others would be judged.

For the next decade, while working at the newly established British Sound Archive, Lucy continued to visit Gambia, play the kora, and bring Jobarteh and other Gambian virtuosos to England for small concert tours. She augmented the musicians' fees by organizing private gatherings where listeners were encouraged to shed their British reserve and stuff five-pound notes into the kora's sound hole. In 1986, things began to speed up; Durán's friend James Fox (author of *White Mischief* and *Life: Keith Richards* and host of a few kora "house concerts") secured a commission for an article on Mandé traditional music from, of all places, *House and Garden* magazine.

Off he and Lucy went to Gambia, where, after long evenings spent with different kora masters, Amadou proposed that they pay a visit to Sidiki, whom he considered the greatest of them all. After a harrowing bush-taxi and sardine-packed, standing-room-only, slow-train journey to Bamako, the two cousins met for the first time. The visitors were soon being dazzled by Sidiki's playing and immersed in the rich musical life of the Malian capital. Back in London, Willie Robson, head of music for BBC Radio 3, commissioned Lucy to produce a series of programs on African classical music. Robson then mounted a festival at the South Bank on the theme "Music of the Royal Courts" and asked Durán to put together an evening on the medieval Mali Empire. On an organising trip to Bamako, she heard Sidiki's kora-playing son, who had been away on tour during her previous visit.

Enter stage left our leading character, Toumani Diabaté. Jalis don't give their offspring formal lessons; children pay attention and play along, and Toumani paid very close attention. At the center of Mandé society there is a cruel irony: their foundation epic tells of Sundiata, the shrunken, crippled, and rejected prince who gains Shaka-like revenge, defeating his enemies and building the medieval Mali Empire. Reverence for Sundiata does not, however, translate into acceptance of those similarly afflicted. As a boy, Toumani suffered an attack of polio that left him with a withered right leg and a crutch-assisted limp; it's difficult to assess how much he suffered from his family's low expectations, but the long hours spent on his own while other kids were playing football were certainly put to good use, endlessly practicing the kora and listening to Jimi Hendrix, Miles Davis, anglophone rock, and Spanish flamenco on his Walkman. Toumani's style is very much in keeping with his father's, but the wide listening nourished an adventurous melodic approach and a worldly subtext to his playing.

Durán brought a strong ensemble to London, including Diabaté father and son, as well as the vocalists Jalimady Sissoko and Kandia Kouyaté. The concert was a triumph, climaxing in Sissoko's performance of the Sundiata epic backed by Sidiki. When the others returned to Bamako, Toumani stayed on; at a WOMAD night in a Bristol club, John Hollis from Gabriel's Real World label heard him and suggested he submit a demo. When Toumani asked Lucy her opinion of his double-tracked-kora-plus-vocal effort, she told him he was the only one who could pull off a pure solo recording with no overdubbing and none of his (somewhat labored) singing. I was summoned to hear him play; what's Bamana for "no-brainer"? We agreed a deal and booked an afternoon in a Camden Town studio.

From this vantage point, a solo kora album may seem like a fairly straightforward idea, but no one had ever attempted anything like *Kaira* before. From hours of tape, Lucy edited a concise, beautiful record that entranced listeners, most of whom had never heard of th;e instrument. She has described to me how the process forced her to abandon much of her ethnographic training; this was not a documentation, in which an outside expert presses "record," stands back, and publishes the results with as little creative interference as possible. Editing *Kaira* quickly became "producing," treating the music with the respect with which a classical producer would approach editing an album of Chopin nocturnes. Durán may have been the only one who could have found edit points in the music's complex patterns. Toumani was thrilled with the result, we put together a jacket design with a photo of a Malian cloth from the Museum of Mankind, Lucy wrote some liner notes, and Hannibal Records became the proud home of a classic.

Outdoor soirées are common in London when the weather is balmy, so a gathering in the genteel surroundings of a communal garden concealed behind some very expensive real estate near the Thames in Chelsea was nothing out of the ordinary. But James Fox was hosting this one, so the musical entertainment was appropriately high-grade: Toumani plus a then-little-known Malian singer named Ali Farka Touré. Ketama, the nuevo flamenco group whose first album Hannibal had just released, were in town doing promotion, and, wanting to keep the four guys entertained, I brought them and Mario Pacheco along to James's party. There was plenty of food, wine, and posh girls in summer frocks, so the Spaniards were happy; then, emanating from an outbuilding in the garden, they heard the sound of the kora. Gathering round, they stared at Toumani's fingers, then began doing *palmas* in time with the music. When the piece finished, Lucy could barely keep up with the questions flying back and forth, translating between Bamana and Spanish. The upshot was an invitation for us all to come to her place the next day for a *jolof paella* lunch.

Having found most cross-cultural jam sessions embarrassing, when the instruments were unpacked after lunch I retreated to another room. As it transpired, the only embarrassment was my aloof absence. Lured back by shouts and whistles, I arrived as Toumani was in the middle of a brilliant solo over Ketama's *rumba flamenca*; those many hours spent listening to Spanish cassettes hadn't been in vain. I had arranged a gig for Ketama that night at London's only flamenco bar, and they insisted Toumani come along and bring his kora. After a rousing set, with the packed club clapping and stomping for an encore, Toumani brought his mysterious instrument onstage as Juan Carmona introduced "*nuestro nuevo amigo.*" The lunchtime scene was repeated, with the audience roaring in amazement. Backstage afterwards, everyone surrounded Mario and me, demanding to know when we were going to make the record.

After a quick huddle, we announced, in chorus, "In three months, in Madrid!"

Songhai, so named (following an over-hasty reading of West African history) in honor of Sahel warriors who helped Muslim crusaders capture half of Spain, wasn't an easy record to make but the sessions were never dull. One problem resembled what I encountered eight years later with Egrem's piano during the ¡Cubanismo! sessions in Havana: just when we had an arrangement worked out and the musicians primed for a take, we'd have to stop for half an hour so Toumani could retune. Most koras now have brass tuning pegs, but this was one of the first times it had ever been part of an ensemble of Western instruments (Ketama's guitars plus Danny Thompson's upright bass), and tuning involved nudging each of the twenty-one leather rings up or down the neck with a small hammer.

Together with *Kaira*, *Songhai* put Toumani and the kora on the world music map, with strong sales, awards, and a BBC TV *Arena* special. We even managed to assemble everyone for a few concerts, but the difficulty of luring flamenco artists out of Spain for the comparatively modest fees on offer was compounded by what happened with one of the *Songhai* tracks. "Vente pa Madrid," a rumba with a catchy chorus and a great kora solo, was clearly a standout on the album, and when Nuevos Medios released it as a single, it ended up in the Spanish Top Ten and all over the radio; even the picky Gitano audience loved "Vente pa Madrid." Ketama were now very expensive Spanish superstars.

I know, I know; I'm supposed to be the arch fusion-o-phobe. But what I dislike is not fusion per se, but artists from great musical cultures performing over generic mid-Atlantic beats. *Songhai* moves between Toumani joining Ketama's flamenco and the group adapting to his Mandé feel, with nothing resembling a pop-rock, jazz-rock, disco, or funk pulse in sight.

Toumani proceeded to tour the world, though his concert career was hindered by occasional no-shows when his marabout advised against traveling on the appointed day. His unpredictability contributed to the fact that from 1988 to 1998 all Hannibal managed to release by him were the excellent (but not so successful) *Songhai 2* and the not so excellent

Djelika. The last year of the century, however, saw the arrival of a pair of albums generally viewed as Toumani's—and the kora's—best.

Most readers will have an array of reasons for regretting that America hasn't had more Democratic presidents in recent decades; my long list includes how keen they seem to be on the Hannibal catalogue. Following on from Bill Clinton's infatuation with Virginia Rodrigues, Barack Obama once named *Kulanjan* as his all-time favorite record. Good choice!

Ever since Toumani and Taj Mahal met and bonded in the late eighties, Lucy and I had wanted to get them into a studio to explore the commonalities between Malian music and the blues. When we finally nailed down a ten-day gap in everyone's schedule so Taj could fly to Bamako and record with Toumani and a traditional ensemble, his agent produced a contract for a concert in Cleveland, Ohio, smack in the middle of that period. I was determined not to let this chance slip away; the Malian mountain would have to come to Taj's Mohammed, somewhere in North America near an airport with flights to Cleveland. When I ran into R.E.M. (for whom I'd produced *Fables of the Reconstruction* fourteen years earlier) at an awards ceremony, they suggested a studio in their hometown of Athens. I still savor the memory of late-afternoon college-town commuters almost falling off their bikes at the sight of a Georgia porch filled with Malians posing for a publicity photo in brightly colored *boubous* and holding koras, a kamelengoni, an ngoni, and a balafon alongside Taj in a lurid Hawaiian shirt.

The album makes a good case for the right sort (well, my sort) of fusion, but also demonstrates the virtues of isolating a group of great musicians with a one-week deadline and a commitment to recording everything live. Ramata Diakité singing a lovely traditional song in counterpoint with Taj performing his signature "Queen Bee" was taped the minute they'd figured out how to fit the two melodies together; Toumani's kora and Taj's guitar blend behind the vocals with equally spontaneous eloquence. You'd never get that feel with an overdub.

Kulanjan saw the emergence of ngoni maestro Bassekou Kouyaté;

the ngoni is a three-stringed, dowel-necked lute that, unlike the kora, *does* have a history extending back into the mists of time. Ibn Batuta heard one during his visit to Timbuktu in 1352 and it's considered the grandfather of the banjo. Taj enjoys recounting his first meeting with Bassekou at a banjo conference in Tennessee in the early nineties, where a roomful of bluegrass players watched his demonstration of African finger-picking techniques in hushed silence.

Taj, Lucy, and the great jali vocalist Kassé Mady Diabaté plumbed their deep combined knowledge of Malian and American music to find songs in which each side could make a telling contribution. At one point, we got Taj to sing the oldest African-American folk song he knew a cappella, letting the Malians create their own guitar-free arrangement. The result is "Ol' Georgie Buck," driven by Dougouyé Coulibaly's kamelengoni, one of my favorite tracks on the record.

Kulanjan features two koras. Lucy and classical engineer Nick Parker had flown to Bamako the year before to record a tribute by Toumani and his cousin Ballaké Sissoko to their fathers' pioneering *Cordes anciennes* from thirty years earlier. When Parker wasn't happy with the studio they'd booked, Lucy wangled permission to use the new Chinese-built Palais de Congrès; they went in at midnight after the city had quieted down and set up their microphones in the marble entrance hall. The result, *New Ancient Strings*, is the most sublime album of pure kora music, showing not just Toumani's brilliance but also Ballaké's; *Kulanjan*, Lucy decided, would have them both.

New Ancient Strings and *Kulanjan* had the sort of impact at the end of the nineties that *Kaira* and *Songhai* had enjoyed a decade earlier. But it wasn't enough to save Hannibal; we'd been rescued from our purgatory of critical applause and modest sales in 1991 by Rykodisc (a far more successful indie), but by the late nineties, changes in the music business were buffeting them, as well. Ryko and Hannibal became briefly part of Chris Blackwell's new Palm Pictures before being subsumed in an investment-bank takeover; it was time for me to get out of the studio and start writing *White Bicycles*.

Toumani continued to flourish; part of our deal was to ship him stocks of cassettes, which he sold in Bamako. Malians were impressed; a track from *Kaira* was picked up by state television for the theme music introducing evening programming. That, combined with his continued international success, made him a powerful figure in the country's music hierarchy, while the shifting winds of world music fashion meant that in the new century it was Toumani, even more than Youssou, who got the guest spots and big-name collaborations. He opened his own music club in Bamako, the Hogon, where jali singers and instrumentalists joined with electric guitars and keyboards to form what Toumani called his Symmetric Orchestra. *Kono* ("birds," as the women singers were known) continued to dominate the wedding parties, but government funds were directed more to Toumani and his fellow jalis. Tradition was suddenly the up-to-date thing.

Bassekou, Ballaké, Kassé Mady, and *Kulanjan*'s balafonist, Lassana Diabaté, also flourished, often aided by Lucy's productions. For a project with the Kronos Quartet, she formed the Trio Da Kali with Lassana, Kassé Mady's daughter, Hawa, and Bassekou's son Mamadou, and added a twist to the transatlantic feedback loop by creating a Bamana version of Mahalia Jackson's "God Shall Wipe Away All Tears"; Hawa's powerful singing turned it into a showstopper.

Even the humble hunter's harp had its moment in the sun; in 2002, Bamako witnessed a spectacular donso gathering, with fearsome-looking hunters eating fire, piercing their cheeks with knives, leading around leashed hyenas, and horrifying the mullahs, who saw the whole thing as a reversion to paganism. Cassettes of the hunters' once-secretive music were piled high in the markets.

Everywhere you turned, it seemed, there were Malian musicians, vocalists, or ensembles performing with Norwegian fiddlers, French cellists, rock bands, jazz groups, and early-music ensembles. Oumou Sangaré became an important festival and concert attraction, while Amadou & Mariam, a Bamako couple who had met at a school for the blind, made a record with Manu Chao that turned them into pop stars in France.

The most influential collaboration, though, was the one that never happened. In the late eighties, a Malian named Babani Sissoko or "Baba

Sora" reappeared in the land of his birth, seemingly determined to emulate the fourteenth-century generosity of King Musa, only with the gold flowing in the other direction this time, from Arab lands to Mali. Baba Sora's exploits as a benefactor included chartering planes for Kandia Kouyaté to fly her from her home village to concerts across Africa, and bestowing houses and automobiles on leading members of the jali musical community. Based for a time in Miami, Sora taught the Americans a thing or two about musical patronage by giving a local high school marching band $300,000 so they could take part in New York's Thanksgiving Day Parade. A group including Djelimady Tounkara and Bassekou Kouyaté were booked to join Ry Cooder and Nick Gold in Havana for a fusion experiment with Cubans, but when word got out that Baba was on his way to Bamako with a Santa's sack full of Mercedes-Benzes, the Malians suddenly lost the will to sort out their visas. Thus was the Havana studio vacuum created into which was sucked *Buena Vista Social Club*.

Everyone assumed that Baba was simply a brilliant and generous businessman until a Dubai bank manager confessed that he'd transferred more than a quarter of a billion (yes, *billion*) dollars into Sora's accounts after being put under a spell by the Malian. Sora retreated to Bamako in reduced circumstances and avoided extradition by getting elected to Parliament. To the day he died, he was revered and beloved by the jalis.

With ancestral musical forms in decline across Africa, it was good to see Mandé traditions defying the laws of time and gravity, though I can't say the results were always for the better. On my first trip to Bamako in 1989, I had heard Habib Koité and his band playing rock 'n' roll: Stones covers, Otis Redding songs, and, as I recall, a Traffic tune. The singer-guitarist had a wonderfully original take on Anglo-American music; if Hannibal hadn't been completely broke at the time, I would have signed him on the spot. A few years later, I saw Koité at a club in Paris; no more blue jeans, his band were dressed in mud cloths and playing acoustic instruments, a kind of singer-songwriter version of the jali tradition and, to my mind, nowhere near as exciting or interesting—or commercial—as what I heard that night by the Niger River.

Malian rock would have its day, but it would emerge not from Bamako but from that gigantic lopsided wedge that appears on maps to be clumsily glued to the top of the country: the arid north.

※

> For some people when you say "Timbuktu," it is like the end of the world, but that is not true. I am from Timbuktu and I can tell you we are right at the heart of the world.
>
> —Ali Farka Touré, quoted on the back of a Hannibal Records promotional T-shirt

As British concert promoter Anne Hunt was preparing to leave for Ghana in the spring of 1986, Andy Kershaw suggested she stop off in Mali and look up Ali Farka Touré. Phone number? Address? No, none of that, just the name, in a country larger than Britain, France, and Germany combined. When Hunt walked into Radio Mali's Bamako studios and asked for help finding Ali, they looked at her blankly. She explained that he was a Malian musician she wanted to bring to London for a concert, that recordings he had made ten years earlier (in that same studio) had been played on Kershaw's show and received a great response. The station manager shrugged and asked the announcer to tell listeners there was a British lady here looking for Monsieur Touré and if anyone knew where he was, to please send him over to the station.

In that moment of kismet—Ali lived hundreds of miles away in the north and just happened to be in Bamako that day—we can pinpoint the start of a movement that has sold more records and concert tickets outside the continent than any other style of African music (*mbqanga* excepted if you count *Graceland*). It encompasses Ali's career as well as that of Tinariwen, Tamikrest, Songhoy Blues, Ali's son Vieux, Bombino, and all the other envoys of "desert blues," plus the Festival in the Desert with its celebrated visitors.

Hunt organized Ali's trip to London (hence his presence at Fox's party) and he was soon in the studio recording for World Circuit Records. The label began life as an adjunct to the concert bureau founded by Hunt and Mary Farquharson; recording their touring artists was, they reckoned, an afterthought that could be left to the intern since he seemed so keen. Nick Gold was the intern, and he would eventually buy out Farquharson and Hunt and build World Circuit into the most successful world music record company ever.

Gold released three Ali Farka Touré albums between 1987 and 1992; all were well received and sold moderately. Touring was sporadic; Ali insisted he was mainly a farmer and a family man with no intention of letting frivolous distractions like the international music business interfere with his life beside the Niger River. One day, Nick got a call from Ry Cooder inquiring about Ali. Both happened to be in London, so Nick invited Ry to his flat, where Touré was staying in the guest room with his Dutch wife (one of three), and hurriedly bought a sofa so they would all have somewhere to sit. There was only one guitar, so the two traded songs, nodding occasionally to affirm cautious admiration; as he left, Ry muttered about how it would be nice to try something in a studio sometime. In the lead-up to Ali's US tour, Nick did two things: he sent Ry demos of some of Ali's unrecorded songs and booked three days at Ocean Way (Ry's favorite LA studio) during a gap purposely built into the tour schedule.

I have always been keen on clarity, though it has not escaped my notice that some of the most successful people I know seem to thrive by keeping things vague. Between Gold's British diffidence and Ry's Californian cool, nothing was arranged, just an offhand invitation for Nick and Ali to drop by Ry's place on their first day off in LA. When they arrived, it became clear that Ry had been studying the demo and that the two enjoyed finally playing together. Ry agreed to come to Ocean Way the next day and mentioned, by the way, that he'd asked John Patitucci and Jim Keltner (the ace Los Angeles rhythm section) to come along, too.

Nick did his best to remain calm as Cooder took charge of the session and the sticker shocks started coming; $1,500 for Patitucci's "bass tech" guy and $200 a reel for tape you could buy down the street for half the price (but weren't allowed to use) plus a few other nasty surprises exploded Gold's budget and forced him to beg promoters for advances on upcoming concert fees. Fortunately, Ry grasped how quickly Ali got bored playing the same song, so the Californians worked fast. As he had on previous collaborations with Hawaiians, Okinawans, the Indian guitarist, and a Tex-Mex group (and would again a few years later in Cuba), Cooder brought a distinct yet restrained presence, cracking open a door for listeners unfamiliar with African music yet never dominating proceedings. Barring a few added tweaks, *Talking Timbuktu* was recorded live in those three allotted days.

Gold knew he had something special. Though World Circuit didn't then have a partner company in America, I had made a (prescient, I like to say) deal one album earlier to release Ali's recordings there, which is how Hannibal won its only Grammy. *Talking Timbuktu* sold a quarter of a million copies and forged the relationship between Gold and Cooder that would lead to *Buena Vista*.

For many, *Talking Timbuktu* settled the issue about the blues' African roots. Starting with his first World Circuit album, critics had been drawing parallels between Ali and John Lee Hooker. Hooker had long been considered the most "African" of American bluesmen, largely because of his resistance to the tonic/subdominant/dominant-seventh cycle of the classic twelve-bar blues; he always seemed happy to make himself at home on one root chord with the odd modal excursion, just as one might imagine an African musician doing. Listeners can certainly be struck by snatches of Ali's music evoking Hooker's, though the closest US equivalent is probably the less well known Robert Pete Williams, a so-called primitive singer first recorded at Louisiana's Angola Penitentiary whose music is marked by loose structures, irregular key changes, and a vaguely pentatonic mode. Touré's recordings seemed to confirm the form's roots in the West African interior, particularly since so many slaves captured there ended up in America.

Cue Gerhard Kubik, always ready to pour an erudite bucket of cold water on facile theories (*roots* being one of Kubik's least favorite words). Comparing a twentieth-century American style with present-day music from Mali, he points out, proves little about connections forged centuries earlier. Gerhard supports the "great man" theory of musical history, that one talented and charismatic figure can have a far greater effect on the music of a region than any tectonic cultural plates. (Franco, Fela, Marley, Arsenio, and Gardel come quickly to mind, and who knows what giants walked the land before the means existed to record them?) In John Lee Hooker and Ali Farka Touré we have a pair of colossi who may be more idiosyncratic than representative.

During his Mississippi boyhood, Hooker's deeply religious father forbade him from listening to anything but church hymns. After his parents separated, his mother married a blues singer with a quirky, modal, no-chord-changes style which he imprinted on the blank slate (from a blues point of view) that was the teenage John Lee. When Hooker moved north after the war, his peculiar style drew enthusiastic crowds and thrust him to the top of the rhythm and blues charts. Did it touch a long-buried Black Atlantic nerve within his audiences? It certainly caught the ear of a few Africans.

Ali Farka Touré's pre–World Circuit life (he was forty-seven when Anne Hunt came to Bamako) had been eventful. His parents were from the Arma community around Timbuktu, descendants of sixteenth-century Moroccan mercenaries who married local Songhai women. After Ali's father was killed while serving with the French Army in 1940, his mother moved back to Niafunké, the riverside town where Touré would be based for the rest of his life. As the only survivor out of eleven children, her family nicknamed him "Farka" (mule) for his stubborn determination to live. A great-aunt who led shamanic ceremonies sensed Ali's musical talent, taught him to play the *njarka* (one-string fiddle), and brought the boy along on her travels around the region. His connection to the music was immediate and intense; he spent one teenage year in rural isolation, recovering from seizures brought on by spirit possession while performing in his aunt's ceremonies.

Ali worked for a while in the mid-fifties in Guinea, where he heard Fodéba Keïta, who had developed Guinea's post-independence template for state-supported music. Keïta's guitar-playing, particularly the way he adapted Mandé traditional music to Kru finger-picking styles, inspired Ali to take up the instrument. This muddies the "desert blues" water somewhat, bringing in the Portuguese and the coast boys as key sources for Ali's playing.

Back in Niafunké, he joined the group representing the region in President Modibo Keïta's annual competitions and received much praise and attention. Following Keïta's overthrow, an ensemble attached to the national radio in Bamako needed someone to represent the cultures of the north, who were feeling marginalized in the Mandé-dominated nation. Ali was perfect for the job; he sings in eleven (mostly northern) languages and had adapted ngoni and other stringed-instrument fingering patterns to the guitar. To augment his salary with the ensemble, he took a job as driver for an ethnographer with a UNESCO grant who traveled the country documenting regional music. Touré became an indispensable sidekick, putting his linguistic skills to use while adding to his own knowledge of the country's vast tapestry of musical styles.

I can attest to Ali's facility with languages; during a gathering at Charlie Gillett's house in 1989, I introduced him to Rumyana Tzintzarska, co-producer of my Bulgarian records, who was in London for a concert we were organizing at the South Bank. Jaws dropped as Ali greeted her eloquently in Bulgarian, explaining that his military service had included six months training on the Danube with the Bulgarian river police when Mali was aligned with the Soviet bloc.

American vinyl, as we have noted, was ubiquitous in seventies Bamako; Touré loved listening to Wilson Pickett, Otis Redding, Albert King, and Motown, and it shows. The guitar motif on "La Drogue," a track he recorded in 1975, is borrowed from the famous lick at the start of "My Girl" by The Temptations, and he also nicked a riff from James Brown's "There Was a Time." When someone played him a John Lee Hooker record, Ali's response was: "I learned he was an American, and then I thought he had stolen our music." He found the blues similar to Tuareg music—"we have the roots and the trunk, and they have the leaves and the branches"—but grew defensive when asked about Hooker's influence on him: "I can teach him things, but he cannot teach me. For ten years I can teach him African tunes without repeating a note." In a later interview, Touré pointed out that Hooker "sings about whiskey, beer, and women. I sing about pastures, forests, nature, the river, the earth and the sky, work, and education against ignorance and racism." Be that as it may, "Amandrai" from Ali's first World Circuit album is a pretty straight-up blues, pitched midway between Hooker and Robert Pete Williams, and bears only passing resemblance to anything African (bar the language and some pentatonic blue notes).

Kubik's view is that American blues and rhythm and blues in Mali are like Cuban rumba in the Congo or Trinidadian calypso in Ghana; local musicians were drawn to those styles because they sounded familiar, creating whirlpools of reciprocal influence that repel any attempt to draw linear conclusions. That seems like a roundabout way of saying, yes, the blues do indeed have at least some roots in West Africa.

A man with a 16 mm projector used to turn up at Tuareg camps in the sands of northern Mali in the mid-sixties and show movies on the side of a tent; it was part of the government's outreach to nomads who felt little connection to the new nation. Ibrahim Ag Alhabib remembers being transfixed as a small boy by a scene in which a cowboy sings a mournful song while strumming a guitar, before grabbing a gun hidden in the neck of the instrument and using it to mow down the bad guys. That, Ibrahim decided, was what he wanted when he grew up, a guitar with bullets.

The Tuareg are the southern branch of the Berbers, original inhabitants of North Africa who were regularly pushed back from the coast and subjugated, first by the Phoenicians, then the Romans, next the Arabs, and finally the French. Berber troops provided much of the manpower for the Islamic conquest of Spain, then battled against their Arab allies as often as they fought the Spaniards, controlling huge swathes of the Iberian Peninsula and the Maghreb for long periods of the region's history. Colonialism wasn't kind to them, with gerrymandered borders ensuring their minority status in a half-dozen nations across North and West Africa. Like Kurds and Ukrainians, Berbers and their culture have long been dismissed and suppressed by ruling majorities, although in recent years the revival of the ancient Tifinagh alphabet has helped carve out more space for their literature and their traditions.

Tuaregs share much culture and blood with darker-skinned peoples to the south, due both to simple proximity and to their past roles as slave traders and slave holders. Most are Muslim, but their society couldn't be more different from that of the Arabs; it is matrilineal and, in many respects, matriarchal, with women taking lead roles in matters of marriage and child-rearing. Fadimata Walett Oumar, leader of the mostly female group Tartit, told Davia Nelson of NPR's *The Kitchen Sisters* that "the divorce party is bigger than the wedding; the more times you divorce, the more beautiful and successful you are. Why remain in a boring marriage?"

France tended to leave nomads alone, but after independence, Mali strove to modernize the economy and control its citizens. While harshly suppressing a rebellion in the early sixties, the army killed Ag Alhabib's father and slaughtered the family's livestock. Ibrahim achieved his boyhood wish; the Tuaregs' long struggle for an independent state has been kept alive, they say, by the bards who fought alongside the MNLA rebels and shared their years of exile in Algerian and Libyan camps. Ibrahim became one of the best, composing songs and playing the guitar—and sometimes fighting—as part of a group of singer-poets who circled back and forth across borders and were known as "the desert boys," or *kel tinariwen* in Tamasheq, the language of the Tuareg. An uprising in the early nineties ended with a French-brokered peace deal, but deep scars remained.

Later in the decade, efforts aimed at improving communication and increasing mutual respect began. In 1998, a Tuareg poetry collective took part in a Bamako theater festival, where they encountered a very un-colonial group of French musicians. Lo'Jo had been formed by a quixotic adventurer named Denis Péan; the group includes two Anjou-born Berber sisters plus a pair of musicians Péan met at the conservatory. Before forming the band and settling down with them in a commune outside Angers in the Loire Valley, Péan had wandered the globe; Lo'Jo continue to seek out intense corners of the map—Chechnya, Reunion Island, Georgia . . . They travel not just to perform, but to participate in street theater and work with local artists. Péan's lyrics fall within the *chanson* tradition, set to melodies spiced with far-flung influence.

In 1998, Angers sponsored Lo'Jo's participation in the event organized by its *ville jumelée* (twinned town) of Bamako. The French city took the event seriously, renting a *maison de la partenariat* to house the delegation and host soirées; during one of these, the group heard a Tuareg singing and playing the guitar. They were transfixed by his music, but the man demurred, insisting he wasn't a performer, that the real poets, the best singers, those that defined Tuareg culture, were far away in the north. Over the next two years, Lo'Jo's indefatigable manager, Philippe Brix, traveled to southern Algeria and Libya and tracked down *kel tinariwen*, recruiting two of them to join a Lo'Jo tour in France. In December 2000, the group's English producer, Justin Adams, engineer Jean-Paul Romann, and Brix flew to Gao in northeastern Mali, drove for two days across the roadless sands to Kidal, and set up recording equipment at the local radio station. Then they waited.

One by one, the desert boys began to arrive; the last to turn up was Ibrahim Ag Alhabib. Adams describes hearing him for the first time, sitting cross-legged on the ground as if by a Sahara bonfire. His touch on the guitar was so tentative, the sound so frail, that Romann doubted it would be possible to record him. Ag Alhabib's singing was equally faint at first, but as he approached the song's chorus, the strokes grow more forceful, his voice filled out, and when the others joined in, the music soared and Justin's arm sprouted goose bumps. Over the next three days, they recorded the first Tinariwen album.

∽

Tonight
I sleep in the ruins
I follow traces of my past
It sometimes befalls me to live like this
My heart oppressed and tight
And I feel the thirst of my soul
Then I hear some music
Sounds, the wind
Some music which takes me far, far away
To the clear light of morning
Where, before my heart,
The brilliance of the stars
Goes out.

— "Ténéré daféo nikchan" (In the Desert by a Wood Fire), by Ibrahim Ag Alhabib of Tinariwen

[W]hen we first started hearing Hendrix . . . we felt something immediately. It was almost as if I had known that music from the day I was born . . . I think that any people who have lived through something that is very hard feel this *asuf*, this pain, this longing. That is what will make their music sound similar to each other.

—Eyadou Ag Leche of Tinariwen

The spiritual gravity of their melodies and grooves demands your attention without offering to reward it—what's sought isn't your affection but your respect. But give them time and eventually affection and even awe will follow.

—Robert Christgau reviewing Tinariwen's *Aman Iman*

Once the recording was done, they all headed east to meet Lo'Jo at a spot in the dunes where a Tuareg gathering was taking place. Brix and "Manny" Ansar, a well-born and well-connected Tuareg, had wangled funds for a stage and sound system as an adjunct to the primary purposes of the occasion: inter-clan courtship and camel-trading, plus a government-backed exchange of weapons for livestock. Tinariwen and Lo'Jo were "headliners" at this first Festival au Désert, playing to a crowd of about sixty (mostly French) foreigners and a thousand Tuaregs.

Despite its modest scale, the event, along with the recording Adams released on his own small label, constituted Tinariwen's coming-out-of-the-desert party. From the minute world music DJs, jam-band promoters, and open-eared rock fans heard them, the group found an audience. Open tunings on their Stratocasters and simple reverb settings on their amps evoked the irresistible sound of Pops's guitar on early Staple Singers recordings (though the Tuaregs had never heard them). Even without a drum kit, their grooves could connect with ZZ Top fans. Able to carry only a few cassettes with them across the sands, the ones they'd kept stayed in heavy rotation: Ali Farka Touré's mid-seventies *Red* album, Hendrix, Algerian *raï* king Cheb Khaled, Boney M., Nass Al Ghiwane from Morocco, Rod Stewart, Oum Kalsoum, and, top of the desert bonfire charts, Dire Straits. Audiences didn't need experts to point out Tinariwen's blues connection; the link is visceral and obvious. Over the next decade, abetted by their English manager Andy Morgan,

Tinariwen established themselves as stars and sold hundreds of thousands of records.

Justin Adams, meanwhile, had joined Robert Plant's new band and intrigued him with tales of the desert; the journey they made together across the sands to perform at the 2003 event was immortalized in a French documentary as well as on Plant's social media postings. Le Festival au Désert became a destination for journalists, adventurous music buffs, and rock stars (Bono and Damon Albarn first in the queue), not to mention the Sahel and Sahara bands hoping to follow in Tinariwen's wake. Volkswagen was inspired to launch an "all-terrain" vehicle called the Touareg. (It proved useless in the sands; Sahara traders, travelers, and fighters use either a Toyota Landcruiser or a camel.) By 2007, the audience ratio between locals and foreigners had tilted towards the latter and the event had become sufficiently mainstream that *Vanity Fair* commissioned a piece by the MTV founder Tom Freston about his journey there.

Reading the article today is sad beyond words. Freston and his friends (including Chris Blackwell and Jimmy Buffett) began their adventure with a spectacular night in Bamako. The city seemed dormant when they arrived, but they wanted music and had the dash to lure performers onto the stage: first, the Rail Band back at the Buffet Hôtel de la Gare, with taxi headlights for illumination, then on to the Hogon for a midnight set by Toumani and his band, and finishing off with a 2 a.m. show by Oumou Sangaré at her nightclub-hotel near the market. Chris said it was the greatest night of music he'd ever experienced (and there's no shortage of competition for that honor). The next day, they flew to Timbuktu, then drove over the dunes to the festival site for three days of music, including a tribute to the recently deceased Ali Farka Touré and appearances by top Malian artists, capped off by a Tinariwen finale. The visitors were startled when someone commended their bravery in ignoring a US State Department travel warning; that was the first they'd heard of it. Optimism ruled; as Freston wrote, "swords turn to guitars, democracy blooms, and music helps bring a sense of national unity."

Two years later, AQIM (Al Qaeda in the Islamic Maghreb) captured a party of Swiss festival-goers who had stayed around afterwards to explore the desert. Most were eventually freed, but when the British refused to release an Al Qaeda prisoner, Edwin Dyer, an Englishman traveling with the Swiss, was beheaded. In 2012, the MNLA relaunched their war for independence; this time they were crushed not by the Malian army but by their Salafist allies, the mostly Arab jihadists with zero tolerance for music, female prerogatives, or Tuareg traditions. Devout Muslim musicians who had felt no need to flee were forced to watch as their instruments and cassette collections were destroyed. A French intervention pushed the invaders back, but intolerance and bigotry spread south far faster than the encroaching desert. The Hogon's landlord evicted Toumani and the site became a mosque as Bamako nights grew ever quieter. The democracy the country had fought so hard to achieve began to fall apart, eroded by corruption and coups. Music could not, after all, hold the nation together.

*

Underneath that burning sun . . .
Do they know it's Christmas time at all?

—"Do They Know It's Christmas?," Band Aid's charity single for Ethiopian famine relief, the 1984 Christmas #1 in Britain

The one thing Ethiopians knew for certain in that fourth week of December 1984 was that it was *not* Christmas. For them, Jesus's birthday falls on the twenty-eighth day in the month of Tahsas (January 7 by our calendar), and they had seniority, having been a Christian country since 330 CE, a time when midwinter festivities in Britain and Ireland could still involve human sacrifice or smearing yourself in woad. Bob Geldof wasn't the first *ferenj* with misapprehensions about Ethiopia; Rastafarians, for example, have been stubborn repeat offenders. Myths and legends about this isolated land hidden behind mountain ranges have persisted since the time of the pharaohs. Until 1985, though, few had much to say about its music.

That spring, as Geldof was discovering that the famine he had raised more than a billion dollars to alleviate wasn't so much a natural disaster as a government tactic in a civil war, a Frenchman arrived in Addis Ababa on a very different mission. A few months earlier, Francis Falceto had heard an album at a friend's house in Poitiers, a provincial city just south of Lo'Jo's Angers, and had been gripped from the first notes. Mahmoud Ahmed's *Ere mela mela* sounded like Memphis soul played in strange minor-key pentatonic melody lines, with Ahmed's powerful singing backed by riffing horns and a churning rhythm section.

The disc had been making the rounds of local music buffs for a while, ever since Bernard Gallodét, a technician traveling with a theater company, had purchased it during a stopover in Addis Ababa because he liked the cover. Falceto was part of a group running Le Confort Moderne, an independent arts center in Poitiers; in their first few years, they brought Sonic Youth, Killing Joke, The Residents, Glenn Branca, and Hannibal's own Defunkt to perform there. Francis was determined to add Mahmoud Ahmed to that list. He made a few cassette copies and sent them to Paris critics and radio DJs; all were stunned by the combination of strangeness and familiarity, the way the music mirrored American soul while seeming to come from another planet, with the singer's voice pitched somewhere between Sam Cooke and Otis Redding.

Encouraged by the reaction, Falceto flew to Addis Ababa and tracked down Ahmed; the singer, though, told him it was pointless applying for an exit visa as the country's Stalinist Derg regime was paranoid about the outside world and hostile not only to Western capitalism but also to music like his, which reminded Ethiopians of happier times. That Geldof's campaign had embarrassed the country's leader, Mengistu Haile Mariam, made things even more difficult. Francis had little choice but to return to Poitiers and hope the Derg would fall. In the meantime, he could study up on the history of this land that had suddenly taken over his life and learn the story behind its addictive music.

The royal line that came to an end when the army overthrew Haile Selassie in 1974 began, according to legend, with the prince who was the fruit of Queen Makeda of Sheba's one-night stand with Israel's King Solomon. Tales such as that have caused Ethiopia to resonate in the world's imagination: pharaohs obsessed about it; Mohammed granted its people a dispensation from jihad in gratitude for sheltering his followers during the seventh-century wars around the birth of Islam; medieval Europeans were intrigued by tales of a Christian kingdom in the wilds of Africa. Emperor Menelik's victory over an invading Italian army in 1896 at the Battle of Adwa put the country in the world's spotlight; no sub-Saharan African army had ever repelled a European force before.

But there's a catch: most Ethiopians don't actually view themselves as "sub-Saharan." As if to prove the point, Menelik immediately began his own "scramble," colonizing outwards from the central highlands with the sort of brutal efficiency France and Britain were demonstrating across the rest of Africa. Like those European powers, the ruling Amharas viewed their conquered peoples as inferior and financed economic growth with the gold and other raw materials they extracted from the captured lands. Amharas, furthermore, kept Black slaves, as they had for millennia.

Haile Selassie's 1924 tour of European capitals to celebrate the country's membership in the League of Nations further emphasized its separation from the rest of the (now fully colonized) continent. Crowds were dazzled by the delegation's colorful finery and the half-dozen lions they brought along as mascots. The climax of the journey—and the start of our musical story—came in Jerusalem, where the Regent (as Selassie was then for his sister, Empress Zewditu) was serenaded by a forty-strong brass band made up of Armenian orphans, survivors of Turkish massacres during the Great War.

Brass instruments intrigued Selassie; he had a storeroom full of them back in Addis Ababa, gifts from Tsar Nicholas of Russia that no one ever played. As in so many cultures, music wasn't a respectable profession, and in any case, Ethiopia had no instructors. The country's own musical instruments were unchanged since the time of Sheba: church ceremonies used large hollow drums and filigreed rattles called *sistra*; bards plucked the *krar*, a harp resembling what cherubs hold in Italian Renaissance paintings; long monophonic horns called *meleket* and *embilta* greeted royalty and drove troops into battle; and the *azmaris*—a cross between griots, troubadours, and street singers—accompanied themselves on the *masenqo*, a one-string bowed instrument similar to the njarka that sent young Ali Farka Touré into a trance.

Selassie offered the orphans a five-year contract to be the official band of the Imperial Palace and hired their fellow Armenian Kevork Nalbandian as coach and conductor. Though Ethiopia is a proud and insular land, it has a long history of bringing in foreign experts and its people are always eager to learn. Nalbandian did well, improving the orphans' techniques while also training locals; when half the band left at the end of the contract, he was able to replace them, mostly with students from Ethiopia's newly conquered lands. With the (suspiciously convenient) death of the empress in 1930, Selassie became emperor and the band strutted its stuff for the international guests attending his coronation (and caused a diplomatic furore by refusing to play the Turkish anthem). In the wake of all those parades and ceremonies, the Ethiopian public went mad for brass bands, just as the rest of the world had done in the previous century.

The country's love affair with that bravado-filled sound was put on hold for a few years when Mussolini sent an army to avenge Adwa. Il Duce left nothing to chance, employing poison gas to defeat the Ethiopians, though Italian rule proved so brief that it doesn't really count as colonization. The British and East African soldiers who turfed out the fascists brought records with them, opening sheltered Ethiopian ears to the sounds of jazz and swing; after the war, rhythm and blues and rock 'n' roll got added to the mix.

I remember brass band concerts from my childhood that featured a "novelty" interlude where a section of the band would step forward to play a bit of jazz or calypso as a change of pace. Addis now also boasted brass bands sponsored by the police and the army, and they were no different, with special "boogie-woogie" numbers popular with audiences and the musicians. These subgroups began moonlighting at the bar of the National Theatre or in one of the hotel lounges, mirroring similar evolutions from marching to dancing that had taken place in the Gold Coast and other African colonies a half-century earlier. The Golden Age of Ethiopian music had begun.

The capital's nightlife expanded in leaps and bounds, three of them to be precise. The first arrived in 1950 with the placing of the former Italian colony of Eritrea on the Red Sea coast under Ethiopian jurisdiction. This would have dire long-term geopolitical consequences, but it brought many Eritreans to Addis, and their love of cafés, bars, and parties transformed the previously staid capital. Next, having survived an attempted overthrow in 1960, Selassie loosened restrictions and invested in schools and universities; the country began breathing freer air and its youth was energized. Then, in 1963, the newly founded Organisation of African Unity made Addis Ababa its headquarters, triggering a building boom while delegates on expense accounts fueled a rash of new hotels and nightclubs. With Peace Corps workers and US airmen spinning their record collections on late-night radio and local teenagers developing a taste for Vespas and miniskirts, youth culture was evolving at dizzying speed to a soundtrack of modern, mostly American music.

The rhythms of Addis's heyday bore little resemblance to parallel years in Accra, Lagos, Kinshasa, Dakar, or Bamako. Cuban and Trinidadian records rarely made it to Ethiopia; rumba and highlife bands never toured. Since the country had never been a source of slaves for America, soul and rhythm and blues were exciting novelties with zero connection to local folklore. Thanks to Kevork Nalbandian and his nephew Nerses, plus a few displaced Jewish teachers and conductors from Eastern Europe who had found their way to Addis, local musicians developed the skills to play their own version of what they were hearing. And, since being part of a brass band had become a prestigious civil service position, Amharas now joined in. The result was a greenhouse hybrid, a grafting of Ethiopian melodies, scales, beats, and lyrics onto an American stem using Armenian string.

A typically arbitrary edict from the palace had granted the Imperial Heritage Society a monopoly on record production; since that organization hadn't the slightest interest in popular culture, the music's evolution across the fifties and sixties went unrecorded. Footage from the seventies shows singer Alemayehu Eshete doing a convincingly wild version of Presley's "You're So Square (Baby I Don't Care)," demonstrating how Ethiopians had thrown themselves full tilt into playing rock 'n' roll with a high level of musicianship. Every New Year's Eve (Ethiopian calendars end in our mid-September), there was a "battle of the bands," with thousands dancing until dawn. For weeks prior, soldiers would stand guard outside rehearsals to prevent eavesdropping as each orchestra sought to dazzle the crowd with a fresh repertoire. The two Nalbandians and other imported arrangers were big-band enthusiasts; with skilled brass and reed players at their disposal, they were able to wed swing-era grandiosity to rock 'n' roll energy, funk guitar riffs, Ethiopian village dances, and traditional pentatonic melodies. Photos from the era show bands in natty matching suits with pegged trousers and coiffed hair, the sax sections swivelling in lockstep, as if they were in a fifties chitlin'-circuit roadhouse.

The supply chain bringing imported vinyl to Addis was haphazard at best, so fans relied on the radio and a few determined store owners; when a box of American discs arrived, it would sell out within days, if not hours. In 1969, a twenty-four-year-old retailer named Amha Eshete (no relation to the Elvis impersonator Alemayehu) decided to challenge the authorities by launching his own label; appropriately, the other Eshete was the only singer brave enough to show up for the first session. By that time, he was no longer channeling the King, nor doing his equally popular James Brown impression, but singing original compositions in Amharic; English lyrics had become passé. After sending the tapes off to Bombay to be pressed onto discs, Amha went nervously to the airport to collect the first shipment, but the customs agent simply asked for a free copy and waved the boxes through.

The prime of the Ethiopian record industry lasted barely seven years. During that time only a few discs sold as many as a thousand copies and none more than five thousand. The trail leading to an afterlife in which hundreds of thousands of CDs were sold and streaming plays numbered in the millions began with a boy hustling in the Addis market to help out his mother, just like Franco. This was Mahmoud Ahmed, born to a family of Gurages, an ethnic group noted for being skilled traders. When Mahmoud failed to show any interest in schoolwork, his mother got him a job shining shoes and washing dishes at the Arizona Club, nocturnal home of the Imperial Bodyguard Band. One night in 1962, their vocalist failed to turn up and teenage Mahmoud convinced the bandleader that he knew the repertoire inside out. Ahmed never looked back; over the course of the sixties, he became a star, renowned for his powerful voice and sexy *eskista*, the shoulder-quivering move you see on any Ethiopian dancefloor. He began recording in the early seventies and seemed to improve with each release; the 1975 album that found its way to France was a culmination of everything that had made the past decade "golden." By the time Falceto and his pals discovered it, however, drum machines, bootleg cassettes, and Derg curfews had brought down the curtain on this glorious era; if it hadn't been for Bernard Gallodét's impulse buy, the world might never have heard this music at all.

Those paltry sales figures speak to the inequality of Ethiopian society and the terrible poverty in the countryside; only salaried urbanites and their teenage offspring could afford record players. The 1973 famine that destabilized the throne was a symptom of century upon century of near feudal conditions and the repeated failures of Selassie's attempts at land reform. Rebellions by junior officers and their ill-fed troops began in early 1974 and by the end of that year, the Emperor was in prison and the country was being led by the Derg ("Committee" in Amharic). The revolution's leadership was chosen from a group of delegates sent by regional army units; the Harar barracks chose an officer who was so universally loathed that the troops voted for him just to get rid of him. This was Mengistu Haile Mariam. Under his leadership, the Derg slowly tightened its noose around Ethiopian life; curfews were imposed, from midnight at first, then earlier, while censorship was applied to newspapers, radio, and, eventually, recordings. Joy was drained from what remained of Addis's nightlife as the Derg enforced their rule with arrests, torture, and summary executions.

Amha Eshete was out of the country in the spring of 1975 when his sound engineer and one of his artists were jailed and his family advised him not to return. A half-Yemeni coffee trader known as "Ali Tango," who had started releasing records in the wake of the Amha label's success, moved into the vacuum, producing *Ere mela mela* later that year. In

1987, Falceto returned to Addis and made a deal with Ali and Mahmoud to release the LP in Europe with a few added tracks. Crammed Discs was on board straight away; our Congo friend Vincent Kenis created the master by dubbing straight off vinyl originals. After hearing it once—and seeing the beautiful cover art—I persuaded Francis and Marc Hollander to grant Hannibal a licence for the UK and North America. Critics loved it, a few radio presenters played it, and Ahmed maneuvered an exit visa to perform at a festival in France. A cult following slowly began to grow. Mengistu had resisted Geldof's relief efforts because he didn't want outsiders prowling the Tigray province in the north; those who reached the area encountered an active anti-Derg rebellion allied with an Eritrean independence movement. By the end of the decade, the army was in retreat and not even masses of Soviet arms could save it. On May 21, 1991, Mengistu fled into Zimbabwean exile; soon, bars and nightclubs reopened and music was heard once more in the streets of Addis Ababa. But it wasn't the same. After seventeen years with no state salaries for musicians and just a few cocktail-hour nightclubs, the live scene was comatose. Weddings were celebrated with singers backed by keyboardists who cued up a rhythm section with the flick of a switch; cassette releases were quickly bootlegged, so production needed to be cheap. Ethiopians were happy just to be freed from the Derg's puritan purgatory, so cheesy sounds worked just fine in the home market; only a few critics and old-timers grumbled about the music's flimsiness. The outside world was another story; if word was to spread, it would need some game-changing events.

Hailing a taxi at Union Station in Washington DC, it's a pretty safe bet the driver will speak Amharic. What Paris is to francophone Africans and London is for Ghanaians and Nigerians, Washington DC is to Ethiopians, who seem to dominate the city's taxi business. There are bars and restaurants with signs in Amharic lettering and nightclubs where you can hear modern or traditional Ethiopian music; the country's two greatest stars, Mahmoud Ahmed and Aster Aweke, now make their homes in DC. It was there that Falceto eventually tracked down

Amha Eshete, though it took a few visits to convince him that there could be a market for Ethiopian music. Once he was persuaded, Eshete and Falceto had to locate the artists and secure permissions; both men have strict views on the need for everyone to have full consultation and fair treatment. Amha then had to figure out where he'd left the masters. In February 1997, armed with a letter of authorization, Francis left a warehouse in the suburbs of Athens (Greece, not Georgia) clutching a suitcase full of tapes: "It was one of the most beautiful days of my life."

As I write this, Falceto is preparing *Éthiopiques 31*. Hannibal and Crammed both had their chance to host the series but Buda Records in Paris was probably his ideal partner (and heaven forfend that Francis might have had to navigate Warner Music's legal department after their purchase of Hannibal). I don't think it over-romantic to suggest that in the record business, more than in most fields of commerce, virtue can be rewarded; no one in his wildest dreams would have imagined that a thirty-disc series devoted to a musical form few had ever heard of would sell in such numbers. Much of that success is down to the collection's stylish and colorful graphics, the wit and rigor of Falceto's bilingual notes, his tireless promotion of the artists and their tours, and his unceasing engagement with the country and its musical culture. But the arresting effect of those pentatonic scales is central; they make the music instantly recognizable and even, if one isn't careful, addictive.

There are many ways to trace the inexorable "Africanization" of Western popular music over the centuries; most of them are rhythmic, but the ever-expanding use of pentatonic modes, scales, and melodies is also central. Ali Farka Touré's appropriation of the "My Girl" figure may constitute an emblematic full-circle moment, but it's just the tip of that iceberg; a musician named David Bennett has a concise online demonstration in which he cites Stevie Wonder's "Superstition," Jackie Wilson's "Higher and Higher," Pink Floyd's "Money," Muddy Waters's "Hoochie Coochie Man," "Amazing Grace," and the guitar riff in "Whole Lotta Love." As with any stimulant, regular consumption can lead to a craving for stronger doses, and Ethiopian music provides them. It uses four pentatonic scales—Bati, Ambassel, Anchihoye, and Tezeta—

with variants (major/minor etc.) within each one. While the pentatonic nature of, for example, most Malian music may not be immediately obvious to the Western ear, Ethiopian modes contain such distinctively wide intervals that they call out instantly to any listener, regardless of whether they have ever heard the term or know what it means.

> Ah, that's nice. Ethiopian sounds. It's good for the heart.
>
> —Winston (Jeffrey Wright) to Don (Bill Murray) in Jim Jarmusch's film *Broken Flowers*

Jim Jarmusch burst onto the independent film scene in 1984 with a Cannes Festival award for *Stranger Than Paradise*, in which he used Screamin' Jay Hawkins's hysterical classic "I Put a Spell on You" to accompany an immigrant girl's deadpan, black-and-white exploration of America. Twenty years later, *Broken Flowers* earned the director another Cannes prize by matching Bill Murray's rent-a-car *hejira* tracking down ex-girlfriends through the Technicolor blandness of American suburbs with music plucked from *Éthiopiques 4: Ethio-Jazz*.

The earworm melodies that fill Murray's car each time he begins another leg of the journey multiplied the audience for Ethiopian music. The tracks are all instrumentals, so no tricky foreign lyrics to deal with, plus they're cool and jazzy, built around Mulatu Astatke's keyboards and vibraphone. Astatke is a patrician Amhara who arrived at Trinity College in 1960, just as Fela Kuti was leaving. London introduced Mulatu to jazz and Latin music and he soon moved on to New York to get closer to the sources. Early releases of what he was already calling "Ethio-Jazz fusion" (inspired, perhaps, by Joe Harriott's "Indo-Jazz fusion") are interesting, but not as compelling as these recorded for Amha Eshete after he returned to Addis at the end of the sixties. Thanks in part to *Broken Flowers*, Astatke would go on to become Ethiopia's most widely known musician, flourishing in the twenty-first century on international concert and festival circuits.

Instigating foreign tours for other Golden Age figures was not so easy. Falceto had been able to cobble together backing groups for early ventures abroad by Ahmed and Alemayehu Eshete, but not without difficulty; most musicians rendered obsolescent by synths and curfews had simply given up. The Walias Band was Addis's equivalent of Motown's Funk Brothers; they played on many of the greatest records of the 1970s and survived as a unit until 1981. They managed to secure exit visas that year to perform for expats in America on condition they keep the trip secret back home; half came back, half decided to stay. The group's keyboard player (and the Golden Age's leading non-Armenian arranger) Girma Beyene set himself up in DC, but became depressed after the death of his wife and ended up pumping gas in a Washington suburb. By the turn of the century, as European and American audiences for the music grew, the country's best musicians were scattered to the winds.

Ethiopians can be wild dancers, but the action is mostly above the waist: shoulders shimmy, heads twirl, arms flex. Afro-Cuban dance is all hips and feet, mirroring how the music lives in the drums; you can take almost any tune and, with the right rhythm section, turn it into a mambo. Ethiopian music is the opposite, defined by its scales and melodies. With rhythmic authenticity less crucial, Europeans and North Americans who might sound lame playing Afro-Cuban styles can make a convincing fist of Ethiopian music. For some jazz players, those pentatonic modes were a siren call, like the allure of bossa nova four decades earlier.

In 2001, Francis noticed that the latest album by Boston's Either/Orchestra included three Ethiopian covers; he invited them to perform at his 2004 festival in Addis Ababa and they began backing Mahmoud Ahmed on tours. The French band Le Tigre des Platanes, Dutch group The Ex, and Switzerland's Imperial Tiger Orchestra joined the parade, coming to Ethiopia, collaborating with local musicians and singers, and helping spread the pentatonic gospel. All four bands come from a generation with jazz chops and rock attitudes (or vice versa) and are open to genre-hopping. Dengue Fever, another promising outfit, contributed a pentatonic track to *Broken Flowers* before being lured away into sixties Cambodian surf music. Hearing all these *ferenj* inspired (or shamed) some young Ethiopians into taking up Golden Age styles and repertoire, leading to a modest revival on home ground. Visitors wanting to hear the sort of music they know from their *Éthiopiques* listening have inspired a few Addis Ababa clubs to present live music with no drum machines.

∽

> I thought it was some kind of Cajun record played backwards. There's something great about hearing music that's so obviously passionate and so obviously good, and not being able to understand the words. I like to imagine this is what my records might sound like to someone in a country that doesn't speak English.
>
> —From Bob Dylan's notes to his 2008 Starbucks compilation, which included "Tezeta" by Getachew Kassa

Mahmoud Ahmed may have played Carnegie Hall, others including Alemayehu Eshete and Tilahoun Gessesse have traveled the globe, and Girma Beyene has finally been able to leave his gas pump, but the primary impact remains with the reissued original recordings. Inside the booklets, alongside witty narratives, compact biographies, and period photographs, all laid out with post-punk elan, are translated lyrics. The Amharic language gives no homophonous clues to meanings, so most listeners would otherwise have no clue about the songs' subject matter. Female beauty seems to be a favorite topic:

> *Your eyes are fascinating, your hips, your legs. Wow! . . . Your breasts are like mandarins. People who see you fall down dead.*
> *My stomach is trembling because I am remembering you.*
> *Her eyes wounded me . . . through her smile [her teeth] shattered me.*
> *My desire is overpowering, like a craving for coffee or qat.*

Such intense yearning is followed, naturally, by heartbreak:

> *I don't eat, I don't drink anymore . . . I don't even recognize my friends.*
> *I am torturing myself so much that I forget to exist.*
> *You are my sickness, because you are not with me . . . I snack on anything.*
> *I don't want anyone to speak to me about her anymore.*

While men were singing of hungry gazes and post-breakup suffering, the few women who recorded were often bolder in celebrating the carnal delights of the affair itself; the climax of Tigist Assefa's "Toutouyé" would make Betty Wright or Missy Elliott blush.

Falceto devotes the entire *Éthiopiques 10* to *tezeta*, which is at once a song, a scale, a form, and a word expressing mournful nostalgia. Many cultures—Portugal with *fado*, Bosnia and its *sevdah*, Albania's *saze*, and Greece with *rembetiko* to name a few—have plaintive styles that critics enjoy comparing to the blues. Tezeta might actually come the closest of all. Like blues, tezeta has a structure that invites singers to improvise and borrow, then goes one better by having its own scale. Mahmoud Ahmed is "Tezeta Negus" (King of Tezeta); his twelve-minute rendition on Vol. 10 is thrilling and chilling, fit to stand beside slow-tempo classics by B.B. King or Bobby "Blue" Bland, with Tewodros Meteku's sax assuming the answering role of the guitar. Equally remarkable is another version Ahmed recorded with the Imperial Bodyguard Band (Vol. 26); most Golden Era tracks feature the stripped-down line-ups heard in nightclubs and after-hours bars, but here, what sounds like the full ceremonial outfit evokes a New Orleans funeral march on its way to the cemetery, complete with swooning trombones.

The era's biggest-selling disc was the one Dylan chose, "Tezeta" by Getachew Kassa from 1972. Side A is played in a traditionally slow 6/8, with Kassa soulfully complaining that *"melancholy haunts my spirit constantly."* The flip side's acceleration to a galloping 4/4 caused a sensation, a symbol of the youthful rebellion then filling the streets of Addis Ababa with protests.

Much of the power of these recordings is attributable to the Armenian arrangers and bandleaders. Descendants of the Nalbandians and other members of the Armenian-Ethiopian musical community have spoken of how profoundly their feelings as exiles connected with the sadness expressed in tezetas. When the Derg's brutal clampdown began, longing came into its own as Ethiopians watched the Golden Age fade in the rearview mirror. The unmistakable notes of the minor tezeta scale signaled censor-proof defiance of a government that demanded everyone face forward into a glorious future that never arrived. Eighties lock-ins at hotel bars, when singers would improvise verse after tezeta verse until curfew's end at dawn, are still talked about in Addis Ababa.

> *Outdoing yesterday, shouldering on today*
> *Borrowing from tomorrow, renewing yesteryears,*
> *Comes tezeta, bearing burdens*
>
> —Mahmoud Ahmed, "Tezeta"

⌒

Hiding one meaning behind another is deeply embedded in Ethiopian culture, a tradition known as "wax and gold." The term is derived from the ancient "lost wax" method of creating jewelry and other artifacts, in which a shape is crafted from beeswax, then covered in clay; as the mold is baked, the wax melts away and molten gold is poured in to replace it. Waxen words inspire the listener's imagination to pour in the gold of their true meaning.

The post-Derg explosion of Addis's nightlife was dominated, at first, by discos. They were the obvious wave of the future, a symbol of the country's reconnection to the modern world. But then something curious happened; in backstreet shacks, sometimes in shadows cast by the Hilton and other tall, modern hotels, *azmari bets* flourished while disco after disco went bust. *Bet* means "house," an etymological connection linking Amharic to an ancient family of Middle Eastern languages, in which *lehem*, for example, signifies "bread," making the location of Christ's birth the "House of Bread." Azmaris were wanderers by nature, but the Derg abhorred such individualistic behavior; the few able to survive in the capital during those years based themselves in the humblest bars. Rulers have long been suspicious of these witty improvisers and conduits of news and gossip; the Italians shot many, while the Derg often sent them for "re-education." With azmaris now free to praise or insult customers regardless of rank (depending on the size of the tip) and to provide a running commentary on current events, *azmari bets* became, against all odds, among the modern city's most popular night-time destinations.

I was in Addis for Falceto's 2004 festival and spent some memorable evenings in *azmari bets*. I recall looking around a small, rectangular room, taking in the earthen, carpeted floor, the narrow benches along the walls and the small, low tables, the few bottles behind the bar at the far end, the azmari standing in the center with the large, crude-looking masenqo strapped to his chest, bowing a counterpoint to his improvised verses, a hand-drummer seated in the corner next to a pair of girls who could be "dashed" to dance or perhaps, I was told, negotiate other services. There were, I felt certain, archaeologists somewhere in Africa or the eastern Mediterranean at that moment, dusting off cup and ewer shards taken from the deeply buried foundations of a similarly shaped building and wondering what went on there three or four thousand years ago. "This," I thought, "is the sort of joint where Gilgamesh would have gone to drown his Sumerian sorrows."

Among the thinly scattered accomplishments of Derg rule was the imposition of (theoretical) sexual equality; female vocalists flourished during those years, from khaki-clad propagandists belting out songs encouraging rural workers, to new stars such as Aster Aweke. Launched in 1977 by Ali Tango, Aweke caught the ear of Iain Scott from UK label Triple Earth (thanks to a tip from—who else?—Lucy Durán). He recorded her in 1989 in Washington with Ethiopian musicians and persuaded the giant Columbia to release the album in the US (not that they did much to promote it, of course). Aweke has never managed to expand her audience much beyond Ethiopians home and away, but remains a stadium-filling superstar.

As a girl growing up in northern Ethiopia, Ejigayehu Shibabaw modeled herself on Aweke. In the nineties, she followed Aster to the US, where she took the stage name "Gigi" and made a reggae-inflected album with musicians from the DC diaspora. (Young Ethiopians were often fascinated when they discovered their country's mythological status in Jamaica and that, combined with Selassie's Rastafarian land grant, lured many into the one-drop.) Chris Blackwell heard it, signed Gigi to his Palm Pictures label, and teamed her up with producer Bill Laswell. She and two siblings were already committed to making a group album for the German label Network; the two recordings were produced back-to-back in 2001–2002 and make for an illuminating contrast.

The Palm album, *Guramayle*, is a pretty straight-up, Laswell-dominated jazz-fusion record; about the only Ethiopian things about it are Gigi's wonderful singing and the Amharic words. Released just as Francis's *Éthiopiques* series was building interest in the real thing, it (unsurprisingly) failed to make an impact. Network's album was billed as *Zion Roots* by "Abyssinia Infinite featuring Ejigayehu 'Gigi' Shibabaw." By the time production began, Gigi and Bill were a couple, so Laswell was locked in as producer. The two kept delivering masters and Network kept rejecting them, demanding removal of the electronics. They finally (and reluctantly) delivered a very good record that sold far better than the Palm CD and generated a European tour. Critics praised it, but reviews from the tour complained that Laswell was imposing his fusion aesthetic on the live shows, leaving audiences underwhelmed and Gigi's career unlaunched. Bill may be having the last laugh, however, as Spotify figures show *Guramayle* with far bigger streaming numbers now than *Zion Roots*.

Neither Aster nor Gigi can claim the title of "most successful Ethiopian female artist ever." That honor belongs to the late Yewubdar Guebrou, whose father (an advisor at the royal court) sent her off in 1929 at age six [*sic*] to a Swiss boarding school. She returned four years later with a passion for music and an obvious gift for the piano. After the war, she spent a few years in Cairo, studying with a former Vilnius classmate of Jascha Heifetz before fleeing Egypt's heat for the mountain air of home. The story became more complicated when she was offered a place at London's Royal Academy of Music and one of Selassie's sons offered to sponsor her. Amid rumors of a romance, Selassie stepped in to forbid the arrangement. With her dreams of a musical career crushed by imperial caprice, Yewubdar sank into a deep depression, ceasing to eat and becoming so weak that she was given the last rites. The brush with death brought her back to life and she vowed to devote herself to the Church, taking the name Emahoy Tsegue-Maryam Guebrou and spending the next ten years at a remote monastery in the northern highlands.

Returning to Addis Ababa, she began work in an orphanage and gave a fundraising concert attended by her many old friends from the court. The program surprised them; instead of the Chopin she had been known for, she performed her own compositions. The palace was impressed and (perhaps guiltily) funded two recording trips to Germany, with the resulting discs sold among the Addis elite for the benefit of the orphanage. Fluent in English, French, German, Italian, and Hebrew as well as Amharic and the ancient liturgical language Ge'ez, Emahoy became an invaluable aide to officials of the Ethiopian Orthodox Church, first in Addis Ababa and then in Jerusalem, where she lived from 1984 until her death in 2023. Music remained a sideline to her religious calling, but one she loved and was proud of.

"Do you know this record?" Falceto heard that fateful question once again in Paris in the early 2000s at the house of Ethiopian friends who owned a rare copy of an Emahoy charity disc. The simple beauty of the music set Francis off on another quest that led him to Jerusalem and the release in 2006 of *Éthiopiques 21: Piano Solo*. Over the next decade, her music invaded hipster enclaves from Brooklyn to Berlin and has been streamed millions of times; in terms of international exposure, no other Ethiopian artist comes close.

How can it be described? Somewhere between Erik Satie and the blues minimalist Jimmy Yancey perhaps, though Emahoy has always denied any American influence. (What we hear as "blue notes" are probably the result of setting pentatonic ecclesiastical and folkloric melodies over chords shaped by years of playing Chopin.) She provided Francis with notes describing the inspiration for each composition: *"the homeless wanderer plays on his flute"*; *"the wind goes around the world and has so many stories to tell "*; *"she experiences her tears as a relief from her sorrow"*; *"the [Jordan] river flowing relates the sad stories of its surrounding drama."* Emahoy delighted in her music's popularity and was very pleased with the income (which all goes to charity).

The *Éthiopiques* catalogue is dizzying in its breadth: singers, regions, periods, styles, labels, instruments. Would the music of any other country reward such a thorough investigation? For millennia, the heartland's high-altitude isolation shielded it from outside influence, allowing something rich and strange to grow relatively undisturbed. When fate threw Armenians into the mix followed by rhythm and blues and jazz, it was as if destiny was a bored kid getting lucky with a chemistry set.

⌒

Éthiopiques opened a floodgate; in the wake of the untimely demises of Franco, Fela, and vinyl (of which only the last would rise again from the grave), the series' success granted compilation producers—and their consumers—permission to accept that an era had ended, that they could stop wasting energy on new artists and focus on undiscovered gems from the past. Analog Africa, Awesome Tapes from Africa, and Retro Afric have mostly stuck to their designated continent, while Network, Soul Jazz, Dust-to-Digital, Soundway, Mr Bongo, and Honest Jon's are more ecumenical. Stern's and Earthworks had been plowing this furrow for years, of course, while the aesthetics and parameters of the compilation had been honed and expanded by the likes of Luaka Bop, Putamayo, and Riverboat's *Rough Guide* series (not to mention the high standards set by Ace Records with American rhythm and blues, the Bear Family with country music, and countless jazz reissue labels). Buda tried to catch lightning in a bottle a second time with its *Zanzibara* series, but despite the music being interesting and the cover art nicely echoing *Éthiopiques*, it generated little of the sales heat of its predecessor and only reached Vol. 9.

One resurrection that briefly flirted with the profile of Falceto's series (and with World Circuit's reissue and revival of Orchestra Baobab) was Luaka Bop's effort with William Onyeabor. Compilers seem to have found seventies Nigerian funk particularly fascinating, though I suspect obscurity, combined with the novelty of hearing Motown filtered through a kitsch (and, I might add, pentatonic) Igbo psychedelia, was responsible for the brief Onyeabor cult.

Post-independence African music promised and delivered much, but the new century has so far spawned few giants. Though international successes have been plentiful, ranging from Senegalese rappers to duets between kora maestros and Norwegian violinists, I'd be surprised if audio archaeologists fifty years from now spend much energy on "overlooked African classics 2000–2020." Our task here, though, is a historical one, not a buyers' guide; generalities can never compete with specifics, so we'll depart the continent in a flourish of dialectics.

∽

A line drawn northeast from the Bight of Bonny to what's left of Lake Chad forms a neat cultural, ethnological, linguistic, and musical boundary. From their original homes along that line, across the millennium from 500 BCE to 500 CE, the Bantu people spread out across central, eastern, and southern Africa, pushing the area's original inhabitants (including Baka "pygmies" and Xan "bushmen") deep into rainforests, deserts, and swamps.

To devise a formula for creating the biggest-selling record in African history, you would want to incorporate elements from either side of that line, Bantu and non-Bantu. No musicological pie charts or cultural diagrams were to hand, of course, when a bar band named Rocafil Jazz went into Decca's studios in Lagos in 1976 to record their new single. But the band's leader, Nico Mbarga, had a Nigerian mother and a Cameroonian father and had been working both sides of that divide for years, playing to crowds who, like him, enjoyed both the highlife on Nigerian radio and the rumba emanating from Brazzaville and Kinshasa.

The song they planned to record had been rejected as "too childish" by the head of EMI's branch office in Onitsha, the commercial hub of the border area in southeastern Nigeria. Mbarga had composed "Sweet Mother" as a paean to maternal love in general and to his own long-suffering single parent in particular. When a local independent producer named Rogers All Stars heard the song, he saw it as a welcome change from the usual agonizing over sex and romance. Mbarga and All Stars worked on the song with the band for months, trying different feels, slowing down the tempo and adjusting lyrics while always keeping Nico's Congo-style guitar chiming away over a highlife beat.

"Sweet Mother" might have sunk without trace if it weren't for Benson Idonije. In those balmy radio days, disc jockeys could play whatever they fancied, and when Idonije heard this ten-minute-long track in a bar, he made a note of the title and looked it up in the NBC library. Months after the record's release, he became the first to ever sign it out; when he played it, phone calls and letters poured in. "Sweet Mother" ended up selling over thirteen million copies across former French, British, Portuguese, and American (meaning Liberia) colonies; Rocafil Jazz toured the continent in its wake, from Dakar to Maputo. In 2017, when the BBC's Africa Service polled listeners to choose the continent's all-time greatest record, "Sweet Mother" won in a landslide.

"Prince" Nico and Rocafil Jazz never made it to London or Paris, and "Sweet Mother" didn't sell much *outside* the continent. The winner in that category sold hardly any copies *inside* Africa. But it was also conceived and recorded along the same dividing line as "Sweet Mother" and its path to glory was just as unlikely.

Manu Dibango had a tortured relationship with Africa. He revered his Cameroonian heritage and wanted to "give back" to the culture into which he was born, but when he tried working there, or in the Congo or the Ivory Coast, he found himself battling jealousies and corruption; fellow musicians and cultural bureaucrats seemed to resent his suave French ways, his blond Belgian wife, and his sophisticated skills. He did enjoy occasional breakthroughs, such as in 1972, when he persuaded the minister for sport to give him four thousand dollars to record a theme tune for the African football championship being held that year in Cameroon. Everyone was happy enough with the song and it got plenty of play in the stadiums and on local radio, but when people turned it over and played the B side, heads were scratched—*what the hell is that?* He'd had the idea while fooling around during rehearsals, coming up with an instrumental track that mixed elements of American funk with what he had to admit was a pretty superficial take on a favorite local rhythm. "Poor *makossa* really took a blow," Manu said afterwards.

Six months later, while finishing an album in Paris, he pondered including that B side. So what if everyone hated it? He owned the tape and he liked it; how bad could it be if he slipped "Soul Makossa" onto the new album? No one complained and few even noticed. But a Brooklyn DJ bought the album in an Atlantic Avenue shop specializing in African and Caribbean imports and started spinning that track at parties. Other New York jocks picked up on it, and when Aristotle Onassis danced to it at a swank Manhattan disco, he demanded to hear it again. And again. And again.

No one else has ever lived a life remotely like the late Ahmet Ertegun's. As the son of Turkey's ambassador to Washington in the 1930s, he grew up entranced by African-American music and, after the war, helped found Atlantic, one of America's greatest-ever labels. I ran into him at a club in London one night in 1970, when he was in town negotiating US rights to the Eric Clapton–Steve Winwood supergroup, Blind Faith. The previous evening, he and his wife, Mica, a Romanian aristocrat, had been high-table guests of President Pompidou at a state banquet in Paris; the next morning, he told me, he would fly to Cleveland, Ohio, with a bag of cash for an influential rhythm and blues DJ who was refusing to play the new Aretha Franklin single unless he got his bribe straight from Ahmet's own hand. If there was anyone whose ear to the ground would hear that a moneyed crowd on the Upper East Side and some street-party animals in Bed-Stuy were all mad for a track called "Soul Makossa," it would have been Ahmet. He licensed Dibango's album for North America and turned the Atlantic promotion team loose. Frankie Crocker (New York's top Black radio DJ, who, a few years later, wouldn't play Bob Marley) jumped on it, and the next thing Dibango knew, he was putting a band together to open for The Temptations at the Apollo Theater. Manu was scared to death, but survived with honors. (All those afros and dashikis on 125th Street in 1973, though, didn't stop Harlemites quizzing him about elephants and hippos in his backyard in Cameroon.)

Some say Dibango's Louis Armstrong–inspired scatting at the start of the record is a key moment in the genesis of rap. It has also been suggested that the "Soul Makossa" beat points the way to disco. Michael Jackson sampled it, as, much later, did Rihanna. Kool and the Gang went into the studio intending to cover it, but changed enough notes to call it "Jungle Boogie" and claim the publishing income. "Soul

Makossa" remained ubiquitous on American and European dancefloors through the seventies (though never in Africa) and was covered again and again, the only slice of African vinyl to ever truly connect with an African-American audience.

∽

In 1989, New York's pioneering Dance Theater Workshop embarked on something adventurous even for them: they organized a tour of North America by two of Africa's greatest bands. The groups came from opposite sides of the "Bantu line"; one was francophone, one anglophone; one had developed with government support and encouragement, the other emerged from a laissez-faire world of dance halls and bars. One comprised devout Muslims who were shocked by how American girls dressed, while the other practiced a mixture of traditional religion and Christianity, passed spliffs and beers around the dressing room, and welcomed groupies. Both were symbols of their respective cultures' efforts to reconcile modernity and tradition.

Bembeya Jazz National were the paramount example of Fodéba Keïta's vision for Guinean culture. Keïta (who was credited, you may recall, with inspiring Ali Farka Touré to pick up the guitar) came from a classic French colonial background. Having followed Léopold Senghor from an elite school in Dakar to the post-war Left Bank, where he performed his songs and read his poetry, Keïta created the Ballets Africains to showcase traditional music and dance. The company toured widely in the fifties, culminating in a two-month Broadway run in 1959. I saw them in London in 1964 and remember being knocked out, particularly by their guitarist, whose playing reminded me of Mississippi John Hurt's. The French colonial office viewed Keïta as a dangerous pro-independence radical and did their best to make his life difficult.

That Guineans would reject de Gaulle's "Greater France" vision should have come as no surprise. Ever since the Fulani arrived in the area in the eighteenth century and converted most of the population to Islam, Guineans had never shown the slightest interest in being part of a francophone Christian world. In the late nineteenth century, the northeast of the country was the stronghold of Samori, the greatest

African military leader since Shaka. (Some historians believe Samori would have defeated the French had he been able to persuade his troops to aim down the sights of their rifle barrels instead of shooting from the hip.) When the result of the 1958 plebiscite was announced, the French bolted for the exit, stripping Guinea of everything from turbine generators to light bulbs and leaving the country in near total darkness. Sékou Touré, who had led the anti-French campaign (and who claimed descent from Samori), assumed leadership of the suddenly independent country. His friend Fodéba "donated" the Ballets Africains to his homeland and returned to Conakry to lead the most ambitious program of cultural *authenticité* in all of Africa.

Every district in the large and varied country held annual musical competitions, with winning ensembles traveling to the capital for the finals. Bembeya Jazz began as an acoustic group from a remote area near the border with Côte d'Ivoire but were soon acclaimed as the country's best and granted the "National" suffix. (Africans seem to have enjoyed the mouth-feel of the word *jazz* as much as people from the Americas relished saying "rumba" or "tango.") By 1963, the group's young guitarist, Sékou Diabaté, had plugged in a Stratocaster and they had added a traditional wood carver named Demba Camara, who was soon hailed as the country's greatest singer. Their style was characteristic of West Africa at the time: local tradition adapted to a Cuban template, enhanced in Bembeya's case by an eight-week stay in Havana as guests of Fidel.

Government support and fierce competition produced results; Guinean bands were tight, inventive, in tune, and emulated across West Africa. But there were shadows, the biggest cast by President Touré. His vision for the country was passionate but blinkered; he abhorred "foreign" dances with a passion equal to his hatred of "fetishistic" traditional beliefs. Guinea, he believed, must turn away from Europe and cherish its heritage while shedding its superstitions and backwardness. Keïta's choreography fit the vision: traditional dances divorced from the ancestral spirits that inspired them.

One Bembeya recording epitomized the aesthetic: *Regard sur le passé*, a fifty-minute single-track album in which Camara delivers an era-defining performance, extolling the exploits of Samori while linking

Touré to the great man. Camara's mixture of speech and song and the band's leisurely jali rhythms meant the record was never going to open doors in Europe or America, but it had a huge influence across West Africa.

By 1989, when Bembeya arrived in America, three key figures in their story were gone. Mourners had turned out en masse across West Africa when Demba Camara perished in a 1976 car crash. Fodéba Keïta met a more sinister end; the acclaim he and Guinean music received (in contrast to the country's disastrous economic performance) made Touré jealous. Accused of plotting against his old friend, Keïta was executed in 1969, during a period in Guinean politics comparable to the Stalin-era show trials of the late thirties. Touré himself expired in 1984 while being treated in a Cleveland, Ohio, hospital, deep in the heart of the imperialist, capitalist enemy.

Bembeya was still a great band in 1989, but somewhat adrift. Touré's death brought about the collapse of the state record label, Syliphone (*syli* means "elephant," a reference to the president's nickname "the big elephant"), and the group was struggling to navigate a new free-market, pirate-rampant world. Their star was now Sékou Diabaté, who'd gained the nickname "Diamond Fingers," a flashy player with the skills to join Docteur Nico, Franco, Barthélémy Attisso, and Djelimady Tounkara in our pantheon of African guitar heroes. Not long after the end of the US tour, though, the band called it a day.

Sharing the bill with Bembeya was the Zimbabwean group Blacks Unlimited, led by Thomas Mapfumo. When Mapfumo started out as a teenager in the sixties, the idea of drawing inspiration from the traditional music of his Shona heritage would have seemed ludicrous. Groups in what was then Southern Rhodesia mimicked American soul or Congolese rumba; Mapfumo was of the former school and excelled at channeling Otis Redding.

While Guinea in the sixties had virtually no White people, Southern Rhodesia was full of them and they were in charge. The country had been founded in the late nineteenth century by Cecil Rhodes with an invasion that resembled the "settling" of the American West. Expecting to find riches to match the gold and diamonds Rhodes was mining in South Africa, the interlopers soon realized that the fertile topsoil was worth a lot more than the mostly barren rocks beneath. After killing or evicting thousands of Shona and Ndebele "natives," they forced the survivors to work on their farms. As for culture, the plan was to remake the inhabitants into a diminished, Christianized version of Englishmen; anything smacking of traditional religion was dismissed as pagan "mumbo-jumbo."

Colonial administrators never paid much attention to "tribal" music, though in some districts churchmen were able to persuade local authorities to ban the *mbira*, an instrument missionaries recognized as their enemy. The mbira is the Shona lamellophone; it's larger and more complex than the equivalent in most African cultures, with as many as thirty-two metal "tongues" or "keys" organized in layers along a seven-tone scale that approximates the Mixolydian mode. It is mounted inside the shell of a calabash, which takes the edge off the sound while also amplifying it, with the added virtue of hiding players' nimble thumbs from the gaze of rivals. The mbira is central to Shona spiritual practice; its heady, circular patterns can lead adherents into a state of trance in which they are visited by the spirits of their ancestors.

When the mbira wasn't getting banned, it was being tamed; folklorist Hugh Tracey's son Andrew was fascinated by it, took lessons from a master player, and showed off his dexterity in *Wait a Minim!*, a "folk revue" that had a good run on Broadway a few years after Ballets Africains. Father and son went into business manufacturing mbiras, which they renamed *kalimbas* and marketed as a fun way for children to learn about African music.

Growing up in the Mbare township outside Salisbury, Mapfumo knew that sound well. Most sacred sites had been destroyed by the settlers, but rituals had migrated to backyards in the shantytowns. The Traceys were alarmed by what they saw as the "disappearance" of Shona traditional music in the face of jazz, rock 'n' roll, and soukous, but they can't have spent much time in the vast townships around Salisbury and Bulawayo or they would have found days-long *bira* ceremonies alive and well (though hardly easy for outsiders to penetrate). These often involved trance possession, which resembled being "ridden" by the spirit at *macumba* ceremonies in Brazil or in African-American Holiness churches.

In 1972, the news that Jimi Hendrix had died shocked and depressed Mapfumo, adding to a general malaise caused by years of playing rock 'n' roll and rhythm and blues covers to drunken crowds. Much of the next year was spent at a mining camp far from the capital, with little to do all day but rehearse; one afternoon, when the group's guitarist picked out the unmistakable triplets of an mbira pattern, the others locked into the groove with ease. That night they played a traditional song, "Ngoma yarira" (The Drums Are Sounding), that way and the miners went crazy. It became their first hit single. Mapfumo's wasn't the only band to make use of mbira patterns but he would take it further and deeper than anyone else. As his biographer, Banning Eyre, put it in *Lion Songs*: "Thomas and his coterie of musicians have succeeded in commingling a world of beer halls, rock 'n' roll bands, journalists, poets, and politicians with the more shrouded realm of bira ceremonies, spirit mediums and ancestors."

We have seen how the interlocking patterns of lamellophones can inform how guitarists in Congolese and other styles play off each other, but this was different. Jonah Sithole, the most creative of Mapfumo's guitarists, developed a way of replicating mbira sequences directly onto an electric guitar and integrating those patterns into the sound of a powerful band. Like so many others around the globe, over the course of the seventies, Thomas went from being inspired by Hendrix to following Marley, digging into his own roots, reducing his aesthetic dependence on Anglo-American music, and developing a political awareness. He also grew dreadlocks.

When Rhodesia's White rulers unilaterally declared their independence from Britain, the war of liberation began. Under the leadership of Robert Mugabe, the revolutionary ZANU party paid as little attention to music as did the Whites; for soldiers in the bush, though, it was a lifeline. As the struggle became more intense, Mapfumo released a series of "Chimurenga" singles, a reference to the Shona rebel leader

Murenga Sororenzou and his valiant but failed resistance against Rhodes's invasion in the last years of the nineteenth century. The tracks were broadcast from Mozambique by rebel pirate radio and many were also playlisted by the state-run RBC, which had no clue that resistance fighters found the songs inspiring. The lyrics seemed innocuous, and when, very late in the day, government censors tried to figure them out, they encountered double meanings, obscure imagery, ancient forms, and mystical references in what Mapfumo calls "deep Shona."

What the government failed to grasp was that subversion was woven into the music itself. With his voice's dark undertones and the intricate, mbira-like backing from bass and guitars, Mapfumo was bringing the spirit of bira, of timeless Shona culture, proudly to the surface. For nearly a century, people had been told their religious practices were infantile and pointless (in contrast to the perfectly rational Christian ancestor worship and disputes about the nature of the Trinity, of course); the sound of Blacks Unlimited contradicted that message and inspired fighters risking their lives far from home.

Robert Mugabe may have begun with good intentions but it didn't take long after victory for him to turn as paranoid and controlling as Sékou Touré. Mapfumo moved from being an avid supporter who performed at government rallies to becoming one of the few calling out high-level corruption and incompetence. In 1988, a year before arriving in the US, he released "Corruption," a single that pointed a finger straight at ZANU; party leaders, who had long celebrated Thomas as "one of them," didn't know how to react.

Mapfumo was too popular to be "disappeared" (as other dissidents often were), but he was harassed and threatened and his life in Zimbabwe became progressively less comfortable. Fortunately, Thomas's dreadlocks, the miasma of marijuana smoke emanating from the stage, and the deep groove of his music forged a connection with a North American fan base of world music enthusiasts, reggae buffs, and stoners. On future tours, he would integrate amplified mbiras into the band, giving it a unique sound. They played America again and again; when Mugabe's thugs began threatening his family, Mapfumo moved with his wife and kids to Eugene, Oregon.

Mugabe is gone, but Zimbabwe's economy and politics have barely improved. In twenty-first-century Guinea, the top bands are mostly acoustic, which is convenient, given that electrical power there is still, six decades after independence, intermittent. These two countries bookended the various ways of dealing with tradition and culture in African colonialism's wake. In nation after nation, regardless of cultural policy or lack thereof, music triumphed, which is one of the few commodities about which that can be said. Musicians able to connect with ancient spiritual forces could never sleep easily, though; such powers unnerve dictators, particularly when they can't keep the lights on.

> Viewed one-dimensionally, [the guitar's] introduction might seem a marker of Western musical imperialism, but the guitar's true history in Africa has been a prismatic, syncretic dialogue between Western popular music and indigenous musical traditions. In its electrified form, the guitar would acquire as many subtle shadings during the early decades of African popular music as it had during the birth of rock and roll: postwar Africa was a constellation of guitar dialects carved out of the raw fusion of melody, rhythm, tone, and electricity.
>
> —Michael E. Veal, *Punk Ethnography*

The Mauritanian, Kevin Macdonald's film about the fourteen-year Guantanamo imprisonment (and eventual exoneration) of Mohamedou Ould Slahi, opens at a marriage celebration in Mauretania's capital, Nouakchott. The wedding singer is the country's best known, Noura Mint Seymali, accompanied by her husband, Jeiche Ould Chighaly, a legend among local guitarists. I was looking forward to the film for a number of reasons, not least because the attorney who smuggled out Slahi's prison diary (written on toilet paper), found a publisher for it and eventually secured his release is my brother Warwick's law partner Nancy Hollander (played by Jodi Foster). Another reason was that I'd heard that it included a live scene of Nouakchott guitar.

Matthew Lavoie, a reporter based in Dakar, had gone to a concert one evening in 1996 to hear Toumani Diabaté's dad, Sidiki. Sidiki was as great as anticipated, but for Lavoie the evening belonged to the opening act from Mauretania, the desert land to the north across the Senegal River. "Their forty-five-minute set remains the most stunning musical experience of my life. The dialogue between the female singer's voice and her young accompanist's electric guitar playing had an immediate physical effect on me. I sat slack-jawed, with tears of ecstasy running down my cheeks." Ignoring warnings from his Senegalese friends, Lavoie paid a visit to Nouakchott; on his first night there he sneaked into a wedding party, becoming the only male besides the musicians to witness the bride and her friends dancing and ululating to music even more exciting than he had hoped. Over the years, he kept going back, inveigling his way into the local music scene, learning the history and context of the manic energy generated by guitarists such as Chighaly.

He tried recording a few of them at a radio station, but found it impossible to capture the intensity of a live show. Lavoie eventually culled a compilation entitled *Wallahi Le Zein!!* from his collection of 700 wedding-party cassettes dubbed to order at storefronts known as *standards*, a royalty-free business model that flourished across the developing world during the quarter-century heyday of the cassette. The CD booklet includes vivid notes giving the backstories of the artists and chronicling the evolution of the music out of local griots' playing of the *tidinitt*, an ngoni-like lute, via Moroccan *gnawa*, Tuareg desert blues, Malian jalis, Wolof mbalax, and flanged rock guitar.

Hearing the avalanche of notes generated by a Nouakchott guitar hero for the first time can be dizzying, but for me the sound called to mind a couple of tracks Andy Kershaw played on his BBC show in 1997. I was so stunned by Jean-Noël's machine-gun style that I paid a singer I knew in his capital city to go and check him out. (This was back when ¡Cubanismo! and Muzsikás were selling well and, thanks to the Frank Zappa catalogue and rock bands Sugar and Morphine, Rykodisc could afford speculative scouting trips.) Jean-Noël is from Tulear near the southern tip of Madagascar, just about the farthest point in Africa from Nouakchott; he played a style known as *tsapiky* that grew out of the ritual music of the island's arid southwest that is performed during marriage and circumcision ceremonies, or when shrouded cadavers are periodically dug up and danced with, a tradition imported centuries ago by seaborne migrants from the Malay Archipelago. I knew Hanitrarivo Rasoanaivo from her time with the group Tarika that toured Europe and America in the nineties; bus journeys to the southwest coast from Antananarivo, she said, were long and arduous, but she was willing to fly to Tulear.

Hanitra rang me when she landed back in the capital; she'd gone straight from the airport to the neighborhood where musicians lived, locating Jean-Noël's bungalow around midday and finding it filled with sleeping bodies. A woman roused herself and said that Jean-Noël was "out of town for a gig." Detective work at a local bar revealed that he was performing that night at an illegal sapphire mine deep in the bush. She hired a driver with a four-by-four, followed directions down miles of single-track dirt road, turned onto an unmarked side road, talked her way past guards wielding AK-47s, and eventually, as the sun was setting, arrived at a vast pit surrounded by tin-roofed buildings beside a landing strip with a couple of unmarked planes. A makeshift stage faced a buzzing crowd of miners, guards, and prostitutes. The show was wild, she said, with roars of approval for guitar solos and shouts for Jean-Noël's sexy pair of girl singers. During a break, she was able to tell him that a cassette of his (which was barely available outside the southern region of the island) had been played on the BBC.

There's no romantic punch line to the story. Rykodisc began its slow-motion implosion and I was in no position to fly to Madagascar with an engineer and an envelope full of cash as I had to Havana a few years earlier. By the time of Lavoie's and Hanitra's journeys, Nouakchott wedding music and tsapiky were already fading, outmuscled by the computer, with tsapiky being further curbed by gangs of cattle rustlers who made it dangerous to move around the region. Jeiche Ould Chighaly, Jean-Noël, and their many compatriot guitar heroes remain evanescent footnotes in African music history, five thousand miles apart in places few outsiders ever visit and with virtually no distribution for their music.

Wallahi Le Zein!! was preceded by Stern's 2003 *Tulear Never Sleeps* compilation, so investigation by the curious can be rewarded. I have generally given short shrift to easy generalizations about this vast and varied continent, but much in Veal's quote rings true: an electric guitar in the hands of an African virtuoso has an ability to evoke ancient instruments and styles, keeping tradition alive and bringing it up to date. For a while, anyway.

It also shows how modern media shrunk the globe; Jimi Hendrix and Bob Marley were idols and exemplars in both Mauretania and Madagascar. And if you cock an ear to tsapiky's chord progressions, you may recognize something familiar—the sound of mbaqanga flying through the airwaves across the Mozambique Channel from South Africa. Jean-Noël and Paul Simon, musicians at opposite ends of the financial hierarchy, both found inspiration in that Zulu drive. Which brings us back to where we began.

IX

How we begin to remember

Guillaume Apollinaire was rarely bored. His friends couldn't figure out where he found the time to see so many exhibitions, take so many drugs, read so many books, chase so many women, write so many articles, and explore so many obscure Paris neighborhoods. No one ever suggested he was a great poet or painter, but he had a nose for ideas and people; history confirms that most of those he embraced and promoted in his short life were among the era's most important.

Walking with Pablo Picasso one day in 1907 down one of those Paris backstreets, they passed a junk shop with some African carvings in the window. It's unclear if this was by accident or design, but African art was certainly one of Apollinaire's latest enthusiasms. They stopped to look at the figures. Picasso was fascinated; he'd never shared the Parisian art world's enthusiasm for exoticism, but something about those pieces struck a chord. A few days later, Guillaume took Pablo to the Ethnographic Museum in the Trocadéro to view its collection of African masks. This is the famous encounter that altered the course of Western culture: the inspired painter began working on *Les Demoiselles d'Avignon*, a canvas generally considered to be the starting pistol for modernism in painting. Eighteen years earlier, Claude Debussy had stood in that same building listening to a Javanese gamelan ensemble, a moment cited as one of musical modernism's many beginnings. The experience altered Debussy's ideas about scales, harmonies, and rhythms, leading to music that caught the ear of Igor Stravinsky in Russia and Béla Bartók in Hungary, luring them towards a modernism as radical and tradition-inspired as Picasso's. The Trocadéro was the place for epiphanies. Perched on a hill across the Seine from the Eiffel Tower, it was a Byzantine structure originally built for the 1878 Exposition Universelle, then torn down in 1935 to make way for the Mussolini-modern Palais de Chaillot. The 1878 Expo was one of those "giant new rituals of self-congratulation" encountered in the first chapter, where Europeans and North Americans celebrated the triumphs of the Industrial Revolution and exhibited "natives" as if they were animals in a zoo. Nineteenth-century Europe had conflicted notions about traditional cultures. While politicians, generals, and financiers used Darwin's theory of evolution to justify conquering and exploiting African and Asian societies that lacked the modern weaponry to resist, many poets and philosophers believed Western culture had reached a dead end and needed invigorating by the "primitive." Johann Herder had started it with his theory that the soul of a people lay in the music and stories of the peasantry, Goethe added his admiration for the freedom of the "gypsy" life, and Baudelaire suggested that uncorrupted sources would aid the "wilful recovery of childhood wonder." Observers of the crowds at those world's fairs described a wistfulness, a feeling that the mocked-up rustic villages represented something the rapidly industrializing West had lost. Such notions infuriated Charles Dickens; his anti-Zulu rant insisted that the quicker everyone was propelled into the Victorian notion of progress, the better, that industrialized societies had absolutely nothing to learn from less "developed" ones.

As cultural elites pondered and debated these ideas, millions of blissfully unaware young Europeans were putting them into practice on the dancefloor. Couples had been voting with their feet for "roots" music since the turn of the century, when they borrowed the waltz from Tyrolean peasants. They looked east for the mazurka and the polka before seizing on the Africa-derived dance beats arriving from America: the Cakewalk, the Turkey Trot, and the Grizzly Bear. In the new century, as critics and the more adventurous bourgeoisie were trying to get used to modernism in galleries and concert halls (and being shocked half out of their wits by *The Rite of Spring*), everyone, starting with the Parisians, went crazy for the tango.

When a Zulu troupe performed in the French capital in 1878, it wasn't in a sober recital hall like their predecessors in London but at the Folies Bergère, where they were followed a few years later by an Ashanti outfit from the Ivory Coast. Among French audiences and intellectuals there was always tension between a craving for the "exotic" and the straightforward appreciation of musical or artistic brilliance. Apollinaire tried to persuade the Ethnographic Museum to let him reconfigure their African displays based on beauty and aesthetic appeal rather than as anthropological specimens, and described an iron sculpture from Dahomey as "the most unexpected and graceful object of art to be found in Paris."

When colonial officials failed to keep Brazza's report on inhuman practices in French Africa hidden, the furor it caused brought an outpouring of sympathy for the peoples of France's new empire as well as an increased interest in Black culture in general. Jack Johnson's victory over Jim Jeffries in the 1910 world championship boxing match caused rioting across the US by outraged Whites, but was celebrated in France. Johnson became one of many Black figures who caught the imagination of the French public during the decades bracketed by those malign bookends, the Dreyfus affair and the German occupation. The most illustrious was Josephine Baker, but as beloved as she became, the French could never quite decide if they adored her for her charm, intelligence, Francophilia, and sophisticated performing skills or for her banana-skirted "primitivism."

Things were different across the Channel. After the Zulus left town, the British public showed little interest in unfamiliar music; despite having such a vast and varied empire, the closest popular culture came to falling for something foreign was Gilbert and Sullivan's *Mikado*. As the French embraced jazz, tango, samba, and "rhumba," the British Musicians' Union made it impossible for Argentine, Brazilian, Cuban, or US bands to tour. We have seen how the London public turned up their noses at Uday Shankar's troupe and how struggling tango dancers were forced to admit that they were simply too British for it.

Parisians recognized that musical modernity was being defined by African rhythms; anything else was starting to sound old-fashioned. Tango, *son*, and samba had to overcome racism and snobbery on home ground before setting off to win hearts and feet in Europe, but African-American music went through an even more intense and bizarre struggle before arriving in the French capital. It is difficult to look back objectively at minstrel shows or at the *bufo* blackface of the Hispanic world, but both tell an important story of White fascination with Black music. Post–Civil War American audiences were hungry for it but weren't ready to take it straight; it had to be drip-fed in the guise of a racist clown show. Like Moiseyev's jazz and rock 'n' roll parodies, minstrel and bufo shows opened a trap door to the real thing; behind the emotional shield of burnt cork and ridicule, there was a lot going on, both on the stage and in the audience. In *Doo-dah!*, Ken Emerson's biography of composer Stephen Foster, he quotes from a White performer's diary which describes being "swept away by a liberating rapture" when he appeared on stage in blackface for the first time. In that moment, Emerson suggests, lies a central drama of the West's popular music. He draws a line directly from there to the exuberance of White rockers a century later, transfigured by their immersion in Black rhythms.

Minstrel shows were finally put out of their misery by Black entertainers corking up and joining the circuit; that may sound ridiculous, but the practice of African-American performers applying black makeup along with exaggerated lips and eyes was widespread in the US during the last decades of the nineteenth century. These thick-skinned pioneers eventually gained the upper hand, imitating themselves better than any Whites could (and subtly taking the piss out of White performers while they were at it). Black artists singing "coon songs" to a ragtime beat were among the biggest draws of the 1890s; they steadily diluted the form's lurid racism until Black performers were established as a foundational element of the US entertainment industry. In music halls and vaudeville theaters across the country, they showed Whites much more than just the right way to do the buck-and-wing and the Cakewalk; they made comedy more sophisticated, transformed the energy of vaudeville, and, along the way, modernized American popular music.

∽

When louder, more vivid electrical recordings and cheaper, better Victrolas arrived in the late twenties, it changed how people experienced music. Most audiences had previously encountered sounds from other cultures only when performers themselves appeared: Roma wagons setting up camp outside town, slaves parading through colonial streets on saints' days, Joseph Kekuku's Hawaiian troupe touring the American heartland as a vaudeville act, visiting performers at one of those Universal Expositions or the Harlem Hellfighters' marching band introducing Europeans to the brilliance of African-American musicianship during World War One. Musical excitement was suddenly flying around the globe in the grooves of 78 rpm discs: Louis Armstrong's trumpet and Jimmie Rodgers's yodels were heard loud and clear across oceans and continents, Cuban discs set off the Congo's rumba explosion, Carlos Gardel was lifted to his Franco-Latin pedestal, Trinidadian calypsos delighted anglophone Africa, and Carmen Miranda, Bing Crosby, and Marlene Dietrich began their journeys to international stardom . . .

Technology in the service of music did more than just spread the sounds. Michael Denning makes the case, in his book *Noise Uprising*, that recordings of the music evolving in the commercial hubs of colonial empires—Accra, Saigon, Calcutta, Kinshasa, Port-of-Spain, Fort-de-France, Lagos—transformed how colonized peoples perceived themselves. The simple act of hearing their own music coming from the same grooves as the Americans and Cubans boosted their self-awareness and confidence and inspired their demands for independence.

Allied victory in World War Two cleared the way for a vision of modernity defined by American prosperity: appliances, advertising, chewing gum, Technicolor, suburbs, chrome fins on cars . . . but not music, at least not immediately. Big-band jazz had been the war's soundtrack, but few orchestras survived into peacetime and swing's successor, bebop, was regarded with suspicion both at home and abroad. Music is like weather; low-pressure zones invite new fronts to move in, and the dancefloor wind blowing into many cities, the new world capital New York in particular, was Afro-Cuban. When the Yanks finally came up with a world-beating sound in the mid-1950s, it was seen as a true American melting pot. On the surface, rock 'n' roll was a Black and White checkerboard; but it also included sizable helpings of sentimental Italian melody and Yiddish wit, while much of its power lay in the habanera syncopation absorbed through New Orleans.

Rock 'n' roll gave the world the electric guitar, a vehicle that transformed popular music as dramatically as electrical recording had extended its reach. It was loud, it was phallic, it was rhythmically adaptable, its sustained tones could evoke the human voice, you could play it in any key or scale, and its strings could be bent to seek out sub-Saharan notes between the frets. From the late fifties through the mid-seventies, it invaded every corner of the globe. Guitarists acted as funnels, blending rhythms, scales, chords, riffs, and techniques borrowed from Hawaii, Cuba, Mississippi, Andalusia, Nashville, Calcutta, Buenos Aires, Chicago, and La Zone into a sound that exuded youth, virtuosity, rebellion, modernity, and freedom all in one. The instrument's dominance created a high-pressure field that, for a quarter of a century, limited the number of new musical winds blowing into Europe or North America. But towards the back end of the seventies, with punk and disco having dug a sufficiently deep creative trough, something was bound to arrive from over the horizon.

Friedrich Nietzsche's contribution to those nineteenth-century debates about culture included an essay called *The Birth of Tragedy out of the Spirit of Music*, in which he describes the human psyche as divided between Apollonian and Dionysian impulses. Plato's and Socrates's favorite instrument was the gentle lyre, bestowed on the Greeks by the god Apollo for accompanying poetry. They both hated the *aulos*, the forked pipe you see youths blowing on the sides of Greek pottery in museums, which, with its drone and melody barrels, sounded like a bagpipe. *Aulete* were the rock stars of ancient Greece; they wore leather head-straps to keep the instrument in place during wild, days-long Dionysian revelries and were accused of "leading women astray." The two philosophers worried that these raves would have a destabilizing effect on society, but Nietzsche thought the Greeks had achieved an ideal balance between Apollo and Dionysus, the lyre and the aulos, order and chaos, or, as Freud put it, between the super ego and the id. Dionysus had lost a lot of ground over the long centuries of dominance by those killjoy religions Christianity and Islam, and the rhythmic revolutions I've described had only clawed some of it back. But if there was ever a year in which the god of excess was clearly surging forward, it was 1967. And if there was anywhere on earth where the sort of music and ritual that so disturbed the two philosophers could still be found, it was up in the foothills of Morocco's Rif Mountains, just south of Tangier.

The village of Joujouka is home to the Attars, a clan who trace their origins back to Damascus before the time of Mohammed. Chased away by music-hating mullahs, they followed Ziryab the Blackbird to Cordoba, where generations of Attars performed for the sultans until 1492, when the *reconquista* sent them fleeing across the Gates of Hercules to northern Morocco. The group play drums, flutes, and *rhaitas*, double-reed pipes that sound like those ancient *auloi*, with as many as thirty blowing at once. They also smoke a lot of *kif*. Their most important celebration is an eight-night-long fertility rite that starts on the last day of Ramadan each year, a syncretic sleight-of-hand worthy of the orishas who masquerade as Catholic saints in Brazil and Cuba. A boy wearing the still-warm skin of a slaughtered goat dances the Pan-like figure of Boujeloud into life, chastising women with a branch from an ageless tree that is said to make the barren fruitful. Over relentless pounding from the drums, the pipers improvise drone-based, trance-inducing patterns, employing a circular breathing technique as old as ancient Greece. Not only is Joujouka the closest we will come to knowing what a days-long party sounded like in Athens in the fifth century bce, the Boujeloud ceremony and the Attars' drumming are precisely the kind of thing the Pope demanded that the Visigoths chase out of Spanish Christendom.

An expat painter named Brion Gysin had been living in Tangier since 1951 and often took visitors up into the hills to experience Boujeloud. One recent guest had been the high priest of Dionysian ecstasy,

Timothy Leary. Next up would be the Rolling Stones' tragic Orpheus, Brian Jones. You'd have thought Brian would never want to see Morocco again after Anita Pallenberg broke his heart in Marrakech by running off with Keith Richards. But Brian was a true music hound and he'd been intrigued by what he heard during that ill-fated 1966 trip; he returned a year later with a sound engineer and a new girlfriend who looked a lot like Anita. The three headed for Tangier to meet Gysin, who'd promised to take them up to Joujouka.

The Attars were very welcoming to visitors. This is partly down to the all-embracing spirit of Sufism, but also to the fact that their support system had crumbled. For centuries, annual gifts from a sheik and tithing by local farmers had allowed them to do nothing but play music and get high. The end of the French occupation in 1956 had cut the legs out from under that; not only did the new nation strip back feudal practices, but the country's rulers and most of its citizens aspired to modernity, and if there was anything that was the opposite of shiny 1950s modernity, it was the Master Musicians of Joujouka. Gysin raised money to help keep traditions and players alive, but his resources were limited. The arrival of a pop star with a tape recorder opened up new possibilities.

Jones's timing wasn't ideal; he'd missed the big feasts, so Gysin organized a skeleton group to gather around Brian and the engineer for an afternoon and then spent two weeks with him back in Tangier going through the tapes. It was Gysin who had invented the "cut-up" technique for random juxtaposition of text and sound, so it's unsurprising that when Jones went into a London studio, he felt free to mess around with the tapes, making arbitrary joins, running some tracks backwards (which he thought sounded much the same as forwards), and having fun with the latest studio gadget, the phaser. Soon after the record was finished, Brian was kicked out of the Stones. His first response was to form a group that would play Joujouka-inspired trance music, but as the musicians arrived for their first rehearsal, they found ambulances and police surrounding the house. Brian had drowned in his swimming pool.

The album was released in 1971 to modest sales and attention; *Brian Jones Presents: The Master Musicians of Joujouka* wasn't something hippies could make love to like Ravi Shankar or get stoned and enjoy through headphones like the Koutev Ensemble, but it marked the start of something, the moment an emissary from the pop world started to look beyond African-American music for a new source of influence, the sort of thing academics and obsessives had been doing ever since Bartók bought his first wind-up wax recorder and headed into the Carpathian Mountains.

Patti Smith really liked the album; her "Radio Ethiopia" track sounds like a punk-rock tribute to Joujouka. The critic Robert Palmer, who was among the first to point out the connection between Delta blues and the Sahel, persuaded *Rolling Stone* to send him to Morocco. He threw himself into the music and the ceremony and wrote a piece that matched Michael Thomas's Jamaican article for opening readers' eyes to the wider musical world. Palmer returned the following year accompanied by Ornette Coleman, who was thrilled by the experience of jamming with the Attars. Whatever anchor Ornette had to the tempered Western scale was left somewhere behind a bush outside Joujouka. Bill Laswell also made the pilgrimage, producing *Apocalypse Across the Sky*, an excellent, straightforward documentation. The author and musician Brian Cullman, who assisted him on that adventure, described the music as "like the world's best horn section jamming with an ambulance, like chaos sitting in with darkness, like the four horsemen of the apocalypse auditioning for a gig as eternity's house band."

As is often the case, the most impactful visit wasn't by a VIP. When Mohamed Hamri, the Attars' man in Tangier, encountered a newly arrived British Deadhead named Rikki Stein, he asked, "Where you be? I wait you long time!" and took him straight up to Joujouka. It makes sense that Stein, who had immersed himself in San Francisco acid tests and organized tours by the Grateful Dead (and would later manage Fela Kuti), would be the one to bring the Master Musicians out into the world. He organized a tour across Europe in 1980, during which they performed on concert stages, in parks, in clubs, and in front of Glastonbury Festival founder Michael Eavis's barn. Crowds everywhere were mesmerized by the power and strangeness of their music. In 2023, before Elton John, Lana Del Rey, and Guns n' Roses took their turns on stage, the Glastonbury Festival opened with a set by the Master Musicians of Joujouka.

∽

"Heard any good music lately?" The journalist and filmmaker Mark Kidel had once interviewed Peter Gabriel, so when he ran into him at the bar of the Hammersmith Odeon on December 2, 1980, during the interval of a Talking Heads concert, their conversation picked up where it had left off. Kidel's day job was teaching at Dartington Hall, the progressive institution that had served as a British base for, among others, Rabindranath Tagore, Uday Shankar's troupe, and, decades later, little brother Ravi. Mark had been working his way through Dartington's complete set of the *UNESCO Collection of Traditional Music of the World* and had hosted Rikki Stein and the Joujouka team there, so he had plenty to report. For his part, Gabriel had included a tribute to Stephen Biko on his latest album and was immersing himself in African vinyl. Of all the sounds the two enthused about that night at the bar, none contained any English lyrics.

On stage, Talking Heads were performing songs from *Remain in Light*, their third Brian Eno–produced album. Eno, you may recall, was among the first outside West Africa to notice Tony Allen's genius. He and David Byrne had absorbed the lessons of Tropicália; they weren't mimicking Africa 70 on the new album, they'd simply "eaten" its rhythms. *Remain in Light* was a breakthrough record, a breath of rhythmic fresh air that had critics throwing their hats in the air. Eno and Byrne also had *My Life in the Bush of Ghosts* up their sleeves, ready for release early in the new year. *Ghosts* was a startlingly original collagist project involving mysterious snatches of sound laid over afrobeat/funk tracks that the two had put together between Talking Heads albums. Jon Hassell, a colleague of Terry Riley's and devotee of Pandit Pran Nath, had left the project following creative differences, but his fingerprints—and those of an outward-looking avant-garde world—were all over the album. *Ghosts* is abstract but infectious; it didn't sell millions, but it was hugely influential, and not just along the cutting edge of pop. It made sampling fashionable; when Jiggs Chase and Duke Bootee were putting together their revolutionary rap masterpiece "The Message," *My Life in the Bush of Ghosts* was in constant rotation on their turntable.

Peter and Mark parted that night vowing to do something about the fact that the world was full of great music that few people in Britain ever got to hear. The remedy was already forming in Gabriel's mind; a year and a half on from that evening would see the first "World of Music and Dance"—WOMAD—festival. Kidel and Stein helped Gabriel and the festival's producer Thomas Brooman lay the event's conceptual foundations but would remain footnotes in its history. The notion of a weekend-long celebration of music from faraway lands might, until very recently, have seemed a bit nerdy and academic, but thanks to Joujouka, *My Life in the Bush of Ghosts*, and Peter Gabriel's star power, the idea now sounded unassailably cool.

> In order to understand, it is immensely important for the person who understands to be *located outside* the object of his or her creative understanding—in time, in space, in culture . . . We raise new questions of a foreign culture, ones that it did not raise itself; we seek answers to our own questions in it; and the foreign culture responds to us by revealing to us new aspects and new semantic depths . . . Such a dialogic encounter does not result in merging or mixing. Each retains its own unity and *open* totality, but they are mutually enriched.
>
> —Mikhail Bakhtin, *Speech Genres and Other Late Essays*

One of my favorite WOMAD experiences took place in 1983, the festival's cautious second year following a red-ink bath in its first. In the reduced circumstances of London's Institute of Contemporary Arts, I joined a small crowd for one of the most remarkable concerts I've ever seen; the music wasn't particularly exciting, but the thought behind it was so extraordinary I couldn't stop smiling. The first half was a group from Arnhem Land in northern Australia whose music was so elemental they didn't even use didgeridoos or clapsticks or bullroarers, just rocks banged together as they chanted. After the interval came Frank Chickens, a pair of Japanese women whose songs were based on fifties monster movies, with synth backing tracks coming from a ghetto blaster at their feet. All the world's music, I felt, could be contained between these two bookends.

An assortment of indie labels (including Hannibal) spent the mid-eighties trying to fill that space, licensing existing recordings and producing their own. The fringes of press and radio joined in: Ian Anderson's *Southern Rag* reviewed a concert by a Chinese ensemble in 1979 (before renaming itself *Folk Roots*, then *fRoots*), while in the US, Tom Schnabel's *Morning Becomes Eclectic* on KCRW in Santa Monica played me my first Carlos Gardel track and campus radio stations across the country gave nerds with exotic record collections late-night slots to share their obsessions. Dance clubs started mixing in Latin and African records with the funk and disco, and it wasn't only DJs looking for the next "Soul Makossa" who could be spotted thumbing through the bins at shops in immigrant neighborhoods. I remember a busy open-air stall in Islington Market where you could find Nigerian and Ghanaian pressings, while at the other end of the spectrum was the dignified hush of Collet's in Charing Cross Road, where Ian Anderson picked up "A Lambkin Has Commenced Bleating." Robert Urbanus took over Stern's African Record Centre, David Byrne's and my New York favorite, the no-frills Soho Music Gallery, was up and running, and you could find almost anything at Aron's in Hollywood.

Those GLC African concerts in 1985 cranked everything up a couple of notches before *Graceland* multiplied the market at a stroke, bringing increased press and radio coverage and a surge in orders from shops. Most retailers, however, were stuck in a time when "foreign" music came mostly from sober ethnographic labels like Folkways, Topic, Ocora, et al. Record shops lived by bin dividers; you could see the titles peeking up above the endless racks of vinyl like meerkats: "Jazz," "Disco," "Classical," "Pop," with subsections: "Police," "Queen," "Rolling Stones," "P-Q-R Misc."

. . . Our records? Tucked behind un-sexy barricades like "International Folk" or "Ethnic." Thanks to Marley, Blackwell, and John Peel, "Reggae" had earned its own bin by then, and it would have been nice if we could have persuaded the HMV chain and Virgin Megastores to establish separate sections for "African," "Flamenco," "Latin," "Indian," etc., but sales were too small for such a leap. We knew that precious few customers would move from picking out the latest Talk Talk to hunting for Abdul Aziz El Mubarak or Trio Bulgarka; potential buyers for these albums were more likely to be looking for Nusrat or Salif or cumbia. We needed our own corner to capitalize on the hipness bestowed by *Bush of Ghosts*, by those GLC African concerts, by Ofra Haza soaring up the pop charts, and now by *Graceland*. So the heads of these small labels, plus our key allies Lucy Durán, Charlie Gillett, Andy Kershaw, and the *Guardian*'s Robin Denselow, met in a room above a London pub and voted for dividers called "World Music." Each label paid £50 into a promotion fund for every album they wanted listed in a stocking guide supplied to the shops; with that £3,700 we manufactured the dividers, paid for a *New Musical Express* giveaway compilation cassette, and hired a PR person, Suzanne Parks, with the leftovers. She told us that £1,500 wouldn't stretch very far, but she'd have a go.

It turned out to be the most effective £1,500 of PR money ever spent. Within six months, most large record shops from Paris to Tokyo had World Music sections, concert halls were booking artists for World Music seasons, radio stations scheduled World Music shows (some even starting before midnight), newspapers and magazines added regular columns of World Music reviews, WOMAD started negotiating globe-spanning offshoots, bucolic spots in Western Europe and North America announced World Music festivals, and within a couple of years we had WOMEX, our annual convention. All of this flowed from a couple of meetings organized by middle-class White people in London, the former beating heart of colonialism, about how best to label music that came largely from the "Global South." What could possibly go wrong?

For over a decade, very little. It all worked brilliantly: wonderful artists toured Western Europe and North America, outstanding records were produced and licensed (and often sold in respectable quantities), artists and composers who had rarely, if ever, received decent concert fees or royalties got well paid, audiences swelled, ears were opened and virtuosity acclaimed. There were also grumbles; promoters of African music felt that the likes of Balkan and Andean music were riding Africa's coattails. Over time, the biggest issue for many—including David

Byrne, who stated how much he hated the term—was lumping all those artists and cultures under a heading that implied, essentially, "Other." Categories shouldn't be imposed on musicians, they insisted, particularly when power is so skewed in favor of those doing the categorizing. Music is simply music and shouldn't be put in a box.

Those are all good points. But we small labels, with our modest ambitions and budgets, were dealing with the real world [*sic*] landscape of record retailing. For most people, music serves as a soundtrack for their lives, with words and textures that reflect their experience. Customers interested in music from other cultures, sung in languages they don't understand, are a self-selecting minority; how many albums would Thomas Mapfumo have sold had he been filed under "M-N-O" and stuck behind Mudhoney? We weren't defining the music so much as identifying an audience and steering them to records they might want to buy. Some artists felt, as Youssou N'Dour did, that they were being held back in their broader pop ambitions by getting thrown in with traditional musicians from the four corners of the globe. But how many tickets would have been sold for tours by Byrne's favorite Susana Baca if there hadn't existed a specialized infrastructure of press, radio, arts-center seasons, awards, and festivals with their mailing lists? Virgin Megastores and Tower Records would never have stocked Mapfumo's albums without a marketing hook aimed at a targeted audience. Placing them in a category designed to attract likely record and ticket buyers was the only way he or Baca could have had a career outside their homelands. Most artists understood that, even if the critics didn't. Any other term we might have chosen would have run up against the same issues—who was doing the naming and what did that imply? The Grammys and other organizations and media outlets would eventually opt for the self-satirizing solution of swapping "world" for "global." (Yes, reader, as did I in this book's subtitle.) World music as a concept turned out, in the end, to be flawed, but in a different way.

One evening in the late eighties, I went to a London concert by Abdel Aziz El Mubarak. Charlie Gillett had been playing his records and plugging the gig for weeks, and the promoter had done a good job of reaching out to London's Sudanese community, so the place was full: half Sudanese, half Gillett-listeners. El Mubarak walked out to center stage carrying his oud, while the other musicians filled a semi-circle of chairs behind him. He opened with a beautiful slow *taqsim*, answering his vocal lines with slinky runs on the oud. Then he paused, looked over his left shoulder, and nodded. The guy in the end chair pushed a button and the snap and thump of a beat box came blasting out of the PA speakers. The Sudanese cheered, raised their arms, and began swaying from side to side; the rest of the audience exchanged glances. The records Charlie had been playing are driven by *tarambouka* hand drums, but now, on stage, the taramboukas were following the box. As more than a few White faces began moving towards the exits, the Sudanese looked at us in bewilderment: *what's your problem?*

Our problem is that a computer-generated rhythm feels completely different from one created in real time by humans. What happens when a drummer and bass player lock eyes across a stage or a studio might barely measure on an oscilloscope, but without such nuanced human interactions, music loses something fundamental. Few of the forms featured in this book have found a place in their hearts for the drum machine; tango, flamenco, csardas, *son*, rumba, manouche jazz, samba, and Hindustani classical music contain too many subtle and variable nuances for it to work and all have suffered severe downsizing as their host communities embrace local and international iterations of modern machine pop and rap. Some have evolved hybrid forms which sacrifice the rhythms but keep the vocal techniques and melodies (Spain's Rosalía being a good example), but in order to fully embrace that technology, a traditional rhythm would have to do as reggae did and radically alter its nature. Balkan *chalga* and American R&B have eagerly taken up the new technology; few of R&B's movers, shakers, or listeners seem to miss the way Howard Grimes and the Hodges Brothers leaned so elegantly to the back of the beat on those great Al Green records.

In Africa, home of the drum, many have voted with their beats for the digits. John Collins told me of a conversation he had in Accra in the early 1990s; highlife was dead by then, strictly an "oldies" phenomenon, as youth turned to hip-hop. Local producers used the cheapest Casio drum machines and synths, and Collins found them hard to listen to. When he asked one of his students about the tinny vibe, he was told that flimsiness was part of the appeal; what had the legacy of highlife ever given the young generation? The economy sucked, jobs were scarce, and they saw no bright future, so the shoddy modernity of bootleg cassettes served as a defiant reflection of their situation.

That exchange proved prophetic. One slow afternoon in 1998, a London sound engineer was fooling around with an Autotune device, a gadget designed to silently shift off-pitch vocals back where they belonged. Just for a laugh, he tried spinning the dial way past the normal setting to see what it might do to Cher's voice and was so tickled by the weird result that he played it for her. Producers and label execs hated it, but Cher loved it, so it stayed in the final mix of "Believe." Thus was the ultimate cheap, inauthentic sound let loose upon the world. It's hard to walk down any city street these days without hearing this unabashedly fake, proudly populist effect. For me, the Autotune works like the Bach and Vivaldi that shopping malls once used to keep out loitering youths or how looped owl hoots chase away pigeons and mice.

The eighties turned out to be an evanescent moment in time, when Western audiences with money to spend and disco-sized holes in their record collections were drawn to the musical cultures I've written about in this book, as well as others from Portugal, Mexico, Cape Verde, Scandinavia, Georgia, the Maghreb, and Colombia, to name a few. Not only were many great performers still at the height of their powers, but technology in the form of electric guitars, good microphones, drum kits, and multitrack recording was being used in the service of music, modernizing it without entombing its rhythms. But, as Paul Simon learned in that Soweto bar, much of what the West was discovering was already out of date. On home ground, world music's biggest sellers—*Le Mystère des Voix Bulgaires, Buena Vista Social Club*, Ladysmith Black Mambazo—were considered old-fashioned, even reactionary. African, Afro-Cuban, African-American, and Roma rhythms, scales, vocal styles, and instrumental techniques had once transformed Western popular music into something dazzlingly modern. (Ann Douglas's book *Terrible*

Honesty: Mongrel Manhattan in the 1920s eloquently makes the case that our twentieth-century culture emerged from a confluence of Freudian psychology, skyscrapers, post-war anger, Madison Avenue, and Black music.) By the 1990s, though, modernity's banner was being carried by the new technologies that were reshaping music, and World Music, to many, sounded like the past.

The beast had been brought to life, however, and its infrastructure of concert series, agencies, festivals, labels, and radio shows—and their audiences—needed to be fed. DJs and producers laid "global" sounds on top of mid-Atlantic beats—*Buddha Bar*, Deep Forest, *One Giant Leap*, and the rest—while those working the traditional side of the street roamed the world, highlighting one culture after another until few were left un-celebrated. The French, naturally, led the way, with Cesária Évora and Cheb Khaled shrugging off the limitations of what even the FNAC chain labeled "World" to become mainstream stars. Parisian venues presented an endless stream of brilliantly curated concerts, while the regional network of Maisons de la Culture turned generous subsidies into wide-ranging programming. Germany and the Netherlands were also on the front foot, with the visionary promoters Horst Lippmann and Fritz Rau following up their pioneering blues packages with tango, flamenco, and bossa nova tours, while WDR in Cologne opened the ears of viewers and listeners to music from around the world. The programming at Amsterdam's Melkweg, Paradiso, and Tropical Institute was equally adventurous. The US, as Kanda Bongo Man's appearance at the New Orleans Jazz and Heritage Fair demonstrated, remained the most resistant of the major markets; with so much homegrown "roots" music to choose from, it was hard for musicians from abroad to get a look-in, and the costly and complex visa system didn't help.

With music traditions no longer so central to the life of most societies, performers worthy of festival and concert stages became harder to find. Presenters and concert promoters often did a great job, but not many had the budgets or obsessive focus of such as Orezzoli and Segovia or Theodore Levin and the Aga Khan Foundation; when independent record labels organized tours and concerts, their commitment to the artists and attention to detail often made for great shows, but such creative determination was hard to maintain. Musicians and producers from the global south tried to fill the gap by forming revivalist groups, but most couldn't resist adding contemporary touches and textures, which was usually the last thing the new audiences wanted to hear. New combinations kept emerging as World Music became its own genre, blander than what had come before, with rhythmic edges sanded off and complexities dumbed down. (Festival audiences love to clap along.)

Every autumn, artists showcased at WOMEX would be slotted into the following year's festivals and touring seasons across the northern hemisphere. All this energy and funding couldn't alter the fact that the best-sellers in those notorious World Music bins and those most praised by critics continued to be the unfused expressions of a particular tradition, either classic recordings or new ones produced by outsiders, since local producers tended to make their recordings sound as hi-tech as possible. This is a dialectic that plays out in many areas besides music, how the "developed" world's middle class craves the "authentic" and the "natural" while those in so-called emerging economies prefer the most modern and up-to-date.

One of the movement's accomplishments was the opportunities it opened up for female musicians. Cosmopolitan audiences inspired and encouraged women from conservative societies to master instruments long reserved for men, to lead groups and use traditions as the basis for songs that addressed issues around gender equality, political repression, and the environment. Many of the biggest stars to emerge during World Music's later years were female. The Portuguese singer Mariza represents an ideal balance between a tradition—fado—and the new audiences, a winning ambassador for Lusophone culture and a hall-filling star at home and abroad. Angélique Kidjo, on the other hand, left Benin and its music behind, moved to New York, and became the queen of fusion. Her albums often have clever themes (including tributes to Celia Cruz and *Remain in Light*) and win repeated Grammys, but I've never found them particularly memorable. Eliza Carthy, a daughter of English folk royalty, forced her way onto the World Music stage with an impassioned talk at the 2004 WOMEX that broke down the walls between "World" and "Folk," convincing festivals and presenters to stop treating British traditional music as a kind of contraband.

In the new millennium, the World Music movement began to lose momentum: fewer stars meant smaller crowds, resulting in fewer concerts and tours, while criticism of the concept resonated with more critics, artists, and audiences. Post-9/11 paranoia made visas harder to obtain. Press outlets suffered (*fRoots* closed), radio programming was reduced (the BBC canceled Lucy Durán's weekly *World Routes* show), and, along with the rest of the music industry, record sales dried up. Labels, venues, festivals, and the media began tiptoeing around the term. The years leading up to the start of the new century and those immediately after it were, nonetheless, a golden time, when audiences were introduced to so many extraordinary artists. The World Music movement may have been at the heart of much of it, but it was just one part of something far larger.

A case could be made that the Johann Herder of the twentieth century was Harry Smith. Smith kept his vast collection of late-1920s 78s in his room at the Chelsea Hotel (which had to install a joist in the room below to keep the ceiling from collapsing) and from it compiled his *Anthology of American Folk Music*, a six-disc collection released in 1952. The set convinced a generation of folk singers and many among their audiences that traditional music should be taken straight and unpolished and that wondrous beauty could be found in the most remote and unexpected corners. Just as Bartók had undermined the idea that folk music must pass through the pen of a composer before becoming listenable outside its home valley, Smith's collection subverted the leftist vision of folk music as a unifying form made up of songs that everyone could sing around a campfire. (Fun fact: Bartók's son Peter became a New York sound engineer, and it was he who cut the master lacquers for the Harry Smith albums.) The ramifications of this were many; the days of genteel renditions of folk songs by coffee-house balladeers were numbered, as were those of kitsch arrangements by Moiseyev-style ensembles. In his autobiographical book *Chronicles*, Bob Dylan recounts how Smith's collection fueled his rebellion against the folk establishment, leading to Newport 1965 and the birth of "rock." When roots-music aficionados had heard their fill of blues and hillbilly records, many decided it was time to explore the rest of the world. Which is how Brian Jones ended up in Joujouka, and how—in person or in spirit—Peter Gabriel, Brian Eno, Tony Allen, David Byrne, and Mark Kidel converged at the Hammersmith Odeon in December 1980.

Across the eighties, the ripples spread, often to unlikely places. 1982 not only saw the first WOMAD festival, but, a week later in Mexico City, a UNESCO conference declared "intangible cultural heritage" to be something worth preserving and that there must be no hierarchy of cultures based on power or population size. Looking back, Heidi Berg handing that South African cassette to Paul Simon to play in his car may have made the biggest waves of all. Three years on, and right after *Graceland*, Linda Ronstadt (who had sung harmony on "Under African Skies") startled her fans with *Canciones de mi padre*, an album honoring the border-straddling Mexican-American music she had grown up with; it sold two million copies and helped shift the narrative about a culture often treated by the mainstream media with cartoonish disrespect. In that same year, Benny Andersson and his accordion went out on the road with Orsa Spelmän, a traditional *polska* outfit from northern Sweden. Their albums never sold as well as Linda's, but they helped revive the region's beautiful fiddle music. (And some of those melodies sound a lot like ABBA hits.) Andersson still performs with them in the long Swedish summer evenings, while his avatar packs in the crowds at a London theater.

In the late eighties, near the end of a banquet in his honor, the Korean film director Im Kwon-taek was confronted by a *p'ansori* singer and her percussionist kneeling in front of him on the traditional low table. Like most Koreans at the time, Im viewed p'ansori (which bears some resemblance to pre-guitar flamenco) as an old-fashioned form out of step with the rapid modernization of post-war Korea; not seeing any graceful exit, he stayed for the (very long) performance and was moved to tears. During a gap between productions a few years later, he shot *Seopyeonje*, a low-budget but very moving drama about three traditional musicians. A film the director saw as a personal indulgence became a surprise smash, Korea's biggest-grossing local production to date, which set off a p'ansori revival that reconnected South Koreans to a cornerstone of their cultural past. Today there are festivals, theater seasons, more feature films, and, if not K-pop-level record sales, at least pride and respect.

The Garifuna people are descended from Africans who rebelled against slavery in the Windward Islands, made their way across the Caribbean through many arduous obstacles, intermarried with Arawak people, and created a distinct community along the coasts of Belize, Honduras, and Nicaragua. Andy Palacio had been a teenage rocker in Belize, but a trip to London in the late eighties inspired him to use Garifuna rhythms and melodies as the basis for what he called "punta rock." His albums achieved that rare feat of being popular both at home and with world music audiences; in 2007, WMEX made him their Artist of the Year. A year later, aged only forty-seven, Palacio died suddenly of heart failure. His work endures, however; the Garifuna language is now taught in schools and a generation of artists are carrying on his musical legacy.

"*Sevdah* will be sung after every war," predicted singer Zaim Imamović in an interview during the Siege of Sarajevo, which lasted from 1992 to 1996. *Sevdah* is a Bosnian song tradition that grew out of the country's long heritage of Slavic, Ottoman, Sephardic, and Central European influences; during the Tito years, Imamović had been one of its greatest stars. By the time the Wall fell in 1989, the younger generation had turned to rock, punk, and heavy metal, but under the guns of the Serbian snipers, *sevdah* took on a new meaning. During long hours in the shelters, many began playing the old recordings, then picking up guitars and learning the songs, as the music served to unite those who left and those who remained. After the war, it became part of the search for a new Bosnian identity, with Zaim's grandson Damir Imamović a key figure in its revival. Damir is a charismatic performer and a tireless researcher, teacher, and composer who finds fresh meanings in old *sevdalinka* and whose own songs carry messages of tolerance, secularism, and peace beyond Bosnia to the rest of the Balkans and the wider world.

The power of music to unify communities and inspire cultural pride has always unnerved autocrats and big-nation nationalists. Like Franco with the Catalans, Turkey today tries hard to block the dissemination of Kurdish music. Israeli authorities accuse Palestinian folklore groups of subversion for promoting what they insist is a fictional heritage. China hasn't (so far as we know) gone to the lengths Stalin did when he murdered all those Ukrainian bandura players, but Beijing's suppression of Uighur, Tibetan, and Mongolian cultures follows the Soviet playbook, treating traditional music as the expression of a subversive ideology (Islam, Buddhism, or "splittism"). President Xi's actions provide ample evidence that the claimed supremacy of Mao Tse-tung's thought is simply a mask for Han racial and cultural domination. As of this writing, leading Uighur musician Sanubar Tursun has been forced to undergo "re-education," and traditional music scholar Rahile Dawut remains in jail.

Lest North American and Antipodean readers get too comfortable with these citations of oppression by nationalist regimes, they mustn't forget the lengths to which settler states Canada, Australia, and the US have gone in separating Native children from their heritage, or that such practices continued into the 1970s. And that into the late 1940s, Louisiana schoolchildren were punished for speaking (or singing) in Cajun French. Or how Condoleezza Rice traversed the globe in 2003, frantically trying to bully countries into agreeing provisions in the GATT treaty that would outlaw local content quotas for radio stations and film-funding bodies. (Thankfully, she failed.)

If governments are made uneasy by music's unifying power, religions can be terrified by its sensuality and power to connect body and spirit. Salafist mullahs have appeared in this book as music-banning villains, and rightly so, but throughout its history, Christianity hasn't been much different. Barbara Ehrenreich's *Dancing in the Streets: A History of Collective Joy* gives chapter and verse on the Church's obsession with preventing women from moving their bodies; the headscarf, for example, was introduced to keep their hair from swaying during services. The Protestant reformation was conflicted: Martin Luther loved to dance, but John Calvin warned that "venom and corruption are distilled to the very depths of the heart by melody." Calvin's heirs in Evangelical Protestantism insist that all music other than approved hymns is a pagan wedge opening the door to sin. Just as Roma are forced to give up secular music as the price of admission to their Light and Life church, evangelism's converts continue to be threatened with perdition if they try to keep their musical traditions alive.

⌇

> Tradition is not the worship of ashes, but the preservation of fire.
>
> —Gustav Mahler

> Music expands the heart's capacity. It can make emotional connections across barren distances and frontiers of culture and language. It can create empathy where none would otherwise exist.
>
> —Andy Morgan, *Music, Culture and Conflict in Mali*

Repressive governments and censorious preachers can strangle traditional music, but allowing technology to seize control of the rhythm may be a more insidious threat. The irony is that machine beats grew out of a desire to capture and replicate spontaneous moments of human inspiration. In 1973, while Kool Herc was in a Bronx basement figuring out how to repeat the sizzling drum break in James Brown's "Give It Up or Turnit a Loose" by using two copies on adjacent turntables, a hundred blocks south in midtown Manhattan, Paul Simon and the pioneering engineer Phil Ramone were copying and looping the best bars from a backing track of "Kodachrome," the ones that crackled with the most energy. Kool Herc's turntable revolution begat hip-hop, while Ramone's ingenuity foreshadowed how digital technology would be used to construct tracks like building Lego sets. From replicating and multiplying those indelible moments, creating drum parts from scratch wasn't such a leap. And like so many brilliant inventions (particularly digital ones), it quickly became like the broom in *Fantasia*, helping out by carrying buckets of water but impossible to stop as the waters rose.

The democratic appeal of the gadgets isn't hard to understand; they allow anyone, megastar or unknown, to make records alone at home.

Stars can email their master files to the best session players money can buy, while others simply download a pulse from the internet. Either way, the magic of collective inspiration is lost. The same goes for live shows; some at the high end, including Dua Lipa, Beyoncé, and Taylor Swift, have dispensed with musicians altogether, while those who still tour with a band often use click tracks to keep dancers, lighting—and drummers—in rigid sync. Full live groups were once common at weddings and other celebrations, but many now opt for a DJ or a singer backed by a keyboard with a rhythm switch. This not only starves musicians of a key source of income but drains communities of those occasions for connection with their most resonant traditions.

In the studio or on stage, programmed beats threaten to put an end to the sort of transcendent moments that once lived forever, on record or in the memories of those who were there. I have tried to bring some of those to life in this book: Miguelito Valdés's orchestra not missing a note or beat as they filled those last six wax discs in Havana in 1937; Django Reinhardt and Stéphane Grappelli drawing crowds to their backstage jams at the Claridge Hotel; Dmitri Pokrovsky and his group singing open-throat for the first time at the Gnessin Institute; Zuluboy and the Jazz Maniacs leaving their White rivals in the dust outside a Johannesburg courtroom; Rodolfo Biagi's teatime piano-pounding at the Chanticleer; Alla Rakha and Mickey Hart chasing rhythmic complexity around a Marin County motel room; Scratch Perry turning on the tape machine the minute Marley, Tosh, or Livingston finished writing a song; Stevie Wonder cheering Fela on at the Shrine during FESTAC . . . Metaphors are tempting: are modern productions a kind of sonic fast food, tasty, briefly satisfying, but unhealthy? Is music unaided by digits the equivalent of natural fibers? Comparisons to biodiversity are more apt; we may not notice, at first, that birds and insects are disappearing from the countryside, but we'll pay dearly for it in the long run, with a chain reaction of lost links and functions in our natural world. Handmade local music is still very much alive; communities have their own dance steps, their sense of musical movement, feet linked to drums or the scales and patterns of instruments and voices. Clips regularly posted by the admirable Dust-to-Digital label display the wondrous diversity of humanity's music, joyful, virtuosic, sometimes hilarious, touching, extraordinary . . . and hardly a drum machine in sight.

How music from across the globe has been interwoven over the centuries is fundamental to how our world sounds. Humanity's sense of pulse, of what constitutes musical excitement, has been shaped at village dances, in ceremonies, parades, and dockside bars, by captives, migrants, and travelers. The twentieth century added shellac grooves and radio waves to these channels of exchange, enabling the virtuous circles of connection and bringing forth era-defining stars. It may appear that technology has opened up even more possibilities, but sampling doesn't count. On the contrary, sampling is a sign that we're cannibalizing what we have for parts, like a rusting auto up on cinder blocks in the backyard. Music will always remain an indefinable mystery: why do humans need it and how does it transform us? The stories in this book show how unstoppable it is, how heedless of oceans and borders. They remind us that no culture has evolved in isolation, and of how very diverse yet inseparably linked we are. In times of division and fragmentation, the connections music can provide are needed more than ever.

Recordings from the golden age that lasted from 1925 to the end of the century remind us how music shifted and changed, how rhythms, scales, and melodies flowed across the globe, constantly altering what the world danced and listened to. Like the Arabic libraries that preserved the writings of Greek philosophers, those recordings constitute our shared heritage to treasure and learn from. New technologies may divert our attention, but music created in the moment can still be found where it always has been, in the feet, fingers, voices, and spirits of musicians in every corner of the world. Like the song says, that's where the roots of rhythm remain.

Acknowledgments

This book might never have been finished were it not for my extraordinary wife, Andrea Goertler. Over the course of a decade, she has read and listened, praised and criticized, brought me new ideas and sources, and always cheered me on. As the deadline approached, it was her energy, determination, and attention to detail that got it over the finish line. During the years in which the book came to dominate our life together (aside from her own challenging and satisfying professional life), Andrea's enthusiasm and unshakable tolerance were remarkable. I am grateful beyond measure for her loving support.

In my research, I was able to rely on a group of supremely knowledgeable friends and colleagues, experts who never failed to make themselves available, answering questions, suggesting sources, and setting me straight. Those I called upon most often include Chris Albertyn, Rob Allingham, Ian Anderson, Simon Broughton, Robin Denselow, Acho Estol, Banning Eyre, Francis Falceto, Nick Gold, Dániel Hamar, Marc Hollander, Mark Kidel, Theodore Levin, Martin Meissonnier, Alfredo Russo, Iain Scott, Rikki Stein, and Robert Urbanus, with special "above and beyond the call of duty" badges for Lucy Durán and Ned Sublette. Special thanks are also due to Ruy Castro, Alma Guillermopietro, Mark Hudson, and Maxine McGregor for generously allowing me to borrow extended passages from their own writing.

After waiting for months as American editors took their time reading this book, worried about its length, and dithered, Michael Zilkha of ZE Books got the manuscript on a Friday and by Monday we had a deal. Since then, everything about working with ZE has been like that: enthusiastic, energetic, creative. Michael's warmth, deep love of music, and generosity of spirit has been a tonic, while Nathan Rostron has brought wise counsel, great ideas, and attention to detail at every turn. The wider ZE-associated team, from Chris Heiser of Unnamed Press, to copy editor John McGhee and text designer Anna Moschovakis, to

ACKNOWLEDGMENTS

creative director Jiminie Ha and her With Projects crew, have been an absolute pleasure to work with. I am very thankful to Julian Mash for making the connection.

For the past five years this book's home base has been with Faber in the UK, during which time they have provided a deft combination of freedom and discipline, keeping me on a loose rein while bringing to bear their legacy of high standards and strict rules. From the brilliant duo of Popular Music Director Dan Papps and Managing Editor Anne Owen to my astute and always encouraging editor Bill Swainson, text editor and tireless fact-checker Mark Sinker, proofreader Ian Bahrami, photo sleuth Amanda Russell, legal advisor Sean McTernan, and production designer Kate Ward, I have been in great hands. Much gratitude to Alexa von Hirschberg for bringing me there, to Alex Bowler for welcoming me to the fold. In the pre-Faber years, much-needed encouragement, advice, and belief was provided by Pete Ayrton and Claire Conrad.

Profuse thanks are due my tireless and sagacious agent, Matthew Hamilton, who has expertly navigated this book's path to publication.

As befits a book of this size and breadth, the list of those who have helped me in significant ways, from interviews and advice to timely encouragement and oblique connections, is long. The manner and nature of their assistance varied widely, but all are greatly appreciated: Justin Adams, Jesús Alemañy, Tony Allen, Peregrine Andrews, Gwen Ansell, Harriet Armstrong, John Armstrong, Roger Armstrong, Ben Ayres, Lucy Bailey, Stuart Baker, Christopher Ballantine, Peter Barakan, Lisa Barkley, Emily Bingham, David Bither, Chris Blackwell, Hilary Blecher, Sara Blecher, Kanda Bongo Man, Adrian Boot, Christoph Borkowsky Akbar, Jerry Boys, Bill Bragin, Thomas Brooman, Robert Browning, Kim Burton, John Bush, Kate Bush, Pikey Butler, David Byrne, Andreas Campomar, Garth Cartwright, Javier Casalla, Eric S. Charry, Sam Charters, Alexander Cheparukhin, Johnny Clegg, Jonathan Clyde, Deborah Cohen, John Collins, Steve Collins, Dick Connette, Caroline Coon, Mary Corey, Graeme Counsel, Martin Cradick, Brian Cullman, William Dalrymple, Catherine Daly, Emmanuel de Buretel, David Defries, Marjorie Lynn Devon, Violet Diallo, Rob Dickins, Cary

ACKNOWLEDGMENTS

Diez, Petr Dorůžka, Justin Dowling, Beco Dranoff, Michael Dregni, Merlyn Driver, Michel Duval, Fernanda Eberstadt, Chris Eckman, Lu Edmonds, Tim Eriksen, Veit F. Erlmann, Viktor Erofeyev, Kieran Evans, Yale Evelev, John Fenton, William Ferris, Paul Fisher, Isabel Fonseca, James Fox, Andrew Franklin, João Franklin, Marisa Gandelman, Paul Geoghegan, Frances Giguette, Jody Gillett, Vivian Goldman, Xenia Goloubovitch, Hanna Gorjaczkowska, Arthur Gorson, Boris Grebenchikov, Dominique Green, Peter Guralnick, Edward Haber, Justine Henzell, Sally Henzell, Trevor Herman, Mike Heron, Adam Hochschild, Tony Hollingsworth, Jac Holzman, David Howard, Chris Howe, Ken Hunt, Damir Imamović, Angela Impey, Eric Jeitner, Josh Jelly-Shapiro, Robert Johnson, David Jones, Vinod Joshi, Ashley Kahn, Alexander Kan, Yasen Kazandjiev, Vincent Kenis, Andy Kershaw, Jon Kertzer, Tom Killingbeck, Elizabeth Kinder, Christopher King, Kalin Kirilov, Frank Klaffs, Claudio Kleiman, Dana Kletter, Kosta Kolev, Remy Kolpa Kopoul, Marie Korpe, Elena Kouteva, Basseku Kouyate, Philippe Krumm, Peter Kulesh, Hanif Kureishi, Albert Kuvezin, Fred Lawton, Carolina Le Port, Aaron Levinson, Karl Lippegaus, Katerina Lobeck, Csaba Lökös, Connie Lopes, Meny Lopes, John Lyons, Tom Luddy, Alastair Macaulay, Kevin Macdonald, Geraldinho Magalhaes, Kálmán Magyar, Taj Mahal, Ben Mandelson, Yazid Manou, Peter Manuel, Mariza, David Mattacks, Cerys Matthews, Charles Maynes, Louise Meintjes, Barry Miles, Malcolm Mills, Andy Morgan, Guy Morris, Michele Mortimer, Christian Mousset, Ian Nagoski, Litto Nebbia, Borimira Nedeva-Moore, Davia Nelson, Helmut Neumann, Ben Okri, Jeff Opland, Bryn Ormrod, Maria Pacheco, Ricardo Pachón, Philip Page, Leslie Palmer, Ivo Papasov, Silvana Paternostro, Katerina Pavlakis, Martin Perna, John Potter, Edit Pula, Jerry Rappaport, Hanitrarivo Rasoanaivo, Rita Ray, Jerome Reese, Sally Reeves, Max Reinhardt, Cristóbal Repetto, Timothy Rice, Lewis Robinson, Jeff Rosen, Lloyd Ross, John Ryle, Frank Rynne, Kate St John, Gustavo Santaolalla, Mark Satlof, Katherine Schofield, Christian Scholze, Márta Sebestyén, Corrina Seddon, Gerald Seligman, Harry Sepulveda, Vyacheslav Shchurov, Steve Shehan, Polina Shepherd, Jo Shinner, Alex Shoumatoff, Susan Sillins, Carol Silverman, Jennifer Silverstone,

ACKNOWLEDGMENTS

Paul Simon, Bintou Simporé, Faith Singh, Tjinder Singh, Anthony Smith, Salamon Soma, Cosima Spender, Roger Steffens, Catherine Steinmann, Neil Storey, Stephen Strauss, David Suff, Philip Sweeney, Bintou Sylla, Ibrahim Sylla, Fruzsina Szép, Jaïr Tchong, Jose Teles, Yosvany Terry, Johannes Theurer, Richard Thompson, Carole Tongue, Pierre Toureille, Geoff Travis, Artemy Troitsky, Eric Trosset, Jean Trouillet, Sean Twomey, Rumyana Tzintzarska, Ahmet Uluğ, Tony Van der Eecken, Jumbo Vanrenan, Caetano Veloso, Moreno Veloso, Julián Viñuales, Joop Visser, Anthony Wall, Alain Weber, Hannah Westland, Vicki Wickham, Richard Williams, Nigel Williamson, Michel Winter, Trevor Wyatt, Jody Yebga, and Yuri Yunakov.

Part-time assistance from Sarah Golden, the late, much-missed Claudia Mower, Alexis Osborn, and Georgie Pope enabled my life to continue on a relatively even keel while also providing important support for my work on the book.

I began this project fifteen years ago and over that time have seen progressively less and less of friends and family. I am grateful that they continued to support my monomaniacal task in ways both direct and indirect, particularly Warwick Boyd and Roberta Price, Mark and Sian Cooper, Ernie Eban, Alan Elliott, Petra and Wilfried Goertler, Pierre Hodgson, Nick Laird-Clowes and Angelica von Hase, Jenni Muldaur, Melissa North and Tchaik Chassay, Marie-Cécile Renauld, Alex Shulman and David Jenkins, Chaim and Susannah Tannenbaum, Michael Thomas, Ed Vulliamy, Nigel Waymouth, and Trevor Wyatt.

Many whom I held in my thoughts as I wrote this book are no longer with us, including three dear friends with whom I shared great times listening to music and who so inspired me. In memoriam: Charlie Gillett, Mario Pacheco, and John Singh.

From an early age, I have never stopped listening to music. Changes in the musical landscape that I describe in this book plus my own focus on the task at hand has meant that I've experienced far less live music in recent years than at any time since I was a teenager. The shaft of musical light that has brightened my life is the time Andrea and I have spent in Albania, where many pages of this book were written. We've passed memorable evenings listening to polyphonic singing, crossed the border into Greece to hear the wonderful, closely related music of Epirus, joined the dancing at friends' celebrations, and, above all, recorded, toured with, and listened, both on stage and off, to the eight marvelous southern Albanian musicians whom, with our friend Edit Pula, we united under the name Saz'iso. The story of Albanian music may not have fit into the narratives I constructed for this book, but seeing how moved their European audiences were and witnessing the way enthusiasm for traditional music at home spread, especially among younger listeners, confirmed my belief in the power of music grown from ancient roots.

Notes on Sources

vii   *This is the story of how we begin to remember*: lyrics to "Under African Skies".
Words and music by Paul Simon
Copyright © 1986 Paul Simon (BMI)
International Copyright Secured
All Rights Reserved. Used by Permission.
Reprinted by Permission of Hal Leonard LLC.

I Mbube

2   *On the contrary, technology will liberate*: author's recollection of a 1979 Trevor Horn interview; in a 2023 interview, Horn stated: "it was a revelation—the idea that you could make a record without having a group there . . . You could make music all by yourself, because of the new technology" (Rob Tannenbaum, "The Buggles' Song Launched MTV. After 45 Years, They're Going on Tour," *New York Times*, Apr. 7, 2023).
cesspool of nations: Malcom McLaren to Trevor Horn, quoted in Craig Bromberg, *The Wicked Ways of Malcolm McLaren* (New York: Harper & Row, 1989), p. 260.
That's a tribe: Malcom McLaren, quoted in Bromberg, p. 265.
slept with a few Zulu girls: Malcom McLaren, quoted in Bromberg, p. 266.

3   *Over that summer . . . you haven't heard this before!*: author's conversations with Paul Simon, with additional information from his album notes for *Graceland* (Warner Bros. Records, 9 25447-1, 1986).

5   *Do you think it will sell?*: author's conversation with Paul Simon, London, 1985.
This music contravenes: Robert Christgau, "South Africa Romance," *Village Voice*, Sept. 23, 1986 (www.robertchristgau.com/xg/rock/simon-86.php).

6   *I realized immediately*: author's conversation with a friend, Moscow, 1991.
strengthening the people: Neo Mnumzana of the African National Congress (ANC), quoted in Christgau.

7   *We used Paul as much*: Ray Phiri, quoted in Mark Beaumont, "Graceland at 35: How Paul Simon Recorded a Masterpiece in Apartheid South Africa," *Independent*, Aug. 25, 2021.

8   *I'm not a good "angry" songwriter*: author's conversation with Paul Simon.

10   *no one escapes being a member*: quoted in Louise Meintjes, *Sound of Africa! Making Music Zulu in a South African Studio* (Durham and London: Duke University Press, 2003), p. 195.
more than fourteen thousand: Greg Marinovich, *The Bang-Bang Club: Snapshots from a Hidden War* (New York: Basic Books, 2000), pp. 212–13.

NOTES ON SOURCES

11   *Miriam Makeba resented . . . on-the-spot cattle slaughtering*: author's conversation with Paul Simon.
If you sing the truth: Joseph Shabalala interviewed in *Paul Simon: Graceland*, dir. Jeremy Marre, BBC Four *Classic Albums* (1997).
In the decade before the 1976 uprising: author's interview with Trevor Herman of Earthworks Records.

12   *In the jungle:* lyrics to "The Lion Sleeps Tonight" by Hugo Peretti, Luigi Creatore, George Weiss, and Albert Stanton, based on the song "Wimoweh" by Solomon Linda and Paul Campbell.

13   *By 1948, it had sold over 100,000:* Rian Malan, "In the Jungle," *Rolling Stone*, no. 841, May 25, 2000, p. 56.

18   *Charles Dickens's response*: Charles Dickens, "The Noble Savage," *Reprinted Pieces*, Project Gutenberg eBook #872, 2014 (www.gutenberg.org/files/872/872-h/872-h.htm#page391).
giant new rituals of self-congratulation: E. J. Hobsbawm, *The Age of Capital 1848–1875* (London: Abacus, 1993), p. 47.

19   *Critics were befuddled*: Veit Erlmann, *Music, Modernity, and the Global Imagination: South Africa and the West* (New York and Oxford: Oxford University Press, 1999), p. 135.

20   *Many of the native songs*: quoted from W. C. Scully's "By Veldt and Kopje" (1907), in David B. Coplan, *In Township Tonight! South Africa's Black City Music and Theatre* (London and New York: Longman, 1985), p. 29.

21   *insufferable to the musical ear . . . little better than a deadened howl . . . low monotonous native air*: quoted in Erlmann, p. 127.
pray with their faces on the ground: quoted in Barbara Ehrenreich, *Dancing in the Streets: A History of Collective Joy* (London: Granta Books, 2008), p. 159.
The missionaries stepped up: Steve Biko, *I Write What I Like* (Johannesburg: Picador Africa, 2004), p. 103.

22   *I turn my back on the many shames*: Xhosa poet Jonas Ntsiko in 1884, quoted in Erlmann, pp. 147–48.
At first we had the land: quoted from social anthropologist Monica Hunter, in Freda Troup, *South Africa: An Historical Introduction* (Harmondsworth: Penguin Books, 1975), p. 173.
Just our coons: quoted in Gwen Ansell, *Soweto Blues: Jazz, Popular Music, and Politics in South Africa* (New York and London: Continuum, 2004), p. 13.

23   *as if they were lifting up*: quoted in Erlmann, p. 149.
uniform movements under the control: quoted in Coplan, p. 72.

27   *We cannot afford a wage*: Witwatersrand Chamber of Mines in 1907, quoted in Ansell, p. 21.
the bare . . . necessities of life: quoted in Troup, p. 244.

28   *Drink my dear*: Modikwe Dikobe's poem "Shebeen Queen," quoted in Ansell, pp. 80–81.
The atmosphere was obscene: poet, playwright, and journalist Herbert Dhlomo, quoted in Christopher Ballantine, *Marabi Nights: Early South African Jazz and Vaudeville* (Johannesburg: Ravan Press, 1994), p. 28.

NOTES ON SOURCES

29 *pathological, nerve-irritating*: quoted from a 1922 *New York American* article in Ballantine, p. 81.
32 *Taking aborigines to London*: from a letter to the South African press, quoted in Ballantine, p. 69.
33 *ill suited to city life*: Nelson Mandela, *Long Walk to Freedom* (London: Little, Brown and Co., 2008), p. 89.
Sophiatown was like a Mediterranean city: *Drum* magazine photographer Jürgen Schadeberg, quoted in Ansell, p. 64.
34 *people felt very positive*: quoted in Ansell, p. 69.
35 *You tell such lovely lies*: lyric from "Lovely Lies" by Tom Glazer; original song and lyrics to "Lakutshona iLanga" by Mackay Davashe.
38 *Have you heard*: lyric from "Meadowlands," written by Strike Vilakazi, quoted in Ansell, pp. 79–80.
He used to go at the typewriter: Anthony Sampson, quoted in Mike Nicol, *A Good-Looking Corpse: The World of DRUM—Jazz and Gangsters, Hope and Defiance in the Townships of South Africa* (London: Secker & Warburg, 1991), p. 85.
Her first name is Amaren: Todd Matshikiza, quoted in Nicol, pp. 143–44.
41 *The government despised our joy*: Hugh Masekela and D. Michael Cheers, *Still Grazing: The Musical Journey of Hugh Masekela* (New York: Three Rivers Press, 2004), p. 70.
Natives will be taught from childhood: Hendrik Verwoerd, head of the Native Affairs Department, quoted in Masekela and Cheers, p. 67.
42 *Here comes the black man*: lyric from "Ndodemnyama we Verwoerd" (Watch Out, Verwoerd) by Vuyisili Mini, translated in *Amandla! A Revolution in Four-Part Harmony*, dir. Lee Hirsch (2002).
44 *Give us jazz and film stars*: interview with Anthony Sampson in Ansell, p. 65.
a particularly dirty basin: Yvonne Huskisson, SABC music director, quoted in Ansell, p. 110.
45 *We dropped our corn bread*: Todd Matshikiza, quoted by Ansell, p. 59.
It's a . . . very strong food: West Nkosi, quoted in Hank Bordowitz, *Noise of the World: Non-Western Musicians in Their Own Words* (Brooklyn, New York: Soft Skull Press, 2004), p. 222.
47 *My father died when I was seven*: Simon "Mahlathini" Nkabinde, quoted by Trevor Herman in album notes to Mahlathini, *King of the Groaners* (Earthworks/Caroline, CAROL 2428-2, 1993). Used by permission.
48 *We made one good solid rhythm*: West Nkosi, quoted in Meintjes, p. 28.
the hurrying of people in Durban: lyrics to the Hanover Brothers' song, quoted in Rob Allingham and Gregory Mthembu-Salter, "South Africa: Popular Music," in Simon Broughton, Mark Ellingham, and Jon Lusk (eds.), *The Rough Guide to World Music Vol. 1: Africa and the Middle East*, 3rd ed. (London and New York: Rough Guides, 2006).
51 *If you play some of that shit*: Miles Davis to Hugh Masekela, quoted in Masekela and Cheers, p. 165.
It was the only place in Johannesburg: Maxine McGregor, *Chris McGregor and the Brotherhood of Breath: My Life with a South African Jazz Pioneer* (Flint, Michigan: Bamberger Books, 1995), p. 27. Used by permission.

NOTES ON SOURCES

54 *music saved us*: Abdullah Ibrahim, interviewed in *Amandla!*
55 *That what you do doesn't really matter*: McGregor, p. 98.
56 *a Transkei evening with herders*: Chris McGregor's brother Tony McGregor, writing in the South African jazz magazine *Twotone*, quoted in McGregor, p. 237.
57 *the first step is . . . to infuse*: Biko, p. 31.
58 *In confidence we lay our cause*: inscription below a statue of Paul Kruger, former president of the Republic of the Transvaal, outside the courthouse in Pretoria, quoted in Mandela, p. 417.
   I want to join your revolution: Dizzy Gillespie, quoted in Bordowitz, p. 254.
59 *putting in an AK-47 here*: interview in *Amandla!*
   we didn't want the singing: interview in *Amandla!*
60 *We're trapped, man*: Hugh Masekela, quoted in Ansell, p. 198.
64 *To be with the Zulus*: Johnny Clegg, quoted in Jeremy Marre and Hannah Charlton, *Beats of the Heart: Popular Music of the World* (New York: Pantheon Books, 1985), p. 39.
65 *She's a rich girl*: lyric from "Diamonds on the Soles of Her Shoes," written by Paul Simon (beginning by Paul Simon and Joseph Shabalala).
66 *How does it happen*: lyric from "Diamonds on the Soles of Her Shoes," written by Paul Simon (beginning by Paul Simon and Joseph Shabalala), translation from isiZulu by Erlmann, p. 170.
   Strong wind destroy our home: lyric from "Homeless," written by Paul Simon and Joseph Shabalala.
   We are the conquerors: lyric from "Homeless," written by Paul Simon and Joseph Shabalala, translation from isiZulu by Erlmann, pp. 227–28.
67 *the best I ever did*: author's interview with Paul Simon.
68 *Then you had to stay an African*: interview with Hilda Tloubatla, leader of the Mahotella Queens, by Robin Denselow, "They're Going to Graceland," *Guardian*, June 9, 2006.
70 *turn rural people into subjects*: Nomboniso Gasa, quoted in Lydia Polgreen, "South Africa Debates Law to Support Tribal Courts," *New York Times*, June 16, 2012.

II Babalú-Ayé

74 *full of improper contortions*: Desidero Arnaz, mayor of Santiago, quoted in Ned Sublette, *Cuba and Its Music: From the First Drums to the Mambo* (Chicago: Chicago Review Press, 2004), pp. 370–71.
76 *I hear a drum, Mama*: lyrics to "Conga de Los Dandys" by Chano Pozo, translated and quoted in album notes by Jordi Pujol for *Chano Pozo: El tambor de Cuba (Life and Music of the Legendary Cuban Conga Drummer)* (Tumbao Cuban Classics, TCD 305, 2001), p. 106.
78 *Yo son carabalí*: lyrics to "Bruca manigua," written by Arsenio Rodríguez, translated and quoted in Sublette, p. 445.
79 *They are responsible*: Tito Puente 1992 interview, quoted in Josephine Powell, *Tito Puente: When the Drums Are Dreaming* (Bloomington, Indiana: AuthorHouse, 2007), p. 52.

NOTES ON SOURCES

82 *this gorgeous hunk of a man*: Frank "Machito" Grillo, quoted in Max Salazar, *Mambo Kingdom: Latin Music in New York* (New York: Schirmer Trade Books, 2002), p. 43.
smallpox-afflicted, Dahomeyan god: Sublette, p. 581.
84 *like being crushed*: Dizzy Gillespie, quoted in Pujol, p. 112.
85 *already figured out*: Dizzy Gillespie, in Dizzy Gillespie and Al Fraser, *To Be, or Not . . . to Bop* (Minneapolis and London: University of Minnesota Press, 2009), p. 321.
87 *[A]ll those guys are like babes*: Dizzy Gillespie to Mario Bauzá, quoted in Leonardo Padura Fuentes, *Faces of Salsa: A Spoken History of the Music*, trans. Stephen J. Clark (Washington and London: Smithsonian Books, 2003), p. 22.
88 *[Miguelito] Valdés is the one responsible*: Charlie Palmieri, quoted in Salazar, p. 196.
89 *With the Arabs expelled*: Fernando Ortiz, quoted in Sublette, p. 71.
91 *If there had been no drum*: informant of Cuban ethnographer Lydia Cabrera, quoted in Sublette, p. 58.
92 *Havana, maritime capital*: from Fernando Ortiz's essay "La Clave xilofónica de la música cubana," quoted in Alejo Carpentier, *Music in Cuba*, ed. Timothy Brennan, trans. Alan West-Durán (Minneapolis: University of Minnesota Press, 2001), pp. 95–96.
95 *there is not a more industrious people*: writer Robert Campbell, who visited Nigeria in 1859, quoted in Sublette, p. 210.
96 *Jesus Christ does not get drunk*: Sublette, p. 224.
101 *caged but not tamed*: Billy Bergman, *Reggae and Latin Pop: Hot Sauces* (Dorset: Blandford Press, 1985), p. 11.
The power the black race has: 1881 newspaper article in *La Aurora de Yumurí*, quoted in John Charles Chasteen, *National Rhythms, African Roots: The Deep History of Latin American Popular Dance* (Albuquerque: University of New Mexico Press, 2004), p. 81.
Africanism is the secret sickness: 1882 newspaper article in *El Triunfo*, quoted in Chasteen, p. 109.
A European musician can play: 1830s columnist El Lugareño, quoted in Chasteen, p. 158.
Who does not know: private letter of 1837, quoted in Chasteen, p. 158.
executed every night: J. B. Rosemond de Beauvallon in 1844, quoted in Sublette, p. 125.
103 *[Cuban men] express fear*: article from *La Habana elegante*, quoted in Chasteen, p. 81.
Prends garde à toi!: lyrics to aria "L'Amour est un oiseau rebelle," from *Carmen* by Georges Bizet.
St. Louis woman: lyrics to "St. Louis Blues" by W. C. Handy.
104 *The black musician was elusive*: Carpentier, p. 158.
You could call it syncopation: Sublette, p. 135.
105 *French opera and popular song*: Alan Lomax in *Mister Jelly Roll*, quoted in John Storm Roberts, *The Latin Tinge: The Impact of Latin American Music on the United States* (New York and Oxford: Oxford University Press, 1999), p. 34.
107 *Now you has—jazz*: lyrics to "Now You Has Jazz" by Cole Porter.
109 *To be brief and emphatic*: US Army surgeon, quoted in Tom Gjelten, *Bacardi and the Long Fight for Cuba: The Biography of a Cause* (New York: Penguin Books, 2009), p. 77.
To the faults of the parent: from an 1889 article, quoted in Gjelten, p. 52.

110 *[Havana's] immorality is worn*: Charles Pepper, a late-nineteenth-century visitor to Havana, quoted in Chasteen, p. 125.
111 *at once the characteristics of giants*: José Martí, quoted in Gjelten, p. 52.
114 *[Cuban] music should not be sacrificed*: Sánchez de Fuentes, quoted in Robin Moore, *Nationalizing Blackness: Afrocubanismo and Artistic Revolution in Havana, 1920–1940* (Pittsburgh: University of Pittsburgh Press, 1997), p. 204.
If you are young: John Storm Roberts, *Black Music of Two Worlds* (New York: Praeger Publishers, 1972), p. 28.
116 *group of highly original*: Fernando Ortiz, quoted in Pujol, p. 97.
117 *Son de la loma*: lyrics to "Mamá, son de la loma" by Miguel Matamoros, translated in Sublette, p. 368.
119 *With our music we Cubans*: from Fernando Ortiz, *La Africanía en la musíca folklórica de Cuba*, quoted in Hernando Calvo Ospina, *¡Salsa!: Havana Heat, Bronx Beat*, trans. Nick Caistor (London: Latin America Bureau, 1998), p. 19.
120 *revision of all false and wasteful values*: Grupo Minorista manifesto, quoted in Timothy Brennan, "Introduction to the English Edition," in Carpentier, p. 11.
There is nothing more contemporary: Alejo Carpentier's 1922 text "Sóngoro consongo . . . en Paris," quoted in Brennan, p. 4.
121 *cone of nuts:* lyrics to "El Manisero" by Moisés Simons, translated and quoted in Sublette, p. 398.
masterworks of the human spirit: quoted in Moore, *Nationalizing Blackness*, p. 171.
betrayed European culture: Oswald Spengler, *The Decline of the West*, quoted in Moore, *Nationalizing Blackness*, p. 172.
Even the pallid daughters of Albion: Alejo Carpentier's 1922 text "Sóngoro consongo . . . en Paris," quoted in Brennan, p. 4.
122 *hollow like a maraca*: Fernando Ortiz, quoted in Roberto González Echevarría, *Cuban Fiestas* (New Haven and London: Yale University Press, 2010), p. 125.
I gave the Americans: Xavier Cugat, quoted in Roberts, *The Latin Tinge*, p. 87.
124 *fifty million little monkeys:* lyrics to "The Peanut Vendor" by Moisés Simons, Marion Sunshine, and L. Wolfe Gilbert.
125 *come starve with me*: Bauzá writing to Grillo in 1937, quoted in Bergman, p. 101.
126 *In black music*: Fernando Ortiz, quoted in Pujol, p. 122.
We still remember: Alejo Carpentier, quoted in Carpentier, p. 228.
With any kind of object: quoted in Carpentier, pp. 228–29.
128 *wooden raindrop*: translated and quoted in Raul A. Fernandez, *From Afro-Cuban Rhythms to Latin Jazz* (Berkeley, Los Angeles and London: University of California Press, 2006), p. 26.
129 *does not even have to be played*: Sublette, pp. 170–71.
A European ear would analyse: Sublette, p. 96.
131 *I couldn't get that little island*: Meyer Lansky, quoted in T. J. English, *Havana Nocturne: How the Mob Owned Cuba . . . and Then Lost It to the Revolution* (New York, London, Toronto, and Sydney: Harper, 2008), p. 19.
The colors, the music: Celia Cruz and Ana Christina Reymundo, *Celia: My Life*, trans. José Lucas Badué (New York: Rayo/HarperCollins, 2004), p. 21.

stands out as the musician: Fernandez, pp. 107–8.
133 *Cuban music is voices and drums*: Orlando Marin, paraphrased in Roberts, *The Latin Tinge*, p. 124.
137 *I would have liked to sing opera*: Ignacio Villa, quoted in Sublette, p. 485.
138 *If Cachao and Arsenio Rodríguez*: Bebo Valdés, quoted in "Israel 'Cachao' Lopez Biography," AllMusic (www.allmusic.com/artist/israel-cachao-lopez-mn0000108790/biography).
141 *You want the green*: Federico Pagani, quoted in Bergman, p. 103.
Looking back, it seems: Palladium dancer Jose Torres, quoted in Vernon W. Boggs, *Salsiology: Afro-Cuban Music and the Evolution of Salsa in New York City* (New York: Excelsior Music Publishing, 1992), p. 130.
142 *My feeling for Latin music grew*: Bill Graham and Robert Greenfield, *Bill Graham Presents: My Life Inside Rock and Out* (New York: Da Capo Press, 2004), p. 47.
145 *My biggest ambition*: Graham and Greenfield, pp. 49–50.
We began with the danza: Osvaldo Castillo Faílde, translated and quoted in Moore, *Nationalizing Blackness*, p. 24.
147 *Our ideas of dance*: quoted in Carpentier, p. 198.
[Afro-Cuban dance] always represents: Frederika Bremer, quoted in Chasteen, p. 112.
What fondlings! What liberties!: quoted in Chasteen, p. 130.
The whole year is one big dance: quoted in Chasteen, p. 155.
148 *The talent, for the female dancer*: Moreau de Saint-Méry (1789), quoted in Carpentier, p. 102.
Se armó la rumba: translated and quoted in Alicia Castro, Ingrid Kummels and Manfred Schäfer, *Anacaona: The Amazing Adventures of Cuba's First All-Girl Dance Band*, trans. Steven T. Murray (London: Atlantic Books, 2007), p. 257.
151 *[Y]ou have to be born*: Cachao *López* interview in Padura Fuentes, p. 97.
rotating hips and shimmying shoulders: "Obituary: Alicia Parla," *Daily Telegraph*, Oct. 20, 1998.
there's a great big crack: lyrics to "South America, Take It Away," written by Harold Rome, quoted in Roberts, *The Latin Tinge*, p. 110.
Caramba! It's the samba: lyrics to "Caramba! It's the Samba," written by Edward Eddie Pola, George Wyle, and Irving Taylor, quoted in Roberts, *The Latin Tinge*, p. 110.
153 *Cuban, a good dancer*: quoted in Fernandez, p. 39.
Life is a dream: Lyrics to "La Vida es un sueño" by Arsenio Rodríguez, translated and quoted in Sublette, p. 533.
154 *Arsenio dressed like a prince*: Mario Bauzá interview in Padura Fuentes, p. 24.
158 *If there is such a thing as a magic word*: Sublette, p. 585.
smooth and suave: Sublette, p. 560.
aggressive, jumpy, and violent: Sublette, p. 560.
Who invented the mambo: lyrics to "Locas por el mambo" by Benny Moré, translated in Sue Steward, *¡Musica!: Salsa, Rumba, Merengue, and More: The Rhythm of Latin America* (San Francisco: Chronicle Books, 1999), p. 34.
Possibly the mambo is an outrage: Gabriel García Márquez (writing as "Septimus") in *El Heraldo*, Barranquilla, January 1951, quoted in Sublette, p. 547.
159 *Don't play*: interview with Bebo Valdés's cousin Josefina Barreto, in *Old Man Bebo*, dir. Carlos Carcas (2008).

NOTES ON SOURCES

160 *I couldn't believe my eyes*: Tito Puente, quoted in Powell, p. 185.
161 *Arsenio created the mambo*: Pérez Prado during a show, as reported by Arsenio Rodríguez in a 1964 radio interview, quoted in David F. García, *Arsenio Rodríguez and the Transnational Flows of Latin Popular Music* (Philadelphia: Temple University Press, 2006), pp. 77–78.
163 *[Havana is an] American playground*: Ava Gardner, quoted in Robin D. Moore, *Music and Revolution: Cultural Change in Socialist Cuba* (Berkeley, Los Angeles, and London: University of California Press, 2006), p. 33.
We are in Havana: Steve Allen, quoted in English, p. 249.
[Havana] was being debased: Arthur Schlesinger, quoted in Moore, *Music and Revolution*, p. 33.
167 *What a diff'rence*: lyrics to "What a Diff'rence a Day Makes" by María Grever and Stanley Adams.
168 *By the late fifties, the president's*: John Radanovich, *Wildman of Rhythm: The Life and Music of Benny Moré* (Gainesville: University Press of Florida, 2009), p. 96.
I approved the proclamation: John F. Kennedy, interviewed on Oct. 24, 1963, by French journalist Jean Daniel, quoted in Jean Daniel, "Unofficial Envoy: An Historic Report from Two Capitals," *The New Republic*, Dec. 14, 1963.
169 *We shouldn't have killed Giovanni*: Santo Trafficante to his attorney Frank Ragano, as quoted in English, p. 326.
Per ha de llegar el día: lyrics of 1910 Columbia recording, quoted in Sublette, p. 306.
170 *We are not only disposed*: quoted in English, p. 309.
Havana has become: unsigned article quoted in Moore, *Music and Revolution*, pp. 61–62.
It is the same thing as squeezing: quoted in Gjelten, p. 245.
172 *a voice of clarity*: Cachao López, quoted in Padura Fuentes, p. 101.
173 *part American hep-cat*: Radanovich, p. 83.
175 *A truly revolutionary party*: Leon Trotsky essay, quoted in Moore, *Music and Revolution*, p. 16.
What do our homeland's pain: quoted in English, p. 161.
The [buildings] revalidated: Alma Guillermoprieto, *Dancing with Cuba: A Memoir of the Revolution*, trans. Esther Allen (New York: Pantheon Books, 2004), p. 270.
176 *Fidel doesn't dance*: author's conversation in Havana.
177 *Que se acabe la rumba!*: recounted in Guillermoprieto, *Dancing with Cuba*, p. 59.
commercial structures designed to exploit: 1967 article by Alfredo Muñoz-Unsain in Bohemia, quoted in Moore, *Music and Revolution*, pp. 110–11.
contribute to crudeness: José Ardévol, translated and quoted in Moore, *Music and Revolution*, p. 109.
178 *lumpen*: quoted in Moore, *Music and Revolution*, p. 108.
Nikita, you little faggot: song lyrics, translated from the Spanish "Nikita, mariquita, lo que se da no se quita" and quoted by Moore, *Music and Revolution*, p. 72.
179 *How tasty the cane is*: lyrics to "Bailando mozambique me voy a cortar caña" (Dancing Mozambique I'm going to cut cane) by Pedro Izquierdo; episode recounted in Moore, *Music and Revolution*, p. 184.
[T]he Revolution had not yet progressed: quoted in Richard Gott, *Cuba: A New History* (New Haven and London: Yale University Press, 2004), p. 173.
I'll give my life for you: quoted in Gott, p. 173.

181 *Son, rumba, mambo*: Castro, p. 343.
183 *being* prostituted *and presented*: Carlos Moore, quoted in Moore, *Music and Revolution*, p. 187.
185 *It's clear that salsa*: Willie Colón, quoted in Padura Fuentes, p. 32.
 In Fania we had Dominicans: Johnny Pacheco, quoted in Padura Fuentes, p. 59.
 His musicians were really scary-looking: Johnny Pacheco, quoted in Padura Fuentes, p. 56.
189 *Did we, the politicians*: quoted in Moore, *Music and Revolution*, p. 153.
191 *squares . . . who didn't trust the young*: quoted in Moore, *Music and Revolution*, p. 152.
193 *I admit that the graduates*: quoted in Castro, p. 375.
 The songo *thing is just a distillation*: interview by Larry Birnbaum, as quoted in Boggs, p. 294.
194 *We valorize most*: from Fidel Castro's 1972 speech, translated by and quoted in Moore, *Music and Revolution*, p. 14.
 The Revolution cannot wipe out: Miguel Barnet interview, "*What's Cuba Playing At?*" dir. Mike Dibb, BBC *Arena* (1985).
203 *It was like washing the windscreen*: author's interview with Jerry Boys.
204 *I think you'll be pleased*: author's interview with Nick Gold.
205 *Hernández and his wife*: author's conversation with witness.
206 *I decided . . . to do to their music*: interview quoted in Padura Fuentes, p. 130.

III Catch a Fire

213 *Late one hot Saturday afternoon . . . never again be the same*: author's interview with Chris Blackwell.
215 *By 1860, the 400,000 slaves*: Adam Hochschild, *Bury the Chains: The British Struggle to Abolish Slavery* (London: Macmillan, 2005), p. 67.
216 *take me money and run Venezuela*: lyrics to "Matilda" by Harry Thomas (alias Harry Belafonte).
217 *Day-o . . . daylight come*: Lyrics to "Day-O (The Banana Boat Song)," traditional, arranged by Harry Belafonte, William Attaway, and Lord Burgess.
219 *It seem like to be a teenager*: Derrick Harriott, quoted in Lloyd Bradley, *This Is Reggae Music: The Story of Jamaica's Music* (New York: Grove Press, 2000), p. 3.
 greasin' da crease: Timothy White, *Catch a Fire: The Life of Bob Marley* (New York: Henry Holt and Co., 2006), p. 124.
219 *a lively dating agency*: Bradley, *This Is Reggae Music*, p. 5.
224 *It's ska we play*: Heather Augustyn, "What's in a Name? The Skatalites," Skabook blog (skabook.com/2016/05/29/whats-name-skatalites/), May 29, 2016.
226 *[Y]ou can hear ska unfurl*: John Jeremiah Sullivan, "That Chop on the Upbeat," *Oxford American*, Nov. 17, 2013.
231 *sufferah's jamboree*: White, p. 204.
 we gonna rule this land: lyrics to "Jail House" by Bob Marley and Coxsone Dodd.
 The beginnings of ska: Linton Kwesi Johnson, "Introduction," in album notes for *The Story of Jamaican Music (Tougher Than Tough)* (Mango, IBXCD 1—518 399-2, 1993).

NOTES ON SOURCES

232 *strong like lion:* lyrics to "Rudie Don't Fear" by Derrick Morgan.
235 *Garvey shouted words:* Claude McKay, quoted in Colin Grant, *Negro with a Hat: The Rise and Fall of Marcus Garvey* (New York: Oxford University Press, 2008), p. 185.
dark but comely ... dark and comely: Grant, p. 308.
236 *Some Afric chief will rise:* Thomas Thistlewood, quoted in Trevor Burnard, *Mastery, Tyranny and Desire: Thomas Thistlewood and His Slaves in the Anglo-Jamaican World* (Chapel Hill and London: University of North Carolina Press, 2004), p. 262.
And Babylon shall become: Jeremiah 51:37, King James Bible, quoted in Stephen Foehr, *Jamaican Warriors: Reggae, Roots & Culture* (London: Sanctuary Publishing, 2000), p. 62.
237 *Princes shall come out of Egypt:* Psalm 68, King James Bible, quoted in White, p. 7.
238 *Red, fe de bloodshed:* quoted in White, p. 169.
He causeth the grass to grow: quoted in White, p. 13.
239 *there shall no razor:* Numbers 6:5, King James Bible, quoted in Foehr, p. 175.
he shall be holy: Leviticus 21:5, King James Bible, quoted in Foehr, p. 175.
It helps you to think faster: The First Rasta (Le Premier Rasta), dir. Hélène Lee (2011).
241 *I want you to know:* lyrics to "Bam Bam."
Words and Music by Frederick Hibbert
Copyright © 1980 UNIVERSAL—SONGS OF POLYGRAM INTERNATIONAL, INC.
All Rights Reserved. Used by Permission
Reprinted by Permission of Hal Leonard Europe Ltd.
These islanders are disturbed: V. S. Naipaul, quoted from the 1970 essay "Power to the Caribbean People" in Joshua Jelly-Schapiro, "The Bob Marley Story," *New York Review of Books,* Apr. 9, 2009.
What somebody should have foreseen: Michael Thomas, in Michael Thomas and Adrian Boot, *Jamaica: Babylon on a Thin Wire* (London: Thames and Hudson, 1976), p. 88.
243 *Get-up-in-the-morning:* lyrics to "Israelites" by Desmond Dekker and Leslie Kong.
Brook Benton and Sarah Vaughan: Bob Marley, quoted in Billy Bergman, *Reggae and Latin Pop: Hot Sauces* (Dorset: Blandford Press, 1985), p. 28.
Me don't dip on the black man's side: Bob Marley, quoted in Jelly-Schapiro.
246 *When the people hear what I-man do:* 1977 Lee "Scratch" Perry interview with Bruno Blum, quoted in David Katz, *People Funny Boy: The Genius of Lee 'Scratch' Perry* (London: Omnibus Press, 2006), p. 112.
He was the one who taught: Jimmy Riley, quoted in Katz, p. 112.
250 *Forty years after the event ... played the first local acetate:* author's conversation with Sally Henzell.
251 *The next move came from Paul Simon ... wrote lyrics to fit the track:* author's conversation with Paul Simon.
253 *A week earlier:* author's conversation with Chris Blackwell.
256 *Reggae is where it's at!:* Paul McCartney to a British newspaper, quoted in White, p. 261.
260 *make a ghetto uptown:* Bob Marley, quoted in Jelly-Schapiro.
261 *get out of the contract:* author's conversation with Chris Blackwell.
263 *Bob Marley played Adelaide:* quoted in Timothy D. Taylor, *Beyond Exoticism: Western Music and the World* (Durham and London: Duke University Press, 2007), p. 156.

NOTES ON SOURCES

Something in the rhythm: quoted in Adam McGovern (ed.), *MusicHound World: The Essential Album Guide* (Detroit and London: Visible Ink Press, 2000), p. 141.
In his words I heard my own: Lemn Sissay, *My Name Is Why: A Memoir* (Edinburgh: Canongate, 2019), pp. 113–14.
I ventured cocaine: Ken Boothe, quoted in Foehr, p. 167.

268 *As soon as they had to stop*: Dennis Bovell, quoted in Lloyd Bradley, *Sounds Like London: 100 Years of Black Music in the Capital* (London: Serpent's Tail, 2013), p. 243.
270 *he'd have to know everybody*: Bradley, *Sounds Like London*, p. 254.
271 *A good idea attempted*: Don Letts, quoted in David Nobakht, "Foreword," in Don Letts and David Nobakht, *Culture Clash: Dread Meets Punk Rockers* (London: SAF Publishing, 2007), p. 13.
273 *bastardised reggae*: Stewart Copeland interview in *Reggae Britannia*, dir. Jeremy Marre, BBC Four *Britannia* series (2011).
reggae that wouldn't frighten: Boy George, quoted in Neil Spencer, "Reggae: The Sound That Revolutionised Britain," *Observer*, Jan. 30, 2011.
275 *The sun hadn't gone down yet*: Nelson George, quoted in Alex Ogg and David Upshall, *The Hip Hop Years* (London: Macmillan, 1999), p. 17.
277 *A happy face*: Bradley, *Sounds Like London*, p. 329.
There is a downside: Letts and Nobakht, p. 204.
279 *Why do you look so sad*: lyrics to "Coming in from the Cold" by Bob Marley.
284 *I don't write nursery rhymes*: author's interview with Toots Hibbert.
Etty in the room a-cry: lyrics to "Sweet and Dandy."
Words and Music by Frederick "Toots" Hibbert
Copyright © 1980 UNIVERSAL—SONGS OF POLYGRAM INTERNATIONAL, INC.
All Rights Reserved. Used by Permission
Reprinted by Permission of Hal Leonard Europe Ltd.

IV Latcho Drom

287 *put the listener in a relaxed mood*: Richard Bock, quoted in Oliver Craske, *Indian Sun: The Life and Music of Ravi Shankar* (London: Faber & Faber, 2020), pp. 183–84.
289 *the slow and reflective beginning*: David Crosby, interviewed by and quoted in Peter Lavezzoli, *The Dawn of Indian Music in the West* (New York and London: Continuum, 2007), p. 163.
Wow, man, you can dance to that!: Richard Clayton, "How The Byrds transformed Bob Dylan's 'Mr Tambourine Man,'" *Financial Times*, July 25, 2016.
290 *Ringo who?*: Ajana Angadi, quoted in Craske, p. 292.
292 *endowed with one of the most perfect bodies*: Anna Pavlova, quoted in Craske, p. 32.
293 *an alarming cacophony*: recounted in Amit Chaudhuri, "Indian Classical Music, the Beatles and the Blues," *Guardian*, Sept. 21, 2012.
a maze of noises: narrator of E. M. Forster's novel *A Passage to India*, quoted in Craske, p. 4.

NOTES ON SOURCES

294 *music is a form of listening*: Amit Chaudhuri, *Finding the Raga: An Improvisation on Indian Music* (London: Faber, 2021), p. 65.

295 *That's simple, dear king*: recounted in Namita Devidayal, *The Music Room* (New Delhi: Random House India, 2007), p. 27.

296 *Nada Brahma*: quoted in Lavezzoli, p. 140.

298 *very emotional and sexual*: David Crosby, interviewed by and quoted in Lavezzoli, p. 163.

300 *[T]he eruption of Indian music*: Laurent Aubert, The Music of the Other: New Challenges for Ethnomusicology in a Global Age, trans. Carla Ribeiro (Hampshire: Ashgate, 2007), p. 79.

301 *Did anyone realise they didn't change chords?*: quoted in Craske, p. 296.

The Indian drone as brought into First World culture: quoted in Ian MacDonald, *Revolution in the Head: The Beatles' Records and the Sixties* (Chicago: Chicago Review Press, 2007), p. 192.

302 *My heart melted with love for him*: quoted from Ravi Shankar's autobiography *Raga Mala* in Ajoy Bose, *Across the Universe: The Beatles in India* (Hayana, India: Penguin Books, 2021), p. 80.

This music is thousands of years old: quoted from the Beatles' *Revolver* album notes in Bose, p. 52.

306 *When you get the message*: quoted in Craske, pp. 343–44.

308 *Raindrops on roses*: lyrics to "My Favorite Things" by Richard Rodgers and Oscar Hammerstein II.

309 *pentatonic sonority*: 1963 John Coltrane interview in Paris, quoted in Lavezzoli, p. 282.

310 *complex rhythms of Indian music*: David Fricke, "100 Greatest Guitarists: David Fricke's Picks," *Rolling Stone*, Dec. 3, 2010.

311 *The Grateful Dead was a rhythm machine*: Mickey Hart, interviewed by and quoted in Lavezzoli, p. 92.

the Einstein of rhythm: Mickey Hart, interviewed by and quoted in Lavezzoli, p. 84.

allowed for modal playing: Mickey Hart, interviewed by and quoted in Lavezzoli, p. 94.

314 *the best he's ever fucking played*: Simon Leng, *While My Guitar Gently Weeps: The Music of George Harrison* (Milwaukee, Wisconsin: Hal Leonard, 2006), p. 109.

315 *[Ravi looks like] a man who has patiently endured*: quoted in Craske, pp. 323–24.

Melodically and rhythmically, Indian music: Yehudi Menuhin in his autobiography *Unfinished Journey*, quoted in Lavezzoli, p. 48.

Ours is the song of personal solitude: translation by Rosinka Chaudhuri quoted in Chaudhuri, *Finding the Raga*, p. 35.

316 *had the most incredible ability*: quoted in Craske, p. 520.

317 *like a loaf of bread ... strings them together like beads*: Philip Glass, quoted in Lavezzoli p. 130.

intentionless: Philip Glass, quoted in Lavezzoli, p. 130.

318 *The frequencies in the raga*: Terry Riley, interviewed by and quoted in Lavezzoli, p. 262.

319 *like iron filings to a magnet*: La Monte Young, quoted in Lavezzoli, p. 247.

320 *the greatest living musician of our time*: La Monte Young, quoted in Lavezzoli, p. 249.

once Indian music came to the West: Terry Riley, quoted in Lavezzoli, p. 255.

322 *There are many ways to the Divine*: verse by Rumi.

All day and night, music: *The Essential Rumi*, trans. Coleman Barks with John Moyne, A. J. Arberry, and Reynold Nicholson (New York: Quality Paperback Book Club, 1998), p. 46.
Let your throat-song: *The Essential Rumi*, p. 244.

327 *There's dancing, behind movie scenes*: Lyrics to "Brimful of Asha."
Words and Music by Tjinder Singh
Copyright © 1997 SONGS OF UNIVERSAL, INC., and MOMENTUM MUSIC 2 LTD.
All Rights in the U.S. and Canada Controlled and Administered by UNIVERSAL—SONGS OF POLYGRAM INTERNATIONAL, INC.
All Rights Reserved. Used by Permission
Reprinted by Permission of Hal Leonard Europe Ltd.

329 *There's been a significant amount of Islamophobia*: quoted in Fatima Bhutto, "Superheroes, Jazz, Queer Art: How Pakistan's Transgressive Pop Culture Went Global," *Guardian*, Dec. 19, 2022.

330 *effortless command of intertonal pitching*: Mike Senior, "Mohabbat by Arush Aftab," *The Mix Review* (themixreview.org/reviews/mohabbat/), Feb. 11, 2022.

331 *O Pabuji, the cows' little calves are weeping*: excerpt from the Pabuji epic, quoted in William Dalrymple, *Nine Lives: In Search of the Sacred in Modern India* (London: Bloomsbury, 2010), p. 82.

336 *descendants of the Pharaohs*: quoted in Bálint Sárosi, *Gypsy Music*, trans. Fred Macnicol (Budapest: Corvina Press, 1978), p. 56.

337 *the German musicians almost chewed up*: quoted from a 1790 *Magyar Kurir* report quoted in Sárosi, p. 70.

338 *takes the theme of a song or a dance . . . diatonic and chromatic scales*: Franz Liszt, quoted in Sárosi, p. 146.
bind the notes together: Carl Philipp Emanuel Bach, quoted in Sárosi, p. 107.

339 *When they think to be able to improve*: Franz Liszt, quoted in Sárosi, p. 140.
They excite the hatred *of the bourgeois*: Gustave Flaubert, in a letter to George Sand, quoted in Michael Dregni, *Gypsy Jazz: In Search of Django Reinhardt and the Soul of Gypsy Swing* (New York: Oxford University Press, 2008), p. 24.

341 *goose-feather bed / raggle taggle gypsies, oh*: lyrics to traditional folk song "The Raggle Taggle Gypsies Oh."

344 *played incredible, complicated things . . . who were unable to follow him!*: Jean Vaissade, quoted in Dregni, p. 43.

345 *These ones are real*: Sophie "Naguine" Ziegler, quoted in Dregni, p. 51.

349 *Django's ideas . . . lit up my brain*: B.B. King, quoted in Dregni, p. 8.

350 *O Lord, where should I go?*: excerpt from 1970 poem "Weszo, Dadoro miro" (Oh Forest, My Father) by Bronisława Wajs, quoted in Isabel Fonseca, *Bury Me Standing: The Gypsies and Their Journey* (London: Vintage Books, 2006), p. 4.

356 *In every village there are Gypsies*: quoted in William Blacker, *Along the Enchanted Way: A Romanian Story* (London: John Murray, 2009), p. 157.
You don't learn this job, you steal it: Nicolae Neacşu, quoted from *Honourable Brigands* album notes in Garth Cartwright, *Princes Amongst Men: Journeys with Gypsy Musicians* (London: Serpent's Tail, 2005), p. 199.

NOTES ON SOURCES

357 *to bring gypsy musicians to Belgium*: author's interview with Michel Winter.
359 *a naked slave standing*: quoted in Ned Sublette, *Cuba and Its Music: From the First Drums to the Mambo* (Chicago: Chicago Review Press, 2004), p. 8.
361 *There is no such thing as a stupid gypsy man*: La Preciosa, heroine of *La Gitanilla* by Miguel de Cervantes, quoted in Giles Tremlett, *España: A Brief History of Spain* (London and New York: Bloomsbury Publishing, 2022), p. 134.
The poor payos don't understand: quoted in Claus Schreiner, "Introduction," in Claus Schreiner (ed.), *Flamenco: Gypsy Dance and Music from Andalusia*, trans. Mollie Comerford Peters (Portland, Oregon: Amadeus Press, 1990), p. 16.
362 *prodigality, a hair-trigger temper*: Bernard Leblon, *Gypsies and Flamenco: The Emergence of the Art of Flamenco in Andalusia*, trans. Sinéad ní Shuinéar (Hatfield: University of Hertfordshire Press, 2003), p. 43.
364 *That night in January*: quoted in Will Kirkland (ed.), *Gypsy Cante: Deep Song of the Caves*, selected and trans. Will Kirkland (San Francisco: City Lights Books, 1999), p. 78.
I climbed up to the town walls: quoted in Jason Webster, *Duende: A Journey in Search of Flamenco* (London: Doubleday, 2003), p. 133.
Your mother keeps on saying: quoted in Kirkland, p. 74.
Man goes through his days: quoted in Kirkland, p. 19.
366 *the drunkest, wildest, most argumentative*: quoted in biography "Manolo Caracol," andalucia.com (www.andalucia.com/flamenco/musicians/manolocaracol.htm).
367 *There is nothing more delicate than a rhythm*: Federico García Lorca, quoted in Michael Chanan, *Repeated Takes: A Short History of Recording and Its Effects on Music* (London and New York: Verso, 1995), p. 12.
[The guitar] has lurked upon the dark: Federico García Lorca, *In Search of Duende*, trans. Chistopher Maurer (New York: A New Directions Pearl, 1998), p. 29.
372 *a Republican Gitano*: interview with El Farruco in "An Andalucian Journey: Gypsies and Flamenco," dir. Jana Bokova, episode 9, BBC *Arena* (1988).
Their swarthy complexion brings out the clarity: quoted in Jean-Paul Clébert, *The Gypsies*, trans. Charles Duff (Harmondsworth, UK: Penguin Books, 1970), p. 124.
377 *music they were ashamed to listen to*: Mario Pacheco in *Revelando a Mario: El hombre detrás de la revolución musical*, dir. Simó Mateu (2020).
379 *a 1920s-style tango voice*: Holger Mende, "Flamencos—Pictures and Notes from Andalusia," in Schreiner, *Flamenco*, p. 156.
380 *The duende does not come at all*: García Lorca, *In Search of Duende*, p. 67.
Olé! that has duende: García Lorca, *In Search of Duende*, p. 57.
Where did you foreigners ever get this idea: Juan Talega, quoted in Schreiner, "Introduction," p. 26.
[W]hat can a history student say of an art: Don Benito Cuesta, quoted in Gerald Howson, *The Flamencos of Cádiz Bay* (London: The Bold Strummer, 1994), p. 206.
381 *When I sing as I please*: Tía Anica la Piriñaca, quoted in Kirkland, p. xv.
The Castilians on the corners: flamenco song lyrics, quoted in Kirkland, p. 8.
382 *Oh Mary, don't you weep*: lyrics to "Oh Mary, Don't You Weep," traditional African-American spiritual.

NOTES ON SOURCES

383 *Your daddy he's an outlaw:* lyrics to "One More Cup of Coffee (Valley Below)."
Words and Music by Bob Dylan
Copyright © 1975 UNIVERSAL TUNES
Copyright Renewed
All Rights Reserved. Used by Permission
Reprinted by Permission of Hal Leonard Europe Ltd.

386 *When the party is on*: Rafael Ruiz, quoted in Giles Tremlett, *Ghosts of Spain: Travels Through a Country's Hidden Past* (London: Faber and Faber, 2006), p. 165.

V Chega de saudade

390 *now I understand samba*: author's conversation with Alexander Shoumatoff.
Who invented Brazil?: lyrics to "História do Brasil" by Lamartine Babo, translated and quoted in Bryan McCann, *Hello, Hello Brazil! Popular Music in the Making of Brazil* (Durham and London: Duke University Press, 2004), p. 1.

391 *Afterwards / Ceci loved Peri:* lyrics to "História do Brasil" by Lamartine Babo, translation based on McCann, p. 1, and Maris Jones, "'Quem foi que inventou Brasil?' The Symbolic Role of Music and Race in the Development of Brazilian National Identity," *Yale Historical Review: An Undergraduate Publication* V, issue II, spring 2016.

392 *Sex across the divide*: Peter Robb, *A Death in Brazil: A Book of Omissions* (London: Bloomsbury, 2005), p. 24.
Gilberto's work leaves us all: Jorge Amado, quoted in Robb, p. 28.

393 *There began . . . those lewd dances*: quoted from de Saint-Hilaire's Brazilian field books in Peter Fryer, *Rhythms of Resistance: African Musical Heritage in Brazil* (Hanover: Wesleyan University Press, 2000), p. 101.
While most instruments may have been imported: quoted in Claus Schreiner, *Música Brasileira: A History of Popular Music and the People of Brazil*, trans. Mark Weinstein (New York and London: Marion Boyars, 2002), p. 76.
A mestizo culture is taking shape: Jorge Amado, *Tent of Miracles*, trans. Barbara Shelby (London: Collins Harvill, 1989), p. 254.

394 *When the 1976 census . . . like a shadow in the water*: Brazilian Institute of Geography and Statistics, "What Color Are You?" in Robert M. Levine and John J. Crocitti (eds.), *The Brazil Reader: History, Culture, Politics* (London: Latin America Bureau, 1999), p. 386.
Inventories of Brazilian instruments: "Glossary," in Chris McGowan and Ricardo Pessanha, *The Brazilian Sound: Samba, Bossa Nova and the Popular Music of Brazil* (Philadelphia: Temple University Press, 1998), pp. 207–13.
A catalogue of indigenous groups: Wikipedia, "List of indigenous peoples in Brazil" (en.wikipedia.org/wiki/List_of_indigenous_peoples_of_Brazil).

395 *the Negroes appear to possess*: quoted in Fryer, p. 134.
treated them very well: narration in *The Miracle of Candeal (El milagro de Candeal)*, dir. Fernando Trueba (2005).
a stranger . . . might imagine: English botanist Clarke Abel, quoted in Fryer, p. 6.

NOTES ON SOURCES

Africa has civilised America: Brazilian senator Bernardo Pereira de Vasconcelos, quoted in Fryer, p. 9.
[A]n original sort of music: quoted in Fryer, p. 143.

397 *The best way to explain*: quoted in Fryer, p. 127.
398 *Let's face it*: quoted in John Krich, *Why Is This Country Dancing? A One-Man Samba to the Beat of Brazil* (New York: Simon & Schuster, 1993), p. 173.
401 *pedantic . . . negroid and ridiculous*: writer quoted in Marc A. Hertzman, *Making Samba: A New History of Race and Music in Brazil* (Durham and London: Duke University Press, 2013), p. 107.
they will take us for Guinea Blacks: quoted in McCann, p. 64.
samba . . . is a far more serious thing: quoted in McCann, p. 64.
403 *a black Pan [playing]*: Orestes Barbosa in a 1923 article quoted in Hertzman, p. 157.
Samba was like this: quoted in McCann, p. 47.
a more syncopated style of samba: quoted in McCann, p. 47.
407 *[Music had] the pre-national and national spirit*: quoted in Hermano Vianna, *The Mystery of Samba: Popular Music and National Identity in Brazil*, ed. and trans. John Charles Chasteen (Chapel Hill and London: University of North Carolina Press, 1999), p. 14.
I'm one of those who have always believed: quoted in Vianna, p. 91.
The negroid music in Brazil: quoted in Hertzman, p. 164.
409 *despotism mitigated by sloppiness*: a visiting political scientist, quoted in "The Vargas Era," in Levine and Crociti, p. 151.
take me, carry me to the hill: lyrics to "Me larga" by Marília Batista, translated and quoted in McCann, p. 52.
410 *tricky mulato*: translated and quoted in McCann, p. 71.
411 *I don't use folklore*: Heitor Villa-Lobos, quoted in Ricardo Averbach, *Villa-Lobos and Modernism: The Apotheosis of Cannibal Music* (Lanham: Lexington Books, 2022), p. 47.
Chattanooga choo choo: lyrics to "Chattanooga Choo Choo" by Harry Warren and Mack Gordon.
dear old Southland: lyrics to "Dear Old Southland" by Henry Creamer and Turner Layton.
beat their feet on the Mississippi mud: lyrics to "Mississippi Mud" by Harry Barris and James Cavanaugh.
412 *I say money, money, money*: quoted in Ruy Castro, *Carmen: Uma Biografia* (São Paulo: Companhia das Letras, 2005), p. 201.
413 *annex the USA to the kingdom of samba*: quoted in Castro, *Carmen*, p. 314.
417 *You are jealous, yes?*: Castro, *Carmen*, p. 343.
420 *Boom parará chim*: quoted in McCann, p. 235.
423 *[I]ndependent prostitutes*: quoted in Ruy Castro, *Bossa Nova: The Story of the Brazilian Music That Seduced the World*, trans. Lysa Salsbury (Chicago: Chicago Review Press, 2000), p. 52.
424 *I could write a piece*: quoted in McGowan and Pessanha, p. 60.
429 *He discovered that the acoustics*: Ruy Castro, *Bossa Nova*, trans. Lysa Salsbury, p. 102. Used by permission. From *Chega de Saudade* by Ruy Castro, published in 1990 by

NOTES ON SOURCES

Companhia das Letras, and published in English in the US in 2000 by Chicago Review Press as *Bossa Nova*. New, revised English edition forthcoming.

430 *João Gilberto did the following*: quoted in Schreiner, *Música Brasileira*, pp. 138–39.

431 *Third-world countries usually produce*: quoted in John Lewis, "Why Bossa Nova Is 'the Highest Flowering of Brazilian Culture,'" *Guardian*, Oct. 1, 2013.

432 *No, I haven't got a good voice*: quoted in Castro, *Carmen*, p. 322.

433 *bossa nova evening . . . a bossa nova group*: quoted in Castro, *Bossa Nova*, pp. 150–51.

["Chega de saudade"] sounded like: quoted in Julian Dibbell, "Foreword" to Castro, *Bossa Nova*, p. xii.

How fabulous: quoted in Castro, *Bossa Nova*, p. 254.

Bossa nova is serene: quoted in McGowan and Pessanha, p. 62.

[Bossa nova lyrics] must never speak about death: quoted in Schreiner, *Música Brasileira*, p. 140.

He was like Oscar Niemeyer: Artur da Távola interview in *This Is Bossa Nova* (*Coisa Mais Linda: Histórias e Casos da Bossa Nova*), dir. Paulo Thiago (2005).

434 *It's mine!*: quoted in Castro, *Bossa Nova*, p. 153.

435 *We're not going to "sell"*: translated by and quoted in Hertzman, p. 230.

macumba for tourists: translated and quoted in Hertzman, p. 230.

[Bossa nova turned] classic samba: Dibbell, "Foreword," in Castro, *Bossa Nova*, p. xii.

We were looking for new ways: Roberto Menescal interview in *This Is Bossa Nova*.

I'd really like to know what it felt like: quoted in Schreiner, *Música Brasileira*, p. 189.

You see those yachts, kid?: author's conversation with music publisher Chuck Kaye in 1968.

440 *Her marvellous passing*: quoted in *Songlines*, episode 7/8, presented by John Cavanagh, BBC Radio Scotland (2007).

it would be better if all three of us sang: quoted in Castro, *Bossa Nova*, p. 238.

[the] poetry was all but destroyed: quoted in John Lewis, "Gilberto Gil and Caetano Veloso in London," *Guardian*, July 15, 2010, including song lyrics to "Garota de Ipanema" by Antônio Carlos Jobim and "The Girl from Ipanema" by Norman Gimbel.

442 *The last time I sang so softly*: quoted in Castro, *Bossa Nova*, p. 329.

443 *I'm part of the bourgeoisie*: quoted in Castro, *Bossa Nova*, p. 200.

443 *I'm the bravest woman I know*: quoted in Castro, *Bossa Nova*, p. 272.

After João opened up the gates: João Donato interview in *This Is Bossa Nova*.

444 *Nara whipped our butts*: Roberto Menescal in *This Is Bossa Nova*.

446 *the blackest white man in Brazil . . . son of Xangô*: quoted in McGowan and Pessanha, p. 65.

I want nothing, and I mean nothing, to do . . . making a little bossa nova to sell: quoted in Castro, *Bossa Nova*, pp. 268–69.

447 *[I] thought he was a very interesting guy*: quoted in Alex Robinson, "Gilberto Gil: 'We Wanted to Question How Brazilian Society Was Constituted—The Ethnic Make-Up of Brazil,'" *Songlines*, Feb. 16, 2018.

[W]e were being faithful to bossa nova: Caetano Veloso, *Tropical Truth: A Story of Music and Revolution in Brazil*, ed. Barbara Einzig, trans. Isabel de Sena (New York: Alfred A. Knopf, 2002), p. 102.

NOTES ON SOURCES

I am going to do that when I grow up: quoted in Robinson, "Gilberto Gil."
a cross-dressed Katy Jurado: Veloso, p. 28.
the big surdo *drum*: Veloso, p. 25.

448 *A crisis of insecurity*: quoted in Vianna, p. 96.
449 *If you leave, I'll leave, too*: quoted in Krich, p. 182.
São Paulo is the samba's graveyard: quoted in Schreiner, *Música Brasileira*, p. 178.
450 *É que aprendemos com João*: lyrics to "Saudosismo" by Caetano Veloso, translated and quoted in Castro, *Bossa Nova*, p. xiv.
We were influenced by the Beatles: quoted in Krich, p. 183.
451 *In Tropicália, anything went*: McGowan and Pessanha, p. 84.
The critics thought we were rock and rollish: quoted in Krich, p. 182.
The idea of cultural cannibalism: Veloso, p. 156.
452 *You are the youth*: quoted in McGowan and Pessanha, p. 85.
Both. And even more: quoted in Schreiner, *Música Brasileira*, p. 171.
453 *If you're the same in politics*: quoted in Jonathan Blitzer, "How Caetano Veloso Revolutionized Brazil's Sound and Spirit," *The New Yorker*, Feb. 7, 2022.
Pay attention: lyrics to "Divino, Maravilhoso" by Gilberto Gil and Caetano Veloso, translated by Christopher Dunn, "Tropicalism and Brazilian Popular Music Under Military Rule," in Levine and Crocitti, p. 246.
455 *Um país que vai pra frente . . . Um país de absurdo*: Schreiner, *Música Brasileira*, p. 2.
457 *father, take from me this chalice*: lyrics to "Cálice" by Chico Buarque and Gilberto Gil.
458 *It would be better to play rock 'n' roll*: quoted in Castro, *Bossa Nova*, p. 302.
Sprung from an ultra-cool attitude: John Storm Roberts, *Black Music of Two Worlds* (New York: Praeger Publishers, 1972), p. 80.
[T]he kind of soul and harmonic beauty: quoted in McGowan and Pessanha, p. 67.
461 *in all fusion bands*: quoted in McGowan and Pessanha, p. 173.
463 *Because everyone enjoyed*: Amado, p. 81.
464 *Alas, I am far too French for that*: quoted in John Ryle, "Miracles of the People: How a French Ethnologist Became a Magician in Brazil," *Times Literary Supplement*, July 31, 1998.
Thank God, I wasn't born up north: quoted in Krich, p. 152.
465 *In Bahia, the conditions in which*: Amado, p. 288.
[A Filhos de Gandhy procession] makes you feel: quoted by McGowan and Pessanha, p. 122.
467 *We're postmodern*: quoted in Vianna, p. 103.
471 *As for Brazilian music, let's just say*: quoted in Krich, p. 172.
476 *HOW TO SAMBA (WOMEN'S VERSION)*: Alma Guillermoprieto, *Samba* (New York: Vintage Departures, 1991), pp. 37–38. Used by permission. Originally published by Knopf/Vintage. Copyright © 1990 by Alma Guillermoprieto. All rights reserved.
477 *HOW TO SAMBA (MEN'S VERSION)*: Guillermoprieto, *Samba*, pp. 97–99. Used by permission. Originally published by Knopf/Vintage. Copyright © 1990 by Alma Guillermoprieto. All rights reserved.
479 *Only intellectuals like misery*: quoted in Guillermoprieto, *Samba*, p. 90.
That's something very strange: quoted in Guillermoprieto, *Samba*, p. 195.
Samba . . . propels and ignites the lower body: David Byrne's album notes to *Brazil Classics Vol. 2: O Samba* (Luaka Bop/Sire, CD 26019-2, 1989).

482 *To reach the people*: interview in *Brasil, Brasil!*, prod. Robin Denselow, BBC Four mini-series, "3—A Tale of Four Cities" (2007).
482 *Why complain? I drive a VW bug*: lyrics to "País Tropical" by Jorge Ben Jor, translated and quoted in Krich, p. 54.
482 *[M]oney makes you white*: Amado, p. 342.
483 *The bomb blew up*: lyrics to "Nega maluca" by Fernando Lobo, translated and quoted in Hertzman, p. 220.
Who invented the mulata?: Guillermoprieto, *Samba*, p. 180.
483 *as a mulata*: Guillermoprieto, *Samba*, p. 180.
477 *I think of myself as mulato*: quoted in "A Politically Correct Brazilian Carnival," *The Economist*, Feb. 9, 2017.
484 *There is no folklore*: quoted in Robinson, "Gilberto Gil."
486 *creating high art on its own terms . . . selling that art around the world*: quoted in Lewis, "Why Bossa Nova Is."

VI Mano a mano

488 *silhouettes that glide by silently*: from "Tango," poem by Ricardo Güiraldes, translated and quoted in Artemis Cooper, "Tangomania in Europe and North America 1913–1914," in Simon Collier, Artemis Cooper, María Susana Azzi, and Richard Martin, *¡Tango! The Dance, the Song, the Story* (London: Thames and Hudson, 2002), p. 76.
The tango is in Buenos Aires: Enrique Rodriguez Larreta, quoted in Jo Baim, *Tango: Creation of a Cultural Icon* (Bloomington and Indianapolis: Indiana University Press, 2007), p. 88.
Argentina? . . . Oh yes, the tango!: quoted in Cooper, p. 96.
489 *[A country] which has such a national dance*: quoted in Cooper, p. 96.
Is one supposed to dance it: Comtesse Mélanie de Pourtalès, quoted in Cooper, p. 76.
tango transformed conventions: Adry de Carbuccia, quoted in Cooper, p. 77.
490 *our grandmothers fought tooth and nail*: 1913 article, quoted in Cooper, pp. 83–84.
The tango as danced in England: 1914 article, quoted in Baim, p. 56.
Whether we like it or not: 1914 London *Times* article "The Cult of the Tango," quoted in Baim, p. 61
491 *[T]heir brazen, immoral, abdominal localisations*: translated and quoted in Kate Flakoll (St John), *The Porteno Tango*, unpublished thesis for City University London, 1981, p. 3.
Within the chaste contours of the tango: quoted in Richard Martin, "The Lasting Tango," in Collier et al., p. 173.
Del fango viene el tango: quoted in Flakoll (St John), p. 1.
Tango was also danced by carters: quoted in album notes by Jorge Montes for *Historia del Tango, Vols. 1 & 2* (Music Hall, MH 10.001/2-2, 1988), p. 6.
492 *Maidens and other innocents*: Buenos Aires public prosecutor, quoted in John Charles Chasteen, *National Rhythms, African Roots: The Deep History of Latin American Popular Dance* (Albuquerque: University of New Mexico Press, 2004), p. 101.

NOTES ON SOURCES

a proper understanding of their own lowness: Buenos Aires city council official, quoted in Chasteen, p. 100.

496 *The bandoneón is a hellish instrument*: quoted in Cooper, p. 113.

499 Weltschmerz *and cool*: quoted in Robert Farris Thompson, *Tango: The Art History of Love* (New York: Pantheon Books, 2005), p. 183.
Tango is a sad thought: quoted in Farris Thompson, *Tango*, p. 26.
The basis is rhythm: translated by and quoted in Baim, p. 43.
The tango appears to be: Julie Taylor, *Paper Tangos* (Durham and London: Duke University Press, 1998), pp. 65–66.
My girl's got a gift: lyrics to "Cuerpo de alambre" by Ángel G. Villoldo, translated by and quoted in Farris Thompson, *Tango*, p. 29.

500 *The quadrilles were danced*: Lucio Vicente López, quoted in Chasteen, p. 131.
with stop-pattern flourishes: Ignacio H. Fotheringham, quoted in Farris Thompson, *Tango*, p. 127.

501 *In a lengthy 1913 article*: from a *Crítica* article, summarized in Simon Collier, "The Tango Is Born," in Collier et al., p. 44.
[gloried] . . . in quick subtle tricks: quoted in Farris Thompson, *Tango*, p. 129.
This is called being stuck together . . . This corte will leave Uncle cross-eyed: quoted in Farris Thompson, *Tango*, p. 234.

502 *to season it with candombe*: recounted in Robert Farris Thompson, *Aesthetic of the Cool: Afro-Atlantic Art and Music* (Pittsburgh and New York: Periscope Publishing, 2011), p. 151.

505 *the true poetry of our time*: quoted in María Susana Azzi, "The Golden Age and After: 1920s–1990s," in Collier et al., p. 132.

506 *You dribbled* [gambeteabas] *. . . should the occasion arise*: excerpts from lyrics to "Mano a mano" by Celedonio Flores, Carlos Gardel, and José Razzano, translated by Alfredo Rosso and the author.

507 *For example*: song synopses to "Mano cruel" by Armando Tagini and Carmelo Mutarelli / "Malevaje" by Enrique Santos Discépolo and Juan de Dios Filiberto / "Seguí mi consejo" by Juan Fernández, Salvador Merico, and Eduardo Trongé / "La Cumparsita (Si supieras)" by Pascual Contursi, Enrique P. Maroni, and Gerardo Hernán Matos Rodríguez, translated and paraphrased by Simon Collier in album notes for *Carlos Gardel: The King of Tango, Vol. 1* (Nimbus Records, NI 7896, 1999), pp. 14–17. Used by permission. Text by Simon Collier (NI7896) courtesy of Nimbus Records, www.wyastone.co.uk.

509 *[A] real showcase of mischief*: lyrics to "Cambalache" by Enrique Santos Discépolo, translated and quoted in Azzi, "The Golden Age and After," p. 137.
. . . through your complicated tango steps: excerpts from the poem "El Entrerriano" by Carlos de la Púa, translated by and quoted in Baim, p. 102.

510 *I do not like the woman to talk*: dancer interview from Julie M. Taylor, *Tango: Theme of Class and Nation*, quoted in Baim, p. 87.

514 *Tango, once you were happy*: "Alguien le dice al tango" by Jorge Luis Borges. Copyright © 1996, Maria Kodama, used by permission of The Wylie Agency (UK) Limited. Translated and quoted in Farris Thompson, Tango, pp. 27–28.

NOTES ON SOURCES

514 *Qué booa?*: private recording by audience member provided to the author.
516 *No, my boy, that isn't tango*: translated and quoted in Azzi, "The Golden Age and After," p. 158.
is the real *Astor Piazzolla*: Farris Thompson, *Tango*, p. 208.
519 *the kind of vivid, meticulous, serious*: quoted in Christine Denniston, *The Meaning of Tango: The Story of the Argentinian Dance* (London: Portico, 2007), pp. 93–94.
520 *Tango in Argentina is like ice*: quoted in Uki Goñi, "How Argentina's Gravel-Voiced Crooner Put the Soul Back into Tango for the Rap Generation," *Guardian*, Oct. 23, 2016.
Tango is against anything that may be: quoted in album notes by Jorge Montes to *Historia del Tango, Vols 1 & 2* (Music Hall, MH 10.001/2-2, 1988), p. 4.
522 *every comma, every period*: interview with Roberto Goyeneche in *Tributo al polaco*, dir. Eduardo Berti, Luis Barros and Alejandro Siskos (1995).
Very young, in that backyard: excerpts from the poem "Elolaco" by Horacio Ferrer, translated by Litto Nebbia, Alfredo Rosso, and the author. Used by permission.
524 *ni milonga, ni tango*: Carlos Gardel in the film *Cuesta abajo*, dir. Louis J. Gasnier (1934).
525 *tango is waiting for you*: author's correspondence with Litto Nebbia.
526 *Tango doesn't need reviving*: author's correspondence with Acho Estol.
[T]he French or Spanish composer who: Jorge Luis Borges, *The Total Library: Non-Fiction 1922–1986*, ed. Eliot Weinberger, trans. Esther Allen, Suzanne Jill Levine, and Eliot Weinberger (London: Penguin Books, 2001), p. 401.
528 *The man who cannot make the woman feel*: quoted in Kapka Kassabova, *Twelve Minutes of Love: A Tango Story* (London: Granta, 2019), p. 282.
I'm delighted that we have: quoted in Kassabova, p. 277.
530 *follows the follower*: Denniston, p. 23.
giving her back her body: Taylor, p. 20.
laugh and forget your troubles . . . all about *your troubles*: Kassabova, p. 2.
At its best, the milonga makes: Kassabova, p. 193.
531 *dance partners exchange leadership*: Martin, "The Lasting Tango," p. 179.
How do you take responsibility: Farris Thompson, *Aesthetic of the Cool*, p. 155.
[taking] the woman's hand: Farris Thompson, *Aesthetic of the Cool*, p. 155.
always fifty-fifty: María Nieves, quoted in Farris Thompson, *Tango*, p. 25.
move differently from the rest of us: quoted in Kassabova, p. 275.
532 *the cigarette smoke and the barbecue*: Julio Cortázar, *Blow-Up and Other Stories*, trans. Paul Blackburn (New York: Pantheon Books, 1985), p. 111.
bound into tight black suits: Cortázar, p. 106.
slowly without speaking: Cortázar, p. 107.
Don't come back here with that: Farris Thompson, *Tango*, p. 260.
533 *the staggered, shuffling, cheeky*: Kassabova, p. 293.
Milonga is daughter of candombe: quoted in Kassabova, p. 293.
the only thing that united them: Kassabova, p. 294.
Tango is a product of crisis of identity: quoted in Kassabova, p. 96.
Freud said that the aim of psychotherapy: quoted in Kassabova, p. 176.

534 *If nostalgia is a country*: Farris Thompson, *Tango*, p. 25.
I've never been held like that before: Farris Thompson, *Aesthetic of the Cool*, p. 155.
when we grow up: reference to previous Litto Nebbia quote.

VII Szerelem, szerelem

535 *While music will obligingly serve*: Mark Slobin, "Introduction," in Mark Slobin (ed.), *Retuning Culture: Musical Changes in Central and Eastern Europe* (Durham and London: Duke University Press, 1996), p. 4.
OK, on one condition: author's conversation with Jac Holzman.
544 *saw all the wrong things*: Solomon Volkov, *St. Petersburg: A Cultural History* (New York: The Free Press, 1995), p. 53.
545 *an inquisitive savage*: Claude Debussy, quoted in Peter Fletcher, *World Musics in Context: A Comprehensive Survey of the World's Major Musical Cultures* (Oxford and New York: Oxford University Press, 2001), p. 463.
546 *The study of the people*: quoted in Orlando Figes, *Natasha's Dance: A Cultural History of Russia* (London: Allen Lane, 2002), p. 222.
we, the lovers of the people: quoted in Figes, p. 224.
There is more love of humanity: quoted in Figes, p. 207.
547 *In Europe we were hangers-on*: quoted in Anna Reid, *The Shaman's Coat: A Native History of Siberia* (London: Phoenix, 2003), p. 11.
Drinking is the joy of the Russes: quoted in Philip Marsden, *The Spirit-Wrestlers and Other Survivors of the Russian Century* (London: Flamingo, 1999), p. 164.
548 *a fairytale land*: quoted in Figes, p. 384.
a hedonistic kingdom: quoted in Figes, p. 384.
549 *these new sounds were a sort*: quoted in Volkov, p. 102.
Only a Russian could have composed it: quoted in Figes, p. 391.
Take my hand, I'm a stranger: lyrics to "Stranger in Paradise" by Robert Wright and George Forrest, with music by Alexander Borodin, from the musical *Kismet*.
550 *languorous undulation*: Richard Taruskin, *Defining Russia Musically: Historical and Hermeneutical Essays* (Princeton and Oxford: Princeton University Press, 2000), p. 168.
had been surrounded with Oriental impressions: Vladimir Stasov, quoted in Figes, p. 392.
551 *the finest living relics*: Fedor Buslaev, quoted in Figes, p. 396.
We had enough of the Orient . . . Art isn't a pastime: Modest Mussorgsky, quoted in Richard Taruskin, "'Entoiling the Falconet': Russian Musical Orientalism in Context," *Cambridge Opera Journal* 4, no. 3, Nov. 1992, p. 280.
552 *A steppe is a steppe is a steppe*: Dimitri Tiomkin, as quoted in Harlow Robinson, *Russians in Hollywood, Hollywood's Russians* (2007), referenced in "Dimitri Tiomkin" Wikipedia (en.wikipedia.org/wiki/Dimitri_Tiomkin).
554 *In our hearts, the needle of a seismograph*: Alexander Blok in 1908, translated and quoted in Taruskin, *Defining Russia Musically*, p. 378.
555 *I say to all: abandon love*: Kazimir Malevich, quoted in Palko Karasz, "At Malevich Exhibition, a Journey of Ideas," *New York Times*, Mar. 16, 2015.

556 *[T]he whole of the Russian intelligentsia*: quoted in Lynne Viola, *Peasant Rebels Under Stalin: Collectivization and the Culture of Peasant Resistance* (New York and Oxford: Oxford University Press, 1996), p. 31.
Any peasant who . . . has emerged: quoted in Viola, p. 17.
557 *I can't listen to music too often*: Vladimir Ilyich Lenin, quoted in Alex Ross, *The Rest Is Noise: Listening to the Twentieth Century* (London: Fourth Estate, 2012), p. 238.
558 *defeat peasant darkness . . . overcome rural backwardness*: quoted in Viola, p. 13.
the half-savage, stupid, ponderous people: quoted from Maxim Gorky's "On the Russian Peasantry" in Viola, p. 13.
558 *Communism was modernity*: quoted from Baumann's *Intimations of Postmodernity* in Slobin, "Introduction," p. 2.
the idiocy of rural life: Karl Marx, quoted in Tony Judt, *Postwar: A History of Europe Since 1945* (London: Penguin Books, 2005), p. 365.
A way of life which has not changed: Vladimir Mayakovsky, quoted in Figes, p. 467.
559 *13,000 "riots" in 1930*: Viola, p. 4.
2,796 assaults on Party officials: Viola, p. 155.
561 *Folk songs . . . [have] nothing in common*: quoted from *Sovetskoe Iskusstva (Soviet Art)*, no. 1, 1927, in S. Frederick Starr, *Red and Hot: The Fate of Jazz in the Soviet Union 1917–1980* (New York: Oxford University Press, 1983), p. 94.
recognise themselves, their thoughts: quoted in Laura J. Olson, *Performing Russia: Folk Revival and Russian Identity* (London and New York: RoutledgeCurzon, 2004), p. 54.
563 *the music and literature of a country*: from the translation of Plato's *The Republic* by Desmond Lee, quoted in Laurent Aubert, *Music of the Other: New Challenges for Ethnomusicology in a Global Age*, trans. Carla Ribeiro (Hampshire, UK: Ashgate, 2007), p. 1.
564 *You must forget the phrase*: recounted in Sjeng Scheijen, *Diaghilev: A Life* (London: Profile Books, 2010), p. 15.
565 *Diaghilev's boundless energy*: quoted in Scheijen, p. 101.
[W]hat could be more destructive: Sergei Diaghilev, quoted in Scheijen, p. 100.
The demand that art should serve society: Sergei Diaghilev, quoted in Scheijen, p. 99.
subversive art in a lavish setting: Scheijen, p. 89.
things . . . coming to an end: quoted in Scheijen, p. 134.
566 *carry the torch that she lit*: Sergei Diaghilev, quoted in Scheijen, p. 173.
grand homosexual: composer and collaborator Nicolas Nabokov, quoted in Oliver Winchester, "Diaghilev's Boys," in Jane Pritchard (ed.), *Diaghilev and the Golden Age of the Ballets Russes 1909–1929* (London: V&A Publishing, 2010), p. 46.
567 *It was as if Creation*: quoted in Scheijen, p. 183.
I could never have dreamt: quoted in Scheijen, p. 184.
To enter Poiret's salons: quoted in Claire Wilcox, "Paul Poiret and the Ballets Russes," in Pritchard (ed.), *Diaghilev and the Golden Age*, p. 65.
568 *Oh excellently. I've already bought*: quoted in Scheijen, p. 192.
fairy tale for grown-ups: Alexander Benois, quoted in Figes, p. 275.
569 *sonic halo*: Ross, p. 13.
a solemn pagan rite: Igor Stravinsky, quoted in Scheijen, p. 212.

NOTES ON SOURCES

I am the vessel: quoted in Tom Service, "The Rite of Spring: 'The Work of a Madman,'" *Guardian*, Feb. 12, 2013.

570 *Till the end, my dear!*: quoted in Scheijen, p. 263.
The old upright piano: quoted in Figes, p. 265.
I am an Egyptian: quoted in John E. Bowlt, Nicoletta Misler, and Evgenia Petrova, "Fire and Ice," in John E. Bowlt, Nicoletta Misler, and Evgenia Petrova (eds.), *The Russian Avant-Garde, Siberia and the East* (Milan: Skira Editore, 2013), p. 26.

571 *the most dazzling [audience]*: quoted in Scheijen, p. 271.
a dentist! . . . two dentists!: quoted in Scheijen, p. 272.
During the whole performance: quoted in Scheijen, p. 271.

572 *nerveless as a crocodile*: Igor Stravinsky, quoted in Service, "The Rite of Spring."
Did you recognize it: as recounted by Edwin Evans, quoted in Jane Pritchard, "Creating Productions," in Pritchard (ed.), *Diaghilev and the Golden Age*, p. 82.
The prize bull that inseminated: Robert Craft, quoted in Richard Taruskin, "Shocker Cools into a 'Rite' of Passage," *New York Times*, Sept. 14, 2012.
exactly what I wanted!: quoted in Scheijen, p. 272.
un ballet biologique . . . forehead against the bars: Jacques Rivière, quoted in Taruskin, *Defining Russia Musically*, p. 379.

573 *The spirit of the music was modern*: from one of T. S. Eliot's "London Letter" essays published in *The Dial* LXXI, no. 4, Oct. 1921 (theworld.com/~raparker/exploring/tseliot/works/london-letters/london-letter-1921-10.html), pp. 452–55.
I realized that I prefer "Le Sacre": quoted in Richard Taruskin, "Shocker Cools into a 'Rite' of Passage."

574 *the perfect musical approach . . . [R]ational complexity is far less disquieting*: Taruskin, *Defining Russia Musically*, p. 385.
a kind of apotheosis of Russian rural music: quoted in Ross, p. 98.

575 *What extraordinary resolve!*: quoted in Marsden, p. 14.
Yes, we are Scythians: excerpt from the poem "Scythians" by Alexander Blok, quoted in Marsden, p. 14.
You have forgotten such love exists: excerpt from the poem "Scythians" by Alexander Blok, quoted in Marsden, p. 33.

576 *beautiful, healthy barbarism*: quoted in Ross, p. 94.
an organic, preternatural unanimity: Taruskin, *Defining Russia Musically*, p. 412.
legalism: Taruskin, *Defining Russia Musically*, p. 394.
quell the voice of reason: quoted in Taruskin, *Defining Russia Musically*, p. 424.
realer than the real: quoted in Taruskin, *Defining Russia Musically*, p. 431.

577 *incomparably compelling aesthetic integrity*: Taruskin, *Defining Russia Musically*, p. 448.
harsh implacable machine: Alastair Macaulay, "A Latter-Day American Answer to Stravinsky's 'Rite of Spring,'" *New York Times*, June 16, 2023.
perfectly impersonal, perfectly homogeneous: quoted from Robert Craft's interviews with Igor Stravinsky in Taruskin, *Defining Russia Musically*, p. 448.
The knowledge that you live: Pyotr Suvchinsky, quoted in Taruskin, *Defining Russia Musically*, p. 399.

NOTES ON SOURCES

I don't believe that anyone venerates Mussolini: quoted in Taruskin, *Defining Russia Musically*, p. 451.
Mussolini of music: Taruskin, *Defining Russia Musically*, p. 452.
578 *tonal masses . . . sculptured in marble*: Igor Stravinsky, quoted in Taruskin, *Defining Russia Musically*, p. 467.
a great Russian artist: quoted in Ross, p. 104.
[m]usic needs no help: quoted in Taruskin, *Defining Russia Musically*, p. 366.
He was . . . a Dionysian pagan: quoted in Scheijen, p. 443.
579 *There's absolutely no fooling around*: Henri Matisse, quoted in Scheijen, p. 352.
[T]he art of man isn't simply birdsong: quoted in Scheijen, p. 5.
580 *decadence and unhealthy exoticism*: quoted in Richard Stites, *Russian Popular Culture: Entertainment and Society Since 1900* (Cambridge: Cambridge University Press, 1995), p. 47.
582 *The proletarian culture does not abolish*: 1925 speech by Joseph Stalin, quoted in Aubert, p. 50.
584 *remnants of bourgeois ideology*: Olson, p. 54.
went away a nightingale: quoted in Theodore Levin, *The Hundred Thousand Fools of God: Musical Travels in Central Asia (and Queens, New York)* (Bloomington and Indianapolis: Indiana University Press, 1996), p. 25.
584 *like you're listening to funeral music*: quoted in Levin, *The Hundred Thousand Fools of God*, p. 65.
585 *[A] Russian girl in our school dances*: Igor Moiseyev, quoted in Anthony Shay, *Choreographic Politics: State Folk Dance Companies, Representation and Power* (Middletown, Connecticut: Wesleyan University Press, 2002), p. 78.
586 *union of free republics sealed forever*: 1943–55 lyrics of the "State Anthem of the Union of Soviet Socialist Republics," written by Sergei Mikhalkov and Gabriyel' Arkadyevich Ureklyan, with music by Alexander Alexandrov.
587 *All this energy could be invested*: quoted in Stites, p. 133.
588 *No one knew him by sight*: Yuri Vdovin, quoted in Alexei Yurchak, *Everything Was Forever, Until It Was No More: The Last Soviet Generation* (Princeton and Oxford: Princeton University Press, 2006), p. 181.
In the 1950s the impact of the one hundred: Shay, p. 4.
590 *Finally they've shown us Moscow invalids*: quoted in Olson, p. 84.
591 *I will NOT have men with beards*: author's interview with Vyacheslav Shchurov.
I remember where they were standing: quoted in Olson, p. 82.
593 *[s]uch men . . . through those songs*: Zhanna Kabanova, quoted in Olson, p. 93.
stillborn forgeries of folk creation: reviewer, quoted in Olson, p. 73.
594 *something that's appropriate in a kitchen*: quoted in Theodore Levin, "Dimitri Pokrovsky and the Russian Folk Music Revival Movement," in Slobin (ed.), *Retuning Culture*, p. 28.
595 *The wound is still open*: Roger Bartra, *The Cage of Melancholy*, quoted in Donna Buchanan, "Metaphors of Power, Metaphors of Truth: The Politics of Music Professionalism in Bulgarian Folk Orchestras," *Ethnomusicology* 39, no. 3, autumn 1995, p. 404.

598 *interferential diaphony*: Gerald Florian Messner's study "Interferential Diaphony in the Village of Bistritsa: Research on the Polyphonic Song Forms of a Village in Central Western Bulgaria," quoted in Stoyan Djoudjev, "The Diaphony of Bistritsa," *Obzor: A Bulgarian Quarterly Review of Literature and Arts*, issue 74, 1986, p. 91.
602 *The people don't like the people's music*: quoted in Timothy Rice, *May It Fill Your Soul: Experiencing Bulgarian Music* (Chicago and London: University of Chicago Press, 1994), p. 260.
605 *a gripping, stirring evening of music*: John Rockwell, "Review/Folk Music: The Songs of Bulgaria," *New York Times*, May 18, 1988.
607 *I thought I told you there was no folklore*: head of Yambol district Committee for Culture, quoted in Rice, p. 18.
608 *resurgence of Bulgarian identity*: quoted in Donna A. Buchanan, "Wedding Musicians, Political Transition, and National Consciousness in Bulgaria," in Slobin (ed.), *Retuning Culture*, p. 215.
610 *[I]t's about time the government paid attention*: quoted in Carol Silverman, "Contemporary Wedding Music in Bulgaria," unpublished manuscript, 1988, p. 14.
611 *Bulgarian folk music [has] become an organic necessity*: culture ministry official, quoted in Carol Silverman, *Balkanology*, 33 1/3 Europe series (New York and London: Bloomsbury Academic, 2021), p. 68.
They have created a style: scholar, quoted in Silverman, *Balkanology*, p. 69.
613 *play like a man*: quoted in Carol Silverman, *Romani Routes: Cultural Politics and Balkan Music in Diaspora* (Oxford and New York: Oxford University Press, 2012), p. 135.
Have you ever seen how a hunted wild rabbit: Yuri Yunakov, quoted in Silverman, *Balkanology*, p. 37.
614 *A wedding is equal to a dozen concerts*: Papasov, quoted in Silverman, *Romani Routes*, p. 312.
616 *a bell, sunken in a mountain lake*: excerpt from poem "Bartók's String Quartet No. 5" by Géza Képes, translated in Peter Laki and Claire Lashley, "A Selection of Poems Inspired by Béla Bartók," in Laki (ed.), *Bartók and His World*, p. 300.
617 *They did not beat us up*: Béla Halmos, quoted in Judit Frigyesi, "The Aesthetic of the Hungarian Revival Movement," in Slobin (ed.), *Retuning Culture*, p. 62.
618 *We must drink our fill*: quoted in Ross, p. 83.
619 *I shall collect all the most beautiful Hungarian folk songs*: quoted in Jean-François Boukobza, "Entre avant-garde internationale et identité nationale: le folklore au cœur de la création de Bartók," in *Allegro Barbaro, Béla Bartók et la modernité hongroise, 1905–1920* (Paris: Editions Hazan, 2013), p. 107.
620 *attains an unsurpassable degree of perfection*: quoted in Leon Botstein, "Out of Hungary: Bartók, Modernism, and the Cultural Politics of Twentieth-Century Music," in Laki, p. 15.
620 *came to understand rural music*: Ross, p. 89.
showed me how I could free myself: quoted in Boukobza, p. 105.
621 *the art of the Hungarian people*: quoted in Botstein, p. 33.
[W]e are dealing with an individual gone astray: quoted in Peter Laki, "The Gallows and the Altar: Poetic Criticism and Critical Poetry about Bartók in Hungary," in Laki, p. 87.

NOTES ON SOURCES

622 *These melodies are meant for the tavern*: singer Jenő Takács, quoted in Mrs Pál Voit, née Éva Oláh Tóth, "Recollections of Béla Bartók," trans. Peter Laki, in Laki, p. 267.
Bartók has become the servant: critic Emil Haraszti in *Budapesti Napló*, quoted in Boukobza, p. 106.
I never liked his music anyway: quoted in David E. Schneider, "Bartók and Stravinsky: Respect, Competition, Influence, and the Hungarian Reaction to Modernism in the 1920s," in Laki, p. 172.
completely objective . . . devoid of human expression: Igor Stravinsky, quoted in Schneider, p. 180.
Now I know quite exactly what the new direction is: quoted in Schneider, p. 184.
I never could share his lifelong gusto: quoted in Schneider, p. 173.
All the tangled chaos: quoted in Schneider, p. 186.

623 *discomfort with the truth*: Hans Eisler, quoted in Botstein, p. 11.
the apparently "logical" consequences: Botstein, p. 5.
shameful: Theodor W. Adorno, quoted in Botstein, p. 5.
narcotic illusionism and an aesthetic inducement: Adorno, paraphrased in Botstein, p. 7.
ethical power: Adorno, paraphrased in Botstein, p. 8.
to make our souls function again: Arnold Schoenberg, quoted in Botstein, p. 8.

624 *the representative of our perishing world's*: Bence Szabolcsi, "Two Bartók Obituaries," trans. Peter Laki, in Laki, p. 293.

626 *came into my heart*: Dániel Hamar interview in *Muzsikás Story (Muzsikás Történet)*, dir. Péter Pál Tóth (2009).

627 *People think folk music is for old situations*: quoted in Simon Broughton, "The Rough Guide to World Music: Hungary," *Songlines*, July 17, 2018.

630 *Amazing scenes last night*: Michael Tumelty, "A Hair-Raising Brew: BBC Scottish Symphony and Folk Group Muzsikás Explore Bartók's Roots," *Glasgow Herald*, Mar. 8, 2004.

640 *Singing two notes at once*: AT&T promotional brochure, quoted in Theodore Levin and Valentina Süzükei, *Where Rivers and Mountains Sing: Sound, Music, and Nomadism in Tuva and Beyond* (Bloomington and Indianapolis: Indiana University Press, 2006), p. 205.

645 *You mustn't broadcast this nonsense*: author's conversation with Olga Solovyova.
This is sex together with culture: quoted in Olson, p. 136.

646 *an alternative symbolic universe*: quoted in Olson, p. 183.
strengthening the foundations of the nation . . . foreign sounds negatively impact: journalist Natal'ia Sapozhnikova, quoted in Olson, p. 123.

647 *The Cossack revival is a disaster*: Neal Ascherson, *Black Sea: The Birthplace of Civilisation and Barbarism* (London: Vintage, 1996), p. 106.

648 *like drinking a cooling glass of water*: Yevgeni Yefremov to Bruce Clark of the *Times*, quoted in Ascherson, p. 110.

648 *Now you understand this country!*: author's conversation with Viktor Erofeyev.

649 *The USA is a chimerical, anti-organic*: Alexander Dugin, quoted in Anton Barbashin and Hannah Thoburn, "Putin's Brain: Alexander Dugin and the Philosophy Behind Putin's Invasion of Crimea," *Foreign Affairs*, Mar. 31, 2014.

651 *My guiding philosophy has always been*: quoted album notes by Muzsikás, trans. Nicholas Jenkins, for Muzsikás Featuring Márta Sebestyén & Alexander Balanescu, *The Bartók Album* (Hannibal Records, HNCD 1439, 1999).

652 *Muzsikás and Tina Turner*: Viktor Orbán speech during a Fidesz party congress on Feb. 7, 1992.

653 *All politicians are liars*: author's conversation in Hungary.

In those villages, you were judged by: author's conversation with Dániel Hamar.

ulcers on the body of the motherland: quoted in Benedict Anderson, *Imagined Communities: Reflections on the Origin and Spread of Nationalism* (London and New York: Verso, 1992), p. 103.

[G]uests . . . bring with them: quoted in Anderson, p. 109.

VIII Tezeta

654 *Are you hearing this!?*: author's interview with Tony Allen.

656 *We should have been playing*: Tony Allen, in Tony Allen and Michael E. Veal, *Tony Allen: An Autobiography of the Master Drummer of Afrobeat* (Durham and London: Duke University Press, 2013), p. 46.

660 *I'm telling you—it was fantastic*: Allen and Veal, p. 32.

661 *We are civilised people*: quoted from Antonio Olinto's *The Water House* in Christopher Alan Waterman, *Jùjú: A Social History and Ethnography of an African Popular Music* (Chicago and London: University of Chicago Press, 1990), p. 32.

662 *air of authority, a compelling manner*: quoted from a 1951 Ransome-Kuti family portrait in *West Africa* magazine in Michael E. Veal, *Fela: The Life and Times of an African Musical Icon* (Philadelphia: Temple University Press, 2000), p. 30.

663 *penis of a poison rat / vagina's head will seek vengeance*: quoted in Veal, *Fela*, p. 32.

sophisticated, magically powerful: Waterman, *Jùjú*, p. 94.

665 *utilitarian syncretism*: based on Robert Baron's 1977 article "Syncretism and Ideology," in Waterman, *Jùjú*, p. 15.

I don't think anyone kicked my ass: quoted in Veal, *Fela*, p. 30.

666 *looked like a . . . perfect square*: J. K. Braimah, quoted in Veal, *Fela*, p. 34.

I forgot everything: Fela Kuti, quoted in Michael Archangel, *Rule by Love: Rhythms and Consent—The Definitive Fela Biography* (Sydney: Sazimor, 1998), p. 28.

I was playing the piano: Fela Kuti, quoted in Archangel, p. 32.

667 *[A]n extraordinary fellow*: a fellow student, quoted in Veal, *Fela*, p. 45.

Oh wow. These white people: Fela Kuti, quoted in Veal, *Fela*, p. 43.

I kept blowing nonsense: Fela Kuti, quoted in Veal, *Fela*, p. 43.

It was really colonial: Fela Kuti, quoted in Veal, *Fela*, p. 45.

668 *[G]irlfriends, he always had them*: Remilekun (Remi) Anikulapo-Kuti, quoted in Veal, *Fela*, pp. 45–46.

it was far too complicated: Veal, *Fela*, p. 54.

Fela Ransome Kuti knows music: journalist Peter Enahoro ("Peter Pan"), quoted in album notes by John Armstrong for *Nigeria 70: The Definitive Story of 1970s Funky Lagos* (Afrostrut, STRUTCD 013, 2001), p. 4.

NOTES ON SOURCES

669 *The whole place was alien*: Sarduna of Sokoto, quoted in Martin Meredith, *The State of Africa: A History of Fifty Years of Independence* (London: Free Press, 2006), p. 75.
672 *Our Yoruba tradition*: quoted in Waterman, *Jùjú*, p. 2.
673 *[Brown's] rhythms*: John Miller Chernoff, quoted in Veal, *Fela*, p. 57.
proof that black people: Thulani Davis, quoted in Veal, *Fela*, p. 58.
This man was tearing Lagos to pieces: Fela Kuti, quoted in Jason Ankeny, "Geraldo Pino Biography," AllMusic (www.allmusic.com/artist/geraldo-pino-mn0000650864/biography).
A lot of the local bands: witness, quoted in Veal, *Fela*, p. 65.
675 *let's get our asses out*: quoted in Allen and Veal, p. 67.
Look, I never came all the way: Fela Kuti, quoted in Allen and Veal, p. 69.
676 *I felt ashamed that a woman*: Fela Kuti, quoted in Archangel, p. 45.
Man, I used to just stand there: Fela Kuti, quoted in Veal, *Fela*, p. 54.
677 *the old Fela was gone overnight*: quoted in Allen and Veal, pp. 77–78.
It was the first African tune: Fela Kuti, quoted in Veal, *Fela*, p. 72.
678 *[R]oll, land on the other pillow . . . "You fucking got it!"*: Allen and Veal, p. 75.
that I should not try to impress foreigners: Fela Kuti, quoted in Veal, *Fela*, p. 75.
Because of Sandra: J. K. Braimah, quoted in Christopher A. Waterman, "Chop and Quench," *African Arts* 31, no. 1, winter 1998, p. 4.
679 *We have so many women . . . should be about reality*: Fela Kuti, interviewed by and quoted in John Collins, *Fela: Kalakuta Notes* (Amsterdam: KIT Publishers, 2009), p. 135.
threw the drum to the ground: phrase used by Yoruban talking drummers, quoted in Waterman, "Chop and Quench," p. 6.
like a symphony: Fela Kuti, quoted in Gary Stewart, *Breakout: Profiles in African Rhythm* (Chicago: University of Chicago Press, 1992), p. 117.
680 *Like a great boxer*: Michael E. Veal, "Introduction," in Allen and Veal, p. 11.
681 *I sit straight*: Tony Allen, in Allen and Veal, p. 90.
I had been using jazz: John Collins interview with Fela Kuti, quoted in Collins, *Fela*, p. 135.
682 *Today I'm not the slave*: Tony Allen, in Allen and Veal, p. 106.
3 P.M.: Fela Kuti: Carlos Moore and Sylviane Kamara, quoted in Veal, *Fela*, p. 126.
684 *Tell our parents we were going*: Yomi Gbolagunte, quoted in Veal, *Fela*, p. 137.
He is . . . certainly not handsome: journalist John Darnton, quoted in Veal, *Fela*, p. 100.
When you are the king: Fela Kuti interview in *Fela Kuti: Music Is the Weapon (Musique au poing)*, dir. Jean-Jaques Flori and Stéphane Tchalgadjieff (1982).
We were the only white people: Paul McCartney, quoted in *Finding Fela*, dir. Alex Gibney (2014).
686 *[H]e weaves local and world events*: Archangel, p. 128.
One can easily and without exaggeration: quoted in Waterman, *Jùjú*, p. 4.
Pen get power gun no get: lyrics to "Authority Stealing" by Fela Kuti.
Some will rob you: lyrics to "Pretty Boy Floyd" by Woody Guthrie.
687 *Go and kill*: lyrics to "Zombie" by Fela Kuti.
688 *[T]he man turned Nigeria*: unidentified Nigerian fan, quoted in Veal, *Fela*, p. 121.

691 *them regular trademark:* lyrics to "Sorrow Tears and Blood" by Fela Kuti.
692 *[He] has lost nothing musically:* Fola Arogundade, quoted in Veal, *Fela*, p. 170.
an exasperated and unknown soldier: quoted from an April 1977 *Daily Times* article by Veal, *Fela*, p. 156.
693 *The gods do not want the music:* quoted in Veal, *Fela*, p. 181.
695 *I would never work with musicians:* Bill Laswell, quoted in Veal, *Fela*, p. 209.
697 *Put it in, please:* lyrics to "Na Poi" by Fela Kuti, translated by and quoted in Veal, *Fela*, p. 134.
698 *Every day, every day:* lyrics to "Unnecessary Begging" by Fela Anikulapo-Kuti used with the kind permission of the Estate of Fela Anikulapo-Kuti.
I have opened the eyes: quoted in Veal, *Fela*, p. 260.
699 *I have to undo:* Fela Kuti, quoted in Collins, *Fela*, p. 134.
sick pilgrims and brainwashed Africans: Fela Kuti, quoted in Veal, *Fela*, p. 163.
Me, I'm a born-again "pagan": Fela Kuti, quoted in Archangel, p. 139.
702 *It was almost like he created a beat:* quoted in Ben Beaumont-Thomas, "'His Drums Were Singing, You Know?' Tony Allen Remembered by His Collaborators," *Guardian*, May 4, 2020.
Tony Allen gets what a boy can do: lyrics to "Music Is My Radar" by Damon Albarn, Graham Coxon, Alex James, and Dave Rowntree.
Questlove, Chris Dave, Moses Boyd: quoted in Beaumont-Thomas.
703 *But before I let your steam drill:* lyrics to American folk song "John Henry."
Totally boring, really, really boring: author's interview with Tony Allen.
704 *human zoo:* quoted in album notes by Mwana Mafuta for *Congo Revolution: Revolutionary and Evolutionary Sounds from the Two Congos 1955–62* (Soul Jazz Records, SJR CD437, 2019), p. 38.
705 *to see if [my color] came off:* Roger Izeidi, quoted in Gary Stewart, *Rumba on the River: A History of the Popular Music of the Two Congos* (London and New York: Verso, 2003), p. 84.
706 *[I]t was not the natives:* quoted in Stewart, *Rumba on the River*, p. 10.
708 *The Belgians were awful:* anonymous diplomat, quoted in Michela Wrong, *In the Footsteps of Mr Kurtz: Living on the Brink of Disaster in the Congo* (London: Fourth Estate, 2001), p. 51.
710 *still an African city:* John Gunther, quoted in Stewart, *Rumba on the River*, pp. 3–4.
714 *We are no longer your monkeys:* Patrice Lumumba, quoted in Meredith, p. 102.
[The guitars'] lustrous melodies: Michael E. Veal, "Dry Spell Blues: Sublime Frequencies Across the West African Sahel," in Michael E. Veal and E. Tammy Kim (eds.), *Punk Ethnography: Artists and Scholars Listen to Sublime Frequencies* (Middletown, Connecticut: Wesleyan University Press, 2016), p. 215.
715 *[T]he best way to achieve happiness:* Mobuto Sese Seko, quoted in Bob W. White, *Rumba Rules: The Politics of Dance Music in Mobutu's Zaire* (Durham and London: Duke University Press, 2008), p. 80.
a doctor of his craft: quoted in Stewart, *Rumba on the River*, p. 84.
eroticized the rumba: Florent Mazzoleni, *Afro Pop: L'Âge d'or des grands orchestres africains* (Bègles: Castor Music, 2011), p. 12.

NOTES ON SOURCES

716 *An insignificant matter:* lyrics to "Mass Media" by Tabu Ley Rochereau, translated in Wolfgang Bender, *Sweet Mother: Modern African Music*, trans. Wolfgang Freis (Chicago and London: University of Chicago Press, 1991), p. 56.

720 *On entre OK:* lyrics to "On entre OK, on sort KO" by Franco Luambo Makiadi. *Congolese Balzac:* quoted in White, p. 79
vay-way, vay-way: lyrics to "Azda" by Franco Luambo Makiadi.

721 *I cannot sleep at all*: Mobuto Sese Seko, quoted in Wrong, p. 214.

722 *He [Mobutu] was so different*: quoted in Wrong, p. 63.
There are no opponents in Zaire: quoted in Wrong, p. 83.
[W]e are proud: quoted in Meredith, p. 308.

723 *Does Rochereau realize . . . But a song goes everywhere*: quoted in Frank Tenaille, *Music Is the Weapon of the Future: Fifty Years of African Popular Music*, trans. Stephen Toussaint and Hope Sandrine (Chicago: Lawrence Hill Books, 2002), p. 5.
They were giving cattle herds: José Endundu, quoted in Wrong, p. 93.

724 *This is going to be the greatest show*: quoted in Hugh Masekela and D. Michael Cheers, *Still Grazing: The Musical Journey of Hugh Masekela* (New York: Three Rivers Press, 2004), p. 277.

727 *the beauty of a New York in miniature*: Manu Dibango and Danielle Rouard, *Three Kilos of Coffee: An Autobiography*, trans. Beth G. Raps (Chicago and London: University of Chicago Press, 1994), p. 41.
With Lumumba's assassination: White, pp. 250–51.

729 *If as a leader you're not hard*: J. P. Busé, quoted in White, p. 257.

730 *We imagine corruption*: quoted in Richard Dowden, *Africa: Altered States, Ordinary Miracles* (London: Granta, 2019), p. 230.
Inside each of us: quoted in White, p. 227.
[I]n their desire for splendour: quoted in White, p. 250.
Most peoples measure: "The King of the Rumba," *The Economist*, Apr. 30, 2016.
1,200 working bands: Tenaille, p. 63 (footnote).

733 *A sapeur's walk*: Wrong, p. 175.

734 *Listen my love:* lyrics to "Matebu" by Papa Wemba, translated in Margalit Fox, "Papa Wemba, Congolese King of 'Rumba Rock,' Is Dead at 66," *New York Times*, Apr. 25, 2016.
La sape is a movement: Paul Goodwin, "Introduction," in Daniele Tamagni, *Gentlemen of Bacongo* (London: Trolley Books, 2009), pp. 7–9.

735 *We are not scared of Parisians*: quoted in Tamagni, p. 172.

736 *Versace for jackets*: quoted in Wrong, p. 179.

739 *What we'll never be able to recapture*: Tabu Ley Rochereau, quoted in Stewart, *Breakout*, p. 19.

740 *Why did we fight:* lyrics to "Le Glas a sonné" by Tabu Ley Rochereau, translated in Wrong, p. 165.
Evening arrives, the day disappears: lyrics to "Mabele (Ntoto)" by Simaro Lutumba, translated in Stewart, *Rumba on the River*, p. 203.

742 *Kinshasa is a very loud town*: Mingiedi Mawangu, quoted in Alexis Petridis, "Assume Crash Position," *Guardian*, Apr. 4, 2006.

746 *All of the money to build them*: author's interview with Tony Van der Eecken.
Vive la France: Léopold Sédar Senghor, quoted in Meredith, p. 60.

NOTES ON SOURCES

748 *Everyone strum your koras:* lyrics of "Le Lion rouge," national anthem of Senegal, by Léopold Sédar Senghor.

749 *simply pounce:* Tsitsi Ella Jaji, *Africa in Stereo: Modernism, Music, and Pan-African Solidarity* (New York: Oxford University Press, 2014), p. 91.

752 *I'm not the one who changed:* quoted in Lucy Durán, "Key to N'Dour: Roots of the Senegalese Star," *Popular Music* 8, no. 3, "African Music," Oct. 1989, p. 277.

We are people of the dance: Léopold Sédar Senghor, quoted in Jenny Cathcart, *Hey You! A Portrait of Youssou N'Dour* (Witney Fine: Line Books, 1989), p. 32.

[I]n griot families, we sing: Youssou N'Dour, quoted in Cathart, p. x.

753 *Have all these albums:* Mark Hudson, *The Music in My Head* (London: Vintage, 1998), p. 143.

Big record companies don't know: Youssou N'Dour, quoted in Stephen Moss, "I'm Bringing a Message," *Guardian,* Mar. 21, 2007.

755 *keep me as an exhibit:* author's conversation with Lieven Van den Broeck.

756 *the greatest catastrophe:* author's conversation with a band member.

757 *Mansour Seck will always be:* Baaba Maal, interviewed by and quoted in Johannes Waechter, "Afrika ist sehr modern," *Süddeutsche Zeitung Magazin,* July 9, 2009.

We are like the baobab tree: Rudy Gomis, quoted in Mark Hudson, Doudou Sarr, Paul Hayward, and Lucy Durán, "Senegal and The Gambia: A Tale of Two Countries," in Simon Broughton, Mark Ellingham, and Jon Lusk (eds.), *The Rough Guide to World Music Vol. 1: Africa and the Middle East,* 3rd ed. (London and New York: Rough Guides, 2006), p. 330.

766 *Swiss Army knife . . . repository of traditional knowledge:* Andy Morgan, *Finding the One: The Strange and Parallel Lives of the West African Kora and the Welsh Harp* (Ceredigion: Theatr Mwldan and Astar Artes, 2013), p. 23.

767 *We were entering a new era:* Malick Sidibé interview, quoted in Jon Henley, "Malick Sidibé Photographs: One Nation Under a Groove," *Guardian,* Feb. 27, 2010.

768 *[We] knew the names of all:* Manthia Diawara, quoted in Veal, "Dry Spell Blues," in Veal and Kim, p. 217.

770 *A Mandé-style girlie chorus:* Hudson, p. 63. Used by permission.

771 *Unlike . . . Fela Kuti, [Mory] Kanté:* 1988 review in *Melody Maker,* quoted in Lucy Durán, "Techno-Griot," *Folk Roots,* issue 175, Jan./Feb. 1998, p. 40.

worked the crowd like Buddy Guy: author's correspondence with Banning Eyre.

772 *Sundays in Bamako:* lyrics to "Beaux Dimanches" by Amadou Bagayoko. Used by permission. "Beaux Dimanches" (Bagayoko) © Reva Sons/Sony Music Publishing France.

774 *Wait for me, my love:* lyrics to "Diaraby nene."
Words and Music by Oumou Sangaré
Copyright © 1989 BMG Rights Management (UK) Limited
All Rights Administered by BMG Rights Management (US) LLC
All Rights Reserved. Used by Permission
Reprinted by Permission of Hal Leonard Europe Ltd.

The music of the spheres . . . I'm busy now: author's interview with Lucy Durán.

775 *[T]here's life in the kora:* Seckou Keita, quoted in Andy Morgan, *Finding the One,* p. 56.

785 *For some people when you say "Timbuktu":* Ali Farka Touré, quoted on the back of a Hannibal Records promotional T-shirt.

789 *I learned he was an American . . . leaves and the branches*: Ali Farka Touré, quoted in Tenaille, p. 102.
we have the roots: Ali Farka Touré, quoted in Tenaille, p. 102.
I can teach him things: Ali Farka Touré, quoted in Banning Eyre, *In Griot Time: An American Guitarist in Mali* (London: Serpent's Tail, 2002), p. 202.
789 *sings about whiskey, beer*: Ali Farka Touré, quoted in Tenaille, p. 102.
791 *the divorce party is bigger*: interview with Fadimata Walett Oumar, from group Tartit, for the Kitchen Sisters' NPR radio series *The Hidden World of Girls*.
792 *Tonight / I sleep in the ruins*: lyrics to "Ténéré Daféo Nikchan" by Ibrahim Ag Alhabib, translation from author's correspondence with Andy Morgan.
793 *[W]hen we first started hearing Hendrix*: Eyadou Ag Leche, quoted in Larry Rohter, "Blues from the Desert, Recorded On-Site," *New York Times*, Aug. 31, 2011.
The spiritual gravity of their melodies: Robert Christgau's review of Tinariwen's *Aman Iman* (World Village) (www.robertchristgau.com/get_artist.php?id=5036), 2007.
794 *swords turn to guitars*: Tom Freston, "Showtime in the Sahara,'" *Vanity Fair*, July 2007, p. 169.
795 *Underneath that burning sun*: lyrics to "Do They Know It's Christmas?" by Bob Geldof and Midge Ure.
803 *It was one of the most beautiful days*: quoted in Andy Morgan, "Swingin' Addis," *Songlines*, Sept./Oct. 2007, p. 30.
804 *Ah, that's nice. Ethiopian sounds*: Winston to Don in *Broken Flowers*, dir. Jim Jarmusch (2005).
806 *I thought it was some kind of Cajun record*: Bob Dylan on "Tezeta (Fast)" by Getachew Kassa, in album notes to *Bob Dylan (Music That Matters to Him)*, Artist's Choice series (Starbucks Entertainment, CDS-132, 2008), p. 25.
Your eyes are fascinating: lyrics to "Ene negn bay manesh" by Getatchew Degefu and Girma Beyene, translated by Amaretch Tesfaye Guilbert, Francis Falceto, and Karen Louise Albrecht in album notes for *Éthiopiques 8: Swinging Addis, 1969–1974* (Buda Musique, 82982-2, 2000), p. 20.
My stomach is trembling: lyrics to "Almokerkum neber" by Hirut Bekele, translated by Francis Falceto and Karen Louise Albrecht in album notes for *Éthiopiques 3: Golden Years of Modern Ethiopian Music, 1969–1975* (Buda Musique, 82963-2, 1998), p. 24.
Her eyes wounded me: lyrics to "Gud aderegetchegn" by Ayalew Mesfin, translated by Francis Falceto and Karen Louise Albrecht in album notes for *Éthiopiques* 13: Ethiopian Groove—The Golden Seventies (Buda Musique, 82255-2, 2002), p. 19.
My desire is overpowering: lyrics to "Amlak abet abet" by Teshome Sissay, translated by Francis Falceto and Karen Louise Albrecht in album notes for *Éthiopiques 13: Ethiopian Groove—The Golden Seventies* (Buda Musique, 82255-2, 2002), p. 20.
I don't eat . . . I don't drink: lyrics to "Tessassategn eko" by Bahta Gebre-Heywet, translated by Amaretch Tesfaye Guilbert, Francis Falceto, and Karen Louise Albrecht in album notes for *Éthiopiques 8: Swinging Addis* (Buda Musique, 82982-2, 2000), p. 21.
I am torturing myself: lyrics to "Hasabe" by Ayalew Mesfin, translated by Amaretch Tesfaye Guilbert, Francis Falceto, and Karen Louise Albrecht in album notes to *Éthiopiques 8: Swinging Addis* (Buda Musique, 82982-2, 2000), p. 20.

You are my sickness: lyrics to "Ere mela mela" by Mahmoud Ahmed, translated by Francis Falceto and Karen Louise Albrecht in album notes for Mahmoud Ahmed, *Éthiopiques 7: Ere Mela Mela* (Buda Musique, 82980-2, 1999), p. 10.

I don't want anyone to speak: lyrics to "Atawurulegn lela" by Mahmoud Ahmed, translated by Francis Falceto and Karen Louise Albrecht in album notes for Mahmoud Ahmed, *Éthiopiques 7: Ere Mela Mela* (Buda Musique, 82980-2, 1999), p. 11.

807 *melancholy haunts my spirit constantly*: lyrics to "Tezeta Slow/Fast" by the Shebeles, translated by Francis Falceto and Karen Louise Albrecht in album notes for *Éthiopiques 10: Tezeta—Ethiopian Blues and Ballads* (Buda Musique, 82222, 2002), p. 28.

808 *Outdoing yesterday, shouldering on today:* lyrics to "Tezeta" by Shewalul Megistu and Mahmoud Ahmed/Trad., amended from the translation by, and quoted in, Dagmawi Woubshet, "Tizita: A New World Interpretation," *Callaloo* 32, no. 2, part 2, spring 2009, p. 629.

811 *Do you know this record?*: author's conversation with Francis Falceto.

the homeless wanderer ("The Homeless Wanderer") / the wind goes around the World ("The Story of the Wind") / she experiences her tears ("A Young Girl's Complaint"), the [Jordan] river flowing ("The Jordan River Song"): song notes by Emahoy Tsegue-Maryam Guebrou, translated by Francis Falceto and Karen Louise Albrecht in album notes for Emahoy Tsegue-Maryam Guebrou, *Éthiopiques, Vol. 21: Piano Solo* (Buda Musique, 86012-2, 2006).

813 *too childish*: quoted in *Music Extra: Sweet Mother*, presented by DJ Edu, BBC World Service (2017).

814 *Poor* makossa: Dibango and Rouard, p. 82.

820 *Thomas and his coterie of musicians*: Banning Eyre, *Lion Songs: Thomas Mapfumo and the Music That Made Zimbabwe* (Durham and London: Duke University Press, 2015), p. 53.

822 *Viewed one-dimensionally*: Veal, "Dry Spell Blues," in Veal and Kim, p. 214.

823 *Their forty-five-minute set*: Matthew Lavoie in album notes for *Wallahi Le Zein!!— Wezin, Jakwar and Guitar Boogie from the Islamic Republic of Mauritania* (Latitude, 07, 2011), p. 3.

IX How we begin to remember

828 *giant new rituals of self-congratulation*: E. J. Hobsbawm, *The Age of Capital 1848–1875* (London: Abacus, 1993), p. 47.

830 *swept away by a liberating rapture*: John Alexander Joyce, quoted in Ken Emerson, *Doo-dah!: Stephen Foster and the Rise of American Popular Culture* (New York: Simon & Schuster, 1997), p. 252.

835 *like the world's best horn section*: Brian Cullman, "Jajouka: Burning a Hole in the Night," *The Journal of the Plague Years*, autumn 2022 (www.journaloftheplagueyears. ink/blog/jajouka-burning-a-hole-in-the-night).

where you be?: author's conversation with Rikki Stein.

836 *Heard any good music lately?*: author's conversation with Mark Kidel.

NOTES ON SOURCES

837 *In order to understand*: Mikhail Bakhtin, quoted in Richard Taruskin, *Defining Russia Musically: Historical and Hermeneutical Essays* (Princeton and Oxford: Princeton University Press, 2000), p. xxiii.

847 Sevdah *will be sung after every war*: Damir Imamović quoting his grandfather Zaim Imamović in Garth Cartwright, "Damir Imamović—The Sevdah Master of Sarajevo," *The Attic*, July 3, 2020 (theatticmag.com/features/2338/damir-imamovi%C4%87-_-the-sevdah-master-of-sarajevo.html).

849 *Tradition is not the worship of ashes*: Gustav Mahler, believed to be paraphrasing Thomas More (1477/78–1535).
Music expands the heart's capacity: Andy Morgan, *Music, Culture and Conflict in Mali* (Copenhagen: Freemuse 2013), pp. 211–12.

Photo Credits

t = top, c = center, b = below, l = left, r = right

SECTION 1 (PAGES 1–16)
1t © Michael Graham-Stewart/Bridgeman Images. 2cl Photo by Jurgen Schadeberg/Getty Images. 2cr Photo by Jurgen Schadeberg/Getty Images. 2b © Val Wilmer. 3a Photo by Clayton Call/Redferns via Getty Images. 3b Photo by Reggie Lewis/NBC/NBCU Photo Bank via Getty Images. 4tr Photo by Stanley Kubrick. X2011.4.11302.18. Museum of the City of New York. 4c Allan Grant/The LIFE Picture Collection/Shutterstock. 4b RKO/Kobal/Shutterstock. 5t Danvis Collection/Alamy. 5b © Frank Driggs. Lincoln Center for the Performing Arts. 6t Photo by Ibrahim Arce (Narcy Studios, Havana.) 6cl The Ministry of Culture, Cuba. 6cr Photograph [Cuban singer Benny Moré on stage], ca. 1953, 9.5 x 6 inches (24 x 15 centimeters), The Wolfsonian–Florida International University, Miami Beach, Florida, Promised Gift of Vicki Gold Levi, XC2016.01.1.44. 6b © Max Borges. 7t Yale Joel/The LIFE Picture Collection/Shutterstock. 7cl Glasshouse Images/Alamy. 7c KCET/PBS Social. 7cr Allan Grant/The LIFE Picture Collection/Shutterstock. 8t © BMG Rights Management (UK) Limited. 8cl © Astley Chin. 8cr Photo by Express/Hulton Archive via Getty Images. 8b Photo by Michael Ochs Archives/Getty Images. 9t Photo by James Van Der Zee/Michael Ochs Archives/Getty Images. 9cl Lynn Pelham/The LIFE Picture Collection/Shutterstock. 9cr Lynn Pelham/The LIFE Picture Collection/Shutterstock. 9b © Adrian Boot/Urban Image. 10tl © Dennis Morris. 10tr © Dennis Morris. 10b © Adrian Boot/Urban Image. 11t National Museum, New Delhi, India. 11c Museum Rietberg Zürich, Legat Alice Boner ABF O-47. 11b The Hindu Archive. 12t Photo by Hulton Archive/Getty Images. 12cl Photo by Don Nelson/Fotos International via Getty Images. 12cr Photo by Jorgen Angel/Redferns via Getty Images. 12b Photo by Clive Arrowsmith, Camera Press, London. 13cl Jak Kilby/ArenaPAL. 13b Courtesy of Menil Archives, The Menil Collection, Houston. 14tl Hungarian National Museum. 14tr © Masataka Hashida. 15t Photo © Leonard de Selva/Bridgeman Images. 15c, 1–4 ©Paco Manzano. 15bl Archivo de Manuel Cerrejón. 15br Alamy. 16t Alamy. 16cl Nijs, Jac. de/Anefo National Archives, Amsterdam. 16cr © Mario Pacheco. 16b © Denis Brihat.

NOTES ON SOURCES

SECTION 2 (PAGES 16–32)
1tl Gilberto Ferrez/Instituto Moreira Salles. 1tr Photo by Hollywood Photo Archive/Mediapunch/Shutterstock. 1c Acervo Sérgio Cabral / MIS-RJ. 1b MIS/SP, Chico Albuquerque Collection. 2t Hart Preston/The LIFE Picture Collection/Shutterstock. 2br Photo by PoPsie Randolph/Michael Ochs Archives/Getty Images. 3a Photo by Samuel Elyachar. 3cl Instituto Gilberto Gil, Brazil. 3clb National Archives, Correio da Manhã, BR RJANRIO PH.0.FOT.35970. 3br Taken from *Tropicalia. A Brazilian Revolution in Sound* (Soul Jazz Records), design by Adrian Self and Toothé Grim, adapted from original image taken from *Tropicalia Ou Panis et Circenses* (Odeon, 1968). 4tl Maria del Carmen Obella Collection. 4tr Alamy. 4c Maurice-Louis Branger. Roger-Viollet/TopFoto. 4b National Archives, Argentina. 5t National Archives, Argentina. 5cr Alamy. 5bl Eduardo Comesaña/Alamy. 5br © Kike. 6b Courtesy of Acho Esto. 7t Ryhor Bruyeu/Alamy. 7cl Lebrecht Music & Arts/Alamy. 7cr Photo by Apic/Getty Images. 7bl Photo by AFP/Getty Images. 7br Photo by Evening Standard/Hulton Archive via Getty Images. 8t Photo: Cordo. 8cl © Karen Sherlock. 8cr © Andrey Gaidabura. 8b Courtesy of the Koutev Estate. 9t Photo John Bush. 10t Bartók Archives, Institute for Musicology, HUN-REN Research Center for the Humanities. 10c © Mario Pacheco. 10b © BENKŐ Imre, *Dance Hall Meeting*, Budapest, 1982. 11t Photo by Leni Sinclair/Michael Ochs Archives via Getty Images. 11bl © Gilles Verdili/Paris Match. 11br © Bernard Benant. 12tl © Estate of Jean DEPARA/courtesy *Revue Noire*, Paris. 12tr © Estate of Jean DEPARA/courtesy *Revue Noire*, Paris. 12bl © Benoit Van Maele. 12br © Daniele Tamagni, Courtesy of Giordano Tamagni. 13bl Photo by Michael Ochs Archives/Getty Images. 13br Photo by Frans Schellekens/Redferns via Getty Images. 14cl Photo by Dave Peabody/Redferns via Getty Images. 14cr © Claus Bunks/afrobrasil. de. 14b Malick Sidibé, *Nuit de Noël (Happy Club)*, 1963/2008, silver gelatin print, 37.5 x 38 inches image size. © Malick Sidibé. Courtesy of the artist and Jack Shainman Gallery, New York. 15t 2nd Police Band 1965–66 (Coll. éthiopiques.) 15cl Photo by Frans Schellekens/Redferns via Getty Images. 15cr ©Véronique Guillien. 15b © Gali Tibbon. 16t Photo by Mondadori/Getty Images. 16c © The Trustees of the British Museum. 16bl © Justin Gardner. 16br © Herman Vanaerschot.

Bibliography

I Mbube

BOOKS

Allingham, Rob, and Gregory Mthembu-Salter, "South Africa: Popular Music," in Simon Broughton, Mark Ellingham, and Jon Lusk (eds.), *The Rough Guide to World Music Vol. 1: Africa and the Middle East*, 3rd ed. (London and New York: Rough Guides, 2006)

Ansell, Gwen, *Soweto Blues: Jazz, Popular Music, and Politics in South Africa* (New York and London: Continuum, 2004)

Ballantine, Christopher, *Marabi Nights: Early South African Jazz and Vaudeville* (Johannesburg: Ravan Press, 1994)

Biko, Steve, *I Write What I Like* (Johannesburg: Picador Africa, 2004)

Bordowitz, Hank, *Noise of the World: Non-Western Musicians in Their Own Words* (Brooklyn, New York: Soft Skull Press, 2004)

Bromberg, Craig, *The Wicked Ways of Malcolm McLaren* (New York: Harper & Row, 1989)

Broughton, Simon, Mark Ellingham, and Jon Lusk (eds.), *The Rough Guide to World Music Vol. 1: Africa and the Middle East*, 3rd ed. (London and New York: Rough Guides, 2006)

Coplan, David B., *In Township Tonight! South Africa's Black City Music and Theatre* (London and New York: Longman, 1985)

Ehrenreich, Barbara, *Dancing in the Streets: A History of Collective Joy* (London: Granta Books, 2008)

Erlmann, Veit, *Music, Modernity, and the Global Imagination: South Africa and the West* (New York and Oxford: Oxford University Press, 1999)

Fletcher, Peter, *World Musics in Context: A Comprehensive Survey of the World's Major Musical Cultures* (Oxford and New York: Oxford University Press, 2001)

Hobsbawm, E. J., *The Age of Capital 1848–1875* (London: Abacus, 1993)

Makeba, Miriam, and Nomsa Mwamuka, *Makeba: The Miriam Makeba Story* (Johannesburg: STE Publishers, 2004)

Mandela, Nelson, *Long Walk to Freedom* (London: Little, Brown and Company, 2008)

Marinovich, Greg, *The Bang-Bang Club: Snapshots from a Hidden War* (New York: Basic Books, 2000)

Marre, Jeremy and Hannah Charlton, *Beats of the Heart: Popular Music of the World* (New York: Pantheon Books, 1985)

Masekela, Hugh, and D. Michael Cheers, *Still Grazing: The Musical Journey of Hugh Masekela* (New York: Three Rivers Press, 2004)

McGregor, Maxine, *Chris McGregor and the Brotherhood of Breath: My Life with a South African Jazz Pioneer* (Flint, Michigan: Bamberger Books, 1995)

Meintjes, Louise, *Sound of Africa! Making Music Zulu in a South African Studio* (Durham and London: Duke University Press, 2003)

BIBLIOGRAPHY

Nicol, Mike, *A Good-Looking Corpse: The world of DRUM—Jazz and Gangsters, Hope and Defiance in the Townships of South Africa* (London: Secker & Warburg, 1991)
Ritter, E. A., *Shaka Zulu* (Harmondsworth: Penguin Books, 1978)
Ross, Robert, *A Concise History of South Africa* (Cambridge and New York: Cambridge University Press, 2007)
Troup, Freda, *South Africa: An Historical Introduction* (Harmondsworth: Penguin Books, 1975)

ARTICLES, PAPERS, MISCELLANEOUS TEXTS

Allingham, Rob, "From 'Noma Kumnyama' to 'Pata Pata': A History," *African Music* 8, no. 3, 2009
Beaumont, Mark, "Graceland at 35: How Paul Simon Recorded a Masterpiece in Apartheid South Africa," *Independent*, Aug. 25, 2021
Boustany, Nora, "The Bushman's Advocate," *Washington Post*, Dec. 18, 1995
Boyd, Joe, "Sing When You're Winning," *Guardian*, Dec. 12, 2003
Bradshaw, Melissa, "Techno from the Townships," *Guardian*, Aug. 12, 2011
Christgau, Robert, "South Africa Romance," *Village Voice*, Sept. 23, 1986 (www.robertchristgau.com/xg/rock/simon-86.php)
Connor, Pearl, "Obituary Nathan Mdledle: Sing Freedom," *Guardian*, May 24, 1995
Denselow, Robin, "They're Going to Graceland," *Guardian*, June 9, 2006
Dickens, Charles, "The Noble Savage," *Reprinted Pieces*, Project Gutenberg eBook #872, 2014 (www.gutenberg.org/files/872/872-h/872-h.htm#page391)
Dugger, Celia W., "When a Song Is Not Just a Song," *New York Times*, May 2, 2011
Duval Smith, Alex, "South African Townships Take Stick-Fighting Tradition into New Future," *Guardian*, Jan. 30, 2011
Duval Smith, Alex, "Thousands Face Agony or Death After Zulu King's Decree on Circumcision," *Observer*, Jan. 17, 2010
Ewens, Graeme, "Obituary: Miriam Makeba," *Guardian*, Nov. 11, 2008
Eyre, Banning, "Interview: Louise Meintjes," *Afropop Worldwide*, June 6, 2007 (afropop.org/articles/interview-louise-meintjes)
Hammer, Joshua, "Will He Rule South Africa," *New York Review of Books*, Feb. 12, 2009
Impey, Angela, "Songs of the Night: Isicathamiya Choral Music from KwaZulu Natal," *1997 Festival of American Folklife Program Book*, Smithsonian Institution, June/July 1997
"Joseph Shabalala Obituary," *The Times*, Feb. 14, 2020
Kinder, Elizabeth, "The Recording Men," *fRoots*, issue 282, Dec. 2006
Malan, Rian, "The Fabulous Alcock Boys," *Observer Magazine*, June 24, 2007
Malan, Rian, "In the Jungle," *Rolling Stone*, no. 841, May 25, 2000
McNeil, Donald G., Jr., "Obituary: Simon Mahlathini Nkabinde, 62, Zulu Singer," *New York Times*, July 30, 1999
Pareles, Jon, "Obituary: West Nkosi, 58, a Producer of South African Musicians," Oct. 13, 1998
Pietilä, Tuulikki, "Whose Creativity and What Kinds of Rewards? South African Artists and the Recurring Questions of Ownership and Exploitation," *World Music and Small Players in the Global Music Industry Seminar*, Danish Institute for International Studies, Copenhagen, Aug. 19–20, 2005

Polgreen, Lydia, "South Africa Debates Law to Support Tribal Courts," *New York Times*, June 16, 2012
Prince, Rob, "Indestructible Beat," *Folk Roots*, issue 60, June 1986
Sinclair, David, "Global Music Pulse: The Latest Music from Around the Planet—South Africa," *Billboard*, Nov. 11, 1995
Spencer, Neil, "Fifa's World Cup Kick-Off Concert," *Observer*, June 6, 2010
Steinberg, Johnny, "End of the Rainbow," *Guardian*, Oct. 4, 2008
Tannenbaum, Rob, "The Buggles' Song Launched MTV. After 45 Years, They're Going on Tour," *New York Times*, Apr. 7, 2023

ALBUM NOTES

Allingham, Rob, *Miriam Makeba and the Skylarks Volume 1* (Teal Records, TELCD 2303, 1991)
Allingham, Rob, The Manhattan Brothers, *The Very Best of the Manhattan Brothers: Their Greatest Hits (1948–1959)* (Gallo, CDZAC 77, 1999)
Allingham, Rob, John Moriri, and the Manzini Girls, *Isikhova* (Gallo, CDGB 65, 2007)
Ewens, Graeme, *Township Jazz'n'Jive* (Nascente, NSCD 022, 1997)
Frederking, Klaus, *Drum: South African Jazz and Jive 1954–1960* (Line/Monsun Records, MSCD 9.01092 O, 1991)
Herman, Trevor, *Thunder Before Dawn: The Indestructible Beat of Soweto Vol. 2* (Earthworks/Caroline, CAROL 2428-2, 1987)
Herman, Trevor, Mahlathini, *King of the Groaners* (Earthworks/Caroline, CAROL 2428-2, 1993)
Scurfield, Harry, *Squashbox: Le concertina Zoulou et Sotho en Afrique du Sud 1930–1965* (Silex Memoire—Y225107, 1993)
Simon, Paul, *Graceland* (Warner Bros. Records, 9 25447-1, 1986)
Topp Fargion, Janet, *Gumboot Guitar: Zulu Street Guitar Music from South Africa* (Topic Records, TSCD923, 2003)
Wrasse Records, *Long Walk to Freedom: A Celebration of 4 Decades of South African Music* (Wrasse Records, WRASS 080, 2002)

FILM, TELEVISION, RADIO

Amandla! A Revolution in Four-Part Harmony, dir. Lee Hirsch (2002)
AmaZulu: The Children of Heaven, dir. Hannan Majid and Richard York (2006)
Beats of the Heart: Rhythm of Resistance, dir. Jeremy Marre (1979)
Come Back, Africa, dir. Lionel Rogosin (1959)
Mandela: Long Walk to Freedom, dir. Justin Chadwick (2013)
Paul Simon: Graceland, dir. Jeremy Marre, BBC Four *Classic Albums* (1997)
Under African Skies, dir. Joe Berlinger (2012)
Zulu, dir. Cy Endfield (1964)
Zulu Dawn, dir. Douglas Hickox (1979)

INTERVIEWS, CONVERSATIONS, CORRESPONDENCE

Chris Albertyn, Rob Allingham, Steve Collins, David DeFries, Robin Denselow, Trevor Herman, Tony Hollingsworth, Louise Meintjes, Christian Mousset, Paul Simon

II Babalú-Ayé

BOOKS

Arnaz, Desi, *A Book* (New York: William Morrow and Co., 1976)
Bergman, Billy, *Reggae and Latin Pop: Hot Sauces* (Dorset: Blandford Press, 1985)
Bethell, Leslie (ed.), *Cuba: A Short History* (New York: Cambridge University Press, 1994)
Boggs, Vernon W., *Salsiology: Afro-Cuban Music and the Evolution of Salsa in New York City* (New York: Excelsior Music Publishing, 1992)
Brennan, Timothy, "Introduction to the English Edition," in Alejo Carpentier, *Music in Cuba*, ed. Timothy Brennan, trans. Alan West-Durán (Minneapolis: University of Minnesota Press, 2001)
Brenneman, Eric Silva, "Havana and Miami: A Music Censorship Sandwich," in Marie Korpe (ed.), *Shoot the Singer! Music Censorship Today* (London and New York: Zed Books, 2004)
Calvo Ospina, Hernando, *¡Salsa! Havana Heat, Bronx Beat*, trans. Nick Caistor (London: Latin America Bureau, 1998)
Carpentier, Alejo, *Music in Cuba*, ed. Timothy Brennan, trans. Alan West-Durán (Minneapolis: University of Minnesota Press, 2001)
Castro, Alicia, Ingrid Kummels, and Manfred Schäfer, *Anacaona: The Amazing Adventures of Cuba's First All-Girl Dance Band*, trans. Steven T. Murray (London: Atlantic Books, 2007)
Charters, Samuel, *A Language of Song: Journeys in the Musical World of the African Diaspora* (Durham and London: Duke University Press, 2009)
Chasteen, John Charles, *National Rhythms, African Roots: The Deep History of Latin American Popular Dance* (Albuquerque, New Mexico: University of New Mexico Press, 2004)
Cruz, Celia, and Ana Christina Reymundo, *Celia: My Life*, trans. José Lucas Badué (New York: Rayo/HarperCollins, 2004)
English, T. J., *Havana Nocturne: How the Mob Owned Cuba . . . and Then Lost It to the Revolution* (New York, London, Toronto, and Sydney: Harper, 2008)
Fernandez, Raul A., *From Afro-Cuban Rhythms to Latin Jazz* (Berkeley, Los Angeles, and London: University of California Press, 2006)
García, David F., *Arsenio Rodríguez and the Transnational Flows of Latin Popular Music* (Philadelphia: Temple University Press, 2006)
Gillespie, Dizzy, and Al Fraser, *To Be, or Not . . . to Bop* (Minneapolis and London: University of Minnesota Press, 2009)
Gjelten, Tom, *Bacardi and the Long Fight for Cuba: The Biography of a Cause* (New York: Penguin Books, 2009)
González Echevarría, Roberto, *Cuban Fiestas* (New Haven and London: Yale University Press, 2010)
Gott, Richard, *Cuba: A New History* (New Haven and London: Yale University Press, 2004)
Gottschalk, Louis Moreau, *Notes of a Pianist: The Chronicles of a New Orleans Music Legend*, ed. Jeanne Behrend (Princeton and Oxford: Princeton University Press, 2006)
Graham, Bill, and Robert Greenfield, *Bill Graham Presents: My Life Inside Rock and Out* (Cambridge, Massachusetts: Da Capo Press, 2004)

Guillermoprieto, Alma, *Dancing with Cuba: A Memoir of the Revolution*, trans. Esther Allen (New York: Pantheon Books, 2004)
Jelly-Schapiro, Joshua, *Island People: The Caribbean and the World* (Edinburgh: Canongate, 2016)
Laferl, Christopher F., *"Record It, and Let It Be Known": Song Lyrics, Gender, and Ethnicity in Brazil, Cuba, Martinique, and Trinidad and Tobago from 1920 to 1960* (Vienna: Lit Verlag, 2005)
Lindop, Grevel, *Travels on the Dance Floor* (London: André Deutsch, 2010)
Lomax, Alan, *The Land Where the Blues Began* (New York: Pantheon Books, 1993)
Lomax, Alan, *Mister Jelly Roll: The Fortunes of Jelly Roll Morton, New Orleans Creole and "Inventor of Jazz"* (New York: Duell, Sloan and Pearce, 1950)
Lowinger, Rosa, and Ofelia Fox, *Tropicana Nights: The Life and Times of the Legendary Cuban Nightclub* (Orlando, Austin, New York, San Diego, Toronto, and London: Harcourt, 2005)
Mazor, Barry, *Ralph Peer and the Making of Popular Roots Music* (Chicago: Chicago Review Press, 2015)
Montejo, Esteban, *The Autobiography of a Runaway Slave* (Harmondsworth: Penguin Books, 1970)
Moore, Robin D., *Music and Revolution: Cultural Change in Socialist Cuba* (Berkeley, Los Angeles, and London: University of California Press, 2006)
Moore, Robin D., *Nationalizing Blackness: Afrocubanismo and Artistic Revolution in Havana, 1920–1940* (Pittsburgh: University of Pittsburgh Press, 1997)
Ortiz, Fernando, *Cuban Counterpoint: Tobacco and Sugar*, trans. Harriet De Onís (New York: Alfred A. Knopf, 1947)
Padura Fuentes, Leonardo, *Faces of Salsa: A Spoken History of the Music*, trans. Stephen J. Clark (Washington and London: Smithsonian Books, 2003)
Powell, Josephine, *Tito Puente: When the Drums Are Dreaming* (Bloomington, Indiana: AuthorHouse, 2007)
Radanovich, John, *Wildman of Rhythm: The Life and Music of Benny Moré* (Gainesville: University Press of Florida, 2009)
Rathbone, John Paul, *The Sugar King of Havana: The Rise and Fall of Julio Lobo, Cuba's Last Tycoon* (London: Penguin Books, 2010)
Roberts, John Storm, *Black Music of Two Worlds* (New York: Praeger Publishers, 1972)
Roberts, John Storm, *The Latin Tinge: The Impact of Latin American Music on the United States* (New York and Oxford: Oxford University Press, 1999)
Salazar, Max, *Mambo Kingdom: Latin Music in New York* (New York: Schirmer Trade Books, 2002)
Steward, Sue, *¡Musica! Salsa, Rumba, Merengue, and More: The Rhythm of Latin America* (San Francisco: Chronicle Books, 1999)
Sublette, Ned, *Cuba and Its Music: From the First Drums to the Mambo* (Chicago: Chicago Review Press, 2004)
Sublette, Ned, *The World That Made New Orleans: From Spanish Silver to Congo Square* (Chicago: Lawrence Hill Books, 2009)
Tuchman, Barbara W., *The Proud Tower: A Portrait of the World Before the War 1890–1914* (London: Folio Society, 1997)

BIBLIOGRAPHY

ARTICLES, PAPERS, MISCELLANEOUS TEXTS

Barton, Laura, "The Sweet Sound of Cuba," *Guardian*, Mar. 23, 2015
Daniel, Jean, "Unofficial Envoy: An Historic Report from Two Capitals," *New Republic*, Dec. 14, 1963
Denselow, Robin, "Hasta la vista," *Guardian*, Oct. 10, 2008
Fairley, Jon, "Revolutionary Art," *Folk Roots*, issue 67, Jan. 1989
Herrera, Isabelia, Jon Pareles, and Giovanni Russonello, "'Buena Vista Social Club' at 25," *New York Times*, Sept. 22, 2021
Jelly-Shapiro, Joshua, "An Empire of Vice," *The Nation*, June 29, 2009
Lakhani, Nina, "Young Mexicans Embrace the Seductive Charms of the Dance That Cuba Forgot," *Observer*, Aug. 18, 2013
"Obituary: Alicia Parla," *Daily Telegraph*, Oct. 20, 1998
Paternostro, Silvana, "Communism Versus Prostitution: Sexual Revolution," *New Republic*, July 10, 2000
Pujol, Jordi, "Chano—La Havane à l'Opéra Comique," dir. Jérôme Savary, program note, trans. Tommy Meini, *L'Opéra Comique*, May–June 2002
Ratliff, Ben, "Obituary: Graciela Peréz-Gutierrez, Afro-Cuban Singer, Dies at 94," *New York Times*, Apr. 9, 2010
Ryle, John, "From Polka to Polyrhythm," *Times Literary Supplement*, July 6, 2001

ALBUM NOTES

Garcia, David F., Arsenio Rodríguez, *El alma de Cuba: Grabaciones completas RCA Victor 1940–1956* (Tumbao Cuban Classics, TCD-315, 2007)
Pujol, Jordi, Chano Pozo, *Chano Pozo: El tambor de Cuba (Life and Music of the Legendary Cuban Conga Drummer)* (Tumbao Cuban Classics, TCD 305, 2001)

FILM, TELEVISION, RADIO

Beats of the Heart: Salsa, dir. Jeremy Marre (1979)
Buena Vista Social Club, dir. Wim Wenders (1999)
Cachao: Uno más, dir. Dikayl Rimmasch (2008)
Chico & Rita, dir. Fernando Trueba, Javier Mariscal and Tono Errando (2010)
El Son es lo más sublime: Ignacio Piñero y el Septeto Nacional, dir. Ileana Rodríguez (2004)
Old Man Bebo, dir. Carlos Carcas (2008)
Our Latin Thing (Nuestra Cosa Latina), dir. Leon Gast (1972)
Son cubano: Une histoire de la musique cubaine, dir. Jean-Christophe Hervé and Dominique Roland (1993)
We Are the Music (Nosotros, la música), dir. Rogelio París (1964)
What's Cuba Playing At?, dir. Mike Dibb, BBC *Arena* (1985)

INTERVIEWS, CONVERSATIONS, CORRESPONDENCE

Jesús Alemañy, David Bither, Jerry Boys, Lucy Durán, Nick Gold, Jesse Moskovitz, Mario Pacheco, Silvana Paternostro, Alfredo Rodríguez, Harry Sepulveda, Ned Sublette, Yosvany Terry

III Catch a Fire

BOOKS

Augustyn, Heather, *Ska: The Rhythm of Liberation* (Plymouth: Scarecrow Press, 2013)
Belafonte, Harry, with Michael Schnayerson, *My Song: A Memoir of Art, Race and Defiance* (Edinburgh: Canongate, 2012)
Bergman, Billy, *Reggae and Latin Pop: Hot Sauces* (Dorset: Blandford Press, 1985)
Bilby, Kenneth M., *True-Born Maroons* (Kingston and Miami: Ian Randle Publishers, 2006)
Bradley, Lloyd, *Sounds Like London: 100 Years of Black Music in the Capital* (London: Serpent's Tail, 2013)
Bradley, Lloyd, *This Is Reggae Music: The Story of Jamaica's Music* (New York: Grove Press, 2000)
Burnard, Trevor, *Mastery, Tyranny and Desire: Thomas Thistlewood and His Slaves in the Anglo-Jamaican World* (Chapel Hill and London: University of North Carolina Press, 2004)
Charters, Samuel, *A Language of Song: Journeys in the Musical World of the African Diaspora* (Durham and London: Duke University Press, 2009)
De Koningh, Michael and Marc Griffiths, *Tighten Up: The History of Reggae in the UK* (London: Sanctuary Publishing, 2003)
Echols, Alice, *Hot Stuff: Disco and the Remaking of American Culture* (New York and London: W. W. Norton & Co., 2010)
Farley, Christopher John, *Before the Legend: The Rise of Bob Marley* (New York: Amistad, 2006)
Foehr, Stephen, *Jamaican Warriors: Reggae, Roots & Culture* (London: Sanctuary Publishing, 2000)
Grant, Colin, *Negro with a Hat: The Rise and Fall of Marcus Garvey* (New York: Oxford University Press, 2008)
Hochschild, Adam, *Bury the Chains: The British Struggle to Abolish Slavery* (London: Macmillan, 2005)
Jelly-Schapiro, Joshua, *Island People: The Caribbean and the World* (Edinburgh: Canongate, 2016)
Katz, David, *People Funny Boy: The Genius of Lee "Scratch" Perry* (London: Omnibus Press, 2006)
Lee, Hélène, *The First Rasta: Leonard Howell and the Rise of Rastafarianism*, trans. Lily Davis (Chicago: Lawrence Hill Books, 2003)
Letts, Don, and David Nobakht, *Culture Clash: Dread Meets Punk Rockers* (London: SAF Publishing, 2007)
McGovern, Adam (ed.), *MusicHound World: The Essential Album Guide* (Detroit and London: Visible Ink Press, 2000)
Ogg, Alex, and David Upshall, *The Hip Hop Years* (London: Macmillan, 1999)
Shapiro, Peter, *Turn the Beat Around: The Secret History of Disco* (London: Faber and Faber, 2009)
Sissay, Lemn, *My Name Is Why: A Memoir* (Edinburgh: Canongate, 2019)
Steffens, Roger, and Peter Simon, *Reggae Scrapbook* (San Raffael, California: Insight Editions, 2007)
Stolzoff, Norman C., *Wake the Town and Tell the People: Dancehall Culture in Jamaica* (Durham and London: Duke University Press, 2000)

Taylor, Timothy D., *Beyond Exoticism: Western Music and the World* (Durham and London: Duke University Press, 2007)
Thomas, Michael, and Adrian Boot, *Jamaica: Babylon on a Thin Wire* (London: Thames and Hudson, 1976)
White, Timothy, *Catch a Fire: The Life of Bob Marley* (New York: Henry Holt and Company, 2006)

ARTICLES, PAPERS, MISCELLANEOUS TEXTS
Augustyn, Heather, "What's in a Name? The Skatalites," Skabook blog, May 29, 2016 (skabook.com/2016/05/29/whats-name-skatalites/)
Bradley, Lloyd, "Obituary: Peter Tosh 'Volatile,'" *Q*, Nov. 1987
Grant, Colin, "Marley's Ghosts," *Frontline*, issue 5, winter 2010
Jelly-Schapiro, Joshua, "The Bob Marley Story," *New York Review of Books*, Apr. 9, 2009
Katz, David, "Obituary: Nearlin 'Lyn' Taitt," *Guardian*, Feb. 11, 2010
Martin, Kevin, "Echo Chamber Odysseys," Interview with Lee Perry, *The Wire*, May 1995
Perrone, Pierre, "Obituary: Sister Mary Ignatius Davies," *Independent*, Mar. 3, 2003
Simpson, Dave, "How We Made: Musical Youth's "Pass the Dutchie'," *Guardian*, Aug. 20, 2018
Spencer, Neil, "Reggae: The Sound That Revolutionised Britain," *Observer*, Jan. 30, 2011
Stelfox, Dave, "Vinyl Has Been Eliminated," *Guardian*, Jan. 18, 2008
Sullivan, John Jeremiah, "That Chop on the Upbeat," *Oxford American*, Nov. 17, 2013
White, Timothy, "Days of Dying," *Musician*, Oct. 1989
Williams, Richard, "Bob Marley's Funeral, 21 May 1981: A Day of Jamaican History," *Guardian*, Apr. 24, 2011

ALBUM NOTES
Barrow, Steve, *The Story of Jamaican Music (Tougher Than Tough)* (Mango, IBXCD 1—518 399-2, 1993)
Kwesi Johnson, Linton, "Introduction," in Steve Barrow, *The Story of Jamaican Music (Tougher Than Tough)* (Mango, IBXCD 1—518 399-2, 1993)

FILM, TELEVISION, RADIO
The First Rasta (*Le Premier Rasta*), dir. Hélène Lee (2011)
The Harder They Come, dir. Perry Henzell (1972)
Marley, dir. Kevin Macdonald (2012)
Reggae Britannia, dir. Jeremy Marre, BBC Four *Britannia* series (2011)
Rocksteady: The Roots of Reggae, dir. Stasha Bader (2009)
This Is Ska!, Iva/Maverick Productions (1964)
Toots and the Maytals: From the Roots, dir. Kieran Evans (2017)
Toots and the Maytals: Reggae Got Soul, dir. George Scott, BBC Four (2011)

INTERVIEWS, CONVERSATIONS, CORRESPONDENCE
Chris Blackwell, Vivien Goldman, Sally Henzell, Toots Hibbert, Leslie Palmer, Paul Simon, Roger Steffens, Trevor Wyatt

IV Latcho Drom

BOOKS

Attlee, Helena, *Lev's Violin: An Italian Adventure* (Milton Keynes: Particular Books, 2021)
Aubert, Laurent, *The Music of the Other: New Challenges for Ethnomusicology in a Global Age*, trans. Carla Ribeiro (Hampshire: Ashgate, 2007)
Bharucha, Rustom, *Rajasthan: An Oral History—Conversations with Komal Kothari* (New Delhi: Penguin Books, 2003)
Blacker, William, *Along the Enchanted Way: A Romanian Story* (London: John Murray, 2009)
Blas Vega, José, *Silverio: Rey de los cantaores* (Córdoba: Ediciones de la Posada, 1995)
Bose, Ajoy, *Across the Universe: The Beatles in India* (Hayana, India: Penguin Books, 2021)
Cartwright, Garth, *Princes Amongst Men: Journeys with Gypsy Musicians* (London: Serpent's Tail, 2005)
Chanan, Michael, *Repeated Takes: A Short History of Recording and Its Effects on Music* (London and New York: Verso, 1995)
Chaudhuri, Amit, *Finding the Raga: An Improvisation on Indian Music* (London: Faber & Faber, 2021)
Clébert, Jean-Paul, *The Gypsies*, trans. Charles Duff (Harmondsworth: Penguin Books, 1970)
Craske, Oliver, *Indian Sun: The Life and Music of Ravi Shankar* (London: Faber & Faber, 2020)
Dalrymple, William, *Nine Lives: In Search of the Sacred in Modern India* (London: Bloomsbury, 2010)
Dalrymple, William, *White Mughals: Love and Betrayal in Eighteenth-Century India* (London: Harper Perennial, 2004)
Devidayal, Namita, *The Music Room* (New Delhi: Random House India, 2007)
Dregni, Michael, *Django: The Life and Music of a Gypsy Legend* (New York: Oxford University Press, 2006)
Dregni, Michael, *Gypsy Jazz: In Search of Django Reinhardt and the Soul of Gypsy Swing* (New York: Oxford University Press, 2008)
Eberstadt, Fernanda, *Little Money Street: In Search of Gypsies and Their Music in the South of France* (New York: Vintage Books, 2007)
Fletcher, Peter, *World Musics in Context: A Comprehensive Survey of the World's Major Musical Cultures* (Oxford and New York: Oxford University Press, 2001)
Fonseca, Isabel, *Bury Me Standing: The Gypsies and Their Journey* (London: Vintage Books, 2006)
Fraser, Angus, *The Gypsies* (Oxford: Blackwell Publishing, 2005)
García Lorca, Federico, *Deep Song and Other Prose*, ed. and trans. Christopher Maurer (London and Boston: Marion Boyars, 1980)
García Lorca, Federico, *In Search of Duende*, trans. Chistopher Maurer (New York: New Directions, 1998)
Howson, Gerald, *The Flamencos of Cádiz Bay* (London: The Bold Strummer, 1994)
Kahn, Ashley, *The House That Trane Built: The Story of Impulse Records* (London: Granta Books, 2006)
Kenrick, Donald, and Grattan Puxon, *The Destiny of Europe's Gypsies* (New York: Basic Books, 1972)

BIBLIOGRAPHY

Kirkland, Will (ed.), *Gypsy Cante: Deep Song of the Caves*, selected and trans. Will Kirkland (San Francisco: City Lights Books, 1999)
Lavezzoli, Peter, *The Dawn of Indian Music in the West* (New York and London: Continuum, 2007)
Leblon, Bernard, *Gypsies and Flamenco: The Emergence of the Art of Flamenco in Andalusia*, trans. Sinéad ní Shuinéar (Hatfield, UK: University of Hertfordshire Press, 2003)
Leng, Simon, *While My Guitar Gently Weeps: The Music of George Harrison* (Milwaukee, Wisconsin: Hal Leonard, 2006)
MacDonald, Ian, *Revolution in the Head: The Beatles' Records and the Sixties* (Chicago: Chicago Review Press, 2007)
Miles, Barry, *Ginsberg: A Biography* (New York: HarperPerennial, 1990)
Sárosi, Bálint, *Gypsy Music*, trans. Fred Macnicol (Budapest: Corvina Press, 1978)
Schreiner, Claus, "Introduction," in Claus Schreiner (ed.), *Flamenco: Gypsy Dance and Music from Andalusia*, trans. Mollie Comerford Peters (Portland, Oregon: Amadeus Press, 1990)
Schreiner, Claus (ed.), *Flamenco: Gypsy Dance and Music from Andalusia*, trans. Mollie Comerford Peters (Portland, Oregon: Amadeus Press, 1990)
Silverman, Carol, *Romani Routes: Cultural Politics & Balkan Music in Diaspora* (Oxford and New York: Oxford University Press, 2012)
Tremlett, Giles, *España: A Brief History of Spain* (London and New York: Bloomsbury Publishing, 2022)
Tremlett, Giles, *Ghosts of Spain: Travels Through a Country's Hidden Past* (London: Faber and Faber, 2006)
Wald, Elijah, *Global Minstrels: Voices of World Music* (New York: Routledge, 2007)
Washabaugh, William, *Flamenco: Passion, Politics and Popular Culture* (Oxford and Washington DC: Berg, 1996)
Webster, Jason, *Duende: A Journey in Search of Flamenco* (London: Doubleday, 2003)
Yoors, Jan, *The Gypsies* (Prospect Heights, Illinois: Waveland Press, 1987)

ARTICLES, PAPERS, MISCELLANEOUS TEXTS

Bartal, Yossi, "Flamenco's Repression and Resistance in Southern Spain," Truthout, Dec. 14, 2014 (truthout.org/articles/flamenco-under-attack/)
Bhutto, Fatima, "Superheroes, Jazz, Queer Art: How Pakistan's Transgressive Pop Culture Went Global," *Guardian*, Dec. 19, 2022
Chaudhuri, Amit, "Indian Classical Music, the Beatles and the Blues," *Guardian*, Sept. 21, 2012
Clayton, Richard, "How The Byrds Transformed Bob Dylan's 'Mr Tambourine Man,'" *Financial Times*, July 25, 2016
Cornwell, Jane, "Gypsy Kings," *Songlines*, July 2008
Dalrymple, William, "Homer in India," *The New Yorker*, Nov. 12, 2006
Fox, Margalit, "Obituary: Enrique Morente, 67, Singer Who Made a New Flamenco," *New York Times*, Dec. 17, 2010
Fricke, David, "100 Greatest Guitarists: David Fricke's Picks," *Rolling Stone*, Dec. 3, 2010
Hunt, Ken, "A Straight Bhatt," *Folk Roots*, issue 136, Oct. 1994

Joshi, Vinod, "Folk Arts in Folk Lives," pamphlet, Jaipur Virasat Foundation, 2005
Kirkup, James, "Obituary: Camarón de la Isla," *Independent*, July 7, 1992
Minder, Raphael, "Flamenco's Foreign Saviors," *New York Times*, Mar. 16, 2013
Minder, Raphael, "Obituary: Paco de Lucía, Flamenco Guitarist, Dies at 66," *New York Times*, Feb. 27, 2014
Rorke, Bernard, "Hate Is Where the Heart Is: Time for Europe to Confront Anti-Gypsyism," openDemocracy, May 2, 2013 (www.opendemocracy.net/en/can-europe-make-it/hate-is-where-heart-is-time-for-europe-to-confront-anti-gypsyism/)
Rush, Phil, "Rock Con Raices," *Folk Roots*, issue 66, Dec. 1988
Sen, Amartya, "Tagore and His India," *New York Review of Books*, June 26, 1997
Senior, Mike, "Mohabbat by Arush Aftab," *The Mix Review*, Feb. 11, 2022 (themixreview.org/reviews/mohabbat/)
Singh, Faith, "Anokhi," talk during "Creative Industries: A Symposium on Culture-Based Development Strategies," *India Seminar No. 553: The Monthly Symposium*, Sept. 2005
Singh, John, "Manganiyar Community Annual Get-Together," pamphlet, Jaipur Virasat Foundation, District Jaisalmer, Feb. 24–26, 2012
Tremlett, Giles, "Gypsies: The Nomads Who Settled 1,500 Years Ago," *Guardian*, Dec. 8, 2012
Tremlett, Giles, "Painting Roma Tradition with a Modern Twist," *RA Magazine*, winter 2022
Yee, Amy, "The Art of an Indian Tradition," *New York Times*, May 27, 2011

ALBUM NOTES

Leroux, Thibault, *Nostalgique Bollywood: Chansons mémorables, de films, d'amour et de dévotion 1939–1959* (Buda Musique, 860375, 2022)
Romero, Angel (ed., written, and compiled), *Duende: From Traditional Masters to Gypsy Rock—The Passion & Dazzling Virtuosity of Flamenco*, Mini-Book (Ellipsis Arts, CD3350, 1994)

FILM, TELEVISION, RADIO

An Andalucian Journey: Gypsies and Flamenco, dir. Jana Bokova, episodes 9 and 10, BBC Two *Arena* (1988)
Apu Trilogy, dir. Satyajit Ray: *Pather Panchali* (1955), *Aparajito* (1956), *The World of Apu* (1959)
Gadjo dilo (*The Crazy Stranger*), dir. Tony Gatlif (1997)
Latcho drom, dir. Tony Gatlif (1993)
Monterey Pop, dir. D. A. Pennebaker (1968)
Papusza, dir. Joanna Kos-Krauze and Krzysztof Krauze (2013)
Revelando a Mario: El hombre detrás de la revolución musical, dir. Simó Mateu (2020)
Time of the Gypsies (*Dom za vešanje*), dir. Emir Kusturica (1988)
When the Road Bends Tales of a Gypsy Caravan, dir. Jasmine Dellal (2006)

INTERVIEWS, CONVERSATIONS, CORRESPONDENCE

Dániel Hamar, Marc Hollander, Damir Imamović, Vinod Joshi, Carolina Le Port, Peter Manuel, Mario Pacheco, Ricardo Pachón, Katherine Schofield, Faith Singh, John Singh, Michel Winter

V Chega de saudade

BOOKS

Amado, Jorge, *Tent of Miracles*, trans. Barbara Shelby (London: Collins Harvill, 1989)
Averbach, Ricardo, *Villa-Lobos and Modernism: The Apotheosis of Cannibal Music* (Lanham: Lexington Books, 2022)
Brazilian Institute of Geography and Statistics, "What Color Are You?," in Robert M. Levine and John J. Crocitti (eds.), *The Brazil Reader: History, Culture, Politics* (London: Latin America Bureau, 1999)
Castro, Ruy, *Bossa Nova: The Story of the Brazilian Music That Seduced the World*, trans. Lysa Salsbury (Chicago: Chicago Review Press, 2000)
Castro, Ruy, *Carmen: Uma Biografia* (São Paulo: Companhia das Letras, 2005)
Castro, Ruy, *Rio de Janeiro: Carnival Under Fire*, trans. John Gledson (London: Bloomsbury, 2004)
Charters, Samuel, *A Language of Song: Journeys in the Musical World of the African Diaspora* (Durham and London: Duke University Press, 2009)
Chasteen, John Charles, *National Rhythms, African Roots: The Deep History of Latin American Popular Dance* (Albuquerque, New Mexico: University of New Mexico Press, 2004)
Da Cunha, Euclides, *Rebellion in the Backlands*, trans. Samuel Putnam (Chicago and London: University of Chicago Press, 2010)
Dibbell, Julian, "Foreword," in Ruy Castro, *Bossa Nova: The Story of the Brazilian Music That Seduced the World*, trans. Lysa Salsbury (Chicago: Chicago Review Press, 2000)
Dunn, Christopher, "Tropicalism and Brazilian Popular Music Under Military Rule," in Robert M. Levine and John J. Crocitti (eds.), *The Brazil Reader: History, Culture, Politics* (London: Latin America Bureau, 1999)
Fausto, Boris, *A Concise History of Brazil*, trans. Arthur Brakel (New York: Cambridge University Press, 2006)
Freyre, Gilberto, *The Masters and the Slaves: A Study in the Development of Brazilian Civilization* (New York: Alfred A. Knopf, 1964)
Freyre, Gilberto, *New World in the Tropics* (New York: Alfred A. Knopf, 1966)
Fryer, Peter, *Rhythms of Resistance: African Musical Heritage in Brazil* (Hanover: Wesleyan University Press, 2000)
Guillermoprieto, Alma, *Samba* (New York: Vintage Departures, 1991)
Hanchard, Michael George, *Orpheus and Power: The Movimento Negro of Rio de Janeiro and São Paolo, Brazil 1945–1988* (Princeton, New Jersey: Princeton University Press, 1998)
Hertzman, Marc A., *Making Samba: A New History of Race and Music in Brazil* (Durham and London: Duke University Press, 2013)
Krich, John, *Why Is This Country Dancing? A One-Man Samba to the Beat of Brazil* (New York: Simon & Schuster, 1993)
Levine, Robert M., and John J. Crocitti, "The Vargas Era," in Robert M. Levine and John J. Crocitti (eds.), *The Brazil Reader: History, Culture, Politics* (London: Latin America Bureau, 1999)
Levine, Robert M., and John J. Crocitti (eds.), *The Brazil Reader: History, Culture, Politics* (London: Latin America Bureau, 1999)

McCann, Bryan, *Hello, Hello Brazil! Popular Music in the Making of Brazil* (Durham and London: Duke University Press, 2004)
McGowan, Chris, and Ricardo Pessanha, *The Brazilian Sound: Samba, Bossa Nova and the Popular Music of Brazil* (Philadelphia: Temple University Press, 1998)
Morin, France, and John Alan Farmer (eds.), *The Quiet in the Land: Everyday Life, Contemporary Art and Projecto Axé*, trans. Sabrina Gledhill with Lavinia Sobreira de Magalhães and Alejandro Rejes (Salvador: Museu de Arte Moderna da Bahia, 2000)
Robb, Peter, *A Death in Brazil: A Book of Omissions* (London: Bloomsbury, 2005)
Roberts, John Storm, *Black Music of Two Worlds* (New York: Praeger Publishers, 1972)
Schreiner, Claus, *Música Brasileira: A History of Popular Music and the People of Brazil*, trans. Mark Weinstein (New York and London: Marion Boyars, 2002)
Veloso, Caetano, *Tropical Truth: A Story of Music and Revolution in Brazil*, ed. Barbara Einzig, trans. Isabel de Sena (New York: Alfred A. Knopf, 2002)
Vianna, Hermano, *The Mystery of Samba: Popular Music and National Identity in Brazil*, ed. and trans. John Charles Chasteen (Chapel Hill and London: University of North Carolina Press, 1999)

ARTICLES, PAPERS, MISCELLANEOUS TEXTS

Blitzer, Jonathan, "How Caetano Veloso Revolutionized Brazil's Sound and Spirit," *The New Yorker*, Feb. 7, 2022
Jere-Malanda, Regina, "Brazil: The Fall of a 'Racial Paradise,'" *New African*, Feb. 2008
Jones, Maris, "'Quem foi que inventou Brasil?' The Symbolic Role of Music and Race in the Development of Brazilian National Identity," *Yale Historical Review: An Undergraduate Publication* V, issue II, spring 2016
Lewis, John, "Gilberto Gil and Caetano Veloso in London," *Guardian*, July 15, 2010
Lewis, John, "Why Bossa Nova Is 'The Highest Flowering of Brazilian Culture,'" *Guardian*, Oct. 1, 2013
Marriage, Zoë, "Capoeira and Security: The View from Upside-Down," openDemocracy, Feb. 1, 2012 (www.opendemocracy.net/en/opensecurity/capoeira-and-security-view-from-upside-down/)
Miranda, Beatriz, "Obituary: Johnny Alf: A Bossa Nova Giant Who Fell from Sight," *New York Times*, Aug. 10, 2020
Phillips, Tom, "Samba Rings Out Instead of Gunfire as Rio Favela Is Purged of Drug Gangs," *Observer*, Feb. 13, 2011
"A Politically Correct Brazilian Carnival," *The Economist*, Feb. 9, 2017
Robinson, Alex, "Gilberto Gil: 'We Wanted to Question How Brazilian Society Was Constituted—The Ethnic Make-Up of Brazil,'" *Songlines*, Feb. 16, 2018
Ryle, John, "Miracles of the People: How a French Ethnologist Became a Magician in Brazil," *Times Literary Supplement*, July 31, 1998
"Slavery's Legacies," *The Economist*, Sept. 10, 2016
Vernon, Paul, "Sambaphones," *Folk Roots*, issue 153, Mar. 1996

ALBUM NOTES

Baker, Stuart, *Bossa Nova and the Rise of Brazilian Music in the 1960s* (Soul Jazz Records, SJR CD239, 2011)

Baker, Stuart, *Tropicália: A Brazilian Revolution in Sound* (Soul Jazz Records, SJR CD118, 2006)
Byrne, David, *Brazil Classics Vol. 2: O Samba* (Luaka Bop/Sire, CD 26019-2, 1989)

FILM, TELEVISION, RADIO
Black Orpheus (*Orfeu Negro*), dir. Marcel Camus (1959)
Beyond Ipanema: Brazilian Waves in Global Music (*Ondas brasileiras na música global*), dir. Béco Dranoff and Guto Barra (2009)
Brasil, Brasil!, prod. Robin Denselow, BBC Four miniseries, 1: "Samba to Bossa," 2: "Tropicalia Revolution," 3: "A Tale of Four Cities" (2007)
Favela Rising, dir. Jeff Zimbalist and Matt Mochary (2005)
Flying Down to Rio, dir. Thornton Freeland (1933)
The Girl from Ipanema: Brazil, Bossa Nova and the Beach, dir. Andy Dunn (2016)
It's All True, dir. Orson Welles (1942, unfinished)
The Life Aquatic with Steve Zissou, dir. Wes Anderson (2004)
The Man Who Bottled Clouds (*O Homem que engarrafava nuvens*), dir. Lírio Ferreira (2009)
The Miracle of Candeal (*El Milagro de Candeal*), dir. Fernando Trueba (2004)
Saludos Amigos, dir. Norman Ferguson, Wilfred Jackson, Jack Kinney, Hamilton Luske, and Bill Roberts (1942)
The Secret History of Bossa Nova, prod. Simon Hollis, pres. Monica Vasconcelos, BBC Radio 4 (2013)
Songlines, episodes 7/8, pres. John Cavanagh, BBC Radio Scotland (2007)
Taking Iacanga (*O Barato de Iacanga*), dir. Thiago Mattar (2019)
This Is Bossa Nova (*Coisa mais linda: Histórias e casos da Bossa Nova*), dir. Paulo Thiago (2005)

INTERVIEWS, CONVERSATIONS, CORRESPONDENCE
Deborah Cohen, Béco Dranoff, Chuck Kaye, Geraldinho Magalhães, Alex Shoumatoff, Caetano Veloso

VI Mano a mano

BOOKS
Azzi, María Susana, "The Golden Age and After, 1920s–1990s," in Simon Collier et al., *¡Tango! The Dance, the Song, the Story* (London: Thames and Hudson, 2002)
Baim, Jo, *Tango: Creation of a Cultural Icon* (Bloomington and Indianapolis: Indiana University Press, 2007)
Borges, Jorge Luis, *The Total Library: Non-Fiction 1922–1986*, ed. Eliot Weinberger, trans. Esther Allen, Suzanne Jill Levine, and Eliot Weinberger (London: Penguin Books, 2001)
Brown, Jonathan C., *A Brief History of Argentina* (New York: Checkmark Books, 2004)
Castle, Irene, *Castles in the Air* (New York: Da Capo Press, 1980)
Chasteen, John Charles, *National Rhythms, African Roots: The Deep History of Latin American Popular Dance* (Albuquerque: University of New Mexico Press, 2004)
Cohen, Donald (ed.), *Tango Voices: Songs from the Soul of Buenos Aires & Beyond* (London: Wise Publications, 2007)

BIBLIOGRAPHY

Collier, Simon, *Carlos Gardel: Su vida, su música, su época* (Buenos Aires: Plaza & Janés, 2003)
Collier, Simon, "The Tango Is Born," in Simon Collier et al., *¡Tango! The Dance, the Song, the Story* (London: Thames and Hudson, 2002)
Collier, Simon, Artemis Cooper, María Susana Azzi, and Richard Martin, *¡Tango! The Dance, the Song, the Story* (London: Thames and Hudson, 2002)
Cooper, Artemis, "Tangomania in Europe and North America, 1913–1914," in Simon Collier et al., *¡Tango! The Dance, the Song, the Story* (London: Thames and Hudson, 2002)
Cortázar, Julio, *Blow-Up and Other Stories*, trans. Paul Blackburn (New York: Pantheon Books, 1985)
Denniston, Christine, *The Meaning of Tango: The Story of the Argentinian Dance* (London: Portico, 2007)
Eichelbaum, Edmundo, *Carlos Gardel: L'Âge d'or du Tango* (Paris: Denoël, 1984)
Farris Thompson, Robert, *Aesthetic of the Cool: Afro-Atlantic Art and Music* (Pittsburgh and New York: Periscope Publishing, 2011)
Farris Thompson, Robert, *Tango: The Art History of Love* (New York: Pantheon Books, 2005)
Flakoll, Kate (St John), *The Porteño Tango*, unpublished thesis for City University London (1981)
Flores Montenegro, Rafael, *Carlos Gardel: The Voice of the Tango*, trans. Donald Snowden (Los Angeles: Mundo Gardeliano Editions, 2019)
Kassabova, Kapka, *Twelve Minutes of Love: A Tango Story* (London: Granta, 2019)
Lavocah, Michael, *Tango Stories: Musical Secrets* (Norwich: Milonga Press, 2020)
Martin, Richard, "The Lasting Tango," in Simon Collier et al., *¡Tango! The Dance, the Song, the Story* (London: Thames and Hudson, 2002)
Taylor, Julie, *Paper Tangos* (Durham and London: Duke University Press, 1998)
Winter, Brian, *Long After Midnight at the Nino Bien: A Yanqui's Missteps in Argentina* (London: William Heinemann, 2008)

ARTICLES, PAPERS, MISCELLANEOUS TEXTS

Goñi, Uki, "How Argentina's Gravel-Voiced Crooner Put the Soul Back into Tango for the Rap Generation," *Guardian*, Oct. 23, 2016
Goñi, Uki, "Strictly Tango for the Dance Tourists," *Guardian*, Nov. 18, 2007
Lusk, Jon, "Tango Territory," *fRoots*, issue 300, June 2008
Sayle, Alexei, "Tango & Cash," *Guardian*, Nov. 29, 2014
Smith, Helena, "Stepping Away from Austerity with a Tango," *Guardian*, Nov. 17, 2015

ALBUM NOTES

Collier, Simon, *Carlos Gardel: The King of Tango, Vol. 1* (Nimbus Records, NI 7896, 1999)
Montes, Jorge, *Historia del Tango* (Music Hall, MH 10.001/2-2, 1988)
Schuhmann, Till and Gigi Backes, *Tango Alla Romanesque: Old World Tangos Vol. 2* (Oriente Musik, RIEN CD 40, 2002)

FILM, TELEVISION, RADIO

Carlos Gardel: El Gardel que conocí, dir. Eduardo Morera (Universal Music Argentina, 635 110-9, 2000)

Cuesta abajo, dir. Louis J. Gasnier (1934)
Si sos brujo: una historia de Tango (*Si Sos Brujo: A Tango Story*), dir. Caroline Neal (2005)
Sur (*The South*), dir. Fernando E. Solanas (1988)
Tango, un giro extraño, dir. Mercedes García Guevara (2004)
Tangos: El exilio de Gardel (*Tangos: The Exile of Gardel*), dir. Fernando E. Solanas (1985)
Tributo al polaco, dir. Eduardo Berti, Luis Barros and Alejandro Siskos (1995)

INTERVIEWS, CONVERSATIONS, CORRESPONDENCE
Javier Casalla, Acho Estol, Claudio Kleiman, Litto Nebbia, Cristóbal Repetto, Alfredo Rosso, Gustavo Santaolalla

VII Szerelem, szerelem

BOOKS
Allegro Barbaro: Béla Bartók et la modernité hongroise, 1905–1920 (Paris: Editions Hazan, 2013)
Anderson, Benedict, *Imagined Communities: Reflections on the Origin and Spread of Nationalism* (London and New York: Verso, 1992)
Ascherson, Neal, *Black Sea: The Birthplace of Civilisation and Barbarism* (London: Vintage, 1996)
Aubert, Laurent, *The Music of the Other: New Challenges for Ethnomusicology in a Global Age*, trans. Carla Ribeiro (Hampshire: Ashgate, 2007)
Botstein, Leon, "Out of Hungary: Bartók, Modernism, and the Cultural Politics of Twentieth-Century Music," in Peter Laki (ed.), *Bartók and His World* (Princeton, New Jersey: Princeton University Press, 1995)
Boukobza, Jean-François, "Entre avant-garde internationale et identité nationale: le folklore au cœur de la création de Bartók," in *Allegro Barbaro: Béla Bartók et la modernité hongroise, 1905–1920* (Paris: Editions Hazan, 2013)
Bowlt, John E., Nicoletta Misler, and Evgenia Petrova, "Fire and Ice," in John E. Bowlt et al. (eds.), *The Russian Avant-Garde, Siberia and the East* (Milano: Skira Editore, 2013)
Bowlt, John E., Nicoletta Misler, and Evgenia Petrova (eds.), *The Russian Avant-Garde, Siberia and the East* (Milano: Skira Editore, 2013)
Buchanan, Donna A., "Wedding Musicians, Political Transition, and National Consciousness in Bulgaria," in Mark Slobin (ed.), *Retuning Culture: Musical Changes in Central and Eastern Europe* (Durham and London: Duke University Press, 1996)
Cartwright, Garth, *Princes Amongst Men: Journeys with Gypsy Musicians* (London: Serpent's Tail, 2005)
Figes, Orlando, *Natasha's Dance: A Cultural History of Russia* (London: Allen Lane, 2002)
Fletcher, Peter, *World Musics in Context: A Comprehensive Survey of the World's Major Musical Cultures* (Oxford and New York: Oxford University Press, 2001)
Frigyesi, Judit, "The Aesthetic of the Hungarian Revival Movement," in Mark Slobin (ed.), *Retuning Culture: Musical Changes in Central and Eastern Europe* (Durham and London: Duke University Press, 1996)

Jávorsky, Béla Szilárd, *The Story of Hungarian Folk*, trans. Abel Petneki (Budapest: Kossuth Kiadó, 2015)
Judt, Tony, *Postwar: A History of Europe Since 1945* (London: Penguin Books, 2005)
King, David, *Red Star Over Russia: A Visual History of the Soviet Union from 1917 to the Death of Stalin* (London: Tate Publishing, 2009)
Koestler, Arthur, *The Thirteenth Tribe: The Khazar Empire and Its Heritage* (London: Hutchinson, 1976)
Laki, Peter, "The Gallows and the Altar: Poetic Criticism and Critical Poetry about Bartók in Hungary," in Peter Laki (ed.), *Bartók and His World* (Princeton, New Jersey: Princeton University Press, 1995)
Laki, Peter (ed.), *Bartók and His World* (Princeton, New Jersey: Princeton University Press, 1995)
Laki, Peter, and Claire Lashley (trans.), "A Selection of Poems Inspired by Béla Bartók," in Peter Laki (ed.), *Bartók and His World* (Princeton, New Jersey: Princeton University Press, 1995)
Lenoe, Matthew, *Closer to the Masses: Stalinist Culture, Social Revolution, and Soviet Newspapers* (Cambridge, Massachusetts, and London: Harvard University Press, 2004)
Levin, Theodore, "Dimitri Pokrovsky and the Russian Folk Music Revival Movement," in Mark Slobin (ed.), *Retuning Culture: Musical Changes in Central and Eastern Europe* (Durham and London: Duke University Press, 1996)
Levin, Theodore, *The Hundred Thousand Fools of God: Musical Travels in Central Asia (and Queens, New York)* (Bloomington and Indianapolis: Indiana University Press, 1996)
Levin, Theodore, and Valentina Süzükei, *Where Rivers and Mountains Sing: Sound, Music, and Nomadism in Tuva and Beyond* (Bloomington and Indianapolis: Indiana University Press, 2006)
Marsden, Philip, *The Spirit-Wrestlers and Other Survivors of the Russian Century* (London: Flamingo, 1999)
Olson, Laura J., *Performing Russia: Folk Revival and Russian Identity* (London and New York: RoutledgeCurzon, 2004)
Polonsky, Rachel, *Molotov's Magic Lantern: Uncovering Russia's Secret History* (London: Faber and Faber, 2010)
Pritchard, Jane, "Creating Productions," in Jane Pritchard (ed.), *Diaghilev and the Golden Age of the Ballets Russes 1909–1929* (London: V&A Publishing, 2010)
Pritchard, Jane (ed.), *Diaghilev and the Golden Age of the Ballets Russes 1909–1929* (London: V&A Publishing, 2010)
Reid, Anna, *The Shaman's Coat: A Native History of Siberia* (London: Phoenix, 2003)
Rice, Timothy, *May It Fill Your Soul: Experiencing Bulgarian Music* (Chicago and London: University of Chicago Press, 1994)
Ross, Alex, *The Rest Is Noise: Listening to the Twentieth Century* (London: Fourth Estate, 2012)
Scheijen, Sjeng, *Diaghilev: A Life* (London: Profile Books, 2010)
Schneider, David E., "Bartók and Stravinsky: Respect, Competition, Influence, and the Hungarian Reaction to Modernism in the 1920s," in Peter Laki (ed.), *Bartók and His World* (Princeton, New Jersey: Princeton University Press, 1995)

Shay, Anthony, *Choreographic Politics: State Folk Dance Companies, Representation and Power* (Middletown, Connecticut: Wesleyan University Press, 2002)

Silverman, Carol, *Balkanology*, 33 1/3 Europe series (New York and London: Bloomsbury Academic, 2021)

Silverman, Carol, *Romani Routes: Cultural Politics and Balkan Music in Diaspora* (Oxford and New York: Oxford University Press, 2012)

Slobin, Mark, "Introduction," in Mark Slobin (ed.), *Retuning Culture: Musical Changes in Central and Eastern Europe* (Durham and London: Duke University Press, 1996)

Slobin, Mark (ed.), *Retuning Culture: Musical Changes in Central and Eastern Europe* (Durham and London: Duke University Press, 1996)

Starr, S. Frederick, *Red and Hot: The Fate of Jazz in the Soviet Union 1917–1980* (New York and Oxford: Oxford University Press, 1983)

Stites, Richard, *Russian Popular Culture: Entertainment and Society Since 1900* (Cambridge: Cambridge University Press, 1995)

Szabolcsi, Bence, "Two Bartók Obituaries," trans. Peter Laki, in Peter Laki (ed.), *Bartók and His World* (Princeton, New Jersey: Princeton University Press, 1995)

Taruskin, Richard, *Defining Russia Musically: Historical and Hermeneutical Essays* (Princeton and Oxford: Princeton University Press, 2000)

Troitsky, Artemy, *Back in the USSR: The True Story of Rock in Russia* (London: Omnibus Press, 1987)

Viola, Lynne, *Peasant Rebels Under Stalin: Collectivization and the Culture of Peasant Resistance* (New York and Oxford: Oxford University Press, 1996)

Voit, Mrs. Pál, "Recollections of Béla Bartók," trans. Peter Laki, in Peter Laki (ed.), *Bartók and His World* (Princeton, New Jersey: Princeton University Press, 1995)

Volkov, Solomon, *St. Petersburg: A Cultural History* (New York: The Free Press, 1995)

Wilcox, Claire, "Paul Poiret and the Ballets Russes," in Jane Pritchard (ed.), *Diaghilev and the Golden Age of the Ballets Russes 1909–1929* (London: V&A Publishing, 2010)

Winchester, Oliver, "Diaghilev's Boys," in Jane Pritchard (ed.), *Diaghilev and the Golden Age of the Ballets Russes 1909–1929* (London: V&A Publishing, 2010)

Yurchak, Alexei, *Everything Was Forever, Until It Was No More: The Last Soviet Generation* (Princeton and Oxford: Princeton University Press, 2006)

ARTICLES, PAPERS, MISCELLANEOUS TEXTS

Alekseyeva, Anna, "The Russian Politics of Multiculturalism," openDemocracy, Mar. 30, 2015 (www.opendemocracy.net/en/odr/russian-politics-of-multiculturalism/)

Barbashin, Anton, and Hannah Thoburn, "Putin's Brain: Alexander Dugin and the Philosophy Behind Putin's Invasion of Crimea," *Foreign Affairs*, Mar. 31, 2014

Broughton, Simon, "The Rough Guide to World Music: Hungary," *Songlines*, July 17, 2018

Buchanan, Donna, "Metaphors of Power, Metaphors of Truth: The Politics of Music Professionalism in Bulgarian Folk Orchestras," *Ethnomusicology* 39, no. 3, autumn 1995

Coleman, Nick, "Bulgarian Rhapsody," *Time Out*, Apr. 13–20, 1988

Djoudjev, Stoyan, "The Diaphony of Bistritsa," *Obzor: A Bulgarian Quarterly Review of Literature and Arts*, issue 74, 1986

Eliot, T. S., "London Letter," *The Dial*, New York, vol. LXXI, no. 4, Oct. 1921 (theworld.com/~raparker/exploring/tseliot/works/london-letters/london-letter-1921-10.html)
Figes, Orlando, "From Russia: Local Heroes," RA, spring 2008
Frank, Joseph, "Idealists on the Run," *New York Review of Books*, June 12, 2008
Karasz, Palko, "At Malevich Exhibition, a Journey of Ideas," *New York Times*, Mar. 16, 2015
Kárpáti, János, "The Living Tradition of Bartók's Sources (The Bartók Album by the Muzsikás Ensemble)," *Hungarian Quarterly* 40, no. 154, summer 1999
Macaulay, Alastair, "A Latter-Day American Answer to Stravinsky's 'Rite of Spring,'" *New York Times*, June 16, 2023
Pareles, Jon, "Bulgarian Instruments and Vocals," *New York Times*, May 13, 1988
Pomerantsev, Peter, "2012: The Year the Kremlin Lost Control of the Script," openDemocracy, Dec. 28, 2013 (www.opendemocracy.net/en/odr/2012-year-kremlin-lost-control-of-script/)
Prina, Federica, "Russia for the Russians—A Putative Policy," openDemocracy, Apr. 5, 2013 (www.opendemocracy.net/en/odr/russia-for-russians-putative-policy/)
Rockwell, John, "Review: Folk Music: The Songs of Bulgaria," *New York Times*, May 18, 1988
Scott, Roger, "Interview with Kate Bush," *The Kate Bush Club*, official club magazine, 1989
Service, Tom, "The Rite of Spring: 'The Work of a Madman,'" *Guardian*, Feb. 13, 2013
Silverman, Carol, "Contemporary Wedding Music in Bulgaria," unpublished manuscript, 1988
Taruskin, Richard, "'Entoiling the Falconet': Russian Musical Orientalism in Context," *Cambridge Opera Journal* 4, no. 3, Nov. 1992
Taruskin, Richard, "Shocker Cools into a 'Rite' of Passage," *New York Times*, Sept. 14, 2012
Tumelty, Michael, "A Hair-Raising Brew: BBC Scottish Symphony and Folk Group Muzsikás Explore Bartók's Roots," *Glasgow Herald*, Mar. 8, 2004

ALBUM NOTES
Muzsikás, trans. Nicholas Jenkins, Muzsikás Featuring Márta Sebestyén & Alexander Balanescu, *The Bartók Album* (Hannibal Records, HNCD 1439, 1999)

FILM, TELEVISION, RADIO
Burnt by the Sun, dir. Nikita Mikhalkov (1994)
Genghis Blues, dir. Roko Belic (1999)
Muzsikás Story (*Muzsikás Történet*), dir. Péter Pál Tóth (2009)
The Singing Revolution, dir. Maureen Castle Tusty and James Tusty (2006)
Stravinsky: Once at a Border, dir. Tony Palmer (1982)

INTERVIEWS, CONVERSATIONS, CORRESPONDENCE
Ian Anderson, David Bither, Simon Broughton, Garth Cartwright, Alexander Cheparukhin, Lu Edmonds, Viktor Erofeyev, Dániel Hamar, Brad Hill, Jac Holzman, Martin Koenig, Andrei Kotov, Elena Kouteva, Theodore Levin, Csaba Lőkös, Borimira Nedeva-Moore, Ivo Papasov, Márta Sebestyén, Vyacheslav Shchurov, Polina Shepherd, Carol Silverman, Olga Solovyova, Artemy Troitsky, Rumyana Tzintzarska, Yuri Yunakov

VIII Tezeta

BOOKS

Agawu, Kofi, *Representing African Music: Postcolonial Notes, Queries, Positions* (New York and London: Routledge, 2003)

Allen, Tony, and Michael E. Veal, *Tony Allen: An Autobiography of the Master Drummer of Afrobeat* (Durham and London: Duke University Press, 2013)

Andriamirado, Sennen, and Virginie Andriamirado, *Mali Today* (Paris: Les Éditions du Jaguar, 1997)

Appiah, Kwame Anthony, and Henry Louis Gates, Jr. (eds.), *Africana: The Encyclopedia of the African and African American Experience* (New York: Basic Civitas Books, 1999)

Archangel, Michael, *Rule by Love: Rhythms and Consent—The Definitive Fela Biography* (Sydney: Sazimor, 1998)

Arnaud, Gérald, and Henri Lecomte, *Musique de toutes les Afriques* (Paris: Fayard, 2006)

Bender, Wolfgang, *Sweet Mother: Modern African Music*, trans. Wolfgang Freis (Chicago and London: University of Chicago Press, 1991)

Broughton, Simon, Mark Ellingham, and Jon Lusk (eds.), *The Rough Guide to World Music Vol. 1: Africa and the Middle East*, 3rd ed. (London and New York: Rough Guides, 2006)

Cathcart, Jenny, *Hey You! A Portrait of Youssou N'Dour* (Witney: Fine Line Books, 1989)

Charters, Samuel, *A Language of Song: Journeys in the Musical World of the African Diaspora* (Durham and London: Duke University Press, 2009)

Charters, Samuel, *The Roots of the Blues: An African Search* (New York: Da Capo Press, 1981)

Chernoff, John Miller, *African Rhythm and African Sensibility: Aesthetics and Social Action in African Musical Idioms* (Chicago and London: University of Chicago Press, 1981)

Collins, John, *African Pop Roots: The Inside Rhythms of Africa* (Slough, UK: W. Foulsham & Co., 1985)

Collins, John, *Fela: Kalakuta Notes* (Amsterdam: KIT Publishers, 2009)

Davidson, Basil, *The African Genius: An Introduction to African Social and Cultural History* (Boston, Toronto, and London: Little, Brown and Co., 1969)

Diawara, Manthia, *In Search of Africa* (Cambridge, Massachusetts, and London: Harvard University Press, 2000)

Dibango, Manu, and Danielle Rouard, *Three Kilos of Coffee: An Autobiography*, trans. Beth G. Raps (Chicago and London: University of Chicago Press, 1994)

Diop, Cheikh Anta, *The African Origin of Civilization: Myth or Reality*, trans. and ed. Mercer Cook (Chicago: Lawrence Hill Books, 1974)

Dowden, Richard, *Africa: Altered States, Ordinary Miracles* (London: Granta, 2019)

Durán, Lucy, "Mali: Gold Dust by the River," in Simon Broughton, Mark Ellingham, and Jon Lusk (eds.), *The Rough Guide to World Music Vol. 1: Africa and the Middle East*, 3rd ed. (London and New York: Rough Guides, 2006)

Ewens, Graeme, ":Congo: Heart of Danceness," in Simon Broughton, Mark Ellingham, and Jon Lusk (eds.), *The Rough Guide to World Music Vol. 1: Africa and the Middle East*, 3rd ed. (London and New York: Rough Guides, 2006)

Eyre, Banning, *In Griot Time: An American Guitarist in Mali* (London: Serpent's Tail, 2002)

BIBLIOGRAPHY

Eyre, Banning, *Lion Songs: Thomas Mapfumo and the Music That Made Zimbabwe* (Durham and London: Duke University Press, 2015)

Eyre, Banning, *Playing with Fire: Fear and Self-Censorship in Zimbabwean Music* (Copenhagen: Freemuse, 2005)

Falceto, Francis, *Abyssinie Swing: A Pictorial History of Modern Ethiopian Music*, trans. Karen Louise Albrecht (Addis Ababa: Shama Books, 2001)

Falceto, Francis, "Ethiopia: Land of Wax and Gold," in Simon Broughton, Mark Ellingham, and Jon Lusk (eds.), *The Rough Guide to World Music Vol. 1: Africa and the Middle East*, 3rd ed. (London and New York: Rough Guides, 2006)

Farris Thompson, Robert, *Aesthetic of the Cool: Afro-Atlantic Art and Music* (Pittsburgh and New York: Periscope Publishing, 2011)

Farris Thompson, Robert, *Flash of the Spirit: African and Afro-American Art and Philosophy* (New York: Vintage Books, 1984)

French, Howard W., *Born in Blackness: Africa, Africans and the Making of the Modern World, 1471 to the Second World War* (New York: Liveright Publishing Corp., 2021)

Gates, Henry Louis, Jr., "Europe, African Art and the Uncanny," in Tom Philips, *Africa: The Art of a Continent* (London: Royal Academy of Arts; Munich and New York: Prestel, 1996)

Gilroy, Paul, *The Black Atlantic: Modernity and Double Consciousness* (Cambridge, Massachusetts: Harvard University Press, 1993)

Goodwin, Paul, "Introduction," in Daniele Tamagni, *Gentlemen of Bacongo* (London: Trolley Books, 2009)

Gorer, Geoffrey, *Africa Dances* (London: Eland, 2003)

Hochschild, Adam, *King Leopold's Ghost: A Story of Greed, Terror, and Heroism in Colonial Africa* (New York: Houghton Mifflin Company, 1998)

Hudson, Mark, *The Music in My Head* (London: Vintage, 1998)

Hudson, Mark, Doudou Sarr, Paul Hayward, and Lucy Durán, "Senegal and The Gambia: A Tale of Two Countries," in Simon Broughton, Mark Ellingham, and Jon Lusk (eds.), *The Rough Guide to World Music Vol. 1: Africa and the Middle East*, 3rd ed. (London and New York: Rough Guides, 2006)

Jaji, Tsitsi Ella, *Africa in Stereo: Modernism, Music, and Pan-African Solidarity* (New York: Oxford University Press, 2014)

Josephy, Alvin M., Jr. (ed.), *The Horizon History of Africa* (New York: American Heritage Publishing Co., 1971)

Kubik, Gerhard, *Africa and the Blues* (Jackson: University of Mississippi, 1999)

Kubik, Gerhard, *Jazz Transatlantic: Jazz Derivatives and Developments in Twentieth-Century Africa, Volume II* (Jackson: University Press of Mississippi, 2017)

Levine, Donald N., *Wax and Gold: Tradition and Innovation in Ethiopian Culture* (Chicago and London: University of Chicago Press, 1972)

Lobeck, Katharina, "Guinea: Move Over Mali," in Simon Broughton, Mark Ellingham, and Jon Lusk (eds.), *The Rough Guide to World Music Vol. 1: Africa and the Middle East*, 3rd ed. (London and New York: Rough Guides, 2006)

Masekela, Hugh, and D. Michael Cheers, *Still Grazing: The Musical Journey of Hugh Masekela* (New York: Three Rivers Press, 2004)

Mazzoleni, Florent, *Afro pop: L'Âge d'or des grands orchestres africains* (Bègles: Le Castor Astral, 2011)
Mazzoleni, Florent, *Musiques modernes et traditionnelles du Mali* (Bègles: Le Castor Astral, 2011)
Meredith, Martin, *The State of Africa: A History of Fifty Years of Independence* (London: Free Press, 2006)
Morgan, Andy, *Finding the One: The Strange and Parallel Lives of the West African Kora and the Welsh Harp* (Ceredigion: Theatr Mwldan and Astar Artes, 2013)
Morgan, Andy, *Music, Culture and Conflict in Mali* (Copenhagen: Freemuse 2013)
Oliver, Paul, *Savannah Syncopators: African Retentions in the Blues* (London: Studio Vista, 1970)
Pakenham, Thomas, *The Scramble for Africa: White Man's Conquest of the Dark Continent from 1876 to 1912* (New York: Avon Books, 1991)
Palmer, Robert, *Deep Blues: A Musical and Cultural History of the Mississippi Delta* (New York: Penguin Books, 1981)
Pankhurst, Richard, *The Ethiopians: A History* (Malden, Oxford and Carlton: Blackwell Publishing, 2001)
Stewart, Gary, *Breakout: Profiles in African Rhythm* (Chicago: University of Chicago Press, 1992)
Stewart, Gary, *Rumba on the River: A History of the Popular Music of the Two Congos* (London and New York: Verso, 2003)
Sublette, Ned, *Cuba and Its Music: From the First Drums to the Mambo* (Chicago: Chicago Review Press, 2004)
Tamagni, Daniele, *Gentlemen of Bacongo* (London: Trolley Books, 2009)
Tenaille, Frank, *Music Is the Weapon of the Future: Fifty Years of African Popular Music*, trans. Stephen Toussaint and Hope Sandrine (Chicago: Lawrence Hill Books, 2002)
Veal, Michael E., "Dry Spell Blues: Sublime Frequencies Across the West African Sahel," in Michael E. Veal and E. Tammy Kim (eds.), *Punk Ethnography: Artists and Scholars Listen to Sublime Frequencies* (Middletown, Connecticut: Wesleyan University Press, 2016)
Veal, Michael E., *Fela: The Life and Times of an African Musical Icon* (Philadelphia: Temple University Press, 2000)
Veal, Michael E., and E. Tammy Kim (eds.), *Punk Ethnography: Artists and Scholars Listen to Sublime Frequencies* (Middletown, Connecticut: Wesleyan University Press, 2016)
Waterman, Christopher Alan, *Jùjú: A Social History and Ethnography of an African Popular Music* (Chicago and London: University of Chicago Press, 1990)
White, Bob W., *Rumba Rules: The Politics of Dance Music in Mobutu's Zaire* (Durham and London: Duke University Press, 2008)
Wrong, Michela, *In the Footsteps of Mr Kurtz: Living on the Brink of Disaster in the Congo* (London: Fourth Estate, 2001)

ARTICLES, PAPERS, MISCELLANEOUS TEXTS
Beaumont-Thomas, Ben, "'His Drums Were Singing, You Know?' Tony Allen Remembered by His Collaborators," *Guardian*, May 4, 2020

Birrell, Ian, "In the Heart of the Congo," *Independent*, Feb. 29, 2008
Christgau, Robert, "Review of Tinariwen's *Aman Iman*," *World Village*, 2007 (www.robertchristgau.com/get_artist.php?id=5036)
Cornwell, Jane, "African Music the Actual African Diaspora Likes," *Guardian*, Sept. 9, 2010
Cumming, Tim, "Orchestral Manoeuvres," *Independent*, Nov. 16, 2007
Denselow, Robin, "Made in Dakar," *Guardian*, Sept. 28, 2007
Diallo, Violet, "Sounding Out . . . Bamako," *Songlines*, Mar./Apr. 2005
Doyle, Rachel B., "In Ethiopian Capital, Jazz Takes Back the Night," *New York Times*, Nov. 15–16, 2014
Durán, Lucy, "Djely Mousso," *Folk Roots*, issue 75, Sept. 1989
Durán, Lucy, "Key to N'Dour: Roots of the Senegalese Star," *Popular Music* 8, no. 3, African Music, Oct. 1989
Durán, Lucy, "Royal Blues," *Songlines*, May 2007
Durán, Lucy, "Techno-Griot' "*Folk Roots*, issue 175, Jan./Feb. 1998
Falceto, Francis, "Alfanalech? Gigi Between Past and Future," *Les nouvelles d'Addis*, lesnouvelles.org, Feb. 22, 2012 (web.archive.org/web/20120222192034/http:// www.lesnouvelles.org/P10_magazine/16_analyse02/16088_gigifalceto-eng.html)
Fernandes, Sujatha, "The Day the Music Died," *New York Times*, May 21, 2013
Fox, Margalit, "Papa Wemba, Congolese King of 'Rumba Rock,' Is Dead at 66," *New York Times*, Apr. 25, 2016
Freston, Tom, "Showtime in the Sahara," *Vanity Fair*, July 2007
"Getachew Kassa and His Tezetas," *Ethiopia Observer*, Dec. 19, 2016
Henley, Jon, "Malick Sidibé Photographs: One Nation Under a Groove," *Guardian*, Feb. 27, 2010
Hepworth, David, "There's a Griot Going On," *The Word*, Mar. 2008
Honigmann, David, "Singing Out as Africa's 'Head of Culture,'" *Financial Times*, Oct. 13–14, 2007
Howe, John, "Fela Anikulapo Kuti: A Honest Man," *New Left Review*, issue 225, Sept./Oct. 1997
Isherwood, Charles, "Feeling Unsettled at a Feel-Good Show," *New York Times*, Jan. 31, 2010
Khan, Aina J., "A Hallowed Tradition That Wasn't Meant to Include Women," *New York Times*, Sept. 21, 2021
Kinder, Elizabeth, "Rift Valley Home," *fRoots*, issue 286, Apr. 2007
Lobeck, Katharina, "Addis Swinger," *fRoots*, issue 268, Oct. 2005
Lobeck, Katharina, "Stars & Hopes," *fRoots*, issue 305, Nov. 2008
Lobeck Kane, Katharina, "Guinea 2008," *fRoots*, issue 301, July 2008
Lobeck Kane, Katharina, "Wasulu Goes City Style," *fRoots*, issue 309, Mar. 2009
Lusk, Jon, "Overcoming All the Odds," *fRoots*, issue 338/9, Sept. 2011
Lusk, Jon, "Tony Allen 70: Nigeria 50," program note, Barbican, London, Oct. 6, 2010
Morgan, Andy, "Mali: Three Years After the Music Ban," *Freemuse*, Dec. 15, 2015
Morgan, Andy, "Mali's Desert Nomads Turn Up," *Observer*, Aug. 21, 2011
Morgan, Andy, "Swingin' Addis," *Songlines*, Sept./Oct. 2007
Morgan, Andy, "We Won't Let Islamists Get Away with It. Mali Without Music Is an Impossibility," *Guardian*, Oct. 25, 2012

Moss, Stephen, "I'm Bringing a Message," *Guardian*, Mar. 21, 2007
Muggs, Joe, "Q&A: Senegalese Groovemaster Baaba Maal–Where Dakar Meets the Royal Festival Hall," *The Word*, July 2009
O'Dair, Marcus, "Congotronics vs Rockers," program note, Barbican, London, July 12, 2011
"Papa Wemba: The King of the Rumba," *The Economist*, Apr. 30, 2016
Pareles, Jon, "Expanding the Boundaries of a West African Instrument," *New York Times*, July 27, 2010
Pareles, Jon, "Obituary: Mory Kante; He Fused African Music with Styles from Western Pop," *New York Times*, May 26, 2020
Pareles, Jon, "Obituary: Tabu Ley Rochereau; Spread Sounds of Afro-Pop Worldwide," *New York Times*, Dec. 9, 2013
Petridis, Alexis, "Assume Crash Position," *Guardian*, Apr. 4, 2006
Prince, Rob, "Candid Kanda," *Folk Roots*, issue 82, Apr. 1990
Rohter, Larry, "Blues from the Desert, Recorded On-Site," *New York Times*, Aug. 31, 2011
"Rumba in the Jungle," *The Economist*, Dec. 20, 2003
"Songlines Presents . . . The Music of West Africa," *Songlines*, Nov. 18, 2021
Spencer, Neil, "Out of Africa," *Observer*, May 18, 2008
Stewart, Gary, "Soukous: Birth of the Beat," *The Beat* 8, no. 6, 1989
Stoudmann, Elisabeth, "Ethiopian Stripes," *fRoots*, issue 338/9, Aug./Sept. 2011
Sweeney, Philip, "Ibrahima Sylla Obituary," *Guardian*, Jan. 30, 2014
Waechter, Johannes, "Afrika ist sehr modern," *Süddeutsche Zeitung Magazin*, July 9, 2009
Waterman, Christopher A., "Chop and Quench," *African Arts* 31, no. 1, winter 1998
Williams, Murphy, "Songs of Experience," *Telegraph Magazine*, Jan. 20, 2007
Williamson, Nigel, "Beginner's Guide: Youssou N'Dour," *Songlines*, Nov./Dec. 2002
Woubshet, Dagmawi, "Tizita: A New World Interpretation," *Callaloo* 32, no. 2, part 2, spring 2009

ALBUM NOTES

Armstrong, John, *Nigeria 70: The Definitive Story of 1970s Funky Lagos* (Afrostrut, STRUTCD 013, 2001)
Bensignor, François, *20 Years History: The Very Best of Syllart Productions* (Syllart Productions, CDS 8911, 2002)
Braun, Ken, Franco, and Le TPOK Jazz, *Francophonic—Africa's Greatest: A Retrospective, Vol. 1—1953–1980* (Sterns Africa, STCD3041-42, 2008)
Braun, Ken, Franco, and Le TPOK Jazz, *Francophonic—Africa's Greatest: A Retrospective, Vol. 2—1980–1989* (Sterns Africa, SRCD3046-47, 2009)
Counsel, Graeme, *Authenticité: The Syliphone Years—Guinea's Orchestres Nationaux and Federaux 1965–1980* (Stern's Music, STCD3025-26, 2007)
Dylan, Bob, *Bob Dylan (Music That Matters to Him)*, Artist's Choice series (Starbucks Entertainment, CDS-132, 2008)
Ewens, Graeme, *Golden Afrique Vol. 2* (Network Medien, 29.076, 2005)
Eyre, Banning, and Brett J. Bonner, *Mali to Memphis: An African-American Odyssey* (Putmayo World Music, PUTU 145-2, 1999)

Falceto, Francis, trans. Karen Louise Albrecht, *Éthiopiques 1: Golden Years of Modern Ethiopian Music, 1969–1975* (Buda Musique, 82951-2, 1997)

Falceto, Francis, trans. Karen Louise Albrecht, *Éthiopiques 2: Tetchawet! Urban Azmaris of the 90's* (Buda Musique, 82952-2, 1997)

Falceto, Francis, trans. Karen Louise Albrecht, *Éthiopiques 3: Golden Years of Modern Ethiopian Music, 1969–1975* (Buda Musique, 82963-2, 1998)

Falceto, Francis, trans. Karen Louise Albrecht, *Éthiopiques 4: Ethio Jazz & Musique Instrumentale 1969–1974* (Buda Musique, 82964-2, 1998)

Falceto, Francis, trans. Karen Louise Albrecht, Mahmoud Ahmed, *Éthiopiques 6: Almaz* (Buda Musique, 82979-2, 1999)

Falceto, Francis, trans. Karen Louise Albrecht, Mahmoud Ahmed, *Éthiopiques 7: Ere Mela Mela* (Buda Musique, 82980-2, 1999)

Falceto, Francis, trans. Karen Louise Albrecht, *Éthiopiques 8: Swinging Addis, 1969–1974* (Buda Musique, 82982-2, 2000)

Falceto, Francis, trans. Karen Louise Albrecht, *Éthiopiques 10: Tezeta—Ethiopian Blues and Ballads* (Buda Musique, 82222, 2002)

Falceto, Francis, trans. Karen Louise Albrecht, *Éthiopiques 13: Ethiopian Groove—The Golden Seventies* (Buda Musique, 82255-2, 2002)

Falceto, Francis, trans. Karen Louise Albrecht, Emahoy Tsegue-Maryam Guebrou, *Éthiopiques, Vol. 21: Piano Solo* (Buda Musique, 86012-2, 2006)

Falceto, Francis, trans. by Karen Louise Albrecht and Sayem Osman, *Éthiopiques 24: Golden Years of Modern Ethiopian Music 1969–1975* (Buda Musique, 860176, 2008)

Gretz, Günter, and Jean Trouillet, *Golden Afrique Vol. 1* (Network Medien, 27.677, 2005)

Lavoie, Matthew, *Wallahi Le Zein!!—Wezin, Jakwar and Guitar Boogie from the Islamic Republic of Mauritania* (Latitude, 07, 2011)

Lecomte, Henri, Sidiki Diabaté, Batourou Sekou Kouyaté, Djelimady Sissoko, and N'fa Diabaté, *Mali: Cordes Anciennes—Mali: Ancient Strings*, Musique du Monde series (Buda Musique/Records, 1977822, 1970/1999)

Leroux, Thibault, *Kongo Ya Nostalgic—Nostalgique Kongo: Rumbas Lingala, Swahili, Kikongo & Douala 1950–1960* (Buda Musique, 860339, 2019)

Mafuta, Mwana, *Congo Revolution: Revolutionary and Evolutionary Sounds from the Two Congos 1955–62* (Soul Jazz Records, SJR CD437, 2019)

Murphy, William, Abyssinia Infinite Featuring Ejigayehu 'Gigi' Shibabaw, *Zion Roots* (Network Medien, 24.971, 2003)

Razafintsalama, Jean-Paul, and Ian Anderson, *Tulear Never Sleeps: Tsapiky Guitars from South Western Madagascar* (Stern's Music/Earthworks, STEW49CD, 2003)

Toublanc, Pierre-Olivier, and Pierre René-Worms (eds.), *Africa: 50 Years of Music—1960/2010: 50 Years of Independence* (Discograph, 3218462, 2010)

Ward, Jonathan, *Opika Pende: Africa at 78 RPM* (Dust-to-Digital, DTD 22, 2011)

FILM, TELEVISION, RADIO

Benda Bilili!, dir. Renaud Barret and Florent de la Tullaye (2010)

Broken Flowers, dir. Jim Jarmusch (2005)

Dolce Vita Africana, dir. Cosima Spender, BBC Four *Storyville* (2008)

Ethiopiques: Revolt of the Soul (*Ethiopiques: Muzyka Duszy*), dir. Maciej Bochniak (2017)
Fela Kuti: Music Is the Weapon (*Musique au poing*), dir. Jean-Jaques Flori and Stéphane Tchalgadjieff (1982)
Félicité, dir. Alain Gomis (2017)
Finding Fela, dir. Alex Gibney (2014)
The Importance of Being Elegant, dir. George Amponsah and Cosima Spender, BBC Four Storyville (2004)
Lumumba, dir. Raoul Peck (2000)
Music Extra: Sweet Mother, pres. DJ Edu, BBC World Service (2017)
Soul Power, dir. Jeffrey Levy-Hinte, prod. Leon Gast (2008)
Soul to Soul, dir. Denis Sanders (1971)
La Vie est belle (*Life Is Rosy*), dir. Mwezé Ngangura and Benoît Lamy (1987)

INTERVIEWS, CONVERSATIONS, CORRESPONDENCE
Tony Allen, Ian Anderson, Jerry Boys, John Collins, Lucy Durán, Brian Eno, Banning Eyre, Francis Falceto, James Fox, Nick Gold, Marc Hollander, Mark Hudson, Kanda Bongo Man, Vincent Kenis, Martin Meissonnier, Andy Morgan, Davia Nelson, Martín Perna, Christian Scholze, Iain Scott, Rikki Stein, Ibrahima Sylla, Robert Urbanus, Tony Van der Eecken

IX How we begin to remember

BOOKS
Abbott, Lynn, and Doug Seroff, *Ragged but Right: Black Traveling Shows, "Coon Songs," and the Dark Pathway to Blues and Jazz* (Jackson: University Press of Mississippi, 2007)
Anderson, Benedict, *Imagined Communities: Reflections on the Origin and Spread of Nationalism* (London and New York: Verso, 1992)
Archer-Straw, Petrine, *Negrophilia: Avant-Garde Paris and Black Culture in the 1920s* (New York: Thames & Hudson, 2000)
Berlin, Isaiah, *The Roots of Romanticism*, ed. Henry Hardy (London: Pimlico, 2000)
Blanning, Tim, *The Triumph of Music: The Rise of Composers, Musicians and Their Art* (Cambridge, Massachusetts: Belknap Press of Harvard University Press, 2008)
Brooman, Thomas, *My Festival Romance* (London: Tangent Books, 2017)
Chanan, Michael, *Repeated Takes: A Short History of Recording and Its Effects on Music* (London and New York: Verso, 1995)
Denning, Michael, *Noise Uprising: The Audiopolitics of a World Musical Revolution* (London and New York: Verso, 2015)
Douglas, Ann, *Terrible Honesty: Mongrel Manhattan in the 1920s* (New York: Farrar, Straus and Giroux, 1995)
Ehrenreich, Barbara, *Dancing in the Streets: A History of Collective Joy* (London: Granta Books, 2008)
Emerson, Ken, *Doo-dah!: Stephen Foster and the Rise of American Popular Culture* (New York: Simon & Schuster, 1997)
Gioia, Ted, *Music: A Subversive History* (New York: Basic Books, 2019)

Gray, Louise, *The No-Nonsense Guide to World Music* (Oxford: New Internationalist Publications, 2009)
King, Christopher C., *Lament from Epirus: An Odyssey into Europe's Oldest Surviving Folk Music* (New York and London: W. W. Norton & Co., 2018)
Knowles, Mark, *The Wicked Waltz and Other Scandalous Dances: Outrage at Couple Dancing in the 19th and Early 20th Centuries* (Jefferson, North Carolina, and London: McFarland & Company, 2009)
Mac Sweeney, Naoíse, *The West: A New History of an Old Idea* (London: W. H. Allen, 2023)
Morgan, Andy, *Music, Culture and Conflict in Mali* (Copenhagen: Freemuse, 2013)
Nietzsche, Friedrich, *The Birth of Tragedy: Out of the Spirit of Music*, ed. Michael Tanner, trans. Shaun Whiteside (London: Penguin Books, 1993)
Palmer, Robert, *Blues & Chaos: The Music Writing of Robert Palmer*, ed. Anthony DeCurtis (New York and London: Scribner, 2009)
Puchner, Martin, *Culture: A New World History* (London: Ithaka, 2023)
Richards, Keith, with James Fox, *Life* (London: Weidenfeld & Nicolson, 2010)
Said, Edward W., *Orientalism* (London: Penguin Books, 2003)
Samaltanou-Tsiakma, Ekaterini, *Guillaume Apollinaire: Catalyst for Primitivism, for Picabia and Duchamp* (PhD thesis) (University of Virginia Dissertations Publishing, 1981)
Taruskin, Richard, *Defining Russia Musically: Historical and Hermeneutical Essays* (Princeton and Oxford: Princeton University Press, 2000)

ARTICLES, PAPERS, MISCELLANEOUS TEXTS

Cullman, Brian, "Jajouka: Burning a Hole in the Night," *The Journal of the Plague Years*, autumn 2022 (www.journaloftheplagueyears.ink/blog/jajouka-burning-a-hole-in-the-night)
Gabriel, F. R., "What Western Art Owes to the World," *Arcadia*, Mar. 7, 2022 (www.byarcadia.org/post/what-western-art-owes-to-the-world)
Leighten, Patricia, "The White Peril and *L'Art négre*: Picasso, Primitivism, and Anticolonialism," *The Art Bulletin*, vol. LXXII, no. 4, Dec. 1990
Moss, Chris, "The Great Musical Genres of the 20th and 21st Centuries," *Songlines*, Nov. 2022
Sullivan, Caroline, "How We Made: Jiggs Chase and Ed Fletcher on 'The Message,'" *Guardian*, May 27, 2013

ALBUM NOTES

Gysin, Brion, *Brian Jones Presents the Pipes of Pan at Joujouka* (Rolling Stones Records, COC 49100, 1971)

FILM, TELEVISION, RADIO

Seopyeonje, dir. Im Kwon-taek (1993)

INTERVIEWS, CONVERSATIONS, CORRESPONDENCE

Ian Anderson, Thomas Brooman, Simon Broughton, John Collins, Robin Denselow, Rob Dickins, Alan Elliott, Brian Eno, Jodie Gillett, Damir Imamović, Mark Kidel, Theodore Levin, Ben Mandelson, Barry Miles, Bryn Ormrod, Rikki Stein

Index

A&M Records, 459–60
Abakuá societies, 96, 112, 130, 149
Abeokuta, Nigeria, 653, 655–56, 685
Abidjan, 769, 771
Abyssinian Baptist Church, 23
Adams, Justin, 792, 794
Adès, Thomas, 595
Adorno, Theodor, 580, 623
Afanasiev, Alexander, 568
Afra, Tybee, 143
Africa Express, 703–704, 745
Africa 70 (band), 677–79, 681, 687–89, 692, 697, 700
African Americans, geographical origins, 97–99
African Fiesta, 717–720
African Jazz, 705–706, 714, 717–18
African Jazz & Variety Show, 40, 47
African National Congress (ANC), 8–10, 32–33, 58–60, 53, 65, 67, 69–71
Africando, 763
Afro-Argentines, 492–93, 498, 500
afrobeat, x, 668, 672, 674, 685, 693–94, 696–97, 699–701, 703–704
Afro-Cuban music, 73–80, 82, 84–85, 89, 96–97, 100–105, 108– 109, 111, 113–123, 125–26, 129–30, 135, 137–140, 143, 151, 192– 97; musical instruments, 126–29
AfroReggae, 482
Aftab, Arooj, 329–30
Ag Alhabib, Ibrahim, 790–92
Aga Khan Foundation, 642, 843
Aguabella, Francisco, 132
Aguilar, "Cuban Pete," 143, 154
Ahmed, Mahmoud, 796, 800–802, 805–808
AIDS, 67, 96, 698, 740
Aitken, Laurel, 222–23, 266–67
Akan culture, 215, 217, 225
Albarn, Damon, 703, 745, 794
Alemañy, Jesús, ix, 199, 201
Alexander, Bill, 711
Alexander VI, Pope, 390–91
Alf, Johnny, 426
Ali, Muhammad, 676, 725, 727
Ali, Nazakat and Salamat, 321, 324, 366
Allen, Steve, 163, 168
Allen, Tony, 655–56, 659–62, 666, 668–70, 673, 678, 680–82, 691– 93, 696, 701–704, 738
Allingham, Rob, 69
Almeida, Mauro de, 400

Almirante, 404, 421–22
Alpert, Herb, 459–60
Alpha Boys Home, 226–27, 230, 267, 281
Alphonso, Roland, 226
Álvarez y su Son, Adalberto, 207
Alves, Franciso, 409
Amado, Jorge, 392, 394, 463, 463, 465, 474, 482, 484
Amadou & Mariam, 703, 772, 783
Amandla, 61
Amaral, Tarsila do, 451
Amaya, Carmen, 374
AME (African Methodist Episcopal) Church, 23, 34, 53
American Federation of Musicians, 160
Amsterdam, Morey, 216
Andalusia, 358, 360–63, 365–68, 370–71, 373–74, 376, 378–79
Anderson, Ian, 537, 756
Anderson, Lindsay, 719
Andersson, Benny, 846
Andreev, Vasily, 554
Andrews Sisters, 7, 40, 46, 124, 216
Angadi, Ayana and Patricia, 290–91
Anges Noires, Les (Brussels nightclub), 704–706, 714–15
Angola, 183
Anjos do Inferno, 422
Anka, Paul, 442
Anthology of American Folk Music (compilation albums), 845
Antibalas, 700
Antibes Jazz Festival (1964), 53–54
Apaches, Los, 113
Apollinaire, Guillaume, 827, 829
Arcaño, Antonio, 133, 138–40, 153, 157–58
Argentina: Black Argentines, 492–94, 498, 500–501; *canyengue*, 502; dance instruction, 501–502, 529; exiles in Paris, 517, 521; Falklands (Malvinas) War and aftermath, 518–19; habanera in, 487, 494–95, 497; Juan Perón, 512–14; *malambos*, 500; milongas, 486, 488, 493, 494, 506, 512, 523–24, 526; musical instruments and styles, 495–97, 511–12, 525; and Nazi Germany, 156, 414, 418; pampas communities, 496, 498, 500–502; poverty, 506–507; pre- war economy, 489; radio local content rule, 513, 523; state oppression, 512–15, 518, 520, 523; tango clubs, 517, 527–29, 531; Western dance embellishment, 500–501; White Argentines, 491, 494–96, 500–501; *see also* tango; tango canción
Arienzo, Juan d', 511–12
Armenteros, Alfredo "Chocolate," 136
Armstrong, Louis, x, 7, 136, 659
Arnaz, Desi, 73–75, 81–84, 88–89, 117
"Asa branca" (song), 420
Assefa, Tigist, 807
Astatke, Mulatu, 804
Aswad, 268, 270, 277
Atlantic Records, 261, 459

INDEX

Attenborough, Richard, 316
Attisso, Barthélémy, 758–60
Autotune, 842
Auvergnois music, 343–44
Avakian, George, 287–88
Aweke, Aster, 802, 809
Azpiazú, Don, 123, 151

Baba Sora (Babani Sissoko), 783
Babakhanov, Leviche, 584
"Babalú" (song), 81–82
Babo, Lamartine, 390–91, 413
Bach, Carl Philipp Emmanuel, 338
Baker, Josephine, 120–21, 151, 508, 829
Bakst, Leon, 564, 566–67, 572, 579
Balakirev, Mily, 545, 549
balalaika (instrument), 543, 553–54
Balanescu Quartet, 629
Balkana, 604–605, 607
Balkanton (record label), 602, 611
Ball, Lucille, 83, 88
ballet, 564–73
Ballets Russes, 489, 564, 569, 571, 577–80
Bamba, Cheikh Amadou, 754, 759
Bambaataa, Afrika, 2
Band, Heinrich, 496
Bando de Tangarás, 404
Bando do Lua, 413
bandoneón (instrument), 493, 496–98, 512
Bang Records, 163
Bangladesh, charity concert in Madison Square Garden (1971), 312
Bapa, Sayan, 640
Barbieri, Gato, 516
Barbosa, Domingos Caldas, 396
Barrett, Aston "Family Man," 246–49, 265
Barretto, Ray, 188, 726
Barrister, Sikiru Ayinde, 682, 701
Barroso, Ary, 410–12, 415, 437
Bartók, Béla: collection of Transylvanian folk songs, 120, 579; folk music and modernism, 616–25; and Hungarian folk music, 357; international outlook, 650, 652; on *The Rite of Spring*, 574; use of recording technology, 545
Bartók Album, 627
Bartók Ensemble, 616–17, 625
Batista, Fulgencio, 134, 164, 167–68
Batista, Wilson, 404, 409
Bauzá, Mario, 84, 87, 124–25, 142, 144, 153, 154
Beat, The, 271
Beatles, The, 184, 289–90, 303–308, 313, 435, 462
Beaton, Cecil, 567
bebop movement, 33, 84–85, 87, 659–60
Beckford, Theophilus, 224
Beethoven, Ludwig van, 338–39, 542, 544
Belafonte, Harry, 3, 49, 103, 215–18, 242
Belgium, colonial rule in Congo, 704–708, 711–13, 746

Bembeya Jazz National, 816–18
Ben, Jorge, 450, 455–56, 466, 472, 482
Benavent, Carles, 376
Bennett, David, 803
Benton, Brook, 60
Berlin, Irving, 553, 581
Berlin Jazz Festival (1978), 690
Berns, Bert, 162–63
Bethânia, Maria, 447–48, 451, 455
Beyene, Girma, 805–806
Bhatt, Mohan, 314
Bhengu, John, 25, 46, 60
Bhosle, Asha, 328
Bhundu Boys, 737–38
Bhutto, Fatima, 329–30
Biagi, Rodolfo, 510–11
Bihari, János, 338, 618
Biko, Steve, 21, 57
Bither, David, 203–204
Bizot, Jean-François, 694–95
Black Orpheus (Orfeu Negro) (film), 438
Blacker, William, *Along the Enchanted Way*, 358
Blacks Unlimited, 818, 821
Blackwell, Chris, 213–14, 223–24, 227–230, 243, 249–50, 252–55, 260–61, 280–83, 694–95, 757, 809
Blades, Rubén, 188–89, 208
Blakey, Art, 87
Blavatsky, Madame, 575–76, 649
Blecher, Hilary, 62–63
Blok, Alexander, 554, 575
Blondie, 272
Bloomfield, Mike, 301
Blue Beat Records, 266
"blue notes," 314, 660, 765, 790, 811
Blue Notes, 52–56
Bob & Marcia, 253, 267
Bock, Richard (Dick), 287–90, 306, 309, 315
Boeck, Egide de, 709
Bola de Nieve (Ignacio Villa), 80, 137, 139, 156, 166, 190
Bollywood, 325–332
Boneva, Stoyanka, 603
Boney M, 272
Bonfá, Luiz, 428, 438–39
bongo drums, 126–27
Bopape, Rupert, 46–47
Borges, Jorge Luis, 502, 505, 514, 526
Borodin, Alexander, 545; *Prince Igor*, 549–50
Bôscoli, Ronaldo, 430–31, 438, 444, 446, 458
Bosnia, *sevdah* (song tradition), 847
bossa nova, 424, 426–27, 429–36, 438, 442–50, 455–56
Botha, P. W., 64
Botswana, 61, 70
Boulanger, Nadia, 137, 317, 516
Bovell, Dennis, 268
Bowane, Henri, 711, 719

INDEX

Boy George, 273
Boyd, Pattie, 290
Boyoyo Boys, 2–3, 47, 66
Boys, Jerry, 199, 204, 760
Bradley, Lloyd, 219
Braimah, J. K., 666
Brand, Adolph "Dollar" (later Abdullah Ibrahim), 41, 53
Brando, Marlon, 127
brass bands: in Ethiopia, 798–99; in New Orleans, 106–107; Serbian, 355
Brazil: African influences, 394–95; Amazon warriors, 389; *baião*, 419–20; *baile funk*, 482; coup (1964), 448; favelas, 408, 480–83; MPB (Música Popular Brasileiro), 455–57, 472–73, 476; musical instruments and styles, 395–95; Portuguese colonization, 392–97; Rio Carnival, 404–06, 411–12; *trio elétrico*, 465, 469, 470; *see also* bossa nova; samba
"Brazil" (song), 410, 415, 437
Brazil Classics (compilation albums), 473, 479
Brazzaville, Congo, 710, 713
break-dancing, 276
Bregović, Goran, 355
Brevett, Lloyd, 226
Brezhnev, Leonid, 591, 633
Britain: and dance music, 277–78; and Indian music, 290–91; Jamaican musical influence, 266–69; West Indian immigration, 265–68; WOMAD concert (1983), 837
Brix, Philippe, 783, 784
Broken Flowers (film), 804
Brook, Michael, 325
Brooks, Baba, 226
Brooman, Thomas, 837
Brotherhood of Breath, 56
Brown, Carlinhos, 468–69
Brown, James, 155, 672–73, 718, 726
Brown, Ray, 85
Buarque, Chico, 441, 456–57
Buda Records, 803, 812
Buena Vista Social Club (group), 119, 124, 199, 203
Buena Vista Social Club (studio album), 9, 204, 206, 763
Buenos Aires: and the tango, 488–89, 491, 498, 509–15, 531–33
Bulgaria: collectivization and musical decline, 599; Koprivshtitsa festival, 537–39, 602; Koutev Ensemble, 535–36, 540, 587–89, 600; Roma wedding bands, 607–09, 643; Trio Bulgarka, 595, 603, 605; vocal singing, 598
Bulgarian Radio Choir, 603–604, 607, 644
Burke, Elena, 139
Burman, Rahul Dev, 328–29
Burman, Sachin Dev, 328–29
Burna Boy, 701
Burnt by the Sun (film), 648
Burru drumming, 217, 225, 232–33
Bush, Kate, 605

Buslaev, Fedor, 546
Buster Campbell, *see* Prince Buster
Buthelezi, Chief Mangosuthu, 10–11, 33
Butterfield, Paul, 301, 535
Byrd, Charlie, 436
Byrds, The, 289, 301, 607
Byrne, David, 420, 471–73, 479, 836, 840

Cabral, Pedro, 390
Cádiz, 359
Cadogan, Susan, 268
Cage, John, 128
cajón (instrument), 129
Caldas, Sílvio, 409
Cale, John, 318
"Cálice" (song), 457
Calloway, Cab, 86, 125
Calmon, Pedro, 401
Caluza, Reuben, 27
calypso, 216–17
Camara, Demba, 817–18
Camarón de la Isla (José Monje Cruz), 367, 377–76, 377, 381–82
Campbell, Ambrose, 672
Campbell, Ian, 273
Campos, Augusto de, 435, 448
Canaro, Francisco, 498, 509
Candomblé, 399, 464, 466
Candrix, Alfons "Fud," 712
Cantón, Edgardo, 517
Capeman, The (musical), 208–209
Capitol Records, 163, 166
Caracol, Manolo, 366–67
Carbuccia, Adry de, 489
Carlos, Roberto, 449
Carmichael, Stokely, 51, 181, 688
Carnegie Hall, bossa nova concert (1962), 438–39, 442
Caro, Julio de, 498
Carpentier, Alejo, 104, 116, 120, 121, 126, 149
Carthy, Eliza, 844
Carthy, Martin, 4
Casalla, Javier, 525
Casas, Bartolomé de las, 90
cassette players, 290, 385, 610, 736, 762
cassette tapes: bootlegged/pirate, 191, 324, 610, 687, 736, 762, 795, 796, 801, 842; destruction by extremists, 795; field recordings, 617, 626, 743; in mobile/rural communities, 47, 389; as new technology, 290; "revolution" of, 385, 773, 823
Castle, Vernon and Irene, 398, 490
Castro, Fidel, 115, 168–70, 175–77, 180–81, 183, 189, 194, 205–206
Castro, Ruy, Bossa Nova, 429
Catherine the Great, 541, 548
Cavos, Catterino, *Ilya Bogatyr* (opera), 544
Caymmi, Dorival, 412, 419, 421, 431, 437, 470
Cedrón, Juan "Tata," 517

925

INDEX

Cele, Solomon "Zuluboy," 29, 30, 32
Cele, Willard, 36
Cellier, Marcel, 536, 607
Celluloid Records, 695
Cendrars, Blaise, 401–402
Central Asia, Soviet suppression of music in, 584–86
Chacón, Antonio, 365, 366
Chaka Chaka, Yvonne, 61
Chalyapin, Fyodor, 555, 565
Chappotín, Félix, 76, 80, 136
Charisma Records, 2, 3
Charles I, King, 90
"Chega de saudade" (song), 427–28, 431, 433
Chekhov, Anton, 546
Cheparukhin, Sasha, 640
Chernoff, John, 673
Cherry, Neneh, 753
Chico, Igo, 680
Chico Science, 471
Chighaly, Jeiche Ould, 822–24
Chile, 190
China, cultural suppression, 848
Chocolate, El (Antonio Núñez Montoya), 371
Cigala, Diego el (Diego Jiménez Salazar), 379
Cissoko, Issa, 760
Clapton, Eric, 255, 267
Clark, Gene, 288–89
Clarke, Kenny, 85, 87
Clarke, Michael, 289
Clash, The, 270
Clegg, Johnny, 64
Cliff, Jimmy, 227, 229, 242–43, 250, 253, 260
Cocteau, Jean, 402
Coetzee, Basil, 54
Cole, Allan "Skill," 261–62
Cole, Nat "King," 166–67
Coleman, Nick, 606
Coleman, Ornette, 835
Collier, Simon, 507
Collins, John, 756, 841
Colón, Willie, 185, 188
Coltrane, John, 308–310
Columbia Records, 118, 163, 287–88, 809
Columbus, Christopher, 89
Come Back, Africa (film), 39–40
Communist Party, Cuban, 139
conga drum, 73, 75, 78, 89, 130, 131
conga line, 73–75
Congo: becomes Zaire, 723; Belgian colonialism, 706–708, 710; Brazzaville, 710, 713, 720, 735, 748; Congolese rumba, 706, 710, 715, 736, 746, 758, 818; *Missa Luba*, 719; Mobutuism, 723–25, 731; OK Jazz Band, 748; and Patrice Lumumba, 705, 714; record companies, 706, 708–11; *sapeurs*, 733–37; soukous (musical style), 737–39, 741
Conover, Willis, 587
Contursi, Pascual, 504
Cooder, Ry, 201–204, 314, 784

Copacabana, 398, 417, 423–24, 458
"Copacabana" (song), 422
Copeland, Stewart, 273
Copes, Carlos, 515, 519, 531
Corea, Chick, 461
Cortázar, Julio, 517, 532
Costa, Gal, 450, 455
Costello, Elvis, 270
Count Ossie, 225
Covaci, Gheorghe, 629
Crammed Discs, 357, 475, 745, 802
Crosby, Bing, 510
Crosby, David, 288–89, 607
Cruz, Celia, 131, 132, 138, 139, 166, 171–72, 186, 725
Cruz, José Monje, *see* Camarón de la Isla (José Monje Cruz)
Csángáló, Ferenc, 632
Csoóri, Sándor, 626
CTI Records, 460
Cuba: Afro-Cuban music, 76–90; Arab-Spanish influence, 78; bolero, 167; British occupation, 93; carnival and conga, 73–75; cha- cha-cha, 162; claves (instrument), 127–29; Cuban Jam Sessions, 175; cultural censorship, 176–79, 192; danzón (dance form), 100– 103, 109, 113, 132, 133, 145–48; economic collapse (1930s), 134; ethnicity, 114–15; French refugees, 93–94; guaguancó (rumba style), 149–51, 161, 165, 209; King's Day parades, 74, 92; Latin jazz, 84–85; nueva trova, 189–91, 195, 199; Radio Mil Diez (1010), 139–40, 154, 157; radio stations, 138–39; Ten Years' War (1868– 78), 102; timba, 129, 152, 194–99, 206–207, 210; US occupation, 109–11; War of Independence, 107–10; Yorùbá slaves deported to, 95
Cuban Revolution: cultural censorship, 171, 176–79; and homosexuals, 183–84; and race, 180–83; suspicion of foreign music, 184
¡Cubanismo!, ix, 171, 179, 199–201, 205–206; *Jesús Alemañy's ¡Cubanismo!*, 201
Cueva, Julio, 139
Cugat, Xavier, 73, 75, 82–84, 122–23, 143
Cui, César, 545, 549
Cullman, Brian, 835
Culture Club, 273
Curbelo, José, 144

Dahomey, 95
Dairo, I. K., 672, 699
Dalrymple, William, 293, 332
Dammers, Jerry, 8, 271
Dankó, Pista, 339
d'Arienzo, Juan, 511–512
Darmstadt Festival, 623
Davashe, Mackay, 35
Davis, Angela, 181
Davis, Miles, 51, 289, 309, 310, 460
Davis, Ronny, 142
Davis, Thulani, 673

INDEX

Dawut, Rahile, 848
de Falla, Manuel, 366
de Klerk, F. W., 65
de Lucía, Paco, 129, 367, 369–70, 375, 376, 381
de Noailles, Anna, 567
Dean, Eric, 226
Debussy, Claude, 545, 569, 570, 574, 578–79, 827
Decca Records, 13, 693, 813
Dekker, Desmond, 242–43, 266
Delaunay, Charles, 346–47, 349
Denning, Michael, *Noise Uprising*, 831
Denniston, Christine, *The Meaning of Tango*, 529–30
Denselow, Robin, 9, 279, 839
Deodato, Eumir, 460, 462
"Desafinado" (song), 420, 434, 437, 459
"desert blues," 785, 788–90, 823
Desilu Productions, 88
Dhlomo, Herbert, 28
Di Sarli, Carlos, 512
Diabaté, Kassé Mady, 782, 783
Diabaté, Lassana, 783
Diabaté, Sékou, 817
Diabaté, Sidiki, 776–78, 822
Diabaté, Toumani, 777–78, 779–81, 782–83, 794–95
Diaghilev, Sergei, 80, 366, 551, 564–71, 572, 574;
    Ballets Russes, 489, 564, 569–77, 578–80
Diakité, Ramata, 781
Diawara, Manthia, 768
Dibango, Manu, 704–705, 725, 727; "Soul Makossa," 814–816
Dickens, Charles, 18, 828
Dickson, Jim, 288–89
digital technology, 849–51
Dikobe, Modikwe, 28
Dirty Dancing (film), 146
Discépolo, Enrique, 499, 509
discos, rise of, 274–75
DJs, rise of, 260, 274
Dlamini, Ezekiel, 38
Dlamini, Mose, 60
Dodd, Clement "Coxsone," 218–19, 221–23, 224, 225, 226, 231, 242, 244, 247, 268; see also Studio One Records
Donaldson, Eric, 272
Donato, João, 424, 443
Donay, Millie, 143, 154
Donga (Ernesto Joaquim Maria dos Santos), 400–401, 402, 407, 426
Doors, The, 300
Dostoyevsky, Fyodor, 544, 546, 547, 551, 575
Downey, Wallace, 408, 412, 437
drones (musical), 290, 299, 301, 302, 303, 309, 318, 330, 598, 598–99
drug trafficking, 277
Drum (magazine), 33–34, 35, 40
Drummond, Don, 226, 230, 267
dub (musical style), 227, 258, 260, 268, 269–70, 273, 276–79, 281

Dugin, Alexander, 649
Dumakude, Thuli, 62
Dundee Wandering Singers, 50
Dunham, Katherine, 83, 151, 749
Duprat, Rogério, 451, 452
Durán, Gustavo, 775
Durán, Lucy, 199, 202, 756, 774–79, 781–83, 809, 839, 845
Dutra, Eurico, 418
Dyani, Johnny, 56
Dylan, Bob, 289, 304, 312, 383–84, 806, 846
Dynamic Sounds (studio), 229, 251

Earthworks Records, 3, 7, 69, 812
Edinburgh Festival, 62, 321
Edmonds, Lu, 641
Edwards, Jackie, 252
Eecken, Tony van der, 743, 746
Effrosse, Georges, 348
Egba people, Nigeria, 663–64
EGREM Studios, 175, 178, 184, 200–201, 203, 205
Egypt 80 (band), 692–93, 694–95, 698
Ehrenreich, Barbara, *Dancing in the Streets*, 848
El Fillo, Diego, 363–65
El Farruco (Antonio Montoya Flores), 371
"El Manisero" (song), 121, 123–24
El Mubarak, Abdel Aziz, 839
Elektra Records, 535
Eliot, T. S., 573
Ellington, Duke, 87, 223
Elliott, Ramblin' Jack, 50
Ellis, Alton, 233
Emerson, Ken, 830
Eno, Brian, 472, 656, 697, 836
Éri, Péter, 617, 626
Ertegun, Ahmet, 815
Eshete, Alemayehu, 799–800
Eshete, Amha, 800, 801
Ethiopia: azmaris, 808; Derg era, 802, 807–809; history, 795–97; musical evolution, 797–801; musical instruments, 797–98; tezeta (musical style), 807–808
Éthiopiques (compilation CDs), 803, 804, 806–807, 810–812
Evans, Bill, 572
Evora, Cesária, 843
Ezra Collective, 702

Fademolu, Tunde, 675–76
Faílde Pérez, Miguel, 103, 148
Falceto, Francis, 796, 801–803, 804, 807, 808, 811, 812
Falla, Manuel de, 366
falsetto singing, 12, 14, 34, 637
Fania All-Stars, 187, 725, 726
Fania Records, 186–89
Fanon, Frantz, 109, 699
Farkas, Ilona, 627

927

INDEX

Farkas, Zoltán "Batyu," 630
Farney, Dick, 422–23
Farris Thompson, Robert, 493, 497, 499, 502, 531, 534, 735
Farruco, El (Antonio Montoya Flores), 371
Farruquito, El, 372
Fassie, Brenda, 61
Faustino, Tio, 404
Fela! (musical), 700
female musicians, 844
Fenton, John, 321
Fernández, Joseíto, 139
Fernandez, Raul, 131
Ferrer, Horacio, 522
Ferrer, Ibrahim, 203, 759
FESMAN (Festival Mondial des Arts Nègres), 749
FESTAC '77, 685–89
Festival au Désert (Mali), 793–94
Feynman, Richard, 637–38
Feza, Mongezi, 53, 56
Ficowski, Jerzy, 351
Figari, Pedro, 533
Figes, Orlando, 543, 548
Fillo, Diego El, 363–64
Fiorentino, Francisco, 512
Fire Island, New York, 275
Firpo, Roberto, 498
Fitzgerald, Ella, 40, 53, 124, 423
flamenco: dance, 372–74; guitar, 367–69; *nuevo flamenco*, 377–78; origins, 359–60; *rumba flamenca*, 385, 779; singing, 363–68; and tourism, 370
Flatley, Michael, 589
Flores, Celedonio, 505–506
Flying Down to Rio (film), 414–15
Fokine, Michel, 568
Folkes Brothers, 225
folk-rock, 289
Fonior (record distributor), 706, 721, 744
Ford, Vincent, 256
Foreman, George, 725, 726
Formell, Juan, 133, 191–92
Fox, James, 777, 779
Fox, Martín, 165, 166, 168, 173
France: *bal-musettes*, 343–44; interest in Black culture, 829–30; Saintes-Maries-de-la-Mer, 383–84; *see also* Paris
"Franco" (François Luambo Makiadi), 719–24, 725, 727–29, 739– 44
François, Claude, 443
Franconetti, Silverio, 365
Frazer, James George, *The Golden Bough*, 573
Freston, Tom, 794
Frey, Sidney, 438–39
Freyre, Gilberto, 402; *The Masters and the Slaves*, 391–93
Frutos, Lina, 150
Fugard, Athol, 43, 62
Fuqua, Harvey, 245

Gabriel, Peter, 324–25, 736, 739, 754–55, 836–37
Gadjo dilo (film), 356
Gallo, Eric, 13, 14, 35, 37
Gandhi (film), 316
ganja (marijuana): America, 277; Brazil, 423, 428; Jamaica and Rastafarians, 215, 219, 229, 237, 240, 242, 254, 256, 259, 277; Nigeria, 677, 683, 693; Soviet Union, 634; United Kingdom, 240, 701; United States, 51, 814
Gardel, Carlos, 503–508, 510, 515–16
Garifuna people, 847
Garvey, Marcus, 234–39
Gasa, Nomboniso, 70
Gast, Leon, 726
Gatlif, Tony, 356
Gaye, Barbie, 228
Geldof, Bob, 795–96
Genghis Blues (film), 638
George, Nelson, 275
Georgieva, Eva, 603–604
Gergiev, Valery, 595
Germany, cultural censorship, 274
Gershwin, George, 124
Getz, Monica, 439, 441
Getz, Stan, 436–37, 439–41
Ghana: highlife (musical genre), 655–59, 660, 666; independence, 656–57; Koola Lobitos in, 674–75
Gieco, León, 525
Gigi (Ejigayehu Shibabaw), 809–10
Gil, Gilberto, 398, 447–49, 450, 452–53, 454, 456–57, 465, 466, 467, 471
Gilberto, Astrud, 441–42, 444
Gilberto, Bebel, 475
Gilberto, João, 428–35, 439–42, 456, 463
Gillespie, Dizzy, 58, 84–87, 142, 659–60
Gillett, Charlie, 839, 840–41
Gimbel, Norman, 440, 475
Gippius, Yevgeny, 591
Gipsy Kings, 386, 643
"Girl from Ipanema" (song), 440, 441–43, 445, 446
Gitanos, 361–77, 385, 494
Glass, Philip, 317
Glastonbury Festival, 454, 703, 835
Glinka, Mikhail, 558
Gnattali, Radamés, 418, 422, 424
Gnessin Institute, Moscow, 591
Gold, Nick, 199, 201, 759, 784, 786–87
Goldner, George, 162; *see also* Gone Records
Gomis, Rudy, 758–60
Goncharova, Natalia, 577
Gone Records, 163
Gonzaga, Chiquinha, 405–406
Gonzaga, Luiz, 419–21, 424
González, Andy, 738
González, Celina, 194
González, Juan de Marcos, 199, 202
Goodall, Howard, 580
Goodman, Benny, 30

928

INDEX

Gordine, Sacha, 426, 437–38
Gordon, Rosco, 221, 223, 225
Gorer, Geoffrey, 747
Gorjaczkowska, Hanna, 745
Gorky, Maxim, 554–56, 558, 563, 581, 619
Gottschalk, Louis Moreau, 105, 147
Goyeneche, Roberto, 521–22
Graceland (album), 5–7, 8, 46, 66–67, 71–72
Graham, Bill, 142, 145, 155
Grand Kallé, Le (Kabasele, Joseph), 705–706, 714, 715, 717–18, 721, 727, 740
Granz, Norman, 142
Grappelli, Stéphane, 346–47
Grateful Dead, 311
Grau, Ramón, 134
"Great Awakening" religious revival, 98
Great Exhibition (1899), 19
Grela, Roberto, 523–24
Grennan, Winston, 251, 283
Grillo, Frank "Macho," 125, 144
Grossman, Albert, 289, 535, 607
"Guajira Guantanamera" (song), 139
Guebrou, Emahoy Tsegue-Maryam, 810–11
Guerrero, Félix, 137
Guetta, David, 274
Guevara, Ernesto "Che," 169, 178, 741
Guido Haazen, Father, 718
Guillermoprieto, Alma, 175, 183; *Samba*, 429, 476–79
Guillot, Olga, 139
Guinea, 51, 748, 788, 816–17, 818, 822
Guinle, Arnaldo, 401
Güiraldes, Ricardo, 487–88
güiro (musical gourd), 127
Gullo, Ustad Hussain Bakhsh, 330
Gunther, John, 710
Guy, Michel, 517–18
Gwangwa, Jonas, 41, 61
"gypsy music," 339, 357, 358, 556, 580, 597, 601, 609, 619; see also Roma
Gysin, Brion, 833–34

habanera (dance rhythm), 103–104, 106, 107, 170, 385, 487, 494–95, 494–95, 497, 832
Haitian Revolution, 94
Halee, Roy, 4, 66
Haley, Bill, "Rock Around the Clock," 587
Halmos, Béla, 617, 651
Hamar, Dániel, 625–26, 653
Hammond, John, 131
Hanim, Seyyan, 527
Hannibal Records, 5, 201, 203, 204, 321, 474–75, 536–37, 605, 628, 738, 779, 780–82, 784–85, 796, 802–803, 838
Hanover Brothers, 48
Harder They Come, The (film), 232, 250–53, 284
Hare Krishna chanters, 312
Harlow, Larry, 188, 189
Harriott, Joe, 226

Harris, Jet, 46
Harrison, George, 288–91, 302–305, 307, 310–14
Harry J, 254, 266, 268
Hart, Mickey, 311
Hatuey (Taíno king), 114
Havana, Cuba, 75–83, 92–95, 100, 105, 109–10, 130–31, 138–39, 152–53, 163–66
Havel, Václav, 611
Hawaiien, Jhimmy l' (Zacharie Elenga), 715
Haynes, Jah Jerry, 226
Hénault, Charles, 718
Hendrix, Jimi, 305, 640, 793, 820, 825; *Jimi Hendrix* (film), 725
Henzell, Perry, 249–51
Henzell, Sally, 250
Herder, Johannes, 541, 544, 551, 596, 828
Heredia, Ray, 381
Hernández, Orlando "El Duque," 205
Hernández, José, *The Gaúcho Martín Fierro*, 500
Heron, Mike, 302
Herrera, Lazaro, 136, 193
Hierrezuelo, Lorenzo, 119
Higgs, Joe, 243, 244, 255
highlife (musical genre), 655–60, 666–75
Higuelin, Jacques, 753
Hill, Virginia, 82–83, 87
Hillman, Chris, 289
Hindi film music, 325–26
Hindustani music, 294–95
hip-hop, 1, 149, 275–76, 329, 534, 842, 849
HMV, GV series, 708–709, 711
Hobsbawm, Eric, 18
Hochschild, Adam, 707
Hodson, Millicent, 572
Hoffman, E. T. A., 338
Hollander, Marc, 475, 745, 802
Hollingsworth, Tony, 8–9
Holzman, Jac, 535
homosexuals, in Cuba, 183–84
Hooker, Earl, 223
Hooker, John Lee, 787–88
Hoover, J. Edgar, 50
Hopkins, John "Hoppy," 269
Horn, Trevor, 7
Hourdebise, Jean, 709
How the Beatles Rocked the Kremlin (film), 6
Howell, Leonard, 237–40
Howson, Gerald, 380
Huddleston, Trevor, 40–41, 43
Hudson, Mark, *The Music in My Head*, 753, 770
Human Rights Tour (1988), 754
Hungary: 1956 uprising, 618; Bartók's folk-music collecting, 616–20; Liszt's *Hungarian Rhapsodies*, 340, 618; Roma musicians, 336–40, 354, 607–609, 629; *táncház* movement, 617, 624–26, 627–28, 631–33, 651–53
Hunt, Anne, 785–86
Hurok, Sol, 588

INDEX

Huskisson, Yvonne, 44, 49, 58
Hussain, Zakir, 311
Huun-Huur-Tu, 638, 640
Hylton, Jack, 345

Idonije, Benson, 813–14
Ifang Bondi, 751
Imamović, Damir, 847
Imamović, Zaim, 847
Incredible String Band, 190, 301, 307, 454, 603
Indian music: arrival in the West, 287, 290–91, 295–98, 310; history, 290–91
Invader, Lord, 216
Ipi Tombi (musical), 43, 62
Irakere, 191
Islam: Aga Khan Foundation, 642, 843; Ali Brothers and, 321–22; Bulgaria, 596, 603; conversion to, 297, 329, 547, 761, 764, 816; and dance, 589; extremism, 794–95, 848; Guinea, 816; Iberian peninsula, 89, 359–60, 367; India, 326; Mali, 772, 791, 794; Nigeria, 660, 665, 689, 699; *qawwali* singing, 323–25; Russia, 547, 577, 583; Sahel, 761; Senegal, 754; Senegambia, 90; and slavery, 90–91, 95, 97, 660; Yorùbá people, 95; *see also* Sufism
Islamophobia, 91, 329, 583–84, 590
Island Records, 214, 228–29, 243, 248, 250, 252–53, 254–55, 261, 266–67, 281–82, 694

Jackson, Milt, 85
Jacobs, Nancy, 38
Jagger, Mick, 301, 332
Jaipur Virast Foundation, 333
jam bands, 311
Jamaica: Bob Marley effect, 246; history and character, 230; Maroon communities, 214–17; "sound system" boom, 219; violence during 1970s, 259–60; visit of Haile Selassie, 233–34
James, Lloyd "Prince Jammy," 280
Jaques-Dalcroze, Emile, 570
Jara, Víctor, 190
Jaraizbhoy, Nazir, 302
Jarmusch, Jim, 804
Jaro Records, 607
Jazz Epistles, 41
Jazz Maniacs, 29–30, 32, 850
"jazz-rock fusion," 71, 311, 461
Jean-Noël (Jean-Noël Gaston), 823–25
Jelly-Schapiro, Josh, 281
Jeronimidis, Nicolas, 711
Jewish song, in Russia, 553
jitterbug swing, 79, 152, 155, 208, 274, 587
Jobarteh, Amadou Bansang, 776–77
Jobim, Antônio Carlos, 424–25, 427, 431, 433–36, 438–40, 442, 455, 459–60
Joffrey Ballet, 572
Johns, Vere, 222, 228, 230
Johnson, Jack, 829
Jolson, Al, 123, 508

Jones, Brian, 301, 834, 846
Jones, Norah, 318, 330
Jones, Quincy, 3, 317, 460
Jones, Richard M., 223
Jorge, Seu, 475
Joujouka, Morocco, *see* Master Musicians of Joujouka
Jubilee choirs, 23

Kabanov, Ivan, 591
Kabasele, Joseph (Le Grand Kallé), 705–706, 714, 715, 717–18, 721, 727, 740
Kabila, Laurent, 741
Kaempfert, Bert, 44, 50
Kaira (album), 778–79, 780
Kamzamalov, Yuri, 614
Kanda Bongo Man, 737–38, 744, 745, 843
Kandinsky, Wassily, 551, 579
Kanté, Mory, 769, 772
Karadjova, Nadka, 537
Karafizieva, Maria, 612, 614, 615
Karakos, Jean, 695
Kardec, Allan, 566
Karnatic music, 294, 297
Karo, Stéphane, 357
Kasaï Allstars, 743, 745
Kasanda, Nico, 715, 717
Kassa, Getachew, 806
Kassabova, Kapka, *Twelve Minutes of Love*, 528, 529, 533
Kassé, Ibrahim, 761
Kazakhstan, Azia Dausy music festival, 634–35
Kazakov, Radi, 614–615
Keita, Fodéba, 788, 816–818
Keita, Modibo, 766, 772
Keita, Salif, 48, 769–70
Kekana, Fana, 63
Kékélé, 763
Kekuku, Joseph, 313, 831
Keltner, Jim, 786
Kenis, Vincent, 743–44, 745, 802
Kennedy, John F., 169, 170
Kenton, Stan, 85, 159, 160, 422, 423, 429, 459
Kershaw, Andy, 737, 785, 823, 839
Kessel, Barney, 444
Kessler, Harry, 567, 571
Ketama, 377, 378, 525, 779
Khaled, Cheb, 843
Khan, Ali Akbar, 294, 296, 299–300, 312–13
Khan, Allaudin, 293, 296–97
Khan, Annapurna, 294, 299
Khan, Nusrat Fateh Ali, 320, 324–25
Khan, Wahid, 320
Khouri, Ken, 222–23
Khoza, Rufus, 35
Kidel, Mark, 836, 846
Kidjo, Angélique, 70, 844
Ki-Kongo (language), 78, 96, 130, 194, 396, 398, 492, 493, 494, 495, 502, 724
King, Anthony, 774–75

INDEX

King, B.B., 350
King, Don, 724
King, Pete, 228
King Kong (musical), 38, 42
Kingston, Jamaica, 218–21, 257–58, 274–75
Kinks, The, 301
Kinshasa, Congo (formerly Léopoldville), 710, 713–27, 730–36
Kismet (musical), 549
kitsch aesthetic, 339, 451, 457, 540, 564, 587
Kitt, Eartha, 166
Klaasen, Thandi, 39
Klerk, F. W. de, 65
Knibb, Lloyd, 226
Kodály, Zoltán, 620, 627, 629
Kodály Chamber Dance Ensemble, 630
Koellreutter, Hans-Joachim, 424
Koenig, Martin, 605
Koité, Habib, 784
Kolev, Kosta, 540
Kolosoy, Wendo, 711
Kong, Leslie, 227, 242
Kongo culture, 91–92, 100, 135, 149, 709, 731
Konono No1, 742, 743, 745
Kool Herc (Clive Campbell), 275–76, 849
Koola Lobitos, 667, 668–69, 672, 674
Koprivshtitsa (Bulgarian music festival), 537–39, 601, 602–603, 644
kora (instrument), 769–75
Koussevitsky, Serge, 553
Koutev, Maria, 540
Koutev, Philip, 316, 535–36, 540, 554, 597, 599
Koutev Ensemble, 535–36, 591–92, 597–98, 600, 603–604, 607, 643
Kouteva, Elena, 540
Kouyaté, Bassekou, 202, 781, 782, 783
Kouyaté, Kandia, 778
Kozlovsky, Alexei, 586
Kraftwerk, 278
Krivopolenova, Maria, 555
Kronos Quartet, 328, 783
Kru people, 670, 716, 788
Kruger, Paul, 17, 58
Krupa, Gene, 656
Kubik, Gerhard, 660, 716, 787–88, 790
Kubitschek, Juscelino, 426, 434, 436
Kulanjan (album), 781–82
Kurdish music, 848
Kusturica, Emir, *Time of the Gypsies* (film), 354
Kuti, Fela: 1970s popularity, 684–86; and Africa 70 (band), 677–79; and the "African Shrine," 682–84; and afrobeat, 668; arrests and beatings, 693; attitude to women, 699; background and musical education, 666; death from HIV, 698; and Egypt 80 (band), 692–95; European tour, 694; legacy, 698–99; macho posturing, 717; move to Accra, 689; and sex, 663; in the USA, 676–80
Kuti, Femi, 698, 699

Kuvezin, Albert, 636, 637, 638, 640

La Chicana, 525–26
Ladysmith Black Mambazo, 5–6, 45, 49, 70, 72, 537, 842
Lagos, Nigeria, 660–61
Lai, Francis, 459
Lamarque, Libertad, 513–14
lamellophone (instrument), 671, 819–20
Land, Harold, 223
Lane, Abbe, 122, 143
Lansky, Meyer, 131, 163–64, 170
Lanza, Mario, 222
Las Vegas, 80, 87, 143, 264
Laswell, Bill, 695, 809–10, 835
Latcho drom (film), 358
Latin dance, 145–55, 159–62, 185–90
Latin jazz, 85–87, 89, 174, 198
Latin music, 78–79, 81, 83–89, 93–94, 132, 143–45, 184–88, 199
Lavelli, Jorge, 517
Lavoie, Matthew, 822–24
Le Pera, Alfredo, 508, 510
Leão, Nara, 443–48, 551, 463
Leary, Timothy, 834
Leblon, Bernard, 362
Lecuona, Ernesto, 120
Lecuona, Margarita, 81
Lee, Byron, 229
Lee, Spike, 755
Leighton, Ralph, 637–38, 640
Lenin, Vladimir, 556–57, 563, 583–85
Lennon, John, 244, 289–90, 302, 307–8, 425
Lerole, Elias, 36
Lerole, Jack, 46
Leschenko, Pyotr, 527–28
Leskova, Tania, 80
Lesotho, 47, 61
Letts, Don, 270–71, 274, 277
Levin, Theodore, 639, 642–43, 853
Levine, Stewart, 725
Lewis, Hopeton, 231
Lewis, Jerry, 88, 173, 220, 224, 462
Lewis, John, 85–87, 517
Linda, Solomon, 12–14, 31, 35, 48–49, 72, 216
Lindsay, Arto, 469
Lindy Hop (dance), 152, 154, 163
Lins de Rego, José, 401
Linyova, Yevgeniya, 568, 576–77
Lion King, The (film), 14
"Lion Sleeps Tonight, The" (song), 12, 14
Lippmann, Horst, 843
Liszt, Franz, 105, 338–40, 618, 620
Livingston, Bunny, 214, 242, 244, 255, 261
Lo'Jo, 791–93, 796
Lomax, Alan, 13, 98, 105, 536
London: Brixton Academy, 695; evolution of dance music, 277; GLC concerts (1985), 696, 737,

INDEX

838–39; Nigerian music in, 695– 701; and the tango, 490–91
López, Israel "Cachao," 87, 133, 137–38, 151, 157–58, 174
Lorca, Federico García, 128, 365, 367, 551
Louisiana, 99, 787, 848
Love, Mike, 307
lovers' rock, 268, 270, 273, 277
Luaka Bop Records, 472, 812
Luampasi, Albert "Papa," 719
Lucey, Roger, 64
Lucía, Paco de, 129, 367, 369–70, 375–76, 381–82, 385
Lucky Stars, 32
Lucumí (ritual language), 95, 132, 135, 172–73, 180, 182, 195
Lula da Silva, 483
Lumumba, Patrice, 705, 714, 720, 722, 727, 741
Lunacharsky, Anatoly, 580
Lutumba, Simaro, 721, 740
Lvov, Nikolai, 542, 545, 552–53, 569, 651
Lyceum Theatre, London, 255
Lyn, Warwick, 282
Lynch, Ventura, 501
Lyra, Carlos, 432, 443, 445, 484

Maal, Baaba, 703–4, 756–57, 770
Macaulay, Alastair, 577, 855
MacDonald, Kevin, 244, 822, 855
Macedo, Osmar, 464
Machado, Gerardo, 117, 134, 151
Machín, Antonio, 123–24
Machito and His Afro-Cuban All-Stars, 75, 82–83, 87–88, 125, 141–42, 144, 154–55, 161
Machuki, Count, 258
Madness, 271, 273
Maglio, Juan "Pacho," 512
Maharishi Mahesh Yogi, 306
Mahavishnu Orchestra, 310, 461
Mahfood, Margarita, 230
Mahlasela, Vusi, 68, 70–72
Mahlathini (Simon Nkabinde), and the Mahotella Queens, 7–11, 16, 46–49, 68–69, 72
Maiga, Boncana, 763
Mailer, Norman, 727
Maimane, Arthur, 34
Makeba, Miriam, 7, 9, 11, 21, 38–40, 43, 49–50, 70, 72, 688, 725, 750
Makgona Tsohle, 7, 46, 60
Makwela, Joseph, 46, 48
Malan, Rian, 14
Malema, Julius, 70
Malevich, Kazimir, 545, 555
Mali: independence, 763; kora (instrument), 769, 772; Mandé culture, 751, 765–66; military coup (2012), 795; Rail Band, 48, 201, 768–69, 771–72, 794; Toumani Diabaté, 777–78, 782–83; Tuareg people and culture, 768, 789–92, 795; *see also*

Sangaré, Oumou; Touré, Ali Farka
mambo, 96, 134, 155–63
Mambo All-Stars, 209
Mandela, Nelson, 8–11, 27, 33, 42, 44, 56, 58, 65, 67, 69, 313; birthday concert (Wembley Stadium, 1988), 8
Manganyar (Indian musical clan), 334–35
Mangeshkar, Lata, 328
Mango Records, 757
Mangwana, Sam, 695, 721, 737, 740
Manhattan Brothers, 35–36, 39–40, 43
"Manisero, El" (song), 121, 123–24, 137, 708
Manitas de Plata (Ricardo Baliardo), 384
Mankwane, Marks, 46, 48
Manley, Michael, 259, 279
Mann, Herbie, 87, 198, 436, 439, 461
"Mano a mano" (song), 505–6
Mapfumo, Thomas, 818–21, 840
maracas (instrument), 112, 127, 136, 138, 659, 731, 736
Máramaros: The Lost Jewish Music of Transylvania (album), 629
Marcelo D2, 482
Marchena, Pepe, 379–80
Maredi, Selaelo, 62
Maria, Antônio, 423
marijuana, 28, 51, 141, 283, 423, 428, 634, 677, 683, 693, 701, 821 *see ganja* (marijuana)
Mariza (Marisa dos Reis Nunes), 844
Marković, Boban, 355
Marley, Bob, 62, 214–15, 243–47, 249, 253–56, 260–63, 265, 267, 270, 273, 279–80, 695, 700, 716, 750, 815, 825
Martí, José, 109–10
Martin, Dean, 88, 167
Martin, George, 290, 451, 462
Martin, György, 616
Martin, Richard, 531
Martínez, Rogelio, 171
Mary Ignatius Davies, Sister, 226
Masekela, Hugh, 6–7, 9, 31, 40–41, 43, 50–51, 54, 60–61, 68, 70– 72, 688, 697, 725–26
Mashiyane, Spokes, 37, 72
Massine, Léonide, 574, 580
Master Musicians of Joujouka, 834, 836
Masucci, Jerry, 186–89, 725
Masuka, Dorothy, 40, 50
Matisse, Henri, 574, 579–80
Matshikiza, Todd, 38, 43, 45, 51
Matsoua, André, 733–34
Matumba, Cuthbert, 42
Matumbi, 268
Mauretania, 822–23, 825
Mauritanian, The (film), 822
Mawangu, Mingiedi, 742
Mayakovsky, Vladimir, 555, 558, 580
Mayfield, Curtis, 231, 245, 283
Mbarga, Nico, 813

INDEX

mbira (thumb piano), 737, 819–21
M'boup, Laye, 758
"Mbube" (song), 12–13, 32, 39
McAdoo, Orpheus, 23
McCann, Bryan, 403
McCartney, Paul, 12, 256, 269, 302, 684, 687
McCook, Tommy, 226
McDowell, Malcolm, 719
McGregor, Chris, 52–54, 56, 72
McGregor, Maxine (née Lautré), 52–53, 56, 853
McGuinn, Roger (Jim), 135, 288–90
Mchunu, Sipho, 64
McKay, Claude, 235
McKibbon, Al, 85, 143
McLaren, Malcolm, 1–4, 12, 20, 24, 271
McLaughlin, John, 310–11, 376
McNair, Harold, 226
Mehta, Zubin, 316
Meissonnier, Martin, 694–95, 743, 769, 853
Mejía, Sebastián Ramos, 496
Melingo, Daniel, 520, 526
Mendes, Sérgio, 439, 443, 445–46, 455, 459, 469
Mendonça, Newton, 434
Menencier, Alfonso, 74, 109
Menescal, Roberto, 430–32, 436, 444, 446, 460
Mensah, E. T., 659
Menuhin, Yehudi, 287, 298, 315–17
Merchant, Natalie, 605
Mercury, Daniela, 468, 470–71
merengue (musical genre), 207, 479, 762
Mérimée, Prosper, 372
Merry Blackbirds, 30
Messner, Gerald, 598
Mexico, Cuban music in, 156–57
Mgcina, Sophie, 62
"Mi noche triste" (song), 504, 524
Midani, André, 431–32, 457
Mikhalkov, Nikita, 648
Mikhalkov, Sergei, 586
Mil Diez (Radio 1010), Cuba, 139, 157, 174
Milanés, Pablo, 190
Milhaud, Darius, 402, 411
Mills Brothers, 30, 35, 46, 49, 59, 346
Mini, Vuyisile, 42
minstrel shows, 22, 106, 830
Miranda, Carmen, 399, 405, 408, 410–17, 423, 425, 431–33, 437, 444, 453, 455, 470–71, 480, 750, 831
Mitchell, Joni, 606
mixtape, birth of, 275
Mkhize, Alson, 50
Mnyele, Thami, 61
Mobutu Sese Seko, 722, 724
Modern Jazz Quartet, 85
modernism, 573, 578, 827–28
Moeketsi, Kippie, 41, 43
Mohammed, Murtala, 684
Mohapeloa, J. P., 31

Moholo, Louis, 53, 56
Moinuddin, Khwaja, 323
Moiseyev, Igor, 540, 562, 564, 645
Moiseyev Dance Company, 562, 574, 587–89, 645
Molina, Manuel, 376
Monk, Thelonious, 58, 309, 435, 749
Monroe, Marilyn, 49
Montaner, Rita, 76, 80, 119–23, 137–39, 156, 165, 169, 173
Monterey Pop Festival (1967), 305
Monteux, Pierre, 570, 572–73
Montoya, Dolores, 376
Montoya, Ramón, 369, 371–72
Moore, Carlos, 183, 682
Moraes, Vinícius de, 417, 424–27, 430, 433–35, 437–38, 440, 445–46, 449
Moré, Benny, 79, 88, 138, 150, 156, 158–59, 162, 172–74, 186, 208, 244, 265
Moreira, Airto, 460
Morente, Enrique, 381
Morgan, Andy, 766, 793, 849, 855
Morgan, Derrick, 232, 243
Moriri, John, 61
Morocco, Master Musicians of Joujouka, 834–36
Morton, Jelly Roll, 106–7
Moskowitz, Jesse, 198
Motsieloa, Griffiths, 13, 31
Moulton, Tom, 275
Mozambique, LM Radio, 57
Mozart, Wolfgang Amadeus, 106, 185, 316, 325, 338, 369, 544, 565, 586
Msomi, Reggie, 50
Mubarak, Abdel Aziz El, 839–41
Mugabe, Robert, 820–22
Mulligan, Gerry, 287, 439, 442, 516
Muñequitos de Matanzas, Los, 151, 209
Murphy, David, 316
Murray, Arthur, dance schools, 156, 161–62, 229, 515
Music of Bulgaria (album), 535
music publishing, royalties, 437–39
music technology, 831, 841–42, 849
musical instruments: African, 127, 680–81, 797; Afro-Cuban, 97, 113, 129; Argentine, 494; Brazilian, 394, 423, 432; Cuban, 97, 129; Egyptian, 776; forbidden, 97, 113, 129; Iberian, 104, 670; Indian, 293–94, 308, 316, 319–20, 330–31; Persian, 294; played by North American slaves, 97; South African, 7, 98; temperament, 319; Ukrainian, 568
Musical Youth, 274
Musicians' Union: American, 81, 140, 349; British, 55, 829; Mexican, 156
Muslims, 89, 91, 323, 360–61, 664–65, 695, 816, *see* Islam; Islamophobia
Mussorgsky, Modest, 545, 549, 551, 564, 566; *Boris Godunov*, 545, 565
Muzsikás, 626–32, 651–54, 823
Mwamba, Charles "Déchaud," 715

INDEX

"My Way" (song), 443
Mystère des Voix Bulgares, Le (album), 473, 536, 595, 605, 607

Nalbandian, Kevork, 798–800
Napier-Bell, Simon, 443
Nascimento, Adolfo "Dodo," 464
Nascimento, Milton, 457–58, 460, 462
Nash, Johnny, 246, 254
Nath, Pandit Pran, 319–21, 836
N'Dour, Youssou, 48, 695, 750–56, 759–60, 769–770, 840
Nebbia, Litto, 521–22, 855
Nedeva, Borimira, 606, 855
Nelson, Davia, 791
Neshev, Neshko, 615
Nestrovski, Arthur, 440–41
New Ancient Strings (album), 782
New Orleans, 18, 88, 94, 99–100, 105–7, 136, 224, 309, 659, 807
New Orleans Jazzfest (1989), 739, 843
Newport Folk Festival (1965), 37, 289, 414, 672
Newport Jazz Festival (1965), 9, 54, 441, 672
Neyra, Roderico ("Rodney"), 165
Ngoma Records, 711, 715
ngoni (instrument), 97, 772–74, 781–82, 789, 823
Nicol, Simon, 55
Niemand, Bernoldus, 64
Niemeyer, Oscar, 427, 433, 468
Nietzsche, Friedrich, 575, 832–33
Nieves, María, 515, 519, 531–32
Nigeria: Biafran war, 674, 678; British rule in, 664; *fuji* (musical genre), 679, 701; highlife (musical genre), 655–56, 659–61, 666–67, 669–70, 672, 674–75; independence, 669–70; juju music, 670, 672, 674–75; military regime (1970s), 688; *see also* Kuti, Fela
Nijinska, Bronislava, 577
Nijinsky, Vaslav, 567, 570–74, 580, 588
Nkabinde, Simon "Mahlathini," 46; *see* Mahlathini (Simon Nkabinde), and the Mahotella Queens
Nkosi, West, 45–46, 48, 66
No Doubt, 272
Noailles, Anna de, 567
Nonesuch Records, 203–4, 535, 605, 759
Notting Hill Carnival, 269
Nouakchott (musical style), 822–23
Ntsiko, Jonas, 22
Nuevos Medios (record label), 377–78, 381, 780
Nunes, Clara, 471–72
Nureyev, Rudolf, 588
Nurkadilov, Zamanbek, 634, 636
Nyabinghi drums, 225

Obesanjo, General Olusegun, 685–88, 692
Ocora (record label), 357, 838
O'Farrill, Chico, 138
Oito Batutus, 401–402, 407, 410–11, 419

OK Jazz Band, 720; *see also* TPOK Jazz
Okudzhava, Bulat, 587
Olatunji, Michael, 309, 688
Olinto, Antonio, *The Water House*, 661
Olodum, 467–68, 474
Olson, Laura, 645
Olympia Records, 718
Omar, Nelly, 514
Ondar, Kongar-ol, 638, 640
one-drop (drum pattern), 232, 248, 273, 403
Onyeabor, William, 812
open-throat singing, 537, 543, 554, 561, 591, 598, 615, 645–46, 650, 850
Oppenheim, David, 384
Orbán, Viktor, 652–53
Orchestra Baobab, 757–58, 771, 812
Orezzoli, Héctor, 373, 518–19, 843
Orfeu de Conceição (musical theatre production), 426–27, 437
Orientalism, 489, 551, 568, 570, 579
Original Evening Birds, 12, 35; *see also* Linda, Solomon
Ortiz, Fernando, 90, 92, 116, 119, 126
Os Cariocas, 422, 426
Oumar, Fadimata Walett, 791
Our Latin Thing (film), 187–89
overtone singing, 639

Pacheco, Johnny, 185–86, 725, 768
Pacheco, Mario, 370, 377, 525, 762, 779, 856
Pachón, Ricardo, 376, 378–79, 855
Pacific Jazz Records, 287–89
Pagani, Federico, 89, 140–41, 144, 185, 618
Page, Jimmy, 301, 310, 474
Pakenham, Thomas, *The Scramble for Africa*, 766
Pakistan, 329–31
Palacio, Andy, 847
Palermo, Pibe, 502
Palladium (New York City), 89, 141–46, 148, 150–51, 153–55, 160–62, 174, 185–86, 188–89, 198, 207, 209
Palmer, Robert, 85, 835
Palmieri, Charlie, 88, 186
Palmieri, Eddie, 79, 184, 189, 210
p'ansori (Korean opera), 846–47
Papasov, Ivo, 354, 612–14, 643, 654, 855
Papusza (Bronisława Wais), 350–52
Paramount Studios, 508
Paris: Cuban music in, 120–22; Diaghilev in, 564–68; Django Reinhardt in, 343–48; Exposition Universelle (1878), 828; and the tango, 487–89, 516–19
Parker, Charlie, 84, 127, 142, 216, 435, 574, 614
Parla, Alicia, 151
Pásztory, Ditta, 622–23
Pata Negra, 378
Paternostro, Silvana, 196
Patitucci, John, 786
Péan, Denis, 791

INDEX

Peel, John, 269, 538, 737, 838
Peer Southern Music (music publisher), 80–81, 157, 437
Pello El Afrokán, 179, 182, 184
"Pelo telefone" (song), 400, 403, 505
Pena, Paul, 638
Penev, Dimitar, 606
Pennebaker, D. A., 305
pentatonic scales: afrobeat, 701; anhemitonic, 577; Ethiopian music, 795; *fuji* music, 679, 701; Hungarian songs, 619; instrument tunings to, 776; as lacking corruption, 577; Nguni songs, 21; Phrygian mode, 549; Russian songs, 549, 552, 577; Stravinsky's use of, 549, 577; universality, 309; *see also* "blue notes"
Peraza, Armando, 127, 132
Pereira, Geraldo, 418
Perna, Martín, 700
Perón, Eva, 425, 513–14
Perón, Juan, 512–514
Perry, Lee "Scratch," 221, 246, 850
Phiri, Ray, 7, 59, 72
Piazzolla, Astor, 317, 516, 521
Picasso, Pablo, 120, 384, 574, 579–80, 827–28
Pickett, Wilson, 60, 726, 789
Pieterson, Hector, 58
Piñeiro, Ignacio, 118, 133, 193
Pink Floyd, 311, 450, 595, 635, 803
Pino, Geraldo, 673, 751
Pixinguinha, 400, 402–3, 407–8, 418, 422
Planet Drum project, 311
Planno, Mortimo, 234, 241, 244–46
Plant, Robert, 794
Platters, The, 221, 223
Plovdiv, Bulgaria, school of folklore, 601–2, 608, 610–12, 614
Poiret, Paul, 567
Pokrovsky, Dmitri, 591–95, 644–47, 649, 651, 653–54, 850
Police, The, 273
Poppie Nongena (musical), 43, 62, 64, 72
Portugal, colonization of Brazil, 367, 396
Posadas, Carlos, 495–97
Potemkin, Grigory, 542
Powell, Baden, 430, 446
Pozo, Chano, 76–77, 79–80, 83–84, 86, 89, 125, 130–31, 136, 205, 309, 749
Prado, Pérez, 124, 157–62, 173, 422
Presley, Elvis, 88, 243, 799
Previn, André, 316
Prieto, Dafnis, 210
Prince Buster (Buster Campbell), 221–22, 224, 231, 250, 266, 268, 274
Prokofiev, Sergei, 568, 580–81
Protestantism, and cultural suppression, 849
psychedelic drugs, 301, 305–6, 317
Púa, Carlos de la, 509
Puente, Tito, 79, 87, 132–3, 144–45, 160, 188–89, 208–9, 681

Puerto Rico, 105, 125, 154, 207, 311, 367
Pugliese, Osvaldo, 513, 515, 521
Pukwana, Dudu, 36, 53, 55, 72, 282
punk music, 270–71
Pussy Riot, 560, 640, 650
Putin, Vladimir, 512, 574, 576, 595, 645, 647–51
Pyatnitsky, Mitrofan, 554–55, 558, 561, 564
Pyatnitsky Ensemble, 540, 557, 560, 563

qawwali singing, 323–25
Quad Sisters, 39
Quatres Etoiles, Les, 695, 737
Quersin, Benoît, 389–90, 743
Quintet of the Hot Club of France, 347

Rachabane, Barney, 3, 11
Radebe, Mark, 31
Radio Brazzaville, 659, 673, 710
Radio Mil Diez (1010), Cuba, 139, 157, 174
Raft, George, 37, 124
raga, 294–98, 316–20
Ragavoy, Jerry, 50
ragtime, 104–7, 319, 408, 495, 830
Rahman, Allah Rakha, 329
Rail Band, 48, 768–69, 771–72, 794
Rajasthan International Folk Festival, 332
Rakha, Alla, 297, 305, 311, 317, 850
Ramone, Phil, 849
Ranglin, Ernest, 225, 228
Ransome-Kuti, Funmilayo, 662–63, 665–66
rap, 815
RAPM (Russian Association of Proletarian Musicians), 581
Rasoanaivo, Hanitrarivo, 824, 855
Rastafarianism, 236, 239–40, 242, 256, 270
Ratliff, Ben, 475
Rau, Fritz, 843
Razzano, José, 503–04
RCA Victor Records, 77, 404
Reagan, Ronald, 6–8, 206
Red Army Choir, 588
Redding, Otis, 283, 305, 784, 789, 796, 818
Redzepova, Esma, 352–54, 358
reggae, 222–23, 242–43, 246–57, 263, 265, 268–73
Reggae Got Soul (album), 282
Regina, Elis, 449, 455, 457–58, 471
Reicha, Anton, 618
Reid, Arthur "Duke," 220–22, 225, 227, 231–32, 257, 266, 274
Reinhardt, Django, 54, 310, 345–49, 383, 386, 465, 523, 614, 712, 758, 850
Repetto, Cristóbal, 525, 855
Repilado, Francisco, 119
Retief, Piet, 18
Revé, Elio, 192–93
Revolver (album), 303
Reyes, José, 384–85
Rezant, Peter, 30

935

INDEX

Rhodes, Cecil, 17, 818
Rhone, Trevor, 249–50
Ricardo, José, 504, 508
Ricardo, Niño, 369
Rice, Condoleezza, 848
Rice, Tim, 604, 607, 611, 855
Richmond, Howie, 14
Riley, Terry, 318–19, 836
Rimsky-Korsakov, Nikolai, 545, 549, 551–52, 564, 566, 568–69, 573
Rio de Janeiro: Carnival, 392; history, 392
Ríos, Luciano, 495, 497
Riverdance (show), 589
Rivière, Jacques, 572
Roach, Max, 87, 655–56, 658
Robbins Music, 437
Robinson, Dave, 273
Robson, Willie, 777
Rocafil Jazz, 813–14
Rochereau, Tabu Ley, 48, 716–21, 723, 725, 730, 736, 739–40, 743–44, 746, 763
Rock Against Racism, 270, 277
Rockefeller, Nelson, 414–15
rock'n'roll, 166–67, 447–48, 832
rocksteady, 231–33, 245, 248, 251, 272
Rodgers, Paul, 254
Rodrigues, Virginia, 469, 474, 781
Rodríguez, Alfredo, 180, 199
Rodríguez, Arsenio, 78, 80, 130, 133, 135–40, 149, 152–54, 157– 58, 161, 185
Rodríguez, Rico, 267, 272, 282
Rodríguez, Silvio, 190–91
Rodríguez, Tito, 87, 144–45
Roerich, Nicholas, 564, 569, 571
Rogers, Ginger, 168, 414
Rogosin, Lionel, 39–40, 43
Rolling Stone (magazine), 14, 252
Rolling Stones, 272, 310, 462, 834, 838
Roma: in the Balkans, 336, 353–55, 527; Bulgarian, 340, 356, 536, 596–97, 643; Gitanos in Spain, 361, 373; "gypsy music," 337, 339, 357–58, 586, 597, 609, 643; in Hungary, 336–40; influence on German and Austrian composers, 338–39, 36; migration into Western Europe, 341; murdered by the Nazis, 348, 350; origins, 336; pilgrimage to Saintes-Maries-de-la-Mer, 383; post-war, 349; in Russia, 553–54; *see also* Bihari, János; Redzepova, Esma; Reinhardt, Django; Taraf de Haïdouks
Romeu, Armando, 165
Ronnie Scott's (club), 55, 228
Ronstadt, Linda, 846
Rooney, Mickey, 417–18
Roosevelt, Franklin D., 109, 117, 134, 235, 540, 712
Ros, Edmundo, 122, 659
Ros, Lázaro, 182
Rosa, Noel, 404, 471
Ross, Alex, *The Rest Is Noise*, 580, 620
Ross, Sanford, 50

Rossi, Tino, 717
Rotten, Johnny, 269–70
Rubinstein, Anton, 544–45
Ruddock, Osborne "King Tubby," 257
rumba, 112–15, 129–31, 149–51
rumba flamenca, 385, 779
Rumba Timba, 210
Rumi, Jelaluddin, 323, 330
Rupkina, Yanka, 595, 603
Russell, George, 54, 85
Russia: Asian cultural influence, 543, 649; Cossack songs and dance, 552, 647–48; female protest, 559–60; folk revival, 590, 593– 94, 645–48; folksong collection, 542, 544–46, 552–54; Orientalism, 551, 568, 570; revolution and collectivization, 556–57; rise of nationalism, 597, 649; serf choirs, 543, 545, 553–55; Soviet censorship and suppression, 588, 618, 640; state folk ensembles, 540, 561–62; Turanianism, 575, 577
Rykodisc, 201, 203–4, 782, 823–24

Sacasas, Anselmo, 79, 81–82
Sacko, Fanta, 772
Saddler, Joseph, 276
Sagoo, Baljit "Bally," 324–25
Sahel region, Africa, 90, 97, 761–65
St. Petersburg, Russia, 488, 541, 543, 555, 566
Saintes-Maries-de-la-Mer, France, 383
Saint-Saëns, Camille, 571
Salazar, Cucha, 377
Salgán, Horacio, 517, 519
salsa, 88–89, 119, 124, 135, 146, 184–87, 189, 193, 197–99, 207–9
Saludos Amigos (film), 415
Salvador, Brazil, 474, 484
samba: and Brazilian broadcasting, 408; broadcast to Nazi Germany, 392; and Carmen Miranda, 399, 405, 408, 410–11, 413–15, 417; dancing, 476, 478–80; definitions, 398–99; origins, 392–94, 398; "Pelo telefone," 400, 403, 505; racial spectrum, 406, 409
samba-reggae, 467–68
Sampson, Anthony, 38, 44
Sánchez, Antonio, 369
Sangaré, Oumou, 203, 703, 772–73, 783, 794; *Moussolou*, 773
Santamaría, Mongo, 80
Santana, Carlos, 132, 138, 145, 187, 378, 726, 758
Santaolalla, Gustavo, 525, 855
Santería, 81, 95–96, 113, 116–18, 130–31, 165, 171–72, 182, 185
Santiago carnival, 73–74
São Paulo, Brazil, 448–52
Sayan Ring Festival, Siberia, 650
Schadeberg, Jürgen, 33
Schnittke, Alfred, 590, 594
Schoenberg, Arnold, 574, 578, 580, 607, 620, 623, 660
Schreiner, Claus, 374

INDEX

Schwartz, Tony, 217
Scorsese, Martin, *The Last Temptation of Christ* (film), 324
Scott, Iain, 809, 853
Scott, James, 646
Scriabin, Alexander, 566
Seaga, Edward, 222–23, 227, 229, 248, 259, 279–80
Sebestyén, Márta, 537, 627–28, 651, 654, 855
Sebó, Ferenc, 617
Sechenov, Ivan, 562
Seck, Mansour, 757
Second Viennese School, 424, 580, 620
Seeger, Pete, 14, 50, 139, 590–91, 594
Segovia, Claudio, 518–19
Selassie, Haile (Ras Tafari), 233–34, 237–42, 259, 263, 796–99, 801, 809–10
Selecter, The, 271
Senegal: independence, 748; *mbalax*, 696, 752–53, 755; Mourides, 754, 759, 761; Orchestra Baobab, 757–58, 771, 812; Youssou N' Dour, 695, 750–56, 759–60, 769–70, 840
Senegambia, 90, 97–98, 100
Senghor, Léopold, 685, 746–49, 752–54, 758, 761, 816
Sephardic Jews, 360, 492, 847
Sepulveda, Harry, 198, 855
serial music, 578, 580, 623
sevdah (song tradition), 807, 847
Sevilla, Ninón, 157–58, 169
Sexteto Nacional, 118, 120
Seymali, Noura Mint, 822
Shabalala, Joseph, 7, 11, 16, 48–49, 66, 71
Shadows, The, 46
Shaka (Zulu king), 15–16, 18, 25, 34
Shakti, 300, 310–11
Shalit, Emil, 266
Shankar, Anoushka, 318, 328
Shankar, Ravi: background and career, 297–98, 300, 313; and the Beatles, 288–90, 302, 313; collaboration with Philip Glass, 317; film music, 298–99, 313, 316; and George Harrison, 288–91, 302, 305, 312–14, 317; and John Coltrane, 290, 308, 310–11; at the Monterey Pop Festival, 305, 311; in New York (1957), 287, 290, 298, 300, 311; pupil of Allaudin Khan, 293, 297; and Western classical music, 287, 311
Shankar, Uday, 292–93, 299, 327, 830, 836
Shchurov, Vyacheslav, 590–91, 645, 855
Shearing, George, 127, 142–43, 230
Shembe, Isaiah, 23
Shepherd, Polina, 646, 855
Shirinda, Mdjadji, 2
Shostakovich, Dmitri, *Lady Macbeth of Mtsensk*, 582
Shoumatoff, Alex, 390, 856
Shubert, Lee, 411–413, 417, 437
Sibanda, Seth, 63
Siberia, Soviet censorship and suppression, 557, 585–86, 588, 590

Sidibé, Balla, 758
Sidibé, Malick, 767
Siegel, Bugsy, 82, 87
Siegel, Jay, 12, 14
Sierra Maestra, 168, 199, 202, 210
Sigler, Vicente, 123
Silva, Ismael, 403
Silva, Orlando, 409, 428–29, 431
Simon, Barney, 63
Simon, Paul, 3–7, 11–12, 37, 60, 249, 453, 467–68, 484, 620, 744, 825, 842, 846, 849, 856; *The Capeman* (musical), 208–9; *Graceland*, 5–7, 11, 65–66, 71, 208, 251
Simons, Moisés, 120–22
Sims, Danny, 246, 255–56
Sinatra, Frank, 83, 143, 163, 166–67, 243, 422–23, 429, 442–43, 458–59, 509, 667
Singh, John and Faith, 333, 856
Sinhô (José Barbosa da Silva), 407
Sipos, Mihály, 626
Sirin (Russian choir), 647
Sissoko, Babani (Baba Sora), 783
Sissoko, Jalimady, 778
sitar: and George Harrison, 289–91, 302, 304–5, 313–14; and Indian melody, 290, 301, 313–14, 316; and Ravi Shankar, 287, 289–91, 293, 297, 299, 301–2, 305, 313–14, 316; in rock'n'roll, 301
Sithole, Jonah, 820
ska, 222–31, 233, 245, 251–53, 266, 268, 271–73, 276
skank (dance rhythm), 221, 223, 252
Skatalites, The, 226, 229–31, 268
Skylarks, 40
Slahi, Mohamedou Ould, 822
slave trade, 93, 99, 108
Sledge, Percy, 59, 355, 603
Slickers, The, 232
slide guitar, 313–14, 325
Slumdog Millionaire (film), 329
Small, Millie, 228–29
Smith, Harry, 845
Smith, Sandra, 675–76, 690
Smith, Solly, 63
Smith, Wayne, 280
Sol negro (compilation album), 474
Solanas, Fernando, 521
Solovyova, Olga, 644
Solzhenitsyn, Alexander, 593, 648
son (folk music), 111–125, 127–28, 130, 133–36, 139, 199
Songhai (album), 780, 782
Sonora Matancera, 132, 171–72
Sontonga, Enoch, 26
Sophiatown, Johannesburg, 32–33, 35, 37–39, 41, 45, 50–51, 62, 71
Sosa, Mercedes, 523
Sosimi, Dele, 701
Soul II Soul, 277
"Soul Makossa," 814–15, 838

937

INDEX

soul music, 59
Soul Power (film), 726–27
Soul to Soul (film), 725–26
South Africa: Anti-Apartheid Movement, 8–9, 43, 55–59, 61–63, 67; apartheid, 5, 16–17, 26, 32–34, 39, 54, 58–59, 62, 65, 67–68, 183, 706; arrival of Christianity, 20–23; Bantu Radio, 48–49, 60; Black Consciousness Movement, 21, 57; Boers, 16–18, 44, 57–58, 63, 65; British colonialism, 16–17, 19–20, 747; *Drum* (music magazine), 33–35, 38, 40, 44; and *Graceland*, 5–9, 11–12, 46, 48, 59, 63, 66–67, 71–72, 206, 208, 251, 737, 785, 838–39, 846; Grahamstown, Battle of (1819), 21; gumboot dances, 24, 30–31; "iLand Act," 26; Isandlwana, Battle of (1879), 18–20; *isicathamiya*, 11, 34–35, 44, 47–49, 60, 65–66, 264; *isigubudu*, 13; jazz in, 40–41; *kwaito* (musical genre), 67; *kwela* (musical genre), 30, 36–37, 41, 45–46, 48, 50, 54–55; *marabi* (musical genre), 27–29, 32, 36, 41, 45, 56, 60; *maskanda* (Zulu guitar style), 24–25, 27, 60, 64, 737; *mbaqanga*, 2–5, 7, 9, 11, 15, 25, 45–49, 51, 55, 59–62, 64–67, 71, 253, 825; "Mbube," 12–14, 32; *ngomas* (song competitions), 34; Nguni song, 21, 23–24, 29–31, 46, 72; "Nkosi Sikelel iAfrika," 26–27, 58, 62, 72; pennywhistles, 37; Robben Island prison, 21; Sharpeville massacre (1960), 37; shebeens, 2, 11, 28–29, 38, 44; *tsaba-tsaba* (dance move), 33, 50; Zulu Inkatha movement, 10–11, 61, 65, 67, 69; *see also* Xhosa people; Zulu people
South African Broadcasting Corporation (SABC), 43–44, 48, 57, 59, 61
Soweto, Johannesburg, 2, 38
Soyinka, Wole, 682, 749
Spain: Cádiz, 359; "Reconquista" (expulsion of Moors and Jews), 89, 833; *see also* flamenco
Spassov, Teodosi, 611–12
Special, Lemmy, 37, 50
Specials, The, 271
Spelmän, Orsa, 846
Spencer Davis Group, 252
Spender, Cosima, 767, 856
Spengler, Oswald, 121, 575
spirituals, 23
Springfield, Dusty, 443
Staff Benda Bilili, 744
Stalin, Joseph, 115, 540, 555, 557–58, 560, 562, 582–84, 586–87, 596, 603, 623–24
Stambolovo Festival, Bulgaria, 610
Stanley, Henry Morton, 707
Stapleton, Chris, 738
Starr, Ringo, 290–91, 307
Stasov, Vladimir, 549–51, 575
steel bands, 654
Steel Pulse, 268, 270, 277
Stefani, Gwen, 272
Stein, Rikki, 835–36, 853
Stewart, Rod, 456, 462, 793
Stiff Records, 273

Sting, 273
Stravinsky, Igor: on Bartók's folk-music collecting, 595, 599, 622; *Firebird*, 568–69; *Le Chant du Rossignol*, 571; *Les Noces*, 568–69, 577, 595; *Rite of Spring*, 545, 549–50, 569–70, 572–74, 588; and Turanianism, 575–78
Strummer, Joe, 269–70
Studio One Records, 242, 245
Sublette, Ned, 82, 95, 99, 104, 129, 155, 158, 195, 209, 360, 762, 853
Sufism, 320, 322–23, 834; *qawwali* singing, 323–27, 329
Sugar, Dick, 143
Sullivan, John Jeremiah, 223, 227, 283
"Summer of Love" (1967), 304
Sunny Ade, King, 672, 682, 695, 699, 757
Sunshine, Marion, 123
Super Etoiles, 48
Sur (South), (film), 521
Sylla, Ibrahima, 761–63, 769–70
syncopation: American jazz, 224; *baião*, 413–14; bebop, 84–85, 87, 660; bossa nova, 432, 436; habanera and tango, 104, 107, 487, 494– 95, 497, 527; *kwela*, 46; Milhaud on, 402; *modinha*, 396; rhythm and blues, 155, 162–63, 221–22; rock'n'roll, 88, 163, 220; samba, 400; ska, 222–33, 245
syncretism, 92, 95, 665
Szabolcsi, Bence, 624
Szörényi, Levente, 628

Tagore, Rabindranath, 292, 315, 836
Taíno people, 90, 94, 112, 114–15
Tait, Nerlynn "Lynn," 232
Taj Mahal (musician), 781, 855
Taking Iacanga (documentary), 463
Talega, Juan, 380
Talking Heads, 473, 687, 836
Talking Timbuktu (album), 201, 203, 787
tango: books on, 493, 507, 529; Buenos Aires tango clubs, 517, 529; and Carlos Gardel, 25, 173, 244, 253, 380, 425, 503–5, 507–10, 515, 522, 750, 831, 838; in Europe, 524; Golden Age, 511–12; guitar-based, 525; in Japan and China, 503, 528; and nostalgia, 503, 517, 534; origin of word, 96, 146; origins and evolution, 493–94; and Piazzolla, 317, 516, 521; in pre-war Europe and America, 292, 487– 88, 490, 571; in Uruguay, 491, 532–33
Tango argentino (show), 519–21, 528
tango canción, 112, 396, 505–7, 509
Tangos: El exilio de Gardel (film), 521
Tansen, Mia, 295
Tanto tempo (album), 475
Taraf de Haïdouks, 356–57, 745
Taruskin, Richard, 550, 574–75, 577–78, 595
Taylor, Creed, 436, 439, 441, 460
Taylor, Don, 261–62
Taylor, Julie, *Paper Tangos*, 499, 529
Taylor, Lance, 276

938

INDEX

Teixeira, Humberto, 419–21
Telles, Sylvia, 444, 471
Teodosievski, Stevo, 352–53
Terry, Yosvany, 206, 210, 856
Thandiswa (Thandiswa Mazwai), 71
Thomas, Michael, 241, 252, 835, 856
Thompson, Leopoldo, 495, 499
Thompson, Richard, 55, 537, 856
thumb pianos (lamellophones), 671, 742, 820
Tia Ciata (Hilária Batista de Almeida), 398–400, 405–6
Tibetan monks, 637
Tidbits, 251
Tight Fit, "The Lion Sleeps Tonight" (video), 12, 14
timbales (instrument), 79, 126, 128, 132, 248, 467, 681
Time of the Gypsies (film), 354–56
Tinariwen, 70, 97, 785, 792–94
Tiomkin, Dimitri, 552
Tjader, Cal, 87, 127, 132, 142–43
Tloubatla, Hilda, 68
toasting, 258, 260, 276
Todorov, Manol, 610
Tokens, The, "The Lion Sleeps Tonight," 12, 14
Tolbert, Stephen, 725–26
Tolstoy, Leo, 546, 564, 586
Toni, Árpád, 629
Toots and the Maytals, 56, 229, 242, 247, 254, 281–82
Torin, "Symphony Sid," 143, 198
Tosh, Peter, 214, 242, 253, 255, 261, 265, 279, 850
Tóth, Ildikó "Fecske," 630
Tounkara, Djelimady, 201, 771, 784, 818
Touré, Ali Farka, 97, 201, 779, 785–86, 788, 793–94, 798
Touré, Sékou, 51, 688, 817, 821
Townshend, Pete, 305, 319
TPOK Jazz, 721, 728; *see also* Franco; OK Jazz Band
Tracey, Hugh, 45, 50, 819
Trakia, 613–14
Translyvania, 120, 199, 340, 346, 353, 357–59, 617, 619, 621, 624–26, 629–32, 651, 653, 773
Trenchtown, Kingston, 242, 244, 252, 256–57, 262, 276–77
tres (instrument), 78–79, 130, 133, 135–36, 187, 199
Treton, Bernard, 743
Treurnicht, Andries, 57
Trinidad: calypso, 112, 216–17; musical exports to Britain, 277
Trio Bulgarka, 595, 603, 605, 611, 839
Trio Matamoros, 119, 156, 671, 708, 750
Triple Earth Records, 809
Troilo, Aníbal, 512, 515–16, 521, 523
Troitsky, Artemy, 634, 636, 856
Trojan Records, 267
Tropicália movement, 190, 447–49, 451–53, 455–56, 472, 836
Tropicana (Havana nightclub), 80, 143, 157, 164–67, 171, 173–74, 178

Trueba, Fernando, 379
Trujillo, Rafael, 207
Trump, Donald, 272
trumpet, in Cuban music, 136, 138
Tulear Never Sleeps (compilation album), 824
Tumelty, Michael, 630
Turner, Tina, 652, 700, 726
Tursun, Sanubar, 848
Tuvan throat-singing, 635–36, 638, 640
twelve-bar blues, 128, 787
twelve-tone music, 294, 424, 580, 620, 623, 660
Tzara, Tristan, 120
tzigane (use of word), 336, 347, 386; *see also* Roma
Tzintzarska, Rumyana, 539, 603, 645, 789, 856

UB40, 273, 324
Ukraine, massacre of *banduristy* (1938), 582
uMabatha (Zulu *Macbeth*) (play), 43, 62
Under African Skies (film), 71, 846
"Under Mi Sleng Teng" (song), 280
Underground (film), 355
UNESCO, "intangible cultural heritage," 749, 789, 836, 846
Uruguay, 365, 421, 438, 491, 532–33
Uighur music, 848
Uzbekistan, Soviet suppression of music in, 583, 586, 636

Valdés, Bebo, 79, 138, 157–59, 161, 166, 174, 379
Valdés, Carlos "Patato," 131–32
Valdés, Merceditas, 139
Valdés, Miguelito, 77–79, 81–84, 86–89, 132, 135, 140, 143, 152–53, 159, 195, 200, 750, 850
Vale, João de, 446, 448
Van Van, Los, 133, 192, 194–95, 199–200, 207
Varela, Adriana, 522
Vargas, Getúlio, 391–92, 402, 406–11, 413, 416, 418, 421–25–26, 461, 512, 723
Varimezov, Kostadin, 604, 609
Vasconcelos, Naná, 461–62
Vasilev, Ognyan "Jimmy," 604
Vasnetsov, Viktor, 545
Vedder, Eddie, 327
Veloso, Caetano, 420, 431, 433–34, 447–56, 462, 465, 468–70, 472–74, 483–85, 514–15, 856
Vera, María Teresa, 118
Verger, Pierre, 464
Vertinsky, Alexander, 587
Verwoerd, Hendrik, 32–33, 41–42
Village Gate, 132, 197, 205
Villa-Lobos, Heitor, 410–11, 424; *Bachianas Brasileiras No. 5*, 410
Villoldo, Angel, 497, 499
Virgin Records, 755, 838, 840
Virginia Jubilee Singers, 23
Volkov, Ilan, 630–31
voodoo, 95, 99
Vysotsky, Vladimir, 587

939

INDEX

Wailers, The, 222, 231, 242, 244–45, 247–49, 254–55, 261, 279, 720; *see also* Marley, Bob
Wajs, Bronisława ("Papusza"), 350–51
Wallahi Le Zein!! (compilation album), 823–24
Wanderers, The, 545, 564
Warren, Guy, 658, 674
Washington, Dinah, 167, 243
Waters, Muddy, 9, 343, 803
Weather Report, 194, 461, 703
Weavers, The, 13–14, 35, 594; *see also* Seeger, Pete
Webb, Chick, 124
Weiss, George David, 14
Welles, Orson, 415
Wells, H. G., 490
Wemba, Papa, 733–34, 736, 739
Wenders, Wim, 204
West Indies Records Ltd (WIRL), 222–23, 229
Westwood, Vivienne, 2–3
White, Bob, 716, 727
Whiteman, Paul, 124, 345, 435, 581
Wickham, Vicki, 443, 856
Williams, Robert Pete, 787, 790
Williamson, Robin, 301
Wilson, Delroy, 259
Wilson, Roy, 244
"Wimoweh" (song), 13–14, 35, 39, 72, 139
Winchell, Walter, 83
Windrush generation, 228, 265, 267, 269, 277
Winter, Michel, 357, 856
Winter, Paul, 436, 458
Winwood, Steve, 252, 282, 815
Withers, Bill, 725, 746
WOMAD festival, 199, 325, 566, 778, 837, 839, 846
WOMEX (convention), 642, 839, 844–45
Wonder, Stevie, 8, 688, 803, 850
Woodstock festival, 187, 306, 724, 768
World Circuit Records, 199, 203–4, 759, 785, 789, 812
"World Music," as musical category, 838–40, 842–45, 847
WR (studio and label), 468–69
Wrong, Michela, 708, 722, 733, 736

Xaba, Michael, 45
Xhosa people: dance, 27; impact of missionaries, 20–22; language, 20, 43, 62–63; music, 20–23, 26, 27–28, 32, 35, 40–41, 49, 52–54, 56, 61, 63; and politics, 10, 20, 44, 65; stick-fighting, 69; *see also* South Africa

Yakut people, 635–36
Yardbirds, The, 301
Yorùbá culture and religion, 82, 95–96, 100, 126, 182, 191–192, 194–195, 237, 309, 464, 466, 484, 663–66, 670, 672–73, 677, 681, 690, 696–97, 701
Yorùbá music, 75–76, 79, 81, 131, 665-66, 679–80
Yorùbá people, 118, 130, 215, 659, 662, 669
Young, La Monte, 318–20

Yunakov, Yuri, 613, 615, 856
Yupanqui, Atahualpa (Héctor Chavero Aramburu), 523
Yurlov, Alexander, 591

Zaiko Langa Langa, 731, 733
Zaire, *see* Congo, 695, 708, 722–24, 727, 729–30, 733, 736, 738, 741
Zamfir, Gheorghe, 536
Zhivkov, Todor, 540, 608–09, 614, 616, 633
Zimbabwe, 3, 47, 59, 70, 264, 730, 737, 741, 802, 818, 821–22
Ziryab (Abu al-Hasan Ali ibn Nafi), 360, 367, 833
Zulu (film), 2, 24
Zulu Dawn (film), 18
Zulu Nation (group), 1, 2
Zulu people: nineteenth-century performances, 18–19, 21, 43–44, 552–53, 825; and Christianity, 23; language, 14, 31; music, 2, 5, 7, 10–13, 15, 18, 24–32, 34–35, 39, 41, 45–49, 60–61, 64–66, 71; musical instruments and styles, 24–25; and politics, 10, 65, 68–69; Radio Zulu, 60; as "savages," 18–19; Shaka's rulership (and successors), 15–16, 18; stick-fighting, 69; suppression and displacement, 19–20, 26, 28, 31; violence, 10–11, 25, 30, 32, 60, 65, 68; *see also* South Africa
Zuma, Jacob, 65, 67, 69–70

About the Author

Joe Boyd is a record producer and writer, known for his memoir, *White Bicycles: Making Music in the 1960s*. Artists he has produced include Nick Drake, Pink Floyd, R.E.M., Taj Mahal, Fairport Convention, Richard and Linda Thompson, Maria Muldaur, Kate and Anna McGarrigle, and 10,000 Maniacs among many over the course of a nearly sixty-year career. As a film producer, his credits include *Amazing Grace*, *Scandal*, and *Jimi Hendrix*.

After graduating from Harvard in 1964, he tour-managed Muddy Waters, Sister Rosetta Tharpe, Sonny Rollins, Stan Getz and Astrud Gilberto, and others, then served as production manager for the 1965 Newport Folk and Jazz Festivals. After Newport, he moved to London to open Elektra Records' office there, then started the legendary UFO club, original home to Pink Floyd and Soft Machine and center of London's psychedelic revolution. Through his work with the Incredible String Band, Fairport Convention, Nick Drake, John and Beverley Martyn, and Sandy Denny, his production company, Witchseason, set a new course for folk and folk-rock music in Britain.

Boyd moved to Los Angeles in 1971 to become Director of Music Services for Warner Brothers Films, where he supervised scores for *Deliverance* and *A Clockwork Orange* and co-created the documentary *Jimi Hendrix*. In the mid-to-late '70s, he produced records by Maria Muldaur ("Midnight at the Oasis"), Kate and Anna McGarrigle, Toots and the Maytals, and James Booker.

After spending 1979 in charge of Lorne Michaels's start-up film production company, Broadway Pictures, he launched his own label, Hannibal Records, which he ran for twenty years. Hannibal released albums by a diverse mix of Anglo-American artists ranging from Defunkt and John Cale to Richard Thompson and Robert Wyatt. Joe

ABOUT THE AUTHOR

and Hannibal were also at the forefront of independent labels bringing global artists to Western audiences, including ¡Cubanismo! and Alfredo Rodriguez, Toumani Diabaté and Ali Farka Touré, Virginia Rodrigues and Moreno Veloso, Trio Bulgarka and Ivo Papasov, Muzsikás and Márta Sebestyén, Ketama and Songhai.

He left Hannibal in 2001 and wrote *White Bicycles*. Since its publication, he has traveled widely, lecturing, reading, and performing in a double-act with singer Robyn Hitchcock.

During the years spent writing *And the Roots of Rhythm Remain*, he has co-produced records with his wife, Andrea Goertler, by Albanian group Saz'iso and Bosnian sevdah artist Damir Imamović. His popular podcast, *Joe Boyd's A-Z*, takes listeners on musical adventures from around the world. In 2019, he completed unfinished business from his time at Warner Brothers Films by serving as Executive Producer on *Amazing Grace*, Alan Elliott's acclaimed film of Aretha Franklin's 1972 recording session which had lain unseen in the vaults for forty-seven years. A gifted raconteur, he appears frequently on the BBC and other global radio and television outlets.